THE ULTIMATE
CODE BOOK
CHEATING MADE EASY

Prima Games

A Division of Random House, Inc.

3000 Lava Ridge Court
Roseville, CA 95661
(916) 787-7000
www.primagames.com

Project Editor: Teli Hernandez

Editorial Assistant: Carrie Ponseti

Associate Product Manager: Christy L. Curtis

Special thanks to: Michael Knight

All products and characters mentioned in this book are trademarks of their respective companies.

Important:

ISBN: 0-7615-4064-4

Library of Congress Catalog Card Number: 2002109759

Printed in the United States of America

01 02 03 04 DD 10 9 8 7 6 5 4 3 2 1

Contents

HOW TO USE THIS BOOK

Number in Parentheses

Throughout this book there are numbers in parenthesis after button presses, like this: X(3). This tells you to press the button the number of times written in the parenthesis. For example, if you see Circle (3), Square (2), press the Circle button three times, then press the Square button two times.

Command Line Codes

Some PC games have Cheat codes that require you to add a command line parameter to the end of the .exe file name. For example, in Half-Life, in order to get to the place where you can enter codes, load the game using hl.exe -console. To do this, go to your computer's MS-DOS prompt. Then go to the Half-Life folder and type hl.exe console. Or you can right-click on Start in the Windows task bar, select the game folder, right-click on the hl.exe file, then select Properties. Change hl.exe to hl.exe -console. Create a shortcut by going to the game folder and right-clicking on the hl.exe file. Select Create Shortcut, right-click on the shortcut file, then change hl.exe to hl.exe -console.

PC

 Numbers

101ST AIRBORNE IN NORMANDY

Soldiers Re-Jump into Normandy
Type AirNormandy during gameplay.

Soldiers Are Given Food
Type AngryManDinners during gameplay.

Display All Germans, Equipment Bags, and Insides of Buildings
Type Iknow during gameplay.

Current Soldier Surrenders
Type TraitorTraitor during gameplay.

Remove All Parachutes
Type PrisonPod during gameplay.

All Soldiers on the Map Are Made Available
Type Weasel during gameplay.

Kill All Germans on the Map
Type YouGoSquishNow during gameplay.

All the Germans on the Map Surrender
Type Ihaveyounow during gameplay.

Kill All Cows on the Map
Type Beef during gameplay.

Turn Off Iknow
Type Heknows during gameplay.

Make Your Soldier Go Berserk
Type Robocop3 during gameplay.

Give Your GI a Brand New MG42 Plus Two Ammo Belts
Type Hohoho during gameplay.

Cheat Mode
During gameplay, hold Control+Shift+Alt+W. Type 2061 at the prompt that appears at the screen's bottom left corner and press Enter. Now press A and press Enter again to enable Cheat mode.

Money
Enable Cheat mode and press Shift+M.

Bricks
Enable Cheat mode and press Shift+Z.

Cannon
Enable Cheat mode and press Shift+K.

Wood
Enable Cheat mode and press Shift+H.

Tools
Enable Cheat mode and press Shift+T.

All Buildings
Enable Cheat mode and type fastgame.

1602 A.D.

Level 2 Password
JOURNEYMAN

Level 3 Password
SILHOUETTE

Level 4 Password
REMUNERATE

3001: SPACE SURVIVAL

God Mode
Start the game with 3001 GOD.

See the Programmer
Start the game with 3001 PROG.

3D HUNTING GRIZZLY

Show Where the Bear Hides
In the game, type GHBEAR.

Faster Bears
Press F1+F2+F3+F4.

3D ULTRA RC RACERS

Extra Springy Vehicles and Track Boundaries
When in a race, type bouncy.

Increased Traction for All Cars
When in a race, type sticky.

Loss of Traction
When in a race, type slippery.

Double Your Normal Car Speed
When in a race, type turbo.

Unlimited Bottle Rockets for Everyone
When in a race, type war.

No Collisions
When in a race, type ghost.

Aggressive Computer Drivers
When in a race, type hitme.

Reduced Gravity
When in a race, type moon.

Increased Gravity
When in a race, type heavy.

Get 200
Enter the name i cheat, then at the Upgrade menu, type money.

4 GET IT

Level 1 Password
PRISONER

Level 2 Password
FISHHEAD

Level 3 Password
MOREFISH

Level 4 Password
FISHFISH

Level 5 Password
TINYFISH

Level 6 Password
FREDFISH

Level 7 Password
BIGFISHY

Level 8 Password
EATDEATH

Level 9 Password
EATFISHY

Level 10 Password
SLOWFISH

Level 11 Password
FISHFAST

Level 12 Password
PLUNGERS

Level 13 Password
MOPHAPPY

Level 14 Password
JANITORS

Level 15 Password
THROMULI

Level 16 Password
PARAKEET

Level 17 Password
FUZZYDOG

Level 18 Password
SPAMKEET

Level 19 Password
BABYHEAD

Level 20 Password
FISHNOSE

Level 21 Password
FOOTFISH

Level 22 Password
FISHBONG

Level 23 Password
ABCDEFGH

A

A-10 CUBA

500 Feet Altitude Increase
Press Control+Tab.

Access Cheat Mode
Activate the control setting to Invincible Aircraft.

Joystick Enabled
Press Control+Tab+X (use the keypad to move around).

Slow Motion
Press Control+Tab+S.

ABARON

Access Cheat Mode
When in the game, type OUTLAW.

Skip Level
Access Cheat mode and press /.

Make Your Ship Immune
Access Cheat mode and press I.

Choose Weapons for Player 1/2
Access Cheat mode and press 1-7, F1-F7.

ABOMINATION

Unlimited Ammo
Go into Multiplayer and host a new game. At the game settings, set unlimited ammo. Start the multiplayer game, then quit. Start a new game or load an old game.

ACCELERATOR

Add $130,000
When in the game, hold Control and type muchmoney.

All Weapons
When in the game, hold Control and type allweapons.

Repair Damage
When in the game, hold Control and type helpme.

Unlimited Weapons
When in the game, hold Control and type agressor.

Extra Acceleration
When in the game, hold Control and type booster.

ACE OF ACES

Unlimited Lives
At the High Score screen, type DUSTY BUG on the first position.

ACTUA SOCCER

Enhanced Team
Start a game with soccer -01142475549 as command line parameter.

Italian Teams
Type itscomminghome at the title screen.

ACTUA SOCCER 2

Big Players
Type bigdaddy at the main screen.

Brian Clough
Type brianclough at the main screen.

Fooseball
Type twisycontrol at the main screen.

Italian Teams
Type itscominghome at the main screen.

Tiny Players
Type bilbobaggins at the main screen.

ACTUA SOCCER 3

Activate 24 Gag Teams
At the main screen, press Enter, type tff teams, then press Enter again.

Activate 24 More Teams
At the main screen, press Enter, type prem clubs, then press Enter again.

Activate 5 Nations Select Team
At the main screen, press Enter, type rule brittania, then press Enter again.

Activate Actua Soccer Web Team
At the main screen, press Enter, type spit n spin, then press Enter again.

Activate Arsenal 70-90 Team
At the main screen, press Enter, type tea total, then press Enter again.

Activate Arsenal Ladies Team
At the main screen, press Enter, type longdon girls, then press Enter again.

Activate Best of Spurs Team
At the main screen, press Enter, type diamond lights, then press Enter again.

Activate Blackburn 94-95 Team
At the main screen, press Enter, type down down down, then press Enter again.

Activate Boat Racers Team
At the main screen, press Enter, type tff hobby, then press Enter again.

Activate Boro Stars Team
At the main screen, press Enter, type emmersons woe, then press Enter again.

Activate Busby Babes Team
At the main screen, press Enter, type sir matt, then press Enter again.

Activate Chalton Stars Team
At the main screen, press Enter, type valley boys, then press Enter again.

Activate Chelsea Stars Team
At the main screen, press Enter, type foreign legion, then press Enter again.

Activate Classic Ipswitch Team
At the main screen, press Enter, type bald fritz, then press Enter again.

Activate Coventry Stars Team
At the main screen, press Enter, type lady godiva, then press Enter again.

Activate Cyborg Rovers Team
At the main screen, press Enter, type metal heads, then press Enter again.

Activate Derby Stars Team
At the main screen, press Enter, type ram raiders, then press Enter again.

Activate Dicks Picks N Mix Team
At the main screen, press Enter, type candy man, then press Enter again.

Activate Doncaster Rovers Team
At the main screen, press Enter, type shame, then press Enter again.

Activate Dons Stars Team
At the main screen, press Enter, type flash the cash, then press Enter again.

Activate Dud's Spuds Team
At the main screen, press Enter, type miss wilko, then press Enter again.

Activate Everton Stars Team
At the main screen, press Enter, type duncnnomore, then press Enter again.

Activate FC Gremlin Team
At the main screen, press Enter, type i made this, then press Enter again.

Activate Fighting Forth Team
At the main screen, press Enter, type flagstoning, then press Enter again.

Activate Food Group Team
At the main screen, press Enter, type bin man, then press Enter again.

Activate Forest Stars Team
At the main screen, press Enter, type men in tights, then press Enter again.

Activate Greenhouse Test Team
At the main screen, press Enter, type ozone layer, then press Enter again.

Activate Gremlin Staff 1Team
At the main screen, press Enter, type wide boys, then press Enter again.

Activate Gremlin Staff 2 Team
At the main screen, press Enter, type double trouble, then press Enter again.

Activate Heavenly HTFC Team
At the main screen, press Enter, type lee the pig, then press Enter again.

Activate Ledbury FC Team
At the main screen, press Enter, type sink or swim, then press Enter again.

Activate Leeds Stars Team
At the main screen, press Enter, type bremners boot, then press Enter again.

Activate Leicester Stars Team
At the main screen, press Enter, type fruit n veg, then press Enter again.

Activate Liverpool 77-98 Team
At the main screen, press Enter, type scouse perms, then press Enter again.

Activate Maddness Friday Team
At the main screen, press Enter, type impossibility, then press Enter again.

Activate Newcastle Stars Team
At the main screen, press Enter, type down the toon, then press Enter again.

Activate Pattis Shandi Men Team
At the main screen, press Enter, type cpu spud, then press Enter again.

Activate Shearer XXX Team
At the main screen, press Enter, type sexy football, then press Enter again.

Activate Skellington United Team
At the main screen, press Enter, type grim reaper, then press Enter again.

Activate Soton Stars Team
At the main screen, press Enter, type dell boys, then press Enter again.

Activate the Hardmen Team
At the main screen, press Enter, type shadwell town, then press Enter again.

Activate Top 50 Babes 1 Team
At the main screen, press Enter, type yes please, then press Enter again.

Activate Top 50 Babes 2 Team
At the main screen, press Enter, type no thanks, then press Enter again.

Activate Villa Stars Team
At the main screen, press Enter, type bit of claret, then press Enter again.

Activate Virtual Blades Team
At the main screen, press Enter, type chip butty, then press Enter again.

Activate Wednesday Stars Team
At the main screen, press Enter, type barmy army, then press Enter again.

Activate West Ham Stars Team
At the main screen, press Enter, type wright buy, then press Enter again.

Activate Wigan 98-98 Team
At the main screen, press Enter, type egg chasers, then press Enter again.

ACTUA TENNIS

Big Balls
Type bigballs at the main menu.

Large Heads
Type selfimportant at the main menu.

Super Shots Increase
Type morespeed at the main menu.

ADDAMS FAMILY

Bird Defeated, Energy Heart Password
&1Y1M

Snow Monster Defeated, Energy Heart Password
?1J14

Wednesday Rescued Password
?ZR1K

Uncle Fester Rescued Password
VGJ1Y

Grandma Rescued Password
VLKKV

Level 2 Password
?ZR9R

Level 3 Password
1ZYKF

Level 4 Password
VDJ15

Level 5 Password
?DY9M

Level 6 Password
VDH9C

AERO DANCING

More Options
Enter the name TASCAS and select "Special" in Options.

AFRICAN SAFARI

Activate Flying
Type vulture in 3D mode.

All Animals Marked
Type flagevery in 3D mode.

All Unlicensed Animals Marked
Type flagall in 3D mode.

Build Herds
Type spawnall in 3D mode.

Current Location Marked
Type gps in 3D mode.

Kill Zone Display
Type xray in 3D mode.

License to Hunt Elands
Type license1 in 3D mode.

License to Hunt Elephants
Type license3 in 3D mode.

License to Hunt Kudus
Type license4 in 3D mode.

License to Hunt Zebras
Type license2 in 3D mode.

More Money
Press Control+4 with the cursor placed at the screen's top left corner.

Part Invisibility
Type hgwells in 3D mode.

Unlimited Ammo
Type hugeguns in 3D mode.

AGE OF EMPIRES

600 Hit Points and Six Speed Points for Priest
During a game, press Enter and type hoyohoyo.

Add Laser Gunner
After creating an Empire, click on the town center, press Enter, and type photon man.

Beat Scenario
During a game, press Enter and type home run.

Camouflaged Archer
During a game, press Enter and type dark rain.

Car Rockets
During a game, press Enter and type bigdaddy.

Command Animals
During a game, press Enter and type gaia.

Destroy Player
During a game, press Enter and type kill and player 1 to 8.

Enhance Range of Ballista
During a game, press Enter and type icbm.

Enhanced Range and Power of Catapult
During a game, press Enter and type big bertha.

Food Up 1,000
During a game, press Enter and type pepperoni pizza.

Gold Up 1,000
During a game, press Enter and type coinage.

Change Horse Archers to Black Riders
During a game, press Enter and type black rider.

Immediate Building
During a game, press Enter and type steroids.

Kill Everyone
During a game, press Enter and type diediedie.

Land-Mobility for Juggernauts
During a game, press Enter and type flying dutchman.

No Fog
During a game, press Enter and type no fog.

Peasant-Shooting Catapults
Select the cannon, press Enter, and type jack be nimble.

Quit Game
During a game, press Enter and type resign.

Stone Up 1,000
During a game, press Enter and type quarry.

Suicide
During a game, press Enter and type hari kari.

Trooper as Nuclear Weapon
During a game, press Enter and type e=mc2 trooper.

View Entire Map
During a game, press Enter and type reveal map.

Change a Dead Villager to a Black Rider, Then to a Heavy Catapult
During a game, press Enter and type medusa.

Wood Up 1,000
During a game, press Enter and type woodstock.

AGE OF EMPIRES II

1,000 Food
During a game, press Enter and type cheese steak jimmy's.

1,000 Gold
During a game, press Enter and type robin hood.

1,000 Stone
During a game, press Enter and type rock on.

1,000 Wood
During a game, press Enter and type lumberjack.

Instant Victory
During a game, press Enter and type i r winner.

Kill All Opponents
During a game, press Enter and type black death.

Full Map
During a game, press Enter and type marco.

Instant Loss
During a game, press Enter and type resign.

Commit Suicide
During a game, press Enter and type wimpy-wimpywimpy.

Cobra Car
During a game, press Enter and type how do you turn this on.

Build Fast
During a game, press Enter and type aegis.

No Shadows
During a game, press Enter and type polo.

Control the Animals
During a game, press Enter and type natural wonders.

Saboteur Unit
During a game, press Enter and type to smitherenes.

Slay Selected Opponent
During a game, press Enter and type torpedo [x]. Replace [x] with a number between 1 and 8.

Fast Construction
During a game, press Control+Q for faster building.

Build Immutable Structure
During a game, press Control+P.

New Resource Menu
During a game, press Control+T.

View the Ending
During a game, press Control+C to see the ending.

800 x 600 Resolution
Type 800 at the command line.

1024 x 768 Resolution
Type 1024 at the command line.

1280 x 1024 Resolution
Type 1280 at the command line.

Auto Save
Type AUTOMPSAVE at the command line.

Disable Music
Type NOMUSIC at the command line.

Disable Sounds
Type NOSOUND at the command line.

Fix Sound Problems
Type AWE FREEZES MSYNC at the command line. This only works for some hardware.

Fix Display Problems
Type MFILL at the command line. This only works for some video cards.

Disable FMV Sequence
Type NOSTARTUP at the command line.

Disable Terrain Sounds
Type NOTERRAINSOUND at the command line.

Default Mouse Driver
Type NORMALMOUSE at the command line.

AGE OF EMPIRES: THE RISE OF ROME

Access Cheat Mode
Go into Talk mode, then press Enter.

600 Hit Points and Six Speed Points for Priest
Activate Cheat mode, then type hoyohoyo.

Add Laser Gunner
After creating an Empire, click on the town center, activate Cheat mode, then type photon man.

Beat Scenario
Activate Cheat mode, then type home run.

Car With Rocket Launcher
Activate Cheat mode, then type bigdaddy.

Command Animals
Activate Cheat mode, then type gaia.

Destroy Player
Activate Cheat mode, then type kill and player 1 to 8.

Change Eagle into 999 Hp Dragon
Activate Cheat mode, then type king arthur.

Enhanced Range and Power of Catapult
Activate Cheat mode, then type big bertha.

Enhanced Range of Ballista
Activate Cheat mode, then type icbm.

Food Up 1,000
Activate Cheat mode, then type pepperoni pizza.

Gold Up 1,000
Activate Cheat mode, then type coinage.

Immediate Building
Activate Cheat mode, then type steroids.

Kill Everyone
Activate Cheat mode, then type diediedie.

Land Mobility for Juggernauts
Activate Cheat mode, then type flying dutchman.

Lethal Animal Bite
Activate Cheat mode, then type grantlinkspence.

Missile Launcher Car
Activate Cheat mode, then type big momma.

No Fog
Activate Cheat mode, then type no fog.

Peasant-firing Catapult
After selecting the cannon, activate Cheat mode, then type jack be nimble.

Priest Division
Activate Cheat mode, then type convert this!.

Quit Game
Activate Cheat mode, then type resign.

Robot
Activate Cheat mode, then type stormbilly.

Stone Up 1,000
Activate Cheat mode, then type quarry.

Suicide
Activate Cheat mode, then type hari kari.

Tricycle-Riding Gun-Toting Baby
Activate Cheat mode, then type pow.

Trooper as Nuclear Weapon
Activate Cheat mode, then type e=mc2 trooper.

View Entire Map
Activate Cheat mode, then type reveal map.

Change a Dead Villager to a Black Rider, Then to a Heavy Catapult
Activate Cheat mode then type medusa.

Wood Up 1,000
Activate Cheat mode, then type woodstock.

AGE OF RIFLES

Debug Mode
Start the game with the command line parameter DEBUG.

No Time Delays
Start the game with the command line parameter QUICK -.

Slower Reaction to Orders
Start the game with the command line parameter REACTIONS-.

Faster Reaction to Orders
Start the game with the command line parameter REACTIONS+.

Unambiguous Status Reports
Start the game with the command line parameter REPORTS-.

No Sound
Start the game with the command line parameter QUIET.

AGE OF SAIL 2

Mission Skip
Type qsww during game play to complete the current mission.

Mission Skip
Type qswd during game play to lose the current mission.

AGE OF WONDERS

Access Cheat Mode
Set the command line to aow.exe beatrix and start a game. During the game, press Control+Shift+C and you should hear a sound.

Fog Toggle On or Off
Activate Cheat mode and type fog.

Gold Up 1,000
Activate Cheat mode and type gold.

Level Loss
Activate Cheat mode and type lose.

Level Victory
Activate Cheat mode and type win.

Mana Up 1,000
Activate Cheat mode and type mana.

Move Anywhere
Activate Cheat mode and type freemove.

Receive All Spells
Activate Cheat mode and type spells.

Research Spells
Activate Cheat mode and type research.

Town Independence
Activate Cheat mode and type towns.

View Toggles
Activate Cheat mode and type explore.

AGE OF WONDERS 2

Access Cheat Mode
Press Control + Shift + C during game play. A sound will confirm correct entry. Enter one of the codes given below to activate the corresponding cheat function. Note: The codes do not work between the Fire and Life stages.

Explore Map
Activate Cheat mode and type explore.

Fog Toggle On or Off
Activate Cheat mode and type fog.

Gold Up 1,000
Activate Cheat mode and type gold.

Level Loss
Activate Cheat mode and type lose.

Level Victory
Activate Cheat mode and type win.

Mana Up 1,000
Activate Cheat mode and type mana.

Move Anywhere
Activate Cheat mode and type freemove.

Receive All Spells
Activate Cheat mode and type spells.

Research Spells
Activate Cheat mode and type research.

Summon New Hero Spell
Activate Cheat mode and type emergehero.

Toggle Instant Production
Activate Cheat mode and type instantprod.

Toggle Instant Research
Activate Cheat mode and type instantres.

Toggle Your Player's AI
Activate Cheat mode and type ai.

Toggle Spying of Enemy Cities
Activate Cheat mode and type cityspy.

Upgrade Your Hero
Activate Cheat mode and type upgradehero.

View All Towns
Activate Cheat mode and type towns.

AGILE WARRIOR

Enable Cheat Mode
During a game, press Escape, then C.

Become Invincible
Enable Cheat mode and type 14214.

Finish All Missions
Enable Cheat mode and type 33124.

Highest Fuel and Armor
Enable Cheat mode and type 13593.

Highest Weapons
Enable Cheat mode and type 25245.

Select Level
Enable Cheat mode and type 17357.

AIRFIX DOGFIGHTER

God Mode
During a game, type hybris.

All Weapons
During a game, type hefaistos.

Highest Tech Level
During a game, type athena.

Get Medals
During a game, type admiral.

Autopilot
During a game, type autopilot.

Drive Car
During a game, type racerwagen.

Slow Motion
During a game, type slomo.

Faster
During a game, type birgeroco.

Lose Mission
During a game, type hades.

AIRLINE TYCOON

All Helpers Working
During a game, type mentat.

Choose Level
During a game, type atmissall.

Make Airport Bigger
During a game, type expander.

More Money
During a game, type donaldtrump.

No Debts
During a game, type nodebts.

Notebook
During a game, type thinkpad.

Skip to Next Level
During a game, type winning.

View All Flights
During a game, type showall.

ALADDIN

Level Skip
Pause the game and type ABBAABBA.

ALIEN BREED

Level 2 Password
AAJIGDDC

Level 3 Password
GGHDGGDG

Level 4 Password
HDICICCII

Level 5 Password
IDHEHDGCC

Level 6 Password
IJIIDIHEC

Level 7 Password
CFDFEFEFJ

Level 8 Password
JIIJIIIIC

Level 9 Password
AAAABAAAA

Level 10 Password
CCGDGBBBB

Level 11 Password
HHIAAJJIG

Level 12 Password
GGDDJJHFD

Level 13 Password
JIECBFGFF

Level 14 Password
HGGEDDCCB

Level 15 Password
HHHGFGDCC

Level 16 Password
IHDCHGHFF

ALIEN BREED: SPECIAL EDITION

Power Sub-System Deck Two Password
55955

Oval Zone Deck Four Password
48361

Engineering Sub-System Deck Six Password
63556

Powermech Systems Deck Eight Password
86723

Reactor Core Deck Ten Password
25194

ALIEN NATIONS

Reveal Map
During a game, type magiceye.

Max Lollypops
During a game, type lolly.

Max Mushroom Juice
During a game, type juice.

Max Chocolate Cake
During a game, type choco.

Max Weapons
During a game, type wartime.

Max Food
During a game, type iamhungry.

Max Iron
During a game, type ironman.

Max Stone
During a game, type stonemason.

Max Lumber
During a game, type lumberjack.

Max Maggot
During a game, type rain.

Add $5,000
During a game, type cashcow.

Lose Mission
During a game, type winner.

ALIEN VS. PREDATOR

Cheat Mode
First install the save game patch. Using the avp.exe -debug command line, load the game. Then press ~ while playing as the specified character.

Add CPU Alien (Any)
Activate Cheat mode and type alienbot.

Add CPU Marine (Any)
Activate Cheat mode, type marinebot, then the class number.

Add CPU Praetorian Alien (Any)
Activate Cheat mode and type praetorianbot.

Add CPU Predator (Any)
Activate Cheat mode, type predobot, then the class number.

Add CPU Predator-Alien (Any)
Activate Cheat mode and type predalienbot.

Add CPU Zenoborg (Any)
Activate Cheat mode and type xenoborg.

Add Species
To force the game to have the desired character type, use the avp.exe -debug -l[ampcxtr] command line when you start the game: a=alien, m=marine, p=predator, c=civilian, x=xenoborg, t=praetorian alien, and r=predator-alien. Do this before creating characters that do not normally exist in the level.

Adjust Blue Tint in Sky (Any)
Activate Cheat mode, type sky_blue, then a number.

Adjust Green Tint in Sky (Any)
Activate Cheat mode, type sky_green, then a number.

Adjust Red Tint in Sky (Any)
Activate Cheat mode, type sky_red, then a number.

Adjust Speed of Game (Any)
Activate Cheat mode, type timescale, then a number from 0.0 to 1.0.

Adjust Speed of Motion Tracker (Marine)
Activate Cheat mode, type motiontracker-speed, then a number from 0 to 16.

Adjust Volume of Motion Tracker (Marine)
Activate Cheat mode, type motiontracker-volume, then a number from 0.00 to 1.00.

Alien Sound Doppler Shift (Any)
Activate Cheat mode and type dopplershift then 0 or 1.

All Ammunition and Weapons (Any)
Activate Cheat mode and type giveallweapons.

Alter Sidestepping Tilt (Any)
Activate Cheat mode, type leanscale, then a number.

Cheat List (Any)
Activate Cheat mode and type listcmd.

Crouch/Crawl Toggle (Alien)
Activate Cheat mode, type crouchmode, then 0 or 1.

God Mode (Alien)
Activate Cheat mode and type theonedeadly-creatureevercreated.

God Mode (Any)
Activate Cheat mode and type god.

God Mode (Marine)
Activate Cheat mode and type freakoftheunivers.

God Mode (Predator)
Activate Cheat mode and type skullcollector.

Help List (Any)
Activate Cheat mode and type listvar.

Invisibility (Any)
Activate Cheat mode and type observer.

Light Aura (Any)
Activate Cheat mode and type light.

Play as Final Xenomorph (Alien)
Activate Cheat mode and type winneroftheonegreatbattleoftheuniverse.

Refill Energy (Predator)
Activate Cheat mode and type gimme_charge.

View Coordinates of Level (Any)
Activate Cheat mode and type showcoords.

View Frame Rate (Any)
Activate Cheat mode and type showfps.

View Rendered Polygons Count (Any)
Activate Cheat mode and type showpolycount.

Wire Frame Mode (Any)
Activate Cheat mode, type wireframemode, then 0 or 1.

ALIEN VS. PREDATOR II

Cheat Mode
Press Enter during game play, type one of the codes given below, then press Enter again to activate the corresponding cheat function. The sound of the predator's mask switching vision types will confirm correct code entry.

All Weapons and Ammo
Activate Cheat mode and type mpschuckit.

Change Health to Indicated Number
Activate Cheat mode and type mpdoctordoctor <number>.

Change into Indicated Character Type
Activate Cheat mode and type mpmorph <character type>.

Full Armor
Activate Cheat mode and type mpsmithy.

Full Ammo
Activate Cheat mode and type mpstockpile.

Level Select for All Three Species
Activate Cheat mode and type mpxfiles.

Teleport to Level Start with Default Conditions
Activate Cheat mode and type mpbeamme.

Toggle Invincibility
Activate Cheat mode and type mpcanthurtme.

Toggle Rotation Display
Activate Cheat mode and type mpgrs.

Toggle Size Display
Activate Cheat mode and type mpsizeme.

Toggle Speed Display
Activate Cheat mode and type mptachometer.

Toggle No Clipping
Activate Cheat mode and type mpsixthsense.

Toggle Third-Person View
Activate Cheat mode and type mpicu.

Unlimited Ammo
Activate Cheat mode and type mpbunker.

ALIEN VS. PREDATOR GOLD

Cheat Mode
Type -debug as command line parameter and load the game. Then press ~ while playing as the specified character.

Add CPU Alien (Any)
Activate Cheat mode and type ALIENBOT.

Add CPU Marine (Any)
Activate Cheat mode, type MARINEBOT, then the class number.

Add CPU Praetorian Alien (Any)
Activate Cheat mode and type PRAETORIANBOT.

Add CPU Predator (Any)
Activate Cheat mode, type PREDOBOT, then the class number.

Add CPU Predator-Alien (Any)
Activate Cheat mode and type PREDALIENBOT.

Add CPU Zenoborg (Any)
Activate Cheat mode and type XENOBORG.

Adjust Speed of Game (Any)
Activate Cheat mode, type TIMESCALE, then a number from 0.0 to 1.0.

Adjust Speed of Motion Tracker (Marine)
Activate Cheat mode, type MOTIONTRACKERSPEED, then a number from 0 to 16.

Adjust Volume of Motion Tracker (Marine)
Activate Cheat mode, type MOTIONTRACKERVOLUME, then a number from 0.00 to 1.00.

All Ammunition and Weapons (Any)
Activate Cheat mode and type GIVEALLWEAPONS.

Cheat List (Any)
Activate Cheat mode and type LISTCMD.

Crouch/Crawl Toggle (Alien)
Activate Cheat mode, type CROUCHMODE, then 0 or 1.

God Mode (Any)
Activate Cheat mode and type GOD.

Help List (Any)
Activate Cheat mode and type LISTVAR.

Light Aura (Any)
Activate Cheat mode and type LIGHT.

Refill Energy (Predator)
Activate Cheat mode and type GIMME_CHARGE.

View Frame Rate (Any)
Activate Cheat mode and type SHOWFPS.

View Rendered Polygons Count (Any)
Activate Cheat mode and type SHOWPOLYCOUNT.

ALIEN TRILOGY

Cheat Codes
Enter these codes while playing.

All weapons
comeandhaveago

Unlimited Ammo
ifyouthinkyouarehardenough

Warp to level
nadiapopov##

Infinite Energy
takeonallcomers

Restore Energy
theironlady

God Mode
ripleydoesitwithbigguns

ALPHA CENTAURI

Add Discovery Technology
Press Control+K during a game, then press Shift+F2.

Add Unit
Press Control+K during a game, then press Shift+F1.

Adjust Amount of Energy Credits
Press Control+K during a game, then press Shift+F4.

Change Sides and Point of View
Press Control+K during a game, then press Shift+F3.

Choose Different Year
Press Control+K during a game, then press Shift+F5.

Destroy Enemy
Press Control+K during a game, then press Shift+F6.

Edit Faction Skills
Press Control+K during a game, then press Shift+F9.

Show All FMVs
Press Control+K during a game, then press Shift+F8.

Show Entire Map
Press Control+K during a game, then press Y.

Show Replay
Press Control+K during a game, then press Shift+F7.

ALPHA CENTAURI: ALIEN CROSSFIRE

Firaxian Faction
In the Faction Editor, click on Open, type sid, and save it as sid or brian. Then click on Add Faction.

AMAZON TRAIL

Enable Management
Type the password dream at the Enable Management option.

AMERICAN DEER HUNTER 2000

Enable Console
In the Text Editor, add the command line consoleenabled = 1 to the <l>config.scr<l> file in the game directory.

Choose Level
Enable Console, press ~ during a game, then type level and a number from 1 to 15.

Move Fast
Enable Console, press ~ during a game, then type runfast.

Show Animal Locations on Map
Enable Console, press ~ during a game, then type showanimalsonmap.

Show Animals
Enable Console, press ~ during a game, then type showanimals.

Show Bedding
Enable Console, press ~ during a game, then type showbedding.

Show Bedding Locations on Map
Enable Console, press ~ during a game, then type showbeddingsonmap.

AMERICAN MCGEE'S ALICE

To access the codes for the full version, enable the console window in the game options. During gameplay press the ~ and Esc keys.

Toggle God Mode
god

Toggle No Clip Mode
noclip

All Weapons
Wuss

Give Health
health

Enemies Cannot See You
Notarget

All Weapons and Ammo
give

Level Select

Type map, then type one of the following levels:

centipede1
centipede2
facade
fortress1
fortress2
funhouse
garden1
garden2
garden3
garden4
grounds1
grounds2
gvillage
hedge1
hedge2
hedge3
jlair1
jlair2
keep
pandemonium
potears1
potears2
potears3
qlair
rchess
skool1
skool2
tower1
tower2
tower3
utemple
wchess1
wchess2
wforest

Set Health Level
health # (# is the amount of health you want)

First Person View
cg_cameradist –45

Default View
cg_cameradist 128

Change the Frame Rate
fps

Spawn Knife
give_knife.tik

Spawn Card
give_cards.tik

Spawn Mallet
give_mallet.tik

Spawn Jackbomb
give_jackbomb.tik

Spawn Eyestaff
give_eyestaff.tik

Spawn Icewand
give_icewand.tik

Spawn Jacks
give_jacks.tik

Spawn Blunderbuss
give_blunderbuss.tik

Spawn Demon Dice
give_demondice.tik (Use multiple times to get all three Demon Dice.)

Spawn Rage Box
give_ragebox.tik

Spawn Watch
give_watch.tik

AMOK

God Mode
For code mode, go to the Options screen and type "babyxx."

Level Select
Enter the password "ZZZCYX" to start the game at any level.

ANCIENT CONQUEST

More Amber and Fish
Press Enter during a game, type exiton, then press Enter again.

ANDRETTI RACING

Indy Cars
Begin a new career with the name CHAO BROS.

Stock Cars
Begin a new career with the name PEACEFUL OCEAN.

ANTS!

Create Ant
During a game, type Control+H.

APACHE LONGBOW

Invincibility and Unlimited Ammo
In Campaign mode, type MONTY BARRYMORE as the pilot name.

AQUANOID

Skip to Final Level
Type the password GYPSUM.

ARES RISING

Become Invincible
Press Shift+C in a single-player game, type BigAssShields, then press Escape.

Become Invisible
Press Shift+C in a single-player game, type WonderWoman, then press Escape.

Destroy Target
Press Shift+C in a single-player game, type DieDieDie, then press Escape.

Finish Mission
Press Shift+C in a single-player game, type IamTheMaster, then press Escape.

Unlimited Ammunition
Press Shift+C in a single-player game, type ShootEmUp, then press Escape.

Unlimited Fuel
Press Shift+C in a single-player game, type GoingAndGoing, then press Escape.

ARMORED FIST 2 M1A2 ABRAMS

All Weapons, Unlimited Fuel, and Health
During the game, push Backspace and type KYLE.

Full Ammunition
Alt+Shift+R

Repair Damage
Alt+Shift+D

Toggle Overview
Ctrl+F12

Selected Tank is Indestructible
Alt+Shift+I

ARMY MEN

Activate Explosions, Opponent Point of View, and Invincible Sarge
Press Escape during a game, type Kahuna, then click on Back.

Air Fighter Backup
Press Escape during a game, type Aeroballistics, then click on Back.

Explosion Toggle
Press Escape during a game, type Pyromancer, then click on Back.

Maximum Ammunition
Press Escape during a game, type Plethora, then click on Back.

Opponent Point of View Toggle
Press Escape during a game, type Omnisicient, then click on Back.

Paralyze Enemies
Press Escape during a game, type Paralysis, then click on Back.

Sarge Invincibility
Press Escape during a game, type Invulnerable, then click on Back.

Sarge Teleportation
In Scroll mode, choose a destination, press Escape during a game, type Telekinetic, then click on Back.

Scenario Loss
Press Escape during a game, type Succumb, then click on Back.

Scenario Victory
Press Escape during a game, type Triumph, then click on Back.

Stealth
Press Escape during a game, type Occultation, then click on Back.

ARMY MEN 2

Cheat Mode
Press Backspace during a game and type !when all else fails….

End of Phoenix Ending
Enable Cheat mode and type !cliche ending.

Acquire Aerosol Spray
Enable Cheat mode and type !roach spray.

Acquire Bazooka
Enable Cheat mode and type !no rocket launcher.

Acquire M-80
Enable Cheat mode and type !fourth of july.

Acquire Magnifying Glass
Enable Cheat mode and type !ruby ray.

Acquire Medical Kit
Enable Cheat mode and type !rubber cement.

Acquire Sniper Rifle
Enable Cheat mode and type !beautiful nikita or !god of gamblers.

Acquire Vulcan Gun
Enable Cheat mode and type !a better tomorrow.

Add Mine Sweeper
Enable Cheat mode and type !pooper scooper.

Add Sudden Enemies
Enable Cheat mode and type !surprise party.

Air Attack
Enable Cheat mode and type !geronimo!

Acquire Flak Jacket
Enable Cheat mode and type !aluminum foil.

Acquire Flame Thrower
Enable Cheat mode and type !village people.

Armageddon
Enable Cheat mode and type !armageddon.

Become Invincible
Enable Cheat mode and type !santini.

Complete Mission
Enable Cheat mode and type !veni vidi vinci.

Different Background Music
Enable Cheat mode and type !techno.

Fly
Enable Cheat mode and type !jumpjets.

Gray Cover
Enable Cheat mode and type !metal sheeting.

Heal
Enable Cheat mode and type !doctor doctor.

Investigating Flights
Enable Cheat mode and type !watchtower in the sky.

Mission Loss
Enable Cheat mode and type !i give up.

More Explosives
Enable Cheat mode and type !gnomish inventions.

More Fog
Enable Cheat mode and type !moleman.

More Grenades
Enable Cheat mode and type !i have a rock.

More Mines
Enable Cheat mode and type !acme discs.

More Paratroopers
Enable Cheat mode and type !paper dolls.

Promotion of Men to Five Stars
Enable Cheat mode and type !patton's speach.

Sarge on Fire
Enable Cheat mode and type !phoenix!

Show All FMVs
Enable Cheat mode and type !fond memories.

Show Entire Map
Enable Cheat mode and type !spidey senses tingling.

Shrink Wrap Disguise
Enable Cheat mode and type !shrink wrap.

Smorfs Disguise
Enable Cheat mode and type !smorfs.

Stealth
Enable Cheat mode and type !ninja arts.

Suicide
Enable Cheat mode and type !suicide kings.

Turn Bodies into Zombies
Enable Cheat mode and type !night of the walking dead.

ARMY MEN 3: TOYS IN SPACE

Cheat Mode
Press Backspace while playing, then type !throw me a frickin bone here. Then hit Backspace and type one of the following codes.

Win Scenario
Enable Cheat mode and type !cut to the chase.

God Mode
Enable Cheat mode and type !captain scarlet.

God Mode and All Items
Enable Cheat mode and type !full monty.

Infinite Air Attacks
Enable Cheat mode and type !roody-pooh.

Infinite Bazooka
Enable Cheat mode and type !i like to keep this handy.

Three Air Attacks
Enable Cheat mode and type !heavenly glory.

Three Hammer Mines
Enable Cheat mode and type !spiny norman.

Three Baseballs
Enable Cheat mode and type !one time.

Three Napalm Air Strikes
Enable Cheat mode and type !this one goes to eleven.

Three Paratroopers
Enable Cheat mode and type !johnny ricco.

Three Recons
Enable Cheat mode and type !peep show.

Three Space Troopers
Enable Cheat mode and type !scotty.

Nine Blue Disguises
Enable Cheat mode and type !i woke up this morning.

Nine Gray Disguises
Enable Cheat mode and type !incognito.

Nine Tan Disguises
Enable Cheat mode and type !no sunblock.

10 TNT
Enable Cheat mode and type !haunt haunt haunt!

20 Fly Swatters
Enable Cheat mode and type !harsh language.

30 Mines
Enable Cheat mode and type !sprinkles.

30 Insecticide Spray
Enable Cheat mode and type !henry.

Invisibility
Enable Cheat mode and type !its dark.

Lots of Enemy Troops
Enable Cheat mode and type !no one expects.

Laser
Enable Cheat mode and type !hello neo.

Freeze Everyone
Enable Cheat mode and type !oh behave.

Extinguish Sarge's Fire
Enable Cheat mode and type !disco is dead.

Low Health for Sarge
Enable Cheat mode and type !let me down.

Large Explosion Around Sarge
Enable Cheat mode and type !italian job.

Display Frame Rate
Enable Cheat mode and type !rate me.

Zombie Enemies
Enable Cheat mode and type !halloween.

Sarge Has a Laser Rifle
Enable Cheat mode and type !mib.

Sarge Has a Flak-Jacket
Enable Cheat mode and type !whistle and flute.

Sarge Has a Force Field
Enable Cheat mode and type !stay frosty.

Lose Scenario 1
Enable Cheat mode and type !the meek.

Lose Scenario 2
Enable Cheat mode and type !time for bed.

Random Item
Enable Cheat mode and type !mona lisa.

Reveal Enemies on Map
Enable Cheat mode and type !there is no spoon.

Infinite Aerosol
Enable Cheat mode and type !hey dante.

Infinite Flame Napalm
Enable Cheat mode and type !here's a lockpick....

Infinite Flame Thrower
Enable Cheat mode and type !patty melt.

Infinite Glue
Enable Cheat mode and type !hey stifler.

Infinite Grenades
Enable Cheat mode and type !you want some.

Infinite M80s
Enable Cheat mode and type !penny.

Infinite Magnifying Glass
Enable Cheat mode and type !the sun.

Infinite Medi Kit
Enable Cheat mode and type !florence.

Minesweeper
Enable Cheat mode and type !i got two words for ya....

Sniper Rifle
Enable Cheat mode and type !yippee!!!

Teleport Sarge to Pointer Location
Enable Cheat mode and type !door.

ARMY MEN: AIR TACTICS

Full Health
Press Backspace during a game and type !ripoff blue.

Mission Loss
Press Backspace during a game and type !ripoff white.

Red Levels for All Amounts
Press Backspace during a game and type !plastic surgery.

Unlimited Health
Press Backspace during a game and type !ripoff red.

ARMY MEN: WORLD WAR

Cheat Mode
Press Backspace during a game and type !throw me a frickin bone here.

Activate AI
Enable Cheat mode, press Backspace during a game, and type !mojo.

Choose Random Item/Effect
Enable Cheat mode, press Backspace during a game, and type !mona lisa.

Deactivate AI
Enable Cheat mode, press Backspace during a game, and type !oh behave.

Debug
Enable Cheat mode, press Backspace during a game, and type !rate me.

Destroy Specified Units
Enable Cheat mode, press Backspace during a game, and type !time for bed.

Fail Mission
Enable Cheat mode, press Backspace during a game, and type !the meek.

Finish Mission
Enable Cheat mode, press Backspace during a game, and type !cut to the chase.

Flak Jacket for Unit
Enable Cheat mode, press Backspace during a game, and type !whistle and flute.

Nine Blue Disguises for Unit
Enable Cheat mode, press Backspace during a game, and type !i woke up this morning.

Nine Gray Disguises for Unit
Enable Cheat mode, press Backspace during a game, and type !incognito.

No Disguises
Enable Cheat mode, press Backspace during a game, and type !let me down.

Sniper Rifle Ammo for Unit
Enable Cheat mode, press Backspace during a game, and type !yippee!!!.

Three Bombing Airstrikes for Unit
Enable Cheat mode, press Backspace during a game, and type !heavenly glory.

Three Napalm Airstrikes for Unit
Enable Cheat mode, press Backspace during a game, and type !this one goes to eleven.

Three Recons for Unit
Enable Cheat mode, press Backspace during a game, and type !peep show.

Unlimited Air Attack for Unit
Enable Cheat mode, press Backspace during a game, and type !roody-pooh.

Unlimited Health Kits
Enable Cheat mode, press Backspace during a game, and type !florence.

ARSENAL

Clear Area Around Specified Device
During a game, type bullit.

Demolish All Buildings and Units (Except Bulldozers)
During a game, type sucker.

Destroy Specified Units
During a game, type youdie.

Fanato Headquarters
During a game, type fanato.

Finish Research
During a game, type eureka.

Normo Headquarters
During a game, type normo.

One Million Civilians
During a game, type babyboom.

One Million Fuel
During a game, type koweit.

One Million Gold
During a game, type 1,000,000 gold.

One Million Iron
During a game, type maggy.

Parano Headquarters
During a game, type parano.

Psycho Headquarters
During a game, type psycho.

Schyzo Headquarters
During a game, type schyzo.

ASTEROIDS

All Weapons
For all power-ups, type "issallgood" while playing.

AstroRock 2000

All Guns Password
kickass

Level Select Password
togotforme

BFPG9000 Password
outofbubblegun

Rapid Fire Password
morebullets

Show Frame Rate Password
fps

ATOMIC ROBOKID

Cheat Mode
At the title screen, type TUESDAY 14TH. Then press Fire to start the game.

ATOMIX

Disable Timer
During a game, type time.

AVERY CARDOZA'S CASINO 2000

See Winning Numbers in Keno
Set your clock back five minutes to see the winning numbers on the past game console for Keno.

AXIS

God Mode
During a game, press ` and type god.

All Weapons
During a game, press ` and type weapons.

Restore Health
During a game, press ` and type healthr.

Ammo
During a game, press ` and type ammo.

AXIS & ALLIES

Unlimited Lives
At the main screen, type neverdie.

B-HUNTER

Pilot BAT Vehicle
During a game, type IABAT.

God Mode On/Off
During a game, type IADQD.

All Weapons and Full Ammo
During a game, type IAKFA.

BACKTRACK

Access Cheat Mode
During a game, press Escape, A(2). You see a monitor. Press A and type one of the following codes. Press B to exit.

God Mode
Enable Cheat mode and type god.

Full Ammo
Enable Cheat mode and type ammo.

All Weapons
Enable Cheat mode and type weapons.

BACKYARD BASEBALL

Play as Mr. Clanky
At the Trophy Case in the clubhouse, hold Shift and click on him.

BACKYARD FOOTBALL

Play as Dummies
Name your coach MRCLANKY.

Special Kid
At the Draft Players screen, type superkid.

Secret Plays
During a game, type moreplays.

More Speed
During a game, type superspeed.

Improved Passes
Before passing, type sharpeye.

Improved Tackles
Before tackling, type whatatackle.

BACKYARD SOCCER

Get Mr. Clanky
At the Trophy Case in the clubhouse, hold Shift and click on him.

BALDUR'S GATE

Enable Cheat Mode
In the game directory, find the <I>Baldur.ini<I> file and make a backup copy. Then using a text editor, open the file, and under Game Options type Cheats=1.

Get Gold
Enable Cheat mode. During game, press Control+Tab. Type Cheats:Midas(); and press Enter and Control+Tab.

Create Cow Kill Spell (If Cow Nearby)
Enable Cheat mode. During game, press Control+Tab. Type Cheats:CowKill(); and press Enter and Control+Tab.

Summon Friendly Drizzt
Enable Cheat mode. During game, press Control+Tab. Type Cheats:DrizztDefends(); and press Enter and Control+Tab.

Summon Hostile Drizzt
Enable Cheat mode. During game, press Control+Tab. Type Cheats:DrizztAttacks(); and press Enter and Control+Tab.

All Main Quest Items
Enable Cheat mode. During game, press Control+Tab. Type Cheats:CriticalItems(); and press Enter and Control+Tab.

Show Full Map
Enable Cheat mode. During game, press Control+Tab. Type Cheats:ExploreArea(); and press Enter and Control+Tab.

10 Friendly Berserk Chickens
Enable Cheat mode. During game, press Control+Tab. Type Cheats:TheGreatGonzo(); and press Enter and Control+Tab.

Teleport to Get Unstuck
Enable Cheat mode. During game, press Control+Tab. Type Cheats:Hans(); and press Enter and Control+Tab.

Healing Items
Enable Cheat mode. During game, press Control+Tab. Type Cheats:FirstAid(); and press Enter and Control+Tab.

Change Experience Points
Enable Cheat mode. During game, press Control+Tab. Type CLUAConsole:SetCurrentXP ([desired number]) and press Enter and Control+Tab.

Cheat Keys
Enable Cheat mode. During game, press Control+Tab. Type CLUAConsole:EnableCheat-Keys() and press Enter and Control+Tab. Use the following Cheat Keys:

Jump to Pointer
Enable Cheat mode and Cheat Keys, then press Control+J.

View Final FMV Sequence
Enable Cheat mode and Cheat Keys, then press Control+B.

Select FMV Sequence
Enable Cheat mode and Cheat Keys, then press Control+S.

Play Selected FMV Sequence
Enable Cheat mode and Cheat Keys, then press Control+A.

View Game Statistics
Enable Cheat mode and Cheat Keys, then press Control+D.

Turn Around
Enable Cheat mode and Cheat Keys, then press Control+F.

Spawn NPC or Creature
Enable Cheat mode. During game, press Control+Tab. Type one of the following codes, then press Enter and Control+Tab.

Gibberling
CLUAConsole:CreateCreature(Ray)

Khalid
CLUAConsole:CreateCreature(Khalid)

Jaheira
CLUAConsole:CreateCreature(Jaheir)

Noober
CLUAConsole:CreateCreature(Noober)

Rufie
CLUAConsole:CreateCreature(Rufie)

Flaming Fist Mercenary
CLUAConsole:CreateCreature(Flame)

Angelo
CLUAConsole:CreateCreature(Angelo)

Guard
CLUAConsole:CreateCreature(Guard)

Ogre Mage
CLUAConsole:CreateCreature(Droth)

Flaming Fist Wizard
CLUAConsole:CreateCreature(Flamwiz)

Dilos
CLUAConsole:CreateCreature(Flma13)

Drizzt
CLUAConsole:CreateCreature(Drizzt)

Elminster
CLUAConsole:CreateCreature(Elmins)

Create Selected Item
Enable Cheat mode. During game, press Control+Tab. Type one of the following codes and press Enter and Control+Tab.

+1 CHR Manual
BOOK07

+1 CON Manual
BOOK03

+1 DEX Manual
BOOK05

+1 INT Manual
BOOK06

+1 STR Manual
BOOK04

+1 WIS Manual
BOOK08

Acid Arrow
AROW04

Agannazar's Scorcher
SCRL1B

Agni Mani Necklace
AMUL06

Amulet of Metaspell Influence (+1 2nd Level Spell)
AMUL16

Amulet of Protection+1
AMUL14

Andar Gem
MISC22

Angel Skin Ring
RING16

Animate Dead
SCRL2D

Ankheg Plate Mail
PLAT06

Ankheg Shell
MISC12

Antidote
POTN20

Antidote
POTN32

Aquamarine Gem
MISC33

Armor
SCRL67

Arrow
AROW01

Arrow+1
AROW02

Arrow+2
AROW11

Arrow+2 (Different Graphic)
AROW1A

Arrow of Biting
AROW05

Arrow of Detonation
AROW06

Arrow of Fire
AROW08

Arrow of Ice
AROW09

Arrow of Piercing
AROW10

Arrow of Slaying
AROW03

Arrow or Dispelling
AROW07

Bandit Scalp
MISC86

Bastard Sword
SW1H01

Bastard Sword+1
SW1H02

Bastard Sword+1, Shapeshifters
SW1H03

Battle Axe
AX1H01

Battle Axe+1
AX1H02

Battle Axe+2
AX1H03

Black Opal
MISC38

Blindness
SCRL71

Bloodstone Amulet
AMUL13

Bloodstone Gem
MISC20

Bloodstone Ring
RING15

Bluestone Necklace
AMUL05

Blur
SCRL85

Bolt
BOLT01

Bolt+1
BOLT02

Bolt+2
BOLT06

Bolt of Biting
BOLT04

Bolt of Lightning
BOLT03

Bolt of Polymorphing
BOLT05

Boo (GO FOR THE EYES BOO!)
MISC84

Boots of Avoidance
BOOT04

Boots of Grounding
BOOT05

Boots of Speed
BOOT01

Boots of Stealth
BOOT02

Boots of the North
BOOT03

Bottle of Wine
MISC61

Bowl of Water Elemental Control
MISC53

Bracers
BRAC05

Bracers of Archery
BRAC04

Bracers of Defense AC 6
BRAC03

Bracers of Defense AC 7
BRAC02

Bracers of Defense AC 8
BRAC01

Broken Armor
MISC58

Broken Miscellaneous
MISC59

Broken Shield
MISC57

Broken Weapon
MISC56

Buckler
SHLD08

Buckler
SHLD09

Buckler
SHLD10

Bullet
BULL01

Bullet+1
BULL02

Bullet+2
BULL03

Chainmail
CHAN01

Chainmail+1
CHAN02

Chainmail+2
CHAN03

Charm Person
SCRL69

Chew Toy
MISC63

Child's Body
MISC54

Chill Touch
SCRL82

Chromatic Orb
SCRL83

Chrysoberyl Gem
MISC30

Clairvoyance
SCRL1D

Cloak of Balduran
CLCK05

Cloak of Displacement
CLCK03

Cloak of Non-Detection
CLCK06

Cloak of Protection +1
CLCK01

Cloak of Protection +2
CLCK02

Cloak of the Wolf
CLCK04

Cloudkill
SCRL2E

Club
BLUN01

Color Spray
SCRL70

Composite Long Bow
BOW01

Composite Long Bow +1
BOW02

Cone of Cold
SCRL2F

Confusion
SCRL1U

Contaminated Iron
MISC87

Cure Critical Wounds
SCRL61

Cure Serious Wounds
SCRL56

Cursed Scroll of Stupidity
SCRL18

Cursed Scroll of Weakness
SCRL10

Dagger
DAGG01

Dagger +1
DAGG02

Dagger +2
DAGG03

Dagger +2, Longtooth
DAGG04

Dart
DART01

Dart +1
DART02

Dart of Stunning
DART03

Dart of Wounding
DART04

Dead Cat
MISC62

Delorna's Statue
MISC70

Detect Evil
SCRL86

Detect Invisibility
SCRL87

Diamond
MISC42

Dimension Door
SCRL1V

Dire Charm
SCRL1S

Dispel Magic
SCRL1E

Duke Eltan's Body
MISC55

Eagle Bow
BOW08

Elixir of Health
POTN17

Emerald
MISC43

Female Body
MISC79

Fire Agate Gem
MISC16

Fire Opal Ring
RING18

Fireball
SCRL1G

Flail
BLUN02

Flail +1
BLUN03

Flame Arrow
SCRL1F

Flame Strike
SCRL62

Flamedance Ring
RING17

Free Action
SCRL58

Friends
SCRL72

Full Plate Mail
PLAT04

Full Plate Mail +1
PLAT05

Garnet Gem
MISC34

Gauntlets of Dexterity
BRAC07

Gauntlets of Fumbling BRAC08	**Helmet** HELM01	**Light Crossbow** XBOW04
Gauntlets of Ogre Power BRAC06	**Helshara's Artifact Fragment** MISC69	**Light Crossbow +1** XBOW05
Gauntlets of Weapon Expertise BRAC10	**Hold Person** SCRL1I	**Light Crossbow of Speed** XBOW06
Gauntlets of Weapon Skill BRAC09	**Horn Coral Gem** MISC35	**Lightning Bolt** SCRL1K
Ghost Armor SCRL1T	**Horror** SCRL89	**Lock of Nymph's Hair** MISC51
Ghoul Touch SCRL1C	**Identify** SCRL75	**Long Bow** BOW03
Girdle BELT01	**Idol** MISC48	**Long Bow +1** BOW04
Girdle of Bluntness BELT03	**Improved Invisibility** SCRL1Y	**Long Bow of Marksmanship** BOW07
Girdle of Piercing BELT04	**Infravision** SCRL76	**Long Sword** SW1H04
Girdle of Sex Change BELT05	**Invisibility** SCRL90	**Long Sword +1** SW1H05
Gold Necklace AMUL10	**Iol Gem** MISC26	**Long Sword +2** SW1H06
Gold Piece MISC07	**Jade Ring** RING13	**Luck** SCRL93
Gold Ring RING10	**Jasper Gem** MISC23	**Lynx Eye Gem** MISC17
Golden Girdle BELT02	**Key to River Plug** MISC83	**Mace** BLUN04
Golden Pantaloons MISC47	**Kings Tears** MISC44	**Mace +1** BLUN05
Grease SCRL66	**Knock** SCRL91	**Magic Missile** SCRL77
Greenstone Ring RING14	**Know Alignment** SCRL92	**Magical Book** BOOK01
Halberd HALB01	**Laeral's Tear Necklace (3,000 gp)** AMUL12	**Male Body** MISC80
Halberd +1 HALB02	**Large Shield** SHLD05	**Medium Shield** SHLD03
Halberd +2 HALB03	**Large Shield** SHLD15	**Medium Shield** SHLD13
Haste SCRL1H	**Large Shield** SHLD16	**Medium Shield** SHLD14
Heavy Crossbow XBOW01	**Large Shield +1** SHLD06	**Medium Shield +1** SHLD04
Heavy Crossbow +1 XBOW02	**Large Shield +1, +4 vs. Missiles** SHLD07	**Melf's Acid Arrow** SCRL95
Heavy Crossbow of Accuracy XBOW03	**Larloch's Minor Drain** SCRL84	**Melicamp the Chicken** MISC49
Helm of Balduran HELM07	**Leather Armor** LEAT01	**Minor Globe of Invulnerability** SCRL1Z
Helm of Charm Protection HELM06	**Leather Armor +1** LEAT02	**Mirror Image** SCRL96
Helm of Defense HELM04	**Leather Armor +2** LEAT03	**Mithril Chain Mail +4** CHAN06
Helm of Glory HELM03	**Letter** SCRL2I	**Monster Summoning I** SCRL1L
Helm of Infravision HELM05	**Letter** SCRL2J	**Monster Summoning II** SCRL2A
Helm of Opposite Alignment HELM02	**Letter** SCRL3D	**Monster Summoning III** SCRL2G

Moonbar Gem MISC40	**Potion of Freedom** POTN45	**Protection from Fire** SCRL06
Moonblade SW1H13	**Potion of Frost Giant Strength** POTN04	**Protection from Magic** SCRL07
Moonstone Gem MISC27	**Potion of Genius** POTN29	**Protection from Normal Missiles** SCRL1N
Morning Star BLUN06	**Potion of Healing** POTN08	**Protection from Petrification** SCRL15
Morning Star +1 BLUN07	**Potion of Healing** POTN25	**Protection from Petrification** SCRL73
Mulahey's Holy Symbol MISC85	**Potion of Heroism** POTN09	**Protection from Poison** SCRL08
Necklace AMUL02	**Potion of Hill Giant Strength** POTN03	**Protection from Undead** SCRL09
Necklace of Missiles AMUL01	**Potion of Infravision** POTN30	**Quarterstaff** STAF01
Neutralize Poison SCRL59	**Potion of Insight** POTN43	**Quarterstaff +1** STAF02
Non-Detection SCRL1M	**Potion of Insulation** POTN31	**Rabbit's Foot** MISC88
Normal Book BOOK09	**Potion of Invisibility** POTN10	**Rainbow Obsidian Necklace** AMUL07
Nymph Cloak CLCK07	**Potion of Invulnerability** POTN11	**Raise Dead** SCRL63
Oil of Fiery Burning POTN13	**Potion of Invulnerability** POTN40	**Red Potion** POTN15
Oil of Speed POTN14	**Potion of Magic Blocking** POTN33	**Resist Fear** SCRL94
Oil of Speed POTN23	**Potion of Magic Protection** POTN34	**Ring** RING01
Pearl MISC36	**Potion of Magic Shielding** POTN35	**Ring of Animal Friendship** RING03
Pearl Necklace AMUL11	**Potion of Master Thievery** POTN36	**Ring of Clumsiness** RING04
Plate Mail +1 PLAT02	**Potion of Mind Focusing** POTN37	**Ring of Energy** RING20
Plate Mail Armor PLAT01	**Potion of Mirrored Eyes** POTN38	**Ring of Fire Resistance** RING02
Potion of Absorption POTN18	**Potion of Perception** POTN39	**Ring of Folly** RING23
Potion of Agility POTN19	**Potion of Power** POTN41	**Ring of Free Action** RING09
Potion of Clarity POTN21	**Potion of Regeneration** POTN42	**Ring of Holiness** RING22
Potion of Cloud Giant Strength POTN06	**Potion of Stone Form** POTN46	**Ring of Infravision** RING21
Potion of Cold Resistance POTN22	**Potion of Stone Giant Strength** POTN12	**Ring of Invisibility** RING05
Potion of Defense POTN24	**Potion of Storm Giant Strength** POTN07	**Ring of Protection +1** RING06
Potion of Explosions POTN26	**Potion of Strength** POTN44	**Ring of Protection +2** RING07
Potion of Fire Giant Strength POTN05	**Protection from Acid** SCRL03	**Ring of Wizardry** RING08
Potion of Fire Resistance POTN02	**Protection from Cold** SCRL04	**Rogue Stone** MISC45
Potion of Firebreath POTN27	**Protection from Electricity** SCRL05	**Ruby Ring** RING19
Potion of Fortitude POTN28	**Protection from Evil** SCRL78	**Samuel (Body)** MISC13

Sclmltar +3, Frostbrand
SW1H15

Shadow Armor
LEAT08

Shadow Door
SCRL2H

Shandon Gem
MISC32

Shield
SCRL79

Shield Amulet
AMUL15

Shocking Grasp
SCRL80

Short Bow
BOW05

Short Bow +1
BOW06

Short Sword
SW1H07

Short Sword +1
SW1H08

Short Sword +2
SW1H09

Short Sword of Backstabbing
SW1H10

Silver Necklace
AMUL09

Silver Ring
RING11

Skull
MISC50

Skull Trap
SCRL1P

Skydrop Gem
MISC21

Sleep
SCRL81

Sling
SLNG01

Sling +1
SLNG02

Slow
SCRL1O

Small Shield
SHLD01

Small Shield
SHLD11

Small Shield
SHLD12

Small Shield +1
SHLD02

Spear
SPER01

Spear +1
SPER02

Spear +3, Backbiter
SPER03

Spell Book
BOOK02

Spell Scroll
SCRL02

Sphene Gem
MISC37

Spider Body
MISC60

Spider's Bane
SW2H06

Splint Mail
CHAN04

Splint Mail +1
CHAN05

Star Diopside Gem
MISC31

Star Saphire
MISC41

Stinking Cloud
SCRL97

Strength
SCRL98

Studded Leather Armor
LEAT04

Studded Leather Armor +1
LEAT05

Studded Leather Armor +2
LEAT07

Studded Leather Armor +2, Missile Attraction
LEAT06

Studded Necklace with Zios Gems
AMUL04

Sunstone Gem
MISC18

Tchazar Gem
MISC24

Telescope
MISC64

The Candle
MISC74

The Claw of Kazgaroth
MISC72

The Horn of Kazgaroth
MISC73

Throwing Axe
AX1H04

Throwing Axe +2
AX1H05

Throwing Dagger
DAGG05

Tiger Cowrie Shell Necklace
AMUL08

Turquoise Gem
MISC19

Two-Handed Sword
SW2H01

Two-Handed Sword +1
SW2H02

Two-Handed Sword, Berserking
SW2H03

Vampiric Touch
SCRL1Q

Violet Potion
POTN16

Wand of Fear
WAND02

Wand of Fire
WAND05

Wand of Frost
WAND06

Wand of Lightning
WAND07

Wand of Magic Missiles
WAND03

Wand of Monster Summoning
WAND10

Wand of Paralyzation
WAND04

Wand of Polymorphing
WAND09

Wand of Sleep
WAND08

Wand of the Heavens
WAND11

War Hammer
HAMM01

War Hammer +1
HAMM02

War Hammer +2
HAMM03

Water Opal
MISC39

Waterstar Gem
MISC28

Web
SCRL99

Winter Wolf Pelt
MISC01

Wraith Form
SCRL1R

Wyvern Head
MISC52

Ziose Gem
MISC29

Zircon Gem
MISC25

BALDUR'S GATE II: SHADOWS OF AMN

Access Cheat Mode
Backup the file <l>Baldur.ini<l> then open it with any text editor. Under the Program Options heading, type Debug Mode=1. Now start the game and press Control+Space to bring up the console.

XP for Selected Character or Group, Cap Is 2950000
Enable Cheat mode and type CLUAConsole:Set-CurrentXP(amount).

Gold
Enable Cheat mode and type CLUAConsole:-AddGold(amount).

Reveal Map
Enable Cheat mode and type CLUAConsole:-ExploreArea().

Max Stats
Enable Cheat mode and press Control+Shift+8.

Heal a Character
Enable Cheat mode and press Control+R.

Jump to Mouse Cursor Location
Enable Cheat mode and press Control+J.

Heal Party
Enable Cheat mode and press Control+T.

Kill Person or Monster Cursor Is On
Enable Cheat mode and press Control+Y.

Change Armor Class of Selected Character
Enable Cheat mode and press Control+1.

Change the Model of Selected Character
Enable Cheat mode and press Control+6 and 7.

BANG! GUNSHIP ELITE

Level 2
At the New Game menu, type your player name as mayday.

Level 3
At the New Game menu, type your player name as victory.

Level 4
At the New Game menu, type your player name as challenger.

Level 5
At the New Game menu, type your player name as azimuth.

Level 6
At the New Game menu, type your player name as revealed.

Level 7
At the New Game menu, type your player name as stoneage.

Level 8
At the New Game menu, type your player name as warfare.

Level 9
At the New Game menu, type your player name as oxygen.

Level 10
At the New Game menu, type your player name as skyhigh.

Level 11
At the New Game menu, type your player name as sunshine.

Level 12
At the New Game menu, type your player name as blowup.

Level 13
At the New Game menu, type your player name as neuftrois.

Level 14
At the New Game menu, type your player name as baracuda.

Level 15
At the New Game menu, type your player name as giveaway.

Level 16
At the New Game menu, type your player name as waterfall.

Level 17
At the New Game menu, type your player name as seventeen.

Level 18
At the New Game menu, type your player name as neartheend.

Level 19
At the New Game menu, type your player name as y2k.

Activate God Mode Control at In-Game Cheat Menu
At the New Game menu, type your player name as dogmode.

Infinite Shield Control
At the New Game menu, type your player name as stoneskin.

Enemy Shot Control
At the New Game menu, type your player name as pianist.

Infinite Boost Control
At the New Game menu, type your player name as boooost.

String Input in Cheat Menu
At the New Game menu, type your player name as kinput.

Infinite Flux Beam Ammo
At the New Game menu, type your player name as reflux.

Infinite Phase Shift Cannon Ammo
At the New Game menu, type your player name as greens.

Infinite Hellfire Ammo
At the New Game menu, type your player name as firecrackers.

Infinite Titans Hammer Ammo
At the New Game menu, type your player name as nails.

Infinite Magma Cannon Ammo
At the New Game menu, type your player name as volcano.

Infinite Electronic Laser Ammo
At the New Game menu, type your player name as lightning.

Infinite Stasis Cannon Ammo
At the New Game menu, type your player name as staystill.

Infinite Sonic Cannon Ammo
At the New Game menu, type your player name as listener.

Infinite Plasma Cannon Ammo
At the New Game menu, type your player name as bloody.

Infinite All Weapons Ammo
At the New Game menu, type your player name as stormfire.

Infinite Ammo on No Weapon
At the New Game menu, type your player name as getridof.

BATTLE BEAST

Access Cheater Menu
At the Battle Beast Order Form, type YOYOYO.

Access All Bonus Doors
At the Cheater menu, type =D259

Beast Morphing Off
At the Cheater menu, type EATEE.

Toggle Flying in Bonus Rooms
At the Cheater menu, type EHRTRR.

Fight All Opponents
At the Cheater menu, type ERHNE.

Weaken Toadman
At the Cheater menu, type ERHYHRLY.

Activate 2 Out of 3 Bouts
At the Cheater menu, type ITIHFO.

Engage Auto-Flying in Lab
At the Cheater menu, type OAOAEIOA.

Double Bonus Room Time
At the Cheater menu, type OFOVH.

Activate Tadpole Attacks in Lab
At the Cheater menu, type OIVNNFOF.

God Mode in Bonus Rooms
At the Cheater menu, type ORUFO.

BATTLE CHESS

Distraction Piece
During a game, type DISTRACTIONPIECE.

BATTLEZONE

Unlimited Shields
bzbody

Unlimited Pilots and Resources
bzfree

Full Map
bzradar

Unlimited Ammo
bztnt

Comsat Link Without Having to Power or Build One
bzview

BATTLEZONE 2

Cheat Mode
During a game, hold Control and press ~ to display the console screen.

Infinite Ammo
Activate Cheat mode, type game.cheat bztnt, and press Enter.

All Units on the Map and Radar
Activate Cheat mode, type game.cheat bzradar, and press Enter.

Infinite Shields
Activate Cheat mode, type game.cheat bzbody, and press Enter.

Infinite Pilots and Resources
Activate Cheat mode, type game.cheat bzfree, and press Enter.

Instant Comsat Link
Activate Cheat mode, type game.cheat bzview, and press Enter.

Win the Mission
Activate Cheat mode, type ai.winmission, and press Enter.

Play as ISDF After Mission 14
Activate Cheat mode, type play isdf, and press Enter.

Play as Scion After Mission 14
Activate Cheat mode, type play scion, and press Enter.

BATTLEZONE: THE RED ODYSSEY

Cheat Mode
During a game, hold Shift+Alt to display the console screen.

God Mode
Activate Cheat mode, type tebuffy, and press Enter.

Infinite Ammo
Activate Cheat mode, type tedeadite, and press Enter.

Full Map
Activate Cheat mode, type tedontdie, and press Enter.

Satellite Without Com Tower
Activate Cheat mode, type tenerd, and press Enter.

Infinite Shields
Activate Cheat mode, type terat, and press Enter.

BEAST WARS

Enable All Missions Except Rescue
When at the Logo Start/Exit screen, type ilikeiteasy. If you did it correctly, you will hear "Beast Wars!"

Enable Unlimited Special Weapon Uses
When at the Logo Start/Exit screen, type weloveithot. If you did it correctly, you will hear "Beast Wars!"

Enable Access to All Rescue Missions
When at the Logo Start/Exit screen, type rescueme. If you did it correctly, you will hear "Beast Wars!"

BEAVIS AND BUTT-HEAD DO U

Cheat Mode
Type gosanta while playing or at any screen. Then while playing, press F2 to bring up a Cheat menu.

BERNIE BOULDER

Level 2 Password
GTOUF

Level 3 Password
GNOMO

Level 4 Password
FNUFI

Level 5 Password
TRULK

Level 6 Password
VOLTO

Level 7 Password
WUMON

Level 8 Password
OLUHK

Level 9 Password
ZUMBL

Level 10 Password
BNOK

Level 11 Password
DRIGO

Level 12 Password
ACIDA

Level 13 Password
BUMSI

Level 14 Password
ALOSA

Level 15 Password
KNUFF

Level 16 Password
NILOU

Level 17 Password
MUBLO

Level 18 Password
BTAGM

Level 19 Password
JUMER

Level 20 Password
KRUBO

Level 21 Password
KREWA

Level 22 Password
GORFA

Level 23 Password
KNIRL

Level 24 Password
HRNZF

Level 25 Password
HULAM

Level 26 Password
MOIRA

Level 27 Password
KAYOM

Level 28 Password
ZIRFA

Level 29 Password
ORNIM

Level 30 Password
FROBI

Level 31 Password
QUOLA

Level 32 Password
ZNALG

Level 33 Password
EXIRO

Level 34 Password
NOLIR

Level 35 Password
TZULI

Level 36 Password
ROLOK

Level 37 Password
EPOLM

Level 38 Password
URLIM

Level 39 Password
KLIMB

Level 40 Password
PLOFO

Level 41 Password
HATZI

BIRD HUNTER: WILD WINGS EDITION

Go to Nearest Flock of Birds
wwflock

Go to Nearest Covey of Upland Birds
wwcovey

Go to Nearest Animal
wwcallin

Birds Do Not Fear You
wwnofear

Money
During a game, press F3 and type SYNCASH.

All Adventures
During a game, press F3 and type SYNADV.

All Characters
During a game, press F3 and type SYNHEAL.

Province Characters to Fly
During a game, press F3 and type SYNFLY.

BLACK AND WHITE

April Fools!
Set your computer's clock to April Fool's Day and your creature leaves happy face footprints on the ground.

Infinite Food and Wood
Instead of activating a food or wood miracle above the appropriate location, place your hand above the door and continuously tap the action button. The miracle never runs out and you receive enormous amounts at a time.

Fun Day at the Beach
During the game, press F2. There are two islands on the screen. The smaller of the two islands have two Beach Balls, two bowling balls, and a set of bowling pins. Look to the rear of the smaller island to find the toys.

BLACK DAHLIA

P8 Stained Glass Puzzle
leadhead

P11 Winslow's Safe Puzzle
masterlock

P14 Wooden House/Lockbox Puzzle
loghouse

P15 Dresser in Louie's Loft Puzzle
turnkey

P21 Raven Room Circular Table Puzzle
arthur

P22 Seal Puzzle
ringding

P26 Bag of Runes Puzzle
gemstone

P27 Dream Archway Puzzle
cancan

P32 Pressure Gauges Puzzle
pressure

P34 Sewer Levers/Bars Puzzle
barbell

P35 Raven Room Door Plates Puzzle
triangle

P36 Candlestick in Raven Room Puzzle
nimble

P38 Sun/Planets/Door Puzzle
sunspot

P39 Gearshift Puzzle: Treasure Door 1
ladybug

P40 Key Puzzle: Treasure Door 2
keypunch

P41 Half-A-Gear Puzzle: Treasure Door 3
gearoil

P44 Main Chamber Column Puzzle
temple

P46 Slider Puzzle
blockhead

P47 Stone Blocks Puzzle
rock33

P59 Luggage Crate on Train Puzzle
boxtop

P67 Cane Lock Puzzle
candycane

P68 Telegram Puzzle
teleport

P73 Telescope Puzzle
peeper

P76 Cuckoo Clock Puzzle
bongo

BLADE OF DARKNESS

Note that you may need to complete the game before you can activate these codes.

Maximum HP and Stamina
almighty

All Weapons
tothepoint

All Items
itemsgalore

All Keys for Current Level
doorsnomore

Level Skip
levelend

Maximum Level Gain
levelheaded

BLADE RUNNER

Cheat Mode
Play a game at Easy difficulty. As soon as the spinner lands at the pet store, click on McCoy and load a new game at Easy difficulty again. You gain infinite money, you can more easily kill enemies, and it becomes harder for you to be killed.

BLAIR WITCH PROJECT VOL 2: COFFIN ROCK

God Mode
During a game, press F10 and type IWORK-FORGOD.

All Weapons
During a game, press F10 and type GETINTO-MYBELLY.

Big Head Mode
During a game, press F10 and type BIGHEAD.

Gratuitous Dismemberment
During a game, press F10 and type GIBN-PLENTY.

Terminator Skin
During a game, press F10 and type T2000.

Restore Health
During a game, press F10 and type GIVEMEFAITH.

Invisibility
During a game, press F10 and type NOD3D.

Freeze Enemies
During a game, press F10 and type HELL-FREEZEOVER.

Get Shotgun
During a game, press F10 and type BIGSTICK-OFDEATH.

Get Crossbow
During a game, press F10 and type MEDIUMRARE.

Get Dynamite
During a game, press F10 and type GOOD-TIMESMAN.

Get Flamethrower
During a game, press F10 and type BURNY-OURASSOFF.

Get Tommygun
During a game, press F10 and type MEETMY-PALTOMMY.

Get Elephant Gun
During a game, press F10 and type SMILEYNOMORE.

Get Charge Radiance Emitter
During a game, press F10 and type SUNOFGOD.

100 Bullets
During a game, press F10 and type IAMAW-IMPFORTHIS.

Restore Flashlight Battery
During a game, press F10 and type RECHARGE.

Gas Mask
During a game, press F10 and type THEDOGFARTED.

Night Vision Goggles
During a game, press F10 and type ICANSEE.

Get Silver Bullets
During a game, press F10 and type WWBE-WARE.

Get Lith Bullets
During a game, press F10 and type VAMPBEWARE.

Get Mercy Bullets
During a game, press F10 and type DEMON-BEWARE.

Easy Difficulty
During a game, press F10 and type ISUCK.

Hard Difficulty
During a game, press F10 and type IRULE.

Easy Combat
During a game, press F10 and type COMBAT-ISSCARY.

Easy Puzzles
During a game, press F10 and type PUZZLE-SARESCARY.

Crash the Game
During a game, press F10 and type INSTANTCRASH.

Create Storm (Even Inside)
During a game, press F10 and type THUN-DERSTORM.

Snowflakes Fall
During a game, press F10 and type SNOWSTORM.

Flaming Ammo
During a game, press F10 and type FLAME-ONASTICK.

Slow or Speed Up Time
During a game, press F10 and type TIME.

Darker Graphics
During a game, press F10 and type DARK.

BLAIR WITCH VOLUME 1: RUSTIN PARR DEMO

God Mode
During a game, press F10 and type godgames.

More Ammo
During a game, press F10 and type moreammo.

Hidden Message
During a game, press F10 and type goldmode.

BLAIR WITCH PROJECT VOL. 2: COFFIN ROCK

God Mode
During a game, press F10 and type godgames.

All Weapons
During a game, press F10 and type winblows.

Auto-Aim Weapons
During a game, press F10 and type autoaim.

Get Skeleton Key
During a game, press F10 and type skeletonkey.

Get More Ammo
moreammo

Gratuitous Dismemberment
goremode

BLAIR WITCH VOLUME 3: THE ELLY KEDWARD TALE

God Mode
godgames

All Weapons and Ammo
winblows

Get Skeleton Key
skeletonkey

More Ammo
moreammo

Elephant Gun
dumbogun

Get Flaming Tip Arrows
buringstake

Rains Outside
thunderstorm

Snows Outside
snowstorm

Big Head Mode
bighead

Restores Health
healme

Get 500 Silver Bullets
silver

Get 500 Aqua Vampire Bullets
aqua

Get 500 Mercury Bullets
mercury

Different Hat
oldhat

Gas Mask
ifarted

Enable Bigboom Code
headofhorrors

Instant Kill
bigboom

Renew Battery
recharge

Secret Message
goldmode

Shotgun and/or 500 Shells
shotgunshell

Stranger Wears Old Hat
oldhat

Summons Baron Samedi
baronsaturday

Toggles Enemy Freezing
freezer

Toggles Gratuitous Dismemberment
goremode

Tommy Gun
gimmecrap

BLEIFUSS FUN

All Tracks
At the main menu, type surmule.

All Cars
At the main menu, type slasktratt.

Extra View
At the main menu, type svinpole.

Four Wheels Only
At the main menu, type skunk.

BLOOD

View Music Video
Look for the Music folder on the disk, then, double click the *Typeonegative* file.

God Mode
While playing, press T and type I wanna be like Kevin, cap in my ass, or mpkfa.

Disable God Mode
While playing, press T and type no cap in my ass.

100 Percent Health
While playing, press T and type clarice.

200 Percent Health
While playing, press T and type spork.

200 Percent Health, Diving Suit
While playing, press T and type cousteau.

200 Percent Health, on Fire
While playing, press T and type krueger.

200 Percent Armor
While playing, press T and type griswold.

All Items
While playing, press T and type montana or satchel.

All Keys
While playing, press T and type keymaster.

All Weapons
While playing, press T and type idaho.

All Weapons and Infinite Ammo
While playing, press T and type lara croft or hong kong. The game doesn't recognize this as a cheat, but it works.

Clipping
While playing, press T and type eva galli.

Display Frame Rate
While playing, press T and type rate.

Display Full Map
While playing, press T and type goonies.

Drunk Mode
While playing, press T and type jojo.

Invisibility
While playing, press T and type onering.

Allow Two of Same Weapon
While playing, press T and type bunz.

Jump Higher
While playing, press T and type funnyshoes.

Level Skip
While playing, press T and type calgon, luigi, or mario.

Level Skip and Cheats Disabled
While playing, press T and type spielberg.

Drunk Mode and No Weapons
While playing, press T and type fork broussard.

Suicide
While playing, press T and type edmark or kevorkian.

Suicide by Fire
While playing, press T and type mcgee.

Temporary Blindness
While playing, press T and type sterno.

BLOOD 2: THE CHOSEN

All Items
Press T and type mpgoshopping.

All Weapons
Press T and type mpkfa.

Full Ammo
Press T and type mpammo.

Triple Damage
Press T and type mpherkermur.

God Mode
Press T and type mpgod.

25 Armor
Press T and type mpward.

25 Health Points
Press T and type mpnicenurse.

100 Armor
Press T and type mpnewcroward.

300 Health Points
Press T and type mpreallynicenurse.

Assault Rifle
Press T and type mpassaultrifle.

Beretta
Press T and type mpberetta.

Flare Gun
Press T and type mpflaregun.

Howitzer
Press T and type mphowitzer.

Laser Rifle
Press T and type mplaserrifle.

Shotgun
Press T and type mpshotgun.

Sniper Rifle
Press T and type mpsniperrifle.

Mini-Gun
Press T and type mpminigun.

Sub-Machine Gun
Press T and type mpsubmachinegun. Re-type this to put a weapon in the other hand.

Become Caleb
Press T and type mpcaleb.

Become Gabriella
Press T and type mpgabby.

Become Ishmael
Press T and type mpishmael.

Become Ophelia
Press T and type mpophelia.

Bug Buster
Press T and type mpbugbuster.

Full Health
Press T and type mphealthy.

Full Armor
Press T and type mparmor.

Increase Power and Gore
Press T and type mpbeefcake.

Invisibility
Press T and type mptakeoffshoes.

Kill All Monsters
Press T and type mpkillemall.

Life Leach
Press T and type mplifeleach.

Napalm Cannon
Press T and type mpnapalmcannon.

Display Coordinates
Press T and type mpwhereami.

Hide Coordinates
Press T and type mphideme.

Change Camera Angles
Press T and type mpcamera.

Change Lighting
Press T and type mplightscape.

Clipping On
Press T and type mpclip.

Clipping Off
Press T and type mpnoclip.

Select Weapon
Press T and type mpbeansofcoolness.

Singularity Generator
Press T and type mpsingularity.

The Orb
Press T and type mptheorb.

Tesla Cannon
Press T and type mpteslacannon.

Voodoo Doll
Press T and type mpvoodoo.

Will Power-Up
Press T and type mpcarbonfiber.

Increase Power

Press T and type mpstronger[x]. (Replace [x] with a number from 1 to 5).

Increase Speed

Press T and type mpspeedup[x]. (Replace [x] with a number from 1 to 5).

Message 1

Press T and type mptotaro.

Message 2

Press T and type mpscorpio.

Message 3

Press T and type mpgoble.

Unknown

Press T and type mpsuperzug.

BLOOD OMEN: LEGACY OF KAIN

Full Health

During a game, press Up, Right, Attack, Action, Up, Down, Right, Left.

Full Magic

During a game, press Right, Right, Attack, Action, Up, Down, Right, Left.

Preview Dark Diary

During a game, press Left, Right, Attack, Action, Up, Down, Right, Left.

BLOODBATH

All Weapons

badass

God Mode

sgtrock

BRIAN LARA CRICKET

Always Rains During Test Match

In Classic Match, type CATSDOGS.

Super Batsmen

In Classic Match, type CMBRLARA.

All Classic Matches Enabled

In Classic Match, type FINISHED.

Unbreakable Wickets

In Classic Match, type NONOTOUT.

Fast Match

In Classic Match, type TIMEWARP.

Large Cricket Ball

In Classic Match, type MEDICINE.

Make Fielders Drop Catches

In Classic Match, type SLIPPERY.

Use Left-Control and Alt to Rotate the Mouse for Free Look

In Classic Match, type SETMOUSE.

Add World XI Team

In Classic Match, type OLDTIMER.

Beach Around the Field on Friendly Matches

In Classic Match, type SUNSHINE.

Open Classic Matches

In Classic Match, type SILLYBOY.

First Seven Classic Matches

In Classic Match, type COPYCATS.

BOARDER ZONE

Unlock Hard Tracks

Type elee or lee at a menu.

Unknown

Type exterminaattori at a menu.

Debug Menu

Type imhotepmaailmojentuhoaja at a menu. Then, press E during a game to bring up the Debug menu.

Screen Shot

Type seivaavideograbbi at a menu.

Guide Boarder

Type hiihtoope or ope at a menu.

BOWLING U.S.A.

Perfect 300 Game

Start a game and press F3 to display the Practice menu. Remove all the pins and resume the game. Now, throw gutter balls in every frame and the game scores them as strikes.

BRAVEHEART

Destroy All Opponents

Press Delete in 3D mode and type bannockburn.

All Cheats

Press Delete in 3D mode and type sesquipidilian.

All Walls Breached

Press Delete in 3D mode and type bastille day.

Disable Blood

Press Delete in 3D mode and type heamorrhage.

All Troops Retreat

Press Delete in 3D mode and type bucks fizz.

Troops are Harder to Defeat

Press Delete in 3D mode and type steve reeves.

All Buildings on Fire

Press Delete in 3D mode and type dresden.

Kill Your Own Troops

Press Delete in 3D mode and type the five hundred.

Disable the Camera

Press Delete in 3D mode and type killcam.

BUBBLE BOBBLE NOSTALGIA

Run Faster

faster

Bubbles Fly Farther

farbubbles

Bubbles Fly Faster

powerspit

Blow Bubbles Faster

blowmachine

Combo Cheat: Bubbles

equipment

All Enemies Turn into Crystals

countdown

All Three Rings

champions

Add Lightning to Your Bubbles

zeus

Pass Three Levels

travel

Invisibility

hidden

Fire Breath

dangerous

Episode I: Level 10

pretty good

Episode I: Level 20

take it easy

Episode I: Level 30

steel spring

Episode I: Level 40

smile

Episode I: Level 50

its a magic

Episode I: Level 60

you scared

Episode I: Level 70

success

Episode I: Level 80

relax

Episode I: Level 90

dont cry

Episode II: Level 110

new journey

Episode II: Level 120

go

Episode II: Level 130

house

Episode II: Level 140

cocktail

Episode II: Level 150

half

Episode II: Level 160

hard trick

Episode II: Level 170

forest

Episode II: Level 180

cup of cofee

Episode II: Level 190

finish

BUBBLE HERO 2

One Player: Stage 2

green, yellow, blue, yellow

One Player: Stage 3

red, green, blue, yellow

One Player: Stage 4

blue, green, yellow, blue

One Player: Stage 5

blue, yellow, red, green

One Player: Stage 6

red, yellow, red, blue

One Player: Stage 7

yellow, green, green, red

Two Player: Stage 2

yellow, blue, red, blue

Two Player: Stage 3

green, yellow, red, blue

Two Player: Stage 4

red, yellow, blue, red

Two Player: Stage 5

red, blue, green, yellow

Two Player: Stage 6

green, blue, green, red

Two Player: Stage 7

blue, yellow, yellow, green

BUGRIDERS

Constant Energy
At the Game Resume menu, type altoparlan.

View Credits
At the Game Resume menu, type creditroll.

Large Bugs
At the Game Resume menu, type largebugs.

Small Bugs
At the Game Resume menu, type smallbugs.

Stop Timer
At the Game Resume menu, type trssensinc.

CABELA'S BIG GAME HUNTER 2

$2,000
At the Catalog screen, press Alt+Control+M.

Display the Frame Rate
While playing, press Alt+Control+F.

Full Health
While playing, press Alt+Control+H.

Weapon Sighting Coordinates
At the target range, press Alt+Control+T. Fire to display coordinates in an X-Y format. Adjust the coordinates to 0-0 and the weapon is now sighted correctly.

Toggle Rifle Sight
While playing, press Alt+Control+J.

Lightning
While playing, press Alt+Control+L.

Activate the Scope
While playing, press Alt+Control+V.

Wind
While playing, press Alt+Control+W.

Snow
While playing, press Alt+Control+S.

Rain
While playing, press Alt+Control+R.

Status of the Hunting Field
While playing, press Alt+Control+B. The green areas indicate big game, yellow areas indicate animals moving in or out of the area, and red areas are devoid of game.

Camera Focus
While playing, press Alt+Control+C.

More Hunting Time
Go back to camp before 8 p.m. Then, repeatedly walk from the lodge to the camp until midnight.

More Tags
Go to the lodge and click on the Buy Tags option. Type in coyote or giraffe to hunt that animal.

CABELA'S BIG GAME HUNTER 3

Cheat Mode
Switch to Wilderness Tracking view. Press Control+Enter. Type footwork at the Console window. Press Control+Enter again. A message confirms correct entry. Enable this code only once per game.

$1,000
With Cheat mode on, press Control+Enter and type coupon.

Full Health
With Cheat mode on, press Control+Enter and type tonic.

Snow
With Cheat mode on, press Control+Enter and type flurry.

Rain
With Cheat mode on, press Control+Enter and type sprinkle.

Animals Are Green Dots on the Map
With Cheat mode on, press Control+Enter and type thereitis.

Remove Selected Animal
With Cheat mode on, press Control+Enter and type destroy.

Go to Next Stand
With Cheat mode on, press Control+Enter and type nextstand.

Teleport to Practice Range
With Cheat mode on, press Control+Enter and type popup.

Toggle Time
With Cheat mode on, press Control+Enter and type cuckoo.

Teleport to Map Location
With Cheat mode on, at the Map screen, press Control+Enter and type getthere.

Display Offset Setting
With Cheat mode on, at the Wilderness Tracking screen, press Control+Enter and type offset.

Display Target Coordinates
With Cheat mode on, at the Map screen, press Control+Enter and type hereiam.

Display Kill Spots
With Cheat mode on, at the video screen, press Control+Enter and type bullseye.

Successful Kill
With Cheat mode on, at the video screen, press Control+Enter and type mytrophy.

CAESAR

Unbreakable Walls
Use wells to create an outer wall.

CAESAR II

Faster Time
Hold A while you are in City or Providence mode.

Create Diseases
Click on the Build Prefecture button. Then, right click on a house to infect it with disease.

Increasing Land Value
Build gardens and parks at the beginning of the game.

CAESAR III

Cheat Mode
Right click on a well. Press Alt+K to activate Cheat mode.

Instant Victory
Enable Cheat mode. While playing, press Alt+V.

More Money
Enable Cheat mode. While playing, press Alt+C. This only works if you have less than 5,000 denarii.

CANNON FODDER

Level Skip
To skip levels, go to the map screen. Hold Ctrl and type "Fodder." A white border appears around the screen. Exit the map and return to the game.

CARMAGGEDON

1,000 Credits
Kill the guy with the flag at the beginning of a race.

All Cars and Levels
Type KEVWOZEAR at the Car Select, View Info, Start Race, and Change Race screens. A clanking noise confirms correct entry.

All Cars in Network Mode
Type JOYRIDER at the Host Network screen. The host may play any car, even cheat cars. The client has access to any car except cheat cars.

Invincibility
While playing, type SPOONREASON.

Instant Repairs
While playing, type INTHEWAR.

Instant Handbrake
While playing, type SPAMFORREST.

Time Bonus
While playing, type MILKYSMILES.

Super Turbo
While playing, type SOAPYTITWANKS.

Grip Tires
While playing, type BOYSFROMTHEBUSH.

Greasy Tires
While playing, type BENFORMARIO.

Final Lap
While playing, type MRCURSORSCOOL.

Five Recovery Vouchers
While playing, type ICECREAMHOLE.

Giant Pedestrians
While playing, type SMALLUDDERS.

Blind Pedestrians
While playing, type HAMSTERSEX.

Pedestrians are Stuck to the Ground
While playing, type SPAMSPAMSPAMSPAM.

Pedestrians on the Map
While playing, type ILOVENOBBY.

Pedestrian Electro-Blast Ray
While playing, type RUSSFORMARIO.

Pedestrians Re-Spawn
While playing, type NAUGHTYTORTY.

Explosive Pedestrians
While playing, type SUPERHOOPS.

Turbo Pedestrians
While playing, type FUNNYJAM.

Pedestrian Harvest
While playing, type TRAMSARESUPER.

Bounce Mode
While playing, type CHICKENFODDER.

Damage Magnifier
While playing, type WEHATEMARIO.

Damaged Body
While playing, type BIGBOTTOM.

Disable Timer
While playing, type SEXWITHFISH.

Drugs
While playing, type INTHELOFT.

Extra Money
While playing, type GIVEMELARD.

Fast Opponents
While playing, type YUMMYLARD.

Fast Police
While playing, type YAKATTACK.

Free Repairs
While playing, type SPAMFRITTERS.

Self-Repair
While playing, press Backspace.

Frozen Opponents
While playing, type SPAMACCIDENTS.

Wall Climber
While playing, type SECRETCOWS.

Volcanic Corpses
While playing, type ISLANDRULES.

Underwater Ability
While playing, type GOOGLEPLEX.

Strange Gravity
While playing, type IHAVESOMESPAM.

Pinball Mode
While playing, type MOOSEONTHELOOSE.

Mines
While playing, type BILLANDBEN.

Lunar Gravity
While playing, type RABBITDREAMER.

Loose Suspension
While playing, type BUYOURNEXTGAME.

Hot Rod
While playing, type IGLOOFUN.

Granite Car
While playing, type KEEPITHAPPINESS.

Frozen Police
While playing, type NASALSMEAR.

CARMAGGEDON 2: CARPOCALYPSE NOW

Bonus Cars
Beat all the levels in the game to unlock every car you've seen.

Extra Armor
While playing, type OSOSTRONG.

Extra Power
While playing, type OSOFAST.

Invincibility
While playing, type SUPACOCKS.

Mega Turbo
While playing, type SUPAWHIZ.

Instant Repairs
While playing, type MINGMING.

Instant Handbrake
While playing, type EYEPOPPER.

Credit Bonus
While playing, type WETWET.

Hot Rod
While playing, type CLINTONCO.

Mega Bonus
While playing, type GLUGGLUG.

Five Recovery Vouchers + C1049
While playing, type PILLPOP.

Afterburner
While playing, type HOTASS.

Angry Pedestrians
While playing, type LARGEONE.

Bonus Armor Slot
While playing, type THATSALOTOFARMOR.

Bonus Armor Slot (2)
While playing, type STRONGBONES.

Bonus Offensive Slot
While playing, type THATSALOTOFOFFAL.

Bonus Offensive Slot (2)
While playing, type NASTYBONES.

Bonus Power Slot
While playing, type THATSALOTOFPOWER.

Bonus Power Slot (2)
While playing, type FAST BONES.

Bonus Slots All Around
While playing, type THATSALOTOFSLOTS.

Bonus Slots All Around
While playing, type LOADSABONES.

Bounce Mode
While playing, type JIGAJIG.

Cloaking Device
While playing, type GOTOINFRARED.

Disable Pedestrian AI
While playing, type LEMMINGIZE.

Maximum Power
While playing, type VASTNESSES.

Maximum Armor
While playing, type STRINGVEST.

Maximum Offense
While playing, type FISTNESSES.

Maximum Everything
While playing, type SKEGNESSES.

Wire Frame Bugs
While playing, type BLOODYARTISTS.

Wall Climber
While playing, type STICKYTIRES.

Frozen Opponents
While playing, type BLUEBALLZ.

Frozen Police
While playing, type BLUEPIGS.

Kangaroo On Command
While playing, type SLIPPYPOOS.

Jupiter Gravity
While playing, type LEDSLEDS.

Underwater Capability
While playing, type WATERSPORT.

Turbo Police
While playing, type PIGSMIGHTFLY.

Turbo Opponents
While playing, type SWIFTYSHIFTY.

Turbo
While playing, type WHIZZ.

Turbo Bastard Nutter Nitros
While playing, type FURKINELL.

Pedestrian Annihilator
While playing, type ZAZAZ.

Pedestrian Electro-Blast Ray
While playing, type FRYINGTONIGHT.

Pedestrian Flame Thrower
While playing, type FRYFRY.

Pedestrian Repulsificator
While playing, type COWCOW.

Mini-Pedestrians
While playing, type TINYTOSS.

Pedestrian Valium
While playing, type INEEDAPILL.

Explosive Pedestrians
While playing, type TWATOFF.

Fat Pedestrians
While playing, type HIPPOTART.

Fast Pedestrians
While playing, type FASTBAST.

Clown Pedestrians
While playing, type GOODHEAD.

Immortal Pedestrians
While playing, type ANGELMOLESTERS.

Suicide Pedestrians
While playing, type TAKEMETAKEME.

Pedestrians are Stuck to the Ground
While playing, type STICKITS.

Pedestrians on the Map
While playing, type DOTACTION.

Pedestrians Re-Spawn
While playing, type XRAYSPEAKS.

Damage Magnifier
While playing, type STUFFITUP.

Damaged Body
While playing, type CLANGCLANG.

Disable Timer
While playing, type STOPSNATCH.

Dismemberfest
While playing, type OHMESSYMESS.

Drugs
While playing, type BLOODYHIPPY.

Drunk Driving
While playing, type EVENINGOFFICER.

Finish the Race
While playing, type SMARTBASTARD.

Flight Mode
While playing, type IWISHICOULDFLYRIGHTUPTOTHESKY.

Free Repairs
While playing, type TINGTING.

Time Bonus
While playing, type TIMMYTITTY.

Stiff Springs
While playing, type TUFFRIDE.

Slippery Tires
While playing, type WOTATWATAMI.

Hot Rod
While playing, type CINTONCO.

Lunar Gravity
While playing, type MOONINGMINNIE.

Slaughter Mortar
While playing, type BONBON.

Pinball Mode
While playing, type TILTY.

Panicked Pedestrians
While playing, type MRMAINWARING.

Opponent Repulsificator
While playing, type POWPOW.

Oil Slicks
While playing, type LIQUIDLUNGE.

No Power-Ups
While playing, type OYPOWERUPNO.

Mutant Tail
While playing, type BIGDANGLE.

Mines
While playing, type DIDEDODI.

Loose Suspension
While playing, type MRWOBBLEY.

Grip Tires
While playing, type RUBBERUP.

Granite Car
While playing, type BIGTWAT.

Giant Pedestrians
While playing, type MEGABUM.

CARMAGEDDON TDR 2000

Access Cheat Mode
During a game, press ` and type hereComes-Trouble.

All Levels
Enable Cheat mode, press ` again, and type openLevelsGuv.

Increase Money (+$10,000)
Enable Cheat mode, press ` again ,and type cash.

God Mode
Enable Cheat mode, press ` again, and type invincible.

AI On/Off
Enable Cheat mode, press ` again, and type ai on/off.

Change Your Car to [CARNAME]
Enable Cheat mode, press ` again, and type setCar [CARNAME].

Create Opponent [CARNAME]
Enable Cheat mode, press ` again, and type makeai [CARNAME].

Destroy All Cars
Enable Cheat mode, press ` again, and type WasteAll.

Start on Final Lap
Enable Cheat mode, press ` again, and type lastlap.

All Checkpoints Checked Except Last
Enable Cheat mode, press ` again, and type lastcheckpoint.

Text Adventure Minigame
Enable Cheat mode, press ` again, and type adventure.

Increase Damage to #
Enable Cheat mode, press ` again, and type damage_multiplier #.

Add Power-Up (#=Name)
Enable Cheat mode, press ` again, and type addPowerup #.

Damage Car (#=Name)
Enable Cheat mode, press ` again, and type breakCar #.

Pedestrians On/Off
Enable Cheat mode, press ` again, and type peds on/off.

Allows You to Buy All Cars
Enable Cheat mode, press ` again, and type enablebuy.

CARNIVORES

Debug Mode
During a game, type debugon to activate Debug mode. Your character now has infinite ammo, is hidden from dinosaurs, and won't be harmed by lava.

Fast Running
Enable Debug mode. Press Control.

Full Map
Enable Debug mode. Press Tab.

Swim
Enable Debug mode. Press Spacebar before entering water.

Longer Jumps
Enable Debug mode. Press Control+N.

Slow Motion
Enable Debug mode. Press Control+S.

Frame Rate Display
Enable Debug mode. Press Control+T.

CARNIVORES 2

Flight Mode
While playing, press Shift+L.

Toggle 3D Objects
While playing, press Shift+M.

Toggle Fog
While playing, press Shift+F.

Debug Mode
During a game, type in debugup to activate Debug mode. Dinosaurs can't detect your character until you shoot.

Fast Running
Enable Debug mode. Press Control.

Full Map
Enable Debug mode. Press Tab.

Swim
Enable Debug mode. Press Spacebar before entering water.

Longer Jumps
Enable Debug mode. Press Control+N.

Slow Motion
Enable Debug mode. Press Control+S.

Frame Rate Display
Enable Debug mode. Press Control+T.

CARNIVORES: ICE AGE

Debug Mode
During gameplay, type debugup. After Debug mode is enabled, use the following key commands:

Run Faster
Ctrl

Slow Motion
Shift+S

Shows Frame Rate
Shift+T

CENTIPEDE 3D

Skip Level
Type goto during a game.

Unlimited Lives
Type getalife during a game.

Slow Motion
Type slow during a game.

Slower Motion
Type sloww during a game.

Very Slow Motion
Type slowww during a game.

Maximum Slow Motion
Type slowwww during a game.

Normal Speed
Type normal during a game.

God Mode (Toggle)
Type wimp during a game.

Fly Mode (toggle)
Type fly during a game.

Make Centipede Nearby
Type pede during a game.

Screen Modes
Type showz during a game.

Clear Caches
Type clearc during a game.

Time Codes (Toggle)
Type times during a game.

Go to Windows
Type dload during a game.

Show Diagnostic Codes
Type diags during a game.

Computer Controls Character
Type robot during a game.

Delete Message
Type purge during a game.

Objects Have Collision Boxes (Toggle)
Type boxes during a game.

Report Files Created
Type report during a game.

CHASE ACE 2

All Weapons
At the title screen, type I WANT THE LOT and press Enter.

CHASM: THE RIFT

Full Ammo
During a game, press Backspace and type ammo.

Full Map
During a game, press Backspace and type fullmap.

Kill All Monsters
During a game, press Backspace and type kill.

God Mode
During a game, press Backspace and type choji.

All Weapons
During a game, press Backspace and type weapon.

200 Armor
During a game, press Backspace and type armor.

Invisibility
During a game, press Backspace and type invisible.

Skip Level
During a game, press Backspace and type next.

Get All Keys
During a game, press Backspace and type keys.

CIVILIZATION

Cheat Mode
Hold Shift and type 1234567890 during the game.

View Full Map
Type Shift+5+6 during the game.

Generate Random Enemy Leaders
During the game press Alt+R.

Infinite Turns
Save and Quit the game after moving all units except one. Reload game. You can move those units again.

CIVILIZATION 2

Toggle God Mode
While holding shift, type 123456. Release Shift and press T.

Remodel Throne Room
Press Q during the game.

Alter Council Time and Attitude
Press Control+Shift+T during the game.

Alter Unit
Press Control+Shift+U during the game.

Edit Enemy City
When moving diagonally into an enemy city, press V, then Enter. The city can now be changed.

CIVILIZATION: CALL TO POWER

Cheat Mode
To activate the Cheat menu, start a new game and press Esc.

CLANS

God Mode
During the game, press T and type /godmode.

Skip to Next Level
During the game, press T and type /nextlevel.

Tiny Players
During the game, press T and type /tiny-players.

Tiny Enemies
During the game, press T and type tiny monsters.

More Money
During the game, press T and type /moregold.

Repeat Last Code
During the game, press T and type /repeat.

Enemies Fight Each Other
During the game, press T and type /insanity.

Go to Selected Room
During the game, press T and type /room[##].

Create Selected Item
During the game, press T and type /spawn[object #]. Select an object number from the following list.

Sword +1
0

Sword +2
1

Sword +3
2

Sword +4
3

Sword +5
4

Shield +1
5

Shield +2
6

Shield +3
7

Shield +4
8

Shield +5
9

Ring of Agility
10

Ring of Fire (+3 Fire Magic)
11

Ring of the Sword (+3 Sword)
12

Ring of Destruction (+3 explosion)
13

Ring of the Axe (+3 Axe)
14

Health Potion
15

Mana Potion
16

Strength Potion
17

Magic Potion
18

Life Potion
19

Poison
20

Key
21

Key
22

Key
23

Key
24

Key
25

Key
26

Axe +1
27

Axe +2
28

Axe +3
29

Axe +4
30

Axe +5
31

Armor +1
32

Armor +2
33

Armor +3
34

Armor +4
35

Armor +5
36

10 Gold
37

15 Gold
38

20 Gold
39

25 Gold
40

30 Gold
41

Gold Bar
42

Gold Bar
43

Gold Bar
44

Ruby
45

Emerald
46

Diamond
47

Ruby Necklace
48

Pearl Necklace
49

Confusion Scroll Level 1
50

Confusion Scroll Level 2
51

Confusion Scroll Level 3
52

Confusion Scroll Level 4
53

Confusion Scroll Level 5
54

Explosion Scroll Level 1
55

Explosion Scroll Level 2
56

Explosion Scroll Level 3
57

Explosion Scroll Level 4
58

Explosion Scroll Level 5
59

Fireball Scroll Level 1
60

Fireball Scroll Level 2
61

Fireball Scroll Level 3
62

Fireball Scroll Level 4
63

Fireball Scroll Level 5
64

1 Gold
65

2 Gold
66

3 Gold
67

4 Gold
68

5 Gold
69

Meteor Rain Scroll Level 1
70

Meteor Rain Scroll Level 2
71

Meteor Rain Scroll Level 3
72

Meteor Rain Scroll Level 4
73

Meteor Rain Scroll Level 5
74

Lightning Scroll Level 1
75

Lightning Scroll Level 2
76

Lightning Scroll Level 3
77

Lightning Scroll Level 4
78

Lightning Scroll Level 5
79

Extra Life Potion
80

CLIVE BARKER'S UNDYING

Press Tab then type one of the following codes
at the chat window:

God Mode
eh

All Weapons and Spells
addall

Spawn Donkey Joke
assall

Toggle Unlimited Mana
infinitemana <0 or 1>

Toggle Extra Light
becomelight <0 or 1>

Set Health to 999
set aeons.patrick health 999

Set Mana to 999
set aeons.patrick mana 999

Flight Mode
flight

Display Frame Rate
showfps

Increase Selected Spell Level
ampattspell

3rd Person Perspective
behindview1

Slow Motion
slowmo (1-5)

Level Select
Use one of the following level names with the
start code. Note: Maps that start with "CU" are
intermission sequences.

Start [map name here]
Aeons
Catacombs_Cisterns
Catacombs_Cliffs
Catacombs_Entrance
Catacombs_Exit
Catacombs_Exit_After
Catacombs_LairOfLizbeth
Catacombs_LairOfLizbethPostCU
Catacombs_LowerLevel
Catacombs_SaintsHall
Catacombs_Tunnels
Catacombs_WellRoom
Catacombs_WindChamber
CU_01
CU_02
CU_03
CU_04
CU_05
CU_06
CU_07
CU_08
CU_09
CU_10
CU_11
CU_12
CU_13
Entry
EternalAutumn_FinalFight_Arch
EternalAutumn_FinalFight_Arena
EternalAutumn_FinalFight_ArenaBattle
EternalAutumn_FinalFight_Ruins
EternalAutumn_Ravines_Airie_Interior
EternalAutumn_Ravines_Bridge
EternalAutumn_Ravines_Chase
EternalAutumn_Ravines_Chieftain
EternalAutumn_Ravines_Forest
EternalAutumn_Transition
EternalAutumn_Waterfall_Dwellings_Lower
EternalAutumn_Waterfall_Dwellings_Upper
EternalAutumn_Waterfall_Gauntlet
Grounds_Cottage
Grounds_dock_night
Grounds_Lighthouse
Grounds_Mausoleum_Approach
Grounds_Mausoleum_Entrance
Grounds_Mausoleum_Tunnels
Grounds_OldCemetery
Manor_CentralLower

Manor_CentralLower_After
Manor_CentralLower_Night
Manor_CentralLower_Storm
Manor_CentralUpper
Manor_CentralUpper_After
Manor_CentralUpper_PostOneiros
Manor_CentralUpper_Storm
Manor_Chapel
Manor_Chapel_Night
Manor_Crypt
Manor_EastWingLower
Manor_EastWingLower_After
Manor_EastWingLower_Night
Manor_EastWingUpper
Manor_EastWingUpper_After
Manor_EastWingUpper_Night
Manor_EntranceHall
Manor_EntranceHall_FromKitch
Manor_EntranceHall_Intro
Manor_EntranceHall_Night
Manor_EntranceHall_Night_ReturnfromCove
Manor_EntranceHall_Storm
Manor_EntranceHall_ToKitch
Manor_FrontGate
Manor_FrontGate_Night
Manor_FrontGate_Night_Return
Manor_Gardens
Manor_Gardens_Night
Manor_Gardens_Storm
Manor_GreatHall_Night
Manor_GreatHall_Storm
Manor_InnerCourtyard
Manor_InnerCourtyard_Storm
Manor_NorthWingLower
Manor_NorthWingLower_After
Manor_NorthWingLower_Night
Manor_NorthWingLower_Storm
Manor_NorthWingUpper
Manor_NorthWingUpper_Night
Manor_NorthWingUpper_PostOneiros
Manor_NorthWingUpper_Storm
Manor_PatricksRoom
Manor_TowerRun_Night
Manor_TowerRun_Storm
Manor_WestWing
Manor_WestWing_Hall1
Manor_WestWing_Night
Manor_WidowsWatch_Storm
Monastery_Past_Church
Monastery_Past_Exterior
Monastery_Past_Interior
Monastery_Past_LivingQuarters
Monastery_Present_Church
Monastery_Present_Cove
Monastery_Present_Entrance
Monastery_Present_InnerSanctum
Monastery_Present_Tunnels
Oneiros_Amphitheater
Oneiros_City1
Oneiros_City2
Oneiros_HowlingWell
Oneiros_Intro
Oneiros_Oracle

Oneiros_RetreatBath
Oneiros_RetreatExterior
Oneiros_RetreatSecondFloor
Oneiros_RetreatStudio
Oneiros_ZigguratInterior
Oneiros_ZigguratLower
Oneiros_ZigguratUpper
PiratesCove_Barracks
PiratesCove_Exterior
PiratesCove_Pier
PiratesCove_Pool
PiratesCove_TreasureRoom
Playground
SmokeTest
StandingStones_FirstVisit
StandingStones_KingFight

CODENAME EAGLE

200% Armor
Press Alt+S, then type: armorgod.

All Weapons
Press Alt+S, then type: weaponmaster.

Extra Items
Press Alt+S, then type: itemgod.

God Mode
Hit Alt+S, then type: codenamegod.

COLIN MCRAE RALLY

Extra Cars
Type the name LOTTOWIN.

Unlock All Tracks
Type the name FREEWAY.

Unlock All Night Tracks
Type the name DARKSIDE.

Tracks in Reverse
Type the name BACKAGAIN.

Customized Replay
Type the name SPECIALED.

Nicky Grist as Driver
Type the name PASSEDOUT.

High-Voiced Nicky Grist
Type the name CHOIRBOY.

Foggy Track
Type the name WHITEOUT.

Increased Power
Type the name BIGGUNS

Accelerate by Tapping Keys
Type the name PRESSFAST.

Steer With Rear Wheels
Type the name TURNBACK.

Turbo Boost
Type the name ROCKETMAN.

Bonus Green Car
Type the name ALIENGOO.

Get Concept Car
Type the name HIPPO.

Hidden Track 1
Type the name INTHECLOUDS.

Hidden Track 2
Type the name QUARRYVILLE.

Hidden Track 3
Type the name TROLLEYPARK.

Hidden Track 4
Type the name WILDAYWORLD.

Tiny Cars
Type the name BORROWERS.

Toyota Celica GT4
Type the name BEEFCAKE.

Steer with All Wheels
Type the name ALLWHEELS.

View Credits During Demo
Type the name XCREDITSX.

Low Gravity
Type the name GIANTLEAP.

Hover Mode
Type the name DELOREAN.

Mirror Mode
Type the name ONTHEWALL

COLIN MCRAE RALLY 2

Type one of the following names at the Create New Driver Profile screen to activate the corresponding cheat function:

All Cars
ALLTHEBUTTONS

All Tracks
GREATNEWS

Mini Cooper S
MINIME

Car Stereo
TURNONTHEICE

Escort mk1
MORRISMODE

Shiny Cars
SHINYBUTTONS

Faster Cars
GOFASTERSTRIPES

Turbo Boost
CURRYFORME

Aggressive Cars
NUTTYNETS

Bouncy Collisions
BOUNCYBOUNCY

Monster Truck Wheels
WHEELYBIG

Bouncer Mode
BOINGBOINGBOING

Mirrored Tracks
WAWEYOURLEFTS

Fireballs in Arcade Mode
EATTHIS

Ford Puma
GARYWILDASS

Lancer Road
EVILEVO

Open All Game Options
LETMEWIN

COMANCHE 3

Repair Damage
During the game, press R and type cat9.

Reload Weapons
During the game, press R and type dog9.

Increase Ammo
During the game, press R and type ipig.

Invisibility (Temporary)
During the game, press R and type ratz.

Freeze Enemy (Temporary)
During the game, press R and type cowz.

GPS Hellfires
During the game, press R and type bat9.

COMANCHE GOLD

Fix Damage
During the game, press R and type fixme.

Freeze Time
During the game, press R and type imacow.

Refill Ammo
During the game, press R and type loadme.

Invisibility
During the game, press R and type imarat.

GPS Hellfires
During the game, press R and type harmony.

Enemies Fight Each Other
During the game, press R and type cheat=mercenary or type 6969.

Kill Team Member
During the game, press R and type die team mate! or type x666.

More Ammo Per Weapon
During the game, press R and type PIGSOINK.

COMANCHE: MAXIMUM OVERKILL

Reload/Fix Damage Options
At the main menu, type kyle while holding Backspace.

COMMAND & CONQUER

Bonus Missions
In MS-DOS mode, type c&c funpark under the *C&C* directory. Start new game.

COMMAND & CONQUER: COVERT OPERATIONS

Bonus Missions (MS-DOS)
In MS-DOS mode, type c&c funpark under the *C&C directory*. Start new game.

Bonus Missions (Win95)
Type C&C95 funpark.

COMMAND & CONQUER: RED ALERT

20 Tanks
When game loads, type XPEINA518.

View Credits
At title screen, click on Westwood logo.

COMMAND & CONQUER: RED ALERT AFTERMATH

Bonus Missions
In MS-DOS mode, type ra funpark under the *C&C directory*. Start new game.

View Credits
At title screen, click on Westwood logo.

COMMAND & CONQUER: RED ALERT COUNTERSTRIKE

Giant Ant Missions
Hold left Shift at title screen, click left mouse button on round speaker.

Keep Units Moving/Firing
Hold Q, select units, and click on enemy unit. Continue to hold Q.

View Credits
At title screen, click on Westwood logo.

COMMAND & CONQUER: RENEGADE

Activate Cheat Mode
Press ~ during gameplay to display the console window. Enter the following codes to activate the corresponding cheat function.

All Weapons
Enable Cheat mode and type allguns.

Enable Extras Cheat
Enable Cheat mode and type extras fnkqrrm.

Different Practice Map
You don't need to be online when you do this. Go into the game menu and click on "Multiplayer LAN" (even if you don't have a LAN), then click on "Host Game." Enter your game name, set your "Players Limit" to "1" and continue with the remaining settings. Make sure you have a different map than "CNC_Under.mix", then click "Start Game." You'll be able to blow up bases and do everything that you could normally do in a regular multiplayer game.

Extra Units in Multiplayer Mode
In multiplayer practice or non-laddered mode, you can get extra units for characters and vehicles by pressing F8 and typing extras fnkqrrm or extras quantifigon (in the unpatched version). The message "Extras enabled" confirms correct code entry. Go to the Purchase Terminal and hold down Alt the entire time that you are looking for something to buy. There should be four new characters and two new vehicles for each side. For GDI, the new characters are General Locke, Elana Petrova, Logan, and Lieutenant Maus. The new vehicles are a sedan and a pickup truck. For NOD, the new characters are mutants, a chef, Mutated Petrova, and Kane. You'll only see the new units. Release Alt to see the normal units. This doesn't work in a laddered game.

Unlimited Skirmish Mode Time
This procedure involves editing a game file; create a backup copy of the file before proceeding. Use a text editor to edit the "svrcfg_skirmish.ini" file in the "\westwood\renegade\data" directory. Change the "gametime" value to zero to remove the time limit. You also can edit the amount of starting money.

COMMANDOS 2

Activate Cheat Mode
Enter GONZOANDJON as your name to enable cheat mode. Then, use the key combinations given below during gameplay to activate the corresponding cheat function. Cheat mode also can be activated during a mission typing GONZOANDJON after selecting a commando (you can't see what you type and there will be no confirmation).

Destroy All Opponents
Control + Shift + X

Display Frame Rate
Control + Minus

Invincibility
Control + I

Invisibility
Control + V

Mission Skip
Control + Shift + N

Teleport Selected Commandos to Position Under Cursor
Shift + X

Level 2 Password
WKUC4

Level 3 Password
YSM51

Level 4 Password
B7D8F

Level 5 Password
3GHSL

Level 6 Password
AZLM1

Level 7 Password
JAHSG

Level 8 Password
UN63A

Level 9 Password
VAZ2P

Level 10 Password
9TT5W

COMMANDOS: BEHIND ENEMY LINES

Enable Cheat Mode
Type gonzo1982 during the game.

Skip Level
Enable Cheat mode and press Control+Shift+N during the game.

See Enemy's View
Enable Cheat mode and press Shift+V during the game.

Annihilate Everything
Enable Cheat mode and press Control+Shift+X during the game.

God Mode
Enable Cheat mode and press Control+I during the game.

Pointer on Selected Commandos
Enable Cheat mode and press Shift+X during the game.

Level 2 Password
NS2B7

Level 3 Password
BFQBF

Level 4 Password
YGF1J

Level 5 Password
JJTCG

Level 6 Password
NT1WN

Level 7 Password
Y3YWX

Level 8 Password
B3WJO

Level 9 Password
HIAXT

Level 10 Password
G4CM3

Level 11 Password
GDODW

Level 13 Password
65UWX

Level 14 Password
CT34V

Level 15 Password
YN9PD

Level 16 Password
BY4MD

Level 17 Password
Y14PW

Level 18 Password
8POJ8

Level 19 Password
8WGJ0

Level 20 Password
88U4V

COMMANDOS: BEYOND THE CALL OF DUTY

Invincibility
Type gonzoopera while playing then press Control+L.

Invisibility
Type gonzoopera while playing then press Control+I.

Mission Skip
Type gonzoopera while playing then press Control+Shift+N.

Annihilate Everything
Type gonzoopera while playing, then press Control+Shift+X.

Pointer on Selected Commandos
Type gonzoopera while playing, then press Shift+X.

User Traced
Type gonzoopera while playing, then press Shift+V.

View Debug Info
Type gonzoopera while playing, then press Control+F9.

Picte Interface
Type gonzoopera while playing, then press Alt+I.

Edit Missions
Type gonzoopera while playing, then press Shift+E, or press Control+E.

Write Info to *memact.dat*
Type gonzoopera while playing, then press Alt+Shift+M.

Write Info to *memlin.dat*
Type gonzoopera while playing, then press Alt+Shift+L.

View Terrain Info
Type gonzoopera while playing, then press F9.

Choose Video Mode
Type gonzoopera while playing, then press Shift+F1, F2, F3, or F4.

Level 2 Password
YBN9J

Level 3 Password
XAPIB

Level 4 Password
QDOAU

Level 5 Password
IIWAY

Level 6 Password
EW82M

Level 7 Password
SJ8S1

Level 8 Password
V6J27

CONFLICT ZONE

Cheat List
During gameplay, press "C." Press Backspace before entering the codes here:

WIN: Win the mission
- REPLAY ALL MISSIONS: Access all of the missions
- MY TAYLOR IS RICH: Get 20,000 points and 100% popularity

COSSACKS: EUROPEAN WARS

Fog of War On/Off
During a game, press Enter and type supervizor.

Give Resources
During a game, press Enter and type money.

Switch Player with NumPad Keys 1-9
During a game, press Enter and type izmena.

Press P to Access All Units
During a game, press Enter and type multitvar.

Activate Fog of War, Switch Player with Numpad, and Press P to Access All Units Cheats
During a game, press Enter and type www.

CRASH KIDS 2

Improved Weapons
At the main menu, press Alt+Tab and load a saved game. Pause and type russian-attack.

Kill Almost Everyone in Level 2
At the main menu, press Alt+Tab and load a saved game. Pause and type no-world.

Enemies Ignore You
At the main menu, press Alt+Tab and load a saved game. Pause and type 456love321peace.

CRIMSON SKIES

Play Any Mission
At the Campaign menu, left-click on the microphone on the left and type idaho. A menu appears in the top right.

CROC: THE LEGEND OF THE GOBBOS

Unlimited Lives
During the game, type argolife.

Level Select
During the game, type argoskip.

Unlock All Levels
At the password screen, enter Left (4), Down, Right (2), Left (2), Down, Right, Down, Left, Up, Right.

CRUSADER: NO REGRET

Activate Cheat Mode
Type loosecannon16 during the game.

God Mode
Activate Cheat mode and press Control+F10.

Restore Energy, Health, Weapons
Activate Cheat mode and press F10.

Show Grid 1
Activate Cheat mode and press F7.

Show Grid 2
Activate Cheat mode and press Alt+F7.

Show Grid 3
Activate Cheat mode and press Control+F7.

Dump Screen with Backspace
Activate Cheat mode and press pix.

Move Items by Holding Shift
Activate Cheat mode and press H.

Miscellaneous Info
Activate Cheat mode and press Alt+V.

View Framework
Activate Cheat mode and press F.

Christmas Mode
Start a game after setting the system date to 12/24 or 12/25.

Refill Ammo
While playing, drop a gun by pressing Alt+L, then pick it up again.

View Secret Movie
Type jassica16 during gameplay and press F10.

Choose Difficulty
When starting the game, use the command line parameter: -skill [skill level 1-4].

Choose Level
When starting the game, use the command line parameter: -warp [level 1-10].

Easter Egg Room
When starting the game, use the command line parameter: -egg 250.

CRUSADER: NO REMORSE

Level Select
Start the game with -warp # in the command line parameter. Replace # with a number between 1 and 15.

Continuous Intro
Start the game with -demo in the command line parameter.

Enabling ENHANCED Mode. (Not!) Message
Start the game with -asylum in the command line parameter.

You DO Need Help! Message
Start the game with -? in the command line parameter.

Difficulty Select
Start the game with -skill # in the command line parameter. Replace # with a number between 1 and 4.

Weapons Room Cheat
Start the game with -egg 250 in the command line parameter. Use this with the Level Select code.

Ammunition Refill
To refill your gun, press Control+D to drop a gun. Pick it up again and the clip is refilled.

Access Cheat Mode
While you are playing, type in JASSICA16. A voice confirms correct entry.

Full Health, Weapons
Enable Cheat mode. Press F10.

Change Playing Grids
Enable Cheat mode. Press F.

Invincibility
Enable Cheat mode. Press Alt+F10.

Alternate Grid 1
Enable Cheat mode. Press F7.

Alternate Grid 2
Enable Cheat mode. Press Alt+F7.

Alternate Grid 3
Enable Cheat mode. Press Control+F7.

Display Stats
Enable Cheat mode. Press Control+L.

Display Version
Enable Cheat mode. Press Control+V.

Transfer Display Toggle
Enable Cheat mode. Press Control+Q.

Toggle Cheat Mode On/Off
Enable Cheat mode. Press ~.

Show Current Location
Enable Cheat mode. Press Control+C.

Glide Across Floor and Spin
Enable Cheat mode. Press F10+Up, Down, Right, or Left.

Hack Mover
Enable Cheat mode. Press [H]. Hold Shift and use the mouse to move items around.

CRUSADERS OF MIGHT AND MAGIC

All Spells and Mana
While playing, press Enter then type -crazyguy

God Mode
While playing, press Enter then type -embiggenme

See Debug Info
During the game, press Enter and type -debug.

View Frame Rate
During the game, press Enter and type -showfps.

Figure Out Frame Rate
During the game, press Enter and type -calcfps.

Go to Random Level
During the game, press Enter and type -uberload.

Flight Mode
During the game, press Enter and type -whoah. Use left and right mouse buttons to fly faster and slower.

Landscape Toggle
During the game, press Enter and type -cswire.

AMD 3DNow! Support Toggle
During the game, press Enter and type -3dnow!.

Boxes Surround Objects
During the game, press Enter and type boundingbox.

CULTURES

Speed Up
During a game, press F2 and type funspeedup. To disable, press Pause.

CURSE OF MONKEY ISLAND

Automatic Win
Press Shift+W anytime in the game.

CYBERMERCS

Cheat Mode
While playing, press Alt+F12 to bring up a key prompt. Type in wlrnwhdakf or doomsday to enable Cheat mode. A Cheatcode Enable message appears if you did it correctly. Press Alt+F12, Enter. Then type one of the following codes:

Invincibility
Enable Cheat mode. Type invulnerable on to activate invincibility. Type invulnerable off to disable it.

One Hit Kills
Enable Cheat mode. Type onekill on to activate one hit kills. Type onekill off to disable it.

Extra Money
Enable Cheat mode. Type money and a number between 1 and 999.

Modify Character's Strength
Enable Cheat mode. Type str and a number between 1 and 999.

Modify Character's Dexterity
Enable Cheat mode. Type dex and a number between 1 and 999.

Modify Character's Intelligence
Enable Cheat mode. Type int and a number between 1 and 999.

Modify Character's Damage Strength
Enable Cheat mode. Type hit and a number between 1 and 999.

CYBERSTORM 2

New Pilot Face
Press Control+[or Control+] at the BioDerm facility.

Cheat Codes
Find and back up the *storm.ini* file in the game directory. Then use a text editor to add one of the following lines under the SPECIAL header. Start a game and press Control+O at the indicated screen to activate the cheat.

Invincibility
Type THERE CAN BE ONLY ONE under the SPECIAL header. Press Control+O during a mission.

1 Credit
Type I'LL BUY THAT FOR A CREDIT under the SPECIAL header. Press Control+O at Herc Base.

1,000 Credits
Type WILL WORK FOR CREDITS under the SPECIAL header. Press Control+O at Herc Base.

10,000 Credits
Type MO MONEY under the SPECIAL header. Press Control+O at Herc Base.

100,000 Credits
Type TOO MUCH WHEAT under the SPECIAL header. Press Control+O at Herc Base.

1,000,000 Credits
Type YOU MAY HAVE ALREADY WON under the SPECIAL header. Press Control+O at Herc Base.

Mega Credits
Type CUC under the SPECIAL header. Press Control+O at Herc Base.

Back to Normal Technologies
Type IT WAS NICE WHILE IT LASTED under the SPECIAL header. Press Control+O at Herc Base.

All Technologies
Type HE WHO DIES WITH THE MOST TOYS under the SPECIAL header. Press Control+O at Herc Base.

Max-O-Commander Mode
Type YOU DA MAN under the SPECIAL header. Press Control+O at Herc Base.

Max-O-Chassis Mode
Type MUST HAVE! under the SPECIAL header. Press Control+O at Herc Base.

Max-O-Repair Mode
Type AS GOOD AS IT GETS under the SPECIAL header. Press Control+O at Herc Base.

Max-O-Facilities Mode
Type HOME IS WHERE THE HEART IS under the SPECIAL header. Press Control+O at Herc Base.

Crush All Enemies
Type DEATH TO ALL WHO OPPOSE US under the SPECIAL header. Press Control+O during a mission.

Repair Selected Vehicles
Type IT'S JUST A FLESH WOUND under the SPECIAL header. Press Control+O during a mission.

Reset Selected Vehicles
Type GO GO POWER RANGER under the SPECIAL header. Press Control+O during a mission.

Single Touch of Death
Type DID I BREAK YOUR CONCENTRATION under the SPECIAL header. Press Control+O during a mission.

Multi Touch of Death
Type THAT MUST HURT under the SPECIAL header. Press Control+O during a mission.

Fog of War
Type LET THERE BE LIGHT under the SPECIAL header. Press Control+O during a mission.

No Fog of War
Type LET THERE BE LIGHT V2 under the SPECIAL header. Press Control+O during a mission.

Become Another Player
Type FREAKY FRIDAY under the SPECIAL header. Press Control+O during a mission.

Cure Selected Pilots
Type TARSUS under the SPECIAL header. Press Control+O during a mission.

Restock Selected Vehicles
Type FEEL MY WRATH under the SPECIAL header. Press Control+O during a mission.

Mega Turn-Based Move Points
Type FLY AWAY under the SPECIAL header. Press Control+O during a mission.

Mega Turn-Based Action Points
Type VENGEANCE IS MINE under the SPECIAL header. Press Control+O during a mission.

DAEDALUS ENCOUNTER

Select Scene
Highlight Game Option and press Alt+F5. Then select "Jump" to start a scene.

Skip Puzzle
During gameplay, hold Alt+Shift and type the first letter of the puzzle name, except for the Orbit puzzle, which is Alt+Shift+I.

DAGGERFALL: ELDER SCROLLS 2

Cheat Mode
Locate and back up the file z.cfg in the Daggerfall directory, then open it with any text editor and add the line cheatmode 1. During gameplay, while in a dungeon press Ctrl+F4 to toggle God Mode. Or press Alt+F11 to return to the last thing you were standing on.

DAIKATANA

Access Cheat Mode
Start the game with the command line parameter +set console 1. During gameplay, press ~ and type a cheat code.

Advance All Attribute Levels
Type boost all in the console.

Advance Attribute Level
Type boost (attribute) in the console.

Cycle Through Three Camera Views
Type cam_toggle in the console.

Disable Cheats
Type cheats 0 in the console.

Focus Camera on Next Enemy
Type cam_nextmon in the console.

Give Weapon # (1 to 10)
Type weapon_give_# in the console.

God Mode
Type god in the console.

Increase Health by
Type health # in the console.

Invisibility
Type notarget in the console.

Kill All Enemies on Level
Type massacre in the console.

No Clipping
Type noclip in the console.

Rampage
Type rampage in the console.

Take Screenshot
Type screenshot in the console.

Unlimited Ammo
Type g_unlimited_ammo 1 in the console.

DAMAGE INCORPORATED

Access Cards
During gameplay, hold Ctrl and type axes. The sound of breaking glass confirms correct entry.

Alternate View
During gameplay, hold Ctrl and type phish. The sound of breaking glass confirms correct entry.

Complete Mission Objectives
During gameplay, hold Ctrl and type qed. The sound of breaking glass confirms correct entry.

Extraction Zone Area
During gameplay, hold Ctrl and type ext. The sound of breaking glass confirms correct entry.

Field of View is 170 Degrees
During gameplay, hold Ctrl and type vomit. The sound of breaking glass confirms correct entry.

Flamethrower
During gameplay, hold Ctrl and type tozt. The sound of breaking glass confirms correct entry.

Freeze Opponents
During gameplay, hold Ctrl and type klatu. The sound of breaking glass confirms correct entry.

Full Armor
During gameplay, hold Ctrl and type arm. The sound of breaking glass confirms correct entry.

God Mode
During gameplay, hold Ctrl and type atheist. The sound of breaking glass confirms correct entry.

Grenades
During gameplay, hold Ctrl and type horse. The sound of breaking glass confirms correct entry.

Infrared Vision
During gameplay, hold Ctrl and type acid. The sound of breaking glass confirms correct entry.

Locations Displayed on Map
During gameplay, hold Ctrl and type blue. The sound of breaking glass confirms correct entry.

M16 Machine Gun with Ammo
During gameplay, hold Ctrl and type xse. The sound of breaking glass confirms correct entry.

Mandatory Suicide Missions
At the main menu, hold Alt+M.

MP5N Machine Gun with Ammo
During gameplay, hold Ctrl and type vent. The sound of breaking glass confirms correct entry.

Opponents and Items Displayed on Map
During gameplay, hold Ctrl and type godeye. The sound of breaking glass confirms correct entry.

Oxygen
During gameplay, hold Ctrl and type oxy. The sound of breaking glass confirms correct entry.

Restore Health of Squad Members
During gameplay, hold Ctrl and type medic. The sound of breaking glass confirms correct entry.

Restore Your Health
During gameplay, hold Ctrl and type hell. The sound of breaking glass confirms correct entry.

Rocket Gun with Ammo
During gameplay, hold Ctrl and type deth. The sound of breaking glass confirms correct entry.

Select Mission
At the main menu, hold Alt+Ctrl.

Skip Mission
During gameplay, hold Ctrl and type soia. The sound of breaking glass confirms correct entry.

Slay Squad Member 1
During gameplay, hold Ctrl and type ksa. The sound of breaking glass confirms correct entry.

Slay Squad Member 2
During gameplay, hold Ctrl and type ksb. The sound of breaking glass confirms correct entry.

Slay Squad Member 3
During gameplay, hold Ctrl and type ksc. The sound of breaking glass confirms correct entry.

Slay Squad Member 4
During gameplay, hold Ctrl and type ksd. The sound of breaking glass confirms correct entry.

Squad Members Go Beserk
During gameplay, hold Ctrl and type hdcs. The sound of breaking glass confirms correct entry.

Squad Members Have All Weapons
During gameplay, hold Ctrl and type thrill. The sound of breaking glass confirms correct entry.

Squad Members Revolt
During gameplay, hold Ctrl and type nimrod. The sound of breaking glass confirms correct entry.

Squad Members Talk
During gameplay, hold Ctrl and type chat. The sound of breaking glass confirms correct entry.

Super Jump
During gameplay, hold Ctrl and type asd. The sound of breaking glass confirms correct entry.

Two Pistols with Ammo
During gameplay, hold Ctrl and type woo. The sound of breaking glass confirms correct entry.

Two Shotguns with Ammo
During gameplay, hold Ctrl and type freedom. The sound of breaking glass confirms correct entry.

Dark Ages

Auto Fire
Press F10+Backspace, then press =.

Dark Angael

Cheat Mode
When you hear Azrael's voice say Dark Angael, press Shift+G for God Mode, Unlimited Ammo, and Ammo. Press Shift+I for full inventory. Press Shift+P for full set of superpowers. These codes don't work in multiplayer.

Dark Colony

Get 10,000 Petra
In the Chat Bar, type WE NEED EQUIPMENT.

View All Map
In the Chat Bar, type SLAG NET.

Dark Earth

Access Cheat Mode
Pause game with P, then type fortytwo.

Arkhan Relieves Himself
Enable Cheat mode, pause, and type much-better.

Big Feet
Enable Cheat mode, pause, and type bigfoot.

Big Head
Enable Cheat mode, pause, and type bighead.

Big Hands
Enable Cheat mode, pause, and type baffe.

Decrease Opponent's Life to One
Enable Cheat mode, pause, and type D.

Normal Character
Enable Cheat mode, pause, and type normal.

Refill Arkhan's Life Gauge
Enable Cheat mode, pause, and press Ctrl+D.

Small Character
Enable Cheat mode, pause, and type dwarf.

Dark Forces

Accessories
During gameplay, type LAUNLOCK.

Add Weapons, Ammo, and Power-Ups
During gameplay, type LAPOSTAL.

Anoat City
During gameplay, type LASEWERS.

Coordinate Information
During gameplay, type LADATA.

Detention Center
During gameplay, type LADTENTION.

Disable Height Checking
During gameplay, type LAPOGO.

Force Successful Level Completion
During gameplay, type LASKIP.

Freeze Enemies
During gameplay, type LAREDLITE.

Fuel Station
During gameplay, type LAFUELSTAT.

Full Inventory
During gameplay, type LAUNLOCK.

Gromas Mines
During gameplay, type LAGROMAS.

Imperial City
During gameplay, type LAIMPCITY.

Insect Mode
During gameplay, type LABUG.

Jabba's Ship
During gameplay, type LAJABSHIP.

Map Supermode
During gameplay, type LACDS.

Max Out All Items
During gameplay, type LAMAXOUT.

Nar Shaddaar
During gameplay, type LANARSHADA.

Ramsees Hed
During gameplay, type LARAMSHED.

Research Facility
During gameplay, type LATESTBASE.

Robotic Facility
During gameplay, type LAROBOTICS.

Secret Base
During gameplay, type LASECBASE.

Talay: Tak Base
During gameplay, type LATALAY.

The Arc Hammer
During gameplay, type LAARC.

The Executor
During gameplay, type LAEXECUTOR.

Weapon Super Charge
During gameplay, type LARANDY.

Dark Rift

Sonork
Type the code kronos.

DARK SUN: THE SHATTERED LANDS

Access Cheat Mode
Start the game with the command line parameter -K911.

Increase Attack Power
Enable Cheat mode, then during gameplay, press Alt+F2.

Learn All Spells
Enable Cheat mode, then during gameplay, press Alt+F4.

Raise Level
Enable Cheat mode, then during gameplay, press T.

Restore All Magic
Enable Cheat mode, then during gameplay, press M.

DARKLIGHT CONFLICT

Invincibility
During gameplay, hold Tab+Page-Up. Release the buttons and press P. If you did it correctly, "Cheat Enabled" appears at the screen's bottom.

DARKSUN 2: WAKE OF THE RAVENGER

No Intro
Start the game with the command line parameter -k911, and use dsun and not ravager. For more options, add the command line parameter -a.

No Music
Start the game with the command line parameter -k911, and use dsun and not ravager. For more options, add the command line parameter -m.

Make the Party the God Party
During gameplay, press Alt+F2.

Spell Casters Memorize All Spells
During gameplay, press Alt+F4.

Memorize All Spells
During gameplay, press m/M.

Raise One Character's Level During His/Her Combat Turn
During gameplay, press t.

Raise Party Level by One
During gameplay, press T.

Start with All Psyonics
Start the game with the command line parameter -k911, and use dsun and not ravager. For more options, add the command line parameter -p.

Start with All Spells
Start the game with the command line parameter -k911, and use dsun and not ravager. For more options, add the command line parameter –s.

DAVE MIRRA'S FREESTYLE BMX

Amish Boy
Beat the game with Dave Mirra, Ryan Nyquist, Joey Garcia, Troy McMurray, Mike Laird, Chad Kagy, Tim Mirra, Kenan Harkin, Shaun Butler, and Leigh Ramsdell.

Big-Crashes Option
Beat the game with Leigh Ramsdell to enable the option at the Cheat menu.

Sticky-Crashes Option
Beat the game with Kenan Harkin to enable the option at the Cheat menu.

Silly-Grunts Option
Beat the game with Tim Mirra to enable the option at the Cheat menu.

First-Person View
Beat the game with Mike Laird to enable the option at the Cheat menu.

Unlock the Ghost Rider
Beat the game with Joey Garcia to enable the option at the Cheat menu.

Unlock Exorcist Mode
Beat the game with Troy McMurray to enable the option at the Cheat menu.

Bike-Suspension Mode
Beat the game with Chad Kagy to enable the option at the Cheat menu.

Night-Vision Mode
Beat the game with Shaun Butler to enable the option at the Cheat menu.

All Bikes
At the Bike Selection screen in Pro Quest mode, press Up, Left, Up, Down, Up, Right, Left, Right, Modifier Airs to unlock all bikes. Note: Each time you select a new bike, you must re-type this code.

All Styles
At the Style Selection screen in Pro Quest mode, press Left, Up, Right, Down, Left, Down, Right, Up, Left, Modifier Airs to unlock all styles.

Play as Slim Jim
At the Rider Selection screen in Pro Quest mode, press Down (2), Left, Right, Up (2), Modifier Airs to unlock Slim Jim. Alternately, beat the game with any rider to unlock a bonus bike and Slim Jim.

DAYS OF THUNDER

Fly Mode
Pause gameplay during the qualifying round and type COMEFLYWITHME.

DEADLOCK

Complete Current Research Project
ghoti

Gain 5,000 Credits and 100 of Every Resource
makeitso

Increase Population
frodo

View Any Video Scene
touche

DEADLOCK 2

Add Resources
During a game, press Ctrl+F12 and type PILE IT ON at the prompt. This doesn't work in Campaign mode.

Research Everything
During a game, press Ctrl+F12 and type Q40 at the prompt. This doesn't work in Campaign mode.

Complete Research on the Current Project
During a game, press Ctrl+F12 and type GREEBLIE at the prompt. This doesn't work in Campaign mode.

Max Population
During a game, press Ctrl+F12 and type WALL2WALL at the prompt. This doesn't work in Campaign mode.

Show Resources/Military Units in Enemy Territories
During a game, press Ctrl+F12 and type LEO at the prompt. This doesn't work in Campaign mode.

View Any Territory
During a game, press Ctrl+F12 and type BIGBRO at the prompt. This doesn't work in Campaign mode.

Be Friends with All Computer Players
During a game, press Ctrl+F12 and type CHARISMA at the prompt. This doesn't work in Campaign mode.

Skirineen Appears Immediately
During a game, press Ctrl+F12 and type S-MART at the prompt. This doesn't work in Campaign mode.

Win Scenario
During a game, press Ctrl+F12 and type SQUISH at the prompt. This doesn't work in Campaign mode.

DEADLY TIDE

All Levels
Type the player name poseidon.

DEATH MASK

Level 2 Password
22428

Level 3 Password
84843

Level 4 Password
22087

Level 5 Password
38641

Level 6 Password
6395

Level 7 Password
33224

Level 8 Password
35527

Level 9 Password
48962

Level 10 Password
65074

Level 11 Password
62438

Level 12 Password
28283

Level 13 Password
85325

Level 14 Password
10769

Level 15 Password
25324

Level 16 Password
43542

Level 17 Password
62156

Level 18 Password
84678

Level 19 Password
57093

Level 20 Password
29264

Level 21 Password
47446

Level 22 Password
75330

Level 23 Password
82855

Level 24 Password
58474

Level 25 Password
38392

Level 26 Password
55276

Level 27 Password
68163

Level 28 Password
75156

Level 29 Password
70948

Level 30 Password
54334

Level 31 Password
39814

Level 32 Password
52262

Level 33 Password
73164

DEATH RALLY

Drop 10 points
At the menu, type DROP.

Get $1,000
At the menu, type DRAW.

Get $500,000
At the menu, type DROOL.

Get 10 Points
At the menu, type DRIVE.

Mushroom Effect
During a race, type DRUG.

No Damage
During a race, type DRUB.

Rocketfuel
During a race, type DRINK.

Unlimited Ammo
During a race, type DREAD.

Unlimited Turbo
During a race, type DRAG.

DEATHDROME

Citadel
SHORT4TIME

Purgatory
LASTMEAL8

The Abyss
2REVOLT

The Inferno
5GETAWAYS

The Outpost
3ACCUSED

The Spike
ARREST7

The Wall
BOLT6DOWN

DEATHKEEP

Additional Key
LEPIK

Experience Mode
LEOLD

Fly
LEBUZ

Full Map, Also Teleport
LEGEO

Full Spells
LEHAT

Invincible
LENEE

Level Select
Shift+Left-Click on Gargoyle's eye on the main menu.

Skip Level
LESKP

DEATHTRAP DUNGEON

Unlimited Health
During gameplay, type elvis.

DEEP SEA TROPHY FISHING

Allow a Fish to Be Caught Immediately
During gameplay, type dscatchnow.

Attract 10 Times as Many Fish as Normal
During gameplay, type ds10x.

Keep the Line from Breaking
During gameplay, type dsnobreak.

Make the Next Fish Caught Be a Blue Marlin
During gameplay, type dsbluemarlin.

DEER AVENGER

Create Another Hunter
During gameplay, hold Left-Shift and select Fart.

DEER HUNT CHALLENGE

Deer Finder
During gameplay, press X.

DEER HUNTER

Attract a Doe
At the Overhead map, type dhdeermate.

Better Accuracy
At the Overhead map, type dhrambo.

Bigger Bucks
At the Overhead map, type dhbigbucks.

Bigger Deer
At the Overhead map, type dhsportaxi.

Deer Can't See You
At the Overhead map, type dhstealth.

Deer Don't Run Away When Shot At
At the Overhead map, type dhbuckdown.

Hit the Deer Anywhere and It'll Die
At the Overhead map, type dhviper.

Locate Deer
At the Overhead map, type dhbambi.

Lure Deer Toward You
At the Overhead map, type dhdoeinheat.

Monster Buck
At the Overhead map, type dhmonsters.

Quiet Hunter
At the Overhead map, type dhhunter.

Reload Faster
At the Overhead map, type dhfastgun.

DEER HUNTER 2

ArrowCam
During gameplay, type dh2deadeye.

Attach Yourself to a Deer
During gameplay, type dh2circle.

Attract Deer
During gameplay, type dh2honey.

Crowcam
During gameplay, type camera set crow#.

Cycle Weather More Quickly
During gameplay, type dh2blizzard.

DeerCam
During gameplay, type camera set deer#.

Fly Mode
During gameplay, type dh2wright.

Foxcam
During gameplay, type camera set fox#.

Giant Deer
During gameplay, type dh2deerzilla.

Make It Lightning
During gameplay, type dh2light.

Make It Rain
During gameplay, type dh2rain.

Make It Snow
During gameplay, type dh2snow.

Make It Thunder
During gameplay, type dh2thunder.

Normal View
During gameplay, type camera set player.

Be in Shooting Range of Nearest Deer
During gameplay, type dh2shoot.

Run Fast
During gameplay, type dh2flash.

Run Very Fast
During gameplay, type dh2supaflash.

Shows the Deer on the Map and GPS
During gameplay, type dh2tracker.

Sight-In Your Weapon Without Target Range
During gameplay, type dh2sightin.

Don't Spook Animals
During gameplay, type dh2doolittle.

DEER HUNTER 3

Animals Are Not Afraid of You
During gameplay, press F2 and type the following, then press F2 again: dh3nofear.

Go to Nearest Animal
During gameplay, press F2 and type dh3find, then press F2 again.

Clear All Weather
During gameplay, press F2 and type dh3dryv, then press F2 again.

Enable All Cheats
During gameplay, press F2 and type dh3super, then press F2 again.

Flight Mode
During gameplay, press F2 and type dh3skyhook, then press F2 again.

Force Time of Day to Noon
During gameplay, press F2 and type dh3noon, then press F2 again.

Hunter Never Dies
During gameplay, press F2 and type dh3homegym, then press F2 again.

Large Deer
During gameplay, press F2 and type dh3monster, then press F2 again.

Make It Lightning
During gameplay, press F2 and type dh3zeus, then press F2 again.

Make It Rain
During gameplay, press F2 and type dh3water, then press F2 again.

Make It Snow
During gameplay, press F2 and type dh3ice, then press F2 again.

Become Irresistible to Animals
During gameplay, press F2 and type dh3beacon, then press F2 again.

More Gore
During gameplay, press F2 and type dh3f13, then press F2 again.

No Animals
During gameplay, press F2 and type dh3plague, then press F2 again.

No Clipping
During gameplay, press F2 and type dh3truck, then press F2 again.

No Noise
During gameplay, press F2 and type dh3damper, then press F2 again.

Show Info on Active View Models
During gameplay, press F2 and type dh3vmwatch, then press F2 again.

Show Info on Nearest Deer
During gameplay, press F2 and type dh3deerwatch, then press F2 again.

Show Info on All
During gameplay, press F2 and type dh3breakdown, then press F2 again.

Sight-In Your Gun
During gameplay, press F2 and type dh3sightin, then press F2 again.

Stop Slope Effect
During gameplay, press F2 and type dh3climber, then press F2 again.

Thunder
During gameplay, press F2 and type dh3thor, then press F2 again.

View Bullet Paths
During gameplay, press F2 and type dh3tracers, then press F2 again.

View Deer on Map
During gameplay, press F2 and type dh3showme, then press F2 again.

Walk Around in Target Range
During gameplay, press F2 and type dh3caddyshack, then press F2 again.

View Follows Projectile
During gameplay, press F2 and type dh3leadeye, then press F2 again.

DEER HUNTER 4

Brings You to Nearest Animal
During a game, press F2 and type dh3find, then press F2 again.

Animals Are Not Afraid of You
During a game, press F2 and type dh3nofear, then press F2 again.

Makes You Irresistible to Animals
During a game, press F2 and type dh3beacon, then press F2 again.

Sights in Your Gun
During a game, press F2 and type dh3sightin, then press F2 again.

Your View Follows the Projectile
During a game, press F2 and type dh3leadeye, then press F2 again.

Make It Rain
During a game, press F2 and type dh3water, then press F2 again.

Make It Snow
During a game, press F2 and type dh3ice, then press F2 again.

Make It Lightning
During a game, press F2 and type dh3zeus, then press F2 again.

Large Deer
During a game, press F2 and type dh3monster, then press F2 again.

No Clipping
During a game, press F2 and type dh3truck, then press F2 again.

Hunter Never Dies
During a game, press F2 and type dh3homegym, then press F2 again.

More Gore
During a game, press F2 and type dh3f13, then press F2 again.

View Deer on Map
During a game, press F2 and type dh3showme, then press F2 again.

Flight Mode
During a game, press F2 and type dh3skyhook, then press F2 again.

Walk Around in Target Range
During a game, press F2 and type dh3caddyshack, then press F2 again.

No Animals
During a game, press F2 and type dh3plague, then press F2 again.

Enable All Cheats
During a game, press F2 and type dh3super, then press F2 again.

No Noise
During a game, press F2 and type dh3damper, then press F2 again.

Thunder
During a game, press F2 and type dh3thor, then press F2 again.

View Bullet Paths
During a game, press F2 and type dh3tracers, then press F2 again.

Stops Slope Effect
During a game, press F2 and type dh3climber, then press F2 again.

Show Info on Nearest Deer
During a game, press F2 and type dh3deerwatch, then press F2 again.

Show Info on Active View Models
During a game, press F2 and type dh3vmwatch, then press F2 again.

Clear All Weather
During a game, press F2 and type dh3dry, then press F2 again.

Force Time of Day to Noon
During a game, press F2 and type dh3noon, then press F2 again.

Shows Info on All
During a game, press F2 and type dh3breakdown, then press F2 again.

DEFIANCE

Enemies/Objects On/Off
Pause gameplay with Pause/Break key, then type HIDEENEMIES.

Free Ammo for All Weapons
Pause gameplay with Pause/Break key, then type ALLGUNS.

God Mode On/Off
Pause gameplay with Pause/Break key, then type IAMGOD.

Show Frame Rate
Pause gameplay with Pause/Break key, then type FPS.

Wall Collisions On/Off
Pause gameplay with Pause/Break key, then type GHOST.

DELTA FORCE

Allow Call for Arty < 5 Shots > Can Be Re-Entered for More
During gameplay, press ` and type raindropskeepfallinonmyhead.

CPU Is Good
During gameplay, press ` and type hitmewithyourbestshot.

God Mode
During gameplay, press ` and type iwillsurvive.

Invisible to Enemies
During gameplay, press ` and type closetoyou.

Level Select
During gameplay, press ` and type letmego.

Reduced Sky Details
During gameplay, press ` and type sky.

Run Faster
During gameplay, press ` and type turbo.

Set Gamma to #
During gameplay, press ` and type gamma #.

Unlimited Ammo
During gameplay, press ` and type takeittothelimit.

DELTA FORCE 2

God Mode
Press ~ then type thetrooper then press Enter.

Infinite Ammo
Press ~ then type diewithyourbootson then press Enter.

DELTA FORCE 2 DEMO

Invincibility and Unlimited Ammo
During a game, press ' and type imnotafraidtofight.

DELTA FORCE: LAND WARRIOR

Full Ammo
During a game, press ~ and type drury.

Unlimited Ammo
During a game, press ~ and type kariya.

God Mode
During a game, press ~ and type roy.

Invisibility
During a game, press ~ and type corbet.

Artillery Strikes
During a game, press ~ and type domi.

DEMOLITION RACER

All Cars and Tracks
Type the name BIG CHEAT, then type your normal name.

All Cars in Demolition League
Type the name LEAGUE CHEAT, then type your normal name.

DEPTH DWELLERS

All Weapons
During gameplay, press Ctrl+Alt+F.

Extra Lives
During gameplay, press Ctrl+Alt+L.

Invulnerability
During gameplay, press Ctrl+Alt+I.

Warp to Next Level
During gameplay, press Ctrl+Alt+N.

DESCENT

All Keys
During gameplay, type GABBAGABBAHEY to enable Cheat mode. Then type MITZI.

Cloak On/Off
During gameplay, type GABBAGABBAHEY to enable Cheat mode. Then type GUILE.

Exit Path Illuminated
During gameplay, type GABBAGABBAHEY to enable Cheat mode. Then type FLASH.

Extra Life
During gameplay, type GABBAGABBAHEY to enable Cheat mode. Then type BRUIN.

Full Map (at Map Screen)
During gameplay, type GABBAGABBAHEY to enable Cheat mode. Then type ALT+F.

Ghosty Mode On/Off
During gameplay, type GABBAGABBAHEY to enable Cheat mode. Then type ASTRAL.

Invulnerability On/Off
During gameplay, type GABBAGABBAHEY to enable Cheat mode. Then type RACERX.

Level Warp
During gameplay, type GABBAGABBAHEY to enable Cheat mode. Then type FARMERJOE.

Mega Wowie Zowie Weapons
During gameplay, type GABBAGABBAHEY to enable Cheat mode. Then type PORGYS.

Robot Firing Off
During gameplay, type GABBAGABBAHEY to enable Cheat mode. Then type AHIMSA.

Robot Painting with Texture 001 to 999
During gameplay, type GABBAGABBAHEY to enable Cheat mode. Then type PLETCH###.

Robots Move fast, Fire Seldom
During gameplay, type GABBAGABBAHEY to enable Cheat mode. Then type LUNACY.

Activate Self Destruct Sequence
During gameplay, type GABBAGABBAHEY to enable Cheat mode. Then type BIOPSYTOYS.

Shields Recharged
During gameplay, type GABBAGABBAHEY to enable Cheat mode. Then type TWILIGHT.

Super Wowie Zowie Weapons
During gameplay, type GABBAGABBAHEY to enable Cheat mode. Then type BIGRED.

Turbo Mode On/Off
During gameplay, type GABBAGABBAHEY to enable Cheat mode. Then type BUGGIN.

Wowie Zowie Weapons
During gameplay, type GABBAGABBAHEY to enable Cheat mode. Then type SCOURGE.

DESCENT 2

Accessories
During gameplay, type ALIFALAFEL.

All Keys
During gameplay, type ALGROOVE.

Bouncing Weapons
During gameplay, type DUDDABOO.

Displays Frames per Second
During gameplay, type FRAMETIME.

Full Map
During gameplay, type ROCKRGRL.

Guide Bot Attacks the Robots
During gameplay, type GOWINGNUT.

Homing Weapons
During gameplay, type LPNLIZARD.

Invulnerability
During gameplay, type ALMIGHTY.

Level Warp
During gameplay, type FREESPACE.

Lose All But One Percent of Shields and Energy
During gameplay, type GABBAGABBAHEY.

Make It Easier to Destroy Robots by Running into Them
During gameplay, type GODZILLA.

Psychedelic Walls
During gameplay, type BITTERSWEET.

Spawn Additional Guide Bots
During gameplay, type HELPVISHNU.

Toasts All Robots in the Mine
During gameplay, type SPANIARD.

Warp You to Exit and Blows Reactor
During gameplay, type FOPKJEWA.

Wowie Zowie Weapons
During gameplay, type HONESTBOB.

DESCENT 3

210 Damage
During gameplay, type TubeRacer.

All Weapons, Energy, Shield
During gameplay, type IveGotIt.

Chase View
During gameplay, type ByeByeMonkey.

Cloak
During gameplay, type Testicus.

Destroy All Bots
During gameplay, type DeadOfNight.

FPS Display
During gameplay, type FrameLength.

Full Map
During gameplay, type TreeSquid.

God Mode
During gameplay, type BurgerGod.

Level Jump
During gameplay, type MoreClangv.

Secret Boss Level
During gameplay, type Deadmanwalking.

Sun Changes to Teletubbies Version
During gameplay, type Teletubbies.

Take Off Energy and Shields; Never Regain Thrusters
During gameplay, type Gowingnut.

Weird Textures
During gameplay, type Shananigans.

DESCENT 3 DEMO

God Mode
During a game, type YUMMYFUNYON.

Kills All Enemies in the Mine
During a game, type FREEITUP.

Full Shield, Energy, All Weapons, 500 Missiles
During a game, type BLIMPIEBEST.

Show FPS
During a game, type FRAMETIME.

Chase View Mode
During a game, type LONGCHIMP.

Cool Texture Mode
During a game, type WEIRDTEXTURE.

Cloak
During a game, type MIGHTYAPHRODITE.

Permanent Cloak Mode
During a game, type APHRODITE.

All Demo Weapons
During a game, type DUMPIEBEST.

Permanent God Mode
During a game, type QEZIRESR.

DESCENT: FREESPACE

Access Cheat Mode
Type WWW.VOLITION-INC.COM to enable Cheat mode. You can advance with Cheat mode enabled.

10 Percent Damage to Yourself
Enable Cheat mode, then hold ~ and press Alt K.

Destroy Targeted Subsystem
Enable Cheat mode, then hold ~ and press Shift K.

Infinite Weapons for ALL ships, including yours
Enable Cheat mode, then hold ~ and press Shift W.

Infinite Weapons for Just Your Ship
Enable Cheat mode, then hold ~ and press W.

Invulnerability
Enable Cheat mode, then hold ~ and press I.

Issue Rearm Request for Target
Enable Cheat mode, then hold ~ and press R.

Kill Target
Enable Cheat mode, then hold ~ and press K.

Mark All Bonus Goals Complete
Enable Cheat mode, then hold ~ and press Alt G.

Mark All Primary Goals Complete
Enable Cheat mode, then hold ~ and press G.

Mark All Secondary Goals Complete
Enable Cheat mode, then hold ~ and press Shift G.

Scroll Backward Through All Secondary Weapons
Enable Cheat mode, then hold ~ and press Shift 9.

Scroll Backward Through All Secondary Weapons
Enable Cheat mode, then hold ~ and press Shift 0.

Scroll Forward Through All Primary Weapons
Enable Cheat mode, then hold ~ and press 0.

Scroll Forward Through All Secondary Weapons.
Enable Cheat mode, then hold ~ and press 9.

Send Message to Enemies
Enable Cheat mode, then hold ~ and press C.

Toggle Availability of Countermeasures for All Ships
Enable Cheat mode, then hold ~ and press Shift C.

Toggle Descent-Style Physics
Enable Cheat mode, then hold ~ and press O.

Toggle Invulnerability for Target
Enable Cheat mode, then hold ~ and press Shift I.

DESCENT: FREESPACE 2

Access Cheat Mode
During gameplay, type www.freespace2.com to enable cheat mode. The message "Cheats activated" appears. You cannot advance to the next level with Cheat mode enabled.

10 Percent Damage to Yourself
Enable Cheat mode, then hold ~ and press Alt K.

Destroy Targeted Subsystem
Enable Cheat mode, then hold ~ and press Shift K.

Infinite Weapons for All Ships, Including Yours
Enable Cheat mode, then hold ~ and press Shift W.

Infinite Weapons for Just Your Ship
Enable Cheat mode, then hold ~ and press W.

Invulnerability
Enable Cheat mode, then hold ~ and press I.

Issue Rearm Request for Target
Enable Cheat mode, then hold ~ and press R.

Kill Target
Enable Cheat mode, then hold ~ and press K.

Mark All Bonus Goals Complete
Enable Cheat mode, then hold ~ and press Alt G.

Mark All Primary Goals Complete
Enable Cheat mode, then hold ~ and press G.

Mark All Secondary Goals Complete
Enable Cheat mode, then hold ~ and press Shift G.

Scroll Backward Through All Secondary Weapons
Enable Cheat mode, then hold ~ and press Shift 9.

Scroll Backward Through All Secondary Weapons
Enable Cheat mode, then hold ~ and press Shift 0.

Scroll Forward Through All Primary Weapons.
Enable Cheat mode, then hold ~ and press 0.

Scroll Forward Through All Secondary Weapons
Enable Cheat mode, then hold ~ and press 9.

Send Message to Enemies
Enable Cheat mode, then hold ~ and press C.

Toggle Availability of Countermeasures for All Ships
Enable Cheat mode, then hold ~ and press Shift C.

Toggle Descent-Style Physics
Enable Cheat mode, then hold ~ and press O.

Toggle Invulnerability for Target
Enable Cheat mode, then hold ~ and press Shift I.

DESERT STRIKE

Cheat Mode
While playing, press Esc, then type "Waterfall." Press Esc again to return to the game and activate the code. You now have infinite numbers of everything except lives. Double your speed at any time by pressing T. To deactivate the code, press F12.

DESPERADOS: WANTED DEAD OR ALIVE

Cheat List
To activate the Cheat menu, press and hold Left Shift, then press F11. This brings up a Cheat menu. Enter the following phrases to unlock the cheats.

Show Dialogues
fidel castro

Turn Victory Condition Display On/Off
epitaph

Win the Current Level
clint

More Ammo
jackal

Show All Objects
show me all

Turn Invisibility On/Off
hollow man

Freeze Time
timeless

Press Alt to Kill Enemies with Flashlight
zeus

Turn Hint Display On/Off
medic

Turn Short Briefings On/Off
whats my destiny

Turn Sound Zone Display On/Off
supersonic

New Weapon
powerman

Exit the Game
schneider

DESTROYER IV

Change Products with Your Opponent
During gameplay, type operation.

Change with Your Opponent
During gameplay, type daltonien.

DESTRUCTION DERBY

Invincibility
Type the name !DAMAGE!

Secret Track
Type the name REFLECT.

Select Number of Opponents
Type the name NPLAYER.

DESTRUCTION DERBY 2

All Tracks
Type the name MACSrPOO. Then start the race, quit, and go into Practice mode.

Animated Credits
Type the name CREDITZ! Then start the race, quit, and go into Practice mode.

Video Credits
Type the name ToNyPaRk. Then start the race, quit, and go into Practice mode.

DETHKARZ

Cheat Screen
At the main screen, hold Shift+Ctrl+C to open the Cheat screen.

All Cars
Type DEV 6 at the Cheat Screen.

All Seasons in Championship Mode
Type RACE CORPS at the Cheat Screen.

All Tracks
Type GLOBAL at the Cheat Screen.

DEUS EX

Access Cheat Mode
Locate and backup the file user.ini, in the deusex/system folder, then open it with any text editor. Change all occurrences of "t=" to "t=talk." During gameplay, press T and a line at the screen's bottom appears. Remove "Say:" and type set DeusEx.JCDentonMale bCheatsEnabled True to activate Cheat mode.

10,000 Credits
Enable Cheat mode, then type allcredits.

All Basic Augmentations
Enable Cheat mode, then type allaugs.

All Images
Enable Cheat mode, then type allimages.

Full Energy
Enable Cheat mode, then type allenergy.

Full Health
Enable Cheat mode, then type allhealth.

Give All Weapons
Enable Cheat mode, then type allweapons.

Give All Skill Points
Enable Cheat mode, then type allskillpoints.

God Mode
Enable Cheat mode, then type god.

Invisibility
Enable Cheat mode, then type invisible.

Kill Current Target
Enable Cheat mode, then type tantalus.

Refill Ammo
Enable Cheat mode, then type allammo.

Secret Menu
Enable Cheat mode, then type legend.

Spawn a Mass of Enemies
Enable Cheat mode, then type spawnmass.

Summon Lockpick
Enable Cheat mode, then type summon Lockpick.

Summon Basketball
Enable Cheat mode, then type summon basketball.

Summon MultiTool
Enable Cheat mode, then type summon MultiTool.

Summon Acoustic Sensor
Enable Cheat mode, then type summon AcousticSensor.

Summon 10mm Ammo
Enable Cheat mode, then type summon Ammo10mm.

Summon Dart Ammo
Enable Cheat mode, then type summon AmmoDart.

Summon Poison Dart
Enable Cheat mode, then type summon AmmoDartPoison.

Summon Flare Dart
Enable Cheat mode, then type summon AmmoDartFlare.

Summon Napalm
Enable Cheat mode, then type summon AmmoNapalm.

Summon Plasma Rifle Ammo
Enable Cheat mode, then type summon AmmoPlasma.

Summon 30-06 Ammo
Enable Cheat mode, then type summon Ammo3006.

Summon Rocket Ammo
Enable Cheat mode, then type summon AmmoRockets.

Summon Pistol
Enable Cheat mode, then type summon WeaponPistol.

Summon Rifle
Enable Cheat mode, then type summon WeaponRifle.

Summon Stealth Pistol
Enable Cheat mode, then type summon WeaponStealthPistol.

Summon Shuriken
Enable Cheat mode, then type summon WeaponShuriken.

Summon Sawed-off Shotgun
Enable Cheat mode, then type summon WeaponSawedOffShotgun.

Summon Riot Prod
Enable Cheat mode, then type summon WeaponProd.

Summon Plasma Rifle
Enable Cheat mode, then type summon WeaponPlasmaRifle.

Summon Assault Shotgun
Enable Cheat mode, then type summon WeaponAssaultShotgun.

Summon Flamethrower
Enable Cheat mode, then type summon WeaponFlameThrower.

Summon Gas Grenade
Enable Cheat mode, then type summon WeaponGasGrenade.

Summon LAM
Enable Cheat mode, then type summon WeaponLAM

Summon Accuracy Modification
Enable Cheat mode, then type summon Weaponmodaccuracy.

Summon Clip Modification
Enable Cheat mode, then type summon Weaponmodclip.

Summon Laser Modification
Enable Cheat mode, then type summon Weaponmodlaser.

Summon Range Modification
Enable Cheat mode, then type summon Weaponmodrange.

Summon Recoil Modification
Enable Cheat mode, then type summon Weaponmodrecoil.

Summon Scope Modification
Enable Cheat mode, then type summon Weaponmodscope.

Summon Silencer Modification
Enable Cheat mode, then type summon Weaponmodsilencer.

Summon Ballistic Augmentation
Enable Cheat mode, then type summon AugBallistic.

Summon Cloak Augmentation
Enable Cheat mode, then type summon AugCloak.

Summon Datalink Augmentation
Enable Cheat mode, then type summon AugDatalink.

Summon EMP Augmentation
Enable Cheat mode, then type summon AugEMP.

Summon Enviro Augmentation
Enable Cheat mode, then type summon AugEnviro.

Summon IFF Augmentation
Enable Cheat mode, then type summon AugIFF.

Summon Item Shield Augmentation
Enable Cheat mode, then type summon AugShield.

Summon Item Stealth Augmentation
Enable Cheat mode, then type summon AugStealth.

Summon Target Augmentation
Enable Cheat mode, then type summon AugTarget.

Turn on EMP Field
Enable Cheat mode, then type iamwarren.

Unlock Targeted Door
Enable Cheat mode, then type opensesame.

DEVIL'S ISLAND PINBALL

Ball Blocker On/Off
During gameplay, press Print Screen, then type none shall pass.

Big Ugly Head Ready
During gameplay, press Print Screen, then type easter island.

Cannibal Attack Lit
During gameplay, press Print Screen, then type 1 green bottle.

Cannon Ready
During gameplay, press Print Screen, then type peashooter.

Idol Ready
During gameplay, press Print Screen, then type false gods.

Into the Lair Lit
During gameplay, press Print Screen, then type 5 green bottles.

Jungle Pursuit Lit
During gameplay, press Print Screen, then type 3 green bottles.

Kickback Lit
During gameplay, press Print Screen, then type field goal.

Last Ingredients Enabled
During gameplay, press Print Screen, then type donut.

Mystery Lit
During gameplay, press Print Screen, then type miss marple.

Next Ingredient Enabled
During gameplay, press Print Screen, then type mixmaster.

Pirate Gold Lit
During gameplay, press Print Screen, then type 2 green bottles.

Points Added
During gameplay, press Print Screen, then type debate team.

Powerball Enabled
During gameplay, press Print Screen, then type transwarp.

Scorpion Hunt Lit
During gameplay, press Print Screen, then type 7 green bottles.

Set to Final Ball
During gameplay, press Print Screen, then type checkmate.

Snake Slaying Lit
During gameplay, press Print Screen, then type 4 green bottles.

Time Decreased
During gameplay, press Print Screen, then type juvenile.

Time Increased
During gameplay, press Print Screen, then type geriatric.

Video Mode Ready
During gameplay, press Print Screen, then type idiot box.

Volcano Ready
During gameplay, press Print Screen, then type pompeii.

Voodoo Curse Lit
During gameplay, press Print Screen, then type 6 green bottles.

Witchdoctor Ready
During gameplay, press Print Screen, then type ooga-booga.

Zombie Ball Enabled
During gameplay, press Print Screen, then type deadman.

DIE HARD: NAKATOMI PLAZA

Activating Cheats
To activate the cheats, you must edit a game file. Create a backup copy of the file before proceeding. Use a text editor to edit the "autoexec.cfg" file in the game folder and change specific lines as designated below.

God Mode
Change the "PlayerTakeDamage 1" entry to "PlayerTakeDamage 0".

No Clipping
Change the "PlayerClip 0" entry to "PlayerClip 1".

Invincible Enemies
Change the "AITakeDamage 1" entry to "AITakeDamage 0".

Enemies Take More Damage
Change the "AITakeDamage 1" entry to "AITakeDamage 99".

DIE HARD TRILOGY 2

All Weapons
Pause gameplay in Action/Adventure mode and type weapons.

Become a Skeleton
Pause gameplay in Action/Adventure mode indicated and type mrbones.

Become Electric
Pause gameplay in Action/Adventure mode and type shocked.

Freeze Enemies
Pause gameplay in Action/Adventure mode and type freeze.

Jump as High as You Want
Pause gameplay in Action/Adventure mode and type followterrain.

Toggle Auto Targeting
Pause gameplay in Action/Adventure mode and type targeting.

Toggle Laser Targeting
Pause gameplay in Action/Adventure mode and type laser.

Unlimited Ammo
Pause gameplay in Action/Adventure mode and type ammo.

Walk Through Walls
Pause gameplay in Action/Adventure mode and type ghost.

Fogging On/Off
Pause gameplay in any mode and type fogging.

God Mode
Pause gameplay in any mode and type painless.

Move Camera
Pause gameplay in any mode and type followme.

Drive Faster
Pause gameplay in Driving mode and type chantastic.

Drive Only With Tires
Pause gameplay in Driving mode and type susonly.

Drive Through Walls
Pause gameplay in Driving mode and type ghost.

Snow
Pause gameplay in Driving mode and type snow.

Toggle Time Limit
Pause gameplay in Driving mode and type freeze.

Unlimited Nitro
Pause gameplay in Driving mode and type nitro.

All Weapons
Pause gameplay in Sharpshooting mode and type weapons.

Autofire On/Off
Pause gameplay in the Sharpshooting and type autofire.

Autoreload On/Off
Pause gameplay in the mode and type autoreload.

Enemies Are Slower
Pause gameplay in Sharpshooting mode and type slowmo.

Rockets Are Slower
Pause gameplay in Sharpshooting mode and type slowrocket.

Unlimited Ammo
Pause gameplay in Sharpshooting mode and type ammo.

DIONAKRA

Level 2 Password
PADDLE

Level 3 Password
CAVERN

Level 4 Password
ASTEROID

Level 5 Password
TEMPLE

Level 6 Password
METEOR

Level 7 Password
GLACIER

Level 8 Password
PEAK

Level 9 Password
VALLEY

Level 10 Password
FANTASY

Level 11 Password
TREASURE

Level 12 Password
ISLAND

Level 13 Password
TWISTER

Level 14 Password
BUTTERFLY

Level 15 Password
CANNON

Level 16 Password
THUNDER

Level 17 Password
LIGHTNING

Level 18 Password
OCEAN

Level 19 Password
TERRAIN

Level 20 Password
OAK

Level 21 Password
FORGE

Level 22 Password
CASTLE

Level 23 Password
TOMB

Level 24 Password
WATERFALL

Level 25 Password
POTION

Level 26 Password
MAGIC

Level 27 Password
STABLE

Level 28 Password
HEAVEN

Level 29 Password
FORCE

Level 30 Password
ARMORY

Level 31 Password
CLIFF

Level 32 Password
TIDE

Level 33 Password
SNOWCAP

Level 34 Password
JUNGLE

Level 35 Password
SERPENT

Level 36 Password
AIRCRAFT

Level 37 Password
POWDER

Level 38 Password
COMPASS

Level 39 Password
ARROW

Level 40 Password
CORE

Level 41 Password
REACTOR

Level 42 Password
GRAVEYARD

Level 43 Password
WATERHOLE

Level 44 Password
SPEEDBOAT

Level 45 Password
BEACH

Level 46 Password
SILVER

Level 47 Password
AMNESIA

Level 48 Password
METAPHOR

Level 49 Password
CHAMBER

Level 50 Password
JUDGEMENT

DISCIPLES: SACRED LANDS

5000 Mana and Gold
givememoney

Able to Build Again
iwanttobuildagain

Alliance with Everyone
wouldyou?

At Peace with Everyone
iloveallofyou

At War with Everyone
iwanttokilleverybody

Become Invisible
playhideandseek

Hide Map
whoturnedoffthelights

Instant Loss
whataloseriam

Instant Win
nobodycanbeatme

Next Fight Will Level Up Your Leader and Units
upgrademe

Recover Health
makemestronger

Refill Units Movement
letmemove

Reveal Enemy/Monster
iwillkeepaneyeonyou

Reveal Map
nowicanseeyou

Revive Dead Units
givemeanotherchance

DOGS OF WAR

Turn Off Sprite Detection
During a game, type TIMBO.

DOMINANT SPECIES

Create a Dog
During gameplay, press ~ and press Enter. Type spawn cisco 1.

Selected Creatures Invincible
During gameplay, press ~ and press Enter. Type armorofgod 10000.

DOOFUS

Stage 2.1 Password
CURCHILL

Stage 3.1 Password
HIGHBALL

Stage 1.2 Password
TOREADOR

Stage 2.2 Password
EUROKISS

Stage 3.2 Password
PARADISO

Stage 1.3 Password
SUNDRIES

Stage 2.3 Password
ANANASIA

Stage 3.3 Password
NIGHTCAP

Stage 1.4 Password
MANDARIN

Stage 2.4 Password
DAIQUIRI

Stage 3.4 Password
KORNKIRI

DOMINION

Extra Money
During a game, press Enter and type TILT.

No Radar
During a game, press Enter and type SETI.

Increase Resources
During a game, press Enter and type LUSHEE.

Reveal Map
During a game, press Enter and type INFRARED.

Kill Enemy Units
During a game, press Enter and type COMBUSTION.

Speed Build
During a game, press Enter and type ZIPPER.

DOOM

Chainsaw
During gameplay, type idchoppers.

Display Your Bearing and Coordinates in Hex
During gameplay, type idmypos.

Display Full Automap
During gameplay, type idbeholdA.

Gain Temporary Invisibility
During gameplay, type idbeholdil.

Gain Temporary Light Amplification Visors
During gameplay, type idbeholdL.

Gain Temporary Radiation Suit
During gameplay, type idbeholdR.

Gain Temporary Invulnerability
During gameplay, type idbeholdV.

Temporarily Go Berserk
During gameplay, type idbeholdS.

Full Ammo, 200 Percent Armor, All Weapons and Keys
During gameplay, type idkfa.

Full Ammo, 200 Percent Armor, and All Weapons
During gameplay, type idfa.

God Mode
During gameplay, type iddqd.

No Clipping
During gameplay, type idspispopd.

Toggles Automap Modes (at Automap)
During gameplay, type iddt.

Warp to Level
During gameplay, type idclevxx (replace xx with a number from 01 to 19).

DOOM 2

All Weapons, Full Ammo, All Keys
During gameplay, type IDKFA.

God Mode
During gameplay, type IDDQD.

Warp to Level
During gameplay, type IDCLEV## (replace ## with a number from 01 to 32).

No Clipping
During gameplay, type IDCLIP.

Gain Temporary Invisibility
During gameplay, type IDBEHOLDI.

Temporarily Go Berserk
During gameplay, type IDBEHOLDS.

Gain Temporary Invulnerability
During gameplay, type IDBEHOLDV.

Gain Temporary Radiation Suit
During gameplay, type IDBEHOLDR.

Display Full Automap
During gameplay, type IDBEHOLDA.

Gain Temporary Light Amplification Goggles
During gameplay, type IDBEHOLDL.

DRAKAN DEMO

God Mode
During a game, press the Talk button and type sanctuary, then press Enter.

Full Health
During a game, press the Talk button and type smeghead, then press Enter.

Debug Mode On
During a game, press the Talk button and type debug on, then press Enter.

Debug Mode Off
During a game, press the Talk button and type debug off, then press Enter.

DR. BRAIN: PUZZLE MADNESS

Flash Gun
At the main menu, type #5L0s7.

Gas Mask
At the main menu, type #0m0sk.

Ice Gun
At the main menu, type #on824.

Signal Jammer
At the main menu, type #90m4r.

Wire Cutters
At the main menu, type #2ut8t.

DR. GOO

Disable Medicine Box Collection
Type the password 1212.

Disable Radioactive Barrels and Green Zapper
Type the password 6024.

Disable Timer
Type the password 7345.

DR. GOO 2

Disable Medicine Box Collection
Type the password 1212.

Disable Radioactive Barrels and Green Zapper
Type the password 6024.

Disable Timer
Type the password 7345.

Level 2 Password
2258

Level 3 Password
3691

Level 4 Password
4990

Walk on Water
Type the password 0750.

DR. GOO 3: THE RUBBLEBUM WAR

Collect All Stars
Type the password 1272.

Disable Death Box
Type the password 6024.

Disable Green Zapper
Type the password 7545.

Disable Radioactive Barrels
Type the password 9602.

Disable Security Shield
Type the password 4455.

Level 2 Password
2002

Level 3 Password
3392

Level 4 Password
4056

Level 5 Password
5152

Level 6 Password
6543

Level 7 Password
7470

Walk on Water
Type the password 0750.

DRAGONFIRE: WELL OF SOULS

Change Level
/changelevel

Clan 69
/clan69

God Mode
/godmode

Invisibility
/invisible

Restore Life
/restorelife

DRAKAN: ORDER OF THE FLAME

Enable/Disable Debug Mode
During gameplay, press \ to talk, then type debug on/off.

Full Health
During gameplay, press \ to talk, then type smoghead.

Get Item
During gameplay, press \ to talk, then type gimme ####.

List Weapons in Debug Mode
During gameplay, press \ to talk, then type all weapons.

Get Weapon #### (Listed in the All Weapons Code)
During gameplay, press \ to talk, then type give ####.

God Mode
During gameplay, press \ to talk, then type iamgod.

God Mode on Final Stage
During gameplay, press \ to talk, then type iamgoddess.

DRIVER

Fast Cars
At the High Score screen, type NJW280172.

Invincibility
At the High Score screen, type RUS3L.

No Police
At the High Score screen, type WAC271074.

DUKE NUKEM 3D

God Mode Toggle
During a game, type DNKROZ.

God Mode Toggle
During a game, type DNCORNHOLIO.

All Weapons, Ammo, and Key Cards
During a game, type DNSTUFF.

All Weapons and Ammo
During a game, type DNWEAPONS.

All Items and Key Cards
During a game, type DNITEMS.

All Items
During a game, type DNINVENTORY.

All Key Cards
During a game, type DNKEYS.

No Clipping Mode
During a game, type DNCLIP.

Full Map
During a game, type DNSHOWMAP.

Steroids
During a game, type DNHYPER.

Open All Doors
During a game, type DNUNLOCK.

Change Skill to Level
During a game, type DNSKILL#.

Level Warp
During a game, type DNSCOTTYell (where e is the episode # and ll is the two-digit level #).

Chase Plane View
During a game, type DNVIEW.

Monsters Disappear When They See Duke
During a game, type DNMONSTERS.

Duke Throws Money When You Press the Spacebar
During a game, type DNCASHMAN.

Displays the Frame Rate
During a game, type DNRATE.

Displays Current Coordinates
During a game, type DNCOORDS.

Displays Debugging Info
During a game, type DNDEBUG.

Displays Message: Register Cosmo Today!
During a game, type DNTODD.

Displays Message: Pirates Suck!
During a game, type DNBETA.

Displays Message: Buy Major Stryker
During a game, type DNALLEN.

DUKE NUKEM 3D: ATOMIC EDITION

All Items
DNINVENTORY

All Items and Key Cards
DNITEMS

All Key Cards
DNKEYS

All Weapons and Ammo
DNWEAPONS

All Weapons, Ammo, and Key Cards
DNSTUFF

Change Skill to Level
DNSKILL#

Chase Plane View
DNVIEW

Display Current Coordinates
DNCOORDS

Display Debugging Info
DNDEBUG

Display Message: Buy Major Stryker
DNALLEN

Display Message: Pirates Suck!
DNBETA

Display Message: Register Cosmo Today!
DNTODD

Display the Frame Rate
DNRATE

Full Map
DNSHOWMAP

Level Warp
DNSCOTTYxyy (where x = episode, y = level)

Monsters Disappear When They See Duke
DNMONSTERS

No Clipping Mode
DNCLIP

Opens All Doors
DNUNLOCK

Press Space Bar to Make Duke Throw Money
DNCASHMAN

Steroids
DNHYPER

Toggle God Mode
DNKROZ

DUKE NUKEM: MANHATTAN PROJECT

Activate Cheat Mode
Press ~ during gameplay to display the console window. Then, enter one of the codes given below to activate the corresponding cheat function.

All Weapons and Items
give all

Maximum Ammunition
give ammo

All Keys
give keys

Jet Pack
give jetpack

Force Field
give forcefield

Extra Life
give life

10 Nukes
give nuke

100 Ego
give health

Mark Secret Found
give secret

Spawn Extra Babe
give bomb

Matrix-Style Pause
pause

God Mode Toggle
g_p_god

Suicide
kill

Display Map Information Toggle
g_map_info

Display Game Statistics Toggle
r_stats

Debug Mode Toggle
g_debug

Camera Can Explore Level
camera camera

Return Camera to Normal
camera player

DUNE II

Accurate Harkonnen Deathhand
When you play as House Harkonnen, you receive a palace in later levels. This palace contains the Deathhand missile. While extremely powerful, it is also the most inaccurate projectile. However, if you put the pointy end of your cursor on the top of a structure's flag when aiming and simultaneously hold down T, the missile destroys that structure and those around it in a single shot.

DUNGEON KEEPER 2

All Magic
Press Ctrl+Alt+C then type I believe its magic.

All Rooms
Press Ctrl+Alt+C then type this is my church.

All Rooms and Traps
Press Ctrl+Alt+C then type fit the best.

DUNGEON SIEGE

Activate Cheat Mode
Press Enter during gameplay and type + followed by one of the following codes to activate the corresponding cheat function. To disable a code, type - followed by the code.

150 More Demons
sixdemonbag

999999 Gold
checksinthemail

Always Chunky
chunkey

Big Character
maxjooky

Chunk Factor
superchunky

Clicks Not Required
shootall

Display Game Version
version

Enable Mouse
mouse

Enable Selection Rings
rings

Invincibility
zool

Maximum Damage
drdeath

Record a Movie
movie

Remove Fog of War
loefervision

Remove Textures
xrayvision

Small Character
minjooky

Full Set of Badger Weapons, Armor, & Items
faertehbadgar

100 Meter Range for All Bows
sniper

Three Super Health and Three Super Mana Potions
potionaholic

Slightly Larger Labels over Head (only if character labels are active)
resizelabels

DYNASTY WARS

Skip Level
Type "cheat mode" at the title screen. Press F2 during game to skip the current level.

EARTH 2140

Access Cheat Mode
Start the game with the command line parameter x640 KR MS MW WW MD or x800 KR MS MW WW MD depending on your resolution.

Destroy All Selected Units
Enable Cheat mode, then during gameplay, hold Shift and type RTHKILL.

Heal All Your Selected Units or Enemy Structure
Enable Cheat mode, then during gameplay, hold Shift and type RTHHEALTH.

Reveal Mission Area
Enable Cheat mode, then during gameplay, hold Shift and type RTHSHOWMP.

$5,000 to All Teams
Enable Cheat mode, then during gameplay, hold Shift and type RTHCSHE.

Four Times Income Per Crate from Mines
Enable Cheat mode, then during gameplay, hold Shift and type RTHMN4.

Two Times Income Per Crate from Mines
Enable Cheat mode, then during gameplay, hold Shift and type RTHMN2.

Allows Another Call for Help
Enable Cheat mode, then during gameplay, hold Shift and type RTHRNFRCMNT.

Complete Mission
Enable Cheat mode, then during gameplay, hold Shift and type RTHVCTR.

Up One Research Level for All Teams
Enable Cheat mode, then during gameplay, hold Shift and type RTHRSRCHE.

Complete All Levels of Research for All Teams
Enable Cheat mode, then during gameplay, hold Shift and type RTHRSRCHLL.

Max Strength to Armor and Firepower for T100 and ST01B
Enable Cheat mode, then during gameplay, hold Shift and type RTHPVR.

Jump to Level ##
Enable Cheat mode, then during gameplay, hold Shift and type RTHGLX## (replace ## with the level number).

EARTH 2150

Damage All Near Units
During gameplay, press Enter and type I_wanna_cheat. Then press Enter and type bad_time_bad_place.

Destroy All Visible Units/Objects
During gameplay, press Enter and type I_wanna_cheat. Then press Enter and type hasta_la_vista_enemigos.

Destroy Selected Unit
During gameplay, press Enter and type I_wanna_cheat. Then press Enter and type see_you_next_life.

Fast Explore Player Only, 0=Off, 1=On
During gameplay, press Enter and type I_wanna_cheat. Then press Enter and type help_me_please!!! 0/1.

Fast Explore, 0=Off, 1=On
During gameplay, press Enter and type I_wanna_cheat. Then press Enter and type einstein 0/1.

Fog
During gameplay, press Enter and type I_wanna_cheat. Then press Enter and type let_be_darkness.

Full Map
During gameplay, press Enter and type I_wanna_cheat. Then press Enter and type no_more_secrets.

Full Repair/Reload Ammo
During gameplay, press Enter and type I_wanna_cheat. Then press Enter and type x-mas_pack.

Give # of CR
During gameplay, press Enter and type I_wanna_cheat. Then press Enter and type i_love_this_game #.

Kill All Enemies at Range of 8
During gameplay, press Enter and type I_wanna_cheat. Then press Enter and type the_hammer_of_thor.

Kill Everything at Range of Eight
During gameplay, press Enter and type I_wanna_cheat. Then press Enter and type massacre.

Meteor Shower
During gameplay, press Enter and type I_wanna_cheat. Then press Enter and type armageddonv.

Mines
During gameplay, press Enter and type I_wanna_cheat. Then press Enter and type fireworks.

See All
During gameplay, press Enter and type I_wanna_cheat. Then press Enter and type eagle_eye.

See All Units
During gameplay, press Enter and type I_wanna_cheat. Then press Enter and type no_one_hides.

Set Unit Limit to # CR
During gameplay, press Enter and type I_wanna_cheat. Then press Enter and type i_hate_limits #.

EARTH 2150: MOON PROJECT

During gameplay, press TAB to access the command console. Type one of the following codes to activate the cheat:

Enable Cheat Mode
Cheater 1

Disable Cheat Mode
Cheater 0

Faster Research
mybrainisfaster 1

Increases Units to # (Replace # With a Number)
limit_up #

Increases Money to # (Replace # With a Number)
moneyfornothing #

Lose Scenario
byebye

Deliver a Meteor Shower
Shower

Damage All Visible Enemies
Tromaville

Destroy Selected Building
gohome!

Destroy Selected Enemy Building
smash

Destroy All Enemies in View
judgementday

Research Is Free
Sciencefornothing

Show Entire Map
beautifulmoon 1

Place Mines
hotground

Show All Enemies in View
hereyouare!

Replace Fog of War
hide

Remove the Fog of War
moonlight

Research Everything
nobelprize

EARTHSIEGE 2

Access Cheat Mode
Start the game with the command line parameter -SPRUNKNOWN. Cheat mode might crash the game.

Play Cockpit Warnings and Announcements
Enable Cheat mode, then during gameplay, press Alt+< or >.

Send Herc 12 Meters in That Direction
Enable Cheat mode, then during gameplay, press Alt+Up or Down.

Face Herc in That Direction
Enable Cheat mode, then during gameplay, press Alt+Left or Right.

Nuke Enemy
Enable Cheat mode, then during gameplay, press Alt+Ctrl+N.

View Herc Textures
Enable Cheat mode, then during gameplay, press Alt+Ctrl+S.

Select Combat Viewpoint One
Enable Cheat mode, then during gameplay, press Ctrl+N.

Toggle AI
Enable Cheat mode, then during gameplay, press Alt+S.

Advance One Frame Forward When AI Disabled
Enable Cheat mode, then during gameplay, press Alt+Keypad Plus.

EARTHWORM JIM

Get 1,000 Ammo
POPQUIZHOTSHOT

Make Jim an Afro
BLOATED

Jim Has Big Lips
SWEATY

Nice Picture!
IDKFA

Gains New Life
ITSAWONDERFUL

New Coordinates
BEAMMEUP

Turns Jim into a Hatman
HATMAN

Another Funny Picture
IDDQD

First Five Levels Free
SLAUGHTERHOUSE

Enable All Levels
GETTHECHEESETOSICKBAY

Max Energy
THREEMILEISLAND

EAT THIS

God Mode On/Off
During gameplay, type ETGOD.

Got All the Stuff You Need
During gameplay, type ETSTUFF.

Got Wings, Chicken/Fly Mode Off
During gameplay, type ETFLY.

End Current Level and Go to Next Level
During gameplay, type ETWIN.

Battledrone/Upgrade
During gameplay, type ETDRONE.

Display Map On/Off
During gameplay, type ETSCAN.

Play as Alien
During gameplay, type ETALIEN.

Restart Current Level
During gameplay, type ETRESTART.

Play in a Rainstorm
During gameplay, type ETRAIN.

Check User Maps Menu
During gameplay, type ETMAPS.

A Cat Runs Off
During gameplay, type ETCAT.

Throws a Cat
During gameplay, type ETPULL.

DEATHWISH?
During gameplay, type ETBOOM.

EMERGENCY: FIGHTERS FOR LIFE

Mission Select
At the Accident scene, place your mouse pointer over Options and type sixteen.

E-MOTION

One Level Up
When the picture of Albert Einstein appears, type MOONUNIT then press F1.

One Level Down
When the picture of Albert Einstein appears, type MOONUNIT then press F2.

10 Levels Up
When the picture of Albert Einstein appears, type MOONUNIT then press F3.

10 Levels Down
When the picture of Albert Einstein appears, type MOONUNIT then press F4.

EMPIRE OF THE ANTS

Access Cheat Mode
Start the game with the command line parameter /11.

Reveal Map
During the game in Cheat mode, press F11 and type showmap.

Turns Anthill into Disco Party
During the game in Cheat mode, press F11 and type Disco.

Freeze Ants
During the game in Cheat mode, press F11 and type marche.

Win the Level
During the game in Cheat mode, press F11 and type WinLevel.

Lose the Level
During the game in Cheat mode, press F11 and type LoseLevel.

Get Food
During the game in Cheat mode, press F11 and type wannaFood.

EMPIRE STRIKES BACK

Cheat Mode
At the title screen, hold Help and type XIFARGROTCEV.

ENTREPRENEUR

Get $10,000,000
In single player, press Tab and type zeropercentinterest.

Get $100,000,000
In single player, press Tab and type canyouspareadime.

Get $100,000,000
In single player, press Tab and type nomoneydown.

Research All Regions
In single player, press Tab and type iseelondoniseefrance.

Get 10 of Each Resource
In single player, press Tab and type feelthatmojorising.

Get 99 of Each Resource
In single player, press Tab and type idkfa.

Get One Action Card
In single player, press Tab and type hitmeagain.

Get Full Hand of Cards
In single player, press Tab and type upmysleeve.

Current Research Project Completed
In single player, press Tab and type impressme.

EQUESTRIAD 2001

Select "Options" from the game's opening menu. Then select "Cheats." Type the cheat and press Enter.

No Dressage Failures
MR HAPPY

Big Head Mode
BIGHEAD

ESCAPE: OR DIE TRYING

Level Select
At the main menu, type LACRIMOSA.

Add Sophia to Playable Characters
At the main menu, type SOPHIA.

Add Karma to Playable Characters
At the main menu, type KARMA.

Full Energy (Red Bar)
Pause gameplay and type XUL.

Full Mana (Purple Bar)
Pause gameplay and type BOZ.

Full Capacity on All Four Weapons
Pause gameplay and type JBB.

Increase Power Slightly on All Four Weapons
Pause gameplay and type MATH.

Increase Armor, Weapon, and Spirit Levels Slightly
Pause gameplay and type GRABO.

Increase Experience to Maximum
Pause gameplay and type MUMU.

Set Number of Lives to 50
Pause gameplay and type ALEX.

All Spells Acquired
Pause gameplay and type RIK.

Add One Star to Each Acquired Spell
Pause gameplay and type VINCE.

Full Energy, Full Mana, Full Experience, 50 Lives, Full Capacity and Power for All Four Weapons, Increase Armor, Weapon, and Spirit Slightly, All Spells Acquired, All Four Stars on Spells
Pause gameplay and type CACHOU.

ESPN NFL PRIMETIME 2002

Activate Cheat Mode
Enter one of the codes below to activate the corresponding cheat function.

Unstoppable Ball Carrier
can't touch this

Super Jumps and Dives
superman

Fumbles (Press L during Gameplay to Cause a Fumble)
ready to fumble

Aloha Stadium and Pro Bowl Teams
aloha

Reliant Stadium
howdy

Weather in Domed Stadiums
shake it up

Controller Scoring
scorebox

Show Everyone
show everyone

E-SWAT

99 Credits
Pause gameplay and type JUSTIFIED ANCIENTS OF MU MU.

EUROPA UNIVERSALIS

Press F12 during gameplay, then type one of the following phrases to get the corresponding cheat:

God Mode
difrules

Bring All Military Units Under Your Control
richelieu

Set Stability to +3
oranje

Get Rid of Natives
cortez

Get Rid of Revolts
alba

Turn Fog of War On/Off
pappenheim

Explore Every Province
Columbus

Increase Level of Land Technology
gustavus

Increase Level of Naval Technology
drake

Increases the level of the Infrastructure
Cromwell

Increases the Level of Trade
polo

No Computer Declarations of War
tilly

Adds 50,000 Ducats to Your Treasury
Montezuma

Add 10 Colonists
Pocahontas

Add 10 Diplomats
Vatican

Add 10 Merchants
dagama

Add 10,000 people to Capitol Province
swift

Limits Troops
peterthegreat

Add Cannon Fodder
russianhordes

Closing Japan
shogun

Starts Reformation Effects
luther

Starts John Calvin Effects
calvin

Create Events
During gameplay, press F12, then type event #. Instead of #, type the number corresponding to the Event you wish to unlock.

Create Random Revolt in Province
1

Create Random Revolt in Colony
2

Create Religious Revolt
3

Religion
7

Heretics
8

Death
9

Excellent
10

Insanity
11

Scandal
12

Gift
13

Gold Lost
14

Obscuritism
15

Except Year
16

Colonist
17

Demand
18

Bank
20

Stock Exchange
21

Trade Company
22

Closure of Port
23

Diplomacy
24

Pressure
25

Col Dyn
26

Inventions
27

Merchants
28

Sea Charts Stolen
29

Plague
30

Naval Disaster
31

Dessertion
32

Land Tech
33

Naval Tech
34

Enthusiastic Army
35

Enthusiastic Navy
36

Annex
37

Agriculture
38

Fire
39

Good Government
40

Poor Government
41

Unhappy Clergy
42

Unhappy Artists
43

Unhappy Peasants
44

Unhappy Merchants
45

Mineral
46

Crisis
47

Corruption
48

Deflation
49

Dip Insult
50

Favored Trade Union
51

Industrial Development
52

New Center of Trade
53

Trade Restrictions
54

Fortification
55

Explorer
56

Conquistador
57

Explorer with Ship
58

Conquistador and 1,000 Troops in Random City
59

EUROPA UNIVERSALIS II

Activate Cheat Mode
Press F12 during gameplay, enter one of the following codes at the console window, and press Enter. Press Ctrl+F12 to close the console window and activate the corresponding cheat function.

Toggle Revolts
alba

Toggle John Calvin Mode
calvin

Explore All Provinces (Cannot be Deactivated)
columbus

Toggle Natives
cortez

Increase Infrastructure Level
cromwell

Additional 10 Merchants
dagama

God Mode
difrules

Increase Naval Technology Level
drake

Increase Land Technology Level
gustavus

Additional Six Missionaries
loyola

Toggle Reformation Mode
luther

Additional 50,000 Ducats to Treasury
montezuma

No Pause during Events
ney

Set Stability to +3
oranje

Toggle Fog of War
pappenheim

Additional Ten Colonists
pocahontas

Increase Trade Level
polo

Toggle Control of All Military Units
richelieu

Change Domestic Policy Freely
robespierre

More Cannon Fodder
russianhordes

Additional 10,000 Population to Capital Province
swift

Toggle Ability of CPU to Declare War
tilly

Toggle Treaty of Tordesillas Mode
tordesillas

Toggle Council of Trent Mode
trent

Additional Ten Diplomats
vatican

Toggle Province Status Review
wallenstein

Trigger Indicated Event
event <number>; where <number> is one of the event codes listed below.

Reformation
100

Jean Calvin
101

Council of Trent
102

Edict of Tolerance
103

Treaty of Tordesillas
110

English Pirates
1000

One Province Revolts Unprovoked
1001

Religious Turmoil; One Revolt
1002

Conversion of Heretics; Changes Religion in One Province
1003

Gift to the State; +200 Gold
1004

Temporary Insanity of Monarch; ADM, DIP, MIL Set to 2 for 12 Months
1005

Excellent Minister; ADM, DIP, MIL Set to 9 for 12 Months
1006

Scandal at Court
1007

Wave of Obscurantism; +3 Revolt Risk
1008

Exceptional Year; -5 Inflation, +100 Gold
1009

Rush of Colonists; +3 Colonists
1010

Diplomatic Move; +50 Relation, +1 Diplomat
1011

Great Reputation; +10 Relation with Seven Countries
1012

Colonial Dynamism; +1 Conquistador, +3 Colonists
1013

Unexpected Invention; +1 Manufacturing
1014

Rush of Merchants
1015

Plague; -5000 People in Province
1016

Reformation of Army; +250 Land Tech
1017

Reformation of Navy; +250 Naval Tech
1018

Enthusiasm for Army; +5000 Troops
1019

Enthusiasm for Navy ; +5 Warships
1020

Agricultural Revolution
1021

Devastating Fire; -1 Manufactory
1022

Good Government Policies; +1 Stability, +250 Infrastructure and Trade Tech
1023

Poor Government Policies; -1 Stability, -250 Infrastructure and Trade Tech
1024

Unhappiness with Clergy
1025

Unhappiness among Artisans
1026

Unhappiness among Peasants
1027

Unhappiness among Merchants
1028

Valuable Mineral
1029

Political Crisis
1030

Corruption
1031

Deflation
1032

Diplomatic Insult
1033

Fortification Effort; +1 Fort to Province
1034

Creation of Bank; -5 Inflation, +200 Gold
1035

Creation of Stock Exchange; -2 Inflation, +100 Gold, +500 Infrastructure Tech
1036

Creation of Company of Trade; +2 Merchants, +500 Trade Tech
1037

Colonial Uprising; a Colony Rebels
1038

Heretic Uprising
1039

Explorer; +1 Explorer, +0 Colonists
1040

Conquistador; +1 Conquistador, +0 Colonists
1041

Nobles; -2 Stability
1042

Trading Company Disaster
1043

Internal Trade
1044

Meteor Sighted
1045

Fire Ordinance
1046

Saint Performs Miracle; +1 Stability, -3 Revolt Risk
1047

Medical
1048

Noble Feud
1049

Nobles Ally with Foreign Power; -2 Stability, Casus Belli (Nation)
1050

Assassination of Noble
1051

Cessation of Church Functions to Nobility
1052

Sale of Offices
1053

Monopoly Company Formed
1054

Nobles Demand Increased Pensions
1055

Grant Export Licenses
1056

New Land Claimed
1057

Establish Cantonments
1058

Nobles Demand Old Rights
1059

Cities Demand Old Rights
1060

Nonenforcement of Ordinances
1061

Bourgeoisie Request Privileges
1062

Italian Engineer Available
1063

Foreign Drill Instructor; -250 Gold, +1 Offensive Doc, +1 Quality/-1 Victory Points
1064

Build a Great Palace
1065

Indulgence Peddler
1066

Uncooperative Philosopher
1067

Regional Heresy
1068

Boundary Dispute
1069

Merchants Harassed
1070

Regional Population Boom; +2 Colonists/+2000 Population
1071

Petition for Redress; -4 Stability, +1 Centralization/-1 Stability, -1 Tax, Revolt (Province)
1072

Noble Family Requests Aid
1073

Support for Dissidents Abroad
1074

Foreign Trade Competition Rises; +1 Mercantilism/-1 Merc
1075

Exceptional Court Painter Available
1076

Catholic Influence in Africa
1077

Christian Influence in South Africa
1078

Mali Returns to Paganism
1079

Moslem Influence in Africa
1080

Moslem Influence in Nubia
1081

Catholic Influence in America; +1 Stability /Convert to Catholic and Four Colonies
1082

Protestant Influence in America
1083

Moslem Influence in Southeast Asia
1084

Newton Publishes *Principia Mathematica*; +200 to Land, Naval, Infrastructure, and Trade Tech
1500

Newton Publishes *Optica*; +250 to Land and Naval Tech
1501

Hungarian Vampire; -1 Stability, -1 Innovativeness
1503

Gerard Mercator de Kremer; +500 to Naval Tech
1506

All Life Is Holy; -2 Stability
1508

The Lollard Heresy; +3 Revolt Risk, -2 Stability, -50g/-100 to 2 Countries
3001

War of the Roses; +1 Artist, Serf, -1 Central, Land, -3 Stability
3002

Bosworth Field; +3 Stability, Central, -3 Serf, Merc, -5 Artist
3003

End of the 100 Years War; +1 Stability, +150 Relations with France
3004

Justices of Peace; +1 Cent, +6 Tax Collectors, +1 Stability, -200g +1 Serf, Artist, +2 Stability, +100g
3005

Support Middle-Class Bureaucrats; +1 Innov, -1 Artist, Merc, Land, Stability -1 Innov, +1 Artist, Serf, Stability, +2 Land, +100g
3006

Court of the Star Chamber; +2 Cent, Innov, +1 Stability, +3 Revolt Risk, +2 Artist, +1 Stability, -1 Cent, Innov
3007

The Enclosure Movement; -3 Stability, +1 Revolt Risk/-1 Central, -2 Serf, +1 Stability
3008

EUROPEAN AIR WAR

Faster Missions
When taxiing on the runway, press A to engage autopilot. When you're airborne, press Alt+N. This takes you directly to the mission directive.

EVEN MORE INCREDIBLE MACHINE

All Level Select
Type the password PASSWORD.

EVIL ISLANDS: CURSE OF THE LOST SOUL

To Activate Cheats
To activate cheats, open the console and type `, then type thingamabob. Press Enter, then type one of the following codes:

God Mode 1
@godmode(0,1)

Skip to New Green Clan's Residence
Type @leavetozone(0,"name",0). Instead of "name," type one of the following codes to transport to various zones. Typing @leaveto-zone(0,"bz1g",0) brings you to the village on the first island.

Skip to Abandoned Mines
bz11k

Skip to Fortress
bz13h

Skip to Last Shelter
bz14h

Skip to Old Necromancer's Tower
bz15h

Skip to Secret Trading Place
bz16h

Skip to Meeting Place
bz18h Cave

Skip to Village
bz1g

Skip to Witch's Cave
bz2g

Skip to Dragon's Lair
bz3g

Skip to Khadaganian Expedition Camp
bz4g

Skip to Lizard Hermit's Home
bz5g

Skip to Sheivar Settlement
bz6g

Great Mage's Catacomb
bz7g

Skip to City of Ingos
bz8k

Skip to Green Clan's Residence
bz9k

Skip to Tunnel
gz10g

Skip to City Environs
gz11k

Skip to Abandoned Mines
gz12k

Skip to Karansul's Domain
gz13k

Skip to Forbidden Catacombs
gz14k

Skip to Death Canyon
gz15h

Skip to Wormheads' Cave
gz16h

Skip to Necromancers' Desert
gz17h

Skip to the City of Suslanger and Its Environs
gz18h

Skip to the Portal
gz19h

Skip to the Ruins
gz1g

Skip to the Catacombs
gz20g

Skip to the Road to the Witch
gz2g

Skip to Foothills
gz3g

Remote Mountains
gz4g

Cave
gz5g

Middle Mountains
gz6g

The River and the Islands
gz7g

Sands
gz8g

Dead City
gz9g

EXCESSIVE SPEED

All Cars
At the main menu, type allcars.

All Tracks
At the main menu, type alltracks.

Full Missile
At the main menu, type addmissile.

Full Turbo
At the main menu, type addturbo.

Full Life
At the main menu, type addlife.

Full Shield
At the main menu, type addshield.

Little Earthquake
At the main menu, type addearthquake.

Full Energy
At the main menu, type addenergy.

Full Pack
At the main menu, type addmine.

GhostCar
At the main menu, type addghost.

Win
During gameplay, type winrace.

Fly
During gameplay, type winflygame.

EXHUMED

All Weapons
lobocop

God Mode
lobodeity

All Items Loaded to 99
loboswag

All Keys
lobopick

EXPENDABLE

Hodspodkins Mode
Start the game with the command line parameter -mumford.

Rockhard Mode
Start the game with the command line parameter -whostayedlate.

EasterEgg Mode
Start the game with the command line parameter -whostayedlateagain.

Enable Cheat Mode
Now during gameplay, press - on the numeric keypad and type bod.

Skip Level
Now during gameplay, press - on the numeric keypad and type mrbenn.

God Mode
Now during gameplay, press - on the numeric keypad and type zippy.

Behind View
Now during gameplay, press - on the numeric keypad and type bucketofchicken.

Extra Credits
Now during gameplay, press - on the numeric keypad and type babapapa.

Extra Life
Now during gameplay, press - on the numeric keypad and type crystaltips.

Instant High Score
Now during gameplay, press - on the numeric keypad and type dunky.

Grenade Power-Up
Now during gameplay, press - on the numeric keypad and type albertofrog.

Disable Cheat Mode
Now during gameplay, press - on the numeric keypad and type bing.

EXTREME G2

Tron Appearance
Type your name as neutron.

Popup Distance Lowered
Type your name as pixie.

Rotating View Camera
Type your name as spiral.

Unlimited Nitro
Type your name as nitroid.

Better Weapons on Tracks
Type your name as misplace.

Unlimited Missiles
Type your name as mistake.

Unlimited Weapon and Shield Charge
Type your name as xcharge.

Airship View
Type your name as spyeye.

Futuristic Cars
Type your name as 2064.

Speed Up Game
Type your name as xxx.

Display Only One-Quarter of the Screen
Type your name as flick.

EXTREME PAINTBRAWL

Access Cheat Mode
Type the team name MAFIA.

Play as a Royal Canadian Mounted Policeman
Press Ctrl+Alt+Shift and type Aye! Yo mother was a mounty! and press Enter.

Walk Through Walls
Press Ctrl+Alt+Shift and type dnclip and press Enter.

F1 2000

Double Speed
Make a new profile with the name Damon Hill.

F-16 MULTIROLE FIGHTER

Unlimited Ammo
During gameplay, press T for the message prompt and type you got what i need.

Reload Plane
During gameplay, press T for the message prompt and type food goes here.

Refuel Plane
During gameplay, press T for the message prompt and type big gulp.

Invincible
During gameplay, press T for the message prompt and type youre here forever.

Can't Crash
During gameplay, press T for the message prompt and type damn that corner.

Repair Plane
During gameplay, press T for the message prompt and type chiliburger.

Can't Be Hit
During gameplay, press T for the message prompt and type spindive.

Auto Level Fly Upside-Down
During gameplay, press T for the message prompt and type upside down.

Paper Airplane
During gameplay, press T for the message prompt and type paperairplane.

F-22 AIR DOMINANCE FIGHTER

Full In-Air Refuel and Reload
Hold Ctrl+Alt+Shift+Insert.

Invincibility
Hold Ctrl+Alt+Shift+Home.

F-22 LIGHTNING 3

Unlimited Ammo
During gameplay, press Ctrl+Enter and type the truth is out there.

Replenish Current Ammo
During gameplay, press Ctrl+Enter and type fight the future.

Refuel
During gameplay, press Ctrl+Enter and type black oil.

God Mode
During gameplay, press Ctrl+Enter and type trust no one.

No Crash
During gameplay, press Ctrl+Enter and type i want to believe.

Heal
During gameplay, press Ctrl+Enter and type this isnt happening.

Invisible Plane
During gameplay, press Ctrl+Enter and type ghostpit.

F-22 RAPTOR

Complete Mission
During gameplay, press T for the message prompt and type it's not my fault.

Can't Be Hit
During gameplay, press T for the message prompt and type never tell me the odds.

Repair Damage
During gameplay, press T for the message prompt and type we can rebuild him.

Invulnerable
During gameplay, press T for the message prompt and type there can be only one.

Reload Stores
During gameplay, press T for the message prompt and type i'll be back.

F-29 RETALIATOR

Full Firepower
Inscribe as CIARAN and your name will change to OCEAN OK.

FALCON 1.0

Fully Rearm
Ctrl+X

Change Time of Day
Shift+T

FALCON 3.0

Increase Altitude
Pause gameplay, press Tab, then resume and press PgUp.

Decrease Altitude
Pause gameplay, press Tab, then resume and press PgDn.

Increase Movement Factor
Pause gameplay, press Tab, then resume and press +.

Decrease Movement Factor
Pause gameplay, press Tab, then resume and press -.

Rotate Right
Pause gameplay, press Tab, then resume and press F3.

Debug Mode (Displays Coordinates)
Pause gameplay, press Tab, then resume and press D.

Enter Coordinates to Transport
Pause gameplay, press Tab, then resume and press T.

Change Time of Day
Pause gameplay, press Tab, then resume and Shift+T.

Rotate Up
Pause gameplay, press Tab, then resume and Shift+F3.

Rotate Down
Pause gameplay, press Tab, then resume and Shift+F4.

Fine tune rotation keys above
Pause gameplay, press Tab, then resume and press Ctrl.

FALCON 4.0

Restore Ammo
During gameplay, type revenge.

FATAL ABYSS

Level Skip
Start the game with the command line parameter iwannaextrafunctions. During gameplay, press * on the numeric keypad.

FALLEN HAVEN

Two Secret Units (Random)
Start the game with MQWIERDSTUFF in the command line.

Increase/Decrease Credits (Ctrl +/-)
Start the game with MQCASH in the command line.

FANTASY EMPIRE

Cheat Mode
Create a character named JIM WARD.

FIFA '96

Special Teams
Select "Quit to DOS" and type xplay during the credits. The Friendly Game menu appears with five extra teams.

Enhanced Play Modes
Enable the "Special Teams" code. Then assign Vancouver to the team on the left and Canada to the team on the right. Now press Ctrl+Alt+Insert to display the menu. Return to this menu by pressing F1.

FIFA '98

Big Head Mode
Type eac rocks as any player's name and a Special Options box will appear.

Take a Dive
Type johnny atomic as any player's name and a Special Options box will appear.

Crazy Ball
Type dohdohdoh as any player's name and a Special Options box will appear.

Invisible Walls
Type urlofus as any player's name and a Special Options box will appear.

Hot Potato
Type xplay as any player's name and a Special Options box will appear.

Silly Moves
Type footy as any player's name and a Special Options box will appear.

FIFA 2000

Unlimited Funds
MOMONEY

Bonus Teams
HOOLIGAN

EAC Pitch
BURNABY

Lightning Mode
SIZZLE

Alien Mode
DIZZY

Glow Mode
LIGHTSOUT

FIFA 2001

Add Money
At the main menu, type Gimmethemoney.

Free Players
At the main menu, type Playersmaybe.

Big Head Mode
At the main menu, type Bigheads.

FINAL DOOM

Strength
During gameplay, type idbehold, then press S.

Invulnerability
During gameplay, type idbehold, then press V.

Partial Invisibility
During gameplay, type idbehold, then press I.

Full Automap
During gameplay, type idbehold, then press A.

Anti-Radiation Suit
During gameplay, type idbehold, then press R.

Light Amplification Visors
During gameplay, type idbehold, then press L.

Get Chainsaw
During gameplay, type idchoppers.

Level Warp
During gameplay, type idclevxyy (x = episode, y = level).

No Clipping
During gameplay, type idclip.

God Mode
During gameplay, type iddqd.

Toggles Automap Mode (at Automap)
During gameplay, type iddt.

Gives Full Ammo, 200 Percent Armor, and All Weapons
During gameplay, type idfa.

Very Happy Ammo (Full Ammo, 200 Percent Armor, All Weapons and Keys)
During gameplay, type idkfa.

Change Background Music to Track ##
During gameplay, type idmus## (replace ## with track number).

Displays Your Bearing And Coordinates in Hex
During gameplay, type idmypos.

FIREFIGHT

Cheat Menu
During gameplay, press C, W, and + on the keypad. Then press F12 to access the Cheat menu.

FLESH FEAST

End Level
During gameplay, hold Left-Shift, Left-Ctrl, Left-Alt, Home.

FLIGHT OF THE AMAZON QUEEN

Info
During gameplay, type GRIMLEY.

Choose Room to Go To
During gameplay, type ZEROXPARK.

High Speed
During gameplay, type KOWAMORI.

Play Tune
During gameplay, type NEUROTOX.

Check CD-Sample
During gameplay, type GRIMLEYZ.

FLY HARDER

Level 2 Password
PHO

Level 3 Password
MET

Level 4 Password
BLA

Level 5 Password
SUP

Level 6 Password
TRA

Level 7 Password
QUA

Level 8 Password
NEO

FLYING HEROES

Full Ammo
During gameplay, type OMMALLUF.

Full Health
During gameplay, type HTLAEHLLUF.

Full Mana
During gameplay, type ANAMLLUF.

Fire Boost
During gameplay, type TSOOBERIF.

Get Metal Star
During gameplay, type RATSLATEM.

Get Teleporter
During gameplay, type RETROPELET.

Get Cloak
During gameplay, type KAOLC.

Get Gas Barrel
During gameplay, type LERRABSAG.

Get Xemines
During gameplay, type SENIMEX.

Get Agmines
During gameplay, type SENIMGA.

Get Invisible
During gameplay, type ELBISIVNI.

Get Disorientate
During gameplay, type TSOOBERIF.

Get Acid Rain
During gameplay, type NIARDICA.

Get Armageddon
During gameplay, type NODDEGAMRA.

Get Death Cloud
During gameplay, type DUOLCHTAED.

Get FallFire
During gameplay, type ERIFLLAF.

Get Fireball
During gameplay, type LLABERIF.

Get Iceball
During gameplay, type LLABECI.

Get Flash
During gameplay, type HSALF.

FLYING SHARK

Unlimited Lives
At the High Score table, type HSC.

Invulnerability
At the High Score table, type KDJ.

FLYING TIGERS

Change Level
Pause gameplay with Tab and type ocellaris1q, then use up/down arrow to change level.

Player One Extra Life
Pause gameplay with Tab and type ocellaris1l.

Extra Health
Pause gameplay with Tab and type ocellaris1h.

Fireball Shots
Pause gameplay with Tab and type ocellaris1f.

Laser Shots
Pause gameplay with Tab and type ocellaris1z.

Napalm Shots
Pause gameplay with Tab and type ocellaris1n.

Missile Shots
Pause gameplay with Tab and type ocellaris1m.

One Shield
Pause gameplay with Tab and type ocellaris1s.

One C-Bomb Shot
Pause gameplay with Tab and type ocellaris1c.

Player Two
Type any of the above codes, replacing 1 with a 2.

FORCE 21

No Trees
amazon

Yellow Boxes Around Vehicles, Buildings
avatar

No Clouds
london

Instant Loss
hasselhoff

No Fog of War
ispy

Invincibility for Everyone
polytheism

Kill All Enemies
killenemy

Display Grid
grid

100 Percent Radar
chessmatch

Disable Commanders Effects
commanders

Change View
stratperspective

Disable Victory Results
novictory

Hurt First Vehicle in Present Platoon
hurt

Lock Vehicle in Place
chillout

Disable Horizon
seattle

Instant Win
gameoverman

Center Camera on Unit
centermass

Exit Directly to Windows
exit

Show Selected Targets
targetlist

Vehicle Selected
id Identify

FORD RACING

All Cars
Type your name as GIMMEGIMME.

FOREVER LEGEND

Access Cheat Mode
Buy the Morph Potion and drink it. Don't leave the current screen or map you're on. Once Kilgaly looks like Link, type one of the following codes. To disable the code, retype it.

Put Kilgaly in a Bubble
Enable Cheat mode and type KSLENSBOY.

Give Max Money
Enable Cheat mode and type KSGIVEME.

Gives Max HP
Enable Cheat mode and type KSLIVEITUP.

Gives Max MP
Enable Cheat mode and type KSBADPOWER.

No Fights on Field
Enable Cheat mode and type KSCHICKEN.

Instant Death
Enable Cheat mode and type KSLIFESUCKS.

End the Game
Enable Cheat mode and type KSITSTOEASY.

Max Attack
Enable Cheat mode and type KSWOAHBABY.

Get All Four Spells
Enable Cheat mode and type KSIAMGOD.

Give It a Try
Enable Cheat mode and type KSROSHAMBO.

Give It a Try
Enable Cheat mode and type KSWHODIDIT.

FORGOTTEN WORLDS

Go to Shop
At the title screen, type ARC and press HELP. During gameplay, press S.

Next Level
At the title screen, type ARC and press HELP. During gameplay, press N.

FORMULA 1

Enable Bonus Track (Start a Quick Race, Quit)
When saving a game, use the name SPEEDY.

Change In-Game Voices
When saving a game, use the name MUZFRANK.

Lava Mode
When saving a game, use the name ASHCAKES.

FORSAKEN

Level Select
At any menu, type bubbles to enable Cheat mode. Then type thefullmonty.

God Mode, Full Weapons, Unlimited Ammo and Nitro, Four Powerpods, Two Unknown Weapons
At any menu, type bubbles to enable Cheat mode. Then type iamzeus.

Access Special Ship and Turn on Adult Textures
At any menu, type bubbles to enable Cheat mode. Then type titsoot.

Missile Toggle
At any menu, type bubbles to enable Cheat mode. Then type lumberjack.

Beam Toggle
At any menu, type bubbles to enable Cheat mode. Then type jimbeam.

FREEDOM: FIRST RESISTANCE

After installing the game, run it at least one time before modifying files to enable the cheat mode. Then close the game and access the game folder in Windows Explorer.

Once at this window, locate two files. First locate Freedom.cfg. Save a copy of this file before you modify it. Open it (use NotePad), then at the very bottom, add this line of code: showmissions true. Save and close the file.

Next locate and open Action.cfg. Save a copy of this file before you modify it. At the top of this file, type this line of code: bind tilde console. Save and close the file.

Close Windows Explorer and launch the game again. Select Load Game to see a screen showing a list of levels. Choose a level and play! During gameplay, you can press ~ and type one of the following codes to manipulate your game.

Freeze the AI
Toggleai

Reverse the State of All Doors
Toggledoors

Turn Off All Damage
Toggledamage

AI Will Not Detect You
Toggledetection

Reduce the Accuracy of the Enemy
Badguysarelousyshots.01

Spawn Toolkit
Gimmi Toolkit

Spawn Rifle
Gimme Rifle

Spawn Rifle Ammo (10 Rounds)
Gimme Rifle ammo

Spawn Catteni Pistol
Gimme Catteni Pistol

Spawn Catteni Pistol Ammo (15 Rounds)
Gimme Catteni pistol ammo

Spawn Allergen Grenades
Gimme Allergen grenades

Spawn Catteni Blaster
Gimme Catteni blaster

Spawn Catteni Blaster Ammo (10 Rounds)
Gimme Catteni Blaster Ammo

FREEDOM FORCE

Activate Cheat Mode
This procedure involves editing a game file; create a backup copy of the file before proceeding. Use a text editor to edit the "init.py" file in the game folder. Add the following lines to the file: import ffff.CON_ENABLE=1

Begin gameplay and press ~ at the database screen to display the console window. Type one of the following case-sensitive codes to activate the corresponding cheat function.

Invincibility for Entire Party
god()

Disable Invincibility
mortal()

Enemies Do Not Move or Attack
peace()

Enemies Move and Attack Again
war()

Win Current Mission
Mission_Win()

Unlock All Character Powers in Current Mission
DEBUG_ALLPOWERS=1

Add CP to Specified Character
Campaign_AddCP('<name>',<number>)

Automatically Recruit Specified Character
Campaign_Recruit('<name>')

Unlock Specified Built-in Character's Origin
Campaign_UnlockOrigin('<name>')

Set Prestige Amount
Campaign_AddPrestige(<number>)

FROGGER 3D

Infinite Lives
Pause gameplay and type NO MORE ROAD SPLATS.

All Zones Open
Pause gameplay and type SHOW ME MORE ZONES PLEASE.

All Levels Open
Pause gameplay and type WAY TOO HARD FOR THE LIKES OF ME.

Infinite Time
Pause gameplay and type TIME FLIES WHEN YOURE HAVING TROUBLE.

FURY 3

Invincibility
TRYMEON

All Weapons
GIVITIUP

Turbo
URDUSTD

Skip to the Next Level
JUMPNIT

Level Skip (Replace X with Level Number)
WORMITx

Servo Laser
PACKIN1

Isokenetic Gun
PACKIN2

Rapid Laser
PACKIN3

DOM
PACKIN4

Viper
PACKIN5

Baryon
PACKIN6

Superbomb
PACKIN7

FUTURE COP L.A.P.D.

Access Cheat Mode
During gameplay, hold F10 and type one of the following codes. Then hold F10 and press F5 to activate the code as much as necessary. If you want to type another code, hold F10 and press F6 to disable the current code

Turn Blue Player to Black
Enable Cheat mode and press F2, F1, F4, F3 (2), F4, F1, F2.

Restore Shield
Enable Cheat mode and press F2, F1, F4, F3.

Reload Weapon 0
Enable Cheat mode and press F2, F4, F1, F3, F1, F3, F4, F2.

Reload Weapon 1
Enable Cheat mode and press F4, F3, F1, F2, F4, F3, F1, F2.

Reload Weapon 2
Enable Cheat mode and press F2, F1, F2, F4, F2, F1, F3.

Level 2 Password
TAFRGYBIRR

Level 3 Password
CRGRGYBLRY

Level 4 Password
FUMRGYBLRL

Level 5 Password
SIFUGOBLLR

Level 6 Password
TAGUGOBLLY

Level 7 Password
CRMUGOBLLL

Level 8 Password
FEMUGOBYSL

GALAXY FORCE 2

End of Level
During gameplay, type DONKEY, then press F3.

GANGSTERS

Get $50,000
At the Lieutenant Section, type I LOVE HANSON.

GAZILLIONAIRE DELUXE

The Buyer's Cheat
While inside the Marketplace Menu, Ctrl-B to bring up a random commodity for you to buy. Sometimes this pays off and other times you'll get worthless goods. Don't worry; this cheat cannot backfire on you. If you don't like the random commodity, you don't have to buy it. The cheat increases the choice of products available to you.

The Passenger Cheat
From the Passenger menu or the main menu, you can press Ctrl-P. This randomly generates a new group of passengers waiting to be picked up. Use this cheat if the original number of passengers waiting to be picked up is very low. In this case, there is a high probability that you will increase the number of passengers for the week. However, if the number of passengers waiting to travel on your ship is reasonable, don't use this cheat. It may backfire on you.

The Voyager Cheat
From the Voyager Insurance menu or from the main menu, you can press Ctrl-V. This randomly generates a new insurance price. Use this cheat if the original insurance price is high. In this case, there is a high probability that you will save some kubars. However, if the price of insurance is already low, don't use this cheat. It may backfire on you.

GEARHEADS

Level 2 Password
3518

Level 3 Password
6382

Level 4 Password
8427

Level 5 Password
2385

Level 6 Password
5924

Level 7 Password
1267

Level 8 Password
7208

Level 9 Password
6532

Level 10 Password
5012

Level 11 Password
6511

Level 12 Password
8562

GEARWORKS

Level 2 Password
3518

Level 3 Password
6382

Level 4 Password
8427

Level 5 Password
2385

Level 6 Password
5924

Level 7 Password
1267

Level 8 Password
7208

Level 9 Password
6532

Level 10 Password
5012

Level 11 Password
6511

Level 12 Password
8562

GENE WARS

Access Cheat Mode
During gameplay, type SALMONAXE.

Win Immediately
Enable Cheat mode and press W.

Instantly Build or Upgrade
Enable Cheat mode and press B.

Improve Technology
Enable Cheat mode and press S.

Access All Purebreds and Hybrids
Enable Cheat mode and press C.

Summon Monoliths
Enable Cheat mode and press L.

Translucent Buildings
Enable Cheat mode and press T.

Memory Stats
Enable Cheat mode and press D.

Reveal Map
Enable Cheat mode and press Shift+Z.

Duranium Bulb at Cursor
Enable Cheat mode and press F5.

Drop Bombs from Cursor
Enable Cheat mode and press F6.

Shoot at Creature
Enable Cheat mode and press F7.

Adds Money
Enable Cheat mode and press F10.

GENOCIDE: REMIXED EDITION

God Mode
During gameplay, press Tab to access the console and type god.

Framesync On/Off
During gameplay, press Tab to access the console and type framesync.

Show Framerate
During gameplay, press Tab to access the console and type fps.

Give [Item]
During gameplay, press Tab to access the console and type give [item].

GET MEDIEVAL

God Mode
mpkfa

Global Position
mppos

Frames per Second
mpfps

Player Takes Zero Damage
mpbodyguard

99 Lives
mphighlander

Level Skip
mpthewolf

Go Back a Level
mpbadmofo

Go to Next Boss Level
mpbringthegimp

Get Keys
mpignition

Get Scrolls
mpturbocharger

Health
mppetrol

Armor
mparmorall

Weapons
mpglovebox

99 Souls
mpshoes

Thief Can't Steal from You
mpironpockets

Health Stops Fading Away
mpbandaid

Get Skull Key
mplockpick

Get Fire Shield Artifact
mpomar

Get Speed Boost Artifact
mptroadrunner

Get Super Scroll Artifact
mpwinturbo

Get Freak Artifact
mpbadbreath

Get Worship Artifact
mpmintybeath

GEX

Cemetery Password
SVZFKHGP

Cemetery Password
BXRFYHGP

Cemetery Password
ZVTCYHGP

Jungle Password
KXVKRHKP

Jungle Password
CVHCSHKP

Jungle Password
SVKLPHKP

Jungle Password
CVBLPHKP

Toonville Password
RVTCSHGP

Toonville Password
XVVBRHKP

Kung Fu Land Password
YTCHPHKP

Kung Fu Land Password
ZTDHPHKP

Kung Fu Land Password
DXVGRHKP

Rezopolis Password
GYVYRHKP

All Levels, Including Planet X Password
PZYPRXYL

GHOST RECON

Activate Cheat Mode
Press Keypad Enter to display the console window. Then, enter one of the following codes to activate the corresponding cheat function.

Achieve Objectives One at a Time
cisco

All Inventory Items
refill

Change Your Kit to Specified File
kit <kit file>

Chicken Grenades
chickenrun

Disable Constant Shaky Screen
rumbleoff

Enable Constant Shaky Screen
rumbleon

Exit Game
quit

Faster Movement
run

God Mode
superman

Hide Corpse Names
hidecorpse

Invisibility
shadow

Lose Current Mission
autolose

Mark Location on Map for Teleport
mark

Paintball Mode
extremepaintball

Report Current Location
loc

Screen Shakes
boom

Squirrel Launcher
squirrelkite

Suicide
god

Take Over Enemy Bases
rock

Team God Mode
teamsuperman

Team Invisibility
teamshadow

Teleport
teleport

Teleport to Preset Locations
spawn

Toggle Actor Stats
toggleshowactorstats

Toggle AI
toggleai

Toggle Display of Tracers
tracers

Toggle Freezing Trees
togglemovetrees

Toggle User Interface
toggleui

Unlimited Ammunition
ammo

Unlock Hero Characters
unlockheros

Win Current Mission
autowin

GIANTS: CITIZEN KABUTO

Game Cheats
During gameplay, press T or Y, enter in one of the following codes. and hit enter.

Display Frame Rate
Fr

Full Base Energy
Basefillerup

Full Health
Pleasehealme

Instant Gift Shop
Gimmiegifts

Instant Party House
Itsmyparty

Instant Smarty Work Force
Basepopulate

Show Entire Map
Mapshowitall

Speedy Base Construction
Basegoveryfast

Unlimited Mana
Ineedspells

Unlock All Levels
allmissionsaregoodtogo

G-NOME

All Single Player Missions
Press Ctrl+F1 at the Mission Computer. Now type Redtop Trod.

Activate Teleport Key (Ctrl+B)
Press Ctrl+F1 at the Mission Computer. Now type Half Libel.

Activate Invincibility Key (Ctrl+I)
Press Ctrl+F1 at the Mission Computer. Now type Had A Nude On.

Activate Ammunition Key (Ctrl+Z)
Press Ctrl+F1 at the Mission Computer. Now type Brass Clue.

Change Mountain on Mission 1-5 to Mt. Rushmore with Programmers' Faces.
Press Ctrl+F1 at the Mission Computer. Now type Mother Mourn Us.

View End Video Sequences
Press Ctrl+F1 at the Mission Computer. Now type Chaste Coed.

Activate Destroy Target (Ctrl+F)
Press Ctrl+F1 at the Mission Computer. Now type Rotted Drop.

Activates All Targets on Radar Key (Ctrl+P)
Press Ctrl+F1 at the Mission Computer. Now type Horny Elk Leer.

Gives Sergeant in Training Missions Irish Accent.
Press Ctrl+F1 at the Mission Computer. Now type O'Sarge.

Changes Citadel Building into Seventh Level Headquarters
Press Ctrl+F1 at the Mission Computer. Now type Swiss Throat.

Take a Screenshot with Shift+Ctrl+ Right-Click
Press Ctrl+F1 at the Mission Computer. Now type A Scramble On.

All Levels
Press Ctrl+F1 at the Mission Computer. Now type Range Goes Gory.

Recording Session Outtakes
Press Ctrl+F1 at the Mission Computer. Now type Dunk It Here.

Activate Ion-Strike Key (Ctrl+X)
Press Ctrl+F1 at the Mission Computer. Now type Oh No! Less Japan.

GOBLINS

Level 1 Password
VQVQFDE

Level 2 Password
DWNDGbW

Level 3 Password
DCPLPMG

Level 4 Password
KKKPURE

Level 5 Password
ICIGCAA

Level 6 Password
JCJCJHM

Level 7 Password
EWDGONK

Level 8 Password
NGOGKSP

Level 9 Password
ECPQPCC

Level 10 Password
ICVGCGT

Level 11 Password
TCNGTOV

Level 12 Password
NNGWTTO

Level 13 Password
FTWKFEN

Level 14 Password
HNWVFKA

Level 15 Password
TCVQRPM

Level 16 Password
LGWFGUS

Level 17 Password
HQWFTFW

Level 18 Password
FTQKULD

Level 19 Password
IQDNKQO

Level 20 Password
TQNGFVC

GOD OF THUNDER

Refill Energy
Start the game with the command line parameter /VOLSTAGG' Then during a game, press Z.

GODFATHER

Invulnerable
Type HOLIDAY INN.

GORKY 17

Win Fight
Start the game with the command line parameter -760722. Then during a game, press Q.

GP500

Become a Ghost
Type the name Ghostriders on the Single Race screen.

Get Doohan's NSR '94 #4
Type the name !Maate! on the Single Race screen.

New Bikes
Type the name BeamTeam on the Single Race screen.

Ride a Scooter
Type the name !Scooter! on the Single Race screen.

Ride in Your Underwear
Type the name RedJocks on the Single Race screen.

G-POLICE

Havoc Sirens
At the main menu, type WOOWOO.

Enemy FallCam
At the main menu, type SUPACAM.

Benny Hill Cars
At the main menu, type BENIHILL.

All Secret Missions (in Training Menu)
At the main menu, type PANTALON.

Infinite Shields (Can't Advance Mission)
At the main menu, type DOOBIES.

Infinite Weapons (Can't Advance Mission)
At the main menu, type MRTICKY.

In-game Info
At the main menu, type STATTOE.

Level 2
DOLMAN

Level 3
SONAGAV

Level 4
ACEDUF

Level 5
JOJOGUN

Level 6
WENSKI

Level 7
SAEGGY

Level 8
MAZMAN

Level 9
DAZMAN

Level 10
DELUCS

Level 11
ANDOOOO

Level 12
KIMBCHS

Level 13
ANDYMAC

Level 14
YERMAN

Level 15
OLLIEB

Level 16
THEYOLK

Level 17
TONYMASH

Level 18
ANDYCROW

Level 19
BIONIC

Level 20
TSLATER

Level 21
IAINTHOD

Level 22
JONRITZ

Level 23
CLAIREC

Level 24
STEVEBOT

Level 25
ANGUSF

Level 26
EUANLEC

Level 27
EDFIRE

Level 28
STUBOMB

Level 29
THONBOY

Level 30
JIMMAC

Level 31
PUGGER

Level 32
ROSSCO

Level 33
CAKEBOY

Level 34
NIKNAK

Level 35
SAGLORD

GRAND PRIX 2

Extra Speed
Pause gameplay and type GIVE ME SPEED.

Turbo
Pause gameplay and type GIVE ME BOOST.

GRAND PRIX MANAGER 2

Cheat Mode
On the Start screen, type iamacheat.

GRAND SLAM TURKEY HUNT

View Turkeys on Map
During gameplay, type gstracker.

Approach Nearest Turkey
During gameplay, type gsfind.

Many Turkeys Appear
During gameplay, type gscallin.

Attach to a Turkey
During gameplay, type gslock.

Hunter Moves Quickly
During gameplay, type gsflash.

Arrow Cam
During gameplay, type gsdeadeye.

GRAND THEFT AUTO

All Levels and All Cities
Type the name itsgallus.

No Police
Type the name iamthelaw.

999,999,999 Points
Type the name itcouldbeyou.

All Weapons, Armor, "Get Out of Jail Free" Card
Type the name suckmyrocket.

Unlimited Lives
Type the name itstantrum.

Raise Pont Values
Type the name hatemachine.

View FMV Sequences
Type the name heartofgold.

Press Keypad * for All Weapons
Type the name buckfast.

Enable Extra Offensive Language
Type the name iamgarypenn.

Disable Extra Offensive Language
Type the name iamnotgarypenn.

Current Status and Coordinates
Type the name porkcharsui, then during gameplay, press C.

Screen Capture in .TGA Format
Type the name porkcharsui, then during gameplay, press D.

Zoom Out
Type the name porkcharsui, then during gameplay, press K.

Zoom In
Type the name porkcharsui, then during gameplay, press L.

Change Screen Mode
Type the name porkcharsui, then during gameplay, press R.

Restart Level
Type the name porkcharsui, then during gameplay, press F12.

Alternate Zoom Out
Type the name porkcharsui, then during gameplay, press].

Alternate Zoom In
Type the name porkcharsui, then during gameplay, press [.

Center Camera View
Type the name porkcharsui, then during gameplay, press Home.

Pan Camera Down
Type the name porkcharsui, then during gameplay, press Numpad 2.

Pan Camera Left
Type the name porkcharsui, then during gameplay, press Numpad 4.

Pan Camera Right
Type the name porkcharsui, then during gameplay, press Numpad 6.

Pan Camera Up
Type the name porkcharsui, then during gameplay, press Numpad 8.

Pause and Advance Single Frame
Type the name porkcharsui, then during gameplay, press Numpad Plus.

All Weapons with Full Ammo
Type the name porkcharsui, then during gameplay, press Numpad *.

GRAND THEFT AUTO 2

All Cities
Type GOURANGA as a name then type BEMEALL as a name.

All Weapons
Type GOURANGA as a name then type BLASTBOY as a name.

Get Out of Jail
Type GOURANGA as a name then type JAILBAIT as a name.

Invincibility
Type GOURANGA as a name then type RSJABBER as a name.

Level Select
Type GOURANGA as a name then type itsallup as a name.

No Police
Type GOURANGA as a name then type LOSEFEDS as a name.

GRAND THEFT AUTO 3

Activate Cheat Mode
Enter one of the following codes during gameplay to activate the corresponding cheat function. The message "Cheat Activated" confirms the correct code entry. The codes also can be activated at the menu screen (press Escape during gameplay) to avoid having your character moving around while the codes are being entered.

All Weapons
guns

Extra Money
ifiwerearichman

Full Health
gesundheit

Higher Wanted Level
morepoliceplease

Lower Wanted Level
nopoliceplease

Tank (Rhino)
giveusatank

Destroy All Cars
bangbangbang

Change Costume
ilikedressingup

Crazy Pedestrians
itsallgoingmaaad

All Pedestrians Attack You
nobodylikesme

Pedestrians Fight Each Other
weaponsforall

Time Advances Quicker
timeflieswhenyou

Very Fast Game Clock
madweather

Faster Gameplay
booooring

100% Armor (unpatched version)
turtoise

100% Armor (patched version)
tortoise

Clear Weather
skincancerforme

Cloudy Weather
ilikescotland

Rainy Weather
ilovescotland

Foggy Weather
peasoup

Invisible Cars; Wheels Only
anicesetofwheels

Flying Car
chittychittybb

Improved Car Handling
cornerslikemad

Gore Mode
nastylimbscheat

GRAND THEFT AUTO: LONDON 1969

Press * for All Weapons
Type the name deathtoall.

Level Select
Type the name flashmotor.

Unlimited Lives
Type the name 6661970.

No Police
Type the name tithead.

10 Times Multiplier
Type the name iamgod.

999,999,999 points
Type the name averyrichman.

All Items
Type the name uaintnuffin.

Press Horn to Change Colors
Type the name psychadelic.

Turn Off Police Radio
Type the name silence.

Driveby
Type the name driveby.

Super Code
Type the name herc.

Debug Mode
Type the name rommel.

Unlimited Lives, Press * for All Weapons
Type the name asawindow.

GRAND TOURING

All Cars
Type GIMME8CARS as your name, then press Enter.

Make Your Car Faster
Type MOREWELLY as your name, then press Enter.

Get an Extra Car
Type BONUSMOTA as your name, then press Enter.

Always Catch Up to Other Cars After a Spin
Type CATCHUP as your name, then press Enter.

GRAVITY FORCE

Level Select
Type the password WARPxx (replace xx with the level number).

GREED

Full Health
RAVEN

Full Map
OMNI

God Mode
ALLAHMODE

Skip Ahead to 100 Points from Level Finish
BEAVIS

Make enemies Small
GULLIVER

Full Ammo
KMFDM

Kill All Enemies
BELFAST

GRID RUNNER

Nimbus Password
2278231788

Circe Password
4073571036

Aquar IV Password
3738142412

Glacia Password
2579585725

Ash Password
3049463469

Hexol Password
3234189981

Aquar II Password
3972503181

Virion Password
3470355070

Ferrinar Password
3806015086

Forge Password
2547901022

Trepidaria Password
3151996494

Iris Password
4241586751

Lair Password
3503504943

Fortress Password
2782261791

GROUND CTRL

Access Cheat Mode
At the main menu, press M+S+V.

Bring Up Console with ~
Enable Cheat mode and type console.

God Mode for All Units
Enable Cheat mode and type god.

Disable God Mode
Enable Cheat mode and type not god.

Play All Campaign Missions (in Custom Game Menu)
Enable Cheat mode and type gimme maps.

Flashlight GUI Mode
Enable Cheat mode and type flashlight.

Funny Textures
Enable Cheat mode and type from massive with love.

Play Secret Sabotage Mission in "Custom Game" Menu
Enable Cheat mode and type the new generation of rts-games.

GRUNTZ

Traitor Mode
During gameplay, press Enter and type mptraitor, then press Enter.

Zombie Mode
During gameplay, press Enter and type mpback2life, then press Enter.

Selected Grunt Is Faster
During gameplay, press Enter and type mpmeepmeep, then press Enter.

Selected Grunt Kills Instantly

During gameplay, press Enter and type mpohmygodtheykilledkenny, then press Enter.

Invisibility for Selected Grunt

During gameplay, press Enter and type mpcloakingdevice, then press Enter.

Bonus Level: High on Sweetz

During gameplay, press Enter and type mplemonbuttercremez, then press Enter.

Bonus Level: High Rollerz

During gameplay, press Enter and type mpyouresomoney, then press Enter.

Bonus Level: Honey I Shrunk the Kidz

During gameplay, press Enter and type mpmakemesomepie, then press Enter.

Bonus Level: Trouble in the Tropics

During gameplay, press Enter and type mpriorio, then press Enter.

GULF WAR: OPERATION DESERT HAMMER

Full Health, Weapons, Strikes

During gameplay, press Enter and type power me.

Full Health

During gameplay, press Enter and type regen me.

Call in Remote Strike Against Enemies

During gameplay, press Enter and type call strike.

Skip Level

During gameplay, press Enter and type done.

Toggle Keymap 1 and 2 Settings

During gameplay, press Enter and type goodkeys.

Toggle HUD On/Off

During gameplay, press Enter and type hud.

GUNMETAL

Full Ammo

During gameplay, press F8 and type MADMECHASTREISAND.

Full Life

During gameplay, press F8 and type MADCOSMODNA.

Full Shields

During gameplay, press F8 and type MADDUCTTAPE.

Flight Mode (A,Z)

During gameplay, press F8 and type MADRUBYSLIPPERS.

Disable Flight Mode

During gameplay, press F8 and type MADBANANAPEEL.

Turbo Mode

During gameplay, press F8 and type MADBUCKETOWEASELS.

Disable Turbo Mode

During gameplay, press F8 and type MADGETOUTANDWALK.

GUNMAN CHRONICLES

Start the game with the command-line parameters: -dev -console -game rewolf (example: c:\gunman\gunman.exe -dev -console -game rewolf). To do this, make a shortcut for the game on your desktop and right-click on it. Click on properties and in the target field plug in -dev -console -game rewolf after whatever is already there. Make sure you have a space between the command line and what is already in the target field. Now use any of the codes listed after pressing ` to bring down the console:

God Mode

/god

No Clipping Mode

/noclip

All Weapons and Ammo

/impulse357

Invisibility

/notarget

Go to a Certain Map

Use one of the following entries with /map:

Takeoff
rusted
meltdown
highnoon
frontier
cinematic1
cinematic2
cinematic3
cinematic4
city1a
city1b
city2a
city2b
city3a
city3b
end1
end2
mayan0a
mayan0b
mayan1
mayan3a
mayan4
mayan6
mayan8
rebar0a
rebar0b
rebar2a
rebar2b
rebar2c
rebar2d
rebar2e
rebar2f
rebar2g
rebar2h
rebar2i
rebar2j
rebar2k
rebar2l
rebar3b
rebar3d
rebar3e

rust1
rust2a
rust2b
rust3a
rust4a
rust4b
rust4c
rust5a
rust6a
rust6b
rust6c
rust6d
rust7a
rust7b
rust7c
rust7d
rust7e
rust8a
rust9a
west1
west2
west3a
west3b
west4a
west4b
west5b
west6a
west6b
west6c
west6d
west6e

Item Codes

Use one of the following entries with /item:

weapon_fists, weapon_gausspistol, weapon_shotgun, weapon_minigun, weapon_beamgun, weapon_dml, weapon_spchemicalgun, ammo_gaussclip, ammo_buckshot, ammo_minigunclip, ammo_beamgunclip, ammo_dmlclip, ammo_chemical, item_healthkit, item_armor, player_armor, or vehicle_tank.

GUTS N GARTERS

All Weapons

Start the game with the command line parameter \DAVESCHEAT.

GUY SPY

Level Skip

Type GETVONMAXGUY. Then press F1 to skip levels.

H2O

Level 2

RQROVVPWTQ

Level 3

ORVSTWUKMS

Level 4

PMVXMQXVOS

Level 5

VWRPXPSLQQ

Level 6
UNRUQQQTRM

Level 7
TNOPVSORWT

Level 8
TXRUPRNQWO

Level 9
SSOOQVWNRW

Level 10
XRTNKVNSSV

Level 11
WUNQPMRRWO

Level 12
WUQQRVWSQT

Level 13
RQVRWXTTSX

Level 14
ORPPSORVUO

Level 15
OWNSRORLNT

Level 16
UTUVOMNLSP

Level 17
PXSMSTQVOR

Level 18
QQNRNONVQM

Level 19
PWUSTQKSPY

Level 20
VVPQOSLTPN

Level 21
PSPOONOUOW

Level 22
RQKRYNXNNV

Level 23
RTOTOUXWSW

Level 24
SQQVNPPSOY

Level 25
RMRQSQNLSO

Level 26
XPPMQRONMP

Level 27
SMTUWSWRTS

Level 28
VVMRPKTRUQ

Level 29
TQSUONTSRU

Level 30
LRUUSVRTVT

Level 31
MPPRLVTONV

Level 32
OQROUSLPST

Level 33
RSXUSLRXOL

Level 34
PMWTROQSSS

Level 35
SRUQOWVKWR

Level 36
PRRTWTRSPV

Level 37
NTPURUXUUW

Level 38
NMTPVRPOWW

Level 39
ONKTOPPULS

Level 40
NSWOLQWMLW

H.E.D.Z.

God Mode
Press T for the message prompt and type OH MY GOD.

AI Off
Press T for the message prompt and type TOO HARD FOR ME.

HALF-LIFE

Command Line Parameters
Right-click on Start button in Windows, select "Open," find the Half-Life icon, and right-click on it. Select "Properties," then add the parameter to the end of the TARGET or CMD_LINE field. An example might look like: C:\Sierra\Half-Life\hl.exe [desired parameter].

Eliminate IPX Error (LAN)
Type -noipx as parameter.

Start Game in Window
Type -startwindowed as parameter.

Disable Direct Sound
Type -wavonly as parameter.

Select Amount of RAM
Type -heapsize X as parameter, where x = RAM (do not assign more RAM than your computer has).

Skip Introduction Movies
Type -nointro as parameter.

Remove DUN box (LAN)
Type -noip as parameter.

Enable Console
Type -console as parameter.

Developer's Mode
Type -dev as parameter.

Enable Cheat Mode
Start game with -DEV -TOCONSOLE as command line parameter. Press ~ during game, type sv cheats, and reload game or die.

All Weapons and Ammo
Activate Cheat mode, press ~ and type /impulse 101.

Create Item
Activate Cheat mode, press ~ and type give [XX]. Replace [XX] with one of the following: Item_security, Item_sodacan, Item_suit, Item_battery, Item_healthkit, Item_longjump, Item_airtank, Item_antidote.

Create Weapon
Activate Cheat mode, press ~ and type give [XX]. Replace [XX] with one of the following:

Weapon_Shark, Weapon_Shotgun, Weapon_Tripmine, Weapon_QuantumDestabilizer, Weapon_RPG, Weapon_Satchel, Weapon_Hornetgun, Weapon_MP5, Weapon_Python, Weapon_Gauss, Weapon_Glock, Weapon_Handgrenade, Weapon_Crossbow, Weapon_Crowbar, Weapon_Egon, Weapon_357, Weapon_9mmAR, Weapon_9mmHandgun.

Create Ammo
Activate Cheat mode, press ~ and type give [XX]. Replace [XX] with one of the following:

Ammo_RPGclip, Ammo_Glockclip, Ammo_MP5clip, Ammo_MP5grenades, Ammo_Crossbow, Ammo_Egonclip, Ammo_Gaussclip, Ammo_9mmclip, Ammo_Argrenades, Ammo_Buckshot, Ammo_357, Ammo_9mmAR, Ammo_9mmbox.

God Mode
Activate Cheat mode, press ~ and type /god.

Opponents Ignore You
Activate Cheat mode, press ~ and type /notarget.

Adjust Gravity
Activate Cheat mode, press ~ and type sv gravity [1-800].

Disable Clipping and Flight Modes
Activate Cheat mode, press ~ and type /noclip.

HALF-LIFE: COUNTER-STRIKE

Adjust Gravity
Enter this code from the host server. During gameplay, access your console (default key is the ~ button). Now type sv_gravity and a number between −999 and 999,999.

Auto Reload
+reload

Deactivate Auto Reload
-reload

Faster Forward Speed
cl_forwardspeed# (Type # between 0 and 999.)

Faster Backward Speed
cl_backwardspeed# (Type # between 0 and 999.)

Faster Strafe Speed
cl_sidespeed# (Type # between 0 and 999.)

Level Select
Changelevel[map name]

Set the C4 Timer
Enter this code from the Host Computer. Hit ~ (by default). Type Mp_c4timer and a # between -1000 and 1000.

Spawn Weapons
Give weapon_awp

Give weapon_ak47

Give weapon_tmp

Give weapon_mp5navy

Give weapon_p90

Give weapon_xm1014

Give weapon_m3
Give weapon_scout
Give weapon_m4a1
Give weapon_sg551
Give weapon_g3sg1
Give weapon_m249
Give weapon_assaultsuit
Give weapon_c4
Give weapon_deagle
Give weapon_usp
Give weapon_p228
Give weapon_glock18

HALF-LIFE: OPPOSING FORCE

Cheat Mode
Load game with -CONSOLE –GAME GEARBOX as a command line parameter. Press ~ to activate.

Disable Clipping and Flight Modes
Activate Cheat mode, press ~ and type /noclip.

Invincibility
Activate Cheat mode, press ~ and type /god.

All Weapons and Ammo
Activate Cheat mode, press ~ and type impulse 101.

Third Person Perspective
Activate Cheat mode, press ~ and type /third-person.

Create Item
Activate Cheat mode, press ~ and type give [XX]. Replace [XX] with one of the following:

Weapon_Sniperrifle,
Weapon_SporeLauncher,
Weapon_pipewrench, Weapon_eagle,
Weapon_M249, Weapon_displacer,
Weapon_grapple, Weapon_knife,
Weapon_Shockrifle, Ammo_556,
Ammo_722.

HARD TRUCK 2

Money and License
Pause gameplay and type hardtruckisthebest.

Money and License
Pause gameplay and type wininalottery.

Open All Roads
Pause gameplay and type openallroads.

See Hidden Containers on Map
Pause gameplay and type advancedmap.

HARLEY DAVIDSON: RACE ACROSS AMERICA

Access Cheat Mode
Type HEDGEHOG0 (the last character is a zero) as your name to enable Cheat mode. Do not press Enter after entering the name. Press Backspace to delete the name and type one of the following codes. This doesn't work in Practice mode.

NOGAS
unlimited gasoline

CLASSIC 1956
KHK Bike

HARRY POTTER AND THE SORCERER'S STONE

Activate Cheat Mode
Enter one of the following codes during gameplay to activate the corresponding cheat function.

Debug Mode (press F7 to disable)
harrydebugmodeon

Restore Health
harrygetsfullhealth

Super Jumps
harrysuperjump

Big Jumps
harrynormaljump

15 Beans
harrytriggercheat

Invisibility
harrykoresh

Silent Walking
harrykorwalk

HAVE A N.I.C.E. DAY

Add Money
During gameplay, hold Ctrl and type MUCHMONEY.

All Weapons and Extras
During gameplay, hold Ctrl and type ALLWEAPONS.

Repair Pack
During gameplay, hold Ctrl and type HELPME.

Infinite Weapons and Extras
During gameplay, hold Ctrl and type AGRESSOR.

More Acceleration
During gameplay, hold Ctrl and type BOOSTER.

HAVE A N.I.C.E. DAY 2

New Car with Max Speed of 600 km/h
Pause gameplay and type MACHTHREE.

Unlimited Ammo in Deathmatch
Pause gameplay and type IMPACT.

Weapon Mode in Championship.
Pause gameplay and type OVERKILL.

Disable Cheats
Pause gameplay and type ALLOFF.

Debug Mode
Pause gameplay and type BUGGYBOY

Auto-Pilot
In Debug mode, type A.

Display Framerates
In Debug mode, type F.

Switch Between Cars
In Debug mode, type G.

Information System
In Debug mode, type I.

Screenshot
In Debug mode, type P.

HEAVY GEAR

God Mode
During gameplay, hold Ctrl+Alt+Shift and type bedouinprince.

Auto Win Mission
During gameplay, hold Ctrl+Alt+Shift and type checkmatein2.

Unlimited Ammo
During gameplay, hold Ctrl+Alt+Shift and type hesbackandhesgotagun.

Free-Eye Mode
During gameplay, hold Ctrl+Alt+Shift and type deplikespudding. Navigate using Ctrl+arrow keys.

HEAVY GEAR 2

Invincibility
Press ~ then type set camti.

HEAVY METAL: F.A.K.K.2

Game Cheats
Before you can use any of these codes, go into the "Video/Audio" menu. Select "Advanced" and from the right-hand side select "Console." Now, when you play the game, you can hit the ~ button to access the console. From "Console," enter one of the following codes.

God Mode
god

All Weapons and Items
give all

Restore Health
health 100

No Clipping Mode
noclip

Disable Enemy AI
notarget

Display Console Commands
eventlist

HELL: A CYBERPUNK THRILLER

Extra Options
During a game, hold down the left mouse button and press Alt+Ctrl+G. When asked for a password, type NATAS LIVE.

HELLBENDER

God Mode
STEROID

All Weapons
IMPUMPD

Go to Next Level
IMSTUCK

Increase Strength to 100 Percent
MAXMEUP

Increase Health to 100 Percent
TOTLPWR

Go to Level
AUTEM# (Replace # with level number.)

Get Gun
URDEAD# (Replace # with gun number.)

HERETIC

All Weapons
rambo

God Mode
quicken

Full Key Ring
ravskel

All Artifacts
gimme

Kill All
massacre

Power Book
shazam

Map
ravmap

Warp Level
engage

Heal
ponce

No Clipping
kitty

Keys
ravskel

Map
map

Turn into a Chicken
cockadoodledoo

Turn on Devparm Mode
ticker

HERETIC 2

Toggle God Mode
During gameplay, press ~ and type playbetter.

Toggle Power-Up
During gameplay, press ~ and type twoweeks.

Kill All Nonboss Monsters
During gameplay, press ~ and type meatwagon.

Kill All Monsters, Including Boss
During gameplay, press ~ and type victor.

Monsters Get Angry
During gameplay, press ~ and type angermonsters.

Monsters Out for Blood
During gameplay, press ~ and type crazymonsters.

Toggle Clipping
During gameplay, press ~ and type kiwi.

Show Coordinates
During gameplay, press ~ and type showcoords.

Select Previous Weapon
During gameplay, press ~ and type weapprev.

Select Next Weapon
During gameplay, press ~ and type weapnext.

Turn into a Chicken
During gameplay, press ~ and type suckitdown chicken.

All Useful Items
During gameplay, press ~ and type suckitdown all.

Max Health
During gameplay, press ~ and type suckitdown health.

Max Offensive and Defensive Mana
During gameplay, press ~ and type suckitdown mana.

Get Silver/Gold Armor
During gameplay, press ~ and type suckitdown armor (repeat code for gold armor).

Get a Tome of Power Power-Up
During gameplay, press ~ and type suckitdown powerup.

HEROES CHRONICLES: CLASH OF THE DRAGONS

Fill Empty Slots with 10 Black Knights
During a game, press Tab and type nwcagents.

Gain All War Machines
During a game, press Tab and type nwclotsofguns.

Gain a Level
During a game, press Tab and type nwcneo.

Fill Empty Slots with Five Archangels
During a game, press Tab and type nwctrinity.

Maximize Luck
During a game, press Tab and type nwcfollowthewhiterabbit.

Unlimited Movement
During a game, press Tab and type nwcnebuchadnezzar.

Maximize Morale
During a game, press Tab and type nwcmorpheus.

Reveal Puzzle Map
During a game, press Tab and type nwcoracle.

Reveal World Map
During a game, press Tab and type nwcwhatisthematrix.

Hides World Map
During a game, press Tab and type nwcignoranceisbliss.

Gain 100,000 Gold and 100 of Each Resource
During a game, press Tab and type nwctheconstruct.

Lose Game
During a game, press Tab and type nwcbluepill.

Win Game
During a game, press Tab and type nwcredpill.

Gain 999 Mana and All Spells
During a game, press Tab and type nwcthereisnospoon.

Gain All Buildings
During a game, press Tab and type nwczion.

Change Game's Colors to a Weird Color Scheme
During a game, press Tab and type nwcphisherprice.

HEROES CHRONICLES: CONQUEST OF THE UNDERWORLD

Fill Empty Slots with 10 Black Knights
During a game, press Tab and type nwcagents.

Gain All War Machines
During a game, press Tab and type nwclotsofguns.

Gain a Level
During a game, press Tab and type nwcneo.

Fill Empty Slots with Five Archangels
During a game, press Tab and type nwctrinity.

Maximize Luck
During a game, press Tab and type nwcfollowthewhiterabbit.

Unlimited Movement
During a game, press Tab and type nwcnebuchadnezzar.

Maximize Morale
During a game, press Tab and type nwcmorpheus.

Reveal Puzzle Map
During a game, press Tab and type nwcoracle.

Reveal World Map
During a game, press Tab and type nwcwhatisthematrix.

Hides World Map
During a game, press Tab and type nwcignoranceisbliss.

Gain 100,000 Gold and 100 of Each Resource
During a game, press Tab and type nwctheconstruct.

Lose Game
During a game, press Tab and type nwcbluepill.

Win Game
During a game, press Tab and type nwcredpill.

Gain 999 Mana and All Spells
During a game, press Tab and type nwcthereisnospoon.

Gain All Buildings
During a game, press Tab and type nwczion.

Change Games Colors to a Weird Color Scheme
During a game, press Tab and type nwcphisherprice.

HEROES CHRONICLES: MASTER OF THE ELEMENTS

Fill Empty Slots with 10 Black Knights
During a game, press Tab and type nwcagents.

Gain All War Machines
During a game, press Tab and type nwclotsofgun.

Gain a Level
During a game, press Tab and type nwcneo.

Fill Empty Slots with Five Archangels
During a game, press Tab and type nwctrinity.

Maximize Luck
During a game, press Tab and type nwcfollowthewhiterabbit.

Unlimited Movement
During a game, press Tab and type nwcnebuchadnezzar.

Maximize Morale
During a game, press Tab and type nwcmorpheus.

Reveal Puzzle Map
During a game, press Tab and type nwcoracle.

Reveal World Map
During a game, press Tab and type nwcwhatisthematrix.

Hides World Map
During a game, press Tab and type nwcignoranceisbliss.

Gain 100,000 Gold and 100 of Each Resource
During a game, press Tab and type nwctheconstruct.

HEROES CHRONICLES: WARLORDS OF THE WASTELAND

Fill Empty Slots with 10 Black Knights
During a game, press Tab and type nwcagents.

Gain All War Machines
During a game, press Tab and type nwclotsofguns.

Gain a Level
During a game, press Tab and type nwcneo.

Fill Empty Slots with Five Archangels
During a game, press Tab and type nwctrinity.

Maximize Luck
During a game, press Tab and type nwcfollowthewhiterabbit.

Unlimited Movement
During a game, press Tab and type nwcnebuchadnezzar.

Maximize Morale
During a game, press Tab and type nwcmorpheus.

Reveal Puzzle Map
During a game, press Tab and type nwcoracle.

Reveal World Map
During a game, press Tab and type nwcwhatisthematrix.

Hides World Map
During a game, press Tab and type nwcignoranceisbliss.

Gain 100,000 Gold and 100 of Each Resource
During a game, press Tab and type nwctheconstruct.

Lose Game
During a game, press Tab and type nwcbluepill.

Win Game
During a game, press Tab and type nwcredpill.

Gain 999 Mana and All Spells
During a game, press Tab and type nwcthereisnospoon.

Gain All Buildings
During a game, press Tab and type nwczion.

Change Games Colors to a Weird Color Scheme
During a game, press Tab and type nwcphisherprice.

HEROES OF MIGHT & MAGIC

Crystals
Type 844690 as code.

Diamonds
Type 899101 as a code.

Full Map
Type 101495 as a code.

Gold
Type 101496 as a code.

Hasten Army
Type 1011111 as a code.

Ore
Type 844691 as a code.

Plutos
Type 991001 as a code.

HEROES OF MIGHT & MAGIC II

Five Black Dragons
Type 32167 as a code.

Crystals
Type 844690 as a code.

Debug Menu
Press F4.

Final Battle
Type 1911 as a code.

Full Map
Type 8675309 as a code.

Gems
Type 899101 as a code.

Gold
Type 101111 as a code.

Increase Probability of Winning
Type 123456789 as a code.

Lose Battle
Type 1313 as a code.

Obelisk Map
Type 101495 as a code.

Ore
Type 844691 as a code.

Win Battle
Type 911 as a code.

HEROES OF MIGHT & MAGIC III

All Magic, Spell Points
Press Tab and type nwctim.

Brighter Screen
Press Tab and type nwcphisherprice.

Build All Buildings in Castle
Press Tab and type nwconlyamodel.

Fail Scenario
Press Tab and type nwcsirrobin.

Gain One Level Up
Press Tab and type nwcigotbetter.

Get Archangels
Press Tab and type nwcavertingoureyes.

Get Death Knights
Press Tab and type nwcfleshwound.

Get Tent, Ballista, Ammo
Press Tab and type nwcantioch.

Highest Luck
Press Tab and type nwccastleanthrax.

Increase All Sources
Press Tab and type nwcshrubbery.

See Full Map
Press Tab and type nwcgeneraldirection.

See Full Secret Item Map
Press Tab and type nwcalreadygotone.

Top Morale
Press Tab and type nwcmuchrejoicing.

Unlimited Move Points
Press Tab and type nwccoconuts.

Win Scenario
Press Tab and type nwctrojanrabbit.

HEROES OF MIGHT & MAGIC III: ARMAGEDDON'S BLADE

10 Death Knights
Press Tab and type nwcdarthmaul.

100 Resources, 1,0000 Gold
Press Tab and type nwcwatto.

100 Resources, 100,000 Gold
Press Tab and type nwcshrubbery.

Five Archangels
Press Tab and type nwcpadme.

All Spells, 999 Spell Points
Press Tab and type nwcmidichlorians.

Ballista, Ammo Cart, Tent
Press Tab and type nwcwr2d2.

Complete Castle Build-Up
Press Tab and type nwccoruscant.

Display Obelisk Map
Press Tab and type nwcprophecy.

Display Terrain Map
Press Tab and type nwcrevealourselves.

Full Castle Facilities
Press Tab and type nwconlyamodel.

Hero Level Up
Press Tab and type nwcquigon.

Unlimited Movement
Press Tab and type nwcpodracer.

HEROES OF MIGHT & MAGIC III: THE SHADOW OF DEATH

Fill Empty Slots with 10 Black Knights
During a game, press Tab and type nwcagents.

Gain All War Machines
During a game, press Tab and type nwclotsofguns.

Gain a Level
During a game, press Tab and type nwcneo.

Fill Empty Slots with Five Archangels
During a game, press Tab and type nwctrinity.

Maximize Luck
During a game, press Tab and type nwcfollowthewhiterabbit.

Unlimited Movement
During a game, press Tab and type nwcnebuchadnezzar.

Maximize Morale
During a game, press Tab and type nwcmorpheus.

Reveal Puzzle Map
During a game, press Tab and type nwcoracle.

Reveal World Map
During a game, press Tab and type nwcwhatisthematrix.

Hide World Map
During a game, press Tab and type nwcignoranceisbliss.

Gain 100,000 Gold and 100 of Each Resource
During a game, press Tab and type nwctheconstruct.

Lose Game
During a game, press Tab and type nwcbluepill.

The Ultimate Code Book: Book of Secrets

Win Game
During a game, press Tab and type nwcredpill.

Gain 999 Mana and All Spells
During a game, press Tab and type nwcthereisnospoon.

Gain All Buildings
During a game, press Tab and type nwczion.

Change Games Colors to a Weird Color Scheme
During a game, press Tab and type nwcphish-erprice.

HEXEN

All weapons
CONAN

Warp
GATEXX (Replace XX with 01 to 41.)

God Mode
MARTEK

Change Class
ZELIGXX (Replace XX with 0 to 2.)

No Clipping
ANGEL

Full Health
MCCOY

All Artifacts
GREED

All Keys
JANITOR

Receive All Puzzle Pieces
PUZZLER

Destroy All Enemies
CARNAGE

Automap
REVEAL

Pig
DELIVERANCE

X Y Coordinates
WHERE

Show Frag Count in DM
KILLS

HIDDEN & DANGEROUS

Cheat Mode
To enable Cheat mode in the American retail version, type "iwillcheat" or "iamcheater" while playing. A click confirms the code.

All Weapons and Items
Enable Cheat mode, then type "allloot."

Big Head Mode
Enable Cheat mode, then type "Funnyhead" in the cheat box.

Change Wardrobe
Enable Cheat mode, then type "Lauracroft" in the cheat box.

Complete Mission Instantly
To instantly win the current mission, enable Cheat mode, then type "gamedone."

Display Player Coordinates
To display your current position, enable Cheat mode, then type "playercoords."

Invulnerability
Enable Cheat mode, then type "cantdie" or "nohits" for invulnerability. Type it again to return to normal.

Lose Mission
To instantly lose the current mission, enable Cheat mode, then type "gamefail."

Restore Health
Enable Cheat mode, then type "Goodhealth" and push Enter.

Resurrection
Enable Cheat mode (if you haven't already done so), then type "resurrect" to revive a fallen companion. Do not do this if you've drowned or the game may crash.

Slaughter Foes
Enable Cheat mode, then type "killthemall" and push Enter. Warning! This will kill any hostages as well. Be careful!

Unlock All Doors
To open all doors within a mission, enable Cheat mode, then type "openalldoor" and push Enter.

View Ending Sequence
To see the concluding CG scenes, enable Cheat mode, then type "showtheend" and push Enter.

View Enemy Locations
To view the enemy, enable Cheat mode, then type "enemyf" to display the enemy in front of you or "enemyb" to view enemies behind you.

Wire Frame Mode
Enable Cheat mode, then type "debugdrawvolumes" or "debugdrawwire" to enable wire frame mode. Enter the code again to return to normal.

HIDDEN BELOW

Level Skip
Type BLOSS RAUS HIER.

HIGH HEAT MAJOR LEAGUE BASEBALL 2002

Fight
Press Keypad Period after getting hit by a pitch to clear the bench and start a fight. Note: Your batter will be ejected.

HI-OCTANE

Destroy Yourself
Alt+F1

Destroy All Enemies
Alt+F2

Full Fuel
Alt+F3

Max Ammo
Alt+F4

Max Shield
Alt+F5

One More Lap
Alt+F6

Autopilot On
Alt+Y

Autopilot Off
Alt+C

HITMAN: CODENAME 47

Access Cheat Mode
Find and back up the file *hitman.ini* in the Hitman directory. Then open it with any text editor and add the line enableconsole 1.

God Mode
During a game in Cheat mode, press ~ and type god 1.

All Weapons and Max Ammo
During a game in Cheat mode, press ~ and type giveall.

HOCUS POCUS

Full Health
feelgood

Laser Shots
banana

All Keys
blake

Rapid Fire
quark

HOME ALONE

Fly Mode
During gameplay, hold Ins+F1+F2+F3 and keep pressing F to fly.

HOMEWORLD

Cheat Codes
Start the game with one of the following command line parameters to activate the corresponding cheat function:

Enable Debug mode—/debug

Disable int 3 after fatal error—/nodebugInt

Disable galaxy backgrounds—/noBG

Disable default CPU players—/noCompPlayer

Disable tactics—/notactics

Disables retreat tactics—/noretreat

Disable FMV sequences—/disableAVI

Fatal errors do not generate int 3 before exiting—/nodebugInt

Sets global memory heap size—/heap

Sets path to search for opening files—/prepath

Sets path to CD-ROM—/CDpath

Press F11 to toggle free mouse—/freemouse

Do not use anything from bigfile(s)—/ignoreBigfiles

Create log of data files loaded—/logFileLoads

Do not use KNI even if support is—/disableKatmai

Force usage of KNI even if determined to be unavailable—/forceKatmai

Turn off all sound effects —/noSound

Turn off all speech —/noSpeech

Swap the left and right audio channels—/reverseStereo

Force mixer to write to Waveout—/waveout

Force mixer to write to DirectSound driver—/dsound

Disable bi-linear filtering of textures—/noFilter

Do not use polygon smoothing—/noSmooth

Do not load textures—/nilTexture

Turn off front end textures—/NoFETextures

Enable stipple alpha (software renderer)—/stipple

Disable ship damage effects—/noShowDamage

Reset rendering system to defaults at startup—/sw

Display full screen with software renderer (default)—/fullscreen

Display in a window—/window

No border on window—/noBorder

Use slow screen blits—/slowBlits

Select an rGL device by name (sw, fx, d3d)—/device

Select default OpenGL as renderer—/gl

Select Direct3D as renderer—/d3d

Disable usage of OpenGL perspective correction hints—/nohint

No pausing with Alt+Tab—/noPause

No minimize with Alt+Tab—/noMinimize

Show dock lines—/dockLines

Show gun lines—/gunLines

Show light lines in debug mode—/lightLines

Render bounding bowties on the ships—/boxes

Enable text feedback in game commands—/textFeedback

Enable AI Player logging—/aiplayerLog

CPU players are deterministic—/determCompPlayer

Enable gathering of stats—/gatherStats

Turn off captaincy log file—/captaincyLogOff

Turn on captaincy log file—/captaincyLogOn

Turn off network logging file—/logOff

Turn on network logging file—/logOn

Turn on verbose network logging file—/logOnVerbose

Generate game stats log file—/statLogOn

Generate int 3 when a sync error occurs—/intOnSync

Autosaves game frequently, records packets—/debugSync

Allow LAN play regardless of version—/forceLAN

Enables NIS testing mode using [nisFile]—/testNIS

Enables NIS testing mode using [scriptFile]—/testNISScript

Record a demo—/demoRecord

Play a demo—/demoPlay

Record packets of multiplayer game—/packetRecord

Play back packet recording—/packetPlay

Do not use the packed textures if available—/disablePacking

Center the SM world plane at 0,0,0 rather than the camera—/smCentreCamera

Close captioning—/closeCaptioned

HOUSE OF THE DEAD
Enable Cheat and Edit Status
At the main menu, hold Ctrl and type SKIDMARX.

Enable Creature Test
At the main menu, hold Ctrl and type CREATURE.

HUMANS
Level 2 Password
ANDIE PANDY

Level 3 Password
GET A LIFE

Level 4 Password
CARLOS

Level 5 Password
HOWIE

Level 6 Password
MOOBLE

Level 7 Password
CSL

Level 8 Password
THE HUMBLE ONE

Level 9 Password
PIXIE

Level 10 Password
MILESTONE

Level 11 Password
WAR WAR WAR

Level 12 Password
J MCKINNON

Level 13 Password
UNLUCKY

Level 14 Password
BLUE MONKEY

Level 15 Password
RED DWARF

Level 16 Password
BAD TASTE

Level 17 Password
THE KITCHEN

Level 18 Password
CJ

Level 19 Password
SORT IT OUT

Level 20 Password
SMART

Level 21 Password
VILLA3BORA2

Level 22 Password
EARLY MORNING

Level 23 Password
BORO4LEEDS1

Level 24 Password
EASY LIFE

Level 25 Password
JIMS TIES

Level 26 Password
PARKVIEW

Level 27 Password
NICENEASY

Level 28 Password
GREEN CARD

Level 29 Password
COOKIE

Level 30 Password
MALCY MALC

Level 31 Password
RAVING BURK

Level 32 Password
YOU GOT IT

Level 33 Password
SGNIMMEL

Level 34 Password
MINISTRY

Level 35 Password
MAD FREDDY

Level 36 Password
BIZARRE

Level 37 Password
FREE SCOTLAND

Level 38 Password
APPLE JUICE

Level 39 Password
PAYDAY

Level 40 Password
BANANNA MOON

Level 41 Password
BONUS

Level 42 Password
BOUNCING

Level 43 Password
NO MONEY

Level 44 Password
A S F

Level 45 Password
VISION

Level 46 Password
SISTERS

Level 47 Password
FAST FASHION

Level 48 Password
CARGO

Level 49 Password
RAB C NESBITT

Level 50 Password
RANGERS

Level 51 Password
RAINBOW

Level 52 Password
DOODY

Level 53 Password
MIGHTY BAZ

Level 54 Password
TIRED

Level 55 Password
CONSOLIDATED

Level 56 Password
STAY HAPPY

Level 57 Password
AMERICA

Level 58 Password
ANOTHER DAY

Level 59 Password
ISOLATION

Level 60 Password
PROMISED LAND

Level 61 Password
DAEMONSLATE

Level 62 Password
BIG RAB

Level 63 Password
MIAMI VICE

Level 64 Password
MARGARET M

Level 65 Password
A34732473

Level 66 Password
HELP ME

Level 67 Password
THE EXILES

Level 68 Password
EIGHTLANDS

Level 69 Password
WINE AND DINE

Level 70 Password
NIN

Level 71 Password
TECHNOPHOBE

Level 72 Password
GETTING THERE

Level 73 Password
TIME IS

Level 74 Password
RUNNING OUT

Level 75 Password
LORDS OF CHAOS

Level 76 Password
NOW ITS DONE

Level 77 Password
IM OUT OF HERE

Level 78 Password
HERES TO A

Level 79 Password
BETTER LIFE

Level 80 Password
BYE BYE BYE

HUMANS 3: EVOLUTION—LOST IN TIME

Level 2 Password
FLOORS ON FIRE

Level 3 Password
CAMERA TOASTY

Level 4 Password
JUMPING BEANS

Level 5 Password
SPANNER EATER

Level 6 Password
CHALK N CHEESE

Level 7 Password
EYEBROW JUMPER

Level 8 Password
MAD HEAD FRED

Level 9 Password
SPACE CHOMPERS

Level 10 Password
A BIG BEATING

Level 11 Password
GOING TO MARS

Level 12 Password
HUGE TURNIPS

Level 13 Password
PINK PEA SOUP

Level 14 Password
LUMPS OF MUD

Level 15 Password
PILES OF SPUDS

Level 16 Password
GLENZ VECTORS

Level 17 Password
HUNKY DORY

Level 18 Password
RASTER TUNNEL

Level 19 Password
LICKERTY SPLIT

Level 20 Password
PORK CHOP CITY

Level 21 Password
CANNIBAL BOB

Level 22 Password
BABOON CASES

Level 23 Password
SHOTGUN DODGER

Level 24 Password
DRAGON BALLS

Level 25 Password
INTERFERENCE

Level 26 Password
BEEEEEEEEEEEF

Level 27 Password
MUSHROOM SOUP

Level 28 Password
THE SLAM DUNK

Level 29 Password
IN TURKEY TOWN

Level 30 Password
KING KEV HMMMM

Level 31 Password
MAN DINGA SHOP

Level 32 Password
SPIT N POLISH

Level 33 Password
PIE DOMINATION

Level 34 Password
DANCING DINGO

Level 35 Password
RED EGG TIMER

Level 36 Password
DONUT DIMPLE

Level 37 Password
FLAPS

Level 38 Password
KOMBO LICKERS

Level 39 Password
BOMB BANGERS

Level 40 Password
DONKEY WARRIOR

Level 41 Password
BUNS ARE GOOD

Level 42 Password
SNAKES IN TOWN

Level 43 Password
KING PIN BEAST

Level 44 Password
CRUSTY BOFFIN

Level 45 Password
BLUE TREE TOPS

Level 46 Password
PURPLE BULLET

Level 47 Password
BACON SQUASHER

Level 48 Password
HELL AND BACK

Level 49 Password
TROUSER TRICKS

Level 50 Password
MASTER JODEZ

Level 51 Password
CONCRETE BREAD

Level 52 Password
SLIMEY TEACUP

Level 53 Password
TASTY BRICKS

Level 54 Password
FLICKER

Level 55 Password
TABLE OF SKIDS

Level 56 Password
DREGS OF A CAT

Level 57 Password
HOPPING CABLES

Level 58 Password
LIGHT NOODLES

Level 59 Password
HOWLING GARAGE

Level 60 Password
TACTIC

Level 61 Password
CARPET KICKERS

Level 62 Password
PLASMA DRIVER

Level 63 Password
ZOK OF ROCK

Level 64 Password
BEANS ALIVE

Level 65 Password
TEACAKE BLISS

HUMANS: INSULT TO INJURY

Level 2 Password
SPYDER

Level 3 Password
BILLS

Level 4 Password
OUR SHELF

Level 5 Password
MR PARROT

Level 6 Password
BLIZARD

Level 7 Password
KEEF

Level 8 Password
ITS TOSH

Level 9 Password
O O CHILDREN

Level 10 Password
LEOPARD

Level 11 Password
DANNEEE

Level 12 Password
KATIEWOOH

Level 13 Password
IDONTLIKEBRAWN

Level 14 Password
HOW MUCH

Level 15 Password
MRS T

Level 16 Password
GALLOWS FIELD

Level 17 Password
CANDLESTICKS

Level 18 Password
BABBLE

Level 19 Password
TRADER

Level 20 Password
BOILED EGGS

Level 21 Password
TURBO NUTTER

Level 22 Password
RICK NINJA

Level 23 Password
TASH

Level 24 Password
WHINGEING

Level 25 Password
CRAMP

Level 26 Password
HASSLED

Level 27 Password
IMAGITEC

Level 28 Password
DRAKEEAR

Level 29 Password
LURCH

Level 30 Password
JUST TAKES

Level 31 Password
3 NEGATIVES

Level 32 Password
BLOAT ON

Level 33 Password
I LOVE ME

Level 34 Password
AAAAAARGH

Level 35 Password
NIKKI

Level 36 Password
MR FISTIE

Level 37 Password
ARIES

Level 38 Password
FATEANDFORTUNE

Level 39 Password
WHAT WE PUT

Level 40 Password
SEE YA

Level 41 Password
DOOM

Level 42 Password
480

Level 43 Password
BROKE AGAIN

Level 44 Password
NO SUPPORT

Level 45 Password
7 MILE WALK

Level 46 Password
MINI EGGS

Level 47 Password
WORLDOFOUROWN

Level 48 Password
BESTEST BUDS

Level 49 Password
BLUE STUFF

Level 50 Password
UNCLE JOSEF

Level 51 Password
LOOWEEZ

Level 52 Password
RADCLIFFE

Level 53 Password
GILL N GEDS

Level 54 Password
THE SLOBS

Level 55 Password
ALMANBURIE

Level 56 Password
PLAGUE PIT

Level 57 Password
BROWN SUGAR

Level 58 Password
BLATHER

Level 59 Password
SCARY MAN

Level 60 Password
NEED MORE

Level 61 Password
PERFECT PETE

Level 62 Password
WAYNE

Level 63 Password
POUCH

Level 64 Password
SAD BOYS

Level 65 Password
GLUM

Level 66 Password
GOLD LABEL

Level 67 Password
ATARI CORP

Level 68 Password
SOURFACE

Level 69 Password
ENDOSCOPY

Level 70 Password
HAVE A BREAK

Level 71 Password
GIMME SHELTER

Level 72 Password
STAGGER HOME

Level 73 Password
WHO D YOU LOVE

Level 74 Password
SOS

Level 75 Password
PYTHON LEE

Level 76 Password
SISTER BLUE

Level 77 Password
TAURUS

Level 78 Password
DOES IT MATTER

Level 79 Password
THIS IS IT

Level 80 Password
FOREVER

HYPE: THE TIME QUEST

Full Life
leben

Full Magic Power
druidik

Restore Shield
protek

Give 1 to 99 Plastyks
frik

Restore Life Points When Idle
littletroll

Restore Magic Points When Idle
littlegogoud

+10 Blue Arrows
youngelf

+10 Red Arrows
oldelf

+1 of Everything in Inventory
grolot

Destroy Shield
toutundefi

Change Camera
tunnel

Add Boots to Inventory
pouletfrit

Run Very Fast
wonderful

Free Money
glittergold

God Mode
thundergod

Infinite Magic
hermetik

Infinite Arrows
houdini

One Hit to Defeat Barnak
end02

Epok 1 Finished
epok1

Epok 2 Finished
epok2

Epok 3 Finished
epok3

HYPERBLADE

Immunity and Increased Attack
During gameplay, type MDMKSB.

Enable Hidden Teams
During gameplay, type SHUIN.

Changes Character to Gorilla
During gameplay, type GORILLA.

Turn Character Upside-Down.
During gameplay, type SPICYBRAINS.

Decrease Character Size
During gameplay, type POTATO.

ICEWIND DALE: HEART OF WINTER

To enable Cheat mode, go to the Start Bar, Programs, then Black Isle. Select Icewind Dale Configuration. Enable the Game Console under Game Options. Open the game console by pressing Ctrl+Tab. Once the console is open, type the following codes:

Resurrect or Heal Character
GETYOURCHEATON:EnableCheatKeys(Ctrl+R)

Kill Monster
GETYOURCHEATON:EnableCheatKeys(Ctrl+Y)

Display Triggers, Traps
GETYOURCHEATON:EnableCheatKeys(Ctrl+4)

Displays Boundary Boxes
GETYOURCHEATON:EnableCheatKeys(Ctrl+9)

Reveal the Entire Map
GETYOURCHEATON:ExploreArea ();

First Aid Cheat
GETYOURCHEATON:FirstAid()

IGNITION

Flat Opponent Cars
STRINGS

Drop Camera Viewpoint
SVINPOLE

Just Wheels
SKUNK

Flips Screen
FILMJOLK

All Cars
SLASKTRATT

All Tracks
SURMULE

Stretch Cars
BANARNE

IMPERIUM GALACTICA

Access Cheat Mode
During gameplay, hold Shift and type KAROLY.

All Colonies and Inventions
Enable Cheat mode and press C.

Cheats on Planets
Enable Cheat mode and press C again.

+$100,000 Credits
Enable Cheat mode and press V.

Rank 1 (LT)
Enable Cheat mode and press 5.

Rank 2 (CPT)
Enable Cheat mode and press 6.

Rank 3 (CMDR)
Enable Cheat mode and press 7.

Rank 4 (ADM)
Enable Cheat mode and press 8.

Rank 5 (GR ADM)
Enable Cheat mode and press 9.

IMPOSSAMOLE

Three Full Power Bars
At the High Score table, type HEINZ.

Low Energy Refill
At the High Score table, type ANNFRANK.

Double-Length Energy Bar
At the High Score table, type LUMBAJAK.

Walk on Deadly Surfaces
At the High Score table, type OOCHOUCH.

No Weapon Time Limit
At the High Score table, type COMMANDO.

Worms Give Double Health
At the High Score table, type JUGGLERS.

IMPOSSIBLE MACHINE 2025

Level 1 Password
ROCKYI

Level 2 Password
ROCKYV

Level 3 Password
ROCKYX

Level 4 Password
CHAIRI

Level 5 Password
CHAIRV

Level 6 Password
CHAIRX

Level 7 Password
ROBBYI

Level 8 Password
ROBBYV

Level 9 Password
ROBBYX

Level 10 Password
MICROI

Level 11 Password
MICROV

Level 12 Password
MICROX

Level 13 Password
FINALI

Level 14 Password
FINALV

Level 15 Password
FINALX

Level 16 Password
EMPTYI

Level 17 Password
IROCKY

Level 18 Password
VROCKY

Level 19 Password
XROCKY

Level 20 Password
ICHAIR

Level 21 Password
VCHAIR

Level 22 Password
XCHAIR

Level 23 Password
IROBBY

Level 24 Password
VROBBY

Level 25 Password
XROBBY

Level 26 Password
IMICRO

Level 27 Password
VMICRO

Level 28 Password
XMICRO

Level 29 Password
IFINAL

Level 30 Password
VFINAL

Level 31 Password
XFINAL

Level 32 Password
IEMPTY

INCOMING

Cheat Menu
At the main menu, type NUMBERONEDACRE-STREET.

Turn Off Textures
During gameplay, hold Shift and type WIREWEWAITING.

Turns Graphics to Dots
During gameplay, hold Shift and type WHATS-THEPOINT.

Invulnerability
During gameplay, hold Shift and type SOLI-DASAROCK.

No Shading
During gameplay, hold Shift and type FLATBROKE.

Gouraud Shading On
During gameplay, hold Shift and type GOURAUD.

Protect Farm from Jumping Cows
During gameplay, hold Shift and type OLDMACDONALD.

Racing in the Moon
During gameplay, hold Shift and type FLYMETOTHEMOON.

Get Everything
During gameplay, hold Shift and type HAVEALL.

One Shot Kills
During gameplay, hold Shift and type SUPER-DAISY.

Infinite Lives
During gameplay, hold Shift and type INFINITELIVES.

Infinite Weapons
During gameplay, hold Shift and type INFINITEWEAPONS.

INCREDIBLE HULK

Level 2 Password
10C82E5E54

Level 3 Password
80D82E206E

Level 4 Password
00D02702BA

INCUBATION

All Locations Visible
At the City Map, type ix1.

10 Skill Points for Every Marine
At the City Map, type ix2.

500 Equipment Points for Your Squad
At the City Map, type ix3.

Next Mission
At the City Map, type ix4.

INDEPENDENCE WAR

Dock with Any Vessel
In flight, type darkgoat then hold Left-Shift and press K.

Destroy Targeted Ship
In flight, type darkgoat then hold Left-Shift and press 0.

Force Next Mission Event
In flight, type darkgoat then hold Left-Shift and press S.

Freeze Target
In flight, type darkgoat then hold Left-Shift and press ;.

Invulnerability
In flight, type darkgoat then hold Left-Shift and press I.

Jump to Lagrange Point
In flight, type darkgoat then hold Left-Shift and press J.

Jump to Target
In flight, type darkgoat then hold Left-Shift and press 8.

Match Target's Velocity
In flight, type darkgoat then hold Left-Shift and press 9.

Superspeed
In flight, type darkgoat then hold Left-Shift and press A.

View Previous Movie
In flight, type darkgoat then hold Left-Shift and press Backspace.

Win the Mission
In flight, type darkgoat then hold Left-Shift and press W.

INDIANA JONES AND THE INFERNAL MACHINE

All Weapons
Press F10, type urgon_elsa, then press Enter.

God Mode
Press F10, type taklit_marion on, then press Enter.

INTERSTATE '76

Play as the Helicopter
Type RETPOCILEH as a name and select Phaedra Rattler.

Play as the Tank
Type KNAT as a name and select Phaedra Rattler.

INTERSTATE '76: NITRO PACK

Blow Up Quickly
During gameplay, press Ctrl+Alt+X.

Front Right Flat Tire
During gameplay, display the map, hold Ctrl+Shift and type frflat.

Front Left Flat Tire
During gameplay, display the map, hold Ctrl+Shift and type flflat.

Back Right Flat Tire
During gameplay, display the map, hold Ctrl+Shift and type brflat.

Back Left Flat Tire
During gameplay, display the map, hold Ctrl+Shift and type blflat.

Larger Radar Parameter
During gameplay, hold Ctrl+Shift and type thirdnostril.

Level Skip
During gameplay, hold Ctrl+Shift and type GETDOWN. Now die to advance.

Save a Vehicle
Press F12 twice.

Screen Shake
During gameplay, hold Ctrl+Shift and type wiggleburger.

Hot-Air Balloon
Type HOTAIR as a name and select Phaedra Rattler.

UFO
Type THETRUTHISHERE as a name and select Phaedra Rattler.

Helicopter
Type RETPOCILEH as a name and select Phaedra Rattler.

Tank
Type KNAT as a name and select Phaedra Rattler.

INTERSTATE '82

Full Ammo
Press Esc then type caress then press Esc again.

God Mode for Current Car
Press Esc then type cuddle then press Esc again.

JACK NICKLAUS 4

Gale Force Winds
During gameplay, type gonewiththewind.

Jupiter Gravity
During gameplay, type triplegee.

Ball Bounces Very High and Long
During gameplay, type superball.

High Bounce
During gameplay, type superball.

Big Hills
During gameplay, type molehill.

Play Wack-A-Nerd
During gameplay, type waxanerd.

Secret Opponent
Create a female player who is a pro and plays from the black tee. Name the player Barbara Nicklaus.

JAGGED ALLIANCE 2

Access Cheat Mode
At the Tactical screen, hold Ctrl and type G A B B I.

Make All Characters (Enemies and NPCs) and Items Visible
At the Tactical screen, press Alt+E.

Kill All Enemies in Current Sector
At the Tactical screen, press Alt+O.

Teleport Selected Character to Cursor Location
At the Tactical screen, press Alt+T.

Hurt Character Under Cursor Location
At the Tactical screen, press Ctrl+H.

Refresh APs of Selected Character
At the Tactical screen, press Alt+D.

Reload Selected Character's Gun
At the Tactical screen, press Alt+R.

Heal All Characters' Health and Energy
At the Tactical screen, type Ctrl+U.

Abort Enemies' Turn
At the Tactical screen, type Alt+Enter.

In Travel Mode, Teleport Squad to Sector Under Cursor
At the Map screen, type Ctrl+T.

Kill All Enemies in Sector
At the Map screen, type Alt+AUTO RESOLVE.

Increase Funds by $100,000
At the laptop, type +.

Decrease Funds by $10,000
At the laptop, type -.

Left-Clicking Merc Forces Any "Away" Character to Join Team
At the laptop, type Space.

Enemy Appears at Cursor
At any other screen, type Alt+B.

Civilian Appears at Cursor
At any other screen, type Alt+C.

Item Appears at Cursor
At any other screen, type Alt+I.

Mustard Gas Explosion at Cursor
At any other screen, type Alt+K.

100 Points of Damage to All Enemies in Sector
At any other screen, type Alt+O.

Character Changes to Monster
At any other screen, type Alt+5.

Create New Character
At any other screen, type Alt+G.

Create Robot
At any other screen, type Alt+V.

Character Uses Wheelchair
At any other screen, type Alt+4.

JAMES BOND JR.

Level 2 Password
33481

Level 3 Password
258600

Level 4 Password
320370

JAMES POND 2: OPERATION ROBOCOD

Level Select
Start the game with the command line parameter /RECxx (replace xx with the level number).

JAMES POND 3

Cheat Menu
During gameplay, type NIGHTMARE, then press F10.

JAZZ JACKRABBIT

HAHAHA Displayed
During gameplay, press P, then Backspace. Now type ddarjan.

AWESOME Displayed
During gameplay, press P, then Backspace. Now type ddtim.

Displays Numbers Onscreen
During gameplay, press P, then Backspace. Now type ddcheck.

Opens an Arjan Greetz Window
During gameplay, press P, then Backspace. Now type ddgreetz.

Jump to Next Level
During gameplay, press P, then Backspace. Now type ddlamer.

Lose life and Start Over
During gameplay, press P, then Backspace. Now type ddmark.

Toggles Between 16 Colors and Normal
During gameplay, press P, then Backspace. Now type ddapogee.

Get Every Weapon with 100 Rounds for Each and Five Rounds of TNT
During gameplay, press P, then Backspace. Now type ddgunhed.

Make It Harder to Destroy Enemies and Collect Ammo
During gameplay, press P, then Backspace. Now type dddoom.

Warp to Bonus Stage After Finishing Current Level
During gameplay, press P, then Backspace. Now type ddhooker.

Teleport If an Enemy Is Below or Above You
During gameplay, press P, then Backspace. Now type ddhocus.

Hip-Hop Bird
During gameplay, press P, then Backspace. Now type ddbad.

Super Sonic Speed
During gameplay, press P, then Backspace. Now type ddsable.

Air Board
During gameplay, press P, then Backspace. Now type ddcstrike.

Temporary Invincibility
During gameplay, press P, then Backspace. Now type ddbouf.

Exit Game
During gameplay, press P, then Backspace. Now type ddken.

JAZZ JACKRABBIT 2: THE SECRET FILES

God Mode
jjgod

All Weapons
jjguns

All Ammo
jjammo

Sugar Rush
jjrush

Helicopter Ears, Again for Hoverboard
jjfly

Self Destruct
jjk

Power Shield
jjshield

Level Skip
jjnext

Fully Light Level
jjlight

Bird Assistance
jjbird

Get Coins
jjcoins

Get Gems
jjgems

Return to Main Menu
jjending

Quit to Desktop
jjq

Change into Spaz, again for Bird, again for Frog, again for Jazz
jjmorph

JAZZ JACKRABBIT: X-MAS '95

All Guns
Rabbit

JEDI KNIGHT: DARK FORCES 2

All Items
Press T, type wamprat, then press Enter.

All Weapons
Press T, type red5, then press Enter.

Invincibility
Press T, type jediwannabe1, then press Enter.

Level Skip
Press T, type thereisnotry, then press Enter.

JEFF GORDON XS RACING

Access Cheat Mode
At the main menu, type icancheat and press Enter.

Unlock Wraith Car
Enable Cheat mode, then at the Car Selection screen, type wildone.

Unlock X-Wave Car
Enable Cheat mode, then at the Car Selection screen, type widebodyopen.

Expert Mode
Enable Cheat mode, then at the Car Selection screen, type takemeon.

Jeff Gordon's Car
Enable Cheat mode, then at the Car Selection screen, type redfury.

No Clipping
Enable Cheat mode, then at the Car Selection screen, type clipped.

Reckless Mode
Enable Cheat mode, then at the Car Selection screen, type reckless.

Set Number of Laps
Enable Cheat mode, then at the Car Selection screen, type lapset.

Cloverleaf and Pepsi Planet Tracks
Enable Cheat mode, then at the Car Selection screen, type freeride.

All Other Tracks
Enable Cheat mode, then at the Car Selection screen, type freedrive.

JETFIGHTER 3

Refill Fuel
During gameplay, press Shift+F.

Refill Ammo
During gameplay, press Shift+M.

Destroy Airborne Target
During gameplay, press Ctrl+X or Ctrl+W.

JURASSIC WARS

5,000 Foods
During gameplay, press Enter and type FOOD.

Skip Level
During gameplay, press Enter and type NEXT.

KATHARSIS

1-2 Password
SHIELD

1-3 Password
WHIRLWIND

1-4 Password
ELECTRICITY

2-1 Password
BOMBSHELL

2-2 Password
BORER

2-3 Password
SWITCH

2-4 Password
HEAT

3-1 Password
LEVIATHAN

3-2 Password
RAINBOW

3-3 Password
SPRINGER

3-4 Password
BAD DREAM

4-1 Password
ANTENNAE

4-2 Password
SLEDGEHAMMER

4-3 Password
CAVITY

4-4 Password
BULLET RAIN

5-1 Password
GIANTS

5-2 Password
PRIME TEAM

5-3 Password
XL SHIPS

5-4 Password
BLOOD BATH

KEEN DREAMS

God Mode
F10+G

Free Items
F10+I

Jump Cheat
F10+J

Warp
F10+W

Slow Down Game
F10+S

KINGPIN: LIFE OF CRIME

Access Cheat Mode
Start the game with the command line parameter+developer 1. Then during gameplay, press ` to bring down the console and type one of the following codes:

God Mode
At the console, type IMMORTAL.

Clipping Mode
At the console, type NOCLIP.

Onscreen Enemies Catch on Fire
At the console, type EXTRACRISPY.

Rearview Mirror
At the console, type CL_REARVIEWMIRROR 1.

Enemies Cannot See You
At the console, type NOTARGET.

Get All Items (Except Cash)
At the console, type GIVE ALL.

Get Money
At the console, type GIVE CASH ### (replace ### with amount).

Get Coil
At the console, type GIVE COIL.

Get Watch
At the console, type GIVE WATCH.

Get Battery
At the console, type GIVE BATTERY.

Get Whiskey
At the console, type GIVE WHISKEY.

Get Chemical Plant Key
At the console, type GIVE CHEM_PLANT_KEY.

Get Fuse
At the console, type GIVE FUSE.

Get Bait-Shop Key
At the console, type GIVE SHOP_KEY.

Get Warehouse Key
At the console, type GIVE WAREHOUSE_KEY.

Get Lizzy's Head
At the console, type GIVE LIZZY HEAD.

Get Shipyard Key
At the console, type GIVE SHIPYARD_KEY.

Get Moker's Office Key
At the console, type GIVE OFFICE_KEY.

Get Valve Handle
At the console, type GIVE VALVE.

Get Skytram Ticket
At the console, type GIVE TICKET.

Get Flashlight
At the console, type GIVE FLASHLIGHT.

Get All Weapons
At the console, type GIVE WEAPONS.

Get All Ammo
At the console, type GIVE AMMO.

Get Weapon
At the console, type GIVE CROWBAR.

Get Weapon
At the console, type GIVE PISTOL.

Get Weapon
At the console, type GIVE SHOTGUN.

Get Weapon
At the console, GIVE TOMMYGUN.

Get Weapon
At the console, type GIVE HEAVY MACHINEGUN.

Get Weapon
At the console, type GIVE GRENADE LAUNCHER.

Get Weapon
At the console, type GIVE BAZOOKA.

Get Weapon
At the console, type GIVE FLAMETHROWER.

Get Bullets
At the console, type GIVE BULLETS ### (replace ### with number desired).

Get Shells
At the console, type GIVE SHELLS ### (replace ### with number desired).

Get 308cal
At the console, type GIVE 308CAL ### (replace ### with number desired).

Get Grenades
At the console, type GIVE GRENADES ### (replace ### with number desired).

Getof Rockets
At the console, type GIVE ROCKETS ### (replace ### with number desired).

Get Gas
At the console, type GIVE GAS ### (replace ### with number desired).

Get Silencer for Handgun
At the console, type GIVE SPISTOL.

Auto-Reload for Handgun
At the console, type GIVE PISTOL RELOAD.

Get Small Medical Kit
At the console, type GIVE SMALL HEALTH.

Get Large Medical Kit
At the console, type GIVE LARGE HEALTH.

Get Adrenaline
At the console, type GIVE ADRENALINE.

Get Full Health
At the console, type GIVE HEALTH.

Get Helmet Armor
At the console, type GIVE HELMET.

Get Jacket Armor
At the console, type GIVE JACKET.

Get Legs Armor
At the console, type GIVE LEGS ARMOR.

Get Full Armor
At the console, type GIVE ARMOR.

Skidrow
At the console, type MAP SR1.

Sewers
At the console, type MAP SEWER.

The Super
At the console, type MAP SR2.

Jax
At the console, type MAP BAR_SR.

Mean Streets
At the console, type MAP SR3.

The Jesus
At the console, type MAP SR4.

Bike
At the console, type MAP BIKE.

Poisonville
At the console, type MAP PV_H.

Club Swank
At the console, type MAP BAR_PV.

Louie's Errand
At the console, type MAP PV_1.

Blanco Industries
At the console, type MAP PV_B.

Nikki Blanco
At the console, type MAP PV_BOSS.

Lizzie's Problem
At the console, type MAP SY_H.

Salty Dog
At the console, type MAP BAR_SY.

Pier Pressure
At the console, type MAP SY1.

Das Boot
At the console, type MAP SY2.

Steeltown
At the console, type MAP STEEL1.

Boiler Room
At the console, type MAP BAR_ST.

Steel Mill
At the console, type MAP STEEL2.

Steel Processing
At the console, type MAP STEEL3.

Moker Shipping
At the console, type MAP STEEL4.

Consequences
At the console, type MAP KPCUT3.

Derailed
At the console, type MAP TY1.

Dark Passage
At the console, type MAP TY2.

Trainyards
At the console, type MAP TY3.

Depot
At the console, type MAP TY4.

The Picnic
At the console, type MAP KPCUT4.

Radio City Station
At the console, type MAP RC1.

Enter the Dragons
At the console, type MAP RC2.

Streets of Fire
At the console, type MAP RC3.

Skytram Station
At the console, type MAP RC4.

Typhoon
At the console, type MAP BAR_RC.

Central Towers
At the console, type MAP RC5.

Crystal Palace East
At the console, type MAP RCBOSS1.

Crystal Palace West
At the console, type MAP RCBOSS2.

Outro
At the console, type MAP KPCUT7.

KISS PSYCHO CIRCUS: THE NIGHTMARE CIRCUS

God Mode
During a game, press ` and type Invuln.

All Weapons
During a game, press ` and type GimmieGimmieGimmie.

No Clipping Mode
During a game, press ` and type NoClip.

Monster Targeting On/Off
During a game, press ` and type NoTarget.

Fly Mode
During a game, press ` and type Spectator.

Chase Camera (Five Different Angles)
During a game, press ` and type ChaseCam.

Cycle Through Four Player Classes
During a game, press ` and type CyclePlayerClass.

Increase Armor and Health
During a game, press ` and type NextArmor.

Decrease Armor
During a game, press ` and type PrevArmor.

Go to Next Monster
During a game, press ` and type NextMonster.

Go to Previous Monster
During a game, press ` and type PrevMonster.

Restart Current Level
During a game, press ` and type RestartLevel.

L

L.A. BLASTER

Easy Mode with No Tourists
/CRYOEASY

Easy Mode with No Mutants
/CRYOEASY2

God Mode
/CRYOGOD

99 Credits
/CRYOCRED

Flamethrower
/CRYOMAD

OD Car
/CRYOOD

SZ Surf
/CRYOSZ

Mini-Car
/CRYOSTEVIETOUR

Motion Blur
/CRYOBLUR

LABYRINTH OF LIGHT

Level 2 Password
124061436

Level 3 Password
1564540

Level 4 Password
116129760

Level 5 Password
337216760

Level 6 Password
670755100

Level 7 Password
622656474

Level 8 Password
144419184

Level 9 Password
490839620

Level 10 Password
1137029855

Level 11 Password
195832962

Level 12 Password
21147399

Level 13 Password
223215104

Level 14 Password
1435947270

Level 15 Password
96832545

Level 16 Password
1634959200

Level 17 Password
1329909957

Level 18 Password
80731294

Level 19 Password
234168704

Level 20 Password
96101376

Level 21 Password
84079436

Level 22 Password
565369545

Level 23 Password
369527410

Level 24 Password
766105110

Level 25 Password
16824452

Level 26 Password
69661248

Level 27 Password
807523290

Level 28 Password
428282252

Level 29 Password
330949960

Level 30 Password
640228371

Level 31 Password
121568714

Level 32 Password
919748875

LAMENTATION SWORD

Access Cheat Mode
During gameplay, press Enter for an input field. Then type one of the following case-sensitive codes.

Go to Unreal World
Enable Cheat mode and type Icompletedthisghostgame.

Get Item ##
Enable Cheat mode and type IfIwantIgotit ##.

Remove Darkness
Enable Cheat mode and type Seethesilverlining.

Release Whole Card, Display Opponents' Positions
Enable Cheat mode and type Showmetheworld.

Increase Magic to 99
Enable Cheat mode and type Thefierceunknownpower 99.

Increase Health to 99
Enable Cheat mode and type Thegreathealthpower 99.

Increase Brain to 99
Enable Cheat mode and type Thehealthyspiritpower 99.

Increase Dexterity to 99
Enable Cheat mode and type Theoriginaldexteritypower 99.

Increase Strength to 99
Enable Cheat mode and type Therealmusclepower 99.

Increase Power to 99
Enable Cheat mode and type ThesoulHunter'sholyPower 10.

Get money
Enable Cheat mode and type Youcansaymoneyiseverything 10000.

Get Weapon
Enable Cheat mode and type Yougainasoneplease ## (replace ## with weapon number).

LAST EICHOF

Unlimited Life
Start the game with the command line parameter /007.1.

Unlimited Time
Start the game with the command line parameter /007.2.

God Mode
Start the game with the command line parameter /007.3.

LEGACY OF KAIN: BLOOD OMEN 2

Invincibility
This procedure involves editing a game file; create a backup copy of the file before proceeding. Use a text editor to edit the "game.erg" file in the "data" folder in the game folder. Remove the hyphen "-" character from the line: "-BO2 Kain Debug Flags\kain's invulnerable"=1 so it now appears as: "BO2 Kain Debug Flags\kain's invulnerable"=1

LEGACY OF KAIN: SOUL REAVER 2

Invincibility
Press Enter, Left, Left, Up, Down, Right, Action. Raziel will speak to confirm correct code entry. To disable this effect, press Enter, Right, Right, Down, Up, Left, Action.

LE MANS 24 HOURS

All Cars in Arcade Mode
Type driver's name as ALLTHECARSNOW.

All Tracks in Arcade Mode
Type driver's name as ALLTRACKSPLEASE.

All Championship Cars
Type driver's name as ENDOFFERS.

Pick from Any GT1, GT2, Etc. in Le Mans Mode
Type driver's name as LEMANSOFFERS.

Race Over One Lap in Le Mans Mode, Others Cars Handicapped
Type driver's name as MAKEITPEASY.

Resets MAKEITPEASY Cheat
Type driver's name as MAKEITNORMAL.

Race for Toyota Team
Type driver's name as TOYOTA1999.

Secret Audi Prototype
Type driver's name as 1999AUDI.

Secret BMW Prototype
Type driver's name as 19BMW99.

Secret Debora Racing Team
Type driver's name as DEBORALM.

Race for Debora Racing Team in Le Mans Mode
Type driver's name as DEBORACING.

All Secret Prototype GT1 and GT2 Cars
Type driver's name as 1999CHEATCARS.

LEATHERNECK

Invulnerability
During gameplay, type CUTHBERTNECH, then press F3.

LEGEND OF THE LOST

Level Select
Type the password EDLER.

LEGO RACERS

Rocket Car
In Build mode, type the driver name FLYSKYHIGH.

No Wheels Car
In Build mode, type the driver name NWHLS.

Fast Mode
In Build mode, type the driver name FSTFRWRD.

No Chassis
In Build mode, type the driver name NCHSSS.

No Driver
In Build mode, type the driver name NDRVR.

Maintain Speed Off Track
In Build mode, type the driver name NSLWJ.

Reversed Rocket Racer Run Track
In Build mode, type the driver name LNFRRRM.

Shooter Attacking Power-Ups Only
In Build mode, type the driver name PGLLRD.

Turbo Power-Ups Only
In Build mode, type the driver name PGLLGRN.

Mine Power-Ups Only
In Build mode, type the driver name PGLLYLL.

Grapple Power-Ups Only
In Build mode, type the driver name RPCRNLY.

Power-Ups Always at Maximum
In Build mode, type the driver name MXPMX.

Disable All Cheats
In Build mode, type the driver name NMRCHTS.

LEGO ROCK RAIDERS

Access All Levels
At the main menu, type LRRWARP.

All Men Become Rock Monsters
At the main menu, type LRRMONTY.

Access All Vehicles
At the main menu, type LRRVE.

LINKS 2001

During gameplay, press Caps Lock, then type:

Power Swing
Hitmania

Lighter Golf Balls
Lighter

LODE RUNNER 2

Access Cheat Mode
During gameplay, press Esc and type glazed donut.

Go Back One level
Enable Cheat mode and press F3.

Advance One Level
Enable Cheat mode and press F4.

Gain Five Lives
Enable Cheat mode and press Alt F12.

Ten Bombs of Each Type
Enable Cheat mode and press Alt 8.

Beach Ball Power-Up
Enable Cheat mode and press Alt K.

Inviso Power-Up
Enable Cheat mode and press Alt I.

Morph Power-Up
Enable Cheat mode and press Alt T.

Cloak Power-Up
Enable Cheat mode and press Alt B.

LOOPZ

Level 6 Password
JRNP

Level 11 Password
LSFH

Level 16 Password
ZMWK

Level 21 Password
BCQX

Level 26 Password
DGPR

Level 31 Password
KXQC

Level 36 Password
BZKG

Level 41 Password
GNPW

Level 46 Password
VJLF

LORDS OF MAGIC

Access Cheat Mode
During gameplay, press Ctrl+\ to display the Cheat prompt and type one of the following case-sensitive codes. These only work in v2.0 or higher and not in multiplayer.

Dragon
Enable Cheat mode and type puff.

200 Gold, Crystal, Ale
Enable Cheat mode and type jackpot.

1,000 Movement Points
Enable Cheat mode and type marathon.

All Spells, 1,000 Mana
Enable Cheat mode and type hocuspocus.

LORDS OF MAGIC: SPECIAL EDITION

Extra Gold, Ale, and Crystals
During gameplay, press Ctrl+C and type bingo.

Free Dragon
During gameplay, press Ctrl+C and type zilla.

1,000 Movement Points for Selected Party
During gameplay, press Ctrl+C and type go far.

All Spells and 1,000 Mana
During gameplay, press Ctrl+C and type all spells.

LOST VIKINGS 2: NORSE BY NORSEWEST

Credits
CR3D

Go to Highest Level You've Reached
W4RP

Invincibility
GHST

Level 2
1STS

Level 3
2NDS

Level 4
TRSH

Level 5
SW1M

Level 6
W0LF

Level 7
BR4T

Level 8
K4RN

Level 9
B0MB

Level 10
WZRD

Level 11
BLKS

Level 12
TLPT

Level 13
GYSR

Level 14
B3SV

Level 15
R3T0

Level 17
Y0VR

Level 18
0V4L

Level 19
T1N3

Level 20
D4RK

Level 21
H4RD

Level 22
HRDR

Level 23
L0ST

Level 24
0B0Y

Level 25
H0M3

Level 26
SHCK

Level 27
TNNL

Level 28
H3LL

Level 29
4RGH

Level 30
B4DD

Level 31
D4DY

LUCKY LUKE

Level 2
Lucky, Dalton, Pferd, Lucky

Level 3
Hund, Lucky, Dalton, Dalton

Level 4
Dalton, Hund, Hund, Dalton

Level 5
Dalton, Dalton, Lucky, Pferd

Level 6
Pferd, Hund, Hund, Dalton

Level 7
Lucky, Pferd, Lucky, Hund

M

MADDEN NFL '99

Better Defensive Back
leech

Better Catching
gloves

Better Kicking
bigfoot

EA Stadium
ea stadiums

Cleveland Stadium
dogpound99

Old Miami Stadium
notafish

RFK Stadium
thehogs

Old Tampa Bay Stadium
sombrero

Astrodome
for rent

Tiburon Stadium
ourhouse

Original Oakland Stadium
stickem

'99 Cleveland Browns
welcomeback

NFC All Stars
bestnfc

AFC All Stars
afcbest

Madden '98
boom

Stats Leaders
imtheman

All '60s
peacelove

All '70s
bellbottoms

All '90s
hereandnow

Madden All Time Greats
turkeyleg

75th Anniversary
throwback

NFL Equipment Team
gearguys

Heroes EA Sports Team
orrs

Old Oilers
jetsons

Town WildWest
ghost

Old Miami Dolphins
dandaman

Tiburon Sports Complex
sharksfin

MADDEN NFL 2000

More Injuries
painful

No Fumbles
maganasave

No Interceptions
no picks

Perfect Passes
qbintheclub

MADDEN NFL 2002

Unlock All Classic Teams
Go to Setting and select Secret Codes. Enter GOLDENGOD.

Unlock 1977 Dallas Cowboys
Go to Setting and select Secret Codes. Enter PICKEDOFF.

Unlock 1972 Oakland Raiders
Go to Setting and select Secret Codes. Enter WILDCARD.

MADSPACE

All Weapons
During gameplay, press ~ and type WEAPON.

No Clipping
During gameplay, press ~ and type CLIP.

God Mode
During gameplay, press ~ and type GOD.

Kill All Monsters
During gameplay, press ~ and type KILL.

Motion Scanner
During gameplay, press ~ and type SCAN.

Full Weapons and Energy
During gameplay, press ~ and type RESTORE.

MAGIC CARPET

Get All Spells
Press I, type RATTY, then press Alt+F1.

Get More Manna
Press I, type RATTY, then press Alt+F2.

All Magicians Die
Press I, type RATTY, then press Alt+F3.

All Hostile Castles Destroyed
Press I, type RATTY, then press Alt+F4.

Balloons Become Fireballs
Press I, type RATTY, then press Alt+F5.

Heal
Press I, type RATTY, then press Alt+F6.

Kill All Creatures
Press I, type RATTY, then press Alt+F7.

Complete Level
Press I, type RATTY, then press Shift+C.

MAGIC CARPET 2

Access All Spells
Press I, type WINDY, then press Alt+F1.

More Mana
Press I, type WINDY, then press Alt+F2.

Destroy All Players
Press I, type WINDY, then press Alt+F3.

Destroy All Castles
Press I, type WINDY, then press Alt+F4.

Destroy All Balloons
Press I, type WINDY, then press Alt+F5.

Heal
Press I, type WINDY, then press Alt+F6.

Kill All Creatures
Press I, type WINDY, then press Alt+F7.

More Spell Experience Points
Press I, type WINDY, then press Alt+F8.

Free Spell Usage On/Off
Press I, type WINDY, then press Alt+F9.

Invincibility On/Off
Press I, type WINDY, then press Alt+F10.

Complete Current Objective
Press I, type WINDY, then press Shift+D.

Complete Level
Press I, type WINDY, then press Shift+C.

MAGIC MARBLE

Level 2
EVERYWHERE

Level 3
TOOTHPASTE

Level 4
CONNECTION

Level 5
CLEVERNESS

Level 6
COPYWRITER

Level 7
TELEVISION

Level 8
CIGARETTES

Level 9
COMPLICATE

Level 10
IMPOSSIBLE

Level END
INTERESTED

MAGIC POCKETS

Level 2
3425

Level 3
8282

Level 4
4476

Level 5
7766

Level 6
8712

Level 7
4757

Level 8
4757

Level 9
2818

Level 10
1960

Level 11
6331

Level 12
3505

Level 13
692

Level 14
1786

Level 15
1786

Level 16
7962

Level 17
4125

Level 18
2219

Level 19
8498

Level 20
3123

Level 21
3541

Level 22
2823

Level 23
1286

Level 24
6067

Level 25
5139

Level 26
4400

MAJESTY

Win Game
During gameplay, press Enter and type victory is mine.

Lose Game
During gameplay, press Enter and type i'm a loser baby.

Add 10,000 Gold
During gameplay, press Enter and type fill this bag.

Reveal Map
During gameplay, press Enter and type revelation.

All Buildings Available
During gameplay, press Enter and type build anything.

All Spells Available
During gameplay, press Enter and type give me power.

Spells Have No Range Limit
During gameplay, press Enter and type cheezy towers.

Restores Hit Points
During gameplay, press Enter and type restoration.

Shows Frame Count
During gameplay, press Enter and type frame it.

Highlighted Hero Gains Five Levels
During gameplay, press Enter and type grow up.

MASTER OF ORION

Get 100 BC
Hold Alt and press M, O, O, L, A.

View Entire Map and Spaceships
Hold Alt and press G, A, L, A, X, Y.

MASTER OF ORION 2: BATTLE AT ANTARES

All Research
During gameplay, hold Alt and type Einstein.

1,000 BC
During gameplay, hold Alt and type Moola.

Another Research Cheat
During gameplay, hold Alt and type Menlo.

Show All Planets and Players
During gameplay, hold Alt and type Iseeall.

Show Score
During gameplay, hold Alt and type Score.

Complete Building Project for Selected Planet
During gameplay, hold Alt and type Crunch.

MAX PAYNE

Cheat List
When you start the game, use the -developer command line. During gameplay, press F12 to bring up the console. After it's there, type the following commands to get their corresponding effects.

God Mode
god

Turn Off God Mode
mortal

Get All Weapons
getallweapons

Get Infinite Ammo
getinfiniteammo

No Clipping Mode
noclip

Turn Off No Clipping Mode
noclip_off

Enable More Bullet Time
getbullettime

Debug Mode
coder

Display Current Framerate
showfps

Baseball Bat
GetBaseball Bat

Beretta
GetBeretta

Dual Beretta
GetBerettaDual

Dual Desert Eagle
GetDesertEagle

Sawed-Off Shotgun
GetSawedShotgun

Pump Shotgun
GetPumpShotgun

Jackhammer
GetJackhammer

Ingram
GetIngram

Dual Ingram
GetIngramDual

MP5
GetMP5

Colt Commando
GetColtCommando

Molotov Cocktail
GetMolotov

Grenade
GetGrenade

M79
GetM79

Sniper Rifle
GetSniper

MDK 2

God Mode
During gameplay, press ~ and at the Omen prompt, type mdkGobSetDamageFilter(mdkGetPlayerGob(),0).

God Mode
During gameplay, press ~ and at the Omen prompt, type God(1).

Jump to Level 1
During gameplay, press ~ and at the Omen prompt, type mdkNewGame(1,12).

Jump to Level 2
During gameplay, press ~ and at the Omen prompt, type mdkNewGame(2,12).

Jump to Level 3
During gameplay, press ~ and at the Omen prompt, type mdkNewGame(3,12).

Jump to Level 4
During gameplay, press ~ and at the Omen prompt, type mdkNewGame(4,12).

Jump to Level 5
During gameplay, press ~ and at the Omen prompt, type mdkNewGame(5,11).

Jump to Level 6
During gameplay, press ~ and at the Omen prompt, type mdkNewGame(6,8).

Jump to Level 7
During gameplay, press ~ and at the Omen prompt, type mdkNewGame(7,11).

Jump to Level 8
During gameplay, press ~ and at the Omen prompt, type mdkNewGame(8,8).

Jump to Level 9
During gameplay, press ~ and at the Omen prompt, type mdkNewGame(9,13).

Jump to Level 10 (Final)
During gameplay, press ~ and at the Omen prompt, type mdkNewGame(10,7).

Jump to Level 10 #1 (Special)
During gameplay, press ~ and at the Omen prompt, type mdkNewGame(11,1).

Jump to Level 10 #2 (Special)
During gameplay, press ~ and at the Omen prompt, type mdkNewGame(12,1).

God Mode On/Off
During gameplay, press ~ and at the Omen prompt, type GodDebugToggle().

Naked Kurt and Start a Level with Kurt in It
During gameplay, press ~ and at the Omen prompt, type KurtGetNaked().

MEATPUPPET

Full Health
During gameplay, type ~ingesth.

Full Energy
During gameplay, type ~ingeste.

Full Ammo
During gameplay, type ~ingestw.

Full Health, Energy and Ammo
During gameplay, type ~ingesta.

Invulnerability
During gameplay, type ~ingesti.

Sniper Cheat
During gameplay, type ~ingests.

Kill All Enemies on Screen
During gameplay, type ~dansmartbomb.

Explosions
During gameplay, type ~boom.

MECHCOMMANDER

Access Cheat Mode
Create a file called buymechcommander.2 in the game directory.

Replenish Ammo
Enable Cheat mode, and during gameplay, type lorrie.

Toggle God Mode On/Off
Enable Cheat mode, and during gameplay, type osmiu.

Reveal Map
Enable Cheat mode, and during gameplay, type mineeyeshaveseentheglory.

Unlimited Artillery, Press B and Left Click on Target To Kill It
Enable Cheat mode, and during gameplay, type Lordbunny.

More Money
Enable Cheat mode, and during gameplay, type poundofflesh.

Unlimited Dropweight
Enable Cheat mode, and during gameplay, type rockandrollpeople.

Max Gunnery Skill on Mechwarriors
Enable Cheat mode, and during gameplay, type deadeye.

Salvage Every Mech (Don't Check Salvage)
Enable Cheat mode, and during gameplay, type lennrocksthehouse.

MECHCOMMANDER GOLD

Access Cheat Mode
In the game directory, rename the file *windows.fit* to *ixtlriimceourl*.

Finish Mission
Enable Cheat mode, and during gameplay, type Ctrl+Alt+W.

Chart the Map
Enable Cheat mode, and during gameplay, type Ctrl+L.

1,000,000 RP (Logistics Phase)
Enable Cheat mode, and during gameplay, type poundofflesh.

Invincibility (Combat)
Enable Cheat mode, and during gameplay, type osmium.

Max Gunnery Skill for MechWarriors (Combat)
Enable Cheat mode, and during gameplay, type deadeye.

No Drop Weight Limit (Logistics Phase)
Enable Cheat mode, and during gameplay, type rockandrollpeople.

Repair and Reload (Combat)
Enable Cheat mode, and during gameplay, type lorrie.

Reveal Map (Combat)
Enable Cheat mode, and during gameplay, type mineeyeshaveseentheglory.

Repair All Mechs in Mech Bay (Combat)
Enable Cheat mode, and during gameplay, type mitchlovesyou.

Salvage All Mechs in a Level (Logistics Phase)
Enable Cheat mode, and Now during gameplay, type glennrocksthehouse.

Show Frame Rate (Combat)
Enable Cheat mode, and during gameplay, type framegraph.

Unlimited Nuke Strikes, Hold A and Left Click (Combat)
Enable Cheat mode, and during gameplay, type lordbunny.

One of Every Weapon
Enable Cheat mode, and during gameplay, type hereitcomes.

Heal Wounded Pilots (Combat)
Enable Cheat mode, and during gameplay, type healall.

MechWarrior 2: 31st Century Combat

Unlimited Ammo
In the cockpit, hold Alt+Shift+Ctrl and type cia.

Heat Tracking Off
In the cockpit, hold Alt+Shift+Ctrl and type coldmiser.

Hallucinations Until You Meet the Programmers
In the cockpit, hold Alt+Shift+Ctrl and type dorcs.

Similar to the Plane
In the cockpit, hold Alt+Shift+Ctrl and type enolagay.

Rearview HUD Camera Becomes a Front Camera
In the cockpit, hold Alt+Shift+Ctrl and type tlofront.

End Mission
In the cockpit, hold Alt+Shift+Ctrl and type icanthackit.

Time Compression Key Enabled
In the cockpit, hold Alt+Shift+Ctrl and type unmeepmeep.

See Bounding Spheres on Debris and Mech Parts
In the cockpit, hold Alt+Shift+Ctrl and type michelin.

Unlimited Jumpjets
In the cockpit, hold Alt+Shift+Ctrl and type mightymouse.

X-Ray Vision
In the cockpit, hold Alt+Shift+Ctrl and type xray.

Time Expansion Enabled
In the cockpit, hold Alt+Shift+Ctrl and type zmak.

Invulnerability
In the cockpit, hold Alt+Shift+Ctrl and type blorb.

Free-Floating External Cameras
In the cockpit, hold Alt+Shift+Ctrl and type tinkerbell.

Destroy Targeted Mech
In the cockpit, hold Alt+Shift+Ctrl and type cgankem.

Give Your Mech Jump Jets
In the cockpit, hold Alt+Shift+Ctrl and type tloflygirl.

MechWarrior 2: Ghost Bear's Legacy

Unlimited Ammo
During gameplay, hold Alt+Ctrl+Shift and type thundros.

Destroy Targeted Mech
During gameplay, hold Alt+Ctrl+Shift and type palex.

Invulnerable
During gameplay, hold Alt+Ctrl+Shift and type kent.

X-Ray Vision
During gameplay, hold Alt+Ctrl+Shift and type clark.

Destroy You and Your Enemies
During gameplay, hold Alt+Ctrl+Shift and type kaboom.

MechWarrior 2: Mercenaries

Invulnerability On/Off
superfunkicalifragisexy

Unlimited Ammo On/Off
iseenfireandiseenrain

Heat Tracking On/Off
ooohhhlllaaalllaaa

Sprout Jumpjets
itsdabombinmybeautifulballoon

End Mission Successfully
tikruleslikethecomstarbaby

Time Compression Key Enabled/Disabled
ontimeeverytime

Bounding Spheres On/Off
bubbleboy

Infinite Jumpjets On/Off
crazysexycool

Free Eye Mode On/Off
beholdmyglory

Time Expansion Enabled/Disabled
antijolt

Auto-Grouping Enabled/Disabled
flashyflashy

Leading Reticle Enabled/Disabled
walkthisway

MechWarrior: The Titanium Trilogy

Invulnerability On/Off
During gameplay, hold Ctrl+Shift+Alt and type su.

Unlimited Ammo On/Off
During gameplay, hold Ctrl+Shift+Alt and type is.

Heat Tracking On/Off
During gameplay, hold Ctrl+Shift+Alt and type oo.

Nuke Current Target
During gameplay, hold Ctrl+Shift+Alt and type it.

Destroy Current Target
During gameplay, hold Ctrl+Shift+Alt and type re.

Get Jump Jets
During gameplay, hold Ctrl+Shift+Alt and type in.

Unlimited Jump Jet Juice
During gameplay, hold Ctrl+Shift+Alt and type cr.

End Mission Successfully
During gameplay, hold Ctrl+Shift+Alt and type li.

Enable Free-Eye Mode
During gameplay, hold Ctrl+Shift+Alt and type be.

MechWarrior 4: Vengeance

During gameplay press and hold Ctrl+Alt+Shift then type:

Invulnerability
IY

Unlimited Ammo
UO

Heat Tracking Off
HF

Destroy Enemy Mech
IB

Win Last Mission
ML

Medal of Honor: Allied Assault

Activate Cheat Mode
Edit the shortcut to the game so it reads as follows:

"C:LOCATION OF GAMEmohaa.exe" +set ui_console 1 +set cheats 1 +set thereis-nomonkey 1

Then, in the game, press ~ to display the console window. Type in one of the following cheats.

God Mode
dog

Full Health
fullheal

All Weapons and Ammunition
wuss

No Clipping Mode
noclip

Remove Target
notarget

Third-Person View
toggle cg_3rd_person

List Inventory
listinventory

Teleport to Indicated Location
tele <x y z coordinates>

Display Current Coordinates
coord

Set Health
health <number>

Suicide
kill

List Models for Allies
playermodel

Spawn Indicated Weapon
giveweapon weapons/"<weapon_name>".tik

The weapon names are:

colt45

m2frag_grenade

p38

steilhandgrenate m1_garand

kar98

shotgun

bazooka

panzerschreck
bar
mp44
thompsonsmg
mp40
springfield
kar98sniper

Level Select
map <map name>

The names of the maps are:

m1l1
m1l2a
m1l2b
m1l3a
m1l3b
m1l3c
m2l1
m2l2a
m2l2b
m2l2c
m2l3
m3l1a
m3l1b
m6l3e

MEGAMAN X3

All Powers, E-Tanks, Health Chip
Type the password 5114-6385-6872-3153.

Code for 9th Chip
Type the password 6414-4155-6872-3356.

Crush Crawfish
Type the password 4478-4863-4627-7358.

Through Intro Stage
Type the password 3721-1281-3751-4456.

Zero's Beam Sabre
Type the password 1454-3535-6162-7162.

MEN IN BLACK

Access Cheat Mode
During gameplay, press Escape to go to the main menu. Type DOUGMATIC a couple times until it puts you back in the game. Press Escape again and type one of the following codes.

Kill Villains
Enable Cheat mode and type KILLEM.

All Weapons
Enable Cheat mode and type GIVEME.

Unlimited Ammo
Enable Cheat mode and type LOADME.

Full Health
Enable Cheat mode type HEALME.

Invulnerability
Enable Cheat mode and type PROTECTME.

Get Saved Games of All Levels
Enable Cheat mode and type MOVEME.

Become Agent J
Enable Cheat mode and type AGENTJ.

Become Agent K
Enable Cheat mode and type AGENTK.

Become Agent L
Enable Cheat mode and type AGENTL.

Become Agent X
Enable Cheat mode and type AGENTX.

Go to Arctic Level
Enable Cheat mode and type ARCTIC.

Go to HQ
Enable Cheat mode and type HQ.

MERCHANT PRINCE II

Get 50,000 Florins
Here's a way to get easy money: Go to the Venice screen and type HDIKASH. You get 50,000 Florins to spend at your leisure and pleasure.

Mobilize Dormant Mercenary Groups
To put inactive mercenary groups into action, go to the Venice screen. At the prompt, type HDIKARNAGE to activate them.

See What Your Opponent's Doing
To monitor your opponent's actions, go to the Venice screen and type HDISPY.

Show Map
Go to the Venice screen and type HDIVIEW to reveal the map.

MESSIAH

Activate God Mode for Bab
During gameplay, press Escape and type (not fast or too slow, with no pausing) ucantkillme.

Deactivate God Mode
During gameplay, press Escape and type (not fast or too slow, with no pausing) fleshnblood.

AI Off
During gameplay, press Escape and type (not fast or too slow, with no pausing) braindead.

AI On
During gameplay, press Escape and type (not fast or too slow, with no pausing) einstein.

AI Vision Off
During gameplay, press Escape and type (not fast or too slow, with no pausing) icantsee.

AI Vision On
During gameplay, press Escape and type (not fast or too slow, with no pausing) icanseeu.

Freeze Camera
During gameplay, press Escape and type (not fast or too slow, with no pausing) freezecam.

Thaw Camera
During gameplay, press Escape and type (not fast or too slow, with no pausing) thawcam.

End Current Game
During gameplay, press Escape and type (not fast or too slow, with no pausing) toohardforme.

Character Wire Frame On
During gameplay, press Escape and type (not fast or too slow, with no pausing) charwireon.

Character Wire Off
During gameplay, press Escape and type (not fast or too slow, with no pausing) charwireoff.

World Wire Frame On
During gameplay, press Escape and type (not fast or too slow, with no pausing) worldwireon.

World Wire Frame Off
During gameplay, press Escape and type (not fast or too slow, with no pausing) worldwireoff.

Polycount On
During gameplay, press Escape and type (not fast or too slow, with no pausing) onpolycount.

Polycount Off
During gameplay, press Escape and type (not fast or too slow, with no pausing) offpolycount.

Spawn Weapon Ammo
During gameplay, press Escape and type (not fast or too slow, with no pausing) gamespot.

Spawn Bazooka
During gameplay, press Escape and type (not fast or too slow, with no pausing) voodooextreme.

Spawn Grenades
During gameplay, press Escape and type (not fast or too slow, with no pausing) softwarebuys.

Spawn Welding Torch
During gameplay, press Escape and type (not fast or too slow, with no pausing) weldme.

Spawn Buzzsaw
During gameplay, press Escape and type (not fast or too slow, with no pausing) buzzbuzz.

Spawn Pumpgun
During gameplay, press Escape and type (not fast or too slow, with no pausing) boomstick.

Spawn Machinegun
During gameplay, press Escape and type (not fast or too slow, with no pausing) rapidfire.

Spawn Maimer
During gameplay, press Escape and type (not fast or too slow, with no pausing) slicendice.

Spawn Flamethrower
During gameplay, press Escape and type (not fast or too slow, with no pausing) lightmeup.

Spawn Pak Gun
During gameplay, press Escape and type (not fast or too slow, with no pausing) cooloff.

Spawn Bazooka
During gameplay, press Escape and type (not fast or too slow, with no pausing) bigbang.

Spawn Maser
During gameplay, press Escape and type (not fast or too slow, with no pausing) coolfx.

Spawn Harpoon Gun
During gameplay, press Escape and type (not fast or too slow, with no pausing) stickaround.

Spawn Weapon Ammo
During gameplay, press Escape and type (not fast or too slow, with no pausing) illbeback.

Spawn Grenades
During gameplay, press Escape and type (not fast or too slow, with no pausing) getsome.

Spawn Light Cop
During gameplay, press Escape and type (not fast or too slow, with no pausing) lcop.

Spawn Medium Cop
During gameplay, press Escape and type (not fast or too slow, with no pausing) mcop.

Spawn Heavy Cop
During gameplay, press Escape and type (not fast or too slow, with no pausing) hcop.

Spawn Riot Cop
During gameplay, press Escape and type (not fast or too slow, with no pausing) rcop.

Spawn Gun Commander
During gameplay, press Escape and type (not fast or too slow, with no pausing) guncmndr.

Spawn Domina
During gameplay, press Escape and type (not fast or too slow, with no pausing) incharge.

Spawn Armored Behemoth
During gameplay, press Escape and type (not fast or too slow, with no pausing) mynightmare.

Spawn Welder
During gameplay, press Escape and type (not fast or too slow, with no pausing) cantseemyface.

Spawn Worker
During gameplay, press Escape and type (not fast or too slow, with no pausing) workinman.

Spawn Scientist
During gameplay, press Escape and type (not fast or too slow, with no pausing) egghead.

Spawn Radiation Worker
During gameplay, press Escape and type (not fast or too slow, with no pausing) glowstick.

Spawn Medic
During gameplay, press Escape and type (not fast or too slow, with no pausing) heydoc.

Spawn Chot 1
During gameplay, press Escape and type (not fast or too slow, with no pausing) smellyguy.

Spawn Chot 2
During gameplay, press Escape and type (not fast or too slow, with no pausing) nohygiene.

Spawn Chot 3
During gameplay, press Escape and type (not fast or too slow, with no pausing) idontdance.

Spawn Chot 4
During gameplay, press Escape and type (not fast or too slow, with no pausing) scumbucket.

Spawn Chot Dwarf
During gameplay, press Escape and type (not fast or too slow, with no pausing) chotling.

Spawn Chot Behemoth
During gameplay, press Escape and type (not fast or too slow, with no pausing) smellysteroids.

Spawn Fungirl
During gameplay, press Escape and type (not fast or too slow, with no pausing) fungirl.

Spawn Prost 1
During gameplay, press Escape and type (not fast or too slow, with no pausing) workit.

Spawn Prost 2
During gameplay, press Escape and type (not fast or too slow, with no pausing) mansdream.

Spawn Hung
During gameplay, press Escape and type (not fast or too slow, with no pausing) specialguy.

Spawn Male Dweller 1
During gameplay, press Escape and type (not fast or too slow, with no pausing) averagejoe.

Spawn Male Dweller 2
During gameplay, press Escape and type (not fast or too slow, with no pausing) averagejack.

Spawn Male Dweller 3
During gameplay, press Escape and type (not fast or too slow, with no pausing) averagejohn.

Spawn Female Dweller 1
During gameplay, press Escape and type (not fast or too slow, with no pausing) janeplain.

Spawn Female Dweller 2
During gameplay, press Escape and type (not fast or too slow, with no pausing) jillplain.

Spawn Subgirl 1
During gameplay, press Escape and type (not fast or too slow, with no pausing) femfatale.

Spawn Subgirl 2
During gameplay, press Escape and type (not fast or too slow, with no pausing) nastyone.

Spawn Rat
During gameplay, press Escape and type (not fast or too slow, with no pausing) varmint.

Spawn Barman
During gameplay, press Escape and type (not fast or too slow, with no pausing) bestfriend.

Spawn Waitress
During gameplay, press Escape and type (not fast or too slow, with no pausing) bringmeadrink.

Spawn Dancer 1
During gameplay, press Escape and type (not fast or too slow, with no pausing) bustamove.

Spawn Dancer 2
During gameplay, press Escape and type (not fast or too slow, with no pausing) cutarug.

Spawn DJ
During gameplay, press Escape and type (not fast or too slow, with no pausing) mixalot.

Spawn Pimp Daddy
During gameplay, press Escape and type (not fast or too slow, with no pausing) tophat.

Spawn Behemoth
During gameplay, press Escape and type (not fast or too slow, with no pausing) onsteroids.

Spawn Offensive Bot
During gameplay, press Escape and type (not fast or too slow, with no pausing) addedfirepower.

Spawn Companion Bot
During gameplay, press Escape and type (not fast or too slow, with no pausing) keepmecompany.

Spawn Bouncer
During gameplay, press Escape and type (not fast or too slow, with no pausing) letmein.

METAL KNIGHT

Full Health for All Units
During gameplay, press Enter and type amitofo.

Show Map
During gameplay, press Enter and type sunshine.

Win Mission
During gameplay, press Enter and type luckybird.

Lose Mission
During gameplay, press Enter and type pitybird.

Receive Cash
During gameplay, press Enter and type richbird.

MICROSOFT BASEBALL 2000

Wizbang Secret Team
Click on Help, then About Baseball 2000. Now right-click on the first occurrence of Wizbang.

MIDTOWN MADNESS

Display All Police Units on the Map
At the Player Selection screen, click on New and type Showme Cops. This also disables race result monitoring and score and you can't unlock new vehicles.

All Traffic Vehicles Are City Buses
At the Player Selection screen, click on New and type Big Bus Party. This also disables race result monitoring and score and you can't unlock new vehicles.

All Traffic Vehicles Are Compact Cars
At the Player Selection screen, click on New and type Tiny Car. This also disables race result monitoring and score and you can't unlock new vehicles.

All Traffic Vehicles Drive Around
At the Player Selection screen, click on New and type amizdA eoJ.

All Traffic Vehicles Are Air Planes
At the Player Selection screen, click on New and type Jet Planes. This also disables race result monitoring and score and you can't unlock new vehicles.

All AI Is 10 Times Faster
At the Player Selection screen, click on New and type Warp Eleven. This also disables race result monitoring and score and you can't unlock new vehicles.

Access to All Races
Start the game with the command line parameter -allrace.

Access to All Cars
Start the game with the command line parameter -allcars.

No Damage Mode
During gameplay, press Ctrl+Alt+Shift+F7 and a box appears. Type /nodamage. This only works in Single-player mode, disables race result monitoring and score, and you can't unlock new vehicles.

Damage Back On
During gameplay, press Ctrl+Alt+Shift+F7 and a box appears. Type /damage. This only works in Single-player mode.

Spinning Sky
During gameplay, press Ctrl+Alt+Shift+F7 and a box appears. Type /dizzy. This only works in Single-player mode.

Toggles Cop Radar
During gameplay, press Ctrl+Alt+Shift+F7 and a box appears. Type /fuzzy. This only works in Single-player mode, disables race result monitoring and score, and you can't unlock new vehicles.

Bridge Very Quickly
During gameplay, press Ctrl+Alt+Shift+F7 and a box appears. Type /bridge. This only works in Single-player mode, disables race result monitoring and score, and you can't unlock new vehicles.

Replace Planes with UFOs
During gameplay, press Ctrl+Alt+Shift+F7 and a box appears. Type /ufo. This only works in Single-player mode.

Swap the Train with a String of 737s
During gameplay, press Ctrl+Alt+Shift+F7 and a box appears. Type /swap. This only works in Single-player mode.

Ambient Cars Have No Friction
During gameplay, press Ctrl+Alt+Shift+F7 and a box appears. Type /slide. This only works in Single-player mode, disables race result monitoring and score, and you can't unlock new vehicles.

Player Experiences No Friction
During gameplay, press Ctrl+Alt+Shift+F7 and a box appears. Type /puck. This only works in Single-player mode, disables race result monitoring and score, and you can't unlock new vehicles.

Half Gravity
During gameplay, press Ctrl+Alt+Shift+F7 and a box appears. Type /grav. This only works in Single-player mode, disables race result monitoring and score, and you can't unlock new vehicles.

Horn Fires Mailboxes
During gameplay, press Ctrl+Alt+Shift+F7 and a box appears. Type /postal. This only works in Single-player mode, disables race result monitoring and score, and you can't unlock new vehicles.

Commentary Plays Fast
During gameplay, press Ctrl+Alt+Shift+F7 and a box appears. Type /talkfast. This only works in Single-player mode.

Commentary Plays Slow
During gameplay, press Ctrl+Alt+Shift+F7 and a box appears. Type /talkslow. This only works in Single-player mode.

Big People
During gameplay, press Ctrl+Alt+Shift+F7 and a box appears. Type /big. This only works in Single-player mode.

Tiny people
During gameplay, press Ctrl+Alt+Shift+F7 and a box appears. Type /tiny. This only works in Single-player mode.

Wheel/Damage Smoke Off
During gameplay, press Ctrl+Alt+Shift+F7 and a box appears. Type /nosmoke. This only works in Single-player mode.

Wheel/Damage Smoke On
During gameplay, press Ctrl+Alt+Shift+F7 and a box appears. Type /smoke. This only works in Single-player mode.

Generic Car
In Cruise mode only, at the Player Selection screen, click on "New," type vasedans, and pick the Cadillac.

Generic Light Car
In Cruise mode only, at the Player Selection screen, click on "New," type vasedan1, and pick the Bullet.

The Van
In Cruise mode only, at the Player Selection screen, click on "New," type vavan, and pick the Ford F350.

The Diesel
In Cruise mode only, at the Player Selection screen, click on "New," type vadiesels, and pick the City Bus.

Rabbit-Type Compact Car
In Cruise mode only, at the Player Selection screen, click on "New," type vacompact, and pick the VW Bug.

Pickup Truck
In Cruise mode only, at the Player Selection screen, click on "New," type vapickup, and pick the Ford F350.

Bus with Paint Job
In Cruise mode only, at the Player Selection screen, click on "New," type vabus, and pick the City Bus.

Delivery Truck
In Cruise mode only, at the Player Selection screen, click on "New," type vadelivery, and pick the Ford F350.

Random Limo
In Cruise mode only, at the Player Selection screen, click on "New," type valimo, and pick the Mustang GT.

Black Limo
In Cruise mode only, at the Player Selection screen, click on "New," type valimoblack, and pick the Mustang GT.

White Limo
In Cruise mode only, at the Player Selection screen, click on "New," type valimoangel, and pick the Mustang GT.

Yellow Cab
In Cruise mode only, at the Player Selection screen, click on "New," type vataxi, and pick the Cadillac.

Green Checkered Cab
In Cruise mode only, at the Player Selection screen, click on "New," type vataxicheck, and pick the Cadillac.

Mini-Jet
In Cruise mode only, at the Player Selection screen, click on "New," type vaboeing_small, and pick the City Bus.

MIG 29 FULCRUM

Unlimited Ammo
During gameplay, press T for the message prompt and type you got what i need.

Reload Plane
During gameplay, press T for the message prompt and type food goes here.

Refuel Plane
During gameplay, press T for the message prompt and type big gulp.

Invincible
During gameplay, press T for the message prompt and type youre here forever.

Can't Crash
During gameplay, press T for the message prompt and type damn that corner.

Repair Plane
During gameplay, press T for the message prompt and type chiliburger.

Can't Be Hit
During gameplay, press T for the message prompt and type spindive.

Auto Level Fly Upside-Down
During gameplay, press T for the message prompt and type upside down.

Paper Airplane
During gameplay, press T for the message prompt and type paperairplane.

MIGHT AND MAGIC III

Easy Money
Type DOE MEISTER as password.

Ultimate Power Orb
Type ORB MEISTER as password.

View Ending
Type BLASTOFF as password.

MIGHT AND MAGIC IV

Find a Hidden Town
Type SHANGRI-LA at teleport mirror.

Get the Magical Sword
Type I LOST IT at teleport mirror.

Go to Dragon's Lair
Type COUNT DU MONEY at teleport mirror.

Go to End of the Game
Type SHOWTIME at teleport mirror.

Go to Lord Xeen
Type LORD XEEN at teleport mirror.

MILITATO

Restore Health and Ammo
During gameplay, press F8 and type mspace.

Level Skip
During gameplay, press F8 and type nextstage.

Additional Communications Device
During gameplay, press F8 and type additem.

MOB RULE

Cheat Mode
During gameplay, type one of the following codes. If you type it correctly, you hear a beep. You may enable as many codes as you wish. After enabling the code, press C to toggle Cheat mode.

Allow Sped Up Game in Network Mode
During gameplay, type speed364 and press Enter.

Allow Buying of Workers at Any Time
During gameplay, type worker928 and press Enter.

Allow Picking Up of Enemy Beacons
During gameplay, type pickup036 and press Enter.

Allow Buying of Any Weapon for Gangster
During gameplay, type weapons563 and press Enter.

Allow Selection of Any Tenant at Any Time
During gameplay, type tenants872 and press Enter.

Allow Borrowing of Any Amount from Bank
During gameplay, type loans458 and press Enter.

Allow Buying of an Estate Without Conditions
During gameplay, type estates216 and press Enter.

Money Trick
Enter the "loans458" code, then borrow any amount up to $21,475,000 from the bank. Now the bank pays you $214,756 each month.

MONSTER TRUCK MADNESS

Race as Tyrannosaurus Rex
During gameplay, type TREX.

MORTYR

God Mode
During gameplay, press ~ and type satan.

Jump to Level Number
During gameplay, press ~ and .jt # (replace # with desired level).

All Weapons and Items
During gameplay, press ~ and type allit. If you use this cheat, you can't progress through the advanced levels.

All Weapons and Items
During gameplay, press ~ and type gimme all. If you use this cheat, you can't progress through the advanced levels.

MOTOCROSS MADNESS 2

Big Head Mode
At the main menu, type big heads.

Quick Recovery
Press Tab to reset the player on the bike.

Rainbow Studios Pattern
During gameplay, press Alt+Tab+A. This switches screens. Return to the game and the ground will is Rainbow Studios' pattern. To reset this, restart the race.

MOTOCROSS MANIA

After installing the game and starting a new championship you're asked to create a new profile. Enter one of the following names at the profile screen to enable your cheats.

Unlock All the Stunts
Mad Dog

Unlock All the Tracks
Beef Cake

Loads of Money
Uncle Bill

Automatically Qualify for Every Race
Vera Champ

MOTOR EXTREME

Unlock Lunar Track
Hold Ctrl and highlight all eight track icons.

MOTORACER 2

Access All Tracks
During gameplay, type CDNALSI.

Extra Tracks, Access at Main Menu
During gameplay, type CESREVER.

Rocket Bikes
During gameplay, type CTEKCOP.

MOTORHEAD

Supercars Mode
In Personal options, type the name Supercars and the team Grem.

Mega-Springs Mode
In Personal options, type the name Demon and the team Grem.

LA-Style Suspension
In Personal options, type the name g-ride and the team west.

Moon Gravity
In Personal options, type the name Buzz Aldrin and the team NASA.

Ignition Mode
In Personal options, type the name Ignition and the team UDS.

Avenger (Hardware Acceleration Only)
In Personal options, type the name Avenger and the team Zx.

Water Mode (Hardware Acceleration Only)
In Personal options, type the name Ramlosa and the team H20.

All Cars and Tracks
In Personal options, type the name R Peterson and the team Swe.

Hell Mode (Hardware Acceleration Only)
In Personal options, type the name Lemmy and the team Ace.

Tron Mode (Glide Only)
In Personal options, type the name tribute to tron.

MYSTERY ISLAND

More Power
During gameplay, type MRBIONIC.

High Jump
During gameplay, type MRPOLO.

Invincible
During gameplay, type MRTOUGH.

Fast Run
During gameplay, type MRSPEED.

Unlimited Lives
During gameplay, type MRGOD.

MYSTERY OF THE SITH

Uber-Jedi
During gameplay, press T and type iamagod.

All Weapons
During gameplay, press T and type diediedie.

Full Inventory
During gameplay, press T and type gimmestuff.

Level Jump
During gameplay, press T and type gameover.

Freeze Enemies On/Off
During gameplay, press T and type statuesque 1/0.

Force Level Up
During gameplay, press T and type trainme.

Fly Mode
During gameplay, press T and type freebird.

God Mode On/Off
During gameplay, press T and type boinga 1/0.

Full Mana
During gameplay, press T and type trixie.

Show Map
During gameplay, press T and type cartograph.

Slow-Mo Mode On/Off
During gameplay, press T and type gospeedgo 1/0.

Warp to Specific Coordinate
During gameplay, press T and type quickzap.

MYTH 2: SOULBLIGHTER

Instant Win
Hold Ctrl+Alt then press +.

Level Select
Hold Shift and select "New Game."

NAM

God Mode
NVAGOD

God Mode
NVACALEB

Show the Whole Map
NVASHOWMAP

All Weapons
NVABLOOD

Toggle All Locks
NVUNLOCK

Something with the Radio
NVAMATT

No Clipping
NVACLIP

Ex. 205 Episode 2, Level 5
NVALEVEL###

Change the Rate
NVARATE

Debug
NVADEBUG

NBA FULL COURT PRESS

Run as Fast as Possible
During gameplay, type TOPSPEED.

Do a Line Dance
During gameplay, type LINEDANCE.

Do a Moving Line Dance
During gameplay, type MOVEDANCE.

NBA INSIDE DRIVE 2000

No Intro Movie
Start the game with the command line parameter -novideo.

Play on Gym Court
Start the game with the command line parameter -floor gym.

High Voltage Parking Lot
Start the game with the command line parameter -floor hvs.

Outside Practice Court
Start the game with the command line parameter -floor outsite.

Easy Alley Oops
Start the game with the command line parameter -EasyAlleyOops.

Huge Players
Start the game with the command line parameter -HugePlayers.

Mini Players
Start the game with the command line parameter -MiniPlayers.

NBA LIVE 2000

Michael Jordan
Play against Jordan, set the match to 11 points and choose Jordan at the Controller Setup screen. Let the other player score 10 points, then switch controllers and score 1 point on Jordan to unlock him on the roster.

Power Dunks
At the main menu, type redrover. If you did it correctly, you hear a noise.

NBA LIVE '99

Europals
In the Create Custom Team option, type EA-Europals.

Coders
In the Create Custom Team option, type Hitmen-Coders.

Earplugs
In the Create Custom Team option, type Hitmen-Earplugs.

Idlers
In the Create Custom Team option, type Hitmen-Idlers.

Pixels
In the Create Custom Team option, type Hitmen-Pixels.

Playground Court
At the Team Selection screen, enter PLAYGROUND before any game.

Secret Internet Setup
At the Main screen, type ILOVELAG, then click Multiplayer.

NBA LIVE 2001

M. Jordan
Beat Michael Jordan in One-on-One to use him in the classic team (1990's). At the start of the game, when you see a guy holding a ball, hold N. When the EA sports screen appears, hold B. And when the screen that shows the teams appears, hold A. When the menu appears, type NBA Live 2001, and there is a team called the Laker's Peacers. The members in the team are awesome; they shoot threes like it's nothing.

NCAA FOOTBALL '99

Tiny Home Team, Huge Away Team
At the Ctrl Select screen, type elah before you select your controller. Select controller and begin gameplay.

NEBULA FIGHTER

Full Shields
Pause gameplay and type onereality.

Extra Ship
Pause gameplay and type holodream.

Warp to Next Level
Pause gameplay and type aelfread.

All Weapons, Max Nukes
Pause gameplay and type terry.

Full Shields, Max Nukes, Power-ups
Pause gameplay and type alan.

NEED FOR SPEED 2

School Bus
At the main menu, type bus.

Volkswagen Beetle
At the main menu, type vwbug.

Volkswagen Fastback
At the main menu, type vwfb.

Truck Cab
At the main menu, type semi.

Mazda Miata
At the main menu, type miata.

Mercedes-Benz
At the main menu, type mercedes.

Volvo Stationwagon
At the main menu, type volvo.

BMW
At the main menu, type bmw.

Mercedes Unimog Army Truck
At the main menu, type armytruck.

Mercedes Unimog Snow Truck
At the main menu, type snowtruck.

Volkswagen Combi Van
At the main menu, type vanagon.

Jeep YJ
At the main menu, type jeepyj.

Toyota Landcruiser
At the main menu, type landcruiser.

Audi Quattro
At the main menu, type quattro.

Commanche Pick-Up Truck
At the main menu, type Commanche.

Monolithic Studios Bus
At the main menu, type drive29.

Limo
At the main menu, type drive30.

Citroen 2CV
At the main menu, type drive31.

Cart
At the main menu, type drive36.

Outhouse
At the main menu, type drive37.

T-Rex
At the main menu, type drive38.

Wagon
At the main menu, type drive39.

Souvenir Stand 1
At the main menu, type drive40.

Souvenir Stand 2
At the main menu, type drive41.

Souvenir Stand 3
At the main menu, type drive42.

Log
At the main menu, type drive43.

Wooden Crate
At the main menu, type drive44.

Monorail
At the main menu, type drive45.

Hoverpolice
At the main menu, type drive46.

UFO
At the main menu, type drive47.

Hovering Sewage Truck
At the main menu, type drive48.

Snowy Wooden Box
At the main menu, type drive49.

Snowy Wooden Box 2
At the main menu, type drive50.

Monolithic Studios: Hollywood Track
At the main menu, type hollywood.

Enable Super Slip and Slide Mode
At the main menu, type slip.

Enable Pioneer Engine in All Cars
At the main menu, type pioneer.

NEED FOR SPEED 2 SE

Rainbow Color Car and Horizon (3Dfx Only)
At the main menu, type kcjones.

Honk with Opponent in Front and He Will Crash
At the main menu, type roadrage.

Cows Fly Behind You (3Dfx Only)
At the main menu, type mad.

Slot Mode
At the main menu, type slot.

Opponent Cars Follow You If in Front
At the main menu, type chase.

Rain Conditions in Proving Ground or Mystic Peaks Track (non-3Dfx)
At the main menu, type rain.

Slippery Tracks
At the main menu, type slip.

Upgrade All Cars' Engines
At the main menu, type pioneer.

Lot of Traffic
At the main menu, type rushhour.

Bonus Track: Monolithic Studios
At the main menu, type hollywood.

Bomber BFS
At the main menu, type bomber.

FZR 2000
At the main menu, type fzr2000.

Tombstone Daytona Racing Car
At the main menu, type tombstone.

NEED FOR SPEED 3

Police Talk on Bullhorn
At any menu, type bullhorn.

Enable El Nino Car
At any menu, type elnino.

Enable Mercedes CLK-GTR
At any menu, type merc.

Enable Jaguar Sports Car
At any menu, type jag.

Enable Empire City Track
At any menu, type empire.

Lots of Traffic
At any menu, type rushhour.

Twice the Speed in Single-Player Mode
At any menu, type gofast.

Enable All Cars Including Pursuit Vehicles
At any menu, type allcars.

Bonus Police Cars
At any menu, type newcars.

Pursuit Diablo SV Bonus Car
At any menu, type dcop.

Pursuit El Nino Bonus Car
At any menu, type ecop.

Manual Transmission with Automatic Functions
At any menu, type monkey.

AI Cars Drive at Maximum Capability
At any menu, type madland.

Colored Cars Mode
At any menu, type ckjones.

All Cars in Pursuit Mode
At any menu, type macr.

Miata
At any menu, type go01.

Toyota Landcruiser
At any menu, type go02.

Cargo Truck
At any menu, type go03.

BMW 5 Series
At any menu, type go04.

'71 Plymouth 'Cuda
At any menu, type go05.

Ford Pickup with Camper Shell
At any menu, type go06.

Jeep Cherokee
At any menu, type go07.

Ford Fullsize Van
At any menu, type go08.

'64/65 Mustang
At any menu, type go09.

'66 Chevy Pickup
At any menu, type go10.

Range Rover
At any menu, type go11.

School Bus
At any menu, type go12.

Taxi (Caprice Classic)
At any menu, type go13.

Chevy Cargo Van
At any menu, type go14.

Volvo Station Wagon
At any menu, type go15.

Sedan
At any menu, type go16.

Crown Victoria Cop Car
At any menu, type go17.

Mitsubishi Eclipse Cop Car
At any menu, type go18.

Grand Am Cop Car
At any menu, type go19.

Range Rover Cop Car/Ranger Vehicle
At any menu, type go20.

Cargo Truck (Same as 03)
At any menu, type go21.

NERF ARENABLAST

God Mode
During gameplay, press ~ and type god, then press Enter.

999 Shots for All Guns
During gameplay, press ~ and type allammo, then press Enter.

Fly Mode
During gameplay, press ~ and type fly, then press Enter.

Walk Through Walls
During gameplay, press ~ and type ghost, then press Enter.

Turns Off Fly and Ghost
During gameplay, press ~ and type walk, then press Enter.

Third-Person View
During gameplay, press ~ and type behindview 1, then press Enter.

Open Asteroid Map
During gameplay, press ~ and type open AR-Asteroid, then press Enter.

Open Barracuda Map
During gameplay, press ~ and type open AR-Barracuda, then press Enter.

Open Luna Map
During gameplay, press ~ and type open AR-Luna, then press Enter.

Open Orbital Map
During gameplay, press ~ and type open AR-Orbital, then press Enter.

Open Sequoia Map
During gameplay, press ~ and type open AR-Sequoia, then press Enter.

Open Sky Map
During gameplay, press ~ and type open AR-Sky, then press Enter.

Open Tut Map
During gameplay, press ~ and type open AR-Tut, then press Enter.

Open Autoplay Map
During gameplay, press ~ and type open Autoplay, then press Enter.

Open Entry Map
During gameplay, press ~ and type open Entry, then press Enter.

Open Plaza Map
During gameplay, press ~ and type open Nerf-Plaza, then press Enter.

Open Amateur Map
During gameplay, press ~ and type open PM-Amateur, then press Enter.

Open Asteroid Map
During gameplay, press ~ and type open PM-Asteroid, then press Enter.

Open Barracuda Map
During gameplay, press ~ and type open PM-Barracuda, then press Enter.

Open Champion Map
During gameplay, press ~ and type open PM-Champion, then press Enter.

Open Luna Map
During gameplay, press ~ and type open PM-Luna, then press Enter.

Open Orbital Map
During gameplay, press ~ and type open PM-Orbital, then press Enter.

Open Sequoia Map
During gameplay, press ~ and type open PM-Sequoia, then press Enter.

Open Sky Map
During gameplay, press ~ and type open PM-Sky, then press Enter.

Open Tut Map
During gameplay, press ~ and type open PM-Tut, then press Enter.

Open Luna Map
During gameplay, press ~ and type open PMX2-Luna, then press Enter.

Open Asteroid Map
During gameplay, press ~ and type open PMX-Asteroid, then press Enter.

Open Luna Map
During gameplay, press ~ and type open PMX-Luna, then press Enter.

Open Orbital Map
During gameplay, press ~ and type open PMX-Orbital, then press Enter.

Open Amateur Map
During gameplay, press ~ and type open RR-Amateur, then press Enter.

Open Asteroid Map
During gameplay, press ~ and type open RR-Asteroid, then press Enter.

Open Barracuda Map
During gameplay, press ~ and type open RR-Barracuda, then press Enter.

Open Champion Map
During gameplay, press ~ and type open RR-Champion, then press Enter.

Open Luna Map
During gameplay, press ~ and type open RR-Luna, then press Enter.

Open Orbital Map
During gameplay, press ~ and type open RR-Orbital, then press Enter.

Open Sequoia Map
During gameplay, press ~ and type open RR-Sequoia, then press Enter.

Open Sky Map
During gameplay, press ~ and type open RR-Sky, then press Enter.

Open Asteroid Map
During gameplay, press ~ and type open SH-Asteroid, then press Enter.

Open Barracuda Map
During gameplay, press ~ and type open SH-Barracuda, then press Enter.

Open Luna Map
During gameplay, press ~ and type open SH-Luna, then press Enter.

Open Orbital Map
During gameplay, press ~ and type open SH, then press Enter.

Open Sequoia Map
During gameplay, press ~ and type open SH-Sequoia, then press Enter.

Open Sky Map
During gameplay, press ~ and type open SH-Sky, then press Enter.

Open Tut Map
During gameplay, press ~ and type open SH-Tut, then press Enter.

NETSTORM: ISLANDS AT WAR

10,000 Storm Power-Up and Battle Select
In One Player, press F2 and type .cheatorama 8675309.

NEVERWINTER NIGHTS

Activate Cheat Mode
This procedure involves editing a game file; create a backup copy of the file before proceeding. Use a text editor to edit the "nwn.ini" file in the game folder. Add the following line under the "Game Options" section:

Debug Mode=1
Then, press ~ during gameplay and type DebugMode 1 (case sensitive) to enable cheat mode. Press ~ again and press Tab to view the debug commands. Press Tab to scroll through the commands. Enter one of the following case-sensitive codes to activate the corresponding cheat function. The message "Success" will confirm correct code entry. If the message "Entered Target Mode" appears, click on the desired character to apply the cheat.

Set Strength Attribute
SetSTR <number>

Set Dexterity Attribute
SetDEX <number>

Set Intelligence Attribute
SetINT <number>

Set Wisdom Attribute
SetWIS <number>

Set Constitution Attribute
SetCON <number>

Set Charisma Attribute
SetCHA <number>

Get Indicated Amount of Gold
dm_givegold <number>

Invincibility
dm_god

Restore All Hit Points
dm_heal

Ride a Hobby Horse
dm_mylittlepony

Killer Flying Cows
dm_cowsfromhell

Get Indicated Amount of Experience Points
GiveXP <number>

Raise Indicated Number of Levels
GetLevel <number>

Set Character's Fortitude Save Modifier
ModSaveFort

Set Character's Reflex Save Modifier
ModSaveReflex

Set Character's Will Save Modifier
ModSaveWill

Set Character's Spell Resistance Modifier
ModSpellResistance <number>

Set Character's Age
SetAge <number>

Set Character's Base Attack
SetAttackBase <number>

Change Character's Race (Human, Elf, etc.)
SetAppearance <race>

NFL BLITZ 2000

Custom Playbook
At the Vs. screen, press Turbo, Jump (2), Pass (2), Left. A sound confirms correct entry, and the code name appears.

Infinite Turbo
At the Vs. screen, press Turbo (5), Jump, Pass (4), Up. A sound confirms correct entry, and the code name appears.

Fast Turbo Running
At the Vs. screen, press Jump (3), Pass (2), Left. A sound confirms correct entry, and the code name appears.

Power-Up Offense
At the Vs. screen, press Turbo (3), Jump, Pass (2), Up. A sound confirms correct entry, and the code name appears.

Power-Up Defense
At the Vs. screen, press Turbo (4), Jump (2), Pass, Up. A sound confirms correct entry, and the code name appears.

Power-Up Teammates
At the Vs. screen, press Turbo (2), Jump (3), Pass (3), Up. A sound confirms correct entry, and the code name appears.

Power-Up Blockers
At the Vs. screen, press Turbo (3), Jump, Pass (2), Left. A sound confirms correct entry, and the code name appears.

Super Blitzing
At the Vs. screen, press Jump (4), Pass (5), Up. A sound confirms correct entry, and the code name appears.

Super Field Goals
At the Vs. screen, press Turbo, Jump (2), Pass (3), Left. A sound confirms correct entry, and the code name appears.

No Interceptions
At the Vs. screen, press Turbo (3), Jump (4), Pass (4), Up. A sound confirms correct entry, and the code name appears.

No Random Fumbles
At the Vs. screen, press Turbo (4), Jump (2), Pass (3), Down. A sound confirms correct entry, and the code name appears.

No First Downs
At the Vs. screen, press Turbo (2) Jump, Up. A sound confirms correct entry, and the code name appears.

No Punting
At the Vs. screen, press Turbo, Jump (5), Pass, Up. A sound confirms correct entry, and the code name appears.

Allow Stepping out of Bounds
At the Vs. screen, press Turbo (2), Jump, Pass, Left. A sound confirms correct entry, and the code name appears.

Fast Passes
At the Vs. screen, press Turbo (2), Jump (5), Left. A sound confirms correct entry, and the code name appears.

Turn Off Stadium
At the Vs. screen, press Turbo (5), Left. A sound confirms correct entry, and the code name appears.

Late Hits
At the Vs. screen, press Jump, Up. A sound confirms correct entry, and the code name appears.

Show Field Goal Percentage
At the Vs. screen, press Pass, Down. A sound confirms correct entry, and the code name appears.

Show Punt Hang Meter
At the Vs. screen, press Pass, Right. A sound confirms correct entry, and the code name appears.

Use Team Plays
At the Vs. screen, press Turbo, Up. A sound confirms correct entry, and the code name appears.

Hide Receiver Name
At the Vs. screen, press Turbo, Pass (2), Right. A sound confirms correct entry, and the code name appears.

Invisible Receiver Highlight
At the Vs. screen, press Turbo (3), Jump (3), Pass (3), Left. A sound confirms correct entry, and the code name appears.

Invisible
At the Vs. screen, press Turbo (4), Jump (3), Pass (3), Up. A sound confirms correct entry, and the code name appears.

Big Football
At the Vs. screen, press Jump (5), Right. A sound confirms correct entry, and the code name appears.

Big Head
At the Vs. screen, press Turbo (2), Right. A sound confirms correct entry, and the code name appears.

Huge Head
At the Vs. screen, press Jump (4), Up. A sound confirms correct entry, and the code name appears.

No Head
At the Vs. screen, press Turbo (3), Jump (2), Pass, Left. A sound confirms correct entry, and the code name appears.

Headless Team

At the Vs. screen, press Turbo, Jump (2), Pass (3), Right. A sound confirms correct entry, and the code name appears.

Team Tiny Players

At the Vs. screen, press Turbo (3), Jump, Right. A sound confirms correct entry, and the code name appears.

Team Big Players

At the Vs. screen, press Turbo, Jump (4), Pass, Right. A sound confirms correct entry, and the code name appears.

Team Big Heads

At the Vs. screen, press Turbo (2), Pass (3), Right. A sound confirms correct entry, and the code name appears.

No Play Selection (Two-Player Agreement Required)

At the Vs. screen, press Turbo, Jump, Pass (5), Left. A sound confirms correct entry, and the code name appears.

Show More Field (Two-Player Agreement Required)

At the Vs. screen, press Jump (2), Pass, Right. A sound confirms correct entry, and the code name appears.

No CPU Assistance (Two-Player Agreement Required)

At the Vs. screen, press Jump, Pass (2), Down. A sound confirms correct entry, and the code name appears.

Power-Up Speed (Two-Player Agreement Required)

At the Vs. screen, press Turbo (4), Pass (4), Left. A sound confirms correct entry, and the code name appears.

Hyper Blitz (Two-Player Agreement Required)

At the Vs. screen, press Turbo (5), Jump (5), Pass (5), Up. A sound confirms correct entry, and the code name appears.

Smart CPU Opponent (Two-Player Agreement Required)

At the Vs. screen, press Turbo (3), Jump, Pass (4), Down. A sound confirms correct entry, and the code name appears.

Tournament Mode (Two-Player Game Only)

At the Vs. screen, press Turbo, Jump, Pass, Down. A sound confirms correct entry, and the code name appears.

Always Quarterback (Two Human Teammates Required)

At the Vs. screen, press Turbo (2), Jump (2), Pass (2), Left. A sound confirms correct entry, and the code name appears.

Always Receiver (Two Human Teammates Required)

At the Vs. screen, press Turbo (2), Jump (2), Pass (2), Right. A sound confirms correct entry, and the code name appears.

Old Day Stadium

At the Vs. screen, press Turbo (5), Pass, Up. A sound confirms correct entry, and the code name appears.

Day Stadium

At the Vs. screen, press Turbo (5), Pass, Down. A sound confirms correct entry, and the code name appears.

City Stadium

At the Vs. screen, press Turbo (5), Pass, Left. A sound confirms correct entry, and the code name appears.

Old Night Stadium

At the Vs. screen, press Turbo (5), Pass (2), Up. A sound confirms correct entry, and the code name appears.

Night Stadium

At the Vs. screen, press Turbo (5), Pass (2), Down. A sound confirms correct entry, and the code name appears.

Old Snow Stadium

At the Vs. screen, press Turbo (5), Pass (3), Up. A sound confirms correct entry, and the code name appears.

Snow Stadium

At the Vs. screen, press Turbo (5), Pass (3), Down. A sound confirms correct entry, and the code name appears.

Roman Stadium

At the Vs. screen, press Turbo (5), Pass (3), Left. A sound confirms correct entry, and the code name appears.

Grass Field

At the Vs. screen, press Turbo (3), Up. A sound confirms correct entry, and the code name appears.

Asphalt Field

At the Vs. screen, press Turbo (3), Pass, Up. A sound confirms correct entry, and the code name appears.

Dirt Field

At the Vs. screen, press Turbo (3), Pass (2), Up. A sound confirms correct entry, and the code name appears.

Astroturf Field

At the Vs. screen, press Turbo (3), Pass (3), Up. A sound confirms correct entry, and the code name appears.

Snow Field

At the Vs. screen, press Turbo (3), Pass (4), Up. A sound confirms correct entry, and the code name appears.

Fog On

At the Vs. screen, press Jump (3), Down. A sound confirms correct entry, and the code name appears.

Thick Fog On

At the Vs. screen, press Jump (4), Pass, Down. A sound confirms correct entry, and the code name appears.

Weather: Clear

At the Vs. screen, press Turbo (2), Jump, Pass, Left. A sound confirms correct entry, and the code name appears.

Weather: Snow

At the Vs. screen, press Turbo (5), Jump (2), Pass (5), Down. A sound confirms correct entry, and the code name appears.

Weather: Rain

At the Vs. screen, press Turbo (5), Jump (5), Pass (5), Right. A sound confirms correct entry, and the code name appears.

Night Game

At the Vs. screen, press Jump (2) Pass (2), Right. A sound confirms correct entry, and the code name appears.

Hidden Player: Beth

In the "Enter Name for Record Keeping" option, type this name/PIN: BETH/7761.

Hidden Player Billz

In the "Enter Name for Record Keeping" option, type this name/PIN: BILLZ/0526.

Hidden Player: Brains

In the "Enter Name for Record Keeping" option, type this name/PIN: BRAIN/1111.

Hidden Player: Brian

In the "Enter Name for Record Keeping" option, type this name/PIN: BRIAN/0818.

Hidden Player: Headless

In the "Enter Name for Record Keeping" option, type this name/PIN: CARLTN/1111.

Hidden Player: Dan Thompson

In the "Enter Name for Record Keeping" option, type this name/PIN: DANIEL/0604.

Hidden Player: D.B.N.

In the "Enter Name for Record Keeping" option, type this name/PIN: DBN/6969.

Hidden Player: Ed

In the "Enter Name for Record Keeping" option, type this name/PIN: ED/3246.

Hidden Player: Dan Forden

In the "Enter Name for Record Keeping" option, type this name/PIN: FORDEN/1111.

Hidden Player: Gatson

In the "Enter Name for Record Keeping" option, type this name/PIN: GATSON/1111.

Hidden Player: Gene

In the "Enter Name for Record Keeping" option, type this name/PIN: GENE/0310.

Hidden Player: Jim Gentile

In the "Enter Name for Record Keeping" option, type this name/PIN: GENTIL/1111.

Hidden Player: The Grinch

In the "Enter Name for Record Keeping" option, type this name/PIN: GRINCH/2220.

Hidden Player: Guido

In the "Enter Name for Record Keeping" option, type this name/PIN: GUIDO/6765.

Hidden Player: Jeff Johnson

In the "Enter Name for Record Keeping" option, type this name/PIN: JAPPLE/6660.

Hidden Player: Jason Skiles

In the "Enter Name for Record Keeping" option, type this name/PIN: JASON/3141.

Hidden Player: Jennifer Hedrick

In the "Enter Name for Record Keeping" option, type this name/PIN: JENIFR/3333.

Hidden Player: Jim K.

In the "Enter Name for Record Keeping" option, type this name/PIN: JIMK/5651.

Hidden Player: John
In the "Enter Name for Record Keeping" option, type this name/PIN: JOHN/5158.

Hidden Player: Josh
In the "Enter Name for Record Keeping" option, type this name/PIN: JOSH/4288.

Hidden Player: LT
In the "Enter Name for Record Keeping" option, type this name/PIN: LT/7777.

Hidden Player: Luis Mangubat
In the "Enter Name for Record Keeping" option, type this name/PIN: LUIS/3333.

Hidden Player: Marka
In the "Enter Name for Record Keeping" option, type this name/PIN: MARKA/1112.

Hidden Player: Mike Lynch
In the "Enter Name for Record Keeping" option, type this name/PIN: MIKE/3333.

Hidden Player: Mitch
In the "Enter Name for Record Keeping" option, type this name/PIN: MITCH/4393.

Hidden Player: Monty
In the "Enter Name for Record Keeping" option, type this name/PIN: MONTY/1836.

Hidden Player: Nico
In the "Enter Name for Record Keeping" option, type this name/PIN: NICO/4440.

Hidden Player: Paula
In the "Enter Name for Record Keeping" option, type this name/PIN: PAULA/0425.

Hidden Player: Paulo
In the "Enter Name for Record Keeping" option, type this name/PIN: PAULO/0517.

Hidden Player: Raiden from *Mortal Kombat*
In the "Enter Name for Record Keeping" option, type this name/PIN: RAIDEN/3691.

Hidden Player: Rog
In the "Enter Name for Record Keeping" option, type this name/PIN: ROG/8148.

Hidden Player: John Root
In the "Enter Name for Record Keeping" option, type this name/PIN: ROOT/6000.

Hidden Player: Ryan
In the "Enter Name for Record Keeping" option, type this name/PIN: RYAN/1029.

Hidden Player: Sal Divita
In the "Enter Name for Record Keeping" option, type this name/PIN: SAL/0201.

Hidden Player: Shinnok from *Mortal Kombat*
In the "Enter Name for Record Keeping" option, type this name/PIN: SHINOK/8337.

Hidden Player: Shun
In the "Enter Name for Record Keeping" option, type this name/PIN: SHUN/0530.

Hidden Player: Skull
In the "Enter Name for Record Keeping" option, type this name/PIN: SKULL/1111.

Hidden Player: Smiley Face
In the "Enter Name for Record Keeping" option, type this name/PIN: SMILE/1111.

Hidden Player: Thug
In the "Enter Name for Record Keeping" option, type this name/PIN: THUG/1111.

Hidden Player: Todd
In the "Enter Name for Record Keeping" option, type this name/PIN: TODD/1122.

Hidden Player: Mark Turmell
In the "Enter Name for Record Keeping" option, type this name/PIN: TURMEL/0322.

Hidden Player: Van
In the "Enter Name for Record Keeping" option, type this name/PIN: VAN/1234.

Hidden Player: ZZ
In the "Enter Name for Record Keeping" option, type this name/PIN: ZZ/1221.

NFL FEVER 2000

Change Head Sizes
On the field after the play is dead, hold Left and press Hurdle (5). The first time this code is typed, it produces little heads; the second time, big heads; the third time reverts to normal.

Large Football
On the field after the play is dead, hold Right and press Hurdle (5).

NFL QUARTERBACK CLUB

Constant Turbo
At the Team Selection screen in Pre-season mode, press F1, F1, F2, F2, F1, F2.

Fumble Mode
At the Team Selection screen in Pre-season mode, press F1, F1, F1, F4, F1, F1.

Landmine Mode
At the Team Selection screen in Pre-season mode, press F1, F1, F1, F3, F1, F1.

Forty-Seven Historic Teams
At the Team Selection screen in Pre-season mode, press F4, F2, F5, F3, F4, F5.

Forty-Seven More Historic Teams
At the Team Selection screen in Pre-season mode, press F4, F2, F5, F4, F4, F5.

Long Range Throw/Kick Mode
At the Team Selection screen in Pre-season mode, press F1, F1, F3, F5, F1, F3.

Shadow Player Mode
At the Team Selection screen in Pre-season mode, press F1, F1, F3, F4, F1, F3.

NFC/AFC Preseason Mode
At the Team Selection screen in Pre-season mode, press F1, F1, F1, F2, F1, F1.

Super Slippery Mode
At the Team Selection screen in Pre-season mode, press F1, F1, F5, F3, F1, F5.

Super Team Mode
At the Team Selection screen in Pre-season mode, press F1, F1, F5, F2, F1, F5.

Super Fast Team Mode
At the Team Selection screen in Pre-season mode, press F1, F1, F4, F4, F1, F4.

NHL 2 ON 2

Unlimited Turbo
At the Face Off screen, press Turbo, Shoot (2), rotate joystick clockwise Top to Top.

Tournament
At the Face Off screen, press Right+Shoot+Pass+Turbo.

Super Goalies
At the Face Off screen, press Down, Down, Down, Down, Pass.

Disable Throws
At the Face Off screen, press Down+Turbo, Up+Shoot.

CPU Assistance Off
At the Face Off screen, rotate joystick clockwise Top to Top (repeat).

Jersey Color
At the Team Select screen, press Pass to select Home or colors.

Random Team Select
At the Team Select screen, press Up+Start in Top-Left Corner (Team 1).

Player Tiny Head
Press Turbo (2), Up, Shoot (2), Up.

Player Normal Head
Press Down+Shoot, Pass.

Player Big Head
Hold Pass and Turbo, press Up.

Player Huge Head
Hold Up+Shoot+Pass, and press Up (repeat three times).

Goalie Tiny Head
Hold Shoot, rotate joystick counterclockwise.

Goalie Normal Head
Press Shoot, Turbo, Pass.

Big Head
(Goalie) Pass, Pass, Turbo, Shoot, Pass

Goalie Huge Head
Hold Pass, rotate joystick counterclockwise Top to Top, rotate joystick clockwise Top to Top.

Baby Size Teams
Rotate joystick counterclockwise from Bottom to Top, hold Turbo, rotate joystick clockwise from Top to Bottom.

Force Fat Head
Rotate joystick clockwise Right to Left, rotate joystick counterclockwise Left to Left.

Big Puck
Up, Up, Down, Down, Turbo

Dark Rink
Press Pass+Turbo, Pass, Pass+Turbo, Pass, Pass+Shoot, Pass, Pass+Shoot, Pass, Pass+Shoot, Pass, Pass+Turbo, Pass.

Disable Top Display
Press Left+Turbo, Left, Left+Turbo, Left, Left+Turbo, Left, Left+Shoot, Left, Left+Shoot, Left, Left+Pass, Left, Left+Pass, Left, Left+Pass, Left.

Hidden Player: Ted Barber
Create a new player with these initials, date: BAR, Dec 5.

Hidden Player: Heather Beach
Create a new player with these initials, date: HAB, Mar 24.

Hidden Player: Steve Beran
Create a new player with these initials, date: SAB, Aug 29.

Hidden Player: Chris Bobrowski
Create a new player with these initials, date: ME_, May 12 ("_" = space).

Hidden Player: Ed Boon
Create a new player with these initials, date: EJB, Feb 22.

Hidden Player: Matt Booty
Create a new player with these initials, date: MVB, Apr 18.

Hidden Player: John Carlton
Create a new player with these initials, date: JMC, Aug 5.

Hidden Player: Jay Cohen
Create a new player with these initials, date: JNC, June 4.

Hidden Player: Matt Cooney
Create a new player with these initials, date: MJC, June 6.

Hidden Player: Xion Cooper
Create a new player with these initials, date: XC_, Aug 9 ("_" = space).

Hidden Player: Steve Correll
Create a new player with these initials, date: RSC, Sept 16.

Hidden Player: Pat Cox
Create a new player with these initials, date: PGC, Apr 11.

Hidden Player: Bill Dabelstein
Create a new player with these initials, date: DOZ, Dec 31.

Hidden Player: Kevin Dale
Create a new player with these initials, date: J_R, Sept 15 ("_" = space).

Hidden Player: Matt Davis
Create a new player with these initials, date: MJD, Aug 19.

Hidden Player: Warren Davis
Create a new player with these initials, date: WBD, Aug 17.

Hidden Player: Sal Divita
Create a new player with these initials, date: SAL, Feb 2.

Hidden Player: Paul Dussault
Create a new player with these initials, date: PGD, Dec 17.

Hidden Player: Brian Eddie
Create a new player with these initials, date: BRE, Apr 20.

Hidden Player: Nik Ehrlich
Create a new player with these initials, date: NIK, Nov 17.

Hidden Player: Joan Faux
Create a new player with these initials, date: JBF, July 17.

Hidden Player: Bridgitte Fedesna
Create a new player with these initials, date: BMF, May 9.

Hidden Player: Jennifer Fedesna
Create a new player with these initials, date: JKF, Feb 25.

Hidden Player: Eddie Ferrier
Create a new player with these initials, date: EF_, June 10 ("_" = space).

Hidden Player: Pat Foley
Create a new player with these initials, date: PJF, Dec 23.

Hidden Player: Ray Gay
Create a new player with these initials, date: RMG, Aug 11.

Hidden Player: Eugene Geer
Create a new player with these initials, date: OEG, Nov 5.

Hidden Player: Jim Gentile
Create a new player with these initials, date: JPG, Jan 23.

Hidden Player: Tony Goskie
Create a new player with these initials, date: TWG, Dec 7.

Hidden Player: Jim Greene
Create a new player with these initials, date: JDG, May 31.

Hidden Player: Evil Hager
Create a new player with these initials, date: JH_, July 13 ("_" = space).

Hidden Player: Jack Haeger
Create a new player with these initials, date: JEH, July 13.

Hidden Player: Jack H. Haeger
Create a new player with these initials, date: HAH, Jan 6.

Hidden Player: Jennifer Hedrick
Create a new player with these initials, date: JJH, May 3.

Hidden Player: Jon Hey
Create a new player with these initials, date: JWH, Sept 20.

Hidden Player: Gordie Howe
Create a new player with these initials, date: G_H, Mar 31 ("_" = space).

Hidden Player: Craig Janney
Create a new player with these initials, date: C_J, Sept 26 ("_" = space).

Hidden Player: Eugene Jarvis
Create a new player with these initials, date: EPJ, Jan 27.

Hidden Player: Jeff Johnson
Create a new player with these initials, date: JBJ, Nov 4.

Hidden Player: Ed Keenan
Create a new player with these initials, date: EJK, Apr 10.

Hidden Player: Al Lasko
Create a new player with these initials, date: AL_, Aug 31 ("_" = space).

Hidden Player: Mark Loffredo
Create a new player with these initials, date: ML_, May 25 ("_" = space).

Hidden Player: John Lowes
Create a new player with these initials, date: JML, Nov 4.

Hidden Player: Andy Lycke
Create a new player with these initials, date: AL_, Nov 23 ("_" = space).

Hidden Player: Mike Lynch
Create a new player with these initials, date: MJL, Feb 28.

Hidden Player: Ray Macika
Create a new player with these initials, date: REM, Mar 26.

Hidden Player: Luis Mangubot
Create a new player with these initials, date: LM_, Apr 18 ("_" = space).

Hidden Player: Martin Martinez
Create a new player with these initials, date: MAM, Aug 7.

Hidden Player: Cary Mednick
Create a new player with these initials, date: CMM, July 2.

Hidden Player: Tony Metke
Create a new player with these initials, date: ARM, July 19.

Hidden Player: Dave Michicich
Create a new player with these initials, date: DLM, Aug 6.

Hidden Player: John Newcomer
Create a new player with these initials, date: JRN, June 18.

Hidden Player: Mike Ossian
Create a new player with these initials, date: OTT, Jan 11.

Hidden Player: Sheridan Oursler
Create a new player with these initials, date: SNO, Jan 3.

Hidden Player: Mark Panache
Create a new player with these initials, date: MDP, Jan 13.

Hidden Player: Carlos Pesina
Create a new player with these initials, date: CCP, Nov 15.

Hidden Player: Jeff Peters
Create a new player with these initials, date: JTP, Dec 15.

Hidden Player: Jim Rohn
Create a new player with these initials, date: JR_, May 22 ("_" = space).

Hidden Player: Maryann Rohn
Create a new player with these initials, date: MAC, July 7.

Hidden Player: Rebecca Scott
Create a new player with these initials, date: RS_, Sept 27 ("_" = space).

Hidden Player: Ross Shaffer
Create a new player with these initials, date: FRS, Apr 13.

Hidden Player: Glenn Shipp
Create a new player with these initials, date: GWS, June 11.

Hidden Player: Jake Simpson
Create a new player with these initials, date: JMS, Feb 22.

Hidden Player: Jason Skiles
Create a new player with these initials, date: JMS, July 29.

Hidden Player: Kevin Stevens
Create a new player with these initials, date: KMS, Apr 15.

Hidden Player: Sidney Strong
Create a new player with these initials, date: SID, Feb 12.

Hidden Player: Dan Thompson
Create a new player with these initials, date: DJT, June 4.

Hidden Player: Art Tianis
Create a new player with these initials, date: AJT, Oct 23.

Hidden Player: Jim Tianis
Create a new player with these initials, date: DJT, Oct 20.

Hidden Player: John Tobias
Create a new player with these initials, date: TOB, Aug 24.

Hidden Player: Josh Tsui
Create a new player with these initials, date: CET, Nov 28.

Hidden Player: Mark Turmell
Create a new player with these initials, date: MJT, Mar 22.

Hidden Player: Mike Vinikour
Create a new player with these initials, date: MJT, Mar 22.

Hidden Player: Mike Waldron
Create a new player with these initials, date: MJW, Jan 9.

Hidden Player: Ken Williams
Create a new player with these initials, date: WKW, May 30.

Hidden Player: Christa Woss
Create a new player with these initials, date: CLW, July 9.

Hidden Player: Dave Zab
Create a new player with these initials, date: ZAB, May 28.

Hidden Player: Zarley Zalapski
Create a new player with these initials, date: ZBZ, April 22.

NHL '98

Players Have Elongated Arms, Legs, and Necks
During gameplay, type MANTIS.

Make Players Kid-Sized
During gameplay, type NHLKIDS.

Give Home Team a Goal
During gameplay, type HOMEGOAL.

Give Away Team a Goal
During gameplay, type AWAYGOAL.

Cause a Penalty
During gameplay, type PENALTY.

Cause an Injury
During gameplay, type INJURY.

Zamboni Emerges
During gameplay, type ZAMBO.

Fireworks
During gameplay, type VICTORY.

Camera Flashes from Stands
During gameplay, type FLASH.

Pre-Game Spotlights
During gameplay, type SPOTS.

Every Player Body Checks Opposing Player Upon Contact
During gameplay, type CHECK.

Every Player Stick Holds upon Contact
During gameplay, type GRAB.

View End of Season FMV
Highlight "Credits" and type STANLEY.

EA Blades Team
Highlight "Credits" and type EAEAO.

Enables TCP/IP as an Available Protocol
Highlight "Credits" and type ULTIMATE-JUDGE.

Increase Game Speed
Select Exit, Credits, then Programming and type warp9.

Enable Internet Play
Select Exit, Credits, then Programming and type eaonline.

Players Have Big Heads
Select Exit, Credits, then Programming and type headbone.

Players Are Huge
Select Exit, Credits, then Programming and type buffed.

Play the Stanley Cup Video
Select Exit, Credits, then Programming and type 1999.

All Players Are Fast and Good
Select Exit, Credits, then Programming and type quicker.

Crowd Leaves
Select Exit, Credits, then Programming and type nobody.

Goalies Are Very Tall
Select Exit, Credits, then Programming and type gulliver.

Unlock All Resolutions for D3D
Select Exit, Credits, then Programming and type crankit.

NHL 2000

Give Away Team a Goal
During gameplay, type awaygoal.

Give Home Team a Goal
During gameplay, type homegoal.

Zamboni Emerges
During gameplay, type zambo.

Show the Pre-Game Spotlights
During gameplay, type spots.

Bring a Penalty to the Team Without the Puck
During gameplay, type penalty.

Cause an Injury
During gameplay, type injury.

Fireworks
During gameplay, type victory.

Camera Flashes from Crowd
During gameplay, type flash.

Auto Check on Contact with Opposing Player
During gameplay, type check.

Auto Stick Hold on Contact with Opposing Player
During gameplay, type grab.

Gives Players Elongated Arms, Legs, and Necks
During gameplay, type mantis.

Makes Players Smaller
During gameplay, type nhlkids.

Faster Players
During gameplay, type quickftr.

Entire Team Fights
During gameplay, type big fight.

Nasty Fights
During gameplay, type bloody.

NHL 2001

Super Players
Enter any programmer's name.

Players Bleed
At the Credits screen, type Broken tomato.

Loose Puck Flies to Goalie if Manual Goalie is Set
At the Credits screen, type Magnet.

Goal for Home Team
During gameplay, type HOMEGOAL.

Goal for Away Team
During gameplay, type AWAYGOAL.

N.I.C.E. 2

600 Km/h Super Car
Pause gameplay and type machthree.

Unlimited Ammo in Deathmatch Mode
Pause gameplay and type impact.

Free Choice in Starting League
Pause gameplay and type clementine.

Enable Weapon Mode in Championship
Pause gameplay and type overkill.

Animated Switches in Menus
Pause gameplay and type mccoy.

Tuning Phase 5 for All Systems
Pause gameplay and type likepamela.

All Additional Systems at 99
Pause gameplay and type liselotte.

All Cars
Pause gameplay and type nalice.

Cheat Mode Off
Pause gameplay and type alloff.

NIGHT SHIFT

Access Next Level
Type MPICKLE at the High Score table.

Level 2
Kirsche, Banane, Banane, Zitrone

Level 3
Banane, Kirsche, Ananas, Pflaume

Level 4
Ananas, Zitrone, Ananas, Ananas

Level 5
Ananas, Ananas, Zitrone, Kirsche

Level 6
Kirsche, Pflaume, Pflaume, Ananas

Level 7
Kirsche, Ananas, Zitrone, Banana

Level 8
Ananas, Banane, Ananas, Kirsche

Level 9
Ananas, Zitrone, Zitrone, Kirsche

Level 10
Zitrone, Banane, Pflaume, Plaume

Level 11
Banane, Ananas, Kirsche, Pflaume

Level 12
Kirsche, Pflaume, Banane, Ananas

Level 13
Pflaume, Kirsche, Banane, Ananas

Level 14
Ananas, Kirsche, Plaume, Banane

Level 15
Pflaume, Pflaume, Ananas, Ananas

Level 16
Banane, Banane, Ananas, Banane

Level 17
Banane, Pflaume, Kirsche, Pflaume

Level 18
Pflaume, Zitrone, Zitrone, Pflaume

Level 19
Zitrone, Ananas, Kirsche, Pflaume

Level 20
Kirsche, Ananas, Ananas, Kirsche

Level 21
Zitrone, Kirsche, Ananas, Ananas

Level 22
Pflaume, Kirsche, Zitrone, Banane

Level 23
Pflaume, Kirsche, Kirsche, Zitrone

Level 24
Pflaume, Ananas, Zitrone, Zitrone

Level 25
Banane, Ananas, Ananas, Zitrone

Level 26
Pflaume, Kirsche, Kirsche, Banane

Level 27
Banane, Kirsche, Zitrone, Banane

Level 28
Pflaume, Banane, Banane, Ananas

Level 29
Kirsche Pflaume, Kirsche, Ananas

Level 30
Kirsche, Kirsche, Banane, Pflaume

NIGHTMARE CREATURES

Access Cheat Mode
At the main menu, type EVERYWHERE for Level Select and to enable Cheat mode. Then type one of the following codes and press Enter. A sound confirms correct entry.

Unlimited
Enable Cheat mode and type BOULON.

Reduce
Enable Cheat mode and type CHICO.

Cut Body
Enable Cheat mode and type GU.

Play Monster
Enable Cheat mode and type BRONKO.

Disable Combos
Enable Cheat mode and type DAVID.

Play Blur
Enable Cheat mode and type BLUR.

Team Greetings
Enable Cheat mode and type LOVDIK.

Debug
Enable Cheat mode and type BES.

CD Track Select
Enable Cheat mode and type MOBY.

All Cheats
Enable Cheat mode and type ALAIN GUYET.

NO ONE LIVES FOREVER

God Mode
During gameplay, press T and type mpimyourfather.

Infinite Ammo
During gameplay, press T and type mpwegotdeathstar.

All Weapons and Items, Unlimited Ammo
During gameplay, press T and type mpkingofthemonstars.

Complete Mission
During gameplay, press T and type mpmaphole.

Full Health
During gameplay, press T and type mpdrdentz.

Full Armor
During gameplay, press T and type mpwonderbra.

Add All Armor Options
During gameplay, press T and type mpyoulooklikeyouneedamonkey.

All Weapon Upgrades
During gameplay, press T and type mpgoattech.

Exit Game
During gameplay, press T and type mpmiked.

Show Game Build
During gameplay, press T and type mpbuild.

Third Person View
During gameplay, press T and type mpasscam.

Spawn Snowtruck
During gameplay, press T and type mprosebud.

Position Display
During gameplay, press T and type mppos.

NOCTURNE

God Mode
iamacheatingbastard

All Weapons and Ammo, God Mode
gimmecrap

Kill Surrounding Creatures
ebola

You Look Like Terminator 2000
t2000

Get Ammo
layitonme

Get Radiance Emitter (Sun Gun)
amonra

Get Tommygun
driveby

Get Flamethrower
torchmyass

Get Dynamite
tntrules

Get Wooden Stake Crossbow
woodenstakegun

Get Shotgun and 500 Shells
shotgunshell

Get Flaming Arrows
torchtip

Get Elephant Gun
dumbogun

Summon Baron
baronsaturday

Freeze Creatures
reallycold

Get Skeleton Key
keysuper

Change Hat
oldhat

Restore Full Health
bandaid

Get 500 Silver Bullets
silver

Get 500 Aqua Vampire Bullets
aqua

Get 500 Mercury Bullets
mercury

Get Gas Mask for Stranger
youfarted

Renew Battery
pinkbunny

NORMALITY

Cheat Mode
During gameplay, type WENDY and press Enter. Now press G to access 100+ Gremlin Digital FMVs. Also, press F1 to access all game locations.

NOX

Access Cheat Mode
During gameplay, type Racoiaws in the console to enable Cheat mode.

God Mode and Unlimited Mana
Enable Cheat mode and type set god.

List Cheats
Enable Cheat mode and type help cheat.

Reset User Abilities
Enable Cheat mode and type cheat ability.

Go to Named Waypoint
Enable Cheat mode and type cheat goto waypoint l x y.

Refill Health
Enable Cheat mode and type cheat health.

Refill Mana
Enable Cheat mode and type cheat mana.

Set Play to Given Level Number
Enable Cheat mode and type cheat level # (replace # with desired level).

Set All Spells to Given Level
Enable Cheat mode and type cheat spells.

Adds Gold to Character
Enable Cheat mode and type cheat gold # (replace # with amount desired).

ODDWORLD: ABE'S EXODDUS

Level Skip
At the main menu, hold Shift and press Down, Right, Left, Right, Left, Right, Left, Up.

Next Path
At the Gameplay menu, hold Shift and press Left, Right, Up, Down, Left, Right.

View Next FMV Sequence
At the main menu, hold Shift and press Up, Left, Right, Left, Right, Left, Right, Down.

ODDWORLD: ABE'S ODDYSEE

Level Select
At the main menu, hold Shift and press Down, Right, Left, Right, Left, Right, Left, Up.

View All Movie Scenes
At the main menu, hold Shift and press Up, Left, Right, Left, Right, Left, Right, Down.

OFFENSIVE

German Level 1
GNBQD

German Level 2
NUCWE

German Level 3
DABDD

German Level 4
GSCGE

German Level 5
NTTDC

German Level 6
HXAME

German Level 7
GTAND

German Level 8
VIALC

German Level 9
GLBJD

German Level 10
IBWDE

German Level 11
BHADE

German Level 12
GXCSE

German Level 13
FQACD

German Level 14
VWAAB

German Level 15
HPBSE

German Level 16
RIATE

German Level 17
GUBEE

German Level 18
NBGSR

German Level 19
SJBED

German Level 20
PKBGC

Allies Level 1
UHFNE

Allies Level 2
FBGBA

Allies Level 3
CHRJN

Allies Level 4
JQHEX

Allies Level 5
GBBXD

Allies Level 6
MUKNN

Allies Level 7
UNGHP

Allies Level 8
ADMKE

Allies Level 9
OGOAB

Allies Level 10
LPCKD

Allies Level 11
MAAHD

Allies Level 12
LOREI

Allies Level 13
SAGUE

Allies Level 14
BCUJI

Allies Level 15
HCGKE

Allies Level 16
LOKIE

Allies Level 17
BHSDE

Allies Level 18
ULCSE

Allies Level 19
DATJU

Allies Level 20
IOGPD

OH NO! MORE LEMMINGS

Level 1: That's a Good Level
TFLCAHVFBD

Level 2: Dolly Simple
FLCIHTTGBK

Level 3: Many Lemmings Make Level Work
LCALUTFHBJ

Level 4: Lemming Express
CILTTFLIBQ

Level 5: 24-Hour Lemathon
CAHRUFLJBE

Level 6: The Stack
IHRUFLCKBN

Level 7: And Now, the End Is Near
LRUFLCALBK

Level 8: Keep on Trucking
RUFLCILMBD

Level 9: On the Antarctic Coast
WNHCEIVNBH

Level 10: Rocky VI
FLCIHVUOBF

Level 11: No Problemming!
LCAMTUFPBR

Level 12: Lemming Friendly
BIMTUNLQBT

Level 13: It's a Trade Off
CAIPTDMBCK

Level 14: Time Waits for No Lemming
IHRTDMCCCF

Level 15: Worra Load of Old Blocks!
LRULICADCH

Level 16: Across the Gap
RVLICILECQ

Level 17: Digging for Victory
TDMCAHVFCD

Level 18: No Problem
DMCIITTGCL

Level 19: Don't Panic
ICAMTVLHCO

Level 20: Ice Ice Lemming
CILVVLIICI

Level 1: Tubular Lemming
GAIPTFLBFS

Level 2: Be More Than Just a Number
IIPTFLGCFL

Level 3: It's the Price You Have to Pay
LPTFLGADFH

Level 4: The Race Against Clichés
RTFLGILEFS

Level 5: There's Madness in the Method
TFLGAHVFFL

Level 6: Now Get Out of That!
FLGIHVTGFE

Level 7: Creature Discomforts
LGALVTFHFR

Level 8: Lemming About Town
GILTNNHIFM

Level 9: Aaaaaarrrrrggggggghhhhhh!!!!!!
GAIPUFLJFL

Level 10: Flow Ctrl
IHRUFLGKFF

Level 11: Welcome to the Party, Pal!
MRWFHFALFQ

Level 12: It's All a Matter of Timing
RUFLGILMFL

Level 13: Highland Fling
UFLGAHVNFE

Level 14: Synchronized Lemming
FLGMHTUOFP

Level 15: Have an Ice Day
LGALVUFPFK

Level 16: Scaling the Heights
GILTUNHQFF

Level 17: Where Lemmings Dare
GAIPVLIBGI

Level 18: Lemmings in a Situation
MHPTDMGCGO

Level 19: Looks a Bit Nippy Out There
MPTDMGADGI

Level 20: Look Before You Lead!
ETDMGILEGS

Level Skip
Type the password SLAMRACING, then press 5 on the keypad during gameplay.

Level 2: Rent-a-Lemming
IHRTDLCCAR

Level 3: Undercover Lemming
LRTDLCADAO

Level 4: Downwordly Mobile Lemmings
RTDLCILEAH

Level 5: Smuggle Up to a Lemming
TDLCAHTFAO

Level 6: Intsy-Wintsy Lemming!
DLCIHUTGAJ

Level 7: Who's That Lemming
LCALUTDHAG

Level 8: Dangerzone
CILUTDLIAP

Level 9: And Now This.
CAHRUDKJAR

Level 10: New Lemmings on the Block
IHRUDLCKAK

Level 11: With Compliments
LRUDLCALAH

Level 12: Citizen Lemming
RUDLCILMAQ

Level 13: Thunder-Lemmings Are Go!
UDLCAHVNAJ

Level 14: Get a Little Extra Help
DLCIITUOAR

Level 15: Not Just a Pretty Lemming
LCALVUDPAP

Level 16: Gone with the Lemming
CILVUDLQAI

Level 17: Honey, I Saved the Lemmings
CAHRTFLBBL

Level 18: Lemmings for Presidents!
IHRTFLCCBE

Level 19: Lemming Productions Presents.
LRTFLCADBR

Level 20: Custom Built for Lemmings
RTFLCILEBK

Level 1: Lemming Tomato Ketchup Facility
UFMCAHTNDN

Level 2: Introducing Super Lemming
NICMHVUOOQ

Level 3: This Corrosion
MCALVUFPDF

Level 4: Oh No! It's the Fourth Dimension!
CILVUFMQDO

Level 5: Chill Out!
GAHRTDHBEM

Level 6: Pop Til You Drop!
IHRTDLGCEJ

Level 7: Last Lemming to Lemming Central
MPTLLFADEM

Level 8: A Towering Problem
PVLHGMMEEI

Level 9: How on Earth?
VLHGAHVFEO

Level 10: Temple of Love
DLGIHTTGEP

Level 11: Rocky road
LGALTTDHEM

Level 12: Suicidal Tendencies
GILVTLHIEL

Level 13: Almost Nearly Virtual Reality
GEHPUDLJEL

Level 14: The Lemming Learning Curve
IHPWLHGKEG

Level 15: Spam, Spam, Spam, Egg, and Lemming
MPUDLGALEO

Level 16: Five Alive
RULHGILMEM

Level 17: Down the Tube
ULHGEITNEI

Level 18: Lots More Where They Came From
DLGIHTUOEI

Level 19: Up, Down or Round and Round
HGAMTWLPEM

Level 20: The Lemming Funhouse
GIMTULHQED

Level 1: Pop Your Top!!!
BAHRWLMJCN

Level 2: Lemming Hotel
IHPUDMCKCL

Level 3: Lemming Rhythms
LPUDMCELCM

Level 4: Meeting Adjourned
PUDMCIMMCS

Level 5: Lemming Head
UDMCAHVNCM

Level 6: Just a Quickly
LICMHVWOCP

Level 7: You Take the High Road
MCALVUDPCS

Level 8: It's a Tight Fit
CILVUDMQEL

Level 9: Ice Station Lemming
CAHRTFMBDO

Level 10: Higgledy Piggledy
IHRTFMCCDH

Level 11: Mutiny on the Bounty
MRTNICADDJ

Level 12: Snow Joke
PTFMCIMEDM

Level 13: Onward and Upward
TNICAHTFDL

Level 14: Ice Spy
NICMHUVGDJ

Level 15: The Silence of the Lemmings
ICEMVVNHDH

Level 16: Take Care, Sweetie
CIMVTNIIDK

Level 17: The Chain with No Name
CAHRUFMJDH

Level 18: Dr. Lemming Good
IHRUFMCKDQ

Level 19: Lemmingpelica
MPUNICELDE

Level 2:0 Got Anything Lemmingy???
PUFMCMLMDI

ONI

To enable Cheat codes for *Oni*, beat the game once. Then start a new game and press F1 during gameplay to bring up the diary. After that, type in the cheat you want to activate.

Change Character During Missions by Pressing the "F8" Key
shapeshifter

Infinite Health
liveforever

Kill Enemies with Only One Shot
touchofdeath

Konoko Can't Be Knocked Down
canttouchthis

All Ammo and Health
Fatloot

Break Everything in the Game
glassworld

Win the Running Scenario
winlevel

Lose the Running Scenario
loselevel

Big Head Mode
bighead

Mini Mode
minime

Gives Konoko Powerful Bullets
superammo

Kumite Mode
reservoirdogs

Gatling Guns Mode
roughjustice

Konoko Becomes Stronger
chenille

Giant Mode
behemoth

Enables Health Regeneration
elderrune

Enables Cloaking Mode
moonshadow

Pile of Weapons
munitionfrenzy

Fists of Legend Mode
fistsoflegend

Ultra Strong and Fast Enemies
killmequick

Slow Motion Mode
carousel

Phase Cloak
moonshadow

Weapons Locker
munitionfrenzy

Enable Developer Mode
Use the thedayismine code, then press ~ to display the console window. Enter one of the following codes to activate the corresponding command.

Cycle Through All Possible Weapons
F7

Change Character
F8

Start Recording
F9

Stop Recording
F10

Playback Recording
F11

Toggle Slow Motion
Ctrl+Shift+G

Toggles Textures
Ctrl+Shift+S

Display Opponent Logic
Ctrl+Shift+B

Display Frame Rate
Crtl+Shift+Y

View Console Commands
dump_docs

All Doors Unlocked
door_ignore_locks

Kill All Nearby AI
ai2_kill

No Clipping Mode
chr_nocollision 1

No Clipping Mode
disabled chr_nocollision 0

OREGON TRAIL 3

Extra Money
During gameplay, type more money. This can only be done once per game.

OUTCAST

Access Cheat Mode
During gameplay, type KOKKUSPOKKUS to enable Cheat mode.

All Weapons
Enable Cheat mode, press F12, and type ARSENAL.

Infinite Ammo
Enable Cheat mode, press F12, and type AMMO_FLOW.

Dynamite
Enable Cheat mode, press F12, and type DYNAMIT.

Kill All Enemies in Level
Enable Cheat mode, press F12, and type KILL_SOLDIERS.

Invisibility
Enable Cheat mode, press F12, and type IAMINVISIBLE.

Fly Mode On/Off
Enable Cheat mode, press F12, and type FLY.

Radar
Enable Cheat mode, press F12, and type TRACKER.

No Clipping
Enable Cheat mode, press F12, and type BENNY.

Show Points
Enable Cheat mode, press F12, and type POINTS.

Quit the Game
Enable Cheat mode, press F12, and type QUIT.

Ranzaar
Enable Cheat mode, press F12, and type NEIGE.

Shamazaar
Enable Cheat mode, press F12, and type TEMPLES.

Okriana
Enable Cheat mode, press F12, and type VILLE.

Motazaar
Enable Cheat mode, press F12, and type MONTAGNE.

Okasankaar
Enable Cheat mode, press F12, and type MARCHES.

Okar
Enable Cheat mode, press F12, and type FOREST.

OUTPOST 2

10% Higher Population
Press Ctrl+F4.

Unlimited Resources
Press Ctrl+F11.

OUTWARS

God Mode
During gameplay, type MACLEOD.

Unlimited Ammo
During gameplay, type DIRTYHARRY.

Glider Wings
During gameplay, type BUZZ.

Frame Rate
During gameplay, type FRAMERATE.

Spy on Creatures Using the F11 and F12 Keys
During gameplay, type PHANTOM.

Reset to Start Position
During gameplay, type GOHOME.

Show Enemy on Radar
During gameplay, type THRASHER.

Remove Mission Timer
During gameplay, type TIMEWARP.

Follow Your Fired Weapons
During gameplay, type WEAPONCAM.

Display a Message: "Singletrac Rules!"
During gameplay, type SINGLETRAC.

Get Armor, Health, and Ammo
During gameplay, type KEYMASTER.

Jump to Oasis Level
During gameplay, type JUMPOASIS.

Jump to Anubis Level
During gameplay, type JUMPANUBIS.

Jump to Ragnarok Level
During gameplay, type JUMPRAGNAROK.

Jump to Juggernaut Level
During gameplay, type JUMPJUGGERNAUT.

Jump to Last Level
During gameplay, type JUMPDEAD.

Show the Entire Map
During gameplay, type SHOWALL.

Change Fighter's Gender
During gameplay, type SNIPSNIP.

OVERDRIVE

Level 25
92018902

Level 50
97943401

Level 75
73654930

Level 100
16136595

Level 125
89628556

Level 150
42925501

Level 175
58465605

Level 200
71088981

P-47

Cheats
At the High Score table, type ZEBEDEE. Press F1 to skip the level, or press F2 to renew your lives.

PACMAN: ADVENTURES IN TIME

Hit Esc and type in a Cheat code:

God Mode
IAINTSCARED

All Levels
SHOWMETHEMAZES

Win the Level
INEEDTHEPOINTS

Win the Level
INEEDANEXIT

Shrink Pacman
HONEYISHRUNKPACMAN

Blow Up Pacman
HONEYIBLEWUPPACMAN

First Person View
UPCLOSEANDPERSONA

First Person View
BEINGPACMANOVICH

Add 1 Life
GETALIFE

Suicide
KILLME

FPS and Other Stats
PACSTATS

God Mode
During gameplay, press Escape and type IAINTSCARED.

All Levels
During gameplay, press Escape and type SHOWMETHEMAZES.

Win Level
During gameplay, press Escape and type INEEDTHEPOINTS.

Win Level
During gameplay, press Escape and type INEEDANEXIT.

Shrink Pacman
During gameplay, press Escape and type HONEYISHRUNKPACMAN.

Blow Up Pacman
During gameplay, press Escape and type HONEYIBLEWUPPACMAN.

First-Person View
During gameplay, press Escape and type UPCLOSEANDPERSONAL.

First-Person View
During gameplay, press Escape and type BEINGPACMANOVICH.

Slomo On/Off
During gameplay, press Escape and type STEVEAUSTIN.

Fast Monsters
During gameplay, press Escape and type MISSIONIMPOSSIBLE.

Add One Life
During gameplay, press Escape and type GETALIFE.

Kill Yourself
During gameplay, press Escape and type KILLME.

FPS and Other Stats
During gameplay, press Escape and type PACSTATS.

PACIFIC AIR WARRIOR

Cheat Mode
During gameplay, type rasta.

PAGANITZU

99 Lives
During gameplay, press F1, then press Ctrl+A+L and type 325 at the prompt.

Invincibility
During gameplay, press F1, then press Ctrl+A+L and type 642 at the prompt. To disable the code, type 643 at the prompt.

PANDEMONIUM

Level 2
NAABEBAI

Level 3
ENAIAKBI

Level 4
PEIAIBBA

Level 5
KFCACICE

Level 6
AFICBAIM

Level 7
NGIAIBJJ

Level 8
EHIIAKAC

Level 9
NIIAIBKB

Level 10
AHICBAJE

Level 11

LOCACMGI

Level 12
KACACIIM

Level 13
OAIAIDLB

Level 14
ELIIAODC

Level 15
OEIAIELJ

Level 16
OGIAJEEB

Level 17
AHMCBCMD

Level 18
AJECBDEF

PANDEMONIUM 2

31 Lives
IMMORTAL

Full Health
HORMONES

Invincibility
NEVERDIE

Level 2: Zorrscha's Lab
OMACCBAI

Level 3: Hot Pants
FAIAGCBI

Level 4: Stan's the Man
FEKAGCCA

Level 5: Oyster Desoyster
LGBFIICE

Level 6: Puzzle Wood
LMBBIIEE

Level 7: Temple of Nori
IEBBIIGF

Level 8: Egg! Egg!
KNBBIIAI

Level 9: Huevos Libertad!
LGBJIICI

Level 10: Pipe Hous
LOBJIIEI

Level 11: Hate Tank
IGBJIIGJ

Level 12: Fantabulous
FFCAGCCC

Level 13: Mr. Schneobelen
FHCAGCCK

Level 14: Collide O Scope
FJKEGCDC

Level 15: The Zoul Train
FLKEGCDK

Level 16: Lick the Toad
ADIKBIIB

Level 17: The Bitter End
ADMIBIID

Level 18: Rub the Buddha
MAECCBEJ

Level Select
GETACCES or OCMCKKEJ

Mutant Mode
GENETICS

Psychedelic Textures

ACIDDUDE

Regenerating Monsters
JUSTKIDN

Rolling Camera View
GONAHURL

Speed Mode
SKATBORD

Weapons
MAKMYDAY

PANG

Choose Any Place You Want
At the Map, type WHAT A NICE CHEAT.

PANZER DRAGOON

Infinite Continues
At the Difficulty menu, press Up, Zoom1, Right, Zoom2, Down, Zoom3, Left, Zoom2, Up, Zoom1.

Invincibility
At the Difficulty menu, press Left, Left, Right (2), Up, Down, Left, Right.

No Dragon
During gameplay, press Up, A, Right, A, Down, A, Left, A, Up, S, D.

Stage Select
At the Difficulty menu, press Up, Up, Down, Down, Left, Right, Left, Right, Zoom1, Zoom2, Zoom3.

Wizard Mode
At the main menu, press Z, C, Z, C, Up, Down, Up, Down, Left, Right.

PAX CORPUS

Prison
During gameplay, type bidytj.

Rocket Silo
During gameplay, type codup.

Space Lab
During gameplay, type benyo.

Temple
During gameplay, type knutw.

PEARL HARBOR

Unlock New Planes
To unlock either the F22 Raptor, a Flying Saucer, or the Japanese Kikka, click on the small plane to the right of the Select Mission menu. You are taken to a menu to select one of the three.

PENTAX PUZZLE

Level 2
RAFTING

Level 3
PAPAGEIEN

Level 4
BALLONS

Level 5
EISHOCKEY

Level 6
MARATHON

Level 7
ERDE

Level 8

Level 9
BUNTSTIFTE

PERFECT WEAPON

All the Power-Ups
During gameplay, type GMPETE and press Enter.

Back to Normal
During gameplay, type GMNORM and press Enter.

Big Head
During gameplay, type GMBIGH and press Enter.

Cyborg
During gameplay, type GMBORG and press Enter.

Enemies Are Easier to Kill
During gameplay, type GMKILL and press Enter.

Invincibility
During gameplay, GMGODM and press Enter.

Level 2
ADDCAADC

Level 3
ACBABBCC

Level 4
ADDDCACC

Level 5
DDBDBBCA

Level 6
CCDBCCDA

Level 7
AADBDDAC

Level 8
CADDCBCC

Level 9
ADAABADB

Level 10
BADDBBBC

Level 11
ABBDADDA

Level 12
DCADCAAC

PHARAOH

Angry Gods
During gameplay, press Ctrl+Alt+Shift+C and type Fury of Seth.

Angry Hippos
During gameplay, press Ctrl+Alt+Shift+C and type Hippo Stomp.

Attack by Land
During gameplay, press Ctrl+Alt+Shift+C and type mockattack1.

Attack by Sea
During gameplay, press Ctrl+Alt+Shift+C and type mockattack2.

Better Inundation
During gameplay, press Ctrl+Alt+Shift+C and type Bounty. Osiris must be worshiped first.

Destroy Farms
During gameplay, press Ctrl+Alt+Shift+C and type Underworld. Osiris must be worshiped first.

Destroy Storage
During gameplay, press Ctrl+Alt+Shift+C and type Grenow. Ptah must be worshiped first.

Destruction
During gameplay, press Ctrl+Alt+Shift+C and type Seth Strikes. Seth must be worshiped first.

Double Harvest
During gameplay, press Ctrl+Alt+Shift+C and type Life From Death. Osiris must be worshiped first.

Free Deben
During gameplay, press Ctrl+Alt+Shift+C and type Treasure Chest.

Full Houses and Bazaars
During gameplay, press Ctrl+Alt+Shift+C and type Cat Nip. Bast must be worshiped first.

Full Stock
During gameplay, press Ctrl+Alt+Shift+C and type Noble Djed. Ptah must be worshiped first.

Increase Export
During gameplay, press Ctrl+Alt+Shift+C and type Pharaohs Glory. Ra must be worshiped first.

Industrial Destruction
During gameplay, press Ctrl+Alt+Shift+C and type Big Dave. Ptah must be worshiped first.

Instant Win
During gameplay, press Ctrl+Alt+Shift+C and type Pharaohs Tomb.

Killer Plague
During gameplay, press Ctrl+Alt+Shift+C and type Kitty Litter. Bast must be worshiped first.

Less Trade
During gameplay, press Ctrl+Alt+Shift+C and type Bird of Prey. Ra must be worshiped first.

More Hippos
During gameplay, press Ctrl+Alt+Shift+C and type Side Show. Hippos must already be present for this to work.

Protect Soldiers
During gameplay, press Ctrl+Alt+Shift+C and type Typhonian Relief. Seth must be worshiped first.

Protection from Invaders
During gameplay, press Ctrl+Alt+Shift+C and type Spirit of Typhon. Seth must be worshiped first.

Super Storage Yard
During gameplay, press Ctrl+Alt+Shift+C and type Supreme Craftsman. Ptah must be worshiped first.

Worse Inundation
During gameplay, press Ctrl+Alt+Shift+C and type Mummys Curse. Osiris must be worshiped first.

PHAROAH'S ASCENT

Walk Through Fire
In a room, type firewalker.

Show First Hint
In a room, type givemehelp.

Show Second Hint
In a room, type helpmeplenty.

Show Final Hint, Completing Room
In a room, type youdoit.

Complete Current Room
In a room, type shazam.

PHARAOH'S REVENGE

Extra Life
During gameplay, press F5.

One Hit Kills
During gameplay, press F7.

PHAROAH'S TOMB

Level Skip
Turn Scroll Lock on and press + on the keypad.

PINBALL ILLUSIONS

Unlimited Tilts
During gameplay, type earthquake or vacuum.

PIPE DREAM

Level Select
Select Level 33 and enter the password FOOZ.

PITFALL: THE MAYAN ADVENTURE

Nine Lives
MEOWMEOWLIKEMEOWMAN

Nine Continues
EATMOREBRAN

Turn into a Stick Figure (Repeat for Everyone Else)
HATMAN

Show Game Developers
IDDQD

Show Framerate
FRAMERATE

Add 99 of Each Item
PUMPYOUUP

First Five Levels Completed
FIVEEASYPEICES

Go to 2600 Game
LETSDOTHETIMEWARP

POLARIS REBELLION

Show Bandits' Movement Path
path

Full Energy
energize

Get 99 Ships
invade

Get $10,000
fortune

Kill All
kill

Max Equipped Ship
gimme

Level 2
WARPDRIVE

Level 3
GRAVITY

Level 4
ICEWORLD

Level 5
LASERBEAM

Level 6
VOLCANO

Level 7
LAVADOME

Level 8
THUNDER

Level 9
METEORS

Level 10
STARSHIP

Level 11
WASTELAND

Level 12
SANDSTORM

Level 13
CARAVAN

Level 14
REBIRTH

Level 15
OASIS

POPULOUS

Level 999
At the title screen, type KILLUSALL.

POPULOUS: THE BEGINNING

Access Cheat Mode
During gameplay, press Tab+F11 and type byrne to activate Cheat mode.

Instant Training Mode
Enable Cheat mode and press Tab+F1.

All Spells
Enable Cheat mode and press Tab+F3.

All Buildings
Enable Cheat mode and press Tab+F4.

Full Mana
Enable Cheat mode and press Tab+F5.

POSTAL

Full Health
HEALTHFUL

Full Armor
THICKSKIN

Double Ammo Capacity
CARRYMORE

Get Everything
GIMMEDAT

Resurrection
HESSTILLGOOD

Grenades, Missiles, Napalm, Flamer
DAWHOLEENCHILADA

Shotgun Ammo
BREAKYOSAK

Makes Chars Smaller
MYTEAMOUSE

SprayCannon
SHELLFEST

Grenades, Missiles, Heatseekers
EXPLODARAMA

Molotovs, Napalm, Flamer
FLAMENSTEIN

Shotgun Ammo
SHOTGUN

SprayCannon
THEBESTGUN

Grenades
LOBITFAR

Missiles, Heatseekers
TITANIII

Napalm
STERNOMAT

Flamer
FIREHURLER

Mines
CROTCHBOMB

Skip Level
THERESNOPLACELIKEOZ

Invulnerability
IAMSOLAME

POWERSLIDE

Alt Key Raises Car
During gameplay, type APOLLO.

Repel Other Cars
During gameplay, type BLAST.

Launch a Bomb from Your Car Onto the Track
During gameplay, type BOMB.

Briefly Ignite a Spot Near Your Car
During gameplay, type BURN.

When in the Air, Car Controls Like a Glider
During gameplay, type GLIDER.

Cars Hover
During gameplay, type HOVER.

Car Acts Like a Missile
During gameplay, type ICBM.

Car Jumps Several Feet in the Air
During gameplay, type JUMP.

Launch and Move Car
During gameplay, type LAUNCH, then press A to launch a car, Z to move in the direction you're facing.

Lighter Car
During gameplay, type LIGHT.

Lunar Gravity
During gameplay, type LUNAR.

AI Cars Don't Steer, Just Accelerate
During gameplay, type SLEEP.

Slippery Surfaces
During gameplay, type SLIPPY.

Car Adheres to Any Surface
During gameplay, type SPIDER.

Stick Surfaces
During gameplay, type STICKY.

Cars Gravitate Toward Each Other
During gameplay, type SUCK.

Slow Time for AI Opponents
During gameplay, type TIMEWARP.

An Invisible Tornado Whips Around AI Cars
During gameplay, type TWISTER.

Other Cars Crawl Over Track
During gameplay, type WARP.

Access Advanced Levels
At the Sign-In screen, type your name as Jeff.

Access Expert Levels
At the Sign-In screen, type your name as AaronFoo.

Access all levels/Ais
At the Sign-In screen, type your name as Megasaxon.

PREHISTORIC 2

Level 2
F372

Level 3
973B

Level 4
CO8B

Level 5
6450

PRIMAL PREY

Get Lots of Money
Go to the Guns and Items screen and press F2. Type "MOMONEY" at the prompt to get enough dough to purchase all the gear you want.

PRINCE OF PERSIA 2

Access Cheat Mode
Start the game with the command line parameter YIPPEEYAHOO.

Add Time
Enable Cheat mode, then during gameplay, press +.

Subtract Time
Enable Cheat mode, then during gameplay, press -.

Kill All Enemies On Screen
Enable Cheat mode, then during gameplay, press K.

Return From Dead
Enable Cheat mode, then during gameplay, press R.

Show Position
Enable Cheat mode, then during gameplay, press F1.

Player On/Off
Enable Cheat mode, then during gameplay, press F3.

Ruler
Enable Cheat mode, then during gameplay, press F6.

Add Energy
Enable Cheat mode, then during gameplay, press Shift+T.

Subtract Energy
Enable Cheat mode, then during gameplay, press Shift+K.

Show Room Number and Jump Right
Enable Cheat mode, then during gameplay, press Shift+R.

Show Room Number and Jump Left
Enable Cheat mode, then during gameplay, press Shift+W.

Turn Screen Upside-Down
Enable Cheat mode, then during gameplay, press Shift+I.

Show Prince Only
Enable Cheat mode, then during gameplay, press Shift+B.

Skip to Next Level
Enable Cheat mode, then during gameplay, press Alt+N.

Pro Bass Fishing

Show All Fish in Fishing Mode
Type pbxray as your name. When done correctly, the name disappears.

Line Won't Break
Type pbpowerpole as your name. When done correctly, the name disappears.

Fish Can't Resist
Type pbsuperbait as your name. When done correctly, the name disappears.

Project IGI

Activate Cheat Mode
Type nada at the main menu to enable cheat mode. Then, enter one of the following codes during gameplay to activate the corresponding cheat function.

God Mode for Player and Team
allgod

Unlimited Ammunition
allammo

Easy Mode
easy

Kill Enemies
ewww

Quake

Access Cheat Mode
Press ~ to access console, then type one of the following codes.

Quad Damage
Enable Cheat mode and type IMPULSE 255.

All Weapons
Enable Cheat mode and type IMPULSE 9.

Display Runes
Enable Cheat mode and type IMPULSE 11.

Gold Key
Enable Cheat mode and type IMPULSE 14.

Monsters Don't Attack Unless Provoked
Enable Cheat mode and type NOTARGET.

Walk Through Walls
Enable Cheat mode and type NOCLIP.

Get Crosshairs
Enable Cheat mode and type CROSSHAIR 1.

Invincibility
Enable Cheat mode and type GOD.

Commit Suicide
Enable Cheat mode and type KILL.

Toggle Flight
Enable Cheat mode and type FLY.

Silver Key
Enable Cheat mode and type IMPULSE 13.

Quake II

Access Cheat Mode
Press ~ to access console, then type one of the following codes.

Invulnerability
Enable Cheat mode and type give invulnerability.

Change Gravity
Enable Cheat mode and type sv_gravity.

Change Crosshairs
Enable Cheat mode and type crosshair.

Combat Armor
Enable Cheat mode and type give combat armor.

Power Cube
Enable Cheat mode and type give power cube.

Slugs
Enable Cheat mode and type give slugs.

Commanders's Head
Enable Cheat mode and type give commander's head.

Power Shield
Enable Cheat mode and type give power shield.

Armor Shard
Enable Cheat mode and type give armor shard.

Blue Key
Enable Cheat mode and type give blue key.

Red Key
Enable Cheat mode and type give red key.

Security Pass
Enable Cheat mode and type give security pass.

God Mode
Enable Cheat mode and type god.

No Target Mode
Enable Cheat mode and type notarget.

No Clip Mode
Enable Cheat mode and type noclip.

Body Armor
Enable Cheat mode and type give armor.

Body Armor
Enable Cheat mode and type give bodyarmor.

Weapon Silencer
Enable Cheat mode and type give silencer.

Health
Enable Cheat mode and type give health.

All Weapons
Enable Cheat mode and type give weapons.

All Ammo
Enable Cheat mode and type give ammo.

All Items
Enable Cheat mode and type give all.

Quake III Arena

Cheat Codes
Press ~ during gameplay to bring up the console. Type /sv_cheats 1 then type /devmap yyyyyyy. Replace yyyyyyy wtih the name of your map, such as q3dm15. Then type one of the following codes.

100 Health Over the Limit
Enable Cheat mode and type /give mega health.

Get Item
Enable Cheat mode and type /give item name. Replace item name with one of the following: ammo, armor, bfg10k, gauntlet, grappling hook, grenade launcher, haste, health, lightning gun, machine gun, medikit, personal teleporter, plasma gun, railgun, regeneration, rocket launcher, shotgun.

Become Invisible
Enable Cheat mode and type /give invisibility.

Run Faster
Enable Cheat mode and type /give speed.

Immune to Lava, Drowning, Acid, etc.
Enable Cheat mode and type /give battle suit.

Quad Damage
Enable Cheat mode and type /give quad damage.

Third-Person Viewpoint
Enable Cheat mode and type /cg_thirdperson 1.

Fly
Enable Cheat mode and type /give flight.

Fly and Go Through Walls
Enable Cheat mode and type /noclip.

Get All Guns
Enable Cheat mode and type /give all.

Get Hidden Sarge Skin
Enable Cheat mode and type /model sarge/krusade.

Unlock All Levels at Skill 1
Enable Cheat mode and type /iamacheater.

Unlock All Levels at Skill 100
Enable Cheat mode and type /iamamonkey.

God Mode
Enable Cheat mode and type /god.

View All FMV Sequences
Type this string at the command line in the DOS prompt: quake3.exe +seta g_spVideos "\tier1\1\tier2\2\tier3\3\tier4\4\tier5\5\tier6\6\tier7\7\tier8\8".

Rage of Mages

Access Cheat Mode
#Chicken

God Mode for Self
#modify self +god

God Mode for Army
#modify army +god

Get Gold
#create gold

Kill All Enemy Units
#killall

Pick All Sacks (Except in Units)
#pickup all

Show Entire Map
#show map

Hide Map
#hide map

Show Conversations from Units in Current Level
#event x (Replace x with any number.)

End Current Round in Victory
#victory

Rage of Mages 2

Access Cheat Mode
Press Enter and type #coward then enter one of the following codes:

All Spells
Enable Cheat mode and type #modify self+spells.

God Mode (Self)
Enable Cheat mode and type #modify self+god.

God Mode (Army)
Enable Cheat mode and type #modify army+god.

RAILROAD TYCOON 2

Win with Gold Victory
BigfootGold

Win with Silver Victory
BigfootSilver

Win with Bronze Victory
BigfootBronze

Win with Gold Victory
Bigfoot

Lose Scenario
BoBo

Give Your Character $100,000
King of the hill

Give Company $100 Million
Powerball

Give Company $1 Million
Slush fund

Access All Denied Territories
Let me in

Double Maximum Train Speeds
Speed Racer

Convert All Engines to AMD-103s at Expense of Profits
AMD103

Crash All Competitors' Trains
Casey Jones

Get All Engines
Show me the trains

Increase City Sizes
Viagra

Give Player 1 Million
Cattle Futures

Never Crash (for v1.53)
nowreck

Stations Double Cargo Output
Overtime

RAINBOW SIX

Team God Mode
During gameplay, press ' and type teamgod.

Player God Mode
During gameplay, press ' and type avatargod.

Stumpy Mode
During gameplay, press ' and type stumpy.

Enlarge Player's Feet and Hands
During gameplay, press ' and type clodhopper.

Mega Head Mode
During gameplay, press ' and type meganoggin.

Big Head Mode
During gameplay, press ' and type bignoggin.

Refill Ammo
During gameplay, press ' and type 5fingerdiscount.

Turn AI Off
During gameplay, press ' and type nobrainer.

Debug Keys Enabled
During gameplay, press ' and type debugkeys.

Flatulent Walking
During gameplay, press ' and type silenbutdeadly.

Change Players from 3D to 2D
During gameplay, press ' and type turnpunchkick.

Heavy Breathing
During gameplay, press ' and type 1-900.

Victory Conditions On/Off
During gameplay, press ' and type explore.

Level Skip
During gameplay, press ' and type debugkeys. Press Enter, then press F10. Now press F12.

Suicide
During gameplay, press ' and type debugkeys. Press Enter, then press F10. Now press F7 or F8.

Change View
During gameplay, press ' and type debugkeys. Press Enter, then press F10. Now press F6.

Adjust Elevation
During gameplay, press ' and type debugkeys. Press Enter, then press F10. Now press Comma, Period, or /.

RAINBOW SIX: ROGUE SPEAR

God Mode
Press Enter then type avatargod.

Team Is Invincible
Press Enter then type teamgod.

RAINBOW SIX: ROGUE SPEAR– URBAN OPERATIONS

Team God Mode
During gameplay, press Enter and type teamgod.

God Mode
During gameplay, press Enter and type avatargod.

Disable AI
During gameplay, press Enter and type nobrainer.

No Victory Conditions
During gameplay, press Enter and type explore.

Refill Inventory
During gameplay, press Enter and type 5fingerdiscount.

Invisibility
During gameplay, press Enter and type theshadowknows.

RALLY CHAMPIONSHIP 2000

A8 Championship Available
Type world class as Player Four's name.

A8 Cars Available in Single Race and Time Trial
Type turbo challenge as Player Four's name.

Secret Citroen WRC Car
Type max power as Player Four's name.

Gives Citroen Saxo WRC
Type throw me a bone as Player Four's name.

One More Minute of Service Time (Press T at Service Screen)
Type give me time as Player Four's name.

Bonus Car
Type group b as Player Four's name.

Bonus Car
Type mooserati as Player Four's name.

Bonus Car
Type lambaaghini as Player Four's name.

Bonus Car
Type spud car as Player Four's name.

Things Bonus Car
Type precious as Player Four's name.

Bonus Car
Type furry dice as Player Four's name.

Bonus Car
Type mf hotback as Player Four's name.

Bonus Car
Type tree hugger as Player Four's name.

R/C Car
Type radio car as Player Four's name.

Energy in Arcade Mode
Type arcade unlimited as Player Four's name.

Arcade Mode Surprises
Type arcade action as Player Four's name.

RAMBO 3

Level Select
Enter the name RENEGADE on the High Score table. Then press 1, 2, or 3.

RAYMAN

99 Lives, All Cages Captured, All Levels Beaten
Enter the password 942KV3W9XD.

RAYMAN 2: THE GREAT ESCAPEAPE

All Powers
During gameplay, type globoxrules.

More Fire Power
During gameplay, press Escape and type glowfist.

Five Extra Lives
During gameplay, press Escape and type gimmelife.

Five Extra Lumz
During gameplay, press Escape and type gimmelumz.

Level Select
During gameplay, press Escape and type gothere.

RAYMAN FOREVER

99 Lives
raylives

Full Power
raypoint

Golden Fist
goldfist

All Normal Powers
power

Free Level Selection
gothere

Five Free Lumz
gimmelumz

Restores Life Bar
gimmelife

Full Energy
During gameplay, hold Tab and type points.

View All Gold Coins
During gameplay, hold Tab and type goldens.

5 Extra Lives
During gameplay, hold Tab, type lives05, and press the Backspace key.

20 Extra Lives
During gameplay, hold Tab, type lives20, and press the Backspace key.

50 Extra Lives
During gameplay, hold Tab, type lives50, and press the Backspace key.

Use Cursor Keys for Free Movement
During gameplay, hold Tab, type moveray, and press the Backspace key.

REAP

Start with Better Weapons
diesheepdie

God Mode
absolutenot

Unlimited Lives
sdivinorum

Tougher Enemies
toughguy

REBEL ASSAULT

Planet Kolaador (Easy)
BOSSK

Star Destroyer Attack (Easy)
ENGRET

Tatooine Attack (Easy)
RALRRA

Asteroid Field Chase (Easy)
FRIJA

Imperial Walkers (Easy)
LAFRA

StormTroopers (Easy)
DERLIN

Protect Rebel Transport (Easy)
MOTLOK

Yavin Training (Easy)
MORAG

Tie Attack (Easy)
TANTISS

Death Star Surface (Easy)
OSWAFL

Surface Cannon (Easy)
KLAATY

Power Relays (Easy)
IRENEZ

Death Star Trench (Easy)
LIANNA

Finale (Easy)
PAKKA

End (Easy)
NORVAL

Planet Kolaador (Normal)
BOTHAN

Star Destroyer Attack (Normal)
HERGLIC

Tatooine Attack (Normal)
LEENI

Asteroid Field Chase (Normal)
THRAWN

Imperial Walkers (Normal)
LWYLL

StormTroopers (Normal)
MAZZIC

Protect Rebel Transport (Normal)
JULPA

Yavin Training (Normal)
MORRT

Tie Attack (Normal)
MUFTAK

Death Star Surface (Normal)
RASKAR

Surface Cannon (Normal)
JHOFF

Power Relays (Normal)
ITHOR

Death Star Trench (Normal)
UMWAK

Finale (Normal)
ORLOK

End (Normal)
NKLLON

Planet Kolaador (Hard)
BORDOK

Star Destroyer Attack (Hard)
SKYNX

Tatooine Attack (Hard)
DEFEL

Asteroid Field Chase (Hard)
JEDGAR

Imperial Walkers (Hard)
MADINE

StormTroopers (Hard)
TARKIN

Protect Rebel Transport (Hard)
MOTHMA

Yavin Training (Hard)
GLAYYD

Tie Attack (Hard)
OTTEGA

Death Star Surface (Hard)
RISHII

Surface Cannon (Hard)
IRZINA

Power Relays (Hard)
KARRDE

Death Star Trench (Hard)
VONZEL

Finale (Hard)
OSSUS

End (Hard)
MALANI

View End Sequence
Enter the password ORGANA.

REBEL ASSAULT 2

Level 2 (Beginner)
Jabba

Level 3 (Beginner)
Endor

Level 4 (Beginner)
Lachton

Level 5 (Beginner)
Borsk

Level 6 (Beginner)
Kroyties

Level 7 (Beginner)
Auril

Level 8 (Beginner)
Kampl

Level 9 (Beginner)
Ferrier

Level 10 (Beginner)
Galia

Level 11 (Beginner)
Denarii

Level 12 (Beginner)
Sadow

Level 13 (Beginner)
Onderon

Level 14 (Beginner)
Aleema

Level 15 (Beginner)
Cathar

Finale (Beginner)
Dominus

Level 2 (Novice)
Ewoks

Level 3 (Novice)
Chewie

Level 4 (Novice)
Dankin

Level 5 (Novice)
Noghri

Level 6 (Novice)
Chamma

Level 7 (Novice)
Bogga

Level 8 (Novice)
Incom

Level 9 (Novice)
Kothlis

Level 10 (Novice)
Krath

Level 11 (Novice)
Siosk

Level 12 (Novice)
Adegan

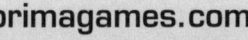

Level 13 (Novice)
Amanda

Level 14 (Novice)
Ambria

Level 15 (Novice)
Sylvar

Finale (Novice)
Miraluka

Level 2 (Standard)
Bantha

Level 3 (Standard)
Katana

Level 4 (Standard)
Dengar

Level 5 (Standard)
Pellaeon

Level 6 (Standard)
Ithull

Level 7 (Standard)
Stenness

Level 8 (Standard)
Myrkr

Level 9 (Standard)
Churba

Level 10 (Standard)
Artoo

Level 11 (Standard)
Satal

Level 12 (Standard)
Lobue

Level 13 (Standard)
Denaba

Level 14 (Standard)
Sturm

Level 15 (Standard)
Crado

Finale (Standard)
Carrack

REBEL MOON RISING

Full Weapons and Ammo
fwpsyko

Full Health and Oxygen
fwmarit

Invincibility
fwmithra

Invisibility
fwkitty

Skip to Mission Number
fwwarp## (Replace ## with the desired number.)

Jetpack (On/Off with F/Z)
fwbert

RECOIL

Access Cheat Mode
During gameplay, press Ctrl+X to enable Cheat mode, then type one of the following case-sensitive codes:

God Mode
Enable Cheat mode and type Cavalry.

All Weapons
Enable Cheat mode and type Hemmit.

Shields at Full Strength
Enable Cheat mode and type Medic.

Free Hover Tech
Enable Cheat mode and type killjoy.

RED FACTION

Activate Cheat Mode
Press ~ during gameplay to display the console window, then enter one of the following codes to activate the corresponding cheat function.

God Mode
vivalahelvig

All Weapons and Ammunition
bighugmug

Flight Mode
heehoo

Suicide
kill

Alternate View
camera<1-3>

REDLINE

Access Cheat Mode
During gameplay, hold G+O+D at the same time to display the command line, then type one of the following codes.

God Mode
Enable Cheat mode and type IMMORTAL.

God Mode Off
Enable Cheat mode and type MORTAL.

Third-Person View On Foot
Enable Cheat mode and type CAMERA.

All On-Foot Weapons Have Max Ammo
Enable Cheat mode and type ALLAMMO.

Targeting for On-Foot Weapons
Enable Cheat mode and type TARGETS.

Double Damage When On Foot
Enable Cheat mode and type DBDAMAGE.

On-Foot Radar
Enable Cheat mode and type RADAR.

All Car Ammo
Enable Cheat mode and type CW.

Full Armor
Enable Cheat mode and type CA.

Running Person in Place of Car
Enable Cheat mode and type STONEAGE.

No Car Geometry
Enable Cheat mode and type CAROFF.

Flip Car Geometry
Enable Cheat mode and type CARFLIP.

Reverse Car Geometry
Enable Cheat mode and type CARREVERSE.

Toggle Car Wheels
Enable Cheat mode and type WHEELSOFF.

REDLINE RACER

All Bikes and Tracks
Enter the name ABODE.

More Stuff
Enter the name dissent.

REDNECK RAMPAGE

Get Everything
During gameplay, type rdall.

Message "Eat Me!"
During gameplay, type rdbeta.

Toggle No Clipping
During gameplay, type rdclip.

Toggle Debug Mode
During gameplay, type rddebug.

Message "Elvis Lives!"
During gameplay, type rdelvis.

Message "Elvis Is Dead!"
During gameplay, type rdhounddog.

Get All Guns
During gameplay, type rdguns.

Get All Inventory
During gameplay, type rdinventory.

Get All Keys
During gameplay, type rdkeys.

Message "Maxx Rules"
During gameplay, type rdmaxx.

Toggle No Monsters
During gameplay, type rdmonsters.

Toggle yyy Moonshine Mode
During gameplay, type rdmoonshine.

Message "For Your Grandpa!"
During gameplay, type rdrafael.

Show Framerate
During gameplay, type rdrate.

Toggle Show Map
During gameplay, type rdshowmap.

Change Skill
During gameplay, type rdskill# (replace # with a number from one to four).

All Locks Toggled
During gameplay, type rdunlock.

Another Debug Mode
During gameplay, type rdyerat.

Level Warp
During gameplay, type rdrdmeadowXYY (X=1-2, Y=01-07).

REDNECK RAMPAGE DEER HUNTIN

You Attract Deer
dhcome

Turbo Mode
spork1

Deer Are Tracked
spork2

Toggle God Mode
rdhounddog

Get Everything
rdall

Level Warp
rdmeadow### (Replace ### with desired level.)

Toggle Show Location
rdyerat

Lock Toggle
rdunlock

Get All Items
rditems

Show Framerate
rdrate

Change Skill Level
rdskill# (Replace # with desired level.)

You Were All Wrong!
rdteachers

Get Moonshine
rdmoonshine

Monster Respawn Toggle
rdcritters

For You Grandpa!
rdrafael

Toggle Show All Map
rdshowmap

Toggle Clip Mode
rdclip

Get All Guns
rdguns

Get All Inventory
rdinventory

Get All Keys
rdkeys

Toggle Debug Mode
rddebug

Get the Motorcycle
rdjoseph

Inflict Heavy Damage on Oneself
rdmrbill

Instant Death
rdrhett

Mushroom Mode
rdaaron

Turn Off All Cheats
rdnocheat

Toggle Drunk Mode
rdwoleslagle

Get the Boat
rdgreg

Alternate Debug Information
rdnoah

Chicken Mode
rdkfc

REQUIEM: AVENGING ANGEL

Access Cheat Mode
During gameplay, press Enter and type csmilton.

God Mode
Enable Cheat mode and type csyhwh.

All Guns, Ammo, Health, Essence, Angelic Powers, and Items
Enable Cheat mode and type csstigmata.

Load Map
Enable Cheat mode and type csmap [mapname] (replace [mapname] with the desired map name).

All Angelic Powers
Enable Cheat mode and type csrosary.

Full Health
Enable Cheat mode and type cshealth.

Full Armor
Enable Cheat mode and type csshroud.

Full Essence
Enable Cheat mode and type csessence.

All Items
Enable Cheat mode and type csitems.

All Guns
Enable Cheat mode and type csguns.

Ammunition
Enable Cheat mode and type csammo.

No Gravity (Flight Mode)
Enable Cheat mode and type cshost.

Wireframe Level Map
Enable Cheat mode and type cswire.

Stop Time
Enable Cheat mode and cshalt.

All Doorways Highlighted Yellow
Enable Cheat mode and csportal.

Kill All Enemies
Enable Cheat mode and csvanish.

Quick Reset from Last Save
Enable Cheat mode and type csback.

RETURN FIRE 2

Unlimited Ammo
During gameplay, press ~ and type ammo!

Impervious Carrier
During gameplay, press ~ and type carrier!

Unlimited Fuel
During gameplay, press ~ and type fuel!

God Mode
During gameplay, press ~ and type god!

Machine Guns Off
During gameplay, press ~ and type guns!

SAM Launchers Off
During gameplay, press ~ and type sams!

Turrets Off
During gameplay, press ~ and type turrets!

Unlimited Vehicles
During gameplay, press ~ and type vehicles!

RETURN TO CASTLE WOLFENSTEIN

Activate Cheat Mode
Edit your Windows 9x/ME Desktop Shortcut for the game and change the "Target" field to:

"C:\Program Files\Return to Castle Wolfenstein\WolfSP.exe" +set sv_cheats 1

If using Windows XP, right click on the single play shortcut. On the "Command Line," make sure the command line is in quotes and add +set sv_cheats after two spaces, so it says: "drive:\path\folder\WolfSP.exe" +set sv_cheats 1

Notice that there are two spaces between the last " and the + in the Windows XP shortcut.

Edit the path as necessary if you installed the game to another location. Start the game. Press ~ during gameplay to display the console window. Enter one of the following codes to activate the corresponding cheat function.

God Mode
/god

Disable Enemy AI
/notarget

No Clipping Mode
/noclip

All Weapons and Ammunition
/give all

100 Armor
/give armor

Set Armor Amount
/give armor <amount>

Full Ammunition for Current Weapons
/give ammo

100 Health
/give health

Set Health Amount
/give health <number>

Stamina
/give stamina

Spawn Indicated Item
/give <item name>

Never Get Tired
/nofatigue

Display Current Map Name
/mapname

List Maps
/dir maps

Advance to Indicated Map
/spdevmap or /devmap <map name>

Show All Commands
/cmdlist

Reconnect to Last Server
/reconnect

Suicide
/kill

Exit Game
/quit

Show Current Server Settings
/serverinfo

Toggle between Windowed and Full Screen (Restart Game when Changed)
/toggle r_fullscreen

Toggle Compass Display
/toggle cg_drawcompass

Toggle HUD Display
/toggle cg_draw2d

Change Field of View
/cg_FOV <number>

Toggle Old Wolfenstein HUD
/cg_uselessnostalgia <0 or 1>

Third-Person View
/cg_thirdperson 1

Show Time Left
/toggle cg_drawtimer

Toggle Gibs
/toggle cg_gibs

Toggle Team Overlays
/toggle cg_drawteamoverlay

REVENANT

God Mode
During gameplay, press Enter while weapon isn't drawn, and type alreadydead.

Receive Many Potions
During gameplay, press Enter while weapon isn't drawn, and type potionsnlotions.

999,999 Gold
During gameplay, press Enter while weapon isn't drawn, and type alchemy.

Kill Monster with One Hit
During gameplay, press Enter while weapon isn't drawn, and type nahkranoth.

Make Character Level 30
During gameplay, press Enter while weapon isn't drawn, and type noamnesia.

Mana Never Decreases and Get All Talismans
During gameplay, press Enter while weapon isn't drawn, and type abracadabra.

Get Five of Each Food Type
During gameplay, press Enter while weapon isn't drawn, and type gimmesomegrub.

Turn Off Monster AI
During gameplay, press Enter while weapon isn't drawn, and type dummies.

Press F12 for an In-Game Editor
During gameplay, press Enter while weapon isn't drawn, and type debug.

RE-VOLT

All Cars
On the name wheel, type carnival.

Select Weapons in Game with Right Shift
On the name wheel, type sadist.

All Tracks
On the name wheel, type tracker.

Change Car During Mid-Race
On the name wheel, type changeling.

Press F6 for No Clipping, Press F6 Twice for Flight Mode
On the name wheel, type makeitgood.

Enables F5 and F6 Cameras
On the name wheel, type tvtime.

Small Cars
On the name wheel, type drinkme.

UFO Selectable
On the name wheel, type urco.

RISK 2

Go Back a Turn
When playing against the computer, press the menu button and quit the game. Then relaunch the game to continue from the beginning of your turn.

RIVAL REALMS

Reveal Entire Map
During gameplay, press Enter and type SEE ALL.

Show Only Explored Map
During gameplay, press Enter and type HIDE ALL.

Add 1,000 Gold
During gameplay, press Enter and type GIVE ME GOLD.

Add 500 Wood
During gameplay, press Enter and type GIVE ME WOOD.

Add 100 Food
During gameplay, press Enter and type GIVE ME FOOD.

Make Units Invincible
During gameplay, press Enter and type MAKE ME INVINCIBLE.

Restore Unit Vulnerability
During gameplay, press Enter and type MAKE ME VULNERABLE.

End Current Mission and Jump to Mission Number
During gameplay, press Enter and type LEVEL.

Raise Experience Levels for Selected Units
During gameplay, press Enter and type STAR ME UP.

Make Upgrades for All Selected Units
During gameplay, press Enter and type UPGRADE ME.

Restore All Hit Points for Selected Units
During gameplay, press Enter and type HEAL ME.

End Current Mission Victoriously
During gameplay, press Enter and type MAKE ME VICTORIOUS.

Change Name of Selected Unit
During gameplay, press Enter and type NAME.

ROAD RASH

Access Cheat Mode
During gameplay, type XYZZY.

Kill Cop
Enable Cheat mode and type YES,OCCIFER.

Kill Cop
Enable Cheat mode and type BRIBE.

Nitro
Enable Cheat mode and type SPOON!

Get Chain
Enable Cheat mode and type THWACK!

Get Club
Enable Cheat mode and type K'THUNK!

Disable Cheats
Enable Cheat mode and type PLUGH.

ROCKY MOUNTAIN TROPHY HUNTER

Rocket Launcher
While hunting, type BGBARBECUE.

Toggle Weather Effects
While hunting, type BGWEATHER.

Infrared-Like Vision
While hunting, type BGPREDATOR.

Stop Gun from Moving
While hunting, type BGSNIPER.

Show Game Onscreen
At the Map screen, type BGSHOW.

Move Faster Onscreen (Stealth)
At the Map screen, type BGTRACK.

Attract Game
At the Map screen, type BGURINE.

Show Blood Trails
At the Map screen, type BGVAMPIRE.

Increase Number of Animals
At the main menu, type BGNOAH.

Only Trophy-Sized Game
At the main menu, type BGSTEROIDS.

Only Sheep
At the main menu, type BGHORNS.

Only Elk
At the main menu, type BGELABONG.

Only Moose
At the main menu, type BGBULLWINKLE.

Only Bear
At the main menu, type BGYOGI.

ROCKY MOUNTAIN TROPHY HUNTER 2

Show All Animals on Map and GPS
At the Hunt screen, type -rmshowon on the console.

Approach Nearest Animal
At the Hunt screen, type -rmshot on the console.

Become Very Fast
At the Hunt screen, type -rmlight on the console.

Become Irresistible to Animals
At the Hunt screen, type -rmgoodstuff on the console.

Sight-In Your Gun
At the Hunt screen, type -rmsharpshot on the console.

Attract Animals
At the Hunt screen, type -rmurine on the console.

Add Animals to Hunting Location
At the Hunt screen, type -rmnoah on the console.

Animals Ignore You
At the Hunt screen, type -rminvisible on the console.

Snow
At the Hunt screen, type -rmsnow on the console.

Rain
At the Hunt screen, type -rmrain on the console.

Cycle Weather
At the Hunt screen, type -rmblizzard on the console.

ROCKY MOUNTAIN TROPHY HUNTER 3

Travel to Nearest Animal
During gameplay, press F2 and type r3find.

Animals No Longer Fear Hunters
During gameplay, press F2 and type r3nofear.

Gun Sighted In
During gameplay, press F2 and type r3sightin.

Attract Animals
During gameplay, press F2 and type r3beacon.

Rainy Weather
During gameplay, press F2 and type r3water.

Snowy Weather
During gameplay, press F2 and type r3blizzard.

Show Animals on Map
During gameplay, press F2 and type r3showme.

ROLLCAGE

Debug Menu
At any menu, type IAMALAZYBASTARD.

Hyper Speed
At any menu, type WARPSPEEDMRSULU.

Mega Speed
At any menu, type WRECKEDONSPEED.

Mirror Mode
At any menu, type REFLECTIONS.

Scorpio League
At any menu, type GIVEMESCORPIO.

Taurus League
At any menu, type GIVEMETAURUS.

High Gravity
At any menu, type JACKIMFLYING.

Medium Gravity
At any menu, type FLYMETOTHEMOON.

Restore Normal Gravity
At any menu, type BRINGMEBACKTOEARTH.

Expert Difficulty
At any menu, type TROTTERS.

Hard Difficulty
At any menu, type BIGANDPINK.

ROLLCAGE STAGE 2

All Cars
At the Bonus Awards menu, type metropolis.

All Campaigns
At the Bonus Awards menu, type mynameisneo.

All Campaigns Minus 1
At the Bonus Awards menu, type mynameismrsmith.

Mirror Mode
At the Bonus Awards menu, type inversion.

All Game Types (Excluding Soccer)
At the Bonus Awards menu, type wreckedonspeed.

ROLLERCOASTER TYCOON

Take Pictures of Rides
Rename any guest to Chris Sawyer.

Paint Pictures of Rides
Rename any guest to Simon Foster.

Increase Guests' Happiness
Rename any guest to Melanie Warn.

Waving Guests
Rename any guest to Katie Brayshaw.

Constantly Think Wow!
Rename any guest to John Wardley.

Pay Double Prices on Rides
Rename any guest to John Mace.

Drive Go-Karts Twice as Fast
Rename any guest to Damon Hill.

Unlimited Cash
Rename any guest to BigBucks.

Eat Lots of Hamburgers
Rename any guest to Tony Day.

Rides Four Times as Fast
Rename any guest to Michael Schumacher.

R-TYPE

Unlimited Lives
Enter SUMITA on the High Score table.

RUGRATS IN PARIS

Level 2
TQMMY QK

Level 3
RQVDHJVV

Level 4
BVBYFJND

Level 5
RJDBCVRT

Level 6
VNGBLJCV

Level 7
BJGSMVSH

Level 8
LJTBWQQD

RUNE

Enable Cheat Mode
During gameplay, press ~ or Tab and type CHEATPLEASE.

God Mode
During gameplay, press ~ or Tab and type GOD.

No Clipping
During gameplay, press ~ or Tab and type GHOST.

Fly Mode
During gameplay, press ~ or Tab and type FLY.

Ghost/Fly Mode Off
During gameplay, press ~ or Tab and type WALK.

First-Person View
During gameplay, press ~ or Tab and type BEHINDVIEW 0.

Pause All Nonplayer Characters
During gameplay, press ~ or Tab and type PLAYERSONLY.

Kill All Enemies
During gameplay, press ~ or Tab and type KILLPAWNS.

Full Screen Mode On/Off
During gameplay, press ~ or Tab and type TOGGLEFULLSCREEN.

Advanced Options
During gameplay, press ~ or Tab and type PREFERENCES.

Show FPS
During gameplay, press ~ or Tab and type STAT FPS.

SACRIFICE

Full Heal
During gameplay, press Ctrl+Shift+~ and type @ bythepowerofgrayskull.

Full Mana
During gameplay, press Ctrl+Shift+~ and type @ ihavethepower.

Wizard Is Invincible
During gameplay, press Ctrl+Shift+~ and type @ yourbulletscannotharmme.

Adds Souls
During gameplay, press Ctrl+Shift+~ and type @ dontfearthereaper.

Wizard Can Collect Red Spirits
During gameplay, press Ctrl+Shift+~ and type @ castratetheheathens.

Resets the Spell Timers
During gameplay, press Ctrl+Shift+~ and type @ timeisonmyside.

Summon Four [Monster Name]
During gameplay, press Ctrl+Shift+~ and type @ aplethoraof [monster name].

Summon One [Monster Name]
During gameplay, press Ctrl+Shift+~ and type @ alliwantforxmasisa [monster name].

Get [Spell Name]
During gameplay, press Ctrl+Shift+~ and type @ gimmegimmegimme [spell name].

SANITY: AIKEN'S ARTIFACT

God Mode
During gameplay, press Enter and type mptedthehead, then press Enter again.

Add Health, Mana
During gameplay, press Enter and type mpjuiceme, then press Enter again.

Enable All Levels
During gameplay, press Enter and type mpshipit, then press Enter again.

SAVAGE

Level 2
SABATTA

Level 3
PORSCHE

SCREAMER

All Normal Tracks Available
At any menu, type VTELO.

All Normal Plus Inverted Tracks
At any menu, type INVER.

New Obstacles Set 1
At any menu, type MONTY.

New Obstacles Set 2
At any menu, type JOINT.

Stop Clock
At any menu, type CLOCK.

Bullet Car Available
At any menu, type TAZOR.

Turns Graphics Upside Down
At any menu, type UPDOW.

Mirror Mode
At any menu, type MIRRO.

SCREAMER RALLY

All Tracks
At the main menu, type TRAMO.

All Cars
At the main menu, type CARBO.

Access All Leagues
At the main menu, type LEALL.

SCUD: IE

Level 2
OLD MAN

Level 3
SHORT BUT TALL

Level 4
DIET MNIP

Level 5
TITHES

Level 6
POPCORN

Level 7
NOT POODLE

Level 8
PACKET OF CRISPS

Level 9
MEDICINE

Level 10
SNOWBOARDING

Level 11
216BIT

Level 12
RENDERING

Level 13
BEAR GAME

Level 14
HORSE

Level 15
KIDDYWINKS

Level 16
JALLABALLABON

Level 17
HOT BEVERAGE

Level 18
MUNTRESS

Level 19
PANTERA ROSA

Level 20
RENNAISSANCE WEDDING

Level 21
HECTIC MAN

SEA DOGS

Ship Repaired, Full Crew
While at sea, press Ctrl+Z and type have live.

Extra Experience
While at sea, press Ctrl+Z and type expu mne.

Extra Money
While at sea, press Ctrl+Z and type deneg day.

Extra Cannon Damage
While at sea, press Ctrl+Z and type get me magic.

No Cannon Damage
While at sea, press Ctrl+Z and type make screen shots.

Move Camera with Ctrl+F
While at sea, press Ctrl+Z and type now i flying.

Fire from Camera with 0 on Keypad
While at sea, press Ctrl+Z and type fire from camera.

Teleport Ship to Camera Location with Ctrl+L
While at sea, press Ctrl+Z and type teleport.

SEPTERRA CORE

Access Cheat Mode
During gameplay, press F12 and type imarealweenie, then press Enter, F12.

List Enemy Hit Points
Enable Cheat mode and type enemies.

Show Line of Sight
Enable Cheat mode and type sight.

Show Debug numbers
Enable Cheat mode and type spy.

Kill All Enemies
During gameplay, press F12 and type WTSWWT-BGIOB and press Enter. Press F12 and type IMAREALWEENIE and press Enter. Now press Ctrl+F3 to kill all enemies.

Enemies Don't Attack
Press F12 and type makethemstopmommie.

Hide Spoken Text
Press F12 and type hidetext.

Show Frames per Second
Press F12 and type fps.

Displays Map in BMP Format
Press F12 and type mapmaker.

SERIOUS SAM

Press the ~ key during play and type:

All Weapons
Please giveall

Fly Mode
Please fly

No Clipping
Please ghost

All Items
Please giveall

God Mode
Please god

Invisibility
Please invisible

All Enemies Dead
Please killall

All Doors Open
Please open

Max Health
Please refreash

Kill All Enemies
Please killall

All Data Available in NETRICSA
Please tellall

SERIOUS SAM: THE SECOND ENCOUNTER

Activate Cheat Mode
Press ~ to display the console window. Enter one of the following codes, then press Enter to activate the corresponding cheat function.

God Mode
please god

Restore Energy
please refresh

Flight Mode
please fly

No Clipping Mode
please ghost

View All Messages
please tellall

All Weapons and Ammunition
please giveall

Kill All Monsters on Level
please killall

Open All Doors
please open

Invisibility
please invisible

SETTLERS

Level 2
STATION

Level 3
UNITY

Level 4
WAVE

Level 5
EXPORT

Level 6
OPTION

Level 7
RECORD

Level 8
SCALE

Level 9
SIGN

Level 10
ACRON

Level 11
CHOPPER

Level 12
GATE

Level 13
ISLAND

Level 14
LEGION

Level 15
PIECE

Level 16
RIVAL

Level 17
SAVAGE

Level 18
XAVER

Level 19
BLADE

Level 20
BEACON

Level 21
PASTURE

Level 22
OMNUS

Level 23
TRIBUTE

Level 24
FOUNTAIN

Level 25
CHUDE

Level 26
TRAILER

Level 27
CANYON

Level 28
REPRESS

Level 29
YOKI

Level 30
PASSIVE

SETTLERS IV

Cheat List
To activate the cheat console, type !wqsa during gameplay. Type in the following code to activate these cheats.

Defeat the Current Level
!win

Go One Minute Forward in Time
Press F12.

SEVEN KINGDOMS

Access Cheat Mode
During gameplay, type !!!@@@### to enable Cheat mode. This reduces your score to 0.

Add $1,000 to Your Cash
Enable Cheat mode and press C.

Add 1,000 to Your Food Reserves
Enable Cheat mode and press \.

All Technological Advances and Scrolls
Enable Cheat mode and press T.

Reveal Map
Enable Cheat mode and press M.

Increase Population in Selected City and Random Nationality
Enable Cheat mode and press ;.

Increase Prayer Points in Selected Seat of Power
Enable Cheat mode and press =.

Finish Selected Building
Enable Cheat mode and press B.

Toggle On/Off Fast Build Mode
Enable Cheat mode and press Z.

King is Immortal
Enable Cheat mode and press U.

SEVEN KINGDOMS 2

Access Cheat Mode
During gameplay, type '!!##%%&&' to enable Cheat mode.

Reveal Map
Enable Cheat mode and press Ctrl+M.

Know All Technology
Enable Cheat mode and press Ctrl+T.

Toggle Mortal/Immortal King Mode
Enable Cheat mode and press Ctrl+U.

Toggle Debug Messages
Enable Cheat mode and press Ctrl+A.

Toggle AI Info
Enable Cheat mode and press Ctrl+D.

Add 1,000 Food
Enable Cheat mode and press Ctrl+\.

Add 1,000 Treasure
Enable Cheat mode and press Ctrl+C.

Fast Build Mode
Enable Cheat mode and press Ctrl+Z.

Add 10 Population in Selected Town
Enable Cheat mode and press Ctrl+;.

Seat of Power Full
Enable Cheat mode and press Ctrl++ (Ctrl+Plus Key).

Minus 10 Reputation
Enable Cheat mode and press Alt+Ctrl+E.

Plus 10 Reputation
Enable Cheat mode and press Alt+Ctrl+R.

Minus 20 Damage to Selected Building
Enable Cheat mode and press Alt+Ctrl+K.

Plus 20 Damage to Selected Building
Enable Cheat mode and press Alt+Ctrl+J.

Minus 1,000 Treasure
Enable Cheat mode and press Alt+Ctrl+X.

Minus 1,000 Food
Enable Cheat mode and press Alt+Ctrl+C.

SHADOW COMPANY

God Mode for Every Soldier
During gameplay, press Enter and type DOLEMITE.

Show All Enemy Soldiers
During gameplay, press Enter and type PAUL HANEY SEES ALL.

Bottom Display On/Off
During gameplay, press Enter and type TOGGLE BOTTOMBAR.

Instant Win
During gameplay, press Enter and type AUTOWIN!.

SHADOW WARRIOR

Toggle God Mode
During gameplay, press T and type SWCHAN.

All Items
During gameplay, press T and type SWGIMME.

Enable Every Cheat
During gameplay, press T and type SWGREED.

Save Current Map on Disk as *SWSAVE.MAP*
During gameplay, press T and type SWSAVE.

Warp to Level
During gameplay, press T and type SWTREKxy (x=episode, y=level).

Change Resolution
During gameplay, press T and type SWRES.

Restart Level
During gameplay, press T and type SWSTART.

Toggle Clipping Mode
During gameplay, press T and type SWGHOST.

Toggle Automap
During gameplay, press T and type SWMAP.

Turn on Bunny Rockets with Rocket Launcher
During gameplay, press T and type SWTRIX.

Win Pachinko Game and Gain an Item
During gameplay, press T and type WINPACHINKO.

Change Name in Multiplayer Game
During gameplay, press T and type SWNAME.

Plays Sound File 0 to 999
During gameplay, press T and type SOUND x (x=Sound File).

Show Framerate, Repeat to Show Location in Level
During gameplay, press T and type SWLOC.

SHADOWMASTER

Access Cheat Mode
At the main menu, press F2+F3. The message "Cheats On" appears. Now hold + and press Backspace for a prompt, then type one of the following codes:

Enable Playtester Keys
Enable Cheat mode and type SCOUSER.

Turbo Mode
Enable Cheat mode and type TURBO.

Can Save After Every Level
Enable Cheat mode and type EVERY LEVEL SAVE.

Single Player on Multilevel
Enable Cheat mode and type ALLOW SINGLE.

Press Insert to Save a Screenshot (in *C:\TEMP\PIX*)
Enable Cheat mode and type PAPARAZZI.

All Cheats Off
Enable Cheat mode and type THE WHOLE OF CREATION.

Skip Level
Shift+F9

Ammo cheat
F11

Health Cheat
F12

SHOGO: MOBILE ARMOR DIVISION

Full Ammo, Armor, Health
During gameplay, press T and type mpkfa.

God Mode
During gameplay, press T and type mpgod.

SID MEIER'S ALPHA CENTAURI

Change Year
During gameplay, press Ctrl+K and press Shift+F5.

Create Unit
During gameplay, press Ctrl+K and press Shift+F1.

Discover Technology
During gameplay, press Ctrl+K and press Shift+F2.

SimANT

Ten Fertilized Black Queen Ants
Pause, then type oops.

Ten Fertilized Red Queen Ants
Pause, then type OOPS.

Ten Queen Ants
Pause, then type just.

Always Beat Red Ants
Pause, then type will.

Ant Colony in All Patches
Pause, then type jeff.

Be the Spider
Press X and click on the spider to control it.

Full Health for Yellow Ants
Pause, then type rand.

Funny Picture
Pause, then type joke.

Get Additional Red Queen Ant
Pause, then type Queen or QEEN.

Money
Pause, then type FUND.

More Black Ant Eggs
Pause, then type eggs.

More Holes for Black Ants
Pause, then type holes.

More Holes for Red Ants
Pause, then type HOLE.

More Red Ant Eggs
Pause, then type EGGS.

Unlimited Health for Black Ant Colony
Pause, then type jenn.

Unlimited Health for Yellow Ant Colony
Pause, then type susi.

Watch Ending Sequence
Pause, then type fred.

SimCITY

Loan Money
Hold down Shift and type FUND. This gives you $10,000 as a loan to be paid back with interest.

SimCITY 2000

$10,000 Bond
Type fund during gameplay to receive a $10,000 bond with 25 percent interest.

$500,000 Extra Money
Type imacheat or buddamus during gameplay.

Change Residential Areas to Churches
Type damn, darn, or heck during gameplay.

Debug Menu
Type priscilla during gameplay.

Extra Money
Type FUND and agree to the 25 percent interest. Type FUND again and agree to receive a second bond. Then go to the Budget window and issue a real bond. Select to repay one bond, take out another bond, and then repay one bond. This should give you $1,000,000.

Funny Picture
Type joke during gameplay.

Get a Military Base
Type gilmartin during gameplay.

Helicopter Shootings
Select the centering tool and then click on the helicopter to shoot it down.

Nuclear Meltdown
Type gomorrah to start a nuclear disaster.

Start a Fire
Type mrsoleary during gameplay.

Start a Flood
Type noah during gameplay.

Stop a Flood
Type moses during gameplay.

SimCITY 3000

Access Cheat Mode
Press Ctrl+Shift+Alt+C during gameplay. In the console window, type one of the following codes.

$250,000 Money Donation
Enable Cheat mode and type call cousin vinnie.

1234 Message
Enable Cheat mode and type 1234.

Advisor Message
Enable Cheat mode and type advisor.

Bat Message
Enable Cheat mode and type bat.

Birds Fly Around Your City
Enable Cheat mode and type the birds.

Broccoli Message
Enable Cheat mode and type broccoli.

Deals with Neighbors
Enable Cheat mode and type let's make a deal.

EA Message
Enable Cheat mode and type electronic arts.

Easter Egg Message
Enable Cheat mode and type easter egg.

Erts Message
Enable Cheat mode and type erts.

Fresh Water
Enable Cheat mode and type salt off.

Fund Message
Enable Cheat mode and type fund.

Hello Message
Enable Cheat mode and type hello.

Help Message
Enable Cheat mode and type help.

Llama Message
Enable Cheat mode and type llama.

Load Grayscale Picture as Terrain
Enable Cheat mode and type load terrain.

Lower Construction Costs
Enable Cheat mode and type i am weak.

Lower Terrain by One
Enable Cheat mode and type terrain one down.

Lower Terrain by Ten
Enable Cheat mode and type terrain ten down.

Maxis Message
Enable Cheat mode and type maxis.

Mayor Message
Enable Cheat mode and type mayor.

Money Message
Enable Cheat mode and type money.

More Secret Messages
Enable Cheat mode and type simant, simmars, simcopter, simearth, or Broccoli Education Foundation.

Moremoney Message
Enable Cheat mode and type moremoney.

No More Advice
Enable Cheat mode and type stop forcing advice.

Porntips Message
Enable Cheat mode and type porntipsguzzardo.

Raise Terrain by One
Enable Cheat mode and type terrain one up.

Raise Terrain by Ten
Enable Cheat mode and type terrain ten up.

Receive a SimCastle
Enable the $250,000 donation code and refuse Vinnie's offer. Then enable Cheat mode and type zyxwvu.

Reduce Pollution and Traffic
Enable Cheat mode and type traffic lights.

Salt Water
Enable Cheat mode and type salt on.

SC3K Message
Enable Cheat mode and type sc3k.

Scurk Message
Enable Cheat mode and type scurk.

Sim Message
Enable Cheat mode and type sim.

SimCity Message
Enable Cheat mode and type type simcity.

Ticker Message
Enable Cheat mode and type ticker.

Transform Low-Tech to High-Tech
Enable Cheat mode and type nerdz rool.

UFOs in Your City
Enable Cheat mode and type ufo swarm. Then set disaster to UFO.

Unlock All Buildings
Open and close the Power Plant window. Open and close the Rewards and Opportunities window. Open and close the Garbage Disposal window. Then open the Landmarks menu and all buildings are available.

Unlock All Extra Gifts
Enable Cheat mode and type pay tribute to your king.

Unlock All Garbage Buildings
Enable Cheat mode and type garbage in, garbage out.

Unlock All Ordinances
Enable Cheat mode and type i love red tape.

Unlock All Power Plants
Enable Cheat mode and type power to the masses.

Unlock All Water Buildings
Enable Cheat mode and type water in the desert.

Will Wright Message
Enable Cheat mode and type type will wright.

SIM COASTER

Polar Zone
Play the Land of Invention, and beat the first objective. After a little more gameplay, the president grants you the ability to open the Polar Zone theme park.

Arabian Knights
Play the Polar Zone, and beat a few of the objectives. The president informs you that Arabian Knights open for you, but you must complete a few more objectives. Train your staff for some of the objectives.

Golden Tickets
Certain people offer you challenges, and if you win, you earn two Golden Tickets!

Earn Training Room
Beat the first objective in Land of Invention and you can build a training center to train your staff.

Earn Research Lab
Beat the first objective in Land of Invention. Now you can hire scientists and research new things for your park.

SIMCOPTER

Big Helicopters
Press Ctrl+Alt+X during gameplay. Then type Make me big.

Camera Follows Car
Press Ctrl+Alt+X during gameplay. Then type Out on a Sunday drive.

Day or Night Code
Press Ctrl+D to change between day and night.

Drive-In Movies
Press Ctrl+Alt+X during gameplay. Then type Lights, Camera, Action!.

Ending Sequence
Press Ctrl+Alt+X during gameplay. Then type Gort.

Fly Faster
Press Ctrl+Alt+X during gameplay. Then type superpower multiply. Hold down the Shift key to fly faster. If you exit your helicopter and press Shift, you transform into a dog.

Infinite Lives
Press Ctrl+Alt+X during gameplay. Then type Gas does grow on trees.

Invincibility
Press Ctrl+Alt+X during gameplay. Then type Shields up.

Map Code
Press Ctrl+Alt+X during gameplay. Then type The map, please.

Megaphone Code
Press Ctrl+Alt+X during gameplay. Then type A megaphone in the hand is worth two in the bush.

Money Code
Press Ctrl+Alt+X during gameplay. Then type Give me bucks or give me death, then type a number between 1 and 50,000.

Nuclear Explosion
Press Ctrl+Alt+X during gameplay. Then type Radioactivity.

Programmer's Wife on Billboards
Press Ctrl+Alt+X during gameplay. Then type PAMCAREYGOLDMAN.

Return to Hangar Without Your Helicopter
Press Ctrl+Alt+X during gameplay. Then type There's no place like home.

Return to Helicopter
Press Ctrl+Alt+X during gameplay. Then type I love my helicopter.

Save City Map in ASCII format
Press Ctrl+Alt+X during gameplay. Then type Stop and ask for directions.

Select Level
Press Ctrl+Alt+X during gameplay. Then type Warp me to carrier, then type a number between 0 and 30.

Select a Helicopter
Press Ctrl+Alt+X during gameplay. Type I'm the CEO of McDonnell Douglas. Activate a helicopter by pressing the corresponding numeric key.

Skip Level
Press Ctrl+Alt+X during gameplay. Then type Been there, done that.

SIMEARTH

Extinct Plants and Animals
Put your mouse pointer in the toolbox, and type erad.

Flat Terrain
Type SMOOTH during gameplay.

Joke Window
Pause, then type JOKE.

More Money
Put your mouse pointer in the toolbox and type fund.

Random Altitudes
Type rand at the Map window.

SIMFARM

$10,000 More Money
During gameplay, type corn.

Three Cows in Perfect Health
During gameplay, type poultry.

Display Version Number
During gameplay, type v.

Donate $10,000
During gameplay, type fund.

Llama Screen
During gameplay, type llama.

Test Mode
During gameplay, type t.

SIMGOLF

Cheat Mode
Press Ctrl+S during game. Then release both keys and type bombsheep.

SIMISLE

200 Random Additions
Pause and type catsndogs.

Agents Work for Free
Save island as marksanchovypizza then reload game.

AT Disaster
Save island as duhdun then reload game.

Change Plants into Earth Tiles
Pause and type paveme.

Display Alien Message
Pause and type hialiens.

Drug-Peddling Village
Save island as jennerdrawgoodpictures then reload game.

Earthquakes
Save island as quakerattleandroll then reload game.

Enable All Cheats
Save island as al'sfetish then reload game.

Increase Building Materials by 1,000
Save island as deesextrapixel then reload game.

Increase EMUs by 10,000
Save island as iaintestedtico then reload game.

Increase Food by 5,000
Save island as ragschocolatesach then reload game.

Increase Heavy Machinery by 100
Save island as simonchickenb then reload game.

Instant Travel
Save island as cheatingnotme then reload game.

Islanders Turn Blue
Pause and type beauregard.

Maximum Amount of Money
Pause and type warbucks.

More Skilled Laborers
Save island as chinslovetreats, then reload game.

No Money
Save island as marysecosystem, then reload game.

Oil Spill at Terminal
Save island as peanutbettertoast, then reload game.

Oil Tanker Spill
Save island as pinkeyandperkyeatchease, then reload game.

Portside Disaster
Save island as headlesstourists, then reload game.

Rizzo Appears on Demand
Pause and type rizme.

SIMLIFE

Disable Ultra-Food Sources
Type food.

Display "$10,000 Richer" Message
Type fund.

Display Funny Joke
Type joke.

Mountain Tool Increases Soil Quality
Type weiss.

Plants Germinate Throughout World
Type seed.

Rocks Become Walls
Type wall.

Selected Species Give Birth
Type baby.

Strange Noises
Type just.

THE SIMS

1,000 Simoleans
Press Ctrl+Shift+C and type klapaucius. This works only for the unpatched version of the game (version 1.0). The code for version 1.1 (patched) is rosebud instead of klapaucius.

Display Personality and Interests
Select Sim, press Ctrl+Shift+C and type interests.

Draw All Frames
Press Ctrl+Shift+C and type draw_all_frames on.

Island Home
Press Ctrl+Shift+C and type water_tool.

Map Editor
Press Ctrl+Shift+C and type map_edit on.

Route Balloons
Press Ctrl+Shift+C and type route_balloons on.

Set Event Logging Mask
Press Ctrl+Shift+C and type log_mask.

Set Free Thinking Level
Press Ctrl+Shift+C and type autonomy # (replace # with a number from 1 to 100).

Set Grass Growth
Press Ctrl+Shift+C and type grow_grass # (replace # with a number from 1 to 150).

Set Time of Day
Press Ctrl+Shift+C and type SET_HOUR # (replace # with a number from 0 to 23).

Tile Information
Press Ctrl+Shift+C and type tile_info on.

Toggle Ticks
Press Ctrl+Shift+C and type sweep on or sweep off.

THE SIMS: HOUSE PARTY

Activate Cheat Mode
Press Ctrl + Shift + C during gameplay to display a prompt in the upper left corner of the screen. Enter one of the following codes to activate the corresponding cheat function.

1000 Simoleons
rosebud

Add New Family History Stat to the Current Family
hist_add

Automatically Import and Load Indicated FAM File
import <FAM file>

Automatically Load Indicated House
house <house number>

Crash Game
crash

Create Moat or Streams
water_tool

Create-a-Character Mode
edit_char

Display Personality and Interests
interests

Enable Debug Flag to Show Outcome Choice Dialogs for Social Interactions
debug_social

Map Editor Disabled
map_edit off

Map Editor Enabled
map_edit on

Move Any Object
move_objects on

Quit Game
quit

Rotate Camera
rotation <0-3>

Save Currently Loaded House
save

Save Family History File
history

Say "plugh"
plugh

Say "porntipsguzzardo"
porntipsguzzardo

Say "xyzzy"
xyzzy

Set Free Thinking Level
autonomy <1-100>

Set Game Speed
sim_speed <-1000-1000>

Set Grass Growth
grow_grass <0-150>

Set Lot Size
lot_size <number>

Set Time of Day
set_hour <1-24>

Toggle Allowing Visitors to Be Controlled Using the Keyboard
visitor_control

Toggle Camera Mode
cam_mode

Toggle Music
music

Toggle Sounds
sound

Toggle Web Page Creation
html

THE SIMS: VACATION

Activate Cheat Mode
Press Ctrl + Shift + C during gameplay to display a prompt in the upper left corner of the screen. Enter one of the following codes to activate the corresponding cheat function.

1000 Simoleons
rosebud

Add New Family History Stat to the Current Family
hist_add

Automatically Import and Load Indicated FAM File
import <FAM file>

Automatically Load Indicated House
house <house number>

Crash Game
crash

Create Moat or Streams
water_tool

Create-a-Character Mode
edit_char

Display Personality and Interests
interests

Enable Debug Flag to Show Outcome Choice Dialogs for Social Interactions
debug_social

Map Editor Disabled
map_edit off

Map Editor Enabled
map_edit on

Move Any Object
move_objects on

Quit Game
quit

Rotate Camera
rotation <0-3>

Save Currently Loaded House
save

Save Family History File
history

Say "plugh"
plugh

Say "porntipsguzzardo"
porntipsguzzardo

Say "xyzzy"
xyzzy

Set Free Thinking Level
autonomy <1-100>

Set Game Speed
sim_speed <-1000-1000>

Set Grass Growth
grow_grass <0-150>

Set Lot Size
lot_size <number>

Set Time of Day
set_hour <1-24>

Toggle Allowing Visitors to Be Controlled Using the Keyboard
visitor_control

Toggle Camera Mode
cam_mode

Toggle Music
music

Toggle Sounds
sound

Toggle Web Page Creation
html

SIM THEME PARK

Infinite Cash Code
Press Backspace during gameplay and type GIMMECASH.

SIMTOWER

Automatically Remove Old Units
Hold Shift when placing new unit on top of old one.

Build Three-Story Lobby
Hold Shift+Ctrl when placing lobby.

Build Two-Story Lobby
Hold Shift when placing lobby.

SIMTOWN

Disappearing Rabbit Trick
When rabbit appears, type wolfdog.

Flying Pigs
Zoom in on pig and type bacon.

More Resources
Pause and type cheatercheaterwhimpwhimp.

Parachuting Kid
Type uspa87419.

Toaster
Type toast when mobile home appears.

SIN

All Weapons
During gameplay, press ~ and type wuss.

God Mode
During gameplay, press ~ and type superfuzz.

SINISTAR UNLEASHED

God Mode
During gameplay, press ~ and type cheatnodmg.

More Crystals
During gameplay, press ~ and type cheatfreecrystal.

SLAMSCAPE

Invincibility
During gameplay, type SHAZAM.

Full Power-Up
During gameplay, type KABLASTROPHE.

SLAVE ZERO

Upgrade Weapons
During gameplay, press T and type goodies.

Win Mission
During gameplay, press T and type I win.

SMALL SOLDIERS

Access Cheat Mode
During gameplay, hold Ctrl+Shift+X+S. Release S, then the other keys. Type one of the following codes at the flashing red line in the screen's lower left corner.

Set Number of Max Toys Available
Enable Cheat mode and type toys # (replace # with the desired number).

Disable Fog of War
Enable Cheat mode and type clear.

Set Max Number of Your Team
Enable Cheat mode and type team # (replace # with the desired number).

Enable God Mode
Enable Cheat mode and type mcleod 1.

Disable God Mode
Enable Cheat mode and type mcleod 0.

Click on Enemy for Instant Kill
Enable Cheat mode and type kill.

SOLDIER OF FORTUNE

Access Cheat Mode
Start the game with the command line parameter +set console 1. Then during gameplay, press ~ and type one of the following codes:

God Mode
Enable Cheat mode and type heretic.

Walk Through Walls
Enable Cheat mode and type phantom.

Enemies Don't See You
Enable Cheat mode and type ninja.

Default Weapons
Enable Cheat mode and type defaultweapons.

Weapons 1 to 5
Enable Cheat mode and type elbow.

Weapons 6 to 10
Enable Cheat mode and type bigelbow.

Timescale
Enable Cheat mode and type matrix # (replace # with 1 to 10).

More Ammo
Enable Cheat mode and type updateinvfinal.

Kills All Enemies
Enable Cheat mode and type killallmonsters.

Go to Level
Enable Cheat mode and type map X and enter one of the following level names: tut1, tsr1, tsr2, trn1, arm1, arm2, arm3, kos1, kos2, kos3, sib1, sib2, sib3, irq1a, irq1b, irq2a, irq2b, irq3a, irq3b, ger1, ger2, ger3, ger4, nyc1, nyc2, nyc3, sud1, sud2, sud3, jpn1, jpn2, jpn3.

9mm
Enable Cheat mode and type GIMME item_weapon_pistol.

Shotgun
Enable Cheat mode and type GIMME item_weapon_shotgun.

Sniper Rifle
Enable Cheat mode and type GIMME item_weapon_sniper_rifle.

Silenced 9mm
Enable Cheat mode and type GIMME item_weapon_machinepistol.

SMG
Enable Cheat mode and type GIMME item_weapon_assault_rifle.

Machinegun
Enable Cheat mode and type GIMME item_weapon_machinegun.

Slugthrower
Enable Cheat mode and type GIMME item_weapon_autoshotgun.

Rocket Launcher
Enable Cheat mode and type GIMME item_weapon_rocketlauncher.

Flamethrower
Enable Cheat mode and type GIMME item_weapon_flamethrower.

MicrowavePulseGun
Enable Cheat mode and type GIMME item_weapon_microwavepulse.

9mm
Enable Cheat mode and type GIMME item_ammo_sp_pistol.

0.44
Enable Cheat mode and type GIMME item_ammo_sp_pistol2.

Shells
Enable Cheat mode and type GIMME item_ammo_sp_shotgun.

Slugs
Enable Cheat mode and type GIMME item_ammo_sp_slug.

Rockets
Enable Cheat mode and type GIMME item_ammo_sp_rocket.

Flamer
Enable Cheat mode and type GIMME item_ammo_sp_gas.

MPG
Enable Cheat mode and type GIMME item_ammo_sp_battery.

Body Armor
Enable Cheat mode and type GIMME item_equip_armor.

MedKit
Enable Cheat mode and type GIMME item_equip_medkit.

C4 Explosive
Enable Cheat mode and type GIMME item_equip_c4.

Flashbangs
Enable Cheat mode and type GIMME item_equip_flashpack.

Hand Grenades
Enable Cheat mode and type GIMME item_equip_grenade.

Night Vision
Enable Cheat mode and type GIMME item_equip_light_goggles.

Claymore Mines
Enable Cheat mode and type GIMME item_equip_claymore.

SOLDIER OF FORTUNE 2

Activate Cheat Mode
Press ~ to display the console window. Type sv_cheats 1 and press Enter to enable cheat mode. Then press ~ to bring up console and type one of the following codes to activate a cheat.

Toggle God Mode
god

Toggles No Clipping Mode
noclip

All Weapons and Ammunition
give all

Spawn Indicated Item
give <item name>

Armor
give armor

Full Ammunition for Current Weapons
give ammo

Health
give health

Stamina
give stamina

Unlimited Power
pinkspider

Disable Enemy AI
notarget

Never Get Tired
nofatigue

List Console Commands
cmdlist

Display Current Map Name
mapname

List Maps
dir maps

Advance to Indicated Map
map, spdevmap or devmap <level name>

Level Select Icon at Main Menu
raven 1

Change Gravity; 800 Is Default, Set to 0 to Fly
g_gravity <0-800>

Change Movement Rate; 320 Is Defeault, Lower Is Slower
g_speed <number>

Change Player's Name
name <text>

Toggle Windowed and Full Screen; Will Restart Game
toggle r_fullscreen

Show Current Server Settings
serverinfo

Reconnect to Last Server
reconnect

Suicide
kill

Exit Game
quit

SONIC AND KNUCKLES COLLECTION

Level 2
2965 3192 9023

Level 3
3610 2354 7327

Level 4
2921 0274 3999

Level 5
3737 7423 1487

Level 6
3053 9029 9071

Level 7
3698 8191 7375

Level 8
3009 6111 4047

Level 9
3482 7286 3167

Level 10
2809 6267 2575

Level 11
3454 5929 0879

Level 12
2765 3348 7551

Level 13
3582 0497 5039

Level 14
2898 2104 2623

Level 15
3543 1266 0927

Level 16
2853 9185 7599

Level 17
4014 2308 3455

Level 18
3319 6540 9215

Level 19
3964 5702 7519

Level 20
3275 3622 4919

Level 21
4092 0771 1679

Level 22
3408 2377 9263

Level 23
4053 1539 7567

Level 24
3363 9449 4239

Level 25
3837 0634 3359

Level 26
3163 9615 2764

Level 27
3808 8777 1068

Level 28
3119 6696 7740

Level 29
3936 3845 5228

Level 30
3252 5452 2812

Level 31
3897 4614 1116

Level 32
3208 2533 7788

Level 33
2994 5155 4236

Level 34
3673 9888 9404

Level 35
2944 5155 4236

Level 36
3629 6970 4380

Level 37
3072 0223 8396

Level 38
3762 5728 9452

Level 39
3033 0992 4284

Level 40
3718 2807 4428

Level 41
2817 0087 0076

Level 42
3518 2963 2956

Level 43
2788 8229 7788

Level 44
3474 0044 7932

Level 45
2916 3298 1948

Level 46
3606 8800 3004

Level 47
2877 4066 7836

Level 48
3562 5881 7480

Level 49
3348 5109 0364

Level 50
4028 3236 9596

Level 51
3298 8503 4428

SOUTH PARK

Access Cheat Mode
During gameplay, press Escape, select Options and click in the lower left corner.

Big Enemy Heads
Enable Cheat mode and type EGOTRIP.

God Mode
Enable Cheat mode and type BEEFCAKE.

All Weapons and Unlimited Ammo
Enable Cheat mode and type SWEET.

Show Frame Rate
Enable Cheat mode and type FRAMERATE.

All Cheats Enabled
Enable Cheat mode and type BOBBYBIRD.

SPAWN

Boss Code
At the main menu, type GIMMEJIM.

First-Person View
At the main menu, type VIRTUAL1.

Big Heads
At the main menu, type FUNNYHEADS.

Special Moves (# Keys)
At the main menu, type LIFEISUNFAIR.

SPEED BUSTERS

Unlimited Nitro
At the beginning of a race, type fulofit.

Chopper View
At the beginning of a race, type choperview.

Arcade Mode Checkpoints Off
At the beginning of a race, type notimelim.

Bumped Racers Get Sent Back to Start
At the beginning of a race, type tagkiller.

Poor Ctrl
At the beginning of a race, type blackice.

No Brakes
At the beginning of a race, type crazyedie.

All Cars
At the beginning of a race, type hwy69.

SPELLCROSS

Reset Troops Action Points
At the Battle screen, type againagain.

Increase Funds by 100
At the Upgrade, Research, etc., screens, type cashiup.

SPORTS CAR GT

Access Cheat Mode
At the main menu, type isi-cheeseman.

GT3 League
Enable Cheat mode and type isi-plague.

Access All Tracks and Vehicles
Enable Cheat mode and type isi tbone.

Awards Credits
Enable Cheat mode and type isi-aardvark.

All Car Parts to Maximum
Enable Cheat mode and isi-corsica.

KittyCat Mode
Enable Cheat mode and isi-delicate.

STAR TREK: ARMADA

Skip to Next Mission
During gameplay, press Enter and type kobayashimaru.

Increases Money
During gameplay, press Enter and type showmethemoney.

Chat List in Multiplayer Mode
During gameplay, press Enter and type phonehome.

Boot List in Multiplayer Mode
During gameplay, press Enter and type screwyouguysimgoinghome.

Activate Limited AI Over Your Ships
During gameplay, press Enter and type canofwhoopass.

Enter Gamma Quadrant
During gameplay, press Enter and type imouttastepwithreality.

Faster Ship Production
During gameplay, press Enter and type youstopmecold.

Faster Crew Production
During gameplay, press Enter and type avoidance.

STAR TREK: AWAY TEAM

Type cheater during gameplay to enable Cheat mode. Then type one of the following codes:

Heal Your Team
medic

Win Mission
iwin

STAR TREK: BIRTH OF THE FEDERATION

Access Cheat Mode
Start the game with the command line parameter -Mudd.

Add 100 Percent to Overall Research
During gameplay, enable Cheat mode and press F9.

10,000 Credits
During gameplay, enable Cheat mode and press F10.

Reveal Map On/Off
During gameplay, enable Cheat mode and press F11.

STAR TREK: BORG

Previous Scene
BORG

Next Screen
OBEY

Selects Optimal Answer
HUGH

STAR TREK: HIDDEN EVIL

Unlimited Health
During gameplay, type kirk.

Skip Level
During gameplay, type spock.

Add Hypospray to Inventory
During gameplay, type bones.

All Keys and Passcards
During gameplay, type scotty.

STAR WARS: DARK FORCES

All Items, Weapons, Ammo
lamaxout

Disable Height Checks
lapogo

Display Coordinates
ladata

Enemies Freeze When Killed
laredlite

Five AP Mines
labrady

Full Inventory
launlock

Full Map
lacds

Insects
labbug

Invincibility
laimlame

Level 1
lasecbase

Level 2
lataley

Level 3
lasewers

Level 4
latestbase

Level 5
lagromas

Level 6
ladtention

Level 7
laremshed

Level 8
larobotics

Level 9
lanarshada

Level 10
lajabship

Level 11
laimpcity

Level 12
lafuelstat

Level 13
aexecuter

Level 14
laarc

Restore Health and Shields
lapostal

Skip Level
laskip

Supercharge Weapons
larandy

STAR WARS: EPISODE 1—THE BATTLE OF NABOO

Go to Options/Passcodes and use the codes from the list (you hear a short click if the cheat is accepted).

All Regular Levels
GPAYQWAJ

All Regular and Bonus Levels
JHGNRGAS

Dark Side Level
FMRYLDAD

Development Team Photo
EOWXZGAS

Show Credits
DIWMZIAR

Advanced Shields
HRDTOKIL

AAT Tank (Some Levels)
RQORACAQ

Art Gallery in Show Room
JOBXXFAI

Concert Hall in Show Room
RECTVBAH

Dark Side Bonus Level
FMRYLDAD

Double Secondary Weapon
UYCZNCAX

Expert Mode
CXSJMIAA

Guided Missiles
ABVUSEAY

Infinite Lives
LFZWKXAA

Sith Infiltrator (Some Levels)
FRBPTDAY

Swamp Speeder (Some Levels)
XFIIYBAY

All Naboo Side Ships
NIZWAGAO

STAR WARS: EPISODE 1—THE PHANTOM MENACE

#3 Weapon Fires Tank Rounds
Press Backspace, type happy, and press Enter.

60 Frames Per Second
Press Backspace, type 60fps, and press Enter.

All Weapons
Press Backspace, type i like to cheat, and press Enter.

Big Jawas on Mos Espa
Press Backspace, type turn tables, and press Enter.

Darth Maul's Force Push
Press Backspace, type but i feel so good, and press Enter.

Deflect Blaster Shots Perfectly
Press Backspace, type perfection, and press Enter.

Display Credits
Press Backspace, type gurshick, and press Enter.

Drain All Health
Press Backspace, type kill me now, and press Enter.

Full Health
Press Backspace, type heal it up, and press Enter.

Letterbox Mode
Press Backspace, type beyond cinema, and press Enter.

Lower Difficulty
Press Backspace, type i stink, and press Enter.

Over-Shoulder Camera
Press Backspace, type naughty naughty, and press Enter.

Play as Captain Panaka
Press Backspace, type iampanaka, and press Enter.

Play as Obi-Wan
Press Backspace, type iamobi, and press Enter.

Play as Qui-Gon Jinn
Press Backspace, type iamquigon, and press Enter.

Play as the Queen
Press Backspace, type iamqueen, and press Enter.

Raise Difficulty
Press Backspace, type i rule the world, and press Enter.

Super Slowmo Mode
Press Backspace, type slowmo, and press Enter.

Top View Camera
Press Backspace, type from above, and press Enter.

Wireframe Mode (Level Models)
Press Backspace, type perf, and press Enter.

Wireframe Mode (Menus)
Press Backspace, type rex, and press Enter.

Wobble Version
Press Backspace, type drop a beat, and press Enter.

STAR WARS: FORCE COMMANDER

All Missions
Start a new game with the character name "TheWorldIsYours," then double-click on it to access all missions.

Extra Command Points
With version 1.1, start a new game with the character name "TheGalaxyIsYours," then press M in the game to get 500 command points.

Special Troops
You must have the version 1.1 patch in order for this to work. Create a new file called "TheGalaxyIsYours" (case-sensitive)! Enter any mission (even a skirmish) and press Ctrl+0 and at the bottom of the screen. The screen will read "stormtrooper." Press up or down until you find the unit you want. Then press left to get what you chose.

Get 999,999 for Selected Unit
Press Num Lock+Keypad *.

STAR WARS: GALACTIC BATTLEGROUNDS

Activate Cheat Mode
Press Enter during gameplay to display the chat window. Enter one of the following codes to activate the corresponding cheat function.

1000 Food
forcefood

1000 Ore
forceore

1000 Carbon
forcecarbon

1000 Nova Crystals
forcenova

Remove Fog of War
forcesight

Full Map
forceexplore

Instant Construction and Research
forcebuild

Destroy Indicated Enemy
darkside<1-8>

Destroy All Enemies
tarkin

Win Mission
skywalker

Killer Ewok
simonsays

Press Comma for Invisible Naval Ship (Screen Must Be over Water when Activated)
forceboat

Speed Boat with Increased Firepower (Screen Must Be over Water when Activated)
scaryneighbor

Hear Star Wars Quote
<1-58>

STAR WARS: GALACTIC BATTLEGROUNDS: THE CLONE CAMPAIGNS

Activate Cheat Mode
Press Enter during gameplay to display the chat window. Enter one of the following codes to activate the corresponding cheat function.

1000 Food
forcefood

1000 Ore
forceore

1000 Carbon
forcecarbon

1000 Nova Crystals
forcenova

Remove Fog of War
forcesight

Full Map
forceexplore

Instant Construction and Research
forcebuild

Destroy Indicated Enemy
darkside<1-8>

Destroy All Enemies
tarkin

Win Mission
skywalker

Killer Ewok
simonsays

Imperial Star Destroyer
imperial entanglements

Death Star
that's no moon

Corellian Corvette
tantive iv

Press Comma for Invisible Naval Ship (Screen Must Be over Water when Activated)
forceboat

Speed Boat with Increased Firepower (Screen Must Be over Water when Activated)
scaryneighbor

Hear Star Wars Quote
<1-58>

STAR WARS: JEDI KNIGHT: DARK FORCES 2

All Force Powers
traccoonking

All Items
twamprat

All Weapons
tred5

Dark Jedi
tsithlord

Disable AI
twhite flag on

Disable God Mode
tjediwannabe off

Enable AI
twhite flag off

End Current Level
tthereisnotry

Flight Mode
teriamjh

Full Health
tbactame

Full Mana
tyodajammies

God Mode
tjediwannabe on

Level Skip
tdeeznuts

Light Master
timayoda

Normal Speed
tslowmo off

Reveal Map
t5858lvr

Slow Motion
tslowmo on

Upside-Down Mode
tiamthebestjedi

Warp to Level Number
tpinotnoir # (Replace # with desired number.)

STAR WARS: JEDI KNIGHT II: JEDI OUTCAST

Activate Cheat Mode
Press Shift + ~ during gameplay to display the console window. Type helpusobi 1 or devmapall to enable cheat mode. Then, enter one of the following codes at the console window to activate the corresponding cheat function.

God Mode
god

No Clipping Mode
noclip

Disable Enemy AI
notarget

Suicide
kill

All Weapons, Maximum Health, and Armor
give all

Full Health
give health

Full Armor
give armor

Full Ammunition
give ammo

All Weapons
give weapons

Spawn Indicated Weapon
give weaponnum <weapon number>

Spawn Seeker Drone
give item_seeker

Spawn Indicated NPC
npc spawn <character name>

Level Select
map <level name>

Spawn Indicated Item
spawn or give <item name>

Drive AT-ST in Third-Person View
drive_atst

Destroy All AT-STs
use atst_death

Set Game Speed; 1 Is Default, 0.5 Is Half Speed, 2 Is Double Speed
timescale <number>

Crash Game
fly_xwing

999 Health
undying

Cut Off People's Heads, Legs, and Arms
/g_saberrealisticcombat <1-20>

Use Force Heal Ability
force_heal

Set Skill Level; 0 Is the Easiest
g_spskill <0-2>

Fourth Lightsaber Move; Dessan's Stance
setforce 500

Tavion's Lightsaber Moves; Change Lightsaber Style to Blue and Choose the First One
setforceall 600

Tweak Force Ability
setforceall 1138

Desann's Strong Red Lightsaber Style
setsaberoffense 4

Tavion's Fast Yellow Lightsaber Style
Setsaberoffense 5

Max Payne-Style Bullettime
thereisnospoon

Kill All NPCs
npc kill all

Kill Indicated NPC Group
npc kill team <NPC team name>

Kill Selected NPC
npc kill <NPC target name>

Show Number of Kills per NPC
npc score <NPC target name>

Quit Game
quit

Kyle Taunts
taunt

Kyle Does Victory Pose
victory

Holster Weapon
weapon

Reveal where Indicated Entity Is Located
where <classname>

Full Force Bar
give force

Full inventory
give inventory

Full Battery Bar
give batteries

All Weapons
give weapons

Control Any Ally that Is Following You
control <NPC name>

List Commands

NAV STAR WARS: JEDI KNIGHT– MYSTERIES OF THE SITH

All Force Powers
tiamagod

All Weapons
tdiediedie

Disable AI
tstatuesque 0

Display Full Map
tcartograph

Enable AI
tstatuesque 1

Flight Mode
tfreebird

Force Level Up
ttrainme

Free Mana
ttrixie

Full Inventory
tgimmestuff

Invincibility Off
tboinga off

Invincibility On
tboinga on

Level Skip
tgameover

Normal Speed
tgospeedso 1

Slow Motion
tgospeedso 0

STAR WARS: REBEL ASSAULT

Easy Mode Level 02
BOSSK

Easy Mode Level 03
ENGRET

Easy Mode Level 04
RALRRA

Easy Mode Level 05
FRIJA

Easy Mode Level 06
LAFRA

Easy Mode Level 07
DERLIN

Easy Mode Level 08
MOTLOK

Easy Mode Level 09
MORAG

Easy Mode Level 10
TANTISS

Easy Mode Level 11
OSWAFL

Easy Mode Level 12
KLAATY

Easy Mode Level 13
IRENEZ

Easy Mode Level 14
LIANNA

Easy Mode Level 15
PAKKA

Easy Mode Level End
MALANI

Normal Mode 02
BOTHAN

Normal Mode 03
HERGLIC

Normal Mode 04
LEENI

Normal Mode 05
THRAWN

Normal Mode 06
LWYLL

Normal Mode 07
MAZZIC

Normal Mode 08
JULPA

Normal Mode 09
MORRT

Normal Mode 10
MUFTAK

Normal Mode 11
RASKAR

Normal Mode 12
JHOFF

Normal Mode 13
ITHOR

Normal Mode 14
UMWAK

Normal Mode 15
ORLOK

Normal Mode End
NKLLON

Hard Mode Level 02
BORDOK

Hard Mode Level 03
SKYNX

Hard Mode Level 04
DEFEL

Hard Mode Level 05
JEDGAR

Hard Mode Level 06
MADINE

Hard Mode Level 07
TARKIN

Hard Mode Level 08
MOTHMA

Hard Mode Level 09
GLAYYD

Hard Mode Level 10
OTTEGA

Hard Mode Level 11
RISHII

Hard Mode Level 12
IRZINA

Hard Mode Level 13
KARRDE

Hard Mode Level 14
VONZEL

Hard Mode Level 15
OSSUS

Hard Mode Level End
NORVAL

View End Sequence
ORGANA

STAR WARS: REBEL ASSAULT II

Computer Plays (Yoda Mode)
Alt+P

Dark Side Mode
Press Alt+V in Yoda Mode and type JOINME.

Debug Mode (Dark Side Mode)
Alt+D

Extra Life (Force Mode)
Alt+E

Force Mode
Press Alt+V, type LETGO, and press Escape.

Hidden Cutscene
Hold down A+C+T at the end of level 12, after killing the last stormtrooper, and until the elevator shuts.

Increase/Decrease Damage (Force Mode)
Press + or -.

Beginner Level 01
jabba

Beginner Level 02
endor

Beginner Level 03
lachton

Beginner Level 04
borsk

Beginner Level 05
kroyies

Beginner Level 06
auril

Beginner Level 07
kampl

Beginner Level 08
ferrier

Beginner Level 09
galia

Beginner Level 10
denarii

Beginner Level 11
sadow

Beginner Level 12
onderon

Beginner Level 13
aleema

Beginner Level 14
cathar

Expert Level 01
anakin

Expert Level 02
kenobi

Expert Level 03
fortuna

Expert Level 04
modon

Expert Level 05
ommin

Expert Level 06
rekkon

Expert Level 07
shazeen

Expert Level 08
kiirium

Expert Level 09
gundark

Expert Level 10
dianoga

Expert Level 11
atuarre

Expert Level 12
essada

Expert Level 13
paploo

Expert Level 14
nashtah

Expert Level 15
pestage

Level Skip (Yoda Mode)
Alt+J

Screenshot (Dark Side Mode)
Alt+C

Super Pilot (Dark Side Mode)
Alt+S

Unlimited Lives (Force Mode)
Alt+L

View Cutscenes (Yoda Mode)
Alt+M

Yoda Mode
Activate Force Mode, press Alt+V and type ISNOTRY.

STAR WARS: ROGUE SQUADRON

Enable Force Feedback
Type LEIAWRKOUT as password in Settings screen.

Expert Mode
Type ACE as password in Settings screen.

Free Technology Upgrades
Type TOUGHGUY as password in Settings screen.

Infinite Lives
Type IAMDOLLY as password in Settings screen.

Play as AT-ST
Type CHICKEN as password in Settings screen.

Sound Test
Type MAESTRO as password in Settings screen. Access "Concert Hall" under High Scores.

View All Cutscenes
Type DIRECTOR as password in Settings screen. Access "At the Movies" under High Scores.

View Credits
Type CREDITS as password in Settings screen.

STAR WARS: SHADOWS OF THE EMPIRE

Ctrl AT-ST Walker
Hold down 4+6+8 on first level and press Tab until view switches to AT-ST.

Level Select
Hold each letter pair for one second: R+U, N+O, T+T, W+I, T+H, X+I, Z+O, R+S.

STARCRAFT

Any Structure Can Be Built
Press Enter, type modify the phase variance, and press Enter.

Build Units Beyond Supply Limit
Press Enter, type food for thought, and press Enter.

Disable Fog of War
Press Enter, type war aint what it used to be, and press Enter.

Faster Building
Press Enter, type operation cwal, and press Enter.

Free Minerals
Press Enter, type whats mine is mine, and press Enter.

Free Minerals and Vespene
Press Enter, type show me the money, and press Enter.

Free Vespene
Press Enter, type breathe deep, and press Enter.

All Available Upgrades
Press Enter, type something for nothing, and press Enter.

Free Upgrades for Units
Press Enter, type medieval man, and press Enter.

God Mode
Press Enter, type power overwhelming, and press Enter.

Keep Playing After Victory
Press Enter, type staying alive, and press Enter.

Lose Mission
Press Enter, type game over man, and press Enter.

Show Entire Map
Press Enter, type black sheep wall, and press Enter.

Skip to Any Mission
Press Enter, type ophelia, and press Enter. Then type the mission you wish to skip to and press Enter. The mission name is the race followed by a number, e.g. terran1, or zerg1, or protoss1.

Use Special Abilities with No Energy Cost
Press Enter, type the gathering, and press Enter.

Win the Mission
Press Enter, type there is no cow level, and press Enter.

STARCRAFT: BROOD WAR

Any Structure Can Be Built
Press Enter, type modify the phase variance, and press Enter.

Build Units Beyond Supply Limit
Press Enter, type food for thought, and press Enter.

Disable Fog of War
Press Enter, type war aint what it used to be, and press Enter.

Faster Building
Press Enter, type operation cwal, and press Enter.

Free Minerals
Press Enter, type whats mine is mine, and press Enter.

Free Minerals and Vespene
Press Enter, type show me the money, and press Enter.

Free Vespene
Press Enter, type breathe deep, and press Enter.

All Available Upgrades
Press Enter, type something for nothing, and press Enter.

Free Upgrades for Units
Press Enter, type medieval man, and press Enter.

God Mode
Press Enter, type power overwhelming, and press Enter.

Keep Playing After Victory
Press Enter, type staying alive, and press Enter.

Lose the Mission
Press Enter, type game over man, and press Enter.

Show Entire Map
Press Enter, type black sheep wall, and press Enter.

Skip to Any Mission
Press Enter, type ophelia, and press Enter. Then type the mission you wish to skip to and press Enter. The mission name is the race followed by a number, e.g. terran1, or zerg1, or protoss1.

Use Special Abilities with No Energy Cost
Press Enter, type the gathering, and press Enter.

Win the Mission
Press Enter, type there is no cow level, and press Enter.

Zerg Theme Song
This code only works if you are playing as the Zerg race. Press Enter, type radio free zerg, and press Enter.

STREET WARS: CONSTRUCTOR UNDERWORLD

Buy Workers Anytime
When selecting your team color, type worker928.

Pickup Enemy Beacons
When selecting your team color, type pickup036.

Buy Weapons for Gangsters
When selecting your team color, type weapons563.

Select Tenants Anytime
When selecting your team color, type tenants458.

Borrow Any Amount from Bank
When selecting your team color, type loans458.

Buy an Estate Without Conditions
When selecting your team color, type estates216.

Choose Any Mission
When selecting your team color, type maps029.

Select Any Building
When selecting your team color, type houses426.

Buildings Appear Directly
When selecting your team color, type build830.

Work on House Immediately
When selecting your team color, type upgrade934.

Speed Up Network Games
When selecting your team color, type speed364.

STREETS OF SIM CITY

Full Ammo
In Player's Choice, press Ctrl+Alt+X and type lock and load.

$999,999
In Player's Choice, press Ctrl+Alt+X and type sampo.

Repair Damage
In Player's Choice, press Ctrl+Alt+X and type im back.

Invincibility
In Player's Choice, press Ctrl+Alt+X and type mr fabulous.

Jupiter Gravity
In Player's Choice, press Ctrl+Alt+X and type jupiter.

Earth Gravity
In Player's Choice, press Ctrl+Alt+X and type earth.

Mars Gravity
In Player's Choice, press Ctrl+Alt+X and type mars.

Moon Gravity
In Player's Choice, press Ctrl+Alt+X and type moon.

Enable Cruise Ctrl
In Player's Choice, press Ctrl+Alt+X and type cruise control.

Display Cow Frags in Scenario Progress Window
In Player's Choice, press Ctrl+Alt+X and type cow frags.

All Weapons and Mods
In Player's Choice, press Ctrl+Alt+X and type beefcake beefcake.

SUBMARINE TITANS

Reveal Map
During gameplay, press Enter and type FOW.

All Techs
During gameplay, press Enter and type TECH.

Full Energy
During gameplay, press Enter and type ENERGY.

Full Air
During gameplay, press Enter and type AIR.

Full Silicon
During gameplay, press Enter and type SILICON.

Metal +1,000
During gameplay, press Enter and type METAL.

Gold +1,000
During gameplay, press Enter and type GOLD.

Corium +5,000
During gameplay, press Enter and type CORIUM.

Gold +1,000, Corium +5,000, Metal +1,0000
During gameplay, press Enter and type EXITON.

SUDDEN STRIKE

Press Enter during gameplay, then type in the code:

Spaceships Replace Bombers
starcraft

Invincibility
superman

Reveal Map
nofog

Hide Map
staticfog

THE SUM OF ALL FEARS

Activate Cheat Mode
Press Keypad Enter during gameplay, then type one of the following codes to activate the corresponding cheat function.

Invisibility for Character
shadow

Invincibility for Team
teamshadow

God Mode for Character
superman

God Mode for Team
teamsuperman

Unlimited Ammunition
ammo

Refill Ammunition
refill

Run Faster
run

Suicide
god

SUMMONER

Eliminate Casting Time
Right after casting a spell, go to the Inventory screen. When you return to the game, the spell instantly takes effect. Use this trick if you need to get off a spell immediately.

Dungeons & Dragons Spoof
At the main menu choose to view the credits and then press X. You are taken to a hilarious animated skit of a few of the characters from Summoner playing *Dungeons & Dragons*.

SWAT 3: CLOSE QUARTERS BATTLE

Complete All Objectives, Win Current Mission
During gameplay, press ~ to access the console and type iamleet.

Slows Entire Game Process
During gameplay, press ~ to access the console and type johnwoo.

God Mode For Entire Team
During gameplay, press ~ to access the console and type swatlord.

Unlimited Ammo
During gameplay, press ~ to access the console and type biggerpockets.

Team Missing Pants and Shirts
During gameplay, press ~ to access the console and type casual.

Fire Weapon Faster
During gameplay, press ~ to access the console and type doubleshot.

Bodies Bleed More When Injured
During gameplay, press ~ to access the console and type nc17.

Night Missions Play as If During the Day
During gameplay, press ~ to access the console and type noshades.

Teammates Fire Weapons
During gameplay, press ~ to access the console and type whosyourboss.

Suspects Are Harder to Kill
During gameplay, press ~ to access the console and type hotstuff.

Suspects Never Surrender
During gameplay, press ~ to access the console and type justin.

Killer Rats (When Shot)
During gameplay, press ~ to access the console and type rabies.

AI Becomes Smarter
Press Shift and ~ during play to bring up the command menu. Type HOTSTUFF and press enter to activate the cheat. To exit from the menu, press Esc.

AI Never Surrenders
Press Shift and ~ during play to bring up the command menu. Type JUSTIN and press enter to activate the cheat. To exit from the menu, press Esc.

Faster Rate of Fire
Press Shift and ~ during play to bring up the command menu. Type DOUBLESHOT and press enter to activate the cheat. To exit from the menu, press Esc.

God Mode
Press Shift and ~ during play to bring up the command menu. Type SWATLORD and press enter to activate the cheat. To exit from the menu, press Esc.

Infinite Ammo
Press Shift and ~ during play to bring up the command menu. Type BIGGERPOCKETS and press enter to activate the cheat. To exit from the menu, press Esc.

More Blood
Press Shift and ~ during play to bring up the command menu. Type NC17 and press enter to activate the cheat. To exit from the menu, press Esc.

Night Missions Become Day
Press Shift and ~ during play to bring up the command menu. Type NOSHADES and press enter to activate the cheat. To exit from the menu, press Esc.

Plain Clothes
Press Shift and ~ during play to bring up the command menu. Type CASUAL and press enter to activate the cheat. To exit from the menu, press Esc.

Rats Become Rabid When Shot
Press Shift and ~ during play to bring up the command menu. Type RABIES and press enter to activate the cheat. To exit from the menu, press Esc.

Slow Mo
Press Shift and ~ during play to bring up the command menu. Type JOHNWOO and press enter to activate the cheat. To exit from the menu, press Esc.

Win Mission
Press Shift and ~ during play to bring up the command menu. Type IAMLEET and press enter to activate the cheat. To exit from the menu, press Esc.

SYSTEM SHOCK 2

Full Psi Points
During gameplay, press : and type psi_full.

Turn Player into Homo Superior
During gameplay, press : and type ubermensch.

Give Player Additional Build Pool Points
During gameplay, press : and type add_pool.

Display Version in Game Mode
During gameplay, press : and type show_version.

Toggle Inv Panel
During gameplay, press : and type toggle_inv.

Cycle Through Available Ammo Types
During gameplay, press : and type cycle_ammo.

Toggle Compass State
During gameplay, press : and type toggle_compass.

Query Cursor 1 = On 0 = Off
During gameplay, press : and type query.

Split Cursor 1 = On 0 = Off
During gameplay, press : and type split.

Jump the Player
During gameplay, press : and type shock_jump_player.

Put Cursor into Look Mode
During gameplay, press : and type look_cursor.

Reload Weapon Out of Inventory
During gameplay, press : and type reload_gun.

Switch Primary and Secondary Weapons
During gameplay, press : and type swap_guns.

Toggle Weapon Settings
During gameplay, press : and type wpn_setting_toggle.

Bring up Psi Power Selection MFD
During gameplay, press : and type select_psipower.

Search Inventory for Weapon and Equip It
During gameplay, press : and type equip_weapon.

Cycle to Next Equippable Weapon, 1 for Forward, -1 for Back
During gameplay, press : and type cycle_weapon.

Acts Like the 1 to 5 Level Buttons
During gameplay, press : and type psi_power.

Open an MFD by Overlay Constant
During gameplay, press : and type open_mfd.

Stop Any Currently Playing Email/Log
During gameplay, press : and type stop_email.

Clear Any Existing Teleport Marker
During gameplay, press : and type clear_teleport.

Bind a Quick Slot
During gameplay, press : and type quickbind.

Activate a Quick Slot
During gameplay, press : and type quickuse.

Use an Object By Name
During gameplay, press : and type use_obj.

Toggle Message History
During gameplay, press : and type msg_history.

Play an Unread Log
During gameplay, press : and type play_unread_log.

Switch Between Mouselook and Cursor Modes
During gameplay, press : and type toggle_mouse.

Switch Between Modes, Frobbing Current Selection
During gameplay, press : and type frob_toggle.

Simple Frob of Selected Object
During gameplay, press : and type frob_object.

Simple Frob of Selected Object, in World or Inventory
During gameplay, press : and type frob_object_inv.

Use an Item
During gameplay, press : and type interface_use.

Fire Weapon 1=Start 0=Finish
During gameplay, press : and type fire_weapon.

Drag and Drop 1=Start 0=Finish
During gameplay, press : and type drag_and_drop.

Drag and Drop 1=Start 0=Finish
During gameplay, press : and type drag_and_drop_frob.

Drag and Drop 1=Start 0=Finish
During gameplay, press : and type drag_and_drop_mode.

Save to Current Subdirectory
During gameplay, press : and type quicksave.

Load from Current Subdirectory
During gameplay, press : and type quickload.

TACHYON: THE FRINGE

Access Cheat Mode
During gameplay, press 7 on the keypad to bring up the command window. Then type IM A CHEATER.

Add 5,000 Credits
Enable Cheat mode and type ONE MILLION DOLLARS.

God Mode
Enable Cheat mode and type QUICKENING.

Full Ammo
Enable Cheat mode and type COME GET SOME.

Full Energy
Enable Cheat mode and type DILITHIUM.

Return to Starbase to Win
Enable Cheat mode and type THERE IS NO SPOON.

All Items Available
Enable Cheat mode and type BOOM STICK.

All Ships Available
Enable Cheat mode and type RAGTAG.

Enhance Ship
Enable Cheat mode and type KESSEL RUN.

TACTICAL OPS: ASSAULT ON TERROR

Activate Cheat Mode
Press ~ to display the console, then enter iamtheone to enable cheat mode. Then, enter one of the following codes at the console to activate the corresponding cheat function.

God Mode
god

Flight Mode
fly

No Clipping Mode
ghost

TARZAN

Skip Level
stlevel

Select Level
ststage

Kill All Unwanted Animals
stanimals

Save Game
stsave

Load Game
stload

Change to Tarzan
sttarzan

Change to Jane
stjane

Brighter Colors
stcolour

TEAM FORTRESS CLASSIC

Get Any Weapon
To get any weapon, the server must type "sv-cheats 1." In battle, go to the console (~) and type "give tf_weapon_???". replace the ??? with the code for the weapon you want:

    auto cannon=ac
    rocket launcher=rl
    grenade launcher=gl
    pipe bomb launcher=pl
    wrench=spammer
    knife=knife
    tranquilizer gun=tranq
    chain gun=ac
    rocket launcher=rpg
    medkit=medikit
    super shotgun=supershotgun
    flamethrower= flamethrower
    railgun=railgun

Gravity
Host your own game and set your console command window as the button ~. Press it and a window comes down. Type sv_gravity ***. Fill in the *** with as many numbers as you want. The normal gravity is 600–700.

Heavy Powered Sniper
Join a game that has a level with a stationary machine game (total war). Join the game as a sniper. Walk to the gun with your sniper gun out, gain control of the machine gun, and sniper in. your accuracy will be a lot better with this cheat.

TERMINAL VELOCITY

Invincibility
TRIGODS

Shield Restore
TRISHLD

Power Up All Weapons
3DREALM

Skip to Next Level
TRINEXT

Warp to Level
TRWARP# (Replace # with the desired level.)

Hover While Firing
TRIHOVR

Speed Up Afterburner
TRIBURN

1,000 Afterburner Ammo
MANIACS

Oscilloscope
TRSCOPE

FPS Ticker
TRFRAME

Temporary Invincibility
TRIFIR0

PAC Ammo
TRIFIR1

ION Ammo
TRIFIR2

RTL Ammo
TRIFIR3

MAM Ammo
TRIFIR4

SAD Ammo
TRIFIR5

SWT Ammo
TRIFIR6

DAM Ammo
TRIFIR7

200 Afterburner Ammo
TRIFIR8

Temporary Invisibility
TRIFIR9

TEST DRIVE 4

No AI Racers in LAN Game
Enter NOAICARS in Slot 10 on the Save Game screen, then press Enter. You may use multiple codes.

No 3D Collisions
Enter STICKIER in Slot 10 on the Save Game screen, then press Enter. You may use multiple codes.

All Collisions Off
Enter AARDVARK in Slot 10 on the Save Game screen, then press Enter. You may use multiple codes.

No Special Effects (3Dfx Version Only)
Enter ITSLATE in Slot 10 on the Save Game screen, then press Enter. You may use multiple codes.

Show Credits with Cool Pics
Enter CREDITZ in Slot 10 on the Save Game screen, then press Enter. You may use multiple codes.

Unlock All Cars
Enter SRACLLA in Slot 10 on the Save Game screen, then press Enter. You may use multiple codes.

Unlock All Tracks
Enter LEVELLLA in Slot 10 on the Save Game screen, then press Enter. You may use multiple codes.

Test Drive on Acid
Enter SPAZZY in Slot 10 on the Save Game screen, then press Enter. You may use multiple codes.

Black and White Mode
Enter BANDW in Slot 10 on the Save Game screen, then press Enter. You may use multiple codes.

Big Cars
Enter MIKTROUT in Slot 10 on the Save Game screen, then press Enter. You may use multiple codes.

Mini Cars
Enter MPALMER in Slot 10 on the Save Game screen, then press Enter. You may use multiple codes.

Fast Forward Mode
Enter GONZON in Slot 10 on the Save Game screen, then press Enter. You may use multiple codes.

FF Mode Off
Enter GONZOFF in Slot 10 on the Save Game screen, then press Enter. You may use multiple codes.

View from Above
Enter BIRDVIEW in Slot 10 on the Save Game screen, then press Enter. You may use multiple codes.

Nitro Boost with Horn Button
Enter NITROyyy in Slot 10 on the Save Game screen, then press Enter. You may use multiple codes.

Extra Credits
Enter BOBCRED in Slot 10 on the Save Game screen, then press Enter. You may use multiple codes.

Return to Color Screen
Enter COLOUR in Slot 10 on the Save Game screen, then press Enter. You may use multiple codes.

TEST DRIVE 5

Unlock All Cup Races
At the Options menu, type cup of choice.

Backward Mode
At the Options menu, type that takes me back.

Unlock All Cars and Tracks
At the Options menu, type i have the key.

Drive Police Cars
At the Options menu, type i carry a badge.

Nitro (Press Horn)
At the Options menu, type lone crusader in a dangerous world.

Freeze Opponents (Press Horn)
At the Options menu, type remote braking.

Reverse Tracks
Have a fast enough time to get on the High Score table, then type knacked.

Nitros (Press Horn)
Have a fast enough time to get on the High Score table, then type whoooosh.

Tiny Cars
Have a fast enough time to get on the High Score table, then type mjcim.rc.

Bonus Cars
Have a fast enough time to get on the High Score table, then type sausage.

TEST DRIVE 6

$6 Million
Type your name as AKJGQ.

All Cars
Type your name as DFGY.

All Tracks
Type your name as ERDRTH.

All Quick Race Tracks
Type your name as CVCVBM.

No Quick Race Tracks
Type your name as OCVCVBM.

Shorter Tracks
Type your name as QTFHYF.

All Challenges
Type your name as OPIOP.

No Challenges
Type your name as OPOIOP.

Disable Checkpoint Times
Type your name as FFOEMIT.

Enable Checkpoint Times
Type your name as NOEMIT.

Stop the Bomber Mode
Type your name as RFGTR.

Honda Bike
Type your name as Honda XR.

TEST DRIVE OFFROAD 3

All Cheat Options and Vehicles
Enter the name ZAKARY X.

THEME PARK

$500,000 Cash
Enter the HORZA to enable Cheat mode, then during gameplay, press C.

Get All Rides
Enter the HORZA to enable Cheat mode, then during gameplay, press Alt+Z.

Get All Shops
Enter the HORZA to enable Cheat mode, then during gameplay, press Ctrl+Z.

Get All Facilities
Enter the HORZA to enable Cheat mode, then during gameplay, press Shift+Z.

Ultimate Theme Park
Enter the name DEMO.

THIEF 2: THE METAL AGE

Level Skip
During gameplay, press Ctrl+Alt+Shift+End.

THIEF GOLD

Level Skip
During gameplay, press Ctrl+Alt+Shift+End.

THIEF: THE DARK PROJECT

Level Skip
During gameplay, press Ctrl+Alt+Shift+End.

TIMELINE

God Mode
During gameplay, press ~ and type GOD. You will be vulnerable until you are down to 10 health points. Then your health will hold at 10, and you can't be killed.

THRUST, TWIST, & TURN

All Tracks and Shadow Tracks
Start the game with the command-line parameter -accs.

TNN OUTDOORS PRO HUNTER

Get 10-Point Buck
During gameplay, press ~ and type DEER.

Get Turkey
During gameplay, press ~ and type TOM.

God Mode
During gameplay, press ~ and type GOD.

Flight Mode
During gameplay, press ~ and type FLY.

Walk Through Walls
During gameplay, press ~ and type GHOST.

Unlimited Ammo
During gameplay, press ~ and type ALLAMMO.

TOCA: TOURING CAR CHAMPIONSHIP 2

Make Things Hazy
Type the name TOPDOWN to enable Cheat mode. Then type your name as HANGOVER.

Other Cars Move Out of Your Way
Type the name TOPDOWN to enable Cheat mode. Then type your name as REPEL.

All Tracks
Type the name TOPDOWN to enable Cheat mode. Then type your name as DOUBLE.

All Cars
Type the name TOPDOWN to enable Cheat mode. Then type your name as CARTASTIC.

Battle Mode
Type the name TOPDOWN to enable Cheat mode. Then type your name as OUCH.

Bouncy Crashes
Type the name TOPDOWN to enable Cheat mode. Then type your name as RUBBER.

Silly Crashes
Type the name TOPDOWN to enable Cheat mode. Then type your name as MOVIE.

Low Gravity
Type the name TOPDOWN to enable Cheat mode. Then type your name as HIGHJUMP.

Blurred Horizon
Type the name TOPDOWN to enable Cheat mode. Then type your name as HANGOVER.

Wheels Only View
Type the name TOPDOWN to enable Cheat mode. Then type your name as SKINNY.

Double Speed, Brake, and Grip
Type the name TOPDOWN to enable Cheat mode. Then type your name as SKATES.

Higher Decors and Walls, Side of Road Higher, Narrower Roads, and Shortcomings Amplified

Type the name TOPDOWN to enable Cheat mode. Then type your name as GIRDLE.

Full Championship Distances

Type the name TOPDOWN to enable Cheat mode. Then type your name as TIMEOUT.

Unlock Extra Track

Type the name TOPDOWN to enable Cheat mode. Then type your name as ECKLOCK.

Turbo On

Type the name TOPDOWN to enable Cheat mode. Then type your name as FASTBOY.

Micro Machines Mode

Type the name TOPDOWN to enable Cheat mode. Then type your name as MINICARS.

Psychedelic Mode

Type the name TOPDOWN to enable Cheat mode. Then type your name as TRIPPY.

No Season Kick-Out

Type the name TOPDOWN to enable Cheat mode. Then type your name as POSHKID.

TOM CLANCY'S SSN

Access Cheat Mode

During gameplay, press B, type CISCO SEZ, and press Enter.

Targeted Ship or Sub Becomes Ally

Enable Cheat mode, press B, and type BE MY BUDDY.

Turn Sub Around

Enable Cheat mode, press B, and type FLIP HER.

Sub Flies Like a Blimp

Enable Cheat mode, press B, and type ZEPPLIN.

Stop Sub

Enable Cheat mode, press B, and type DROP ANCHOR.

Fix Sub

Enable Cheat mode, press B, and type HEAL ME.

Change Torpedo

Enable Cheat mode, press B, and type EAT LEAD.

Explode Targeted Object

Enable Cheat mode, press B, and type BOOM.

Improve Sonar

Enable Cheat mode, press B, and type SEE THEM.

Hide Sub from Enemy Sonar

Enable Cheat mode, press B, and type ENGAGE CLOAKING DEVICE.

TOMB RAIDER I

All Weapons

Step forward, step backward (using Shift), turn around three times to the left, jump backward.

Extra Ammo

Step forward, step backward (using Shift), turn around three times to the left, flip backward.

Level Skip

Step forward, step backward (using Shift), turn around three times to the left, jump forward.

TOMB RAIDER II

All Weapons

Take out flare, step forward, step backward (holding walk key), turn around three times, jump backward.

Exploding Lara

Take out any weapon, step forward, step backward (holding walk key), turn around three times, jump backward.

Level Skip

Take out flare, step forward, step backward (using Shift), turn around three times, jump forward.

TOMB RAIDER III

All Weapons

Take out pistols, step back, step forward, crouch, stand, turn around three times, jump backward.

Level Skip

Take out pistols, step back, step forward, crouch, stand, turn around three times, jump forward.

TOMB RAIDER: THE LAST REVELATION

All Items

Turn Lara exactly north according to her compass. Confirm this by checking the inventory screen: If the red portion is transparent, then Lara is facing north. Enter the Inventory screen and highlight the Small Medipack. Press and hold G+U+N+S.

All Weapons

Enable the All Items code first. Turn Lara exactly north, go to the inventory screen and highlight the Large Medipack. Press and hold W+E+A+P+O+N+S.

TOMB RAIDER CHRONICLES

For the following cheats you MUST be facing ABSOULTE NORTH.

Level Skip

Go to the Inventory screen and then, to load game, press and hold L+I+F+T.

All Weapons

Go to the Inventory screen, then to the large medipak, and press and hold C+T+R+L, in sequence.

All Items

Go to the Inventory screen, then to the small medipak, and press and hold A+L+T+G+R, in sequence.

God Mode

Go to the Inventory screen, then to the flares, and press and hold F+I+R+E, in sequence.

TONY HAWK'S PRO SKATER 2

All Cheats

Pause the game and hold 7 on the numpad, then press Spacebar (3), C, V, Up, Down, Left, Up, C, V, Spacebar, V, B, Spacebar, V, B.

Thin Skater

Pause the game and hold 7 on the numpad, then press Spacebar (4), C, Spacebar (4), C, Spacebar (4), C.

Neversoft Skaters

At the main menu, hold 7 on the numpad and press Up, C (2), V, Right, Up, B, V. Now create a skater and give him a name of a Neversoft Dev Team member.

Special Meter Always Full

Pause the game and hold 7 on the numpad, then press Spacebar, V, B (2), Up, Left, V, C.

Raise Stats to 10

Pause the game and hold 7 on the numpad, then press Spacebar, V, B, C, V, Up, Down.

Turbo Mode

Pause the game and hold 7 on the numpad, then press Down, C, V, Right, Up, B, Down, C, V, Right, Up, B.

Fat Skater

Pause the game and hold 7 on the numpad, then press Spacebar (4), Left, Spacebar (4), Left, Spacebar (4), Left.

Big Head Mode

Pause the game and hold 7 on the numpad, then press C, B, Up, Left (2), C, Right, Up, Left.

Blood Mode

Pause the game and hold 7 on the numpad, then press Right, Up, C, V.

TOTAL ANNIHILATION

Gain 1,000 Energy and Metal
+ATM

Turn on CD Music Player
+CDSTART

Enable In-Game Clock
+CLOCK

3D Game Contours
+CONTOUR # (Replace # with a number from 1 to 15.)

Ctrl Different Enemy AI
+CONTROL #

Dithering
+DITHER

Double Weapon Damage
+DOUBLESHOT

Half Weapon Damage
+HALFSHOT

You Lose
+ILOSE

You Win
+IWIN

Kill Player
+KILL #

Remove All Energy
+NOENERGY

Remove All Metal
+NOMETAL

Stop Screen Shaking (Very Useful)
+NOSHAKE

See Entire Map
+NOWISEE

100 Percent Radar Coverage
+RADAR

Units Sing Responses
+SING

Toggle Squad Selection to Alt+# Keys
+SWITCHALT

Show Another Player's Resources
+VIEW #

Enable All Missions from Single-Player Screen
DRDEATH

Toggle 3D Antialiasing
+ANTIALIAS

Units Respond Differently
+BIGBROTHER

TOTAL ANNIHILATION: KINGDOMS

Instant 5,000 Mana
+ATM

Double Weapon Damage
+DOUBLESHOT

Half Weapon Damage
+HALFSHOT

Toggle On/Off LOS
+LOS

See Entire Map
+NOWISEE

Toggles On/Off Full Radar
+RADAR

Computer Cycles Through Units
+BIGBROTHER

See Playing Time
+CLOCK

Show 3D Contour Lines
+CONTOUR #

Change Fog Color on RGB Scale
+FOGCOLOR ### (replace # with a number from 1 to 256)

Toggle On/Off Full Screen Radar
+FSR

Change Lighting Rendering
+LIGHTRANGE # (replace # with a number from 1 to 20)

Change Your Race's Color
+LOGO # (replace # with a number from 1 to 9)

Add Blood
+LOTSABLOOD

Create Enormous Game Screenshot (Slow)
+MAKEPOSTER

Rename Selected unit
+NAMEUNIT [name]

Toggle On/Off the On-Screen Score Card
+NETSCORECARD

Toggle Fog to Speed Game (3D Only)
+ROLLINGFOG

Send Selected Unit(s) out of Your Command
+SELFDESTRUCT

Toggle On/Off Shadows
+SHADOWS

Toggle On/Off Splattering Blood
+SHOWBLOOD

Show Area Effect Damage Radii (Hold Shift)
+SHOWRANGES

Units Sing
+SING

Try It Yourself
+SING JERSEY

Toggle On/Off Unit Damage Bars
+TOGGLEDAMAGEBARS

Keep Selected Unit in Screen Center
+TRACKUNIT

Toggle Wavy Fog to Speed Game (3D Only)
+WACKYFOG

Toggle Wavy Water to Speed Game (3D Only)
+WACKYWATER

TOY STORY

Level Select
At the Opening screen, when "Press Start" appears, type abracadabra.

TRESPASSER

Jump High, Run Slow
During gameplay, press Ctrl+F11 and type BIONICWOMAN.

God Mode
During gameplay, press Ctrl+F11 and type INVUL.

Location
During gameplay, press Ctrl+F11 and type LOC.

Enhance Blood
During gameplay, press Ctrl+F11 and type GORE 2.

Freeze Dinosaurs
During gameplay, press Ctrl+F11 and type DINOS.

Unlimited Ammo
During gameplay, press Ctrl+F11 and type WOO.

Transport to Important Locations
During gameplay, press Ctrl+F11 and type TNEXT.

Ending Movie
During gameplay, press Ctrl+F11 and type WIN.

TRIBAL RAGE

Reveal Map
During gameplay, press Shift+Ctrl+R.

Auto Victory
During gameplay, press Shift+Ctrl+V.

Add 1,000 Credits
During gameplay, press Shift+Ctrl+Z.

TRICKSTYLE

Always Win
At the Options screen, select "Cheats," and enter TEAROUND.

Win Everything
At the Options screen, select "Cheats," and enter CITYBEACONS.

Never Run Out of Time
At the Options screen, select "Cheats," and enter IWISH.

Power-Up Moves
At the Options screen, select "Cheats," and enter TRAVOLTA.

Big Head Mode
At the Options screen, select "Cheats," and enter INFLATEDEGO.

TRIPLE PLAY '97

Cornfield
At the Stadium Select screen, press Up, Down, Right, Up, Down, Left, Up.

Mystery Stadium
At the Stadium Select screen, press Right, Left, Up, Left, Down, Right, Left.

TROPICO

Hold down the Ctrl key and type:

+10 Happiness
contento

+ $20,000
pesos

Faster Building
rapido

TUROK 2: SEEDS OF EVIL

Big Hands and Feet Mode
TROMPEM

Big Head Mode
BIGBADNOODLE

Stick Mode
HELLOSTICKY

Tiny Mode
LILLIPUTIAN

Pen and Ink mode
PICASSO

Gouraud Mode
HENRYSBILERP

Juans Cheat
YOQUIEROJUAN

Do Nothing
MRNOPRULEZ

Zach Attack Cheat
LEGOMANIAC

Blackout Mode
INEEDAUPS

MMMM.. Tasty Frooty Stripes
WIZARDOFOZ

Big Cheat
OBLIVIONISOUTTHERE

Janes Cheat
JANESSPECIALWORLD

TZAR: BURDEN OF THE CROWN

Access Cheat Mode
During gameplay, press Enter and type HMPRETTYPLEASEWITHSUGARONTOP.

God Mode for Currently Selected Unit
Enable Cheat mode and type HMGOD.

Show Entire Map
Enable Cheat mode and type HMREVEAL.

Remove Fog of War
Enable Cheat mode and type HMNOFOG.

50,000 for All Resources
Enable Cheat mode and type HMPETLEVA.

10,000 for All Resources
Enable Cheat mode and type HMDVALEVA.

The Ultimate Code Book: Book of Secrets

Show Timer
Enable Cheat mode and type HMTIMER.

Fast Build
Enable Cheat mode and type HMBUILDOZER.

Lose Ctrl of Main Buildings
Enable Cheat mode and type HMUSURP.

Buildings/Units Don't Depend on Upgrades
Enable Cheat mode and type HMNOTECH.

Selected Unit Becomes Part of Player X's Unit
Enable Cheat mode and type HMKINGDOM # (replace # with a number from 1 to 9).

Spawn Any Unit
Enable Cheat mode and type HMSPAWN.

Population Limit Increased to 1,000
Enable Cheat mode and type HMNOPOP.

Lose the Game
Enable Cheat mode and type HMRESIGN.

UNCHARTED WATERS 2: NEW HORIZONS

No Pirate Will Attack
Name yourself Black Beard.

UNREAL

Access Cheat Mode
During gameplay, press Tab. Then enter one of the following codes.

Add More Bots
Enable Cheat mode and type ADDBOTS # (replace # with the number of bots wanted).

All Weapons
Enable Cheat mode and type LOADED.

Ammo
Enable Cheat mode and type ALLAMMO.

Broadcast Message
Enable Cheat mode and type SAY [text] (replace [text] with desired message).

Deathmatch Map: Radikus
Enable Cheat mode and type OPEN DmRadikus.

Deathmatch Map: Tundra
Enable Cheat mode and type OPEN DmTundra.

Deathmatch Map: Night Op
Enable Cheat mode and type OPEN DkNightOp.

Deathmatch Map: Fith
Enable Cheat mode and type OPEN DmFith.

Deathmatch Map: Heal Pod
Enable Cheat mode and type OPEN DmHealPod.

Deathmatch Map: Morbias
Enable Cheat mode and type OPEN DmMorbias.

Deathmatch Map: Death Fan
Enable Cheat mode and type OPEN DmDeathFan.

Deathmatch Map: Deck 16
Enable Cheat mode and type OPEN DmDeck16.

Deathmatch Map: El Sinore
Enable Cheat mode and type OPEN DmElSinore.

Deathmatch Map: Ariza
Enable Cheat mode and type OPEN DmAriza.

Deathmatch Map: Curse
Enable Cheat mode and type OPEN DmCurse.

Disable Flight Mode
Enable Cheat mode and type WALK.

Enable Clipping
Enable Cheat mode and type WALK.

Fix Garbled Graphics
Enable Cheat mode and type FLUSH.

Flight Mode
Enable Cheat mode and type FLY.

Freeze Players
Enable Cheat mode and type PLAYERSONLY.

God Mode
Enable Cheat mode and type GOD.

Immune to Drowning
Enable Cheat mode and type AMPHIBIOUS.

Kill All Enemies
Enable Cheat mode and type KILLPAWNS.

Kill All Indicated Enemies
Enable Cheat mode and type KILLALL [actor] (replace [actor] with character class or race).

Local Machines Map 01: Vortex Riders
Enable Cheat mode and type OPEN Vortex2.

Local Machines Map 02: Nyleve's Falls
Enable Cheat mode and type OPEN NyLeve.

Local Machines Map 03: Skaaj Mine of Rrajigar
Enable Cheat mode and type OPEN Dig.

Local Machines Map 04: Depths of Rrajigar
Enable Cheat mode and type OPEN Dug.

Local Machines Map 05: Sacred Passage
Enable Cheat mode and type OPEN Passage.

Local Machines Map 06: Chizra Nali Water God Temple
Enable Cheat mode and type OPEN Chizra.

Local Machines Map 07: Ceremony
Enable Cheat mode and type OPEN Ceremony.

Local Machines Map 08: Dark Arena
Enable Cheat mode and type OPEN Dark.

Local Machines Map 09: Harobed Village
Enable Cheat mode and type OPEN Harobed.

Local Machines Map 10: Terraniux Underground
Enable Cheat mode and type OPEN TerraLift.

Local Machines Map 11: Terraniux
Enable Cheat mode and type OPEN Terraniux.

Local Machines Map 12: Noork's Elbow
Enable Cheat mode and type OPEN Noork.

Local Machines Map 13: Temple of Vandora
Enable Cheat mode and type OPEN Ruins.

Local Machines Map 14: Trench
Enable Cheat mode and type OPEN Trench.

Local Machines Map 15: ISV Kran Deck 4
Enable Cheat mode and type OPEN IsvKran4.

Local Machines Map 16: ISV Kran Decks 3 and 2
Enable Cheat mode and type OPEN IsvKran32.

Local Machines Map 17: ISV Kran Deck 1
Enable Cheat mode and type OPEN IsvDeck1.

Local Machines Map 18: Spire Village
Enable Cheat mode and type OPEN SpireVillage.

Local Machines Map 19: The Sunspire
Enable Cheat mode and type OPEN TheSunspire.

Local Machines Map 20: Gateway to Na Pali
Enable Cheat mode and type OPEN SkyCaves.

Local Machines Map 21: Na Pali Heaven
Enable Cheat mode and type OPEN SkyTown.

Local Machines Map 22: Outpost 3J (Mountain Forest)
Enable Cheat mode and type OPEN SkyBase.

Local Machines Map 23: Velora Pass (Sleeping Giant)
Enable Cheat mode and type OPEN VeloraEnd.

Local Machines Map 24: Bluff Eversmoking
Enable Cheat mode and type OPEN Bluff.

Local Machines Map 25: Dasa Mountain Pass
Enable Cheat mode and type OPEN DasaPass.

Local Machines Map 26: Cellars at Dasa Pass
Enable Cheat mode and type OPEN DasaCellars.

Local Machines Map 27: Nali Castle Canyon
Enable Cheat mode and type OPEN NaliBoat.

Local Machines Map 28: Nali Castle
Enable Cheat mode and type OPEN NaliC.

Local Machines Map 29: Nali Castle Warlord
Enable Cheat mode and type OPEN NaliLord.

Local Machines Map 30: D Crater
Enable Cheat mode and type OPEN Dcrater.

Local Machines Map 31: Mothership Basement
Enable Cheat mode and type OPEN ExtremeBeg.

Local Machines Map 32: Mothership Lab
Enable Cheat mode and type OPEN ExtremeLab.

Local Machines Map 33: Mothership Core
Enable Cheat mode and type OPEN ExtremeCore.

Local Machines Map 34: Skaarj Generator
Enable Cheat mode and type OPEN ExtremeGen.

Local Machines Map 35: Illumination
Enable Cheat mode and type OPEN ExtremeDGen.

Local Machines Map 36: The Darkening
Enable Cheat mode and type OPEN ExtremeDark.

Local Machines Map 37: The Source Antechamber
Enable Cheat mode and type OPEN ExtremeEnd.

Local Machines Map 38: The Source
Enable Cheat mode and type OPEN QueenEnd.

Local Machines Map 39: End Game
Enable Cheat mode and type OPEN EndGame.

No Clipping
Enable Cheat mode and type GHOST.

Play Dead
Enable Cheat mode and type FEIGNDEATH.

Set Field of Vision
Enable Cheat mode and type FOV # (replace # with desired angle).

Set Game Speed
Enable Cheat mode and type SLOMO # (replace # with speed from 1 to 10).

Show Network Sockets
Enable Cheat mode and type SOCKETS.

Spawn Object
Enable Cheat mode and type SUMMON UNREALI.object (replace object with interactive item to be spawned).

Third-Person Perspective
Enable Cheat mode and type BEHINDVIEW1.

UNREAL TOURNAMENT

Access Cheat Mode (1P)
Press ~ and type iamtheone. Then type one of the following codes.

Add More Bots
Enable Cheat mode and type ADDBOTS # (replace # with the number of bots wanted).

All Weapons
Enable Cheat mode and type LOADED.

Ammo
Enable Cheat mode and type ALLAMMO.

Broadcast Message
Enable Cheat mode and type SAY [text] (replace [text] with desired message).

Disable Flight Mode
Enable Cheat mode and type WALK.

Enable Clipping
Enable Cheat mode and type WALK.

Fix Garbled Graphics
Enable Cheat mode and type FLUSH.

Flight Mode
Enable Cheat mode and type FLY.

Freeze Players
Enable Cheat mode and type PLAYERSONLY.

God Mode
Enable Cheat mode and type GOD.

Kill All Enemies
Enable Cheat mode and type KILLPAWNS.

Kill All Indicated Enemies
Enable Cheat mode and type KILLALL [actor] (replace [actor] with character class or race).

No Clipping
Enable Cheat mode and type GHOST.

Set Game Speed
Enable Cheat mode and type SLOMO # (replace # with a speed from 1 to 10).

Spawn Object
Enable Cheat mode and type SUMMON UNREALI.object (replace object with interactive item to be spawned).

Third-Person Perspective
Enable Cheat mode and type BEHINDVIEW1.

UPRISING

Invincibility
During gameplay, press M, type CHUMP, then press Enter.

Unlimited Weapons
During gameplay, press M, type DANGEROUS, then press Enter.

Super Weapons
During gameplay, press M, type TUFF ASS, then press Enter.

Super Speed, Invincibility (Enable Invincibility First)
During gameplay, press M, type CHUMP, then press Enter.

Unlimited Weapons, Invincibility (Enable Invincibility First)
During gameplay, press M, type DANGEROUS, then press Enter.

Super Weapons, Invincibility (Enable Invincibility First)
During gameplay, press M, type TUFF, then press Enter.

Unlimited Weapons, Super Speed, Invincibility (Enable Unlimited Weapons, Invincibility First)
During gameplay, press M, type DANGEROUS, then press Enter.

Unlimited Weapons, Super Weapons, Super Speed, Invincibility (Enable Unlimited Weapons, Super Speed, Invincibility First)
During gameplay, press M, type TUFF ASS, then press Enter.

UPRISING 2

Invincibility
During gameplay, press M and type CHUMP, then press Enter.

Unlimited Weapons
During gameplay, press M and type DANGEROUS, then press Enter.

Super Weapons
During gameplay, press M and type TUFF ASS, then press Enter.

Super Speed, Invincibility
During gameplay, press M and type CHUMP, then press Enter.

Unlimited Weapons, Invincibility
During gameplay, press M and type DANGEROUS CHUMP, then press Enter.

Rainy Weather
During gameplay, press M and type STORMY, then press Enter.

Increase Money by 5,000
During gameplay, press M and type WAY MO MONEY, then press Enter.

Die
During gameplay, press M and type SLICK, then press Enter.

Win Scenario
During gameplay, press M and type DONE, then press Enter.

Invincible
During gameplay, press M and type YOYO, then press Enter.

Clear Weather
During gameplay, press M and type CLEARSKY, then press Enter.

Snow
During gameplay, press M and type FLURRY, then press Enter.

URBAN ASSAULT

New Vehicle and Bonus Weapon
During gameplay, hold Shift and type SWEAPON.

URBAN CHAOS

Access Cheat Mode
During gameplay, press F9 and type BANGUNSNOTGAMES to enable cheats and become invulnerable.

Cluster of Explosions
Enable Cheat mode, press F9, and type BOO.

Turn Crinkles on/off
Enable Cheat mode, press F9, and type CRINKLES.

Ctrl Officer D'Arci
Enable Cheat mode, press F9, and type DARCI.

Ctrl Roper
Enable Cheat mode, press F9, and type ROPER.

Set Fog Fade Level
Enable Cheat mode, press F9, and type FADE # (replace # with any number).

Select Music
Enable Cheat mode, press F9, and type WORLD.

Set Ambient Light
Enable Cheat mode, press F9, and type AMBIENT # # # (replace # with values for R,G,B).

Win the Level
Enable Cheat mode, press F9, and type WIN.

Lose the Level
Enable Cheat mode, press F9, and type LOSE.

Turn Everything Fluorescent Green
Enable Cheat mode, press F9, and type CCTV.

Go to Important Game Point
Enable Cheat mode, press F9, and type TELW # (replace # with game point number).

Save Waypoint on Map
Enable Cheat mode, press F9, and type TELS.

Return to Saved Waypoint
Enable Cheat mode, press F9, and type TELR.

Show Car Paths
Press Q.

Make Rain Ripples
Press W.

Make Random Vehicle
Press E.

Make Explosive Barrel
Press R.

Show Pedestrian Walking Areas
Press I.

Toggle Enemy View
Press [.

Toggle Enemy View
Press].

Enemy View On/Off
Press P.

Slow Motion
Press ;.

Pause Action
Press '.

Fart Smoke
Press >.

Stealth Debug
Press /.

Show Statistics
Press Ctrl.

Move Forward 10 Feet or Onto Ledge
Press G.

Coordinate Grids Show
Press J.

Create Light
Press L.

Clouds On/Off
Press F11.

Create Game Weapons
Press F12.

Exit Game
Press F3.

Select Game Effect
Press Keypad 7.

Execute Game Effect
Press Keypad 5.

Weird Orange Fog
Press Keypad 3.

VAMPIRE: THE MASQUERADE-REDEMPTION

Access Cheat Mode
Start the game with the command line parameter -console. Then during gameplay, press ~ for the console and type one of the following codes.

God Mode
Enable Cheat mode and type god 0/1 (1 = God mode on, 0 = God mode off).

Change Cash Amount
Enable Cheat mode and type cash # (replace # with the desired amount).

Drop Cash Amount
Enable Cheat mode and type dropcash # (replace # with the desired amount).

Add to XP
Enable Cheat mode and type xp # (replace # with the desired amount).

Cast Disciplines Without Blood
Enable Cheat mode and type freecasting 0/1 (1 = On, 0 = Off).

Turn Off AI for Enemy and Your Party
Enable Cheat mode and type ai.

Increases All Disciplines
Enable Cheat mode and type addalldisciplines # (replace # with the desired amount).

Full Health (Can Be Done After Death)
Enable Cheat mode and type revive.

Open Personal Vault from Anywhere
Enable Cheat mode and type vault.

No Need for Ammo
Enable Cheat mode and type freeammo.

Stake Self
Enable Cheat mode and type stakme.

True Death (Revive Cannot Bring Back)
Enable Cheat mode and type killme.

List Scene Info (XP, Gold, Etc.)
Enable Cheat mode and type totals.

Spawn Item
Enable Cheat mode and type addthing # (replace # with an item, such as Vitae, Dagger, etc.).

Bring Up Advancement Window
Enable Cheat mode and type advancement.

Framerate
Enable Cheat mode and type framerate 0/1 (1 = Show, 0 = Off).

Poison Self
Enable Cheat mode and type poisonme.

Disease Self
Enable Cheat mode and type diseaseme.

Damage Self
Enable Cheat mode and type damage me.

Location Stats
Enable Cheat mode and type whereis.

Put Christof into Frenzy
Enable Cheat mode and type frenzyme.

Set Maximum FPS
Enable Cheat mode and type maxfps # (replace # with a number).

Shapeshift
Enable Cheat mode and type shapeshift # (replace # with a creature, such as bat).

Shapeshift Back to Normal
Enable Cheat mode and type shapeshift.

Freeze Body
Enable Cheat mode and type freeze. You can still move around the level.

Pause Action
Enable Cheat mode and type pause.

Resume Action
Enable Cheat mode and type resume.

Emit Something from Character's Feet
Enable Cheat mode and type emit # (replace # with an item, such as gas or fire).

VANGERS

Money
During gameplay, type bolshedeneg.

All Locks Open
During gameplay, type hochutuda.

Increased Luck
During gameplay, type udacha.

Increased Dominance
During gameplay, type avtoritet.

VENOM WING

Infinite Lives
At the Thalamus logo, type IDJ.

VENUS

Level 2
Mantids

Level 3
Cicadas

Level 4
Psyllids

Level 5
Pierids

Level 6
Satyrid

Level 7
Lycaenid

Level 8
Pyralid

Level 9
Noctuid

Infinite Time
JUPITER

Infinite Ammo
PLUTO

All Weapons
MARS

Constant Flying Ability
MERCURY

VIETNAM BLACK OPS

God Mode
During gameplay, press T for the console and type god.

No Clipping Mode
During gameplay, press T for the console and type noclip.

All Weapons
During gameplay, press T for the console and type weapons.

All Ammo
During gameplay, press T for the console and type ammo.

Remove Enemy
During gameplay, press T for the console and type removeai.

Easy Mode
During gameplay, press T for the console and type easy.

Normal Mode
During gameplay, press T for the console and type normal.

Hard Mode
During gameplay, press T for the console and type hard.

VIGILANCE

God Mode with Unlimited Ammo
During gameplay, press Enter and type *cheat.

Show Player's Current Action
During gameplay, press Enter and type *state.

Show Credits
During gameplay, press Enter and type *thunderdome.

Show Frames Per Second
During gameplay, press Enter and type *fps.

Show MAX Frames Per Second
During gameplay, press Enter and type *maxfps.

Commit Suicide
During gameplay, press Enter and type *suicide.

Show Current Coordinates
During gameplay, press Enter and type *coords.

Ctrl Enemy
During gameplay, press Enter and type *other.

Walk Through Walls
During gameplay, press Enter and type *ghost.

Freeze Hit Points
During gameplay, press Enter and type *freeze.

Show Message
During gameplay, press Enter and type *HoneyBunny.

VIGILANTE

Extra Lives
At the Scroe screen, type GREEN CRYSTAL, then press F1.

Skip Levels
At the Scroe screen, type GREEN CRYSTAL, then press F8.

VIPER RACING

Drive Lamborghini
In Options, choose "Hacks," then type Morepowerthebetter.

VIRTUA FIGHTER 2

Play as Dural
Highlight Akira and press Down, Up, Right, Left, A.

Play as Gold Dural
At the Fighter Selection screen, press Down, Up, Left, Guard/Kick, Right, but not too fast.

Play as Silver Dural
At the Fighter Selection screen, press Down, Up, Right, Guard/Kick, Left, but not too fast.

VIRUS 2000

Activate All Cheats
During gameplay, type CHEATSEQ.

Weapons
During gameplay, type HHROQTAT.

Repair
During gameplay, type CCHASERQ.

Level Skip
During gameplay, type TERHSRER.

Complete Current Level
During gameplay, type HERHSORE.

Complete All Levels
During gameplay, type QHEROEST.

Cargo
During gameplay, type HTARSREC.

VR POWERBOAT RACING

Small Boat Mode
Type your name as SML.

Big Head Mode
Type your name as BIG.

Big Engine Mode
Type your name as POW.

Auto Pilot
Type your name as BAA.

Always Win
Type your name as WIN.

Catamarans (Minnow)
Type the password FAN.

Catamarans (Pike)
Type the password DIP.

Catamarans (Barracuda)
Type the password URN.

Championship Mode
Type the password EPS.

Slalom
Type the password PBR.

Hidden Track
Type the password PDL.

Fast Boats
Type the password BIF.

Slow Boats
Type the password BAD.

WAR GAMES

Extra Zoom Level on Lower Level Machines
During gameplay in single-player mode, press T and type eyeofgod.

Choose Level
During gameplay in single-player mode, press T and type saladtossed, then exit current game. Press Ctrl+W for WOPR or Ctrl+H for Human and click load game.

Build Unit
During gameplay in single-player mode, press T and type twobyfour x (replace x with the desired unit).

Build Units Faster
During gameplay in single-player mode, press T and type hermes.

Shoot Jeeps Instead of Missiles
During gameplay in single-player mode, press T and type donkeys.

Removes Fog of War
During gameplay in single-player mode, press T and type morningafter.

Build Everything, Even Without Command Center
During gameplay in single-player mode, press T and type gimmiegimmie.

God Mode
During gameplay in single-player mode, press T and type unclejohn.

Add 10,000 Cash
During gameplay in single-player mode, press T and type chaching. Repeat until desired amount is reached.

Upgrade Player's Armor
During gameplay in single-player mode, press T and type mrmuscle.

Downgrade Enemy Armor
During gameplay in single-player mode, press T and type bigsofty.

Upgrade Player's Speed
During gameplay in single-player mode, press T and type coffee.

Downgrade Enemy Speed
During gameplay in single-player mode, press T and type beer.

Upgrade Player's Firepower
During gameplay in single-player mode, press T and type shaft.

Downgrade Enemy's Firepower
During gameplay in single-player mode, press T and type shank.

WAR GODS

Free Play On
Go to the Advanced options and type 2504.

Player 1 Invincible
Go to the Advanced options and type 1971.

Player 2 Invincible
Go to the Advanced options and type 1515.

Finish Game After First Round
Go to the Advanced options and type 4774.

Play as Grox
Go to the Advanced options and type 3871.

Play as Exor
Go to the Advanced options and type 9021.

Secret Level
Go to the Advanced options and type 9997.

Easy Fatalities
Go to the Advanced options and type 1037.

WAR OF THE WORLDS

All Research
When at the Battle or War map, type ICOMEBACK.

Purge All Martians
When at the Battle map, type ATCHOOO.

Purge All Humans
When at the Battle map, type PUNYHUMANS.

Efficiency to 100 Percent
When at the Battle map, type YOULIKEIT.

WARCRAFT

Gain 10,000 Gold, 5,000 Lumber
Pot of Gold

All Spells
Eye of Newt

All Units Invincible (1P)
Type Corwin of Amber, then type there can be only one.

Entire Map
Sally Shears

Faster Game
Type CHRONUS and press +.

Final Sequence (1P)
Type Corwin of Amber, then type ides of march.

Loss Sequence (1P)
Type Corwin of Amber, then type crushing defeat.

Speed Up Building
Hurry up Guys

Update Technology
Iron Forge

Victory Sequence (1P)
Type Corwin of Amber, then type yours truly.

Warp to Level (1P Human)
Type Corwin of Amber, then type human# (replace number with desired level).

Warp to Level (1P Orc)
Type Corwin of Amber, then type orc# (replace number with desired level).

WARCRAFT 2: BATTLE.NET EDITION

All Weapon/Armor Upgrades
During single-player gameplay, type Deck me out.

All Spell Upgrades
During single-player gameplay, type Every little thing she does.

Increase Resources
During single-player gameplay, type Glittering prizes.

Cut Down Trees with Two Chops
During single-player gameplay, type Hatchet.

Make Your Units Ultra-Powerful
During single-player gameplay, type It is a good day to die.

Speed Building and Unit Production
During single-player gameplay, type Make it so.

Show Entire Map
During single-player gameplay, type On screen.

Go to Campaign Victory Sequence
During single-player gameplay, type There can be only one.

Instantly Win Scenario
During single-player gameplay, type Unite the clans.

Enable Level Jumping
During single-player gameplay, type Tigerlily.

WARCRAFT II: BEYOND THE DARK PORTAL

Funky Music
Press Enter and type disco.

WARCRAFT II: TIDES OF DARKNESS

"Go Bruins" Display
ucla

5,000 Oil
valdez

Allow Surrender (MP)
allowsync

Demo Start Faster
fastdemo

Disable Magical Traps
noglues

Display "Fief"
day

Display Network Performance
netprof

Enable/Disable Cheats (MP)
title

Fast Build
make it so

God Mode
it is a good day to die

Instant Defeat
you pitiful worm

Level Skip
unite the clans

More Gold, Lumber, Oil
glittering prizes

Quick Ending
there can be only one

Quicker Lumber Harvest
hatchet

Remove Victory Sequence
never a winner

Reveal Map (1P)
showpath

Reveal Map (MP)
on screen

Upgrade Everything
deck me out

Upgrade Mages
every little thing she does

Warp to Level #
tigerlily # (Replace # with the desired level.)

WARGASM

Level 2
TOAST

Level 3
BUTTIES

Level 4
KEBAB

Level 5
GATEAUX

WARLORDS: BATTLECRY

God Mode
During gameplay, type IAMATANK.

Reveal Map
During gameplay, type IAMASEER.

Lose Scenario
During gameplay, type IAMALOSER.

Win Scenario
During gameplay, type IAMAWINNER.

All Spells
During gameplay, type IAMANARCHMAGE.

WARTORN

Show Enemy Buildings and Vehicles
During gameplay, press C and type debugcheatshowenemy=1, then press Enter.

Fast Build For Vehicles
During gameplay, press C and type debugcheatfastbuild=1, then press Enter.

WARZONE 2100

Stop/Start Mission Timer
During gameplay, press T and type time toggle.

Kill All Enemy Units on Map
During gameplay, press T and type get off my land.

Get 1,000 Extra Power
During gameplay, press T and type show me the power.

Infinite Power
During gameplay, press T and type whale fin.

Skip to Next Mission
During gameplay, press T and type hallo mein schatz.

Complete All Currently Active Research Topics
During gameplay, press T and type work harder.

All Your Units Become Twice as Tough
During gameplay, press T and type double up.

Show Framerate and Gfx Engine Data
During gameplay, press T and type timedemo.

Kill Selected Units
During gameplay, press T and type killselected.

Easy Difficulty Level
During gameplay, press T and type easy.

Normal Difficulty Level
During gameplay, press T and type normal.

Hard Difficulty Level
During gameplay, press T and type hard.

Show When Game Code Was Compiled
During gameplay, press T and type version.

Toggle Weather: Snow, Rain, Clear
During gameplay, press T and type john kettley.

Units Almost Indestructible
During gameplay, press T and type biffer baker.

Screen Shakes When Units Explode
During gameplay, press T and type shakey.

Display Game Speed
During gameplay, press T and type how fast.

Stronger Units
During gameplay, press T and type sparkle green.

WCW NITRO

All Wrestlers
At the Character Selection screen, press V (4), Space (4), Q (4), T (4), H.

Big Head Mode
At the Select Mode screen, press V (7), Q, H.

Big Head, Hands, Feet
At the Select Mode screen, press Q (7), V, H.

Instant Win
Highlight a character and press Space, V, T, Q, Space, V, T, Q, H.

Ring Select
At the Options menu, press V, Q, V, Q, H. Press H to advance the ring by one.

Secret Rings
At the main menu, press Space, T, V, Q, Space, T, V, Q, H.

Swelling Head
At the Select Mode screen, press Space (7), T, H.

WET ATTACK

Destroy All Opponent Ships
In the 3D Area, type ARMAGEDDON.

Destroy Opponent Ships with One Hit
In the 3D Area, type BOMBERMAN.

No Pirates Attack
In the 3D Area, type PEACE.

Your Ship Is Invincible
In the 3D Area, type DIFFUSE.

Stops Opponent Ships
In the 3D Area, type FREEZE.

One Million Dollars
In the Adventure Area, type JACKPOT.

Game Runs Faster
In the Adventure Area, type MAKEITFASTER.

Clock Runs 60 Times Faster
In the Adventure Area, type LIKEARABBIT.

WHEEL OF TIME

God Mode
During gameplay, press ~ and type god.

Breathe Underwater
During gameplay, press ~ and type amphibious.

Finish All Levels
During gameplay, press ~ and type completelovol.

All Guns, Ammo
During gameplay, press ~ and type allammo.

Walk Through Walls
During gameplay, press ~ and type ghost.

Fly Mode
During gameplay, press ~ and type fly.

Walk Mode
During gameplay, press ~ and type walk.

View Character from Behind
During gameplay, press ~ and type behindview 1.

Normal View
During gameplay, press ~ and type behindview 0.

Freeze Time, Repeat to Unfreeze
During gameplay, press ~ and type playersonly.

Become Invisible
During gameplay, press ~ and type invisible 1.

Become Visible Again
During gameplay, press ~ and type invisible 0.

Kill All Actors of a Certain Class
During gameplay, press ~ and type killall [class] (replace [class] with the desired class).

Kill All Monsters
During gameplay, press ~ and type killpawns.

Set Gamespeed
During gameplay, press ~ and type slomo # (replace # with the desired speed; 1.0 is normal).

Spawn Actor of the Specified Class
During gameplay, press ~ and type summon [class] (replace [class] with the desired class).

Switch Server to New Level with Coop Style Weapon Carrying
During gameplay, press ~ and type switch-cooplevel [new level] (replace [new level] with the level desired).

Switch to a New Level
During gameplay, press ~ and type switchlevel [new level] (replace [new level] with the level desired).

WHO WANTS TO BE A MILLIONAIRE?

Easier Questions
When Regis asks for your name, don't type anything. He types Kathie Lee. The questions will now be easier.

Harder Questions
To have harder questions, type your name as John Carpenter. You will have harder questions

Make Regis Mad...Method 1
During the fastest finger contest, if nobody answers the question right in a long period of time, Regis gets mad and the game turns off.

Make Regis Mad...Method 2
When Regis asks how many players are playing, do not answer. Regis makes three or four funny comments and the game turns off.

Repeated Questions
To have easier questions, type your name as Regis Philbin. You will have questions you have had before.

WILD WILD WEST: STEEL ASSASSINS

All Weapons
During gameplay, type Kill them All.

WIPEOUT XL

Silly Ships
At the title screen, type RUSH.

Enable Piranha Team
At the main menu, type XTEAM.

Enable Phantom Class
At the main menu, type XCLASS.

All Tracks
At the main menu, type XTRACK.

Infinite Weapons
During gameplay, pause and type PSYMEGA.

Infinite Energy
During gameplay, pause and type PSYPROTECT.

Infinite Time
During gameplay, pause and type PSYTICKER.

Machine Gun
During gameplay, pause and type PSYRAPID.

Display Frame Rate
During gameplay, pause and type FRAMERATE.

WORLD WAR II: G.I.

God Mode
ww2god

All Items
ww2blood

Level Skip
ww2level

FPS
ww2rate

Mad Cow Mode
ww2matt

Show Map
ww2showmap

God Mode
ww2ryan

No Clipping
ww2clip

Debug Mode
ww2debug

X-COM: ENFORCER

Ghost Mode
During gameplay, press ~ to activate a drop-down menu. In dropdown, enter the following code to activate Ghost mode: ghost.

Invulnerability
During gameplay, press ~ to activate a drop-down menu. In dropdown, enter the following code for Invulnerability: xgod.

Learnin' to Fly
During gameplay, press ~ to activate a drop-down menu. In dropdown, enter the following code to Fly: fly.

Level Upgrades
During gameplay press ~ to activate a drop-down menu. In dropdown, enter the following code to bring all levels to upgrade level 1: upgrademe 1 (same works with 2, 3, 4[EM]do "upgrademe 4" to max out everything).

Open All Levels
During gameplay, press ~ to activate a drop-down menu. In dropdown, enter the following code to Open Levels: open map00 (number between 00 and 40).

Beat This Level
During gameplay, press ~ to activate a dropdown menu. In dropdown, enter the following code to activate "Beat This Level" Mode: icandoit.

Return to Normal
During gameplay, press ~ to activate a drop-down menu. In dropdown, enter the following code to return everything to normal: walk.

X-COM: INTERCEPTOR

Enable In-Flight Cheats
During gameplay, press Ctrl+E and listen for the low double beep, then type battlecheat.

Invincibility
During gameplay, press Ctrl+E and listen for the low double beep, then type canttouchthis.

Unlimited Flight Range
During gameplay, press Ctrl+E and listen for the low double beep, then type fillerup.

All Research Is Yours
During gameplay, press Ctrl+E and listen for the low double beep, then type knowitall.

Finish All Bases Under Construction
During gameplay, press Ctrl+E and listen for the low double beep, then type quickbase.

Money
During gameplay, press Ctrl+E and listen for the low double beep, then type payday.

ZERO DEGREE FIGHTER COMBAT

Add Single Enemy
During gameplay, type ADD-MRCRANKY in the console.

Add 10 New Enemies
During gameplay, type ADD-MOB in the console.

Start Writing DEMO File
During gameplay, type DEMOWRITE in the console.

Stop Writing DEMO File
During gameplay, type DEMOSTOP in the console.

Play Demo File
During gameplay, DEMOPLAY in the console.

Add Nuke
During gameplay, IAMBECOMEDEATH in the console.

Add Meson Cannon
During gameplay, type NOHEISENBERG in the console.

Add EMD
During gameplay, type BETTERTHANTESLA in the console.

Add HIVE MISSILES
During gameplay, type ONESHOTONEKILL in the console.

Toggle Autopilot
During gameplay, type TAKETHESTICK in the console.

Show Credits
During gameplay, type CUETHECREDITS in the console.

Set Wuss to Mission Complete
During gameplay, type IMAWUSS in the console.

Toggle Success/Fail State
During gameplay, type IMASISSYCRYBABY in the console.

Toggle Autocannon
During gameplay, type ZEUS-23 in the console.

Add Camouflage
During gameplay, type GO-ME-THE-GHILLIE in the console.

Add Avionics Package
During gameplay, type WHO-DAT-WHO-DAT-HUH in the console.

ZEUS: MASTER OF OLYMPUS

Add 1,000 Coins
During gameplay, press Ctrl+Alt+C and type Delian Treasury.

Win Scenario
During gameplay, press Ctrl+Alt+C and type Ambrosia.

Strike Ground with Fireball
During gameplay, press Ctrl+Alt+C and type Fireballs from Heaven.

Towers Shoot Cows
During gameplay, press Ctrl+Alt+C and type Bowvine and Arrows.

Cheese Suits for Dairy Workers
During gameplay, press Ctrl+Alt+C and type Cheese Puff.

ZEUS OFFICIAL EXPANSION: POSEIDON

Instantly Win Current Episode
Type Ctrl-Alt-C, then Ambrosia.

Adds 1,000 Dr to the Treasury if Your Balance Is Less Than 15,000 Dr
Type Ctrl-Alt-C, then Delian Treasury.

Left-Click to Rain Fireballs on Your City
Type Ctrl-Alt-C, then Fireballs from Heaven.

Tower Guards Shoot Cows at Enemies
Type Ctrl-Alt-C, then Bowvine and Arrows.

Replaces the Usual Cheesemakers with Their Mascot, Wedgie
Type Ctrl-Alt-C, then Cheese Puff.

ZPC

God Mode
During gameplay, hold Ctrl and type TETSUO.

Health
During gameplay, hold Ctrl and type ACK.

PlayStation

NUMBERS

007 RACING

Pre-Mission Replay
Successfully complete the Pre-Mission in less than 90 seconds at Agent level. Player is able to see the pre-mission replay instead of the CG sequence.

Slippery Track
Knock out all 11 fire hydrants on the "Gimme a Brake" Mission at 00 level (you must also complete the mission successfully). All track surfaces are slippery. You will have difficulty controlling your vehicle.

No Radar
Successfully complete "Ambush" with at least 85% health at Agent level. No Radar is present on the HUD during Two-Player gameplay.

Unlock all Missions
Successfully complete the "Highway Hazard" Mission at 00 level without hitting any traffic cars. All Missions are available to play in any order in 00 Agent Mode.

Red Sea
Disable all three tanks on the "Survive the Jungle" Mission at Agent level (you must complete the mission must successfully). All water in the levels turns red.

Funky Missile Trail
All "empty" tents (those not containing power-ups) must still be intact when the level is completed successfully at 00 level. Smoke trails on Hellfires and Stingers are multi-colored, shifting rapidly through several hues.

Crazy Skids
Successfully complete the "Escape" Mission with 100% score at Agent level. Skid marks appear bright green as opposed to their usual black.

Double Health
Successfully complete the "Break Out" Mission with 100% health at 00 level. All Medical kits are worth double their original value: 50 points.

Double Damage
Collect all Nitro and TSP-6060 pickups in the "River Race" Mission, and successfully complete it at Agent level. In Two-Player, any damage inflicted on the opposing player is worth double its original value.

Purple Explosions
Complete the "Download" Mission with a perfect score at 00 level. All explosions in all levels appear purple instead of orange.

Blue Goggles
Successfully complete the "Submerged" Mission with 100% health at Agent level. The security cameras in Mission 8 "Break Out" (usually green) and the IRGoggles in Mission 11 "Submerged" (usually red) are tinted blue.

All Gadgets
Complete the "Showdown" Mission in less than 2:00 at 00 level. All weapons in the game are available in all levels.

Unlock Aston Martin Vantage in 2P
Press the following button combination on the title screen: L1, R1, Triangle, O, X. The Aston Martin Vantage is unlocked for use in Two-Player gameplay.

Unlock Two-Player Arena: Compound
Successfully complete Mission 7 (Escape) in Agent mode. This will unlock the previously-unavailable "Compound" Two-Player track.

Unlock Two-Player Arena: Rooftops
Successfully complete Mission 10 (Download) in 00 Agent mode. This will unlock the previously-unavailable "Rooftops" Two-Player track.

1 ON 1

Play as Oscar and Mash
Start a game in one-player Story mode. Then meet Oscar and Mash.

Play as King
Beat the game with all characters, including Oscar and Mash.

Omake Mode
Beat the game with any character to get three pictures of the character in Omake mode. Omake mode will appear in the main menu.

Basketball Tricks
Press Triangle to control the basketball at the main menu. Continue bouncing the ball to view comments.

Play as Dr. T
Start a game in one-player Story mode. Then meet Dr. T (but remember that Dr. T's appearance is random).

2XTREME

Infinite Energy
Your energy level must be full already. Hold R2 to keep your energy bar full. If you let go, your energy level will start to fall.

Bonus Track
Perform the following code in sequence on any track. Get to the first ramp and perform an easy trick (Square, Triangle). At the second ramp, perform a medium trick (Square, Circle, Triangle). Perform a hard trick (Square, Circle, X) at the third ramp. At the fourth ramp, hit this button sequence: Square, X, Triangle, Circle. Finish the race and the Japan bonus track will load.

Turbo Start
Tuck and press Up when you start a race to start more quickly.

Mountain Bike Special
Use the mountain bike and press X, Square, Triangle, Circle or X, Circle, Square, Triangle to perform a special trick.

Rollerblade Special
Use the rollerblades and press Circle, Square, X, Triangle to perform a special trick.

Skateboard Special
Use the skateboard and press Triangle, X, Square, Circle to perform a special trick.

Snowboard Special
Use the snowboard and press Triangle, Square, X, Circle to perform a special trick.

3XTREME

Unlock All Exhibition Tracks
Highlight "Memory Card" at the main menu. Press Right or Left to access the Codes menu. Enter "VOUYEUR" to unlock the tracks.

Unlock All Freestyle Tracks
Highlight "Memory Card" at the main menu. Press Right or Left to access the Codes menu. Enter "TRIXXY" to unlock the tracks.

Unlock All Alien Characters
Highlight "Memory Card" at the main menu. Press Right or Left to access the Codes menu. Enter "ASTROMEN."

Unlock All the Monsters
Highlight "Memory Card" at the main menu. Press Right or Left to access the Codes menu. Enter "SCREAM."

Unlock All Humans
Highlight "Memory Card" at the main menu. Press Right or Left to access the Codes menu. Enter "RATPACK."

Unlock All Cars
Highlight "Memory Card" at the main menu. Press Right or Left to access the Codes menu. Enter "SMOKEY."

Unlock All Characters
Highlight "Memory Card" at the main menu. Press Right or Left to access the Codes menu. Enter "GENEPOOL."

Play as Dominique
Highlight "Memory Card" at the main menu. Press Right or Left to access the Codes menu. Enter "DOMINIQUE."

Play as Lugnut
Highlight "Memory Card" at the main menu. Press Right or Left to access the Codes menu. Enter "LUGNUT."

Play as TP
Highlight "Memory Card" at the main menu. Press Right or Left to access the Codes menu. Enter "TP."

Play as Bink
Highlight "Memory Card" at the main menu. Press Right or Left to access the Codes menu. Enter "BINK."

Play as Geep
Highlight "Memory Card" at the main menu. Press Right or Left to access the Codes menu. Enter "GEEP."

Play as Nyub
Highlight "Memory Card" at the main menu. Press Right or Left to access the Codes menu. Enter "NYUB."

Play as Red Car
Highlight "Memory Card" at the main menu. Press Right or Left to access the Codes menu. Enter "REDLINE."

Play as Blue Car
Highlight "Memory Card" at the main menu. Press Right or Left to access the Codes menu. Enter "BLUELINE."

Play as Black Car
Highlight "Memory Card" at the main menu. Press Right or Left to access the Codes menu. Enter "BLACKLINE."

Play as White Car
Highlight "Memory Card" at the main menu. Press Right or Left to access the Codes menu. Enter "WHITELINE."

Play as White Car with 99% Stats
Highlight "Memory Card" at the main menu. Press Right or Left to access the Codes menu. Enter "WHITECAR."

Play as Blue Car with 99% Stats
Highlight "Memory Card" at the main menu. Press Right or Left to access the Codes menu. Enter "BLUECAR."

Play as Red Car with 99% Stats
Highlight "Memory Card" at the main menu. Press Right or Left to access the Codes menu. Enter "REDCAR."

Haunted Mansion Track
Beat the Pro Circuit with any character to unlock the Haunted Mansion track in Freestyle mode.

Ultraspank Video
Go to Options in the main menu and press Right, X to check out the Ultraspank video.

3D BASEBALL

Secret Mini-Game
Hold R1+Circle as the game loads. When CDs fly across the screen, press Up, Left, Down, Right. A character will appear at the lower left to tell you the code was entered correctly, and a secret game will appear the next time the game loads something.

40 WINKS

Big Heads
Pause the game. Hold Select and press L1, Up, Right, L2, Up. Release Select. Hold Select and press L1, Up, Right, L2, Up.

Full Cogs
Pause the game. Hold Select and press Down, R2, L1, Up, R2.

Restore Lives
Pause the game. Hold Select and press L1, Up, Right, L2, Up.

Restore Moons
Pause the game. Hold Select and press Up, L2, Left, R2, Left.

Restore Zzz's
Pause the game. Hold Select and press Right, L1, Up, R1, L1.

All Winks
Pause the game at the House Hub. Hold Select and press Left, Down, Right, Right, Right.

All Dream Keys
Pause the game at the House Hub. Hold Select and press Circle, L1, L2, L1, L2.

4TH SUPER ROBOT WARS SCRAMBLE

Reset the Game
Press L1+L2+R1+R2+Select+Start during gameplay to return to the main menu.

70'S ROBOT ANIME GEPPY-X

Star Geppy X
At the title screen, press Down, Left, Left, Down, Down, Right, Right, Triangle.

Wild John Mode
At the title screen, press Up, Down, Right, Up, Down, Right, Up, Triangle.

View FMV Sequences
At the title screen, press Down (2), Left, Down (2), Left, Down, Triangle.

Queen Fairy Mode
At the title screen, press Left, Right, Left, Down (2), Right (2), Triangle.

64/74 Shiki Mode
At the title screen, press Up (2), Down (2), Right, Left, Right, Triangle.

Atlancer Mode
Press Left, Right (2), Down, Left (2), Right, Triangle.

A BUG'S LIFE

99 Lives
In the main menu, hold R1 and press X, O, and L2.

Bonus Level
Complete all training level objectives; then kill all the spiders.

Extra Lives
Collect letters F, L, I, C, and K in the training level. Repeat this as often as you like before resuming a regular game.

A-TRAIN

Infinite Money
In the title screen, press L1+L2+R1+R2. Then press Square+Triangle. Press Start, and then hold down L1+L2+R1+R2 and press Circle.

ACE COMBAT 2

Normal Ending
Make your way to the 19th mission, "Kingpin." Beat the mission without destroying the skilled enemy pilot Z.O.E.

Bad Ending
Make your way to the 19th mission, "Kingpin." Beat the mission and destroy the skilled enemy pilot Z.O.E. At the 20th mission, "Last Resort," don't shoot down the cruise missile and you'll view a different ending.

Bonus Ending
Make your way to the 20th mission, "Last Resort." Shoot down the cruise missile to advance to the 21st level, "Fighter's Honor." Beat that mission to view the bonus ending.

Different Mission Map Views
Place the cursor over "Mission" at the Mission Select screen. Press Select to choose from up to three different viewing angles.

Hidden Level
A new mine level opens when you destroy the C-5 transport on the first Raven level.

Music Test
Beat the game with a rank above First Lieutenant to unlock a Music Player mode in the Options menu. You may play all the game music there. Use the controller buttons to select music.

Pause during Replay
Press and hold Square during a replay to stop the camera.

Free Mission Mode
Beat the game to see the normal or bonus ending. A Free Mission option appears after the opening menu.

Bonus Aircraft
Beat the game to see the normal or bonus ending. Select the new option that appears and you may buy new airplanes when you play another game.

XFA-27 Fighter
Beat the game at Normal difficulty. Then play the game again at Hard difficulty. Make your way to the "Dead End" mission. Destroy the four YF-23As in the special Fox Force Four squadron south of the target to unlock the XFA-27 and a medal at the Debriefing screen.

View 3D Aircrafts
Shoot down all Skilled enemy pilots (planes labeled "Danger" in the Briefing screen) and collect all medals in the Statistics screen. A new option appears in the Options menu that lets you view all the planes you've encountered.

ACE COMBAT 3: ELECTROSPHERE

Unlock Mission 36
Earn a "B" or better in the regular game's 35 missions to unlock the 36th mission.

Japanese Movie
Beat the game at Hard difficulty.

Music Test
Beat the game at Easy difficulty.

Mission Simulator
Beat the game at Normal difficulty.

Unlock the XR-900 Geopelia
Beat Mission 36 with an "A" in the mission simulator.

Unlock the X-49 Night Raven
Beat all 36 missions with an "A" in the mission simulator at Normal difficulty.

Unlock the U14054 Aurora
Beat all 36 missions with an "A" in the mission simulator at Normal or Hard difficulty.

Unlock the Orbital Satellite Laser (OSL)
Beat all 36 missions with an "A" in the mission simulator at Hard difficulty.

Control the Replay
Press Square, Circle, X, Triangle, L1, or R1 during a replay to change camera angles. Press L2 to add a filter. Press R2 to use motion blurring.

ACTION BASS

Extra Lures
Toggle through the lure selections and catch a bass on every lure five times. Quit the game, choose challenge, and finish first, second, and third in the challenge three times in a row. Catch a free fish, and every time you cast, you get an extra lure.

Win Challenge
If you do a challenge after the free fish, you will catch one fish that will win the challenge every time!

ACTUA GOLF

Longer Shots
Enter "Hacker" As Your Name.

ACTUA ICE HOCKEY

Extra Teams
Press and hold L1+L2+R1+R2 at the title screen.

ACTUA SOCCER

Bonus Player
Hold Select+Upper-left.

Gremlin Dream Team
Press R2+L2+Select+Upper-left to unlock the "Gremlin" dream team.

ACTUA SOCCER 2

Beach Ball
Press Left, Right, Left, Up, Left, Right, Square (2) at the Start menu.

Super Fury Animals Team
Press Left (2), Square, Right (2), Circle, Up, Down at the Start menu.

Break Reflectors
Press Left (3), Circle, Right (3), Square at the Start menu.

Ghost Ball
Press Square (2), Left (2), Right (2), Circle (2) at the Start menu.

Giant Players
Press Up, Down (2), Right, Square (2), Circle (2) at the Start menu.

Invisible Players
Press Square, Circle, Down, Circle, Up, Right, Square, Left at the Start menu.

B&W Color TV Mode
Press Up, Down, Up, Square, Circle, Up, Down, Up at the Start menu.

Small Players
Press Circle, Down (2), Square, Up (2), Left, Right at the Start menu.

Gremlin 11 Team
Press Left, Right, Square, Circle, Up, Down, Square, Circle at the Start menu.

ACTUA SOCCER 3

Giant Head Players
Enter "TOP HATS" as a custom team name.

Classic Ipswich Team
Enter "BALD FRITZ" as a custom team name.

Wednesday Stars Team
Enter "BARMY ARMY" as a custom team name.

Food Group Team
Enter "BIN MAN" as a custom team name.

Villa Stars Team
Enter "BIT OF CLARET" as a custom team name.

Leed's United All-Stars Team
Enter "BREMNERS BOOT" as a custom team name.

Dicks Pick N Mix Team
Enter "CANDY MAN" as a custom team name.

Virtual Blades Team
Enter "CHIP BUTTY" as a custom team name.

Pattis Shandi Men Team
Enter "CPU SPUD" as a custom team name.

Southampton Stars Team
Enter "DELL BOYS" as a custom team name.

Best of Spurs Team
Enter "DIAMOND LIGHTS" as a custom team name.

Gremlin Staff 2 Team
Enter "DOUBLE TROUBLE" as a custom team name.

Blackburn 94-95 Team
Enter "DOWN DOWN DOWN" as a custom team name.

Newcastle Stars Team
Enter "DOWN THE TOON" as a custom team name.

Everton Stars Team
Enter "DUNCNNOMORE" as a custom team name.

Wigan 98-98 Team
Enter "EGG CHASERS" as a custom team name.

Boro Stars Team
Enter "EMMERSONS WOE" as a custom team name.

Dons Stars Team
Enter "FASH THE CASH" as a custom team name.

Fighting Forth Team
Enter "FLAGSTONING" as a custom team name.

Chelsea Stars Team
Enter "FOREIGN LEGION" as a custom team name.

Leicester Stars Team
Enter "FRUIT N VEG" as a custom team name.

Skellington Stars Team
Enter "GRIM REAPER" as a custom team name.

Gremlin Team
Enter "I MADE THIS FC" as a custom team name.

Madness Friday Team
Enter "IMPOSSIBILITY" as a custom team name.

Coventry Stars Team
Enter "LADY GODIVA" as a custom team name.

Heavenly HTFC Team
Enter "LEE THE PIG" as a custom team name.

Arsenal Ladies Team
Enter "LONDON GIRLS" as a custom team name.

Forest Stars Team
Enter "MEN IN TIGHTS" as a custom team name.

Cyborg Rovers Team
Enter "METAL HEADS" as a custom team name.

Dud's Spuds Team
Enter "MISS WILKO" as a custom team name.

Top 50 Babes 2 Team
Enter "NO THANKS" as a custom team name.

Green House Test Team
Enter "OZONE LAYER" as a custom team name.

Bonus Teams
Enter "PREM CLUBS" as a custom team name.

Derby Stars Team
Enter "RAM RAIDERS" as a custom team name.

Nations Select Team
Enter "RULE BRITTANIA5" as a custom team name.

Liverpool 77-78 Team
Enter "SCOUSE PERMS" as a custom team name.

Shearer's XXX Team
Enter "SEXY FOOTBALL" as a custom team name.

The Hardmen Team
Enter "SHADWELL TOWN" as a custom team name.

Doncaster Rovers Team
Enter "SHAME" as a custom team name.

Ledbury FC Team
Enter "SINK OR SWIM" as a custom team name.

Busby Babes Team
Enter "SIR MATT" as a custom team name.

Actua Soccer Web Team
Enter "SPIT N SPIN" as a custom team name.

Arsenal 70-90 Team
Enter "TEA TOTAL" as a custom team name.

Boat Racers Team
Enter "TFF HOBBY" as a custom team name.

Joke Teams
Enter "TFF TEAMS" as a custom team name.

Chalton Stars Team
Enter "VALLEY BOYS" as a custom team name.

Gremlin Staff 1 Team
Enter "WIDE BOYS" as a custom team name.

West Ham Stars Team
Enter "WRIGHT BUY" as a custom team name.

Top 50 Babes 1 Team
Enter "YES PLEASE" as a custom team name.

ADIDAS POWER SOCCER

Female Announcer
In Arcade mode, press Circle+Square at the Commentator option to change to a female announcer. Press Left or Right to choose a different language.

Dream Team
Press L2, R2, Square, X at the Player Select or Formations screen. Keep pressing the buttons until your team name changes to "Dream Team."

Pull Shirt Move
During gameplay in Arcade mode, press Triangle+Circle while you're on defense.

Push Move
During gameplay in Arcade mode, press Triangle+X while you're on defense.

Danger Kick Move
During gameplay in Arcade mode, press Square+X while you're on defense.

Running
During gameplay in Arcade mode, press Square+Circle while you're on offense.

Back Heel
During gameplay in Arcade mode, press Square+X while you're on offense.

Mega Shot
During gameplay in Arcade mode, press Triangle+X while you're on offense.

Back Flick

During gameplay in Arcade mode, press Circle+Triangle while you're on offense.

ADIDAS POWER SOCCER 98

Cheat Mode

Press and hold L1+L2+R1+R2 at the start screen to display the Cheat Entry screen.

Hidden Stadium

Execute the Cheat mode code. Then press Square, Circle, Square, Triangle (2), Circle, X (2).

Bonus Teams

Execute the Cheat mode code. Then press X, Triangle, X, Square, Circle, Square, X, Triangle.

Win Match

Execute the Cheat mode code. Then press X, Triangle (2), Circle, X, Square, Circle, Triangle. Pause the game to win the match.

Big Head Mode

Execute the Cheat mode code. Then press Square, Circle (2), X, Triangle, X, Square, Circle.

View Credits

Execute the Cheat mode code. Then press Circle, Square, Triangle, Circle, X, Triangle (2), Square.

ADVAN RACING

Transparent Car

Hold Start and press Up (2), Right, Left, Down (2), Left, Up, Right (2), Up, Down, Left (2), Down as the main menu appears.

Big Tracks

Hold X+Select and press Right, Down, Left, Up, Right, Down, Left, Up, Down, Right, Up, Left, Down, Right, Up as the main menu appears.

Wide Turns

Hold Circle and press Down (2), Left, Down (3), Left, Down, Up, Down, Right, Left, Right, Left, Up as the main menu appears.

Deformed Cars

Hold X and press Right (2), Up (2), Down, Left, Down, Left, Right, Up, Down, Left, Right, Up, Right as the main menu appears.

Lower Gravity

Hold Start+Circle and press Right, Up, Down, Left, Right, Up, Down, Left, Right, Up, Down, Left, Right, Up, Left as the main menu appears.

Monochrome Mode

Hold Select and press Right (4), Up (4), Down, Right, Up, Down, Right, Up, Left as the main menu appears.

Unlock Bonus Tracks

Place first on all levels in STC and SSS mode to reveal more tracks.

Unlock NC Mode Bonus Cars

Place first on all levels in NC mode to unlock nine bonus cars. Place second or third in all levels in NC mode to unlock six bonus cars. Place fourth, fifth, or sixth in all levels on NC mode to unlock three bonus cars.

Unlock TC Mode Bonus Cars

Place first on all levels in TC mode to unlock nine bonus cars. Place second or third in all levels in TC mode to unlock six bonus cars. Place fourth, fifth, or sixth in all levels in TC mode to unlock three bonus cars.

ADVANCED VARIABLE GEO

Unlock K1 and K2

Complete Story mode at Hard difficulty to unlock K1 and K2 in Versus mode.

ADVANCED VARIABLE GEO 2

Unlock Miranda

Complete the game in Normal mode.

Unlock Material

Complete the game in Story mode.

Extra Options

Unlock Material and Miranda using the previous codes to unlock an extra option in the Config screen.

ADVENTURES OF LOMAX

Level Select

During game, hold Down+Start. Hold Up while pressing Triangle, Circle, X, Square. Use L1+Select to change level and L1+Start to start the level.

Flying Lomax

Insert the Level Select code; then press L1+Square.

Level 3 Password

Enter Square (3), Triangle, X, Square, Circle, Triangle at the Password screen.

Level 4 Password

Enter Triangle, Circle, Square, Triangle, Circle, Square, Circle, X at the Password screen.

Level 5 Password

Enter X, Circle, X, Triangle, X, Square, Circle, X at the Password screen.

Level 6 Password

Enter Square, X, Triangle, Circle (4), X at the Password screen.

Level 7 Password

Enter X, Triangle, Circle, (3), Square, Circle, X at the Password screen.

Level 8 Password

Enter Triangle (2), Square, Circle (2), Square, Circle, X at the Password screen.

Level 9 Password

Enter X, Circle, X, Circle, X (2), Circle, X at the Password screen.

Level 10 Password

Enter Triangle, Square, Triangle, Square, X (2), Circle, X at the Password screen.

Level 11 Password

Enter Circle, Square, Circle, Square, X (2), Circle, X at the Password screen.

Level 12 Password

Enter Square (4), X, Square, Circle, Square at the password screen.

Level 13 Password

Enter X (3), Square, X (2), Circle, Square at the Password screen.

Level 14 Password

Enter Square, Triangle, Circle, X (2), Triangle, Square, X at the Password screen.

Level 15 Password

Enter Circle, Triangle, Square, X (2), Triangle, Circle, Square at the Password screen.

Level 16 Password

Enter Triangle (2), X (3), Triangle, Square, X at the Password screen.

Level 17 Password

Enter Square, X, Triangle (2), Square, Triangle, Square, X at the Password screen.

Level 18 Password

Enter X (2), Circle, Triangle, Square, Triangle, Square, X at the Password screen.

Level 19 Password

Enter Triangle, X, Square, Triangle, Square, Triangle, Square, X at the Password screen.

Level 20 Password

Enter Circle, X, X, Triangle, Square, Triangle, Square, X at the Password screen.

Level 21 Password

Enter Square (2), Triangle, Circle, Square, Triangle, Square, X at the Password screen.

Level 22 Password

Enter X, Square, Circle (2), Square, Triangle, Square, X at the Password screen.

AGENT ARMSTRONG

Cheat Mode

Begin a game and move to the right immediately. Keep moving right to find a location with a teddy bear. Face the wall and press Circle to jump in that direction. You'll hear a soft sound if you do it correctly. Move forward and walk through the next room (just right of this location) into another small room. Press Circle to access a platform. Use the platform to reach a playroom and activate Cheat mode. Then enter any of the following codes.

All Weapons

Press Circle (3), Triangle (2), X (2), Square on Controller 2 during gameplay.

Level Select

Press Triangle (3), Square (3), X (2), Circle on Controller 2 during gameplay.

Invincibility

Press X (4), Triangle, Circle, X, Square on Controller 2 during gameplay.

AGILE WARRIOR

B-1 Airstrike

Pause and press Left, Square (4), Up, Triangle (3), Right, Circle, Down, X (6).

Debug Info

Pause the game and press Left, Square (4), Up, Triangle (3), Right, Circle, Down, X, L2, R2.

Enable Ground Crash

Pause and press Left, Square (4), Up, Triangle (3), Right, X, Down, X, Square, X (2), Square.

Hidden Camera Angles

Pause and press Left, Square (4), Up, Triangle (3), Right, Circle, Down, X, Up, Down, Left, Right.

Long Camera Views

Pause the game and press Left, Square (4), Up, Triangle (3), Right, Circle, Down, X (4), Circle, X (3).

Hover

Pause and press Left, Square (4), Up, Triangle (3), Right, Circle, Down, X, Triangle (3), X.

Invincibility
Pause and press Left, Square (4), Up, Triangle (3), Right, Circle, Down, X, Triangle (3), Square.

Maximum Weapons
Pause and press Left, Square (4), Up, Triangle (3), Right, Circle, Down, X, R1 (4), L1 (4), R2 (4), L2 (4).

Mesh Fog Editor
Pause and press Left, Square (4), Up, Triangle (3), Right, Circle, Down, X, Down (3), Triangle (3).

Mission Complete
Pause the game and press Left, Square (4), Up, Triangle (3), Right, Circle, Down, X, Triangle (3), Down (3).

Overhead Map
Pause the game and press Left, Square (4), Up, Triangle (3), Right, Circle, Down, X, Circle (5).

Strip Tease
Pause and press Left, Square (4), Up, Triangle (3), Right, Circle, Down, X, Down, X, Down, X, Down, X, Down, X, Down, X.

Maximum Fuel and Shields
Pause the game and press Left, Square (4), Up, Triangle (3), Right, Circle, Down, X, Triangle (3), Circle.

Unlock All Missions
Pause and press Left, Square (4), Up, Triangle (3), Right, Circle, Down, X, Select, X (3), Select, Triangle (3), Select (3).

Level Passwords
Enter these passwords to go to your desired level.

Level 1
5433

Level 2
0007

Level 3
1213

Level 4
1224

Level 5
7154

AIR COMBAT

Cheat Menu
To activate Cheat mode, press and hold R1+Circle as the bird logo appears before the Now Loading screen. When you do this correctly, the screen becomes black, with CDs bouncing across the background. Then you may enter the following codes.

999,999,000 Credits
Enable Cheat mode. As the game loads, press Up, Circle, Triangle (3), Circle, Triangle, Circle, Triangle. Press Circle+Triangle, then hold Circle+Triangle.

Extra Credits
Enable Cheat mode. As the game loads, press Right, Circle, Triangle (3), Circle, Triangle, Circle, Triangle, Circle+Triangle, then press and hold Circle+Triangle.

Mini Game
Enable Cheat mode. As the game loads, press Up, Left, Down, Right.

Original Paint job
Enable Cheat mode. Press Up, Down, Left, Right, Up, Down, Left, Right, R1 while game loads.

Secret Sub-Game
Enable Cheat mode. Press Up, Left, Down, Right while game loads.

Undecorated Wingman
Enable Cheat mode. Hold R1 and press Start (10).

AIR RACE CHAMPIONSHIP

Unlock the Light Flyer Jet
Use Limit 500 or Unlimited modes and beat the game with the normal ending.

Unlock the Leo Copter Jet
Use Unlimited, Mirror, or Reverse modes and beat the game with the good ending.

Unlock the Foo Fighter Jet
Use Unlimited, Mirror, or Reverse modes and beat the game with the Light Flyer and Leo Copter bonus jets.

Unlock the Fly Jet
Use Unlimited, Mirror, or Reverse modes and beat the game with the Foo Fighter bonus jet.

AKUJI THE HEARTLESS

Debug Mode
Pause the game. Hold L2 or R2 and press Left, Up (2), Triangle, Right, Square, Left, Triangle, Up, Down, Right (2).

Infinite Spirit Spells
Pause the game. Hold L2 or R2 and press Left, Triangle, Left (2), Circle, Left, Triangle, Right, Circle, Up (2), Down.

Invincibility
Pause the game. Hold L2 or R2 and press Right (2), Left, Triangle, X, Up, Circle, Left.

ALEXI LALAS INTERNATIONAL SOCCER

Unlock All-Time Players
Press L2 (3), Right at the main menu.

Unlock the 1970 Brazil Team
Press R1 (3), Right at the Team Selection screen.

Use Azzuri (Best Italian Players)
Press L2, Up (2), Right at the main menu.

ALIEN RESURRECTION

Cheat Mode
At the main menu, press Circle, Left, Right, Circle, Up, R2, then enter the Cheats menu from the Options menu.

Research Mode
At the main menu, press Square, Up, Down, Circle, Left, R1, then enter the Research mode from the Options menu.

ALIEN TRILOGY

Level Select
Enter "G0LVL xx," where xx represents the level you want. For example, if you want to go to Level 14, enter "G0LVL14."

Ultimate Cheat
Enter "1GOTP1NK8C1DBOOTSON" as a password.

Ending Sequence
Enter "FLYTO35" as a password.

Instant Shotgun
Pause the game. Press Triangle, Circle (2), Square.

Level 1-2 Password
Enter "J3BBBBBBDWP8903BBBBBBBBMBB-BXJBBB" to reach that level at Xenomania difficulty.

Levels 1-3 Password
Enter "LZBBBBBKCPB9N3DBBBCGBBMBB-CD1BBB" to reach that level at Xenomania difficulty.

Level 1-4 Password
Enter "FBBBBBBBMCPB9XLDBBBFBBBM-BBCX1BBB" to reach that level at Xenomania difficulty.

Level 1-5 Password
Enter "7LBB7BBB84PB9K3GBBBDLBLMBB-DB1BBB" to reach that level at Xenomania difficulty.

Level 1-6 Password
Enter "1LBBBBBB6WPB7F3GBBBJ2BBBBB-DX1BBB" to reach that level at Xenomania difficulty.

Level 1-7 Password
Enter "YGBJLBBB70PB9R3CQVCBG9BBD-BQFJ9CLB" to reach that level at Xenomania difficulty.

Level 1-8 Password
Enter "WGBBBBBB0HPBJLBLL3BTGBLM-BVFX9DVB" to reach that level at Xenomania difficulty.

Level 1-9 Password
Enter "XQBJLBBBMHPBJNVFQVBTGBLM-CBGD9HBB" to reach that level at Xenomania difficulty.

Level 1-10 Password
Enter "4BBBGBBBFWPBQHLPN2BTLBLJCG-G29FBB" to reach that level at Xenomania difficulty.

Level 1-11 Password
Enter "3ZBJLBBB4HPBQQ3PQVBTLBLJCG-HJ9FBB" to reach that level at Xenomania difficulty.

Level 1-12 Password
Enter "03BJGBBBHWPB9BB0H3BTLBLDCB-HZ9GVB" to reach that level at Xenomania difficulty.

Level 2-1 Password
Enter "Z3BBSBBB74PB9GVTJVBBBBBDB7-JG9BVB" to reach that level at Xenomania difficulty.

Level 2-2 Password
Enter "4BBLGBBBB8PB91B4PVBBBBBMB-3JZ9C3B" to reach that level at Xenomania difficulty.

Level 2-3 Password
Enter "4GBKVBBBZRPB9BB5QVBBBBBKC-GKG9GLB" to reach that level at Xenomania difficulty.

Level 2-4 Password
Enter "2BBQGBBBSRPBBBBB5BBBBBBBB-BBKZ9GVB" to reach that level at Xenomania difficulty.

Level 2-5 Password
Enter "0ZBBBBBD9V8PB9QWDHBBTLBLBC-GLH9G3G" to reach that level at Xenomania difficulty.

Level 2-6 Password
Enter "03BQVBD9VHPB9QWJM7BTLBLGCG-L09HBD" to reach that level at Xenomania difficulty.

Level 2-7 Password
Enter "1LBHXBD354PBJBCLPQBTBBLBB3-MH9HBD" to reach that level at Xenomania difficulty.

Level 2-8 Password
Enter "RQBBBBD988PBJCCVDBBTBBLBBV-M09CBH" to reach that level at Xenomania difficulty.

Level 2-9 Password
Enter "4BBQVBFGX4PBJJMVQGBTLBLBCG-NH9FVK" to reach that level at Xenomania difficulty.

Level 2-10 Password
Enter "77BQVBDMYMPBJ24XPQBRLBLBBZ-NY9HBD" to reach that level at Xenomania difficulty.

Level 3-1 Password
Enter "8ZBCLBC8RMPBDKMPB3BS1BLBB3-PF9HBF" to reach that level at Xenomania difficulty.

Level 3-2 Password
Enter "H7BBBBCSFRPB9DWLP3BC7BBLBL-P09GVB" to reach that level at Xenomania difficulty.

Level 3-3 Password
Enter "NQBBBBCSLMPBQHCLP3BC7BBLB-QQH9GVB" to reach that level at Xenomania difficulty.

Level 3-4 Password
Enter "0GBBBBFGK8PBLH4KK2BBBBBLB7-Q09CBC" to reach that level at Xenomania difficulty.

Level 3-5 Password
Enter "KBBBBBFGCWPBLH4KJVBBBBBLB3-RH9B3C" to reach that level at Xenomania difficulty.

Level 3-6 Password
Enter "KVBBBBBRL0PB9BBBCLBSQBBMB3-R099CLB" to reach that level at Xenomania difficulty.

Level 3-7 Password
Enter "03BBBBB8CPB9BBXDQBSQBBMC-BSK9CLB" to reach that level at Xenomania difficulty.

Level 3-8 Password
Enter "WVBBBBBBY8PB9BBXL33BN3BLMB-7509CBB" to reach that level at Xenomania difficulty.

Level 3-9 Password
Enter "TQBBBBBB4MP9P3BDQBBBBBMCG-TH9BBB" to reach that level at Xenomania difficulty.

Level 3-10 Password
Enter "4VBJLBFGDMP89XVNQVBJLBBMCB-T49F3J" to reach that level at Xenomania difficulty.

Level 3-11 Password
Enter "4VBFNBCSZ4PB94BNF7BQVBBMB-7VH9F3J" to reach that level at Xenomania difficulty.

Level 3-12 Password
Enter "S3BBBBFGS0PB94BNKZBQVBBMBZ-V09HBL" to reach that level at Xenomania difficulty.

Level 3-13 Password
Enter "Q3BQVBDXRCPB94BNQVBTLBLMB-GWH9GBL" to reach that level at Xenomania difficulty.

ALL-STAR TENNIS '99

Big Head and Feet
Choose any player and court. Start a normal game. Hold L1+L2+R1+R2+Start during gameplay. When you enter the code correctly, you'll hear a sound.

ALONE IN THE DARK 2

Cheat Mode
Press L1, L2, Left at the main menu.

ALUNDRA

Get Jess's Armor Fixed for Free
After you get Jess's broken armor, you can take it to Lurvy and get it fixed, but for a large sum of money. Instead, climb the cliffs behind his house until you are the highest you can go on the right side. From there, jump down a few cliffs to the treasure chest on the cliff directly behind Lurvy's house. From that cliff, jump to his roof. On the top of his chimney, you will fall into his house. You catch Lurvy doing something, and he says he'll fix anything of yours for free if you don't tell anyone about his secret. Give him the broken armor and walk out with a new shiny piece of armor.

Get the Legend Sword
To get the Legend Sword (the most powerful weapon in the game) Jess must give you the "Power Glove." Die and use the "Quick Restart" feature over 16 times (you can do this at any time in the game even before you get the power glove). Head for the statue of King Snow (east of Inoa Village) and use the power glove to lift the large rock blocking your way to the statue. Walk to the statue and the screen darkens, if you have done all of the above correctly, King Snow pities you and gives you the Legend Sword.

Listen to the Music
After completing a number of your quests, go to the Inoa Mine. There is a house by the stream. If you go inside and upstairs, you meet Rohei. This great composer lets you listen to some of his music, which is in fact the music from the game.

Playing Tips
When fighting Melzas, pay attention to where he pops up. The last clone to come from the ground is the creature himself. Wait in the middle of the screen and pick him off. When fighting the final brain creature, run to the brain and perform repeated jump attacks.

The Silver Armor
After the town has been burnt to the ground, go to the item shop in Inoa and try to buy the armor. The woman will finally give you the armor.

ALUNDRA 2

Infinite Gold Coins
In the city of Torledo, go into a house that says "villagers home." Go upstairs and into the room containing the guy. Go to your left until you see a pig. Break the pig to get three gold coins. Return downstairs, then go up to the same room to see that the pig is there again. Break it and you will have three gold coins. Repeat this as many times as you want.

ANDRETTI RACING

Bonus Stock Cars
Enter "Go Bears!" at the register screen for a new career.

Bonus Formula One Cars
Enter "Go Bruins!" at the Register screen.

Change Car Color
During a race, press Pause and go to Race Strategy screen. Press and hold L1+L2+R1+ R2+X+Circle+Select.

Master Options
Pause the race. Go to the Race Standings screen and press Circle+X.

ANGEL BLADE: NEO TOKYO GUARDIANS

Picture Test
Press Down (2), Up (2), Right, Left, Right, Left, Triangle, Square.

Sound Test
Press X (2), Triangle (2), Circle, Square, Circle, Square, Up, Left.

ANGEL EYES

Unlock Special Raiya
Beat Story mode with Raiya at Normal difficulty.

Unlock Anime Reika
Beat Story mode with Reika at Normal difficulty.

Unlock Robo C
Beat Story mode with Chibi at Normal difficulty.

Unlock Panda
Beat Story mode with Marie at Normal difficulty.

Unlock Akane
Beat Story mode with Kiriko at Normal difficulty.

Unlock Lina2
Beat Story mode with Lina at Normal difficulty.

Unlock Critical H Star
Beat Story mode with H Star at Normal difficulty.

Unlock H Mysp
Beat Story mode with M Pow at Normal difficulty.

Unlock Anime Kiriko, Anime Lina, Anime Bin C
Unlock all the foregoing characters. Then beat Arcade mode with all the same characters at Hard difficulty.

ANIMANIACS TEN PIN ALLEY 2

300 Game Tournament
In sixth saved game space, enter "Vllooma" as a name.

Anna Kournikova's Smash Court Tennis

See All End Sequences
Press Up (4), Down (4), Left (4), Right (4) on Controller 2 as Press Start appears at the main menu.

Unlock Bonus Equipment
Win a Grand Slam tournament to receive a new piece of equipment.

Unlock Bonus Characters
Win a Street tournament to receive a new character.

Ape Escape

Collect More Explosive Bullets
Pause the game. Press R2, Down, L2, Up, Right, Down, Right, Left.

Rearview Mirror
Press L1+R1 during the Ski mini-game to get a rearview mirror.

Never Lose a Life
Press Start and exit whenever you're falling off a cliff. You'll go to the time station with the number of lives you had before you fell.

Extra Mini-Game Boxers
Defeat the extra boxers in the Specter Boxing mini-game at Championship mode.

Apocalypse

Level Select
Pause the game. Hold L1 and press Triangle, Up, X, Down.

Debug Mode
Pause the game. Hold L1 and press Down (2), Triangle.

Invincibility
Pause the game. Hold L1 and press Down, Up, Left (2), Triangle, Up, Right, Down.

Infinite Lives
Pause the game. Hold L1 and press Triangle, Circle, X, Square.

All Weapons
Pause the game. Hold L1 and press Square, Circle, Up, Down, X, Square.

All Weapons and Infinite Ammo
Pause the game. Hold L1 and press X, Triangle, Circle.

Refill Health
Pause the game. Hold L1 and press Square, X, Triangle, Circle.

Falls Never End
Pause the game. Hold L1 and press X (6). Enter the code again to disable it.

Return to Last Place of Death
Pause the game. Hold L1 and press Square, Circle, X.

Select Checkpoint
Pause the game. Hold L1 and press Triangle, Square, Circle, X.

Lingering Smart Bombs
Pause the game. Hold L1 and press L1, L1, R1, R2.

Disable Weapon and Health Display
Pause the game. Hold L1 and press Up, Square, Up, X.

Arcade's Greatest Hits: Atari Collection Vol. 1

Cheat Menu
Start any game and press L1+L2. Press X to view the Cheat menu when the Options screen appears.

Tempest Level Skip
Press Select at the Demonstration and High Score screens. Use the game options to enable Demonstration mode. Start a game and press R1 or L1 to change levels.

Gauntlet Bonus Energy
When the game begins or when you restart a level, press the Credit button repeatedly for extra health. (Press no other buttons.)

Arcade's Greatest Hits: The Atari Collection 2

Gauntlet Health Trick
Normally in *Gauntlet*, if you press the credit button to get more health, your score decreases. However, there is a way around this. When you start, don't touch anything. Press the credit button rapidly to rake in loads of health. When you reach your desired amount, grab a treasure and get going. This also works if you die and have to restart on a level in which you died.

Arcade's Greatest Hits: The Williams Collection Vol. 1

Cheat Menu
Start any game and press L1+L2. The Options screen appears. Press X to access the Cheat menu.

Area 51

Hidden Level Warp
Go to the main menu and click on Arcade mode to view a screen with two boxes. Click on the blank, black area around the box to warp to another level far ahead in the game.

Best Ending
Shoot all the panels from the Mothership.

Worst Ending
Don't shoot any panels and let the Mothership escape.

Start with a Shotgun
Pause the game. Press Triangle, Square, Triangle, Left, R1.

Kronn Hunter Mode
Shoot only the first three STAAR members you see.

Level 1 Secret Room
Shoot both blue lights.

Level 2 Secret Room
Shoot out all the upper windows of the hangar's rearmost wall. To find another secret, shoot all the yellow barrels when you ride on the forklift.

Level 4 Secret Room
Shoot all the yellow boxes when you ride in the STAAR jeep.

Level 5 Secret Room
Shoot the doorplate of the second door (marked "General Weatherby") as it opens.

Level 7 Secret Room
Shoot all the yellow barrels at the first area, where four purple zombies throw barrels down a hill.

Arkanoid Returns

Level Select
Highlight "Continue." Then press X+Circle.

Armored Core

Fixed Camera View
Press Circle+X+Start to pause the game. Resume playing to use the fixed camera angle.

Change Background
Design a background using the Edit Emblem option. Then hold L1+R1+Select.

First-Person View
Press Triangle+Square+Start to pause the game. Resume playing to see the new view.

Change Pilot Name
Enter the garage and highlight "Change AC Name." Hold L2+R2+Right. Then hold Square and quickly tap X. When you do this correctly, "Change AC Name" becomes "Change Pilot Name."

Death Enhancements
Fail all the missions until you fall below -50,000 credits. The game will restart from the first level with all the items from your previous game. When you do this correctly, "Rebel" becomes your pilot name. You'll unlock something every time you use this cheat. Do this six times to unlock all bonus enhancements.

Armored Core: Master of Arena

Fixed Camera Angle
Press Circle+X+Start to pause the game. Resume playing to see the fixed camera angle.

Change Emblem Backgrounds
Make an emblem in the Edit Emblem screen. Then press and hold L1+R1+Select.

First-Person View
Press Triangle+Square+Start to pause the game. Resume playing to see the new view.

Return to Default View
Pause the game and press Start to resume to return the view to normal.

Armored Core: Project Phantasma

First-Person View
Press Start+Triangle+Square to pause the game. Resume playing to see the fixed camera angle.

Weird Camera Angle
Hold X+Circle and press Start twice while you're playing a mission or versus game in One-player mode. Pause and unpause the game to disable the camera angle.

Change Pilot Name
Highlight "Change AC Name." Hold Select and press X.

Change Emblem Backgrounds
Make an emblem in the Edit Emblem screen. Then press and hold L1+R1+Select.

ARMY MEN 3D

Level Select
Press Square, Circle, R1, L1, L1+R1 at the main menu.

Invincibility
Pause and quickly press Square, Circle, L1, L1+L2.

All Weapons
Pause and quickly press Square, Circle, R1, L1, R1+R2.

All War Zones
Enter the Difficulty screen via the Options screen. Hold Triangle+Square+Circle and press L1+L2.

More Damage in Multiplayer
Tap X to inflict greater flame-thrower damage in Two-Player mode.

Run Faster in Multiplayer
Hold Square+Triangle to run quicker in a multiplayer game.

Secret Level
Pause the game. Press Square five times, but with a one-second delay between each press. Unpause the game to go to one of the three secret levels.

ARMY MEN: AIR ATTACK

All Co-Pilots
Up, Down, Up, Down, Up, Down, Up, Down as a password.

Fly Apache
Beat Mission 14, "Pick Up the Pieces."

Fly Super Stallion
Beat Mission 8, "Saucer Attack."

Fly Chinnok
Beat Mission 4, "Tan Terror Troy."

Mission Passwords
Enter the following passwords to go to the level you want.

Mission 2
X, Down, Left, Left, Square, Circle (2), Right

Mission 3
Triangle, Up, Left, Right, Down, Triangle, Circle, Up

Mission 4
Down (2), Square (2), Left, Right, Circle, X

Mission 5
Right (2), X, Circle, Down, Up, Down, Up

Mission 6
Square, Circle, X, Square, Triangle, Left, Up, Right

Mission 7
Square, Circle, X, Square, Left, Up, Right

Mission 8
Right, Down, Left, Up, Triangle, Down, Up, Down

Mission 9
Circle (2), Right, Up, Right, Up, X (2)

Mission 10
X, Down (4), X, Left, Right

Mission 11
Triangle, Up, Circle, Down, Square, Left, X, Right

Mission 12
Up (2), Triangle (2), Left (2), Circle (2)

Mission 13
Left, Down, Left, Down, Square, Circle, Square, Circle

Mission 14
Down (4), X (2), Circle (2)

Mission 15
Square, Right, Left, Circle (2), Up, Down, Square

Mission 16
Triangle, Down, Triangle, Down, Square, Up, Square, Up

Multiplayer Mission Passwords
Enter the following passwords to play the mission you want.

Mission 2 (Multiplayer)
Right, Up, Square, X, Up, Circle, Up, Right

Mission 3 (Multiplayer)
Left, Down, Left, Down, Up (4)

Mission 4 (Multiplayer)
Square, X (2), Square, Circle, Triangle (2), Square

Mission 5 (Multiplayer)
Circle (2), Square, Down (2), Square, X (2)

Mission 6 (Multiplayer)
X, Up, Circle, Down, Triangle, Left, Square, Right

Mission 7 (Multiplayer)
Up, Down (3), Right, Left (3)

Mission 8 (Multiplayer)
Left (2), Triangle, Right (2), Triangle, Up (2)

Mission 9 (Multiplayer)
Square (3), Circle, Down (3), Left

Mission 10 (Multiplayer)
Circle, Up, Left, Square, Up, Left, Down (2)

Mission 11 (Multiplayer)
Triangle, Circle, Triangle, Circle, Up (2), Down (2)

Mission 12 (Multiplayer)
Up, Down, Left, Right, Circle (2), Up, Square

Mission 13 (Multiplayer)
X, Left (3), Square, Triangle, Circle, X

Mission 14 (Multiplayer)
Left, Down, Left, Down, Square, Circle, Square, Circle

Mission 15 (Multiplayer)
Down (3), Down, X (2), Circle (2)

Mission 16 (Multiplayer)
Triangle, Down, Triangle, Down, Square, Up, Square, Up

ARMY MEN: AIR ATTACK 2

At the main menu, choose "Continue Game," then choose "Password." At the Password menu, enter the following codes:

Skip to Level 3
Triangle, Circle, Down, Left, Square (2), Up (2)

Skip to Level 4
X, Right, Left, X, Circle, Square (2), Triangle

Skip to Level 5
Down (2), Circle, Square, Circle, Square, Right, X

Skip to Level 6
Triangle, X, Up, Left, Right, Left, Circle, Triangle

Skip to Level 7
Right, Square, Right, Down, Circle, X (2), Right

Skip to Level 8
Triangle, Right, Square (2), Circle, Down (2), X

Skip to Level 9
Up, X, Square, Left, Right, Circle, Left (2)

Skip to Level 10
Triangle, Up, Circle, X, Square, Down (3)

Skip to Level 11
Circle (2), Up, Left, Right, X, Triangle, Square

Skip to Level 12
Right, Up, X, Right, Circle, Square, Triangle, Circle

Skip to Level 13
Left (2), Triangle, Circle, X (2), Down, Right

Skip to Level 14
Square, Right, Circle, Up, Down, Square, Down, X

Skip to Level 15
Left, Right, Circle, X, Square, Down (2), Circle

Skip to Level 16
Triangle, Circle, X, Right (2), Circle, Square, Down

Skip to Level 17
Square, Up (2), Right, Left, Square, Down, X

Skip to Level 18
Circle, X, Right, Triangle, Square, Up, X (2)

Skip to Level 19
Down, Right, X, Square, Right, Up, Circle (2)

Skip to Level 20
Up, X, Circle, Up, Left, Square, Circle, X

Skip to Level 21
Left, Circle, Triangle, Down, X (3), Circle

Skip to Level 22
Triangle, X, Down, Left, Right, X, Circle, Square

Unlock All levels
Triangle, Circle, X, Right (2), Circle, Square, Down, Start

ARMY MEN: SARGE'S HEROES

All Weapons
Pause the game and press Square, Circle, R1, L1. When you enter the code correctly, you'll hear a sound.

All Levels
Hold Square+L1+R1 and press Up, Down, Left, Right at the main menu. When you enter the code correctly, you'll hear a sound.

ARMY MEN: SARGE'S HEROES 2

Invincibility
Pause game, then press Square, Circle, L1, R1. The word "INVINCIBLE" appears if you did it correctly.

All Weapons and Ammo
Pause game, then press Square, Circle, R1, L1. The words "POWER UP" appear if you did it correctly.

Tin-Foil Uniform
Enter TNMN.

All Levels
Hold L1+R1+S, then press Up, Down, Left, Right.

Mission 2 (Bridge)
fllngdwn

Mission 3 (Fridge)
gtmlk

Mission 4 (Freezer)
chllb

Mission 5 (Inside Wall)
clsngn

Mission 6 (Graveyard)
dgths

Mission 7 (Castle)
frnknstn

Mission 8 (Tan Base)
bdbz

Mission 9 (Revenge)
lbbck

Mission 10 (Desk)
dskjb

Mission 11 (Bed)
gtslp

Mission 12 (Blue Town)
smllvll

Mission 13 (Cashier)
chrgt

Mission 14 (Train)
ntbrt

Mission 15 (Rockets)
ndglr

Mission 16 (Pool Table)
fstnls

Mission 17 (Pinball Table)
whswzrd

ARMY MEN: WORLD WAR

All Levels
Press R1+R2, L1+L2, Circle, Square at the main menu.

All Weapons and Ammo
Pause. Press Square, Circle, R1, L1. The word "POWER UP" appears if you did it correctly.

Invisible Player
Press R1, L1, X, Circle (2), Square (2), R1, Circle at the main menu.

All Weapons
Press X (2), Triangle, Circle, Up (2), Down, Square, Triangle at the main menu.

ARYTON SENNA KART DUEL 2

Bonus Track
Enter "SENNA 1" to gain access to the Extra Classic track.

Bonus Karts
Place first on the Extra Classic track to unlock the first bonus cart. Use it to win two consecutive rounds in Championship mode to get a second bonus cart.

ASSAULT: RETRIBUTION

Goodies Option
At the Press Start screen, press Triangle, Square, Circle, Left, Square, Triangle, Square, Circle, Left, Square within three seconds.

Stage Select
Execute the Goodies Option code. At the Press Start screen, press Left, Right, X, Triangle, Left, Up within three seconds.

Turbo Mode
At the Press Start screen, press X, Square, Triangle, Circle, X, Square, Triangle, Circle, L2, R2 within three seconds. Then, during gameplay, press Circle to run faster.

Grayscale Graphics
At the Press Start screen, press X (2), Triangle (2), Square (2), Circle (2), Up, Down within three seconds.

Big Head Player
At the Press Start screen, press Square, Circle (2), Square, Up, Square, Circle (2), Square, Triangle within three seconds.

Nakomi Mode
At the Press Start screen, press Up (2), Down (2), Left, Right, Left, Right, X, Circle within three seconds.

Big Head Aliens
At the Press Start screen, press Square, Circle (2), Square, Up, Square, Circle (2), Square, X within three seconds.

Sephia Graphics
At the Press Start screen, press Left (10) within three seconds.

ASSAULT RIGS

All Weapons and Items
During gameplay, press Left, Right, Left (2), Right, Left, Right (2), Up, Down, Up (2), Down, Up, Down (2).

Invincibility
During gameplay, press Left, X, Left, X, Left (2), X, Right, X, Right, X (2).

Level 1 Password
Circle (6)

Level 2 Password
Square, X, Square, X, Triangle, Square

Level 3 Password
Triangle, Square (2), Circle (2), Triangle

Level 4 Password
Triangle, Square, Triangle (2), Circle, Triangle

Level 5 Password
Square, Triangle (3), X, Triangle

Level 6 Password
Triangle, Square, Circle (2), X, Square

Level 7 Password
X, Square (3), Circle, Triangle

Level 8 Password
Triangle, Square, X, Square, Triangle (2)

Level 9 Password
Square, Triangle, Square, X, Triangle, X

Level 10 Password
Triangle (2), Circle, Square, X, Square

Level 11 Password
Triangle (2), X, Triangle, Circle, Square

Level 12 Password
Circle, Square, Triangle (3), Circle

Level 13 Password
Triangle, Square, Circle, X, Triangle, Square

Level 14 Password
Triangle (2), X, Square (2), X

Level 15 Password
Circle, X, Triangle (4)

Level 16 Password
Circle, Square, Circle (3), Square

Level 17 Password
Triangle (3), Circle, Triangle, Square

Level 18 Password
Square, Circle, Square, X, Square, Triangle

Level 19 Password
X (2), Square, X, Triangle, Circle

Level 20 Password
X, Square, X, Triangle (2), Square

Level 21 Password
Triangle, Square, Triangle, Square, Triangle (2)

Level 22 Password
Square (2), Triangle, Circle, Square, Triangle

Level 23 Password
Circle, X (4), Triangle

Level 24 Password
Triangle, Square (2), Triangle (3)

Level 25 Password
Triangle, Circle, Triangle (2), Circle, Square

Level 26 Password
Square, Circle (2), X, Circle, X

Level 27 Password
X, Circle, Square, Triangle (2), Square

Level 28 Password
Square, Circle, Square (4)

Level 29 Password
Triangle, Square, Circle, X, Circle (2)

Level 30 Password
Square, Circle, X, Circle, X, Triangle

Level 31 Password
Circle, Square, X, Triangle, Circle, Triangle

Level 32 Password
Triangle, Square, X, Circle, Square, X

Level 33 Password
X (2), Triangle, X (2), Square

Level 34 Password
X, Circle, Square, Circle (2), Square

Level 35 Password
Circle, Triangle, X, Triangle, X, Triangle

Level 36 Password
X, Triangle (2), X (2), Square

Level 37 Password
X, Triangle (2), X, Triangle, Square

Level 38 Password
Square, Triangle, Square, Triangle, Square, X

Level 39 Password
Square, X, Triangle, X (2), Triangle

Level 40 Password
Triangle, X, Triangle, Circle, Square, X

Level 41 Password
Circle, X, Triangle, Circle, Triangle, Square

ASTERIX

Cheat Mode
At the language selection screen, hold Triangle and press Up, Right, Down, Left (2), Down, Right, Up. A "Cheat Mode Active" message appears when you input the code correctly. Start a new game to access the Cheat menu.

ASTEROIDS

Cheat Menu
At title screen, hold Select and press Square, Triangle, Circle, Triangle (2), Square, Circle. Press Start+Select to activate the Cheat menu during a game.

Play Classic Asteroids
Hold Select at the title screen and press Circle (3), Triangle, Square (2), Circle.

99 Lives (Classic Asteroids)
Pause the game. Press Up, X, Down, Triangle, Left, Square, Right, Circle.

Invincibility (Classic Asteroids)
Pause the game. Press Down (2), Up (2), Circle, Square, Triangle (2).

Extra Life (Classic Asteroids)
Pause the game. Press Up, Down, Left, Right, Circle, Square, X, Triangle.

Excalibur Ship
At the title screen, hold Select and press Triangle, Circle (2), Triangle, Square, Circle, Square. When you enter the code correctly, you'll hear a sound.

ASTRO TROOPER VANARK

Invincibility
Hold L1, R2, Select, and Triangle at the Start Up Engine Screen.

ASUKA 120% BURNING FEST

Unlock Shinobu
Beat the game using no continues at a difficulty of two or three stars. Fight Shinobu to complete the game. When you select a character in Versus mode, press R1 or R2 to play as Shinobu.

Secret Character
After you hear "Suta Ato, Oshite ne," press Up (2), Down (2), Left, Right, Left, Right, X, Circle, Up (2), Down (2), Left, Right, Left, Right, X, Circle, Up (2), Down (2), Left, Right, Left, Right, X, Circle. When you enter the code correctly, you'll hear a sound. Enter the Character Selection screen and press R1 for the secret character.

AUBIRD FORCE

Play as Captain Henshin
Enter "Sugokueraihito" as a player name.

AUTO DESTRUCT

Cheat Menu
During gameplay, press Pause, Up, Down, Left, Right, Down, Right, L1, R1 (2) to access the Cheat menu.

Blood Mode
Execute the Cheat Menu code. Then press L1, Down, R1, Left, L1, Right, R1.

Angel Mode
Execute the Cheat Menu code. Then enter the Blood Mode code. Finally, press Up, R1, Down, L1, Up, Left, R1, Right, L1.

Immortal
Execute the Cheat Menu code. Then press Left, R1, Up, L1, Up, Right, R1, Down, L1.

Double Laser
Execute the Cheat Menu code. Then press R1, L1, R1, L1, Up, Down, Up, Left, Right.

Unlimited Fuel
Execute the Cheat Menu code. Then press L1, Circle, Left, L1, Circle, R1, L1, Up, R1, Down.

Add One Minute to Time
Execute the Cheat Menu code. Then press Down, L1 (2), Circle, Circle, R1, Up, Square, L1.

Extra Money
Execute the Cheat Menu code. Then press L1, R1, Up, Circle, Down, Square, Right, R1, L1.

Extra Tune
Execute the Cheat Menu code. Then press Down, L1 (2), O (2), R1, Up, Square, L1.

More Nitros
Execute the Cheat Menu code. Then press L1, O, Down, L1, Up, Square, O, R1.

Invulnerability
Execute the Cheat Menu code. Then press L1 (4), Left, O (2), Square, L1.

Next Mission
Execute the Cheat Menu code. Then press L1, Right, Down, Left, Up, R1.

Car Select (Tune Up Menu)
Execute the Cheat Menu code. Then press Left, R1, Right, R1, Left, R1, Right, R1.

All Time Trials
Execute the Cheat Menu code. Then press R1, L1, O, Left, O (2), Right, L1, O.

Unlock New York Time Trial
Execute the Cheat Menu code. Then press L1, Right, Down, Left, Up, R1.

Unlock Tokyo Time Trial
Execute the Cheat Menu code. Then press L1, Left, Right, R1, Left, Right, L1.

Unlock Subway Time Trial
Execute the Cheat Menu code. Then press L1, Left, L1, R1, Right, R1.

Mission Select
Execute the Cheat Menu code. Then press Up, Down, O, L1, R1, L1, O, Up, Down.

Tune-Up Menu
Execute the Cheat Menu code. Then press L1, R1, L1, Up, Down, O, Down, Right, Left, Square, R1.

Debug Mode
Pause, Up, Right, Left, Down, Circle, L1, R1, R1, L1, Circle, Down, Left, Right, Up.

Level 1
sSFTgfCnZ

Level 2
rnLVbbJnY

Level 3
frJKZYCPf

Level 4
rmKKFFfnk

Level 5
gvLKCgkmp

Level 6
gvLKBgkmb

Level 7
gvJVCskmp

Level 8
gvBVYshNv

Level 9
kRfXrWYPs

Level 10
gFFVkrFVY

Level 11
sSSPhtZNb

Level 12
gSTBXrfmq

Level 13
gXTCTTZmY

Level 14
gXWBXWfrz

Level 15
sSSFJWLNZ

Level 16
gSTRghCfm

Level 17
gSFXTMBKH

Level 18
sVHtsMMKC

Level 19
gSFXTMBKH

Level 20
gSBMVMFKS

Level 21
sPCgfghggr

Level 22
gSFMgkHZP

Level 23
sPHgfgfgS

Level 24
gXBTgshCM

Level 25
gSJVfVYZN

AYRTON SENNA KART DUEL 2

Unlock Hidden Karts
Enter "SENNA 1" as your name. Then enter an Extra Classic track. To get an extra kart, get 1st place on this extra track. Use this extra kart to win two rounds continuously in Championship Mode. You'll get the second hidden kart.

AZITO 2

9,999,999 Dollars
During gameplay, press and hold Square and press R2 (2), L1 (2), Triangle, L2 on Controller 2.

AZURE DREAMS

Refill Life
Stand in any corner and press X+Circle repeatedly.

Easy Money
Build a racetrack. Go inside and bet $1,000 on the "3-4" combination once the track is built. If the odds aren't high, you can leave and come back. When the race starts, speed up and get in Horse 2's way. Horse 2 will slow down. Horse 3 and Horse 4 will lead. Lose the race to get this easy money.

BACKSTREET BILLIARDS

Enable All Opponents and Locations
Defeat all opponents, complete Story mode, and return to check each area. Defeat Dean, the Boss, then enter the Options screen, select "Memory Card," and save. If "Auto Loading" appears when resetting or powering off the game, new locations and characters won't be present, so return to the "Memory Card" menu in the Options screen and reload.

BAKURETSU HUNTER

Skip Mah Jong Game
While talking to an enemy in Story mode, hold L1+R1+Circle+Left to defeat the enemy without playing Mah Jong.

BALDY LAND

Level Select
Enter the password: Up (2), Triangle, Down, R2, L1.

BALLBLAZER CHAMPIONS

Enable Scoring in Own Goal
Enter the following password: X (4), Square, X, Circle, X (2), Circle, X, Square, X, Triangle, X (3), Square, X (2), Triangle, X (2), Square, X (4), Square, X.

Play Old Version of Ballblazer
Enter the following password: Square (2), X (4), Square (4), X (2), Square (6), X (2), Square (2), X (2), Square (6).

Play as Xarta
Enter the following password: X, Circle (3), X, Square, Circle, X, Triangle, X, Circle, Square, Circle, Triangle, X, Triangle, Circle, Square, Circle, X, Triangle, X, Circle, Square, X, Circle (3), X, Square.

Play in Master Dome (Easy)
Enter the following password: Circle, L1 (2), R1, R2, L2, X, Square (2), R1, R2, R1, R2, Triangle, L2, R1, L2, Circle, L2, R2, R1, X, L1, R2, Square, L2, R1, X, R1 (2).

Get Shrinking Rotofoil
Enter the following password: X, Circle, X (2), Circle, X (9), Triangle (2), X (2), Square, X, Square (4), X.

Upside-Down Field
Enter the following password: X, Square (4), X, Square, X (4), Square, X (2), Triangle (2), X (9), Circle, X (2), Circle, X.

BASES LOADED 96

Cheat Mode
Pause. Press (on controller two) Triangle, Square, X, Circle (2). A piano sound confirms correct entry.

Computer vs. Computer
Enter Cheat mode. Press L2 to have CPU vs. CPU. To disable, reenter Cheat mode and press L2.

Automatic Home Run
Enter Cheat mode. Press L1 to make every hit a home run. To disable, reenter Cheat mode and press L1.

Inning Select
Enter Cheat mode. Press X and "Let's go to Inning" pops up. Keep pressing X to select the desired inning.

BASS LANDING

Free a Stuck Lure
Press X+Circle.

BATMAN FOREVER: THE ARCADE GAME

Play as Villains
At the Player Select screen, hold X+Circle+L2 on controller two.

BATMAN & ROBIN

Invincibility
At title screen, hit L1, R2, R1, L2, Select, X, Circle.

Limited Invincibility
Press Circle (2). A yellow meter (below your health meter) shows how long you'll be invincible.

BATTLE ARENA TOSHINDEN

Additional Camera Controls
Pause and press Square+Circle+Triangle+X, Select (2). Pan and zoom with L1, L2, R1, R2. To disable, press Square+Circle+Triangle+X, Select.

Get Extra Costumes
When selecting a character, highlight a fighter and press Select.

Use Desperation Moves
While using a controller configuration that sets L1, L2, R1, and R2 as the special attack buttons, simultaneously press all four top buttons when your character's energy bar is flashing.

Get Sho
Enable the "Play as Gaia" code, then enter Demonstration mode. During the demo, press Start on controller two. While the words slide onto the title screen, press Left, Right, Left, Right, Left+Square on controller two. You hear "fight" and the screen's text turns blue. Then while selecting a character, highlight Kayin and press Down+Square.

Final Battle Rewards
Defeat Gaia at a difficulty setting below Normal to receive a "desperation" move. Reach Sho without using continues at a difficulty of Normal or harder to receive a secret move. Continues can be used in the battle against Sho.

Get Gaia
Press Down, Down-Left, Left, Square at title screen. Highlight Eiji at the Player Select screen, hold Up+Attack button.

BATTLE ARENA TOSHINDEN 2

Get Uranus and Master
At title screen, press R1, R2, X, L1, R2, Circle. A sound confirms a correct entry. Go to the Random Character option and press Select to slow the display. The characters appear after Chaos. Or beat the game in single-player on a difficulty of four or higher, then press Select at the Random Character option to choose the new characters.

Get Special Moves on High Difficulty
Use controller one to set the difficulty to level three, then use controller two to set all second player's controls to "Special." Start a single-player game using controller two and the special move buttons are available. In a two-player game, player two can use the special move buttons on any difficulty level.

Enable Camera Control
Select control type "H2" from the Options menu, then select "Camera Action" and the "Your Self" option. Choose a control type, and L1, L2, R1, and R2 now control the camera angles. Start a new fight and pause. When changing camera angles, use Select to switch between the rotate/tilt and zoom/pan functions.

Get Extra Costumes
Beat the game then hold Select to slow the character cycling. Press Weak Punch or Weak Kick when your character appears to select alternate outfits.

Get Sho and Vermillion
Enable the Get Uranus and Master code. At the title screen, press Circle, R2, L1, X, L2, R1 with controller two. A sound confirms a correct entry and the Option button turns red. Go to Random Character Selection and hold Select to slow the display. The new characters appear after Chaos. Or, beat the game with Master in One-player mode on a difficulty of six or higher. Then go to the Random Character Select option and press Select to choose new characters.

Remove Power Bar
Pause. Hold Circle+Square+Triangle+X and press Select (2).

Warp to Final Boss
At title screen press Up, Down, Up, Down, Up+Triangle.

BATTLE ARENA TOSHINDEN 3

Change "Loading" Color
At Loading screen, rapidly press X.

Get Sub-Bosses
Finish the game with each basic character on a difficulty level of three or higher to enable that character's sub-boss.

Get Sho
After unlocking all the sub-bosses, finish the game with Vermillion on a difficulty level of three or higher.

Get Abel
Finish the game with Sho on level seven.

Get Veil
Finish the game with Abel on level seven.

Get Naru
Finish the game with Veil on level seven.

Get Extra Costumes
Finish the game with Naru on level seven, then highlight a character at the Selection screen and press Square or X.

Enable Instant Secret Moves
Finish the game with Naru, then configure two or more of the top buttons for special moves. While fighting, press all special move buttons at once to use a secret move. This doesn't work with all characters.

PLAYSTATION

Hide Display

Pause the game then hold Circle+Triangle+Square+X and press Select to remove the Continue, Options, and Reset Items. While still holding the buttons, press Select again to remove the Life and Over Drive bars. To redisplay the items, repeat the code and press Select once.

Random Character Select

Inside the Character Selection screen, hold L1+L2+R1+R2 and press Square, Triangle, X, or Circle when the selection box is moving.

BATTLE HUNTER

Better Movement, Attack, and HP

When creating your hunter, enter the name SHUICHI.

Better Attack and HP

When creating your hunter, enter the name VIKEIF.

BATTLE STATIONS

Level Skip

Hold L1+L2+R1+R2+Select and press Start+X during gameplay in Single-player mode.

BATTLETANX: GLOBAL ASSAULT

All Tanks

Enter the password THRTN.

All Weapons

Enter the password SRTHMB.

Invincibility

Enter the password MSTSRVV.

Level Select

Enter the password BCKDR.

More Tank Bucks

Enter the password DPPCKTS.

Brandon Gang

Enter the password SMSLGNG.

Custom Gang 1

Enter the password TRDDYBRRKS.

Campaign Mode Bonus Level

Enter the password WRDRB.

Cassandra Gang

Enter the password NSTYGRL.

BEAST WARS: TRANSFORMERS

Level Skip

Pause and hold L2. Press Up, Down, Left, Right, Triangle, X (2), Triangle, Right, Left, Down, Up, then unpause.

Power Up Weapons

Pause and hold L2. Press Up, Down, Left, Right, Triangle, X, Square. Let go of L2 and unpause.

BEAT MANIA

Hidden Mode 1

When Press Start button appears, hold L+R on the Beat Mania controller and press Start. Release the buttons and press Left+X. A sound confirms a correct entry.

Double Play Mode

When Press Start button appears, hold Left+Square+X and press Start. Release the buttons and press L+R on the Beat Mania controller. A sound confirms correct entry.

BEATMANIA: 2ND MIX

Secret Stages

Go to arcade. When you pick expert, hold the select button, push the Circle button, and pick either classic for rave 2nd remix or techno for hard techno.

BEYOND THE BEYOND

Double Deadly Attack

Hit X repeatedly.

Secret Intro

Hold Triangle+Up before title screen appears.

Extra Items and Party Members

When "Press Start" appears, hold Right and press Circle, Triangle, X, Square, X, Triangle, Circle, X, Circle, Square, Start.

BIG AIR

Race Shawn Palmer

At the main menu, quickly press Square (8). Place first in the first track in World Tour mode.

Race Mike Beallo

At the main menu, quickly press Square (6), Circle (2). Place first in the first track in World Tour mode.

Race Fabien Rohrer

At the main menu, quickly press Square (5), Circle, Square, Circle. Place first in the first track in World Tour mode.

Race Ian Spiro

At the main menu, quickly press Square (6), Circle, Square. Place first in the first track in World Tour mode.

Race Ross Powers

At the main menu, quickly press Square (5), Circle, Square (2). Place first in the first track in World Tour mode.

Race Nicola Thost

At the main menu, quickly press Square (7). Place first in the first track in World Tour mode.

Accolade Board

Press Right, Left, Right, Left, Square, Circle (2), Square at main menu. Select Pitbull board.

All Courses

Press Right, Left, Right, Left, Circle, Square, Circle, Square at main menu. Choose Freeride mode.

Angel Board

Press Right, Left, Right, Left, Square, Circle, Square, Circle at main menu. Select Pitbull board.

Big Air Board

Press Right, Left, Right, Left, Square (3), Circle at main menu. Select Pitbull board.

Daniel's Board

Press Right, Left, Right, Left, Circle, Square (2), Circle at main menu. Select Pitbull board.

Fire Board

Press Right, Left, Right, Left, Square, Circle, Square (2) at main menu. Select Pitbull board.

Huge Air in Freestyle

Using Fire Board, find course's largest jump. Press Circle (3), Square, Triangle, L1, L2, L1, R2 at highest place in the air.

Jimmy's Board

Press Right, Left, Right, Left, Square, Circle (3) at main menu. Select Pitbull board.

John's Board

Press Right, Left, Right, Left, Circle, Square (3) at main menu. Select Pitbull board.

Steve's Board

Press Right, Left, Right, Left, Square (2), Circle (2) at main menu. Select Pitbull board.

TD5 Board

Press Right, Left, Right, Left, Square (2), Circle, Square at main menu. Select Pitbull board.

BIO F.R.E.A.K.S.

Fight Clonus Opponent

Hold Select when choosing an opponent.

Alternate View

During gameplay, hold L2+R2 and press Away. To revert, hold L2+R2 and press Down.

Taunts

Press Left Punch+Right Kick while fighting.

BIO-HAZARD: DIRECTOR'S CUT

Easy Arrange Mode

At the title screen, highlight Arrange, then press and hold Right for at least three seconds. The word "Arrange" changes to green. You will now play in Easy Arrange mode.

BLACK DAWN

2P Mode

At title screen, press Select+R2 on both controllers.

Cycle Gun Modes

Pause, then press Select, L2, Select, R2, Select (3).

Disable Collision Detection

Pause, then press Select, L2, Select, R2, Square (4).

Hidden Atari Classic

On both controllers, hold Select+R2 at title screen.

Invincibility

Pause, then press Select, L2, Select, R2, Triangle (3), Square.

Maximum Fuel and Armor

Pause, then press Select, L2, Select, R2, Triangle (3), Circle.

Maximum Weapons

Pause, then press Select, L2, Select, R2, L1, L2, R1, R2.

Mission Complete

Pause, then press Select, L2, Select, R2, Triangle (3), Down (3).

Remove Pause Menu

Pause, then press Select, L2, Select, R2, Down, R1, R2.

Select Mission

Hold Left+L2 and press Select at main menu.

Summon Wingman

Pause, then press Select, L2, Select, R2, Square (3), Circle.

Upgrade Current Weapon

Pause, then press Select, L2, Select, R2, L1 (2), R1 (2).

Extra FMV Movie
Beat the game under Rockin difficulty to see extra background footage from the development team.

Urban Shield Level Password
1018

Black Out Level Password
1006

Ice Storm Level Password
1213

Desert Fury Level Password
0203

Tiger Trap Level Password
0917

Crack Down Level Password
0354

BLADE

Master Code
Hold L1 then press Right, Left, Up, Down, L2 (2), R2 (2) at the main menu. Then press Start during gameplay and activate any option at the Cheat menu.

Unlimited Ammunition
Down, Right, Up, Left, L2, L1, R2, R1

Unlimited Life
Left (3), Right, L2, L1, R2, R1

All Items
Right, Left, Up, Down, L2 (2), R2 (2)

BLAST CHAMBER

Infinite Lives
Press Square, Left, Square, Right, Circle, Down, Circle, Up at the main menu. Select Sole Survivor mode in Games menu.

Bonus Level Password
JODPEGEA

Ziggurat Level Password
NAEMMAAB

Backstab Level Password
MAGDIEAH

Fall N Arch Level Password
NINKPDME

Fugitive Level Passwords
MJKKAMKC

Rainbow Level Password
JODPIGEH

Bonus Level Password
JODPEGEA

Lavapalooza Level Password
ICJPABNA

BLAST RADIUS

Hidden Levels
Press L1, Left, L2, Down, Select, Left, Down, R2 (3), Select, Up at the main menu. This code doesn't work if you entered the Wraith Ship/Sector 8 and Powered Up Ships/Sector 5 codes.

Powered Up Ships/Sector 5
Press Right, L1, Up (2), Down, Right, R2, L2, R2, Down, Up, Down at the main menu. Choose any ship, start game, then quit game.

Programmer Backgrounds
Press Down, Up, L1, Right, L1, Up, Right, Select, Right, R2, L1, L2 at the main menu. This code doesn't work if you entered the Wraith Ship/Sector 8 and Powered Up Ships/Sector 5 codes.

Wraith Ship/Sector 8
Press Left, Right, L1, Left, Right, L1, R2 (2), L2, Left, Right, Up at the main menu.

BLASTO

Swim Without Air
At the start screen, press Down (3), Left, Right, Down, Right, Up, Right (2).

Alternate Costumes
Press Up (2), Down, X, Triangle, Circle at the main menu.

All Weapons
Press Up (2), Down (2), Right, Up, Right, Down, Left (2) at Start menu after beating the game.

Play as Evil Blasto
After beating the game, press Up, Down, Up, Down, Left, Right, Up, Down, Right, Left at Start menu.

Powered Up Gun
Press Right, Up, Down, Left, Down, Left, Right, Up, Down, Right at main menu.

BLAZE AND BLADE

Duplicate Equipment
Sell equipment to anyone at an auction, then save only the person that received the equipment. Reset to double the equipment.

BLAZING DRAGONS

50 Percent Complete
Enter the password LW26UL XAU%HR ?4AWQB to start halfway through the game.

Final Password
Enter the password V?U5MK 4N6LUL OHW5CB to go to the final level.

BLOOD LINES

Play as Annor
Enter the password CLAWEDFIST.

Play as Daria
Enter the password DOMINATION.

Play as Joe
Enter the password JUJOFEVRY1.

Play as Jon
Enter the password UNMASKED.

Art Gallery Option
Enter the password LEONARDO.

Voice Mode
Enter the password TONGUEBATH.

Expert Mode
Enter the password SKUPASTYLE.

BLOOD OMEN: LEGACY OF KAIN

Blood Refill
Press Up, Right, Square, Circle, Up, Down, Right, Left during gameplay.

Full Magic
Press Right (2), Square, Circle, Up, Down, Right, Left during gameplay.

View All Videos
Press Left, Right, Square, Circle, Up, Down, Right, Left during gameplay. Then press Select and view Dark Diary sequences.

BLOODY ROAR

Extra Alice Costume
Select Time Attack mode and defeat all enemies in less than 10 minutes.

Extra Replay Views
Hold Select to hit your opponent during the winning sequence.

Show Bonus Graphics
Finish the game in Arcade mode and press Left or Right to view different scenes in the characters' endings.

Enable Shadow Mode
Finish the game with all characters.

Enable Psychedelic Mode
Finish the game with all characters at difficulty level four or higher.

Disable Guard Mode
Finish the game with Gada at difficulty level four or higher.

Remove Character Lighting
Finish the game with Long at difficulty level four or higher.

Enable Camera Control
Finish the game with Alice at difficulty level four or higher.

Remove Energy Bars
Finish the game with Yugo at difficulty level four or higher.

Regenerating Energy
Finish the game with Bakuryu at difficulty level four or higher.

Invisible Walls
Finish the game with Fox at difficulty level four or higher.

Disable Ring Walls
Finish the game with Mitsuko at difficulty level four or higher.

Small Stage
Finish the game with Greg at difficulty level four or higher.

Big Stage
Select Survival mode and beat 10 opponents in a row.

Big Arms
Select a character while holding L1+L2.

Change Costume
Use Circle to select your character.

Meaty Arms
Select character while holding L1+L2.

Change Costume/Big Head
Select character with Circle while holding L2.

Change Costume/Kid
Select character with Circle while holding R2.

Big Head
Select character with X while holding L2.

Kid
Select character with X while holding R2.

Giant Characters
Select character while holding L2.

BLOODY ROAR 2: THE NEW BREED

Expert Mode
Hold L1+L2+R1+R2 at the title screen and pick any option.

Get Gado
Finish the game with any character in Arcade mode.

Fight Shen Long
Finish the game with any character in Arcade mode without using continues.

Get Shen Long
Defeat Shen Long in the special stage.

Enable Model Type Option
Finish the game with any character in Story mode.

Enable Recovery Speed Option
Finish the game with any character in Story mode without using continues.

Enable Any Cancel Point Option
Defeat 15 or more characters in Survival mode.

Extra Costume
Finish the game with all characters in Arcade mode and press Start to select a character in a fourth costume.

Enable Custom Option
Finish Arcade mode with any character.

Remove Menu on Pause Screen
Pause and hold R2.

Unlock Dash Mode
Beat Story mode with Shen Long.

Movies and Pictures
Beat Story mode with every character at a difficulty level of four or more to unlock all pictures and movies.

BLUE SABRE KNIGHTS

Alternate Camera Views
Pause gameplay during a battle. Hold R1+R2 and use the D-Pad to move the camera around. Press L1 and L2 to zoom in and out.

BODY HAZARD

All Weapons
Pause and press R1+Square, Triangle, Circle, X.

Big Head
Pause and press L1+L2+R2+Down.

Hidden Boss
Enter Circle, Square (2), X, Circle, X (2), Circle as a password.

Increase Clean Points
Pause and press L1+L2+Circle+Square.

Invincibility
Pause and press Circle, Square, Left, Right+R1+R2.

Special Mode
Pause and press R1+R2+Triangle+Circle.

BOGEY DEAD 6

Unlimited Continues
Choose training option from the game menu and select the "Wolves Awakening" mission. Change your heading to north 010 degrees and accelerate. Continue flying north until a yellow blip shows on the radar. Load air to ground missiles and fire at the mountain they lock on. Gold bars appear here. Fire another missile and destroy the gold bars. Crash to end the mission and return to the main menu. The word "INFINITY" replaces the aircraft icons on the Continue Game screen if you correctly activated this code.

Air-to-Air Missile Invincibility
Hold L1+L2+R1+R2 and rotate the D-Pad counterclockwise at the Now Loading screen.

All Missions
Press Up, Down (2), Right, Left, Down, Up, Triangle at the Mission Select screen.

All Fighters
Press Left (2), Right, Down, Up, Down, Right, Select at the Plane Selection screen.

Chase View
Highlight aircraft and select holding L1+L2+R1 +R2+Select. Press Select to change view.

More Time
Hold L1+L2+R1+R2+X+Triangle+Square+Left at the Now Loading screen.

BOMBERMAN

Alternate Block Locations
In Battle mode, enter the password 56565656 for beginner, 16161616 for normal, or 49894989 for hard.

Level 1 (Full Power) Password
46224622

Level 11 (Full Power) Password
10191019

Level 21 (Full Power) Password
12221222

Level 31 (Full Power) Password
26572657

Level 41 (Full Power) Password
38793879

Level 10 (Show Time Event) Password
3G59E326

Level 20 (Show Time Event) Password
3D5D49C4

Level 30 (Show Time Event) Password
8D5A4B26

Level 40 (Show Time Event) Password
8D5A4BCE

BOMBERMAN FANTASY RACE

50 Saved Game Positions
Select New System Data, hold L1+L2+R1+R2+Select+Start and press Circle.

Mirror Tracks
Place first in all tracks. Then at the Track Selection screen, press Right.

Alternate Footstep Sound Effect
Pause gameplay and press L1 (2), R1 (2), Down, Up, Circle.

View Ending Sequence
Win all mirror tracks. Then at the title screen, press Select.

Double Money
Save the game in two different slots. Enter the bank and transfer the money from one slot to the other.

Hidden Animals
Buy all five kangaroos and dinosaurs. The black kangaroo and white dinosaur become available.

BOMBERMAN WARS

View the Bomber Prince
In Quest mode, finish 10 stages, then enter the practice room. Put all characters in the hallway and go back to the practice room. The Bomber Prince appears half the time.

Faster Game
At the title screen, hold Circle and press Start.

Bonus Levels
Win Quest mode once.

Best Equipment
Area 5: 3623

Level 1-1 Password
8010

Level 1-2 Password
1180

Level 1-3 Password
8086

Level 1-4 Password
2919

Level 1-5 Password
1021

Level 2-1 Password
0127

Level 2-2 Password
1220

Level 2-3 Password
1018

Level 2-4 Password
0804

Level 2-5 Password
0714

Level 3-1 Password
1027

Level 3-2 Password
2413

Level 3-3 Password
3009

Level 3-4 Password
6502

Level 3-5 Password
6809

Level 4-1 Password
0627

Level 4-2 Password
8808

Level 4-3 Password
3674

Level 4-4 Password
4891

Level 4-5 Password
0605

Level 5-1 Password
0730

Level 5-2 Password
2151

Level 5-3 Password
3562

Level 5-4 Password
3812

Level 5-5 Password
2203

Bonus Versus Level Password
5656

Bonus Battle Level Password
4989

Battle Royale Password
1616

Maniac Mode Password
4622

Two Secret Levels Password
3636

BOMBERMAN WORLD

Extra Bonus Levels
Type 3636 as a password. The new stages are Under the Sea and Bomber Shock.

BOOMBOTS

Unlock Characters and Levels
At the BoomBot Selection screen, press Square (4), Circle (4), Square (4), Select (3).

Cheat Mode
At the BoomBot Selection screen, press Square, Circle (2), Square, Circle (2), Square, Circle (2), Square, Circle (2), Select (3).

One Hit Kills CPU Opponent
Enter Cheat mode, pause gameplay, and press Circle+Square+Triangle.

CPU Opponent Has 100 Less Health
Enter Cheat mode, then pause gameplay and press Circle+Square.

BRAHMA FORCE

Easier Game
Hold Up-Right+X+Square at the Press Start screen and press Start.

Flight Mode
Complete the game before 1:30:00. Hold L2+R2 and press X on controller two. While playing, fly with R2 and L2.

Harder Game
Press L1, R1, L2, R2, Square, X, Triangle, Circle at the title screen.

Level Skip
Load a saved game and keep tapping Start until the saved game message appears. Pick "No" to continue at the next level.

Reset Game
Press L1+L2+R1+R2+Select during gameplay.

Control the Map
Pause. Enter the Map option. Press Select to stop the map movement. Press R1, R2, L1, L2, or the D-Pad to control the map movements.

Extra Options
Beat the game before 1:30:00. Enter the "Special" option after the title screen to access all the bonus options.

BRAINDEAD-13

Final Room
Enter AAAABLFJSIMON as a password to jump to the final room. You can then enter one of the following ending codes.

Normal Ending
Press Left (4), Down, Up, Left (2), Right (2), Down, Left, Right, Down, Fire, Right, Up, Down, Fire, Down, Fire (4).

Alternate Ending
Press Left, Right (2), Down, Left, Right, Down, Fire, Right, Up, Down, Fire, Down, Fire (4).

BRAVE FENCER MUSASHI

Burning Plants
In the Ice Palace, and in a few other places, there are plants. If you use the Fire Scroll, you can set them on fire. This causes repeating damage in increments of 8.

Giant Plants
On Twinpeak Mountain, there are Blue Plants growing out of pots. Walk to them and use the Water Scroll. Throw bubbles on them, and they grow to three times the normal size.

Mom Minku
After you capture all the minku, go to the entrance of the Meandering Forest. The Mother Minku will be there. Stock up on BP- and HP-restoring food.

Unlimited Money
In the village bar, which is open in game time from 6:00pm until 2:00am, you can play a high-low game with a character named Macho. The game costs 100 to play and will return doubled amounts in this sequence: 200, 400, 800, 1,600, 3,200, 6,400, 12,800, 25,600, 51,200, and lastly 102,400. However, if you get 102,400, he will no longer play the game with you. If he picks a number less than 7, select high. If he picks 7 or higher, select low. Starting with a few hundred for a loss cushion, you can quickly become extremely wealthy. Always stop your winnings at 51,200, though, or you can't keep raking it in!

BRAVO AIR RACE

Change Plane Color
While the race is loading, hold R2+L1.

Turbo GeeBee
Pick the GeeBee for a game. At the Now Loading screen, repeatedly tap X until the GeeBee flies to the top of the screen. "Good" appears on the screen if you entered the code correctly. The GeeBee will fly faster now.

Bonus Planes
At the title screen, hold R1+L2 and quickly press Select (20) on controller two. A sound confirms correct entry. The F16 and Stealth jet become available.

BREATH OF FIRE III

Beat Gaist
You can make your confrontation with the sole living guardian (besides Garr) simpler by getting rid of the two torches on either side of Ryu. At first it seems that they replenish 25HP to Gaist, but it also makes his fire-based attacks more deadly. Have Ryu equip something like Magma Armor that absorbs Fire-based attacks.

Beat the Dragon Zombie
Battling with the Dragon Zombie after Ryu becomes older is a tough battle because of its poisoning abilities. To destroy this monster quickly, have Ryu cast all his best heal spells on the Creature. This takes care of him in no time. This trick works on any undead creatures, except vampires.

Beat the Dragon Zombie: Method 2
When you get to the Dragon Zombie after you grow up, have Garr cast kyrie on him, and he dies instantly.

Change Names
In your Faerie Village, put three Faeries in a casino. Talk to the one on the left and she'll let you change the names of your party members, including those not with you, and other Faeries.

Control the Kaiser Form
When you choose the Kaiser, Ryu will be out of control. For better results, choose Infinity + Trance + Radiance as your only genes.

Deis
To get Deis, go to Zublo Mountain after you free her. Go up the stairs when you enter Zublo Mountain, go up to the slab and press X. She will ask if you would like to be her apprentice.

Easy Experience
Later in the game, develop the Faerie Village until you have a copy shop, and copy an Ivory Dice until you have 12. Use those dice in battle on an enemy. Depending on what enemy you use them, you'll get 20,000 to 80,000 experience!

Easy Ghosts
If you're having trouble beating the ghosts in McNeil Manor, use Heal on them. This even works on the boss.

Free Berries
For free berries, go to the coffee shop and kick the apple tree.

Get the Beast Spear
As soon as you beat Gaist, search his ashes.

Get the Ding Frog Fishing Lure
To get the ding frog, you have to be a "MASTER OF FISHING++." The ding frog is a lure that attracts everything. The man only gives you three. He is at the cliff South of Steel Beach.

Get the Royal Sword and the Life Armor
Fish near Kombinat with the Deep Diver lure until you have two Whales, four Spearfish and four Barandy. (The Barandy fish is at the spot south of the Northern Checkpoint. You need a Frog lure for these fish.) After you get all the fish, return to Kombinat and use a Coin lure to reel in the big, fat creature swimming around. He asks if you want to buy something. Say yes, and the sword and armor are yours!

Master of Agility

To get the Faerie Meryleep to become your master, go east of Wyndia where there is a spring that is home of the Faeries. Have Peco run and knock a rock into the middle of the pool, and a Faerie appears. She sends you on a mission to get an object that a crow stole from her. Go to the mountain west of the Arena. If you walk behind the mountain, a "?" appears. Enter and have Peco hit the tree with the crow on it. Take the object back to the Faerie, and she offers to be your master. Your agility goes up +2, but your HP, Power, and Defense go down 1.

The Magic Master (Mygus)

After you have gone a ways through the game, go north of McNeil to see a tree stump on the map (a question mark shows). Enter it and go up to see an old man. Talk to him. Whichever character that is apprenticed with him will gain more INT and AP, but gain a little less Attack Power and Defense during level-ups.

The Master D'Lonzo

Near Windia, there is a coffee shop. Go behind it to see a girl walking around. You need 15 kinds of weapons to get her.

The Master Emitai

After you get older, you can get Emitai as one of your Masters. (Emitai is the leader of the second team you fight in the Tournament of Champions.) After you get older, go near Ogre Road go down the northern path. There is a hut. Talk to Emitai, and he tells you that if you pay him 10,000 zenny for his mortgage, he will teach you some of his spells.

The Secret Master

After you go to Windia the second time, there is a Master. There is a pathway between the walls surrounding Windia. Go this way to enter a little house. In this house is a Master.

The Strength Master (Bunyan)

After you get farther in the game, go back to Bunyan's Cabin to make him a Master for one of your characters. Any character apprenticed to Bunyan will gain more Attack Power and Defense, and less Intelligence and HP when gaining a level.

BRIAN LARA CRICKET '98

Always Win
Classic Match Password: GETBRIBE

Cricket on the Beach
Classic Match Password: SUNSHINE

Large Hands
Classic Match Password: BIGHANDS

Large Heads
Classic Match Password: BIGHEADS

Play with Beach Ball
Classic Match Password: BIGBALLS

Slippery Ball
Classic Match Password: DROPBALL

Stronger Batsmen
Classic Match Password: SUPERMAN

Wickets Never Fall Over
Classic Match Password: SOLIDOAK

World Team in Friendly Matches
Classic Match Password: PENSIONS

CPU Fielders Always Drop Ball
Classic Match Password: BUTTERFINGERS

Helmet View
Classic Match Password: CHRISREA

Classic Match Level Passwords
Press Down, X to activate the password option.

Classic Match Level 2 Password
OVERTIME

Classic Match Level 3 Password
SAUSAGES

Classic Match Level 4 Password
DILLBERT

Classic Match Level 5 Password
BATKINGS

Classic Match Level 6 Password
PANCAKES

Classic Match Level 7 Password
FRIEDEGG

Classic Match Level 8 Password
PLACEBO1

Classic Match Level 9 Password
CLUELESS

Classic Match Level 10 Password
NOWAYEAS

BRIGANDINE

Play as Esgares Empire
At the General Select screen, press L2+R1+Start.

BROKEN HELIX

More Ammo
Pause and press Triangle. A sound confirms a correct entry.

More Health and Armor
Pause and press Triangle. Highlight the HELP TEXT option, hold L1+R2 and press X+Circle. A sound confirms a correct entry.

All Items
Pause and press Triangle. Highlight the HELP TEXT option, hold L1+R2+R1+Square and press X. A sound confirms a correct entry.

BUBBLE BOBBLE

Debug Mode
Press Down, Up, Down, Up, Right, Down, Left, Down, Up, Down at the title screen.

Warp to Previous Level
Enter the Debug code first. During gameplay, press L1 to skip to the previous level.

Warp to Next Level
Enter the Debug code first. During gameplay, press R1 to skip to the next level.

View Debug Menu
Enter the Debug code first. During gameplay, press R2 to display the Debug menu. Press R1 to hide the Debug menu.

Various Bonus Effects
Enter SEX, TAK, I.F, KTT, MTJ, NSO, STR, KIM, LSD, or YSH as the initials in the high score screen. Then start another game. The new effects appear when certain bonuses are collected during the game.

Original Game
At the title screen, press Right, Left, Up, Down, Up, Down, Up.

BUBSY 3D

Cheat Codes
Select the Load and Save option, then enter the following passwords.

All Codes
XALLDBUGCR

99 Lives
XMUCHOLIFE

All Rockets
XTOOROCKER

Bonus Round
XBNSCHTMMM

Coordinates
XDBUGLOCNC

Level Select
XLVLCHTMSB

Change Shape
XURASNAKER

Secret Voice Tests
BUBSYHITXA

Secret Voice Tests
BUBSYBOPXA

Secret Voice Tests
BUBSYCNTXA

Secret Voice Tests
BUBSYDOGXA

Secret Voice Tests
BUBSYCARXA

Secret Voice Tests
BUBSYGLDXA

Secret Voice Tests
BUBSYHIHXA

Secret Voice Tests
BUBSYIDLXA

Secret Voice Tests
BUBSYPOWXA

Secret Voice Tests
BUBSYSCRXA

Secret Voice Tests
BUBSYUFOXA

Secret Voice Tests
BUBSYH2OXA

Secret Voice Tests
BUBSYWOOXA

Secret Voice Tests
BUBSYWOLXA

Secret Voice Tests
BUBSYWORXA

Warp
Enter XZOOMMERKB and press Left+Start during gameplay to move around the level.

BUGGY

Slow Cars
Set a track record and enter the name SLO. Press X. At the OK? prompt, hold L1+L2+R1+R2 and press X. A jingle confirms correct entry.

Disable All Graphics Textures
Set a track record and enter the name WOW. Press X. At the OK? prompt, hold L1+L2+R1+R2 and press X. A jingle confirms a correct entry.

Unlock All Views
Set a track record and enter the name CAM. Press X. At the OK? prompt, hold L1+L2+R1+R2 and press X. A jingle confirms a correct entry. During gameplay, press Triangle to change views.

BUGS BUNNY: LOST IN TIME

All Abilities
At the Level Select or Era Select screen, hold L2+R1 and press X, Square, R2, L1, Circle, X, Square, Circle, Square.

Extra Key
At the Level Select or Era Select screen, hold L2+R1 and press X, Square, R2, L1, Circle, X, Circle, Square (2).

Full Energy
At the Level Select or Era Select screen, hold L2+R1 and press X, Square, R2, L1, Circle, X, Square, Circle (2).

Lose a Life
At the Level Select or Era Select screen, hold L2+R1 and press X, Square, R2, L1, Circle, X, Circle (3).

Maximum Carrots
At the Level Select or Era Select screen, hold L2+R1 and press X, Square, R2, L1, Circle, X, Square (2), Circle.

View Complete Ending
At the Level Select or Era Select screen, hold L2+R1 and press X, Square, R2, L1, Circle, X, Circle, Square, Circle.

View Incomplete Ending
At the Level Select or Era Select screen, hold L2+R1 and press X, Square, R2, L1, Circle, X, Circle (2), Square.

Level Select
At the Level Select or Era Select screen, hold L2+R1 and press X, Square, R2, L1, Circle, X, Square (3).

BURNING ROAD

Reversed Tracks
Start a new race in Practice mode. When the race begins, turn and drive in the opposite direction. When you pass the first checkpoint, you will be first and other cars will follow. Three new tracks become accessible.

BUSHIDO BLADE

Hidden Boss and Ending
Win Story mode without getting hit or continuing and following the Bushido code.

Fight as Katze
Beat all 100 opponents in Slash mode without dying.

BUSHIDO BLADE 2

Fight as Sub-Characters
Win in Story mode, keeping both sub-characters alive. They may now be used in any other mode.

Slash Mode
Win in Boss mode without continuing. Slash mode appears on the main menu.

Fight as Katze
Win in Slash mode in less than 15 minutes with a Shainto fighter.

Fight as Tsubame
Win in Slash mode in less than 15 minutes with a Narukagami fighter.

Chanbarra Mode
In Boss mode, beat all 13 bosses without continuing. At the main menu, highlight Link mode and press Down (2).

Hundred Slashes Mode
Beat the game with the six regular characters.

BUST-A-GROOVE

Bonus Level
Complete the first level with Shorty. Then press Up, Down, Left, Right, and Circle to go to a new level.

Level Skip
After beating the game, use L2+Select in Single-player mode.

Play as Alternate Character
Highlight a character. Hold Select and press X.

Play as Capoeira
Win as any character at Normal difficulty.

Play as Robo-Z
Win as any character at Normal difficulty after unlocking Capoeira.

Play as Burger Dog
Unlock Robo-Z first. Then win as Hamm at Normal difficulty.

Play as Columbo
Unlock Robo-Z first. Then win as Shorty at Normal difficulty.

Super Solos
Enter these moves during solo section of dance:

Heat's Super Solo
Up, Down, Up, Circle

Frida's Super Solo
Up, Down, Up, Circle

Strike's Super Solo
Up (2), Left, Circle

Hamm's Super Solo
Down, Right Up, Circle

Kelly's Super Solo
Right, Left, Right, Circle

Shorty's Super Solo
Down (3), Circle

Hiro's Super Solo
Right, Up, Down, Circle

Pinky Diamond's Super Solo
Up, Left, Up, Circle

Gas-O's Super Solo
Left, Down, Right, Up, Circle

Kitty NakaJima's Super Solo
Down (2), Right, Circle

Capoeira's Super Solo
Right, Up, Right, X

Robo-Z's Super Solo
Up, Down, Left Right, Circle

Columbo's Super Solo
Down (3), Circle

Burger Dog's Super Solo
Down, Right, Up, Circle

Winning Pose Close-Up
After winning a stage, hold down Circle.

BUST-A-MOVE

Another World
Press R1, Up, L2, Down at the title screen.

Character Select
Press Left (2), Up, Down, L1+L2+R1+R2, at the Map screen.

More Continues
Highlight "Credits" on the Options screen and press Left, Right, R1, R2, L2, L1, Up, Down. Then press X repeatedly.

BUST-A-MOVE 2: ARCADE EDITION

Another World
When "Press Start" appears at the title screen, press R1, Up, L2, Down. A small green wizard confirms correct entry. Begin a new game and select a regular puzzle game. The levels will be faster and contain newer backgrounds.

Character Select
Start a puzzle game, and at the Map screen, press Left (2), Up, Down, L1+L2+R1+R2.

More Credits
In Options, press Left, Right, R1, R2, L2, L1, Up, Down. A 30-second timer appears in the upper-right corner. Now quickly highlight "Credit" and press X or Circle repeatedly to add up to 29 credits. Returning to Options resets the credits to the default value.

BUST-A-MOVE 2: DANCE TENGOKU MIX

Unlock Pander Bonus Level
Rank at "Fever Time" in each level.

Play as Columbo
Win as Shorty.

Play as Chi Chi and Sally
Win as Capoeira.

Play as Pander
Unlock the Pander bonus level and win as Robo-Z Gold.

Play as Robo-Z Gold
Unlock the Pander bonus level and win in Mix mode.

BUST-A-MOVE 3

Another World
At the title screen, press Circle, Left, Right, Circle. An ant appears in the lower-right, confirming a correct entry.

BUST-A-MOVE 4

Another World in Arcade Mode
At the Start screen, press Triangle, Left, Right, Left, Triangle. A green face in the lower-right corner confirms correct entry. Pick Arcade mode and Puzzle mode to access more puzzles.

Bonus Characters

At Start screen, press Left (2), Triangle, Right (2), Triangle, Left (2). Applause confirms correct entry.

Talking Demo

At the Start screen, press Square, Up, Left, Down, Right, Up, Square, Down, Left, Up, Right, Down, Square. A sound confirms correct entry. The Options menu contains the new option.

Tarot Readings

At the Start screen, press Up, Triangle, Down, Triangle, Up. The Options menu contains the new option.

BUSTER BROTHERS COLLECTION

Bonus Levels

Press X on both controllers while selecting a normal game.

Level Select

When selecting a normal game, press Down+X.

C: THE CONTRA ADVENTURE

Level Select

Press Left, Up, Right, Square (2), Triangle (2), Down at the title screen.

Infinite Lives

Press Up, Right, Square, Triangle, Right, Left, Square, Triangle at the title screen.

FMV Movies

Press Triangle (2), Down, Square, Up (2), Left, Triangle at the title screen.

Machine Gun

Press Right (2), Square, Triangle, Right, Left, Down (2) at the title screen.

Infinite Super Bombs

Press Square (2), Right, Down (2), Left, Square, Triangle at the title screen.

CAPCOM GENERATIONS VOLUME 1

Special Weapons: 1943

Before the level begins, hold the following buttons:

1. Down
2. Weapon 1
3. Up/Right+Weapon 1+Weapon 2
4. Down/Left+Weapon 2
5. Weapon 1
6. Left
7. Up/Left
8. Left+Weapon 1+Weapon 2
9. Down/Right+Weapon 1+Weapon 2
10. Up/Right+Weapon 2
11. Up/Left
12. Right+Weapon 1+Weapon 2
13. Up
14. Up/Left+Weapon 1+Weapon 2
15. Down/Left+Weapon 1
16. Right+Weapon 1

CAPCOM GENERATIONS VOLUME 2

Level Select—Super Ghouls 'n' Ghosts

In Options, highlight "Backup." Hold L1+Start on controller two and press Start on controller one.

CAPTAIN COMMANDO

One Hit Kills

Using Captain or Jennety, hold X+Circle and press the special move button.

Four-Player Mode

On the opening screen, when the warning appears, press Square+Triangle+Circle+X to allow four players.

Stage Select

Highlight "Game Start" and press X+Circle+Left.

CARDINAL SYN

Unlock Kron

At the title screen, press L2 (2), Up (3), Left, Down, Up, Circle, L1. A sound confirms correct entry.

Unlock Syn

At the title screen, press R1, Right, R2, Square, R1, Down, R1, R2 (2), Circle. A sound confirms correct entry.

See Endings

At the title screen, press Down, Up, Down, Right, Left (2), Up, Left, R1, Circle (2), L2. A sound confirms correct entry.

Unlock All Characters

At the title screen, press L1, R2, R1, Square, Down, Circle, Down, L2, Square (4). A sound confirms correct entry.

Orion's Alternate Costume

At the title screen, press R2, Down (2), Circle, Square (2), R2.

Juni's Alternate Costume

At the title screen, press Down, Square, Down, L2, Down (3).

Nephra's Alternate Costume

At the title screen, press Square, L1, Circle, Up, Triangle, Left, Triangle.

Syn's Alternate Costume

At the title screen, press Circle (3), L1, R1, Circle, Left.

Infinite Magic

At the title screen, press Right (3), Left, Triangle, Left (2), Square. A sound confirms correct entry.

Fatalities at Any Time

At the title screen, press Up (2), Right (2), Left, Circle (2), Down. A sound confirms correct entry.

Mongoro's Fatality

During a match, press Forward+Square, Triangle, Square (2), Forward+Square.

Kahn's Fatality

During a match, press Back+Triangle, Back+Triangle, Square (2), Back+Square.

Redemptor's Fatality

During a match, press Back+Square, Square (3), Back+X.

Plague's Fatality

During a match, press Triangle (3), Back+Triangle.

Stygian's Fatality

During a match, press Square, Triangle (2), Back+X.

Juni's Fatality

During a match, press Square (4), Forward+Square, Forward+Square, Back+Square.

McKrieg's Fatality

During a match, press Triangle (3), Square, Forward+Square.

Vanguard's Fatality

During a match, press Triangle, Square (3), Back+Square.

Moloch's Fatality

During a match, press Forward+Triangle, Triangle (2), Square, Up+Square.

Orion's Fatality

During a match, press Forward+Triangle, Forward+Triangle, Square (2), Forward+X.

Finkster's Fatality

During a match, press Square (4), Back+Square, Back+Square, Forward+Square.

Bimorphia's Fatality

During a match, press Square, Triangle, Square (2), Back+Square.

Vodu's Fatality

During a match, press Square (3), Triangle, Back+Square, Up+X.

Hecklar's Fatality

During a match, press Square (3), Triangle, Forward+Square, Up+Triangle.

Nephra's Fatality

During a match, press Square, Triangle, Square (2), Back+Square.

Mongwan's Fatality

During a match, press Forward+Triangle, Forward+Triangle, Square, Triangle, Forward+Triangle.

CARMAGEDDON

Unlock All Cars and Levels

At the initial main menu screen, enter: Up, Down, Up, Down, Left, Right, Left, Right, Triangle, Square, and Start.

CARNAGE HEART

Manual OKE Control

During a battle, press Select (12), then select "Manual" from the menu that appears.

CARNAGE HEART EZ

Manual OKE Control

Before going to battle with your OKE, press Select. Then press Select (10).

Bonus Music

At the Music Options screen, hold L1+L2+R1+R2 to unlock five additional tracks.

CARNAGE HEART SECOND ZEUS

Battle on the Moon

Finish level 22, with 6+ times more destroyed targets than damaged targets.

CART WORLD SERIES

Alternate Paint Jobs

Enter ROOSTER as name.

Sunset Track
Enter SUNNYSKY as name.

Night Track
Enter NIGHTRID as name.

Space Track
Enter SPACERID as name.

Titon Track
Enter EPILEPTI as name.

Cars Only Have Wheels
Enter WHEELS as name.

Increased Gravity
Enter RADBRAD as name.

Maximum Gravity
Enter STONE as name.

Half Gravity
Enter FLOAT as name.

Three-Quarter Gravity
Enter FEATURE as name.

Fat Tires
Enter FAT TIRES as name.

Instant Win
Enter WTFIN as name.

Invincibility
Enter IMMORTAL as name.

No Collisions
Enter BANZAI as name.

Two Laps in Season Mode
Enter GEK as name.

Set Number of Cars
Enter MAXCARSx. Replace "X" with a letter representing the number of cars in the race (A=1, B=2, C=3, etc.). For example, MAXCARSA represents one car.

Light Car
In Single Race or Season modes only, enter FEATHER as a name.

CASPER

Fast Movement
Hold Triangle and press X, R1 (3) during gameplay.

Drift Over Walls
In top-left corner of any room, hold Up+Left+L1+R1+Start to freeze the game. Release Up+Left and L1, then press Down+Right+Triangle. Use R1 and the D-Pad to fly over walls. Press L1 to resume normal gameplay.

CASTLEVANIA: SYMPHONY OF THE NIGHT

Axe Lord Armor
Complete the game once, then enter AXEARMOR as name in a new game. The armor appears in your inventory.

Enhanced Luck
Complete game once, then enter X-X!V"Q as name in a new game. You start with 99 luck, but with reduced strength and hit points.

Extra Options
Enter AXELORD as name, then access the Settings screen.

Control the Now Loading Logo
Use the D-Pad to manipulate the Now Loading logo.

Bonus Music
Place the game disk into an audio CD player. Listen to tracks two and above.

Music Test
Beat the game with a 190 percent or higher ranking with Alucard. Start a new game with Alucard without overwriting the previous saved game. Go to the Librarian to see a Music Select option in the Buy/Sell window.

Play as Richter Belmont
Save a game with one of these attributes: after the final battle in the game, into the middle section of the inverted castle, after beating the final villain, or marked as "clear." Start a new game and enter RICHTER as a name.

CASTROL HONDA SUPERBIKE RACING

Wheelie
Accelerate out of first gear. Once you reach 100 mph, release the throttle for three seconds. Then accelerate again.

CAT THE RIPPER

Chris' Secret Level
Touch the PeRoPePo Candy at hotel room 109.

CD SAMPLER PACK VOLUME 3

Crash Bandicoot Information
At the Crash Bandicoot screen, press Square (2), Triangle.

King of Fighters '95 Information
At the King of Fighters '95 screen, press Triangle, Circle, Square.

NCAA GameBreaker Information
At the NCAA GameBreaker screen, press Circle, Triangle, Circle.

Ridge Racer Revolution Information
At the Ridge Racer Revolution screen, press Circle, Triangle, Square.

Tekken 2 Information
At the Tekken 2 screen, press Triangle (2), Square.

Twisted Metal 2 Information
At the Twisted Metal 2 screen, press Square, Circle, Triangle.

View Horned Owl FMV Sequence
At the Tunnel B1 screen, press Triangle, Square (2).

View Independence Day FMV Sequence
At the Blast Chamber screen, press Triangle, Circle, Triangle.

View Jumping Flash 2 FMV Sequence
At the NHL Faceoff '97 screen, press Square, Triangle, Circle.

View Motor Toon Grand Prix FMV Sequence
At the Formula 1 screen, press Square, Triangle, Square.

View Tobal No. 1 FMV Sequence
At the Jet Moto screen, press Circle (2), Triangle.

View Twisted Metal 2 FMV Sequence
At the 2Xtreme screen, press Circle, Square, Circle.

CD SAMPLER PACK VOLUME 3.5

Crash Bandicoot Information
At the Crash Bandicoot screen, press Square (2), Triangle.

King of Fighters '95 Information
At the NFL Gameday '97 screen, press Triangle, Circle, Square.

NCAA GameBreaker Information
At the NCAA GameBreaker screen, press Circle, Triangle, Circle.

Ridge Racer Revolution Information
At the Ridge Racer Revolution screen, press Circle, Triangle, Square.

Tekken 2 Information
At the Tekken 2 screen, press Triangle (2), Square.

Twisted Metal 2 Information
At the Twisted Metal 2 screen, press Square, Circle, Triangle.

View Carnage Heart FMV Sequence
At the Rally Cross screen, press Triangle, Square (2).

View Independence Day FMV Sequence
At the Blast Chamber screen, press Triangle, Circle, Triangle.

View Jumping Flash 2 FMV Sequence
At the NHL Faceoff '97 screen, press Square, Triangle, Circle.

View Tobal No. 1 FMV Sequence
At the Jet Moto screen, press Circle (2), Triangle.

View Motor Toon Grand Prix FMV Sequence
At the Formula 1 screen, press Square, Triangle, Square.

View Twisted Metal 2 FMV Sequence
At the 2Xtreme screen, press Circle, Square, Circle.

CENTIPEDE

Cheat Mode
Pause in Adventure mode. Press L1 (2), L2, L1, Start. A sound confirms correct entry. Invincibility is enabled when the player has an odd number of lives. For an extra life, pause and press Right.

CHAMPIONSHIP BASS

Level Select
Enter the case-sensitive password EVpUyYy18VoE

Challenge Mode Passwords
2 WK7GuHcbZo7a

3 JZsVh[Star]romb82

4 cMB4UBWVTuB[Triangle]

CHAMPIONSHIP MOTOCROSS

Big Heads
Enter GROSSE TETE in the name entry in Championship mode.

Mirror Mode
Enter OPPOSITE LOCK in the name entry in Championship mode.

Track Unlock
Enter DIRT TRACKS in the name entry in Championship mode.

PLAYSTATION

Unlock All Championships
Enter ALL EVENTS in the name entry in Championship mode.

Unlock Extra Video
Enter LIVE ACTION in the name entry of Championship mode.

CHAMPIONSHIP SURFER

Unlock Every Beach
L2, R1, R2, L1, L2

CHASE THE EXPRESS

Unlimited Ammo
Enter the following code while the game is paused: L1, L2, R1, R2, Square, X, X.

Skip to Next Level
Pause the game at any point, and enter: L1, R1, X, Circle, Square.

CHECKMATE

Bonus Characters
At the title screen, press Left, Up (2), Right (3) to pick a bonus character in Versus mode. For another bonus character, unlock the first, then press L1 (3), R1 (3) at the title screen.

CHESSY

Level Skip
Enter X (2), Square, Circle as a password, then choose "LEVEL SKIP" in the Options menu.

CHICKEN RUN

Bonus Ending
Get a gold medal in every minigame, then go to Hut 1 to get the bonus ending.

CHOCOBO DUNGEON 2

Bonus Sequence
Beat the game and allow the credits to finish. A bonus section begins. Finish this bonus section to view another ending.

CHOCOBO RACING

Instant Speed
Before race starts, hold Up+Square.

Unlock Bahamut Class
Place first in every stage (including the *Final Fantasy 8* track) in the Grand Prix mode of Chocobo and Behemoth class.

Unlock Mirror Mode
Place first in every stage (including the *Final Fantasy 8* track) in the Grand Prix mode of Bahumut class. Choose the Mirror Mode option at the Options screen.

Secret Characters
Each time you beat Story mode, a hidden character is unlocked. To use the bonus character, highlight Squall and press the corresponding buttons. Below is the list of bonus characters.

Squall
Win twice in Story mode. Highlight Squall and press Square, Triangle, Circle, or X.

Cid
Win three times in Story mode. Highlight Squall and press L1.

Mumba
Win four times in Story mode. Highlight Squall and press L2.

Cloud
Win five times in Story mode. Highlight Squall and press R1.

Cactuar
Win six times in Story mode. Highlight Squall and press R2.

Aya
Win seven times in Story mode. Highlight Squall and press L1+L2.

Mini Chocobo
Win eight times in Story mode. Highlight Squall and press R1+R2.

Iben Super Air Ship
Win nine times in Story mode. Highlight Squall and press L2+R2.

Jack
Win 10 times in Story mode. Highlight Squall and press L1+R1.

CHRONICLES OF THE SWORD

Skip First Parts
Enter SADAIN as a password.

Skip to End of Disk 1
Enter MAZOE as a password.

CHRONO CROSS

Always Win Roulette Game
When the roulette pointer starts spinning and the red tip is within the west and the south edges of the wheel, pause and press Circle to resume; make it land on north and double your money.

CIRCUIT BREAKERS

Better Engine (2P Mode)
At the Track Selection screen, press X+Square+Triangle+Circle. An engine appears if you entered the code correctly.

Invincibility
Pause. Press L1, L2, L1 (3), L2 (3), Circle, Triangle, Square, Circle, Triangle, Square. You become an invincible skeleton with everything.

Jumping Bean Cars (2P Mode)
Press Circle+Left at race countdown.

Race at Night
At the Track Selection screen, press L1+L2+R1+R2.

Upside-Down Tracks
At the Track Selection screen, press L2+R2+X+Down. An arrow appears if you entered the code correctly.

All Tracks (1P Mode)
Start a race in One-player mode. Pause. Enter the Sound option and highlight "FX Volume." Press L1+L2.

CIVILIZATION II

Extra Money
Enter _CasH as town name and hold R1 when selecting H.

CLOCK TOWER

Pause (Mouse Mode)
Put the pointer in the upper left corner of the screen. Press both mouse buttons simultaneously.

CLOCK TOWER 2

Change Custom 1
Hold L1+R1+Select+Triangle at the title screen.

Change Custom 2
Hold L1+R1+Select+Square at the title screen.

Sound Test
Press Left, Circle, Down, Triangle, Right, Square, Up, X, L1, R2, L2, R1+Start at the title screen. Sound Test is under Option mode

Unlimited Power Spell
Press L1+L2+R1+R2 at the title screen. Start a new game.

Wear School Uniform
Hold L1+R2+Select+Triangle+Start at the title screen and start a new game.

Extra Mode
Get an A ending rank to reveal "Extra Mode" on the title screen.

View Character Biographies
Unlock all 13 endings. Select Pamphlet mode. A "Guide" option displays each character's data.

CLOCK TOWER: GHOST HEAD

School Uniform
Hold L1+R2+Select+Triangle at the title screen. Start the game and your character is wearing a school uniform.

CODENAME: TENKA

All Weapons
Pause. Hold L1 and press Triangle, R1, Triangle, Square, R1, Circle, Square (2). Release L1.

Level Warp
Pause. Hold L2 and press Circle (2), Square, Triangle, R1, Square, Triangle, Circle. Release L2.

COLIN MCRAE RALLY

Fog
Enter PEASOUPER as name.

Power Accelerator
Enter BUTTONBASH as name.

Squeaky-Voiced Co-Driver
Enter HELIUMNICK as name.

Replays
Enter DIRECTORCUT as name.

Turbo Boost
Enter KITCAR as name.

Double Engine Power
Enter MOREOOMPH as name.

Rear Wheel Steer
Enter FORKLIFT as name.

4 Wheel Steering
Enter TROLLEY as name.

Small Cars
Enter DIDDYCARS as name.

Back-to-the-Future Cars
Enter HOVERCRAFT as name.

Low Gravity
Enter MOONWALK as name.

60 Frames Per Second
Enter SILKYSMOOTH as name.

Green Jelly Car
Enter BLANCMANGE as name.

Metallic Cars
Enter TINFOILED as name.

Nicky Grist as Driver
Enter BACKSEAT as name.

Play in the Dark
Enter NIGHTRIDER as name.

Reversed Tracks
Enter SKCART as name.

Right Side Driver
Enter WHITEBUNNY as name.

Unlock All Tracks
Enter OPENROADS as name.

Unlock All Cars
Enter SHOEBOXES as name.

Wobbly Car
Enter MAGFLOAT as name.

Pursuit Mode
Pause. Press Triangle+Square+Circle six times, L1, L2, R1, R2 six times. Somebody says something if you entered the code correctly.

COLIN McRAE RALLY 2.0

All Cars
At the Create New Driver Profile, enter ONECAREFULOWNER.

Lancer Road Car
At the Create New Driver Profile, enter OFFROAD.

Mini Cooper
At the Create New Driver Profile, enter JOBINITALY.

Sierra Cosworth
At the Create New Driver Profile, enter JIMMYSCAR.

Ford Puma
At the Create New Driver Profile, enter COOLESTCAR.

All Levels
At the Create New Driver Profile, enter HELLOCLEVELAND.

Mirrored Tracks
At the Cheat Options screen, enter RORRIM-SKCART.

Shoot Fireballs
At the Cheat Options screen, enter GREAT-BALLSOF. In Arcade mode, use the Handbrake to shoot fireballs.

Bouncing Collisions
At the Cheat Options screen, enter RUBBERTREES. Only available in Time Trial and Single Stage Rally modes.

Monster Truck Wheels
At the Cheat Options screen, enter EASY-ROLLER. Only available in Time Trial and Single Stage Rally modes.

Low Gravity
At the Cheat Options screen, enter MOON-LANDER. Only available in Time Trial and Single Stage Rally modes.

Turbo Mode
At the Cheat Options screen, enter ROCKET-FUEL. Only available in Time Trial and Single Stage Rally modes.

Faster Game
At the Cheat Options screen, enter PRUNE-JUICE. Only available in Time Trial and Single Stage Rally modes.

Aggressive CPU Cars
At the Cheat Options screen, enter NEURAL-NIGHTMARE. Only available in Arcade mode.

Cat Silhouette
At the Cheat Options screen, enter HELLO RAZU AND FLEA.

COLLEGE SLAM

Enable Dunks
Press Up, Down, Up, Down, Up, Down at Tonight's Match-Up screen.

Hidden Teams
Press Left, Up, Circle, Up, Down, Up, Right, Triangle at the title screen.

High Shots
Press Up (6), Down, at Tonight's Match-Up screen.

Max Power
Press Triangle, Down, Triangle, Right, at Tonight's Match-Up screen.

Power-Up Three-Pointers
Press Up (3), Triangle (3), at Tonight's Match-Up screen.

Power-Up Fire
Press Left, Right, Left, Right, Up, Down (2), at Tonight's Match-Up screen.

Power-Up Goaltending
Press Up (2), at Tonight's Match-Up screen.

Power-Up Offense
Press Right, Up, Down (2), Up, at Tonight's Match-Up screen.

Power-Up Push
Press Up, Triangle, Up, Circle, Up (2), at Tonight's Match-Up screen.

Power-Up Turbo
Press Down, Triangle, Down (2), Up, at Tonight's Match-Up screen.

Push Opponent, Both Fall
Press Up, Left (2), at Tonight's Match-Up screen.

Push Opponent, Teammate Falls
Press Down, Triangle, Down, Triangle, Down, Triangle, at Tonight's Match-Up screen.

Quick Hands
Press Left, Triangle, Circle (2), Up, at Tonight's Match-Up screen.

Small Players
Press Triangle (7), Start, at Player Select screen.

Speed-Up
Press Left (6), Right, at Tonight's Match-Up screen.

Whirlwind
Perform two clockwise circles with the D-Pad at Tonight's Match-Up screen.

COLONIZATION

Cheat Mode
Enter the name CHARLOTTE for one of the cities.

COLONY WARS

Level Select Password
Commander Jeffer

Infinite Primary Weapon Power Password
Tranquillex

Infinite Shields Password
Hestas Retort

All Missions and Endings Password
zX7z15EEvLax7Q0N

Disable All Cheats Password
All*cheats*off

Unlimited Secondary Weapons Password
Memo*X33RTY

COLONY WARS 3: RED SUN

Cheat Code Option
At the Home Station, press R2 (2), L2 (2), R1 (2), Select (2) to enable the Cheat Code option.

All Ships
Perform the Cheat Code option, then enter Greyam Beard.

All Weapons
Perform the Cheat Code option, then enter Armoury.

All Weapons Loaded on Ship
Perform the Cheat Code option, then enter Big Daddy.

Spaceship and Strength
Perform the Cheat Code option, then enter Break and Enter.

Hub Select
Perform the Cheat Code option, then enter Move House.

Indestructible
Perform the Cheat Code option, then enter Awrate.

Unlimited Afterburners
Perform the Cheat Code option, then enter Jalferezi.

Unlimited Ammo
Perform the Cheat Code option, then enter Sly n Devious.

Weapons Do Not Overheat
Perform the Cheat Code option, then enter ROCKWROK.

Mission Skip
Perform the Cheat Code option, then enter Quickie.

Disable All Codes
Perform the Cheat Code option, then enter All Cheat Off.

COLONY WARS: VENGEANCE

Invincibility Password
Vampire

All Weapons Password
Tornado

All Ships Password
Thunderchild

Cheat Mode Password
Blizzard

Disable All Codes Password
Stormlord

Primary Weapons Always Available Password
Dark*Angel

Infinite Secondary Weapons Password
Chimera

Infinite Afterburners Password
Avalanche

Infinite Tokens Password
Hydra

Mission and Ending Select Password
Demon

COMMAND & CONQUER

Covert Operations Password
COVERTOPS

Extra $5,000
Pause. Press Right, Down (2), Left, L1, Left, Right, Down, Left, Start. Repeat as desired.

Instant Air Strike
Pause. Press Right, Down, Left (2), Down, Right (2), Down, Left, X, Square, Circle.

Instant Ion Cannon
Pause. Press Right, Down, Left (2), Down, Right (2), Down, Left, X, Square, Triangle.

Instant Nuclear Strike
Pause. Press Right, Down, Left (2), Down, Right (2), Down, Left, X, Up, X.

Japanese Mode Password
GODZILLA

Secret Level (On GDI Disk) Password
PATSUX

View Entire Map
While starting new game, hold L1+L2+R1+R2+Square+Circle until the mission briefing begins. Alternately, pause and press Circle (3), Up, Circle, Square, R1, Circle (3).

Air Strike and Ion Cannon
Pause. Press Right, Down, Left (2), Down, Right (2), Down, Left, X, Square, Triangle+Circle. Unpause to see both weapons.

GDI Passwords 2
04XFOOP3W

GDI Password 3
W3KIESA3O

GDI Password 4
A8OTO3WIW

GDI Password 5
W1N457LJ4

GDI Password 6
OLXRH5ZUS

GDI Password 7
OX3CS3D4G

GDI Password 8
036Y0TVNY

GDI Password 9
V199PXG5L

GDI Password 10
8PH1NEGII

GDI Password 11
GTJKF2J00

GDI Password 12
T0RMFVVM5

GDI Password 13
AQU7OQ65A

GDI Password 14
KV2UWMZJ9

GDI Password 15
GTJ2PV46O

GDI Special Ops Mission 1 Password
8PHJTYIP1

GDI Special Ops Mission 2 Password
SZ4VH22RY

GDI Special Ops Mission 3 Password
878FR0G1M

GDI Covert Ops Mission "Blackout" Password
GT1BEQHY8

GDI Covert Ops Mission "Hell's Fury" Password
8PH1RPW9W

GDI Covert Ops Mission "Infiltrated!" Password
SHDZUI8ID

GDI Covert Ops Mission "Elemental Imperative" Password
8PZAIF13P

GDI Covert Ops Mission "Ground Zero" Password
GT1TAEXF9

GDI Covert Ops Mission "Twist of Fate" Password
C9RO8NZGU

GDI Covert Ops Mission "Blindsided" Password
W15VEC3SQ

NOD Password 2
C99FAXKW8

NOD Password 3
RZNLQZ3NL

NOD Password 4
W1954XWLF

NOD Password 5
W15DASRS8

NOD Password 6
8PH1MR53W

NOD Password 7
GTJKWOJDK

NOD Password 8
YKK424K3D

NOD Password 9
874LCPUT4

NOD Password 10
A8SHPAHXW

NOD Password 11
OX3UKOP94

NOD Password 12
QGDUMSK2J

NOD Password 13
SZP09VDSB

NOD Special Ops Mission 1 Password
0LXRXJOY5

NOD Special Ops Mission 2 Password
03O5MO802

NOD Covert Ops Mission "Bad Neighborhood" Password
C99X6L0D9

NOD Covert Ops Mission "Deceit" Password
SHVQLLFOX

NOD Covert Ops Mission "The Tiberian Sun" Password
W1N4V4TKB

NOD Covert Ops Mission "Cloak & Dagger" Passwords
C99FJ8DM5

NOD Covert Ops Mission "Hostile Takeover" Password
C99F1A8VH

NOD Covert Ops Mission "NOD Death Squad" Password
0LF0D3T25

NOD Covert Ops Mission "Under Siege: C&C" Password
457E1D682

COMMAND & CONQUER: RED ALERT

Secret Message from Kane
Hold Select and turn the game on.

Cheat Codes
Click on the Teams menu with the Cancel button (Circle by default). Move the cursor over the following icons on the menu bar and press Cancel on each. Use this method for the following codes.

1,000 Credits
Square (2), Circle, X, Triangle, Circle

Nuke Attack
Circle, X, Circle, Triangle, Square, Triangle

Instant Victory
X, Square (2), Circle, Triangle, Circle

Parabomb
Square, X, Circle (2), X, Triangle

Full Map
Square, Triangle, Circle, X, Triangle, Square

Chronoshift
Triangle, Circle (2), Square (2), X

Change Ore or Crystals to Gold
Square, Circle, Square, X, Circle (2)

Change Ore to Civilians
X, Circle, Triangle (2), Circle, X. Enter this code after a refinery is present in multiplayer mode.

Allies Password 2
PJ1OC3IEW

Allies Password 3
EC5NAHTU

Allies Password 4
9BFVYZAZ8

Allies Password 5
P4XS4CZVC

Allies Password 6
FMNAE6U08

Allies Password 7
7XIQW4KQI

Allies Password 8
WPLAGLJ2G

Allies Password 9
4TNT8RJ21

Allies Password 10
FZ0ZY7ZQA

Allies Password 11
X9FJZVJZI

Allies Password 12
5RNHTXLRY

Allies Password 13
J7VEWVT09

Allies Password 14
OLHDAPYHL

Allies Password 17
17LE3FDV

Soviet Password 1
17DUXFJ6C

Soviet Password 2
VMBWOQ284

Soviet Password 3
XN37MCCSO

Soviet Password 4
LH06FZZQL

Soviet Password 5
BUVV20LFF

Soviet Password 6
AVYQ10YA8

Soviet Password 7
LZRJTMQAN

Soviet Password 8
YQX4C9GFH

Soviet Password 9
1QESO8LE0

Soviet Password 10
RKP0UOXJA

Soviet Password 11
CDLKYL7Q4

Soviet Password 12
8T5GGDK25

Soviet Password 13
X5CDE0KN8

Ant Missions
Set the difficulty to Hard, pick "Campaigns," and go to England.

Chronoshift
Place cursor over these controller symbols in sidebar and press Cancel: Square, Circle, Triangle, X, Circle (2).

Easy Money
Place cursor over matching controller symbols in sidebar and press Cancel: X (2), Square, Circle (3).

Instant Win
Place cursor over these controller symbols in sidebar and press Cancel: Circle (2), Triangle, X (2), Square.

Iron Curtain
Place cursor over these controller symbols in sidebar and press Cancel: Square, X, Circle, X, Triangle (2).

Nuclear Attack
Place cursor over these controller symbols in sidebar and press Cancel: Circle, X, Circle (2), X, Square.

Parabombs
Place cursor over these controller symbols in sidebar and press Cancel: X (3), Circle, Triangle, Square.

Reveal Map
Place cursor over these controller symbols in sidebar and press Cancel: Triangle (2), X, Circle, Triangle, Square

Soylent Green Mode
Place cursor over these controller symbols in sidebar and press Cancel: Square, X, Square, X, Square, X, Square, X

Lose Mission
Place cursor over these controller symbols in sidebar and press Cancel: Circle, X, Circle, Square (2), X

Civilians Have Names
Place cursor over these controller symbols in sidebar and press Cancel: Square (2), Circle (2), Triangle

COMMAND & CONQUER: RED ALERT RETALIATION

Chrono Storm
When you chronoshift a couple of times, a strange orb appears on the map, slowly floating around. The orb is a chrono storm that electrocutes anything that comes near. If it heads to your base, kiss a good section of it good-bye. A chrono storm has a 30% chance of being created every chronoshift. It appears randomly on the map, so do not get carried away chrono shifting.

Chronoshift
To get a chronoshifter, enter this code: Place the cursor over the corresponding symbols on the sidebar, then press cancel (the Circle button on the default settings), Square, Circle, Triangle, X, Circle, Circle.

Easy Money
To enter this code, place the cursor over the corresponding symbols on the sidebar, then press cancel (the circle button on the default settings.): X, X, Square, Circle, Circle, Circle.

Instant Win
To enter this code, place the cursor over the corresponding symbols on the sidebar, then press cancel (the circle button on the default settings): Circle, Circle, Triangle, X, X, Square.

Iron Curtain
While playing, look on the sidebar (the right-hand toolbar). Halfway down the bar are four symbols that match your controller. To enter this code, move the cursor over those symbols and press the Cancel button (Circle by default) over each one in the order shown here. Move the cursor over the Square and press Cancel. Move the cursor over X and press Cancel. Move the cursor over Circle and press Cancel. Move the cursor over X and press Cancel. Move the cursor over Triangle and press Cancel. Move the cursor over Triangle and press Circle.

Nuclear Attack
To enter this code, place the cursor over the corresponding symbols on the sidebar, then press cancel (the Circle button on the default settings): Circle, X, Circle, Circle, X, Square.

Parabombs
To get parabombs, enter this code. Place the cursor over the corresponding symbols on the sidebar, then press Cancel (the Circle Button on the default settings), Parabombs: X, X, X, Circle, Triangle, Square.

Reveal Map
To enter this code, place the cursor over the corresponding symbols on the sidebar, press Cancel (the circle button on the default settings), Reveal Map: Triangle, Triangle, X, Circle, Triangle, Square.

Secret England Mission
Beat every level on the allied forces or Soviet discs to enable the hidden England missions. The mission will not light up blue. In this mission, you defend yourself against giant ants.

Soylent Green Mode
With this code, all ore fields turn to civilians, and ore trucks harvest them. To activate, go to the in-game sidebar, go to the team select bar, and enter the following symbols using the Circle button: Square, X, Square, X, Square, X, Square, X.

CONSTRUCTOR

Free Money, Etc.
At the Start menu, press R1, L2, Circle, X, Triangle, Square, Select.

CONTENDER

Main Event Boxers in Versus Mode
In Main Event mode, create a new boxer and immediately save the boxer to a memory card. Then repeat. Now begin a two-player match in Versus mode. At the Character Selection screen, press Square to choose one of the previously saved Main Event boxers.

Hidden Exhibition Mode Boxers
Win the World Championship, then save the game. Then, in Exhibition mode and at the Character Selection screen, press Square (2).

Unlock the Boxing Trainer
Press Square (2) at the Two-player Versus mode Character Selection screen. The boxing trainer appears as a selectable character.

Newspaper Photograph

During a match, turn on the analog and press one of the analog sticks to take a photograph. The photograph appears in the newspaper after the fight.

Contra: Legacy of War

9 Lives

At the title screen, press L2, R2, L1, R1, Down, Up (2), Down. Then, press Triangle+Circle during gameplay.

Bamboo Arcade

At the title screen, press R2, R1, Right, Left, L1, L2.

Bamboo Gyruss

At the title screen, press L2, L1, Left, Right, R1, R2.

Change Weapon

At the title screen, press L2, R2, L1, R1, Up, Down (2), Up. Then, press Square+Triangle during gameplay.

Level Select

At the title screen, press L2, R1, L1, R2, Left, Right, Circle, Square, R2, L2.

Sound Test

At the title screen, press R2, R1, L1, L2, Up, Right, Down, Left.

Unlimited Continues

At the title screen, press L2, R2, L1, R1, Left, Right (2), Left.

View FMV's

At the title screen, press L2, L1, R1, R2, Up, Left, Down, Right.

Cool Boarders

Extra Grabs

Press and hold any direction+R1 or R2.

High-Pitched Announcer

At the Options screen, press Select (40).

Additional Boards

Win the three rankings to use special boards. Each level has three special boards.

Special Course

Obtain three special boards to unlock the hardest course.

Alternate View

Win all rankings on all courses to unlock another view.

Snowman

Win the three rankings of the hardest course. Pick the Alpine board by pressing Up+Circle+Triangle. Snowman becomes accessible and you can save him to the memory card.

Trick Names

Hold L1+L2 between the Selection and Play screens. Then, hold R1+R2 on controller two to see the trick name.

Trick Points

Hold L1+L2 between the Selection and Play screens. Then, press L1 or L2 to view the trick points when you play boards.

Load Time

Press Select between the Selection and Play screens.

Cool Boarders 2

Alternate Clothing (Irin and Cindy)

Highlight Competition mode. Press Down, R1, Up, R1, Down, R2, Up, R2, Up (2), R1, Down (2), R2. This gives Cindy a leather outfit and Irin a school uniform.

Hard Mode

Hold L1 and press X at the game's beginning in Tour Competition mode.

Play as Boss

Place first in Competition Mirror mode.

Play as Gray

Obtain a "Gray" rank in Trick Master mode or score higher than 37.5 in Half Pipe mode.

Play as Snowman

Break all the records (each category on all 10 courses) in Freestyle mode.

Disable the Music

Keep pressing Start repeatedly during gameplay. Stop pressing Start once the music begins playing while the game is paused. Press Start again to resume play without the music.

Bonus Boards

Obtain the top records on all tracks in Freestyle mode.

Unlock the Alpine Board

Place first in the "Time" category on at least five courses in Freestyle mode. This board isn't available in Tour Competition or Half Pipe modes.

Unlock the Freestyle Board

Place first in the "Trick" category on at least five courses in Freestyle mode. This board isn't available in Tour Competition mode.

Unlock the All-Around Board

Place first in the "Total" category on at least five courses in Freestyle mode. This board isn't available in Tour Competition or Half Pipe modes.

Reversed Courses

Beat all nine rounds in Snowboarding Competition mode and obtain any ranking. Then hold R1 and pick Freestyle or Snowboarding Combined mode.

Mirror Mode

Win the Snowboarding Competition. Enter the Options screen and press Select on controller two. Enter the Mode Selection screen and press R1+Square.

Cool Boarders 3

Unlock All Mountains

Enter WONITALL as a name in Tournament mode.

Unlock All Boarders

Enter OPEN_EM as a name in Tournament mode.

Unlock All Boards

Enter GET EM as a name in Championship mode.

Big Heads

Enter BIGHEADS as a name in Tournament mode. Pause, then press L2 to shrink the head and R2 to expand it.

View Current Position

Enter SHOWPOS as a name in Tournament mode.

View Game Completion Date

At the screen that reads "one player or split screen," press L1, L2, R2, R1. The game's completion date is displayed.

Control the Replay Camera

During a replay, hold Left for slow motion, Down to pause.

Control the Camera

Press Select during gameplay.

Play as Burg

Unlock every player, board, and track. Then play in a single event on Powder Hill Downhill. Place first with a score higher than 3,400 points.

Play as Fast Eddie

Race on the mountain. Race on Powder Hill Downhill and get first place with a score that is higher than 3,400 points.

Cool Boarders 4

All Boards, Boarders, and Mountains

Enter ICHEAT as a name. A spoken phrase confirms correct entry.

All Special Events

Enter IMSPECIAL as a name. A spoken phrase confirms correct entry.

Unlock an Extra Mountain

Enter NEWHILL as a name. A spoken phrase confirms correct entry.

Control the Replay Camera

During a replay, hold R1 or R2 and press Down to stop the replay. Hold R1 or R2 and press Left for slow motion replay. Hold R1 or R2 and press Right to fast forward.

Unlock Fast Eddie

Beat Rookie on Trickmaster.

Unlock a Mystery Character

Finish the Colorado Tournament with Jimmy Hallop. A "Cool Man" message is spoken as confirmation.

Play as Bear

Shatter every record in France and win the special event.

Play as a Snowman

Shatter every record in Japan and win the special event.

Cool Boarders 2001

Unlock Everything

Enter the Career Mode and enter your name as GIVEALL. After you enter the last L, a voice will says "Hey, no cheating." You have now unlocked everything.

Courier Crisis

Bonus Level

Press L1+R2 at the Neighborhood Selection screen. A sound confirms correct entry.

Free Mode

Enter HANOILBKJO as a password.

Give Someone the Finger

Press R1+R2 or L1+L2 during gameplay.

Play as Zaskar
Enter FDFKFKHCJK as a password.

Play as Pantera
Enter KFKFKFOEKJ as a password.

Play as Gorilla
Enter SAVAGEAPES as a password.

Play as Alien
Enter XFIFTYONEX as a password.

Play as STS-1
Enter IFKFKFKGKJ as a password.

Play as Fish
Enter FINALSDFIN as a password.

Bonus Music
Press R1, Triangle, R1, L1, Circle, X, R2, L2 during gameplay to unlock three new songs. Press R1, Triangle, R1, L1, Circle, X, R2, L2 to hear a fourth song.

Level 1 Password
eflcifcgkj

Level 2 Password
iflcifccki

Level 3 Password
mflcifcokj

Level 4 Password
aflcifckkj

Level 5 Password
fhclfigcjl

Level 6 Password
flclficcil

Level 7 Password
fpclfiocjl

Level 8 Password
fdclfikcjl

Level 9 Password
kflcifcgii

Level 10 Password
oflcifccii

Level 11 Password
cflcifcoij

Level 12 Password
gflcifckij

Level 13 Password
ffclfigccj

Level 14 Password
fjclficcij

Level 15 Password
fnclfiocjj

COVERT OPS: NUCLEAR DAWN

Infinite Ammo
Beat "Scenario A: Paris" on any difficulty level to play the game a second time with infinite ammo.

CRASH BANDICOOT

Debug Menu
At the Naughty Dog logo, hold Up+X until the title screen appears. Hold Left and press Square, Circle, Square, Start. Then during gameplay, press Down, X (26), Select to display the Debug menu.

Access All Levels, Keys, Gems
At the Password screen, enter Triangle (4), X, Square, Triangle (4), Square, X, Triangle, Circle, Triangle (3), Circle, Square, Triangle, X (4).

Start 2 Percent Complete
At the Password screen, enter Circle, Square, Circle, Square, Circle(2), Triangle, Square.

Start 6 Percent Complete
At the Password screen, enter Circle, X, Square, Triangle, Circle, Square (2), Triangle.

Start 11 Percent Complete
At the Password screen, enter Square (2), X, Square (2), Triangle, X, Triangle.

Start 13 Percent Complete
At the Password screen, enter X, Square, X, Circle, X, Square, Triangle, X.

Start 18 Percent Complete
At the Password screen, enter Square (2), Triangle, X, Circle (2), X, Triangle.

Start 19 Percent Complete
At the Password screen, enter Triangle (2), X, Triangle, Circle (2), Square, X, Square, X, Circle, Square, Circle, Square, X, Triangle, Square, X (2), Square, X (2), Triangle, Square.

Start 22 Percent Complete
At the Password screen, enter Circle, Square (2), Circle (2), X (3).

Start 27 Percent Complete
At the Password screen, enter X, Circle, X, Circle (2), X, Square, Circle.

Start 31 Percent Complete
At the Password screen, enter Square, X, Triangle (2), X, Square, X, Triangle.

Start 36 Percent Complete
At the Password screen, enter X, Circle (3), X, Square, X, Square.

Start 38 Percent Complete
At the Password screen, enter Square (2), X, Triangle, X, Square, Circle, X.

Start 50 Percent Complete
At the Password screen, enter Triangle (3), Square (3), Triangle, Circle (2), X, Square (2), Triangle (2), Circle (3), X, Square (3), Circle, Triangle, Circle.

Start 52 Percent Complete
At the Password screen, enter Triangle (2), Circle, X (2), Square (2), Circle, Square, Triangle (2), X (2), Circle (2), Square, Circle, Square, Triangle, Square, X (3), Circle.

Start 56 Percent Complete
At the Password screen, enter Triangle (5), X, Square (3), Triangle (2), X (2), Triangle, Square, Circle, Triangle, Square, Circle, X, Circle (2), Triangle, X.

Start 57 Percent Complete
At the Password screen, enter Triangle(3), Square(4), Circle, Square, Triangle (2), X (2), Triangle (2), X, Circle, Square (2), X, Square, Triangle, X, Circle.

Start 63 Percent Complete
At the Password screen, enter Triangle (2), X (4), Triangle, Square (2), X (3), Circle, Square, Triangle (2), X, Circle, X, Circle, Triangle (2).

Start 68 Percent Complete
At the Password screen, enter Triangle (2), X (2), Square, Circle, Square, Triangle (2), X (3), Circle, X, Square (2), Triangle (2), Circle (2), Square, X, Circle.

CRASH BANDICOOT 2: CORTEX STRIKES BACK

Revisit Boss Stages
Go to the middle platform of a warp room. Hold L1+L2+R1+R2 and press Triangle, Up when Crash points.

Aku Aku Mask
Hold Up+Circle after losing a life. Release the buttons when Crash loses his second life. Alternately, while in a warp tunnel, press X (2) and then hold Up+X. Release the buttons when Crash loses his second life.

Extra Levels
In the Unbearable level, jump in after the second polar bear falls off the bridge to enter a bonus level. In the Turtle Woods level, locate a menacing face after a checkpoint box. Perform a belly-flop on the face to have Crash fall into the extra level.

Extra Lives
Jump on the baby polar's head in the second warp room (levels 6 to 10) to have Crash collect 10 extra lives.

CRASH BANDICOOT 3: WARPED

Spyro the Dragon Demo
At the title screen, press Up (2), Down (2), Left, Right, Left, Right, Square.

Turbo Starts
On any motorcycle level, when the second red lights up, press and hold X. You do a wheelie and start off faster.

Hot Cold Hidden Level
Go to Level 14 and ride about halfway through the level. Run into the alien crossing sign on the left side to be taken to Level 31.

Eggipus Rex Hidden Level
Go to Level 11 and grab the yellow gem ride. Continue to the area where the big dinosaur chases Crash. Let the second pterodactyl grab Crash to be taken to Level 32.

CRASH BASH

Spyro 3 Demo
At the title screen, press L1, R1, Square, Start.

CRASH TEAM RACING

Invisibility Power-Up
At the main menu, hold L1+R1 and press Down, Left, Right, Up, Down, Right.

Unlock Komodo Joe
At the main menu, hold L1+R1 and press Down, Circle, Left (2), Triangle, Right, Down.

Unlock N. Trophy
At the main menu, hold L1+R1 and press Down, Left, Right, Up, Down, Right (2).

Unlock Papu Papu
At the main menu, hold L1+R1 and press Left, Triangle, Right, Down, Right, Circle, Left (2), Down.

Unlock Penta Penguin

At the main menu, hold L1+R1 and press Down, Right, Triangle, Down, Left, Triangle, Up.

Unlock Pinstripe

At the main menu, hold L1+R1 and press Left, Right, Triangle, Down, Right, Down.

Unlock N. Oxide

Beat N. Oxide's ghost on every track in time trials.

Unlock Ripper Roo

At the main menu, hold L1+R1 and press Right, Circle (2), Down, Up, Down, Right.

Spyro 2 Demo

At the main menu, hold L1+R1 and press Down, Circle, Triangle, Right.

Turbo Counter

At the main menu, hold L1+R1 and press Triangle, Down (2), Circle, Up.

Turbo Pads

At the main menu, hold L1+R1 and press Triangle, Right (2), Circle, Left.

Infinite Masks

At the main menu, hold L1+R1 and press Left, Triangle, Right, Left, Circle, Right, Down (2).

Scrapbook

At the main menu, hold L1+R1 and press Up (2), Down, Right (2), Left, Right, Triangle, Right.

Bonus Tracks

At the main menu, hold L1+R1 and press Right (2), Left, Triangle, Right, Down (2).

Infinite Bombs

At the main menu, hold L1+R1 and press Triangle, Right, Down, Right, Up, Triangle, Left.

Infinite Wumpa Fruit

At the main menu, hold L1+R1 and press Down, Right (2), Down (2).

Three Extra Battle Arenas

Complete One-player Arcade mode on the Easy, Medium, and Hard difficulty settings.

Red Gem Cup

Collect all four red CTR coins in Adventure mode.

Green Gem Cup

Collect all four green CTR coins in Adventure mode.

Purple Gem Cup

Collect all four purple CTR coins in Adventure mode.

Yellow Gem Cup

Collect all four yellow CTR coins in Adventure mode.

Blue Gem Cup

Collect all four blue CTR coins in Adventure mode.

Fake Crash

Win the Purple Gem Cup in Adventure mode.

Unlock N. Oxide's Spaceship

Obtain four Boss Keys to unlock the ship.

CRIME CRACKERS

Animation Select

Press Up (2), Down (2), Left (2), Right (2), Select, at the title screen.

Debug Mode

Press R1 (2), L1 (2), R2 (2), L2 (2), Left, Circle, Right, Square, Select, Start at the title screen.

CRIME KILLER

Level 2 Password

Circle, Square, X, Triangle, Square, Triangle, Square

Level 3 Password

Circle (2), Square, X, Triangle, Circle (5)

Level 4 Password

Circle (2), Square, Triangle, Circle (2), Square, Triangle, Square, X

Level 5 Password

Triangle, Circle (7), Square, Triangle

Level 6 Password

Square, Triangle, Square, Triangle, Circle, Square, X (3), Triangle

Level 7 Password

Circle (4), Square, X, Triangle, Circle (3)

Level 8 Password

Square, Triangle, Square, X, Triangle, Square, X, Triangle, Square, X

Level 9 Password

X (2), Triangle, Circle, Square, X, Triangle, Square, Triangle, Circle

Level 10 Password

Circle, Triangle, Circle (2), Square, X, Triangle, Circle (3)

Level 11 Password

Square, Triangle, Square, Triangle, Circle (2), Square, Triangle, Square, Triangle

Level 12 Password

Square, Triangle, Square, Triangle, Square, Triangle, Circle, Square, Triangle, Square

Level 13 Password

X (3), Triangle, Circle (3), Square, X (2)

Level 14 Password

X (4), Triangle, Circle, Square, X (3)

Level 15 Password

X, Triangle, Square, X (2), Triangle, Circle, Square, Triangle, Square

End Level Password

X, Triangle, Circle, Square, Triangle, Square, X, Triangle, Square, Triangle

CRISIS BEAT

Unlock Free Mode

Beat the game with both Eiji-Julia Team and Keneth-Feisu Team in Single mode or Pair mode. Then you can use any two characters in a two-player game.

Unlock Expert Mode

Beat the game under Normal difficulty.

CRISIS CITY

Unlock Area 6

Choose a character in Versus mode. Highlight the Random option on the Area Selection screen, hold L1, and press Circle.

Unlock Area 7

Choose a character in Versus mode. Highlight the Random option on the Area Selection screen, hold L2, and press Circle.

Extra Option

Press Up, Down, Left, Right, X, Circle at the title screen.

CRITICAL BLOW

Fight as Hagane

Win Theater mode at any difficulty setting.

Fight as Merkuar

Win Tournament mode using any fighter.

Fight as EX Rickey

Win Tournament mode at Hard.

Fight as Sieguei

Win Tournament mode at Easy.

CRITICAL DEPTH

Depth Charge

During gameplay, hold R2 and press Left, Right, Up.

Drop Pods

During gameplay, press L1, R1, L1, R1, Up, Down, Left, Up.

Guided Missiles

During gameplay, hold Triangle and press R1+L1. Control guided missile with the D-Pad. Detonate the missile by pressing R1+L1.

Infinite Weapons

During gameplay, press L1, R1, L1, R1, Up, Down, Left, Down.

Lay Mines

During gameplay, hold R2 and press Right, Left, Down.

Quadruple Damage

During gameplay, press R1, R2, R1, R2, Up, Down, Up, Down.

Stun Blast

During gameplay, hold R2 and press Right, Left, Up.

Invincibility

During gameplay, press L1, R1, L1, R1, Up, Down, Left, Right.

Surface Mine

During gameplay, hold R2 and press Right, Left, Down.

Mr. Phatt Submarine

Beat the game at Medium difficulty.

Agent 326 Submarine

Beat the game using Mr. Phatt at Hard difficulty.

Overseer Submarine

Beat the game using Agent 326 at Hard difficulty.

Abbadon Submarine

Win the game using Agent 326 at Captain difficulty.

CRITICOM

View All Endings

Enter TTAM at the password screen for the person whose ending you want to see.

Dayton (Level 2) Password

SIER

Dayton (Level 3) Password

ETER

Dayton (Access) Password

DIRAT

Delara (Level 2) Password
PHAN

Delara (Level 3) Password
KING

Delara (Access) Password
DCINO

Demonica (Level 2) Password
GONE

Demonica (Level 3) Password
WORL

Demonica (Access) Password
DANAR

Exene (Level 2) Password
SPHE

Exene (Level 3) Password
WING

Exene (Access) Password
ESCIN

Gorm (Level 2) Password
CHAM

Gorm (Level 3) Password
MARV

Gorm (Access) Password
GODNE

Sid (Level 2) Password
ODTH

Sid (Level 3) Password
BATM

Sid (Access) Password
SOBRU

Sonork (Level 2) Password
PLAY

Sonork (Level 3) Password
CHRO

Sonork (Access) Password
SSISE

Yenji (Level 2) Password
SPID

Yenji (Level 3) Password
STAR

Yenji (Access) Password
YAHAM

CROC: LEGEND OF THE GOBBOS

Never Lose a Life by Falling
Pause before Croc starts his yell. Press Select and select the Quit option. Then select "No." Press Down so that "Continue" and "Quit" options are not highlighted. Press X to restart at the current level without losing a life.

Sound Test
Press Select at the Audio Options screen.

Level Select
Enter the password: Up, Left, Down, Left, Right, Left, Down, Up, Left, Right (2), Down, Right (2), Up.

Super Password
Enter the password: Left (4), Down, Right (2), Left (2), Down, Right, Down, Left, Up, Right. You will be playing at the end of the game and have all the secrets.

Level 1-1 Password
Up, Left (4), Down (2), Up, Left, Up, Left, Up, Right (2), Up

Level 1-2 Password
Up, Left (4), Down (2), Up, Left, Up, Right, Down, Right (2) Up

Level 1-3 Password
Right, Up, Left, Up, Left, Up (2) Right, Left, Right, Up, Right, Left, Up, Down

Level 1-B1 Password
Down, Left, Up, Right, Left, Down, Right, Left, Right, Left, Right (2), Down, Left (2)

Level 1-4 Password
Up, Right, Down, Left (2), Down (2), Up, Left, Right (2), Down, Right (2), Up

Level 1-5 Password
Right, Down (2), Up, Left, Up (2), Right, Left, Up (2), Right, Left, Up, Down

Level 1-6 Password
Down, Right (3), Left, Down, Right, Left, Right, Down, Right (2), Down, Left (2)

Level 1-B2 Password
Down, Right, Up, Right (4), Left (4), Right, Up, Left (2)

Level 2-1 Password
Right, Down, Left, Up, Right (2), Up, Right, Left, Right, Up, Right, Left, Up, Down

Level 2-2 Password
Down, Right, Up, Right (2), Left, Right, Left, Right, Left, Right (2), Down, Left (2)

Level 2-3 Password
Right, Left, Right (5), Left (5), Up, Left (2)

Level 2-B1 Password
Up, Left, Down, Left, Right, Left, Down, Up, Left, Right (2), Down, Right (2), Up

Level 2-4 Password
Right, Down (2), Up, Right, Left, Up, Right, Left, Right, Down, Right (2), Up, Down

Level 2-5 Password
Left, Up (3), Left, Up, Down, Up, Down, Right, Up, Left, Up, Left, Down

Level 2-6 Password
Right, Up, Left, Up, Right, Down, Up, Right, Up, Right, Down, Right (2), Up, Down

Level 2-B2 Password
Down, Left, Up, Right (2), Up, Right, Left, Up, Left (3), Up, Left (2)

Level 3-1 Password
Right, Up, Down, Up, Right, Down, Up, Right, Up, Right, Up, Right (2), Up, Down

Level 3-2 Password
Right, Up, Down, Up, Right, Down, Up, Right, Up, Right, Down, Left, Right, Up, Down

Level 3-3 Password
Left (4), Down, Up (2), Left, Up, Down, Up, Down, Left, Up, Right

Level 3-B1 Password
Left, Right, Left (2), Down, Up, Right, Left, Up, Down (2), Up, Left, Up, Right

Level 3-S1 Password
Left (2), Down, Left, Down, Right (2), Left, Down (2), Up (2), Left, Up, Right

Level 3-4 Password
Left (2), Down, Left, Down, Right (2), Left, Down (4), Left, Up, Right

Level 3-5 Password
Left (2), Down, Left, Down, Right (2), Left, Up, Down, Up, Down, Left, Up, Right

Level 3-6 Password
Left, Right, Down, Left, Down, Right (2), Left, Up, Down (2), Up, Left, Up, Right

Level 3-B2 Password
Left (4), Down, Right (2), Left, Down (2), Up, Down, Left, Up, Right

Level 3-S2 Password
Left, Right, Left (2), Down, Right (2), Left, Down (3), Up, Left, Up, Right

Level 4-1 Password
Left, Right, Left (2), Down, Right (2), Left, Up, Down, Up (2), Left, Up, Right

Level 4-2 Password
Left, Right, Left (2), Down, Right (2), Left, Up, Down (3), Left, Up, Right

Level 4-3 Password
Left, Right, Down, Left, Down, Up, Right, Left (2), Down, Right, Down, Left, Up, Right

Level 4-B1 Password
Left (2), Down, Left, Down, Up, Right, Left (2), Down, Left, Up, Left, Up, Right

Level 4-S1 Password
Left (2), Down, Left, Down, Up, Right, Left, Right, Down, Right, Up, Left, Up, Right

Level 4-4 Password
Left (2), Down, Left, Down, Up, Right, Left, Right, Down, Left, Down, Left, Up, Right

Level 4-5 Password
Left (4), Down, Up, Right, Left (2), Down, Right, Up, Left, Up, Right

Level 4-6 Password
Left (4), Down, Up, Right, Left (2), Down, Left, Down, Left, Up, Right

Level 4-B2 Password
Left (4), Down, Up, Right, Left, Right, Down, Right, Down, Left, Up, Right

Level 4-S2 Password
Left, Right, Left, Down, Up, Right, Left, Right, Down, Left, Up, Left, Up, Right

Level 5-1 Password
Left (2), Down, Left, Down, Right (2), Left (2), Down, Right, Up, Left, Up, Right

Level 5-2 Password
Left (2), Down, Left, Down, Right (2), Left (2), Down, Left, Down, Left, Up, Right

Level 5-3 Password
Left (2), Down, Left, Down, Right (2), Left (2), Down, Right, Down, Left, Up, Right

Level 5-4 Password
Left, Right, Down, Left, Down, Right (2), Left, Right, Down, Left, Up, Left, Up, Right

Level 5-B Password
Left (4), Down, Right (2), Left (2), Down, Right, Down, Left, Up, Right

CROC 2

Cheat Mode
Hold L1 and press Triangle, Left (2), Right, Square, Up (2), Left, Circle at the title screen. Then during gameplay, press L2+R2.

Infinite Crystals
Hold L1 and press Square (2), Circle, Down, Left, Right, Left, Right at the title screen. During gameplay, hold R2 and press Square to add 100 crystals to your inventory.

Infinite Lives
Hold L1 and press Circle, Down, Left, Up, Right, Triangle, Down at the title screen.

CROW: CITY OF ANGELS

Debug Mode
Enter the password Square, X, Square, Circle, Triangle (2), Circle, Square, X, Square.

FMV Select
Enter the password Triangle (2), Circle (6), Triangle (2).

Long Neck Mode
Enter the password X, Circle, Triangle, Circle, Square (2), Triangle, Circle, X, Circle.

Skinny Mode
Enter the password Triangle (2), X, Square, Circle (2), Square, X, Triangle (2).

Unlimited Energy
Enter the password Circle, X, Triangle, X, Circle, Triangle, Square, Circle, X, Square. You won't get any passwords when this code is enabled.

Pier Level Password
Triangle, X, Triangle (2), Circle, Square, Triangle, X, Circle

Boat Level Password
X (4), Triangle, Square, X, Circle

Tomb Level Password
Triangle, Circle, Triangle, Circle, Square, Triangle (2), Circle, X, Circle

Grave Level Password
X, Triangle, X, Triangle, Square, X (2), Triangle, Square, Circle

Church Level Password
Triangle (4), Circle, Square, Triangle, Square (2), Circle

Day O' Dead Level Password
X, Triangle, X, Triangle, Square, Circle (2), X, Square, Circle

Club Level Password
Triangle, Circle, Triangle, Circle (2), Triangle, X, Circle, Square, Circle

Tower Level Password
X (2), Circle, X, Square (2), X, Triangle, Circle

Borderland Level Password
Triangle, X (3), Circle, Square, Triangle, Square

Finale Level Password
X (3), Circle, Square (2), X (2), Triangle, Circle

CRUSADER: NO REMORSE

Full Health and Energy
Enter LOSR at the Password screen. A message tells you it is invalid, but Cheat mode is on. Then press Square+R1 during gameplay.

All Weapons and Items
Enable Cheat mode, then press Circle+R1 during gameplay.

Hidden Pictures Password
PPPP

Mama's Boy Mission 02 Password
FWQP

Mama's Boy Mission 03 Password
PLRQ

Mama's Boy Mission 04 Password
SZNF

Mama's Boy Mission 05 Password
TD5S

Mama's Boy Mission 06 Password
J1BT

Mama's Boy Mission 07 Password
K2CV

Mama's Boy Mission 08 Password
N3DW

Mama's Boy Mission 09 Password
M4FX

Mama's Boy Mission 10 Password
X5GZ

Mama's Boy Mission 11 Password
C6H0

Mama's Boy Mission 12 Password
D7J1

Mama's Boy Mission 13 Password
F8K2

Mama's Boy Mission 14 Password
FGK3

Mama's Boy Mission 15 Password
JFM4

Mama's Boy Realtime Level Password
LRTN

Weekend Warrior Mission 02 Password
GWQP

Weekend Warrior Mission 03 Password
QLRQ

Weekend Warrior Mission 04 Password
TZNF

Weekend Warrior Mission 05 Password
VD5S

Weekend Warrior Mission 06 Password
K1BT

Weekend Warrior Mission 07 Password
L2CV

Weekend Warrior Mission 08 Password
P3DW

Weekend Warrior Mission 09 Password
N4FX

Weekend Warrior Mission 10 Password
Z5GZ

Weekend Warrior Mission 11 Password
D6H0

Weekend Warrior Mission 12 Password
F7JI

Weekend Warrior Mission 13 Password
G8K2

Weekend Warrior Mission 14 Password
GGL3

Weekend Warrior Mission 15 Password
KMF4

Weekend Warrior Realtime Level Password
MRTN

Loose Cannon Mission 02 Password
HWQP

Loose Cannon Mission 03 Password
RLRQ

Loose Cannon Mission 04 Password
VZNF

Loose Cannon Mission 05 Password
WD5S

Loose Cannon Mission 06 Password
L1BT

Loose Cannon Mission 07 Password
M2CV

Loose Cannon Mission 08 Passwords
Q3DW

Loose Cannon Mission 09 Password
P4FX

Loose Cannon Mission 10 Password
05GZ

Loose Cannon Mission 11 Password
F6H0

Loose Cannon Mission 12 Password
G7J1

Loose Cannon Mission 13 Password
H8K2

Loose Cannon Mission 14 Password
HGL3

Loose Cannon Mission 15 Password
LFM4

Loose Cannon Realtime Level Password
NRTN

No Remorse Mission 02 Password
JWQP

No Remorse Mission 03 Password
SLRQ

No Remorse Mission 04 Password
WZNF

No Remorse Mission 05 Password
XD5S

No Remorse Mission 06 Password
M1BT

No Remorse Mission 07 Password
N2CV

No Remorse Mission 08 Password
R3DW

No Remorse Mission 09 Password
Q4FX

No Remorse Mission 10 Password
15GZ

No Remorse Mission 11 Password
G6H0

No Remorse Mission 12 Password
H7J1

No Remorse Mission 13 Password
J8K2

No Remorse Mission 14 Password
JGL3

No Remorse Mission 15 Password
MFM4

No Remorse Realtime Level Password
PRTN

CRUSADERS OF MIGHT AND MAGIC

Unlimited Items
Beat the game. Start another game and you have infinite items.

CU-ON-PA

Level Select
At the Player Select screen, choose the "New Entry" option and enter STA, GE, SEL, and ECT as names. A Level Select option shows up for the "ETC" name.

FMV Movies
At the Player Select screen, choose the "New Entry" option and enter DEM, O P, REV, and IEW as names. Then select Movie Test mode.

CYBERBOTS: FULL METAL MADNESS

Unlock Gouki
Enter Versus mode and select any character. At the Area Selection screen, highlight the "Random" option. Hold L2 and press Circle to play as Gouki.

CYBERIA

View Credits
Enter TNRUB_SDC_NOILLIB_A or _REEB_ OROPPAS_KNIRD at the terminal password screen. The "_" represents a space.

Level Select
Enter NEMROSIM as your name.

Level 2 Password
RIG DOCK

Level 3 Password
MEET GIA

Level 4 Password
SKEET SHOOT

Level 5 Password
BIG KISS

Level 6 Password
GOING UP

Level 7 Password
ZAPPED

Level 8 Password
EASY RIDE

Level 9 Password
BIG SHOCK

Level 10 Password
OPEN OCEAN

Level 11 Password
CATWALK

Level 12 Password
ISLAND RUN

Level 13 Password
STEAL PLANE

Level 14 Password
VALLEY RUN

Level 15 Password
ROUGH RIDE

Level 16 Password
PORT FLYBY

Level 17 Password
UNDERGROUND

Level 18 Password
PIT STOP

Level 19 Password
ICE SCREAM

Level 20 Password
COLD FEET

Level 21 Password
DOOR MAN

Level 22 Password
LOCKED OUT

Level 23 Password
SLICEOMATIC

Level 24 Password
NOT FRIENDS

Level 25 Password
LISTEN IN

Level 26 Password
GENIUS

Level 27 Password
RED LIGHT

Level 28 Password
DRUG STORE

Level 29 Password
UNSAFE DOOR

Level 30 Password
GRAFFITI

Level 31 Password
YOU WITH ME

CYBERSLED

Unlock Extra Sleds
Press Up, Left, Down, Right, Up, Triangle, Up, Right, Down, Left, Up, Circle at the title screen. An explosion confirms correct entry.

CYBERSPEED

Cow Ship
Press Up, Left, Down, Up, Left, Down, Right, Left, Down, Right Square, X, Circle at the Ship Selection screen. Enter LLLLLLLLLLLLLL as a password and then press X.

Mystery Car
Enter VVVVVVVVVVVV as a password. Choose the unnamed car at the ship selection screen.

Level 2 Access With Bonus
Enter 4xvhbbbcdbcdbg as a password to reach Level 2 with the super car and a bonus.

Play All Movies
Highlight Options and press Circle, Square, Triangle, Left, Right, Up, Square, Right.

Track 2 Password
JCBQCBBBCBCDBB

Track 3 Password
JDBZCDDCCCDDBB

Track 4 Password
JFB5DFDCCCFGBB

Track 5 Password
JHBCFFFCCCGJBB

Track 7 Password
JJBKFGFCCDHLBB

Track 8 Password
JLBSHGGCDDJLBB

CYBERTIGER

Bonus Clubs
Score an eagle to get forged clubs. Make three birdies in a row to get a rubber-faced putter.

Password Screen
At the course selection screen, press Circle.

Badlands Course Password
HARESO

Canyons Course Password
NAMOPI

Sawgrass Course Password
SECARE

Summerlin Course Password
PORASO

Unlock All Courses Password
POQAKI

D

Alternate Endings
You have two choices when you meet the father at the end of the game. For the good ending, shoot him with your pistol. For the bad ending, walk toward him.

DANCE DANCE REVOLUTION

Eight Hidden Characters
After selecting mode, press Left+Start to release one set of characters or Right+Start to release the other set.

Secret Level: Another
Press Up at Mode Selection screen, then Up (2), Down (2), Up (2), Down (2).

Secret Level: Maniac
Press Up at Mode Selection screen, then Left (2), Right (2), Left (2), Right (2).

Secret Level: Double Another & Maniac
Press Up at Mode Selection screen, then Up (2), Down (2), Left, Right, Left, Right.

Secret Level: Mirror Another & Maniac
Press Up at Mode Selection screen, then Left, Right, Left, Right, Left, Right, Left, Right.

DANCE DANCE REVOLUTION 2ND REMIX

All Songs
Press Start on Arcade mode. Then highlight either Easy, Normal, or Hard and press Right (6).

Different Characters On-Screen
While holding either Right or Left, press Start.

Alter Playing Style
While holding X, press Start.

Nonstop Modes
On Normal difficulty, finish the game 50 times. On Hard difficulty, finish the game 200 times.

Super Mode
At the title screen, press Up (2), Down (2), Left, Right, Left, Right.

Paint Mode
In Options, set Level to 7. Then set Max Stage to 5 for Easy, 3 for Normal, or 1 for Hard. Now set Time Limit to On and Game Over to 2nd Remix. Return to the title screen and press Right, Left, Right, Left, Down (2), Up (2). Then press Select.

Another Mode
Press Down (2) at the Game Mode Selection screen.

Maniac Mode
Enter Another Mode code, then press Down (2) at the Game Mode Selection screen.

Return to Normal Mode
At the Game Mode Selection screen, press Up (2).

Right Mode
Press Select, Right (8), at the Song Selection screen.

Left Mode
Press Select, Left (8) at the Song Selection screen.

Mirror Mode
Press Select, Left, Right, Left, Right, Left, Right, Left, Right at the Song Selection screen.

Shuffle Mode
Press Select, Up, Down, Left, Right, Down, Up, Right, Left at the Song Selection screen.

Hidden Mode
Press Select, Up, Down, Up, Down, Up, Down, Up, Down at the Song Selection screen.

Little Mode
Press Select, Left, Down, Right, Down, Left, Down, Right, Down, Up at the Song Selection screen.

DANCE! DANCE! DANCE!

Play as Yumi
Replace the game disk with the audio CD containing "The Twister" after the game begins.

DANCING BLADE

Unlock Special Skate Park:
The Dream House
When you open the final skate area (Huntington), place third or better in the competition to receive a Dreamhouse in which wings of the Mansion can be unlocked by completing tasks from the courses (High Score, hitting all of a certain object, etc.).

Unlock Every Single Level
During play, pause the game and press Circle, Up, Down, Square, Triangle. All levels, including the Dreamhouse, are now unlocked.

Unlock Every Single Trick
Press pause, Down, Left, Up, Right, Down, Left, Up, Right. The screen will read "all tricks enabled."

DANCING STAGE: FEATURING TRUE KISS DESTINATION

Super Maniac Mode
When "Push Start" appears, press Right, Left, Right, Left, Down (2), Up (2), Left, Right.

Free Mode
When "Push Start" appears, press Up (2), Down (2), Left, Right, Left, Right.

DANGER GIRL

Unlock Level Select and Cheat Menu
L1, R2, L2, R1, Circle, Square, Triangle (2). Next press and hold: L1+L2+R1+R2.

Invincibility
At the pause menu, hold R1 and press X, Circle, X.

DARK FORCES

All Levels, All Guns
Use 205F6HJT0V as a password.

Cheat Menu
Press Left, Circle, X, Right, Circle, X, Down, Circle, X during the game.

Level Select
Use X7P!45QX39 as a password.

Level 2 Password
09VCJGG7WM

Level 3 Password
18WBDP7RMN

Level 4 Password
885BVHMCQ8

Level 5 Password
!32ZNJQHT3

Level 6 Password
GV8KF!G6KL

Level 7 Password
3X8MJ47R3X

Level 8 Password
LMZRK4!R3D

Level 9 Password
BR2WYK2CQJ

Level 10 Password
00GBNLJ4G0

Level 11 Password
T2GDTJG5JT

Level 12 Password
H2DCTKH40S

Level 13 Password
PPYRQP58LD

Level 14 Password
RT2W121V7J

DARKLIGHT CONFLICT

Cheat Menu
In Options, press Down (2), Up, Square, Left (2), L1, R1, Circle. Then select "Extra" under main menu.

Final Level Password
HDVMKXVCK

Password: Mission 2
KXCSSSDSC

Password: Mission 3
PHPPXDDJH

Password: Mission 4
PJVQXHDJH

Password: Mission 5
MHMGTWLBW

Password: Mission 6
HHMTVCMPD

Password: Mission 7
WVCHDWVCK

Password: Mission 8
HKMBVXMPD

Password: Mission 9
QJCSSLDDV

Password: Mission 10
GDQLPPVHT

Password: Mission 11
QLLTSHDDV

Password: Mission 12
LVCVLHDMQ

Password: Mission 13
QCTJSBDDV

Password: Mission 14
QVMXJCLTM

Password: Mission 15
PMLPWCDJH

Password: Mission 16
XKVPBWMGJ

Password: Mission 17
GVJHQTDDV

Password: Mission 18
CVHBSSVVB

Password: Mission 19
LPMCGWVCK

Password: Mission 20
KQPKBBMGJ

Password: Mission 21
GHDMJTLTM

Password: Mission 22
LSMJPSDSC

Password: Mission 23
XVJKBSVCK

Password: Mission 24
LHHBXSVVX

Password: Mission 25
CSDWHMVQP

Password: Mission 26
PQHBHPVQP

Password: Mission 27
MTHLVQDJH

Password: Mission 28
MVXTVSDJH

Password: Mission 29
GCBBPDDDV

Password: Mission 30
LKPJBLVCK

Password: Mission 31
HKTTSKLKS

Password: Mission 32
WKVSDXMGJ

Password: Mission 33
KWCTBBDWL

Password: Mission 34
PDCQVCVLG

Password: Mission 35
QDSJXTLBW

Password: Mission 36
HVLLMDDSC

Password: Mission 37
DHHMXBLBW

Password: Mission 38
HKXLWLVVX

Password: Mission 39
TMQPXSDSC

Password: Mission 40
WPGLLCDWL

Password: Mission 41
VWKTGXDMQ

Password: Mission 42
VBKMJJMGJ

Password: Mission 43
VGVLJDMGJ

Password: Mission 44
MSQVCCLTM

Password: Mission 45
SQDVQHDJH

Password: Mission 46
HGTJWGDSC

Password: Mission 47
HJPGLKVCK

Password: Mission 48
DGGPTXVVB

Password: Mission 49
XCWCSDMPD

Password: Mission 50
SDQTBJVQP

DARKSTALKERS 3

Play as Male Shadow
Highlight "?" at the Character Select screen and press Select (5).

Play as Female Shadow
Highlight "?" at the Character Select screen and press Select (7).

Play as Image Talbain
Highlight "Talbain" at the Character Select screen, then hold Select and press all three Punch or Kick buttons.

Play as Oboro
Highlight "Bishamon" at the Character Select screen, then hold Select+any button.

Alternate Colors
Highlight a character under the Character Select screen. Punch or Kick twice.

DARKSTALKERS 3: VAMPIRE SAVIOR EX

Fight as Shadow
Highlight "?" at the Character Select screen and press Select (5) and any button.

Fight as Marionet
Highlight "?" at the Character Select screen and press Select (7) and any button.

Fight as Original Gallon
Finish the game with Gallon. Highlight Gallon at the Character Select screen and press Select+Punch (2) or Select+Kick (2).

Fight as Hyper Bishamon
Finish the game with Bishamon. Highlight Bishamon at the Character Select screen and press Select+Punch (2) or Select+Kick (2).

Fight as Vampire Hunter Phobos
Hold Select to choose Phobos from the Character Select screen.

Fight Against Hyper Bishamon
During a one-player game, use EX moves to beat at least two opponents and never lose a round.

DAVE MIRRA FREESTYLE BMX

Unlock All Bikes
Begin a Proquest and pick any rider. At the Bike Selection screen, press Up, Left, Up, Down, Up, Right, Left, Right, Circle to pick any bike. Re-enter the code whenever you want to pick a new bike.

Unlock All Levels
Begin a Proquest and pick any rider. At the Style Selection screen, press Left, Up, Right, Down, Left, Down, Right, Up, Left, Circle. Re-enter the code whenever you want to pick a new bike.

Unlock All Styles
Begin a Proquest and pick any rider. Pick any bike. At the Style Selection screen, press Left, Up, Right, Down, Left, Down, Right, Up, Left, Circle. Re-enter the code whenever you want to pick a new bike.

Unlock Amish Boy
Finish the game with all 10 original riders.

Unlock Slim Jim
Begin a Proquest. At the Rider Selection screen, press Down (2), Left, Right, Up (2), Circle.

Unlock Hidden Dave Mirra Movie
Beat the game as Dave Mirra.

Unlock Hidden Ryan Nyquist Movie
Beat the game as Ryan Nyquist.

Unlock Hidden Online Contest Movie
Beat the game as Slim Jim.

Unlock Hidden Programmer Movie
Beat the game as Amish Boy.

Exorcist Mode
Beat the game as Troy McMurray. This cheat appears in the Cheat menu from the Options menu.

First-Person Mode
Beat the game as Mike Laird. This cheat appears in the Cheat menu from the Options menu.

Bike Suspension Mode
Beat the game as Chad Kagy. This cheat appears in the Cheat menu from the Options menu.

Silly Grunt Mode
Beat the game as Tim Mirra. This cheat appears in the Cheat menu from the Options menu.

Sticky Crash Mode
Beat the game as Kenan Harkin. This cheat appears in the Cheat menu from the Options menu.

Night Vision Mode
Beat the game as Shaun Butler. This cheat appears in the Cheat menu from the Options menu.

Big Crash Mode
Beat the game as Leigh Ramsdell. This cheat appears in the Cheat menu from the Options menu.

Ghost Rider Mode
Beat the game as Joey Garcia. This cheat appears in the Cheat menu from the Options menu.

DAVE MIRRA FREESTYLE BMX: MAXIMUM REMIX

Unlock Amish Boy
Beat the game with these riders: Tim Mirra, Dave Mirra, Ryan Nyquist, Mike Laird, Joey Garcia, Chad Kaigy, Troy McMurray, Kenan Harkin, Leigh Ramsdell, and Shaun Butler.

Unlock Big Crashes
To unlock ye olde Big Crashes feature, beat the game with Leigh Ramsdell.

Unlock Exorcist Mode
Beat the game with Troy McMurray.

Unlock First Person View
To open the first person view, beat the game with Mike Laird.

Unlock Ghost Rider
Beat the game with Joey Garcia to open Ghost Rider.

Unlock Grunts
Beat the game with Tim Mirra to open the "Goofy Grunts" cheat.

Unlock Night Vision Mode
To unlock Night Vision Mode, beat the game with Shaun Butler.

Unlock Sticky Crashes
To unlock the Sticky Crashes cheat, beat the game with Kenan Harkin.

DEAD BALL ZONE

All Stadiums and Teams
Highlight "Italian" language and hold R1+L2+Up+Square.

Infinite Weapons
Press Up (2), Down (2), Select, Triangle, Circle, Square (2), Right (2), Left (2), Start (under "French" option).

DEAD HEAD TRIAL

All Cars
At Road GP mode, Highlight F D 7, and press L1+L2+R1+R2+Down+Select+Triangle.

Watch Movie Clips
At the Video Clip screen, press L1+L2+R1+R2+Up+Select+Triangle.

DEAD IN THE WATER

God Mode
Hold Square+Circle, then press R2, L2, R1, R2.

Boats: Level 2
Hold Square+Circle, then press R2, R1 (2), L1.

Boats: Level 3
Hold Square+Circle, then press L1, R2, L2, L1.

Infinite Missiles
Hold Square+Circle, then press L1, R1, L1, L2.

Big Waves
Hold Square+Circle, then press R2, L1, R1 (2).

Unlimited Special Weapons
Hold Square+Circle, then press R1, L1, L2, L2.

Unlimited Turbo
Hold Square+Circle, then press L2, R2, L2, R1.

More Money
Hold Square+Circle, then press L1, R1 (2), R2.

Maximum Boat Upgrade
Hold Square+Circle, then press L1, R2, L2, L1.

RC Mode (mini boats)
Hold Square+Circle, then press L1 (2), L2, L1.

Chicken Boats
Hold Square+Circle, then press R1 (2), R2, L1.

Access All Tracks
Hold Square+Circle, then press L2, L2, R1, L1.

Reversed Tracks
Hold Square+Circle, then press R2 (2), L1 (2).

DEAD OR ALIVE

Fight as Raidou
Unlock all costumes for all characters, then select costume 14 for female characters or 5 for male characters and beat the game under Normal and Default.

Fight as Ayane
Beat the game using Raidou under Normal and Default.

Control Victory Camera
Press Left, Up, Right, Down to move camera during victory pose, and use R1 and L1 to control zoom.

Alternate Costumes
Finish Tournament mode with all options on default settings. Finish game multiple times to unlock multiple costumes.

Instant Replay
Before the victory pose at the end of the round, hold Circle+Square and press Triangle.

Danger Bounce
Accumulate 12 hours of gameplay or complete Kumite mode with a victory record of 80 percent or more. The new option appears under "Extra Config."

Danger Damage
Accumulate nine hours of gameplay, or, using all 10 fighters on the default settings, finish the game, or, go to Survival mode and beat all 10 fighters. The new option appears under "Extra Config."

Fighting Order
Accumulate three hours of gameplay or finish the game with anyone. The new option appears under "Extra Config."

CG Gallery
Use the "Alternate Costumes" code to unlock all of Ayane's costumes. The new option appears under "Extra Config."

Safety Zone Size
Accumulate six hours of gameplay or finish Time Attack mode in less than 5 minutes at Normal difficulty.

System Voice: Wakana
Accumulate 15 hours of gameplay or finish the game with any fighter.

System Voice: Sakura
Accumulate 15 hours of gameplay or play Kasumi 100 times or more.

DEADLY SKIES

Bonus Plane: F19
Press Up, Down, R1, Circle, Square, Left, L1 at Plane Selection screen.

Bonus Plane: F117
Press Square, R1, R2, Square, Up, Square, L2 at Plane Selection screen.

Use Laser Weapon
Press Left, Up, Right, Triangle, Select, Left, Right, X during gameplay.

Increase Homing Missiles
Press Right, Down, Left, Up, Triangle, Select, R1, R2, X during gameplay.

Infinite S. Skill
Press Right, Down, Left, Up, Triangle, Select, Left, Right, X during gameplay.

Level Select
Press L2, L1, Triangle, Up, at title screen.

VS Mode in First Boss Stage
Press L2, L1, Square, Up at VS Mode Selection screen.

VS Mode in 2nd Boss Stage
Press L2, L1, Square, Down at VS Mode Selection screen.

DEATHTRAP DUNGEON

Invincibility
Press Up, Down (2), Up, Left (2), Right, Up at Setup screen.

Level Select
Press L1, R1, Triangle (2), Square, Circle, R1, L1, then Load Game.

DECOTRA THE ART TRUCK BATTLE

Drive Ultra Truck
In Time Attack mode, place first on every track.

DEFCON 5

Asteroids Minigame
Access any VOS terminal in the defense station. Select Communications, then Local Communications. When the message about that option being unavailable appears, press Triangle.

DEFEAT LIGHTNING

Alternate Color Costumes
When selecting your character, hold Select and press Circle, Square, or Triangle.

DEMOLITION RACER

Cheat Mode
Press X (2), Square (2), Triangle (2), Circle (2)

DEPTH

Gold Dolphin
Highlight "Start" on the title screen and press Down, Up, Right, Left+Square.

DESCENT

All Level Keys
During gameplay, press Square, X, Circle, Triangle, X, Triangle (2), X, Triangle, X, Triangle, X.

All Weapons, 10 Lives, Level Select
During gameplay, press Triangle, X, Square (2), Triangle, Circle (2), Square, Triangle, Square, Circle, X.

Brighter Screen
During gameplay, press Square, Triangle, Circle, Square (2), X, Circle, Triangle, Square, Circle, X, Triangle.

Cloaking Device
During gameplay, press Triangle, Square, X, Circle, Square, X, Circle, Triangle, X, Square, X, Triangle.

Invulnerability
During gameplay, press Square, Triangle, Circle, Square (2), Triangle, Circle (2), Square, Triangle, Square, X.

Mega Weapons
During gameplay, press Triangle, Square, Circle, X, Triangle, Square, X, Triangle, Square, X, Circle, Left.

Restore Shields
During gameplay, press Triangle (2), X, Square, Triangle, Circle, Triangle, X, Square, X, Triangle, X.

Strange Colors
During gameplay, press Square, Triangle, Circle, Square (2), Triangle, Circle (2), Square, Triangle, Square, X, Triangle, X, Square, Triangle.

Harder Difficulty/Level Select
Press Triangle, Square (2), Triangle, Circle (2), Square (2), Triangle, Circle, Square (2) during the game. Then quit game and start a new one.

Extra Life
Press Square, Triangle, Circle, Square, Circle, X, Square, Triangle, Circle, Triangle (2), X during gameplay.

More Strange Colors
Press Square, Triangle, Circle (2), Square, Triangle, Square, X, Triangle, X, Square during gameplay.

Odd Robots
Press Square, X, Square, X, Circle, Square, Circle, Square, Triangle, Circle (2), Square during gameplay.

Password: Level 2
DBG4B-JB7S7-DS4#Y-MSBYB

Password: Level 3
QQM#B-7B7S7-DHLTQ-8VBXV

Password: Level 4
SGVFB-JM7TB-GNMXG-JWB5V

Password: Level 5
N*5KB-STLVQ-HC344-62B3B

Password: Level 6
Y8FPB-SL3TB-JAM66-S9D2V

Password: Level 7
XORTB-SQGTB-HBMC8-VBF#B

Password: Level 8
RH2FB-NV70*-GBL5Q-*BBBB

Password: Level 9
8SHKB-9WLT*-JPLD8-NCCKB

Turbo Speed
During gameplay press Square, Triangle, Circle, Square, Circle, X, Square, X, Circle, Triangle, Square, X.

DESCENT MAXIMUM

Last Level Password
2R*8H-9YMBL-3JGCS-NF#WR-WHKG97

Cheat Code: Weapons, Shields, Energy (Enter in Keys Section)
STOS TSX SOTSX ACE

Cheat Code: Weapons, Shields, Energy, Keys, Level Select (Enter in Keys Section)
TSOXT STX TSXO $40

Cheat Code: Invincibility (Toggle) (Enter in Keys Section)
TXTOX TSX TXOT DCD

Cheat Code: Alternate Colors (Enter in Keys Section)
TXO TSOX TXTOX LSD

Cheat Code: Go Wingnut Mode (Toggle) (Enter in Keys Section)
TSOTX STOS TXO 4AD

Cheat Code: Hello Minnie Mode (Enter in Keys Section)
XOXOXOXOXOXO XO

Cheat Code: Acid Mode (Enter in Keys Section)
STOS TSX TX TOX ACID

Cheat Code: All Accessories (Enter in Keys Section)
STXOXX TSXO SOX TOY

Cheat Code: Acid (Enter in Keys Section)
STOS TSX TX TOX

Cheat Code: All Keys (Enter in Keys Section)
STXTO TX TXTSX MIK

Cheat Code: Toggle Cloak (Enter in Keys Section)
XTO SOTSX TXTO RED

Cheat Code: Extra Life (Enter in Keys Section)
TXSO TX SXO XTO +1 UP

Cheat Code: Full Shields (Enter in Keys Section)
TXOS SXO TSXOS BUG

Cheat Code: Robots Move Faster (Enter in Keys Section)
TXS STO SXO STO JAVA

Cheat Codes: Turbo (Enter in Keys Section)
TSOX SXO STOXX SVT

Invulnerability
Triangle, X, Triangle, Circle, X, Triangle, Square, X, Triangle, X, Circle, Triangle.

DESTREGA

Random Level Select
Hit Start at the Level Select menu.

Unlock *Dynasty Warriors* Characters
Use any character at any difficulty to beat Battle mode, then go to the Character Select screen, highlight the same character you used, and press R2.

DESTRUCTION DERBY

Select Number of Opponents
Enter the name NPLAYERS, choose a track from the Track Selection menu, and the option becomes available.

Ridge Racer Track
In Two-player mode, name Player 1 RIDGE and Player 2 RACER.

Cow Appears
Enter the name !CUPCAKE!

Animated Credits
Enter CREDITZ! as name.

Bonus Team
Press L1, Left, Circle at piracy warning.

Easy Points
Press Accelerate+Right prior to start of race.

Invulnerability
Enter !DAMAGE! as name.

Monkey on the Track
Enter MONKEY as name, and do five 360's during game.

Ruined Monastery
Enter REFLECT! as name.

Unfair Advantage
Enter DERBYMAN as name.

DESTRUCTION DERBY 2

All Tracks
Enter MACSrPOO as name in Championship mode.

Animated Credits
Enter CREDITZ! as name in Championship mode.

Invincibility
Enter !DAMAGE! as name.

Video Credits
Enter ToNyPaRk as name in Championship mode.

DESTRUCTION DERBY RAW

Ruined Monastery Track
REFLECT!

Invulnerability
!DAMAGE!

Choose Number of Competitors
NPLAYERS

DETANA! TWIN-BEE YAHOO!

Dark Play
Pause while in Arcade mode and press Up (2), Down (2), Left, Right, Left, Right, X, Circle.

Skip Levels
Get 573,000 or more points in Twin Bee Yahoo mode, pause, and press Left (2), Right (2), Down, Up, Down, Up, Circle (2), Square (2), Triangle, X, Triangle (2).

DEVIL DICE

Bonus Puzzles
Win all 100 puzzles under Puzzle mode. Then at the Stage Selection screen, highlight Random and press X. Now press L2 or R2 to select from 1,000 new puzzles.

Speed Mode
Hit Triangle as soon as life meter runs out in Wars mode.

Audio Rules
Press Right at the title screen. Continue to press Right to get back.

DIABLO

Extra Gold
Begin a new game in multiplayer and give all gold to one character. Save the game for the one with the gold. Restart the game and the other players have the same amount of gold as before. Repeat.

Duplicate Belt Items
Surround your player with items so that you cannot throw down any more items. Throw an item from your belt, which will land two squares from your player. The item you threw from your belt is still there and on the ground. Go pick it up. Repeat as desired.

DIE HARD TRILOGY

***Die Hard 1*: Alter Commentary Speed**
Pause, highlight "Quit," hold R2, and press Down, Square (2), Right.

***Die Hard 1*: Display Coordinates**
Pause, highlight "Quit," hold R2, and press Left, Circle, Down, Square.

***Die Hard 1*: Fat Mode**
Pause, highlight "Quit," hold R2, and press Right, Square (2), Down.

***Die Hard 1*: Floating Dead**
Pause, highlight "Quit," hold R2, and press Down, Square, Triangle, Down.

***Die Hard 1*: Grenades**
Pause, highlight "Quit," hold R2, and press Right, Square, Down, Circle.

***Die Hard 1*: Invincibility**
Pause, highlight "Quit," hold R2, and press Right, Up, Down, Square.

***Die Hard 1*: Reverse Directions**
Pause, highlight "Quit," hold R2, and press Right, Square, Triangle, Right.

***Die Hard 1*: Select Level**
Pause, highlight "Quit," hold R2, and press Down, Circle, Left, Square, Up, Square, Left. Hold Start and press Left or Right to select level.

***Die Hard 1*: Silly Mode**
Pause, highlight "Quit," hold R2, and press Down, Circle (2), Down, Triangle, Down.

***Die Hard 1*: Skeleton Mode**
Pause, highlight "Quit," hold R2, and press Triangle (10), Right (4).

***Die Hard 1*: Strange Death Sounds**
Pause, highlight "Quit," hold R2, and press Circle (2), Square (2), Right.

***Die Hard 1*: Unlimited Ammunition**
Pause, highlight "Quit," hold R2, and press Right, Up, Down (2), Square, Right.

***Die Hard 2*: Extra Ammunition**
Pause, highlight "Quit," hold R2, and press Right, Square, Left, Circle, Triangle, Down.

***Die Hard 2*: Fergus Mode**
Pause, highlight "Quit," hold R2, and press Circle, Down (2), Square, X, Square.

Die Hard 2: Giant Cars
Pause, highlight "Quit," hold R2, and press Left, Triangle, Right, Down.

Die Hard 2: Invincibility
Pause, highlight "Quit," hold R2, and press Down, Triangle, Right, Square.

Die Hard 2: Odd People
Pause, highlight "Quit," hold R2, and press Left, Triangle, Right, Down.

Die Hard 2: Skeleton Mode
Pause, highlight "Quit," hold R2, and press Down, Square, Triangle, Down.

Die Hard 3: 999 Turbos
Pause, highlight "Quit," hold R2, and press Circle (2), Square (2), Down (2), X (2).

Die Hard 3: Cloudy Skies
Pause, highlight "Quit," hold R2, and press Down, Square, Triangle, Right.

Die Hard 3: Debug Mode
Pause, highlight "Quit," hold R2, and press Right, Up, Down, Square.

Die Hard 3: Disable Texture Mapping
Pause, highlight "Quit," hold R2, and press Down, Up, Left (2), Down, Up, Left (2), Down, Up, Left (2).

Die Hard 3: Fergus Mode with Invincibility
Pause, highlight "Quit," hold R2, and press Circle, Down (2), Triangle, X, Square.

Die Hard 3: Flat Shade Mode
Pause, highlight "Quit," hold R2, and press Down, Up, Left (2), Down, Up, Left (2), Down, Up, Left (2).

Die Hard 3: Flying Saucer Level
Pause, highlight "Quit," hold R2, and press Right, Circle, Triangle, Down, X (3).

Die Hard 3: Fuzzy Dice Model Car Ornaments
Pause, highlight "Quit," hold R2, and press Right, Circle, Left (2), Square, Down.

Die Hard 3: Giant Cars
Pause, highlight "Quit," hold R2, and press Left, Triangle, Right, Down.

Die Hard 3: Sky Camera
Pause, highlight "Quit," hold R2, and press Circle, Right, Down, Square, Triangle, Left.

Die Hard 3: "Sky Cam" Option
Pause, highlight "Quit," hold R2, and press Down, Circle, Down, Circle.

Die Hard 3: Slow Motion
Pause, highlight "Quit," hold R2, and press Left, Up, Left (2), Square, Down.

Die Hard 3: Unlimited Lives
Pause, highlight "Quit," hold R2, and press Left, Circle, Up, Down, Square, Right.

Die Hard 3: Warp Camera Lens
Pause, highlight "Quit," hold R2, and press Circle, Down (2), Square, Right.

Die Hard 1: Password Level 2
ZN1!6HTWZJ!HF GK5N5W7CX7JZR V!CYHP-ZRV!CXH KZRV!CYHPZRVJ

Die Hard 1: Password Level 3
T41X_3_4TD1DP 5B9W974MM6DT7 4XMLG-9T74XMMG FT74XMLG9T74J

Die Hard 1: Password Level 4
Q_1WSX3WQK!CD !6FSS!M1FFPQ2 SC1D-5JQ2SC1F5 NQ2SC1D5JQ2S_

Die Hard 1: Password Level 5
Y41!ZDT3YJMZZ Y!BPYY6MW7DY7 NZMV-H9Y7NZMWH FY7NZMVH9Y7NJ

Die Hard 1: Password Level 6
F8279HY3FLM6X 15K1!TGNWWHF9 P6NV-MBF9P6NWM GF9P6NVMBF9P_

Die Hard 1: Password Level 7
74225VHK7WVMW H7GRVLCLH1X74 XMLG-9T74XMLH9 Y74XMLG9T74XJ

Die Hard 1: Password Level 8
TN1ZN9JCSJ_XL 7X5R9N4WL68TR 6XWM-GFTR6XWLG 9TR6XWMGFTR6J

Die Hard 1: Password Level 9
H425H75XGGVRV BXK479!L!3XH5 XRLZCT-H5XRL!C YH5XRLZCTH5XJ

Die Hard 1: Password Level 10
3D231ZZ!23CK! 8BS_QV9Q7JZ3D FKQ6SW-3DFKQ7S !3DFKQ6SW3DFJ

Die Hard 1: Password Level 11
W82GN88TVSCFX WCM79Q5PRZ!WC FFPQ-QVWCFFPRQ ZWCFFPQQVWCF_

Die Hard 1: Password Level 12
942RCHX88Z14N RL3WL4XLM2D95 4NLL-B9954NLMB F954NLLB9954J

Die Hard 1: Password Level 13
TJ2HGH_DSD1DP Z_VN45NTLG9TM 6DTM-6DTM6DTL6 8TM6DTM6DTM6_

Die Hard 1: Password Level 14
DX22HW5SGZPQ7 _Z5NGQZGSM2DY MQG-TW7DYMQGSW 3DYMQGTW7DYMJ

Die Hard 1: Password Level 15
BX21PND98VGP_ 4ZB1QDYGNLLBY CPGP-VRBYCPGNV MBYCPGPVRBYCJ

Die Hard 1: Password Level 16
XJ2BXT9SZXPG5 DJ6S_Z69SH1XM LG9T7-4XMLG9S7 _XMLG9T74XML_

Die Hard 1: Password Level 17
RS2GX9C5P9SCJ S3X65LMYGYWRV !CYHP-ZRV!CYGP VRV!CYHPZRV!_

Die Hard 1: Password Level 18
FS237Z5NHGKQR 871JV7ZXVWCFT R6XW-MGFTR6XVM BFTR6XWMGFTR_

Die Hard 1: Password Level 19
B42_RJ498VGPC 7S8DVXY2P2NB5 8P2NBK-B58P2PB PB58P2NBKB58J

Die Hard 2: Password Level 2
14_JJ2JB144JL 289144JB__F1_ 4JLKT3GS9_L38 F144JL289144J

Die Hard 2: Password Level 3
SS_XHKG5SW3DF KQ6SW3F!QQ1SM 3DDQ-RNCCVDFJQ 2SW3DFKQ6SW3_

Die Hard 2: Password Level 4
F416QVMBF5NQL VC9F5NNSLCHF9 NQM1-W6TDP6LWC FF5NQLVC9F5NJ

Die Hard 2: Password Level 5
N__V38Y3N2JB1 85_N2J955Y1NL JB_1L4Q-7TV195 4N2JB185_N2J_

Die Hard 2: Password Level 6
8N_N8KL68P2NB KB58P2RQ!L581 2NB698-681NBJB 18P2NBKB58P2J

Die Hard 2: Password Level 7
8D142J2_8F1N6 JV38F1JJ3B_8P 1N7BGC-BSV46KV 78F1N6JV38F1J

Die Hard 2: Password Level 8
N_1B58Y3N2JB1 85_N2JHHXP2NZ JB_76L-XXNV195 4N2JB185_N2J_

Die Hard 3: Password Central Park #1
XJ1GFT!7XMLG9 T74XMLD3K72X! LG82RC-8VMZKSH HXWQZWM7GVHSJ

Die Hard 3: Password Chinatown #1
T81XMLG9TC5DP LQBTC5G!VQDT7 5DN9-65F24Y7QQ 7TW1X6CK5JV6J

Die Hard 3: Password Downtown #1
ZS1!CYHPZWWHF YRQZWWF7PRJZR WHD-67TBLVY7QR TZ3!!!BK!_2BJ

Die Hard 3: Password Central Park #2
KS28P3DFKV78Y 3NGKV7BRCN8KQ 78XS4-15M6VCC4 _K63SGSJDFD2J

Die Hard 3: Password Chinatown #2
Z41!5XRLZ7S!3 XHKZ7SY9NHRZC S!27!Z-BGTD7LR J!7XHK!CVWFG_

Die Hard 3: Password Urban #2
!81!MZHT!CYHP ZRV!CYF!QRX!7 YHN57P-C2XX9MH TZ3T!7VPFC4H_

Die Hard 3: Password Downtown #2
5422VBKB54NLL B9954NJS29H58 NLMKT6-KFP6VT1 C48J2198NRN6J

Die Hard 3: Password Aquaduct #1
S82DFJG1SC1D5 JQ2SC1GHSQ4S7 1D4C6-FD2_SM_6 7TW5XQ4QGC62_

Die Hard 3: Password Wharf
7N23LHKZ7NZMV H9Y7NZKJ79W7S ZMWN-TLMY!6ST9 T6_V38MH9T9RJ

Die Hard 3: Password Aquaduct #2
8J24_KV78K248 K248K262T228Y 249BLCXS-3K66L 3996NV535LHKJ

Die Hard 3: Password Simon Gruber
9N24LMLG9P6NV MBF9P6QJWBC9T 6NW8-V2YX72L82 C89248C9MQZN_

DIE HARD TRILOGY 2

All Weapons
Pause and press Square (2), Circle (2), L1 (2).

Turn Off Laser Sight
Pause and press L1 (2), Triangle (2), L1 (3).

Shooter Mode: Auto Reload
Pause and press Square (2), Triangle (2), Circle (2).

Adventure Mode: Electric Man
Pause and press Square (2), L1 (2), R1 (2).

Adventure Mode: First-Person View
Pause and press Circle, Triangle (2), Square.

Invincibility
Pause and press Triangle (2), Circle (2), L1, L2.

Driving Mode: Snake Car
Pause and press Circle, Square, R1 (2), Circle, L1, Circle.

Driving Mode: Unlimited Time
Pause and press L1, R1, Square (2), R1, L1.

Driving Mode: Rain
Pause and press Square (2), L1 (2), Triangle, Circle.

Invisible Body
Pause and press L1, R1 (2), L1 (2), R1.

Slower Rockets
Pause and press L1, R1 (2), L1, Triangle, Square.

Level Select
Press L1 (2), Circle (2), Square (2) while at the main menu.

Darken Camera
Pause and press Triangle (3), Square (3).

Funk Mode
Pause and press Circle (2), Square (2), L1 (2).

Unlimited Ammo
Pause and press L1 (2), R1 (2), Circle (2).

Slo-Mo Mode
Pause and press Triangle, L1, Triangle, L1, Triangle, L1.

Big Head Mode
Pause and press R1 (2), L1 (2), Triangle (2).

Pop Top Mode
Pause and press Square (2), Circle (2), R1 (2).

Skeleton Mode
Pause and press Circle, Square, Triangle (2), Square, Circle.

DIGIMON WORLD

Cheat Mode
Start a new game. Hold Triangle+Square+Circle after the FMV sequence ends. Release the buttons and check your inventory. Feed your Digimon something, and if it shakes its head or eats it, quickly press Triangle+Square+Circle. Depending on what you fed it, it turns into a different monster. Repeat as desired.

DIGITAL LEAGUE

Real Faces
Press Circle, Right, X, Down, Square, Left, Triangle, Up, R1, L1, R2, L2.

DINO CRISIS

Open Chief's Room Door
HEAD

Unlock Door Back to Main Entrance
NEWCOMER

Unlock B1 Hall Door
LABORATORY

Unlock Rest Station Room Door
WATERWAY

Unlock Parts Storage Room Door
DOCTORKIRK

B1 Library Computer Code
3695

Chief's Vault Combo
705037

Gas Experiment Room Keycode
7248

John Doyle's ID Number
57036

Lounge Safe Combo
8159

Management Office Safe Combo
O426

Parts Storage Computer Code
364204

Paul Baker's ID Number
59104

Dr. Kirk's ID Number
31415

Security Pass Room Keychip Code
O392

Security Pass Room Computer Code
31415

Stabilizer Design Access Code 1
O367

Stabilizer Design Access Code 2
O204

Stabilizer Experiment Room Case Combo
1281

Army/Battle Costumes
Beat the game once.

Ancient Costume
Beat the game twice.

Operation: WipeOut Mode
At any difficulty, beat the game within five hours.

Grenade Gun
Beat the game three times.

DINO CRISIS 2

Unlimited Ammo
Beat the game and get all 11 Dino files (you see the EPS Platinum card at the Save screen). You'll have unlimited ammo in your next game.

Unlocking Dino Coliseum
Beat the game once.

Unlocking Dino Duel
Use your Extinct points to purchase Rick, Gail, and the tank. Then you get a new row of dinosaurs to choose from. Buy the dinosaurs with your Extinct points and fight them in Dino Duel.

Unlocking Triceratops and Compsagnathus
These become available after you purchase all the other dinosaurs for Dino Duel and Dino Coliseum.

DISNEY'S HERCULES

Level Password: Hero's Gauntlet
Hydra, Medusa, Shield, Medusa

Level Password: Centaur's Forest
Centaur, Herc's head, Minotaur, Archer

Level Password: Big Olive
Centaur, Shield, Hydra, Herc's Head

Level Password: Hydra Canyon
Shield, Helmet, Shield, Soldier

Level Password: Medusa's Lair
Archer, Pegasus, Archer, Centaur

Level Password: Cyclops Attack
Helmet, Pegasus, Herc's Head, Archer

Level Password: Titan Fight
Soldier, Shield, Shield, Lightning

Level Password: Halls of Eternal Torment
Medusa, Soldier, Centaur, Pegasus

Level Password: Vortex of Souls
Soldier, Lightning, Soldier, Centaur

Level Password: Full Motion Videos
Pegasus, Soldier, Centaur, Soldier

DISRUPTOR

All Weapons
Hold Select and press L1, Square, Triangle, Square (2), Circle, Square, Circle, Triangle.

Full Ammo
Hold Select and press L1, X, Square, Triangle (2), X, Circle, Triangle, X.

Full Health
Hold Select and press L1, Triangle, X (2), Circle, X, Triangle, Square (2).

Invulnerability
Hold Select and press L1, Circle (2), Square, Circle, Triangle, X (2), Circle.

Level Password: Chemical Factory
S,O,X,O,T,T,X,X,O,S,X,S

Level Password: Rooftops
X,T,S,O,S,X,T,O,T,T,T,T

Level Password: Jupiter Station
T,X,T,S,O,O,X,O,X,T,S,S

Level Password: Triton
X,O,T,O,S,T,X,X,S,O,O,T

Level Password: Mars
O,X,O,T,X,X,S,O,O,X,T,X

Level Password: Antarctica
S,O,X,T,T,O,S,T,X,T,S,T

Level Password: Io
O,S,O,X,T,T,X,O,X,T,X,X

Level Password: Reactor
S,X,O,O,T,X,X,S,O,T,O,O

Level Password: Orbiting Habitat
S,O,X,X,S,X,T,O,S,O,T,S

Level Password: Dream
T,T,X,X,O,O,T,T,T,S,S,O

Level Password: Prison
O,S,T,O,X,O,S,T,X,X,O,S

Level Password: Fortress
T,T,X,S,T,T,O,X,O,S,X,O

DO DOI PACHI

Enter Round Two
Finish the game with fewer than three losses, at least 50,000,000 points, five or more Pachi Item Perfects, and the hit rates 270 for Type A, 300 for Type B, and 330 for Type C.

DOKI DOKI PRETTY LEAGUE

A Hidden Character
Save your data during an International Team Tournament game. When the Save Data Loading screen appears, hold L1+R1.

DOOM

Full Guns and Ammo
Pause and press X, Triangle, L1, Up, Down, R2, Left (2).

Full Map
Pause and press Triangle (2), L2, R2, L2, R2, R1, Square.

God Mode
Pause and press Down, L2, Square, R1, Right, L1, Left, Circle.

Level Warp
Pause and press Right, Left, R2, R1, Triangle, L1, Circle, X

Map with Objects
Pause and press Triangle (2), L2, R2, L2, R2, R1, Circle.

Level 2 Password
CR!3WDD3DB

Level 3 Password
3JJCMK8W64

Level 4 Password
03LTJ0Y!02

Level 5 Password
H33!1HFTHK

Level 6 Password
04MSKZX9Z1

Level 7 Password
YTTLCXXLXV

Level 8 Password
09SMBY04YW

Level 9 Password
7KKBLD7V53

Level 10 Password
FM4217GSGJ

Level 11 Password
H!!3WDGLDB

Level 12 Password
07QPDW26WY

Level 13 Password
WTXQ9C3W12

Level 14 Password
RBR4G!LDLN

Level 15 Password
WTXQ9C3W11

Level 16 Password
548C7DFWYX

Level 17 Password
JOC89DZPQS

Level 18 Password
JGB9CT0NRT

Level 19 Password
9QLTKR0!02

Level 20 Password
78M63QX921

Level 21 Password
S!61FHVQJG

Level 22 Password
33QHFTT6WY

Level 23 Password
VBGQPJ!Y46

Level 24 Password
ZYKTLW7V53

Level 25 Password
0DJSM4HW64

Level 26 Password
LS5YPTCRKH

Level 27 Password
ZDJSMVRW64

Level 28 Password
1YKTX4QV53

Level 29 Password
XKF6R8LZ97

Level 30 Password
DJX07Q4HTR

Level 31 Password
C0W1!QNJQS

Level 32 Password
VM!3V1D3DB

Level 33 Password
W394W2DMFC

Level 34 Password
ZQ58ZKJRKH

Level 35 Password
Z758ZKJ8KH

Level 36 Password
5C2V3DQBNL

Level 37 Password
NCKBLX7V53

Level 38 Password
1Q580FCRKH

Level 39 Password
HTMSKZZ9Z1

Level 40 Password
WS58ZKCRKH

Level 41 Password
CSNRG2W820

Level 42 Password
WT670JBQJG

Level 43 Password
DQLTJ1Y!02

Level 44 Password
2N94VFFMFC

Level 45 Password
CQLTJ0Y!02

Level 46 Password
WR492GDSGJ

Level 47 Password
PFFGXH3777

Level 48 Password
JWCJV2X479

Level 49 Password
CJJTM35964

Level 50 Password
M!T174XZXV

Level 51 Password
5770MX2CDF

Level 52 Password
YJLW3PPCPM

Level 53 Password
DKKBLM58J3

Level 54 Password
7L3!266DJK

Level 55 Password
4680Q7B5BD

Level 56 Password
T3QP7W26WY

Level 57 Password
RNSM5YYMYW

Level 58 Password
HWKB!57V53

Level 59 Password
2394VBXMFC

Level 60 Password
N1DHQ7C0!8

Level 61 Password
CRMSKZX9Z1

X-Ray Specs
Pause and press L1, R2, L2, R1, Right, Triangle, X, Right.

DOUBLE DRAGON

Bonus Characters
Highlight Billy for three seconds, then highlight Marian for three seconds, then highlight Chung Fu for three seconds, and finally highlight Jimmy for three seconds.

DOWNHILL SNOW

Bonus Characters
Beat the game under Hard.

Mirror Mode
Beat the game under Normal.

Bonus Costumes
Beat Scenario mode with each character.

DRAGON BEAT: LEGEND OF PINBALL

Extra Balls
Hold L1+L2+R1+R2 at Selection screen and press Start.

DRAGON HEART

Level Skip: Crypt Camelot
XK6DLJTCXT6TBXH

Level Skip: Battleground
PJXWKL34WHK4TZS

Level Skip: Caer Einonoch Entrance
XTGJC4G4WG34DHB

Level Skip: Tower of Caer Einonoch
BBXMQZPCQWCMRZQ

Level Skip: Courtyard
RVHDSLX7QP37CJX

DRAGON SEEDS

Fire Dragon
Start with the phrase "Armageddon is near." This increases your chance to obtain the dragon; repeat to increase chances.

High Stat Dragon
Start with the phrase "The power is eternal." This increases your chance to obtain the dragon; repeat to increase chances.

Special Attack Dragon
Start with the phrase "The Rock is Shining." This increases your chance to obtain the dragon; repeat to increase chances.

Powerful Dragon
Start with the phrase "Life is Beautiful." This increases your chance to obtain the dragon; repeat to increase chances.

Weak Dragon
Start with any obscene word.

Ice Dragon
Name your dragon Ja.

Mutant/Super Dragons
In the clonelab, use the phrase "Life is Eternal."

High Wisdom
Start with the phrase "The Egg is Crying." This increases your chance to obtain the dragon; repeat to increase chances.

DRAGONBALL GT FINAL BOUT

Alternate Costumes
Select character in Training or 2P mode by pressing Square+X+Circle.

Bonus Fighters
Press Right, Left, Down, Up, Right, Left, Down, Up at title screen.

Play as SS4 Goku
Press Triangle (5), Square (9) at title screen.

Play as Super Bebi
When selecting fighter, press Select+Square.

Sound Test
Press L1, L2, R1, R2, Start at the title screen.

Wire Frame Characters
Hold Select when choosing fighter.

DRAGONBALL Z: THE GREAT DRAGONBALL LEGEND

Raise Z Rank in Campaign Mode
Hold Triangle+X+Square+Select at the end of any episode, when the Z Rank screen appears. Then release the buttons and use Up or Down to alter the Z rank.

Special Ending
Use the "Raise Z Rank" code and change the rank to 999 percent.

DRAGONBALL Z: ULTIMATE BATTLE 22

Unlock Additional Characters
Press Up, Triangle, Down, X, Left, L1, Right, R1 at the title screen.

Unlock Super Saya-Jin X3
Use Gokou to beat the game, then start another game. Beat the first opponent but lose to the next opponent. Continue the game with Gokou to find him transformed.

DRIFT KING

9,999,999 Points
Hold Start+L1+L2+R1+Down at "Genki" logo and release at the title screen.

DRIVER

Rear Wheel Steering
Press R1 (3), R2, L2, R1, R2, L2, L1, R2, R1, L2, L1 at the main menu and access Cheats menu.

Long Suspension
Press R2, L2, R1, R2, L2, L1, R2 (2), L2 (2), L1, R2, R1 at the main menu and access Cheats menu.

Inverted Screen
Press R2 (2), R1, L2, L1, R2, L2, L1, R2(2), L2, R2, L1 at the main menu and access Cheats menu.

View Credits
Press L1, L2, R1, R2, L1, R1, R2, L2, R1, R2, L1, L2, R1 at the main menu and access Cheats menu.

Invincibility
Press L2 (2), R2 (2), L2, R2, L2, L1, R2, R1, L2, L1 (2).

No Police
Press L1, L2, R1 4 times, L2 (2), R1 (2), L1 (2), R2.

Mini Cars
Press R1, R2, R1, R2, L1, L2, R1, R2, L1, R1, L2 (3).

DRIVER 2

Observing the World
During gameplay, stand next to a chair and press the action button. Tanner sits down and looks around. Use the right analog stick to change viewpoints.

Baseball Stadium Secret
Activate the switch outside the ticket office building in the Chicago level to unlock the secret area and view a text message.

Mini Car Secret
Activate the switch outside the garage building in the Havana level to unlock the secret area and view a text message.

Army Base Secret
Activate the switch outside the Hidden Switch area in the Havana level to unlock the secret area and view a text message.

Custom Pick-Up Secret
Activate the switch outside the garage building in the Vegas level to unlock the secret area and view a text message.

Construction Site Secret
In the Vegas level, jump into the construction site to unlock the secret area and view a text message.

Invincible Secret
Activate the switch outside the drug store in the Vegas level to unlock the secret area and view a text message.

Truck Secret
Activate the switch outside the docks in the Rio level to unlock the secret area and view a text message.

Immunity Secret
Activate the switch outside the police station in the Rio level to unlock the secret area and view a text message.

DUKE NUKEM: LAND OF THE BABES

All Cheats
Go to the Cheat menu and press L1, L2, R2, R1, L1, L2, R2, R1, L1, L2, R2, R1, L1, L2, R2, R1, Circle (4), X (4), Square (4), Select (4).

Pick Level:
Circle, X, Square (2), X, Circle, Square

All Weapons
R2, X, L1, Square, R1, Circle, L2

Unlimited Ammunition
L2, Circle, R2, Square, Circle, L2, R1

Invincibility
L1, Square, Circle (2), Square, L1, L2

Full Armor
L1 (2), R1 (2), X (2), Circle (2)

Full Ego
R1 (2), Circle (2), L1 (2), R2

Double Damage
Square (3), Circle (3), X

Big Head Duke
Square, X, Circle (2), X, Square

Small Head Duke
Square, X, Circle (2), X, Square (2)

Outtake FMV Sequences
L1, L2, R1, R2, Square (2), Circle (2)

DUKE NUKEM: TIME TO KILL

Invincibility
Pause and press L2, R1, L1, R2, Up, Down, Up, Down, Select (2).

Invisibility
Pause and press L1, R1, L1, R1, L1, R1, L1, R1, L1, R1.

Infinite Ammunition
Pause and press Left, Right, Left, Right, Select, Left, Right, Left, Right, Select.

All Weapons
Pause and press L1, L2, Up, L1, L2, Down, R1, Right, R2, Left.

All Keys
Pause and press Up, Right, Up, Left, Down, Up, Right, Left, Right, Down.

Instant Win
Hold L2+R2 during the game and press Square, Triangle, Circle (2), Start.

All Inventory
Pause and press R1 (5), L2 (5).

2x Damage
Pause and press L2, R2, L2, R2, L2, R2, L2, R2, L2, R2.

Invincibility (Temporary)
Pause and press R1, L2, L1, L2, R1, L1, R1, L2, L1, L2.

Bonus Weapons
Pause and press R1, R2, L2, L1, R1, R2, L2, L1, Select, Select.

Big Head Mode (Duke)
Pause and press R1 (9), Up.

Big Head Mode (Enemies)
Pause and press R1 (9), Left.

Small Head Mode (Duke)
Pause and press Right, R1 (8), Down.

Small Head Mode (Enemies)
Pause and press R1 (9), Right.

Level Select
Pause and press Down (9), Up. Quit game and go to main menu. Choose the "Time to Kill" option, press Left or Right to choose a level and X to begin.

Hidden Movie
Press L1+L2+R1+R2 when the GT Interactive logo appears at the game's start.

View Kilt Sequence
Pause and press Select, Up (9), Select, R2.

View Intro
Pause and press Select, Up (9), Select, L1.

View Victory
Pause and press Select, Up (9), Select, L2.

View Credits
Pause and press Select, Up (9), Select, R1.

DUKE NUKEM: TOTAL MELTDOWN

Access Turbo Kick Mode
During gameplay, hold L1+L2+R1+R2 and press Square multiple times.

DUNE 2000

Show Full Map
While in the sidebar, press X while pressing Square, Circle, X, Triangle (2), Square.

DUKES OF HAZZARD: RACING FOR HOME

More Power-Ups
Grab a power-up. Leave the area then return. The power-up reappears. Collect a maximum of five nitro power-ups.

Level Select
Beat the game and save it to a memory card. Load the game from the Options screen and choose any episode and scene. Return to the main menu and re-save.

Beating the Police
Hit the police cars on the back of the car to escape the police.

Luke Hanging Out of the Window
Drive slowly to keep Luke hanging out the window. He goes back in if you hit anything.

DYNAMITE BOXING

Enable Trainer Mode
Press Down, X, Left, Right, Left, X, Down.

DYNASTY WARRIORS

Fight as Zhuge Liang
Beat the game with Guan Yu, Zhang Fei, and Zhao Yun. Then at the Character Selection screen, press Left.

Fight as Cao Cao
Beat the game with all characters except for Guan Yu, Zhang Fei, and Zhao Yun.

Fight as Lu Bu
Beat the game with Zhuge Liang and Cao Cao.

Fight as Toukichi
Enable Lu Bu. Then at the title screen, quickly press Down (2), Right, Up, Circle, Triangle, R1, R2.

Fight as Nobunaga
Enable Lu Bu. Then at the title screen, quickly press Square, Up, Triangle, Down, Circle.

Fight as Sun Shang Xiang
At the One-player Battle screen, press Left (2), Up, Down, Triangle, Square, L1, R1. Now press L1 or L2 to select this character.

EAGLE ONE: HARRIER ATTACK

Level Select
Enter the Options screen and press R1, L1, R2, L2, Start.

Invincibility
Enter the Options screen and press R1, L1, R2, L2, L1.

Infinite Ammunition
Enter the Options screen and press R1, L1, R2, L2, R1.

EARTH SIEGE

Play as Daruma
Complete Story mode with Haito Kanakura.

Play as Samurai
Complete Story mode with Jin-Emon Hanafusa.

Play as Brute
Complete Story mode with Jushiro Sakaki.

Play as Mugenji
Complete Story mode with Yaci Izanagi.

Play as Iga Ninjas
Complete Story mode with Hanzo Hattori.

Play as Tashon Mao
Complete Story mode with Garyo the Whirlwind.

Play as Oboro's Amazons
Complete Story mode with Saya.

Play as Yuda
Complete Story mode with Mikoto.

Play as Minto
Complete Story mode with Ran Po.

Play as Tohma Kuki
Complete Story mode with Seishiro Kuki.

Play as Mikoto
Complete Story mode with Haomaru.

Play as Seishiro Kuno
Complete Story mode with all characters.

ECW: ANARCHY RULZ!

Big Damage Mode
Beat the Toughman Belt Tournament with "no blocking" on at Hard difficulty.

Big Feet Mode
Beat the Heavyweight Belt Tournament at Set Hard difficulty with Spike Dudley.

Big Head Mode
Beat the Heavyweight Belt Tournament at Hard difficulty with Simon Diamond.

Big Hands Mode
Beat the Heavyweight Belt Tournament at Hard difficulty with Super Crazy.

Ego Mode
Beat the Heavyweight Belt Tournament at Hard difficulty with Jerry Lynn.

Fat Man Mode
Beat the Heavyweight Belt Tournament at Hard difficulty with Big Sal E. Graziano.

Hangman Mode
Beat the Heavyweight Belt Tournament at Hard difficulty with Kid Kash.

Headless Mode
Beat the Heavyweight Belt Tournament at Hard difficulty with New Jack.

Little Head Mode
Beat the Heavyweight Belt Tournament at Hard difficulty with Amish Roadkill.

Random Head Mode
Beat the Heavyweight Belt Tournament at Hard difficulty with Trainer.

Unlock Custom Stuff
Complete the One Player Career mode at Hard difficulty with a custom character.

Unlock Stable Stuff
Beat One Player Career mode with a stable, custom, or featured character.

Unlock Joey Styles
Beat Career mode with any character to unlock the Heavyweight Title option in Tournament mode. Win this title at Hard difficulty with Sandman.

Unlock Joel Gertner
Beat Career mode with any character to unlock the Heavyweight Title option in Tournament mode. Win this title at Hard difficulty with Mikey Whipwreck.

Unlock Lou E Dangerously
Beat Career mode with any character to unlock the Heavyweight Title option in Tournament mode. Win this title at Hard difficulty with "Beautiful" Billy Wiles.

Unlock Paul Heyman
Beat Career mode with any character to unlock the Heavyweight Title option in Tournament mode. Win this title at Hard difficulty with Dusty Rhodes.

Unlock Cyrus the Virus
Beat Career mode with any character to unlock the Heavyweight Title option in Tournament mode. Win this title at Hard difficulty with Rhino.

Unlock John Finegan
Beat Career mode with any character to unlock the Heavyweight Title option in Tournament mode. Win this title at Hard difficulty with Angel.

Unlock Bill Alfonso
Beat Career mode with any character to unlock the Heavyweight Title option in Tournament mode. Win this title at Hard difficulty with Tony Devito.

Unlock Judge Jeff Jones
Beat Career mode with any character to unlock the Heavyweight Title option in Tournament mode. Win this title at Hard difficulty with Jack Victory.

Unlock William F
Beat Career mode with any character to unlock the Heavyweight Title option in Tournament mode. Win this title at Hard difficulty with Balls Mahoney.

Unlock Valkyrie
Beat Career mode with any character to unlock the Heavyweight Title option in Tournament mode. Win this title at Hard difficulty with Jazz.

Unlock Shaman
Beat Career mode with any character to unlock the Heavyweight Title option in Tournament mode. Win this title at Hard difficulty with Chris Chetti.

Unlock Esophicus
Beat Career mode with any character to unlock the Heavyweight Title option in Tournament mode. Win this title at Hard difficulty with Yoshiro Tajiri.

Unlock Doug Gentry
Beat Career mode with any character to unlock the Heavyweight Title option in Tournament mode. Win this title at Hard difficulty with Masato Tanaka.

Unlock Candy Girl
Beat Career mode with any character to unlock the Heavyweight Title option in Tournament mode. Win this title at Hard difficulty with C.W. Anderson.

Unlock Booger
Beat Career mode with any character to unlock the Heavyweight Title option in Tournament mode. Win this title at Hard difficulty with the Prodigy.

Unlock Helia Monster
Beat Career mode with any character to unlock the Heavyweight Title option in Tournament mode. Win this title at Hard difficulty with Jason.

Unlock Lance Storm
Beat Career mode with any character to unlock the Heavyweight Title option in Tournament mode. Win this title at Hard difficulty with Gabe S.

Unlock Rob Feinstein
Beat Career mode with any character to unlock the Heavyweight Title option in Tournament mode. Win this title at Hard difficulty with Danny Doring.

Unlock Martian Boy
Beat Career mode with any character to unlock the Heavyweight Title option in Tournament mode. Win this title at Hard difficulty with Tommy Dreamer.

Unlock Mad Goat
Beat Career mode with any character to unlock the Heavyweight Title option in Tournament mode. Win this title at Hard difficulty with Electra.

Unlock Jester
Beat Career mode with any character to unlock the Heavyweight Title option in Tournament mode. Win this title at Hard difficulty with Francine.

Unlock Jan E. Regan
Beat Career mode with any character to unlock the Heavyweight Title option in Tournament mode. Win this title at Hard difficulty with Little Guido.

Unlock Kid
Beat Career mode with any character to unlock the Heavyweight Title option in Tournament mode. Win this title at Hard difficulty with Steve Corino.

Unlock The D I
Beat Career mode with any character to unlock the Heavyweight Title option in Tournament mode. Win this title at Hard difficulty with Justin Credible.

Unlock Sally M
Beat Career mode with any character to unlock the Heavyweight Title option in Tournament mode. Win this title at Hard difficulty with Dawn Marie.

Unlock Lance Storm
Beat Career mode with any character to unlock the Heavyweight Title option in Tournament mode. Win this title at Hard difficulty with the Trainer.

ECW HARDCORE REVOLUTION

All Jobbers
Successfully defend the ECW World Heavyweight belt five times in Career mode.

Alternate Costumes
At the Character Selection screen, hold L1, L2, or R2 while selecting a character.

Big Feet Mode
Complete Tournament mode with Balls Mahoney.

Big Hands Mode
Complete Tournament mode with Jason.

Big Head Mode
Complete Tournament mode with Rhino.

Custom Superstar Textures
Complete Tournament mode with Tommy Dreamer.

Ego Mode
Complete Tournament mode with Chris Chetti.

Fat Man Mode
Complete Tournament mode with Spike Dudley.

Hangman Mode
Complete Tournament mode with Sal E. Graziano.

Headless Mode
Complete Tournament mode with Taz.

Little Head Mode
Complete Tournament mode with Roadkill.

New Chant
Pause the game after a chant starts. The crowd does a different chant when gameplay resumes.

Random Character
At the Character Selection screen, press R1.

Random Head Mode
Successfully complete Tournament mode with Louie Spicolli.

Play as Beulah McGillicutty
Win the ECW World Tag Team belt in Career mode.

Play as Bill Alfonso
Successfully complete Tournament mode with Rob Van Dam.

Play as Cyrus the Virus
Win the ECW World TV belt in Career mode.

Play as Joel Gertner
Win the Acclaim belt in Career mode.

Play as Joey Styles
Win the Acclaim belt in Career mode.

Play as Judge Jeff Jones
Successfully complete Tournament mode with Mike Awesome.

Play as Louie Spicolli
Win the ECW World Heavyweight belt in Career mode.

Play as Taz
Win the ECW World Heavyweight belt in Career mode.

Play as the Sheik
Win the ECW World Tag Team belt in Career mode.

Play as Tommy Rich
Win the ECW World TV belt in Career mode.

EDGE OF SKYHIGH

Level Select
Pause, hold L1+L2+R1+R2 and press Triangle, Square, Right, Down, Left, Up.

EHRGEIZ: GOD BLESS THE RING

Alternate Costumes
At the Arcade mode Character Selection screen, hold Up while selecting a fighter.

Evil Panel Minigame
Defeat the CPU 10 consecutive times in the "Battle Panel" minigame, then hold L1+L2+R1+R2 and choose "Battle Panel" on the main menu.

Hidden Introduction Sequence
Load the game, but don't press any buttons. Let the introduction sequence play four times without interruption. Enter the Movie Player screen, highlight the "Opening Movie" selection, and press Right to access the new "Extra Opening" selection.

Play as Clair Andrews
Complete Arcade mode with any female character.

Play as Django
Complete Arcade mode with the eight regular non-*Final Fantasy 7* characters.

Play as Koji Masuda
Complete Arcade mode with any male character.

Play as Vincent Valentine
Complete Arcade mode with Tifa.

Play as Yuffie Kisaragi
Complete Arcade mode with Cloud.

Play as Zack
Complete Arcade mode with all *Final Fantasy 7* characters.

EINHANDER

Selene Fighter
Without using continues, win at Hard difficulty. After the final credits, save the game and start a new one. At the Fighter Selection screen, cycle through the ships and find an Unknown Fighter Type II named the Selene. The Selene can carry 9,999 rounds of ammo for any weapon.

Extra Fighters
Unlock a minimum of 15 secrets and win at any difficulty level to fly in a small Earth fighter. Finish the game on Hard difficulty without continuing more than twice to fly in a Moon fighter from the final level.

Extra Option
Finish with a high ranking to open the "Gallery" option from the main menu and view graphics depicting the ships, weapons, and battles.

ELECTRIC IRA IRA ROD RETURNS

Extra Stocks
Highlight "1 Play" at Mode screen and press Right (4), Down (2), Right, Left (8).

ELEMENTAL GEARBOLT

Bonus Options
Finish the game at Normal or higher difficulty. Then "Movie," "Music," "Sound test," and "Libraries" options appear on the Options menu.

ELIMINATOR

All Primary Weapons
At ID Selection, enter GUNCRAZ.

All Secondary Weapons
At ID Selection, enter MAXMEOUT.

All Time Pickups Worth 10 Minutes
At ID Selection, enter WAITABIT.

Bonus Level
At ID Selection, enter WAKYLEVL.

Cadillac Ship
At ID Selection, enter NEWWEELS.

Invincibility
At ID Selection, enter CLEVALAD.

ENIGMA

Play as Mummy
Highlight a character at the Selection screen and press L1+R1+Up+Triangle+Circle.

ERETZVAJU

Gallery Mode and Character Biographies
Beat Story mode.

Congratulations in Extra Options
Beat all game modes with all characters. Choose the "Congratulations" option under Extra Options to view an extra FMV sequence.

Narrator Mode in Extra Options
Beat the game in One-player mode.

Unlock Bonus Stage and Bosses
Beat Story mode with three or more different characters.

ESPN EXTREME GAMES

Bonus First Race Money
Enter 229, 013, 066, 016, 000, 000, 000, 000, 031 and finish race as Paul Dillon.

Final Race of Season
Enter 254, 071, 216, 094, 085, 177, 113, 104.

Start Game With Money
Enter 243, 255, 063, 000, 000, 000, 176, 113, 012.

Super Athlete
Enter Continue Season mode from the Exhibition screen. Select "No" when prompted to load from the memory card. Enter 237 190 190 080 000 000 176 113 219 as a password. You receive a super athlete, $5,030, every vehicle, and first-place ranking for the first two races.

Flight Mode
At the Play/Help screen, highlight "Help" and press Triangle. During a game, jump to fly.

End of Extreme level
Enter 190, 069, 254, 049, 105, 048, 001, 016, 146 as a password.

Money Round
Pass through every gate on a course to enter the bonus Cash Course, with $5 and $10 gates.

Unlimited Money
Go to the TV marked "1" in the equipment room and press X to deactivate the CPU opponent. Then, highlight all the equipment selections and press X again to deactivate them. Then choose a course to begin the race. You always place first. Repeat to collect infinite money.

Hidden Crypt
Midway through the Italy course, look for an area that dips downhill past some columns. Pass through the purple gate on the extreme left side of the screen to make a hidden passageway and additional gates appear.

Race in Reverse
Come to a complete stop and hold Triangle.

ESPN X-GAMES PRO BOARDER

Circuit Level Password
Press X, Circle, X, Triangle (2), Square.

Unlock Super Circuit/Bonus Boarders
Press Triangle, X, Square, X, Triangle, Circle.

Unlock Super Circuits Option
Press Square, Triangle , X, Square, Circle (2).

Unlock All Tracks/ Circuits
Press Square, X, Triangle, Square, Circle (2).

EVIL DEAD: HAIL TO THE KING

Infinite Chainsaw Fuel
Hold L1 and press X (2), Circle, Square, Circle, Square, Triangle.

EVIL ZONE

Play as Ihadurca and Bonus Stage
Finish Story mode with three different characters to unlock Ihadurca and a bonus stage in Versus mode.

Alternate Costumes
Beat the game with any character to unlock his or her alternate costumes in Versus mode or single-player Battle mode.

Character Biographies and Gallery Mode in Extra Options
Beat Story mode.

Narrator Mode in Extra Options
Beat One-player mode.

Congratulations Mode in Extra Options
Obtain all voices in Voice Collection (Extra Options). Choose "Congratulations" to view a special FMV sequence.

Voice Collection in Extra Options
Complete 1P Battle mode with the character and number of wins listed below to unlock each character's voice in Voice Collection.

Gally
37

Danzaiver
42

Al
44

Kakurine
44

Setsuna
46

Erel
49

Midori
50

Keiya
60

Lie
60

Ihadurca
84

EXCALIBUR 2555 AD

Full Health
Pause and press Triangle (3), Square (5).

Full Sword Power
Pause and press Triangle (2), Square (2), Circle (2), Square (2).

Level Skip
Pause and press Square, Circle, Square, Triangle, Circle, Triangle (3).

Level 1 Password
Circle, Square, X, Circle (2), Triangle

Level 2 Password
Square, X, Triangle (2), X, Circle

Level 3 Password
Circle, X, Circle, Triangle, Square, X

Level 4 Password
X, Circle, Triangle, Square, Circle (2)

Level 5 Password
Square (2), Circle (2), X, Triangle

Level 6 Password
Circle, X, Square, Triangle (2), Square

Level 7 Password
Square (2), Circle (2), X, Triangle

Level 8 Password
Circle, X, Square, Triangle (2), Square

Level 9 Password
Triangle, X, Triangle, Circle, Square, Triangle

Level 10 Password
Triangle, Circle (2), Square, Triangle, X

Level 11 Password
X, Square (2), X, Triangle, Square

Level 12 Password
Circle, Triangle, X, Circle, Square, Circle

Level 13 Password
Square, Triangle, Circle, X(3)

Spinning Slice
X, Triangle, Circle, Square

Roundhouse Swing
X, Square, Circle, Triangle

EXECTOR

Level Passwords
35314_DF

Level 2 Password
FBE_723_F

Level 3 Password
8759_AB_3

Level 4 Password
9_A_969_C_0

Level 5 Password
I_FEBD_7_B

EXPENDABLE

More Lives
Pause and press Square, Down, Right, Circle, Square, Left, Up, X.

More Continues
Pause and press X, Up, Down, Triangle, Circle (3), L1.

God Mode
Pause and press Left, Right, Left, Right, L1, R1, L1, R1.

Level Select
Pause and press Up, Down, Right, Left, X (3), Triangle.

First-Person Viewpoint
Pause and press L1, Up, Left, Triangle, X, L2, R1, L2.

EXPLOSIVE RACING

Mirrored Tracks
Enter NARCIS as name.

Super Car
Enter LNCMU as name.

FADE TO BLACK

Cheat Code Password
Square, Triangle, Circle, X, Circle, Triangle

Unlimited Shield
Enter Cheat Code password, exit, then enter Square, Circle (2), Square, Triangle, X.

Invincibility
Enter Cheat Code password, exit, then enter Triangle, X, Triangle (2), Square, Circle.

Cinema Test
Enter Cheat Code password, exit, then enter Square, X, Circle, Triangle, Circle, X.

Level 1 Password
Square, Circle, Triangle, X, Circle, Square

Level 2 Password
Triangle, Circle, X, Circle, Square, X

Level 3 Password
X, Circle, X, Circle, Triangle, X

Level 4 Password
X, Square, Triangle, Circle (2), Triangle

Level 5 Password
Square (2), Triangle, X (2), Triangle

Level 6 Password
Triangle, X (4), Circle

Level 7 Password
Circle (2), Triangle, X, Triangle, X

Level 8 Password
Square (2), X, Triangle, Square (2)

Level 9 Password
Triangle, X (2), Triangle, Circle, Triangle

Level 10 Password
X, Triangle, Square, Circle, Triangle, X

Level 11 Password
Circle, Square, X (2), Square, X

Level 12 Password
Square, Triangle, X, Square, Circle, X

Level 13 Password
X (2), Circle, Triangle, Circle, Triangle

FANTASTIC FOUR

Hidden Options
In the Options menu, highlight Training mode and press L1+L2+R1+R2. New options appear, including invincibility and stage skip.

One Hundred Lives
At the title screen, press Up(2), Down, Left, Right, Down.

Same Character Game
Start a two-player game. Then press Start, Select, choose a new character, and press X. When the new character appears, quickly press Start, Select on the other controller. Now both players play the same character.

FATAL FURY

Play as Mr. Karate
Beat the game without continues and without losing any rounds.

Play as Duck King
Beat the game with every character.

Additional Options
Unlock Duck King as a playable character to open Team Battle and Data modes.

Alternate Geese's Costume
Highlight Geese at the Character Selection screen, then hold Start and press Circle or X for a black suit, Square or Triangle for a dark brown one.

Alternate Geese's Ending
Win the game with Geese in his alternate costume.

Alternate Billy's Ending
Win the game with Billy in his alternate costume.

FEAR EFFECT

Infinite Health
Choose "Credits" on the Options screen. Then press L1, Triangle, Up, Down, Circle (2), Triangle, Square, Right, Square.

Maximum Ammunition
Choose "Credits" on the Options screen. Then press L1, Triangle, Up, Down, Circle (2), Triangle, Square, Left, Triangle.

Instant Death with All Firearms
Choose "Credits" on the Options screen. Then press L1, Triangle, Up, Down, Circle (2), Triangle, Square, Down, R1.

Instant Puzzle Solution
Choose "Credits" on the Options screen. Then press L1, Triangle, Up, Down, Circle (2), Down (3), Up.

Expert Mode
Choose "Credits" on the Options screen. Then press Down (3), Triangle, Down (3), Square, Left, Right for tougher enemies.

FEAR EFFECT 2

Cheat Mode
Finish the game at least once. Begin a new game, and wait until the starting sequence ends. After Rain leaves, you can control yourself and Hana for the first time. Find the small control pad on the left-hand wall immediately after the screen switches. Walk up to it and the "Use" option appears. Press Triangle and enter one of the following codes:

All Weapons
Enter "11692" at the small control pad.

Unlimited Ammunition
61166

Big Head Mode
10397

Concept Art (Disk One)
Left, Right, Up, Down (2), Circle on the title screen. The screen should flash red.

Concept Art (Disk Two)
UP (2), R1 (2)

Concept Art (Disk Three)
L1, R2, L1, R2, L1, Square

Concept Art (Disk Four)
Circle (2), Square, L2, Square

FEDA 2

Invincibility
Hold R1+R2+Square at the title screen and press Select during gameplay.

FELONY 11-79

All Vehicles
Insert a memory card with no saved games. Hold Triangle, then hold L2+R1+R2 on controller two at the main menu. Release L2+R1+R2, then Triangle. You hear an explosion.

All Vehicles and Tracks
At the main menu, quickly press L2+R1+R2, R2, L2, R1+Triangle on controller two. You hear an explosion. Alternately, hold Triangle and quickly press L2+R1+R2, R2, L2, R1 on controller two at the Game Mode Selection screen.

Faster Cars
At the Game Mode Selection screen, hold Triangle, then hold L2+R1+R2 on controller two. Release L2+R1+R2, then quickly press R2, L2, R1 while still holding Triangle. You hear an explosion.

Alternate Camera View
During gameplay, hold Select and press Triangle.

Unlock Bonus 360
Complete the Metro City track with more than $2.5 million.

Unlock Bonus BUS (City Bus)
Complete the Seaside track.

Unlock Bonus CIV (Honda Civic)
Complete the Downtown track within four minutes.

Unlock Bonus DAM
Complete the Metro City track.

Unlock Bonus DBL (Diablo)
Complete the Metro City track within four minutes.

Unlock Bonus DTK (Diesel truck)
Complete the Metro City track.

Unlock Bonus ELS
Complete the Seaside track with over $2.5 million.

Unlock Bonus FD7
Complete the Downtown track within four minutes.

Unlock Bonus FML (Indy Car)
Complete the Downtown track with no accumulated money and no damage.

Unlock Bonus GT1
Complete the Seaside track within four minutes.

Unlock Bonus GTK (Garbage Truck)
Break the speed limit on the freeway section of the Seaside track by at least 60 to 75 mph.

Unlock Bonus GTR
Complete the Seaside track.

Unlock Bonus GTS
Complete the Downtown track with more than $1 million or complete the Seaside track.

Unlock Bonus LIM (Limousine)
Complete the Metro City track.

Unlock Bonus NSR (Acura NSR)
Complete the Downtown track within four minutes.

Unlock Bonus PLC (Police Cruiser)
Complete the Seaside track with no accumulated money and no damage.

Unlock Bonus PCS
Complete the Downtown track within four minutes.

Unlock Bonus RCC (R/C Car)
Destroy the displays on the left wall at the shopping mall in the Metro City level, then complete the track before time runs out.

Unlock Bonus SIR
Complete the Downtown track.

Unlock Bonus SSP (Street Sweeper)
Exceed 144 mph at the speed checkpoint on the Seaside track.

Unlock Bonus TAC
Complete the Metro City track within four minutes.

Unlock Bonus TNK (Tank)
Complete the Metro City track with no accumulated money and no damage.

Unlock Bonus VPR (Dodge Viper)
Complete the Downtown track with more than $1 million. To do this, select the 318 and reverse into the jewelry store when starting at the beginning of the track. Destroy the rest of the jewelry items, worth $80,000 each.

FIFA '96

Invisible Walls
Pause and press X, X, X, Triangle, Square (3), Triangle. Then highlight "Resume," press Square, and start new game.

Curve Ball
Pause and press Triangle, Square, X, Triangle, X, X. Then highlight "Resume," press Square, and start new game.

Crazy Ball
Pause and press X, Square, Triangle, X, X, Triangle, Square, X. Then highlight "Resume," press Square, and start new game.

Super Power
Pause and press Triangle, Square, Triangle (8). Then highlight "Resume," press Square, and start new game.

Super Goalie
Pause and press Square (5), Triangle (5). Then highlight "Resume," press Square, and start new game.

Super Offense
Pause and press Square (5), Triangle, X. Then highlight "Resume," press Square, and start new game.

Super Defense
Pause and press Triangle (5), X, Triangle. Then highlight "Resume," press Square, and start new game.

Shootout
Pause and press Square, Triangle, Square, X, Square, Triangle. Then highlight "Resume," press Square, and start new game.

Stupid Team
Pause and press Square, Triangle, X, Square, Triangle, X. Then highlight "Resume," press Square, and start new game.

Dream Team
Pause and press Square (2), Triangle (2), X, X, Square (2). Then highlight "Resume," press Square, and start new game.

Tuxedoes as Uniforms
Enter Square, Triangle, X, Square, Triangle (2), X, Triangle in Options menu. Then exit game and return to Options menu.

Data and Spock
Enter Square, Triangle, X, Square, Triangle (2), X, X in Options menu. Then exit game and return to Options menu.

Batman and Robin
Enter Square, Triangle, X, Square, Triangle (3), Square in Options menu. Then exit game and return to Options menu.

Default Color Pallet
Enter Square, Triangle, X, Square, Triangle (3), X in Options menu. Then exit game and return to Options menu.

Invisible Players
Enter Square, Triangle, X, Square, Triangle (2), X, Square in Options menu. Then exit game and return to Options menu.

EA Custom Teams
Enter Square, Triangle, X, Square, Triangle (2), Square (2) in Options menu. Then exit game and return to Options menu.

Oktoberfest
Enter Square, Triangle, X, Square, Triangle (4) in Options menu. Then exit game and return to Options menu.

Secret Intro
Press Square, Triangle during intro.

FIFA '99

Unlimited Bankroll
Press L1, L2, R2, R1, Circle, X, Square, Triangle, Start, Select in Team Edit mode.

Unlimited Fouls
Press L1, L2, R1, R2 Circle, X, Square, Triangle, Start, Select in Team Edit mode.

FIFA 2000

EA Sports Teams
When selecting your team, choose "Rest Of World," then cycle through to teams that begin with E. The players on teams EA 1, EA 2, EA 3, and EA 4 have been customized by the EA Sports staff.

Special Guests Team
When selecting your team, choose "Rest Of World," then cycle through to teams that begin with S. The Special Guests team is the same as the EA Sports teams, but with different names. The players are perfect.

Finding Ronaldo
Ronaldo is No. 9 for the Italian side, Inter Milan, and the Brazilian national team.

Finding Pele
Pele is No. 10 on the Classic Brazilian team, Santos '62-'63, and the Classic Brazilian national team, Brazil '58 and Brazil '70.

Finding Romario
Romario is No. 11 and for the Brazilian team, Flamengo.

Finding Youri Djorkaeff
Youri Djorkaeff is No. 14 for the German side, Kaiserslautern.

FIFA SOCCER '97

Instant Replay Zoom
During gameplay, press R1+D-Pad on the Instant Replay screen to change the magnification of the replay.

Moving Shadows
During gameplay, go to the Instant Replay screen and hold L1 or R1.

EA Players
Select a friendly match, choose the USA league, and play as Dallas or New York to play with members of the EA development team.

Hidden Audio
Play track six of the game disk in a CD player to hear singing by John Motson, a member of the EA development team.

FIFA: ROAD TO WORLD CUP '98

Editable Bankroll
Press Square, X, Square, L2, L1 at Team Edit screen.

Toepunt (Hard Kicks)
Press R1, L1, Down, Up, Left at Team Select screen.

Unlimited Player Attributes
Press L1, L2, X, Square, X in Player Edit screen.

Adjust lighting
Pause the game and press Square, Triangle, X, Square, Triangle (2), X (2), Square (6), Triangle (5) at the Options screen.

FIFTH ELEMENT

Level Select +
Press L1, L2, R2, R1, Select, Start, at the main menu.

FIGHTER'S IMPACT

Alternate Costumes
Highlight character, hold Circle+Square, and press Start.

Deformed Characters
Press Select (10) at the title screen.

Paper Cut-out Characters
Press Right (10) at the title screen.

Small Characters
Highlight character, hold Down+X+Circle, and press Start.

Stick Figure Characters
Press Left (10) at the title screen.

Unlock Four Hidden Characters
Beat the game four times.

FIGHTING FORCE

Cheat Mode
At main menu, hold Left+Square+L1+R2.

Extra Weapons
Finish a level, view the destruction bonus, and quickly exit. You'll see a flash and hear a sound. Then a shotgun or handgun appears when the next level begins. In Two-player mode, each player receives a weapon.

FIGHTING FORCE 2

Cheat Mode
Hold L1+L2+R1+Triangle+X+Left at the Press Start screen.

FINAL DOOM

Full Guns and Ammo
Press X, Triangle, L1, Up, Down, R2, Left (2).

Full Map
Press Triangle, Triangle, L2, R2, L2, R2, R1, Square.

Invincibility
Press Down, L2, Square, R1, Right, L1, Left, Circle.

Level Warp
Press Right, Left, R2, R1, Triangle, L1, Circle, X.

Map with Objects
Press Triangle, Triangle, L2, R2, L2, R2, R1, Circle.

Master Level 2 Virgil Password
RBF9D395SQ

Master Level 3 Canyon Password
1L3C!F7XO2

Master Level 4 Combine Password
HLLZTPOKKK

Master Level 5 Catwalk Password
6J1NWHFR64

Master Level 6 Fistula Password
8WWRSSHM79

Master Level 7 Geyron Password
D9SOWVFJFC

Master Level 8 Minos Password
HS9YW3HMFC

Master Level 9 Nessus Password
OSSHCWFVYW

Master Level 10 Paradox Password
HT!OVLXLDB

Master Level 11 Subspace Password
J77VYTMDCF

Master Level 12 Subterra Password
6XDHRW25!8

Master Level 13 Vesperas Password
C33W2YOGHK

**TNT Evilution Password:
Level 14 System Control**
FP62ZMSWJG

**TNT Evilution Password:
Level 15 Human Barbecue**
D5510QKRKH

**TNT Evilution Password:
Level 16 Wormhole**
ZVBKT!O69!

**TNT Evilution Password:
Level 17 Crater**
1CCTV9GQ!9

**TNT Evilution Password:
Level 18 Nukage Processing**
TM4OLJ2ZKJ

**TNT Evilution Password:
Level 19 Deepest Reaches**
HYY4GQ9GSQ

**TNT Evilution Password:
Level 20 Processing Area**
!5NR4W7C20

**TNT Evilution Password:
Level 21 Lunar Mining Project**
1FFGVZ1777

TNT Evilution Password: Level 22 Quarry
SN5YORKIGH

TNT Evilution Password: Level 23 Ballistyx
ZBBST6R89!

TNT Evilution Password: Level 24 Heck
GK25JLV3LL

**Plutonia Experiment Password:
Level 25 Congo**
G224SGYSNL

**Plutonia Experiment Password:
Level 26 Aztec**
TR8WXJVNBD

**Plutonia Experiment Password:
Level 27 Ghost Town**
XBBRT67N8!

**Plutonia Experiment Password:
Level 28 Baron's Lair**
NGZ9HTCMMP

**Plutonia Experiment Password:
Level 29 the Death Domain**
OGGMO6W546

**Plutonia Experiment Password:
Level 30 Onslaught**
99SD40FYVW

X-Ray Specs
Press L1, R2, L2, R1, Right, Triangle, X, Right.

FINAL FANTASY VII

Increase Chocobo Speed
Hold L1+L2+R1+R2.

Increase Chocobo Stamina
Hold R1+R2.

Huge Materia
Use Circle, Square, X, X as Rocket Town passcode.

FINAL FANTASY VIII

SeeD Test 1 Answers
Y, N, Y, Y, Y, N, N, Y, N, N

SeeD Test 2 Answers
Y, N, Y, Y, Y, N, Y, Y, N, N

SeeD Test 3 Answers
N, N, Y, N, Y, Y, Y, N, Y, N

SeeD Test 4 Answers
N, Y, Y, Y, N, N, Y, Y, N, N

SeeD Test 5 Answers
N, N, N, Y, Y, N, N, Y, Y, Y

SeeD Test 6 Answers
Y, N, Y, Y, N, N, Y, Y, N, Y

SeeD Test 7 Answers
Y, Y, Y, Y, Y, N, Y, Y, N, Y

SeeD Test 8 Answers
N, Y, N, N, Y, Y, N, N, Y, N

SeeD Test 9 Answers
N, Y, N, N, N, N, N, Y, N, Y

SeeD Test 10 Answers
Y, N, N, N, N, N, N, N, N, N

SeeD Test 11 Answers
Y, Y, N, Y, Y, N, Y, N, N, Y

SeeD Test 12 Answers
N, Y, N, N, Y, N, Y, N, Y, N

SeeD Test 13 Answers
Y, N, N, N, Y, N, N, N, N, N

SeeD Test 14 Answers
Y, Y, Y, Y, N, Y, Y, N, Y, N

SeeD Test 15 Answers
Y, Y, N, N, N, N, N, Y, N, Y

SeeD Test 16 Answers
Y, N, N, Y, N, Y, N, N, Y, N

SeeD Test 17 Answers
Y, N, N, N, Y, N, N, Y, N, N

SeeD Test 18 Answers
Y, N, N, Y, N, N, N, N, N, N

SeeD Test 19 Answers
Y, N, N, Y, N, N, N, N, N, Y

SeeD 20 Test Answers
Y, Y, Y, N, Y, N, Y, Y, N, N

SeeD Test 21 Answers
Y, Y, Y, Y, N, N, Y, Y, N, N

SeeD Test 22 Answers
N, N, N, Y, N, N, N, Y, Y, N

SeeD Test 23 Answers
Y, N, N, N, Y, Y, Y, Y, Y, Y

SeeD Test 24 Answers
Y, Y, N, N, Y, Y, N, N, N, Y

SeeD Test 25 Answers
Y, N, Y, Y, Y, N, N, Y, N, N

SeeD Test 26 Answers
Y, Y, N, Y, N, Y, N, Y, N, N

SeeD Test 27 Answers
N, N, N, N, N, Y, N, Y, N, N

FINAL FANTASY IX

Get Excalibur 1
Buy the "Magic Finger" item early on at the Treno Auction. After you reach Dargelo, give this item to an elderly man you meet there. He gives you Excalibur in return.

Get Excalibur II
Get to Hades in under 12 hours. After beating Hades, check the farthest right pillar for the sword.

Black Jack Minigame
Beat the game normally and allow the credits to finish. Press R2, L1, R2, R2, Up, X, Right, Circle, Down, Triangle, L2, R1, R2, L1, Square (2) at the "The End" screen.

Squirrel Land Spirit Location
Found around Dali. Offer it an Ore Stone.

Ghost Land Spirit Location
Found in front of Treno (but not too far) or around the South Gate. Offer it an Ore Stone.

Lady Bug Land Spirit Location
Found around the Black Mage Village. Offer it two Ore Stones.

Yeti Land Spirit Location
Found in the forest outside Madain Sari. Offer it two Ore Stones.

Nymph Land Spirit Location
Found in the forest near Iifa. Offer it three Ore Stones.

Jabberwock Land Spirit Location
Found in the forest East of Oeivell. Offer it an Emerald.

Feather Suckle Land Spirit Location
Found on the Ice Continent, on the Chocobo tracks. Offer it a Moonstone.

Galda Land Spirit Location
Found in the forest outside Gizamaluke Cave after climbing the rope. Offer it a Lapis Lazly.

Yan Land Spirit Location
Found on Bile Island (small island near center of map). It keeps running away until you find all other, eight Land Spirits. Offer it a Diamond.

Stellazzio Quest
Talk to the lady in the house north of the Treno Combination Shop. She tells you about a set of 13 Stellazzio that are spread across the world. Find them all and she rewards you every time you return. This quest is required in order to see the game's alternate ending.

Aries Stellazzio Location
Found in Dali, in the windmill all the way to be back (not downstairs).

Cancer Stellazzio Location
Found in Burmecia, behind the overturned cart.

Scorpio Stellazzio Location
Found in Quan Cave spring.

Gemini Stellazzio Location
Found in the fountain at the first screen after you enter Treno. Throw coins 13 times into the fountain.

Taurus Stellazzio Location
Found in Treno, behind the item shop.

Virgo Stellazzio Location
Found in the Black Mage Village Inn, around the beds.

Libra Stellazzio Location
Found in Madain Sari fountain.

Leo Stellazzio Location
Found in Alexandria (after raid), left Tower near Neptune Statue.

Sagittarius Stellazzio Location
Found in Linblum, in the left side of the 3D screen, up from Commerical Square.

Capricorn Stellazzio Location
Found in Dargelo Library, right-hand side.

Aquarius Stellazzio Location
Found in Ipsen Heritage, right-hand pillar at entrance.

Pisces Stellazzio Location
Found in the treasure chest inside Invincible.

13th Stellazzio Location
Return to the Quan Cave east of Treno after collecting and returning all 12 coins.

Renaming Characters
Use the Namingway card during the card tournament in Treno if you go against Mario, or find it in Kuja's Palace. Once you have the Namingway Card, go to Daggereo and get to the middle floor. Here you find a man who wants to see the card. He will rename your characters after seeing the card.

Quan's Dwelling Reunion
If you take Vivi and Quina to Quan's Dwelling, you get a short movie sequence. After that, go to the balcony and examine the clock to get a rare item, the running shoes.

Two-Player Mode
Pause the game (so the menu comes up). Next, go to the "CONFIG" option, then go to "Battle Control." Set it to "Custom" and push X.

FINAL FANTASY CHRONICLES

Secret Developer's Room (*Final Fantasy IV*)
The "Secret Developer's Room" is hidden in the Dwarf Castle in the Underworld. Between the weapon and armor shop is an odd section of wall that is actually a doorway to the "Rally-Ho" pub. On the right side of the pub is a fake wall. Walk through this wall to reach a staircase that leads to the Secret Programmer's Room.

Skip Sealed Cave Event (*Final Fantasy IV*)
When you go to the Underworld and into the Dwarf Kingdom, after you fight the dolls in the secret crystal chamber, Rydia returns and helps you fight. After you are done and in the main chamber, use her warp spell to get to the crystal room. The crystal will still be there. Approach and examine the crystal to take it. Later when you have to go to the Sealed Cave, if you have the Crystal you will not have to enter the cave. Skip that event, and the game automatically goes to the sequence that normally happens as you are coming out.

Double Weapons and Shields for Free
During a battle, select the items menu on the character with whom you wish to double something, then select an empty slot in your items inventory. Press Up until you see the left and right hand equip screen, and select an item. Repeat for both items, then when you exit the battle, select equip. Equip the item you just took off, and it will say "dark sword 2." Unequip the weapon and equip it again to have one equipped and one in your items inventory. Repeat and sell for big bucks.

Experience (On *Final Fantasy IV*)
In the Tower Babel Overworld, after you get an edge and are on your way to fight Rubicant: If you run into a sorcerer and two blade men, kill the two blade men but leave the sorcerer alone. It summons more monsters and so on. After awhile, the more monsters you kill, the more experience you get at the end of the battle

FIRO & KLAUD

Skip to Construction Level
CBOBUNAABAASY65X

Level Password: Back Alley
MOOMIN

Level Password: Back Street
MOONPIG

Level Password: Back Street B
MOONPINGEON

Level Password: Back Roof
SNUFFKIN

Level Password: Main Street
LITTLE_MI

Level Password: Main Street B
LITTLE_MO

Level Password: Vinnie's Scrap Yard
SOUP_DRAGON

Level Password: Vinnie's Scrap Yard B
SUPER_DRAGON

FISHERMAN'S BAIT

Attract Fish
Press Triangle, X, Circle, Square, Up, Down, Left, Right at the title screen.

Total Count List
Press Up (2), Down (2), L1, R1, L1, R1, X, Circle, Start at the title screen. Choose "Total Count List" under Options to see how many times the game has been played

Concave Dam Lake
Play the game at least 50 times. (Use the Total Count List code to know.)

Center Lake
Play the game at least 100 times. (Use the Total Count List code to know.)

FIST OF THE NORTH STAR

Level 2 Password
BCDEKHJ

Level 3 Password
JCGHBFD

Level 4 Password
JGBDECH

Level 5 Password
FBIDGHJ

The Ultimate Code Book: Book of Secrets

Level 6 Password
JBGAFKC

Level 7 Password
BKDFECJ

Level 8 Password
IBFDJHE

Level 9 Password
EFGHCDI

Level 10 Password
FKACDE

Level 11 Password
DGAFEKI

Level 12 Password
CBEHGDK

Level 13 Password
DFGBCEI

Level 14 Password
KBCDGIA

FORD RACING

All Cars
Go into a new career and enter your name as GIMMEGIMME.

Invisible Car
Enter your name as MARK MARTIN in a new career mode

FORMATION SOCCER '97: THE ROAD TO FRANCE

Strongest Team
Finish playing through the Human Cup and save. Enter Exhibition mode. Go through this selection: HOL, USA, MEX, ARG, NGR then, press Square.

New Difficulty
Finish playing through the Human Cup and save.

FORMULA 1

Buggy Mode
Hold Select and press Right, Up, Triangle, Left, Up, Square, Triangle at the Race Qualify screen.

Bike Mode
Hold Select and press Down, Up, Circle, Triangle, Right, Up, Square, Triangle at the Race Qualify screen

Lava Mode
Hold Select and press Square, Circle, Up, Right (2), Circle, X at the Race Qualify screen.

Gibberish Mode
Hold Select and press Left, Circle, Up, Down (2), Right, Circle, Square (2) at the Race Qualify screen.

Bonus Track
Hold Select and press Left, Circle (2), Triangle (2), Circle, Up, Right at the Race Qualify screen.

German Mode
Hold Select and press Down, Up, Left (2), Square, Circle, X at the Race Qualify screen.

Spanish Mode
Hold Select and press Triangle, Circle, Right, Circle, Triangle, Circle, Right, Circle at the Race Qualify screen.

FORMULA 1 '98

Bonus Track
Enter CHEESY POOFS in the Driver Edit option.

Roman Coliseum Track
Enter GO COWS in the Driver Edit option.

FORMULA 1 '99

Ring Mode
Enter RINGS as name on the High Score screen.

Safety Car Mode
Enter SAFETY as name on the High Score screen.

Monaco Nights Track
Enter NIGHTS as name on the High Score screen.

FORMULA 1: CHAMPIONSHIP ED.

VR Style Graphics
Enter VIRTUALLY VIRTUAL as name.

New Sound Effects
Enter SWAP SHOP as name.

Over-Inflated Tires
Enter LITTLE WHEELZ as name.

Wipeout Mode
Enter PI MAN as name.

Helicopter Viewpoint
Enter ZOOM LENSE as name.

Murry & Martin Commentators
Enter BOX CHATTER as name.

Four Extra Tracks
Enter BILLY BONUS as name.

Rain Frogs
Enter CATS DOGS as name.

Round 16 in Championship
Enter OEAN ALESI as name.

Automatic First Place
Enter TOO EASY as name.

Alternate Camera Angles
Drive to the side of the track and press Select on controller two to choose from more views. This is ineffective if your car is in the pits.

1960's Cars
Enter SWINGIND SIXTIES as a name and start an Arcade mode game.

Expert Mode
Enter BLOOMIN ARD as a name.

Reach Championship Round 16
Enter OEAN ALESI (200 points, second place), PEAN ALESI (200 points, third place), QEAN ALESI (200 points, fourth place), or NEAN ALESI (0 points, last place) as a name.

FORMULA KARTS

Hidden Track
Enter WOODSTOCK as a password.

Super Kart
Enter CHIPPIE as a password.

FORSAKEN

All Weapons
Press X, Circle, X, Circle, X, Circle, R1, R2, L2, L1.

Cheat Options
Highlight Options, then press Left, Right, Left, Right, X.

Level 4 Password
5J9DNN1D

Level 5 Password
5N9XNN1F

Level 6 Password
FSBDP43G

Level 7 Password
80BJN8B0

Level 8 Password
G4C4N4CK

Level 9 Password
X8MLP4H2

Level 10 Password
VDX2NXGM

Level 11 Password
XK4QNDH4

Level 12 Password
4PFDN095

Level 13 Password
STFNN8G6

Level 14 Password
NYG4N0F7

FOX HUNT

Free Guns
Enter FBI room and press R1, L2, R1 (2), Triangle, X, L1, Circle, Start.

FREESTYLE BOARDIN' 99

Play as Mr. Chicken
Complete all 10 courses on any stage with each of the five standard characters using the same saved game file to unlock Mr. Chicken.

Game Music
Play all but track one of the game disk in an audio CD player to hear music from the game.

FRENZY

Cheat Menu
Enter PICKLE as password, press Triangle to return to the main menu, and select Cheat menu option.

Level 2 Password
ADRIAN

Level 3 Password
CORRODE

Level 4 Password
GLUGGLUG

Level 5 Password
SNOWBALL

Level 6 Password
FLATPACK

Level 7 Password
SPOOKY!

Level 8 Password
BOSSMAD!

Level 9 Password
RUNAWAY!

FROGGER

Level Select
Pause and press Right, Square, Triangle, Square, Triangle, R1, L1, R1, L1 and Circle.

Infinite Lives
Pause and press Right, Square, Triangle, Square, Triangle, X.

FROGGER 2: SWAMPY'S REVENGE

Level Select
During the game, pause and hold the Square button and enter: Up, Down, Left, Right, Right, Right, Down, Left.

Level Skip
During the game, pause and hold the Square button and enter: Right, Left, Up, Up, Up, Right, Left, Left.

Unlock All Characters
During the game, pause and hold the Square button and enter: Left, Right, Left, Left, Left, Up, Left, Left.

Unlock All Extras and Bonus Levels
During the game, pause and hold the Square button and enter: Right, Up, Up, Down, Right, Down, Right.

Infinite Lives
During the game, pause and hold the Square button and enter: Down, Down, Up, Down, Right, Down, Up, Up.

Temporary Invincibility
During the game, pause and hold the Square button and enter: Left, Left, Up, Left, Down, Right, Right, Right.

FRONT MISSION 2

Be Iyana W. Robot
Enter SCHNECKE at the Network. Enter SN as the password. Then, enter GERMANY as an answer to the question. That allows you to access the Iyana W. Robot.

Play with Your Battle Skills
Beat Emma's or Alisa's story line. Save your game at a final save point after the credits. The title screen appears. Load your memory card file. You can play the same or different story line with all the battle skills from your previous game file.

Special Weapon
In the Alisa missions, after Mission 46, go to the Armored K web site. Check out BBS 3. Notice 555-XKR-224 at the bottom. Go to the Auspend Garbage pit and type that number into the Infernal Dialer. You receive parts for a Hoshun MK112 and a laser weapon. Put it together and upgrade it.

FRONT MISSION 3

Play with Your Battle Skills
When you beat Emma's or Alisa's story line, wait until after the credits to save your game at a final save point. The title screen comes up. Load your memory card file into the game. You are allowed to play the other or the same story line with all the Battle Skills you learned in your previous game file.

Special Weapon
In the Alisa missions, after mission 46, go to the ArmoredK web site and check out BBS 3. At the bottom is a number(555-XKR-224). Go to the Auspend Garbagepit. There is something called the Infernal Dialer. Dial this number in to receive the parts to a Hoshun Mk112 and a laser weapon. Put it together and upgrade it.

FUTURE COP LAPD 2100 AD

Invincibility
Pause and highlight "Sound FX Volume," then press Circle (2), Select (2), Circle, Select, X, Square.

200 Bonus Points
Pause game, highlight "Sound FX," and press Circle, Square, Circle, X, Select, Square, X, select Quit and "yes."

All Levels Completed
DYPYFASRHR

All Levels Done/Bonus Weapons
DYTIFASUHL

All Bonus Weapons
SYMRGOBRRL

Black and White Graphics
Pause game, highlight "Sound FX," and press Square, Select, Circle, X (2), Circle, Select, Square, choose Quit and "yes."

Machine Gun Ammo
Pause game, highlight "Sound FX," and press Square, Circle, Select, X, Select, X, Circle, Square, and choose Quit and "yes."

Machine Gun Power-up
Pause game, highlight "Sound FX," and press Circle (3), X (3), Circle, Select, and choose Quit and "yes."

Level 1 Password
TAFRGYBLRR

Level 2 Password
CRGRGYBLRY

Level 3 Password
FUMRGYBLRL

Level 4 Password
SICUGYBLLI

Level 5 Password
TAFUGYBLLR

Level 6 Password
CRGUGYBLLY

Level 7 Password
FUMUGYBLLR

Level 8 Password
SIFYGYBISR

Super Heavy Weapons
Pause game, highlight "Sound FX," and press Square (3), Circle, X, Circle, X, and select Quit and "yes."

Super Jump
Pause game, highlight "Sound FX," and press Circle (4), Square, X, Select, Square, X, Select, Circle, choose Quit and "yes."

Super Special Weapons
Pause game, highlight "Sound FX," and press Square, Circle, Square, Select, Circle, X, Square, Circle, choose Quit and "yes."

Unlimited Ammo
Press X, R1 (3), R2, L1 (2), L2, X, Square, Select at the title screen.

Precinct Assault Mode 1P Level Password:
Urban Jungle, 5
FUCUGYBIMI

Precinct Assault Mode 1P Level Password:
Urban Jungle, 10
SUHUGYBIDR

Precinct Assault Mode 1P Level Password:
Proving Grounds, 5
SICRRYBLLI

Precinct Assault Mode 1P Level Password:
Proving Grounds, 10
TIFRNYBLSR

Precinct Assault Mode 1P Level Password:
Hollywood Keys, 5
SICRGYDLLI

Precinct Assault Mode 1P Level Password:
Hollywood Keys, 10
TIFRGYPLSR

Precinct Assault Mode 1P Level Password:
Venice Beach, 5
SICRGLBLLI

Precinct Assault Mode 1P Level Password:
Venice Beach, 10
MIFRGIBLSR

G DARIUS

View FMV
At the Options screen, highlight "Movies," press Down, Up, Down, Up, hold L1+L2+R1+R2, and press Start.

View All FMV Sequences
At the Options screen, highlight "Movie." Press Left, Right, Left, Right, then hold L1+L2+R1+R2 and press Start. For the Japanese version, press Down, Up, Down, Up, then hold L1+L2+R1+R2 and press Start.

GALAXIAN 3

Debug Mode
Press L1, R2, R1, L2, Up, Down, Up, Down at the title screen.

GAME OF LIFE

Unlimited Money
Enter GET A LIFE as name.

GAUNTLET LEGENDS

Play as Sumner
Exit through the secret door in the last level of the Trench. Then collect 50 coins in the bonus level to unlock Sumner.

Play as Falconess
In the bonus level of the Castle World, collect 50 coins. Falconess has the same turbo attacks as the Valkyrie.

New Weapon
Reach Level 10 to receive a new weapon, and Levels 50 and 99 for additional new weapons.

Get a Familiar
Reach level 25 to receive a familiar; Valkyrie receives an Eagle, Wizard receives a Dragon, Archer receives a Butterfly, and Warrior receives a Dragonfly. Reach level 50 for better familiars.

Permanent Anti-Death
Finish the game to receive permanent anti-death, which allows you to steal health from death.

G-DARIUS

Infinite Continues
Accumulate more than 100 continues, then enter the Options screen and change the "Credit" option to "Free Play."

View All FMV Sequences
At the Options screen, highlight "Movie." Press Left, Right, Left, Right, then hold L1+L2+R1+R2 and press Start. For the Japanese version, press Down, Up, Down, Up, then hold L1+L2+R1+R2 and press Start.

GEKIDO

Play as Gorilla
Complete Urban Fighters mode with Travis and Michelle to unlock Gorilla in all modes.

Play as Kobuchi
Complete Urban Fighters mode with Tetsuo and Ushi to unlock Kobuchi in all modes.

Play as Kintaro
Complete Urban Fighters mode with Gorilla to unlock Kintaro in Arena Battle mode. Complete Urban Fighters mode at Hard difficulty to unlock Kintaro in Urban Fighters mode.

Play as Angela
Complete Urban Fighters mode with Kobuchi to unlock Angela in Arena Battle mode. Complete Urban Fighters mode at Hard difficulty to unlock Angela in Urban Fighters mode.

Play as Akujin
Complete Urban Fighters mode at Hard difficulty to unlock Akujin in all modes.

Alternate Costumes
Complete Urban Fighters mode at the Normal difficulty setting three times. Then, hold L1, L2, R1, or R2 while selecting a character at the Character Selection screen.

Hard Mode
Complete Urban Fighters mode with all characters at the Normal difficulty setting to unlock the Hard difficulty setting under the Options screen.

Shadow Fighter Mode
Complete Urban Fighters mode once.

Survival Mode
Complete Urban Fighters mode twice.

Team Battle Mode
Complete Urban Fighters mode three times.

Street Gang Battle Mode
Complete Urban Fighters mode at Hard difficulty with Kintaro, Angela, or Akujin.

Deform Mode
Get a hi-score and enter DEFORMANIA as a name to unlock Deform mode under the Options screen.

Skeleton Mode
Get a hi-score and enter BONECRACK as a name to unlock Skeleton mode under the Options screen.

Arena 2
Complete Shadow Fighter mode with Gorilla to unlock Arena 2 in Arena Battle mode.

Arena 5
Complete Shadow Fighter mode with Kobuchi.

Arena 7
Complete Shadow Fighter mode with Kintaro to unlock Arena 7 in Arena Battle mode.

Arena 8
Complete Shadow Fighter mode with Angela to unlock Arena 8 in Arena Battle mode.

Arena 9
Complete Shadow Fighter mode with Akujin to unlock Arena 9 in Arena Battle mode.

GEX

100 Gex Lives
Pause, hold R1, and press Up, Circle, Triangle, Down, Right, Square, Down, Select.

Bolts of Electricity
Pause, hold R1, and press Right, Left, Right, Circle, Triangle, Right, Circle, Down, Right, Select.

Fire Balls
Pause, hold R1, and press X, Up, Right, Up, Right (2), Select.

Ice Balls
Pause, hold R1, and press Circle (2), Left, Down, Circle, Up, Right, Select.

Invulnerability
Pause, hold R1, and press X, Square, Down (2), Up, Down, Right, Select.

Super Jump
Pause, hold R1, and press X, Circle, Up (2), Down, Right (2), Select.

Super Speed
Pause, hold R1, and press Down, Start, Right (2), Down, Up, Start, Select.

Unlimited Lives
Pause, hold R1, and press Up, Circle, Triangle, Down, Right, Square, Down, Select.

Level Select
Press R1+Select at Media Dimension, then press Circle, Start, Right, Up, Square, Left (2), Up, Start.

Level 1-2 Password
SVZFKHGP

Level 1-3 Password
BXRFYHGP

Level 1-4 Password
ZVTCYHGP

Level 2-1 Password
KXVKRHKP

Level 2-2 Password
CVHCSHKP

Level 2-3 Password
SVKLPHKP

Level 2-4 Password
CVBLPHKP

Level 3-1 Password
RVTCSHGP

Level 3-2 Password
XVVBRHKP

Level 4-1 Password
YTCHPHKP

Level 4-2 Password
ZTDHPHKP

Level 4-3 Password
DXVGRHKP

Level 5-1 Password
GYVVRHKP

Level 5-2 Password
PZYPRXYL

Level 6-1 Password
RYYRYXKB

Stage Select
Press R1+Select during game, and press X, Square, X, Right (2), Up, Left, Circle (2), Down (2).

GEX 2: ENTER THE GECKO

All Remotes
Press Square, Circle, R1, Triangle, L1, R1, L1, R1, Circle (2), R1, Triangle, L1, R1, Circle, L1, Triangle, Circle, Triangle, L1, R1, Circle, L1, Triangle, Circle, R1, L1.

Bonus Ending
Press R1, R2, X, L2, Square. X, Square, R2 (2), X, L2, Square, X, R2, Square, L2, R2, X, L2, Square, X, R2, Square, L2, R2, X, Square.

Debug Menu
Pause, highlight "Exit," hold L2, and press Left, Circle, Up, Down, Right (2), Left, Triangle, Up, Down.

Gex One-liners
Pause, highlight "Exit," hold L2, and press Triangle, Left, Circle, Up, Down. (During game, press Select to hear lines.)

Invincibility
Pause, highlight "Exit," hold L2, and press Left, Right, Triangle, Down, Right, Left.

Level Select
Pause, highlight "Exit," hold L2, and press Right (2), Left, Right, Triangle, Down, Right. (During game, press Select to choose a level.)

Level Statistics
Pause, highlight "Exit," hold L2, and press Right, Triangle, Right, Left, Triangle, X. (Select displays game statistics; Square shows records.)

Rambling Gex
Pause, highlight "Exit," hold L2, and press Down, Right, Up, Down, Right, Left, Right, Down (2).

Unlimited Lives
Pause, highlight "Exit," hold L2 and press Up (2), Down, Right, Triangle, Down.

Free Tour
Press L1, R1, L2, L1, X, Circle, R2, R1, L2, R1, L2, L1, X, Circle, Square, Triangle, R2, R1, L2, L1, X, Circle, Square, Triangle, R2, R1, L2, Triangle.

GEX 3: DEEP COVER GECKO

Invincibility
Pause, then hold L2, and press Down, Up, Left (2), Triangle, Right, Down.

Debug Mode
Pause, then hold R2+Up, Circle, Right, Up, Left, Right, Down. You should hear a sound. Resume the game and press Select to display a list of options including Level Select, Sound Debug, and Collectibles. For the European/Australian PAL version, pause, then hold L2, and press Up, Circle, Right, Up, Left, Right, Down.

Gex Quotes
Pause, then hold L2, and press Down, Right, Left, Circle, Up, Right. You should hear a sound. Resume the game and press Select to make Gex talk.

GEXVault Codes
Collect all four secret keys in the hidden levels to open the GEXVault in the GEXCave. In the GEXVault, enter one of the following codes to trigger the corresponding cheat function:

Debug Mode
Enter Square (2), Diamond, Circle, X (2), then press Select.

Level Select
Enter Square, Circle (2), Triangle, X (2).

Invincibility
Enter Square, Star, Triangle, Square, Triangle, Diamond.

Extra Life
Enter Triangle, Circle, Star, Square (2), X.

Ten Lives
Enter Square, X, Circle (2), Triangle, Square.

Eight Hit Paws
Enter Square, Diamond, Triangle (2), Star, Diamond.

Gex Quotes
Enter Square, Triangle, X, Star, Square, X. Press Select to make Gex comment.

Toggle Timer
Enter Square (2), Diamond, Circle, X (2). Turn the timer on or off at the Extras screen.

Play as Alfred
While in the GEXCave, enter Square, X, Triangle, Square, Star (2).

Play as Cuz
While in the GEXCave, enter Square, Diamond, Square (2), Triangle, Diamond.

Play as Rex
While in the GEXCave, enter Square, Star (2), Square, Triangle (2).

Play as DracuGex
While in the GEXCave, enter Star, X (2), Circle, Square, Triangle.

View FMV Sequence
Enter Circle, Triangle, Square, Star, Diamond, Star.

View FMV Sequence 2
Enter Diamond, Star, Square, X, Triangle, Circle.

View FMV Sequence 3
Enter X, Diamond, Star, Triangle (2), Circle.

GHOST IN THE SHELL

All Missions, Training Videos
Press R2, R1, Square (2), Up, Down, Square (2), R2 (2) at the main menu.

Level Select
Press R2, R1, Square (2), Up, Down, Square (2), R2 (2) at the main menu

GLOBAL DOMINATION

Defensive Missiles Times Six
Pause and press R1 (3), Select (2), X (2).

Ammo (Defensive Weapons)
Pause and press L1 (3), Select (4).

Ammo (Special Weapons)
Pause and press X, Select (2), L1 (3), R1, L1, R1, L1.

CPU Aid
Pause and press Select, R1 (3), X, L2 (2).

Fire from All Defense Silos
Pause and press R1, L1, R1, X (4).

Level Skip
Pause and press X, L1 (2), R1 (2), X, L1. (Zoom in/out to change levels, press Triangle to confirm.)

Produce All Mobile Units
Pause and press R1, L1, Select (2), X (2), L1.

Shield Selected Country
Pause and press X, Select (2), R1 (3), L1 (2), R1.

Show Enemy Submarines
Pause and press L1, R1, X (4), L1 (2).

Transform Special Forces
Pause and press Select, X, Select, X, L1 (2), R1.

GLOVER

Cheat Menu
Pause and press R1 (3), L1 (2), L2, L1, L2. A message appears.

Infinite Lives
Pause and press R1 (5), L2, R2, L2. A message appears.

Infinite Health
Pause and press L2 (2), R2, L2 (3), R1, L1. A message appears.

Checkpoint Select
Pause and press R2 (2), L2, L1, R1 (2), R2, L1. A message appears.

Call Ball
Pause and press R1, L1 (2), R1, L2, L1, R2, R1. A message appears.

Disable All Cheats
Pause and press L2 (8). A message appears.

GOAL STORM

Easter Island Heads
Press Up (2), Down (2), Left, Right, Left, Right, Square, Circle at the title screen.

More Camera Modes
Press Up (2), Down (2), Left, Right, Left, Right, Triangle (2) at the title screen.

GOLDEN NUGGET

More Money
Enter the video poker section. Raise the game to 100-dollar coins and start to play. Put in some of your money without touching any cards. Press the pay button. When it shows you being paid, leave video poker. You will have won thousands or millions.

G-POLICE

All Weapons/ Unlimited Ammo
Hold L2+R1+Circle and hit Left after briefing at Weapons screen.

Bonus Camera Angle
SUPACAM

Enable Sirens
WOOWOO

Faster Civilian Traffic
BENIHILL

Unlock Secret Missions
PANTALON

Invincibility
Hold L2+R1+Square and press Left during briefing.

Level 1 Password
MADGAV

Level 2 Password
DOLMAN

Level 3 Password
SONAGAV

Level 4 Password
ACEDUF

Level 5 Password
JOJOGUN

Level 6 Password
WENSKI

Level 7 Password
SAEGGY

Level 8 Password
MAZMAN

Level 9 Password
DAZMAN

Level 10 Password
DELUCS

Level 11 Password
ANDOOOO

Level 12 Password
KIMBCHS

Level 13 Password
ANDYMAC

Level 14 Password
YERMAN

Level 15 Password
OLLIEB

Level 16 Password
THEYOLK

Level 17 Password
TONYMASH

Level 18 Password
ANDYCROW

Level 19 Password
BIONIC

Level 20 Password
TSLATER

Level 21 Password
IAINTHOD

Level 22 Password
JONRITZ

Level 23 Password
CLAIREC

Level 24 Password
STEVEBOT

Level 25 Password
ANGUSF

Level 26 Password
EUANLEC

Level 27 Password
EDFIRE

Level 28 Password
STUBOMB

Level 29 Password
THONBOY

Level 30 Password
JIMMAC

Level 31 Password
PUGGER

Level 32 Password
ROSSCO

Level 33 Password
CAKEBOY

Level 34 Password
NIKNAK

Level 35 Password
SAGLORD

Level 1 (Alternate) Password
SXYLAAAA

Level 2 (Alternate) Password
KJOXAAAA

Level 3 (Alternate) Password
UIXZAAAA

Level 4 (Alternate) Password
MKFHRFAA

Level 5 (Alternate) Password
WHLTMIAA

Level 6 (Alternate) Password
YITSRFAA

Level 7 (Alternate) Password
UWCQAAAA

Level 8 (Alternate) Password
MYKXQFAA

Level 9 (Alternate) Password
YIOQMIAA

Level 10 (Alternate) Password
CJWGRFAA

Level 11 (Alternate) Password
IKFNIVDA

Level 12 (Alternate) Password
GVFSAAAA

Level 13 (Alternate) Password
MGIZAAAA

Level 14 (Alternate) Password
EIQGRFAA

Level 15 (Alternate) Password
QSTZMIAA

Level 16 (Alternate) Password
EEIQRFAA

Level 17 (Alternate) Password
CHYRAAAA

Level 18 (Alternate) Password
UGZKAAAA

Level 19 (Alternate) Password
KFPGRFAA

Level 20 (Alternate) Password
YCQGNIAA

Level 21 (Alternate) Password
ICZINIAA

Level 22 (Alternate) Password
WHCIAAAA

Level 23 (Alternate) Password
KTUWQFAA

Level 24 (Alternate) Password
YQVWMIAA

Level 25 (Alternate) Password
IQEZMIAA

Level 26 (Alternate) Password
EGXTVCAA

Level 27 (Alternate) Password
SRPIMIAA

Level 28 (Alternate) Password
CRAUVCAA

Level 29 (Alternate) Password
ODHDWCAA

Level 30 (Alternate) Password
CPZRMIAA

Level 31 (Alternate) Password
YOVYMIAA

Level 32 (Alternate) Password
YAXTRFAA

Level 33 (Alternate) Password
CRZOVCAA

Level 34 (Alternate) Password
QOAPRFAA

Level 35 (Alternate) Password
OPLRMIAA

G-POLICE 2: WEAPONS OF JUSTICE

Cheat Mode
UTOPIA

Level Select
PLINTH

Infinite Ammunition
Hold L1+L2+R1+R2+Circle at the Weapon screen.

GRADIUS GAIDEN

Power-Up
Press Up (2), Down (2), Left, Right, Left, Right, X, Circle.

Level Select
Beat the game without continues at Normal difficulty. A Level Select option appears on the title screen.

Free Play Mode
Accumulate at least 10 hours of gameplay on any difficulty level and save the game. Then restart the game to access Free Play mode.

GRAN TURISMO

Arcade Mode Bonuses
The following bonuses are awarded in Arcade mode after winning each track. You must do them in A, B, and C order.

High Speed Track
Autumn Ring

Trial Mountain Track
Deep Forest

Grand Valley East Track
SS R5

Clubman Stage 5 Track
Grand Valley Speedway

Autumn Ring Track
the New Dodge cars

Deep Forest Track
TVR cars

SS R5 Track
Toyota cars

Grand Valley Speedway Track
Subaru cars

High Resolution Mode
Earn an International A license, then win all four cups in the GT League. Alternately, successfully complete all Arcade mode tracks at Hard difficulty.

Bonus FMV Sequence
In Arcade mode, place first in all tracks with any car in A, B, and C Class mode at Normal or higher difficulty. A "Staff Video" option appears under Bonus Items.

Chrysler Copperhead Concept Car
Win all gold medals in the B Class license test or place first in the UK vs. US championship.

Toyota TRD3000GT
Win all gold medals in the A Class license test.

Nissan Nismo 400
Win all gold medals in the International A license test.

Conserve Memory Card Slots
Play the game in Arcade mode, exit, then enter Simulation mode and save the game. The Arcade and Simulation mode information is saved together, halving the required number of memory card slots.

Memory Card Battle with Only One Card
Enter Memory Card Battle mode. A message appears stating that player one is loading and that no memory card was found for player two. Wait until the information has loaded for player one, then remove the memory card and insert it into the second memory card slot. Both players can now participate in the memory card battle.

Duplicate Parts

Purchase two identical cars. Buy as many parts as you want for the first car. View the list of fitted parts from the garage. Then switch to the second car, get inside, and view its fitted parts list, which should be empty. In the second car, enter a spot race. At the qualify options, select "Machine Setting," then "Change Parts." The first car's parts should be available. Exit and return to the garage. Note: Only items available on the Change Parts menu may be duplicated. This won't work on awarded cars.

GRAN TURISMO 2

Super License

Earn every license (A, B, Intl. A, Intl. B, Intl. C) to unlock the "Super License" option on the License Test menu.

Event Synthesizer Race

Earn the Super License to open the Event Synthesizer race in Gran Turismo League.

Kiddie Medal

Get a license award if you miss the bronze medal by 3 to 5 seconds (it may take several attempts). It's the small green-and-yellow object on the Status screen under "licenses."

Motor Sports Land Track

Obtain all licenses to open the Motor Sports Land track in Time Trial mode on the arcade disk.

All Tracks in Arcade Mode

Obtain all licenses in Simulation mode on disk two.

FedEx Car

Enter the Gran Turismo League race events until you reach the Pacific League races. Then, enter the Midfield Raceway event to obtain a R*Nissan 300ZX GTS FedEx race car.

Mark Martin's NASCAR #6 Ford Taurus

Purchase a Ford Taurus and perform the Racing modification.

License Test Cars

Get all gold on the indicated licenses to get the following cars:

Gold B

Spoon S2000 (J)

Gold A

Dodge Concept Car (red)

Gold IC

3000GT LM Edition

Gold IB

Del Sol LM Edition

Gold IA

FTO LM Edition

Gold S

Toyota GT-ONE Race Car '99

Ending Credits

Win every race in Gran Turismo League to see the ending credits on the arcade disk. Or place first on all 21 tracks in Arcade mode on Professional difficulty.

Increasing Number of Days

Go to a race. At the "Start Race" selection, choose "Exit" to add a day.

Increasing Completion Percentage

Each victory moves you 4.5 percent toward game completion.

Obtain Licenses Easier

At the main menu in Simulation mode, select "Transfer" or "Communication." Load your licenses from the original *Gran Turismo* here.

More Laps in Max Speed Test

To raise your high speed during this test, drive backward until you reach your desired speed. Then turn back around to finish the race.

More Car Indicator

When shopping for a car, look in the right corner of the screen. Click on the right arrow to see more cars.

Finding Cars

If you cannot find a car you want in the used car lot, check back in about 10 days. Some cars appear only on certain days.

Easy Rally Racing

Use the ESCUDO Pikes Peak version to compete in any of the Rally Races.

GRAND THEFT AUTO

Five Times Multiplier

Enter EXCREMENT as name.

9,999,990 Points

Enter WEYHEY as name.

99 Lives

Enter SATANLIVES as name.

All Cities

Enter CHUFF as name.

All Cities (1 and 2)

Enter TURF or INGLORIOUS as name.

All Weapons

Enter GROOVY as name.

Display Coordinates

Enter BLOWME as name.

Liberty City (1 and 2)

Enter FECK as name.

Liberty City and San Andreas

Enter TVTAN as name.

Maximum Wanted Level

Enter EATTHIS as name and set Wanted to Level 4.

Multiple Cheats

Enter BASTARD or THESHIT as name.

All Cities, Weapons, Money

Enter HANGTHEDJ as name.

All Weapons, Armor, Jail Card

Enter PECKINPAH as name.

Select Level

Enter SKYBABIES as name.

GRAND THEFT AUTO 2

Level Select

ITSALLUP

Invincibility

LIVELONG

All Weapons

NAVARONE

No Police

LOSEFEDS

Turbo Mode

Enter IGNITION as a player name.

Display Coordinates

Enter WUGGLES as a player name.

Maximum Wanted Level

Enter DESIRES as a player name.

Five Times Multiplier

Enter HIGHFIVE as a player name.

One Million Points

Enter BIGSCORE as a player name.

Debug Basic Scripts

Enter NOFRILLS as a player name.

Game Music

Play all but track one of the game disk in a CD player to hear music from the game.

GRAND THEFT AUTO: LONDON 1969

Five Times Multiplier

Enter SIDEBURN as name.

9,999,990 Points

Enter BIGBEN as name.

99 Lives

Enter MCVICAR as name.

All Cities

Enter RAZZLE or READERWIFE as name.

Display Coordinates

Enter SWEENEY as name.

London (1 and 2)

Enter MAYFAIR as name.

London (1-3)

Enter PENTHOUSE as name.

Maximum Wanted Level

Enter OLDBILL as name.

All Weapons, Jail Card

Enter DONTMESS as name.

Multiple Cheats

Enter FREEMANS, HAROLDHAND, or GETCARTER as name.

No Police

Enter GRASS as name.

GRAND TOUR RACING '98

All Switzerland Levels

Use R1 to match the rhythm of "Doe, a deer, a female deer."

All Moscow Levels

Use R1 to match the rhythm of "Jingle bells, jingle bells, jingle all the way."

All Scotland Levels

Use R1 to match the rhythm of "Hark, where the night is falling", from Scotland the Brave.

All Easter Island Levels

Use R1 to match the rhythm of "Happy birthday to you, happy birthday to you."

All Egypt Levels

Use R1 to match the rhythm of "Always look on the bright side of life," from Monty Python's the Life of Brian.

All Hong Kong Levels

Use R1 to match the rhythm of the flute music you hear in front of the monastery.

All Levels

Use R1 to match the rhythm of "Ding dong, the witch is dead, which old witch, the wicked witch," from *The Wizard of Oz*.

Multiplayer Suicide Mode

Use R1 to match the rhythm of "Supercallifragilisticexpialidotious" from *Mary Poppins*. Then, select an A track in Split Screen mode. The players race around the track in opposite directions.

Hong Kong Bonus Level

Drive around the circuit on Hong Kong Level 5 until you reach a dirt track. On that track, find a small low bridge over a small stream. Load the secret level by driving into the orange ball under the bridge in the middle of the stream.

Easter Island Bonus Level

Complete Easter Island Level 1 by finishing in first place to continue to Level 2. On Level 2, find a small sand-colored jump near a red-and-white barrier. Drive around the right side of the barrier to see a small triangular piece of sand with an orange ball at the end. Drive into it to load the secret level.

Moscow Bonus Level

Complete Moscow Level 1 in first place and continue to Level 2. There, drive backward until you get to a small jump. Pass it, turn around, and jump off it at an angle to land over the barrier to its right. Find an orange ball and drive into it to load the secret level.

Switzerland Bonus Level

Select Switzerland Level 1. Drive until you reach a collection of houses and people. Look for buildings with "ski house" signs. Drive behind the farthest one up the hill to find a yellow-and-orange ball. Drive into it to load the secret level.

Egypt Bonus Level

Select Egypt Level 1. Drive through town until you are out in the open desert. Immediately before the first tunnel is a piece of land with some buildings on the right side of the road. Drive to where the piece of land starts, and drive up the shortest side. This is the only way to get up there. Drive on it without steering back on the road. Drive for a few seconds until you reach the end of the piece of land. About at the end is an orange ball. Drive into it to load the secret level.

Use Horn

Press Up to use the horn during a race.

Game Music

Play all but track one of the game disk in a CD player to hear music from the game.

GRANDIA

Unlock Door

Press Right (2), Left (2), Down, Up, Down, Up.

GRID RUNNER

All Flags Mode

Press Down, Triangle, Right, X, Right, Up, Right, Circle, X, Down, Start in the Password screen.

Free-For-All Mode

Press Up, Triangle, X, Right, Up, Triangle, Circle, Down, Right, Down, Start in the Password screen.

Grid Racer Mode

Press X, Triangle, Right, Square, Right, Up, Down, Triangle, Right, Down, Start in the Password screen.

View Ending Sequence

Choose the "Restore Game" option and enter X, Triangle, X, Right, Down, Triangle, Up, Right (2), X.

THE GRINCH

Blue Prints in Town Hall

Go to the bottom level and pull out three of the rugs on the wall. You will notice them by the size difference.

Hammer & Chisel

Go to City Hall and sneak past the guards to the room with the big cabinet in it. Use the Grinch's strength to move the cabinet and reveal a safe. Use the jump attack to open it, then go across the hall and jump over the security poles to turn off the alarm.

More Presents

Shoot the kids with an egg launcher. Presents pop out of them, and the kids run away.

Open the Town Hall

To get into City Hall, shoot the big clock.

Paint Bucket

Go to the walkway along the building and follow it until you come to a pole. Swing on it to another pole, then on to a rafter. Knock off the "Who" by using the jump attack, and you receive the paint bucket.

Powerful Breath

When you are in City Hall, breathe on the alarm system to see the lasers.

Secret Presents

Behind the snowy walls there are at least two presents (you will need the rocket launcher found in level two). On top of the Whoville town Christmas tree is another present.

Slow 'Em Down

When you need to slime the Mayor's skis, shoot the snow from the peak or on the side of the roof onto the dog to stall it for 15 seconds.

Level Skip

Go to the gadget screen and press X while holding R1.

How to Avoid the Lasers on the Statue

Unlock the lasers on the statue in City Hall by using the Grinch's bad breath.

Mini Game Access

Destroy the following number of presents to get the indicated mini game. Go to the upper level of Mount Crumpit to play the games.

    750 presents—Spin N Win Mini Game

    1,500 presents—Pankamania Mini Game

    2,500 presents—Copter Race Mini Game

    3,000 presents—Bike Race Mini Game

The Different Gadgets

    Binoculars—Whoville—four blueprints

    Rotten egg launcher—Whoville—four blueprints

    Rocket spring—whoforest—nine blueprints

    Slime shooter—whoforest—nine blueprints

    Octopus climbing device—the dump—nine blueprints

    Marine mobile—wholake—16 blueprints

    Grinch copter—every level—16 blueprints

GRIND SESSION

All Tricks Unlocked

Enter Tournament mode and pause. Press Down, Left, Up, Right, Down, Left, Up, Right.

GROW LANSER

All items

Press Up, Right, L2, L2, Down, R2, R2, Up, Down, R2, L2, Right, Left, Square, Square, Square during gameplay while walking to get all items. A sound confirms correct code entry.

Instant Victory

Enter the Character menu during a battle, then press Start, Right, Left, Up, Down, R1, Square, R2, Square, Start, Down, Left, X. Resume gameplay and all onscreen enemies will be defeated. This has no effect on Bosses.

The M2

Successfully complete the game to have the M2 available in the next game.

GUITAR FREAKS

Battle Mode

At the Mode Select screen, press Pick, Green (2), Pick.

GTA: LONDON ADD ON

Play Your Own CD

Pause the game and replace the game disk with an audio CD.

Cheat Codes

Enter any of the following codes as a player name. To use combinations, enter and accept a code, then choose "Rename" and enter another code. You can rename your character after the last code is entered.

All Levels, All Weapons, Infinite Ammunition, "Get Out of Jail Free" Card, Armor, Parrot Picture, 9,999,990 Points, Ninety-Nine Lives, Five Times Multiplier, No Cops, Display Coordinates

Enter HAROLDHAND as a player name.

All Levels, All Weapons, Infinite Ammunition, "Get Out of Jail Free" Card, Armor, Ninety-Nine Lives, Five Times Multiplier, Maximum Wanted Level, Display Coordinates

Enter GETCARTER as a player name.

All Levels, All Weapons, Infinite Ammunition, "Get Out of Jail Free" Card, Armor, Five Times Multiplier

Enter FREEMANS as a player name.

All Weapons, Infinite Ammunition, "Get Out of Jail Free" Card, Armor

Enter DONTMESS or "TOOLEDUP" as a player name.

All Levels, All Weapons, Infinite Ammunition, "Get Out of Jail Free" Card, Armor

Enter SORTED as a player name.

All Levels
Enter RAZZLE or READERWIFE as a player name.

London Levels 1 and 2
Enter MAYFAIR as a player name.

London Levels 1 through 3
Enter PENTHOUSE as a player name.

Ninety-Nine Lives
Enter MCVICAR as a player name.

9,999,990 Points
Enter BIGBEN as a player name.

Five Times Multiplier
Enter SIDEBURN as a player name.

Maximum Wanted Level
Enter OLDBILL as a player name.

No Cops
Enter GRASS as a player name.

Display Coordinates
Enter SWEENEY as a player name.

GUARDIAN'S CRUSADE

Reset Game
Press L1+L2+R1+R2+Start+Select during gameplay.

GUILTY GEARS

Hard Mode
Hold Down+Square+L1+R2 and power on the PlayStation. Continue to hold until "Team Neo Blood" disappears. "Normal Mode" is replaced with "Hard Mode" and "Hard" appears above the two player/computer chaos bar.

Alternate Colors
At the Character Selection screen, press Square, Triangle, Circle, or X.

GUNDAM 0079: WAR FOR EARTH

Level 1 Password
Triangle (4), Square, X, Triangle, X

Level 2 Password
Square (2), Triangle (2), Square, X, Triangle, X

Level 3 Password
Circle (2), Triangle (2), Square, Circle, Square, Triangle

Level 4 Password
X (2), Triangle (2), Square, Circle, Square, Triangle

Level 5 Password
Circle, Square, Triangle (2), Square, Circle, Square, Triangle

Playback
X, Circle, Triangle (2), Square, Circle, Square, Triangle

GUNDAM BATTLE ASSAULT

Unlock bosses/hidden characters in Versus mode.

Zaku II Commander Type (Char Aznable)
On the Mode Select, press Left, Up, Right, Down, Square, Triangle, Circle.

Big Zam
Finish Story mode on easy.

Neue Ziel
Finish Story mode on normal.

Psycho Gundam Mark III:
Finish Story mode on hard.

Hydra Gundam
Finish Story mode on hard without continues.

RX-78-2 Gundam
Beat the Story mode on any setting with Z-Gundam, then go back and play through Story mode with any suit but Z-Gundam and AcGuy. The Gundam will randomly appear as you play. Defeat it in battle and go on to finish Story mode and afterward, you can select Gundam.

RB-79 Ball
Beat Story mode with all 12 starting mode suits on hard.

V-Gundam
Beat the game on normal with W-Gundam on Story mode. Then beat game with anyone but AcGuy or W-Gundam.

Bosses
Beat the game in every mode to unlock the last 3 bosses.

GUNNERS HEAVEN

Access Cheat Code Screen
Hold L1+L2+R1+R2 and press Select at the title screen. Then use Up and Down, and Triangle and X to change letters.

Debug Mode
Enter MA, press Select, then enter SV and press Start.

Debug (Boost Weapons)
Press Up on controller two.

Debug (Toggle Voice Mode)
Press Down on controller two.

Debug (Change Gunlock Type)
Press Left on controller two.

Debug (Skip Area)
Press Right on controller two.

Debug (Toggle Invincibility)
Press Triangle on controller two.

Debug (Increase Bombs)
Press Circle on controller two.

Debug (Change Weapon Type)
Press Square on controller two.

Debug (Increase Power-up Time)
Press X on controller two.

Level 2 Select
MA

Level 3 Select
UT

Level 4 Select
RH

Level 5 Select
MK

Level 6 Select
HT

Large Player
QB

Small Player
CM

999 Sec Weapon Power-up Time
SS

Start with 9 Bombs
YI

One Hit Kills Player
TY

GUNSHIP

Invincibility
Hold L1+L2+R1+R2 at the Mission Loading screen.

Unlimited Ammo
Hold L1+L2+R2+X at the Mission Loading screen.

GUNTU WESTERN FRONT JUNE, 1994

Level Select
Enter GUNTU as name after earning a Top 10 score.

HARD BOILED

Level Select
Hold Up+X+Start at game opening. Choose "Load Game."

Battle Level 2 Boss
Activate Level Select code. Hold L1 during loading screen.

Battle Level 5 Boss
Activate Level Select code. Hold R1 during loading screen.

HARD CORE 4X4

Unlock Mini Game
Go to the time trial stage, go to edit names, and type your name in as dutchman. Go to the start where you can choose to continue or go to option. Go to option, then go to credits to play an asteroids-type game.

Raining Frogs
Enter "Rainfrog" at the time trial edit names point.

Unlock Secret Truck
At the setup menu, choose "select race type" and select "time trial." Choose "start race," and enter the "edit names" option. Enter your name as MAINLINE, then return to the setup menu and select "choose truck" to find "MOTHER."

HARD EDGE: THE DISASTER ADVENTURE

Alternate Outfits and Weapons
Load the game after completing it. Choose "Select" from Character screen, then "ARMS." Complete game again for more outfits.

HARVEST MOON: BACK TO NATURE

Get Karen to Marry You
Don't talk to her much. In every season a new flower blooms. Pick all the flowers from each season, then give her each flower until one flower turns her face pinkish-red. In the season that the flower blooms, if you give her one of the same flower per day, she will marry you.

Infinite Water in Water Can

Go to the mine that is only available in winter. Dig down until you see a path. Go through to see a spring. Fill your water can with water from the spring, and from then on you have an infinite amount of water. Every time you upgrade your water can, fill it.

Get Girls to Marry You

When the game begins, at the start of the little movie of you playing with the animals, press X, Triangle, X, X, Square, 0 ,0, X to find that every girl wants to marry you at the start of summer.

HEAVEN'S GATE

Fight as Kurara

In Arcade mode, highlight Nanase, press Select, Up, Down (2), L1+L2, Start, Highlight.

Play as Unknown (Angel Boss)

Win at Normal or higher difficulty using a character with Devil alignment.

Play as Geezer (Devil Boss)

Win at Normal or higher difficulty using a character with Angel alignment.

Fight as Kyohya

Enable Kurara, go to Versus mode, highlight Verny, then press Select, Left, Right, Up, Down, R1+R2, Start.

HERC'S ADVENTURE

1,000 Health

Press R1, R2, R1, R2, L1, L2, L1, L2.

1,000 Strength

Press L1, L2, L1, L2, Right, Left (2), Right.

HERCULES

Hero's Gauntlet

Serpent, Medusa, Coin, Medusa.

Centaur's Forest

Centaur, Hercules' Silhouette, Minotaur, Archer.

The Big Olive

Centaur, Coin, Serpent, Hercules' Silhouette.

Hydra Canyon

Coin, Gladiator Helmet, Coin, Soldier.

Medusa's Lair

Archer, Pegasus, Archer, Centaur.

Cyclops' Attack

Gladiator Helmet, Pegasus, Hercules' Silhouette, Archer.

Titan Fight

Soldier, Coin, Coin, Thunderbolt.

Passageway of Eternal Torment

Medusa, Soldier, Centaur, Pegasus.

Vortex of Souls/Final Boss

Soldier, Lightning Bolt, Soldier, Centaur.

End Movie

Pegasus, Soldier, Centaur, Soldier.

HERMIE HOPPERHEAD

Debug Mode

At the New Game/Load Game screen, hold X+Square+Triangle and start a new game. During gameplay, hold Select and press Start. Use the stars that fall to get more lives. Hold Select and press Start again to clear the stage. On the Map screen, hold Square and Hermie runs across the map.

HIGH HEAT BASEBALL 2000

Eject Pitcher

Select Pitch and press Down+Square while another pitcher waits in bullpen.

HI-OCTANE

Reset

While racing, press Start, then hold A+B+C and press Start again.

HIVE

Level 2 Password

IV73

Level 3 Password

AMQ3

Level 4 Password

NGH3

Level 5 Password

ZN03

Level 6 Password

WVQ3

Level 7 Password

HC13

Level 8 Password

1EZ3

Level 9 Password

UVM3

Level 10 Password

TZ93

Level 11 Password

U6Q3

Level 12 Password

2QJ3

Level 13 Password

KLS3

Level 14 Password

2XS3

Level 15 Password

81H3

Level 16 Password

8HU3

Level 17 Password

J5V3

Level 18 Password

VIH3

HOGS OF WAR

Team Lard

Start a new game and rename your team "Mardy Pigs." The game renames you "Team Lard." There's no difference to gameplay.

HOT SHOTS GOLF

Mirror Courses

Highlight course, hold L1+L2, and press X.

Switch Hitting

Press L1+R1+X when selecting golfer.

Every Character and Course

Remove all memory cards. Using controller two, press and hold L1+L2+R1+R2 when screen flashes (just before Hot Shots logo appears). Continue holding; while Hot Shots logo is in motion, press Up (2), Down, Up, Left, Right (2), Left, Up (2), Down, Up, Left, Right (2), Left on controller two. You'll hear a wood driver.

Reset While Playing

Press L1+L2+R1+R2+Select+Start.

HOT SHOTS GOLF 2

Reset While Playing

Press L1+L2+R1+R2+Select+Start.

HOT WHEELS TURBO RACING

Always Have Turbo

At the main menu, press R2, L1, Square, Triangle, R1, L2, L1, R2.

No Textures on Cars

At the main menu, press L1, R1, L2, R2,L1, R1, L2, R2.

Big Tires

At the main menu, press Square, Triangle, Square, Triangle, R1 (2) L2 (2).

TowJam Car

At the main menu, press Square, Triangle, L1, R1, L2, R2, Square, Triangle. You should hear a sound.

Dude Sounds

At the main menu, press R2, R1, L2, R2, Square, Triangle, L1, R1.

Sol-Aire CX4 (Player 1 Only)

OR8B4ORK8R

Sol-Aire CX4 (Player 1 Only)

3F89JR33LH

Formula 5000 (Player 1 Only)

4WDG84WPDS

Hotwheels 500 (Player 1 Only)

YLKMFFOVNP

Hotwheels 500 (Player 1 Only)

DQBMTODDW8

Slide Out (Player 1 Only)

OM46DOMF4F

Slide Out (Player 1 Only)

9LNDM _CC

Super Van (Player 1 Only)

OP482OPH6B

Super Van (Player 1 Only)

LCPQGPLLJF

Stage Fright (Player 2 Only)

O_JLDO_TJT

Stage Fright (Player 2 Only)

CP6O9_CCVR

Slide Out (Player 2 Only)

OWDG8OWPDJ

Slide Out (Player 2 Only)

7KHXNW77QM

PLAYSTATION

Unlock Twinmill 2
TH4T_ROCKS

HYBRID

Unlimited Weapons
Enter #W@NN@CH#@T69696969* as password.

Full Map
Enter B#RTH*W@RK*S#X*D@@TH as password.

Level Select
Enter #W@N@W@RP6969696969 as password.

HYDRO THUNDER

Far East Shortcut
After the Blue Boost that hangs in the air, you hit a bunch of small waterfalls followed by a tunnel. If you jump on top of the tunnel, you cut your time in half for that section.

Venice Canals Shortcut
When you get to the part with the three hard turns in a row (left, right, left), skip all of this by jumping over the island between them both. This comes shortly after the part with the docks.

HYPER FORMATION SOCCER

100 Percent Fitness
At the Team Condition menu before an exhibition match, press Right, Up, Left, Down, Square.

Two New Teams
At the Team Condition menu before an exhibition match, hold R1+L1+Right+Square and press Triangle, X.

IMAGE FIGHT/XMULTIPLY

Level Select (Image Fight)
At the title screen, hold R1+R2+Start.

Super Weapon (Image Fight)
Pause using Start, then press Square, Circle, Triangle, X.

Music Test (Image Fight)
At the Options screen, press L2 (3). Press L2 to select music.

Level Select (XMultiply)
At the title screen, hold L1+L2+Start.

Super Weapon (XMultiply)
Pause using Start, then press X, Triangle, Circle, Square.

Music Test (XMultiply)
At Options screen, press L2 (2). Press L2 to select music.

IMPACT RACING

All Weapons
ALL.TOOLEDUP

Bonus Levels
BONUS.LEVELS

Final Track
ENDGAMELEVEL

Invincibility
I.AM.IMMORTAL

Debug Mode
RABBITBADGER

Sound Test
JOURNEYS.END

Unlimited Ammo
LOADSOFSTUFF

Level 2: AR12, Double Laser
00OG4KBOMO4Q

Level 2: Destroyer, Double Laser
00OG73K26XK

Level 3: Destroyer, Missiles
01F96MBWA79K

Level 4: AR12, Missiles
1MAT6XCE3OIL

Level 5: Destroyer, Quad Laser
02MO4CCLQ84A

Level 7: Destroyer, Firewall
03HAV2DCMDU2

Level 8: AR12, Quad Laser
0ZMAQKDS0OHG

IN COLD BLOOD

Unlock Debug Menu
At the title screen, press and hold L1, then press Triangle, Triangle, X, X. To view the debug menu, start the game and press Start to pause.

IN THE HUNT

Extra Continues
Hold Triangle+Select and press Start at end of last continue.

Level Select
Hold Up and Left+Select at the title screen and press Circle.

Speed Up
Pause game, hold Triangle+R2, resume game.

Slow Down
Pause game, hold Triangle+L2, resume game.

Extra Lives
Just before you lose your last life, press Start on controller two. Extra lives become available.

IN THE ZONE '98

Alley-Oop
Press Square+X.

Slam Dunk
Drive to basket, hold Turbo, and press Shoot.

INCREDIBLE CRISIS

Big Head Mode
To make the character's head big, connect the second controller. Press Up or Down on the D-Pad of the second controller to grow the head.

Flat Mode
To make the character flat, connect the second controller. Press Left or Right on the D-Pad of the second controller to flatten the man.

INCREDIBLE HULK

Level 2 Password
603ee0c530

Level 3 Password
B08E0F0802

Level 4 Password
000026B698

Level 5 Password
0074DFF12

INDEPENDENCE DAY

More Options/Plane Select
Enter MR HAPPY as name, go to Game Select, and press Left, Right, Square, Circle, Triangle (2), Down.

Cheat Menu
Enter GREG FM as name, exit to main screen, press Left, Right, Square, Circle, Triangle (2), Down.

Level Select: Washington
DBKHN (Easy); DBKMO (Medium); DBKQO (Hard)

Level Select: New York
GBKHW (Easy); GBKMX (Medium); GBKQX (Hard)

Level Select: Paris
LLSHW (Easy); LLSMX (Medium); LLSQX (Hard)

Level Select: Moscow
NL9HW (Easy); NL9MX (Medium); NL9QX (Hard)

Level Select: Tokyo
R39JD (Easy); R39NF (Medium); R39RF (Hard)

Level Select: Oahu
T59HW (Easy); T59MX (Medium); T59QX (Hard)

Level Select: Las Vegas
Z99HY (Easy); Z99MZ (Medium); Z99QZ (Hard)

Level Select: Mothership
399HG (Easy); 399MH (Medium); 399QH (Hard)

Tourist Mode
Enter TOURIST as name, exit to Game Select, and press Left, Right, Square, Circle, Triangle (2), Down.

INDY 500

Access Hidden Track/Car
At the title screen, press Circle, X, Triangle, Square three times.

Alternate Replay View
While replaying, hold Select and press L1, L2, R1, R2, Triangle, Square, or X.

Enable Drag Racing
Highlight the Qualify option on Indy 500 mode screen. In One-player mode, hold L1+L2+R1+R2+Start. In Two-player mode, hold buttons at Handicap screen.

Automatically Win Race
Complete trials, begin race in third-party view. Press Pause, press touch-screen on Timer. At Secret Code List, press D, B, C, D, B, C.

Eliminate Damage
Complete trials, begin race in first-party view. Press Pause, press touch-screen on left tire. At Secret Code List, press B, C, D, B, C, D.

Stop Time
Complete trials, begin race in first-party view. Press Pause, press touch-screen on right tire. At Secret Code List press D (2), B (2), C (2).

Skip Race
Begin Easy trial with Car A. Hold A throughout last lap. After last lap, quickly release and rehold A.

INITIAL D

Unlock Bonus Tracks
Complete Practice mode at Beginner, Intermediate, and Expert levels.

Unlock Bonus Cars
Defeat each driver in Story mode.

INTELLIGENT QUBE

Get Cynthia
Beat the game.

Get Spike
Beat the game with Cynthia and an IQ of at least 400.

Design Your Own Puzzles
Clear Final Stage and save to memory card. In Options set game mode to "System" and press Right to turn on Original mode. Exit Options and select 1P game.

INTERACTIVE CD SAMPLER PACK VOLUME 3

Crash Bandicoot Info
At Crash Bandicoot screen, press Square (2), Triangle.

King of Fighters '95 Info
At King of Fighters '95 screen, press Triangle, Circle, Square.

NCAA GameBreaker Info
At NCAA GameBreaker screen, press Circle, Triangle, Circle.

Ridge Racer Revolution Info
At Ridge Racer Revolution screen, press Circle, Triangle, Square.

Tekken 2 Info
At Tekken 2 screen, press Triangle (2), Square.

Twisted Metal 2 Info
At Twisted Metal 2 screen, press Square, Circle, Triangle.

View Horned Owl Full-Motion Video
At Tunnel B1 screen, press Triangle, Square (2).

View Independence Day Full-Motion Video
At Blast Chamber screen, press Triangle, Circle, Triangle.

View Jumping Flash 2 Full-Motion Video
At NHL Faceoff '97 screen, press Square, Triangle, Circle.

View Motor Toon Grand Prix Full-Motion Video
At Formula 1 screen, press Square, Triangle, Square.

View Tobal No. 1 Full-Motion Video
At Jet Moto screen, press Circle (2), Triangle.

View Twisted Metal 2 Full-Motion Video
At 2 Extreme screen, press Circle, Square, Circle.

INTERNATIONAL SUPERSTAR SOCCER DELUXE

Dog Mode
At title screen, press Up (2), Down (2), Left, Right, Left, Right, X+Circle.

All Stars
On controller two at the title screen, press R, Up, Down, L, X, B, Left, Right, B, A.

Extra Skill Points
Enter Edit Players mode before each match and use all available skill points. Highlight Cancel, then press Y for another 200 skill points.

INTERNATIONAL SUPERSTAR SOCCER PRO '98

World All Stars Team
Highlight Exhibition and press Up (2), Down (2), Left, Right, Left, Right, Circle, X. Highlight Germany at Team Select screen, press R1+L1 and X.

INTERNATIONAL SUPERSTAR SOCCER PRO EVOLUTION

Unlock World and European Classic All-Star
In Master League, choose a team at Normal difficulty with a 10 minute limit. Play and stay at the top of the league after match 14. After the credits, you'll see confirmation that the classic All-Star is playable in Exhibition mode.

Historical Japanese Team
Finish the Olympics with Japan.

Bonus Cup
Finish the game with all the cups.

Bonus Stadium
Win the Konami Cup at any difficulty setting. The Clubhouse stadium becomes unlocked in Exhibition mode.

Listen to Play-By-Play Commentary in Training Mode
Pause the game. Choose "Audio Settings" and turn off the play-by-play option. Resume the game and pause again. Select "Audio Settings" and turn on play-by-play. Return to the game and you'll hear John Kabira.

INTERNATIONAL TRACK & FIELD

Balloon
In the hammer throw, throw for a distance at which the meters and centimeters match (32.32, 14.14, etc.). A balloon appears from the crowd.

Bikini Mode
Highlight "100m Free Style" and press Up (2), Down (2), Left, Right, Left, Right, Circle, X.

Birds
In the discus, throw for a distance at which the meters and centimeters match (32.32, 14.14, etc.). A flock of birds appears above the stadium.

Blimp
Qualify in the high jump on your first try. For your second jump, adjust the bar over 40cm and make the jump. During the third jump, a blimp appears.

Mole
In the triple jump or long jump, get a distance where the last three numbers are the same (23.33, 14.44, etc). A mole appears from where you jumped.

Moves Gauges Off Screen
Select "Start Option" from the title screen. Start any event and pause. Hold L1+L2+R1+R2+Square+X+Triangle+Circle while repeatedly pressing Up or Down.

Space Shuttle
In the pole vault, clear the qualifying height on your first jump. On the second attempt, set the pole to 5.0 meters and clear it. A space shuttle flies by when the pole is reset.

Tyrannosaurus Rex
In the shot put, throw for a distance in which all the digits are the same (11.11, 22.22, etc.). A Tyrannosaurus Rex appears behind the crowd.

UFO
In the javelin, tap Square or Circle once to begin jogging toward the foul line. When the angle meter appears, press and hold X to get it over 60 degrees. When the meter rises, begin pressing the Square or Circle rapidly. Make sure you are running at a high speed and release the javelin before the foul line. Throw the javelin with the maximum power at an angle of more than 60 degrees. A UFO falls into the stadium with the javelin protruding from it.

INTERNATIONAL TRACK & FIELD 2000

Konami Man
At the Events Selection screen, press Up (2), Down (2), Left, Right, Left, Right, Circle, X. A sound confirms correct entry. Konami man appears in some of the events and female appearances change.

INVASION FROM BEYOND

All Ships, Weapons, and Upgrades
Press R1, L1, R2, L2, Up, Down, Right, Left(2), Right, Down, Up at the start screen.

Level Select
Press L1, R1, L2, R2, Triangle, X, Circle, Square (2), Circle, X, Triangle at the start screen.

IRON & BLOOD

Play as Lord of Chaos
Press Up, Up+Left, Left, Down+Left, Down, Triangle+X at the Character Select screen.

Play as Minion of Chaos
Press L1+L2+R1+R2+Up+X at the Character Select screen.

Play as Minion of Order
Press Left+Square, Right+Circle at the Character Select screen.

Play as Strahd
Press Up, Right, Down, Left, R1, R2, L2, L1 at the Character Select screen.

IRON MAN XO: MONOWAR IN HEAVY METAL

Warp to Last Level (1P)
C04A770777777 7777777777777

Warp to Last Level (2P)
C02A77X777777 7777777777777

IRRITATING STICK

Extra Lives (7)
At the Mode screen highlight "1P Play" and press Right (4). Highlight Tournament and press Right. Highlight Course Edit and press Left (2). Highlight Option and press Left (6). Highlight 1P Play and press X.

IZNOGOUD

Level 1 Access Password
CORROD

Level 2 Access Password
FISCHER

Level 3 Access Password
GOGONO

Level 4 Access Password
EXTERN

Level 5 Access Password
XFILES

Level 6 Access Password
GOTERR

Level 7 Access Password
SPECTR

Level 8 Access Password
PICNICI

Level 9 Access Password
POILUS

Level 10 Access Password
FEDODO

Level 11 Access Password
FOURNO

Level 12 Access Password
DIKEPI

J LEAGUE WINNING ELEVEN '97

Bonus Team
Highlight main menu's first choice, then press Up, Up, Down, Down, Left, Right, Left, Right, X, Circle.

Different View
At the title screen, press Up (2), Down (2), Left, Right, Left, Right, X, Circle. You can now adjust the view from a different angle.

JACKIE CHAN: STUNTMASTER

Movie Option
Collect 20 gold dragons to unlock the Jackie Chan movie option.

Unlimited Lives
Press R1, R2, L1, X.

Dizzy Punch
Hold Square.

Kick/Flip/Kick
Hold Triangle.

Triple Punch, Butt Bump
Press Square (2), Triangle (2).

Off-Wall Kick
Run toward a wall and hold Triangle.

Roller Kick
Press Roll/Dive, then immediately hold Triangle.

Roller Punch
Press Roll/Dive, then immediately hold Square.

Style Push
Hold Grab and X, Square, Circle, or Triangle.

JADE COCOON: STORY OF THE TAMAMAYU

Free Mugworts
Enter Beetle Forest for the first time. Talk to Koris then attack and defend. He gives you a Mugwort. Then disobey a training command so you can start over to get another Mugwort.

Easily Beat Bird Man
Fire minions make this easier, but just in case, have plenty of Mugworts ready.

Access New Sub-Quest
Finish game, wait through credits, save game.

JAMES HOWE'S WORLD LEAGUE SOCCER

100% Accuracy
For 100% accuracy, hold R1 when taking a shot. You'll never miss!

JAMPACK VOLUME 1

Pitfall 3D Demo
At the *MDK* screen, press Triangle, Circle, Square.

Mechwarrior 2 Information
At the *NBA Shootout '97* screen, press Circle, Square, Triangle.

NBA Shoot Out '97 Information.
At the *Machine Hunter* screen, press Circle (2), Triangle.

Peak Performance Information
At *The Lost World* screen, press Square, Triangle, Square,

Puzzle Fighter 2 Turbo Two-player Mode
At the title screen, press X or Start simultaneously on controllers one and two to begin a best-two-out-of-three match.

View Ogre Battle FMV sequence
At the *Super Puzzle Fighter* screen, press Square, Triangle, Circle.

View Steel Reign FMV sequence
At the *Thunder Truck Rally* screen, press Circle, Square, Circle.

View Underground CD Volume 2 FMV sequence
At the *Codename: Tenka* screen, press Square, Circle, Triangle.

View Credits
At the *Wild Arms* screen, press Triangle (2), Square.

JAMPACK VOLUME 2

View Gex 2 FMV Sequence
At the *Colony Wars* screen, press Square, Circle, Triangle.

View Pandemonium 2 FMV Sequence
At the *Intelligent Qube* screen, press Circle (2), Triangle.

View One FMV Sequence
At the *NFL Gameday '98* screen, press Square, Triangle, Circle.

View Underground CD FMV sequence
At the *Fighting Force* screen, press Triangle, Circle, Square.

View Credits
At the *Nightmare Creatures* screen, press Square, Triangle, Square.

JARRETT AND LABONTE STOCK CAR RACING

Exploding Curbs
kerbkrawl

Silver Car
T2

Activate the Nitro Button
glycerine

Blur Screen
ethanol

Less Gravity
Europa

705 Springs
vanishing

JEREMY MCGRATH SUPERCROSS '98

Automatic Saved Game Loading
Enter McGrath as a case-sensitive rider name.

Backward Trails
Enter SHOWTIME as name.

Cheat Mode
Enter www.atod.se as a case-sensitive rider name and save to memory card. Pause the game and you can access a Cheat menu on the Options screen. Besides the cheat options, highlight a single race and hold Square, then press X to enable Mirror mode and Master 82cc mode and unlock all the tracks in Single-player mode.

M80cc Bike
Complete the season in first place in Intermediate mode.

Mirrored Tracks
Complete the season in first place using reversed tracks.

Super Bike
Press Square, Circle, Up, Down, Right, X at the main menu.

Yamaha YZ80 Bike
Place first in the first race in Advanced mode. You can also race solo against Jeremy.

JEREMY MCGRATH SUPERCROSS '00

Race Jeremy McGrath
Enter MCGRATH as name.

JERSEY DEVIL

99 Lives
Press Triangle, X, Triangle, Square (2), Circle.

JET MOTO

Enable Codes
In the Options screen, set to "Professional, Laps: 6." At the main menu, press Circle (3), Square, Triangle (2), Square, Triangle.

Air Brakes
Enable Codes, then press R1, R2, Right, L2, Up, Circle, Up, Circle.

Ice Racing
Enable Codes, then press Up, R2, R1, Right, L1, Square, Right (2).

Rocket Racer
Enable Codes, then press Triangle, Up (2), L2 (2), Up (3).

Show-off Cameras
Enable Codes, then press Triangle, Down, Square, Triangle, L1 (2), R1 (2).

Super Agility
Enable Codes, then press Down, Circle, Left, L1, Left, Right, Left, Right.

2P Mode with Other Bikes
Enable Codes, then press Circle, Square, R2, Circle, Triangle, L2, Right, Up.

Unlimited Turbos
Enable Codes, then press Triangle, Circle, Right, R2, Up, Square, Up, Triangle.

Zero Resistance
Enable Codes, then press Square, L1, Triangle, Right, L1, Down, R2, Triangle.

Unlock All Tracks/Play at Master Difficulty
At the Options screen, choose Amateur difficulty, and make the trophy presenter male. Go to the main screen and press Up, Right, Down, Left, Up, Right, Down, Left. Press Left, X, then go back to the Options screen. Select Professional difficulty and make the trophy presenter Rider's Choice. Return to the main screen and press Up, Left, Down, Right, Up, Left, Down, Right. You should hear the sound of coins.

View All Riders
Choose Amateur difficulty, turn off turbos, and disable the grapple. Hold L1 and select "Credits."

View All Endings
Choose Amateur difficulty, turn off turbos, and disable the grapple. Hold L2 and select "Credits."

View Dedication
Select "Dakota," and enter the Options screen. Set laps to 2, and the trophy presenter to female. Hold R2 and select "Credits."

JET MOTO 2

Stay at Turbo Speeds
Keep Triangle held after running out of turbos to keep the speed over 100 mph.

Race as Enigma/Enable Insane Difficulty Level
Complete all 10 tracks at the Master difficulty level.

Enable Trick
Win trophy with Racer.

Enable Cyberspace Cam
Win trophy with Technician.

Enable Upside Down Cam
Win trophy with Lil' Dave.

Enable Ice Racing
Win trophy with the Hun.

Enable Remote Control
Win trophy with Steele.

Enable Super Agility
Win trophy with Vampeera.

Enable Super Brakes
Win trophy with Wild Ride.

Enable TV Cam
Win trophy with Blade.

Enable Unlimited Grapple
Win trophy with Gadget.

Enable Unlimited Turbos
Win trophy with the Max.

Enable Zero Resistance
Win trophy with Bomber.

Fast & Easy Aerial 1
Hold L2+L1+Down-Left.

Fast & Easy Aerial 2
Hold R2+R1+Down-Left.

JET MOTO 3

Race at High Speed
During gameplay, press L1+Right, R1+Down, Square, L1+Triangle, R1+Down, L1+Left, Select.

TV Camera
During gameplay, press Circle, L1+Triangle, L1+X, Triangle, R1+Up.

Stunt Mode
Unlock this One- and Two-player mode by collecting all 10 track coins in season mode.

Granny Racer
Place first at the Professional difficulty setting.

Capt. Ballad Racer
Complete the professional season with all but two of the racers.

Planet X and Ramp Park Tracks
Place first in Circuit mode at Professional difficulty.

Take a Dive
Hold R1+R2+L1+L2.

JGTC ALL JAPAN GRAND TOURING CAR CHAMPION

Enable Old Fuji Track
Place first in Match mode.

Unlock Eight Bonus Cars
Complete all tracks under Champion mode.

JIKKYOU AMERICAN BASEBALL

Enable Big-Head Mode
At the title screen, press Circle, X, Triangle, Square, Select, Up, L1, L2, R1, R2.

Enable Funny-Head Mode
At the title screen, press Circle, X, Triangle, Square, Select, Down, L1, L2, R1, R2.

JOHNNY BAZOOKATONE

God Mode
PILCHARD

Level Select
KRISTIAN

Level 2 Password
AFLEAPIT

Level 3 Password
TEASPOON

Level 4 Password
SEDATION

Level 5 Password
VERYNICE

JOJO'S BIZARRE ADVENTURE

Play as Dio
Move the cursor to Alessy, D'Bo, Chaca, and Milder. Press Start on each character, then press start (3) when you get to Milder.

Play as Shadow Dio
Make Dio a playable character, highlight Dio, then press Start (10)

Play as Young Joseph
Move the cursor to Jotaro, Polnareff, Joseph, Kakyoin, Iggi, Avdol and back to Joseph. Press the Start button on each character, then hold start when you get back to Joseph.

JONAH LOMU RUGBY

Enable Bonus Teams
Win the Territories Cup during normal game play. Use the "Play" option to access a new league with bonus teams.

Enable Bonus Teams 2
Use the "Play" option again after winning the cup from the first bonus league for another league with more bonus teams.

J'S RACING

Advan
On controller two, hold R1+Triangle+Up+Start until the title screen appears. The Advan appears under Free Race mode.

Castrol
On controller two, hold R1+Square+Down+ Start until the title screen appears. The Castrol appears under Free Race mode.

Honda
On controller two, hold R1+Up+Square+Start until the title screen appears. The Honda appears under Free Race mode.

Class 1 Car
On controller two, hold R1+Circle+Up+Start until the title screen appears. The Class 1 appears under Free Race mode.

Dunlop
On controller two, hold R1+Down+Triangle+ Start until the title screen appears. The Dunlop appears under Free Race mode.

JUDGE DREDD

Deformed Characters
Enter !PEMON? as a name on the High Score screen.

Invincibility
Enter !EIKKIN as a name on the High Score screen.

Ten Credits
Enter !BEDSTRAW! as a name on the High Score screen

View Ending Sequence
Enter ?LOVESEXY? as a name on the high score screen.

JUMPING FLASH

Control Cloud Speed
Hold L1+L2+R1+R2 and press Up at title screen.

Level Select
At the main menu, press Up (2), Down (2), X (2), Left, Right, Left, Right, X, Triangle, X, Triangle.

Play Again
Defeat the game and you can play the levels again with added, moved, or missing objects plus a time limit.

Extra Jumps
Defeat the game and go to the Stage Select screen. Scroll through the levels until the word "Extra" shows up. Restart the game and you can jump five times in a row instead of three.

Super Mode
Defeat the game (not including extras) using no continues to enter Super mode, where you can jump six times in a row instead of three. When jumping on enemies, press Triangle to fall faster and do more damage. Press L1 or L2 to run faster and jump farther.

JUMPING FLASH! 2

Enable Rachel as Support AI
At the title screen press Left, Right, R1, L2, L1, R2, Up, Down, Triangle, Select.

Enable Tex as Support AI
At the title screen press Up, Down, L1, R2, R1, L2, Left, Right, SELECT, Triangle.

Super Mode
Finish game in Normal Mode.

Extra Mode
Finish game in Super Mode.

Super Jump (Jump Six Times)
Play in Super Mode.

JUPITER STRIKE

Side View
Pause, hold Start 10 seconds, then press L2+Start.

Top View
Pause, hold Start 10 seconds, then press L1+ Start.

JURASSIC PARK: LOST WORLD

Level Select
Go to password on the main screen, then press Square, X, Circle, Triangle, Circle, Triangle, X, Square, Circle, Triangle. You must do this three times.

JURASSIC PARK: WARPATH

Movie Short
To see the short video, beat arcade mode. You'll get all characters and battle arenas. After you have beat arcade mode, it starts playing.

K-1 REVENGE

Super Fast Fighting
In Tournament mode, start a CPU vs. CPU match. Hold Circle during match.

Fight as Master Ishi or James Harrision
Using any fighter, complete single player game.

Fight as Hidefumi Minatoya
Execute more than 100 combos in combo training.

K-1 THE ARENA FIGHTERS

Alternate Outfits
Hold L1+R1 at title screen to hear three beeps. Then press Start to get different costumes for Musashi, Andy Hug, or Sam Greco.

KAGERO: DECEPTION II

Get Evil Upper and Evil Stomp
Finish the game, making sure to kill everyone in Chapters 17 and 21 (first ending).

Get Magic Sack
Finish the game, sparing at least one person in Chapter 17, and killing Keith in Chapter 24 (second ending).

Ardebaran Mask
Finish the game, sparing at least one person in Chapter 17, and sparing Keith in Chapter 24 (third ending).

Evil Kick
Finish the game, killing everyone in Chapter 17, and sparing at least one person in Chapter 21 (fourth ending).

Suezo
Save all four endings to a memory card.

KAMEN RIDERS

Secret Characters
Save game after getting Digital Card 7. Highlight Kamen Rider No. 1 at the Character Selection screen, hold X+Right, press Triangle. Next, get cards 7 and 74. Save game and highlight Kamen Rider No. 2, then hold X+Right and press Triangle.

KARTIA

Level 20 Characters
In Chapter 2, beat all the enemies except Zakuro. Corner him. He will keep creating phantom miles. Have one character attack the phantoms until they are at Level 20. This is also good for getting the secret phantom items. Make a clear game save from Toxa's quest, so you can use the weapons.

Level 20 with Toxa
In Chapter 7 (when you fight Cross), defeat all the phantoms except the ones near Cross. When all the other phantoms are dead, attack the ones near Cross, but don't kill Cross. After you kill off enough phantoms, Cross will make more. Stand near Cross's move limit and wait there. When he creates the phantoms, they will attack you. Kill them and wait. Cross will do this infinitely. Level up all your people to 20, then kill Cross.

KATTOBI TUNE

CPU Controls Car (Toggle)
During game, press Pause, Select, Pause.

KENSEI: SACRED FIST

Full Pause Screen
Pause and press R2.

Alternate Costumes
Highlight a fighter at the Character Selection screen. Press Circle or X to select his or her first costume or Square or Triangle to get another costume.

Fight as Akira
Successfully complete the game under Normal mode as Yugo.

Fight as Quigtao
Successfully complete the game under Normal mode as Yuli.

Fight as Cindy
Successfully complete the game under Normal mode as Douglas.

Fight as Steve
Successfully complete the game under Normal mode as Allen.

Fight as Arthur
Successfully complete the game under Normal mode as Ann.

Fight as Kornelia
Successfully complete the game under Normal mode as Heniz

Fight as Sessue
Successfully complete the game under Normal mode as Hyoma.

Fight as Mark
Successfully complete the game under Normal mode as David.

Fight as Genya
Successfully complete the game under Normal mode as Saya.

Fight as Zhou
Successfully complete the game under Normal mode as all nine starting characters. Then win Normal mode with any starting character.

Fight as Kaiya
Successfully complete the game under Normal mode as all nine starting characters. Then win Normal mode using a bonus character.

Fight as Jelly/Billy
Successfully complete the game under Normal mode as Kaiya.

Fight as Kazane
Successfully complete the game under Normal mode as Zhou.

Extra Mode
Unlock each of the 22 characters.

KILEAK: THE DNA IMPERATIVE

God Mode
Within five seconds at the title screen, enter the following code three times: Triangle (2), Left, Right, Square (2), Select, L1, L2, R1, R2.

Obtain All Items
Press Circle (6), move D-Pad three times in clockwise circle, and press Triangle, Square (2), Triangle, X, Start at the beginning of the conception sequence at the title screen.

KILLER LOOP

Pulse Class 2
Hold Start and press Up, Left, Up, Left, Down, Left, Up, Left at the main menu.

Pulse Class 3
Hold Start and press Down, Left, Up, Left, Down, Right, Up, Right at the main menu.

Pulse Class 4
Hold Start and press Down, Left, Up, Right, Down, Right, Up, Left at the main menu.

H&K Class 2
Holding Start, press Down, Left, Up, Left, Down, Right, Up, Left at the main menu.

H&K Class 4
Hold Start and press Down, Right, Up, Left, Down, Left, Up, Right at the main menu.

Reac Class 1
Hold Start and press Down, Left, Up, Right, Down, Left, Up, Right at the main menu.

Reac Class 3
Holding Start, press Down, Right, Up, Left, Down, Left, Up, Left at the main menu.

Reac Class 4, Faster Mode
Holding Start, press Down, Right, Up, Left, Down, Right, Up, Right at the main menu.

Sinus Class 2
Holding Start, press Down, Left, Up, Left, Down, Left, Up, Right at the main menu.

Sinus Class 3, Killer Loop Mode
Holding Start, press Down, Left, Up, Right, Down, Left, Up, Left at the main menu.

Sinus Class 4
Holding Start, press Down, Left, Up, Right, Down, Right, Up, Right at the main menu.

All Tracks
Holding Start, press Up, Left, Down, Left, Up, Left, Down, Right at the main menu.

KILLING ZONE

Play as the Boss
At the main menu, hold L1+R2+Circle+Start for five seconds. Then, start a one-player game and choose anybody.

Warp to the Last Level
On Level 2, go to the far left side. Hold Down+Left+R1+L1 and press Start. The screen blanks for about 5 seconds and you warp to the last level.

KING OF FIGHTERS '95

Play as Bosses
At the Character Selection screen, pick "Yes" for the Team Edit option. Hold Start and press Up+Circle, Right+Square, Left+X, Down+Triangle. Rugal and Kunsanagi appear.

Multiple Characters
At the Character Selection screen, hold Start and press Up+Circle, Down+Triangle, Left+X, Right+Square, Up+Circle. A character can be chosen more than once on the same team.

Toggle Win Demos
At the Configuration menu, hold L1+L2+R1+R2. A sound confirms correct entry.

Resetting the Game
Hold Circle+Square+X+Triangle and press Start during gameplay. The game resets to the main menu.

KING OF FIGHTERS '96

Fight as Bosses
Hold Start and press Up+Circle, Square+Right, Left+X, Triangle+Down at the Character Select screen.

Demo Select Mode
Successfully complete the game in Team Play mode under any difficulty setting without losing any matches. Save the game vs. Goenitz to unlock "Demo Select" at the Options screen.

Disable Survivor Mode
In Mode Select screen, press Start on Controller two.

God's Calibur Team
Enter "Fight as Bosses" code. On "God's Calibur Team," choose Iori, Kagura, and Kyo to play.

Goenitz Team
Enter "Fight as Bosses" code and choose Goenitz, plus any two fighters besides Kagura, to play.

KING OF FIGHTERS '97

Activate Orochi Characters
In any game mode, press L1+R1 repeatedly at Character Selection screen.

Fight as Orochi
Enter the "Activate Orochi characters" code. Select Versus or Practice mode. Repeatedly press L2+R2 at the Character Selection screen

Fight as Classic Kyo
Highlight Kyo and press Triangle+Start at Character Selection screen.

Select Victory Pose
Press any of the attack buttons before the victory pose is displayed. Press the attack buttons on controller two to select the pose for the CPU's fighter.

KING OF FIGHTERS '98

Alternate Characters
Highlight a character at the Character Selection screen, hold L1, and press any button.

Fight Shingo Yabuki
Either earn at least 100,000 points in Round 3 before knocking out computer, earn at least 100,000 points in Round 4 before getting a perfect knockout, or beat all computer opponents from Rounds 1 to 5 without losing any teammates.

Play as Omega Rugal
Complete a one-player game with Rugal. Save the game and load it. Then, when selecting Rugal, hold Start.

Stage Select
Press Select while at the Order Select screen.

KING OF FIGHTERS '99

Bonus Characters
Highlight the normal version of a fighter at the Character Selection screen, hold L1, and press any button.

Unlimited Survival Mode Time
Highlight Survival Mode option, hold Triangle+Start, and press Circle.

Fight as Krizalid
Highlight the Random Character icon at the Player Selection screen in Team Versus or Single Versus modes. Hold Select and press Circle, X, Triangle, Square.

KING OF FIGHTERS KYO

All Characters
Using Level 10 Kyo, beat the Asia chapter. At the Character Selection screen, highlight Chris and press L1+L2+R1+R2.

Orochi Iori
Successfully complete all chapters. Then hold L2+R2 and choose Iori at the Character Selection screen.

Orochi Team
Successfully complete all chapters. Then hold L2+R2 and choose all New Face Team members at the Character Selection screen.

Saishu Kusanagi
Successfully complete all chapters. Then hold L1 and choose Kyo at the Character Selection screen.

Sendo Siblings
Successfully complete the Disease chapter, Then hold L2+R2 and choose any Art of Fighting team member at the Character Selection screen.

Souiji Kusangai
Successfully complete the Souji and Aoi chapters. Then hold L1 and choose Kyo at the Character Selection screen.

KING'S FIELD

Moonlight Sword
It is possible to obtain the Moonlight Sword without killing Guyra. First, fill all of your crystal flasks, have at least one key in a guidepost and a gate to match it. Make your way to Guyra's chamber. When you get there, strafe to the left, making sure he doesn't knock you off. Now when you are far left and as far forward, wait until Guyra is facing you. Quickly run toward Guyra's other side and get on the same platform as he. Jump across to the platform where the Moonlight sword is. Quickly grab the sword and use the gate to hightail it before Guyra turns around and knocks you off the platform.

KING'S FIELD II

Powering Up Light Magic Fast
To perform this trick, you need a sword that recovers mana (the Triple fang or the moonlight sword). Equip one of the swords, then cast it (Select button) to cast Light Magic. Rapidly press the Select button until your magic starts to rapidly drain. Each time you press select, it is counted as a successful cast and your light magic rapidly rises. Do this at a Gold fountain so you can quickly restore mana. After your light magic is 500+ without any enhancements, you can take out the final boss with one well targeted spell.

KITCHEN PANIC

Refill Energy
Pause, then on controller two, press Up (2), Down (2), Square, Circle, Square, Circle, L1, R1.

Rocket Potato
Pause, then on controller two, press R1, L2, R2, L1, Left, Right, Up.

Padapada Potato
Pause, then on controller two, press R1, L2, R2, L1, Left, Right, Down.

Fuwafuwa Potato
Pause, then on controller two, press R1, L2, R2, L1, Left, Right, Circle.

Jumping Potato
Pause, then on controller two, press R1, L2, R2, L1, Left, Right, Triangle.

Ice Potato
Pause, then on controller two, press R1, L2, R2, L1, Left, Right, Square.

Marine Potato
Pause, then on controller two, press R1, L2, R2, L1, Left, Right, X.

Unlock All Levels
On controller two, hold Circle+X+Triangle+Square+L1+L2+R1+R2 at the Level Select screen. Press Down (2), Right.

99 Lives
On controller two, hold L2+R2 at the Level Select screen. Press Up, Down, Left, Right. Next on controller two, hold L1+R1 while pressing Right, Left, Down. Press Up after releasing L1+R1.

All Damage Takes One Point
On controller two, hold L1+R1. Press Triangle, X, Square, Circle. Next, hold L2+R2 while pressing Circle, Square, X. Press Triangle after releasing L2+R2.

Invincibility in Caves
On controller two, press R2 (2), L2 (3), R1 (7), L2 (3), R2 (3), R1 (7) at the Level Selection screen.

KKND: KROSSFIRE

Cheat Mode
Hold L1+R1+R2+L2 and press Start during gameplay. Choose the "Display Password" menu option. While current password is showing, press Left, Circle, Square, Right, X, then select the Cheat option.

Level Password: "Evolved"
The Guns of Navaho: HHQQQ4

Level Password: "Evolved"
The Spiders Lair: HUQQQI

Level Password: "Evolved"
The Seven Samurai: HDQQQS

Level Password: "Evolved"
The Rabbit Warren: HLQQQZ

Level Password: "Evolved"
The Birds: IQQQHZ

Level Password: "Evolved"
I'll Be Your Friend: IVQQUZ

Level Password: "Evolved"
Supply Run: IAQQGZ

Level Password: "Evolved"
Napalm Sunday: IGQHGZ

Level Password: "Evolved"
The Wall Of Death: ILQHLZ

Level Password: "Evolved"
Dam It Janet: JUQFLZ

Level Password: "Evolved"
Take the Tower: JDQ6LZ

Level Password: "Evolved"
Aerial Supremacy: JCH6LZ

Level Password: "Evolved"
Operation Donut: JKU6LZ

Level Password: "Evolved"
End 2 Robots: KVG6LZ

Level Password: "Evolved"
End 2 Symmetrics: K8GLLZ

Level Password: "Survivor"
The Great Escape: DTSQSB

Level Password: "Survivor"
Hide And Seek: DUSQSI

Level Password: "Survivor"
Let's Get Technical: DBSQSS

Level Password: "Survivor"
Kamikaze Squad: DJSQSZ

Level Password: "Survivor"
Phoenix River: ESSQGZ

Level Password: "Survivor"
Impending Annihilation: ETSQUZ

Level Password: "Survivor"
Charlie Don't Surf: EOSQHZ

Level Password: "Survivor"
Convoy: ENSQJZ

Level Password: "Survivor"
This Ain't Avalon: EJSHJZ

Level Password: "Survivor"
Robots Must Die!: FGSUJZ

Level Password: "Survivor"
Heavy Weapons Operation: FISGJZ

Level Password: "Survivor"
First to the Middle: F3SLJZ

Level Password: "Survivor"
Con Air/Special Delivery: FNGLJZ

Level Password: "Survivor"
Strike Three: GSULJZ

Level Password: "Survivor"
Death to the Freaks: G1HLJZ

Level Password: "Series 9"
Driving Miss Daisy: L41Q14

Level Password: "Series 9"
Gopher Hunt: LI1Q1I

Level Password: "Series 9"
Divide and Conquer: LQ1Q1Q

Level Password: "Series 9"
Checkpoint Charlie: LZ1Q1Z

Level Password: "Series 9"
Highway to Hell: M11Q4Z

Level Password: "Series 9"
Bridges of Mad Son County: MB1QIZ

Level Password: "Series 9"
Ring a Rosie: MP1QQZ

Level Password: "Series 9"
Grapes of Wrath: M91QZZ

Level Password: "Series 9"
The Glue Lagoon: MZ1HZZ

Level Password: "Series 9"
Mutants Off-Line: N41UZZ

Level Password: "Series 9"
Walls of Jerry Co: NN1GZZ

Level Password: "Series 9"
Islands in the Stream: NF1LZZ

Level Password: "Series 9"
River Runs Through It: N94LZZ

Level Password: "Series 9"
Ground to Air: O1ILZZ

Level Password: "Series 9"
Survivors Go Home: QJQLZZ

KLONOA: DOOR TO PHANTOMILE

Control Title screen
Press L2 and R2 at the title screen to blow the leaves off the screen.

Music Test
Complete the Balue's Tower bonus game. A "Music Test" option appears on the Level Selection screen.

Level Select
After completing the game and returning to the title screen, select the "Continue" and "Vision Clear" options.

Balue's Tower (Extra Vision) Bonus Level
Save all 72 Phantomilians.

KNOCKOUT KINGS

Big Heads (Created Boxers Only)
Press Left+Circle, Left+Triangle, Left+Square, Left+X at the main menu.

Upgrade Boxer
Name a boxer PSIRULES in Career mode and use him to fight one match. Leave Career mode and return to find boxer upgraded.

Taunt Opponent
Press R1+R2+X when fighting.

Gain Back Some Energy
Press L1+L2+R1+R2+X when you knock your opponent down. Continue to hit the opponent.

KNOCKOUT KINGS 2000

Tiny Boxers
In the Boxer Creation screen, enter name as MINIME. (Enter RESETPASS to undo Mini mode.)

Throbbing Boxer Heads
In the Boxer Creation screen, enter name as THROB.

Fight as Judge Mills Lane
View "Cyber Athlete" video under Options screen. Then get disqualified in an Exhibition mode fight, and look for Mills Lane under Middleweight.

Fight as Jermaine Dupri
In the Boxer Creation screen, enter name as JERMAINE_DUPRI. Press Circle at Pre-fight Ranking screen to save character.

Fight as Q-Tip
In the Boxer Creation screen, enter name as Q-TIP. Press Circle at Pre-fight Ranking screen to save character.

Fight as O
In the Boxer Creation screen, enter name as O. Press Circle at Pre-fight Ranking screen to save character.

Fight as Marc Ecko
In the Boxer Creation screen, enter name as MARC_ECKO. Press Circle at Pre-fight Ranking screen to save character.

Fight as Tim Duncan
In the Boxer Creation screen, enter name as TIM_DUNCAN. Press Circle at Pre-fight Ranking screen to save character.

Marlon Wayans
In the Boxer Creation screen, enter name as MARLON_WAYANS. Press Circle at Pre-fight Ranking screen to save character.

Fight as Gargoyle
In the Boxer Creation screen, enter name as GARGOYLE. Press Circle at Pre-fight Ranking screen to save character.

Fight as Alien
In the Boxer Creation screen, enter name as ROSWELL. Press Circle at Pre-fight Ranking screen to save character.

Shamcko The Clown
In the Boxer Creation screen, enter name as SHMACKO. Press Circle at Pre-fight Ranking screen to save character.

Ed Mahone
In the Boxer Creation screen, enter name as ED_MAHONE. Press Circle at Pre-fight Ranking screen to save character.

280-Pound Super Heavyweight Fighter
In the Fighter Attribute screen, select Heavyweight and set to maximum weight. Go to second attributes screen by pressing X, select 2 as body style and press Triangle. Reset fighter's weight to 280 lbs.

Illegal Kick
Press Triangle+Circle+X+Square during fight.

Illegal Head Butt
Press R1+R2, Triangle during fight.

Illegal Low Punch
Press R1+R2, X during fight.

Illegal Kidney Punch
Press R1+R2, Circle during fight.

Illegal Elbow
Press R1+R2, Square during fight.

Get Up Faster
Press Analog stick Down+X after being knocked down.

Super Punch
Hold R1+R2 when opponent is dazed. Release when he comes to.

KNOCKOUT KINGS 2001

Unlock Barry Sanders
In Career mode, enter "SANDERS" as the name of your boxer.

Unlock the Clown
CLOWN

Create an Invincible Boxer
INVINCIBLE

Disable All Codes
RESETPASS

Do Double Damage
DOUBLEDAMAGE

Gerber Ghost Code
NALU

Unlock Owen Nolan
NOLAN

Unlock Steve Francis
FRANCIS

Unlock Baby
BABY

Unlock Bulldog
BULLDOG

Unlock Cyclops
EYE

Unlock Gorilla
GORE

Unlock Ashy Knucks
KNUCKS

Unlock Jason Giambi
GIAMBI

Junior Seau
SEAU

Schmacko Throb
THROB

Full stats
100%

Sepia Tone Mode
SEPIA

Black and White Mode
BAW

KONAMI ANTIQUES: MSX COLLECTION VOLUME 1

TwinBee Mode (Gradius)
Highlight "Gradius" on the game menu, hold Select, then choose that game.

KRAZY IVAN

Level Select
Highlight Russia and press Right at the Level Select screen with the globe. Before the Japanese mission details appear, hold X+Down/Left. The globe bounces through the levels. Release the buttons when desired level is displayed.

True Ending
As the shield generator is blown up on the final level (Japan), walk into the explosion's center.

KURIN-PA!

View Ending
Hold Start+Select on controllers one and two during the Now Loading screen. Next, press either Select, Left, Right, or Square.

KURT WARNER'S ARENA FOOTBALL UNLEASHED

No Boundaries on Field
Press Circle (2), X, Left when game is loading and team match-up is displayed.

Hide Plays
Press Up (2) at the Play Selection screen.

LANGRISSER I & II

Level Select
At the Load screen, highlight any scenario except the first. Press Right, Down, Up, Left, R1, Square, Start, Select, Triangle, Circle.

All Secret Items
At the "Buy" word, press Left, Up, Down, Right, Left, Select, Right, Up, Left, Down, Right, Select, Circle.

Secret Items
At the "Buy" word, press Up, Left, Right, Down, Right, Right, Circle.

Test Mode
At the Load screen, highlight any scenario except the first. Press Up, Down, Up, Down, Left, Right, Select, Circle.

LANGRISSER 4

Level Select (Hard Mode)
Press R1 (2), L1 (2), Square, Left, Triangle, Circle at the Save/Load screen to access previously completed levels.

Level Select (Normal Mode)
Press Square, Up, R1, Triangle, Down, Select at the Save/Load screen to access previously completed levels.

Bonus Shop Items
Press R1, Down, L1, Up, Square, X at the Shop screen.

LANGRISSER 5

Level Select (Normal Mode)
Press Square, Up, R1, Triangle, Down, Select at the Save/Load screen to access previously completed levels.

Level Select (Hard Mode)
Press R1 (2), L1 (2), Square, Left, Triangle, Circle at the Save/Load screen to access previously completed levels.

Bonus Shop Items
Press R1, Down, L1, Up, Square, X at the Shop screen.

LAST BLADE

Bonus Characters
Finish the game once. Go to Character Select screen and press L1+L2+R1+R2.

LEGACY OF KAIN: SOUL REAVER

Move Through Barriers
Hold L1 or R1 while game is paused, press Down, Circle (2), Left, Right, Triangle, Up.

LEGEND OF DRAGOON

Easy Boss Kills
(This requires a turbo controller.) To kill bosses and other enemies easily, get items such as Burnout, Spark net, etc. Use the turbo controller to do a lot of damage. These items aren't magic, so you can use them against Kongol at the end of disk one.

Status Abnormalities Be Gone
If you are deep in a dungeon and have run out of Mind Purifiers or Body Purifiers and currently have a status abnormality, turn into a dragoon, win the fight, and your character returns to normal without the status abnormality.

LEGEND OF LEGAIA

Hidden Movie
Wait at title screen for 30 seconds.

Password for Dr. Usha's Research Center
X (2), Triangle, Circle, Square

Fight Xian in Baka Fighter
Beat the wolf in Stage 4 of Baka Fighter, and press X repeatedly when score appears.

LEGEND OF MANA

Shadow Zero Minigame
On Salamander Day, go to the bar in Domina after beating the Jewel Hunter Quests. Talk to the Shadow Zero near the counter to play.

Land Bopper Minigame
Arrange the world map so that nine lands are in full view. Hold L1 and wait for game to start.

Rename Items
Choose an item and item status from the Equip menu. Press X (2) on the item.

LEGO RACERS

Turbo Start
Before the track appears, hold X. Press X with each number of the countdown, and then hold X to start with an extra boost.

Don't Slow Down Off-road
Make a new driver, create a license, and name the driver NSLWJ.

Always Maximum Pick-ups
Make a new driver, create a license, and name the driver MXPMX.

No Driver
Make a new driver, create a license and name the driver NDRVR.

All Pick-ups Are Grapple
Make a new driver, create a license, and name the driver RPCRNLY.

Green Pick-ups
Make a new driver, create a license, and name the driver PGLLGRN.

Yellow Pick-ups
Make a new driver, create a license, and name the driver PGLLYLL.

Red Pick-ups
Make a new driver, create a license, and name the driver PGLLRD.

No Wheels
Make a new driver, create a license, and name the driver NWHLS.

Get Rid of All Cheats
Make a new driver, create a license, and name the driver NMRCHTS.

LEGO ROCK RAIDERS

Bandit's Mission Completed Password
Down, Triangle, Down, Circle, Up, Down, Square, Triangle, Left, Down, Up, Circle, Triangle, Left, Down (2), Left, Triangle, Left, Square, Circle, Down.

Axle's Mission Completed Password
Circle, Triangle, Right, Triangle, X, Up, Triangle, Right, Circle, Right, Left, Down, Up, Right, Triangle, Circle, Up, Right, Square (2), Circle, Right.

Jet's Mission Completed Password
X, Triangle, Right, Triangle, Up, Down, Square, Triangle, Left, Down, Up, Circle, Triangle, Left, Down (2), Left, Triangle, Left, Up, Circle, Right.

Doc's Mission Completed Password
Up, Square, X, Triangle, Up, Circle, Left, Triangle, Square, Triangle, Left, Down, Circle, Up, Down, Circle, Triangle, Up, Down, Up, Triangle, X.

Spark's Mission Completed Password
Right, Square, Left, Up, X, Down, Circle, Down, Square, Triangle, Up, Down, Circle, Left, Square, Triangle (2), Square, Up, Square, Triangle, Left.

Trapped Mission Completed Password
Triangle, Circle, Right, Triangle, Square (2), Down, Right, Left, Triangle, Circle, Left, Up, Right, Square, Circle, Triangle, Circle, Triangle (3), Right.

LEMANS 24 HOURS

All Cars and Tracks (Quick Race Mode)
Enter name as TATOO. Finish the following race.

1999 Audi RSR Prototype
Enter name as MAYOU. Finish the following race.

1999 Toyota GT1
Enter name as PINOU. Finish the following race.

1999 BMW Prototype
Enter name as POHLIN. Finish the following race.

Quick Race Victory
Enter name as FIRSTON. Finish the following race.

Hot Dog Car and Fast Food Race
Enter name as HOTDOG. Finish the following race.

Cheese Car and Fast Food Race
Enter name as FROMAGE. Finish the following race.

Pie Car and Fast Food Race
Enter name as PIE. Finish the following race.

Pizza Car and Fast Food Race
Enter name as PIZZA. Finish the following race.

Space Race
Enter name as NAIMAR.

Spaceship Car in Moto Mash Cartoon Race
Enter MM1 as a name.

Jet Car in Moto Mash Cartoon Race
Enter MM2 as a name.

Mad Car in Moto Mash Cartoon Race
Enter MM3 as a name.

Taxi Car in Moto Mash Cartoon Race
Enter MM4 as a name.

60's Hippie Bus in Moto Mash Cartoon Race
Enter MM5 as a name.

Ice Cream Truck in Moto Mash Cartoon Race
Enter MM6 as a name.

Submarine in Moto Mash Cartoon Race
Enter MM7 as a name.

Beach Buggy Cars
Enter name as BIGGY1, BIGGY2, BIGGY3, BIGGY4, BIGGY5, BIGGY6, BIGGY7, or BIGGY8.

Alternate Opening Screen
Enter name as JACKPOT.

LEMMINGS 3D

Level Select
Enter LAMPWICK as a password. Highlight "END" and press X. Choose a difficulty level.

View the Space FMV
Enter SPACEAAA at the title screen.

View the Egypt FMV
Enter EGYPTAAA at the title screen.

View the Military FMV
Enter ARMYAAAA at the title screen.

View the Secret FMV
Enter MAZEAAAA at the title screen.

Level 2 Password
BLIMBING

Level 3 Password
FANAGALO

Level 4 Password
DRICKSIE

Level 5 Password
KURTOSIS

Level 6 Password
GREGATIM

Level 7 Password
WALLARCO

Level 8 Password
AVENTAIL

Level 9 Password
GAZOGENE

Level 10 Password
JINGBANG

Level 11 Password
DIALLAGE

Level 12 Password
BUNODONT

Level 13 Password
NAINSOOK

Level 14 Password
YAKIMONA

Level 15 Password
FUMITORY

Level 16 Password
CINGULUM

Level 17 Password
BESLAYER

Level 18 Password
ANABLEPS

Level 19 Password
QUINCUNX

Level 20 Password
TARLATAN

Level 21 Password
KAMACITE

Level 22 Password
GUMMOSIS

Level 23 Password
PRODNOSE

Level 24 Password
NGULTRUM

Level 25 Password
COTTABUS

Level 26 Password
BEDAGGLE

Level 27 Password
EPICALYX

Level 28 Password
HOMALOID

Level 29 Password
LALLYGAG

Level 30 Password
BILABIAL

Level 31 Password
CACOFOGO

Level 32 Password
METAVURT

Level 33 Password
SLOWBURN

Level 34 Password
PELLUCID

Level 35 Password
MAKIMONO

Level 36 Password
KHUSKHUS

Level 37 Password
DISPLODE

Level 38 Password
RACAHOUT

Level 39 Password
ORGULOUS

Level 40 Password
DUNCEDOM

Level 41 Password
CABOCEER

Level 42 Password
GEROPIGA

Level 43 Password
BONTEBOK

Level 44 Password
EMPYREAL

Level 45 Password
LANGLAUF

Level 46 Password
NANNYGAI

Level 47 Password
SARATOGA

Level 48 Password
QUINTAIN

Level 49 Password
MUSQUASH

Level 50 Password
ZOMBORUK

Level 51 Password
SKILLING

Level 52 Password
WOBEGONE

Level 53 Password
BINDIEYE

Level 54 Password
FRAXINUS

Level 55 Password
LINDWORM

Level 56 Password
CURLICUE

Level 57 Password
HANEPOOR

Level 58 Password
IDEMQUOD

Level 59 Password
BLANDISH

Level 60 Password
MALAGASY

Level 61 Password
CHORIAMB

Level 62 Password
GARGANEY

Level 63 Password
KAOLIANG

Level 64 Password
MAROCAIN

Level 65 Password
OBTEMPER

Level 66 Password
TASTEVIN

Level 67 Password
VELLOZIA

Level 68 Password
BORACHIO

Level 69 Password
JACKAROO

Level 70 Password
COOLAMON

Level 71 Password
BANAUSIC

Level 72 Password
FABURDEN

Level 73 Password
RECKLING

Level 74 Password
MIRLITON

Level 75 Password
OPAPANAX

Level 76 Password
BIMBASHI

Level 77 Password
CAATINGA

Level 78 Password
PENSTOCK

Level 79 Password
SPRINGAL

Level 80 Password
BABIRUSA

LET'S GO TO PILOT

Bonus Jet
At the school, choose "Jet Course" and press Right, Left, Right, Left, Up (3), Triangle.

LIBERO GRANDE

Play as Edgard Cailaux, Powel Gardner, Roland, or Gerald Wells.
While at Hard difficulty, win International Cup with all countries.

Play as Gregorio Zonaras
Successfully complete Arcade mode at Normal difficulty.

Play as Arnold Lang
In Challenge 9 mode, earn more than 10,000 points.

Play as Minoru Kai
Score more than 10 points for your character.

Play as Ruprecht Goes
When in Challenge 9 mode, unlock last three options.

Play as David Magellan
In Challenge 9 mode, earn more than 11,500 points under each difficulty setting.

Play as Maurice Poulenc
Using Brazil in "vs CPU" mode, get an overall score of 100.

1998 World Cup France Mode
Highlight "New Game/Continue" under the International Cup menu. Hold X+Circle+Select+Start and press Triangle.

LIGHTNING LEGEND

In-game Reset
Press Select+Start+L1+R1 during gameplay.

LIVEWIRE

Level Select
Hold Triangle and press Left, Down, Up, Right, Left at the Level Select screen. To choose a new starting level on any world, press Up or Down.

LMA MANAGER

Replays with Ninja Costumes
Name player MARTIAL ARTS.

Beach Ball
Name player GOLDEN SANDS.

Sunny Weather
Name player DRY DRY DRY.

Replays with Camera View Select
Name player PRIVATE JET.

All Days with Sunshine
Name player FACTOR 25.

LOADED

Level Select
Press Start during game, hold L1+L2 for 10 seconds, and continue to hold while pressing Up, Right, Down, Left, Triangle, Circle, X, Square, X, Triangle, Square, Circle.

Invincibility
Press Start during game, hold L1+L2 for 10 seconds, and continue to hold while pressing Square, Down (2), Square, Down (2), Circle.

Set Gun's Firepower
Press Start during game, hold L1+L2 for 10 seconds, and continue to hold while pressing Down, Right, Down, Right, Triangle.

Play While Dead
Enter "Restore Health" code. After getting killed, quickly press Pause and use the "Health" option in the Options menu.

PLAYSTATION

LODE RUNNER

Turbo Mode
Choose Legend Returns mode from the main menu and select a single player game. Then, holding R2, press X.

View Movies
Highlight "Options" at main menu. Using the following key (R2=1, L2=2, R1=4, L1=8), hold down the L and R buttons on controller two in the combination that adds up to the number of the desired level FMV sequence. While holding down the desired combination, press X. (Example: For the level 6 movie, hold R1+L2+R2 and press X.)

LONE SOLDIER

Invulnerability
Pause and press Up, Left, Circle, Triangle, Up, Left.

Full Weapons
Pause and press Right, Down, Circle, Triangle, Up, Right.

Level Skip
Pause and press Down, Right, Circle, Triangle, Down, Right.

LOST VIKINGS II: NORSE BY NORSEWEST

Invincibility
Enter CH3T as a password.

Level 2 Password
1STS

Level 3 Password
2NDS

Level 4 Password
TRSH

Level 5 Password
SW1M

Level 6 Password
WOLF

Level 7 Password
BR4T

Level 8 Password
K4RN

Level 9 Password
BOMB

Level 10 Password
WZRD

Level 11 Password
BLKS

Level 12 Password
TLPT

Level 13 Password
GYSR

Level 14 Password
B3SV

Level 15 Password
R3TO

Level 16 Password
DRNK

Level 17 Password
YOVR

Level 18 Password
OV4L

Level 19 Password
T1N3

Level 20 Password
D4RK

Level 21 Password
H4RD

Level 22 Password
HRDR

Level 23 Password
LOST

Level 24 Password
OBOY

Level 25 Password
HOM3

Level 26 Password
SHCK

Level 27 Password
TNNL

Level 28 Password
H3LL

Level 29 Password
4RGH

Level 30 Password
B4RD

Level 31 Password
D4DY

LOONEY TOONS RACING
Enter all of the following cheats at the main menu.

Unlock Foghorn Leghorn
Right (2), L2, Square (2), Select

Unlock Pepe Le Pew
Left, Right, R1, Circle, Square, Select

Unlock Yosemite Sam
Left, Right, R2, Square, Circle, Select

Unlock Sylvester
Left (2), L1, Triangle, Circle, Select

Unlock Rocky
Triangle, Left, R2, Circle (2), Select

Unlock Granny
Circle, Triangle (2), L1, R1, Select

Unlock Gossamer
Triangle, Circle, R2, R1, Square, Select

Unlock Duck Dodgers
L2, Square (2), Triangle, Circle, Select

Unlock Evil Scientist
Square, Circle, L2, R2, Triangle, Select

Unlock Genie
Square, L1, R1, Triangle, Circle, Select

Unlock Hector
Triangle, L2, L1, Triangle, Square, Select

Unlock Garden Speedway
R1, Right, Left, L1, Square, Select

Unlock Planet X Speedway
R1, Square, Circle, L2, Triangle, Select

Unlock Duck Dodgers Speedway
Circle, Left, Square (2), R2, Select

Unlock Forest Speedway
Triangle, R2, Left, Triangle, L1, Select

Unlock Planet Y
Right, Left, Triangle, L2, L1, Select

Unlock Wackyland
L1, Circle, Square, R2, Triangle, Select

Unlock ACME Factory
L2, R1, R2, Triangle, Circle, Select

LOST VIKINGS II: NORSE BY NORSEWEST

Invincibility
Enter the password "CH3T".

Level 2
1STS

Level 3
2NDS

Level 4
TRSH

Level 5
SW1M

Level 6
W0LF

Level 7
BR4T

Level 8
K4RN

Level 9
B0MB

Level 10
WZRD

Level 11
BLKS

Level 12
TLPT

Level 13
GYSR

Level 14
B3SV

Level 15
R3T0

Level 16
DRNK

Level 17
Y0VR

Level 18
0V4L

Level 19
T1N3

Level 20
D4RK

Level 21
H4RD

Level 22
HRDR

Level 23
L0ST

Level 24
0B0Y

Level 25
HOM3

Level 26
SHCK

Level 27
TNNL

Level 28
H3LL

Level 29
4RGH

Level 30
B4RD

Level 31
D4DY

LOST WORLD: JURASSIC PARK
Move Freely
Hold Up+L1 and press Square+X when in Human Hunter or Human Prey levels.

LOST WORLD, THE: SPECIAL EDITION
Debug Menu
Enter the following password twice: Square, X, Circle, Triangle (2), X, Square, Circle, Triangle, Circle, X, Square.

LUNAR: SILVER STAR STORY
View FMV Sequences
On the "Making of Lunar" disk, press Up, Down, Left, Right, Triangle, Start during the FMV sequence. Remove that disk and replace it with a game disk to see movies.

Lords of Lunar Minigame
On the "Making of Lunar" disk, press Up, Down, Left, Right, Triangle, Start during the FMV sequence.

LUCKY LUKE
Train 1 Level Password
Dalton (2), Lucky, Luke, Jolly, Jumper.

Train 2 Level Password
Lucky, Luke, Lucky, Luke, Jolly, Jumper, Rantamplan.

Pueblos Level Password
Dalton, Jolly, Jumper, Lucky, Luke, Rantamplan.

Mine Level Password
Lucky, Luke, Jolly, Jumper, Dalton, Rantamplan.

Indian Desert Level Password
Rantamplan (2), Dalton, Jolly, Jumper.

Saloon Level Password
Dalton (2), Jolly, Jumper, Rantamplan.

Waterfall 1 Level Password
Dalton, Lucky, Luke, Lucky, Luke, Jolly, Jumper

Waterfall 2 Level Password
Rantamplan, Dalton, Lucky, Luke, Lucky, Luke.

Wagon Race Level Password
Rantamplan, Dalton (2), Jolly, Jumper.

Bush Wackers Level Password
Jolly, Jumper, Dalton, Rantamplan. (2)

Dalton City Level Password
Jolly, Jumper, Jolly, Jumper, Lucky, Luke, Rantamplan.

MACHINE HUNTER
Shows Cheat Codes
???HOST???

Unlimited Continues
URANUS

View End Movie
SATURN

Shows Credit
SHOWCREDIT

All Pick-ups
LAZYPLAYER

Fight Bosses Only
GET SACKED

Activates EXIT Areas
NO MISSION

One Shot Kills
GRIMREAPER

Unlimited Upgrades
2UNLIMITED

Invincibility
INVINCIBLE

MACHINEHEAD
Infinite Ammo
Press Circle (4), L1, Circle, L1 (2), Circle, L1, Circle, L1 (2), Circle, L1, Circle, L1 (4).

Infinite Energy
Press Circle, L1 (3), Circle, L1, Circle (2), L1, Circle (3), L1 (5), Circle (2), L1.

Level Select
Press L1, Circle, L1 (3), Circle (4), L1 (2), Circle (2), L1, Circle, L1, Circle (4). (R1 and R2 choose starting level.)

Level 1.2 Password
SQDZFO5TJJ

Level 1.3 Password
HYM7GODECM

Level 1.4 Password
EPPGHOXWDQ

Level 2.1 Password
I54FHOD5BF

Level 2.2 Password
E94FHOLLKJ

Level 2.3 Password
MHLFHODTCM

Level 2.4 Password
ALLFHOXGPU

Level 2.5 Password
BDNJHOLLPU

Level 3.1 Password
5SBGHOXIKJ

Level 3.2 Password
E9GGHOJIQH

Level 3.3 Password
9FOJGOLZJD

Level 3.4 Password
SKAGHO9P4O

Level 4.1 Password
JJOBNN9FCM

Level 4.2 Password
EYWJHOP7BF

Level 4.3 Password
JQNFHOP7BF

Level 4.4 Password
7G9DAOMOCE

Endgame Level Password
6H9DAOQJ2F

MACROSS: DIGITAL MISSION VF-X
Debug Mode
At the Start screen, select a save game slot and press Circle, then quickly hold Select. Press Circle, X, Square, and Triangle repeatedly until you see a Debug screen.

MAD STALKER
All Robots in Story Mode
Press Up, Down, Left, Right, X, and Circle at the title screen.

All Robots in Versus Mode
Enable the robots in Story mode then return to the title screen and press Up, Down, Left, Right, Up, Down, Left, Right, Up, Down, Left, Right, X, Circle.

MADDEN NFL 2000
Five-Yard First Downs
POPWARNER

Ten-Point TDs; Seven-Point FGs
DRBENWAY

Receivers Catch Better
MAGNASAVE

Mummies Team
WRAPPEDUP

100-Yard Field goals
BIGFOOT

Ball Camera
VERTIGO

More Injury Prone
PAINFUL

Old Western Stadium
WILDWEST

Xmas Themed Stadium
XMASGIFT

49ers '94
GOLDRUSH

49ers '88
CALLMESALLY

All-Madden Team
TEAMMADDEN

Bears '85
DOORNOB

Bengals '88
PTMOMENFOGET

Bills '90
SPOON

Broncos '97
EARTHPEOPLE

Broncos '86
BLUESCREEN

Browns '86
KAMEHAMEHA

Chargers '81
BUILDMONKEYS

Clowns (Fantasy Team)
CARNEYS

Comets (Fantasy Team)
ONESMALLSTEP

Colts '95
PREDATORS

Dolphins '85
CHICKEN

Dolphins '81
15MOREMIN

EA Sports Team
WEARETHEGAME

Giants '90
PROFSMOOTH

Industrials (Fantasy Team)
INTHEFUTURE

Junkyard Dogs (Fantasy Team)
MADMADDEN

Madden Millennium Team
TIMELESS

Marshall's (Fantasy Team)
COWBOYS

Monsters (Fantasy Team)
KTHULU

NFL Millennium Team
ALLTIMEBEST

Packers '97
TUNDRA

Patriots '76
HACKCHEESE

Praetorians (Fantasy Team)
DOASWEDO

Raiders '76
GAMMALIGHT

Raiders '72
GETMEADOCTOR

Steelers '95
STEAMPUNK

Steelers '72
DONTGOFOR2

Sugar Buzz (Fantasy Team)
TREMENDOUS1_2

Tiburon (Fantasy Team)
SHARKATTACK

Toy-makers (Fantasy Team)
XMASFILES

Vipers (Fantasy Team)
PLAYWTHHEART

All 60's Team
MOJOBABY

Bullet Passes
FASTFORWARD

Curved Space and Time
EMC2 or MOEBIUS

Defense Earns Points
FRAPLAPRO

Floating Heads
TALKINGWHAT

Easier to Throw Interceptions
PICKEDOFF

Electric Sidelines
STATICCLING

First Downs Are Twenty Yards
FIRSTIS20

Easier to Fumble Football
ROLLERJAM

Interceptions All the Time
PRIMETIME

Large vs. Small Team
MINIME

Players Are Harder to Tackle
TEFLON

Players Fatigue Faster
FINALTIME

Players Have Stiffer Arms
SMACKDOWN

Players Jump Farther
SPRONG

Players Run Faster
NO2

Quarterback Is Never Sacked
QBINTHECLUB

QB Never Throws Interceptions
EXPRESSBALL

Super Jumps
SUPERJUMPS

Team Gets Fewer Penalties
REFISBLIND

MADDEN NFL '97

Block All Field Goal Attempts
Choose 3-4 instead of special teams. Then choose 52 angle man 3 (press X as soon as you enter the 3-4 menu). Press X once before the ball is snapped so that the middle man is being controlled. When the ball is snapped, press Down. He weaves left to get by the lineman. (Don't move him back.) Run toward the ball and, immediately before the kicker kicks it, press Triangle to make him jump. It works every time!

Cinema Screen
During the Start screen press L1+L2+R1+R2 to see Super Bowl highlights.

Hidden Teams
To get eight hidden teams, enter an exhibition game, select two teams, enter the name TIBURON, and press X then Circle.

Secret Menu
At the PlayStation logo, hold Down+L1+L2+ R1+R2 until you see a menu. There's no sound and the Options menu is different.

Video Player
Hold R2 during the Load screen.

MADDEN NFL '98

EA Sports Team
Create player named ORRS HEROES.

Tiburon Team
Create player named LOIN CLOTH.

All Time Leaders
Create player named LEADERS.

All Time All Madden
Create player named COACH.

All 60's Team
Create player named PAC ATTACK.

All 70's Team
Create player named STEELCURTAIN.

All 80's Team
Create player named GOLD RUSH.

NFC
Create player named ALOHA.

AFC
Create player named LUAU.

Better Defensive Back
Create player named LEECH.

Easier Catches
Create player named GLOVES.

Better Kicking
Create player named BIGFOOT.

Better Stiff Arm
Create player named JACKHAMMER.

Astrodome
Create player named JETSONS.

Cleveland Browns Stadium
Create player named DAWGPOUND.

Old Oakland Stadium
Create player named SNAKE.

Old Tampa Bay Stadium
Create player named BIG SOMBRERO.

Old Miami Dolphins Stadium
Create player named DANDAMAN.

RFK Stadium
Create player named OLDDC.

Tiburon Sports Complex
Create player named SHARKSFIN.

Old West
Create player named GHOST TOWN.

EA Sports
Create player named PROBST HOUSE.

MADDEN NFL '99

Astrodome
FOR_RENT

Cleveland Browns Stadium
DOGPOUND99

EA Sports Stadium
EA_STADIUM

Old Miami Dolphins Stadium
NOTAFISH

Old Oakland Stadium
STICKEM

Old Tampa Bay Stadium
SOMBRERO

RFK Stadium
THEHOGS

Tiburon Sports Complex
OURHOUSE

'90s Greats
HEREANDNOW

'80s Greats
SPRBWLSHUFL

'70s Greats
BELLBOTTOMS

'60s Greats
PEACELOVE

75th Anniversary Team
THROWBACK

AFC Pro Bowl
AFCBEST

All-Madden Team
BOOM

All-Time Stat Leaders
IMTHEMAN

Cleveland Browns '99
WELCOMEBACK

EA Sports Team
INTHEGAME

Hall of Fame
TURKEYLEG

NFC Pro Bowl
BESTNFC

NFL Equipment Team
GEARGUYS

Tiburon (Fantasy Team)
HAMMERHEAD

Long-Range Special Teams
LONGLEGS

MAGIC CARPET

Gain All Spells
Pause and press Triangle.

Level Select
Press Triangle (2), Circle, Square, Triangle, Circle, Triangle, Square at the Options screen.

Level Skip
Pause and press Circle.

Replenish Mana
Pause and press Square.

MAGIC THE GATHERING: BATTLEMAGE

Easy Campaign Win
Start a new campaign and pick a fight with the CPU. Press Start and Select to show the Quit menu, then press Triangle to quit and return to the main menu. The screen should crash. Get the All Lands deck then battle in Versus mode. After a victory the Campaign screen shows that you have won that land.

MAGIC: THE GATHERING RULES

To Hide Play Selection from Opponent
Press Up, Up at the play select screen.

No Field Boarders
As the team is matching up while the game is loading, press Circle, Circle, X, Left.

Unlimited Turbo
Press L1, L1, L1, L1, L1, Triangle, Circle, Circle, Circle, Circle.

MAGICAL DROP 3

Play as Bosses
Complete the game in Story mode.

Strength's Father
Select Strength at the character screen, then press Triangle.

MAKERUNA! MAKENDO 2

Play as Makendo Ichigo
Press R1, L1, Circle, and Triangle at the title screen.

Play as Makenpo
Press R2, L1, Circle, and X at the title screen.

Play as Makenpo (Different)
Press R1, L1, Circle, and Square at the title screen.

Desperation Move
When your life bar begins to flash press R1 and R2.

Easy Special Moves
Use the D-Pad and R2 button.

MARCH MADNESS 2000

Bonus Teams
In Exhibition mode enter EASPORTS as your name on the Name Selection screen.

MARCH MADNESS '98

Special Women's Team
At the Calendar screen select Division I vs. New Mexico, then enter Exhibition mode. Then re-choose Division I to access a women's team.

Keep Ball After Dunk
After a successful dunk in Exhibition mode, call a time out while the ball's in the basket. You get the points and keep the ball!

MARCH MADNESS '99

Alien Team
In Exhibition mode enter ROSWELL as your name on the Controller Selection screen.

Classic '60s and '70s Players
In Exhibition mode enter OLDTIME as your name on the Controller Selection screen.

Small Players
In Exhibition mode enter OOMPA as your name on the Controller Selection screen.

Large Players
In Exhibition mode enter FATTONY as your name on the Controller Selection screen.

Song Select
Start in Dynasty mode, pause, and select the Controller Selection screen. Press R1 while the team being played is selected. The selected song plays when the opponent has the ball.

MARVEL SUPER HEROES

Play as Dr. Doom
Complete and save the game under the default setting. Then turn off the "shortcuts" option. At the Character Selection screen, press Down (2), then hold Down. While holding, quickly press X, Circle, R1, holding each button before letting go and pressing the next. The phrase "Captain America" is spoken, and Dr. Doom's name and face appear.

MARVEL SUPER HEROES

Play as Thanos
Save and defeat under the default settings. Turn off the "shortcuts" option. Load to the Character Select screen then press Up, then press and hold Up and press L1, Triangle, and Square quickly. Hold each button until the next button press. The words "Spider Man" are spoken and Thanos's face and name appear.

Play as Anita (Japanese version)
Activate the codes "Play as Thanos" and "Play as Doom." Then turn off the "shortcuts" option. Return to the Character screen and press Up, Right, Down, Left, Up, Right, Down, Left, then hold Up and press Square, Triangle, and L1. Hold each button until the next button press. Up, Square, Triangle, and L1 should be held on the controller.

Disable Vs. Mode Power Gems
Before beginning a match press Select on controllers one and two. "No Gems" is displayed.

Continue Fighting
When the match ends, press Select to keep hitting your enemy.

Alternate Costumes
Disable the "shortcuts" option. At the Character Select screen press and hold Down (for characters on the bottom row) or Up (for characters on the top row) for three seconds, then press any button.

Throw Pumpkins
Get and use a reality gem, then press Select.

MARVEL SUPER HEROES VS. STREET FIGHTER

Cheat Menu
Press R1, Circle, Left, Triangle (2) at main menu.

MARVEL VS. CAPCOM

Change Ryu to Ken or Akuma
Select Ryu. At Level 1, do his hurricane kick (half moon) but instead of pressing kick, press Hard Punch to Akuma, Medium Punch to Ken, Low Punch to Ryu.

Extra Options
Select Options at the main menu, then press and hold Select then Start.

EX Menu
Select Options at the main menu. Hold Select then press Start. EX menu enables human/CPU controls for players one and two, the hyper combo gauge, and vitality recovery of speed.

Play as Lilith
Complete the game with Morrigan at any difficulty setting. At the Character Select screen, press Down at the bottom center. This character can be saved on the memory card.

Play as Roll
Complete the game as Mega Man at any difficulty setting. At the Character Select screen, select Mega Man and press Right. This character can be saved on the memory card.

Play as Gold War Machine
Complete the game with War Machine at any difficulty setting. At the Character Select screen at the screen's top right, press Up. This character can be saved on the memory card.

Play as Shadow Lady

Complete the game with Chun Li at any difficulty setting. At the Character Select screen at the screen's left bottom press Down. This character can be saved on the memory card.

Play as Red Venom

Complete the game with Venom at any difficulty setting. At the Character Select screen at the screen's top corner, press Left. This character can be saved on the memory card.

Play as Orange Hulk

Complete the game with the Hulk at any difficulty setting. At the Character Select screen at the screen's top middle, press Up. This character can be saved on the memory card.

Play as Onslaught

Complete the game with any character at any difficult setting. At the Character Select screen choose Wolverine and press Down. During the match with his second form (Big Onslaught) press Select. This helps you to control and learn Big Onslaught's moves.

Play as Mech Zangief

At the Character Select screen choose Zangief, then hold Select and press any other button.

Fight with Akuma's Moves

In any mode, at the Character Select screen choose Ryu, hold Start, and press any button.

Fight with Ken's Moves

In any mode, at the Character Select screen choose Ryu, hold Select and press any button.

Switch Starting Character

Select your characters then hold L1 until the game begins.

Use Sentinel as a Special Tag Partner

Beat the game with Onslaught. At the Special Partner Select screen, select Colossus and press Down.

Use Shadow as a Special Tag Partner

Choose either Shadow Lady or Chun Li and complete the game. At the Special Partner Select screen, select Iceman and press Down.

Rockman's Magnetic Shockwave

Complete the game with Rockman. At the Character Selection screen choose Rockman and hold Select plus any other button. During a match press Down (2)/Back (2) and 2P to perform Rockman's magnetic shockwave move. This takes a level from your gauge.

MASS DESTRUCTION

All Weapons

Enter AMMO as name.

Level Select

Enter the password TTTTTTTTTTTGP.

MASTER OF MONSTERS

All Weapons

Enter AMMO as name. (Doesn't work with the level select code.)

Level Select

Enter the password TTTTTTTTTTTTGP.

MAT HOFFMAN'S PRO BMX

Add Time to Your Run

During Career Mode, extra time significantly enhances your chance of whipping a tight run. To gain eight more minutes of trick time, pause the game, hold L1 and press Square, Up, Circle, X. Now go ride.

Mega Points

To multiply all your tricks scores by 10, pause the game and hold L1, then press Square, Circle, Circle, Up, Down, Down. Enter the code again to erase its effects.

Infinite Balance

Press and hold L1 at the pause screen, then enter Square, Left, Up, Right.

Infinite Special

To ensure that you will never be out of special sauce, pause the game, hold L1, and press Left, Down, Triangle, Circle, Up, Left, Triangle, Square. You meter for Special Tricks will never deplete. Enter the code again to erase its effects.

Make It Hard on Yourself

To divide all your tricks scores by 10, pause the game, hold L1, and press Up, Down, Up, Circle, Circle, Square. Now you'll have to work 10 times as hard. Enter the code again to erase its effects.

Maxed Out Bikes

To earn a new bike with maxed out stats, get two Gold Medals in the competition levels. This unlocks your pro's top bike.

Phat Tires

To play with big wheels, press and hold L1 at the pause screen, then enter Down, Circle, Circle, Down.

See How You're Grinding

At the pause menu, press and hold L1, then enter Left, Circle, Square, Triangle, Square, Circle, X. This displays a special grind meter so you can see how you're balancing.

Unlock Grandma

Retry any Career Mode level 10 times without letting the timer run out. On the tenth try, the game will tell you "You ride like a grandma." This unlocks the geriatric for your next run (and every one thereafter). Grandma, like Tony, has three new bikes (Old School, Basket Case, and Mag Wheels) and three special moves. When you end your first run with her, the screen will say "Granny's going in for a cup of tea now." Now you can ride with her any time and take her through Career Mode.

Unlock Tony Hawk

Beat the game with any rider—with 30 Covers and two Gold Medals—to unlock Tony Hawk. Tony has three of his own bikes and his own stable of special tricks.

Unlock Warehouse from THPS

To unlock the Warehouse level from the original *Tony Hawk's Pro Skater*, pull off a string of tricks worth 200,000 points or more (without cheating). The screen will say "Your Massive Combo Has Unlocked a Secret Level."

Unlocking Burnside from THPS

To unlock the Burnside level from the original *Tony Hawk's Pro Skater*, beat the game with all eight riders with everything (meaning 30 Covers and two Gold Medals).

Unlocking Grandma's Video

To unlock Grandma's video, place in each of the two competition levels with the geezer. A scary movie awaits.

Unlocking Rider Videos

To unlock a rider's video, earn any Medal on both of the two competition levels in the game.

Unlocking the Bails Video

Grab any two Medals on the Competition Levels with Tony Hawk to score the Bails video.

MAX POWER RACING

Max Power track

Choose Arcade mode, select the Peru course, and press Circle, Square, R2 (2), R1 (2). A sound confirms correct entry.

All Tracks

Choose Arcade mode, select the Africa course, and press R1, R2, L1, Square, L1. A sound confirms correct entry.

GTI Cars

Choose Arcade mode, select the Rome course, and press L1, Circle, R1, Square, L2, Square. A sound confirms correct entry.

Performance Cars

Choose Arcade mode, select the U.K. course, and press R1, Square, L1, Circle, R2, Circle. A sound confirms correct entry.

Sports cars

Choose Arcade mode, select the USA course, and press R1, Square, L2, Circle, R2, Circle. A sound confirms correct entry.

R/C Cars

Choose Arcade mode. Select the USA course and press Square, L1, R2, L2, Circle, R1. A sound confirms correct entry.

Reversed Tracks

Successfully complete all 38 tracks.

MAX SURFING 2000

Hidden Surfer

When at the Loading screen hold R1, R2, Square.

Bonus Surfboards

Successfully completing the game unlocks a hidden surfboard. Complete the game with the new surfboard to unlock another (can be done five times). Unlock five more in Season mode the same way.

MAXIMUM FORCE

Arcade Mode

Press Select, Start, Select (2), Start, Select (3), Start, Select (4), Start at Options screen.

MDK

God Mode

Pause and press Down, L1, Up, Square, Start (2), Circle, Triangle (2), Circle, Right, Up, Left, L1, Square.

Level Select

Press Left, Circle, Triangle, Up, Square at the title screen.

Bonus Airstrike
Pause and press Down, R1, Up, Square, Down, Up, Circle, Down, Up, Down, R1.

Cow Drop
Pause and press Down, R1, Up, Square, Up, Down (2), R1, Right.

Dummy Decoy
Pause and press Down, R1, Up, Square, X, R1, Right, Circle, X, Up, Square.

Invincibility
Pause and press Down, R1, Up, Square, Circle, Triangle (2), Circle, Right, Up, Left, R1, Square.

Mortar
Pause and press Down, R1, Up, Square, Left, R1, Triangle, Square, Right, Circle, Left (2).

Nuke
Pause and press Down, R1, Up, Square, Down, Up, Square, Triangle, Down, Circle (2), Right.

Sniper Grenade
Pause and press Down, R1, Up, Square, Up, Square, R1, Left, Circle, Triangle, Square.

Super Chain Gun
Pause and press Down, R1, Up, Square, Left, R1, Down, Square, Triangle, Up, Down.

Super Speed
Pause and press Down, R1, Up, Square, Right, Circle, Triangle, Circle, X.

Thumper
Pause and press Down, R1, Up, Square, Down, Up, Left (2), Triangle, Up, Right, Down.

Tornado
Pause and press Down, R1, Up, Square, Down, R1, Square, Triangle, Right, Up, X.

Interesting Bomb
Pause and press Down, R1, Up, Square, Down, Right, Circle (2), Left (2), Up, Square, Triangle.

Strange Mode
Pause and press L1, Up, Square. Unpause and immediately pause again, then press Left, Circle, X.

No Opponents
Pause and press L1, Up, Square. Unpause and immediately pause again, then press Up, Square, L1, Left, L1, Square (2).

Display Coordinates
Pause and press L1, Up, Square. Unpause and immediately pause again, then press Down (2), Triangle (2), L1, X, Triangle.

MechWarrior 2

Elemental Chassis
T/XO/AZ<#*

Tarantula Chassis
#/XO/A4<LY

Unlock All Missions
T<XO/AXA<=

Extra Weapons
T#XO/AX<<<

Extra Heat Sinks
#XXO/A4>Y+

Continuous Throttle
#AXO/A4YYA

Invincibility
##XO/A><UZ

Unlimited Ammo
TOXO/AX>TU

Use Any Mech
#OXO/A>>O/

Jump Jets (All Mechs)
#YXO/A>YOL

Trial of Refusal Mission 1 Password
T#00A0X++0

Trial of Refusal Mission 2 Password
#/00A04+0#

Trial of Refusal Mission 3 Password
T/00A0Z+T=

Trial of Refusal Mission 4 Password
#000A0>4LA

Trial of Refusal Mission 5 Password
T000/0X4L>

Trial of Refusal Mission 6 Password
#X00/044LA

Trial of Refusal Mission 7 Password
TX00/0Z4UT

Trial of Refusal Mission 8 Password
#Y00/0>U#/

Trial of Refusal Mission 9 Password
TY00=0XU

Trial of Refusal Mission 12 Password
#<00*0>=T#

Trial of Refusal Mission 13 Password
T<00*0X=0=

Trial of Refusal Mission 14 Password
#>00*04=+4

Trial of Refusal Mission 15 Password
T>00*0Z=Y0

Freebirth Trials Mission 1 Password
TL00A0XZUZ

Freebirth Trials Mission 2 Password
#Z00A04Z#*

Freebirth Trials Mission 3 Password
T*00A0ZLY*

Wolf's Dragoons Mission 1 Password
TT00A0XL0/

Wolf's Dragoons Mission 2 Password
#*00A04L+X

Wolf's Dragoons Mission 3 Password
T*00A0ZLY+

Clan Jade Falcon Mission 1 Password
T#X0A0X<

Clan Jade Falcon Mission 3 Password
T/X0A0Z<#L

Clan Jade Falcon Mission 4 Password
#0X0A0>>00

Clan Jade Falcon Mission 5 Password
T0X0>0X>Y0

Clan Jade Falcon Mission 6 Password
#XX0>04>T#

Clan Jade Falcon Mission 7 Password
TXX0>0Z>0=

Clan Jade Falcon Mission 8 Password
#YX0>0>Y+Y

Clan Jade Falcon Mission 9 Password
TYX0/0XY0Z

Clan Jade Falcon Mission 10 Password
#AX0/04Y+*

Clan Jade Falcon Mission 11 Password
TAX0/0ZYYY

Clan Jade Falcon Mission 12 Password
#AL/

Clan Jade Falcon Mission 13 Password
TX0X04AU+

Clan Jade Falcon Mission 15 Password
T>X0X0ZA

Crusader Trials Mission 1 Password
TTX0A0X0LL

Crusader Trials Mission 2 Password
#*XOA040

Inner Sphere Trials Mission 1 Password
TLX0A0XXYU

Inner Sphere Trials Mission 2 Password
#ZX0A04X++

Inner Sphere Trials Mission 3 Password
TZXOA0ZXOX

MEDAL OF HONOR

Invincibility
MOSTMEDALS

Infinite Ammunition
BADCOPSHOW

Captain Dye Mode
CAPTAINDYE

Enable Noah in MP
BEACHBALL

Enable Bismark Dog in MP
WOOFWOOF

Enable Evil Col. Muller in MP
BIGFATMAN

Enable Felix in MP
HOODDOWN

Enable Gunther in MP
GUNTHER

Enable Nutcracker in MP
NUTCRACKER

Enable Otto in MP
HERRZOMBIE

Enable Velociraptor in MP
SSPIELBERG

Enable Werner von Braun in MP
ROCKETMAN

Enable Shakespeare in MP
PAYBACK

Enable Churchill in MP
FINESTHOUR

Enable Wolfgang in MP
HOODUP

Everyone Speaks English
SPRECHEN

History and Making of Level 1
INVASION

History and Making of Level 2
BIGGRETA

History and Making of Level 3
DASBOOT

History and Making of Level 4
STUKA

History and Making of Level 5
KOMET

History and Making of Levels 6 and 7
TWOSIXTWO

History and Making of Level 8
VICTORY DAY

Kill Yourself
Press R1, R2, L2, R1 (3), R2, L2, L1 (2) then press Square.

MP Power-ups
DENNISMODE

Mission 1 Password
RETTUNG

Mission 2 Password
ZERSIOREN

Mission 3 Password
BOOTSINKT

Mission 4 Password
SENFGAS

Mission 5 Password
SCHWERES

Mission 6 Password
SICHERUNG

Mission 7 Password
EINSICKERN

Mission 8 Password
GESAMTHEIT

Picture of Adrian Jones
AJRULES

Picture of Lynn Henson
COOLCHICK

Picture of Development Team
DWIMOHTEAM

Pictures of Staff
DWIGALLERY

Rapid-fire
ICOSIDODEC

Reflecting Shots
GOBLUE

Unlock MP Map
MACOOCOO

Wire Frame Mode
TRACERON

MEDIEVIL

Cheat for European Version
Pause, then hold L2 and press Down, Square, Triangle, Circle, Down, Up, Square, Triangle (dust to dust). (Only works with PAL version.)

Cup of Souls
Go through a tunnel at the level's start. A shaded wall is right of the merchant gargoyle. Use your Daring Dash, hammer, or club to break down the wall. Go down a tunnel and look carefully in the shaded area.

Dragon Armor
First you need the dragon gems. The pumpkin witch gives the first, the mayor in the Asylum gives the second. Go to the crystal caves and past a green door to a waterfall. Look at the dragon face on the wall; the dragon awakens and tries to attack you with fire. Use your hammer to collapse the roof on his head. You can also hit the platform you're standing on.

Easy Cash
Enter Sleeping Village and enter a room with a blue rune, then enter the pillow shop. Don't harm any innocent civilians. When you see rats, attack them with your hammer or club. Each rat gives you two or three gold pieces.

Easy Gold
Every time you hit one of the hands that follow you in graveyards with a club or hammer you receive two pieces of gold.

Expanded Ending
Get all 19 cups in all 19 boards. Then return to Enchanted Earth and use a rune to bring a witch to the pot. Make yourself small, enter an ant hill, rescue the fairies, and get at least seven amber pieces. Kill the ant queen and leave. Return and the fairy lets you into the hall of heroes where you see a statue of gold, and the witch gives you a drumstick. At the game's end you'll see an expanded ending.

Life Bottle 1
Dan's Crypt

Life Bottle 2
The Graveyard

Life Bottle 3
Hall of Heroes

Life Bottle 4
Hall of Heroes

Life Bottle 5
Scarecrow Fields

Life Bottle 6
Pools of Ancient Dead

Life Bottle 7
Hall of Heroes

Life Bottle 8
Time Machine

Missing Cog
To start the corn harvester you need the missing cog. Play until you have enough for a cup of souls. Descend until you reach the last mechanical grinder (right before the end). Behind it is a small space; enter it to find a cog and a gourd. Use the cog on the harvester, then get the cup of souls.

Powerful Attack
Use the dagger instead of the crossbow. Charge it up with Square and attack when the enemy is the most vulnerable. The dagger doesn't require much ammo or money and does plenty of damage.

Secret Area
After you get either the Daring Dash, club, or hammer, reenter Dan's Crypt. In the starting room is a visibly weak wall. Break it down to find a secret room.

Secret Area 2
Enter the Graveyard and cross a bridge that collapses. Floating downstream are some coffins. Jump on a coffin and it floats you to a secret area.

Secret Area 3
Go to the level area containing the Pools of the Ancient Dead. When you come upon the gate with the red hand, look to the side to see a small hidden island that contains energy vials, gold, and a life bottle.

Shadow Demon Talisman
Enter the Enchanted Forest, go to the bird's nest, and get the green key. Open the green door with the key. Go through the mushrooms and kill everything. Go up to the door, use a Shadow Artifact, follow it down, then do the combination for the doors (fire, spiral, water, and tree). Let the Shadow Demons out and you get the talisman. Enter the place that shocks you. Go to the sign near it and use the talisman to enter. Kill the flying creatures to end the level.

Super Cheat Menu for Euro-Version
Pause, hold L2, and press Triangle, Circle, Triangle, Circle (2), Triangle, Left, Circle, Up, Down, Right, Circle, Left (2), Triangle, Right, Circle, Left (2), Triangle, Circle, Down, Circle (2), Right.

Canny Tim Has
Life bottle and crossbow

Stanyer Has
Three gold chests and hammer

Woden Has
Gold chests and broad sword

Warrior Queen Has
Two vials and spear

Ravenhooves Has
Life bottle, flaming longbow, longbow, and magic longbow

Sturnguard Has
Magic shield

Bloodmonath Has
Three gold chests and axe

Dirk Has
Magic Sword

Dame Fortune Has
Lightning Bolts

Cheat Mode (PAL version)
Pause, hold L2, and press Down, Up, Square, Triangle (2), Circle, Down, Up, Square, and Triangle.

Extended Mode (PAL version)
Pause, hold L2, and press Triangle, Circle, Triangle, Circle (2), Triangle, Left, Circle, Up, Down, Right, Circle, Left (2), Triangle, Right, Circle, Left (2), Triangle, Circle, Down, Circle (2), and Right.

Level Select (PAL Version)

Pause and enter the "extended mode" and the "cheat mode" codes. Go to the Camera option and pick "plug in 8." Press Start and resume. After the game starts, a sword and text appear. Use R1, R2, L1, or L2 to zoom and move the camera. Use the D-Pad to point the sword, then pause. Go to Camera options and press X. Press Start to resume and you can pick the levels.

MEDIEVIL 2

Ultimate Cheat Menu

Pause, hold L2 and Triangle, Circle, Triangle, Circle (2), Triangle, Left, Circle, Up, Down, Right, Circle, Left (2), Triangle, Right, Circle, Left (2), Triangle, Circle, Down, Circle (2), Right. Press Pause to access the Cheat menu.

MEGA MAN X4

Mega Man's Armor

Highlight Mega Man at the Character Select screen, press Circle (2), Left (6), hold L1+R2, and press Start.

Zero's Ultimate Armor

Highlight Zero at the Character Select screen, hold R1 and press Right (6), then hold Circle and press X.

MEGA MAN X5

Start with Ultimate Armor X

Highlight "Mega Man X," then press Up (2), Down (9).

Start with Ultimate Armor Zero

Highlight "ZERO," then press Down (2), Up (9).

X Buster's Super Nova Armor

At the Character Selection screen, highlight "X Buster," then press Up (2), Down (9).

Zero's Black Armor

At the Character Selection screen, highlight "Zero," then press Down (2), Up (9).

Zero's Supreme Slash

Repeatedly press Forward+Square as quickly as possible.Megaman 8

Extra Health in Stage One

When you reach the water in stage one, walk backward until you find a group of trees. Kill the trees to get the health.

Extra Life

Kick a mega ball into the clown's mouth at the Clown Man's level.

How to Kill the Bosses

To defeat Grenade Man, use the Thunder Claw. To defeat Frost Man, use the Flash Bomb. To defeat Tengu Man, use the Ice Wave. To defeat Clown Man, use the Tornado Hold. To defeat Aqua Man, use the Astro Crush. To defeat Sword Man, use the Water Balloon. To defeat Search Man, use the Flame Sword. To defeat Astro Man, use the Homing Sniper.

MEGAMAN LEGENDS

100 Zenny

In the Apple Market, kick a can into the big bread store to get a 100 Zenny.

Become DarkMega Man

Kick all the vending machines until they explode or kick a can into the Jetlag Bakery at the Apple Market. Eventually Mega Man darkens. Or when you receive the running shoes, watch TV in the Flutter. During the robbery, shoot the red car that police are chasing. Find the briefcase and go to the gate. Try to leave and say "yes" when asked if you want to keep the money. You turn black instantly. The darkness wears off in time; to get it back kick a vending machine until it explodes.

Lots of Cats

When you see a cat in front of the main gate press Circle. Say "yes" when asked if you wish to take the cat back to Flutter. Every time you enter Flutter, more cats appear.

Free Drinks

Go to a vending machine and press Circle. When asked if you want a drink, say "no," then kick the machine and it gives a free drink.

Hard Mode

After beating the game, return to the Start screen to see a new option for harder play.

Hospital Girl

Ira is the little girl in the hospital in a wheelchair. Give the mayor 15,000 Zenny to help the hospital with technology for Ira's treatment and Ira will give you a flower pearl item.

Bomb Scare

Talk to the police department inspector and he sends you to look for bombs. Defuse the two bombs (on the roof and on the ground) in the Downtown area and you'll get a bomb and Plastque items.

Lost Cash

Return to the inspector and he asks you to help find a man's lost money. Talk to the guy and follow the clues in this order: Electronic Store, Bakery, Library, Downtown Soda machine; talk to a kid with red hair outside the library and check the garbage can to get the Bag item. The inspector gives you an Arm Supporter item.

Rescue

To find the missing grocer's wife, enter the Cardon Forest and talk to her; take her to the hospital. The husband gives you a sunlight item.

MEN IN BLACK

Level Skip

At the Options screen press Left (2), Right, Left, Right, Left (3), Square.

METAL FIST

View FMV Sequences

At the main menu hold L1, L2, R1, and R2 and press Select.

METAL GEAR SOLID

Change Title Screen Colors

At the title screen press Up, Down, Left, or Right on the D-Pad.

Destroy the Generator

Use a Nikita in first-person view for better aim.

Extra Modes

VR Training mode is built-in. After defeating all 10 stages you get Time Attack mode. Beat the game in Time Attack mode to receive Gun Shooting mode. Complete all 10 stages in Gun Shooting mode to get Survival Mission mode.

Fast Travel

Hide inside a box on the cargo truck. Remain still and soon a guard takes the box to the area posted on it. The three boxes go to three locations.

First-Person Nikita Missile

Launch the missile then press Triangle. This only lasts a short time before it explodes.

Get the Bandana

Play until you wreck the Ocelot's Torture Rack without giving up or dying. When you beat the game, Meryl gives you the bandana. After the credits, save the game. When you restart the game, you have the bandana.

Get the Camera

When you get a Level 6 keycard, go the Tank Hanger and take the elevator to basement 2. Enter the hall before the room where you battled Ocelot. Find a spot to blow a hole in the wall and find two rooms, one of which contains a camera.

Jail Break

When one of the guards leaves, crawl under the bed. When he opens the door, knock him over. Otacon gives you some ketchup. When the guard is gone lie on the floor with the ketchup in your items. The guard assumes you are dead. When he opens the door, knock him out and leave.

Knockout Punch

To get a very strong punch press Triangle and Square five times to charge, then use a rapid punch. Usually 10 such punches defeat any boss.

Nice Wolves

Kill all the wolves except the very small one when you enter the caves and also with Meryl. Shoot Meryl with a Socom, then quickly equip a cardboard box. The little wolf urinates on the box. Every time you run into the wolves, equip the box and they leave you alone. Another way to do this is to equip Sniper's Wolf handkerchief.

See Through Mantis's Eyes

When fighting Mantis in First-person mode, hold Triangle to see through Mantis's eyes instead of Snake's.

Silent, Deadly, and Quick Neck Snap

Sneak up behind a guard unarmed, and quickly press Square (10).

Stats When Fighting Liquid

Press Circle on the second controller to see the fight's stats.

Stealth Suit

Go to Ocelot's Torture Rack and press Select. You get the bad ending. After the credits Otacon gives you his suit. Save the game, and when you restart, the suit is in your inventory.

Thermal Goggles

Use the thermal goggles to see mines as well as bosses.

METAL GEAR SOLID INTEGRAL

First-Person Mode
Beat the game in any mode except "very easy" to unlock First-person mode (main menu under "specials"). Quickly press Triangle (2) to switch to first person.

Infinite Ammo
Complete the game without submitting to Ocelot. Get the bandana, save, then restart. Equip the bandana for unlimited ammo.

Stealth Camouflage
Complete the game submitting to Ocelot. Receive the camouflage and save. Once you restart you have the camouflage. Also, cameras and enemies (except bosses) cannot detect you.

Alternate Costumes
Complete the game twice at any difficulty level and save to the same file. The third time, Snake wears a tuxedo, Meryl wears Snake's outfit, and Ninja wears a blue-and-red cyborg costume.

Alternate Title screen
At the title screen, press the D-Pad to change the background color.

METAL GEAR SOLID: VR MISSIONS

Mei Ling Photo Session
Beat Sneaking mode with a best time in all 30 attack time levels. Then the Extras menu contains a photo session option.

METAL OF HONOR: UNDERGROUND

Cartoon Gallery
Enter MOHDESSINS as a password.

Team Gallery
Enter MOHUEQUIPE as a password.

Dreamworks Interactive Personal Screens
Enter DWIECRANS as a password.

Invincibility
Enter PUISSANCE as a password.

Quadruple Firing Rate
Enter BALLESVITE as a password.

Bouncing Bullets
Enter RICOCHET as a password.

Podoski Mode
Enter LATIREUSE as a password.

Wacky Taxi Mode:
Enter AUTODINGUO as a password.

Grand Cheat Select
Select "Options" from the main menu, then select "Password." Enter ENTREZVOUS. Go back to the Password screen and enter PORTECLEFS.

METAL SLUG

Cheat Menu
Press X, Circle, Square, Triangle (2), X, Circle, Square at the Options screen.

METAL SLUG X

Unlock Levels Arcade & Another Mission
Beat the game in Arcade Mission mode to unlock all the levels in the "Arcade Mission" and "Another Mission" options.

Chatty Kathy
Select Combat School, and while it is loading, rapidly press Square until the menu appears. The instructor will ask if you want to chat with her.

METROPOLITAN HIGHWAY BATTLE

Maximum Money
On controller two, press Up, Triangle, X, Right, Square, Left, Circle, Select, Start at the title screen.

All Parts
On controller two, press Right (2), Down, Up (2), Left, Down, Left, Circle, Triangle at the title screen.

Secret Parts
On the second controller press Up, Down (2), Up, Left, Right, Left, Right at the title screen.

Alternate Car Display
At the Car Selection screen press L1 or R2 to show the vehicle's dimensions.

MICHELIN RALLY MASTERS RACE OF CHAMPIONS

Unlock Everything
From the main menu, select Options, then choose the Code Entry screen. From there, enter: J20X4CRFL4ZT.

MICRO MACHINES V3

Any Object
Pause and press Down (2), Up (2), Right (2), Left (2).

Behind Car View
Pause and press Left, Right, Square, Circle, Left, Right, Square, Circle

Big Bounces
Pause and press Square, Right (2), Down, Up, Down, Left, Down (2).

Double Speed
Pause and press Square, X, Circle, Square, Triangle, X (4).

Floating Objects
Pause and press Square, Triangle, Square (2), Triangle, Square (2), Triangle, X.

Slow CPU Cars
Pause and press Circle, Triangle, Square, X, Circle, Triangle, Square, X.

Debug Mode
Pause and press Square, Up, Down (2), Square, Circle (2), Triangle, X.

Change Camera Angle (Debug Mode)
Hold Select and press Up, Down, Left, or Right.

Change Camera Zoom (Debug Mode)
Hold Select and press L2 or R2.

Player into Computer (Debug Mode)
Hold Select and press Square.

Blow Up All Cars (Debug Mode)
Hold X+Triangle+Circle+Square.

Quit Race and Win (Debug Mode)
Press Select+X.

Nine Lives in 1P Mode
CATLIVES

All Tracks in MP Mode
GIMMEALL

Tanks Cannot Shoot
NOTANKS

Tanks Used on Tracks
TANKS4ME

Slippery Roads
WINTERY

MICRO MANIACS

Specials at Maximum Power
At the Options screen, pick "secret options," hold Select, and press Square, X, R1, Circle, Up, Square, Down, Up, Down, X, Square.

Motion Blur Mode
At the Options screen, pick "secret options," hold Select, and press Triangle, Circle, Right, Triangle, Up, Right, Circle, Up, Square.

Increase Options
At the Options screen, pick "secret options," hold Select, and press Circle, Up, Triangle, Circle, Left, Triangle, Square (2), X, Down.

MIKE TYSON BOXING

Unlock Jimmy Flex and the Disco Stadium
Select World mode, then choose a boxer. Rename your Boxer as CLUBFUD. After you type the name, place the cursor on Enter and press the Triangle button.

Unlock John L. Sullivan and Docks Stadium
Select World mode, then choose a boxer. Rename your Boxer as OLD MAN. After you type the name, place the cursor on Enter and press the Triangle button.

Boxer's Heads Will Grow When You Punch Them
Select World mode, then choose a boxer. Rename your Boxer as OUCH. After you have typed the name, place the cursor on Enter and press the Triangle button.

Boxer's Heads Will Spin When You Hit Them
Select World mode, then choose a boxer. Rename your Boxer as HURTS. After you type the name, place the cursor on Enter and press the Triangle button.

Boxer's Necks Will Stretch When You Hit Them
Select World mode, then choose a boxer. Rename your Boxer as NECK. After you type the name, place the cursor on Enter and press the Triangle button.

Unlock the Invisible Boxer
Select World mode, then choose a boxer. Rename your Boxer as GONE. After you type the name, place the cursor on Enter and press the Triangle button.

Small-Headed Boxers
Select World mode, then choose a boxer. Rename your Boxer as BINGY. After you type the name, place the cursor on Enter and press the Triangle button.

Big-Headed Boxers
Select World mode, then choose a boxer. Rename your Boxer as BONGY. After you type the name, place the cursor on Enter and press the Triangle button.

Big Hands and Feet

Select World mode, then choose a boxer. Rename your Boxer as STUPID. After you type the name, place the cursor on Enter and press the Triangle button.

De-Activates All Cheats

Select World mode, then choose a boxer. Rename your Boxer as NORMAL. After you type the name, place the cursor on Enter and press the Triangle button.

MINI 4WD BROS. ETERNAL WINGS

Phantom-Blade Car
Complete Story mode with Knuckle Breaker. Defeat the Phantom-Blade car in the next challenge.

Vise-Intruder Car
Complete Story mode with Max Breaker. Defeat the Vise-Intruder car in the next challenge.

Ray Stinger Car
Complete Story mode with Fire Stinger. Once the end sequence finishes, restart and pick "continue" to start a Ray vs. Stinger match. Beat Ray.

Secret Mode Two Option
Complete Story mode with Berkaiser (Esien Wolf). At Secret mode, two sections appear under "continue." Beat the new option to unlock the last two Berkaisers.

Secret Shop
Defeat Level 6 in Story mode, then move the pointer to the right upper corner of the screen and select that location.

MINNA NO GOLF 2

In-game Reset
During gameplay, press L1, L2, R1, R2, Select, Start.

MISSION: IMPOSSIBLE

Developer Notes
TTOPFSECRETT

Disable AI
SCAREDSTIFF

Level 2
HILKJTKUMLBF

Level 3
PMCQEQPJQQDQ

Level 4
KNDPFTPLQYDO

Level 5
LDEESUVPRWGB

Level 6
LFERHGVRXJGP

Level 7
LBEHSFVNRTGG

Level 8
LPEKSMVQXOGC

Level 9
NIQNKRQUSLHF

Level 10
NQQQKLRHSNHJ

Level 11
AMRQMQSJNQPQ

Level 12
BBMENISNNTKG

Level 13
CENHOQGWIVLD

Level 14
CINKPTGUILLF

Level 15
BQMMTUGHUNKJ

Level 16
BOMNOGGVURKL

Level 17
MEPHFQTWVVJD

Level 18
MIPKGTTUVLJF

Level 19
FLNNEPTITPIK

Level 20
MGNQFHTKTSIM

Level 21
DHIJLSIRKJFP

Level 22
DKILMIUMKXFH

Level 23
OMGSKPIIJPNK

Level 24
DNGOLHIKJSNM

Slow Motion
IMTIREDTODAY

Super Jumps
BIONICJUMPER

Turbo Mode
GOOUTTAMYWAY

View FMV Sequences
SEECOOLMOVIE

MICHELIN RALLY MASTERS RACE OF CHAMPIONS

Unlock Everything
From the main menu, select "Options," then choose the Code Entry screen. From there enter: J20X4CRFL4ZT.

MITSUMETI KNIGHT

Bonus Minigames
At the Options screen, press Up (2), Down (2), Up, Right, Left, Down, Square, Select. A wizard flies across the screen and five hidden minigames appear on the menu.

MLB '98

142 Mph Fastball
Choose the Arizona Diamond Backs, put in pitcher Rex Baca, and throw a fast ball.

Automatic Homeruns
Pick the Arizona Diamond Backs or the Tampa Bay Devil Rays. Scott Murray or Mark Meenahan always hit homers.

Easier Homeruns
At bat, press and hold Up and Left; also hold these after you hit.

Perfect Pitcher
Make a pitcher named "A," format him to be 60 inches tall, small size, and drop all abilities to zero. He pitches 151 mph in Season or Exhibition mode.

MLB '99

Super Player
Enter Scott Murray (or any development team name) as a player name.

More Homeruns
Create a player that is 60 inches tall, zero abilities, and small build.

Baseball Bloopers FMV Sequence
At the Start menu let the demo run. Once half an inning ends, a FMV sequence shows along with credits.

Easy Strikes
Aim for the batter's head; they usually swing at it.

Funny Announcements
When you are the pitcher, remain still. The announcer makes several amusing comments until you move.

MLB 2000

Hit a Homerun
In the batter's box, use the power swing, and press Up-Left, L2, R1, and X once the ball is thrown. Any hit becomes a homerun.

Big Heads
At the Start menu, press R1+X+R2+Select. A sound confirms correct entry.

Blooper Sequence
At the Start menu let the demo run. Once half an inning ends, a FMV sequence shows along with credits.

Super Player
Enter Scott Murray (or any development team name) as a player name.

MLB 2001

Spring Training Stadiums
At the Stadium Select screen in Exhibition mode, move left or right until the spring stadiums display.

Easy Homeruns
At bat, press and hold Up and Left; also hold these after you hit.

Great Player
Enter Scott Murray (or any development team name) as a player name.

MLB 2003

Super Player
Enter Scott Murray as a player name at the Player Creation screen. He can hit 606-foot homeruns.

MLB PENNANT RACE

Super Player
Create a new pitcher with the last name BACA and the first name REX. This player throws 140 mph and always hits a homerun.

Super Batter
Make a new pitcher with a first and last name of "B." He'll always hit a homerun.

MOBILE SUIT GUNDAM: PERFECT ONE YEAR WAR

Hidden Options
At the Bandai logo press Up, Triangle, Left, Square, Down, X, Right, Circle, then hold L1 and R1. A sound confirms correct entry. Release L1 and R1 when the title screen shows. Then press L1, L2, R1, R2 to get Additional mode, which opens narrations, voices, sequences, and 3D demonstrations.

Level Select
When the introduction begins, hold Left+Select+R1+L2, then press Start. Then release Start but continue to hold down the others.

MONKEY HERO

Unlimited Spears and Firecrackers
Return to the room where you learned about the firecrackers and spears. After you finish and pass the test, keep returning to get the items again.

MONOPOLY

Cheaper Property
Playing against one computer, enter an auction and bid one dollar above the computer; the computer always gives up on the second round.

Easy Win
Buy one of each property, starting from purple and moving up to orange.

Start with $4,500
Start a game as usual, but get three players on controller one. When it's your turn, make deals with the player for their money. When it's the player's turn, go bankrupt then play the computer as usual.

MONSTER RANCHER

Bonus Music Track
Play track two of the game disk in an audio CD player.

Ardebaren
Just before you breed a new monster, put in the PSX game Tecno's Deception to reveal the secret character Ardebaran.

Build up Loyalty Levels
Go from town to ranch and check your monster each time. The loyalty should increase by five each time. This is a good way to unspoil your monster.

Committee Permission
Obtain a pure monster that makes up the committee to breed a special monster.

Magic Monster
Get a pure Monol and a pure Gali then combine them with an old mirror item. The lab suggests that this is a bad combination, but proceed anyway to get a magic monster.

Nya Monster
Get to about year 1026, and check the items every so often. The sixth or seventh new item will be a cat doll. Use the doll with any breeding to get the Nya monster.

Skribble, Sketch, and Doodle
To get a Scribble, breed a pure Monol and raise its fame above 80, then play a lower-class tournament until the fame drops below 65. Afterward the monster is covered with graffiti. To get a Doodle, breed a Scribble with another Monol. To get a Sketch, combine a Scribble with any other monster.

Shades
Breed an ape monster and put in Billy Joel's greatest hits CD to get a monster called Shades with excellent stats.

Zombie
You can get a zombie from the Spawn soundtrack with the committee's permission.

MONSTER RANCHER 2

In-game Reset
Hold Start+Select until the game returns to the opening screen.

Secret Monsters
Use the following CDs to create secret monsters: "And Justice For All" from Metallica (Ferious) "Black Album" from Metallica (Monol) "Enema of the State" from Blink 182 (Chef) "Greatest Hits" from Bob Marley (Plant/??? monster) "Hello Nasty" from The Beastie Boys (Unknown) "Licensed to Ill" from The Beastie Boys (Express Worm) "Macarena" from Los Del Rio (Unknown) "Merry Christmas" from Mariah Carey (Satan Clause) "Millennium" from The Backstreet Boys (Happy Mask) "Running with Scissors" from Weird Al Yankovich (Unknown, needs to be class E or D); "The Bridge" from Ace of Base (Gelatine-Mocchi/Gel combination) "The Sign" from Ace of Base or the *Lion King* Original Soundtrack (Bossy-Galli/Ape combination) Disney's *The Little Mermaid* Original Soundtrack (Mermaid) *Men in Black* Soundtrack (Chinosis-Metalner/??? monster) *Star Wars: Episode 1* Soundtrack (Galaxy) *Brave Fencer Musashi* PlayStation game (Shogun) *Bust-A-Move 4* PlayStation game (Cinder Bird) *Devil Dice* PlayStation game (Dice) *Digimon World* (Japanese) PlayStation game (Unknown) *March Madness '99* PlayStation game (Ninja Kato) *Metal Gear Solid: Disk 2* PlayStation game (Soldier Gaboo) *Syphon Filter* PlayStation game (Unknown) *Resident Evil 3* PlayStation game (Unknown) *Diablo* PC game (Unknown, needs to be class E or D).

Free Food
Send your monster the second or third week to avoid buying food for the next month.

Get the Joker
Go with Dr. Talico to the volcano a second time. Take the first right and follow a trail to a large building with stairs. Search until you find a mask. Combine with any monsters to get a Joker.

Get the Phoenix
Join Dr. Talico on his trip to the volcano. On the way you see a building. Search it once and the Phoenix flies out of the volcano. Search the building again to find a fire feather. Combine this with any two monsters to get a 100 percent Phoenix.

Legendary Centaur Monster
Find a spear in the Power Errantry. When you return, a Centaur challenges you. (Make sure your monster is strong or it will be beaten). After the fight, the Centaur runs away but leaves his spear. Use the spear when breeding any two monsters to get a 100 percent Centaur.

MONSTER SEED

All Monsters
At the Options screen at the Soulin Monster Ranch, select "Buy Monster" then press R2, R1, L2, L1, R1, R2, L1, L2 (2).

All Items
At the Options screen press R2, L1, R1, L2, R2, L1, R1, L2 (2).

View Ending
At the title screen press L2, R1, L1, R2, L2, R1, L1, R2 (2).

MORTAL KOMBAT 3

Extended Menu One
Press X, L1, and L2 at the Prepare for Kombat screen. A sound confirms correct entry. Press Start to go to the Kombat Kube screen, then press Up to reveal a question mark. You can choose: Free Play (off/on), Smoke (off/on), Fatality Time (on/off), and Level Select (off/on).

Extended Menu Two
Press X, Circle, Triangle, R1 (2), R2 (2), and R1 (2). Shao Kahn says "You will never win." Press Start to go to the Kombat Kube screen, then press Up to reveal a question mark. You can choose: Round Match (off/on), 1 Hit Death (off/on).

Random Select
Press Up+Start at the Character Selection screen.

Infinite Continues
Press Up (2), Right (2), Left (2), and Down (2), during Story mode.

Ultimate Kombat Kode
Rotate the controller counterclockwise twice during Story mode.

Unlimited Continues
Press Up (2), Right (2), Left (2), Down (2).

Kombat Codes (below)
Enter these codes in Two-player mode using a button to control each of the six boxes on the Versus screen. The numbers indicate how many times each button needs to be pressed. Box 1: Player 1 Low Punch; Box 2: Player 1 Block; Box 3: Player 1 Low Kick; Box 4: Player 2 Low Punch; Box 5: Player 2 Block; Box 6: Player 2 Low Kick.

Winner Fights Shao Kahn
0, 3, 3, 5, 6, 4

Winner Fights Noob Saibot (Black Kano)
7, 6, 9, 3, 4, 2

Winner Fights Smoke
2, 0, 5, 2, 0, 5

Winner Fights Motaro
9, 6, 9, 1, 4, 1

Psycho Kombat (Dark, Randper, No Block, Quick Uppercut Recovery)
9, 8, 5, 1, 2, 5

No Power Bars
9, 8, 7, 1, 2, 3

Blocking Disabled
0, 2, 0, 0, 2, 0

Throwing Disabled
1, 0, 0, 1, 0, 0

Unlimited Run
4, 6, 6, 4, 6, 6

Quazi-Ranper Kombat (Only Changes Player You Are Fighting)
4, 6, 0, 4, 6, 0

Dark Fighting
6, 8, 8, 4, 2, 2

Play Galaga
6, 4, 2, 4, 6, 8

Player One Quarter Energy
7, 0, 7, 0, 0, 0

Player Two Quarter Energy
0, 0, 0, 7, 0, 7

Player One Half Energy
0, 3, 3, 0, 0, 0

Player Two Half Energy
0, 0, 0, 0, 3, 3

Hold Flippers During Casino Run
9, 8, 7, 6, 6, 6

No Fear
2, 8, 2, 2, 8, 2

There Is No Knowledge That Is Not Power
1, 2, 3, 9, 2, 6

Combo System Disabled
7, 2, 2, 7, 2, 2

Player One Inflicts Half Damage
3, 9, 0, 0, 0, 0

Player Two Inflicts Half Damage
0, 0, 0, 3, 9, 0

Inflict Half Damage
3, 9, 0, 3, 9, 0

Fast Uppercut Recovery Enabled
6, 8, 8, 4, 3, 3

Super Run Jumps
3, 2, 1, 7, 8, 9

Special Moves Disabled
5, 5, 5, 5, 5, 6

Regenerating Power Bars
9, 7, 5, 3, 1, 0

Super Endurance
0, 2, 4, 6, 8, 9

Real Kombat
0, 4, 0, 4, 0, 4

Play as Smoke
0, 1, 0, 6, 9, 6

MORTAL KOMBAT 4

Cheat Menu
Select Versus mode and enter the Kombat Kode 302 213. Once you exit the match go to the Options screen. Select "Versus Screen Enabled" and press and hold Block+Run for 10 seconds. Only one cheat option can be enabled at a time.

Endings
Enable Cheat mode and select "Endings" on the Cheat menu. Start the game in Arcade mode then defeat one character to see the character ending.

Fatalities 1
Enable Cheat mode and select "Fatalities 1" on the Cheat menu. In a match, hold Down to finish your opponent, then press High Punch to enable any character's first fatality.

Fatalities 2
Enable Cheat mode and select "Fatalities 2" on the Cheat menu. Hold Down to finish off your enemy, then press High Punch. This performs the second character's fatality.

Level Fatalities
Enable Cheat mode and select "Level Fatalities" on the Cheat menu. When you are about to defeat an opponent, hold Down, then press High Punch. This performs the character's level fatality.

Play as Meat
Starting in Group Mode, beat all 16 characters. Then select any character and begin a match. The character you chose becomes Meat and has all the selected character's moves.

Play as Goro
Complete the game with Shinnok, then save. Enable the Cheat menu. At the Character Selection screen, pick the "Invisible" icon at the screen's bottom. Press Up (3), Left to select Shinnok's icon, then press Run+Block.

Play as Noob Saibot
Complete the game with Reiko. Select Versus mode and enter the Kombat Kode 012 012. Exit a match, go to the Character Selection screen, and pick the "Invisible" icon at the screen's bottom. Press Up (2), Left to select Rieko's icon, then press Run+Block.

New Weapon
Complete the game with Kai. Start a new game with Kai to enable his new weapon: Raiden's lighting staff.

View Biographies
Go to Kombat Theatre mode, select the character, and press Block.

Alternate Costumes
At the Character Select screen, pick a fighter, hold Block, and press any button twice to rotate the picture and enable costumes for everyone except Sonya and Tonya. To get their costumes, rotate the screen three times. Rotating the screen three times for any other character gives you their third costume.

Alternate Weapons
To get alternate weapons for a third character, enable their third costume.

Kombat Kodes
Enable one of the following codes at the Versus mode screen to activate it. At the screen's bottom are three-digit icon boxes. The first box is controlled with the Low Punch, the second by Block, and the third by Low Kick.

One-hit Win
1-2-3-1-2-3

Noob Saibot Mode
0-1-2-0-1-2

Red Rain (on the Rain Stage)
0-2-0-0-2-0

Explosive Kombat
0-5-0-0-5-0

Drawn Weapons Cannot Be Lost
0-0-2-0-0-2

Disable Throws
1-0-0-1-0-0

Disable Max Damage
0-1-0-0-1-0

Disable Throws and Max Damage
1-1-0-1-1-0

Random Weapon Appears
1-1-1-1-1-1

Start with Random Weapon
2-2-2-2-2-2

Start with Weapons Drawn
4-4-4-4-4-4

Many Weapons
5-5-5-5-5-5

Silent Kombat
6-6-6-6-6-6

Big Heads
3-2-1-3-2-1

Fight in Goro's Lair
0-1-1-0-1-1

Fight in Well
0-2-2-0-2-2

Fight in Elder Gods
0-3-3-0-3-3

Fight in Tomb Stage
0-4-4-0-4-4

Fight in Rain Stage
0-5-5-0-5-5

Fight in Snake Stage
0-6-6-0-6-6

Fight in Shaolin Temple
1-0-1-1-0-1

Fight in Living Forest
2-0-2-2-0-2

Fight in Prison
3-0-3-3-0-3

Fight in Ice Pit
3-1-3-3-1-3

Alternate Opponents in Arcade Mode
At the Choose Your Destiny screen, press Start to rotate the character tower to more opponents.

Beat the Game in One Match
First choose a character with the Run and Block buttons. Hold these until the match begins. Hit your dying opponent again to defeat the game.

MORTAL KOMBAT MYTHOLOGIES: SUB-ZERO

Start at the Final Stage
Enter "Zcherry" to begin at the Fortress with 20,000 experience points. If you die before you reach a checkpoint, press L1 to fight Quan or L2 to fight Shinnok.

Invincibility
Enter TDFCLT as a password.

Infinite Urns
Enter NXCVSZ as a password.

Exploding Earth Boss
Enter RCKMND as a password.

View Credits
Enter CRVDTS as a password.

Outtake FMV Sequence
Get to Shinnok with six or more urns of vitality, successfully defeat Shinook, and enter the now-open portal. After the games credits you are treated to a bloopers FMV.

Level 2, Wind
THWMSB

Level 3, Earth
CNSZDG

Level 4, Water
ZVRKDM

Level 5, Fire
JYPPHD

Level 6, Prison
RGTKCS

Level 7, Bridge
QFTLWN

Level 8, Fortress
XJKNZT

MORTAL KOMBAT TRILOGY

Infinite Kredits
Once at the Story screen press Down (2), Up (2), Right (2), and Left (2). A sound confirms correct entry. The credit now reads "Freeplay."

Play as Chameleon
Playing as player one, choose any male ninja character. (Sub-Zero, Reptile, Rain etc.) then hold Left, R1, R2, Square, Triangle until the fight starts. Playing as player two, choose any male ninja and hold Right, R1, R2, Square, Triangle until the fight begins. When the fight begins your ninja changes to Chameleon.

Classic Characters from *MK1*
Press Select when choosing Kano, Kung Lao, Jax, and Rayden.

Stage Select
At the Character screen, select Sonya and press Up and Start when in Versus or One-player mode. You'll see the screen shake and hear a rumble.

Random Character Selection
At the Character Select screen, hold Up and Start.

Enable "?" on Kube
To enable a "?" menu, hold Up, R1, R2, L1, L2 and press Up when the "Konfigure Kombat" square is displayed. The screen will shake. Once the "?" menu is enabled the following options can be set.

Fatality 1
Enable "?," HK

Fatality 2
Enable "?," LK

Brutality
Enable "?," HP

Babality
Enable "?," LP

Animality
Enable "?," Run

Friendship
Enable "?," Block

Kombat Kodes
At the Versus screen, the left player controls the first three boxes and the right player controls the last three boxes at the bottom of the screen. The following numbers can be used for symbols.

0
Dragon

1
MK

2
Yin-yang

3
"3"

4
Question mark

5
Lightning

6
Goro

7
Rayden

8
Shao Kahn

9
Skull

Fast Uppercut Recovery
788-322

No Power
044-440

Silent Kombat
300-300

Throwing Disabled
100-100

Throwing Encouraged
010-010

Blocking Disabled
020-020

Winner Fights Smoke
205-205

Winner Fights Noob
769-342

Winner Fights Shao Kahn
969-141

Winner Fights Mutaro
033-564

Randper Kombat
444-444

No Fear
282-282

Flipper Message
987-666

Wavenet UMK3 Message
550-550

Version Number Message
999-999

"Don't Jump At Me"
448-844

Rain Is in the Graveyard
717-313

"Skunky"
122-221

Ed Boon Message
004-400

No Power Bars
987-123

Dark Fighting
688-422

Psycho Kombat
985-125

Play Hidden Game
642-468

Uppercut Recovery
788-322

Unlimited Running
466-466

Super Run Jumps
321-789

Health Recovery
975-310

Combos Disabled
722-722

Special Moves Disabled
555-556

Special Endurance Kombat
024-689

Automatic Kombos
484-484

Bloody Kombat
109-901

"Babalities Are Reversible"
202-808

Winner Fights Chameleon
123-321

Explosive Kombat/Throwing Disabled
022-220

Explosive Kombat
227-227

Jade's Desert
330-033

Scorpion's Lair
666-444

Bell Tower
091-190

Graveyard
666-333

Scislac Busorez
933-933

Subway
880-088

Noob's Dorfen
050-050

The Roof
343-343

Pit 3
820-028

Khan's Kave
004-700

River Kombat
002-003

Komat Temple
600-040

The Street
079-035

The Soul Chamber
123-901

The Bridge
077-022

Kahn's Tower
880-220

Dead Pool
222-222

The Armory
191-191

The Pit
919-919

Star Bridge
606-606

The Tower
101-010

The Portal
007-007

The Pit 2
166-661

The Courtyard
121-121

The Wasteland
212-212

The Lair
000-666

Bonus Audio
Put the game disk in an audio CD player.

MOTO RACER

Enable All 10 Tracks
At the title screen quickly press Up (2), Left, Right, Down (2) Circle, R2, Triangle, X.

Enable All 10 Reverse Tracks
At the title screen quickly press Down (2), Right, Left, Up (2), Circle, L2, Triangle, X.

Reverse Mode
At the title screen quickly press Left, Right, Left, Right, Circle (2) R1, L1, Triangle, X.

Pocket Bike Mode
At the title screen quickly press Up, Down, R2, L2, Down, Up, L1, X.

50 Km/h All Bikes
At the title screen quickly press Down (3), Circle, L1, Circle, L2, Down (3), X.

Turbo Boosted Bikes
At the title screen quickly press Up (3), Triangle, R1, Triangle, R2, Up (2), X.

Future Vehicles
At the title screen quickly press Up (3), Down, L1, R2, L2, R1, Circle, X.

Night Tracks
At the title screen quickly press Up, Circle, L1, Down, Triangle, L2, Circle, Left, R1, X.

Bike Only, No Rider
At the title screen quickly press Left (2), Triangle, Right (2), Up, Down, L1, R1, X.

Rider Only, No Bike
At the title screen quickly press Right (2), Circle, Left (2), Down, Up, L2, R2, X.

View credits
At the title screen quickly press Circle, Triangle, Circle (2) Triangle, Circle, Up, Right, Left, X.

Victory FMV Sequence
At the title screen quickly press Circle, Triangle, Circle, Triangle, Circle, Triangle, L1, Up, R2, X.

MOTO RACER 2

Bonus Track
Press R1, R2, Up, Left, Triangle.

Faster Bikes
Press Up (3), Right, Left, Triangle, X.

MOTO RACER: WORLD TOUR

In freestyle, press and hold L2 while jumping. Then enter one of these codes and release L2.

Hart Attack
Right, Left, Down, Up, Left

Cliffhanger
Right, Left, Down, Up, Down

Aerial
Left, Right

Double Cancan
Left, Up, Right, Up, Left

Nacnac
Left, Down, Right, Down, Left

Nacnac
Right, Down, Left, Down, Right

Tailstand
Down (2)

Front Fender Grab
Up (2)

Slower Commentaries
At the main menu press Down, Up (2), Right, Triangle, Square, R2.

Unlock Everything
At the main menu press Square, Triangle, Circle (2), Up (2), Left.

MOTOR TOON GRAND PRIX

Advanced Options
Hold L1, L2, R1, and R2, at the Options menu.

Quick Start
Press the gas (X) right when the light turns yellow.

Quick Acceleration
Hold the acceleration button and reverse button.

Ghost Races
Hold R1 while accessing the "memory card" option to watch Sony's best of the best race.

MOTOR TOON GRAND PRIX 2

Super Speed
Hold down reverse while accelerating to get and stay at top speed.

Turbo Start
At the starting line hold down the accelerator when the yellow light comes on.

Advanced Options
When getting items at the Options menu, press and hold L1, L2, R1, and R2.

Perfect Run Mode
When you select "Replay Video," press R1.

Ghost Races
When getting any memory card option, press and hold R1. Now you can race or watch the Sony team's best runs.

View FMV Sequence
Once all the debug codes have been entered, select "Replay Video," then press R1 and X.

Debug Mode
Select "Goodies" at the main menu, hold L1, L2, R1, or R2, and press Select. Four numbers appear in the right lower corner. Enter hexadecimal number combinations in the debug value: R1=1, R2=2, L1=4, and L2=8. For the number 6, enter R2 and L1.

Extra Characters
Debug Number: 4E+43

Extra Tracks
Debug Number: 4154

Tank Combat
Debug Number: 5443

Submarine X
Debug Number: 5358

Motor Toon R
Debug Number: 4631

MOTORHEAD

Division Two Cars and Trucks
Enter COWRULES in the Options menu.

Division One Cars and Trucks
Enter FRAGTIME in the Options menu.

Nobly Hills Track
Enter TURBOMOS in the Options menu.

All Cars and Tracks
Enter LASTCODE in the Options menu.

Faster View
Enter SOFTHEAD in the Options menu.

Overhead View
Enter SUPERCAR in the Options menu.

Alternate Demos
Enter INSANITY in the Options menu.

Disable All Cheats
Enter NOCHEATS in the Options menu.

Alternate Credits
At the credits screen, hold L1+L2+R1+R2+ Square+Circle to change the names.

Bonus Credit Message
Enter SH4 as a name on the High Score screen. A bonus message scrolls on the credits screen.

Bouncing Cars
Find the alley to the left on the outside of the Atlantika Central Station. From here drive to the left corner on the right side of the building in less than 20 seconds.

Jeep-Like Cars
Stop next to the doors of the Black Lotus club for about 15 seconds.

Alternate External View
Stop on the heli-bridge for 10 seconds.

Lunar Gravity
Drive into the left garage door with Digital Illusions signs in Nolby Hills over 75 kph.

MTB DIRT CROSS

Bonus Riders
On Normal difficulty complete the Full Season mode to unlock two new characters.

Bonus Course
On Hard difficulty, remain in first place in all races to unlock the MTB Park course, then place first in that course to unlock other modes.

MTV MUSIC GENERATOR

Jay-Z and Limp Bizkit FMV Sequences
Hold R1 and press Triangle, Circle, Square, Left, Right at the main menu.

MTV SPORTS: SKATEBOARDING FEATURING ANDY McDONALD

Unlock Everything
Enter your name as PASWRD.

MTV SPORTS: SNOWBOARDING

Alaska Level in Challenge
Rant first in the MTV Challenge.

Play as Tsering
In the Alaska challenge, obtain 8,000 points.

MTV SPORTS: T.J. LAVIN'S ULTIMATE BMX

Unlock New Two-Player Tracks
Play TJ's Backyard in the Pro Circuit. Above the van, you see a floating Key. Grab it to unlock the Warehouse Rocks Track in Two-Player Mode. After you have the first Key, another appears in TJ's Backyard. Grab it to unlock the Two-Player Underground Track.

MULAN

Level Skip
Enter L1(2), L2, R1, R2, R2, Square at the main menu. Press X during gameplay to skip levels

THE MUMMY

Unlock Cheats
To enter the cheat codes, pause the game, select Quit, Replay Level, Bonus Game Modes, then press the code.

All Weapons
Circle, Square, Circle, X, X, Triangle, Triangle, Square or finish the game at any percentage.

Unlock Cairo Level
Triangle, X, Triangle, Circle, Square, Triangle, Circle, X or finish the game with a minimum of 50%.

Infinite Ammunition
X, Triangle, X, Square, Circle, Triangle, Square, Triangle or finish the game with a minimum of 55%.

Infinite Lives
Circle, Circle, Triangle, Circle, X, Square, Square, X or finish the game with a minimum of 60%.

Invincibility
Triangle, X, Circle, Circle, Square, X, Triangle, Square or finish the game with a minimum of 65%.

All Cheats
Finish the game with a minimum of 78%.

MUPPET RACE MANIA

All Tracks
Press Circle, Triangle, X, Circle, Triangle, X, Circle, Triangle, Square, X at the title screen.

Reset the Game
Press Triangle, X, Circle, X, Square (2), X, Circle, X, Triangle at the title screen to erase everything you've earned.

Interchangeable Muppets
Press Triangle, Circle, Triangle, Square, Triangle, X, Triangle (2), X, Circle at the title screen. This unlocks all characters and their vehicles and lets you change characters and their vehicles.

Instant Stars on Every Course
Press Square (2), Circle (2), X, Circle, Triangle, Circle, Triangle, Square at the title screen.

Unlock the Studio Bonus Course
Press Square (2), Circle (2), X, Circle, Triangle, Circle, Triangle, Square at the title screen.

Food on Every Course
Press Square, Circle, X, Circle, Square, Triangle, Circle, X, Circle, Triangle at the title screen.

Unlock the Arches Bonus Course
Press Square, Circle, X, Circle, Square, Triangle, Circle, X, Circle, Triangle at the title screen.

All Dozers
Press X, Square, X, Square, X, Square, Triangle, Circle, X, Square at the title screen.

Unlock the Fraggle Rock Bonus Course
Press X, Square, X, Square, X, Square, Triangle, Circle, X, Square at the title screen.

Ending Credits and Extra Courses
Press Circle, Triangle, Square, Triangle, X, Triangle, Square, Circle, Triangle, X at the title screen.

MYST

Secret Message
Begin a new game and turn left immediately to see a door. Go in and head downstairs. Turn around when you reach the bottom. Click on the piece of paper and click on a button at the top left. Two numbers are revealed. Enter 47. Turn around to the cauldron and click on the button for a message.

N GAUGE WORLD TRAIN SIMULATION

Bonus Route
Place first in two routes in Time Attack mode.

N2O: NITROUS OXIDE

Level Select
Press Square, Circle, X, Triangle (2), X, Circle, X as a password. Any level up to 30 is accessible.

Bonus Level Select
Press Square (3), Triangle, Circle, Triangle, Square (2) as a password.

Weapons
Press Square, X, Circle, Square, X, Square, Circle, Square as a password.

Infinite Lives
Press Circle, X (2), Triangle, Square, Triangle, Square, Circle as a password.

Hidden Ship
Press X (3), Square, Triangle, Circle, X, Triangle as a password.

No Bonus Points Reset
Press Square, Triangle, X, Triangle, Circle, Square, Triangle, X as a password.

Firewalls
Press X (2), Square, X (3), Triangle (2) as a password.

H2O Mode
Press Circle, X, Square, Triangle (2), Circle, Triangle, Circle as a password.

Disable Cheats
Press Square (2), X, Circle (4), Triangle as a password.

Level 3
Circle, X, Circle (2), Square, Triangle, X, Triangle

Level 4
Circle (2), Triangle, Circle, Triangle, Circle, Square (2)

Level 5
Square, Triangle, Square, Triangle, Square, Triangle (2), Circle

Level 6
Square (2), Circle, Square, Triangle, X, Triangle, X

Level 7
X, Triangle, Circle, Square, X, Triangle, Circle, Triangle

Level 8
Square, Circle (2), Triangle (2), Square, Triangle, Square

Level 9
Square, Circle, X, Triangle, Square (2), X, Circle

Level 10
X, Triangle, Square, Circle, Triangle, X (3)

Level 11
Circle, Square, Triangle, Square, Circle, Triangle, Square, Triangle

Level 12
Circle, X (3), Triangle, X (2), Square

Level 13
Square, Triangle (2), Circle (2), X, Circle (2)

Level 14
Square (2), Triangle, Circle (2), Triangle, Circle, X

Level 15
Circle, Triangle, X, Square, Circle, Triangle (3)

Level 16
Circle, Square, Triangle, X, Circle (3), Square

Level 17
X, Circle, Triangle, X, Square (3), Circle.

Level 18
Circle, Triangle, Circle (2), Triangle, Square (2), X

Level 19
Square, X, Circle, Square, Circle, X (2), Triangle

Level 20
Circle, Square, Triangle, Square (5)

Level 21
Circle (4), Triangle, X, Triangle, Circle

Level 22
Circle, X, Circle, Triangle, X, Circle, Triangle, X

Level 23
Square (2), Triangle, Circle, Triangle, X, Circle, Triangle

Level 24
Circle (2), Square, Triangle, Square, Triangle (2), Square

Level 25
Circle, X, Triangle, X, Square, Triangle, X, Circle

Level 26
Square, Circle (3), X, Circle, X (2)

Level 27
Square (2), Triangle, Circle, X (2), Square, Triangle

NAGANO WINTER OLYMPICS '98

Medal in All Events
At the title screen press Up, Down, Left, Right, Triangle, Circle, Square, Left (2), Right, Down (2), Up, Triangle, X.

View End Sequence
At the Options screen press L1, R2, Circle, Square, Triangle. A sound confirms correct entry. Then choose a Russian country and enter the name "TWY."

NAMCO MUSEUM VOL. 1

Double Ships
In *Galaga*, when you see the ship with a purplish beam, fly into the beam (make sure you have at least two lives). The beam takes your ship. Shoot the ship that took your ship, then your ship comes back with your other ship and you have a double ship.

Mach Speed *Pac-Man*
With this title there is a *lot* of loading time, but this is a little trick to help pass make the loading time go faster. When you have up the "Now Loading" screen showing the little Pac-Man running around, push any button repeatedly, and he runs faster. Tap the button with super speed, and he becomes a blur!

Safe Mode in *Galaga*
As the ships fly in formation on the screen, don't shoot them. Locate the two blue and yellow ships in the first vertical row on the left. When all the ships are on the screen, shooting, but don't shoot the two mentioned here. After you destroy all but these 2 ships, let them fly around, shooting at you for about 15 minutes. At this point, they stop shooting. Blow them away. From now on, no ships will shoot at you!

Unlimited Lives in *Toy Pop*
In *Toy Pop*, if you die, keep pressing Select, then X.

NAMCO MUSEUM VOLUME 2

Dragon Buster: Increase Vitality
Press Select at the *Dragon Buster* title screen, then press L1 and R1 when your vitality is below 33 to raise it to 128.

Dragon Buster: Level Skip
After loading the game, press Triangle. Press Switch 5 in Box SW2 by hitting X while the switch is lit. Then at the Map screen, hold L1, R1, Circle, and Start until your level appears.

Gaplus: Level Select
Load the game and press Triangle to display the Dip Switch screen. Then, flip Switch 4 in Box SW3 by holding X while it is highlighted. Play the game, then when "Parsec 1" appears, hold L1, R1, Circle, and press Start. Press Up or Down to find the desired level number on the left side of the screen and press Start to begin at that level.

Grobda: Level Select
At the *Grobda* title screen, hold L1, L2, R1, R2, and Start. Choose a level from the Selection screen.

Extra Credit
While playing any game, press Select.

Mappy: Level Skip
Load the game and press Triangle to show the Dip Switch screen. Press Switch 5 in Box SW3 by pressing X while it is highlighted. Begin the game. Press L1, R1, and X to skip to the next level.

Super Pac-Man: Level Skip
Load the game and press Triangle to show the Dip Switch screen. Press Switch 6 in Box SW3 by pressing X while it is highlighted. Play the game until "Ready" appears before the beginning of a level. Then hold L1, R1, Circle, and Start. The screen flashes and you skip a level.

Hidden Game
Select "Cutie Q" from the Start menu and press Circle (7), Square (6), and X (5) to play "Bomb Bee."

NAMCO MUSEUM VOLUME 3

Galaxian: Turbo Mode
During Demo mode, press Select (32) to add to the "Credits" total in the screen's bottom right corner. The number "32" is displayed. Hold Select and press Start to begin in Turbo mode.

Galaxian: Increase Difficulty
Beat Level 9. During the next Demonstration mode, press Triangle. Use the new rank selection on the Options screen to access the new difficulty setting.

Galaxian: Color Trail Mode
Score at least 30,000 points. Press Triangle during the next Demonstration mode. Highlight the "Test" option and press X, then highlight the "Dip Sw" option and press X. Press Up to press Switch 6. Now all the ships have colored trails.

Pole Position 2: Alternate Tracks
Press Triangle to display the Options menu and select "Test." Press Triangle when the "Test" screen appears. Select "Dip Sw" to display the Dip Switch screen. Press Up to press Switch 1 in the left box. Return to the Options screen and select "Game." After the game loads, press Triangle and select the new "Course" option. All four tracks are now different.

The Tower of Druaga: Bonus Machine
In the Museum, hold L1, R1 and press Up, Right, Down, Left, Up, Right, Down, Left, Up, Right, Down, Left. A pickaxe appears in the screen's bottom left. Move forward in the Tower of Druaga area until you see a brick wall. Press X to reveal another Tower of Druaga machine and an FMV sequence.

NAMCO MUSEUM VOLUME 4

Alternate Introduction
While the game is loading and the Namco logo crosses the screen, hold L1 and R1 to see the introduction sequence from the Genji and Heiki Clan.

Hidden Game
Enter the Museum and go to the *Return of Ishtar* room. Then press Right, Left, Up, Down, Circle to start a different version of *Return to Ishtar*.

NANOTEK WARRIOR

Special Weapons
Enter X, Square, Triangle, Circle, Square, Circle, X, Triangle, X as a password.

Black Nanotek Ship
Enter X, Square, X, Square (2), Circle, X, Triangle, X as a password. The ship begins with four lives and all weapons.

Enable Memory Card
Insert a memory card before starting. Then pause and enter Left, Right, Left (2), R2, Circle, L1, X. You hear the power-up sound. Quit the game after completing Level 2 to see a different password screen with five save game slots.

Full Shield
Pause, then press Select, Circle, Right, Up (2), L1 (2), X. You hear the power-up sound.

Warp Speed
Pause, then press Circle, Square, Circle, Square, Triangle (3), X. You hear the power-up sound.

Stop Ship
Pause, then press Triangle, Left, Triangle, Right, Triangle, Up, Triangle, Start. You hear the power-up sound. Now press Triangle to stop your ship.

Random Curving
Pause, then press Circle, Select, Left, Square (2), Down, Up, X. You hear the power-up sound.

Cockpit View
Pause, then press Triangle, Circle, Square (2), Triangle (2), Select, Start. You should hear the power-up sound.

Rotate Enemy and Obstacle Positions
Pause, then press R1 (2), Up, Circle, Square, Triangle, L2, X. You hear the power-up sound. Enemies and obstacles are in different places.

Camera Lock
Pause, then press Circle, Square, Triangle (2), Circle, Square, Triangle, Start. You hear the power-up sound.

Destructible Obstacles
Pause, then press Square, Circle, R2 (2), Left, Up, Down, X. You hear the power-up sound.

Full Story
Insert the game disk into a PC compatible CD-ROM drive. Open the Games folder and select the STORY.TXT file.

Screenshots
Insert the game disk into a PC compatible CD-ROM drive. Open the .JPG files with a graphics program.

Level 2 Password (Normal Difficulty)
Square, Triangle, X, Triangle, Square, X, Square, Triangle, X

Level 3 Password
Triangle, Square, X, Triangle, Square, Triangle, X, Square, X

Bonus 1 Password
Square, Circle, X, Triangle, Square, Circle, Triangle, Circle, X

Level 4 Password
X, Triangle, Square, X, Square, Triangle, X, Square, Circle

Level 5 Password
Circle, Triangle, Square, X, Square, Circle, X, Circle, Square

Level 6 Password
Triangle, Circle, Square, X, Square, Triangle, X, Circle, X

Bonus 2 Password
Square (3), X, Square (2), Triangle (2), Square

Level 7 Password
X, Triangle, X, Circle, Square, X, Triangle, Circle, Square

Level 8 Password
Square, Triangle, X, Circle, Square, X, Triangle, Circle, X

Level 2 Password (Hard Difficulty)
Square, X, Triangle, X, Square, Triangle, X, Square, Circle

Level 3 Password
X, Square, Triangle, X, Square, Circle, X, Square, Triangle

Bonus 1 Password
Square, Circle, Triangle, X, Square, Triangle, Circle, Square, X

Level 4 Password
X, Triangle, Circle, X, Square, Triangle, Circle, Square, Triangle

Level 5 Password
Square, Triangle, Circle, X, Square, Triangle, X, Circle, X

Level 6 Password
Triangle, Square, Circle, Triangle, X, Circle, Square, Circle, Triangle

Bonus 2 Password
Circle, Square, Circle, Triangle, X, Triangle, Square, Circle, X

Level 7 Password
Triangle, X, Triangle, Circle, X, Square, X, Square, Triangle

Level 8 Password
Square, X, Triangle, Circle, X, Square, Triangle, Square, X

NASCAR 2000

Race as Davey Allison
At the Car Selection screen, press R1, L1, R1, L1, Square, R2, L2, R2, L2, Circle.

Race as Bobby Allison
At the Car Selection screen, press L1, R1, L1, R1, Square, L2, R2, L2, R2, Circle.

Race as Alan Kulwicki
At the Car Selection screen, press L1, R1, L2, R2, Square, R1, L1, R2, L2, Circle.

Race as Benny Parsons
At the Car Selection screen, press L1, R2, R1, L2, Square, R2, L1, R1, L2, Circle.

Race as David Pearson
At the Car Selection screen, press L1, R1, R2, L2, Square, R1, L1, L2, R2, Circle.

Race as Cale Yarbaro
At the Car Selection screen, press L1, L2, R1, R2, Square, R1, R2, L1, L2, Circle.

Montana Track
At the Car Selection screen, press L1 (2), R1, R2, Square, L2 (2), R2 (2), Circle.

Waving Driver
In Single-player mode, select "cockpit view," then hold Select until the driver waves.

NASCAR 2001

Black Box Classic Car
Beat the Short Track Challenge.

Black Box Exotic Car
Beat the Half Season.

EA Sports Car
Win the Road Course Challenge.

EA.com Car
Beat the Superspeedway Shootout under either Veteran or Legend Difficulty settings.

Play as Asher Boldt
Go to the credits and select "Development." When the credits roll, enter "Development" as a code, hold L2, and press Square, Circle, Triangle, X.

Treasure Island Track
Beat a season under the Veteran Difficulty setting.

John Andretti's Second Car
Select "Credits", then "Development" at the Options menu. Wait for the FMV sequence to complete, then hold R1 and press Square, Triangle, Square, Triangle when the credits begin to roll.

Proving Grounds Track
Select "Credits," then "Developers" at the Options menu. Wait for the FMV sequence to complete, then hold R1 and press Left, Circle, Down, Right (3).

NASCAR '98

Pinnacle Trading Cards Car
Highlight Bobby Labonte's car at the Car Selection screen in Exhibition mode, then hold X and press Up, Down.

EA Sports Car
Highlight Kenny Wallace's car at the Car Selection screen in Exhibition mode, then hold X and press Up, Down.

Turbo Mode Option
At the Options screen, hold Circle and press Up, Left, Down, Right. The game's frame rate increases at the screen's bottom.

Paintball Mode
Pause, then display the Race Statistics screen. Press L1, L2, R1, R2, Triangle until you hear an engine. Press Triangle to shoot paintballs.

Faster Settings
In the Car Setup screen, adjust the tire pressure to the maximum, wedge to the minimum, rear spoiler to the minimum, and gear ratios to the maximum.

Waving Driver
Select the view in which you can see the driver and the steering wheel. Then while driving, hold Triangle until the driver waves.

NASCAR '99

Race as Bobby Allison
From the main menu, select Single Race and choose Charlotte. Then, from the "Select Car" option, press Left, Up, Right, Square, X, Circle, L1, L2, R2, R1 within four seconds. You hear an engine sound.

Race as Davey Allison
From the main menu, select Single Race and choose Talladega. Then, from the "Select Car" option, press Up, X, Down, R1, Left, Circle, Right, Square, L2, R2 within four seconds. You hear an engine sound.

Race as Alan Kulwicki
From the main menu, select Single Race and choose Bristol. Then, from the "Select Car" option, press R1 (2), R2 (2), Square (2), Circle (2), X (2) within four seconds. You hear an engine sound.

Race as Benny Parsons
From the main menu, select Single Race and choose Richmond. Then, from the "Select Car" option, press R2 (2), L1 (2), L2 (2), R1 (2), R2, L1 within four seconds. You hear an engine sound.

Race as Richard Petty
From the main menu, select Single Race and choose Martinsville. Then, from the "Select Car" option, press Up, R1, Right, Circle, Down, X, Left, Square, L1, R1 within four seconds. You hear an engine sound.

Race as Cale Yarbaro
From the main menu, select Single Race and choose Darlington. Then, from the "Select Car" option, press Up (3), Square (3), Left, Circle (2), Left within four seconds. You hear an engine sound.

Turbo Mode
At the Race Set-up screen, hold down Circle and press Up, Left, Down, Right.

Waving Driver
Select Cockpit view, then hold Select until the driver waves.

NASCAR RACING

Hidden Minigame
Press Start on controller two during the title sequence to play the hidden game.

NASCAR RUMBLE

Unlock All Tracks and Legend Drivers
Select "Game Options" at the main menu, highlight "Load and Save," press Left, then press X to enter the Password screen. Type C9P5AU8NAA.

NBA BASKETBALL 2000

Unlock Larry Bird
Get more than 20 points at the Superstar level in the three-point contest.

NBA FASTBREAK '98

Infinite Money
At the team selection screen, hold Select and press L1, L2, R1 (2), Up (2).

NBA HANGTIME

Cheat Codes
At the Tonight's Matchup screen, press Turbo for the first number, Shoot for the second number, and Pass for the third number. Press these buttons the number of times indicated below.

Tournament Mode
1-1-1

Fast Paced
1-2-0

Stealth Turbo
2-7-3

Maximum Speed
2-8-4

No Pushing
3-9-0

Unlimited Turbo
4-6-1

Hyper Speed
5-5-2

Maximum Block
6-1-6

Quick Hands
7-0-9

Maximum Power
8-0-2

Goal Tending
9-3-7

Hidden Players
Enter the following names and PIN numbers at the Enter Name prompt screen.

Penny Hardaway
AHRDWY 0000

Dan Amrich
AMRICH 2020-

BARDO 6000-

CARLOS 1010

Cliff Robinson
CLIFFR 0000-

DANIEL 0604

Dan Roan
DANR 0000

David Robinson
DAVIDR 0000

Sal Divita
DIVITA 0201

Hakeem Olajuwon
DREAM 0000-

EDDIE 6213

Sean Elliot
ELLIOT 0000-

EUGENE 6767

Patrick Ewing
EWING 0000

Development Team Picture
FUNCOM 1993

Grant Hill
GHILL 0000

Glen Rice
GLENNR 0000

Horace Grant
HGRANT 0000

Jamie Rivett
JAMIE 1000-

JAPPLE 6660-

JASON 0729-

JC 0000-

JIGGET 1010-

JFER 0503

Jon Hey
JONHEY 6000

Larry Johnson
JOHNSN 0000

Shawn Kemp
KEMP 0000

Jason Kidd
KIDD 0000

Ed Boon (*Mortal Kombat* Programmer)
KOMBAT 0004

Karl Malone
MALONE 0000-

MARIUS 1003-

MARTY 1010

Intro Rapper
MDOC 2099-

MEDNIK 6000

Reggie Miller
MILLER 0000-

MINIFE 6000

Air Morris
MORRIS 6000

John Tobias (*Mortal Kombat* Programmer)
MORTAL 0004

Dikembe Motumbo
MOTUMB 0000

Alonzo Mourning
MOURNI 0000

Larry Munday
MUNDAY 5432

Gheorghe Muresan
MURSAN 0000-

MXV 1014-

NICK 7000

Announcer
NFUNK 0101-

NOBUD 1010-

NORTH 5050-

PATF 2000

Joe Perry
PERRY 3500

Scottie Pippen
PIPPEN 0000-

QUIN 0330-

RICE 0000

Dennis Rodman
RODMAN 0000

John Root
ROOT 6000-

SHAWN 0123

Rik Smits
SMITS 0000

S Oursler
SNO 0103

Jerry Stackhouse
STACKH 0000

John Starks
STARKS 0000

Mark Turmell
TURMEL 0322

Spud Webb
WEBB 0000

Chris Webber
WEBBER 0000

NBA HOOPZ

Cheat Mode
Press Square, X, Circle to change the icons on the Versus screen. The numbers in the list below indicate the number of times to press each button. After you change the icons, press the D-Pad in the indicated direction to access the code. The name of the code and a sound will confirm correct code entry. For example, to enter 1-2-3 Left, press Square, X, X, Circle, Circle, Circle, Left.

Infinite Turbo
3-1-2 Up

Beach Court
0-2-3 Left

Street Court
3-2-0 Left

ABA Ball
1-1-1 Right

Granny Shots
1-2-1 Left

Show Shot%
0-1-1 Down

Show Hotspot
1-1-0 Down

No Goaltending
4-4-4 Left

Big Heads
3-0-0 Right

Tiny Heads
3-3-0 Left

Tiny Players
5-4-3 Left

NBA IN THE ZONE

Alley-Oop
Press Square+X while your ball carrier is in the paint and another teammate is nearby.

Fake Pass
Tap Square when you have possession of the ball.

Double Clutch Dunks
Press Left while dunking.

Fade Away Jump Shots
Press Away+Square while shooting.

NBA IN THE ZONE 2

Unlock All-Star Team
Select "Start" on the title screen and hold L1, R2, Select, and Start until the screen fades. The All-Star team becomes available in Exhibition mode.

Play as Magic Johnson
Create a new player, then select model 25.

Play as Larry Bird
Create a new player, then select model 29.

Play as Michael Jordan
Already on the roster, named M.GUARD on the Bulls.

Play as Shaquille O'Neil
Already on the roster, named S.CENTER on the Lakers.

Play as Charles Barkley
Already on the roster, named C.FORWARD on the Rockets.

NBA IN THE ZONE '98

Alley-Oop
Press Square+X while your ball carrier is in the paint and another teammate is nearby.

Dunks
Hold Turbo and press Shoot when you approach the basket.

NBA JAM EXTREME

Big Feet
When exiting the Big Head Selection screen, hold Left.

Short Players with Big Heads
On the Big Head Selection screen, press Up, Down, Left, Right, Down, then hold Up and select "Yes."

Hidden Minigame
When exiting the Select screen in a four-player game, hold Up, Extreme on all four D-Pads.

Marshmallow Treats
Right before the screen dims at the end of the title sequence, hold Up on all D-Pads.

Select Hidden Team
Press Down, Turbo to make cursor and team choices disappear while they are being selected.

Select Random Team
At the Team Selection screen, press Up, Turbo.

Select Random Player
After selecting a random team, press Up, Turbo.

Hidden Stats
On the Team Selection screen, press Left, Extreme to see each player's stats.

Joke Screen
Hold Start while you turn on your PlayStation to see a screen that resembles assembly and C code.

Access All Teams
On the Initials screen, hold L1 and R1 and enter the initials YME and the date May 17.

Hidden Teams
At the Initials screen, hold L1 and R1 and enter one of the following initials and dates.

Sculptured Team
Dwain Skinner
DAS 2/21

Dave Ross
DJR 6/8

Jeff Peters
JBP 5/17

Daren Smith
DRS 4/10

Mike Callahan
MWC 5/1

The TinMan
TIM 1/24

Sculptured Team
Mark Ganus
MMG 9/16

Roy Wilkins
RNW 9/15

Rob Dautel
RAD 3/19

James Hebdon
JPH 4/26

Dean Morrell
DSM 5/9

Mike Peery
MJP 5/26

Squid Team
Melissa Pardike
MAP 3/26

Jane Bradley
JLB 5/23

Jonathan Dansie
JWD 8/2

Lee Phung
LEE 1/1

Jason Greenberg
JAY 4/18

Chris Hawkes
CDH 2/21

Acclaim Team
Weasel
DAN 2/1

Magic Hair
SET 12/8

Samoa
-

Sequioa
SDR 4/10

Air Nick
-

Pistol
WAN 6/10

Acclaim Team
Mark Shafer ("Chaos")
XTL 5/2

Bob Davidson ("Striker")
RAD 10/18

Fumongous
GUN 1/11

Geoff Higgins ("Clouseau")
GCH 4/13

Air Dog
SAM 1/21

Ice Princess
MDK 12/24

Celebrity Team
Junior Seau
JR 6/1

John Elway
WAY 9/30

Frank Thomas
BIG 12/6

Marv Albert
MRV 12/31

Newt Gingrich
NEW 8/12

Samoa
TVH 6/6

Special Sports Team
Cheryl Swoopes
SWO 1/1

Rebecca Lobo
LOB 7/4

Carol Blazejowski ("Blaze")
BLZ 3/1

Bob Lanier
LAN 9/10

Air Nick
ARN 5/18

George Gervin
ICE 4/27

Misfit Team
Stinger
MSS 10/26

Shamrock
JHG 8/26

Diamond Dave
DJP 6/29

Chris Slate ("Hacker")
JCS 12/8

Todd Mowatt ("Cowboy")
TVC 10/3

Richard Szeto ("Richito")
RTS 2/25

Happy Team
Pirate Bill
SAL 2/2

Mr. Happy
MJT 3/22

Dufus the Clown
GRR 6/19

Three Feet Under
TOD 4/17

Mr. Unhappy
GEM 11/3

Ooohh
JLH 1/26

Invisible Team

Who
WHO 1/1

Brained
BCS 1/7

Monkey Boy
PJP 11/2

Howie
BCE 7/10

Jim Jung
JKJ 12/13

Huh
CBR 6/25

Rookie Team (Jason Caffey, Randolph Childress, Kevin Garnett, Alan Henderson, Antonio McDyess, Shawn Respert)
SCT 11/14

Rookie Team (Lawrence Moten, Cherokee Parks, Bryant Reeves, Joe Smith, Kurt Thomas, Ed O'Bannon)
REG 1/17

Rookie Team (Jerry Stackhouse, Gary Trent, Corliss Williamson, Damon Stoudamire, Rasheed Wallace, Antonio McDyess)
BAP 8/11

All-Star East Team (Reggie Miller, Alonzo Mourning, Scottie Pippen, Glen Rice, Juwan Howard, Patrick Ewing)
EST 3/14

All-Star West Team (Clyde Drexler, Sean Elliott, Shawn Kemp, Jason Kidd, Karl Malone, John Stockton)
WST 7/12

All-Star West Team (Dikembe Mutombo, Hakeem Olajuwon, Gary Payton, Mitch Richmond, David Robinson, John Stockton)
RMC 4/21

Keep Record Screen Codes

Enter codes on the Keep Record screen one pair of letters at a time. Enter the first pair, then backspace twice, then enter the next pair and repeat until the code is complete. A sound and flash confirm correct entry.

Start at Playoffs
PL, AY, OF, FS

Start at Finals
FI, NA, LS

Start with 2-0 Playoff Record
CH, EE, SY

Start with 3-0 Finals Record
NO, VI, CE

Shootout for 45 Seconds Before the Game
SH, OO, TO, UT

Sound Test Mode
KA, ZO, O

Pre-game Codes

Begin entering the following codes on the Select screen and complete them on the Versus screen. A sound and player picture confirm correct entry.

Display Shot Percentage
Hold Extreme and Shoot.

Permanent Turbo
Hold Turbo and press Up, Down, Up, Down.

No Turbo Meters
Hold Turbo and Extreme and press Up, Down, Up, Down.

No Crowd
Hold Extreme, Pass, and Up.

Tip-Off Codes

Enter the following codes before the tip-off, while the referee walks out and throws the ball in the air.

No CPU Assistance
Press Extreme, Turbo, Pass (2).

Play with Beach Ball
Press Pass (2), Turbo, Extreme, Turbo, Pass (2).

Play with Soccer Ball
Press Pass (2), Turbo (3), Extreme (3).

Power Push
Press Turbo (2), Pass (2), Turbo (2), Pass (2), Turbo (2), Pass (2), Turbo (2).

Maximum Dunk and Three Points Stat for Each Player
Press Turbo (5), Pass, Extreme, Turbo (6).

Maximum Three Points Stat for Every Player
Press Pass (8), Extreme, Pass (7).

Maximum Rebound Stat for Every Player
Press Pass (2), Extreme, Special, Extreme, Turbo, Extreme, Special, Extreme, Turbo.

Maximum Steal/Block Stat for Every Player
Press Pass (3), Turbo (3), Extreme (3), Pass (3).

Maximum Speed Stat for Every Player
Press Extreme (10), Pass (3).

Goaltending Allowed
Press Extreme (8), Pass, Extreme (9).

High Arc Shots
Press Turbo (5), Pass (2), Turbo (6).

Dribble Under feet
Quickly press Turbo (2).

Dribble Behind back
Quickly press Extreme (2).

Dribble Demo
Quickly press Pass, Turbo, Extreme.

NBA JAM TOURNAMENT EDITION

More Team Players
At the Team Selection screen, hold Select and rotate the D-Pad counterclockwise twice to receive an extended roster.

Infinite Credits
Press Select during the countdown after the game ends.

Quick Hands
At the Tonight's Matchup screen, press Left (4), Circle, Right.

Maximum Power
At the Tonight's Matchup screen, press Right (2), Left, Right, X (2), Right.

High Shots
At the Tonight's Matchup screen, press Up, Down (2), Right, Up, Circle (4), Down.

Push One Opponent and Both Fall
At the Tonight's Matchup screen, press Up (4), Left (4), Circle (2).

Push One Opponent and Teammate Falls
At the Tonight's Matchup screen, press Up (4), Left (4), Circle, Triangle.

Big Head
At the Tonight's Matchup screen, press Triangle, Square, X, Circle, Triangle, Square, X, Circle.

Baby Mode
At the Tonight's Matchup screen, press Circle, Square, Circle, Square, Circle, Square.

Huge Mode
At the Tonight's Matchup screen, press Triangle, X seven times.

Mammoth Head
At the Tonight's Matchup screen, press Circle, X, Square, Triangle four times.

Display Shot Percentage
At the Tonight's Matchup screen, press Up (2), Down (2), Triangle.

Teleport Pass
At the Tonight's Matchup screen, press Up, Right (2), Left, Circle, Down, Left (2), Circle, Square.

Full Court Dunks
At the Tonight's Matchup screen, press Left, Right, X, Circle (2), X.

Powered-Up Defense
At the Tonight's Matchup screen, press Right, Up, Down, Right, Down, Up.

Powered-Up Fire
At the Tonight's Matchup screen, press Down, Right (2), Circle, Triangle, Right.

Powered-Up Three Pointers
At the Tonight's Matchup screen, press Up, Down, Left, Right, Left, Down, Up.

Powered-Up Offense
At the Tonight's Matchup screen, press Square, Circle, Up, Square, Circle, Up, Down.

Powered-Up Turbo
At the Tonight's Matchup screen, press Circle (3), Square, Down (2), Up (2).

Full Court Push
At the Tonight's Matchup screen, press Down (2), X, Circle, X, Right (2).

NBA Jam Champion
At the Initials screen, hold L1+R1 and enter FIN as the initials. Set the date to January 1.

Unlock Adrock
At the Initials screen, hold L1+R1 and enter ADR APRIL 6.

Unlock Alex Delucia
At the Initials screen, hold L1+R1 and enter DEL OCTOBER 19.

Unlock Andy Cattling
At the Initials screen, hold L1+R1 and enter CAT JANUARY 2.

Unlock Asif Chaudri
At the Initials screen, hold L1+R1 and enter CHD MAY 5.

Unlock Barry Hutchinson
At the Initials screen, hold L1+R1 and enter BAR APRIL 9.

Unlock Bill Clinton
At the Initials screen, hold L1+R1 and enter BIL JUNE 3.

Unlock Brett Gow
At the Initials screen, hold L1+R1 and enter GOW JULY 17.

Unlock Carol Blazejowski
At the Initials screen, hold L1+R1 and enter BLZ JANUARY 14.

Unlock Charlotte Hornet
At the Initials screen, hold L1+R1 and enter HOR JUNE 12.

Unlock Chicago Bull
At the Initials screen, hold L1+R1 and enter BEN SEPTEMBER 20.

Unlock Chris Kirby
At the Initials screen, hold L1+R1 and enter CHR DECEMBER 18.

Unlock Darren Falcus
At the Initials screen, hold L1+R1 and enter DAZ AUGUST 6.

Unlock Darren Hodgeson
At the Initials screen, hold L1+R1 and enter HOG DECEMBER 31.

Unlock Darren Tunnicliff
At the Initials screen, hold L1+R1 and enter SAT MAY 7.

Unlock Elizabeth Burgess
At the Initials screen, hold L1+R1 and enter LIZ AUGUST 7.

Unlock Eric Kuby
At the Initials screen, hold L1+R1 and enter KUB APRIL 14.

Unlock Eric Samulski
At the Initials screen, hold L1+R1 and enter AIR JANUARY 21.

Unlock Frank Thomas
At the Initials screen, hold L1+R1 and enter FNK JANUARY 8.

Unlock Fresh Prince
At the Initials screen, hold L1+R1 and enter FRS FEBRUARY 2.

Unlock Hillary Clinton
At the Initials screen, hold L1+R1 and enter HIL NOVEMBER 6.

Unlock Heavy D
At the Initials screen, hold L1+R1 and enter HEA JANUARY 9.

Unlock Jamie Rivett
At the Initials screen, hold L1+R1 and enter REV JULY 6.

Unlock Jason Falcus
At the Initials screen, hold L1+R1 and enter JAS NOVEMBER 16.

Unlock Jason Whitaker
At the Initials screen, hold L1+R1 and enter JAX MARCH 1.

Unlock Jay Moon
At the Initials screen, hold L1+R1 and enter JAY AUGUST 24.

Unlock Jazzy Jeff
At the Initials screen, hold L1+R1 and enter JAZ OCTOBER 9.

Unlock John Carlton
At the Initials screen, hold L1+R1 and enter CAL MARCH 25.

Unlock Kim Gordon
At the Initials screen, hold L1+R1 and enter GOR JULY 3.

Unlock Larry Bird
At the Initials screen, hold L1+R1 and enter LAR JANUARY 15.

Unlock Lee Ronaldo
At the Initials screen, hold L1+R1 and enter REN FEBRUARY 4.

Unlock Mark Thienvanich
At the Initials screen, hold L1+R1 and enter THI NOVEMBER 1.

Unlock Mark Turmell
At the Initials screen, hold L1+R1 and enter TUR JANUARY 31.

Unlock MC Adam Yauch
At the Initials screen, hold L1+R1 and enter MCA APRIL 9.

Unlock Mike D
At the Initials screen, hold L1+R1 and enter M_D JULY 1.

Unlock Mike Muskett
At the Initials screen, hold L1+R1 and enter MUS DECEMBER 24.

Unlock Minnesota Timberwolf
At the Initials screen, hold L1+R1 and enter WOL MARCH 7.

Unlock Nat Gunter
At the Initials screen, hold L1+R1 and enter GUN JANUARY 11.

Unlock Paul McHugh
At the Initials screen, hold L1+R1 and enter BAA JULY 12.

Unlock Pete Wanat
At the Initials screen, hold L1+R1 and enter WAN JUNE 10.

Unlock Phoenix Gorilla
At the Initials screen, hold L1+R1 and enter APE APRIL 2.

Unlock Prince Charles
At the Initials screen, hold L1+R1 and enter CHA MAY 4.

Unlock Rob Gray
At the Initials screen, hold L1+R1 and enter ROB FEBRUARY 24.

Unlock Sal Divita
At the Initials screen, hold L1+R1 and enter DIV JULY 3.

Unlock Seth W. Rosenfield
At the Initials screen, hold L1+R1 and enter STH DECEMBER 8.

Unlock Shawn Liptak
At the Initials screen, hold L1+R1 and enter LIP JANUARY 14.

Unlock Shawn Rosen
At the Initials screen, hold L1+R1 and enter SAW APRIL 10.

Unlock Snake
At the Initials screen, hold L1+R1 and enter SNK JUNE 15.

Unlock Steve Shelly
At the Initials screen, hold L1+R1 and enter SHY JUNE 8.

Unlock Thurston Moore
At the Initials screen, hold L1+R1 and enter MOE JUNE 8.

Unlock Tom Higgins
At the Initials screen, hold L1+R1 and enter TOM FEBRUARY 19.

Unlock Tony Goskie
At the Initials screen, hold L1+R1 and enter GOS JANUARY 6.

Unlock Vaughn Smith
At the Initials screen, hold L1+R1 and enter CCC DECEMBER 2.

Unlock Ziggy Hill
At the Initials screen, hold L1+R1 and enter ZIG APRIL 7.

NBA LIVE '96

Play as Jordan, Barkley, or Magic
Go to the Roster screen before you start a game. Go to the Chicago Bulls and replace one of the current players with "Player." Now Michael Jordan is on the team. Look for "Player" on the Phoenix Suns and Los Angeles Lakers to get Charles Barkley and Magic Johnson, respectively.

NBA LIVE '97

Cheat Menu
At the Game Setup menu, press L1, X (2), L1, X, Square, R1, X, Square, R1, Circle. Ignore the credits screen that may appear. Hold Up-Right+Triangle+Square for five seconds. Then, press Start to load the game. Hold L1+R1+Up+Right+Triangle+X+Square+Circle until the game is loaded. If you did all that correctly, a Cheat menu appears. Use L1 and L2 to control the height of players. Use Up and Down to control the transparency of the player. Use Start and Select on controller one to toggle outdoor courts.

View Credits
Press Circle (4) at the main menu.

Michael Jordan
Put Player #99 on the Chicago Bulls roster.

NBA LIVE '98

Bonus Team One
Enter "EA" as a location and "Europals" as a team name at the Create Custom Team menu.

Bonus Team Two
Enter "Hitmen" as a location and "Coders" as a team name at the Create Custom Team menu.

Bonus Team Three
Enter "Hitmen" as a location and "Allsorts" as a team name at the Create Custom Team menu.

Bonus Team Four
Enter "Hitmen" as a location and "Earplugs" as a team name at the Create Custom Team menu.

Bonus Team Five
Enter "Hitmen" as a location and "Idlers" as a team name at the Create Custom Team menu.

Bonus Team Six
Enter "Hitmen" as a location and "Pixels" as a team name at the Create Custom Team menu.

Bonus Team Seven
Enter "QA" as a location and "Campers" as a team name at the Create Custom Team menu.

Bonus Team Eight
Enter "QA" as a location and "Testubes" as a team name at the Create Custom Team menu.

Bonus Team Nine
Enter "QA" as a location and "DBuggers" as a team name at the Create Custom Team menu.

Bonus Team 10
Enter "TNT" as a location and "Blasters" as a team name at the Create Custom Team menu.

NBA LIVE '99

Bonus Team One
Enter "EA" as a location and "Europals" as a team name at the Create Custom Team menu.

Bonus Team Two
Enter "Hitmen" as a location and "Coders" as a team name at the Create Custom Team menu.

Bonus Team Three
Enter "Hitmen" as a location and "Earplugs" as a team name at the Create Custom Team menu.

Bonus Team Four
Enter "Hitmen" as a location and "Idlers" as a team name at the Create Custom Team menu.

Bonus Team Five
Enter "Hitmen" as a location and "Pixels" as a team name at the Create Custom Team menu.

Bonus Team Six
Enter "Hitmen" as a location and "Rebounds" as a team name at the Create Custom Team menu.

Fake Pass
Press X+R2 while you have the ball.

NBA LIVE 2000

Unlock Michael Jordan
Defeat him one-on-one in Superstar mode.

Unlock Isiah Thomas
Get 15 steals in a Superstar mode game.

Play as Legendary Players
Enter the first name/last name listed below at the Create Player menu. Go to Unlock Legends to activate the player and put him in the free agent pool. The legendary player can be placed on any team.

Andrew Phillip
Whiz/Kid

Bill Sharman
Charity/Stripe

Bob Cousy
B-Balls/Cooz

Bob Pettit
Crash/Boards

Carlo Braun
Hard/Wood

Cliff Hagen
Hook/Shot

Dolph Schayes
Set/Shot

George Yardley
Yard/Bird

Harry Gallatin
Iron/Horse

Larry Costello
Cross/Over

Paul Arizin
Pitchin'/Philli

Richard Guerin
Play/Maker

Bill Russell
All/Defensive

Elgin Baylor
Offensive/Force

Hal Greer
Jump/Shot

Jerry Lucas
Lucas/Layup

Jerry West
The Mr./Clutch

Lenny Winkins
Player/Coach

Oscar Robertson
Bucks/Big O

Sam Jones
Bank/Shot

Tommy Heinsohn
Flat/Shot

Walt Bellamy
No/Comment

Willis Reed
Soft/Touch

Wilt Chamberlain
Big/Goliath

Bill Cunningham
Leaping/Kangaroo

Bill Walton
Shot/Blocker

Bob Lanier
Big/Foot

Dave Bing
The/Duke

Dave Cowens
Red/Head

Earl Monroe
Magic/Pearl

John Havlicek
John/Hondo

Julius Erving
Doctor's/In

Nate Archibald
Big/Tiny

Pete Maravich
Passing/Pistol

Rick Barry
Foul/Shot

Walt Frazier
Cool/Clyde

Wes Unseld
Glass/Cleaner

Charles Barkley
Mound of/Rebound

Dominique Wilkins
High/Light

Earvin Johnson
Magical/Guard

George Gervin
Chilled/Iceman

Hakeem Olajuwon
The Dream/Machine

Isiah Thomas
Bad Boy/Zeke

James Worthy
Big/Game

Karl Malone
Mailman/Delivers

Kevin McHale
Sixth/Man

Larry Bird
Celtics/Pride

Michael Jordan
Come Fly/With Me

Moses Malone
Free/Throws

Patrick Ewing
Player/President

Robert Parish
Celtic/Chief

David Robinson
Spurs/Admiral

Gary Payton
Human/Glove

Grant Hill
Class/Act

John Stockton
Jazz/Man

Mitch Richmond
Live/Coverman

Reggie Miller
Outside/Threat

Scottie Pippen
Complete/Game

Shaquille O'Neal
Little/Warrior

Shawn Kemp
Power/Dunker

NBA SHOOTOUT

View Cheerleaders
Press L1, L2, R1, R2 between quarters or during half time. The stats will be removed and you can see the cheerleaders.

Phoenix All-Star Game
Pick Exhibition mode and press X. At the next screen, press R1, L1, R1, L1, R2, L2, R2, L2. An "All-Star" option appears.

San Antonio All-Star Game
Pick Exhibition mode and press X. At the next screen, press R1 (2), R2 (2), L1, L2, L1, L2. An "All-Star" option appears.

Harder Difficulty
Highlight "Difficulty" on the Options screen and Press L1, R1, L2.

NBA SHOOTOUT '97

All-Star Teams
Select an Exhibition game. At the Team Selection screen, press R1 (2), R2 (2), L1, L2, L1, L2. A fourth option bar appears and you can choose between two different All-Star games.

Players with 100 Percent Attributes
Press and hold Left+Select+Circle+Square at the Create Player Ratings screen.

NBA SHOOTOUT '98

Alley-Oop
When you have the ball and a teammate is near the hoop, press Triangle, Circle, Square, X.

Full Attributes
Create a player with the following characteristics. Enter "NOTHING CAN" as a first name, "SAVE" as a last name, and "YOU" as a college name.

NBA SHOOTOUT 2000

Hidden Easter Egg Menu
While you play the game, press the Start button to pause the game. Now, press L2+R2+Square. You get an Easter Egg menu that you can use.

NBA SHOOTOUT 2001

CD Audio
Place your NBA Shootout 2001 disc into your CD player and advance to track 2. Now you can listen to a few tracks from the game.

NBA SHOWTIME: NBA ON NBC

Different Costumes
Press Up or Down while creating a custom player.

Team Mascots
Enter the name and PIN to play as the team mascot.

Atlanta Hawks
HAWK, 0322

Charlotte Hornets
HORNET, 1105

Chicago Bulls
BENNY, 0503

Denver Nuggets
ROCKY, 0201

Houston Rockets
TURBO, 1111

Indiana Pacers
BOOMER, 0604

Minnesota Timberwolves
CRUNCH, 0503

New Jersey Nets
SLY, 6765

Phoenix Suns
GORILA, 0314

Seattle Sonics
SASQUA, 7785

Toronto Raptors
RAPTOR, 1020

Utah Jazz
BEAR, 1228

NCAA FINAL FOUR '99

Street Court
Pick Exhibition mode and choose to be the visiting team. At the "Shot Meter" selection, press X, then hold L1+L2+R1+R2+X until the game begins.

NCAA FOOTBALL '98

Random Stadium
Press L1+R1 at the Stadium Selection screen.

Bonus Stadiums
Enter COOLSITE as a password at the User Records screen.

FMV at Main Menu
Enter SEE FMV as a password at the User Records screen.

15 Second Quarters
Enter SHORT QUART as a password at the User Records screen.

Fast Players
Enter GB SPEED as a password at the User Records screen.

Electric Table Football Mode
Enter ELECTRICHE as a password at the User Records screen.

Show Team Rankings in Top EA 25
Enter WHOLE POLL as a password at the User Records screen.

NCAA FOOTBALL '99

All Stadiums
Enter OHAMISORE as a name at the User Profile screen. A spoken phrase confirms correct entry.

30 Second Quarters
Enter FASTNFUNKY as a name at the User Profile screen. A spoken phrase confirms correct entry.

See FMV Movies
Enter ILUVMOVIES as a name at the User Profile screen. A spoken phrase confirms correct entry.

Faster Players
Enter CMONGUY as a name at the User Profile screen. A spoken phrase confirms correct entry.

See CPU's Plays
Enter PLAYWIZ as a name at the User Profile screen. A spoken phrase confirms correct entry.

NCAA FOOTBALL 2000

All Exhibition Mode Stadiums
Enter STADSGALORE at the Secret Codes screen.

Maximum Recruiting Points
Enter STAFFUP at the Secret Codes screen.

Super Stats Team
Enter UNSTOPPABLE at the Secret Codes screen.

Maximum Attribute Points
Enter BLUECHIP at the Secret Codes screen.

Receivers Always Catch the Ball
Enter GIMMEDABALL at the Secret Codes screen.

Defense Always Intercepts
Enter PIXGALORE at the Secret Codes screen.

Defense Always Tackles
Enter BRICKWALL at the Secret Codes screen.

Extra Long Kicks
Enter ICBM at the Secret Codes screen.

Faster Game Play
Enter SCRAMBLE at the Secret Codes screen.

Faster Daylight Effects
Enter TIMEFLIES at the Secret Codes screen.

Knock Down Referee for One Point
Enter BADCALL at the Secret Codes screen.

Change Title to NCAA 1900
Enter Y2K at the Secret Codes screen.

Wind at Maximum
Enter SAFETY at the Secret Codes screen.

Complete Poll
Enter CONTROVERSY at the Secret Codes screen.

View CPU Plays
Enter MINDREADER at the Secret Codes screen.

View Entire Rankings
Enter CONTROVERSEY at the Secret Codes screen.

View Introduction Sequence
Enter BIGSCREEN at the Secret Codes screen.

1946 Notre Dame Team
Enter GOLDPAINT at the Secret Codes screen.

1947 Army Team at the Secret Codes screen.
Enter INSIDEOUTSIDE at the Secret Codes screen.

1957 Notre Dame Team
Enter STREAKOVER at the Secret Codes screen.

1959 LSU Team
Enter RIGHTTHISTIME at the Secret Codes screen.

1959 Mississippi Team
Enter HEYREB at the Secret Codes screen.

1962 USC Team
Enter FIGHTFORTROY at the Secret Codes screen.

1962 Wisconsin Team
Enter BUCKY at the Secret Codes screen.

1965 Michigan State Team
Enter BIGGREEN at the Secret Codes screen.

1965 UCLA Team
Enter REVENGE at the Secret Codes screen.

1966 Michigan State Team
Enter NEEDAWIN at the Secret Codes screen.

1966 Notre Dame Team
Enter TAKETHETIE at the Secret Codes screen.

1967 USC Team
Enter WHITEHORSE at the Secret Codes screen.

1967 UCLA Team
Enter PRESSBOX at the Secret Codes screen.

1968 Ohio State Team
Enter 5TITLES at the Secret Codes screen.

1968 USC Team
Enter NICERUN at the Secret Codes screen.

1969 Arkansas Team
Enter WOOPIGSOOEY at the Secret Codes screen.

1969 Texas Team
Enter TEXASFIGHT at the Secret Codes screen.

1970 Ohio State Team
Enter BRUTUS at the Secret Codes screen.

1970 Stanford Team
Enter MVPQB at the Secret Codes screen.

1971 Nebraska Team
Enter GAMEOFCENTURY at the Secret Codes screen.

1971 Oklahoma Team
Enter SCHOONER at the Secret Codes screen.

1973 Alabama Team
Enter PLAYTHEPASS at the Secret Codes screen.

1973 Michigan Team
Enter RUNNERUP at the Secret Codes screen.

1973 Notre Dame Team
Enter GUTSYCALL at the Secret Codes screen.

1973 Ohio State Team
Enter WINNINGVOTE at the Secret Codes screen.

1974 Notre Dame Team
Enter LOSTLEAD at the Secret Codes screen.

1974 USC Team
Enter RALLY at the Secret Codes screen.

1975 Arizona State Team
Enter DEJAVU at the Secret Codes screen.

1975 Nebraska Team
Enter HERBIE at the Secret Codes screen.

1976 Georgia Team
Enter HEDGES at the Secret Codes screen.

1976 Pittsburgh Team
Enter RUSHTD at the Secret Codes screen.

1978 Alabama Team
Enter GOALLINESTAND at the Secret Codes screen.

1978 Penn State Team
Enter SHOULDAPASSED at the Secret Codes screen.

1979 Ohio State Team
Enter JUSTSHORT at the Secret Codes screen.

1979 USC Team
Enter MVPRUN at the Secret Codes screen.

1981 Clemson Team
Enter TOUCHTHEROCK at the Secret Codes screen.

1981 North Carolina Team
Enter NOTHINGFINER at the Secret Codes screen.

1982 Cal Team
Enter THEPLAY at the Secret Codes screen.

1982 Georgia Team
Enter SICEMDAWGS at the Secret Codes screen.

1982 Penn State Team
Enter LIONPRIDE at the Secret Codes screen.

1982 Stanford Team
Enter TROMBONE at the Secret Codes screen.

1983 Miami Team
Enter KNOCKITDOWN at the Secret Codes screen.

1983 Nebraska Team
Enter GOFOR2 at the Secret Codes screen.

1984 Boston College Team
Enter MIRACLE at the Secret Codes screen.

1984 Miami Team
Enter BADLUCK at the Secret Codes screen.

1985 Alabama Team
Enter BLOCKTHATKICK at the Secret Codes screen.

1985 Auburn Team
Enter SMARTBACK at the Secret Codes screen.

1985 Oklahoma Team
Enter UPSETLIONS at the Secret Codes screen.

1985 Penn State Team
Enter SOONERLATER at the Secret Codes screen.

1986 Penn State Team
Enter LINEBACKERINT at the Secret Codes screen.

1986 Miami Team
Enter FATIGUES at the Secret Codes screen.

1987 Miami Team
Enter MONSTERD at the Secret Codes screen.

1987 Oklahoma Team
Enter SLOWSTART at the Secret Codes screen.

1988 Notre Dame Team
Enter LEPRECHAUN at the Secret Codes screen.

1988 UCLA Team
Enter LBBRUINS at the Secret Codes screen.

1988 USC Team
Enter TROJANWAR at the Secret Codes screen.

1988 West Virginia Team
Enter HURTQB at the Secret Codes screen.

1989 Alabama Team
Enter TOOMUCHD at the Secret Codes screen.

1989 Colorado Team
Enter MISSEDCHANCES at the Secret Codes screen.

1989 Notre Dame Team
Enter LIFTOFF at the Secret Codes screen.

1991 Miami Team
Enter SHUTOUT at the Secret Codes screen.

1991 Michigan Team
Enter NICEPOSE at the Secret Codes screen.

1991 Nebraska Team
Enter HITTHEWEIGHTS at the Secret Codes screen.

1991 Washington Team
Enter WILDDOGS at the Secret Codes screen.

1992 Alabama Team
Enter REALMENPLAYZONE at the Secret Codes screen.

1992 Miami Team
Enter TOOTALENTED at the Secret Codes screen.

1993 Florida State Team
Enter TOMAHAWK at the Secret Codes screen.

1993 Nebraska Team
Enter REFUSELOSE at the Secret Codes screen.

1994 Miami Team
Enter RUNOUTSIDE at the Secret Codes screen.

1994 Nebraska Team
Enter STEAMROLLER at the Secret Codes screen.

1994 Oregon Team
Enter GREENGANG at the Secret Codes screen.

1994 Penn State Team
Enter ALMOSTNO.1 at the Secret Codes screen.

1996 Florida Team
Enter PUTINLARRY at the Secret Codes screen.

1996 Florida State Team
Enter GETTHEQB at the Secret Codes screen.

1997 Washington State Team
Enter TURNOVER at the Secret Codes screen.

1997 Nebraska Team
Enter CORNFED at the Secret Codes screen.

1997 Michigan Team
Enter SPLITVOTE at the Secret Codes screen.

1997 Tennessee Team
Enter SMOKEY at the Secret Codes screen.

All Tiburon Team
Enter LASERBEAMS at the Secret Codes screen.

All EA Sports Team
Enter INTHEGAME at the Secret Codes screen.

NCAA FOOTBALL 2001

Change the Date
From the main menu, highlight and enter the Game Settings. Highlight and enter the Secret Codes section. Press Select and enter this code: Y2K. Now you can change the date.

Defense Always Intercepts
From the main menu, highlight and enter the Game Settings. Highlight and enter the Secret Codes section. Press Select and enter this code: OSKIE. This will cause the defense to always intercept the ball.

Increase the Speed of the Daytime Effects
From the main menu, highlight and enter the Game Settings. Highlight and enter the Secret Codes section. Press Select and enter this code: DAYNIGHT. This makes the transition between day and night quicker.

Kick-Butt Receivers
From the main menu, highlight and enter the Game Settings. Highlight and enter the Secret Codes section. Press Select and enter this code: HANDSOFGLUE. Your receivers will always catch the ball.

Max Recruit Points
From the main menu, highlight and enter the Game Settings. Highlight and enter the Secret Codes section. Press Select and enter this code: HEADCOACH. This will grant you Maximum Recruit points to use as you wish.

Maximum Attributes
From the main menu, highlight and enter the Game Settings. Highlight and enter the Secret Codes section. Press Select and enter this code: BALLER. This code boosts your attributes to the maximum.

Maximum Wind

From the main menu, highlight and enter the Game Settings. Highlight and enter the Secret Codes section. Press Select and enter this code: SAFTEY. This maximizes the wind.

Quicker Players

From the main menu, highlight and enter the Game Settings. Highlight and enter the Secret Codes section. Press Select and enter this code: SCRAMBLE. This code increases the speed of the players.

Reveal Plays

From the main menu, highlight and enter the Game Settings. Highlight and enter the Secret Codes section. Press Select and enter this code: MINDREADER. This reveals the play the AI is choosing when you play vs. the Computer.

Slow Players

From the main menu, highlight and enter the Game Settings. Highlight and enter the Secret Codes section. Press Select and enter this code: CEMENTFEET. This makes all of the players slow.

Unlock All Stadiums

Locate the Cheat menu. From the main menu, choose Game Settings, then Highlight the Secret Code option. Press Select to enter this code: OPENSESAME. Now you can choose either Exhibition mode or Situation mode and access any stadium.

Unlock the Juggernaut Team

From the main menu, highlight and enter the Game Settings. Highlight and enter the Secret Codes section. Press Select and enter this code: BULLDOZER. This unlocks the Juggernaut team in the Create a School mode.

View the Whole Poll

From the main menu, highlight and enter the Game Settings. Highlight and enter the Secret Codes section. Press Select and enter this code: POPULARITY. This code allows you to view the entire poll.

NCAA GAMEBREAKER

Alabama All-Time Team

Highlight "Option" at the main menu. Press L1, R1, L2, R2 to access the Code menu. Enter ALA All Stars as a code.

Eastern Michigan All-Time Team

Highlight "Option" at the main menu. Press L1, R1, L2, R2 to access the Code menu. Enter EMU All Stars as a code.

Southern California All-Time Team

Highlight "Option" at the main menu. Press L1, R1, L2, R2 to access the Code menu. Enter USC All Stars as a code.

Ohio State All-Time Team

Highlight "Option" at the main menu. Press L1, R1, L2, R2 to access the Code menu. Enter OSU All Stars as a code.

GameBreaker All-Time Team

Highlight "Option" at the main menu. Press L1, R1, L2, R2 to access the Code menu. Enter GB All Stars as a code.

Michigan All-Time Team

Highlight "Option" at the main menu. Press L1, R1, L2, R2 to access the Code menu. Enter Mich All Stars as a code.

Notre Dame All-Time Team

Highlight "Option" at the main menu. Press L1, R1, L2, R2 to access the Code menu. Enter ND All Stars as a code.

NCAA GAMEBREAKER '98

Win All Simulated Games

Enter SC at the Easter Egg screen.

View Credits

Enter CREDITS at the Easter Egg screen.

Create Gamebreakers

Enter BUILDER at the Easter Egg screen.

Strong Offense

Enter BOOST at the Easter Egg screen.

Switch Teams During A Season

Enter JUMP at the Easter Egg screen.

All Teams

Enter GIMME at the Easter Egg screen.

All Attributes Set to 99

Enter BEAT DOWN at the Easter Egg screen.

1998 Gamebreaker Team

Enter GB98 ALLSTARS at the Easter Egg screen.

NCAA GAMEBREAKER '99

Win All Simulated Games

Enter SC at the Easter Egg screen.

View Credits

Enter CREDITS at the Easter Egg screen.

Better Players

Enter BUILDER at the Easter Egg screen.

Strong Offense

Enter BOOST at the Easter Egg screen.

Unlock All-Time Teams

Enter GREED at the Easter Egg screen.

All Attributes Set to 99

Enter Beat Down at the Easter Egg screen.

Gold Players

Enter GOLDEN at the Easter Egg screen.

Better Passing Game

Enter Pass Attack at the Easter Egg screen.

Better Running Game

Enter Run Attack at the Easter Egg screen.

Equal Teams

Enter Equals at the Easter Egg screen.

NCAA GAMEBREAKER 2000

Win All Simulated Games

Enter SC at the Easter Egg screen.

Better Players

Enter Builder at the Easter Egg screen.

Better Passing Offense

Enter Pass_Attack at the Easter Egg screen.

Better Running Offense

Enter Run_Attack at the Easter Egg screen.

Better Blocking and Tackling

Enter Da_Wall at the Easter Egg screen.

Better Recruits

Enter GOLDEN at the Easter Egg screen.

All Player Attributes Set to 99

Enter Beat_Down at the Easter Egg screen.

Stronger Offense in Simulated Season

Enter Boost at the Easter Egg screen.

Super Team

Enter UNSTOPPABLE at the Easter Egg screen.

Small Fast Team vs. Big Slow Team

Enter David_Goliath at the Easter Egg screen.

NCAA GAMEBREAKER 2001

Excellent Stats

At the main menu, choose "Customize," then "Easter Eggs," and enter Vers as a code.

Strong Defense

At the main menu, choose "Customize," then "Easter Eggs," and enter PHYSICAL as a code.

String Stiff Arm

At the main menu, choose "Customize," then "Easter Eggs," and enter HAMMER as a code.

Better Passing

At the main menu, choose "Customize," then "Easter Eggs," and enter GO DEEP as a code.

Get All Blue Chips

At the main menu, choose "Customize," then "Easter Eggs," and enter MOTIVATE as a code.

All Attributes Set to 99

At the main menu, choose "Customize," then "Easter Eggs," and enter BEAT DOWN as a code.

Better Running Stats

At the main menu, choose "Customize," then "Easter Eggs," and enter REAL ESTATE as a code.

View Credits

At the main menu, choose "Customize," then "Easter Eggs," and enter HOLLYWOOD as a code.

Build Super Players

At the main menu, choose "Customize," then "Easter Eggs," and enter FRANKENSTEIN as a code.

Big Team vs. Small Team

At the main menu, choose "Customize," then "Easter Eggs," and enter BIGandsmall as a code.

Women's Team

Begin a new season. Choose "Division One vs. New Mexico" when the calendar appears. Return to the Exhibition mode screen and choose Division 1.

Big Players

Enter FATTONY at the Team Selection screen in Exhibition mode.

Alien Team

Enter ROSWELL at the Team Selection screen in Exhibition mode.

Small Players

Enter OOMPA at the Team Selection screen in Exhibition mode.

Old Team

Enter OLDTIME at the Team Selection screen in Exhibition mode.

NECTARIS: MILITARY MADNESS

Main Campaign Passwords

Enter one of these passwords to jump to a specific level. If you want to plant the bonus level, then reverse the code. For example, Level 1 is "RANDAL." To get the bonus level, enter "LADNAR" as a password.

Level 1
RANDAL

Level 2
HUNDRA

Level 3
CINBER

Level 4
MARLIN

Level 5
BAYARD

Level 6
WEBLEY

Level 7
PARKER

Level 8
MERKEL

Level 9
ITHACA

Level 10
BAIKAL

Level 11
SAVAGE

Level 12
VALMET

Level 13
MAUSER

Level 14
KIMBER

Level 15
BISLEY

Level 16
MEANEC

Original Campaign Passwords

Enter one of these passwords to jump to a specific level. If you want to plant the bonus level, then reverse the code. For example, Level 1 is "REVOLT." To get the bonus level, enter "TLOVER" as a password.

Level 1
REVOLT

Level 2
ICARUS

Level 3
CRYANO

Level 4
RAMSEY

Level 5
NEWTON

Level 6
SENECA

Level 7
SABINE

Level 8
ARAIUS

Level 9
GALOIS

Level 10
DARWIN

Level 11
PASCAL

Level 12
HALLEY

Level 13
BORMAN

Level 14
APPOLO

Level 15
KAISER

Level 16
NECTOR

NEED FOR SPEED

All Tracks and Warrior Car
Enter MQKZCL as a password in One-player Tournament mode.

Adjust Car Weight
Enter TSYBNS at the password screen. At the Car Selection screen, pick "Car Showcase," "Mechanical," and "Next Slide." Press R1 to add weight to the back of the car and L1 to add weight to the front of the car. The red triangles indicate the amount of weight.

Recover Quick After Crash
Repeatedly press L1+R1.

Lunar Springs Track
Enter MQKZCL as a password in One-player Tournament mode. Press Square to exit Tournament mode. Enter a One-player or Two-player mode. Highlight the Rusty Springs tracks. Hold Triangle+L1+R1 to change it to the Lunar Springs.

Arcade Mode
Enter TSYBNS as a password. At the Lap Selection menu, hold L1+R1 and "Arcade Mode" becomes an option.

Desert Springs Tracks
Enter TSYBNS as a password. Highlight the Rusty Springs track and hold L1+R1. The Rusty Springs track changes to the Desert Springs track.

Lost Vegas and Lost Rally Tracks
Enter TSYBNS as a password. "Lost Vegas" appears as an option at the Track Selection screen. Press L1+R1 while the Lost Vegas track is highlighted in Two-player mode to change Lost Vegas to the Lost Rally track.

Warrior Car
Enter TSYBNS as a password. At the Car Selection screen, hold L1+R1 when you are selecting a car. You can pick the Warrior PTO E/2 car.

Machine Guns
Enter Head-to-Head mode. After you choose your opponent's car, immediately hold Up-Left+L1+Square+Circle until the race begins.

Full Screen Mode
Hold Down when the lights begin the count-down. The gauges disappear if you did it correctly. Hold Down again to make the gauges reappear.

No Mercy Mode
Enter a two-player game. Press L1+R1 at the Head-to-Head Selection screen. This omits oncoming traffic.

Track 1 Password
WRDRTY

Track 2 Password
ZDPBWN

Track 3 Password
MTQRZP

Track 4 Password
JVPZLL

Track 5 Password
ZYMNLH

Track 6 Password
WMRPGZ

Track 7 Password
YXGSJJ

Track 8 Password
KJPQND

Track 9 Password
SDQWCG

Track 10 Password
SLZXDH

Track 11 Password
SPZDFX

Track 12 Password
ZVGRGX

Track 13 Password
XJHVCK

NEED FOR SPEED 2

Better Engine
Enter POWRUP as a password to make your car go faster. Reenter the password to make your car even faster.

Bonus Track
Enter SHOTME as a password to race through a studio.

Drive Ford Indigo Car
Enter LILZIP as a password.

Nine Additional Camera Angles
While the game is loading a race, hold L1+L2+R1+R2+Circle+X+Triangle+Square. Release the buttons when the race begins.

NEED FOR SPEED 3: HOT PURSUIT

Unlock All Regular Cars and Tracks
Enter SPOILT as a name at the Options screen.

Unlock More Camera Views
Enter SEEALL as a name at the Options screen.

Mercedes Benz CLK GTR
Enter AMGMRC as a name at the Options screen.

El Nino
Enter ROCKET as a name at the Options screen.

Jaguar XJR-15
Enter 1JAGX as a name at the Options screen.

NEED FOR SPEED 4: HIGH STAKES

Helicopter
At "Game Options," select "User Name" and enter Whirly.

NEED FOR SPEED: HIGH STAKES

Phantom Car
At "Game Options," select "User Name" and enter Flash.

Titan Car
At "Game Options," select "User Name" and enter Hotrod.

NEED FOR SPEED: PORSCHE UNLEASHED

Unlock All Cars
Enter allporsche as your name.

Game Music
Place the disk into an audio CD player. Listen to track two and higher to hear music from the game.

NEED FOR SPEED: V-RALLY

All Cheats
When the Infogrames logo appears, hold Left+R1+R2+L1+L2 until the logo disappears. A message appears if you entered the code correctly.

Infinite Time
When the Infogrames logo appears, hold Left+L1 until the logo disappears. A message appears if you entered the code correctly.

Infinite Time and Narrow Tracks
When the Infogrames logo appears, hold Left until the logo disappears. A message appears if you entered the code correctly.

NEED FOR SPEED: V-RALLY 2

All Cars, Trophies, and Levels
At the Game Progression screen under the Options menu, press L1, R1, Left, Right, Left, Right, Up, Down, Up, Down, X, X+Select. A sound confirms correct entry. Highlight a square and press X to unlock the corresponding car and trophy.

Fast Acceleration
Enter LDN as your name.

NEWMAN HAAS RACING

Bonus Tracks
Win the championship with Scott Pruett to unlock two tracks.

NEXT TETRIS

Adjust the Music
At the main menu, hold L1+R1 to increase the volume or hold L2+R1 to decrease the volume.

NFL BLITZ

Fat Players
Pause and press Up (2), Left (2), Right (2), Down (2).

Hidden Players
Enter the name and PIN number at the Enter Initials screen.

Mark Turmell
TURMELL, 0322

Jason Skiles
JASON, 3141

Sal Divita
SAL, 0201

Dan Thompson
DANIEL, 0604

Jennifer Hedrick
JENIFR, 3333

Skull
SKULL, 1111

Raiden
RAIDEN, 3691

Shinok
SHINOK, 8337

Headless Guy
CARLTN, 1111

Brain
BRAIN, 1111

Dan Forden
FORDEN, 1111

John Root
ROOT, 6000

Jeff Johnson
JAPPLE, 6660

Luis Magubat
LUIS, 3333

Mike Lynch
MIKE, 3333

Jim Gentile
GENTIL, 1111

NFL BLITZ 2000

Cheat Codes
Change icons accordingly at the VS. screen to enter code.

Infinite Turbo
5-1-4 Up

Super Blitzing
0-4-5 Up

Super Field Goals
1-2-3 Left

No Interceptions
3-4-4 Up

No Random Fumbles
4-2-3 Down

No First Downs
2-1-0 Up

No Punting
1-5-1 Up

Allow Stepping out of Bounds
2-1-1 Left

Fast Passes
2-5-0 Left

Big Head
2-0-0 Right

Huge Head
0-4-0 Up

No Head
3-2-1 Left

Headless Team
1-2-3 Right

Team Tiny Players
3-1-0 Right

Team Big Players
1-4-1 Right

Team Big Heads
2-0-3 Right

NFL BLITZ 2001

Cheat Codes
Change icons accordingly at the VS. screen to enter code.

Punt Hang Time Meter
0-0-1 Right

No CPU Assistance1
0-1-2 Down

Show More Field1
0-2-1 Right

Fast Turbo Running
0-3-2 Left

Huge Head
0-4-0 Up

Super Blitzing
0-4-5 Up

Big Football
0-5-0 Right

Arizona Cardinals Playbook
1-0-1 Left

Atlanta Falcons Playbook
1-0-2 Left

Hide Receiver Name
1-0-2 Right

Baltimore Ravens Playbook
1-0-3 Left

Buffalo Bills Playbook
1-0-4 Left

Carolina Panthers Playbook
1-0-5 Left

Chicago Bears Playbook
1-1-0 Left

Tournament Mode2
1-1-1 Down

Cincinnati Bengals Playbook
1-1-2 Left

Cleveland Browns Playbook
1-1-3 Left

Dallas Cowboys Playbook
1-1-4 Left

No Play Selection1
1-1-5 Left

Denver Broncos Playbook
1-1-5 Right

Detroit Lions Playbook
1-2-1 Left

Green Bay Packers Playbook
1-2-2 Left

Indianapolis Colts Playbook
1-2-3 Up

Super Field Goals
1-2-3 Left

Headless Team
1-2-3 Right

Jacksonville Jaguars Playbook
1-2-4 Left

Kansas City Chiefs Playbook
1-2-5 Left

Miami Dolphins Playbook
1-3-1 Left

Minnesota Vikings Playbook
1-3-2 Left

New England Patriots Playbook
1-3-3 Left

New Orleans Saints Playbook
1-3-4 Left

New York Giants Playbook
1-3-5 Left

New York Jets Playbook
1-4-1 Left

Big Players Team
1-4-1 Right

Oakland Raiders Playbook
1-4-2 Left

Philadelphia Eagles Playbook
1-4-3 Left

Pittsburgh Steelers Playbook
1-4-4 Left

San Diego Chargers Playbook
1-4-5 Left

No Punting
1-5-1 Up

San Francisco 49ers Playbook
1-5-1 Left

Seattle Seahawks Playbook
1-5-2 Left

St. Louis Rams Playbook
1-5-3 Left

Tampa Bay Buccaneers Playbook
1-5-4 Left

Tennessee Titans Playbook
1-5-5 Left

Big Head
2-0-0 Right

Washington Redskins Playbook
2-0-1 Left

Big Head Team
2-0-3 Right

No First Downs
2-1-0 Up

Allow Stepping Out-of-Bounds
2-1-1 Left

Deranged Blitz Mode1
2-1-2 Down

Weather: Clear
2-1-2 Left

Always QB (2P/4P on Same Team)
2-2-2 Left

Always Receiver (2P/4P on Same Team)
2-2-2 Right

Unlimited Throws
2-2-3 Right

Powerup Teammates
2-3-3 Up

Fast Passes
2-5-0 Left

Tiny Players Team
3-1-0 Right

Power-Up Offense
3-1-2 Up

Power-Up Blockers
3-1-2 Left

Smart CPU1
3-1-4 Down

No Highlighting of Receivers
3-2-1 Down

No Head
3-2-1 Left

Ultra Hard Mode1
3-2-3 Up

Red, White, and Blue Football
3-2-3 Left

Cancel "Always QB/Receiver" Code
3-3-3 Up

No Interceptions
3-4-4 Up

Power-Up Speed1
4-0-4 Left

Power-Up Defense
4-2-1 Up

No Random Fumbles
4-2-3 Down

Super Passing Mode1
4-2-3 Right

Invisible
4-3-3 Up

Super Blitz Mode1
0-4-5 Up

Turn Off Stadium
5-0-0 Left

Unlimited Turbo Meter
5-1-1 Up

Unidentified Ball Carrier
5-2-2 Down

Weather: Snow
5-2-5 Down

Hyper Blitz Mode1
5-5-5 Up

Weather: Rain
5-5-5 Right

NFL GameDay

See All Screens
Reset the PlayStation and hold L1+L2+R1+R2.

Access Password Screen
Press Select at the main menu to access the Memory Card screen. Press Select again to enter the Password Screen.

Very Hard CPU
Enter URNOTREDE at the Password Screen.

Strong Offense
Enter OFFENSE at the Password Screen.

Strong Defense
Enter DEFENSE at the Password Screen.

More Injuries
Enter MAYHEM at the Password Screen.

Play as Skeletons
Enter SKELETON at the Password Screen.

More Interceptions
Enter PICK.CITY at the Password Screen.

Speed Burst by Pressing X
Enter JUICE at the Password Screen.

Good Hands
Enter STICKUM at the Password Screen.

Huge Players
Enter BIG.BOYS at the Password Screen.

Massive Hits
Enter CRUNCH.TIME at the Password Screen.

Strong Players
Enter STEROIDS at the Password Screen.

QBs Throw Bullet Passes
Enter CANNON.ARM at the Password Screen.

NFL GameDay 2002

Cheat Codes
Go to the Cheat Code screen and enter the following phrases to unlock the corresponding cheat.

Players Named After 989 Team
989 SPORTS

All Players Will Have the Last Name "Bobo"
ALL BOBO

Players Will Be Named After NBA Superstars
BASKETBALL

Make the Football Large
BIG PIG

Watch the Game's Credits
CREDITS

Give Your Players More Endurance
ENDURANCE

Players Will Be Named After NFL Europe Stars
EURO LEAGUE

Cheerleaders' Pictures Will Appear After the Game
FASHION SHOW

Reduce Your Players' Fatigue
FATIGUE

Unlock the GameDay Stadium
GRUDGE MATCH

Improve Your Defensive Line
LINE BUSTER

Players Will Be Named After Presidents of the United States of America
OVAL OFFICE

All Players Thin and Tall
PENCILS

Players Float Above the Field
POP WARNER

Make Your Running Back Better
SUPER FOOT

Make All Players Big and Fat
TINY

NFL GAMEDAY '97

Access Cheat Codes Area
At the Start Game screen, in either Pre-Season or Season Play, press L1, R1, L2, R2. Then enter the codes below.

Injuries Up
ASSASSIN

Hard Hit Explosions
ATOMIC BOMB

Quarterback with Strong Arm
BAZOOKA

Cheerleaders Are Bigger
BIG GIRLS

Star Players Are Bigger
BIG STARS

More Time to Hit a Receiver and Pop the Ball Out
BLASTERS

Fewer Penalties
BLIND REF

More Snow
BLIZZARD

Shoulder Charge
BO KNOWS

More Injuries
BRITTLE

More Accurate Passes
BROADWAY JOE

More Penalties
BUSY REF

Defense Hits Harder
BUTKAS

Display Credits
CREDITS

Louder Hits
CRUNCHY

Dark Stadium
DARK NIGHT

Better Defense
DEFENSE

Increased Field Goal Range
DEMPSEY

Effective Spins
DERVISH

Delete Last Remaining Code in Menu
DOC

Electric Football
ELECTRIC FB

Most Players Are Equal
EQUALIZER

Small Players
FLEA CIRCUS

Big Players
FRIDGE

Jump Higher
FROG

Faster Gameplay
GB SPEED

CPU Is Hard
GD CHALLENGE

CPU Is Smart
GENIUS

Catch More Passes
GLOVES

Big Players That Sound Like Monsters
GOLIATH

Higher Kicks
HANG TIME

Better Forearm Shivers
HATCHET

Offensive Line Blocks Better
HOGS

Home Team Will Get No Pass Interference or Personal Fouls
HOME COOKING

Slippery Field
ICE SKATES

High Pop Ups When the Receiver Is Hit
INFAMOUS POP UPS

More Injuries
INJURIES UP

Fewer Injuries
INJURIES DOWN

Less Effective One-Handed Catches
JUGGLER

Better Speed Burst
JUICE

Forearm Shiver Is Now a Karate Chop
KARATE

More Fumbles
KRAIG

Players Dive Farther
LONG JUMP

Loud Announcer
LOUD MOUTH

Offensive Line Is At a Disadvantage
MANDARICH

Infinite Time
NO TIME

Swim Move Is Better
NYSE

Better Offense
OFFENSE

Stiff Arm Is Stronger
OUCH

Blockers Knock Over Defenders Frequently
PANCAKE

Stronger Forearm Shiver
PINBALL

Jackhammer Off a Stiff Arm
PISTON

Defensive Players Jump Higher
REJECTION

Better Running Back
SAYERS

Faster Quarterback
SCRAMBLER

Louder Crowd
SHOUT

Slower Play
SLO MO

More Wind with Rain
SQUALL

Harder Hits
STEROIDS

Jump Higher On One-Handed Catches
STRETCH

Dark Stadium
TEMPEST

Better Defensive Pass Coverage
TIGHT COVER

Secondary Plays Farther Off Receivers
TOAST

Quarterback Lobs Passes
TORRETA

Strong Wind
TWISTER

NFL GAMEDAY '98

Access Cheat Codes Area
At the Options screen, choose "Easter Eggs" and enter one of the following codes.

One-Footed Players
AHAB

Quarterbacks Throw Longer and Higher Passes
AIR STRIKE

Better Running Back
BETTIS

Increased Field Goal Range
BIG FOOT

No Penalties
BLIND REF

More Penalties
BUSY REF

Thin Players
COOKIE CUTTER

Better CPU Defense
CPU DEFENSE

Better CPU Offense
CPU OFFENSE

View Credits
CREDITS

Louder Hits
CRUNCH TIME

Smarter Computer
DEEP GRAY

Teams Have Equal Abilities
EQUAL TEAMS

Fast Players
FIRE DRILL

Flat Players
FLAT LAND

Small Players
FLEA CIRCUS

CPU Is Hard
GD CHALLENGE

Catch More Passes
GLOVES

Better Forearm Shivers
HATCHET

No Heads
HORSEMEN

Large Players
HUMONGOUS

Invisible Players
INVISIBLE

Harder Hits
JACKHAMMER

Better Speed Burst
JUICE

Tight Coverage
LEECH

No Hands
LOOK MA

Loud Announcer
LOUD MOUTH

Play as Shadows
MCMAHON

Swim Move Is Better
NYSE

Quiet Crowd
QUIET CROWD

Defensive Players Jump Higher
REJECTION

Dive, Then Press Jump to Roll and Run
SHOW OFF

Make Longer Field Goals
THIN AIR

Secondary Plays Farther Off Receivers
TOAST

Flat Players
VIRTUAL POLYGONS

Stupid CPU
WATERY AI

NFL GAMEDAY '99

Access Cheat Codes Area
At the Options screen, choose "Easter Eggs" and enter one of the following codes.

Large Football
Big Balls

Louder Noises
Big Hits

No Penalties
Blinders

Last Name Is Bobo For All Players
Bobo

Big Players
Bunyon

Better Speed Burst
Coffee Break

CPU Hides Pass Coverage
Con Man

Better CPU Offense
CPU Scores

Better CPU Defense
CPU Stuffs

See Credits
Credits

Better Running Back
Davis

Players Have European Names
Euro League

Equal Players
Even Teams

Small Players
Flea Circus

Flat Players
Flat Land

Bonus Difficulty Level
GD Challenge

Red Redzones, Checkered Touchdown Area, Invisible Field Goals
Grudge Match

Rip a Hamstring After Using Speed Burst
Hamstrung

More Hangtime For Punts
Hangtime

Players Have Basketball Player Names
Hoops

CPU Celebrates in the Open Field
Hot Shot

Frame Rate Changes
Its In The Fps

CPU Knows Your Plays
Mind Reader

Flat Players
Playing Cards

Better Forearm Shivers
Pole Axe

Small, Fast Players
Pop Warner

Players Have Presidents' Names
Presidents

CPU Makes Big Plays
Prime Time

Players Have Red String on Their Heads
Puppets

Players Have Names from Publishers
Red Zone

Ball Carrier Has Speed Bursts
Rocket Man

See Cheerleaders After the Game
Slideshow

All Players Have Names from the Credits
Sports

Better Endurance
Stamina

Longer Field Goal Range
Steel Leg

Better Hands
Stickem

Swim Move Is Better
Swimmers

TVs in Players' Stomachs
Tele Tummy

Quick Fatigue
Weak

NFL GAMEDAY 2000

Access Cheat Codes Area
Enter the Options screen and select "Easter Eggs." Then enter one of the following codes.

989 Studios Players
989SPORTS

Receivers Catch Better
GLOVES

Super Speed
COFFEE BREAK

Super Speed Bursts
JUICE

Super Stiff Arm
PISTON

Super Swim Move
SWIMMERS

Longer and Higher Punts
HANGTIME

Longer Field Goals
STEEL LEG

Harder Tackles
BIG HITS

Players Do Not Fatigue
STAMINA

All Players Have Equal Abilities
EVEN TEAMS

No Penalties for Home Team
HOME COOKING

Better Running Back
BETTIS

Running Back Is Juiced
DAVIS

More Injuries
HAMSTRUNG

Cycle Through Cheerleaders After Game
SLIDESHOW

Hidden Difficulty Level
GD CHALLENGE

Players Have Presidents' Names
PRESIDENTS

Large Football
BIG BALLS

Large Players
GOLIATH

Tall and Thin Players
PENCILS

Tiny Players
FLEA CIRCUS

Very Slow CPU Players
SLOW CPU

View Credits
CREDITS

NFL GameDay 2001

Cheat Codes
Enter the Options screen and select "Easter Eggs," then enter any of the following codes:

Super Speed Burst
ROCKET MAN

Better Receivers
STICKEM

Better Running Back
SUPER FOOT

All Bobo Teams
ALL BOBO

Players Have Equal Abilities
ALL EVEN ALL

Better Defensive Line
LINE BUSTER

Hard Tackles
CRUNCH

Increased Endurance
ENDURANCE

Programmer Names
RED ZONE

Basketball Player Names
BASKETBALL

U.S. President's Names
OVAL OFFICE

989 Studios Players
989 SPORTS

Fast Players
BOOSTER

Large Players
GIANTS

Flat Players
TWO D

Small, Fast Players
POP WARNER

Cycle Through Cheerleaders After Game
FASHION SHOW

Frame by Frame Movement
STROBE LIGHT

Really Small Players
TINY GUYS

Tall Skinny Players
STICK MEN

Expert Mode
SMARTER CPU

Play on the Hidden Gameday Field
GD FIELD

European League Teams
EURO LEAGUE

Extra Hard Mode
UNBEATABLE

Huge Football
BIG PIG

Super Special Moves
SPECIAL MOVE

Fast Gameplay
COFFEE BREAK

Better Stiff Arms
JACK HAMMER

NFL Quarterback Club '97

Enable All Cheats
Press L1 (2), R2 (2), L1, R2 at the Pre-season Team Selection screen.

Bonus Teams
Press L1 (2), L2, R2, L1, L2 at the Pre-season Team Selection screen.

Eight Downs
Press L1, Triangle, L2, Triangle, L1, L2 at the Pre-season Team Selection screen.

Pro Bowl Team
Press L1 (3), Triangle, L1 (2) at the Pre-season Team Selection screen.

NFL Xtreme

Big Players
Enter BIG BEN at the Create Free Agent screen.

Big Head Mode
Enter BIGHEAD BOBBY at the Create Free Agent screen.

Flat Heads
Enter COINHEAD COREY at the Create Free Agent screen.

Long Necks
Enter GEORGE GIRAFFE at the Create Free Agent screen.

Reversed Animations
Enter LAMEBOY LENNY at the Create Free Agent screen.

Long Arms
Enter MONKEY MICKEY at the Create Free Agent screen.

Short Arms
Enter SHRIMPY SEAN at the Create Free Agent screen.

Tiny Players
Enter TINY TOM at the Create Free Agent screen.

NFL Xtreme 2

Play on a Ship
Enter AIRCRAFT CARRIER as a player name at the Player Creation screen, then select "Quick Start."

Big Players
Enter BIG BEN as a player name at the Player Creation screen, then select "Quick Start."

Big Heads
Enter BIGHEAD BOBBY as a player name at the Player Creation screen, then select "Quick Start."

Play in an Urban City
Enter CITYSCAPE as a player name at the Player Creation screen, then select "Quick Start."

Flat Heads
Enter COINHEAD COREY as a player name at the Player Creation screen, then select "Quick Start."

Play in Egypt
Enter EGYPT SPHINX as a player name at the Player Creation screen, then select "Quick Start."

Long Necks
Enter GEORGE GIRAFFE as a player name at the Player Creation screen, then select "Quick Start."

Reversed Animations
Enter LAMEBOY LENNY as a player name at the Player Creation screen, then select "Quick Start."

Play on a Moon
Enter LUNAR FIELD as a player name at the Player Creation screen, then select "Quick Start."

Long Arms
Enter MONKEY MICKEY as a player name at the Player Creation screen, then select "Quick Start."

Play on a Pool Table
Enter POOL TABLE as a player name at the Player Creation screen, then select "Quick Start."

Short Arms
Enter SHRIMPY SEAN as a player name at the Player Creation screen, then select "Quick Start."

Tiny Players
Enter TINY TOM as a player name at the Player Creation screen, then select "Quick Start."

NGEN Racing

More Money
Press R2, L2, R2, L1, R2, R1, R2, L1 at the main menu.

All Tracks and Aircrafts in Arcade Mode
Press R1, L1, R1, R2, L2, R2, L2, L1 at the main menu, then enter Arcade mode to unlock the next three championships and three levels of airplanes.

Extra Airplanes in N.GEN Mode
Press R1, R2, L1, L2, L2, L1, R2, R1 at the main menu.

NHL '97

More Fights
Before the puck falls to ice during a face-off, press L1, L2 (2), R1, Circle. "Entered" displays if you entered the code correctly.

Easier Goals
Before the puck falls to ice during a face-off, press L1, L2, L1, R1, R2. "Entered" displays if you entered the code correctly.

Accurate Shots
Before the puck falls to ice during a face-off, press L1, L2, L1, R1, L2. "Entered" displays if you entered the code correctly.

More Penalty Shots
Before the puck falls to ice during a face-off, press L1, L2, L1, R1 (2). "Entered" displays if you entered the code correctly.

NHL '98

Alternate Uniforms
Enter 3RD or MASKDMAN as a password.

Big Players
Enter BIGBIG as a password.

Big Heads
Enter BRAINY as a password.

EA Blades Bonus Team
Enter EAEAO as a password.

Add Developers to Free Agent List
Enter FREEEA as a password.

Powerplay Given to the Team That Was Scored On
Enter GIPTEA as a password.

Small Players
Enter NHLKIDS as a password.

Small Players, Large Goalies
Enter PLAYTIME as a password.

View FMV of Stanley Cup
Enter STANLEY as a password.

NHL '99

Alternate Uniforms
Enter 3RD as a password.

Big Players
Enter BIGBIG as a password.

Big Heads
Enter BRAINY as a password.

More Fights
Enter DEATHTOALL as a password.

Bonus Teams
Enter FREEEA as a password.

Perfect Player
Enter GREATSKATE as a password.

NHL 2000

Infinite Timeouts
Press Start after a whistle, enter the Strategies screen, then select "Timeout." Immediately press Triangle, enter the screen again, and immediately press X. Repeat until your line is full.

NHL 2001

No Goalie
During a game, press the Start Button to pause the game. Select Controller Setup. Now move your controller to the other team. Return to the previous menu and select your opposing teams' options. Next, select Team Options. Where the screen reads Goalie Status, you can elect to pull the goalie. Return to the Previous menu again and go into Controller Setup. Move your Controller to your original team. When you return to the game, the other team will have no Goalie. If you want to restore the goalie to the other team, repeat all of these steps and elect to return the Goalie to the Net.

Play as "Animal"
On the Create Player screen in the Rosters menu, create a new player and set his first name to Animal. The announcers refer to him as "the Animal" during gameplay.

Play as "the Hammer"
On the Create Player screen in the Rosters menu, create a new player and set his first name to Hammer. The announcers will refer to him as "the Hammer" during gameplay.

Super Defensive Players
Enter the create-a-player screen and enter "Sandis Ozolinsh" or "Chris Pronger" as a name. Answer "Yes" to use his ratings, then adjust them as needed. You can also use NHL Challenge bonus points to boost their attributes. Return to the previous screen and change his name to your choice, but do not change any other setting.

Super Forwards
Enter the create-a-player screen and enter one of the following names "Peter Forsberg," "Jaromir Jagr," "Keith Tkachuk," "Pavel Bure," "Steve Yzerman," "Owen Nolan," "Rob Blake," "Nicklas Lidstrom," or "Olaf Kolzig."

Answer "Yes" to use his ratings, then adjust them as needed. You can use NHL Challenge bonus points to boost their attributes. Return to the previous screen and change his name to your choice, but do not change any other setting.

Super Goalies
Enter the create-a-player screen and enter "Patrick Roy," "Dominik Hasek," or "Ed Belfour" as a name. Answer "Yes" to use his ratings, then adjust them as needed. You can use NHL Challenge bonus points to boost their attributes. Return to the previous screen and change his name to your choice, but do not change any other setting.

NHL Breakaway '98

Access Cheat Mode
Pause and press R1, R2, Right, Left, R1.

Randomly Created Team
Press R1+R2+L1+L2 at the Team Selection screen.

NHL FaceOff

Alternate Team Appearance
When the "Just A Minute" sign appears, hold L2+X+Circle until you hear puck sounds to gain a jersey at the beginning of the game.

NHL FaceOff '97

Super Players
Enter Raja Altenhoff, Josh Hassin, Kelly Ryan, Peter Dille, Tom Braski, Tawn Kramer, Jody Kelsey, Craig Ostrander, Craig Broadbooks, Alan Scales, or Chris Whaley at the Player Creation screen. Set "1" as the jersey number, "Forward" as the player position, and "150" as the weight. Don't change any other attribute. Exit and sign the player as a free agent. The created player will have an overall ranking of 99.

NHL FaceOff '98

Super Players
Enter Raja Altenhoff, Josh Hassin, Kelly Ryan, Peter Dille, Tom Braski, Tawn Kramer, Jody Kelsey, Craig Ostrander, Craig Broadbooks, Alan Scales, Chris Whaley, Steve Braski, Dave Brickhill, or John Rehling at the Player Creation screen. Set "1" as the jersey number, "Forward" as the player position, "Right-handed," and "150" as the weight. Don't change any other attribute. Exit and sign the player as a free agent. The created player will have an overall ranking of 99.

NHL FaceOff '99

Create a Great Player
Go to the Create Player screen. Enter your name, height, and other characteristics. When you reach the attributes, put everything to 99 except for the Fighting, Checking, Aggression, and Endurance areas. If you have leftover points, distribute the points evenly among those four areas. The player has a 99 when you sign him as a free agent.

NHL Open Ice

Big Heads
Press Up+Pass+Turbo at the "Tonight's Game" screen.

Baby Heads
Press Turbo (2), Up, Shoot (2), Up at the "Tonight's Game" screen.

Large Puck
Press Up (2), Down (2), Turbo at the "Tonight's Game" screen.

Big Headed Goalie
Press Pass (2), Turbo, Shoot, Pass at the "Tonight's Game" screen.

Michael Jordan
Enter M J as initials and January 25 as the birthday.

Gordie Howe
Enter G H as initials and March 31 as the birthday.

NHL Powerplay '96

Play as Rad Army Team
Press R2 (3), L2 (3), Select at the Team Selection or Quick Start screen.

NHL Powerplay '98

Bonus Teams
Select "Start Game" from the main menu. Pick Exhibition mode. Immediately hold X+Square+Triangle+Circle until the Team Selection screen appears. Release the buttons to unlock the Rad Army and Virgin Blaster teams.

NHL Rock the Rink

Two-Player King of the Rink Mode
At the title screen, press Select, Triangle, R2, L1, Right, Left, Down, X.

Unlock NHL Teams
Enter BAILEY as a code.

All Boards
Enter POWER SLAM as a code.

Sound Test
Enter NO CHANCE as a code.

Bonus Moves in any Mode
Enter IAMWEAK as a code.

Longer Goal Celebrations
Pause at the front end of the rink. Press Right (2), Up, Down, Left, Square (2), Circle.

Nightmare Creatures

Cheat Mode
As a password, enter Left, Up, Triangle, Down, Triangle (2), X, Up or Left, Up, Triangle, Down, Circle, Triangle, Square, Down. If that didn't work, enter Left, Up, X, Square, Down, Triangle, Square, Down. Start a new game to access the Cheat menu. Infinite lives, weapons, continues, level select, and other options can be enabled.

Ignatius Level 2 Password
Triangle, Circle, Triangle, Left, Triangle, Square, X, Square

Ignatius Level 3 Password
Triangle, X, Circle, Triangle (2), Down, Square, Up

Ignatius Level 4 Password
Triangle, Square, Triangle, Left, Triangle, Down, Up, Square

Ignatius Level 5 Password
Triangle, Up, Triangle, Up, Triangle, Down (2), X

Ignatius Level 6 Password
Triangle, Down, Triangle, X, Triangle, Down, Left, Circle

Ignatius Level 7 Password
Triangle, Left, Triangle, X, Triangle, Left, Triangle, Circle

Ignatius Level 8 Password
Triangle, Right, Triangle, X, Triangle (2), Circle (2)

Ignatius Level 9 Password
Circle, Triangle (2), X, Circle (2), Square, X

Ignatius Level 10 Password
Circle (2), Triangle, Right, Triangle, Up, Down (2)

Ignatius Level 11 Password
Circle, X, Triangle, Right, Triangle, Down, Left, Down

Ignatius Level 12 Password
Circle, Square, Triangle, Square, Triangle, Up, Triangle, Square

Ignatius Level 13 Password
Circle, Up, Triangle, Square, Triangle, Down, Circle, Square

Ignatius Level 14 Password
Circle, Down, Triangle, Right, Triangle, Circle, X, Down

Ignatius Level 15 Password
Circle, Left, Triangle, Square, Triangle (2), Square (2)

Ignatius Level 16 Password
Circle, Right, Triangle, Square, Triangle, Circle, Up, Square

Ignatius Level 17 Password
X, Triangle, X, Square, Triangle, Square, Down, Up

Ignatius Level 18 Password
X, Circle, X, Square, Triangle, Up, Left, Up

Ignatius Level 19 Password
X (3), Square, Circle, Down, Circle, Down

Ignatius Level 20 Password
X, Square, X, Square, Circle, Left, X, Down

Nadia Level 2 Password
Up, Circle, Triangle, Left, Triangle, Square, X, Square

Nadia Level 3 Password
Up, X, Triangle, Up, Triangle, Square (2), X

Nadia Level 4 Password
Up, Square, Triangle, Up, Triangle, Up (2), X

Nadia Level 5 Password
Up (2), Triangle, Up, Triangle, Down (2), X

Nadia Level 6 Password
Up, Down, Triangle, Up, Triangle, Left (2), X

Nadia Level 7 Password
Up, Left, Triangle, Up, Triangle (3), X

Nadia Level 8 Password
Up, Right, Triangle, X, Triangle (2), Circle (2)

Nadia Level 9 Password
Down, Triangle, X (2), Circle, X, Square (2)

Nadia Level 10 Password
Down, Circle, X, Square, Triangle, Square, Down, Up

Nadia Level 11 Password
Down, X (2), Square, Triangle, Up, Left, Up

Nadia Level 12 Password
Down, Square, X, Square, Triangle, Left, Circle, Up

Nadia Level 13 Password
Down, Up, X, Square, Triangle, Left, Circle, Up

Nadia Level 14 Password
Down (2), X, Square, Triangle (2), X, Up

Nadia Level 15 Password
Down, Left, X, Square, Triangle, Circle, Square, Up

Nadia Level 16 Password
Down, Right, X, Square, Triangle, X, Up (2)

Nadia Level 17 Password
Left, Triangle, X, Square, Triangle, Square, Down, Up

Nadia Level 18 Password
Left, Circle, X, Square, Triangle, Up, Right, Up

Nadia Level 19 Password
Left, X (2), Square, Circle, Down, Circle, Down

Nadia Level 20 Password
Left, Square, X, Square, Circle, Left, X, Down

NIGHTMARE CREATURES 2

Walk Through Walls
At the main menu, hold L1+R2+Circle+Square and press Select.

NINJA: SHADOW OF DARKNESS

Level Select
Remove all memory cards from the PlayStation. When "Checking Memory Card" appears on the screen, press L2 (3), R2 (3).

Invincibility and Items
Pause and press L2, R2, L2 (3), R2 (3), Circle, Triangle, Square, Circle, Triangle, Square. You hear a chime and the ninja turns into a skeleton. The skeleton ninja is invincible with infinite items and lives. Repeat the code to turn back into the ninja (you keep the items).

Weapon Select
Pause and press R2 (3), L2 (3), R2 (3), L2 (6). Resume your game to have a new weapon.

Decrease Boss Energy
Pause while fighting a boss, then press L2 (3), R2 (3), Triangle (6).

Big Head, Hands, and Feet
When "Press Start" flashes at the title screen, press Select (3), L2 (3), Select (3).

Baby Mode
When "Press Start" flashes at the title screen, press L2 (3), Select (3), R2 (3).

NO FEAR DOWNHILL MOUNTAIN BIKING

Elite Tracks
Select "Trick Trail" at the main menu, then select "Quit to Menu," then select "Single Race" at the main menu to access the elite tracks. If you highlight over "Pro Tracks," you must start over.

Access Cheat Codes
Go to Time Trial and enter YES as an access code. Then enter the codes below.

Low Gravity
BIGFLOATER

Wire Frame Trail
TYREFRAME

Mirror Mode
EDOMRORRIM

All Riders
GOOBERS

All Upgrades
LOTSOFGEAR

Virtual Reality Trail
JACKED IN

Trick Trail
MONEYBIKE

Cartoon Trail
TOON IT UP

Alien Trail in Pro Mode
ABDUCTION

All Trails
LOTSOFFEAR

NO ONE CAN STOP MR. DOMINO

Play as Bruce
Beat the game with Mr. Domino or Miss Domino.

Play as D/\M*?0
Beat the game with a "best in the US" score on all six levels.

Play as Pierre
Beat the game with a "best in the county" score on all six levels.

NORSE BY NORSEWEST

Level 1 Password
NTRO

Level 2 Password
1STS

Level 3 Password
2NDS

Level 4 Password
TRSH

Level 5 Password
SW1M

Level 6 Password
W0LF

Level 7 Password
T1M3

Level 8 Password
K4RN

Level 9 Password
B0MB

Level 10 Password
WZRD

Level 11 Password
BLKS

Level 12 Password
TLPT

Level 13 Password
GYSR

Level 14 Password
B3SV

Level 15 Password
R3T0

Level 16 Password
DRNK

Level 17 Password
Y0VR

Level 18 Password
0VAL

Level 19 Password
T1N3

Level 20 Password
D4RK

Level 21 Password
H4RD

Level 22 Password
HRDR

Level 23 Password
LOST

Level 24 Password
0B0Y

Level 25 Password
HOM3

Level 26 Password
SHCK

Level 27 Password
TNNL

Level 28 Password
H3LL

Level 29 Password
B4RH

Level 30 Password
B4DD

Level 31 Password
D4DY

Infinite Energy
Enter CH3T, then enter a level password or start a new game to begin with infinite energy.

NOVA STORM

Level Select
Finish with a score that gets you to the High Score screen. Enter "TWIRLY!" Press Start to return to the main menu. The gold icon in the screen's middle takes you to the Select menu. You can select a sub-stage within any level.

NUCLEAR STRIKE

Infinite Armor, Ammunition, Fuel
PACKISBACK

View *Future Strike* FMV sequence
COMMERCIAL

Unlimited Weapon Refill
GOPOSTAL

Faster Vehicles
WARPDRIVE

Infinite Lives
LAZARUS

Easy Mission 1
AVENGER

Four Continues
PHOENIX

Five Continues
WARRIOR

Fly Farther
MPG

Recon Mode
EAGLEEYE

Level 1 Password
JUNGLEWAR

Level 2 Password
CUTTHROATS

Level 3 Password
COUNTDOWN

Level 3B Password
PLUTONIUM

Level 4 Password
PUSAN

Level 5 Password
ARMAGEDDON

Bonus Level Password
LIGHTNING

O.D.T

Play as Sophia
At the main menu, press L1, L2, R2, R1.

Play as Karma
At the main menu, press R1, R2, L2, L1.

Fifty Lives
Pause and press Up, Circle, Right, Select, Square.

Full Ammo
Pause and press Left, Right, Up, Down, Circle+Square and you will get full ammo for all four weapons.

Restore Health
Pause and press Left, Right, Left, Right+Square.

Refill Experience
Pause and press Circle, Square, L1, L2, R1, Select.

Upgrade Spell Level
Pause and press Down, Triangle, Select, L1, R1, Select.

Upgrade Weapon Level
Pause and press R1, L1, R2, L2, Left, Right, Up, Down.

Increase Abilities
Pause and press Square, Circle, Triangle, Select, Left.

Disable Enemy Health
Pause and press Triangle, Square, Circle, Triangle, Circle.

Completing the Game
Play at Hard difficulty to completely finish the game.

Refill Mana
Pause and press Left, Right, Left, Right+Circle.

ODDWORLD: ABE'S ODDYSEE

Level Select
At the Main Options screen, where Abe says "Hello," hold R1 and press Down, Right, Left, Right, Square, Circle, Square, Triangle, Circle, Square, Right, Left.

View FMV Sequences
At the Main Options screen, where Abe says "Hello," hold R1 and press Up, Left, Right, Square, Circle, Triangle, Square, Right, Left, Up, Right.

Invincibility
During gameplay, hold R1 and press Circle, Triangle, Square, X, Down(3), Circle, Triangle, Square, X.

ODDWORLD 2: ABE'S EXODUS

Level Select
At the main menu, hold R1 and press Down, Up, Left, Right, Triangle, Square, Circle, Triangle, Square, Circle, Down, Up, Left, Right.

View FMV Sequences
At the main menu, hold R1 and press Up, Down, Left, Right, Square, Circle, Triangle, Circle, Square, Circle, Up, Down, Left, Right.

Invincibility
During gameplay, hold R1 and press Circle, Triangle, Square, X, Down (3), Circle, Triangle, Square, X.

Level Skip
During gameplay, hold down R1 and press Circle (2), X (2), Square (2).

OFF-WORLD INTERCEPTOR

Level Select
BORNFREE

Invincibility
HARDBODY

31 Extra Lives
VITAMINS

Lots of Hearts
CORONARY

Immortal Enemies
EVILDEAD

Hold L1+L2 to Rotate Screen
TWISTEYE

Quit to Return to the Map
INANDOUT

Hold L2 to Mutate
THETHING

Press Triangle to Swap Characters
BODYSWAP

Unlimited Special Weapons
OTTOFIRE

Pinball Screen When Level Completed
TOMMYBOY

Speed Greed Screen When Level Completed
CASHDASH

OGRE BATTLE

Hidden Stage
At the game's beginning, enter your name as FIRESEAL. Then go through the questions and after some loading, the Map screen appears. Move the cursor to the crossed swords to select Dragon's Heaven.

Music Test
At the game's beginning, enter your name as MUSIC/ON. The game then loads and the Music Mode screen appears.

Faster Gameplay
Start a new game and enter your name as GOTOHELL.

Toggle Load Time Effect
During the game's brief loading, there's a cool graphical effect that sucks in the red squares. Use either the directional pad or the analog stick to control the direction of where it's being sucked.

OMEGA BOOST

U1 Zone
Successfully complete the game at Hard difficulty with 90 AP and without using any continues.

U2 Zone
Successfully complete the game at Hard difficulty with 60 AP.

U3 Zone
Successfully complete the game at Hard difficulty with 50 AP.

U4 Zone
Successfully complete the game at Normal difficulty with 90 AP and without using any continues.

U5 Zone
Successfully complete the game at Normal difficulty with 60 AP.

U7 Zone
Successfully complete the game at Hard difficulty without using any continues.

U8 Zone
Successfully complete the game at Normal difficulty.

U9 Zone
Successfully complete the game at Normal difficulty without using any continues.

V5 Zone
Successfully complete the game with 60 AP.

Inner Level A
Successfully complete the game with 60 AP (with invincibility, all weapons at Level 9).

Inner Level B
Successfully complete the game at Hard difficulty with 90 AP (with unlimited special attacks, all weapons at Level 3).

Inner Level C
Successfully complete the game at Normal difficulty (with highest speed, all weapons at Level 9).

Inner Level D
Successfully complete the game at Normal difficulty with 90 AP (with five-way attack, all weapons at Level 9).

Inner Level E
Successfully complete the game at Hard difficulty (with improved speed when moving up, down, left, right; all weapons at Level 9).

ONE

Debug Mode
Enter HEYBUDDY as a password.

Level Select
Enter HEVYFEET as a password.

All Weapons
Enter MAXPOWER as a password.

Bonus Level
Complete the game then enter 1MORELVL as a password.

Full Pause Screen
Enter THEPRESS as a password.

Level 2 Password
DIYGIXRA

Level 3 Password
KCSVJTJB

Level 4 Password
RWLKLPBC

Level 5 Password
YQFZMLTC

Level 6 Password
FLZNOHLD

ONE ON ONE

Play as Oscar
Beat the game with any character and meet Oscar during the game.

Play as Mash
Beat the game with any character and meet Mash during the game.

Play as King
Beat the game with all characters, including Mash and Oscar.

Unlock Omake Mode
Beat the game with any character to get three pictures of that character.

OPTION TUNING CAR BATTLE

W-Wagon Bonus Car
Select Arcade mode, then choose car type N33 or mines. Press Start to access the W-Wagon.

Supatazen Bonus Car
Select Arcade mode, then choose car type N33 or mines. Press Select to access the Supatazen.

$1 Million
Enter Dai as a name.

OPTION TUNING CAR BATTLE 2

View Ending Sequence
Press R1, Circle, Triangle, Right on controller two at the title screen.

All Cars
Enable the "view ending sequence" code. Then, select Arcade mode and press R1, Circle, Triangle, Right on controller two.

OVERBOARD

Level 1-2 Password
Ship, Skull, Fish, Anchor, Ship, Anchor

Level 1-3 Password
Ship, Anchor, Skull, Ship, Anchor, Fish

Level 1-4 Password
Skull, Ship, Fish, Anchor (2), Ship

Level 2-1 Password
Fish (2), Anchor, Ship, Skull, Anchor

Level 2-2 Password
Skull, Anchor (2), Fish, Anchor, Ship

Level 2-3 Password
Fish, Anchor, Ship (3), Skull

Level 2-4 Password
Anchor, Fish, Ship, Skull (2), Fish

Level 3-1 Password
Ship, Skull (2), Fish, Anchor, Skull

Level 3-2 Password
Fish, Skull, Anchor, Fish, Skull, Fish

Level 3-3 Password
Fish (2), Ship, Skull, Fish, Ship

Level 3-4 Password
Ship, Anchor, Ship, Fish, Anchor, Fish

Level 4-1 Password
Skull (2), Anchor, Ship, Fish (2)

Level 4-2 Password
Ship, Anchor, Skull, Fish (2), Anchor

Level 4-3 Password
Skull, Ship, Skull (2), Fish, Ship

Level 4-4 Password
Ship, Fish, Ship, Fish, Ship, Anchor

Level 5-1 Password
Anchor, Ship, Fish, Skull, Fish, Ship

Level 5-2 Password
Fish, Ship, Anchor, Skull, Ship, Fish

Level 5-3 Password
Ship, Fish, Skull, Anchor (2), Skull

Level 5-4 Password
Skull, Ship, Anchor, Fish, Ship, Skull

OVERBLOOD

All Items Invincibility (Japanese)
Highlight the "Start" option on the main menu. Press Left (2), Right (2), Triangle (3), Square (3), X.

OVERBLOOD 2

Super Jump
Hold X, then press Square and a direction on the D-Pad.

Survive Falls
Display the item menu while falling from a high location. Equip a weapon, then remove it. Your character will not take any damage

PAC-MAN WORLD

God Mode
Pause and press Up, Down, Right, L2 (3), Right, Left, Up.

Extra Continues
Select Classic mode. Before pressing Start, press Select to raise the number of continues to 99.

PANDEMONIUM

31 Lives
Enter VITAMINS as a password.

Bonus Screen
Enter CASHDASH as a password. Then, finish a level to reach a bonus screen.

Extra Hearts for Health
Enter CORONARY as a password.

Immortal Enemies
Enter EVILDEAD as a password.

Invincibility
Enter HARDBODY as a password.

Level Select
Enter BORNFREE as a password.

Pinball Screen
Enter TOMMYBOY as a password. Then, finish a level. You'll reach a pinball screen. You can also enter KNCACKDE as a password.

Restart Without Quitting
Enter INANDOUT as a password. You can quit in the middle of the game and return to the Level Selection screen. To return to the main screen, repeat the quit procedure on the Level Selection screen.

Rotate Screen
Enter TWISTEYE as a password. Hold down L1+L2 and press Left or Right to rotate the screen. Press Down to return to normal.

Special Weapons
Enter OTTOFIRE as a password. This allows access to special weapons that never run out of power.

Switch Characters
Enter BODYSWAP as a password. During gameplay, press Triangle to switch characters.

Warp Body
Enter THETHING as a password. Hold L2+Circle to cycle through different body shapes. Press L2+X to return to normal.

Level 1
ABIAAIIA

Level 2
ACIAEIIC

Level 3
NCAFEBAI

Level 4
KMACBIGA

Level 5
JFACBIAE

Level 6
JNACBICE

Level 7
FEIACCDI

Level 8
JHABBIAI

Level 9
JNAABICI

Level 10
NIABEBCI

Level 11
AHIAEIJG

Level 12
EPAACCC

Level 13
AIIAAIJM

Level 14
NKAAFBLJ

Level 15
NMAAEBE

Level 16
ACMAEIID A

Level 17
KJABBIFA

Level 18
ADMAEIIH

PANDEMONIUM 2

Level Select
Enter GETACCES or OCMCKKEJ as a password.

Invincibility
Enter NEVERDIE as a password.

Full Health
Enter HORMONES as a password.

Weapons
Enter MAKMYDAY as a password.

31 Lives
Enter IMMORTAL as a password.

Rolling Camera View
Enter GONAHURL as a password.

Speed Mode
Enter SKATBORD as a password.

Mutant Mode
Enter GENETICS as a password.

Psychedelic Textures
Enter ACIDDUDE as a password.

Regenerating Monsters
Enter JUSTKIDN as a password.

Level 1, Ice Prison
EMIAGCAI

Level 2, Zorrscha's Lab
OMACCBAI

Level 3, Hot Pants
FAIAGCBI

Level 4, Stan's the Man
FEKAGCCA

Level 5, Oyster Desoyster
LGBFIICE

Level 6, Puzzle Wood
LMBBIIEE

Level 7, Temple of Nori
IEBBIIGF

Level 8, Egg! Egg!
KNBBIIAI

Level 9, Huevos Libertad!
LGBJIICI

Level 10, Pipe Hous
LOBJIIEI

Level 11, Hate Tank
IGBJIIGJ

Level 12, Fantabulous
FFCAGCCC

Level 13, Mr. Schneobelen
FHCAGCCK

Level 14, Collide O Scope
FJKEGCDC

Level 15, The Zoul Train
FLKEGCDK

Level 16, Lick the Toad
ADIKBIIB

Level 17, The Bitter End
ADMIBIID

Level 18, Rub the Buddha
MAECCBEJ

PANZER BANDIT

Get All the Bosses
Enter Options and then go to Story mode. Hold Select and press Up, Down, Right, Left, Square, X, Triangle, Circle.

PARAPPA THE RAPPER

Change Parappa's Voice
Achieve a rating of "Cool!" in the first two levels. Then, press X (3), Triangle, Circle, Triangle, Square (2), Right, Left, Square, X and finish the next level. On Level 4, press X, Square, Triangle, Circle, X to change Parappa's voice. Hold R1 and press Circle or Triangle to cycle through the other characters' voices.

Play as a Beetle
Beat the first board on "Cool!," the second board on "Good!," the third board on "Good!," the fourth board on "Cool!," the fifth board on "Cool!" and the last stage on "Good!" "Cool!" has to be blinking. A new game is selectable: the Beetle Rappa!

Bonus Level
Complete each level with a "Cool!" rating to access a bonus level with Sunny Funny and Katy Kat dancing on a table.

PARASITE EVE

EX Game Mode
Finish the game to enable a new mode option.

Extra Points
Complete one day without saving to receive extra points when the following day begins.

Extra Ammunition
Return to the police station and open the box inside the weapon storage room to collect 30 bullets. This may be done 10 times.

Track the Helicopter
At the City Map screen, press Select to track the helicopter as it flies around the city.

PARASITE EVE II

Hypervelocity Weapon
Get an "A" rating and you can buy this weapon for 20,000 BP (Replay mode only).

Gunblade Weapon
Get an "A" rating and you can buy this weapon from *Final Fantasy VIII* for 10,000 BP (Replay mode only). Use R1 to swing and R2 to shoot at the same time the blade hits the enemy.

Monk Robe
End the game with less than 14,510 EXP and you can buy this armor for 3,000 BP (Replay mode only).

PARODIUS

Invincibility
Pause and press Triangle (2), Right, Left, Right, Left, Down, Left. A sound confirms correct entry. Re-enter the code to disable invincibility.

Power-Ups
Pause and press Up (2), Down (3), L, R, L, R, Right, Left. A sound confirms correct entry. This code enables maximum power.

Level Select
Press Square (5), Triangle (7), Circle (3) at the title screen.

PEAK PERFORMANCE

Special Class Vehicles
At the Car Selection menu, highlight Garage A and press L1+Circle. Highlight Garage B and press L1+Circle. Highlight Garage C and press L1+R1+Circle. Go back to the Car Selection menu and choose the new "Special" option. The bus, truck, McLaren F-1, and scooter are available.

Alternate Car Appearance
Select One-player mode and enter the Car Selection screen. Enter Garage A, hold Circle, and press X. Car A03 now has its top down. Enter Garage B, hold Circle, and press X. Car B04 now has new headlights and new colors. Enter Garage C, hold Circle, and press X. Car C06 now has a sunroof.

Nissan 240 ZX and Bus
Beat the Bay Area track in less than three minutes.

Diablo
Win on the Uptown Driveway track at all three difficulty levels in One-player mode. Then, win on the next level. Race the Uptown Driveway track in Time Trial mode and find the parked Diablo.

Porsche
Win on the Seven Tight Corners track at all three difficulty levels in One-player mode. Then, race the same track in Time Trial mode and find the Porsche at the hotel.

McLaren and Truck
Select a car and Finish the Pikes Peak Hill Climb track in less than two minutes 30 seconds.

Scooter
Race the Northern Country track in Time Trial mode counterclockwise. Go through the gate near the river on the second lap to find the scooter.

Soccer Balls
While using the course editor to turn the cone white, hold X and press Triangle. Repeat until all cones are placed. Start the race. Soccer balls appear where the white cones were placed.

Emergency Flashers
While in any garage, hold L1 and press R1.

PERFECT WEAPON

Level Select
Pause and press R1+Square, Triangle, Circle, X.

Invincibility
Pause and press Circle+Square+Right, Left+R1+R2. An explosion confirms correct entry.

Play as Cyborg Blake
Pause and press R1+R2+Triangle+Circle. The phrase "No Way!" confirms correct entry.

All Sphere Mode
Pause and press L1+L2+Circle+Square.

Big Head Mode
Pause and press L1+L2+R2+Down.

Ice Moon Level
Press X, Square, X, Square (2), Circle, Square, Circle.

Garden Moon Level
Press Circle, X (2), Triangle, Circle (2), X, Triangle.

Forest Moon Level
Press Circle, Triangle, Square, Circle, Square (2), Triangle (2).

Desert Moon Level
Press Circle, X (3), Triangle, Circle, Triangle (2).

Morgone Level
Press X (2), Square, X, Square (2), Triangle, Circle.

PERSONA

Get the Best Ending
When you talk to Mae in the Lost Forest, Mae says, "If I stay here I'll be safe, right?" Respond with, "Stop!" She says, "Why do you fight?" Answer with, "For everyone." She says, "Why must you live?" Respond with, "For finding the answer."

Get Chris to Join You
First, talk to the teacher in the room north of the entrance. Second, search all the rooms on the second floor. Third, talk to the students in room 2-1. Fourth, head to the casino on Joy Street and talk to everyone there. Fifth, visit the abandoned factory. Sixth, head to Yin & Yan and talk to Chris's mother. Say that you know Chris and you'll be his friend. Seventh, leave the hospital and meet Chris in front of the Sebec Building. Then, don't allow Alana, Brad, or Ellen to join you. Meet Chris in Mary's World and he will join you.

PITBALL

First-Person Viewpoint
Highlight "FMV Test" in the Options screen. Press Circle+Square.

Secret Game
Highlight any player video. Press Circle+Square. A different ship is available for each different team.

All FMV Movies
Highlight "FMV Test" in the Options screen. Press Left, Right, Square, Circle. Enter the FMV Test to see any of the game's movies.

PITFALL 3D

Original Pitfall Minigame
Enter CRANESBABY as a password. During the minigame, press one of the following button combinations to activate the corresponding cheat function.

Infinite Lives
Press L1+L2.

Crocodile Message
Press R1+Triangle while on a Crocodile screen.

Change Head to Atari 2600 Programmer
Press R1+R2.

Change Head to Programmer's Daughter
Press R1+Circle.

Invisibility
2DHARRY

Extra Life
GIVEMELIFE

99 Lives
STEVECRANEME

View FMV Sequences
PLAYMOVIES

Show Comic Book Scenes
PITFALLCOMIC

View Credits
CREDITS

Flying Mode
ZEROGHARRY

Big Head Mode
BIGHEADHARY

Start at Level 3 with 56 lives
DISCOLIGHTS5

Disable Comments from Harry
STOPTALKING

Demo Game
VIGILANTE

Level 2, City of Shenrak
METROPOLIS

Level 3, Underground Caverns
DEEPDARK

Level 4, Moku Temple
TEMPLEME

Level 4A, Gladiator
GEEHEISBIG

Level 5, Blister Fields
HOTROCKS

Level 6, Desert into Volcano
GOINGDOWN

Level 7, Blazing Flood
WOWTHATSHOT

Level 7A, Kryll Thular
BIGWORMGUY

Level 8, Cell Blocks
JAILBREAK

Level 9, Life Extraction
THUNDERDOMES

Level 10, Dark Vale
MAGICGARDEN

Level 11, Crystal Matrix
SPOOKYMESAS

End, the Scourge
BESTFORLAST

POCKET FIGHTER

Play as Dan
On the Character Selection screen, highlight Ken and press Right.

Play as Gouki
On the Character Selection screen, highlight Ryu and press Left.

PO'ED

Level Select
At the main menu, press L1+L2+R1+R2+Up. Press Circle to start a new game. At the Difficulty menu, press L1+L2+R1+R2+Down. Choose a difficulty and the level select menu appears.

Fart Sounds
Highlight a game from the Load Game menu and press L1+L2+R1+R2. Exit the Load Game menu. Now levels with the Butthead monster are modified.

Full Inventory
During gameplay, press Square+Select to enter 3D Map mode. Press Left until the map arrow points toward you, then press Start to return to Standard Map view. Press L1+Square+X+Circle while the camera is rotating. Press Select to exit Map mode. Press Triangle for all the weapons and the jetpack.

Full Ammunition
During gameplay, do a back flip by pressing Square+L2. While in the air, press Right+X+ Circle. Ammunition for all weapons is refilled.

Full Health
During gameplay, do a back flip by pressing Square+L2. While in the air, press Down+X+R2. Ox's health refills.

Invincibility
Use the "full inventory" code or find the drill and place it in inventory. Use the frying pan as the current weapon. Enter the Weapon Selection screen and highlight the drill, then press Circle+R1. The number "999" flashes next to the health meter.

Disable Invulnerability
Enter the Weapon Selection screen and press Circle+R1.

View Ending Sequence
Save at least one game. Then, go to the main menu and highlight "Load Game." Hold Right, then press Circle. Release Right and press Triangle to cancel. Next, press Left+Square, then press Triangle to cancel again.

No Collisions
Switch to Jetpack mode and kill an alien. Stand on the alien and press Triangle to display the Weapon Select screen. Then, press L1+Right+Down. Now Ox can fly through the walls and move anywhere in the level.

Disable No Collisions
Switch to Jetpack mode and press Triangle to display the Weapon Select screen. Then, press L1+Right+Down.

POINT BLANK 2

Hidden Options
At the main menu, shoot at the far right side of the screen several times. Then, choose "Options" for more choices.

PONG

Level Select
At the Options screen, press L1, R1, L1, R1, L1, R1. Select the star field beyond what looks like the final level to play the original 1972 Pong.

Unlock First Level in All Zones
At the Zone Selection screen, pause and press L1, R1, L1, R1, then resume.

Unlock Second Level in All Zones
At the Zone Selection screen, pause and press L2, R2, L2, R2, then resume.

Unlock Third Level in All Zones and More
At the Zone Selection screen, pause and hold L1+R1+L2+R2. Resume and the secret power-ups and the three black-and-white Pong versions are available.

POOL HUSTLER

Bowlliards Minigame
At the title screen, press Up (2), Down (2), Triangle (2), X (2), Left, Right, Square, Circle to unlock a bowling/pool game.

POPULOUS: BEGINNING

Cheat Mode
Highlight and press X on every tree in the first level. After that, press Start. The last option should be "Cheat." Select it to access a Cheat menu with options for maximum mana, all spells, and all buildings.

PORSCHE CHALLENGE

All Cars Jump
At the main menu, quickly press Up+Square, Up+X, Up+Square, Up+X, Up+Square, Up+X. You should hear a laugh.

Cheat Menu
At the main menu, press Square, Circle, Square. You should hear a laugh.

Crazy Race
At the main menu, quickly press Up, Left, Right+Select. You should hear a laugh.

Fish-Eye Lens View
At the main menu, quickly press Square+Triangle+Circle, L1, L2, R2, R1. You should hear a laugh.

High Voices
At the main menu, quickly press Up, Triangle, Up, Triangle. You should hear a laugh.

Hyper Car
At the main menu, quickly press Select+Square, Select+Circle, Select+Square+Circle. You should hear a laugh.

Infinite Continues
At the main menu, quickly press L1+L2, R1+R2+Square. You should hear a laugh.

Invisible Car
At the main menu, quickly press Square+X, L2+R2, Square+X, L1+R1, Square+X. You should hear a laugh. Beware: This code might crash the game!

Mirror Mode
At the main menu, quickly press Left+X, Down+Triangle, Right+Square. You should hear a laugh.

More Voices
At the main menu, highlight "Options" and press X, Triangle. Highlight "2 Players" and press X, Triangle. Highlight "1 Player" and press X, Triangle. You should hear a laugh. Select additional voices through a new menu option.

Player's Car Jumps
At the main menu, quickly press Square, X, Square. You should hear a laugh.

Race the Interactive Tracks
At the main menu, quickly press Down+Start, Up+Start, Select, Start. You should hear a laugh.

Race the Long Tracks
At the main menu, quickly press Up+Select, Down+Select, Start, Select.

Super Car
At the main menu, quickly press Select+Square, Select+X, Select+Square+X. You should hear a laugh.

Test Drive Black Porsche
At the main menu, quickly press Right+Square, Left+Circle+Select. You should hear a laugh.

Test Driver Available
At the main menu, quickly press Right+Square, Left+Select+X. You should hear a laugh.

Tune Test Driver
At the main menu, quickly press Left+Circle, Right+Square+Select. You should hear a laugh.

View Credits and Ending Sequence
At the main menu, quickly press Square, X, Left+Select, Right+Select.

POWER INSTINCT 2

Hidden Characters
Enter Team Battle mode. At the Character Selection screen, press Left, Right, Down, Up, Down, Left, Right, Left, Up.

POWER MOVE WRESTLING

Power Warrior Secret Wrestler
While at the title screen, press Square, X, Square, X, Circle, Triangle, Circle, Triangle, Up, Down, Left, Right, Select. You should hear a bell. Highlight Lance and press Select.

Sparrow Secret Wrestler
At the title screen, press Circle, Right, Triangle, Up, Square, Left, X, Down, X, Down, Square, Left, Triangle, Up, Circle, Right, Select. You should hear a bell. Highlight Commandant and press Select.

Ring Announcer Secret Wrestler
At the title screen, press L1 (2), L2, R2 (2), R1, Triangle, Down, X, Up, Select. You should hear a bell. Highlight Agent Orange and press Select.

Referee Secret Wrestler
At the title screen, press Up, Down, Left, Right, Triangle, X, Square, Circle, L1, R1, L2, R2, Select. You should hear a bell. Now highlight the eleventh wrestler listed (El Temblor; Kanemoto in the Japanese version), and press Select.

POWER RANGERS LIGHTSPEED RESCUE

Unlock the Titanium Ranger
Beat the entire game and make sure to save Titanium Ranger at the end. After viewing the credits, save and restart your game. The Titanium Ranger becomes available.

POWER SLAVE

Level Select
At the World Map screen, press Circle, X, Triangle, Square, Right, Down, Up, Left on controller two.

Items
At the World Map, press Select to bring Up the menu. Press Square+Select to add an item. Press Circle to delete an item.

Enhanced Swimming
During gameplay, press Square (2), Triangle (2), X (2), Circle (2). A dolphin icon appears. Your character can now stay underwater longer and swim faster.

Enhanced Flying
During gameplay, press Circle, R1, R2, Square, Right, L1, L2, Left. A vulture icon appears. Press X to fly higher and farther.

Grenade-Propelled Jump
Get the Horus Feather, jump Up, and float just off the ground. Next, look down and toss a grenade. The explosion pushes you Up for a super jump.

Team Dolls
Hidden throughout the game are 23 team dolls. Find 10 dolls to activate Dolphin mode. Your character can swim faster and jump out of the water in this mode. Find 14 dolls to activate Vulture mode. This allows your character to fly.

POWER SPIKE PRO BEACH VOLLEYBALL

Unlock Every Court
In the main menu, highlight "Option" and then enter: Square, Triangle, Circle, Triangle, Square.

POWERBOAT RACING

Tiny Boats
Enter COMPACT as your name.

Turbo Power-Ups on the Course
Enter HELP.ME as your name.

Big Heads
Enter DEFORM as your name.

Big Engines
Enter LARGE as your name.

Faster Boats
Enter ZOOOOOM or SPEEEED as your name.

Championship Mode Password
CUP

Slalom Course Password
L.R

Mines Course Password
U.G

Catamaran and Monohull Boats Password
PLA

Disable Monohull Password
LAS

Minnow Level Catamarans Password
MIN

Barracuda Level Catamarans Password
CUD

Pike Level Catamarans Password
IKE

POY POY

View Character Attributes
At the Character Selection screen, highlight a character and press L1. The number of circles indicates your character's rank in that attribute.

Suicide Bomb
Rapidly tap X, Circle to fill the glove power bar until it explodes.

POY POY 2

Adjust Screen
To adjust the screen, hold down X, Triangle, Circle and Square at the title screen. A grid appears; adjust the screen using the D-Pad, but don't let go of the action buttons!

Easy Upgrades
To by-pass getting enough experience for the gloves, enter and exit the One-player mode until a red-headed man is standing in the place of the usual upgrade. Talk to him, and he offers you upgrades to all your gloves for half price, no matter how much experience you have with it. You will have to enter and exit a few times for this to work.

Suicide Bomb
If your character dies, you can blow yourself up. To do so, press all of the buttons except the directional buttons until your psycho power is full.

PRIMAL RAGE

Hidden Volleyball Game
This code only works in Two-player mode. In the Cove (Sauron's stage), have one player complete a combo. Two humans appear and start to bow. Have the player closest to a human knock him into the air. The other player must volley the human back before he hits the ground. Continue volleying until a net and judge appear. Volleyball with humans is now playable.

Hidden Bowling Game
This code only works in Two-player mode. Both players must be Armadon, and they must perform the Spinning Death (1+3, Away, Toward, Down) move simultaneously three times in a row. If done correctly, both players and their worshippers walk offscreen for a bowling game.

Skydiving Cows
This code only works in Two-player mode. When in the Ruins (Chaos's stage), have one player play as Chaos in a Sudden Death round. Allow the match timer to run down to about two to three seconds. Have the player playing as Chaos perform the Fart of Fury move (2+3, Toward, Up, Away) so that the cloud remains in the air after time expires. The falling meteors turn into falling cows.

Color Change
When selecting your character, press X and Circle, Square, or Triangle.

PRO SKATER

Unlock All Practice Modes
Pause the game, then hold L1 and press Square, Up, left, Up, Circle, Triangle. If you entered the code correctly, the Pause screen shakes. Quit the current level and enter the Selection screen. All practice mode levels will now be unlocked.

Big Head Mode
Pause the game, then hold L1 and press Left, Up, X, Down, Up, X. If you entered the code correctly, the screen shakes. Then, quit the current level and start another game.

Extra Points
While in the air, hold the D-Pad+Circle and release the button before hitting the ground.

Special Moves
Press Left, Left, Square to perform a special move when in the half-pipe in the street course. You need to get enough air to land it. Bob Burnquist does a Fingerflip airwalk, and Tony Hawk does a 540 Board Varial.

PROJECT OVERKILL

Invincibility
Pause and highlight "Sound Volume." Hold Right and press Circle, Square, Triangle. Hold Left and press Circle, Square, and X. "Cheater" appears at the screen's top.

Refill Health
Pause and highlight "Sound Volume." Hold Square and press Circle, X, Triangle. Release Square, hold Circle, and press Square, X, Triangle. Release Circle. "Cheater" appears at the screen's top.

Refill Ammunition
Pause and highlight "Sound Volume." Hold Circle and press Square. Release Circle, hold Triangle, and press X. Release Triangle, hold Circle, and press X. Release Circle, hold X, press Square. Release X. "Cheater" appears at the screen's top.

Shield
Pause and highlight "Sound Volume." Hold Right, and press Circle, Square, Triangle. Release Right, hold Left, and press Square, Circle, X. Release Left and resume the game to have a shield. "Cheater" appears at the screen's top.

Turbo
Pause and highlight "Sound Volume." Hold Up and press Triangle (3). Release Up, hold Down, and press X, Square, Circle. Release Down. "Cheater" appears at the screen's top.

Predator
Pause and highlight "Sound Volume." Hold Triangle and press Square, X (2), Square. Release Triangle, hold X, and press Triangle (2). "Cheater" appears at the screen's top.

Cloaking Device
Pause and highlight "Sound Volume." Hold Triangle and press Square, Circle (2), Square. Release Triangle, hold X, and press Triangle (2). Release X. "Cheater" appears at the screen's top.

End Current Level

Pause and highlight "Sound Volume." Hold X, Up, Down, Up. Hold Square and press Circle. Release Square, hold X, and press Triangle. Release X. "Cheater" appears at the screen's top.

Body Slide

Pause and highlight "Sound Volume." Press Up, Down (2), Up. Hold Square and press Circle. Press Triangle, X (or X, Triangle). "Cheater" appears at the screen's top.

Test mode

Pause and highlight "Sound Volume." Press Left, Right (2), Left. Hold X and press Triangle. Hold Triangle and press X. "Cheater" appears at the screen's top.

Secret Level

In the Throg Breeding Facility is a secret entrance to the Lost City. It's in the lower-right corner of the map. Break through three or four secret doors to find the exit. The Lost City is full of insect-monster larvae and the Throg-Viscerian genetic brain mutations.

PROJECT: HORNED OWL

Extra Options

Beat the game at Very Hard difficulty and the following options become available: Polygon test (view enemies from any angle), Mission select, Movie test (view all FMV sequences), and Audio test.

Extra Continues

Start a game in Single-player mode. Just before losing your last life, press Start on controller two to gain three additional continues.

PSYBADEK

Level Select

Enter GOANYWHERE as a password.

Invincibility

Enter DONDACHAOS as a password.

Nine Lives

Enter DONTDIONME as a password.

Infinite Jelly Wobble

Enter JELLYJELLY as a password.

Faster Dek

Enter DEKPOWERUP as a password.

Slower Dek

Enter CLAPPEDOUT as a password.

Big Xako

Enter INLILLIPUT as a password.

Small Xako

Enter SIZOFANANT as a password.

Extra Slide

Enter GREASEDDEK as a password.

Low Gravity

Enter WALKONMOON as a password.

Upside-Down World

Enter TOPSYTURVY as a password.

PSYCHIC FORCE

Play as Keith

Beat the game with all characters without using any continues in Story mode at "Very Hard" difficulty.

PUZZLE BOBBLE 4X

Another World

Press Triangle, Left, Right, Left, Triangle at the title screen. A sound confirms correct entry and a small face appears.

QUAKE II

Bronze Cheats

Win at Easy difficulty to open "One Hit Kill" and "Weapons Stay" options for Multiplayer modes. You can save these cheats to your memory card.

Silver Cheats

Win at Medium difficulty to open "Game Speed," "Blast Force," "One Hit Kills," and "Weapons Stay" options for Multiplayer mode. You can save these cheats to your memory card.

Gold Cheats

Win at Hard difficulty to open infinite ammo, all weapons, "Game Speed," "Blast Force, "One Hit Kills," and "Weapons Stay" options for Multiplayer mode. You can save these cheats to your memory card.

R4: RIDGE RACER TYPE 4

Turbo Starts

Hold L2+R2 at the race's start.

Bonus Vehicles

Unlock all 320 cars in the game to unlock the Pac-Man car and a new music track, "Eat Em Up."

Unlock Extra Trial Mode

Beat Gran Prix mode to unlock Extra Trial mode.

Rage Racer Banners

Use a memory card that has a saved game file from *Rage Racer*. Your old team information will be displayed on the cars in this game.

Game Music

Place the disk into an audio CD player. Listen to tracks two or higher to hear music from the game.

Four-Player Game

Use a link cable to connect two PlayStations and a "Link Battle" mode appears. This lets you play a four-player game.

RAGE RACER

Mirror Mode

Select a race and hold L1+R1+Select+Start until the race begins. You race in reverse on that track.

Rotate the Logo

In the Logo Painting area, hold L1+R1 and press any D-Pad direction.

Rearview Mirror

Pause the game. Hold Triangle and press L1. This toggles the rearview mirror on and off.

Paint Zoom

In the logo painting area, press L1+L2+R1+R2+Select to get crosshairs.

Additional Paint Colors

Move the cursor out of the painting area. Hold L1+L2+R1+R2+Select. An RGB option appears to the right. Change the values by using Left or Right and R1+Up or R1+Down. Repeatedly tap Select to display the guide markers in the painting area.

Alter Track View

At the Track Selection screen, press L1+R1 to spin the track slower or faster.

Alter Car View

At the Car Selection screen, press L2+R2 to steer the front wheels.

Unlimited Money

Complete the Normal GP mode game on all classes. Watch all the credits. Save in a new slot. Then, play Extra GP mode on Class 1. Pick the only car available. Pick the "Race Start" option and press Start during the countdown. Pick the "Retire" option to quit and you will not lose an attempt. Enter Normal GP mode on Class 1 again and you have unlimited money.

RAGING SKIES

Extra Time

Hold L1+L2+R1+R2+Circle+X+Triangle+Square+Left as the game loads.

RAIDEN PROJECT

Level Select

Select "Settings" and choose the Difficulty option. Hold L1+L2+R1+R2 and press Start.

Play the Demo

Hold L1 during the *Raiden I* demonstration to control the ship. Hold R2 during the *Raiden II* demonstration to control the ship.

Extra Options

Hold L1+L2+R1+R2 during gameplay to see a hidden Options menu.

Infinite Continues

On either game, go into the Options screen, choose "Miscellaneous," and highlight "Credit Limit." Hold Triangle+Circle+Square+X. A "Free Play" option appears if you entered the code correctly.

16 Credits

Set the options to have nine credits. Start a game using controller two. Press Start on controller one once player two's ship launches. Let player two's ship be lost and player one has 16 credits.

RAINBOW ISLANDS

Always Fast Shoes

Enter BLRBJSBJ as a password on the title screen, while the rainbow cycles through colors.

100 Million Counter

Enter SRBJSLSB as a password on the title screen, while the rainbow cycles through colors.

Hidden Food Becomes Money Bags

Enter RRLLBBJS as a password on the title screen, while the rainbow cycles through colors.

Continue After Island Five

Enter LBSJRLJL as a password on the title screen, while the rainbow cycles through colors.

Always Double Rainbows

Enter RJSBJSBR as a password on the title screen, while the rainbow cycles through colors.

Always Fast Rainbows

Enter SSSLLRRS as a password on the title screen, while the rainbow cycles through colors.

Perform the Previous Two Passwords

Enter RRRRSBSJ as a password on the title screen, while the rainbow cycles through colors.

Hint A

Enter BJBJBJRS as a password on the title screen, while the rainbow cycles through colors.

Hint B

Enter LJLSLBLS as a password on the title screen, while the rainbow cycles through colors.

RAINBOW SIX

Unlock All Doors

Pause the game. Hold L1 and press Triangle, Square (2), Triangle, X, Circle, Square, Triangle.

Show the Ending

Pause, hold L1, and press Square, Triangle, Square (2), Circle (2), X, Triangle. This can also be entered at the main menu.

Full Health

Pause, hold L1, and press Triangle (2), X, Circle (2), X, Square (2).

All Maps

Pause, hold L1, and press X, Circle, Square, Triangle (2), Square, Circle, X. This can also be entered at the main menu.

Hostage Can't Be Killed

Pause, hold L1, and press Circle (2), Square, Triangle, X, Triangle, X, Circle. This can also be entered at the main menu.

All Main Guns

Pause, hold L1, and press X, Circle (2), Triangle, Square, X, Square, Circle.

Extra Ammo

Pause, hold L1, and press Square (2), Circle, Triangle, X, Triangle, X, Triangle.

Free For All Mode

Pause, hold L1, and press Circle, Triangle (2), X, Circle, Square, X, Triangle. This can also be entered at the main menu.

No Terrorists

Pause, hold L1, and press Triangle, Circle (2), Triangle, Square, X, Triangle, Circle. This can also be entered at the main menu.

All Secondary Pistols

Pause, hold L1, and press X, Triangle, Square, Circle, Square, X, Triangle, Square.

All Items

Pause, hold L1, and press Triangle, X (2), Circle, Square, Circle, X, Triangle. This can also be entered at the main menu.

Supermen Mode

Pause, hold L1, and press X, Square, Triangle(2), Circle, Square, X (2). This can also be entered at the main menu.

RAINBOW SIX: ROGUE SPEAR

Level Select

Start the game without a memory card. Select campaign mode, choose Load Game, then enter P8H!H!P8P?H!? as a password.

Level 02

4yh8h8pyp?h87

Level 03

wyl8l8xqh?l8z

Level 04

!yp5p5?qh?p8z

Level 05

czt5t5hrf?t8z

Level 06

kzx5v5prf?x8z

Level 07

sz75z5xrf?78z

Level 08

6z?595?rf??8z

Level 09

c6dvbvhsf9d9j

Level 10

k6gvfrpsf9g9j

Level 11

s6kvjrxcf9k9j

RALLY CROSS

Cheat Codes

Only one code can be entered per game.

Fat Tires

Enter fat tires on the High Score screen or when you begin a new season.

No Tires

Enter no wheels on the High Score screen or when you begin a new season.

Extra Tires

Enter wheels on the High Score screen or when you begin a new season.

Heavier Cars

Enter stone on the High Score screen or when you begin a new season.

Lighter Cars

Enter feather on the High Score screen or when you begin a new season.

Low Gravity and Stupid CPU

Enter float on the High Score screen or when you begin a new season.

Reduced Tire Friction

Enter spinner on the High Score screen or when you begin a new season.

Better Acceleration

Enter banzai on the High Score screen or when you begin a new season.

Natural Elements Don't Slow Down the Car

Enter noviscous on the High Score screen or when you begin a new season.

Realistic Gravity

Enter radbrad on the High Score screen or when you begin a new season.

More Skidding on Hard Turns

Enter high_time on the High Score screen or when you begin a new season.

Win the Rookie Season

Enter vet me on the High Score screen or when you begin a new season.

Win the Veteran Season

Enter im a pro on the High Score screen or when you begin a new season.

Win the Normal, Head-On, Mixed-Pro Seasons

Enter weeoo on the High Score screen or when you begin a new season.

RALLY CROSS 2

All Cars

Enter MOOBMOOB as your name when you start a new season.

All Tracks and Most Cars

Enter PREALL as your name when you start a new season.

Low Gravity

Enter AIRFILLED as your name when you start a new season.

Pro Level Tracks and Cars

Enter PREPRO as your name when you start a new season.

Veteran Level Tracks and Cars

Enter PREVET as your name when you start a new season.

Oasis Track

Enter SISAO as your name when you start a new season.

Hillside Track

Enter BSIRHC as your name when you start a new season.

Jungle Track

Enter ELGNUJ as your name when you start a new season.

Little Woods Track

Enter FOSTER as your name when you start a new season.

Dry Humps Track

Enter CIRE as your name when you start a new season.

Rock Creek Track

Enter KCIN as your name when you start a new season.

Frozen Trail Track

Enter NIVEK as your name when you start a new season.

Dusty Road Track

Enter MIT as your name when you start a new season.

No Collisions

Enter INCORPEREAL as your name when you start a new season.

Game Physics

Enter LEADSHOT as your name when you start a new season to play with the physics from the original *Rally Cross* game. Enter MOONEY as a name to return to *Rally Cross 2* game physics.

RAMPAGE 2: UNIVERSAL TOUR

Cheat Option

Enter BVGGY as a password. A Cheat menu becomes added to the Options menu.

Play as George

Enter SM14N as a password.

Play as Lizzie

Enter S4VRS as a password.

Play as Myukus

Enter N0T3T as a password.

Play as Alternate Myukus
Enter B1G4L as a password.

Play as Noobus Myukus
Enter SRY3D as a password.

Play as Ralph
Enter LVPVS as a password.

RAMPAGE WORLD TOUR

Different Character Colors
Press Up to change the color of the character you are choosing.

Infinite Life
Pause, hold R1, and press Triangle, Square (2), Circle (2), X (2), Triangle. A roar confirms correct entry.

RANMA 1/2: BATTLE RENAISSANCE

Alternate Costumes
Hold L1+L2 and pick your character. This only works in Versus and Battle mode.

Play as the Final Boss
Go into Versus mode. Player one needs to highlight Ranma and press Right, Right, Right, Down, Left (3), Up. Then press any key. Player two needs to highlight Ranma and press Left (3), Up, Right, Right, Right, Down. Then press any key.

RAPID RACER

All Boats
Enter /BOA at the player name screen.

Unlock Mirror Tracks
Enter RRIM at the player name screen.

Unlock Day Tracks
Enter _DAY at the player name screen. (The "_" represents a space.)

Unlock Night Tracks
Enter _NIT at the player name screen. (The "_" represents a space.)

Unlock Fractal Tracks
Enter FRAC at the player name screen.

Finish Race
Enter WINR at the player name screen.

Play All Streams
Enter _STR at the player name screen. (The "_" represents a space.)

Duck Cheat
Enter _QAK at the player name screen. (The "_" represents a space.)

Unlock the Hurricane Boat
Enter HURR at the player name screen.

RASCAL

Invincibility
Enter INFIN as a password.

Infinite Ammo
Enter JUICY as a password.

All Rooms and Level Select
Enter HOUSE as a password, then start a new game. During gameplay, press R1 to change the level or R2 to change the room.

RAYMAN

99 Lives
Enter XNB9FM!Z2? as a password.

Simulated Picture-in-Picture
Pause, hold R2, and press Circle (2), Left, Circle (2). Reenter the code to disable it.

Big Rayman
After the Ubi Soft logo appears, hold L1+L2+R1+R2. After you see the animation of the brick wall, hold Start also. Release all the buttons when the screen turns black.

10 Continues
Pause the game when you have fewer than three continues, and press Up, Down, Right, Left.

Disable Levels
Turn on your PlayStation and don't press any buttons. When the screen showing Rayman in bubble letters appears, hold Triangle+Square+Start until you see the screen shake. Then you can pick the levels you want to skip.

Full Power-Up with 99 Lives (Method 1)
Pause, hold R1+R2+L2, and press Circle, Right, Square, Left, Circle. If that didn't work, try Method 2.

Full Power-Up with 99 Lives (Method 2)
Pause, press and hold L2, R1, L1 sequentially, then hold R2. Release L1, L2, R2, R1 sequentially. Press Circle. Hold Left+Circle+Square+Triangle. Release Left, Triangle, Square, and Circle sequentially.

Band Land Completed
Enter J5VLFP58VB as a password (American version only).

Cave of Skop Completed
Enter SM!KV7WSXD as a password (American version only).

Blue Mountain Completed
Enter J5K!ZZC8MD as a password (American version only).

Access to Space Mama
Enter T64H5M!?BB as a password (American version only).

Access to Skops
Enter ?2MC9J!GTB as a password (American version only).

Picture City Completed
Enter SX2!ZP58MD as a password (American version only).

Freed All Electoons
Enter 492kv3w9xd as a password (American version only).

RAYSTORM

Free Play
Hold L1+L2+R1+R2 and press Start when "Press Start" flashes. Continue holding L1+L2+R1+R2 and press Up (7), Down, Up (4). The cursor should be highlighting Option. Press Start. Go to the configuration screen and turn off the credit limit to free play. Otherwise, play the game more than 200 times.

Level Select
Beat the Combat mode game under Arcade mode.

13 Ships
Beat the Combat mode game under Extra mode.

RAY TRACERS

Unlock Tsumuji's Car
Pick Tsumuji as your opponent in Time Attack mode. Place first and his car becomes selectable. This status is saved with the game.

Unlock the White Vestal
Win with all the cars never using a continue.

Unlock the Black Vestal
Win with the White Vestal and without continuing.

RAZOR FREESTYLE SCOOTER

Unlock Everything
Pause the game during gameplay, then press Right, Down, Right, Left, Right, Up, Right(2).

R.C. RACER

Three Alternate Camera Angles
Play on any track in Time Attack mode. Enter CAM as your name. Hold L1+L2+R1+R2 and press X at the OK Confirmation screen. Exit the track and press L1.

All Gates Unlocked
Enter Exploration mode and complete three laps. Enter OPN as a name. Hold L1+L2+R1+R2 and press X at the OK Confirmation screen.

Slow Motion Mode
Enter Exploration mode and complete three laps. Enter SLO as a name. Hold L1+L2+R1+R2 and press X at the OK Confirmation screen.

Enter Gates for Power-Ups
Enter Exploration mode and complete three laps. Enter POW as a name. Hold L1+L2+R1+R2 and press X at the OK Confirmation screen.

R.C. STUNT COPTER

Unlock All Levels
Press Down, Up, Right, Left, Triangle, X, Square, Circle at the title screen. A spoken message confirms correct entry, then the Cheat function displays.

Ending Credits
Press Up, Down, Left (2), X, Square, Triangle, Circle at the title screen. A spoken message confirms correct entry, then the Cheat function displays.

Big Points
Press L2, R2, L1, R1, Triangle, Circle, X, Square at the title screen. A spoken message confirms correct entry, then the Cheat function displays.

Long Name
Press Up, Down, Left, Right, Triangle, X, Square, Circle at the title screen. A spoken message confirms correct entry, then the Cheat function displays.

Unlock All Gold Medals
Press Down, Up, Left, Right, Triangle, X, Square, Circle at the title screen. A spoken message confirms correct entry, then the Cheat function displays.

PLAYSTATION

READY 2 RUMBLE BOXING

Bronze Class Boxers
In Championship mode, enter BRONZE as a gym name to unlock all bronze class boxers in Championship mode. Kemo Claw becomes selectable in Arcade mode also.

Silver Class Boxers
In Championship mode, enter SILVER as a gym name to unlock all silver class boxers in Championship mode. Bruce Blade becomes selectable in Arcade mode also.

Gold Class Boxers
In Championship mode, enter GOLD as a gym name. This unlocks all gold class boxers in Championship mode. Nat Daddy becomes selectable in Arcade mode also.

Championship Class Boxers
In Championship mode, enter CHAMP as a gym name. This unlocks all championship class boxers in Championship mode. Damien Black becomes selectable in Arcade mode also.

Initiate Rumble Mode
Spell out RUMBLE during a round with your character. Press Circle+X to initiate the character's rumble combo.

Alternate Costumes
Press Square+Circle when selecting a character.

Cheap Vitamins
Train your character in Championship mode. At the aerobics screen, press Left, X before the screen scrolls to the other training regimen. Done correctly, this buys $25,000 vitamins for $500. This trick works with other items.

REAL ROBOTS FINAL ATTACK

Play as the Bosses
The robots are numbered 1-7, according to their order from left to right. When you highlight a character, press Triangle.

Boss 1
2,3,4,2,5

Boss 2
4,4,5,2,5

Boss 3
3,7,1,4,2

Final Boss
Boss 1, Boss 2, Boss 3, Boss 1, 1

REBEL ASSAULT II

Skip Level Password
Triangle (2), Circle, Triangle, Square (2)

View Movies Password
Triangle, Square, Circle, Triangle, Circle (2)

All Levels: Easy Password
X, Circle, X, Circle, X, Triangle

All Levels: Medium Password
X, Square, Triangle (2), X, Triangle

All Levels: Hard Password
X, Circle, Square, Triangle, X, Triangle

View Credits Password
Triangle (2), Circle, Triangle, Square (2)

Hard Mode Password
Triangle, Square (3), X, Triangle

Master Mode Password
X, Triangle (2), Square, X, Triangle

Level 2 Password
X, Triangle, X, Circle (3)

Level 3 Password
Triangle, Square, X, Circle (2), X

Level 4 Password
Triangle, Circle, X, Circle (2), Triangle

Level 5 Password
Triangle, X (2), Circle, Square (2)

Level 6 Password
Triangle (2), X, Circle, Square, Circle

Level 7 Password
Square (2), X, Circle, Square, X

Level 8 Password
Square, Circle, X, Circle, Square, Triangle

Level 9 Password
Square, X (2), Circle, Triangle, Square

Level 10 Password
Square, Triangle, X, Circle, Triangle, Circle

Level 11 Password
Circle, Square, X, Circle, Triangle, X

Level 12 Password
Circle (2), X, Circle, Triangle (2)

Level 13 Password
Circle (2), Triangle, X (2), Square

Level 14 Password
Circle, Triangle, X, Circle, X, Circle

Level 15 Password
X, Square, X, Circle, X (2)

Level 16 Password
X, Circle, X, Circle, X, Triangle

REBOOT

Play as Enzo
Press Up, Left, Down, Left, Down, L1, R1, Right, Down, Right at the main menu. Then start a new game.

Play as Dot
Press Left, R1, Right, Up, Down, R2, L1, Right, Up, Down at the main menu.

Full Glitch Energy
Press Right, L1, Up, Right, Down, L1, R1, Up, Down, Left at the main menu. You can't use with the Free Shield code.

Free Shield with Every Glitch Pick-Up
Press Down, R1, Left, Right, Down, L2, R2, Left, Right, Up at the main menu. You can't use this with the Full Glitch Energy code.

Flight Mode
Press Left, Down, Right, Left, Up, R2, L1, Up, Left, Right at the main menu.

Refill All Weapons
Press Up, L1, Down, Up, Left, R1, L2, Down, Left, Right at the main menu.

RECIPRO HEAT 5000

Unlock Two Bonus Planes
Play 1P Player mode and choose any track. Use all 10 planes to finish in first at that same track.

Super Geebee
Pick Geebee as your character. Then, at the loading screen, hold X until the word "Good" appears.

RED ALERT

Secret Message from Kane
Hold Select and turn the game on.

Access Cheat Codes
Click on the Teams menu with the Cancel button (Circle by default).

1,000 Credits
Enable Cheat codes. Press Cancel over Square (2), Circle, X, Triangle, Circle.

Nuke Attack
Enable Cheat codes. Press Cancel over Circle, X, Circle, Triangle, Square, Triangle.

Instant Victory
Enable Cheat codes. Press Cancel over X, Square (2), Circle, Triangle, Circle.

Parabomb
Enable Cheat codes. Press Cancel over Square, X, Circle (2), X, Triangle.

Full Map
Enable Cheat codes. Press Cancel over Square, Triangle, Circle, X, Triangle, Square.

Chronoshift
Enable Cheat codes. Press Cancel over Triangle, Circle (2), Square (2), X.

Change Ore or Crystals to Gold
Enable Cheat codes. Press Cancel over Square, Circle, Square, X, Circle (2).

Change Ore to Civilians
Enable Cheat codes. Press Cancel over X, Circle, Triangle (2), Circle, X. Enter this code after a refinery is present in Multiplayer mode.

Allies Password 2
PJ1OC3IEW

Allies Password 3
EC5NAHTU

Allies Password 4
9BFVYZAZ8

Allies Password 5
P4XS4CZVC

Allies Password 6
FMNAE6U08

Allies Password 7
7XIQW4KQI

Allies Password 8
WPLAGLJ2G

Allies Password 9
4TNT8RJ21

Allies Password 10
FZ0ZY7ZQA

Allies Password 11
X9FJZVJZI

Allies Password 12
5RNHTXLRY

Allies Password 13
J7VEWVT09

Allies Password 14
OLHDAPYHL

Allies Password 15
17LE3FDV

Soviet Password 1
17DUXFJ6C

Soviet Password 2
VMBWOQ284

Soviet Password 3
XN37MCCSO

Soviet Password 4
LH06FZZQL

Soviet Password 5
BUVV20LFF

Soviet Password 6
AVYQ10YA8

Soviet Password 7
LZRJTMQAN

Soviet Password 8
YQX4C9GFH

Soviet Password 9
1QESO8LE0

Soviet Password 10
RKP0UOXJA

Soviet Password 11
CDLKYL7Q4

Soviet Password 12
8T5GGDK25

Soviet Password 13
X5CDE0KN8

RED ALERT RETALIATION

Ant Missions
Set the difficulty to Hard. Pick "Campaigns" and go to England.

Chronoshift
Place cursor over matching controller symbols in sidebar and press Cancel over each one: Square, Circle, Triangle, X, Circle (2).

Easy Money
Place cursor over matching controller symbols in sidebar and press Cancel over each one: X (2), Square, Circle(3).

Instant Win
Place cursor over matching controller symbols in sidebar and press Cancel over each one: Circle (2), Triangle, X (2), Square.

Iron Curtain
Place cursor over matching controller symbols in sidebar and press Cancel over each one: Square, X, Circle, X, Triangle (2).

Nuclear Attack
Place cursor over matching controller symbols in sidebar and press Cancel over each one: Circle, X, Circle (2), X, Square.

Parabombs
Place cursor over matching controller symbols in sidebar and press Cancel over each one: X (3), Circle, Triangle, Square.

Reveal Map
Place cursor over matching controller symbols in sidebar and press Cancel over each one: Triangle (2), X, Circle, Triangle, Square.

Soylent Green Mode
Place cursor over matching controller symbols in sidebar and press Cancel over each one: Square, X, Square, X, Square, X, Square, X.

Lose Mission
Place cursor over matching controller symbols in sidebar and press Cancel over each one: Circle, X, Circle, Square (2), X.

Civilians Have Names
Place cursor over matching controller symbols in sidebar and press Cancel over each one: Square (2), Circle (2), Triangle.

RED ASPHALT

Big Cars
At the main menu, hold L2+R2 and press Up (3), Square (3). A sound confirms correct entry.

Small Cars
At the main menu, hold L1+R1 and press Down (3), Circle (2). A sound confirms correct entry.

Infinite Cash
At the Selection screen, hold L2+R2 and press Left (2), Right (2), Square (2), Circle (2). A sound confirms correct entry.

Showroom Mode
At the title screen, hold L2+R1 and press Triangle (2), Up (2), Left, Right, Down (2), X (2). The screen goes black if you entered the code correctly. Choose the "Car" option to view a car from multiple angles.

Total Chaos Mode
At the title screen, hold L2+R2 and press Down, Right, Down, Right, Circle (3). The screen goes black if you entered the code correctly and you go to the Total Chaos screen.

Unlock Bonus Cars
At the main menu, hold L2 and press Left, Right, Down, Up, Square, Circle, X, Triangle. A sound confirms correct entry.

Invincibility
Pause, hold R1+R2, and press Up, Left, Right, Down, Triangle, Square, Circle, X. A sound confirms correct entry.

Different Car Colors
At the main menu, hold R1 and press Square, Circle, or Triangle to display three more color schemes. A sound confirms correct entry.

Infinite Nitros
Pause, hold R1+R2, and press Down (3), Circle (3). A sound confirms correct entry. You won't see the ending sequence.

Infinite Weapons
Pause, hold R1+R2, and press Left, Up, Right, Down, Square, Triangle, Circle, X. A sound confirms correct entry. You won't see the ending sequence.

REEL FISHING

Easy Reel-In
After the fish bites and starts swimming quickly to the left, tap X once. When the fish slows down, reel it in. It should not struggle. (This does not work on the "Lake" level.)

Quick Reel-In
In the stream creek level, fish as you normally would. When you see the fish ready to bite the bait, look for bubbles that come out of the fish's mouth. When this happens, press X and O simultaneously and the fish will reel in automatically without snapping the line.

RE-LOADED

Extra Ammo
Pause then hold L1+L2 for 10 seconds so the red cursor can't be moved by the D-Pad. Still holding L1+L2, press Triangle, Left (3), Circle, Triangle, Down. From now on, refill your ammo by pausing and selecting the "ammo" option that appears.

Refill Health
Pause then hold L1+L2 for 10 seconds so the red cursor can't be moved by the D-Pad. Still holding L1+L2, press Down, Right, Left, Triangle, Right, Down. From now on, refill your health by pausing and selecting the "health" option that appears.

Weapon Power-Up
Pause then hold L1+L2 for 10 seconds so the red cursor can't be moved by the D-Pad. Still holding L1+L2, press Left, Up, X, Circle. From now on, power-up your weapon by pausing and selecting the "power" option that appears.

Level Skip
Pause then hold L1+L2 for 10 seconds so the red cursor can't be moved by the D-Pad. Still holding L1+L2, press Left, Triangle, X, Right, Circle, Triangle, Down.

Play as Fwank
Highlight Mamma and press L1, Circle, R1, Down (2), R1, Circle, L1 (2). A red balloon appears over Sister Magpie. Move your cursor to her spot and Fwank becomes a playable character.

Play as a Corpse
Enter the Refill Health code first. Then kill yourself. Pause the game right after you die. Use the "health" option to refill the life bar. Your corpse can now move around.

RESIDENT EVIL

Rocket Launcher
Finish the game in less than three hours. A rocket flies by in the credits. Save the game. Wait for the game to restart and begin another game. You begin the new game with a rocket launcher containing infinite ammunition.

Extra Clothes
Rescue the other two players and beat the game. A "You've got the special key" message appears at the end of the credits. Save the game. Wait for the game to restart and start the game that was just saved. Use the key in the room with the large mirror on the second floor of the mansion. Open the door in the back. Go into the closet and move to the back of the clothes. A message comes up saying, "There is an outfit that fits you perfectly, do you want to put it on?" Choose "yes" to change into new clothes.

Reset the Game
Pause and press Start+Select.

RESIDENT EVIL 2

Extra Costumes
Start a new game on Normal difficulty setting. Don't pick up anything on the way to the police station. Get past the zombie in the alley. Collect the shotgun, kill the zombie, and take the key. Use the key to open the lockers in the dark room and get the alternative uniforms.

Rocket Launcher with Infinite Ammo
Beat either character's first scenario with an A or B ranking in under two hours and 30 minutes. The bonus appears in the next game inside the chest.

Gatling Gun with Infinite Ammo
Beat either character's second scenario with an A or B ranking in under two hours and 30 minutes. The bonus appears in the next game inside the chest.

Machine Gun with Infinite Ammo
Beat either character's second scenario with an A or B ranking in under three hours. The bonus appears in the next game inside the chest.

Play as Hunk
Beat either character's first and second scenarios with an A rating in each. Hunk's mission is to get to the rooftop from the sewers.

Play as Tofu
Beat either character's first and second scenarios in less than three hours. Beat the other character's first and second scenarios in less than three hours. Play a third time and complete either character's first and second scenarios in less than three hours. Save fewer than 12 times during each of the six scenarios. Do not use any other codes. Tofu's mission is to get to the rooftop from the sewers.

Film D
Go to the S.T.A.R.S office on the second floor of the police building. Search the desk on the left side of the room. A message says, "It's trashed, someone must have searched it." Keep searching the desk more than 50 times to find a roll of film. Develop the film in the photo lab to see a picture of Rebecca.

Auto-Aim Feature
Pick "Options" from the main menu or by pressing Select during gameplay. Enter the Key Configuration screen, choose "Type C," and exit. Auto-aim is now on. Hold R1 to get the characters to aim at enemies. Hold R1 and press L1 to change targets.

RESIDENT EVIL 2: DUAL SHOCK EDITION

Unlimited Ammo
Press Select during a game to bring up the Options menu. Pick Key Configuration. Hold R1 and Square (10). If you did the code correctly, "Auto" or "Manual" turn red.

Extreme Battle/Survival Mode
Win the game with Leon and save. Now play Claire's second scenario. Win and save. This unlocks Extreme Battle/Survival mode.

Play as Ada Wong
Beat Level 1 of Extreme Battle/Survival Mode.

Play as Chris Redfield
Beat Level 2 of Extreme Battle/Survival Mode.

Extra Costumes
Start a new game at a Normal difficulty setting. Don't pick up anything on your way to the police station. Get past the zombie in the alley. Collect the shotgun, kill the zombie, and take the key. Use the key to open the lockers in the dark room and get the alternative uniforms.

Rocket Launcher with Infinite Ammo
Beat either character's first scenario with an A or B ranking in under two hours and 30 minutes. The bonus appears in the next game inside the chest.

Gatling Gun with Infinite Ammo
Beat either character's second scenario with an A or B ranking in under two hours and 30 minutes. The bonus appears in the next game inside the chest.

Machine Gun with Infinite Ammo
Beat either character's second scenario with an A or B ranking in under three hours. The bonus appears in the next game inside the chest.

Play as Hunk
Beat either character's first and second scenarios with an A rating in each. Hunk's mission is to get to the rooftop from the sewers.

Play as Tofu
Beat either character's first and second scenarios in less than three hours. Beat the other character's first and second scenarios in less than three hours. Play a third time and complete either character's first and second scenarios in less than three hours. Save fewer than 12 times during each of the six scenarios. Do not use any other codes. Tofu's mission is to get to the rooftop from the sewers.

Film D
Go to the S.T.A.R.S office on the second floor of the police building. Search the desk on the left side of the room. A message says, "It's trashed, someone must have searched it." Keep searching the desk more than 50 times to find a roll of film. Develop the film in the photo lab to see a picture of Rebecca.

Auto-Aim Feature
Pick "Options" from the main menu or press Select during gameplay. Enter the Key Configuration screen, choose "Type C," and exit. Auto-aim is now on. Hold R1 to get the characters to aim at enemies. Hold R1 and press L1 to change targets.

RESIDENT EVIL 3: NEMESIS

Boutique Key
Win once and watch the credits. Save the "Next Game" file to receive a key to the Boutique on the first street at the game's start. Use the key to enter the Boutique and change into other uniforms.

Bonus Costumes
Win at Easy difficulty and receive a grade. The grade determines how many new outfits you get from the Boutique: A equals five and F equals only one. The costumes are a police uniform, *Dino Crisis* suit, disco suit, biker outfit, and the original S.T.A.R.S. outfit.

Epilogues
Win at Hard difficulty to unlock one epilogue. Win eight times at Hard difficulty to unlock all eight epilogues.

Mercenary Mode
Win at Hard difficulty. Watch the credits then save your game. The Mercenaries minigame becomes unlocked. Start a new game, choose that saved game, and select the Mercenaries mode. You play as Carlos, Nikoli, or Mikhal in a race against time.

Jill's Diary
Gather all 30 notes and books in the game. Those replace the first book in your file with Jill's diary.

RESIDENT EVIL: DIRECTOR'S CUT

Rocket Launcher with Infinite Ammo
Win with Chris in less than three hours. Save the game. Start a new game using the saved game and Chris's inventory contains a rocket launcher with unlimited ammo.

Reset the Game
Pause the game and press Start+Select.

Double Items
At the title screen, choose a new game. Highlight the Advanced option. Now hold Right until the color of "Advanced" changes. Begin a game and some items will have doubled.

Colt Python with Infinite Ammo
Win with any character on Advanced mode. Save the game. Begin a new game and load that saved game at the title screen. You have the Colt Python with infinite ammo.

Bonus Costumes
Rescue the other two players and beat the game. A "You've got the special key" message appears at the end of the credits. Save the game. Wait for the game to restart and start the game that was just saved. Use the key in the room with the large mirror on the second floor of the mansion. Open the door in the back. Go into the closet and move to the back of the clothes. A message comes up saying, "There is an outfit that fits you perfectly, do you want to put it on?" Choose "yes" to change into new clothes. If you are using the Arrange option, you won't have the key and the door is unlocked.

RESIDENT EVIL: DIRECTOR'S CUT DUAL SHOCK EDITION

Rocket Launcher with Infinite Ammo
Win with Chris in less than three hours. Save the game. Start a new game using the saved game and Chris's inventory contains a rocket launcher with unlimited ammo.

Reset the Game
Pause then press Start+Select.

Double Items
At the title screen, choose a new game. Highlight the Advanced option. Now hold Right until the color of "Advanced" changes. Begin a game and some items will have doubled.

Bonus Costumes

Rescue the other two players and beat the game. A "You've got the special key" message appears at the end of the credits. Save the game. Wait for the game to restart and start the game that was just saved. Use the key in the room with the large mirror on the second floor of the mansion. Open the door in the back. Go into the closet and move to the back of the clothes. A message comes up saying, "There is an outfit that fits you perfectly, do you want to put it on?" Choose "yes" to change into new clothes. If you using the Arrange option, you won't have the key and the door is unlocked.

RESURRECTION

Play as Assault
At the Character Selection screen, press Right, Up (2), Right, Down, Right, Up (2).

Play as Supervisor
At the Character Selection screen, press Down, Right, Down, Up, Right, Down, Left, Down, Up, Right, Up.

Play as Vitriol
At the Character Selection screen, press Left (3), Up (2), Down, Left (2), Down (2).

Play as Mayhem
At the Character Selection screen, press Left, Right, Down, Left, Up, Left, Down, Left, Down.

Play as Anil 8
At the Character Selection screen, press Up, Right, Down, Right (2), Up, Left, Up.

RETURN FIRE

Self Destruct
While a vehicle's out of the hangar, hold Square+X+Circle+Triangle to blow it up.

Hidden Levels
Complete all the levels including the top set. Then, at the Level Selection screen, move past the screen's top to access an extra row of levels.

One-Player Level 2 Password
Umbrella, Bird, Butterfly, Flower

One-Player Level 3 Password
Face, Teapot, Bunny, Umbrella

One-Player Level 4 Password
Bunny, Umbrella, Bird (2)

One-Player Level 5 Password
Flower, Umbrella, Bunny, Teapot

One-Player Level 6 Password
Bird, Teapot, Butterfly (2)

One-Player Level 7 Password
Bear (2), Clover, Bird

One-Player Level 8 Password
Bunny, Teapot, Umbrella, Heart

One-Player Level 9 Password
Clover, Butterfly, Bird, Heart

One-Player Level 10 Password
Heart, Butterfly, Teapot, Heart

One-Player Level 11 Password
Umbrella (2), Bird, Flower

One-Player Level 12 Password
Flower, Teapot, Clover, Butterfly

One-Player Level 13 Password
Heart, Umbrella, Clover, Heart

One-Player Level 14 Password
Bunny, Face, Flower, Clover

One-Player Level 15 Password
Bunny, Face, Bear, Bird Password

One-Player Level 16 Password
Flower, Umbrella, Bird, Bunny

One-Player Level 17 Password
Flower, Bear, Heart, Umbrella

One-Player Level 18 Password
Face, Bird, Heart, Clover

Two-Player Level 2 Password
Butterfly, Umbrella, Bear, Heart

Two-Player Level 3 Password
Bear, Bunny, Flower, Clover

Two-Player Level 4 Password
Umbrella, Heart, Clover, Flower

Two-Player Level 5 Password
Umbrella, Bear, Bunny, Heart

Two-Player Level 6 Password
Teapot, Bird, Butterfly, Flower

Two-Player Level 7 Password
Heart, Flower, Clover, Butterfly Password

Two-Player Level 8 Password
Heart, Bear, Bunny, Heart

Two-Player Level 9 Password
Bear, Bunny, Clover, Flower

Two-Player Level 10 Password
Butterfly, Face, Umbrella, Clover

Two-Player Level 11 Password
Bear, Flower, Face, Flower

Two-Player Level 12 Password
Teapot, Bear, Flower, Umbrella

Two-Player Level 13 Password
Heart, Bird, Flower, Clover

Two-Player Level 14 Password
Face, Bird, Clover, Teapot

Two-Player Level 15 Password
Teapot, Bird, Clover, Bear

Two-Player Level 16 Password
Umbrella, Teapot, Bird, Flower

Two-Player Level 17 Password
Face, Bear, Bunny, Flower

Two-Player Level 18 Password
Bunny, Heart, Flower, Bird

RE-VOLT

All Cars
Enter CARNIVAL as a password.

Easy CPU
While the race is loading on Tournament mode, hold R1+R2+L1+L2+Square+Circle+Select. A laughing sound confirms correct entry.

All Tracks
Enter TRACKER as a password. At the Track Selection screen, press Up to toggle mirrored tracks or Down to toggle reversed tracks.

RIDGE RACER

Play Your Own Music
Start a race and pause the game. Open the PlayStation lid and take out the *Ridge Racer* disk. Insert your own audio CD and then close the lid and resume playing.

Unlock Eight Bonus Cars
Destroy all the ships in the *Galaga* game.

Wave the Flags
At the title screen, hold L1+R1 and press the D-Pad in any direction. Press Start for a transparent flag.

Reverse Tracks
Start a race on any track. Speed up but turn your car around before you get to the main track. Now speed up and drive through the wall at the starting line. You will race backward against the CPU.

Unlock Four Bonus Tracks
Place first on all four tracks. The bonus tracks are reversed versions of the same tracks.

Drive the Lamborghini
Place first in the first four tracks. Then go into the Time Trial mode and defeat the black Lamborghini.

Rotating Cars and Tracks
Hold L1 or R1 to rotate the cars and tracks at their corresponding selection screens.

RIDGE RACER REVOLUTION

Unlock Eight Extra Cars
Destroy all the ships in the *Galaga '88* game.

Laser in *Galaga '88*
Hold L1+R1+Select+Triangle+Down as *Galaga '88* plays. A laser blast destroyed all the aliens.

Small Cars
Do the Laser in *Galaga '88* code first. All your cars appear miniaturized and the commentator will have a child's voice.

Zoom In or Out
Pause while racing with an external view. Hold Triangle and press L1 or R1 to zoom. Press L1+R1 to return to the default view.

Rearview Mirror
Pause while racing with an internal view. Hold Triangle and press L1 or R1 to enable the rearview mirror.

Control the Spotlight
At the title screen, hold L1+R1 and press the D-Pad in any direction.

Unlock Four Bonus Tracks
Place first on all four tracks to unlock reversed tracks. Place first on these tracks to unlock a Scene menu.

Reverse Tracks
Start a race on any track. Speed up but turn your car around before you get to the main track. Now speed up and drive through the wall at the starting line. You will race backward against the CPU.

Secret Cars
Place first in each track (Novice, Advanced, Expert). Then, race each track in Time Trial mode. You receive a car for each track completed.

Spinning Zone

Highlight the Select option at the title screen. Hold Square+X and press Start to choose Game options. Highlight the Start option. Hold Select then hold Square+X+Select, until the race is about to begin. A "Spinning Zone" phrase appears if you did the code correctly. Do some 360 spins on some turns to get a spinning score.

Endings

The game has 12 endings depending on what order you race the tracks. For example, racing in the order of Novice, Expert, Advanced is different than Advanced, Expert, Novice.

RISE OF THE ROBOTS 2: RESURRECTION

Play as Assault

At the Character Selection screen, press Right, Up (2), Right, Down, Right, Up (2).

Play as Supervisor

At the Character Selection screen, press Down, Right, Down, Up, Right, Down, Left, Down, Up, Right, Up.

Play as Vitriol

At the Character Selection screen, press Left (3), Up (2), Down, Left (2), Down (2).

Play as Mayhem

At the Character Selection screen, press Left, Right, Down, Left, Up, Left, Down, Left, Down.

Play as Anil 8

At the Character Selection screen, press Up, Right, Down, Right (2), Up, Left, Up.

RIVAL SCHOOLS

Unlock Kyoko's Office

Beat the Evolution disk game with Kyoko on the highest difficulty setting.

Twenty-Four Bonus Characters

Win 24 times with various characters.

Unlock Service Mode

Beat the Evolution disk game with Natsu on the highest difficulty setting.

Unlock Shoot-Out Mode

Beat the Evolution disk game with Roberto on the highest difficulty setting.

Unlock Home Run Mode

Beat the Evolution disk game with Shoma on the highest difficulty setting.

Unlock Target Mode

Beat the Evolution disk game with any character and difficulty setting.

Different Evolution Mode Outfits

Press Square, Triangle, Circle, X, R1, R2, L1, or L2. This picks one of the eight differently colored outfits for each character.

Different Hinata Costume

Beat Arcade mode with Hinata, Batsu, and Kyosuke. Enable Shortcut mode and this character appears on the bottom row.

Different Tiffany Costume

Beat Arcade mode with Tiffany, Roy, and Boman. Enable Shortcut mode and this character appears on the bottom row.

Different Natsu Costume

Beat Arcade mode with Natsu, Shoman, and Roberto. Enable Shortcut mode and this character appears on the bottom row.

Different Kyoko Costume

Beat Arcade mode with Kyoko and Hideo. Enable Shortcut mode and this character appears on the bottom row.

Easier Way of Alternate Costumes

Beat the game. Hold L2 and choose Natsu, Kyoko, Tiffany, or Hinata to get their alternate costumes.

Rotate the Versus Screen

Disable Shortcuts. When the Versus screen appears on the arcade disk, press any direction on the D-Pad.

RIVAL SCHOOLS 2: UNITED BY FATE

Target Mode

Complete the EVO game disk with any character on any difficult setting.

Service Mode

Complete the EVO game disk with Natsu on the highest difficulty setting.

Home Run Mode

Complete the EVO game disk with Shoma on the highest difficulty setting.

Shoot-Out Mode

Complete the EVO game disk with Roberto on the highest difficulty setting.

Kyoko's Office

Complete the EVO game disk with Kyoko on the highest difficulty setting.

RIVEN: THE SEQUEL TO MYST

View Credits

Start the game and wait until the cyan screen comes up, then press L2 (5), R2 (2). If you are playing with a mouse, press the left mouse button five times and the right mouse button twice. It takes about three seconds to work. Then you can view either of the ending credits.

ROAD RASH

Dismount

Slow your bike down. Once your bike stops completely, press Up+L1+R1. You leap off your bike and can walk around.

ROAD RASH 3D

Special Punch

While racing, hold Up and press Circle. Release Circle to punch.

Special Kick

While racing, hold Down and press Circle. Release Circle to kick.

No Ticket Fines

Pause the game once you are pulled over. Restart the game.

Hitch a Ride

Get behind a car. Press X (2) to pop a wheelie and get on top of the car. Press Square to brake and stay on top of the car as long as desired.

Double Damage

While racing and using the "Far" view, press L2+R2.

Avoid Head-On Collisions

While racing, press X (2) to pop a wheelie before hitting an oncoming car. You use the car as a ramp.

ROAD RASH JAILBREAK

Access Cheat Menu

Highlight "Multiplayer" in the options menu. Hold R1+R2+L1+Right and press X to display Cheat menu. Then enter any of the following codes.

5-0 Mode

Access the Cheat menu and enter BDK.

Jailbreak Mode

Access the Cheat menu and enter KLFSDA.

Four Nitros in Jailbreak Mode

Access the Cheat menu and enter FDMFG.

Sidecar Mode

Access the Cheat menu and enter CMB.

ROBO-PIT

Level Select

At the main menu, hold L1+L2+R1+R2 and press Select. A number appears at the upper-right corner. The left number represents the stage and the right number represents the time. Press Left or Right to change the numbers.

Play as Zio Gagas

Enter h%2SCvWSGWWWG++++ jfX3XnXjVX-ATaXXan as a password.

Play as Kokopeli

Enter zl2r6n+++YgnH+++ XffX3X3JAzmJZY-XXII as a password.

First Place and All Weapons

Enter X57S6LWSWWWWWWWWW WWWW-W6TEnZJWaXXiX as a password.

Fight Zio Gigas

Enter X9y147OMUGWNGXXkX fPX3Xn3jYW-WWaXXdO as a password.

ROBOTRON X

Two-Way Weapon

During gameplay, press Up, Triangle, Up, Triangle.

Three-Way Weapon

During gameplay, press Right (2), Square, X.

Four-Way Weapon

During gameplay, press Down (2), Up, Circle.

Flamethrower

During gameplay, press Down, Right, Down, Right, Circle.

Shield Power-Up

During gameplay, press Down, Left, Square, Circle.

Turbo Power-Up

During gameplay, press Left (2), Right (2), Triangle.

Pulse Wave

During gameplay, press Up, Circle, Down, Right, Square.

ROCKMAN DASH

Easy Money
Go to Shopping Street. Near the Jetlad bakery are a garbage can and a pop can on the floor. If you kick the pop can into the Jetlad bakery, then talk to the lady in the bakery, she gives you $1,000. Do this trick as many times as you want.

Extra Options
Upon beating the game, you receive a new option in the main menu, which is the game's hard mode (green). Beating this mode yields a new easy mode (yellow) which starts you off in the normal difficulty with dash boots and a new part. This new part maxes out your left arm weapon stats!

ROCKMAN X3

Golden Armor
To gain the golden armor, you must have all the sub tanks, hearts, and armor. Don't get the four enhancers, as the golden armor will grant you these. When you have everything you need, go to Doppler's first stage and get the first super armor. Move to where the spikes fall into the first pit, then slide to the left until you enter a secret room. Inside is a pink capsule. Jump on it to gain the golden armor.

Introduction
3721 1281 3751 4456

Gravity Beetle
5623 4888 5851 4221

Blast Hornet
1745 5231 5441 2486

Neon Tiger
3621 4867 5851 2227

Tunnel Rhino
5728 1263 5754 2458

Blizzard Buffalo
7671 2857 2144 1247

Volt Catfish
1778 5253 2444 3488

Crush Crawfish
5718 1266 2727 7458

Dr. Doppler's Lab
5718 1263 2627 7458

Skip to the Endgame
To warp to the endgame, go to the stage select screen. Once there, move your cursor to the X logo and quickly press Down+Square+Cross.

Super Adaptions
After killing the mid-boss in the first Dr. Doppler stage, go to the first pit you see. Now slide along the left wall until you go through it. If you have all of the tanks, weapons, hearts, and full energy, you'll find a capsule that grants you the four Super Adaptations.

Super Password
To have everything except the super adaptations, enter the password 6414 4155 6872 3356.

Zero's Saber
1454 3535 6162 7162.

ROGUE TRIP: VACATION 2012

Cheat Mode
During gameplay, hold L1+R1+R2 and press Select.

God Mode
Enable Cheat mode. Then, during gameplay, hold L1+R1+R2 and press Up, Down, Left, Right.

Invulnerable
Enable Cheat mode. Then, during gameplay, hold L1+R1 and press Up, Down, Left, Right.

Hornet Nest Stingers
Enable Cheat mode. Then, during gameplay, press L1+L2+R1+Triangle+Left.

Infinite Weapons
Enable Cheat mode. Then, during gameplay, hold L1+R1 and press Up, Down, Up, R2.

Powered-Up Weapons
Enable Cheat mode. Then, during gameplay, hold L1+R1+R2+X and press Down.

Play as UFO
On the Password screen, press R1, Square, X, Square, L2, Circle.

Play as Nightshade
On the Password screen, press R1, R2, L1 (2), X, Circle.

Play as Helicopter
On the Password screen, press L1, Triangle, R2, Triangle (2), R1.

Play as Goliath
On the Password screen, press Triangle, L1, R1, X, L2 (2).

Play as Big Daddy
On the Password screen, press Triangle, Square, R2, X, Triangle, R2. Go to Challenge mode and select "Nuke York." Big Daddy appears at the Vehicle Select screen.

Infinite Jump
On the Password screen, press Circle, Square, R2, X, Triangle, R2.

Unlimited Turbos
On the Password screen, press Square, X, Circle, Triangle, R1, R2.

Armor Power-up
On the Password screen, press R1, Triangle, R1, Triangle, L1, Square.

Double Pick-ups
On the Password screen, press L1, L2, Circle, L1, R1, Square.

Duke Nukem Movie
On the Password Screen, press Square (2), Circle (2), Triangle (2).

Funtopia Level (Challenge Mode)
On the Password screen, press X, Circle, L2, X, Square, L1.

Gulch Level (Challenge Mode)
On the Password screen, press X, Square, Circle, L1, L2, Square.

Boss Battle 1
On the Password screen, press Circle, R2, R1, Square, L1, R2. Reenter the password after each challenge battle.

Boss Battle 2
On the Password vacreen, press Circle (2), L2, L1, Triangle (2).

Big Daddy Boss Battle
On the Password screen, press Square, Triangle, Circle (2), R2 (2). Go to Challenge mode and select "Nuke York."

Full Screen
Hold Select+R1 during gameplay and press Up.

Change View
Hold Select+R1 during gameplay and press Down.

ROLL AWAY

Bonus Levels
Finish the game, go to the main menu and select "1 Player," then select "The Final."

Extra Level
Press Triangle, Up, Triangle, L2, L1, L2, Square, X during gameplay.

Extra Level: Clear Screen
Press Right, Circle, Square, L1, Square, Circle (2), Square during gameplay.

Cheat Mode (PAL Version)
On controller 2, press L1+L2+R1+R2+Select during gameplay.

Invulnerable (Temporary)
Press Right, Down, L1, R2, R1, Circle, Triangle, Square during gameplay.

Motion Blur (Toggle)
Press Right, Circle, L2, Circle, R1, Circle, Square, Circle during gameplay.

Time Trial Mode: 30 Extra Seconds
Press Circle, L1, Triangle (2), Circle, X, Triangle, Down during Time Trial mode.

Gain 30,000 Points
Press Square, Up, Down, L2, R1, Triangle, X, Triangle during gameplay.

Checkered Background
Press L1, Circle, Left, Right, L2, Left, R2 (2) during gameplay.

ROLL CAGE

Expert Tracks
Enter the password: HEMPCMDD. Then start a race at Expert difficulty.

Hard Tracks
Enter the password: FAFNOEAP or EEFPHMBC. Then start a race at Hard difficulty.

Hard Tracks and Mirrored Tracks
Enter the password: EADNCMAH or EAFNLEAM or BDGENADM.

Easy Tracks
Enter the password: EEFNIEBA. Then start a race at Easy difficulty.

Maximum Cheat Mode
Enter the password: MAXCHEAT.

Harpoon Deathmatch
Enter the password: HAFIJEAF.

Neoto Deathmatch/All Leagues
Enter the password: KKKJBCFA.

Deathmatch Modes, Extra Car, Mirror Mode, Etc.
Enter the password: HHMPNEED or OGGBEDJE.

Display Development Team Scores
Enter the password: BESTLAPS.

Air Horn
Enter the password: AIRHORNS.

Mirror Mode
Place first in all leagues.

Deathmatch Mode
Place first in all the tracks in a league.

ROLL CAGE EXTREME

All Cars Password
WHEELS,.METAL,.ITS..THE.BIN!

All Tracks Password
NOW.THAT'S.WHAT.I.CALL.RACING.147

All Things Password
I.WANT.IT.ALL.AND.I.WANT.IT.NOW!

ATD Ghost Cars Password
WLL.IF.IT.AINT.THEM.PESKY.KIDS

Super Speed Password
LOOK.OUT!.ITS.ANDY.GREEN

All Combat Tracks Password
YOU.HAVE.A.LOTA.EXPLODING.TO.DO

Increase Masters' Difficulty Password
MASTERS.IS.AS.HARD.AS.NAILS.MON!

Survivor Mode Password
HERE.TODAY,.GONE,.LATE.AFTERNOON

Rubble Soccer Mode Password
IM.OBVIOUSLY.SICK.AS.A.PARROT

Mirror Mode Password
I.AM.THE.MIRROR.MAN,.OOOOOOOOOO!

Pursuit Mode Password
PURSUIT,.A.SUIT.MADE.FROM.CATS

Demolition Mode Password
IS.IT.COLD.IN.HERE.OR.IS.IT.JUST.ME?

ROSCO McQUEEN FIRE FIGHTER EXTREME

Level Select Password: Laundry Stage 2
FLUFFY

Level Select Password: Laundry Stage 3
SWEATY

Level Select Password: Auto Stage 1
HOTROD

Level Select Password: Auto Stage 2
GREASE

Level Select Password: Auto Stage 3
BIGEND

Level Select Password: Harold's Stage 1
SMELLY

Level Select Password: Harold's Stage 2
WIDETV

Level Select Password: Harold's Stage 3
PILLOW

Level Select Password: Leisure Stage 1
TRICEP

Level Select Password: Leisure Stage 2
MOTION

Level Select Password: Leisure Stage 3
HIPHOP

Level Select Password: Residential Stage 1
KENNEL

Level Select Password: Residential Stage 2
BARREL

Level Select Password: Runaround
SPLASH

R-TYPE DELTA

Additional Credits
Play the game for more than three hours.

Unlock Free Play Mode
Play the game for more than six hours.

Refill Force Power
Pause, hold L2, then press Left, Right, Up, Down, Right, Left, Up, Down+Triangle.

Red Power-Up
After obtaining a Force Pod, press Pause. Hold L2 and press Left, Right, Up, Down, Right, Left, Up, Down+Square.

Yellow Power-Up
After obtaining a Force Pod, press Pause. Hold L2 and press Left, Right, Up, Down, Right, Left, Up, Down+Circle.

Blue Power-Up
After obtaining a Force Pod, press Pause. Hold L2 and press Left, Right, Up, Down, Right, Left, Up, Down+X.

Level Select
Use bombs more than 10,000 times. Keep track of your progress at the Notes screen. Look for Stage Select option after the requirement is fulfilled.

Unlock Power Armor Jet
Play the game more than 100 times or complete the game at Human difficulty or higher.

Background Image 2
Use the RX to play the game.

Background Image 3
Use the R13 to play the game.

Background Image 4
Accumulate 20 hours of gameplay. .

Background Image 5
Use the R9 to beat the game at Human difficulty.

Background Image 6
Use the RX to beat the game at Human difficulty.

Background Image 7
Use the R13 to beat the game at Human difficulty.

Background Image 8
Play the game 100 times.

Background Image 9
Use the R9 to beat the game on Bydo difficulty.

Background Image 10
Use the RX to beat the game on Bydo difficulty.

Background Image 11
Use the R13 to beat the game on Bydo difficulty.

Background Image 12
Use the POW to beat the game on Bydo difficulty.

R-TYPES

Level Select
Highlight "R-Type" or "R-Type II" on the main menu and press L2 (10), R2 (10). Start a game and use the Stage Select option.

Slo-Mo Mode
In R-Type or R-Type II, press Pause during gameplay. Hold L2 and press Right, Up, Right, Up, Down, Left, Down, Left, X.

Choose Speed
In R-Type or R-Type II, press Pause during gameplay. Hold L2 and press Right, Up, Right, Up, Down, Left, Down, Left, and use Circle or X to speed up or slow down.

All Weapons
In R-Type or R-Type II, press Pause during gameplay. Hold L2 and press Right, Up, Left, Right, Down, Left, Up, Right. Press Circle, X, Triangle, Square or R1 to access weapons.

RUGRATS: THE SEARCH FOR REPTAR

Secrets from Your PC
Place the CD into your PC CD-ROM drive. Open the data directory, then the hints directory. The 42 text files contain cheats and hints.

Unlock a Secret Level
Get more than 13 Reptar bars and beat the game. You are Reptar in the secret level.

RUNABOUT 2

All Cars
Hold R2 and press Circle, Square, X, Triangle, R1 at the car selection screen.

RUNABOUT CLIMAX

Unlimited Armor
At the Car Selection screen, press R1, L2, Up, Down, Left, Right. Pick a car with automatic transmission.

RUNNING HIGH

Bonus Tracks, Characters
Complete the game once. Then press Down (2), Up (2), Left, Right, Left, Right at the title screen.

RUNNING WILD

Different Outfits
When selecting a character, press L1 or R1.

Difficulty: Medium
On Easy difficulty, finish Challenge mode. Or press Up, Square, R1, L2 (2), Up at Difficulty Select menu.

Difficulty: Hard
On Medium difficulty, finish Challenge mode. Or press L2, Down, L1, R1 at the Difficulty Select menu.

Difficulty: Expert
On Hard difficulty, finish Challenge mode. Or press Square, Down, L2, Down, Circle, L2 at the Difficulty Select menu.

Play as Pyro
Go to the Secret Options menu under the Options screen. Press Up, Down, Circle, Down, L2, Down, R1, L2.

Play as Kostra
Go to the Secret Options menu under the Options screen. Press Up (2), Square, L2, R2, L2, R2, Down.

Play as Lunarr
Go to the Secret Options menu under the Options screen. Press Down(2), L1, Up, Square, R2.

Play as Rex
Go to the Secret Options menu under the Options screen. Press L2, R2, R1, Up, Square, R2. Or use Elephant on Hard difficulty to win Challenge Mode.

Play as Tox
Go to the Secret Options menu under the Options screen. Press Circle, Up, Square, Circle, Square, R1, L1.

Play as Blizzaro
Go to the Secret Options menu under the Options screen. Press Up, Down, L1, Circle (2), R1, R2, L1.

Quicker Game
On Medium difficulty, complete Challenge mode.

Tiny Players
On Easy difficulty, complete Challenge mode.

RUROUNI KENSHIN: ISHIN GEKITOUHEN

Play as Saito Hajime
Beat the game at Hard difficulty to play as Saito Hajime, see all movies, and more.

Play as Kaoru
Beat the game in Story mode or Versus Computer mode.

RUSH HOUR

Extra Track
Press X, Up, Triangle, Down, R1, L1 at the title screen.

Extra Cars
Press Up, Left, Right, X, Circle, Square at the title screen.

Heavy Metal Cars
Press L1, R1, L1, Square, R1, Up at the title screen.

Super Championship
Press Right, Square, Left, Circle, Up, X at the title screen.

Tracks in Reverse
Press Left, Triangle, R1, Circle, L1, Down at the title screen.

RUSHDOWN

All Tracks
Press Up (2), Down (2), Left, Right, Left, Right, Triangle, Circle, Triangle, Circle at the main menu.

SAMMY SOSA HIGH HEAT BASEBALL 2001

3DO Cloud Effects
At the Stadium Selection screen, press L2, R2, L2, R2, Square (2).

Wacky Cloud Effects
At the Stadium Selection screen, press R2, L2, Square, L1, R1, Square.

SAMURAI SPIRITS 1 & 2

Play as Kuroko and Mizuki
Enter Versus mode. At the Character Selection screen, press L1+L2+R1+R2. The Left arrow is for Kuroko and the Right arrow is for Mizuki.

SCARS

All Cars
To unlock all cars, enter the password ALLVID.

All Races
To unlock all grand prix races, enter the password ZDPEAK.

Challenge Mode
To access challenge mode, enter the password XPERTS.

Drive the Cheetah Car
Enter the password RUNNER to gain the Cheetah car.

Drive the Cobra Car
Enter the password RATTLE.

Drive the Panther Car
To drive the Panther car, enter the password MYSTER.

Drive the Scorpion Car
To drive the Scorpion car, enter the password DESERT.

Race in the Crystal Cup
To race in the Crystal Cup, enter the password GLASSX.

Race in the Diamond Cup
To race in the Diamond Cup, enter the password ROCKYY.

Ultimate Password
Enter the password as "ALLVID." This code unlocks all of the game's functions, including four extra vehicles, three additional cup settings, the "Challenge" mode, and the option menu's "Mirror Mode."

SEXY PARODIUS

All Power-Ups
Pause and press Up (2), Down (2), L1, R1, L1, R1, X, Circle. A sound confirms correct entry.

Disable Power-Ups
Enter the All Power-Ups code. Pause and press Up (2), Down (2), Left, Right, Left, Right, X, Circle. Unpause the game and you'll hear a phrase.

SHADOW MADNESS

Bonus Songs
Place any of the CD's in your stereo to listen to some bonus songs.

Easy Level-Ups
When you get to Karillon, go Left until you come to an alleyway containing a cemetery. Past the cemetery are a bunch of guys who will fight you for 100 coins. You can fight them as often as you wish. Each battle earns you 500 to 800 exp.

SHADOW MAN

Play as Ollaflagebbies
Kill the attacking bear on level 7 then press the L2 button to lie Down. You go back to the altar. Quit and Start a new game; you'll be Ollaflagebbies.

SHADOW MASTER

All Weapons
In the first area of the first level, walk forward to a door containing two monsters. Kill the two monsters and, while standing in the room in which they were, press and hold R1+R2+L1+L2+Circle. A red light flashes in front of you if you performed the code Right.

Invincibility and Level Select
Both of these cheats require you to Start a new game on the first mission. After you start, go to the first room and kill the two monsters inside. Now, stay inside the room and enter the following codes.

Invincibility
Press L1+L2+R1+R2+X. A blue light confirms correct entry.

Level Skip
Press L1+L2+R1+R2+Triangle. A green light confirms correct entry. To access the level skip code, press Start and exit the level. When you return to the main menu, you can select your level.

SHADOW STRUGGLE

Hidden Characters
Beat the game with Hagane at Hard difficulty and without continuing to unlock Berserker and Marry P.

SHANE WARNE CRICKET '99

Always Win Code
Enter GETBRIBE as a password.

Improved Batter Skills
Enter BATKINGS as a password.

Horrible Fielders
Enter DROPBALL as a password.

Big Ball Mode
Enter BIGBALLS as a password. When you bowl, the ball will be as big as a beach ball.

Super Batters
Enter SUPERMAN as a password.

Beach Field
Enter SUNSHINE as a password.

Unbreakable Bats
Enter SOLIDOAK as a password.

World XI Team
Enter PENSIONS as a password. Pick Friendly or Test Series to play as the World XI team.

Helmet Cam
Enter CHRISREA as a password.

Level 2 Password
Overtime

Level 3 Password
Sausages

Level 4 Password
Dillbert

Level 5 Password
Batkings

Level 6 Password
Pancakes

Level 7 Password
Friedegg

Level 8 Password

Placebo1

Level 9 Password

Clueless

Level 10 Password

Nowayeas

SHELLSHOCK

Debug Mode

To enter a special debug mode, wait for the Core Design copyright message to appear, then press Up, Down, Left, Right, Down, Down, Right, Right, Triangle.

You are taken to a test menu where you can choose your starting level, max your firepower, view all the videos, see the credits, and improve the game's appearance.

Invincibility

Start a game and quit by pressing Start+Select. At the main title screen, press Up, Up, Up, Down, Down, Down, Right, Right, Triangle. You hear a chime.

SHIPWRECKERS!

Level 1-2 Password

Ship, Skull, Fish, Anchor, Ship, Anchor

Level 1-3 Password

Ship, Anchor, Skull, Ship, Anchor, Fish

Level 1-4 Password

Skull, Ship, Fish, Anchor (2), Ship

Level 2-1 Password

Fish (2), Anchor, Ship, Skull, Anchor

Level 2-2 Password

Skull, Anchor (2), Fish, Anchor, Ship

Level 2-3 Password

Fish, Anchor, Ship (3), Skull

Level 2-4 Password

Anchor, Fish, Ship, Skull (2), Fish

Level 3-1 Password

Ship, Skull (2), Fish, Anchor, Skull

Level 3-2 Password

Fish, Skull, Anchor, Fish, Skull, Fish

Level 3-3 Password

Fish (2), Ship, Skull, Fish, Ship

Level 3-4 Password

Ship, Anchor, Ship, Fish, Anchor, Fish

Level 4-1 Password

Skull (2), Anchor, Ship, Fish (2)

Level 4-2 Password

Ship, Anchor, Skull, Fish (2), Anchor

Level 4-3 Password

Skull, Ship, Skull (2), Fish, Ship

Level 4-4 Password

Ship, Fish, Ship, Fish, Ship, Anchor

Level 5-1 Password

Anchor, Ship, Fish, Skull, Fish, Ship

Level 5-2 Password

Fish, Ship, Anchor, Skull, Ship, Fish

Level 5-3 Password

Ship, Fish, Skull, Anchor (2), Skull

Level 5-4 Password

Skull, Ship, Anchor, Fish, Ship, Skull

SIDEWINDER 2

Strip Tease

Pause and press Left, Square (4), Up, Triangle (3), Right, Circle, Down, X, Down, X, Down, X, Down, X, Down, X.

Level 2 Password

0007

Level 3 Password

1213

Level 4 Password

0224

Level 5 Password

7154

SILENT BOMBER

Advanced Mode

Complete the game one time to unlock the advanced mode, which allows you to select the level on which you wish to play.

SIMCITY 2000

0% Interest Bonds

Open the City Budget window from the menu. At the Budget screen, hold Triangle and press L1, L2, L1, L2, R2, R1, R2, R1.

Cycle Night and Day

To cycle night and day in 3D mode, press Down, Up, Down, Up, Down, L2, R2. To turn it off, press Down, Down, Up, Up, Down, Down, L2, R2.

Fade to Black

To fade the screen to black, press Down, Down, Down, Down, Down, Down, L2, R2. To pause the fade, press Left, Left, Left, Left, Left, Left, L2, R2. To return the screen to normal, press Right, Right, Right, Right, Right, Right, L2, R2.

Maximum Dispatch

Use of any of the dispatch tools (Fire, Police, Military) will yield the maximum number allowable within *SimCity* regardless of the number of stations you have. To activate, use the normal arrow cursor to select and cancel the dispatch tool. Go to the status bar and press Left, Right, Left, Right, Cancel, Accept. Be sure your cursor stays in the status area while doing this.

SIMPSONS WRESTLING

Unlock the Great Ones

There are four secret characters: Moe, Bumble-Bee Man, Frink, and Ned Flanders. To get them, you have to defeat them.

Unlock Itchy & Scratchy, Kang, and Smithers

Beat the game in all three modes to unlock an option to play as Itchy & Scratchy for one level, Kang for another, and Smithers for another.

Unlock Bonus Match Up

Enter the following at the "PRESS Start" screen: Circle, Up (2), Down (2), Left, Right, Left, Right.

Unlock the Mayor

Press R1 (3), Triangle. Now the screen says, "Do you want to save?" Press "Yes." The next time you choose a player, the mayor is there. This cheat only works while you're in a match.

SKELETON WARRIORS

Invincibility

Pause the game and press Down, Circle, Square, Square, Up, X.

Level Select

Start a game on Easy. Pause the game and press Triangle, Circle, Circle, Left, Circle, Up, Down. Restart the game, and a Level Select entry appears on the Options menu.

No Enemies

Press Start to pause the game and press: Up, Down Left, Select, R1, L2, Right, Up, Left, Down. Restart the game, and on the Options menu there is an option for no enemies .

Super Sword

To get the Super Sword, pause the game and press: Circle, Left, Down, Triangle, Right, Circle, Up, Triangle.

Unlimited Hearts

Pause the game and press Left, Up, X, Square, Up, Down, Square. The heart stone count increases to 80 and stays there.

SKULLMONKEYS

1970s Bonus Level

To unlock the 1970s bonus level, enter the password: Square, R1 (2), L1, L2, Triangle, R1, L2, L1, R2, Square, R2.

Cheat Codes

To activate a cheat, pause the game and enter its code.

1970s Icons

Select, Circle, Up, Left, Down, Up, Down, Square

Extra Halo

R2, Circle(2), Down, Left, Circle, Right, Down

Klaymen Are Crazy

Down, Right, Triangle, L2, Up, Left, Triangle, Select

Klaymen Are Fast

Left, Square, R2, Circle, R1, Down, Circle, R2

Klaymen Are Frozen

L2, Left, Circle, R2, Down, Square, Triangle, Down

Klaymen Are Slow

L1, Triangle, Left, Down, R2, Triangle, Left, Select

Klaymen Are Small

R1, Left, Square, Triangle, R1, Left, Square, Triangle

Klaymen Are Tinted

L2, Circle(2), Left, Select, L2, Up, Down

Maximum Lives

L1, Triangle, Down, Left, Circle, Select, Square, Right

More Ammunition

Down, Circle, Up, R2, Left, Triangle, Select(2)

Phart Heads

R1, Left, Up, L1 (2), Square, Right, Select

Phoenix Hand

Square, Triangle, R2, Left, Select, Circle, Triangle, Right

Refill Status Items

L1, Triangle, Down, R1, Circle, Right, Up, Select

Remove Text in Pause Menu
L2, Left, Circle, R2, Down, Square, Triangle, Down

Shoot Head
Down, Square, Triangle, Down(2), Square(2), Right

Skip Current Level
Triangle, L1(2), Square, Right, Circle, Triangle, Down

Super Willies
R1, Left, Square, Triangle, L1, Triangle, R2, Select

Swirly Q Icons
R1, Right, Circle, R2(2), Square, Right, Select

Universe Enema
Left, Triangle, Right, Down, Triangle, Select(3)

World 1: Monkey Shrines
R2(2), Circle, Square

World 2: Hard Boiler
R2, Square, R2, R1, Square, X, R1, X(2), R1, Triangle

World 3: Sno
Circle, Triangle, Square, Triangle, Circle, R1(2), L1, X, R1, Square

World 4: Elevated Structure of Terror
L1(2), Square, L1, Square, R1, Square, L1, Square

World 5: Castle De Los Muertos
Circle, L1, X, Triangle, Square, X(3), L1, R1

World 6: YTN Death Garden
Square, R1, Circle, L1, Circle, R1, Circle, L1, X(2), Square, R2

World 7: YTN Mines
X, Square, X, Triangle, X(2), Square, L1, Square(2)

World 8: YNT Weeds
Triangle, R2, Triangle(2), Square, X, Circle, L1, Square, Triangle, Square(2)

World 9: Evil Engine
X, Triangle, X(2), R1, Square, Circle, X, L1, X

SLAMSCAPE

Full Weapons
To gain all weapons or recharge them, hold Select and press Left, Square, Right, Circle, Up, Triangle.

Invincibility
For invincibility, hold Select and press Square, Square, Circle, Circle, Square, Square, Triangle.

Kill Danger Ranger and Queen Snagger
To take out these annoying villains, hold Select+L1+L2and press Left, Square, Left, Square, Left, Square.

Self Destruct
To kill yourself while playing, hold Select and press Up, Up, Down, Up, Left, Right, L1, L2.

SLED STORM

Cheaper Upgrades
Enter X, L1, Circle, Triangle, Square, Square, Triangle, L2 as a password.

Dance Mix
Enter R2, Triangle, X, R2, Triangle, Square, Circle, X as a password. (Cheat also unlocks Snocross circuits 3-6.)

Demo Track
Enter R2, L1, Triangle, Square, Triangle, R1, Circle, X as a password.

Gio's Sled Storm
Enter Circle, Triangle, Square, L1, R2, L1, X, Triangle as a password.

Jackal's Sled Storm
Unlock Jackal. Enter Circle, Triangle, Square, L2, R2, L1, X, Triangle as a password.

Jay's Sled Storm
Enter Circle, Triangle, Square, Circle, R2, L1, X, Triangle as a password.

Mirrored Tracks
Enter Circle, L1, R2, R2, X, Triangle, L2 as a password.

Nadia's Sled Storm
Enter Circle, Triangle, Square, Square, R2, L1, X, Triangle as a password.

Play as Jackal
Enter L2, L2, Circle, R2, Square, R1, L1, Triangle as a password.

Play as Sergei
Enter Square, L1, Square, L2, Triangle, R2, X, Circle as a password. (In the European version, Sergei is known as Rhine Rider.)

Reversed Tracks
Enter Square, L1, X, Square, R2, X, Triangle, Circle as a password.

Sergei's Sled Storm
Unlock Sergei. Then enter Circle, Triangle, Square, X, R2, L1, X, Triangle as a password. (In the European version, Sergei is known as Rhine Rider.)

Super Snocross 6
Enter Square, X, Triangle, Triangle, L1, R2, Circle, Triangle as a password.

Tracey's Sled Storm
Enter Circle, Triangle, Square, Triangle, R1, L1, X, Triangle as a password.

Travis' Sled Storm
Enter Circle, Triangle, Square, R1, R2, L1, X, Triangle as a password.

Win Open Mountain Championship
Enter Square, X, R2, Square, Circle, R1, Circle, Triangle as a password.

SMALL SOLDIERS

All Weapons
At the code center, press Triangle, Triangle, Circle, Circle, Circle, X, Square, X.

Infinite Ammo
At the password screen, press Triangle, Circle, Circle, Circle, Square, X, Triangle, Square.

Invincibility
At the code center, type Circle, Circle, Triangle, Triangle, Circle, X, Square, X.

Level 1: Gorgon
X, X, Triangle, Square, Square, X, Circle, X

Level 2: Dimensional Temple
Square, X, Triangle, Square, Square, Square, Circle, X

Level 3: Floating Fortress
Circle, X, Triangle, Square, Square, Circle, Circle, X

Level 4: Spirit Bog
Triangle, X, Triangle, Square, Square, Triangle, Circle, X

Level 5: Canyon Village
X, Square, Triangle, Square, Square, X, Triangle, X

Level 6: Creepy Caverns
Square, Square, Triangle, Square, Square, Square, Triangle, X

Level 7: Space Ship
Circle, Square, Triangle, Square, Square, Circle, Triangle, X

Level 8: Hall of Patriots
Triangle, Square, Triangle, Square, Square, Triangle, Triangle, X

Level 9: Graveyard
X, Circle, Triangle, Square, Square, X, X, Square

Level 10: Nuclear Mine
Square, Circle, Triangle, Square, Square, Square, X, Square,

Level 11: Launch Center
Circle, Circle, Triangle, Square, Square, Circle, X, Square

Level 12: Ulhaden Fier
Triangle, Circle, Triangle, Square, Square, Triangle, X, Square

Level 13: Garrison
X, Triangle, Triangle, Square, Square, X, Square, Square

Level 14: Inner Sanctum
Square, Triangle, Triangle, Square, Square, Square, Square, Square

SNATCHER

Special Menu
Go into the Options screen and press Start. Press Up (2), Down (2), Left, Right, Left, Right, X, Circle. Let a few seconds pass and you'll enter a special menu where you can alter some game characteristics.

SNO-CROSS CHAMPIONSHIP RACING

Unlock the ATV
From the main menu, hold the R1 button and enter: Up, Right, Down, Up, Right, Down. Then release the R-trigger. If you entered the code correctly, the screen flickers. Now you can enter any race and select any Snomobile. When you Start the race, you'll have an ATV instead.

Unlock the GoCart
From the main menu hold the R1 button and enter:

Right, Right, Left, Left, Right, Right. Release the R-trigger. If you entered the code correctly the screen flickers. Now you can enter any race and select any Snomobile. When you Start the race you'll have a GoCart instead.

Unlock Secret Cartoon Track
From the main menu, hold the R1 button and enter:

Right, Up, Left, B, Y, X. Release the R-trigger. If you entered the code correctly, the screen flickers. Now you can enter single-player mode and race the Kiruna Track.

PLAYSTATION

Launch The Demo Mode

From the main menu, hold the R1 button and enter:

Up, Up, Up, Down, Down, Down.

Unlock Every League, Snowmobile, and Track

From the main menu, hold the R1 button and enter: Up, Y, Up, Y, Up, Y. You'll then have access to every League, Snowmobile, and Track.

SOUL BLADE

Alternate Costumes

To change your costumes, go to the Character Selection screen, and press one of the following: Square, X + Square, Triangle, X + Triangle, or Circle.

Alternate Endings

When the endings start, press the following buttons for each character when the view shifts to full-screen.

Mitsurugi

Use the control pad to dodge Tanegashima's shots, and use Square or Triangle to deliver the fatal blow.

Seung Mina

Hold X and press Left or Right.

Li Long

Press Square or Triangle repeatedly.

Taki

Press X.

Voldo

Press Up and Down rapidly until Soul Edge breaks (you can also change the camera angle with Triangle while Voldo is speaking to Vercci).

Sophitia

Press Right

Siegfried

Press Triangle

Rock

Press Triangle

Hwang

Press Square

Cervantes

Press Triangle

Hidden Level

After you unlock Evil Siegfried and Han Myong, a new background will unlock.

Namco Voice Trick

At the start of the game, you hear a voice say Namco. Hold L1+L2 then press Up for Seung Mina's voice, Down for a quick voice, or Back for a normal voice.

Play as Evil Siegfried

Find Siegfried's 8th weapon in Edge Master mode.

Play as Han Myong

After Soul Edge becomes selectable, beat Arcade Mode using Hwang, then Seung Mina immediately afterward.

Play as Sophitia in a Bathing Suit

Get every character's 8th weapon in Edge Master mode.

Play as Sophitia without Armor

Find Sophitia's 8th weapon in Edge Master mode.

Play as Soul Edge

To play as Soul Edge, beat Arcade mode with each character, or leave the game running for 12 hours. If you pause mid-game, this "timer" will still run.

Ultimate Weapon

After defeating Cervantes/Soul Edge, your character's Ultimate Weapon appears in one of the stages that can be reached directly from Spain. If you lose the battle where the Ultimate Weapon was, your character performs his/her "loss by time-up" animation on the map screen. If this happens, the Weapon moves to one of the stages adjacent to the one you are on, but it will not move to Spain.

Ultimate Weapon in Arcade Mode

To use the Ultimate Weapons in Arcade mode, highlight the character you want to be and wait until a weapon list appears beside the character. You can also push select. Choose the Ultimate Weapon or any other weapon in battle. You must earn the weapons in Edge Master Mode.

Winning Poses

To change your winning pose, press Triangle, Square, Circle or X after you beat your opponent.

SOUL OF THE SAMURAI

Disappearing Shuriken Trick

When playing the female character in "Soul of the Samurai," she must battle her brother. One of his attacks is to throw several seeking shuriken at her. To negate this attack, hit the Select button (after he has thrown the shuriken). This pauses the action, then choose the ITEM option as if you were going to use an item or change equipment. You don't have to use anything, just enter the ITEM mode, then exit using the Circle button. Exit all the way out by hitting the Circle button again, and action resumes. After you do this, all the seeking shuriken will disappear. It is easier to do this every time he performs this attack rather than dodge or block them all, as some miss you on the first pass, then loop around to strike you from behind.

SOUTH PARK

All Cheats Enabled

Enter the password ZBOBBYBIRD.

Unlock Chef

YLovemachine

Unlock Wendy

Bcheckataco

Unlock Terrence

Sraft

Unlock Phillip

Pphaert

Unlock Jed

Jhawking

Unlock Mr. Macky

Acheatingsbad

Unlock Officer Barbrady

Delvislives

Unlock Big Gay Al

Goutrange

Unlock Starvin Marvin

Mslapupmeal

Unlock Mr. Garrison

Vdorothysfriend

Unlock Pip

Efishnchips

Unlock Jimbo

Qstaringfrog

Unlock Ike

Hkickme

Unlock Ms. Cartman

Kallwoman

Unlock Mephisto

Ngoodscience

Unlock Alien Visitor

Tmajestic

SOUTH PARK: CHEF'S LUV SHACK

Unlock All Mini-Games

To get all of the mini-games, pick Cartman. When you go to the screen where you pick the number of rounds, enter Up, Up, Left, Down, Up, Up. A list of mini-games pops Up. Press X to select one.

SOUTH PARK RALLY

Unlock Everything

Complete the Championship Mode without using any tokens.

Unlock Mr. Garrison

Enter Championship mode and select Chef. Beat the first two levels without using a continuing coin.

SOVIET STRIKE

Cheat Codes

Enter these codes at the password screen.

People Follow You Everywhere

ANGRYLOCAL

Natives Worship Your Chopper

GHANDI

World Peace (No Shooting)

QUAKER

More Powerful Weapons

DAVEDITHER

Double Damage

DRBENWAY

Unlimited Fuel

MOUNTADEW

Infinite Armor

IAMWOMAN

Unlimited Ammo, Fuel, and Attempts

THEBIGBOYS

4 attempts

SADISSA

7 attempts

NOSFERAT

Infinite Ammo

STRANGELUV

Infinite Fuel

EARTHFIRST

Double Fuel Mileage
VULTURE

Infinite Ammo, Infinite Fuel, Infinite Attempts
FUGAZI

Infinite Ammo, Infinite Fuel, Invincible Chopper
MIDNIGHOIL

SPACE INVADERS

Classic SI, Credits, and Ending
Enable Select level code and successfully complete level 00. Hold Right when choosing 1P or 2P game to play classic *Space Invaders*.

Five Shots
Pause game and press Down, Left, Circle, Down, Right(3).

Nine Lives
Pause game and press Right(3), Down, Circle, Left, Down.

Select Level
Press Circle to begin a game (instead of X).

SPACE JAM

More Options
Go to the Options screen, and highlight "GAME OPTIONS" (don't click on it). Next, hold L1+R1+L2+R2+Up and press X.

SPAWN: THE ETERNAL

Cheat Codes
Enter these codes while the game is paused.

Invisibility
Hold L1+R1 and press Square, Square, Circle, Circle, Triangle, X.

Invincibility
Hold L1+R1 and press Triangle, Triangle, X, X, Square, Circle.

All Power-Ups
Hold L2+R2 and press Triangle, Circle, Square, X, Triangle, X.

All Inventory
Hold L2+R2 and press X, Square, Circle, Triangle, Square, Circle.

Reset Physical
Hold L1+R1 and press X, Circle, Triangle, Square, X, Circle.

Reset Magic
Hold L1+R1 and press Triangle, Circle, X, Square, Triangle, Circle.

Level Skip
Hold L1+R1+L2+R2 and press Triangle, X, Square, Circle, Circle, Circle.

Interview
Put the game in a cd player and listen to track 15. It's an excerpt from the Todd McFarlane (the creator of *Spawn*) interview on one of the PlayStation Underground cds.

Play as Overkill
This is a difficult trick to pull off. First get up to Overkill (the first one), then fight him until he falls. But when he is falling, before he hits the ground, hit Start, then hold L1+R2 and press Triangle, Square, Square Circle, X, X, Triangle. When you press Start, Spawn's cape wraps around him. When his cape comes off, Spawn is Overkill.He can punch, kick, and shoot a laser from his eye.

Refill Health
To refill your health, press L1+L2 while playing. This only works a limited number of times.

SPEC OPS

Cheat Codes
Pause your game, then hold: R1+R2+L1+L2. While holding those four buttons, you can enter one of the following codes.

Invincibility
X, Triangle, Square, Circle

All Worlds And Levels
Triangle, Circle, Square, Square

Level Skip
Circle, Square, X, X

Unlimited Ammo
Circle, Square, Triangle, X

Refill Team Health
Triangle, Triangle, X, X

Refill Team Ammo
X, X, Triangle, Triangle

First Special Weapon
Triangle, X, X, X

Second Special Weapon
X, X, X, Triangle

Heavy Weapon
Triangle X, Square, Square

Rocket Boots
Triangle, Square, Square, Triangle

Jet Pack
Square, Square, Triangle, Triangle

All Crates Powered Up
Circle, X, X, Circle

Instant Shape Building
Square, Square, Circle, Circle

Big Feet
Triangle, Square, Square, X

Big Guns
Triangle, Circle, Circle, Triangle

Indestructible Base
X, Triangle, Triangle, X

Easy Gun Build
Circle, Circle, X, X

Easy Buddy Build
Circle, Circle, X, Circle

Animals Don't Attack
Circle, Square, Square, Circle

Invulnerability (God Mode)
Enter ROCKSTAR as your name when you start the game. Press Start during gameplay. You can now toggle Invulnerability on and off from the pause menu.

SPEC OPS RANGER ELITE

Invincibility
To turn on invincibility, enter your name as "ROCKSTAR." A special Invulnerable On/Off selection will be added to the pause menu.

SPEED RACER

Bonus Cars
To Get the extra cars, win each track on the normal level or above in Normal and Endurance racing modes. To get the Demon car, use Racer X's Shooting Star car and win a race in Time trial mode. To get the GRX (the fastest car) use one of the Mach V cars or the Demon on the M track. You need to enter the ruins with this car. Put on your deflector and saws and look for a set of closed doors on your left after you enter the tunnel. Go fast enough so that you will break through the doors. Drive through the Ruins and hang a Left to see the GRX car on display. Then go right and jump over the rail. Go through the water to jump onto the race track. Entering this hidden cave releases the GRX. Use a memory card to save your data so the cars will be available the next time you play.

Bonus Cars the Easy Way
At the car select screen press and hold R1+R2+L1+L2+Select+Down+Triangle. Release everything, then scroll Left or Right to view the other cars.

SPICE WORLD

Giant Spice
At the menu screen where your character walks across the globe, hold the Start button and press Circle, Square, Circle, Square. Your code appears on the screen to confirm it, and your character grows to giant size.

Handbag Code
At the "globe" menu, hold the Start button and press Square, Triangle, Circle, Triangle. With that code on the screen, enter the television studio with your "act" prepared. Instead of standing in a line, the girls will crowd around a pile of handbags on the floor.

Hidden Messages
At the screen where your character walks across the globe, hold the Start button and press Circle, Triangle, Triangle, Circle. The code appears on the screen to confirm. Now hold Start+Select and press Circle, Circle, Circle, Circle. Also press Triangle, Triangle, Triangle, Triangle and Square, Square, Square, Square.

Naked Spice
Enter the first part of the "Hidden Messages" code as described. Press L1+L2+R1+R2+ Select+Start simultaneously to reset the game. You'll get an alternate title screen that shows the Spice Girls naked (except for those chairs).

New Title Screen

At the global screen, hold Start and press Circle, Triangle, Triangle, Circle. Release Start and press L1, L1, R1, R2 and Select.

Spiffy New Dance Moves

Want some new dance moves? Go to the globe menu and while pressing and holding Start, press Square, Triangle, Circle, and Triangle. Enter the dance studio and boogie!

SPIDER

Play as a Flea

Pause the game and press Triangle, Square, Circle, Triangle. The flea jumps better than the spider, but he's very hard to see. To return to normal, enter the code again.

Refill Weapons and Power

Pause the game and press Triangle, X, X, X, Circle, X, Square, Triangle, X, Triangle, Circle.

SPIDER-MAN

Invincibility

At the main menu, select "Special" then "Cheats." Enter RUSTCRST as a password.

Big Head

At the main menu, select "Special" then "Cheats." Enter DULUX as a password.

Level Select

At the main menu, select "Special" then "Cheats." Enter XCLSIOR as a password.

Profanity Filter

At the main menu, select "Special" then "Cheats." Enter a profanity and the game will automatically replace that profanity with a cleaner word.

Unlock All Comic Book Covers

At the main menu, select "Special" then "Cheats." Enter ALLSIXCC as a password.

Unlock All Movies

At the main menu, select "Special" then "Cheats." Enter WATCHEM as a password.

Unlimited Webbing

At the main menu, select "Special" then "Cheats." Enter STRUDL as a password.

Unlock Everything

At the main menu, select "Special" then "Cheats." Enter EEL NATS as a password.

Unlock Joel Jewett

At the main menu, select "Special" then "Cheats." Enter RULUR as a password. Enter the gallery to see Joel Jewett, President of NeverSoft, at the bottom of the character viewer.

Debug Mode

At the main menu, select "Special" then "Cheats." Enter LLADNEK as a password.

Infinite Health

At the main menu, select "Special" then "Cheats." Enter DCSTUR as a password.

All Characters in Character Viewer

At the main menu, select "Special" then "Cheats." Enter CVIEWEM as a password.

Storyboard Viewer

At the main menu, select "Special" then "Cheats." Enter CGOSSETT as a password.

Amazing Bag Man Costume

At the main menu, select "Special" then "Cheats." Enter AMZBGMAN as a password.

Ben Reilly Costume

At the main menu, select "Special" then "Cheats." Enter BNREILLY as a password.

Capt. Universe Costume

At the main menu, select "Special" then "Cheats." Enter SCOSMIC as a password.

Peter Parker Costume

At the main menu, select "Special" then "Cheats." Enter MJSSTUD as a password.

Quick Change Spidey Costume

At the main menu, select "Special" then "Cheats." Enter ALMSTPKR as a password.

Scarlet Spider Costume

At the main menu, select "Special" then "Cheats." Enter LETTERS as a password.

Spidey Unlimited Costume

At the main menu, select "Special" then "Cheats." Enter PARALLEL as a password.

Spidey 2099 Costume

At the main menu, select "Special" then "Cheats." Enter TWNTYNDN as a password.

Symbiote Costume

At the main menu, select "Special" then "Cheats." Enter BLKSPIDER as a password.

SPORTS CAR GT

10 Cars

For 10 additional cars, simultaneously press Square, X, Triangle, and Start.

All Cars

To unlock all cars, press Up, Left(2), Right, Down, Right, L1, Square at the title screen. (This cheat also awards players with additional money!)

Easy Money

In the 2nd class of races, go to the left until you come to the pink and silver Saleen Mustang. Buy it for $30,000, then you can sell it for $55,000. Keep this up to have all the money you want. (It will not work with any other car.)

Unlock Season Races

To unlock additional races, press Down(2), Left, Right, Up, Left, Circle, R2.

SPOT GOES TO HOLLYWOOD

50 Lives

Before using this trick, activate the Level Select code. While playing, pause the game and press Square to gain 50 lives!

Level Select

At the title screen, press Triangle, Up, Right, Down, Left, Triangle, Left, Down, Right, Up, Triangle.

View FMV's

To view all the FMV's, enter the Level Select screen, then hold Square and press Start.

SPYRO THE DRAGON

Crash Bandicoot Warped Demo

Hold L1+Triangle at the New/Load Game menu.

More Lives

Pause and enter the Inventory screen. Press Square (6), Circle, Up, Circle, Left, Circle, Right, Circle, Select to get 99 lives.

Level Select

Pause and enter the Inventory screen. Press Square (2), Circle, Left, Right, Left, Right, Circle, Up, Right, Down. You can access all levels when you go to a balloonist.

SPYRO: YEAR OF THE DRAGON

2D Spyro

To turn Spyro into a flat little dragon, pause the game and enter: Left, Right, Left, Right, L1, R1, L1, R1, Square, Circle.

Extra Lives

This code only works if you're in the first land and haven't moved to another land. Press "Start" and go to the Inventory screen. Then press Square, Circle, Up, Circle, Left, Circle, Right, Circle.

Big-Headed Dragon

To enlarge Spyro's skull, pause the game and enter: Up, R1, Up, R1, Up, R1, Circle (4).

Crash Bash

At the title screen, hold L1+R2 and press Square for a demo of Crash Bash.

Extra Hit Points

To get an extra hit point without going in the Sparx levels, press Circle, R1, Circle, L1, Circle, R2, Circle, L2, Circle.

Game Credits

Press pause during gameplay, then press Left, Right, Left, Right, Left, Right, Square, Circle, Square, Circle, Square, Circle

Make Spyro Black

Pause the game and press Up, Left, Down, Right, Up, Square, R1, R2, L1, L2, Up, Right, Down, Left, Up, Down. To change him back, pause the game and press the same buttons, but replace Down with Left or Right.

Make Spyro Blue

Pause the game and press Up, Left, Down, Right, Up, Square, R1, R2, L1, L2, Up, Right, Down, Left, Up, and X. To change him back, pause the game and press the same buttons, but replace X with Left or Right.

Make Spyro Green

Pause the game and press Up, Left, Down, Right, Up, Square, R1, R2, L1, L2, Up, Right, Down, Left, Up, Triangle. To change him back, pause the game and press the same buttons, but replace Triangle with Left or Right.

Make Spyro Pink

Pause the game and press Up, Left, Down, Right, Up, Square, R1, R2, L1, L2, Up, Right, Down, Left, Up, Square. To change him back, pause the game and press the same buttons, but replace Square with Left or Right.

Make Spyro Red

Pause the game and press Up, Left, Down, Right, Up, Square, R1, R2, L1, L2, Up, Right, Down, Left, Up, and Circle. To change him back, pause the game and press the same buttons, but replace Circle with Left or Right.

Make Spyro Yellow

Pause the game and press Up, Left, Down, Right, Up, Square, R1, R2, L1, L2, Up, Right, Down, Left, Up, Up. To change him back, pause the game and press the same buttons, but replace the last Up with Left or Right.

Skate on a Squid

Press "Start" and go to the Inventory screen. Then, press Up (2), Left (2), Right (2), Down (2), Square, Circle, Square.

Sparx Treasure Finding

Without going to Sparx levels, press "Start" and go to the Inventory screen. Then press Right (2), Left (2), Right (2), Left, (2), Circle (3).

Two-Player

After you beat the yeti in boxing, if you plug in two controllers and attempt to replay the challenge, it will go into Two-Player Boxing mode! One player controls Bentley, the other gets the yeti.

SPYRO 2: RIPTO'S RAGE

Big Head Mode

To make Spyro's head larger, pause the game and press Up(4), R1(4), then Circle.

Fireballs All the Time

In dragon shores, there is a portal that gives you fireballs all the time. Get 100% in the game—64 orbs and 10,000 in treasure.

Flat Mode

To activate Flat Mode, pause the game and hit Left, Right, Left, Right, L2, R2, L2, R2, Square.

Gem Finder

To be zeroed-in instantly on the closest Gem, hold L1+L2+R1+R2 and your little dragonfly buddy Sparks points you in the right direction.

Get All Abilities

To get every ability in the game without working for it, pause the game and hit Circle(4), then Square once.

Make Spyro Black

To turn Spyro black, pause the game and hit Up, Right, Down, Left, Up, Square, R1, R2, L1, L2, Up, Left, Down, Right, Up, Down.

Make Spyro Blue

To turn Spyro blue, pause the game and tap Up, Right, Down, Left, Up, Square, R1, R2, L1, L2, Up, Left, Down, Right, Up, X.

Make Spyro Green

To make Spyro green, pause the game and tap Up, Right, Down, Left, Up, Square, R1, R2, L1, L2, Up, Left, Down, Right, Up, Triangle.

Make Spyro Pink

To turn Spyro pink, pause the game and press Up, Right, Down, Left, Up, Square, R1, R2, L1, L2, Up, Left, Down, Right, Up, Square.

Make Spyro Red

To make Spyro red, pause the game and hit Up, Right, Down, Left, Up, Square, R1, R2, L1, L2, Up, Left, Down, Right, Up, Circle.

Make Spyro Yellow

To change Spyro to yellow, pause the game and press Up, Right, Down, Left, Up, Square, R1, R2, L1, L2, Up, Left, Down, Right, Up(2).

STAR GLADIATOR

Big Heads

After you choose your character, press and hold Right+Start+Circle+Square until the match starts.

Dark Mode

At the Vs. screen, press and hold L2+R2+Down until the fight starts.

Invisible Walls

If you beat the game on Level 4 difficulty or above, you'll find a WALL option in the options menu. If you turn it on, an invisible wall surrounds the arena.

Play as Bilstein

Enter arcade mode, then hold Select, highlight Gore, and press X, Circle, X, Circle, Square, Square, Square, Triangle, Triangle, Triangle, X+Circle.

Play as Blood

Enter arcade mode, then hold Select, highlight Bilstein, and press X, Square, X, Square, X, Square. Highlight Kappa and press Circle, Triangle, Circle, Triangle, Circle, Triangle. To finish, hold L1+R1 and release Select.

Play as Kappah

Enter arcade mode, then highlight Gore and hold Select. Now go to Hayato and press Circle, Square, Triangle, Square, X, Square, Triangle, Square, Circle, Square. To finish, press X+Triangle and release Select.

Reset

To reset the game while playing, press L1+R1+Select+Start.

Small Heads

After you choose your character, immediately press and hold Left+Start+Circle+Square until the match starts.

True Endings

To view the true ending, beat everyone, including Bilstein, in under six minutes if the game is set for best of three rounds per fight (only three minutes if the game is set for one round per fight). After that you will face Super Bilstein. If you beat him, you will see your character's real ending.

Zelkin's Hidden Move

After you do Zelkin's PLASMA FINAL, keep pressing forward when he lights up. If you did it right, he'll spread his wings and move toward his opponent with his sword sticking out. This is great for getting your opponent out of the ring—fly out of the ring, and your opponent chases you, causing a ring-out.

STAR TREK: INVASION

View Credits

At a Mission Briefing screen, press Left, Right, Up, Down (5).

Unlock All

At the Level Select screen, press Up, Left, Down, Right, Up, Right, Down, Left, Up, L1+R1, L2+R2.

STAR WARS: DARK FORCES

Open Secret Cheat Menu

During gameplay, stop and press Left, Circle, X, Right, Circle, X, Down, Circle, X.

STAR WARS: DEMOLITION

Access Cheat Menu

Enter the Options menu and select "Preferences." Press L1+R1 at the Preferences screen. A new sign under Powerups will appear called "Passcode." Scroll through the letters to enter any of the passcodes listed below, and then press X. The game automatically saves the code when you return to the main menu. To remove a code, enter it.

Run Game at Half Speed

Access Cheat menu and enter SLOW_MO_ON.

Reduce Gravity

Access Cheat menu an enter LO_GRAV_ON.

Select a Minimum of Zero Enemies in Battle Mode

Access Cheat menu and enter NO_BADIES.

Invincibility

Access Cheat menu and enter RAISE_THEM.

Show All Victory Movies

Access Cheat menu and enter MOVIE_SHOW.

Both Players in Two-Player Mode Select the Same Vehicle

Access Cheat menu and enter MULTI_CARS.

Unlock All Vehicles

Access Cheat menu and enter WATTO_SHOP.

Change Button Configurations

Access Cheat menu and enter EXTRABUTTS.

Remove Delays on Weapon Firing

Access Cheat menu and enter FIRERATEUP.

Allow Three Enemies to Attack at Once

Access Cheat menu and enter ITS_A_TRAP.

Increase the Mass of Player Vehicles

Access Cheat menu and enter BFM_FEELIT.

Increase the Speed of Player Vehicles

Access Cheat menu and enter THROTTLEUP.

Randomly Select All Opponents and Stages

Access Cheat menu and enter NO_PEEKING.

Show All Defeat Movies

Access Cheat menu and enter SAD_MOVIES.

STAR WARS EPISODE 1: JEDI POWER BATTLES

Play as Captain Panaka

Beat the game on Jedi mode with Plo Koon. Highlight Plo and press Select. Captain Panaka's picture should replace Plo Koon's at the top. Press X to play as Captain Panaka. Both he and Queen Amidala use a blaster and fists.

Play as Queen Amidala

To access Queen Amidala, beat the game on "Jedi Mode" with Obi-Wan Kenobi. Go to the Character Selection screen on the game you beat on "Jedi Mode" with Obi-Wan Kenobi. Highlight Obi-Wan, but do not select him. (In other words, move your green character selector onto Obi-Wan's picture, then stop!) Hold down Select. The picture at the top of the screen changes from Obi-Wan to Queen Amidala. Press X to select the Queen.

Point Trick

In all levels you can easily get thousands upon thousands of extra points. Make sure you have a bunch of extra credits. When you encounter an object that regenerates you when you die, kill everything behind it and near it. Hit the object and die. You will go back to the object and all the enemies will be back. Run as far as you can go and kill everything.

Droidekas

To get this level, beat the game with Plo Koon.

Kaadu Race

Beat the game with Adi Gallia.

Gungan Roundup

Find all three Gungan Artifacts throughout the game.

Survival Challenge

Beat the game as Mace Windu. Beat this level to unlock Ultimate lightsaber mode, and you kill anything in one hit.

Play as Darth Maul

In order to play as Darth Maul, pass the game with Qui-Gon in Jedi mode. He must be level 10 and skill 100. Highlight his character and press Select. You can select Darth Maul as a playable character.

STAR WARS EPISODE 1: THE PHANTOM MENACE

Debug Mode (Level Select, Invincibility, Etc.)

To activate debug mode, highlight Options at the main menu. Then press: Triangle, Circle, Left, L1, R2, Square, Circle, Left. (A tone confirms correct entry.) Hold L1+Select+Triangle to reveal a debug list.

STAR WARS: REBEL ASSAULT II

Unlock All Levels and Endings

Choose "Enter Password" at the Options menu and input one of the following passcodes to gain access to all of the game's stages, including the endings.

Easy Difficulty Level
X, Circle, X, Circle, X, Triangle

Medium Difficulty Level
X, X, Triangle, Circle, X, Triangle

Hard Difficulty Level
Triangle, Square, Square, Square, X, Triangle

STAR WARS: MASTERS OF TERAS KASI

Big Feet, Head, Hands, and Legs

For big feet, hands, legs, and head, hold Down+X+Select while selecting your character. Don't release them until the fight begins.

Big Head Mode

Press and hold Select while choosing a Character. Release Select when the fight starts.

Bouncing Lightsaber

With Luke Skywalker, get the power bar to full, then throw the lightsaber. When the lightsaber comes back, jump up and down and the lightsaber follows you.

Change Uniforms

Press L1 on the character select screen.

Clean Screen

To make the power bars and the force bars disappear, hold Down L1+R2+Select while the match is loading.

Fight Mara Jade

Play the game as Darth Vader, and instead of a mirror match, you fight Mara Jade, a character who uses a blue lightsaber and fights like Darth Vader.

Huge-Headed Thok

When playing in Vs. Mode, select Thok as your character. At the Vs. screen press Down+X+Select+R2 and release when the fight starts. When the characters appear on the screen, Thok will be small. When you get a yellow power bar, press Down, Down, Down, Triangle and Thok will grow into his normal size, only he will have a humongous head. Now you may think that you can pull off this code by using the Big Head Mode, but his head is considerably bigger by doing the code listed here. Also, the code makes Thok fight better.

Invisible Light Saber

When you pick Luke or Mara Jade, throw the lightsaber with the super gold power bar. While the lightsaber is in the air, press R2(2) so you can see the handle on Luke or Mara's leg. When the lightsaber comes back, it is invisible unless you move or attack.

Juggle Your Opponent

With Princess Leia, when you have a super gold power bar, throw your rising tracer out of the ring. After you do that, kick your opponent, and he or she will fly very high into the air. If you have done this correctly, you can juggle your opponent. There is a downside to this, though: After you throw your tracer out of the ring, you cannot get any more power bars.

Level Select

To access level select on Vs. Mode, beat the game using Chewbacca.

Play as Darth Vader

Set the "Player Change at Continue" option to No, then beat the game with Luke Skywalker on the Standard or Jedi setting.

Play as Jodo Kast

Play the survival mode and beat all 10 fighters to unlock Jodo Kast.

Play as Mara Jade

Press and hold L1+L2+R1 when you enter the team battle mode. Be sure the setting is on Jedi and the character change at continue option is off. If you do this correctly, the computer will select fighters for you automatically and the words "Fight for Mara Jade" appear on the screen. Beat the computer, then she will be at your control.

Play as Slave Leia

Set the "Player Change at Continue" option to No, then beat the game with Princess Leia on the Jedi setting.

Play as Speeder-Bike Scout

To do this, you must have the Stormtrooper. At the fighter select screen, highlight the Stormtrooper, then press and hold L1 and tap X.

Play as a Stormtrooper

Set the "Player Change at Continue" option to No, then beat the game with Han Solo on the Jedi setting.

Speed Up the Credits

Whenever you view the game credits, hold down on the control pad. It makes the credits go faster. You can also press up on the control pad to go through the previous credits.

Tiny Players

You can only do this in Vs. mode. Press and hold Down+Select+X+R2. Keep holding until the fight starts.

STARBLADE ALPHA

Rapid-Fire Laser

At the main title screen, press Up, Up, Down, Down, Circle, Triangle, Square while the letters fly together. You will hear a boom. During the game, press X to use the rapid-fire laser.

STARWINDER

Almost All Tracks

Press L1, Triangle, Circle, R2, Square, R1, L1, Triangle to unlock all race mode tracks. Once entered, all tracks but Quadrant 11 will be accessible.

STEEL HARBINGER

All Weapons

Pause gameplay and press X, Triangle, R2, Triangle, X, L2, R2, Down, L2, Square, Right. A beep confirms correct code entry. This code may only be enabled three times during the entire game.

Arctic Card

Pause gameplay and press Up, Right, Triangle, Circle, Down, Left, X, Square. A beep confirms correct code entry. This code may only be enabled once per level.

Full Health

While playing, pause the game and press L2, L2, R2, R2, Up, L1, Up, R1. A beep confirms the code. This code may only be enabled five times during the game.

Level Select

Enter the following codes at the title screen.

Los Angeles
Circle, Circle, R2, R2, Left, Right, Up, L2, L2, Triangle

Los Angeles 7
Circle, Circle, L2, L2, Left, Right, Up, R2, R2, Triangle

Las Vegas
Square, Square, L2, L1, Up, Down, R1, R2, Left, Right

Las Vegas 7
Triangle, Triangle, L2, L1, Up, Down, R1, R2, Right, Left

San Francisco
Circle, Square, L2, R1, Triangle, L1, R2, Down, Up, Left

Houston
L2, L1, R1, R2, Circle, Left, Left, Triangle, Right, Right

Washington
Circle, Circle, L1, R1, L2, R2, Left, Right, Triangle, Square

Florida
L1, R1, Square, Circle, R2, L2, Up, Triangle, Down, Down

Nebraska
Square, Square, Left, Left, Square, Circle, Circle, Up, Up, Square

Moon Base
R1, R1, L2, R1, Square, Triangle, Triangle, Left, Right, R2

M-16 Ammo
Pause gameplay and press Down, Square(3), Circle(2), Up, Right. A beep confirms correct code entry. The M-16 now has 999 rounds of ammunition.

Net Node Card
Pause gameplay and press Left, Triangle. L2, Right, R1, Circle, R1, Down. A beep confirms correct code entry. This code may only be enabled three times during the game.

Rocket Ammo
Pause gameplay and press Left(2), L1, R2, Square, R1, Right(2). A beep confirms correct code entry. This code may only be enabled five times during the game.

Shield
Pause gameplay and press Triangle, X, Triangle, X, Triangle, X Square, Circle, Square, Circle, Up, R1. A beep confirms correct code entry. This code may only be enabled three times during the entire game.

Teleport Credit
Pause gameplay and press L1, R1(2), L2, R2, L2, Circle, Triangle. A beep confirms correct code entry. This code may only be enabled 100 times per level.

View Credits
Press Square(4), Circle(3), Square(2) at the main menu.

View FMV's
Press L2(2), R2(2), L1, R1, Square, Circle, Up, Down at the main menu.

STEEL REIGN

Invincibility
For Super Shields (invincibility), press L2, L1, R2, Circle, Square, Circle, Circle, L1, L2, L1 at the main menu.

Secret Level
To access a secret level, press L1, L2, L1, L2, R2, R1, Square, Circle, Square, Square at the main menu.

Super Tank and More
At the main menu, press L1, L2, L1, Circle, Square, Circle, Circle, L2, L1, R2. This code unlocks a Super Tank with unlimited weapons, and also provides access to all of the other tanks.

STREET FIGHTER ALPHA

Fight Akuma
To fight against Akuma, select any other character, then hold L2+R2+ X until Akuma appears.

Fight Dan
After winning a match, hold Up+L2+R2 until the winning words come up, then release. Repeat this for five matches and your sixth will be against Dan.

Fight M.Bison
This code requires two people to enter it. Hold Start on both controllers. Press Up, Up on both controllers, then release Start. Press Up, Up on both controllers. Simultaneously press Jab on controller one and Fierce on Controller Two.

Play as Akuma
Go to the random box and hold L2. Press Left, Left, Left, Down, Down, Down. Then press Square+Triangle or Circle+X.

Play as Dan
Press and hold L2. Go to the random box and press Triangle, Square, X, Circle, Triangle or do it in the reverse motion for the other color.

Play as M.Bison
Go to the random box and hold L2. Press Left, Left, Down, Down, Left, Down, Down. Press Square and Triangle or Circle+X for the other color.

STREET FIGHTER ALPHA 2

Chun-Li's Original Outfit
To get Chun-li's original outfit, start with any mode of play (arcade, versus, or training). Place the cursor on Chun-li, then hold the Select button for at least five seconds then press any button.

Day-Glo Vega and All-White Dhalsim
Enter training mode and do a teleport move. Pause the game in mid-warp, then go to the menu and select a normal game as Vega or Dhalsim.

Original Zangief Introduction
For Zangief's original arcade intro, hold Select before the bout begins. This only works in versus or training mode.

Secret Stage
To fight in Sagat or M.Bison's secret stage, highlight either Sagat or M.Bison, then hold Start for 5 seconds.

Super Akuma
Highlight Akuma, press and release Select. Then press Down, Right, Right, Down, Left, Down, Left, Down, Right, Right, Right. You end up on Akuma again. Hold Select and press any button. When the fight starts, there is a sign on top of Akuma and he looks black for a second.

Winning Poses
After defeating an opponent, but before the K.O. symbol appears, press and hold select, then one of the punch or kick button.

STREET FIGHTER ALPHA 3

Bonus Modes
Beat Dramatic Battle mode with Ryu/Ken and Juni/Jill to unlock two bonus modes.

Dramatic and Final Battle Modes
Beat Arcade mode on any difficulty level.

Fight Shin Akuma in Final Battle Mode
Select Final Battle mode. Select a character and hold L1+L2 before the versus screen appears.

Fight as Classic Balrog
To play as the arcade version of Balrog, choose a character whose level of experience is below 30. Defeat M.Bison in the final stage of the World Tour.

Fight as Evil Ryu
To play as Evil Ryu, raise a character to an experience level of 31. Defeat Evil Ryu in the first bonus stage of the World Tour.

Fight as Guile
To play as Guile, raise a character to an experience level of 30. Defeat Guile in the second bonus stage of the World Tour.

Fight as Shin Akuma
To play as Shin Akuma, raise a character to an experience level of 32. Defeat Shin Akuma in the final bonus stage of the World Tour. (To select him, hold L2 and choose Akuma.)

Play as Evil Ryu, Evil Ken, and Super Cody
To play as Evil Ryu, Evil Ken, and Super Cody, press L1,L2,R1,R2 then press Start to select them.

STREET FIGHTER COLLECTION

Original Ken and Ryu
In *Street Fighter 2 Alpha Gold*, press Start once and press any button to select them. They will have no power level bars on the bottom, meaning you can't use super moves.

Play Original Characters
All original characters can be selected by pressing Start while selecting the character. This can be used only on characters from the original *Street Fighter*.

Play as Akuma
Put the curser on Ryu, then simultaneously press L1 and R1 to make Akuma appear.

Play as Cammy in *Street Fighter Zero 2*
Select Vega in arcade mode and complete the game in first place with a score greater than 50,000. Enter CAM as initials on the high score screen. Select versus mode, highlight M.Bison, and press Start three times.

Play as Evil Ryu
Highlight Ryu on *Street Fighter Alpha 2 Gold* and press Start twice. Then press any button to select him. He will be able to do Akuma's Teleport and three power bar special move "Raging Demon" by pressing low punch, low punch, low kick, forward, hard punch fast.

Play as Evil Sakura
To play as evil Sakura, highlight Sakura and press Start once so evil Sakura can be selectable.

Play as Gouki in *Super Street Fighter IIX*
In the selection menu, highlight Ryu, hold L1, and press R1. Now you can play as Gouki.

STREET FIGHTER ZERO 3

Alternate Introduction
Accumulate 48 hours of gameplay on the timer in the options menu. Then, instead of showing the arcade characters, the opening sequence shows all the new characters (including Guile and Evil Ryu). Alternatively, unlock all character endings including the bonus characters.

Bonus Modes
Beat Dramatic Battle mode with Ryu and Juni to unlock two bonus modes.

Play as Evil Ryu and Guile
To play as Evil Ryu and Guile, beat them in Dramatic Mode.

STREET RACER

Silver Cup Password
TRAFIK

Gold Cup Password
NEJATI

Silver Cup Password
DOUGAL

Hidden Driver and More
Enter the password "TURGAY" for a hidden driver, a hidden level, and many advanced options.

STREET SK8ER

Play as Bonobo
Finish Street Tour mode twice with Ginger. Or press Right, Circle, Left (2), Circle (2), Square (2) at the main menu.

Play as Mick
Finish Street Tour mode twice with Jerry. Or press Left, Right, Circle, Square, R2, L1, L2, R1 at the main menu.

Play as Saho
Finish Street Tour mode twice with Frankie.

Play as Sarah
Finish Street Tour mode twice with T.J. Or press Left (2), Square, Right (2), Circle, R1 (2) at the main menu.

Bonus Boards
Finish Street Tour mode with a bonus character. Or press Right (2), R1, R2, Left (2), L1, L2 at the main menu.

Mirrored Tracks
Finish Street Tour mode twice with each of the four bonus skaters.

Unlock All Tracks, Open Gates
Press Right, Circle, Square, Left, Square, Circle, R1, L1 at the main menu.

STREET SK8ER 2

Alternate Clothing
At the Skater Select screen, hold L1, L2, R1, or R2 when choosing the "Skate" option.

All Skaters
Press Left (2), Circle (2), L2, Square, Right, R2 at the title screen.

All Boards
Press Circle (2), Square, Circle, Square (2), Circle, R1 at the title screen.

All Tracks
Press Left, Right, Left, Right, Circle (2), R1, Square at the title screen.

View Movies
Press R2 (2), L1, L2, L1, R1 (3) at the title screen. Choose the "Movie" option on main menu.

Full Attributes/Trick Level
Press L1, Square, Left (2), R2, Left, R1, Left at the title screen.

STRIDER 2

Player Set-Up/Stage Select Options (*Strider 1*)
Beat the game once.

Bonus Stage (*Strider 2*)
Beat *Strider 1* and *Strider 2*. The new level is in *Strider 2*.

Play as Strider Hein (*Strider 2*)
Beat the game once.

Unlimited Boost (*Strider 2*)
Beat the game with Strider Hein, then pick "Infinite Boost" under Options.

STRIKE POINT

Play as Ghost
When playing a two-player game, let Player 2 die and complete the level with Player 1. Write down the password before quitting the game. Then enter the password under the Options menu.

STRIKER '96

Unlock Special Cup
Win the World Cup.

STRIKER PRO 2000

Unlock Bonus Stadiums
At the main menu, press Left (2), Up, Circle (2) to unlock extra stadiums.

Unlock Additional Features
At the Cheat screen, press Left, Up, Left, Up, Left, Up, Left, X to unlock new features.

Bird Mode
At the Cheat screen, press Up, Triangle, Left, Square, Right, Circle, X (2) while the game is paused.

SUIKODEN II

Enter Random Name
Press either L1+R1 or L2+R2 at the Name Entry screen.

SUPER LIVE STADIUM

Hidden Ball: Dancing Twister
Press Up, Down, Down-Left, Left, Down, Right+Pitch.

Hidden Ball: Danger Strike
Press Left, Down, Right, Down-Right, Down+Pitch.

Hidden Ball: Lightning Sword
Press Down (3), Up+Pitch.

Hidden Ball: Bracing Tower
Press Up (3), Down+Pitch.

Hidden Ball: Sky Scraper
Press Down (2), Up (2)+Pitch.

Hidden Ball: Star Dust Phantom
Press Right (2), Left, Down-Left, Down, Down-Right, Right+Pitch.

Hidden Ball: Sonic Butterfly
Press Down, Down-Right, Right, Down, Down-Right, Right+Pitch.

Hidden Ball: Highly Cane Ball
Rotate the D-Pad+Pitch.

Hidden Ball: Rising Dragon
Press Left, Right, Down, Up+Pitch.

Hidden Ball: Ultimate Force
Press Right, Down, Left, Right+Pitch.

Hidden Ball: Rolling Thunder
Press Left, Down, Right, Left, Down, Right+Pitch.

Hidden Ball: Splash Wave
Press Left, Right, Down-Right, Down, Down-Left, Left+Pitch.

SUPER PUZZLE FIGHTER II TURBO

Unlock Akuma
Go to the Character Selection screen. Player 1: Highlight Morrigan, hold Select, and press Down (3), Left (3), Circle. Player 2: Highlight Felicia, hold Select, and press Down (3), Right (3), Circle.

Unlock Full-Attack Akuma (Orange CDs Only)
Go to the Character Selection screen. Player 1: Highlight Morrigan, hold Select, and press Up (3), Left (3), Circle. Player 2: Highlight Felicia, hold Select, and press Up (3), Right (3), Circle.

Unlock Anita
Go to the Character Selection screen. Player 1: Highlight Morrigan, hold Select, position the cursor over Donovan, and press Circle. Player 2: Highlight Felicia, hold Select, position the cursor over Donovan, and press Circle.

Unlock Dan
Go to the Character Selection screen. Player 1: Highlight Morrigan, hold Select, and press Left (3), Down (3), Circle. Player 2: Highlight Felicia, hold Selec, and press Right (3), Down (3), Circle.

Unlock Devilot
Go to the Character Selection screen. Player 1: Highlight Morrigan, hold Select, and press Left (3), Down (3), and when the timer gets to 10 seconds, press Circle. Player 2: Highlight Felicia, hold Select, and press Right (3), Down (3), and when the timer gets to 10 seconds, press Circle.

Unlock Full-Attack Devilot (Orange CDs only)
Go to the Character Selection screen. Player 1: Highlight Morrigan, press Down (13), and when the timer gets to 10 seconds, press Circle. Player 2: Highlight Felicia, press Down (13), and when the timer gets to 10 seconds, press Circle.

Unlock Hsien-Ko
Go to the Character Selection screen. Player 1: Highlight Morrigan, hold Select, position the cursor over Lei Lei, and press Circle. Player 2: Highlight Felicia, hold Select, move the cursor left two squares, and press Circle.

Unlock Lei Lei
Go to the Character Selection screen. Player 1: Highlight Morrigan, hold Select, position the cursor over Hsein-Ko, and press Circle. Player 2: Highlight Felicia, hold Select, position the cursor over Hsein-Ko, and press Circle.

Hsien-Ko's Paper Talisman
Go to the Character Selection screen. Highlight Morrigan, hold Start, highlight Lei-Lei, and press Circle.

Level Select: Akuma
After selecting a character, hold Select+L2+R2. Select a handicap, then press L1.

Level Select: Ryu
After selecting a character, hold Select+L2+R2. Select a handicap, then press Left.

Level Select: Chun Li
After selecting a character, hold Select+L2+R2. Select a handicap, then press Down.

Level Select: Ken
After selecting a character, hold Select+L2+R2. Select a handicap, then press Right.

Level Select: Dan
After selecting a character, hold Select+L2+R2. Select a handicap.

Level Select: Sakura
After selecting a character, hold Select+L2+R2. Select a handicap, then press Triangle.

Level Select: Hsien-Ko
After selecting a character, hold Select+L2+R2. Select a handicap, then press X.

Level Select: Donovan
After selecting a character, hold Select+L2+R2. Select a handicap, then press Circle.

Level Select: Felicia
After selecting a character, hold Select+L2+R2. Select a handicap, then press Square.

Level Select: Devilot
After selecting a character, hold Select+L2+R2. Select a handicap, then press R1.

Level Select: Morrigan
After selecting a character, hold Select+L2+R2. Select a handicap, then press Up.

Play Vs. Devilot CPU
Have one or more Super Combos, beat an opponent in one round in under one minute, get a maximum chain of four or above, and a maximum Power Gem with 20 units or above. Do these things, without continuing, before you get to Stage 7.

Play Vs. Dan CPU
Have one or more Super Combos, beat an opponent in one round in under one minute, get a maximum chain of four or above, and a maximum Power Gem with 20 units or above. Do these things, without continuing, before you get to Stage 6.

SUPERCROSS 2000

Access Cheat Mode
While at the Select Event screen, press R1 to display the Cheat screen. Then enter one of the codes below.

Never Crash
N0CR4SH

Big Bikes
B1GB1K3S

Giants on Minibikes
G14NTS

Mercury Gravity
M3RCVRY

Venus Gravity
V3NVS

Moon Gravity
M00N

Mars Gravity
M4RS

Jupiter Gravity
JVP1T3R

Saturn Gravity
S4TVRN

Uranus Gravity
VR4NVS

Neptune Gravity
N3PTVN3

Pluto Gravity
PLVT0

Add a Hop Button
H0P

More Camera Views
M0R3C4MS

Only Bikes, No Riders
N0R1D3RS

No Blockers
BL0CKM3

No Off Track
N00FFTR4CK

No Resetting
SK1PP1NG0K

Big Dirt Spray
B1GSPR4Y

Headless Rider
H34DL3SS

SUPERCROSS 2001

Unlimited Power Clutch
UNLIMITEDPC

All Joke Riders
JOKERIDERS

Invisible Bikes
NOBIKES

Invisible Riders
NORIDERS

Unlimited Turbo
NDFSPD

Low Fences
LOFENCES

Display Riders Weakness
I AM WEAK

Exploding Text
EXPLODE

The Riverbed
OTRATTWTGHWG

The Launching Pad
OSSFMOGLFM

The Washougal
WMXPLIBWWA

Parts Unlimited
NUTSANDBOLTSS

FMF
NEEDNEWEXHAUST

Wrenchead.com
SUPPLIESONLINE

Etnies Freestyle Games
SHOESANDTRICKS

Scott
THROWMEGOGGLES

Etnies Freestyle Games
SHOESANDTRICKS

Unlock Johnny O'Marra
4XUSMXDNCHAMP

Unlock Roger DeCoster
9XBELGIANCHAMP

Unlock Space Overlord
BUNGAVEE

Unlock Bradley G
DTMHBOSS

Unlock Smitty Sugarlegs
ENDZONEDANCE

Unlock Bob Page
FORTYFOUR

Unlock Hot Tub Harvey
HARVEYSAYSRELAX

Unlock Moto Samurai
HONORFIRST

Unlock David Bailey
IRONMAN

Unlock Sir Dirthead
JOUSTER

Unlock EA Gal
LETSGOEAGAL

Unlock The Zombie
LOVESBRAINS

Unlock Doctor Invizzo
LOOKMANOBODY

Unlock Bones
MARROWMAN

Unlock El Luchador
MASKEDMAN

Unlock Tie-Dye Guy
MELLOWOUT

Unlock MR-34 Robot
METALDUDE

Unlock Harry Bigfoot
MMMSQUIRREL

Unlock Astro Nut
ONESMALLSTEP

Unlock Agent Albert
PEANUTBUTTER

Unlock Brave Scotsman
PLAIDROCKS

Unlock Billy Ray MudMullet
POSSUMPANCAKES

Unlock Tricky the Clown
POLKADOT

Unlock Sarcophagus Jones
PYRAMIDSCHEME

Unlock the King
SIDEBURNS

Unlock Marimba
SQWAK

Unlock Spitt Polish
THREEPIECESUIT

Unlock Supercross Avenger
TRIPLELEAPER

Unlock Some Guy
WHOSTHAT

Unlock Ecko Rider
WWWECKOCOM

SUPERCROSS CIRCUIT

Access Cheat Mode
Find the option under Bonus Game Options. Then enter one of the following codes.

Riders Without Heads
SLEEPYHOLLOW

Large Heads
BIG_HELMETS

Invisible Bikes
FLOATING

All Bikes
ALLBIKES

Sheep Race
MUTTON

Freeriding Mode
Place first in local point standings.

SWAGMAN

Invincibility
Pause, then press Circle, Square, X, Square, Circle, Square, Circle, Square, Triangle, Square, Circle, Triangle, Circle, Square, Triangle, Square.

Level Select
At the title screen, Press Square (2), Down (2).

Unlimited Swags
Pause, hold L1, and press Up (2), X.

SWAT 3

Complete All Objectives, Win Current Mission
iamleet

Slow Motion
johnwoo

God Mode for Entire Team
swatlord

Unlimited Ammo
biggerpockets

Team Missing Pants And Shirts
casual

Fire Weapon Faster
doubleshot

Bodies Bleed More When Injured
nc17

Night Mission Like During the Day
noshades

Killer Rats Appear When Shot
rabies

Suspects Never Surrender
justin

Suspects Harder to Kill
hotstuff

SYPHON FILTER

All Weapons and Ammo
Highlight Weapons while paused, hold Right+L2+R2+Circle+Square+X.

Level Select
Highlight Select Mission while paused, hold Left+R1+L1+Select+Square+X.

Expert Mode
Hold Left+L1+R2+Select+Square+Circle+X at the title screen.

Silenced 9mm Super Ammo
Pause, go to "Weapons" and highlight "Silenced 9mm." Hold Left+L1+R2+Select+Square+X.

Make Enemies Weak
Pause, highlight "Map," and hold Right+L2+R1+X.

SYPHON FILTER 2

Unlimited Ammo
On the Map screen enter X (2), Circle (2), Square.

Insta-Kill Flak Jacket Enemies
Press and hold: Select, L2, Circle, Square, X.

Hard Mode
On the title screen, select "New Game," then press and hold: Up, Select, L1, R2, Square, Circle, X

Mission Select
Pause, highlight "Map," then press Right+L2+R2+Circle+Square+X. Now go to the Options screen and select "Cheats."

Super Agent Mode
Pause, highlight "Weaponry," then hold Select+L2+Circle+Square+X.

Skip Level
Pause, then press Right, L2, R2, Circle, Square, X.

View Movies
Pause, highlight "Briefing," and hold Right+L1+R2+Circle+X. Or beat the game on Hard difficulty. Find "Movie Theater" under "Cheats" in the Options screen.

TACTICS OGRE

Unlock Music Mode
Enter name as MUSIC ON.

T'AI FU: WRATH OF THE TIGER

Cheat Mode: Map Screen
Press R2, Triangle, R2, Triangle, Circle, Down, Square at the Map screen.

Level Select/Boss Select
Enter Map Screen Cheat. Then press R2, Triangle, R2, Triangle, Circle, Square, Down, Triangle, Up, Right, Left, Down, Up, L1 at the Map screen.

View Credits
Enter Map Screen Cheat. Then press R2, Triangle, R2, Triangle, Down, Square, Circle, Triangle, Up, Down, Left, Right, Up, R1 at the Map screen.

Style Select/Story Select
Enter Map Screen Cheat. Then press R2, Triangle, R2, Triangle, Square, Circle, Down, Triangle, Up, Left, Right, Down, Up, L2 at the Map screen.

Debug Mode
Start a game and finish one level. Then press L1+L2+R1+R2+Select at the Map screen.

Unlock Map
Press R1+R2 when T'ai Fu walks between levels.

Advance to Final Boss
Use the Unlock Map cheat and, while exploring map, press Circle.

Cheat Mode: Gameplay
Press R2, Triangle, R2, Triangle, Circle, X, Square during gameplay.

Unlimited Lives
Enter Gameplay cheat and press R2, Triangle, R2, Left, Right, X during game.

All Kung Fu Styles
Enter Gameplay cheat and press R2, Triangle, R2, Left, Right, Triangle during game.

Full Health
Enter Gameplay cheat and press R2, Triangle, R2, Left, Right, Circle during game.

Full Chi
Enter Gameplay cheat and press R2, Triangle, R2, Left, Right, Square during game.

Invincibility
Enter Gameplay cheat and press R2, Triangle, R2, Left, Right, R1 during game.

Small Enemies
Enter Gameplay cheat and press R2, Triangle, R2, Left, Right, Down during game.

Big Enemies
Enter Gameplay cheat and press R2, Triangle, R2, Left, Right, Up during game.

Stealth Mode
Enter Gameplay cheat and press R2, Triangle, R2, Left, Right, R2 during game.

Bloody Enemies
Enter Gameplay cheat and press R2, Triangle, R2, Right, Left, Right during game.

TARZAN

Cheat Menu
At the main menu, press Left (2), Right (2), Up, Down, Left, Right, Up (2), Down (2).

Unlimited Lives
At the Cheat menu, press L1, R1, L1, R1, L1, R1, L1, R1, L2, R2. Then begin a game to display a Cheat menu.

Level Select
Enter Cheat Menu code, then press L1, R1, L1, R1, L1, R1, L1, R1, L2, R2.

TEAM BUDDIES

Pause the game in any level. Hold down all four shoulder buttons (L1+L2+R1+R2) and type in one of the following codes:

Level Complete
Circle, Square, Cross (2)

Big Feet
Triangle, Square (2), Cross

Big Guns
Triangle, Circle (2), Triangle

Finish Build Shape
Square (2), Circle (2)

Invulnerable
Cross, Triangle (2), Cross

Team Full Health
Triangle (2), Cross (2)

Team Full Ammo
Cross (2), Triangle (2)

All Crates Build Like Super Crates
Circle, X, Cross, Circle

Free Jetpack
Square (2), Triangle (2)

Return to Sender
Circle (2), Square (2)

Easy Gun Building
Circle (2), X (2)

TECMO WORLD GOLF

Alter Direction of Wind
During gameplay, go to Options menu and select "Function." Under "Time," change clock to 12:34:56 and press Triangle+Square.

Move Ball
During gameplay, go to Options menu and select "Function." Under "Time," change clock to 06:19:56 and press Triangle+X.

Move Cup
During gameplay, go to Options menu and select "Function." Under "Time," change clock to 15:14:38 and press Triangle+Circle.

Metal Golfer
Under "Customize Player," enter "R.Masel" as name and choose Bob Taylor as your golfer. During the loading screen when you start a new game, press Left, Up, Right, Down, R1.

Change Golfer Colors
During gameplay, go to Options menu and select "Function." Turn the "Music Option" off. When ball is in "T-Up" mode, hold Triangle and press R1 or R2.

TEKKEN

View Character Names Instead of Pictures
At the title screen, hold L1+R1 and select "Arcade."

Different Clothing
Press Triangle+Square or Circle+X at the Character Select screen.

Anna Fights in Demonstration Mode
On controller one and/or controller two, during Demonstration mode, press L1+L2+R1+R2+Down.

Armor King Fights in Demonstration Mode
On controller one and/or controller two, during Demonstration mode, press L1+L2+R1+R2+Down-Left.

Ganryu Fights in Demonstration Mode
On controller one and/or controller two, during Demonstration mode, press L1+L2+R1+R2+Left.

Heihachi Fights in Demonstration Mode
On controller one and/or controller two, during Demonstration mode, press L1+L2+R1+R2.

Jack Fights in Demonstration Mode
On controller one and/or controller two, during Demonstration mode, press Down-Right.

Kazuya Fights in Demonstration Mode
On controller one and/or controller two, during Demonstration mode, press Up.

King Fights in Demonstration Mode
On controller one and/or controller two, during Demonstration mode, press Down-Left.

Kunimitsu Fights in Demonstration Mode
On controller one and/or controller two, during Demonstration mode, press L1+L2+R1+R2+Up-Left.

Law Fights in Demonstration Mode
On controller one and/or controller two, during Demonstration mode, press Right.

Lee Fights in Demonstration Mode
On controller one and/or controller two, during Demonstration mode, press L1+L2+R1+R2+Up.

Michelle Fights in Demonstration Mode
On controller one and/or controller two, during Demonstration mode, press Up-Left.

Nina Fights in Demonstration Mode
On controller one and/or controller two, during Demonstration mode, press Down.

P. Jack Fights in Demonstration Mode
On controller one and/or controller two, during Demonstration mode, press L1+L2+R1+R2+Down-Right.

Paul Fights in Demonstration Mode
On controller one and/or controller two, during Demonstration mode, press Up-Right.

Wang Fights in Demonstration Mode
On controller one and/or controller two, during Demonstration mode, press L1+L2+R1+R2+Right.

Yoshimitsu Fights in Demonstration Mode
On controller one and/or controller two, during Demonstration mode, press Left.

Fight as Bosses
Using one character, beat Heihachi and the mid-level boss.

Fight as Sub-Boss
After defeating every fighter in a normal game, defeat a sub-boss.

Fight as Devil Kazuya
Win the eight stages of *Galaga* without restarting the final round. (Stages can be restarted only once, using Select.)

Fight as Heihachi
Defeat Heihachi and all previous characters without continuing.

Camera Views
Press Select when "Select View" pops up.

Heihachi Demo
Hold L1+L2+R1+R2 at the title screen.

Bonus Character
Without getting a double ship, defeat all Galaxian ships.

Two-Player Galaga
When game is loading, hold Up+L1+Triangle+X on controller two.

TEKKEN 2

Big Heads
Hold Select when selecting a character and until fight starts.

Uppercut/Sweep Move Sky Mode
Capture all characters to beat the game, and hold Select+Up when choosing a character, until the fight starts.

Wire Frame Mode
Hold L1+L2 when choosing a character, until the fight starts.

Unlock Anna
Use Nina to finish game.

Unlock Angel
Use Kazuya to beat Devil. Select by pressing Punch.

Unlock Armored King
Use King to finish game.

Unlock Baek
Use Law to finish game.

Unlock Devil
Use Kazuya to beat Devil. Select by pressing Kick.

Unlock Ganryu
Use Michelle to finish game.

Unlock Kazuya
Use any sub-boss to defeat Devil.

Unlock Kunimitsu
Use Yoshimitsu to finish game.

Unlock Kuma
Use Paul to finish game.

Unlock P. Jack
Use Jack-2 to finish game.

Unlock Sub-Bosses
Use each character to defeat Devil.

Play as Alex and Roger
Play in Arcade mode. Get to the third match and wait until your match-winning round to perform this. Let the opponent drain your energy to five percent. Then, defeat your opponent. The announcer says "Great!" if you did this correctly. Your fourth match will be against Alex or Roger, and this unlocks them.

TEKKEN 3

Play as Kuma
Use one fighter to finish Arcade mode.

Play as Julia
Use two fighters to finish Arcade mode.

Play as Gun Jack
Use three fighters to finish Arcade mode.

Play as Mokujin
Use four fighters to finish Arcade mode.

Play as Anna
Use five fighters to finish Arcade mode.

Play as Bryan
Use six fighters to finish Arcade mode.

Play as Heihachi
Use seven fighters to finish Arcade mode.

Play as Ogre
Use eight fighters to finish Arcade mode.

Play as True Ogre
Use nine fighters to finish Arcade mode.

Play as Tiger
Use 18 fighters to finish Arcade mode. Then highlight Eddy at the Character Select screen and press Start.

Play as Panda
Highlight Kuma at the Character Select screen and press Circle.

Play as Dr. Boskonovitch
Finish Tekken Force mode four times and beat Dr. Boskonovitch.

Play as Gon
Pick any character and play either Time Attack or Survival mode. Get a high enough score so it asks for your initials. Write GON as your name.

Different Clothing
In Arcade mode, hold R1+R2+L1+L2 when a character is highlighted. Release when time gets to zero.

Different Intro
Finish game with 10 base fighters or with all fighters, including secret ones.

Play/Record Combo
Select "1P Freestyle" in Practice mode. At Options menu, hold L1+L2+R1+R2 and press Circle. To record or replay, press Down and Select.

Theater Mode
Unlock and view the endings of all fighters.

Jin and Xiaou School Uniforms
Play as Jin and Xiaou 50 times each. Then select them by pressing Start.

Random Team Battle
In Team Battle, select number of players but do not choose any fighters. Press Start.

Jack Wears Tank Top
Play as Jack 10 times. Then select him by pressing Start.

TEMPEST X3

Access Cheat Mode
Press R1+L1+Triangle+Circle+Up-Left+Select+Start at the Select Game Type screen.

Hidden Song
Enable Cheat mode. Hold R1+L2+Triangle+X and press Down at any screen.

MOD Song
Enable Cheat mode. Hold R1+L2+Triangle+X and press Right during game.

Remix Song
Enable Cheat mode. Hold R1+L2+Triangle+X and press Left during game.

Trippy Mode
Enable Cheat mode. Hold R1+L2+Triangle+X and press Up at any screen.

Level Skip
Enable Cheat mode. When Web has no enemies, during gameplay press R1+L2.

A.I. Droid
Enable Cheat mode. Hold L2+R1+Triangle+X and press Down during gameplay. Without dying, finish current level.

Secret Game Options
When entering initials for a high score, use H V S or YIFF!

TEN PIN ALLEY

Bowl Off
Set the play style to "Tournament" and enter "Vllooma" in the sixth slot of the roster. You enter a bowl off with another player. You must get a perfect score of 300 to beat your opponent.

Maui Bowl Music
Enter the name "Adrenalin" in the second or sixth slot of the roster. Play a tournament at Maui Bowl. You hear the music during the eighth and ninth frame.

Bowling Ball Heads
Enter the name Rufus in the fourth slot and Dufus in the fifth slot. Then pick Dutch or Chuckie to fill those spots. They can't both occupy the fourth or fifth spot at the same time.

Taunts
During Team Play mode, hold L1+L2+R1+R2 and press Circle, Square, X, or Triangle to taunt your opponent.

TENCHU: STEALTH ASSASSINS

Access Debug Mode
Pause the game. Hold L1+R2 and press Up, Triangle, Down, X, Left, Square, Right, Circle. Release L1+R2 and press L1, R1, L2, R2. The screen shakes. Press Pause to resume playing and press L2+R2 during gameplay.

Frame by Frame
Enable Debug mode. Enable any debug option and pause the game. Press Select to move through the game frame by frame.

Two Player Mode
Use the "Enemy" option to select any opponent. Select the "Pad-2" option to enable a second player. Move away from the newly created player until a question mark appears near the health bar. Go back toward the newly created player. Now both controllers can used to play in Two-player mode. If any player leaves the screen, the second player is disabled.

Refill Health
Pause the game and press Left (2), Down (2), Square (2), Triangle, Square.

Level Select
Pick a character, proceed to the Mission Selection screen, hold R2, and press Left (2), Down (2), Square (2), Triangle, Square.

All Weapons
At the Item Selection screen, hold R1+L1 and press X, Triangle, Square, Triangle, Square, Circle. Then release and press L1 again.

99 Item Capacity
At the Item Selection screen, hold L1 and press Left (2), Down (2), Square (2), Triangle, Square.

All Items Available
At the Item Selection screen, hold R1 and press Left (2), Down (2), Square (2), Triangle, Circle.

Extra Ayame Costume
Play as Ayame. On the Item Selection screen, press Left (2), Down (2), Square (2), Triangle, Circle. The armor icon will be selected and Ayame has her third costume.

Enable Japanese Voices
Pick a character, proceed to the Mission Selection screen, hold L1, and press Left (2), Down (2), Square (2), Circle. The Japanese voice can be heard after the first level although the narratives are still in English.

Increase Item Inventory
At the Item Selection screen, hold L2 and press Left (2), Down (2), Square (2), Triangle, X.

Layout Select
Pick a character, proceed to the Mission Selection screen, hold R1, and press Left (2), Down (2), Square (2), Triangle, X.

More Costumes
With Rickimaru or Ayame, complete any level without being detected or killing innocent people. A Grandmaster screen appears after the completed level if you did that correctly. Start the next level. When the Item screen appears, look to the far right. Select the object that appeared on the Grandmaster screen to give Ayame or Rickimaru new clothes.

TENCHU II: BIRTH OF THE ASSASSINS

Increase Item Inventory by One
At the Item Selection screen, hold R1+Square and press Right, Down, Left, Up.

Recharge Health to 100
Pause and hold Square and press Left, Right, Up, Down. Your health goes back up, but this automatically counts you as being spotted, so you can't get a perfect score.

Copy Missions from CD in Mission Editor
At the Mission Settings menu, hold Circle and press Up(2), Down (2), Left, Right.

Unlock the Office Level in Mission Editor
At the Mission Selection screen, hold L2 and press Circle, Square, Left, Right, Circle, Square.

Unlock Tatsumaru
At the Stage Selection screen, hold Circle+Square and press R1, R2, L2, L1, Up, Down, Left, Right, Select. Tatsumaru can be used in the mission editor.

Unlock Every Stage
At the Stage Selection screen, hold Circle+Square+Select and press Right (3), Up, Left, Down, R2.

Unlock All Missions in Mission Editor
At the Custom Mission screen, hold R2+Circle and press Up, Down (2), Right, Left (2).

Unlock All Ninja Items
At the Item Selection screen, press Square (3), Circle, Square, Circle (2), Left, Up, Down, Right, R2 (2).

Show All of the Map
During gameplay, hold Select to view the map, then press Circle (5).

TENKA

All Weapons
At the main menu, press R1, R2, L1, L2, X, Triangle, Square (2). Then hold Select and press Start.

TENNIS ARENA

Extra Players and Canyon Court
When the Smart Dog logo appears, press Up, Down, Left, Right, Start. A "Yeah" message confirms correct entry. "Extra Player" and "Canyon Court" are now available in Smash Tennis mode.

Super Backhand
During gameplay, hold R1+R2 and press X, Square, Circle, Square, X, Triangle. Release R1+R2 and press Select.

TEST DRIVE 4

Set Course Record
Set "Checkpoints" on and pick the Jaguar XJ220. Get a time below 11.46 seconds in the quarter mile.

Bonus Cars
Enable the "Traffic" and "Timer" options. Set a course record and enter SAUSAGE as a name.

Faster Cars
Enable the "Traffic" and "Timer" options. Set a course record and enter WHOOOOSH as a name. Use the horn button during a game to get a nitro boost (won't work in first gear).

Tiny Cars
Enable the "Traffic" and "Timer" options. Set a course record and enter MJCIM.RC as a name.

All Tracks
Enable the "Traffic" and "Timer" options. Set a course record and enter KNACKED as a name. This lets you race on mirrored tracks at night.

Extra FMV Movie
Press Up, Left, Circle, X, then select the "Credits" option. The last scene will be altered.

Unlock a Hovercraft
Enable the "Traffic" and "Timer" options. Set a course record and enter FLY as a name. Press Up to move forward and X to hover.

TEST DRIVE 5

All Cars
Enter NOLIFE as a name on the High Score screen. Or enter ROME as a name in Time Trial mode.

All Modes
Enter VRSIX as a name on the High Score screen. Cop Chase and other modes become available.

All Tracks
Enter NUTS as a name on the High Score screen. Or enter NTHREE or MTHREE as a name in Time Trial mode.

Bonus FMV Music
Enter AUXYRAY as a name on the High Score screen. Pick the "Fear Factory Video" option from the main menu.

Super Arcade Mode
Enter SPURT as a name in Time Trial mode.

Daytime Running Lights
Enter YUPS as a name on the High Score screen.

Classic Silverstone Race
Enter QUALITY as a name on the High Score screen.

Extra Cars
Enter SPUNK as a name on the High Score screen.

Quarter Mile Race
Enter FIESTA as a name on the High Score screen.

Raining Question Marks
Select the reverse track of Washington, D.C. Turn around and drive in the opposite direction at the beginning of the race.

No CPU Driver During Cup Race
Complete the first race of any tournament except for Ultimate. Save the game and reset the PlayStation. Reload the saved game and enable "Full Race" and "Time Trial" options. Pick any car and compete in the Time Trial mode. Quit Time Trial mode and choose to continue the race, without loading the previous saved game. Select "Next Cup Race" to start with the car from the time trials and race with no CPU drivers.

TEST DRIVE 6

All Cars
Enter DFGY as a name.

All Tracks
Enter ERERTH as a name.

All Challenges
Enter OPIOP as a name.

All Quick Tracks
Enter CVCVBM as a name.

Enable Checkpoints
Enter NOEMIT as a name.

Short Tracks
Enter QTFHYF as a name.

No Challenges
Enter OPOIOP as a name.

No Quick Tracks
Enter OCVCVBM as a name.

Disable Checkpoints
Enter FFOEMIT as a name.

Stop the Bomber Mode
Enter RFGTR as a name. Or catch all speeders on Paris, New York, Rome, London, and Hong Kong tracks in Cop Chase mode.

Six Million Dollars
Enter AKJGQ as a name.

Preview a Vehicle
Hold L1+R1 while buying or selecting a car. Use the D-Pad to rotate the vehicle.

TEST DRIVE: LE MANS

Unlock All Cars and Tracks in Quick Race Mode
Enter TATOO as a name.

1999 Audi Prototype
Enter MAYOU as a name.

1999 BMW
Enter POHLIN as a name.

1999 Toyota GT1
Enter PINOU as a name.

Hot Dog Car
Enter HOTDOG as a name.

Cheese Car
Enter FROMAGE as a name.

Pie Car
Enter PIE as a name.

Pizza Car
Enter PIZZA as a name.

Spaceship
Enter MM1 as a name.

Jet
Enter MM2 as a name.

Mad Car
Enter MM3 as a name.

Taxi
Enter MM4 as a name.

1960's Bus
Enter MM5 as a name.

Ice Cream Truck
Enter MM6 as a name.

Submarine
Enter MM7 as a name.

Space Race Track
Enter NAIMAR as a name.

Beach Buggy Cars
Enter BIGGY1, BIGGY2, BIGGY3, BIGGY4, BIGGY5, BIGGY6, BIGGY7, or BIGGY8 as a name.

Automatically Win the Race
Enter FIRSTON as a name.

Alternate Loading Screen
Enter JACKPOT as a name. You see a swimsuit model during the loading screens.

TEST DRIVE: OFF-ROAD

All Tracks
Enter ALLTRACK as a name. Press Triangle to go back a screen. Then enter ELVIS as a driver name. This unlocks all circuits and mix league cups.

Drive Monster Truck
Enter BEEFY as a driver name.

Sand Trap Track
Enter CRAZY as a driver name.

No Clipping
Enter DAVON as a driver name.

Tracks Seven Through Nine
Enter DIRTY as a driver name.

Under Construction Track
Enter ELITE as a driver name.

Drive Hot Rod
Enter FIFTY as a driver name.

Dirt Dash Track
Enter FRIENDLY as a driver name.

Drive Stock Car
Enter LOWRIDER as a driver name.

Pharaoh's Curse Track
Enter SANDDUNE as a driver name.

Snowball Express Track
Enter SNOWMAN as a driver name.

Drive Buggy
Enter SPRINTER as a driver name.

Extra Music
Place the disk into an audio CD player. Listen to track two or higher to hear the music.

TEST DRIVE: OFF-ROAD 2

Black Widow Truck
Enter Single Race or World Tour mode. At the Transmission Selection screen, hold Select and press R1, L2 (2), Down (2), Up, L2, L1.

Ice Cream Truck
Enter Single Race or World Tour mode. At the Transmission Selection screen, hold Select and press R2, L2 (2), Down (2), L2 (2), R1.

Nitro Car

Enter Single Race or World Tour mode. At the Transmission Selection screen, hold Select and press L1, Down, Up, L2 (2), R1, Left.

School Bus

Enter Single Race or World Tour mode. At the Transmission Selection screen, hold Select and press L1, Up, L2, Down (2), L2 (2), R2.

Unlock All Cars and Tracks

At the main menu, hold Select and press L1, Left, L2, Right, L2, Left, L1 (2).

View Programmers

Select the reversed Mojave track and begin a race. At the beginning of the race, drive in the opposite direction until you see sand dunes. Make a Right at the sand dunes and keep driving in that direction until you find the Accolade sign.

TEST DRIVE: OFF-ROAD 3

Cheat Mode

Enter ZAKARY X as a name to activate all cheats in the game.

All Divisions

Enter SAD CLOWN as a name.

All Tracks

Enter LEAD TO ROME as a name.

All Upgrades

Enter MAD HOOKUP as a name.

Stunt Mode

Enter TURN TRICKS as a name.

Sumo Mode

Enter YOKOZUNA as a name.

Bonus Vehicles and Tracks

Earn gold medals in the World Tour divisions to unlock bonus tracks and vehicles. The tracks are available in World Tour and Arcade modes. The vehicles are available in Arcade mode.

TETRIS, THE NEXT

Sound Control

At the main menu, hold L1+R1 to raise the music volume; hold R1+L2 to lower the music volume.

TETRIS PLUS

Level Select

Choose Puzzle mode and select the "Password" option. Press Down (2), Right, Up (2), Right, Up (3), Right, Down (2), Right, Up (2), Right, Up (3), Right, X. A "Stage Select" option becomes available as the game starts.

Fast Professor

Beat a level in Puzzle mode. Press R2 after the professor falls to make the professor walk faster.

Access to Secret Puzzle Design Area

Press X (10) when the "Puzzle Design" choice is highlighted.

THEME HOSPITAL

Extra Construction Time

Pause at the beginning of a level. Go to the stop watch symbol. Hold L1 until the indicator reaches the left of the bar. This gives you some extra time to build your rooms.

Clean Hospital

Save the game when the hospital is full. Reload the game and the garbage and patients disappear.

Level 1 Password

Press Square (2), Triangle, Circle, Square, X, Square, X.

Level 2 Password

Press X, Circle, Square, Triangle (2), Circle, Square, X.

Level 3 Password

Press Circle (2), Triangle, Square, X, Triangle, Circle, Triangle.

Level 4 Password

Press Square, Triangle, Circle, Square, X (2), Triangle, Circle.

Level 5 Password

Press Circle, Triangle, Square, Circle, X, Triangle, Circle, Square.

Level 6 Password

Press Square, Triangle, Square, Circle, X, Square, X, Circle.

Level 7 Password

Press Square, Triangle (2), Circle, X, Square, Triangle, Circle.

Level 8 Password

Press X, Triangle, Square, Circle, Triangle, Circle, Square, X.

Level 9 Password

Press Triangle, Square, X, Triangle, Circle, X, Triangle, Square.

Level 10 Password

Press Circle, Square, X, Triangle, Square, X, Circle, Square.

Level 11 Password

Press Triangle, Circle, Square, Circle, Triangle, Square, Circle, X.

Level 12 Password

Press Circle, Square, X (2), Square, Circle, Square, Triangle.

THEME PARK

Super Park

Enter BUD as a nickname. Press Square at the Park Selection screen. Once the game begins, maximum prices can be charged for the concessions, games, and park entrance.

Extra Money and All Rides

Enter BOVINE as a nickname. During gameplay, press X+Square+Circle to get more money.

Clean Park

Save the game when the park is full. Reload the saved game and all of the garbage disappears.

THEME PARK WORLD

Get Everything

While in the park, press Up, Down, Up, Down, Left, Up, Down, Up, Down, Right eight times, Start. A sound confirms correct entry.

Extra Gold Tickets

While in the park, press Up, Down, Left, Right, Circle, Right, Left, Down, Up, Circle four times, Start. A sound confirms correct entry.

No Money Taken Away from Bank

While in the park, press Left, Down, X, Circle eight times, Start. A sound confirms correct entry.

THE MUMMY

To enter these codes, first start a game normally. Then pause and quit out of the game. Go to "Replay Level," then click on "Bonus Features" to get to the screen where you can enter codes.

Hidden Cairo Bonus Level

Triangle, X, Triangle, Circle, Square, Triangle, Circle, X

Infinite Ammo

X, Triangle, X, Square, Circle, Triangle, Square, Triangle

Infinite Lives

Circle (2), Triangle, Circle, X, Square (2), X

Invincibility

Triangle, X, Circle (2), X, Square (2), X

Unlock All Weapons

Circle, Square, Circle, X (2), Triangle (2), Square

THIS IS FOOTBALL

Small Players

Press Square, R2, Right, L2, L1.

Small Heads

Press R2, Down, L2, L1, Circle.

Black-and-White Mode

Press Up, R1, L2, R1, R2.

1970's Mode

Press L1, R2, L2, Circle, R1.

Topless

Press Down, R2 (3), Triangle.

Alternate Clothes

Press Circle, L2, Left, R2, Triangle.

Head Is a Ball

Press Left, L1 (3), R2.

THOUSAND ARMS

Extra Damage

When you are in a battle and plan to use a weapon attack, keep pressing Forward and X at the same time as the options come up. The weapon attack becomes faster or more powerful.

THRASHER: SKATE AND DESTROY

Extra Points

Pause the game and then hold R2+R1+L2+L1 and repeatedly press Circle.

Triple Multiplier

Perform a successful trick while running from a cop, K9, or mugger. The trick value triples.

All Levels

At the main menu, press Square, Triangle, L1, R2, Circle, X, Triangle, Right (2), Left.

Bumble Bee Suit

Pick Roach without a hat. Enter BEESUITGUY as the name. You get a skater wearing a bumble bee suit and having super attributes.

Bonus Moves

Complete the game with a certain character to get a new move. Beat the game with Axl to learn the Darkslide. Beat the game with Cyrus to learn the Impossible. Beat the game with Jasmine to learn the Airwalk. Beat the game with Kahli to learn the Kickflip Casper. Beat the game with Roach to learn the Double Kickflip. Beat the game with Scab to learn the DDP.

Hidden Board 1

Pick Axl and enter SOMBER as a name.

Hidden Board 2

Pick Cyrus and enter MARDUK as a name.

Hidden Board 3

Pick Jasmine and enter TODDLAND as a name.

Hidden Board 4

Pick Kahli and enter ZONTAR as a name.

Hidden Board 5

Pick Roach and enter BYTOR as a name.

Hidden Board 6

Pick Scab and enter VENGE as a name.

Hidden Board 7

Pick any character and enter ROCKSTAR as a name.

Hidden Board 8

Pick any character and enter ZAXIS as a name.

THREE LIONS

Oranje Team

At the Team Selection screen, press L1, Up (2), Right.

Azzuri Team

At the Team Selection screen, press L2, Up (2), Right.

Die Mannschaft Team

At the Team Selection screen, press R2 (3), Right.

All Time Greats Team

At the Team Selection screen, press L2 (3), Right.

Brazil 1970 Team

At the Team Selection screen, press R1 (3), Right.

Aus Asia Stars Team

At the Team Selection screen, press R1, Up (2) Right.

England 1966 Team

At the Team Selection screen, press L1 (3), Right.

African Stars Team

At the Team Selection screen, press R2, Up (2), Right.

South American Stars Team

At the Team Selection screen, press R2, Down (2), Right.

North American Stars Team

At the Team Selection screen, press L1, Down (2), Right.

European Stars Team

At the Team Selection screen, press L2, Down (2), Right.

Z-Axis Team

At the Team Selection screen, press R1, Down (2), Right.

BMG Team

At the Team Selection screen, press L2, Left (2), Right.

All Teams

At the Team Selection screen, press L2, Left, R2, R1, L2, Right. Highlight Europe and press Left to access the bonus teams.

THRILL KILL

Unlock Judas, Cain, Marukka

Beat the game at Medium difficulty.

Maximum Kill Meter

Press L1+L2+R1+R2+Select+Start+Square+ Circle+Triangle+X during a fight.

Extra Costumes

Complete the Practice mode with the character you want the outfit for. Then, go to the Character Selection screen and hold L1+L2 and press X to select your character.

Fight Against the Gimp

Complete Practice mode with all 11 characters. Then, hold L1+L2+R1+R2 and press X when you select your opponent in Practice mode.

THUNDER TRUCK RALLY

Super Car

Press L2, Left, Right, Up, Down, R2 at the main menu. A burp confirms correct entry.

Big Trucks

Press L1, R2, L2, R1, Up at the main menu. A burp confirms correct entry.

Drive an Ice Cream Truck

At the Truck Selection screen, hold L1+L2 while selecting the driver.

Increased Traction

Press Left, L1, R2, R1, Left, R2 (3) at the main menu. A burp confirms correct entry.

Sharp Turns

Press Left, Right, Circle, Square at the main menu. A burp confirms correct entry.

No Damage

Press Left (3), Up, Down, L1, R2 at the main menu. A burp confirms correct entry.

Checkpoint Skip

Press L1 (2), R1 (2), L2 (2), R2 (2) at the main menu. A burp confirms correct entry. Start a race in Endurance mode. Then, press Triangle to be flown to the next checkpoint by a helicopter.

THUNDER FORCE V

Unlimited Continues

Beat the game at Hard difficulty. Go into Options mode and set your credit option to "Free."

Master Mode

Beat the game at Hard difficulty. Go into Options mode and set your difficulty to Master.

Better Ships

Go into the Stage Selection screen. Hold Triangle, Circle, or Square on controller two and select your stages with controller one. Which of three different better ships you get depends on which button you held down on controller two. While the ship's characteristics improve, its appearance doesn't change much.

Time Attack Mode

Beat the game at Normal difficulty.

Extra Continues

Accumulate more than three hours of gameplay to unlock a "Continue" selection at the Options screen.

THUNDERSTRIKE 2

South America (Level 1) Password
ONHV0V6VEBDU55Q

South America (Level 2) Password
2NH70V9VEFDQ592

South America (Level 3) Password
7RH30V7AEFD64BI

South America (Level 4) Password
8NH30V8EEJD24PI

Gulf 2: Oil Dispute (Level 1) Password
VNHR0V0E6JDE53I

Gulf 2: Oil Dispute (Level 2) Password
0RHV0UO66NDA53A

Gulf 2: Oil Dispute (Level 3) Password
IFHD0UOU6RDM5P2

Gulf 2: Oil Dispute (Level 4) Password
NJHP0UKE6VDI5BI

Stealth (Level 1) Password
O7HP0UOQAUDE45A

Stealth (Level 2) Password
U7HL0UNIAUDA5RA

Stealth (Level 3) Password
AFHP0UKUA2DM4HI

Central America (Level 1) Password
FJHL0UGII2CE4KI

Central America (Level 2) Password
G7HH0U72I2CA5R2

Central America (Level 3) Password
2BHP0URQI6CM58A

South China Sea (Level 1) Password
KRG50URQ26GE4J2

South China Sea (Level 2) Password
0RGL0UTI3AGA5UI

South China Sea (Level 3) Password
FRG9S1CM3EGM52I

Panama (Level 1) Password
93G5SD9UNGGE4OA

Panama (Level 2) Password
VVG5SHUENGGA4SQ

Panama (Level 3) Password
JNGH4CPUNKGM5TI

Eastern Europe (Level 1) Password
L3GG4406VOEE5R1

Eastern Europe (Level 2) Password
F7GK5S2QV0EA41A

Eastern Europe (Level 3) Password
27GK50UMV4EM58Q

Gulf 1: Canyon (Level 1) Password
7FGK48T6R8ME4NI

Gulf 1: Canyon (Level 2) Password
8JGK48VUR8MA5JQ

Gulf 1: Canyon (End) Password
T7GK28U2SCMM40I

TIGER WOODS PGA 2000

400 Yard Drive
Go to the create a player screen and name the player JasonZubliac to hit a 400-yard drive!

Easy Course
At the "create player" screen, type in the name OLDSCHOOL. This makes all the courses flat, and easier to hit on.

TIGER WOODS '99 PGA TOUR GOLF

Enable Taunts
During a multiplayer game press L1, L2, R1, R2, X, Square, Triangle or Circle to comment to or taunt your opponent.

Exploding Range Cart
On the driving range, hit the range cart three times to make it explode.

Change Commentator's Voice
While playing, hold either Up or Down and press any other key.

Raise Elevation 200 Percent
On the Player Selection screen, enter a new name of PUMPZ and restart.

Raise Elevation 400 Percent
On the Player Selection screen, enter a new name of MAXIMUMZ and restart.

Flat Terrain
On the Player Selection screen, enter a new name of OLD SCHOOL and restart.

South Park Pilot
Place the disk into your computer's CD-ROM drive and look for a file called *zzdummy.dat* (it only exists on early versions). Open that file with a media player to see a video with the *South Park* characters.

TIGERSHARK

FMV Sequences
Enter KIEV as a password.

Preview Bug Riders
Enter BUGGY as a password.

No Collisions
Enter BURAN as a password.

Infinite Ammo
Enter KIROV as a password.

Invincibility
Enter KURSK as a password.

Random Colored Terrain Boxes
Enter VOLGA as a password.

Powered-Up Weapons
Enter RUBLE as a password.

Low Gravity
Enter SOYUZ as a password.

Sea Hunter Minigame
Enter SNEEG as a password.

Clean Pause
Enter RUSSI as a password.

Disable All Cheats
Enter MINSK as a password.

Random Colored Terrain Polygons
Enter ROGOV as a password.

Disable Enemy Fire
Enter LENIN as a password.

Sound Tests
Enter KAMOV as a password.

Display Collision Boxes
Enter DNEPR as a password.

Level 2 Password
AKULA

Level 3 Password
PASHA

Level 4 Password
MIRAS

Level 5 Password
NAKAT

Level 6 Password
REZKY

Level 7 Password
TUCHA

Level 8 Password
ZARYA

Level 9 Password
VOSTA

TIME COMMANDO

Three Continues
Pause the game and highlight the "Sound FX" option. Press Triangle, Square, Circle, X, Triangle, Circle, Square, X, Triangle, Square, Triangle. A sound confirms correct entry.

All Weapons
Pause the game and highlight the "Sound FX" option. Press Triangle, X, Circle, Square, X, Square, Circle, Triangle, X, Square, Circle. A sound confirms correct entry.

Maximum Energy
Pause the game and highlight the "Sound FX" option. Press X, Triangle (2), Circle, X, Triangle (2), Circle, Square, Circle, X. A sound confirms correct entry.

Refill Health
Pause the game and highlight the "Sound FX" option. Press X, Triangle (2), Circle, X, Triangle (2), Circle, Square (2), X. A sound confirms correct entry.

Maximum Energy Bar Upgrade
Pause the game and highlight the "Sound FX" option. Press Square, Circle (2), Triangle (2), Circle, Square (2), Triangle, Square. A sound confirms correct entry.

Skip Current World
Pause the game and highlight the "Sound FX" option. Press X, Square, X, Triangle, Circle, Square, X, Circle, Triangle (2). A sound confirms correct entry.

Infinite Ammo
Pause the game and highlight the "Sound FX" option. Press Triangle, Circle, Triangle, X, Square, X, Circle, Square, Triangle, X, Square. A sound confirms correct entry.

Weaken the Virus
Pause the game and highlight the "Sound FX" option. Press Triangle (2), Square, Circle, X, Triangle, Circle, Square (3), X. A sound confirms correct entry.

99 Blue Time Chips
Enter ACTIVATE as a password.

Secret Level
Enter COMMANDO as a password.

Level 1 Password
EAUGXTAH

Level 2 Password
DHTKARIZ

Level 3 Password
ZMZZUJKJ

Level 4 Password
PFXMNHHR

Level 5 Password
CBKWSYMY

Level 6 Password
IETDIMGV

Level 7 Password
WTZVUGBX

TIME CRISIS

Bring Up Cheat Menu
On the Arcade, Options, and Special menu, shoot the circle in the middle of the R in the word "Crisis" twice. Now shoot the center of the crosshairs above the title twice. Accuracy is very important. This allows you to enable infinite continues, no reload, and nine lives.

Extra Life
Shoot 50 targets in a row to receive an extra life.

Alternate Reload or Hide Option
Press Circle, Square, X, or Triangle on controller two. You can hide or reload using the second controller.

Level Select
Hold L1+X+Circle for five seconds. A gun sound confirms correct entry. Press Start at the title screen to jump levels.

Easier Story Mode
Pick the first mission from the Mission Selection screen. The next screen offers Normal Play or Time Attack modes. Shoot off the screen. The word "Easy" appears next to Normal Play on the screen. Pick Story mode. This trick gives you extra times and hits.

TIME GAL AND NINJA HAYATE

FMV Sequences
At the title screen, hold L1+L2+R1+R2+Left+Circle on controller two. Then, use controller one and press L2, R1, Left, Start.

TINY TANK: UP YOUR ARSENAL

Access Cheat Mode
At the Options "Stamper" menu, hold L1+L2+R1+R2+Left+Circle+Triangle+Square and press X. The cheat code entry screen appears.

Low Gravity
Access Cheat mode and enter FEATHER.

Level Select
At the New Game "Stamper" menu, hold L1+L2+R1+R2+Left+Circle+Select.

Hidden Sounds
Select the "Sound Test" option and listen to the first six introduction sounds. Then Tiny recites various trivia and miscellaneous sound clips after the instructions and normal reports.

Tiny Toon Adventures: Revenge of the Beanstalk

Downtown Password
Sneezer, Little Beeper, Furrball, Gogo Dodo (2), Buster Bunny, Furrball, Calamity Coyote

Wacky Fairy Tale Kitchen
Sneezer, Plucky Duck, Furrball, Little Beeper, Furrball, Babs Bunny, Elmyra, Sweetie

Wacky Café
Elmyra, Calamity Coyote, Sweetie, Little Beeper, Buster Bunny, Elmyra, Plucky Duck, Little Beeper

TNN Hardcore 4x4

Raining Frogs
Set the weather option to "Severe." Go to Time Trial mode and enter your name as RAIN-FROG. A face appears in the screen's upper corner if you entered the code correctly.

Bonus Game
Go to Time Trial mode. Enter your name as DUTCHMAN. A face appears if you entered the code correctly. Now go to the Credits screen under the Options menu to play an Asteroids minigame.

Hidden Truck
Go to Time Trial mode. Enter your name as MAINLINE. A face appears if you entered the code correctly. This unlocks the hidden truck and two new levels of difficulty: Pro and Extreme.

Tobal 2

Unlock Mufu
Beat the game at Easy difficulty.

Unlock Nork
Beat the game at Normal difficulty.

Unlock Emperor Udan
Beat the game at Hard difficulty.

Shrink or Increase Player's Size
Enter either Vs. CPU or Vs. Player mode. At the Character Selection screen, hold R2+L2+Triangle and pick your character. Continue to hold those buttons until Round 1 appears. Press R2 to increase your character's size. Press L2 to shrink your character's size.

Change Costumes
Press Up at the Character Selection screen.

Control Character's Eyes
Move your character's eyes during the victory pose by using the D-Pad.

Replay Dance
Hold Up-Right+L2 during the match replay, but release the buttons before the replay ends.

Repeat Victory Speech
Press L2+Left after the victory speech.

"F" Monster Practice
Go into Practice mode and highlight the monster above a monster that hasn't been captured yet. Press Circle+Down.

Tobal No. 1

Change Camera View
Press L2+R2 after selecting your character and while the game is loading.

Change Clothing
Hold Up while selecting your character.

Kill Off Hom
Press L1, L2, R1, R2, X, Down or L1+R1+Down during a match.

Unlock Snork
Beat Quest 1.

Unlock Mufu
Beat Quest 2.

Unlock Udan
Beat Quest 3.

Unlock Tori Robo
Beat Quest 4 (Udan's Dungeon).

TOCA Touring Car Championship

Access All Tracks
Enter JHAMMO as a player name.

Extra Cars
Enter CMGARAGE as a player name.

No Collisions
Enter CMNOHITS as a player name.

Helicopter View
Enter CMCOPTER as a player name.

Go-Kart View
Enter CMCHUN as a player name.

Star Background
Enter CMSTARS as a player name.

Cartoon Horizon
Enter CMTOON as a player name.

Overhead View
Enter CMMICRO as a player name.

Disco Fog
Enter CMDISCO as a player name.

Low Gravity
Enter CMLOGRAV as a player name.

UnRain (Falls Up)
Enter CMRAINUP as a player name.

All Cars Speed Doubled
Enter XBOOSTME as a player name.

Trackside View
Enter CMFOLLOW as a player name.

Make Other Drivers Aggressive
Enter CMMAYHEM as a player name.

Big Hands on Wheel
Enter CMHANDY as a player name.

Rain Cats and Dogs
Enter CMCATDOG as a player name.

Increase Difficulty
Enter CMIMPOSS as a player name.

Locks Tracks
Enter CMLOCKS as a player name.

Drive Upside-Down
Enter CMUPSIDE as a player name.

Pink Car
Enter FLEXMOBIL as a player name.

Play Mirror Mode
Enter PATSCREEN as a player name.

Play as a Tank
Enter TANK as a player name.

Flex Car
Enter FLEX as a player name.

Unlock All Cars
Enter GONGOGO as a player name.

TOCA Touring Car Championship 2

All Cars
Enter MECHANIC as a name in Single-player mode.

All Tracks
Enter BIGLEY as a name in Single-player mode.

Bonus Track
Enter TECHLOCK as a name in Single-player mode.

New Option in Challenge Mode
Enter BANGBANG as a name in Single-player mode.

Turbo Mode
Enter FASTBOY as a name in Single-player mode.

Blurred Background
Enter TRIPPY as a name in Single-player mode.

Padded Barriers
Enter PADDED as a name in Single-player mode.

Mini Cars
Enter MINICARS as a name in Single-player mode.

Low Gravity
Enter LUNAR as a name in Single-player mode.

Quicker Damage
Enter DUBBED as a name in Single-player mode.

Disable Championship Disqualification
Enter PUNCHY as a name in Single-player mode.

Bumper Cars
Enter BCASTLE as a name in Single-player mode.

40 Lap Races
Enter LONGLONG as a name in Single-player mode.

Expandable Track
Enter ELASTIC as a name in Single-player mode.

Wheels Only
Enter JUSTFEET as a name in Single-player mode.

Oulton Park Island Circuit
Enter DINKYBIT as a name in Single-player mode.

Turbo Mode
Enter SKATES as a name in Single-player mode.

Tokimeki Battle Puzzle Egg

Play as Sub-Boss
Complete story with all the characters.

Play as Boss
Enable the Play as Sub-Boss code first. Press Up (2), Down (2), Left, Right, Left, Right, X, Circle at the title screen.

TOKIMEKI MEMORIAL DRAMA SERIES VOL. 2

Hard Mode on Space Ring Fighter

Highlight Start at the title screen. Press Up (2), Down (2), Left, Right, Left, Right, X, Circle. Someone speaks, then the game starts.

TOKYO HIGHWAY BATTLE

Free Upgrades

Hold L1+L2+R1+R2+Down+Start at the title screen until the Venue screen appears. Go into the speed shop to have access to every upgrade.

Race the Drift King

Complete Scenario mode and choose Versus CPU mode.

Unlock New Cars

Beat the Drift King to unlock the NSX, Supra, and GT-R.

Different Car Colors

Beat the Drift King again using the NSX, Supra, GT-R. Then go to the Car Selection screen and press R2.

Different Speedometer

Win a race in Scenario mode. Hold L1 and press Select on controller two during gameplay.

Different Car Look

Win a race in Scenario mode. Press L2 at the Car Selection screen.

Debug Info

Win a race in Scenario mode. Hold Down and press Select on controller two during gameplay.

Maximum Points

When the Jaleco logo appears, hold L1+L2+R1+Down+Start on controller two and load the game. Continue holding until the title screen appears.

Lap Display and Best Times

Win a race in Scenario mode. Hold Up and press Select on controller two during gameplay.

TOMB RAIDER

All codes are based on the default control setup.

All Weapons

Press L1, Triangle, R2, L2 (2), R2, Circle, L1 in the Inventory screen (assuming default controls).

Level Skip

Press L2, R2, L1, Circle, Triangle, L1, R2, L2 in the Inventory screen (assuming default controls).

All Weapons, Infinite Ammunition, More Enemies

Beat the game and reload any saved level.

TOMB RAIDER 2

Cheat Information

To walk, hold R1 and press D-Pad in the indicated direction. To sidestep, hold R2 and press D-Pad in the indicated direction. Release R1 and R2 when jumping or spinning.

Level Skip

Perform the following tasks during a game: Sidestep left, sidestep right, sidestep left, walk back one step, walk forward one step. Then release R1 and spin at least three complete circles in any direction. Then, perform a forward jump and do a turn in mid-air by pressing Up+Square, Circle.

All Weapons

Perform the following tasks during a game: sidestep left, sidestep right, sidestep left, walk back one step, walk forward one step. Then release R1 and spin at least three complete circles in any direction. Then, perform a backward jump and do a turn in mid-air by pressing Down+Square, Circle.

Explosion

Perform the following tasks during a game: Walk forward one step, walk back one step. Hold walk while you spin three complete circles in any direction. Then jump backward.

Infinite Flares

Enable the All Weapons or Level Skip code. During gameplay, press Triangle to pull out Lara's guns and then press L2. Even if you don't have any flares in inventory, a flare appears.

CD Music

Put the game disk into an audio CD player. Listen to track two or higher hear the game's music.

TOMB RAIDER 3

All Secrets and Keys

Press L2 (5), R2, L2 (3), R2, L2, R2, L2 (2), R2, L2 (2), R2, L2 (2) during gameplay.

All Weapons, etc.

Press L2, R2 (2), L2 (4), R2, L2, R2 (2), L2, R2 (2), L2 (2), R2, L2 (2), R2 during gameplay.

Level Skip

Press L2, R2, L2 (2), R2, L2, R2, L2, R2, L2 (4), R2, L2, R2 (4), L2 during gameplay.

Racetrack Key

Press R2, L2 (3), R2, L2 (6), R2, L2 (5), R2, L2 (2) during gameplay in Lara's mansion.

Restore Health

Press R2 (2), L2, R2, L2 (6), R2, L2 (3), R2, L2 (4), L2 during gameplay.

TOMB RAIDER: THE LAST REVELATION

All codes must be pressed and held down in sequence.

Turn Lara Exactly North

Have Lara hang or stand on something facing north. The compass turns transparent when she faces exactly north.

Level Skip

Have Lara face north, then press Select to enter the Inventory screen. Highlight "Load Game," press L1, L2, R1, R2, Up, then exit the Inventory screen.

All Weapons

Have Lara face north, then press Select to enter the Inventory screen. Highlight "Small Medipack," press L1, L2, R1, R2, Up, then exit the Inventory screen.

All Items

Have Lara face north, then press Select to enter the Inventory screen. Highlight "Large Medipack," press L1, L2, R1, R2, Down, then exit the Inventory screen.

All Secret Items

Have Lara face north, then press Select to enter the Inventory screen. Highlight "Large Medipack," press L1, L2, R1, R2, Down, Triangle, then exit the Inventory screen.

TOMB RAIDER CHRONICLES

All Items Weapons, Unlimited Ammo, Special Features

Press Select during gameplay, then highlight the Timex-TMX on the Inventory screen. Then hold L1+L2+R1+R2+Down+Circle and press Triangle to exit the Inventory screen. Go back to the Inventory screen to access the extra items.

Unlimited Medkits and Flares

Hold L1+L2+R1+Up+Circle.

Unlimited Health, Ammo, and Weapons

Press Select to bring Up your Inventory screen. Highlight the Timex, hold Up+R1+L1+L2+Circle, and press Triangle.

Unlock All Items for the Level

Press Select to bring up your Inventory screen. Highlight the Timex, hold Down+R1+L1+L2+R2, and press Triangle.

Unlock Special Features, Ammo, and Medical Kits

Press Select to bring up your Inventory screen. Highlight the Timex, hold Down+R1+L1+L2+R2+Circle, and press Triangle. You have unlimited ammo and medical kits. Quit your game and a Special Features menu appears on the main menu. It contains pictures and storyboards for *Tomb Raider* games.

All Items

Hold L1+L2+R1+R2+Down, and press Triangle.

Black Isle Level

At main menu, highlight "New Game," then hold Up+L2, then press X.

View Cutscenes

At the main menu, press Select+R2 for a selection of cutscenes.

TOMBA!

Tomba's Different Hair Color

At the Options screen, hold R1+L1+Select+Square and press Left, Down, Right, Up (2), Right, Down, Left.

Extra Weapons

At the loading screen with dancing pigs, hold R1 and press Select, Right, Left, Down, X, Circle, Start. When the loading has completed, press Start.

Gain Back Health

Save and reload the game. The game doesn't save your health level.

TOMMI MAKINEN WORLD RALLY CHAMPION

Unlock a Bus

Enter STRANGE as a player name. Then, select the "Cheats" option from the main menu.

Unlock a Peugeot
Enter PEUGEOT as a player name. Then, select the "Cheats" option from the main menu.

Rally Jeunes Mode
Enter FFSA as a player name. Then, select the "Cheats" option from the main menu.

Mirror Courses
Enter MIRROR as a player name. Then, select the "Cheats" option from the main menu.

More Money
Enter _Money_ as a player name ("_" represents a space). Then, select the "Cheats" option from the main menu.

Dual Shock Always Vibrates
Enter THRILLS as a player name. Then, select the "Cheats" option from the main menu.

TOMORROW NEVER DIES

Unlock All Missions
At the main menu, press Select (2), Circle (2), L1 (2), Circle, L1 (2).

Invincibility
Pause, then press Select (2), Circle (2), Triangle, Select. Reenter this code to disable it.

View All FMV Sequences
At the main menu, press Select (2), Circle (2), L1 (7). This unlocks a "Mov" selection in the Options screen.

All Weapons and 50 Med Kits
Pause, then press Select (2), Circle (2), L1 (2), R1 (2).

Max Health
Pause, then press Select (2), Circle (2), Up (2), Down.

Run Faster
Pause, then press Select (2), Circle (2), Square (2), Circle (2). Re-enter this code to disable it.

Complete Mission
Pause, then press Select (2), Circle (2), Select, Circle.

View Boundaries
Pause, then press Select (2), Circle (2), Triangle (2), Square (2). Reenter this code to disable it.

Cheat Camera
Pause, then press Select (2), Circle (2), R2 (2). Press R1 to move forward, R2 to move right, Triangle to pan up, L1 to move backward, and L2 to move left. Re-enter this code to disable it.

Minimum Health
Pause, then press Select (2), Circle (2), Down (2), Up.

Ethereal Mode
Pause, then press Select (2), Circle (2), Triangle (4). You can move through objects. Re-enter this code to disable it.

Remove Fire
Pause, then press Select (2), Circle (2), Select (2), R1 (2). Re-enter this code to disable it.

Remove All Objects
Pause, then press Select (2), Circle (2), Select (2), Square (2). Re-enter this code to disable it.

Remove Surface Textures
Pause, then press Select (2), Circle (2), Select (2), Circle (2). Re-enter this code to disable it.

Remove Screen Displays
Pause, then press Select (2), Circle (2), Left, Right, Select.

Freeze Objects
Pause, then press Select (2), Circle (2), Select (2), Triangle (2) to freeze all objects in the game. Re-enter this code to disable it.

Spy Cam
Pause, then press Select (2), Circle (2), R2 (2), L2 (2).

Mission Select
At the main menu, press Select (2), Circle (2), L1 (2), Circle, L1 (2). A sound confirms correct entry.

Infinite Ammo
Pause, then press Select (2), Circle (3), Triangle.

Debug Info
Pause, then press Select (2), Circle (2), L2, R2, L2. Press Select (2), Circle (2), R2, L2, R2 to disable it.

Exit Door at Any Time
Pause, then press Select (2), Circle (2), Square, Triangle, Square. Re-enter the code to disable it.

TONY HAWK'S PRO SKATER

Cheat Mode
Pause, then hold L1 and press Circle, Right, Up, Down, Circle, Right, Up, Square, Triangle. All levels, FMV movies, tapes, full attributes, and Officer Dick are unlocked.

Level Select
Pause the game, then hold L1 and press Triangle, Right, Up, Square, Triangle, Left, Up, Square, Triangle.

Full Special Meter
Pause, then hold L1 and press X, Triangle, Circle, Down, Up, Right.

Slow Motion Mode
Pause, then hold L1 and press Square, Left, Up, Square, Left.

Raise Attributes to 10
Pause, then hold L1 and press X, Square, Triangle, Up, Down.

Raise Attributes to 13
Pause, then hold L1 and press X, Square (2), Triangle, Up, Down.

Big Head Mode
Pause, then hold L1 and press Square, Circle, Up, Left (2).

Play as Officer Dick
Collect all 30 tapes with any character in Career mode.

Play as Private Carerra
Unlock everything with the Cheat Mode code or by earning everything. Start a game in any mode with Officer Dick. Pause, then hold L1 and press Triangle, Up, Triangle, Up, Circle, Up, Left, Triangle. The screen won't shake. Restart and go back to the Character Selection screen. Private Carrera replaces Officer Dick.

Random Start Locations
Pause, then hold L1 and press Square, Circle, X, Up, Down.

Skater's FMV Sequences
Win a gold medal in the three competitions with a specific character to see that skater's videos.

Neversoft Bails FMV Sequence
Use Officer Dick and get a medal in all three competitions to see the developers trying to skate.

Andrew Reynolds's Backflip
When the Special Meter flashes, press Up, Down+Circle.

Andrew Reynolds's Heelflip to Bluntside
When the Special Meter flashes, press Down, Down+Triangle.

Andrew Reynolds's Triple Kickflip
When the Special Meter flashes, press Left, Left+Square.

Bob Burnquist's One-Footed Smith
When the Special Meter flashes, press Right, Right+Triangle.

Bob Burnquist's Backflip
When the Special Meter flashes, press Up, Down+Circle.

Bob Burnquist's Burntwist
When the Special Meter flashes, press Left, Up+Triangle.

Bucky Lasek's Fingerflip Airwalk
When the Special Meter flashes, press Left, Right+Circle.

Bucky Lasek's Kickflip McTwist
When the Special Meter flashes, press Right, Right+Circle.

Bucky Lasek's Varial Heelflip Judo
When the Special Meter flashes, press Down, Up+Square.

Chad Muska's 360 Shove-It Rewind
When the Special Meter flashes, press Right, Right+Square.

Chad Muska's One-Footed 5-0 Thumpin
When the Special Meter flashes, press Right, Down+Triangle.

Chad Muska's Frontflip
When the Special Meter flashes, press Down, Up+Circle.

Elissa Steamer's Primo Grind
When the Special Meter flashes, press Left, Left+Triangle.

Elissa Steamer's Backflip
When the Special Meter flashes, press Up, Down+Circle.

Elissa Steamer's Judo Madonna
When the Special Meter flashes, press Left, Down+Circle.

Geoff Rowley's Backflip
When the Special Meter flashes, press Up, Down+Circle.

Geoff Rowley's Double Hardflip
When the Special Meter flashes, press Right, Down+Square.

Geoff Rowley's Darkside Grind
When the Special Meter flashes, press Left, Right+Triangle.

Jamie Thomas's 540 Flip
When the Special Meter flashes, press Left, Down+Square.

Jamie Thomas's One-Footed Nose Grind
When the Special Meter flashes, press Up, Up+Triangle.

Jamie Thomas's Frontflip
When the Special Meter flashes, press Down, Up+Circle.

Kareem Campbell's Kickflip Underflip
When the Special Meter flashes, press Left, Right+Square.

Kareem Campbell's Casper Slide
When the Special Meter flashes, press Up, Down+Triangle.

Kareem Campbell's Front Flip
When the Special Meter flashes, press Down, Up+Circle.

Officer Dick's Assume the Position
When the Special Meter flashes, press Left, Left+Circle.

Officer Dick's Yeeeehaw Front Flip
When the Special Meter flashes, press Down, Up+Circle.

Officer Dick's Neckbreak Grind
When the Special Meter flashes, press Left, Right+Triangle.

Private Carrera's Ho-Ho-Ho
When the Special Meter flashes, press Left, Up, Square+Circle.

Private Carrera's Somi Spin
When the Special Meter flashes, press Left, Down, Circle.

Private Carrera's Well Hardflip
When the Special Meter flashes, press Right, Left, Square.

Rune Glifberg's Kickflip McTwist
When the Special Meter flashes, press Right, Right+Circle.

Rune Glifberg's Front Back Kickflip
When the Special Meter flashes, press Up, Down+Square.

Rune Glifberg's Christ Air
When the Special Meter flashes, press Left, Right+Circle.

Tony Hawk's 540 Board Varial
When the Special Meter flashes, press Left, Left+Square.

Tony Hawk's 360 Flip to Mute
When the Special Meter flashes, press Down, Right+Square.

Tony Hawk's Kickflip McTwist
When the Special Meter flashes, press Right, Right+Circle.

Tony Hawk's the 900
When the Special Meter flashes, press Right, Down+Circle.

TONY HAWK'S PRO SKATER 2

Cheat Mode
Pause, hold L1, and press X (3), Square, Triangle, Up, Down, Left, Up, Square, Triangle, X, Triangle, Circle, X, Triangle, Circle. The screen shakes if you entered this code correctly and all levels, characters, and other cheats are unlocked.

All Stats at 10
Pause, hold L1, and press X, Triangle, Circle, Square, Triangle, Up, Down.

Toggle Blood/No Blood Code
Pause and hold L1 and press Right, Up, Square, Triangle.

Infinite Special
Pause, hold L1, and press X, Triangle, Circle(2), Up, Left, Triangle, Square.

Faster Gameplay
Pause, hold L1, and press Down, Square, Triangle, Right, Up, Circle, Down, Square, Triangle, Right, Up, Circle.

Fatter Skaters
Pause, hold L1, and press X (4), Left, X (4), Left, X (4), Left. The skater gains some weight. Enter this code multiple times to make the skater even fatter.

Thinner Skaters
Pause, hold L1, and press X (4), Square, X (4), Square, X (4), Square. The skater loses some weight. Enter this code multiple times to make the skater even thinner.

Unlock Private Carrera
Execute every Gap in the nonsecret levels of the game.

Unlock the Neversoft Making Video
Earn three gold medals with Private Carrera.

Unlock Spider-Man
Create your own skater and beat the game with 100 percent. Spider-Man has four costumes.

Unlock the Spider-Man Skate Video
Earn three gold medals with Spider-Man.

Skate Heaven
Earn 100 percent for every level of the game with all skaters, including Officer Dick, Spider-Man, and a custom skater to unlock a new track.

Chopper Drop: Hawaii Level
Earn three gold medals with every character to unlock this track.

Unlock McSqueeb
Beat the game with Tony Hawk at 100 percent. McSqueeb is a 1980's Tony.

Unlock Officer Dick
Clear every goal and collect all the cash on every level and competition to unlock Officer Dick.

Skip to Restart
Clear every goal and collect all the cash on every level and competition twice to pause the game and choose the spawn point.

Kid Mode
Clear every goal and collect all the cash on every level and competition three times to gain better stats and kid-like skaters.

Perfect Balance
Clear every goal and collect all the cash on every level and competition four times to gain better balance to grind for a long time.

Infinite Special
Clear every goal and collect all the cash on every level and competition five times to gain infinite special.

Max Stats
Clear every goal and collect all the cash on every level and competition six times to gain maximum stats.

Weight Cheat
Clear every goal and collect all the cash on every level and competition seven times to alter the skater appearances.

Wireframe Mode
Clear every goal and collect all the cash on every level and competition eight times to use Wireframe mode.

Slow Motion Tricks
Clear every goal and collect all the cash on every level and competition nine times to watch tricks in slow motion.

Big Head Mode
Clear every goal and collect all the cash on every level and competition 10 times to have the skaters appear with big heads.

Sim Mode
Clear every goal and collect all the cash on every level and competition 11 times to gain realistic physics.

Smooth Mode
Clear every goal and collect all the cash on every level and competition 12 times to have no textures.

No Gravity
Clear every goal and collect all the cash on every level and competition 13 times to get lowered gravity.

Disco Mode
Clear every goal and collect all the cash on every level and competition 14 times to get disco lights.

Mirrored Levels
Clear every goal and collect all the cash on every level and competition 15 times to gain mirrored versions of the original levels.

Special Moves
Perform these special moves when your special meter flashes.

Andrew Reynold's Nosegrab Tailslide
Up, Down, Grind

Andrew Reynold's Triple Heelflip
Up, Right, Kickflip

Andrew Reynold's Hardflip Late Flip
Up, Down, Kickflip

Bob Burnquist's Rocket Tailslide
Up, Down, Grind

Bob Burnquist's One Foot Smith
Right, Down, Grind

Bob Burnquist's Racket Air
Left, Down, Grab

Bucky Lasek's Big Hitter
Left, Down, Grind

Bucky Lasek's One Foot Japan
Up, Right, Grab

Bucky Lasek's Fingerflip Airwalk
Left, Right, Grab

Chad Muska's Mute Backflip
Up, Down, Grab

Chad Muska's Hurricane
Down, Right, Grind

Chad Muska's Muska Nose Man
Right, Up, Grab

Elissa Steamer's Madonna Tailslide
Up, Left, Grind

Elissa Steamer's Hospital Flip
Left, Right, Kickflip

Elissa Steamer's Indy Backflip
Up, Down, Grab

Erik Koston's Fandangle
Right, Down, Grind

Erik Koston's Indy Frontflip
Down, Up, Grab

Erik Koston's Pizza Guy
Down, Left, Grab

Geoff Rowley's Rowley Darkslide
Left, Right, Grind

Geoff Rowley's Double Hardflip
Right, Down, Kickflip

Geoff Rowley's Half Flip Casper
Right, Left, Kickflip

Jamie Thomas' Beni F-Flip
Down, Up, Grind

Jamie Thomas' Laser Flip
Down, Right, Kickflip

Jamie Thomas' One Foot Nose Manual
Left, Up, Grab

Kareem Campbell's Casper
Left, Down, Grab

Kareem Campbell's Ghetto Bird
Down, Up, Deck Tricks

Kareem Campbell's Nosegrind to Pivot
Down, Up, Grind

McSqueeb's Pogo Air
Up, Down, Kickflip

McSqueeb's Layback Grind
Up, Down, Grind

Officer Dick's Assume the Position
Left, Down, Grab

Officer Dick's Lazy A. Grind
Down, Up, Grind

Officer Dick's Salute
Left, Right, Grab

Private Carrera's 55 Ho Slide
Left, Right, Grind

Private Carrera's Double Splits
Right, Left, Grab

Private Carrera's Ho-Ho Handplant
Up, Down, Grind

Rodney Mullen's Nollieflip Underflip
Down, Left, Kickflip

Rodney Mullen's Casper to 360 Flip
Down, Right, Grab

Rodney Mullen's Heelflip Darkslide
Right, Left, Grind

Rune Glifberg's One Foot Bluntslide
Left, Up, Grind

Rune Glifberg's Kickflip One Foot Tailslide
Left, Down, Kickflip

Rune Glifberg's Christ Air
Left, Right, Grab

Spider-Man's Spidey Grind
Left, Right, Grind

Spider-Man's Spidey Flip
Up, Down, Grab

Spider-Man's Spidey Varial
Left, Right, Kickflip

Steve Caballero's Hang Ten
Right, Up, Grind

Steve Caballero's Triple Kickflip
Up, Left, Kickflip

Steve Caballero's FS 540
Right, Left, Grab

Tony Hawk's 900
Left, Right, Down, Grab

Tony Hawk's Overturn
Down, Left, Grind

Tony Hawk's Sacktap
Up, Down+Grab

TOP GUN: FIRE AT WILL

No Damage
Press Right, Left, Down, Up, Triangle, X when the mission loads. You hear a "Yes sir, we're definitely underpaid" message if you did it correctly.

Miramar 2
Enter 63631 as a password.

Miramar 3
Enter 86023 as a password.

Miramar 4
Enter 56141 as a password.

Miramar 5
Enter 79523 as a password.

Miramar 6
Enter 07631 as a password.

Cuba 1
Enter 20123 as a password.

Cuba 2
Enter 57131 as a password.

Cuba 3
Enter 70613 as a password.

Cuba 4
Enter 82123 as a password.

Cuba 5
Enter 46464 as a password.

Cuba 6
Enter 75623 as a password.

Cuba 7
Enter 39964 as a password.

Korea 1
Enter 26126 as a password.

Korea 2
Enter 89464 as a password.

Korea 3
Enter 91692 as a password.

Korea 4
Enter 15084 as a password.

Korea 5
Enter 84103 as a password.

Korea 6
Enter 08584 as a password.

Korea 7
Enter 77603 as a password.

Korea 8
Enter 90194 as a password.

Korea 9
Enter 28103 as a password.

Korea 10
Enter 41684 as a password.

Libya 1
Enter 78692 as a password.

Libya 2
Enter 91184 as a password.

Libya 3
Enter 48384 as a password.

Libya 4
Enter 02726 as a password.

Libya 5
Enter 31984 as a password.

Libya 6
Enter 94236 as a password.

Libya 7
Enter 81484 as a password.

Libya 8
Enter 45726 as a password.

TOSHINDEN SUBARU

All Characters
Press Right (2), Left (2), Right (2), R1, R2 at the title screen. A message confirms correct entry.

All Data in Database Mode
Press R1, R2, L1, L2, Left, Right, Select (2) at the title screen. A message confirms correct entry.

All Minigames
Press Left, Right, Left, Right, Left (2), L1, L2 at the title screen. A message confirms correct entry.

TOTAL DRIVIN'

Course Select
Go to the main menu screen where you select all of your options. Tap on R2 to the cadence of "Happy birthday to you" and "Doe, a deer, a female deer." You hear an engine roar if you entered the code correctly. This gives you access to all six tracks in Egypt and Scotland.

TOTAL ECLIPSE TURBO

Extra Continues, Planes, Plasma Shots
Pause the game and select Options. Press Triangle, Square, Circle, Square, Triangle, Square, L1, L1+R1, Select (2). A skull appears to confirm correct entry. Then, press Triangle, Square, L1 (3), Square, Triangle. The game resets, but you have 10 planes, continues, and plasma shots.

Level Select
Go into the Options screen and highlight "Password." Hold Select and press Triangle, L1, Square, then release Select and press Triangle, L1, Square, Triangle, L1, Square. Pick the level by pressing Right or Left in the "Round=" box.

Crystal Dynamics Commercial
Let the demo play through once. Let the demo start again to see the Crystal Dynamics commercial.

Level 1 Password
X, Circle, Triangle, Square, X (3), Square

Level 2 Password
Triangle (2), Circle, X, Triangle (2), X, Square

Level 3 Password
Circle (3), Triangle, X, Triangle, Square (2)

TOUGE MAX 2

Unlock All Cars
Hold L1+L2+R1+R2 at the title screen. A sound confirms correct entry. While still holding those buttons, hold Up+Triangle. Another sound confirms correct entry. With all the buttons held, press Start.

Unlock All Tracks
Hold L1+L2+R1+R2 at the title screen. A sound confirms correct entry. While still holding those buttons, hold Down+X. Another sound confirms correct entry. With all the buttons held, press Start.

TOY STORY 2

Level Select
Press Up (4), Down (2), Up (2), Down (3) at the title screen. This unlocks all the levels, but you still have to complete all the missions.

T.R.A.G.: MISSION OF MERCY

Additional Costumes
Beat and save the game. Load the saved game and use the same character that completed the previous game. Keep beating the game, saving the game, and loading the saved data. Press Select at the Character Selection screen and pick "ARMS" to see new costumes and weapons. The first completion unlocks costumes and music. The second and third completions reveal more costumes and music.

TRAP GUNNER

Alternate Background Music
Press Circle, R2, R1, Triangle, X, Square, Right, L2, L1, Up, Down, Left at the title screen.

Bonus Characters
Press L2, L1, Up, Left, Down, Right, Square, X, Circle, Triangle, R1, R2 at the title screen.

Bonus Level
Press Select (12) at the title screen.

Bonus Costumes
Press R2, R1, Triangle, Circle, X, Square, Right, Down, Left, Up, L1, L2 at the title screen.

Secret Save Icon
Press Left, L2, L1, Up, Down, Right, Square, R1 (2), Triangle, X, Circle at the title screen.

Change Traps
Press L2, R2, L1, R1, Up, Triangle, Left, Right, Square, Circle, Down, X at the title screen.

Unlock Secret Characters
Beat Story mode with Van Reily, Tenrou Ugetsu, and John Bishous to unlock three secret characters.

TRASH IT

Starting Level
Enter TAWK as a password in Quest mode.

Chemical Plant Level
Enter BOGGIN as a password in Quest mode.

Toy World Level
Enter PLEB as a password in Quest mode.

Launchpad Level
Enter BOSTIN as a password in Quest mode.

Planet Core Level
Enter MINGING as a password in Quest mode.

City Level
Enter SHATNER as a password in Quest mode.

Timmy Temple Level
Enter GLITTER as a password in Quest mode.

Moonbeams Lab Level
Enter SMUDGE as a password in Quest mode.

TREASURES OF THE DEEP

Level Select
Pause, then press Down, X, Left, Square, Up (2), Triangle (2), Right (2), Circle (2), Down, Right, Up, Left, Triangle, X.

Play as a Shark
To play as a shark in the California bonus level, beat any normal mission (except for Training mode) after you collect 85 to 90 percent of the level's gold.

Extra FMV Sequences
To get the bonus Atlantis level, beat all levels and collect all tablets pieces. Then beat the bonus level to see a FMV sequence filled with developers.

Level Skip
Pause, then press Down, X, Left, Square, Up (2), Triangle (2), Right (2), Circle (2), Triangle (3), Down (3).

All Equipment
Pause, then press Down, X, Left, Square, Up (2), Triangle (2), Right (2), Circle (2), L1 (4), R1 (4), L2 (4), R2 (4).

All Weapons
Pause, then press Down, X, Left, Square, Up (2), Triangle (2), Right (2), Circle (2), R1 (4), L1 (4), R2 (4), L2 (4).

All Missions Complete
Pause, then press Down, X, Left, Square, Up (2), Triangle (2), Right (2), Circle (2), Square, X (3), Square, Triangle (3), Square, X (3).

Banana Harpoons
Pause, then press Down, X, Left, Square, Up (2), Triangle (2), Right (2), Circle (2), X, Up, Triangle, Down.

Longer Shark Attack Time
Pause, then press Down, X, Left, Square, Up (2), Triangle (2), Right (2), Circle (2), L2 (3), R1 (3), R2, L1.

Extra Continues
Pause, then press Down, X, Left, Square, Up (2), Triangle (2), Right (2), Circle (2), R2 (3), L2 (3).

Extra Gold
Pause, then press Down, X, Left, Square, Up (2), Triangle (2), Right (2), Circle (2), R1, R2, L1, L2, R1, R2, L1, L2.

Tablet Piece
Pause, then press Down, X, Left, Square, Up (2), Triangle (2), Right (2), Circle (2), L1, L2, L1, L2, Square, Circle.

Disabling Fines
Pause, then press Down, X, Left, Square, Up (2), Triangle (2), Right (2), Circle (2), R2, R1, L2, L1.

Infinite Health
Pause, then press Down, X, Left, Square, Up (2), Triangle (2), Right (2), Circle (2), Triangle (2), X (2).

Infinite Air
Pause, then press Down, X, Left, Square, Up (2), Triangle (2), Right (2), Circle (2), Triangle, Circle, X, Square, Up, Right, Down, Left.

Disabling Currents
Pause, then press Down, X, Left, Square, Up (2), Triangle (2), Right (2), Circle (2), R1, L1, L2, R2, X.

Unlock All Doors
Pause, then press Down, X, Left, Square, Up (2), Triangle (2), Right (2), Circle (2), X, Circle, Triangle, Square.

Overhead View
Pause, then press Down, X, Left, Square, Up (2), Triangle (2), Right (2), Circle (2), Triangle, Square, X, Square. Press Select+L1 to zoom out and Select+R1 to zoom in.

Swim Through Objects
Pause, then press Down, X, Left, Square, Up (2), Triangle (2), Right (2), Circle (2), Square (2), Circle (2).

Full Air and Health
Pause, then press Down, X, Left, Square, Up (2), Triangle (2), Right (2), Circle (2), Up, Down, Left, Right, X (2).

Reveal the Map
Pause, then press Down, X, Left, Square, Up (2), Triangle (2), Right (2), Circle (2), Square, X, Circle, X, Square.

Turbo Speed
Pause, then press Down, X, Left, Square, Up (2), Triangle (2), Right (2), Circle (2), R1, R2, R1, R2, R1, R2.

Disable Cross-Hairs and Information Panels
Pause, then press Down, X, Left, Square, Up (2), Triangle (2), Right (2), Circle (2), Right, Circle, Down, X, Triangle, X, Triangle.

Better Frame Rate
Pause, then press Down, X, Left, Square, Up (2), Triangle (2), Right (2), Circle (2), Left (3), Circle (3).

Full Screen Display
Pause, then press Down, X, Left, Square, Up (2), Triangle (2), Right (2), Circle (2), Triangle, X, Up, Down.

Infinite Payload
Pause, then press Down, X, Left, Square, Up (2), Triangle (2), Right (2), Circle (2), Triangle, Up, X, Down.

TRICK N' SNOW BOARDER

Play as *Resident Evil* Characters
At the title screen, press Triangle (2), X (2), Square, Circle, Square, Circle. A sound confirms correct entry. Leon, Claire, or a zombie cop become available as characters.

TRICKY SLIDERS

Play as *Resident Evil* Characters
At the title screen, press Triangle (2), X (2), Square, Circle, Square, Circle. A sound confirms correct entry. Go into Free mode and press R2 or L2 to get Leon, Claire, or a Zombie Cop.

Bonus Tracks
Beat the game in Story mode. Press L1 while selecting a track to see the new tracks.

TRIPLE PLAY 2000

Weather Comments
During gameplay, hold L1+L2+R1+R2 and press X, Down, Triangle, Up.

Announcer Trivia
During gameplay, hold L1+L2+R1+R2 and press Down, X, Right, Circle.

History Comments
During gameplay, hold L1+L2+R1+R2 and press Up, Triangle, Right, Circle.

Additional Batter Information
During gameplay, hold L1+L2+R1+R2 and press Left, Square, Up, Triangle.

Instant Home Run
While in the batter's box, hold L1+L2+R1+R2 and press Triangle, Square, Triangle, Circle, X, Square, Left, Right.

Instant Strike Out
While on the pitcher's mound, hold L1+L2+R1+R2 and press Up, Down, Triangle, Square, Triangle, Circle, X, Square.

Home Run Sounds
Press Triangle, Circle, or Square when you are rounding the bases because of a home run.

Camera Control
During gameplay, hold L1+L2+R1+R2 and press Right, Left, Up, Down, Right, Left. Use L2 to zoom out, R2 to zoom in, Triangle to get a higher view, Square to get a lower view, R1+D-Pad to turn, L1+D-Pad to move faster, and the D-Pad to move the camera.

EA Dream Team
Pick an Exhibition game. Go to the Team Selection screen and press Left, Right (6). A message confirms correct entry. To get the dream team in Home Run Challenge mode, select "Home Run Challenge" from the main menu. Go to the Team Selection screen and hold Up+L1+R1 until a message is spoken.

Remove the Screen Info
During gameplay, hold L1+L2+R1+R2 and press Triangle, Up (3). A thump confirms correct entry.

TRIPLE PLAY 2001

Weather Comments
During gameplay, hold L1+L2+R1+R2 and press X, Down, Triangle, Up.

Announcer Trivia
During gameplay, hold L1+L2+R1+R2 and press Down, X, Right, Circle.

History Comments
During gameplay, hold L1+L2+R1+R2 and press Up, Triangle, Right, Circle.

EA Dream Team
Pick an Exhibition game. Go to the Team Selection screen and press Left, Right (6) or hold L1+R1 and press Left, Right (3), X. A message confirms correct entry. To get the dream team in Big League Challenge mode, select "Big League Challenge" from the main menu. Go to the Team Selection screen and hold Up+L1+R1 until a message is spoken.

Home Run Sounds
Press Triangle, Circle, or Square when you are rounding the bases because of a home run.

Unlock Six Secret Teams
Win the World Series.

Unlock Island Stadium
In Season mode, win 10 games in a row.

Unlock Space Stadium
In Season mode, hit a ground rule double.

Unlock Babe Ruth
In Season mode, hit a home run with a pitcher.

Unlock Cy Young
In Season mode, pitch a complete game shutout.

Unlock Eddie Murray
In Season mode, hit a home run from both sides of the plate in one game with a switch hitter.

Unlock Ernie Banks
In Season mode, perform six double plays in one game.

Unlock Frank Robinson
In Season mode, lead off a game with back-to-back home runs.

Unlock Hank Aaron
In Season mode, hit four consecutive home runs.

Unlock Harmon Killebrew
In Season mode, hit three home runs more than 500 feet.

Unlock Jackie Robinson
In Season mode, steal second and third with the same player in one game.

Unlock Lou Gehrig
In Season mode, hit for the cycle (single, double, triple, home run) in one game.

Unlock Mickey Mantle
In Season mode, hit a home run more than 575 feet.

Unlock Mike Schmidt
In Season mode, hit four home runs in one game with the same player.

Unlock Reggie Jackson
In Season mode, hit an in-the-park home run.

Unlock Satchel Paige
In Season mode, throw three consecutive strike outs.

Unlock Ty Cobb
In Season mode, steal home base.

Unlock Willie Mays
In Season mode, make four diving catches in one game.

Unlock Willie McCovey
In Season mode, hit three consecutive home runs.

Big League Challenge Power Boost
In Big League Challenge mode, hit 10 consecutive home runs to get a boost in power. Hit seven more to get another power boost.

Big Baseball
In Season mode, throw six consecutive strike outs.

Bigger Baseball
In Season mode, throw nine consecutive strike outs.

Flaming Baseball
In Season mode, throw 12 consecutive strike outs.

Big Bat
In Season mode, hit two consecutive home runs.

Pulsating Bat
In Season mode, score five runs in one game with the same player.

Big Glove
In Season mode, perform a diving catch.

Bigger Glove
In Season mode, perform two diving catches in one game.

Pulsating Glove
In Season mode, perform three diving catches in one game.

Big Head
In Season mode, score four runs in one game.

Bigger Head
In Season mode, score eight runs in one game.

Pulsating Head
In Season mode, score 12 runs in one game.

Tiny Head
In Season mode, get 16 hits in one game.

Pencil Head
In Season mode, strike out six consecutives times when you are batting.

Strong Arm
In Season mode, get caught stealing more than twice in one game.

Invisible Players
In Season mode, hit two triples with the same player in one game.

Thin Players
In Season mode, hit a home run with a player weighing less than 160 pounds.

Large Players
In Season mode, hit a home run with a player weighing more than 250 pounds.

Tall Players
In Season mode, get eight hits in one game.

Fast Players
In Season mode, steal all the bases in one game.

Offense Power-Up
In Season mode, hit 10 home runs in one game.

Defense Power-Up
In Season mode, get three double plays in one game.

Speed Power-Up
In Season mode, steal two consecutive bases with the same player.

CPU Assist
In Season mode, win a game by 10 or more runs.

TRIPLE PLAY '97

Instant Home Run
While in the batter's box, hold L1+L2+R1+R2 and press Up (2), Triangle (2), Up (2), X (2). A chime confirms correct entry.

Hidden Stadium
At the Stadium Selection screen, press L1, R1, L1. Then, hold R1 and then press Start.

Super Players
Go into the Custom Player option. Enter any of the case sensitive names from the credits screen, such as: Bruce McMillian, Steve Rechstchattner, Bill McCormick, John Burk, Kevin Loh, Wendall Harlow, Louise Read, Dennis Hirsch, Erik Kiss, Jon Spencer, Chris Johnson, Eric Pauker, Kevin Pickell, Mark Gipson, Mike Swanson, Geoff Coates, Edwin Gomes, Tony Lee, David Demorest, Craig Hui, Mike Sokyrka, Frank Faugno, Gary Lam, Brent Neilsen, or Josh Holmes.

TRIPLE PLAY '98

Instant Home Run
While in the batter's box, hold L1+L2+R1+R2 and press Up, Triangle, Left, Right, Square, Circle, Down, X.

Instant Strike Out
While on the pitcher's mound, hold L2+L2+R1+R2 and press X, Down, Circle, Square, Right, Left, Triangle, Up.

Reveal Three Hidden Stadiums
At the Stadium Selection screen, press L1, R1, L1, R1, Square.

Instant Three Outs
Hold L1+L2+R1+R2 and press Square before you catch a fly ball.

EA Dream Team
At the Team Selection screen, press L2, R2, L2, R2, Circle. The last team is the EA Team, consisting of developers with great attributes.

Jim and Buck
During gameplay, hold L1+L2+R1+R2 and press Circle, Triangle, Square, X (2), Square, X, Circle, Triangle.

Control the Camera
During gameplay, hold L1+L2+R1+R2 and press Right (2), Left (2), Up (2), Down (2).

Crowd Comments
During gameplay, hold L1+L2+R1+R2 and press Square, Circle, Square.

Weather Comments
During gameplay, hold L1+L2+R1+R2 and press Circle, X, Circle.

Sponsor Comments
During gameplay, hold L1+L2+R1+R2 and press Triangle, Circle, Triangle.

Crowd Cheers
During gameplay, hold L1+L2+R1+R2 and press Down, X, Down, X, Triangle.

Crowd Boos
During gameplay, hold L1+L2+R1+R2 and press Down, X, Down, X (2).

Faster Fastball
After throwing a fastball, immediately press Down+Square.

Players in Underwear
Enable the EA Dream Team and Hidden Stadiums codes. Pick the EA Dream Team to be the home team and the San Diego Padres as the visiting team. EA players will be in their underwear.

Modified Players
Enable the Players in Underwear code. Hold L1+L2+R1+R2 and press Circle, Triangle, Square, X (2), Square, X, Circle, Triangle while the players are in their underwear. Physical features of the players will be modified.

Developer Comments: Adrienne Travica
During gameplay, hold L1+L2+R1+R2 and press Right, Circle, Right, Left.

Developer Comments: Alex Garden
During gameplay, hold L1+L2+R1+R2 and press Up, Triangle, Up, Down.

Developer Comments: Anne Geiger
During gameplay, hold L1+L2+R1+R2 and press Left, Square, Left, Right.

Developer Comments: Brent Nielsen
During gameplay, hold L1+L2+R1+R2 and press Left, Square, Left, Circle.

Developer Comments: Chris Johnson
During gameplay, hold L1+L2+R1+R2 and press Up, Triangle, Up, X.

Developer Comments: Chuck Osieja
During gameplay, hold L1+L2+R1+R2 and press Up, Triangle, Up, Square.

Developer Comments: Daniel Ng
During gameplay, hold L1+L2+R1+R2 and press Up, Triangle, Up, Right.

Developer Comments: Darren Stone
During gameplay, hold L1+L2+R1+R2 and press Up, Triangle, Up, Circle.

Developer Comments: Duncan Lee
During gameplay, hold L1+L2+R1+R2 and press Left, Square, Left, Square.

Developer Comments: Edwin Gomez
During gameplay, hold L1+L2+R1+R2 and press Left, Square, Left, Up.

Developer Comments: Erik Kiss
During gameplay, hold L1+L2+R1+R2 and press Up, Triangle, Up, Triangle.

Developer Comments: Ernie Patzel
During gameplay, hold L1+L2+R1+R2 and press Right, Circle, Right, Triangle.

Developer Comments: Frank Faugno
During gameplay, hold L1+L2+R1+R2 and press Right, Circle, Right, X.

Developer Comments: Gary Lam
During gameplay, hold L1+L2+R1+R2 and press Left, Square, Left (2).

Developer Comments: Geoff Coates
During gameplay, hold L1+L2+R1+R2 and press Right, Circle, Right, Up.

Developer Comments: Jon Spencer
During gameplay, hold L1+L2+R1+R2 and press Up, Triangle, Up (2).

Developer Comments: Kirby Leung
During gameplay, hold L1+L2+R1+R2 and press Right, Circle, Right (2).

Developer Comments: Michael Sokyrka
During gameplay, hold L1+L2+R1+R2 and press Right, Circle, Right, Square.

Developer Comments: Mike Swanson
During gameplay, hold L1+L2+R1+R2 and press Up, Triangle, Up, Left.

Developer Comments: Pauline Moller
During gameplay, hold L1+L2+R1+R2 and press Left, Square, Left, X.

Developer Comments: Steven Rechtschaffner
During gameplay, hold L1+L2+R1+R2 and press Left, Square, Left, Triangle.

Developer Comments: Tom Zuber
During gameplay, hold L1+L2+R1+R2 and press Left, Square, Left, Down.

Developer Comments: Tony Lee
During gameplay, hold L1+L2+R1+R2 and press Right, Circle, Right, Circle.

Developer Comments: Wendell Harlow
During gameplay, hold L1+L2+R1+R2 and press Right, Circle, Right, Down.

TRIPLE PLAY '99

Instant Home Run
While in the batter's box, hold L1+L2+R1+R2+ and press Triangle, Square, Triangle, Circle, X, Square, Left, Right. A thump confirms correct entry.

Instant Strike Out
While on the pitcher's mound, hold L1+L2+R1+R2 and press Up, Down, Triangle, Square, Triangle, Circle, X, Square. A thump confirms correct entry.

Unlock Three Hidden Stadiums
At the Stadium Selection screen, press L2, L1, R1, R2 (2), L1, R1, R2. The announcer speaks if you entered the code correctly. Alternately, press L2, R1, L1, R2 at the Stadium Selection screen.

Home Run Sounds
When you are rounding the bases after a home run, press Square, Triangle, X, or Circle.

Stadium Information
During gameplay, hold L1+L2+R1+R2 and press Down, X, Right, Circle.

EA Dream Team
Start a Single-player game. Get to the Team Selection screen and press Left, Right, Left, Right, Left, Right, Left, Right, Left, Right, Left, Right.

Double Designated Hitters
Press Triangle+Up (10) when the FMV sequence begins to play at the beginning of the game. You have two designated hitters and no center fielder when you start a game. Whomever you place in center field gets to hit twice.

Super Players

Enter the "Create a Player" option. Name your player after one of the names in the credits. The player will have outstanding abilities. For example, "Jon Spencer" is an extraordinary pitcher that can throw more than 120 mph. "Erik Kiss" is a great power hitter who hits a home run every time.

Disappointment from the Crowd

During gameplay, hold L1+L2+R1+R2 and press X, Down (2), X.

Soft Cheers from the Crowd

During gameplay, hold L1+L2+R1+R2 and press Triangle, X (2), Triangle.

Loud Cheers from the Crowd

During gameplay, hold L1+L2+R1+R2 and press Square, Left (2), Square.

Boos from the Crowd

During gameplay, hold L1+L2+R1+R2 and press Circle, Right (2), Circle.

Applause from the Crowd

During gameplay, hold L1+L2+R1+R2 and press Triangle, Up (2), Triangle.

Commercials

During gameplay, hold L1+L2+R1+R2 and press Left, Square, Right, Circle.

Announcer Commentary

During gameplay, hold L1+L2+R1+R2 and press Up, Triangle, Right, Circle.

Additional Batter Information

During gameplay, hold L1+L2+R1+R2 and press Left, Square, Up, Triangle.

Announcer Trivia

During gameplay, hold L1+L2+R1+R2 and press Down, X, Right, Circle.

Announcer Nicknames

During gameplay, hold L1+L2+R1+R2 and press Circle, Right, Square, Left.

Crowd Comments

During gameplay, hold L1+L2+R1+R2 and press Up, Triangle, Down, X.

Weather Comments

During gameplay, hold L1+L2+R1+R2 and press X, Down, Triangle, Up.

Developer Comments: Adrienne Travica

During gameplay, hold L1+L2+R1+R2 and press Left, Square, Left, Right.

Developer Comments: Agathat Kuzniak

During gameplay, hold L1+L2+R1+R2 and press Up, Triangle, Up, Down.

Developer Comments: Anne Fouron

During gameplay, hold L1+L2+R1+R2 and press Right, Circle, Right, Down.

Developer Comments: Anne Geiger

During gameplay, hold L1+L2+R1+R2 and press Left, Square, Left, Square.

Developer Comments: Bob Silliker

During gameplay, hold L1+L2+R1+R2 and press Left (4).

Developer Comments: Brent Nielsen

During gameplay, hold L1+L2+R1+R2 and press Up, Triangle, Up (2).

Developer Comments: Brett Marshall

During gameplay, hold L1+L2+R1+R2 and press Down, Triangle, Down (2).

Developer Comments: Carolyn Cudmore

During gameplay, hold L1+L2+R1+R2 and press Down, Triangle, Down, Triangle.

Developer Comments: Chuck Osieja

During gameplay, hold L1+L2+R1+R2 and press Up, Triangle, Up, Square.

Developer Comments: Darron Stone

During gameplay, hold L1+L2+R1+R2 and press Right (4).

Developer Comments: Duncan Lee

During gameplay, hold L1+L2+R1+R2 and press Left, Square, Left, Triangle.

Developer Comments: Edwin Gomez

During gameplay, hold L1+L2+R1+R2 and press Left, Square, Left, X.

Developer Comments: Eric Kiss

During gameplay, hold L1+L2+R1+R2 and press Down (4).

Developer Comments: Frank Faugno

During gameplay, hold L1+L2+R1+R2 and press Right, Circle, Right, Triangle.

Developer Comments: Gary Lam

During gameplay, hold L1+L2+R1+R2 and press Up, Triangle, Up, Circle.

Developer Comments: Jason Lee

During gameplay, hold L1+L2+R1+R2 and press Down, Triangle, Down, Right.

Developer Comments: Jeff Coates

During gameplay, hold L1+L2+R1+R2 and press Right, Circle, Right, X.

Developer Comments: Jen Cleary

During gameplay, hold L1+L2+R1+R2 and press Up (3), Up.

Developer Comments: Jon Spencer

During gameplay, hold L1+L2+R1+R2 and press Up, Triangle, Up, Triangle.

Developer Comments: Kenneth Newby

During gameplay, hold L1+L2+R1+R2 and press Right, Circle, Right (2).

Developer Comments: Kirby Leung

During gameplay, hold L1+L2+R1+R2 and press Right, Circle, Right, Square.

Developer Comments: Louis Wang

During gameplay, hold L1+L2+R1+R2 and press Down, Triangle, Down, Up.

Developer Comments: Mark Dobratz

During gameplay, hold L1+L2+R1+R2 and press Down, Triangle, Down, Left.

Developer Comments: Mark Liljefors

During gameplay, hold L1+L2+R1+R2 and press Right, Circle, Right, Left.

Developer Comments: Michael J. Sokyrka

During gameplay, hold L1+L2+R1+R2 and press Right, Circle, Right, Circle.

Developer Comments: Mike Swanson

During gameplay, hold L1+L2+R1+R2 and press Up, Triangle, Up, Right.

Developer Comments: Mike Rayner

During gameplay, hold L1+L2+R1+R2 and press Triangle (4).

Developer Comments: Mike Sheath

During gameplay, hold L1+L2+R1+R2 and press Right, Circle, Right, Up.

Developer Comments: Pauline Moller

During gameplay, hold L1+L2+R1+R2 and press Up, Triangle, Up, Left.

Developer Comments: Rick Falck

During gameplay, hold L1+L2+R1+R2 and press Down, Triangle, Down, X.

Developer Comments: Rob Anderson

During gameplay, hold L1+L2+R1+R2 and press Square (4).

Developer Comments: Ryan Pearson

During gameplay, hold L1+L2+R1+R2 and press X (4).

Developer Comments: Stan Tung

During gameplay, hold L1+L2+R1+R2 and press Circle (4).

Developer Comments: Stephen Gagno-Cody

During gameplay, hold L1+L2+R1+R2 and press Left, Square, Left (2).

Developer Comments: Steve Rechtschaffner

During gameplay, hold L1+L2+R1+R2 and press Up, Triangle, Up, X.

Developer Comments: Vanessa Gonwick

During gameplay, hold L1+L2+R1+R2 and press Left, Square, Left, Down.

Developer Comments: Wendell Harlow

During gameplay, hold L1+L2+R1+R2 and press Left, Square, Left, Up.

Developer Comments: Yanick Lebel

During gameplay, hold L1+L2+R1+R2 and press Left, Square, Left, Circle.

TRIPLE PLAY BASEBALL

EA Dream Team

Press Left, Right, Left, Right, Left, Right, Left, Right, Left, Right, Left, Right at the Team Selection screen.

Good Hands

Catch a ball that is going over the fence.

Better Hands

Make two diving catches in a single game.

Awesome Hands

Make two to three diving catches in a single game.

Walk Softly

Hit two home runs in a row.

Big Baseball

Throw six strikeouts in a row.

What an Arm

Throw nine strikeouts in a row.

He's On Fire

Throw 12 strikeouts in a row.

Pee Wee League

Get more than 11 hits in a single game.

Fast Players

Steal three bases with the same player in one game.

Power-Up Defense

Make three double plays in a single game.

Big League Challenge Power Boost

Hit 10 consecutive home runs in Big League Challenge to get a boost in power, which is noted with a flaming baseball. After seven more consecutive home runs, you receive another boost in power, which is noted by a pulsating bat.

Home Run Sounds

Press Triangle or Square to hear air horns, or press Circle to hear whistles while running around the bases after hitting a home run. Note: Set the Sound FX volume to maximum for best results.

TUNNEL B-1

Stage Skip

Pause, highlight "Continue," and press Select.

All Weapons and Full Health

Press L1+L2+R1+R2+Square+Circle+X+Triangle during gameplay.

TURBO PROP RACING

Debug Mode

Pause and press Start+Select.

Unlock All Boats

Enter _BOA as a player name ("_" represents a space).

Duck Mode

Enter _QAK as a player name ("_" represents a space).

Hurricane Boat

Enter HURR as a player name. Pick any boat because the Hurricane boat will be used when the race begins.

Play All Streams

Enter _STR as a player name ("_" represents a space).

Unlock All Day Tracks

Enter _DAY as a player name ("_" represents a space).

Unlock All Mirror Tracks

Enter _NIT as a player name ("_" represents a space).

Unlock All Fractal Tracks

Enter FRAC as a player name.

Always Win Race

Enter WINR as a player name.

View FMV Sequences

Enter RUSH as a player name.

Porsche Mode

Enter BXTR as a player name. You must have a saved game file from Porsche Challenge in your memory card for this trick to work.

Race on a Specific Daytime Course

Enter D_[number] as a player name (replace [number] with the desired course number).

Race on a Specific Night Course

Enter N_[number] as a player name (replace [number] with the desired course number).

TWINBEE YAHOO! DELUXE PACK

Dark Play

Pause the game in Arcade mode. Press Up (2), Down (2), Left, Right, Left, Right, X, Circle.

Level Select

Earn a high score greater than 573,000. Then wait until the demo screen appears with Princess Merora, hold R1+L2 and use the D-Pad to select the stages. If you scored more than 1,000,000, then you can repeat this trick twice.

TWISTED METAL

Invincibility

As a level password, enter Square, Triangle, X, Space, Circle.

Unlimited Turbo

As a level password, enter Triangle, X, Triangle (2), Circle.

Unlimited Ammo

As a level password, enter Triangle, Space, Square, Circle (2).

Helicopter View

As a level password, enter Circle (2), Triangle, X, Space. You can only do this on the Arena, Rooftop, and Arena 2 stages. Press Down+Start for another view.

List of Remaining Cars

Hold X and press Start during a One-player game.

Rear View Mirror

Hold Right and press Start during a One-player game.

Secret Level

Find the glass pyramid in the Rooftop stage. Destroy the glass pyramid. Drop down the hole. You can drive around in a hotel with many rooms and areas.

Warehouse District Password

Circle, Triangle, Square, Circle (2)

Freeway Password

X, Square (2), Circle, Triangle

River Park Password

X, Triangle, Square, Circle, Square

Cyburbia Password

X, Square, Triangle (3)

Rooftop Password

Square, Triangle, X, Circle, X

Final Battle Password

Triangle, X, Circle, Square, Triangle

Secret Level Password

Square, Triangle, Circle, Square (2)

TWISTED METAL 2

Invincibility

Hold L1+L2+R1+R2 and press Up, Down, Left, Right (2), Left, Down, Up during gameplay. A sound and text message confirms correct entry.

Infinite Weapons

Hold L2+R2 and press Up, Down, Left, Right (2), Left, Down, Up. A sound and text message confirms correct entry.

Homing Napalm

Obtain two or more napalms. Shoot a napalm, but continue holding the button and press Up, Down (2), Left (3), Right (2). You get extra napalms and you see "Homing Napalm" at the screen's top.

Powered-Up Guns

Hold R2 and press Up, Down, Left, Right (2), Left, Down, Up. A sound and text message confirms correct entry.

No Radar

Press Select+Left during gameplay.

Play as Minion

Press L1, Up, Down, Left at the Car Selection screen.

Play as Sweet Tooth

Press Up, L1, Triangle, Right at the Car Selection screen.

Random Car Select

Press R1 at the Car Selection screen.

More Damage for Axel

Hold R1 and press Up, Down, Left, Right (2), Left, Down, Up during gameplay as Axel. When Axel hits something, a large amount of damage is caused.

Exchange Weapons for Health

Press Down, Up, Right, Left, Up (2), Down (2) during gameplay. All your weapons will be traded in for health.

Jet Moto Level

Start a Two-player Challenge game. At the Track Selection screen, press Up, Down, Right, R1. A sound confirms correct entry.

Rooftop Level

Start a Two-player Challenge game. At the Track Selection screen, press Down, Left, R1, Down. A sound confirms correct entry.

Cyburbia Level

Start a Two-player Challenge game. At the Track Selection screen, press Down, Up, L1, R1. A sound confirms correct entry.

Weapons List

Press Select+Down during gameplay.

Rearview Mirror

Press Select+Right during gameplay.

Change Camera Views

In a One-player game, hold Up and press Select to see a helicopter view. In a Two-player game, hold Up and press Select to change how the screen is split.

Extra FMV Sequence

When the SingleTrac logo changes into its second form, press Up, Down, L1, R1.

Invisibility Move

Press Right, Down, Left, Up during gameplay.

Freeze Move

Press Left, Right, Up during gameplay.

Rear Freeze Move

Press Left, Right, Down, Left, Right, Up during gameplay.

Napalm Move

Press Right, Left, Up during gameplay.

Rear Napalm Move

Press Left, Right, Down, Right, Left, Up during gameplay.

Jump Move

Press Up (2), Left during gameplay.

Mines Move

Press Right, Left, Down during gameplay.

Shield Move
Press Up (2), Right during gameplay.

Rear Attack Move
Press Left, Right, Down during gameplay.

Minion's Attack
Press Up, Down, Up (2), R2 during gameplay.

Extra Energy
Run over 10 people in a stage to gain some extra energy.

Disabling Codes
Reenter a code to disable it.

Axel Moscow Level Password
X, Triangle, X (2), Blank (2)

Axel Paris Level Password
Circle, Triangle, Square, Blank, Triangle, Blank

Axel Amazonia Level Password
Triangle (2), Square, Circle (2)

Axel New York Level Password
Blank, Triangle, Square (2), X, Blank

Axel Antarctica Level Password
X (2), Triangle, Square, Triangle, Circle

Axel Holland Level Password
Circle, X, Circle, Triangle, Circle (2)

Axel Hong Kong Level Password
Triangle, X, Circle, X (2), Circle

Axel Dark Tooth Level Password
Triangle, Square, Triangle, Square, Blank, Square

Grasshopper Moscow Level Password
Triangle, X, Circle, Blank (3)

Grasshopper Paris Level Password
X, Triangle, Circle, Square (2), Circle

Grasshopper Amazonia Level Password
Blank, X, Circle (2), Triangle, Circle

Grasshopper New York Level Password
Circle (2), Square, Circle, Square, Circle

Grasshopper Antarctica Level Password
Square, Triangle, Blank (3), Square

Grasshopper Holland Level Password
Triangle, X, Blank (3), Square

Grasshopper Hong Kong Level Password
X, Triangle (2), Blank (2), Triangle

Grasshopper Dark Tooth Level Password
X, Blank, X, Square (2), Blank

Hammerhead Moscow Level Password
Blank, Triangle, X (3), Blank

Hammerhead Paris Level Password
Blank, X, Triangle, Square, X, Triangle

Hammerhead Amazonia Level Password
Triangle, Blank (3), X, Circle

Hammerhead New York Level Password
Triangle (2), X, Triangle, X (2)

Hammerhead Antarctica Level Password
Triangle, X, Triangle, Circle, X, Square

Hammerhead Holland Level Password
Triangle, Square (2), X, Square, Blank

Hammerhead Hong Kong Level Password
Circle, Triangle, Circle, Square (2), Triangle

Hammerhead Dark Tooth Level Password
Circle (3), Blank, Triangle, X

Mr. Grimm Moscow Level Password
Triangle (2), X (2), Circle, Blank

Mr. Grimm Paris Level Password
Circle, X, Triangle, Circle, Triangle, X

Mr. Grimm Amazonia Level Password
X, Square (2), Triangle (3)

Mr. Grimm New York Level Password
Triangle, Blank (2), Circle, X, Circle

Mr. Grimm Antarctica Level Password
Circle, Triangle, X, Triangle, X, Blank

Mr. Grimm Holland Level Password
X (2), Triangle, Blank, Circle, X

Mr. Grimm Hong Kong Level Password
Blank, X, Circle, Triangle, Square (2)

Mr. Grimm Dark Tooth Level Password
Blank, Square, Triangle, Circle (2), Triangle

Spectre Moscow Level Password
Circle, Triangle, X (2), Triangle, Blank

Spectre Paris Level Password
Blank, Triangle, Square, Circle (2), X

Spectre Amazonia Level Password
Circle, X, Triangle, Square, Triangle, X

Spectre New York Level Password
Blank, X, Circle, X (2), Triangle

Spectre Antarctica Level Password
X, Blank (3), Circle, Triangle

Spectre Holland Level Password
Triangle, Blank, Square, X, Square

Spectre Hong Kong Level Password
X, Triangle, X, Triangle, Circle, Square

Spectre Dark Tooth Level Password
X, Circle (3), Blank, Triangle

Thumper Moscow Level Password
Circle, Blank (2), Triangle, X, Blank

Thumper Paris Level Password
X, Square (2), Circle (2), Triangle

Thumper Amazonia Level Password
Triangle, X, Circle, Blank, Square, Blank

Thumper New York Level Password
X (2), Triangle (2), X, Triangle

Thumper Antarctica Level Password
Triangle (2), Square, Blank (3)

Thumper Holland Level Password
X, Triangle, X, Blank, Square, Triangle

Thumper Hong Kong Level Password
Triangle, Blank (2), Square, Triangle, Blank

Thumper Dark Tooth Level Password
Triangle, Blank, Square (2), X, Circle

Roadkill Moscow Level Password
Circle, X, Triangle, Square (2), Blank

Roadkill Paris Level Password
Triangle, Blank, Triangle, Blank (2), Circle

Roadkill Amazonia Level Password
X (2), Triangle, Circle, Square, Triangle

Roadkill New York Level Password
Circle, Blank (2), X, Blank, X

Roadkill Antarctica Level Password
Blank, Triangle, Square, X, Circle, Blank

Roadkill Holland Level Password
X, Blank (2), Triangle, Square

Roadkill Hong Kong Level Password
Triangle, Square (2), Triangle, Circle, Triangle

Roadkill Dark Tooth Level Password
Triangle, Circle, X, Triangle, Square, X

Shadow Moscow Level Password
Square, Blank (2), Triangle (2), Blank

Shadow Paris Level Password
X (2), Circle, Blank, Triangle, X

Shadow Amazonia Level Password
X, Triangle, X, Square, Circle, Triangle

Shadow New York Level Password
X, Blank (2), X, Circle, Square

Shadow Antarctica Level Password
Circle, X, Circle (2), X, Circle

Shadow Holland Level Password
Circle, Triangle, Square, Triangle, Square

Shadow Hong Kong Level Password
Circle, Blank, Triangle, Blank, Square, X

Shadow Dark Tooth Level Password
Circle, Triangle, Blank, Triangle, Circle, Blank

Outlaw 2 Moscow Level Password
Blank, X, Circle, Blank, Triangle

Outlaw 2 Paris Level Password
Triangle (2), X, Circle, Triangle, Blank

Outlaw 2 Amazonia Level Password
Triangle, Square (3), Triangle, Blank

Outlaw 2 New York Level Password
Circle, X, Triangle (3), Blank

Outlaw 2 Antarctica Level Password
X, Triangle, Circle, X, Triangle, Blank

Outlaw 2 Holland Level Password
X, Square (2), Blank, Triangle, Blank

Outlaw 2 Hong Kong Level Password
Blank, Triangle, X, Square, X (2)

Outlaw 2 Dark Tooth Level Password
Blank, Circle, X, Blank, Triangle, Blank

Twister Moscow Level Password
X, Blank (2), Triangle, Circle, Blank

Twister Paris Level Password
Triangle, X, Circle (2), X, Triangle

Twister Amazonia Level Password
Blank, Triangle, Square, X, Square, Circle

Twister New York Level Password
X, Triangle, X, Circle, X, Blank

Twister Antarctica Level Password
Circle, Blank (2), X, Square, Triangle

Twister Holland Level Password
Blank, X (2), Blank (2), Circle

Twister Hong Kong Level Password
X (2), Triangle, X, Square, Blank

Twister Dark Tooth Level Password
X, Square, Blank, Square, Triangle, Circle

Warthog Moscow Level Password
Triangle, Blank (2), Triangle, Square, Blank

Warthog Paris Level Password
Triangle, Square (3), X, Square

Warthog Amazonia Level Password
Circle, Square (2), Circle, X (2)

Warthog New York Level Password
X, Square (2), Blank, X, Circle

Warthog Antarctica Level Password
Blank, X, Circle, Triangle, Blank, Square

Warthog Holland Level Password
Triangle, X, Triangle, Square, Blank, X

Warthog Hong Kong Level Password
Circle, X, Triangle, Circle, Blank, Circle

Warthog Dark Tooth Level Password
Circle, Square, Blank, Circle (2), Square

Mr. Slam Moscow Level Password
X (2), Triangle, Square, X, Blank

Mr. Slam Paris Level Password
X, Blank (2), Circle, X, Square

Mr. Slam Amazonia Level Password
Circle, Triangle, Square, Blank, Square, X

Mr. Slam New York Level Password
Triangle, X, Circle, Square, Blank, Circle

Mr. Slam Antarctica Level Password
Triangle, Blank, Triangle, Circle, Triangle (2)

Mr. Slam Holland Level Password
Blank, Circle, Blank (2), Circle, Blank

Mr. Slam Hong Kong Level Password
Square, Blank (2), Triangle, Blank, Triangle

Mr. Slam Dark Tooth Level Password
Square, Blank, Square, Triangle, Circle, X

TWISTED METAL 3

All Cheats
At the Password screen, press Triangle (3), L1 (2).

Play as Minion
At the Password screen, press Right (3), Left (2). Minion becomes available at the Car Selection screen.

Play as Sweet Tooth
At the Password screen, press Left (3), Right (2). Sweet Tooth becomes available at the Car Selection screen.

Club Kid's Stage
At the Password screen, press Left (3), Square (2). Return to the main menu and start a Death Match. Pick any car and level and you start in the Club Kid's level.

Warehouse 1 Stage
At the Password screen, press Up (3), Left (2). Return to the main menu and start a Death Match. Pick any car and level and you start in the warehouse.

Warehouse 2 Stage
At the Password screen, press Square (3), Left (2). Return to the main menu and start a Death Match. Pick any car and level and you start in the warehouse.

Flower Power Picture
At the Password screen, press Left, Square (3), Left. Start a One-player game. Pick Flower Power as your character. Highlight Info and press X to see a different picture of Flower Power.

Invincibility
At the Password screen, press L1, Square, X, R1, Start.

Infinite Ammunition
At the Password screen, press Triangle, Circle, Up, Right, Down.

Infinite Specials
At the Password screen, press L1 (2), R1 (3). Return to the main menu, start a game, quit, then restart a new game.

Enhanced Weapons
At the Password screen, press R1 (2), L1 (3).

99 Freeze Missiles
At the Password screen, press Triangle, Up, Circle, Right, Start.

All Pick-Ups Are Power Missiles
At the Password screen, press Start, L1, Start, L1, Start.

All Pick-Ups Are Napalm
At the Password screen, press Start (2), L1 (3).

All Pick-Ups Are Homing Missiles
At the Password screen, press Start, R1, L1, Start (2).

All Pick-Ups Are Remote Bombs
At the Password screen, press L1, R1, Start (2), L1.

CPU Cars Ignore Health Pick-Ups
At the Password screen, press Down, L1, Down, Start, Triangle.

Big Ricochet Bombs
At the Password screen, press Left, Right, Left, Right, Up.

Powered-Up Weapons
At the Password screen, press Triangle, Circle, Down, Left, Up.

Save Game Settings
At the Password screen, press Start (5). Begin a game and the game prompts you to save.

Alone in Deathmatch Mode
At the password screen, press X, Circle (4).

Invisibility Move
Press Up, Down, Left, Right while playing a match.

Rear Fire Move
Press Left, Right, Down while playing a match.

High Jump Move
Press Up (2), Left while playing a match.

Freeze Missile Move
Press Left, Right, Up while playing a match.

Ice World
At the Password screen, press Up (2), X (2), Up.

Enhanced Missiles
At the Password screen, press Triangle, Left, Down, Right, Up. Missiles track your enemies better.

Homing Rain Missiles
At the Password screen, press Up, Down, Up, Down, Up.

No Health Pick-Ups
At the Password screen, press Select, L1, Select, Start, Circle.

No Full Health Pick-Ups
At the Password screen, press L1, Start (3), R1.

No Pick-Ups
At the Password screen, press Select (2), R2, L2, Start.

Better CPU
At the Password screen, press L1, R1, L1, R1 (2). The CPU attacks even harder.

CD Music
Put the disk in an audio CD player. Play track two or higher to hear the game's music.

Auger (Cream Puff Difficulty): D.C.
R1 (2), Right, Select, Down

Auger (Cream Puff Difficulty): Hangar 18
X, Start, X, Up, L1

Auger (Cream Puff Difficulty): North Pole
Select, R1, Left (2), X

Auger (Cream Puff Difficulty): London
Right (2), R1 (2), Right

Auger (Cream Puff Difficulty): Tokyo
Down, R1, L1, X, Right

Auger (Cream Puff Difficulty): Egypt
R2, Start, R2, Right (2)

Auger (Cream Puff Difficulty): Blimp
Triangle, L1, Triangle, Right, Circle

Axel (Cream Puff Difficulty): D.C.
L1, Square, Triangle, Right, Up

Axel (Cream Puff Difficulty): Hangar 18
Right, L2, Select, R2 (2)

Axel (Cream Puff Difficulty): North Pole
L2, R2, Start, Triangle, X

Axel (Cream Puff Difficulty): London
R1, L1, Down, Select, Start

Axel (Cream Puff Difficulty): Tokyo
X, R2, Start, L1, Up

Axel (Cream Puff Difficulty): Egypt
Circle (2), L2, Circle, Right

Axel (Cream Puff Difficulty): Blimp
Select, X (3), R1

Club Kid (Cream Puff Difficulty): D.C.
R2, L2 (3), Start

Club Kid (Cream Puff Difficulty): Hangar 18
Triangle, Select, R1, Left, Up

Club Kid (Cream Puff Difficulty): North Pole
Square, L2, R1, Square, R1

Club Kid (Cream Puff Difficulty): London
Select, Up, Square, R1, Up

Club Kid (Cream Puff Difficulty): Tokyo
Right, L2, Circle, Down, Start

Club Kid (Cream Puff Difficulty): Egypt
L2, Square, Down, R2, Left

Club Kid (Cream Puff Difficulty): Blimp
R1, Left, Select, Circle, R1

Firestarter (Cream Puff Difficulty): D.C.
Left, Up (3), Down

Firestarter (Cream Puff Difficulty): Hangar 18
Up, Square, R1, Left, Down

Firestarter (Cream Puff Difficulty): North Pole
Left, Down, Up, R1, L1

Firestarter (Cream Puff Difficulty): London
R2, X (4)

Firestarter (Cream Puff Difficulty): Tokyo
Triangle, Down, Left, R2, Up

Firestarter (Cream Puff Difficulty): Egypt
Square, X, Select, Right (2)

Firestarter (Cream Puff Difficulty): Blimp
Down, R2 (3), Start

Flower Power (Cream Puff Difficulty): D.C.
L2, Right, Triangle, Select, Circle

Flower Power (Cream Puff Difficulty): Hangar 18
R1, Circle, Right, Start, Right

Flower Power (Cream Puff Difficulty): North Pole
X, Right, X, Left, R2

Flower Power (Cream Puff Difficulty): London
Circle, Left, L1, Circle, Triangle

Flower Power (Cream Puff Difficulty): Tokyo
Up, Right, Select, X, Select

Flower Power (Cream Puff Difficulty): Egypt
Left, Triangle, L1, Circle, Triangle

Flower Power (Cream Puff Difficulty): Blimp
L1, Up, Start, Right, L2

Hammerhead (Cream Puff Difficulty): D.C.
Left, Square, L2, Square, Circle

Hammerhead (Cream Puff Difficulty): Hangar 18
L1 (2), L2, R1, Up

Hammerhead (Cream Puff Difficulty): North Pole
Circle, Square, Down, Left, Up

Hammerhead (Cream Puff Difficulty): London
Square, L1, R1, L1, Triangle

Hammerhead (Cream Puff Difficulty): Tokyo
Up, Down, X, Start (2)

Hammerhead (Cream Puff Difficulty): Egypt
Right, R2, Circle, R2, Down

Hammerhead (Cream Puff Difficulty): Blimp
L2, Down, Circle, Down, R1

Minion (Cream Puff Difficulty): D.C.
X, R2, Start, Circle, Right

Minion (Cream Puff Difficulty): Hangar 18
R2, Left, L1, Start (2)

Minion (Cream Puff Difficulty): North Pole
Up, Select, R1, L1, Right

Minion (Cream Puff Difficulty): London
Left, L2, Up, X, R2

Minion (Cream Puff Difficulty): Tokyo
L1, Select, X, Circle, R2

Minion (Cream Puff Difficulty): Egypt
Circle, L2, Left, Right, Square

Minion (Cream Puff Difficulty): Blimp
Select (3), L2, Up

Mr. Grimm (Cream Puff Difficulty): D.C.
Square, Up, Right, Triangle, Select

Mr. Grimm (Cream Puff Difficulty): Hangar 18
Triangle, Square (2), Up, L1

Mr. Grimm (Cream Puff Difficulty): North Pole
Right, Start, L2, Start, Left

Mr. Grimm (Cream Puff Difficulty): London
L2, R1, Down, R1, Up

Mr. Grimm (Cream Puff Difficulty): Tokyo
R1, Start, L1 (2), Square

Mr. Grimm (Cream Puff Difficulty): Egypt
X, R1, Start, Circle, Start

Mr. Grimm (Cream Puff Difficulty): Blimp
Start, Circle, Left, Start, Up

Outlaw 3 (Cream Puff Difficulty): D.C.
Right, Square (2), Triangle, X

Outlaw 3 (Cream Puff Difficulty): Hangar 18
L2, Left, Triangle, Start, Select

Outlaw 3 (Cream Puff Difficulty): North Pole
R1, Square, Right, Down, Up

Outlaw 3 (Cream Puff Difficulty): London
X, Left, X, L1, L2

Outlaw 3 (Cream Puff Difficulty): Tokyo
X, Left, Circle, Triangle, Start

Outlaw 3 (Cream Puff Difficulty): Egypt
Up, Down, Select, Square, Left

Outlaw 3 (Cream Puff Difficulty): Blimp
Left, X, L1, Up, Start

Roadkill (Cream Puff Difficulty): D.C.
Circle, X, Triangle, R1 (2)

Roadkill (Cream Puff Difficulty): Hangar 18
Select, Right (2), Square (2)

Roadkill (Cream Puff Difficulty): North Pole
Start, Circle, Square, Start, Select

Roadkill (Cream Puff Difficulty): London
Down, Right, R2, Down (2)

Roadkill (Cream Puff Difficulty): Tokyo
L2, Circle, R2, L1 (2)

Roadkill (Cream Puff Difficulty): Egypt
R1, Right, L1, Circle, X

Roadkill (Cream Puff Difficulty): Blimp
X, Circle, Start, Select, Up

Spectre (Cream Puff Difficulty): D.C.
Up, Triangle, Down, Left, L1

Spectre (Cream Puff Difficulty): Hangar 18
Left, Up, Square, R1, X

Spectre (Cream Puff Difficulty): North Pole
L1, Triangle, L2, X, L2

Spectre (Cream Puff Difficulty): London
Circle, Up, Right, Circle, Start

Spectre (Cream Puff Difficulty): Tokyo
Select, R1 (2), Right, R2

Spectre (Cream Puff Difficulty): Egypt
Select (2), Up, R2, Circle

Spectre (Cream Puff Difficulty): Blimp
Down, R1, Circle, Triangle (2)

Sweet Tooth (Cream Puff Difficulty): D.C.
R1 (2), Square, Start, L2

Sweet Tooth (Cream Puff Difficulty): Hangar 18
X, R2, Left, Triangle, R1

Sweet Tooth (Cream Puff Difficulty): North Pole
L1 (2), Select (3)

Sweet Tooth (Cream Puff Difficulty): London
Up, R1, X, Up, Right

Sweet Tooth (Cream Puff Difficulty): Tokyo
Left, L1, Up, L2, L1

Sweet Tooth (Cream Puff Difficulty): Egypt
L1, X, Right, Triangle, Select

Sweet Tooth (Cream Puff Difficulty): Blimp
Circle, R2, Left, L2, Select

Thumper (Cream Puff Difficulty): D.C.
Start, R2 (2), Square, Left

Thumper (Cream Puff Difficulty): Hangar 18
Down, Start, R1, Up (2)

Thumper (Cream Puff Difficulty): North Pole
R2 (2), Triangle, Down, Square

Thumper (Cream Puff Difficulty): London
Triangle, Right, L1, Start, X

Thumper (Cream Puff Difficulty): Tokyo
Square, L2, X, Circle, Left

Thumper (Cream Puff Difficulty): Egypt
Select, Left, Select, L1, L2

Thumper (Cream Puff Difficulty): Blimp
Up, L2, Select, Up, X

Warthog (Cream Puff Difficulty): D.C.
L1, L2, Start, R1, Down

Warthog (Cream Puff Difficulty): Hangar 18
Circle, Square, Triangle, X, L1

Warthog (Cream Puff Difficulty): North Pole
Select, Left, Right, X, L1

Warthog (Cream Puff Difficulty): London
Start, Square, X, Right, Down

Warthog (Cream Puff Difficulty): Tokyo
Down, Left, L2, R2, Right

Warthog (Cream Puff Difficulty): Egypt
R2, Square, Triangle, R2, Select

Warthog (Cream Puff Difficulty): Blimp
Triangle, Down, L1, Select, Circle

Auger (Twisted Metal Difficulty): D.C.
X, Start, Left (2), L2

Auger (Twisted Metal Difficulty): Hangar 18
Up, Down, Triangle, L1, R1

Auger (Twisted Metal Difficulty): North Pole
Left, X, Right, X, Square

Auger (Twisted Metal Difficulty): London
L1, Right, X, Start, Left

Auger (Twisted Metal Difficulty): Tokyo
Circle (2), Left, Right, Left

Auger (Twisted Metal Difficulty): Egypt
Select, Right, L2, L1 (2)

Auger (Twisted Metal Difficulty): Blimp
Circle, L1, Triangle, X, Down

Axel (Twisted Metal Difficulty): D.C.
L2, Triangle (2), Square, Start

Axel (Twisted Metal Difficulty): Hangar 18
R1, Up, Down (2), L1

Axel (Twisted Metal Difficulty): North Pole
X, Triangle, Square, R2, X

Axel (Twisted Metal Difficulty): London
Up, L2, Circle, Square, L1

Axel (Twisted Metal Difficulty): Tokyo
Up, Triangle, Select, Right, Up

Axel (Twisted Metal Difficulty): Egypt
Left, Up, L1, Up, R2

Axel (Twisted Metal Difficulty): Blimp
L1, R1, Up, Left, Circle

Club Kid (Twisted Metal Difficulty): D.C.
Select, R1, Down, X, Right

Club Kid (Twisted Metal Difficulty): Hangar 18
Start (2), Select, R2, X

Club Kid (Twisted Metal Difficulty): North Pole
Right, R1, L2, Right, Triangle

Club Kid (Twisted Metal Difficulty): London
Select, Up, Circle, R1, Up

Club Kid (Twisted Metal Difficulty): Tokyo
R1, L1, R1, Triangle, Up

Club Kid (Twisted Metal Difficulty): Egypt
X, Up, Select, L2, L1

Club Kid (Twisted Metal Difficulty): Blimp
L1, Circle, Start, Triangle, Left

Firestarter (Twisted Metal Difficulty): D.C.
Left, R2, Square, L1, Up

Firestarter (Twisted Metal Difficulty): Hangar 18
L1, R2, X, Left, Down

Firestarter (Twisted Metal Difficulty): North Pole
Circle, R2, R1 (2), R2

Firestarter (Twisted Metal Difficulty): London
Select, R1, Right, Square, Select

Firestarter (Twisted Metal Difficulty): Tokyo
Start, R2, Right, L2, Start

Firestarter (Twisted Metal Difficulty): Egypt
Down, Select, X, Triangle, Left

Firestarter (Twisted Metal Difficulty): Blimp
L2 (2), Left, Square, R1

Flower Power (Twisted Metal Difficulty): D.C.
X, L2, R2, Down, R2

Flower Power (Twisted Metal Difficulty): Hangar 18
Select, Start, L1, Down, X

Flower Power (Twisted Metal Difficulty): North Pole
Up, L2, Triangle, Circle, L1

Flower Power (Twisted Metal Difficulty): London
Left, Square, Right, X, L2

Flower Power (Twisted Metal Difficulty): Tokyo
L1, Left, X, Up, Circle

Flower Power (Twisted Metal Difficulty): Egypt
Circle, Square, Left, L2, Down

Flower Power (Twisted Metal Difficulty): Blimp
Select, Left, R1, R2, Left

Hammerhead (Twisted Metal Difficulty): D.C.
Circle, Right, Circle, X, Select

Hammerhead (Twisted Metal Difficulty): Hangar 18
Select, Circle, Down, Up, Square

Hammerhead (Twisted Metal Difficulty): North Pole
Start, Up, Square, Right, L2

Hammerhead (Twisted Metal Difficulty): London
Down, Triangle, L2, R2, R1

Hammerhead (Twisted Metal Difficulty): Tokyo
R2, Up, Triangle, Square, X

Hammerhead (Twisted Metal Difficulty): Egypt
Triangle (2), R1, Select, Start

Hammerhead (Twisted Metal Difficulty): Blimp
Square, Up (2), Start, Left

Minion (Twisted Metal Difficulty): D.C.
Up, Start, Down, L1, Square

Minion (Twisted Metal Difficulty): Hangar 18
Left, R1, Select, Circle, Left

Minion (Twisted Metal Difficulty): North Pole
L1, Start, R2, Down, Triangle

Minion (Twisted Metal Difficulty): London
Circle, R1, Up, L1, R2

Minion (Twisted Metal Difficulty): Tokyo
Select, Start, R1, L2, Up

Minion (Twisted Metal Difficulty): Egypt
Start, L1, Right, R1 (2)

Minion (Twisted Metal Difficulty): Blimp
Down, X, Square, Down, Select

Mr. Grimm (Twisted Metal Difficulty): D.C.
Down (2), Start, R2, Circle

Mr. Grimm (Twisted Metal Difficulty): Hangar 18
R2, X, Triangle, Down, Right

Mr. Grimm (Twisted Metal Difficulty): North Pole
Triangle, Down, Right, R2 (2)

Mr. Grimm (Twisted Metal Difficulty): London
X (2), Square, Circle (2)

Mr. Grimm (Twisted Metal Difficulty): Tokyo
Down, L2, Select (2), Right

Mr. Grimm (Twisted Metal Difficulty): Egypt
Up, Circle, Up (2), L1

Mr. Grimm (Twisted Metal Difficulty): Blimp
Left, Right, L1, Left, L2

Outlaw 3 (Twisted Metal Difficulty): D.C.
Triangle, Select, Down, Circle, L1

Outlaw 3 (Twisted Metal Difficulty): Hangar 18
Square, L1, R2 (2), Square

Outlaw 3 (Twisted Metal Difficulty): North Pole
Start, Circle, Right, Up, L2

Outlaw 3 (Twisted Metal Difficulty): London
Up, R2, Triangle, Select, R2

Outlaw 3 (Twisted Metal Difficulty): Tokyo
Left, Right, Up, Circle, X

Outlaw 3 (Twisted Metal Difficulty): Egypt
L1, R2, X, Left, Start

Outlaw 3 (Twisted Metal Difficulty): Blimp
Circle, Left, R1, Up, L2

Roadkill (Twisted Metal Difficulty): D.C.
Start, Select, L1, Triangle, L2

Roadkill (Twisted Metal Difficulty): Hangar 18
Down, L2, Start, Right, Select

Roadkill (Twisted Metal Difficulty): North Pole
R2, Select, Triangle, R2, Up

Roadkill (Twisted Metal Difficulty): London
Triangle, L2, Right, Triangle, L2

Roadkill (Twisted Metal Difficulty): Tokyo
Square, Select, Square, Select, Triangle

Roadkill (Twisted Metal Difficulty): Egypt
Left, L2, Start, Square, R1

Roadkill (Twisted Metal Difficulty): Blimp
Right, Square, Left, Start, Select

Spectre (Twisted Metal Difficulty): D.C.
L1, Square, Up, X, R1

Spectre (Twisted Metal Difficulty): Hangar 18
Circle, Left, Circle, Square (2)

Spectre (Twisted Metal Difficulty): North Pole
Select, X, Down, Right, Start

Spectre (Twisted Metal Difficulty): London
Start, Down, Square, L2, Down

Spectre (Twisted Metal Difficulty): Tokyo
Down, X, L2, Triangle, L1

Spectre (Twisted Metal Difficulty): Egypt
R2, Down, Square, X, Up

Spectre (Twisted Metal Difficulty): Blimp
Triangle, X, R1, Start, R2

Sweet Tooth (Twisted Metal Difficulty): D.C.
Circle (2), L1 (2), Start

Sweet Tooth (Twisted Metal Difficulty): Hangar 18
Right (2), Down, Circle, X

Sweet Tooth (Twisted Metal Difficulty): North Pole
L2, Circle, Select, Circle, L2

Sweet Tooth (Twisted Metal Difficulty): London
R1, Right, R2, Up, Right

Sweet Tooth (Twisted Metal Difficulty): Tokyo
Circle, Up, L2, R2, Left

Sweet Tooth (Twisted Metal Difficulty): Egypt
Select, Up, R1 (2), Circle

Sweet Tooth (Twisted Metal Difficulty): Blimp
Start, Triangle, Up, Square, L2

Thumper (Twisted Metal Difficulty): D.C.
R2, Triangle, Left, Down, L2

Thumper (Twisted Metal Difficulty): Hangar 18
Triangle, Up, Select, R2, Triangle

Thumper (Twisted Metal Difficulty): North Pole
Square, R1, R2, Circle, Select

Thumper (Twisted Metal Difficulty): London
Start (2), Select, Up, L1

Thumper (Twisted Metal Difficulty): Tokyo
Right, R1, Triangle, Up, L2

Thumper (Twisted Metal Difficulty): Egypt
L2, Start, Right, Left, Triangle

Thumper (Twisted Metal Difficulty): Blimp
R1 (2), X, L1, Select

Warthog (Twisted Metal Difficulty): D.C.
Select, L1, Left, Start, Left

Warthog (Twisted Metal Difficulty): Hangar 18
Start, L1, Right, R1, L2

Warthog (Twisted Metal Difficulty): North Pole
Down, L1, Start, L2, Square

Warthog (Twisted Metal Difficulty): London
R2, Triangle (2), Start, Left

Warthog (Twisted Metal Difficulty): Tokyo
Triangle, R2, Right, Left

Warthog (Twisted Metal Difficulty): Egypt
Square (2), Start, L1, Triangle

Warthog (Twisted Metal Difficulty): Blimp
R2, L2, Down, X, Left

Auger (Pure Lunacy Difficulty): D.C.
Left, Select, Circle, R2, Up

Auger (Pure Lunacy Difficulty): Hangar 18
L1, L2, L1, Triangle, R2

Auger (Pure Lunacy Difficulty): North Pole
Circle, Select, Start, Up, Select

Auger (Pure Lunacy Difficulty): London
Select, L2, Triangle, L2, Up

Auger (Pure Lunacy Difficulty): Tokyo
Start, Select, Right, R1, L2

Auger (Pure Lunacy Difficulty): Egypt
Down, L2, X, Square, Triangle

Auger (Pure Lunacy Difficulty): Blimp
R2, Square, L2, Select, Start

Axel (Pure Lunacy Difficulty): D.C.
Square (2), L1, R2, Left

Axel (Pure Lunacy Difficulty): Hangar 18
Left, Start, Triangle, R1, Square

Axel (Pure Lunacy Difficulty): North Pole
Up, Square, Triangle, Select, Square

Axel (Pure Lunacy Difficulty): London
Left (2), Down, Start (2)

Axel (Pure Lunacy Difficulty): Tokyo
L1, X, Square, Left (2)

Axel (Pure Lunacy Difficulty): Egypt
Circle, Down, L2, L1, R1

Axel (Pure Lunacy Difficulty): Blimp
Select, X (3), R1

Club Kid (Pure Lunacy Difficulty): D.C.
Down, X, Up, Right, Down

Club Kid (Pure Lunacy Difficulty): Hangar 18
R2, Right, Circle, L2, L1

Club Kid (Pure Lunacy Difficulty): North Pole
Triangle, Circle, Down, Triangle, X

Club Kid (Pure Lunacy Difficulty): London
Square, Right, Square (2), Up

Club Kid (Pure Lunacy Difficulty): Tokyo
Circle, R2, Start, Right, R2

Club Kid (Pure Lunacy Difficulty): Egypt
Right (2), Down, R2, X

Club Kid (Pure Lunacy Difficulty): Blimp
Left, Triangle, R1, L1, Circle

Firestarter (Pure Lunacy Difficulty): D.C.
Circle, Triangle, Circle, Right, Circle

Firestarter (Pure Lunacy Difficulty): Hangar 18
Select, Up, Left, Up, R2

Firestarter (Pure Lunacy Difficulty): North Pole
Start, Triangle, Select, L2, Circle

Firestarter (Pure Lunacy Difficulty): London
Down, Start, R2, R1, Select

Firestarter (Pure Lunacy Difficulty): Tokyo
R2, R1, Square, Up, Square

Firestarter (Pure Lunacy Difficulty): Egypt
Triangle, Start, R1, L2, Down

Firestarter (Pure Lunacy Difficulty): Blimp
Square, R1, Right, Down, Triangle

Flower Power (Pure Lunacy Difficulty): D.C.
Right, R1, Left, Circle, Up

Flower Power (Pure Lunacy Difficulty): Hangar 18
L2, Select (2), Left, L1

Flower Power (Pure Lunacy Difficulty): North Pole
L1 (3), Up, R1

Flower Power (Pure Lunacy Difficulty): London
Circle, Start, Left, Square, Up

Flower Power (Pure Lunacy Difficulty): Tokyo
Select, L1, Triangle, R1, Start

Flower Power (Pure Lunacy Difficulty): Egypt
Start, Right, X, Left, X

Flower Power (Pure Lunacy Difficulty): Blimp
Down, R2, X, R1, Up

Hammerhead (Pure Lunacy Difficulty): D.C.
Start, Left, L1, Right, Down

Hammerhead (Pure Lunacy Difficulty): Hangar 18
Down, Square, Up, L2, Right

Hammerhead (Pure Lunacy Difficulty): North Pole
R2, Left, Circle, Triangle, R2

Hammerhead (Pure Lunacy Difficulty): London
Triangle, Square, Down, Square, Circle

Hammerhead (Pure Lunacy Difficulty): Tokyo
Square, Left, Square, Start, L1

Hammerhead (Pure Lunacy Difficulty): Egypt
Square, R2, Down, Up, Square

Hammerhead (Pure Lunacy Difficulty): Blimp
Right, Down, L1, L2, Up

Minion (Pure Lunacy Difficulty): D.C.
R1, Down, Up, Select (2)

Minion (Pure Lunacy Difficulty): Hangar 18
X (2), Circle, Up (2)

Minion (Pure Lunacy Difficulty): North Pole
Down, Left (2), L2 (2)

Minion (Pure Lunacy Difficulty): London
Start, Circle, Select, R1 (2)

Minion (Pure Lunacy Difficulty): Tokyo
Down, Right, R2, X, Square

Minion (Pure Lunacy Difficulty): Egypt
R2, Circle, Start, Left, X

Minion (Pure Lunacy Difficulty): Blimp
Triangle, Right, R1, Right, Left

Mr. Grimm (Pure Lunacy Difficulty): D.C.
Triangle, R2 (2), X (2)

Mr. Grimm (Pure Lunacy Difficulty): Hangar 18
Square, L1, Triangle, Down, Start

Mr. Grimm (Pure Lunacy Difficulty): North Pole
R2, Start, Select, L1, L2

Mr. Grimm (Pure Lunacy Difficulty): London
Right, Select, Triangle, Start, X

Mr. Grimm (Pure Lunacy Difficulty): Tokyo
L2 (2), Down, Left, X

Mr. Grimm (Pure Lunacy Difficulty): Egypt
R1, Select, Square, L1, Down

Mr. Grimm (Pure Lunacy Difficulty): Blimp
Circle, L2 (2), X, R2

Outlaw 3 (Pure Lunacy Difficulty): D.C.
Up, X, Triangle, Square, Down

Outlaw 3 (Pure Lunacy Difficulty): Hangar 18
Right, Triangle, Left, Select, Start

Outlaw 3 (Pure Lunacy Difficulty): North Pole
L2, Up, Select, Start, Down

Outlaw 3 (Pure Lunacy Difficulty): London
R1, Triangle, L1, Left, L1

Outlaw 3 (Pure Lunacy Difficulty): Tokyo
X, Up, Start, L1, X

Outlaw 3 (Pure Lunacy Difficulty): Egypt
R1, Triangle, X, Square, X

Outlaw 3 (Pure Lunacy Difficulty): Blimp
Up, Start, Right, Down, Up

Roadkill (Pure Lunacy Difficulty): D.C.
R2, Start, L2 (2), Circle

Roadkill (Pure Lunacy Difficulty): Hangar 18
Triangle, R1, Triangle, Up, X

Roadkill (Pure Lunacy Difficulty): North Pole
Square, Start, L1, Square, Right

Roadkill (Pure Lunacy Difficulty): London
L1, Start (2), R2, X

Roadkill (Pure Lunacy Difficulty): Tokyo
Right, Triangle, Down, Circle, Start

Roadkill (Pure Lunacy Difficulty): Egypt
L2, L1, Down, L1, L2

Roadkill (Pure Lunacy Difficulty): Blimp
R1, Square, Circle, Right, Circle

Spectre (Pure Lunacy Difficulty): D.C.
Up, Triangle, Left, Circle, Up

Spectre (Pure Lunacy Difficulty): Hangar 18
Up, R2, L1, L2, Select

Spectre (Pure Lunacy Difficulty): North Pole
Left, Up, R1, Up, Circle

Spectre (Pure Lunacy Difficulty): London
L2, R2, Circle, Square, L2

Spectre (Pure Lunacy Difficulty): Tokyo
Triangle, Down, Triangle, R1, Circle

Spectre (Pure Lunacy Difficulty): Egypt
Square, L2, Square, Down, Square

Spectre (Pure Lunacy Difficulty): Blimp
Select, R2 (2), Start, Right

Sweet Tooth (Pure Lunacy Difficulty): D.C.
L2, Select, R1, Select, R1

Sweet Tooth (Pure Lunacy Difficulty): Hangar 18
R1, L1, Up (2), Square

Sweet Tooth (Pure Lunacy Difficulty): North Pole
X, Square, Circle, Left, Start

Sweet Tooth (Pure Lunacy Difficulty): London
Left (2), R1, Left, X

Sweet Tooth (Pure Lunacy Difficulty): Tokyo
Up, Square, Select, X, L1

Sweet Tooth (Pure Lunacy Difficulty): Egypt
Left (2), R2, X, L2

Sweet Tooth (Pure Lunacy Difficulty): Blimp
L1, Square, Right, Circle (2)

Thumper (Pure Lunacy Difficulty): D.C.
Square, X, Right, Triangle, L1

Thumper (Pure Lunacy Difficulty): Hangar 18
Down, X, Select, X, Triangle

Thumper (Pure Lunacy Difficulty): North Pole
Right, X, Left, Start, Circle

Thumper (Pure Lunacy Difficulty): London
L2, Down, Select, Left, Right

Thumper (Pure Lunacy Difficulty): Tokyo
R1, X, R2, L1, R2

Thumper (Pure Lunacy Difficulty): Egypt
X, Right, Start, Circle (2)

Thumper (Pure Lunacy Difficulty): Blimp
Circle Triangle, Right, Circle, Square

Warthog (Pure Lunacy Difficulty): D.C.
Left, Circle, X, L2, R2

Warthog (Pure Lunacy Difficulty): Hangar 18
L1, Right, L2, R1, Triangle

Warthog (Pure Lunacy Difficulty): North Pole
Circle, Triangle, Square, Select, L1

Warthog (Pure Lunacy Difficulty): London
Select, Up, L1, Up, Square

Warthog (Pure Lunacy Difficulty): Tokyo
Triangle, Start, Down, L2, Up

Warthog (Pure Lunacy Difficulty): Egypt
Right, Up, Triangle, R2, Triangle

Warthog (Pure Lunacy Difficulty): Blimp
L2, Triangle, Down, Circle, Select

TWISTED METAL 4

God Mode
As a password, enter Down, Left, L1, Left, Right. Laughter confirms correct entry.

More Powerful Specials
As a password, enter Up, Start, Circle, R1, Left. Laughter confirms correct entry.

Infinite Specials
As a password, enter Triangle, L1, Down, Triangle, Up. Laughter confirms correct entry.

Faster Weapons
As a password, enter R1, L1, Down, Start, Down. Laughter confirms correct entry.

Faster Health Regeneration
As a password, enter Triangle, L1, Down, Triangle, Up. Laughter confirms correct entry.

No Traction
As a password, enter Down, Triangle, Down, L1, R1. Laughter confirms correct entry.

No Health and Weapon Pick-Ups
As a password, enter Circle, Start, Left, L1, Start. Laughter confirms correct entry.

Infinite Ammo
As a password, enter L1, R1, Up, Square, Circle. Laughter confirms correct entry.

One CPU Ally Vs. Two Human Opponents
As a password, enter Down (2), Right (2), Down. Laughter confirms correct entry.

Harder CPU
As a password, enter Right, Triangle, Right, Triangle, L1. Laughter confirms correct entry.

CPU Ignores Health
As a password, enter L1, Left, Right, Circle, Right. Laughter confirms correct entry.

All Power-Ups Are Homing Missiles
As a password, enter R1, Right, Left, R1, Up. Laughter confirms correct entry.

All Power-Ups Are Remote Bombs
As a password, enter Up, Right, Down, L1, Triangle. Laughter confirms correct entry.

All Power-Ups Are Power Missiles
As a password, enter Down (2), Circle, L1, Left. Laughter confirms correct entry.

All Power-Ups Are Napalms
As a password, enter Right, Left, R1, Right, Circle. Laughter confirms correct entry.

No Health in All Modes
As a password, enter Down, R1, Down, Start. Laughter confirms correct entry.

No Health in Deathmatch Mode
As a password, enter Triangle, Down, Triangle, Circle, Triangle. Laughter confirms correct entry.

No Health in Tournament and Deathmatch Mode
As a password, enter Down, R1, Down, Start, Circle. Laughter confirms correct entry.

Play as Crusher
As a password, enter Down, R1, Right, R1, L1. Laughter confirms correct entry.

Play as Minion
As a password, enter Triangle, L1 (2), Left, Up. Laughter confirms correct entry.

Play as Moon Buggy
As a password, enter Start, Triangle, Right, L1, Start. Laughter confirms correct entry.

Play as RC Car
As a password, enter Up, Down, Left, Start, Right. Laughter confirms correct entry.

Play as Super Auger
As a password, enter Left, Circle, Triangle, Right, Down. Laughter confirms correct entry.

Play as Super Axel
As a password, enter Up, Right, Down, Up, L1. Laughter confirms correct entry.

Play as Super Slamm
As a password, enter Right, L1, Start, Circle, Start. Laughter confirms correct entry.

Play as Super Thumper
As a password, enter Circle, Triangle, Start, Circle, Left. Laughter confirms correct entry.

Play as Sweet Tooth
As a password, enter Start, R1, Right (2), Left. Laughter confirms correct entry.

Freeze Move
Press Left, Right, Up (2) during gameplay.

Rear Freeze Move
Press Left, Right, Down (2) during gameplay.

Hyperspace Move
Press Up (2), Down (2) during gameplay.

Massive Attack Move
Press Up, Down, Up, Down, Up during gameplay.

Rear Massive Attack Move
Press Up, Down, Up, Down (2) during gameplay.

Rear Attack Move
Press Right, Left, Down (2) during gameplay.

Jump Move
Press Up (2), Left during gameplay.

Shield
Press Up (2), Right during gameplay.

Invisibility
Press Down (2), Up (2) during gameplay.

Level 2: Neon City Password
Left, Triangle, Right (2), Left

Level 3: Road Rage Password
Start (2), Down, Circle, L1

Level 4: Bedroom Password
L1, Right, Left (2), L1

Level 5: Amazonia 3000 B.C. Password
Circle, L1, Start, L1, Start

Level 6: The Oil Rig Password
Start, Left, Up, Start, Circle

Level 7: Minion's Maze Password
Start, R1, Left, R1 (2)

Level 8: The Carnival Password
Circle, Left, Down, R1, L1

UEFA CHAMPIONS LEAGUE

Play as the Eliminated Teams
Complete the UEFA Champions League scenarios. Go back and start an Exhibition match. Eliminated Teams appears below Qualified Teams at the Team Selection screen.

ULTRAMAN FIGHTING EVOLUTION

Unlock Gomora
Beat Arcade mode.

Unlock Alien Magma
Beat Arcade mode twice.

Unlock Ace Killer
Beat Arcade mode three times.

Unlock Zetton
Beat Arcade mode four times.

UM JAMMER LAMMY

Bonus Parappa Levels
Beat the game, then return to the Level Selection screen. Press Right until the bonus Parappa levels appear.

Lammy and Parappa Two-Player Levels
Beat all of the bonus Parappa levels.

Special Menu
Beat all the game levels plus the Lammy and Parappa levels to unlock the "Special" option at the title screen.

Customized Lyrics and Notes
Load the game and immediately reset the PlayStation when Lammy appears at the title screen. After reloading the game, a new menu appears next to Lammy's guitar at the title screen.

THE UNHOLY WAR
Unlock All Characters
Enter Mayhem mode and make both teams have all players. Highlight the "Set Teams" option and press Circle+Square, Select (4), Start (3), Square (2), Circle, Circle+Square.

Unlock All One-Player Maps
Enter Strategy mode and highlight the "Set War" option. Press Circle+Square, Select (4), Start (3), Square(2), Circle, Circle+Square.

Unlock Secret Battlefields
Enter Mayhem mode and highlight the "Accept Teams" option. Press Circle+Square, Select (4), Start (3), Square (2), Circle, Circle+Square.

Unlock Super-Prana Devil
Defeat the game with the Arcanes at Hard difficulty.

Unlock Beta Razor
Defeat the game with the Teknos at Hard difficulty. Beta Razor becomes available under Mayhem mode.

Unlock The Maze
Beat the game with the Arcanes at Normal difficulty.

Unlock Menhir Circle
Beat the game with the Teknos at Normal difficulty.

UPRISING X
All Weapons
Enter Right, Circle, Left, Square, Down, Triangle, Down, X as a password.

Bonus Options
Get to level 16. Return to the title screen menu. Two more options become available. Pick the bottom option to display a Hidden Option screen.

Level 2 Password
Left (2), Up, Triangle (2), X, Square, Circle

Level 3 Password
Down (2), Square, Triangle, Down, Triangle, Down, Triangle

Level 4 Password
Circle (3), X (2), Down, X, Circle

Level 5 Password
Right (2), Triangle, Square, Triangle, Left, Right, Triangle

Level 6 Password
Up, Down, Triangle, Square, X, Circle, Left (2)

Level 7 Password
Triangle, Square, Left (2), Right, Up, Down, Circle

Level 8 Password
Triangle (2), Square, Circle, Up (2), Square, Circle

Level 9 Password
Left (2), Right, Up (2), Square (2), Circle

Level 10 Password
X (2), Left, X, Square (2), Triangle, X

Level 11 Password
Square, Triangle (2), Square, Up (2), Right, Up

Level 12 Password
Down (2), Right, Square, X (2), Square, X

URBAN CHAOS
Level Select
Hold R1+L1+Start+Select at the title screen.

Refill Energy and All Weapons
Hold Triangle+Circle+Square+X and press Right during gameplay.

V-FORCE
Secret Options
When you reach level 16, return to the title screen menu to find two new options. The bottom option shows you a Secret Option screen, which allows you to view the FMV sequences, listen to background music, display character biographies, and read the story line.

V2000
Cheat Mode
During gameplay, hold R1 and press Left (2), Square, Circle, R2, Right, Triangle, L2. A sound confirms correct entry. Look for the Cheat option at the bottom of the Options menu.

VAMPIRE: KYUUKETSUKI DENSETSU
Alternate Character/PocketStation Minigame
Keep 80 or more impression points with all the female characters in Stage 3 and restart the game after completion to play as an alternate character or download a minigame to a PocketStation.

VAMPIRE SAVIOR EX EDITION
Play as Dark Gallon
Highlight Gallon at the Character Selection screen. Hold Select and press two punch buttons at the same time.

Play as Marionette
Highlight the "?" at the Character Selection screen. Press Select (7), holding Select the seventh time. Then press any button to select a character and you'll play as Marionette.

Play as Shadow
Highlight the "?" at the Character Selection screen. Press Select (5), holding Select the fifth time. Then press any button to select a character and you'll play as Shadow.

Play as Hanya or Oboro Bishamon
Highlight Bishamon at the Character Selection screen. Hold Select and press two punches or kicks. Or hold L2 and press a punch or kick.

Unlocking Bonus Options
Edit a character in the Original Character mode. Keep playing 1P Battle to gain experience. Once you earn enough experience, you unlock the DX and EX options and images.

VANARK
Invincibility
At the Start Up Engine screen, hold L1+R2+Select+Triangle.

VANDAL HEARTS 2
Advanced Mode
This code, revealed at the end of the game, makes the game much harder. On the Press Start loading screen, quickly press Up (2), Down (2), Left, Right, Left, Right, L1, R1 on controller two. "Advanced Mode" appears onscreen.

VICTORY BOXING
Access Jack-in-the-Box Boxer
In Open Style mode, fight until you are champion.

Access Snake
Defend the Open Style championship title five times.

Access Kiki, Mimi, Roboxer
In Peek-a-Boo mode, fight until you are champion.

Access Edward King and Carrie
Defend the Peek-a-Boo championship title five times.

VICTORY BOXING 2
Change Attributes
During gameplay, press Start+Select.

Automatic Win
While choosing whom to fight in Championship mode, press L1+L2+R1+R2 and then press X on the character you want to fight. "Loading" appears on the screen's bottom right if you entered the code correctly. You go to the Stats screen and have an automatic win.

VIEWPOINT
Skip Level's FMV Sequence
Pause the game and press Square, Circle, Triangle, Right, Down, R1, L2, R2, R1.

Invincibility
During gameplay, pause and press Square (2), Circle (2), Triangle, X, Square, Up (2), Down (2), L1, R1, and Select.

View End of Game Sequence
During gameplay, pause and press Square, Circle, Triangle, Right, Left, Down, R1, L2, R2, R1.

Level 1, Area 2 Code
CLL

Level 1, Area 3 Code
CRR

Level 2, Area 1 Code
FGD

Level 2, Area 2 Code
FLJ

Level 2, Area 3 Code
FRN

Level 3, Area 1 Code
HGD

Level 3, Area 2 Code
HLG

Level 3, Area 3 Code
HRL

Level 4, Area 1 Code
KGG

Level 4, Area 2 Code
KLD

Level 4, Area 3 Code
KRJ

Level 5, Area 1 Code
MGJ

Level 5, Area 2 Code
MLD

Level 6, Area 1 Code
PGL

Level 6, Area 2 Code
PLG

Level 6, Area 3 Code
PRD

VIGILANTE 8

Access Passcode
At the Options menu, select "Game Status," highlight any driver, and press Circle. Now you can enter any of the following codes

All Vehicles and Levels
Access passcode and enter WMNNWLHTSCUCLH. This also unlocks all hidden characters, including "Y" the Alien.

Invincibility
Access passcode and enter I_WILL_NOT_DIE.

Homing Missile Power-Up
Access passcode and enter DEADLY_MISSILE.

All Characters and Extra Levels
Access passcode and enter GIMMIE_DA_WORKS.

Identical Vehicles in 2P Mode
Access passcode and enter SAME_CHARACTER.

Slow Motion
Access passcode and enter SLOW_MOTION_ON.

Sand Factory and Secret Base Levels
Access passcode and enter SECRET_LOCALES.

Unlock Secret Cars
Move the cursor to "Controller Select" in the Options screen. Press Up (2), Down (2), Left (2), Right, Right, X (2), Square (2), Circle (2), Triangle (2) quickly.

Alien Character
Access passcode and enter INVITE_VISITOR.

All Standard Characters
Access passcode and enter GANGS_ALL_HERE.

Monster-Truck Tires
Access passcode and enter MONSTER_WHEELS.

No Enemies
Access passcode and enter GO_SIGHTSEEING.

Low Gravity
Access passcode and enter REDUCE_GRAVITY.

Expert Mode
Access passcode and enter HARDEST_OF_ALL.

Two-Player Mode with Same Vehicles
Access passcode and enter SAME_CHARACTER.

Watch the FMV Sequences
Access passcode and enter SEE_ALL_MOVIES.

Music Change
Once a level has completely finished loading, take out the game CD and replace it with a music CD of your choice. To change music tracks, pause the game. Once the level finishes, you're prompted to put the game CD back in.

Interceptor Missiles
During the game, if you have Halo Decoys in the inventory (though they do not need to be active), press Up (2), then shoot the machine gun. This causes your opponent's missiles or special attacks to lock onto your missiles rather than your vehicle. Requires two Halo Decoys.

Interceptor Missiles II
Requires Turbo and uses two missiles. Press Up (3) and shoot the machine gun. Your vehicle speeds up for a few seconds.

Bull's Eye Rockets
Requires Stampede and uses one through five rockets. Press Up, Down, Up, and then shoot the machine gun. If you hit an enemy, something special happens.

Sky Hammer Mortar
Requires Turtle Turnover and uses two shells. Press Down (3), and shoot the machine gun. This flips opponents' vehicles.

Sky Hammer Mortar II
Requires Crater Maker and uses two shells. Press Down (2), Up, and then shoot the machine gun. This drops a huge bomb, which leaves a crater.

Bruiser Cannon
Requires Cow Puncher and uses two shells. Press Down, Up, Down, and then shoot the machine gun. This pushes opponents' vehicles away.

Bruiser Cannon II
Requires Scatter Blast and uses six shells. Press Down, Up (2), and shoot the machine gun to simultaneously shoot six cannon shells.

Roadkill Mines
Requires Cactus Patch and uses one through six mines. Press Left, Right, Up, and then shoot the machine gun to quickly plant a group of land mines.

Roadkill Mines II
Requires Magnetic Mine and uses two mines. Press Left, Right, Down, and then shoot the machine gun to drop a land mine that pulls nearby vehicles toward it.

Level Password
Chassey Blue 1 AOGIKYFGQQTWGA

Level Password
Chassey Blue 2 YMBEJEOPDHYHZV

Level Password
Chassey Blue 3 RIPJNYEPGFPJAI

Chassey Blue 4 Level Password
HGFTDDNMUBXRLV

Slick Clyde 1 Level Password
TNLCROHSQAZDMQ

Slick Clyde 2 Level Password
QDANNFHMSLBMWF

Slick Clyde 3 Level Password
FYLYRFKEAHGGAW

Slick Clyde 4 Level Password
OIRYEEBGDBNHBJ

Shiela 1 Level Password
EDAOHLJIOUEDBA

Shiela 2 Level Password
HSDNTZSGVOGCLP

Shiela 3 Level Password
NTWZYUQSPXMHMB

Shiela 4 Level Password
BXINCWNWGCQVJF

John Torque 1 Level Password
WSLZFBNQDTFDBF

John Torque 2 Level Password
BXNJRYSXTYACKE

John Torque 3 Level Password
IBXGFDQBSNISJQ

John Torque 4 Level Password
ZCTEAFJVMNDJUT

Dave 1 Level Password
PYQXPDUMJNBOUP

Dave 2 Level Password
OULIUZTJHPKWTD

Dave 3 Level Password
QYDJBUYBZTEUQC

Dave 4 Level Password
WMNNWLHTSCUCLH

Convoy 1 Level Password
AIHJZNIFPZNFWA

Convoy 2 Level Password
UKXCXCOAIGOKVH

Convoy 3 Level Password
KHREIWYIZREYHK

Convoy 4 Level Password
VSNKJVURSUNRWX

Loki 1 Level Password
THLOHJWURONKLQ

Loki 2 Level Password
VIBWYIVGOPAUWX

Loki 3 Level Password
CEJMULWPCYYAVS

Loki 4 Level Password
PGGOVIUNUQEIVU

Houston 3, 1 Level Password
BDPTGXUBXOCCKE

Houston 3, 2 Level Password
GCTPCXCCIWXVUJ

Houston 3, 3 Level Password
CEJMULWPCYYAVS

Houston 3, 4 Level Password
PGGOVIUNUQEIVU

Boogie 1 Level Password
FOJGCRHLWMUQZV

Boogie 2 Level Password
DRFIQVOUYIHGEN

Boogie 3 Level Password
WCHPZDGBCYEDBF

Boogie 4 Level Password
JHAZRUUMTLUYBG

Beezwax 1 Level Password
YUYFNKTAQGLNYW

Beezwax 2 Level Password
TXXKKGEWRONKLQ

Beezwax 3 Level Password
KHUSNNWJXORZHK

Beezwax 4 Level Password
UIBRJCCYSARVH

Molo 1 Level Password
EDDNXIAPNTRDBA

Molo 2 Level Password
ITAHZJRMYTLSJQ

Molo 3 Level Password
NPRJUYRYRAAGMB

Molo 4 Level Password
AKFQPUISMWAHWA

Sid Burn 1 Level Password
LPHPMMDNMPEMVB

Sid Burn 2 Level Password
PEONQGUNUQEIVU

Sid Burn 3 Level Password
XOKIXDXBKQRFOJ

Sid Burn 4 Level Password
OYROHGBDNLSJSI

VIGILANTE 8: SECOND OFFENSE

Password Screen
Enter the Options screen, select "Game Status," then highlight any character and press L1+R1. Then you can enter one of the following passwords.

Super Missiles Password
BLAST_FIRE

Rapid Fire Password
RAPID_FIRE

Quicker Cars Password
MORE_SPEED

Heavier Cars Password
GO_RAMMING

Fast Action Password
QUICK_PLAY

Enemy Magnet Password
UNDER_FIRE

Slow Motion Mode Password
GO_SLOW-MO

Same Cars in Multiplayer Password
MIXED_CARS

Big Wheels Password
GO_MONSTER

No Gravity Password
NO_GRAVITY

High Suspensions Password
JACK_IT_UP

No Wheel Attachment Icons Password
DRIVE_ONLY

All Endings Password
LONG_MOVIE

Invincibility Password
ELBICNIVNI

Get All Characters Password
LLA_KCOLNU

Maximum Stats for All Characters Password
LLA_DORTOH

Light Cars Password
HI_CEILING

Arcade Mode: No Enemies Password
HOME_ALONE

Disable Cheats Password
NO_CODE

Play with Original *Vigilante 8* Levels
During gameplay, pause and insert the original *Vigilante 8* CD. The message "V8 Levels Enabled" appears. Reinsert the *Vigilante 8: Second Offense* CD, quit the game, and you can use the levels from both CDs.

Change Vehicle Color
When selecting a vehicle, use Circle to change colors.

Listen to Alternate Music
During gameplay, pause, take out the *Vigilante 8: Second Offense* CD and replace it with any music CD. Use Pause to switch tracks. When a level ends, you will be prompted to put the V8:SO CD back in.

Bonus Character: Lord Clyde
Complete all the objectives in Quest mode with Nina Loco, Molo, and Dallas 13.

Bonus Character: Obake
Complete all objectives in Quest mode with Lord Clyde.

Bonus Character: Boogie
Complete all objectives in Quest mode with Obake.

Bonus Character: Houston
Complete all objectives in Quest mode with Sheila, John Torque, and the Flying All-Star Trio.

Bonus Character: Convoy
Complete all objectives in Quest mode with Houston.

Bonus Characters: Dave's Cultsmen
Complete all objectives in Quest mode with Convoy.

Bonus Character: Chassey Blue
Complete all objectives in Quest mode with Astronaut Bob O., Garbage Man, and Agent R. Chase.

Bonus Character: Padre Destino
Complete all objectives in Quest mode with Chassey Blue.

Bonus Character: Dusty Earth
Complete all objectives in Quest mode with Padre Destino.

Special Attack: Interceptor Missiles 1
Up (2), Down, Machine Gun

Special Attack: Interceptor Missiles 2
Up (3), Machine Gun

Special Attack: Interceptor Missiles 3
Up (2), Right, Machine Gun

Special Attack: Bull's Eye Rockets 1
Up, Down (2), Machine Gun

Special Attack: Bull's Eye Rockets 2
Up, Down, Up, Machine Gun

Special Attack: Bull's Eye Rockets 3
Up, Down, Right, Machine Gun

Special Attack: Sky Hammer Mortar 1
Down (3), Machine Gun

Special Attack: Sky Hammer Mortar 2
Down (2), Up, Machine Gun

Special Attack: Sky Hammer Mortar 3
Down (2), Right, Machine Gun

Special Attack: Bruiser Cannon 1
Down, Up, Down, Machine Gun

Special Attack: Bruiser Cannon 2
Down, Up (2), Machine Gun

Special Attack: Bruiser Cannon 3
Down, Up, Right, Machine Gun

Special Attack: Roadkill Mines 1
Left, Right, Down, Machine Gun

Special Attack: Roadkill Mines 2
Left, Right, Up, Machine Gun

Special Attack: Roadkill Mines 3
Left, Right, Right, Machine Gun

Special Attack: Brimstone Burner 1
Right, Left, Down, Machine Gun

Special Attack: Brimstone Burner 2
Right, Left, Up, Machine Gun

Special Attack: Brimstone Burner 3
Right, Left, Right, Machine Gun

VIRTUAL GOLF

Extra Hitting Power
Create a new player and name him "Hacker." He hits the ball much farther than normal.

VIRTUAL HIRYU NO KEN

Play as Ryumaou
At the Player Selection screen, hold L2+R2 and press Start.

VIRTUAL POOL

Retry Missed Shot
Hold R1 and press L2.

VMX RACING

Pop a Wheelie
Hold Down+Gas+Brake on a straightaway.

Display Coordinates
During gameplay, press Down, Up, Left, Up, Down, Right, Right, Down, Select.

Gouraud Shaded Circle
During gameplay, press Square (2), X, Triangle, Circle, Square, X, Square, Select.

Paint Trails
During gameplay, press Triangle, X, Triangle, Square (2), Triangle, Circle, X, Select.

Disco Colors
During gameplay, press X, Circle, Square, X (2), Triangle (2), Select.

Random Stunt
Press R1, R2 at the top of a jump. The computer chooses the stunt.

Wave Landscape

During gameplay, press Up, Left, Right, Right, Down, Up, Down, Up, Select.

Techno Music

During gameplay, press Left, Up, Right, Right, Left, Down (2), Right, Select.

View Movies

During gameplay, press Circle, X, Square, Circle, Square, Triangle (2), Circle, Select.

Extra Racetracks

If you do a certain number of tricks during the season, bonus racetracks become available (in this order): Moon, Desert, Figure-8 Supercross.

Trick: Nac Nac

Before a jump, press R2.

Trick: Table-Top

Before a jump, press R1.

Trick: Special Move 1

Before a jump, press R1, R2, R1, R2.

Trick: Special Move 2

Before a jump, press R1 (4).

Trick: Special Move 3

Before a jump, press R2 (4).

VOTOM LIGHTNING SLASH

Get All Parts and Weapons

While the game loads, hold Circle+X+Triangle+Square+Select+Start on controller two until the "Takara" logo appears. Begin a game in Story mode and exchange different items at the factory.

V-RALLY

Access Cheat Mode

When the white Infogrames logo appears, press Up, Down, Triangle+Circle. The words "Lock Off" appear, signifying that the cheat codes lock is off. Quickly press the buttons for one of the following cheats while the Infogrames logo is still visible. If a code is accepted, a message appears onscreen.

Unlimited Time

Access Cheat mode. Hold Left+L1 until you've selected a language.

Narrow Tracks

Access Cheat mode. Hold Left+L2 until you've selected a language.

Roller Coaster Track and Jeep

Access Cheat mode. Hold Left+R1 until you've selected a language.

Restart Race

Access Cheat mode. Hold Left+R2 until you've selected a language.

All Cheats

Access Cheat mode. Hold Left+R1+L1+R2+L2 until you've selected a language.

Debug Mode

When the Infogrames logo appears, press left and then right, followed by Start. This accesses a Memory option, which displays more information.

V-RALLY 2

All Cars and Trophies

At the Game Progress screen, press L1, R1, Left, Right, Left, Right, Up, Down, Up, Down, X, X+Select. A sound confirms correct entry. You can then press X on any car or trophy to unlock it.

Better Acceleration

Use LDN as your driver name.

Fly Coach

Use FLY (with a space before and after) to be able to fly.

Hidden Track 1

Enter CBLC (followed by space) in the name box. Quit and start a new race. Choose your car after entering the code. Pick "Time Trial" from the Game Mode screen. Select "Corsica" and choose any course. You race on a new track.

Hidden Track 2

Enter CBLCA in the name box. Quit and start a new race. Choose your car after entering the code. Pick "Time Trial" from the Game Mode screen. Select "Corsica" and choose any course. You race on a new track.

Hidden Track 3

Enter CBLCB in the name box. Quit and start a new race. Choose your car after entering the code. Pick "Time Trial" from the Game Mode screen. Select "Corsica" and choose any course. You race on a new track.

Hidden Track 4

Enter CBLCC in the name box. Quit and start a new race. Choose your car after entering the code. Pick "Time Trial" from the Game Mode screen. Select "Corsica" and choose any course. You race on a new track.

Hidden Track 5

Enter CBLCD in the name box. Quit and start a new race. Choose your car after entering the code. Pick "Time Trial" from the Game Mode screen. Select "Corsica" and choose any course. You race on a new track.

VR BASEBALL '97

All-Stars

Go to the Options menu and highlight the designated hitter. Press Square, Circle, Square, Circle and then exit the menu. The American League and National League All-Star team players become available.

Bonus Stadium: Field of Dreams

In the Options menu, highlight the Credits option and press Square, Circle, Square, Circle, Triangle. The stadium name turns green and you play in the infamous "Field of Dreams."

Run Outside the Stadium

Play in the King Dome. Have a player run to the right dugout and go to the closest or farthest side of the dugout.

VR GOLF

Longer Drives

Enter "Hacker" as your player's name.

VR POOL

Bonus Players

During gameplay, press R2 (2), L1, Square, Up.

VR POWERBOAT RACING

Champion Mode

Use CUP as a password.

Extra Monohull Boats

Use PLA as a password.

Minnow-Class Catamaran Boats

Use MIN as a password.

Pike-Class Catamaran Boats

Use IKE as a password.

Barracuda-Class Catamaran Boats

Use CUD as a password.

Slalom Level

Use L.R as a password.

Mine Level

Use U.G as a password.

Fast Boats

Go to Challenge mode and enter ZOOOOOM or SPEEEED as your name.

Mini-Boats

In Challenge Mode, use the name COMPACT.

Long Boats

In Challenge Mode, use the name LONGONE.

Big Engines

In Challenge Mode, use the name LARGE.

Automatic Turbo

In Challenge Mode, use the name HELP.ME.

Deformed/Big Head Mode

In Challenge Mode, use the name DEFORM.

VS.

Play as the Bosses

In Challenge mode, beat all gang members, then beat the gang leader (Boss) and save the game. Now you can select that Boss as your character.

Alternate Costumes

Highlight a character and press Start to get a different costume.

V-TENNIS

Hidden Character

Pick a character at the Player Selection screen, then press L2 (2), R1 (3), Down Triangle (4), Circle.

Play as Adversa

At the Player Selection screen, hold L1, R2, Up, Square, X. A bouncing ball sound confirms correct entry.

Play as Mattox

At the Player Selection screen, press L2 (2), R1 (3), Down, Triangle (4), X. A bouncing ball sound confirms correct entry.

Play as Mr. Tonkin

At the Player Selection screen, press L2 (2), R1 (3), Down, Triangle (4), Circle. A shout confirms correct entry.

Play as Mrs. Tonkin

At the Player Selection screen, hold L1+R2+Up+Square and press Circle. A bouncing ball sound confirms correct entry.

WAKU WAKU BOWLING

Level Selection
Choose Party mode, then when selecting a character, hold L2+R2+Select. Go back to the Stage Selection screen and you can choose any level.

WAR GODS

Free Play
At "Cheat Code" on the Options screen, enter 0705 to enable the code. Enter 5070 to disable the code.

Invincibility (Player 1)
At "Cheat Code" on the Options screen, enter 2358 to enable the code. Enter 8532 to disable the code.

Invincibility (Player 2)
At "Cheat Code" on the Options screen, enter 1224 to enable the code. Enter 4221 to disable the code.

Power-Up (Player 1)
At "Cheat Code" on the Options screen, enter 7879 to enable the code. Enter 9787 to disable the code.

Power-Up (Player 2)
At "Cheat Code" on the Options screen, enter 3961 to enable the code. Enter 1693 to disable the code.

Quick Game
At "Cheat Code" on the Options screen, enter 4258 to enable the code. Enter 8524 to disable the code.

Easy Fatalities
At "Cheat Code" on the Options screen, enter 0322 to enable the code. Enter 2230 to disable the code. Press HP+LK to perform the fatality on a defeated opponent.

Fatalities
At "Cheat Code" on the Options screen, enter 7453 to enable the code. Enter 3547 to disable the code.

Play as Grox
At "Cheat Code" on the Options screen, enter 6969 to enable the code. Enter 9696 to disable the code. Only one player may play as Grox.

Play as Exor
At "Cheat Code" on the Options screen, enter 2791 to enable the code. Enter 1972 to disable the code. Only one player may play as Exor.

Level 1 Select
At "Cheat Code" on the Options screen, enter 5550 to enable the code. Enter 5556 to disable the code.

Level 2 Select
At "Cheat Code" on the Options screen, enter 5551 to enable the code. Enter 5556 to disable the code.

Level 3 Select
At "Cheat Code" on the Options screen, enter 5552 to enable the code. Enter 5556 to disable the code.

Level 4 Select
At "Cheat Code" on the Options screen, enter 5553 to enable the code. Enter 5556 to disable the code.

Level 5 Select
At "Cheat Code" on the Options screen, enter 5554 to enable the code. Enter 5556 to disable the code.

Level 6 Select
At "Cheat Code" on the Options screen, enter 5555 to enable the code. Enter 5556 to disable the code.

Level 7 Select
At "Cheat Code" on the Options screen, enter 5557 to enable the code. Enter 5556 to disable the code.

Random Select
Press Up+Start at the Character Selection screen.

WAR GAMES: DEFCON 1

Invincibility
Enter as a password: X, Square, X, Circle, Square (2), Circle, X.

FMV Code
Hold R2, repeatedly press Start before the title screen appears.

Unlock W.O.P.R. Levels
Pick a Two-player W.O.P.R. Co-op mode. Highlight Level 2. Then press Circle, X, Circle (2), X, Circle, X (2), Circle as a password. Go back to the main menu and pick a Single-player W.O.P.R. Co-op mode.

War Games for Player 2
Enter as a password: Circle, Triangle (2), X (2), Triangle (2), Square (2).

Demo Mode
Enter as a password: Square, X, Triangle (2), X, Circle, Square, Circle, X.

Password: Mission 2 (Czech Republic)
Circle, X, Circle / Circle, X (2) / Circle, X, Circle

Password: Mission 3 (Russian Urals)
X (2), Circle / X (3) / X, Circle (2)

Password: Mission 4 (Cairo, Egypt)
Circle, Square, X / Circle (2), Triangle / Circle, X, Square

Password: Mission 5 (Cambodia)
Triangle, X, Circle / Circle, X (2) / Square, Triangle, Circle

Password: Mission 6 (Swiss Alps)
Square, Circle (2) / Square, Circle, X / X, Circle, X

Password: Mission 7 (Libya)
Square, X (2) / X, Circle, Square / Circle, X, Square

Password: Mission 8 (Channel Islands)
Circle (2), X / Square (2), Triangle / Square (2), Circle

Password: Mission 9 (Grenadines)
Square (2), Circle / Triangle, Circle, Triangle / X, Triangle (2)

Password: Mission 10 (Louisiana Bayou)
X, Triangle, Circle / Square, Circle (2) / Circle, X, Square

Password: Mission 11 (China, near Beijing)
Circle, Square, Triangle / X, Square, Triangle / Triangle (2), Square

Password: Mission 12 (Saudi Arabia)
Triangle, Square, Circle / X, Triangle, Circle / Circle, X, Square

Password: Mission 13 (Arctic Circle)
Square (2), Triangle / Square, Triangle, Square / Triangle, X, Triangle

Password: Mission 14 (New York City)
X (2), Circle / Triangle, X, Triangle / Square, X, Square

Password: Mission 15 (Omaha Desert)
Circle, Square, Circle / X, Square, X / Triangle, Circle, X

Password: Mission 2 (Florida Keys)
Circle, X, Circle / Circle, X, Circle / X (2), Circle

Password: Mission 3 (Irian Jaya)
Square, Triangle, X / Triangle, X, Circle / Square, X, Triangle

Password: Mission 4 (New England)
X, Triangle, Circle / X (2), Circle / Circle (2), Triangle

Password: Mission 5 (Russia)
Circle (2), Square / Square, Circle, X / Triangle, X (2)

Password: Mission 6 (Brussels)
X, Circle, X / Triangle (2), Square / Circle, X, Triangle

Password: Password: Mission 7 (South Africa)
Triangle (2), X / X, Square (2) / X (2), Circle

Password: Mission 8 (Hong Kong)
Square, X, Circle / Triangle, X (2) / Square, Circle, Triangle

Password: Mission 9 (Mexico)
Square, Circle, Triangle / Triangle, X, Circle / X (2), Circle

Password: Mission 10 (Bering Strait)
X, Circle, Square / Triangle, Circle, X / Square, X, Triangle

Password: Mission 11 (Kremlin)
Square, Circle, X / Triangle, Square, Triangle / Square, Circle (2)

Password: Mission 12 (Polynesia)
Square, Circle, Triangle / X, Square, Circle / X, Square, Circle

Password: Mission 13 (Congo)
X, Circle, Square / Square (2), X / Circle, X, Circle

Password: Mission 14 (Washington D.C.)
Circle, Triangle, Circle / Circle, Triangle, Square / X, Triangle, Square

Password: Mission 15 (Tokyo)
Triangle, Square, Triangle / Circle, X, Square / Circle (2), Square.

WARCRAFT II: THE DARK SAGA

Access Password Option
During gameplay, press Start, select the "Password" option and enter one of the following codes.

Glittering Resources! (Gain 10,000 Gold, 5,000 Lumber, AND 5,000 Oil)
GLTTRNG

Valdez, Ahoy! (Gain 5,000 Oil)
VLDZ

Gain Invincibility/Boost Units' Strength
TSGDDYTD

Quick Upgrade and Building
MKTS

Gain Full Mana and Access All Spells
VRYLTTL

Upgrade Immediately
DCKMT

Win the Game
THRCNBNLYN

Skip Current Level
NTTHCLNS

Never a Winner
NVRWNNR

Release the Magic Traps
NGLS

See Entire Map
NSCRN

Faster Wood Chopping
HTCHTXNS

Flashing Red Line Background
NTPRF

Lose the Game
YPTFLWRM

Human Level Changing
To get to the following human levels, use these passwords:

Human Level 1 Password
HLLBRD

Human Level 2 Password
MBSHTM

Human Level 3 Password
HSTHSH

Human Level 4 Password
TTCKNZ

Human Level 5 Password
HTLBRD

Human Level 6 Password
DNLGZ

Human Level 7 Password
GRMBTL

Human Level 8 Password
TYRHND

Human Level 9 Password
BTTLTD

Human Level 10 Password
PRSNRS

Human Level 11 Password
BTRYLN

Human Level 12 Password
BTTLTC

Human Level 13 Password
SSLTNB

Human Level 14 Password
GRTPRT

Human Ending Level Password
LLRSJR

Orc Level 1 Password
ZLDR

Orc Level 2 Password
RDTHLL

Orc Level 3 Password
RCSTHS

Orc Level 4 Password
SSLTNH

Orc Level 5 Password
RCTLBR

Orc Level 6 Password
BDLNDS

Orc Level 7 Password
FLLFST

Orc Level 8 Password
RNSTNT

Orc Level 9 Password
RZNGFT

Orc Level 10 Password
DSTRCT

Orc Level 11 Password
DDRSSQ

Orc Level 12 Password
TMBFSR

Orc Level 13 Password
SGFDLR

Orc Level 14 Password
FLLFLR

Orc Ending Level Password
LLRSJR

Human Level 1 Password in "Beyond the Dark Portal"
LLRSJR

Human Level 2 Password in "Beyond the Dark Portal"
BTTLFR

Human Level 3 Password in "Beyond the Dark Portal"
NCMRNT

Human Level 4 Password in "Beyond the Dark Portal"
BYNDTH

Human Level 5 Password in "Beyond the Dark Portal"
SHDWSS

Human Level 6 Password in "Beyond the Dark Portal"
FLLFCH

Human Level 7 Password in "Beyond the Dark Portal"
DTHWNG

Human Level 8 Password in "Beyond the Dark Portal"
CSTFBN

Human Level 9 Password in "Beyond the Dark Portal"
HRTFVL

Human Level 10 Password in "Beyond the Dark Portal"
BTTLFH

Human Level 11 Password in "Beyond the Dark Portal"
DNCFTH

Human Level 12 Password in "Beyond the Dark Portal"
BTTRTS

Orc Level 1 Password in "Beyond the Dark Portal"
SLYRFT

Orc Level 2 Password in "Beyond the Dark Portal"
SKLLFG

Orc Level 3 Password in "Beyond the Dark Portal"
THNDRL

Orc Level 4 Password in "Beyond the Dark Portal"
RFTWKN

Orc Level 5 Password in "Beyond the Dark Portal"
DRGNSF

Orc Level 6 Password in "Beyond the Dark Portal"
NWSTRM

Orc Level 7 Password in "Beyond the Dark Portal"
SSFZRT

Orc Level 8 Password in "Beyond the Dark Portal"
SSLTNK

Orc Level 9 Password in "Beyond the Dark Portal"
DPTMBF

Orc Level 10 Password in "Beyond the Dark Portal"
LTRC

Orc Level 11 Password in "Beyond the Dark Portal"
YFDLRN

Orc Level 12 Password in "Beyond the Dark Portal"
DPDRKP

Introduction Movie
CLMX

"Tides of Darkness" Intro Movie
TDPNNG

"Tides of Darkness" Human II Movie
HKHZMD

"Tides of Darkness" Human III Movie
NRTHLN

"Tides of Darkness" Human IV Movie
RTNTZR

"Tides of Darkness" Human Victory Movie
HTDVCT

"Tides of Darkness" Orc II Movie
RCKHZM

"Tides of Darkness" Orc III Movie
QLTHLS

"Tides of Darkness" Orc IV Movie
TDSFDR

"Tides of Darkness" Orc Victory Movie
RCTDVC

"Beyond the Dark Portal" Intro Movie
DPPNNG

"Beyond the Dark Portal" Human II Movie
DRNRTH

"Beyond the Dark Portal" Human III Movie
HWRNTH

"Beyond the Dark Portal" Human IV Movie
HMSRFV

"Beyond the Dark Portal" Human Victory Movie
HDPVCT

"Beyond the Dark Portal" Orc II Movie
BRNNGF

"Beyond the Dark Portal" Orc III Movie
RCGRTS

"Beyond the Dark Portal" Orc IV Movie
PRLDTN

"Beyond the Dark Portal" Orc Victory Movie
RCDPVC

WARHAMMER: DARK OMEN

Cheats Unlocked
While highlighting the spare book in the caravan, hold Select and press R1, L1, L2, R2.

Skip Battle
At Deployment screen, press Select, R1 (2), L2 (2), R1, R2 then select the "Resume" option.

Mo' Money
At Deployment screen, press Select, R1, L1, R1, L2, R1, R2 then select the "Resume" option.

Tiny Heads
At Deployment screen, press Select, L2 (4), R2, L2, R1 (2) then select the "Resume" option.

Quick Reload
At Deployment screen, press Select, R2, R1, R2, R1, L2, R1 then select the "Resume" option.

Instant Death
At Deployment screen, press Select, R1, L1, R2 (2), R1 (2) then select the "Resume" option.

Chapter Skip
At the main menu, press R2, R1, L2, R2, R1, R2 then select the "Resume" option.

View Credits
At the main menu, press Left, Right, Square, Right, R1, R2.

The Black Grail FMV
At the main menu, press Left, L1, Circle, L2, Triangle, R2.

Carnstein and Jewel FMV
At the main menu, press R1, Triangle, R2 (2), Square, R1.

The Head of Nagash FMV
At the main menu, press R2, Left, R2, Up, Down, Left.

Liber Mortis FMV
At the main menu, press Circle, Triangle, Square, Right, R1, R2.

Victory FMV
At the main menu, press L2, Right, Square, Right, R1, R2.

Long March FMV
At the main menu, press R1, L2, Triangle, Square, Left, R2.

WARHAMMER: SHADOW OF THE HORNED RAT

All Troops
At the Caravan screen, move the hand pointer over the spare book under the pile on the left. Then, hold Select and press R1, L1, L2, R2 to put all units on the troop roster.

Unlimited Magic
At the Caravan screen, move the hand pointer over the magic book. Then, hold Select and press Left, Up, Right, Down, L1, R1. When you cast spells during battle, no points will be deducted.

Free Troops
At the Caravan screen, move the hand pointer over the troop roster. Then, hold Select and press Circle, Triangle, X, Square, Left, Right to have your troops fight at no cost.

WARHAWK

Infinite Weapons and Invincibility
As a password, enter Circle (3), Space, X, Triangle, X (2).

9,999 Flash Bombs
As a password, enter Square, Circle, Square (2), Triangle, X, Triangle (2).

Watch FMVs
As a password, enter Triangle, X, Space, Circle (2), X, Triangle, Square.

Super Swarmers, Ultra-Lockons
As a password, enter X, Circle (2), Square, X, Triangle, Circle, Triangle.

Infinite Weapons
As a password, enter Triangle (2), Circle, Triangle, Square, Triangle (2), X.

Check Special Upgrades Text
As a password, enter Square, Space, Circle, Square, Triangle, X (2), Square.

View Epilogue Text
As a password, enter Square (2), Space, Circle, Square, X, Square, Triangle.

Different Viewpoints
During gameplay, press L1+L2 or R1+R2 to shift the viewpoint.

Face to Face with Kreel
At the Access Code screen, enter Triangle, X, Triangle, Square (3), X, Triangle.

Kreel's Door Is Open
At the Access Code screen, enter Triangle, X, Square, Triangle, Circle, Square, X (2).

Above Third Force Field
At the Access Code screen, enter Triangle, X, Square, Circle, Triangle, X, Triangle, Square.

Above Second Force Field
At the Access Code screen, enter Triangle, X, Triangle (3), X, Circle, Triangle.

Above First Force Field
At the Access Code screen, enter Triangle, X (2), Square, Circle, Square, Circle, X.

Stormland
At the Access Code screen, enter Triangle, X, Triangle, Square, Circle, X, Circle (2).

In with the Gatekeeper
At the Access Code screen, enter Triangle, Circle (2), Triangle (2), X, Square, Triangle.

West Gauntlet Boss
At the Access Code screen, enter Triangle, Circle (2), Square, Triangle, Circle (2), X.

East Gauntlet Boss
At the Access Code screen, enter Triangle, Circle, X, Triangle, Circle, X, Triangle, Square.

Gauntlet Level
At the Access Code screen, enter Triangle, Circle, Triangle, Circle, Triangle, X, Square (2).

Volcano Boss Is Active
At the Access Code screen, enter Square (2), X, Circle, Triangle, Circle, Square, Triangle.

Volcano Level
At the Access Code screen, enter Square, Triangle, X (3), Triangle, Circle, Square.

Airship Rear Hanger Open
At the Access Code screen, enter X, Square, Triangle, Circle, X, Triangle, Square (2).

Post Transformation Airship
At the Access Code screen, enter X, Circle, Triangle (2), Circle (3), X.

Airship Level
At the Access Code screen, enter X, Triangle, X, Square (2), Triangle, Square, Triangle.

Approaching Uma
At the Access Code screen, enter Circle (3), Square, Triangle (2), Square, Triangle.

In Canyon with Crystal
At the Access Code screen, enter Circle, Square, Triangle, Square, Triangle (3), Square.

In Canyon with Belle
At the Access Code screen, enter Circle, Triangle, X, Square, Circle (2), Triangle (2).

In Canyon with Amber
At the Access Code screen, enter Circle, Square, Circle, Square, X, Circle (2), Triangle.

Canyon Level
At the Access Code screen, enter Circle, Triangle (2), X, Circle (2), Square, Circle.

Desert All But Done
At the Access Code screen, enter Triangle, Circle, X, Triangle, Circle (2), X, Square.

Pyramid Has Risen
At the Access Code screen, enter Triangle, Square, X, Triangle, Circle, Square, Circle, X.

Desert Level
At the Access Code screen, enter Triangle, Square, X, Triangle, X (2), Square (2).

WARPATH: JURASSIC PARK

Unlock Six Bonus Characters
Complete Arcade mode on any difficulty setting with each dinosaur. Every following completion unlocks a bonus character.

Survival and Single Mode
Complete Arcade mode on any difficulty setting.

Invulnerability
Complete Survival mode without using any continues.

Unlock Exhibition Mode
Complete Arcade mode on any difficulty setting with eight regular and five bonus characters.

Alternate Appearance
Complete Survival mode to unlock an appearance for the character used. Press Triangle at the Character Selection to change their appearances.

View Extra FMV Video
Complete Arcade mode on any difficulty setting with all 14 characters.

WARZONE 2100

Cheat Mode
Hold Start on controller two, power on the PlayStation, and continue to hold until the main menu appears. Then at the main menu, or while the game is paused, press L1, R1, R2, L1, Select, Start to enable Cheat mode. Menu options for Campaigns 2 and 3 unlock and the following codes may be entered.

God Mode
Enable Cheat mode. During a game, press Triangle on controller 2.

Level Skip
Enable Cheat mode. During a game, press Select on controller 2.

Infinite Power
Enable Cheat mode. During a game, press Circle on controller 2.

All Items
Enable Cheat mode. During a game, press X on controller 2.

Super Unit Strength
Enable Cheat mode. During a game, press Up on controller 2.

Weak Unit Strength
Enable Cheat mode. During a game, press Right on controller 2.

Current Research Completed
Enable Cheat mode. During a game, press Down on controller 2.

Additional Structures
Enable Cheat mode. During a game, press R1 on controller 2.

Additional Units
Enable Cheat mode. During a game, press R2 on controller 2.

WCW BACKSTAGE ASSAULT

Indestructible Weapons
L1, R1, L1, R1, Square (2)

Low Gravity
R1, L1 (3), Square, Triangle

How Rude
R1,L1,R1,L1,Triangle (2)

Big Women
R1 (2), Triangle (2), L1 (2)

Unlock Vampiro
In the Hardcore Challenge, set your opponent on fire in the Truck Arena. Do this by either throwing your opponent into the flame barrel or by setting the 2x4 on fire and hitting your opponent with it. (No specific difficulty level, with any wrestler)

Unlock Billy Kidman
Defeat Kidman in the Hardcore Challenge. Difficulty level must be Medium.

Unlock Brian Adams & Bryan Clark
While in a Hardcore Challenge set your opponent on fire in the Block area. (with any wrestler)

Unlock Lance Storm
Win the Hardcore Gauntlet for the first time. (with any wrestler)

Unlock Lt. Loco (Chavo Guerrero Jr.)
Win the Hardcore Gauntlet for the second time. (with any wrestler)

Unlock Daffney
Win the Hardcore Gauntlet for the third time. (with any wrestler)

Unlock General Rection
Win the Hardcore Gauntlet for the fourth time. (with any wrestler)

Unlock Bret Hart
Win the Hardcore Gauntlet for the fifth time. (with any wrestler)

Unlock Vince Russo
Defeat your opponent by Knockout in the Hardcore Challenge with the briefcase, located in the Green Room. To get to the Green Room, exit the Media Center. The briefcase is on the other side of the Green Room on the floor beside a desk. (with any wrestler)

Unlock Eric Bischoff
Beat the Hardcore Challenge with Vince Russo. Difficulty levels may vary.

Unlock Buff Bagwell
Defeat Buff Daddy in the Hardcore Challenge. Difficulty level must be set on Hard. (World Title, with any wrestler)

Unlock Rey Mysterio Jr.
Defeat Rey Jr. in the Hardcore Challenge. Difficulty level must be set on Medium. (U.S. Title, with any wrestler)

Unlock Johnny the Bull
Defeat Johnny in the Hardcore Challenge. Difficulty level must be set to Easy. (Hardcore Title, with any wrestler)

Unlock Tank Abbott
Defeat your opponent by Knockout in the Block. (with any wrestler)

Unlock Chris Kanyon
Defeat Kanyon in the Hardcore Challenge. Difficulty level must be set to Easy. (Hardcore Title)

Unlock Evan Karagias, Shannon Moore, and Shane Helms (3 Count)
Hit your opponent numerous times with the T.V. in the Green Room. Access the Green Room by exiting the Media Room (Broadcast Room), go to the other end of the Green Room, and the T.V. is sitting on the desk (in the same place you found the briefcase).

Unlock Norman Smiley
In Create a Wrestler mode, create a wrestler with the "Big Wiggle Taunt." After entering a Hardcore Challenge with this created wrestler, use the taunt during a match. Any difficulty level works. (World, U.S., or Hardcore)

Unlock Crowbar
Defeat Crowbar in the Hardcore Challenge. Difficulty level must be set to Easy. (Hardcore Title, with any wrestler)

Unlock Lex Luger (The Total Package)
Defeat Luger in the Hardcore Challenge. Difficulty level must be set to Hard. (World Title, with any wrestler)

Unlock La Parka
Defeat your opponent by Knockout with a chair in the Truck Arena. To get to the chair, run to the corner opposite the arena where the crate and trash can are located. Use any difficulty level. (With any wrestler)

Unlock Scott Hall
Defeat Hall in the Hardcore Challenge. Difficulty level must be set to Hard. (World Title, with any wrestler)

Unlock Don Harris
Defeat Don Harris in the Hardcore Challenge. Difficulty level must be set to Medium. (U.S. Title, with any wrestler)

Unlock Ron Harris
Defeat Ron Harris in the Hardcore Challenge. Difficulty level must be set to Medium. (U.S. Title, with any wrestler)

Unlock Chris Candido
Defeat Candido in the Hardcore Challenge. Difficulty level must be set to Easy. (Hardcore Title, with any wrestler)

Unlock Mike Awesome
In the Hardcore Challenge, put your opponent through a table, bench, or couch. Find tables in storage rooms. Access one storage room by exiting the Block through a door. Find benches in the Locker Room and storage rooms. Find the couch in the Green Room. To access the Green Room, exit the door of the Broadcast Room.

Unlock Shane Douglas (The Franchise)
Defeat Douglas in the Hardcore Challenge. Difficulty level must be set to Medium. (U.S. Title, with any wrestler).

Unlock Kimberly
Beat the Hardcore Challenge with Diamond Dallas Page (DDP). Difficulty level varies.

Unlock Ms. Hancock
In Create a Wrestler, create a wrestler with the "Nasty Hip Swivel" taunt. Enter the Hardcore Challenge on any difficulty level and use the taunt in a match.

Unlock Elizabeth
Win a title with Lex Luger in the Hardcore Challenge. Difficulty level varies.

WCW MAYHEM

Unlock All Backrooms
Enter CBCKRMS as a PPV password. Fight in the backstage areas in a one-on-one match by running to the entrance.

Unlock All Characters
Enter PLYHDNGYS as a PPV password.

Halloween Havoc
Enter td^pKRmZ-<yL as a PPV password.

Starrcade
Enter @KcXKF=W?j^pF as a PPV password.

Thursday Thunder
Enter PLYHDNGYS as a PPV password on the top line. Press X, then enter MSKDLTLRY as a PPV password on the middle line.

World War III
Enter yKh#J$=JQLmFs as a PPV password.

TNT Nitro Set
Enter PLYNTRCLSC as a PPV password.

Momentum Meter
Enter PRNTMMNTM as a PPV password.

Stamina Meter
Enter PRNTSTMN as a PPV password.

Same Characters
Enter DPLGNGRS as a PPV password to play as the same character as your opponent in Versus mode.

Play Rey Mysterio Jr.
Enter MSKDLTLRY as a PPV password.

Better Rankings
Enter CHT4DBST as a PPV password. Go into the Quest for the Best mode and press Right to climb in the rankings.

Unlimited Attribute Points
Enter MKSPRCWS as a PPV password.

Fat Characters
Enter NGGDYNLN as a PPV password.

Unlock Mean Gene Okerland
Beat Quest for the Best mode with a non-Cruiserweight character on Hard difficulty.

Unlock Arn Anderson
Beat Quest for the Best mode with a Cruiserweight character on Hard difficulty.

Unlock Bam Bam Bigelow
Beat Quest for the Best mode with a non-Cruiserweight character on Medium difficulty.

Unlock Barry Windham
Beat Quest for the Best mode with a non-Cruiserweight character on Medium difficulty.

Unlock Bobby Eaton
Beat Quest for the Best mode with a Cruiserweight character on Easy difficulty.

Unlock Bobby Blayze
Beat Quest for the Best mode with a non-Cruiserweight character on Easy difficulty.

Unlock Chris Jericho
Beat Quest for the Best mode, playing in all 13 backstage arenas.

Unlock Doug Dellinger
Beat Quest for the Best mode with a Cruiserweight character on Hard difficulty.

Unlock Eric Bischoff
Beat Quest for the Best mode with a non-Cruiserweight character on Hard difficulty.

Unlock Jimmy Hart
Beat Quest for the Best mode with any character on Hard difficulty.

Unlock Lash LeRoux
Beat Quest for the Best mode with a Cruiserweight character on Medium difficulty.

Unlock Ric Flair
Beat Quest for the Best mode with a non-Cruiserweight character on Hard difficulty.

Unlock Rick Steiner
Beat Quest for the Best mode with any character on Hard difficulty.

Unlock Scott Hall
Beat Quest for the Best mode with any character on Hard difficulty.

Unlock Sgt. Buddy Lee Parker
Beat Quest for the Best mode with any character on Easy difficulty.

Unlock Sony Onoo
Beat Quest for the Best mode with any character on Easy difficulty.

Unlock Wolfpack Sting
Beat Quest for the Best mode with any character on Hard difficulty.

PPV Passwords' Arena Options
In the following match-type PPV passwords, you can replace the first two characters to select a different arena: G6 = Nitro; Qw = Thunder; tS = Superbrawl; 4J = Uncensored; -c = Slamboree; $m = Spring Stampede; Zx = Road Wild; k7 = Fall Brawl; td = Halloween Havoc; 4n = World War III; $K = Starrcade.

Bam Bam Bigelow vs. Lex Luger (Main Event)
td^NmPmQ-<xY

Barry Windham vs. Juvi (Cruiserweight Title)
tdSJKRmZ-<yL

Barry Windham vs. Juvi (TV Title)
tdSJKRmZ-<yL

Barry Windham vs. Rey Mysterio (Cruiserweight Title)
tdSfKRmZ-<yL

Barry Windham vs. Rey Mysterio (TV Title)
tdSfKRmZ-<yL

Barry Windham vs. Wrath (Cruiserweight Title)
tdS4KRmZ-<yL

Barry Windham vs. Wrath (TV Title)
tdS4KRmZ-<yL

Bobby Blaze
tdkDpKRmZ-<yL

Booker T vs. Scott Hall
td^pKxmZ-<yL

Buff Bagwell vs. Kevin Nash
td^pKRmZrhyP

Cruiserweight (Main Event)
td^pKRmZrbyP

Curt Hennig vs. Chris Jericho (Cruiserweight Title)
tdQ6KRmZ-<yL

Curt Hennig vs. Chris Jericho (TV Title)
tdQ6KRmZ-<yL

Curt Hennig vs. Eddy Gurrerro (Cruiserweight Title)
tdQGKRmZ-<yL

Curt Hennig vs. Eddy Gurrerro (TV Title)
tdQGKRmZ-<yL

Curt Hennig vs. Kidman (Cruiserweight Title)
tdQhKRmZ-<yL

Curt Hennig vs. Kidman (TV Title)
tdQhKRmZ-<yL

Disco Inferno vs. Bret Hart
td^pmRmZ-<yL

Disco Inferno vs. Bret Hart, Booker T vs. Hall, Sting vs. Ric Flair, and Savage vs. Steiner
td^pmRmQ-<PY

Disco Inferno vs. Chavo
td^NKRmZ-<yL

Disco Inferno vs. Chavo, Booker T vs. Scott Hall, Rick Steiner vs. Booker T
td^NKxmZ-<ky

Disco Inferno vs. Chris Kanyon
td^pZRmZ-<yL

Disco Inferno vs. Curt Hennig
td^QmPmQ-<YX

Disco Inferno vs. Konnan, Hogan vs. Luger, DDP vs. Rick Flair, and Rick Steiner vs. Booker T
td^NmPmQ-<ky

Disco Inferno vs. La Parka
td^QKRmQ-<ky

Disco Inferno vs. La Parka, Hogan vs. Luger, and DDP vs. Rick Flair
td^QKPmQ-<yP

Goldberg (World Champion)
td^QKYgQrYyP

Horace Hogan
td7QKYgQr-<yP

Horace Hogan vs. Mongo
tdDpKRmZ-xp

Hollywood Hogan
td^QKYgQr-<y*

Randy Savage, Rick Steiner vs. Sting, Ric Flair
td^NKxmQ-<PY

Randy Savage vs. Diamond Dallas Page
td^NmPmQ-<

Randy Savage vs. Diamond Dallas Page (Main Event)
td^pKRmZ-<Yp

Randy Savage vs. Stevie Ray
td^QKRmQ-<YY

Rick Steiner (World Champ) vs. Booker T
td^pKRmZ-<kL

Rick Steiner vs. Diamond Dallas Page
td^QKYgQ-<yP

Rick Steiner vs. Kevin Nash
td^pKRmZ-<kP

Rick Steiner vs. Lex Luger
td^pKYmz-<yL

Scott Hall
td^pKYmz-<yP

Sting (First Match)
td^DpKRmZ-<yL

Sting vs. Hogan
td^QKYgQr<y*

Sting vs. Scott Hall
td^pKYmz-<yP

Sting vs. Sting
td^QKYgQr<yP

WCW NITRO

Unlock All Characters
At the title screen, press R1 (4), L1 (4), R2 (4), L2 (4), Select to unlock 48 bonus characters. A sound confirms correct entry.

Unlock All Rings
At the title screen, press L1, L2, R1, R2, L1, L2, R1, R2, Select.

Turbo Mode
At the title screen, press L2 (4), L1, L2, L1, L2, Select. A sound confirms correct entry.

FMV Sequences
At the title screen, press R2 (4), R1, R2, R1, R2, Select. A sound confirms correct entry.

Big Heads, Hands, and Feet
At the title screen, press R2 (7), R1, Select. A sound confirms correct entry.

Big Heads
At the title screen, press R1 (7), R2, Select. A sound confirms correct entry.

Big Hands
At the Mode Select screen, press L2 (7), L1 (17).

Ring Skip
At the title screen, press R1, R2, R1, R2, Select. Every time you press Select, the ring will advance by one. Move the rings in reverse by pressing L1, L2, L1, L2, Select.

Swelling Heads
At the title screen, press L1 (7), L2, Select. A sound confirms correct entry. Your character's head swells up each time he or she gets hit.

YMCA Dancing
Press L2 while on the Disco stage.

Character Interference
Press Select during a match.

Character Talk
At the Character Selection screen, highlight a character and press Circle.

Special Ending
Beat the game with one of the programmers.

WCW/NWO THUNDER

Unlock All Characters
At the title screen, press R1 (4), L1 (4), R2 (4), L2 (4), Select. A sound confirms correct entry.

Unlock All Rings
At the title screen, press L1, L2, R1, R2, L1, L2, R1, R2, Select. A sound confirms correct entry.

FMV Sequences
At the title screen, press R1 (4), L1 (4), Select. Press Left+X to go to the next sequence, or Right+X to go back, or press Start (2) to exit.

Big Heads, Hands, Feet, and Weapons
At the title screen, press R2 (7), R1, Select. A sound confirms correct entry.

Big Heads
At the title screen, press R1 (7), R2, Select. A sound confirms correct entry.

Cage Ring
At the Option screen, highlight the Random ring and press R1, R2, R1, R2, Select. The word "Cage" confirms correct entry.

Play as Nitro Girls
At the title screen, press L2 (4), R2 (4), L1 (4), R1 (4), Select.

Character Interference
Press Select during a match.

Character Talk
At the Character Selection screen, highlight a character and press Circle.

Might Meter
At the title screen, press L2 (4), R2 (4), L1 (4), R1 (4), Select. A sound confirms correct entry.

Ring Select
At the Option screen, press R1, R2, R1, R2, Select. A sound confirms correct entry. Press Select to move to the next ring in the series. To move in reverse, press L1, L2, L1, L2, Select.

Unlock Individual Bonus Characters
At the Character Selection screen, highlight a character and press L1, R1, L2, R2. A sound confirms correct entry.

Dancing Characters
Press Taunt, Punch, Chop, or Kick while in the USO ring.

WCW VS. THE WORLD

Different Costumes
Highlight Hogan, Sting, Mashiro Chino and press Start.

Random Select
Press Circle at the Character Selection screen.

Unlock the Giant (Andre the Giant)
Beat all the leagues with a Heavyweight character. A Super Heavy league appears. Beat this league and beat the Giant.

Unlock Jaguar (Tiger Mask)
Beat all the leagues with a Lightweight or Juniorweight character. A Super Junior league appears. Beat this league and beat Tiger Mask.

Unlock Shanghai (Karl Gotch)
Defeat the Dead or Alive league with any character.

Unlock Steel Talon (Antonio Anoki)
Defeat the Neo-Strong Wrestling league with any character.

Unlock Major Tom (Terry Funk)
Defeat the Empire Wrestling Federation with any character.

Unlock Jeff Jarrett
Defeat the WCW league with any character.

Unlock Grizz Lee (Bruiser Brody)
Defeat the Independent Union Wrestling league with any character.

Unlock Le Mascarade (Mil Mascaras)
Defeat the Samurai Wrestling Federation with any character.

WHO WANTS TO BE A MILLIONAIRE: 2ND EDITION

Imposter
Enter DAN BLONSKY as your name. The game will give you a new name.

Regis-isms
Enter MILLIONAIRE as your name. Regis will make a comment and change your name.

Regis-isms
Enter REGIS as your name. Regis will make a comment and change your name.

WHO WANTS TO BE A MILLIONAIRE 3RD EDITION

Hear Regis Taunt You
At the name entry screen, sit and leave the name screen blank. Regis makes fun of you for awhile, then he types in a name himself, usually "UNKNOWN."

More Name Fun
If you enter your name as REGIS, Mr. Philbin will change it to something like "PRETENDER" or "BIG FAKER."

WILD 9

Level Select
Pause and press Up, Left, Down, R2, Right, Square, X.

Full Health
Pause and press R1, Triangle, L1, Left, Triangle, Circle, X.

Ten More Missiles
Pause and press X, Circle, R1, Right, Triangle, X, Triangle.

Ten More Grenades
Pause and press R1, X, R1, Right, Square, Right, Square.

Red Beam Mode
Pause and press Right, Up, Left, Circle, Up, Circle (2).

99 Lives
Go to the Centerscape level. Take the extra life behind the pillar on the bridge at the start of the level. Pause and press Select to quit the level. Enter the Centerscape level again and repeat the process to get a maximum of 99 lives.

WILD ARMS

Two-Player Battles
Insert a second controller during a battle. The second controller can use the characters too.

255 Items
Enter a battle. Have the first person to attack use a Heal Berry. Have second person to attack use the Heal Berry also. Then have the third person swap any item you have one of with the Heal Berry. Attack as normal. You must perform all the steps before winning a battle.

WILLIAMS ARCADE'S GREATEST HITS

Cheat Menu
Pick any game. Before the game starts, hold L1+L2+R1+R2 and press Select. Repeat this code twice to get the Operators Options screen. Enter Operator Options to change some game settings such as number of lives and difficulty.

WING COMMANDER 4

Level Select
At the *Wing Commander* copyright screen, press Up, Down (2), Up, R2 to access to a Cheat screen. Press R1 or R2 to select a level.

WING OVER

Unlock All Planes in Free Game Mode
At the Game Mode screen, press Up (2), Down (2), Left, Right, Left, Right, X, Triangle.

WINNING ELEVEN 3: FRANCE '98

Get Extra Romania Team
Pick Romania and finish the World Cup in Hard mode.

"Classic All Stars" Secret Team
At the main menu, highlight Exhibition mode and press Up (2), Down (2), Left, Right, Left, Right, Circle, X. You hear applause. At the Choose Your Country menu, press and hold L1+R1.

WINNING ELEVEN 3: FINAL VERSION

Unlock Secret Teams
Press Up (2), Down (2), Left, Right, Left, Right, X, Circle at the main menu.

WINNING ELEVEN 4

Get Clubhouse Stadium
Win the Konami Cup under any difficult setting.

Get Special Japan Team
Finish Olympic mode with Japan.

WINNING ELEVEN '97

Unlock Bonus Team
At the main menu, enter Up (2), Down (2), Left, Right, Left, Right, X, Circle.

WIPEOUT

Firestar Bonus Track
At the main menu, highlight "One Player" and hold L1+R1+Right+Square+Circle+Start. Press X to select the option that appears.

Get Rapier Ship
At the main menu, highlight "One Player" and hold L2+R2+Left+Select+Start. Press X to select the option that appears.

WIPEOUT 3

Prototype Track
In Single Race mode, complete all tracks with all teams. Then Prototype appears as an option on the main menu.

All Circuits
As a default name, enter WIZZPIG.

All Teams
As a default name, enter AVINIT.

All Challenges
As a default name, enter THEHAIR.

Infinite Hyperthrust
As a default name, enter MOONFACE.

Infinite Thrust and Shields
As a default name, enter GEORDIE.

Unlimited Random Weapons
As a default name, enter DEPUTY.

Unlock Tournaments
As a default name, enter BUNTY.

Phantom Class
As a default name, enter JAZZNAZ.

Changing Blue Turbo Triangles to White
As a default name, enter BEBEDEE.

Prototype Circuits
As a default name, enter CANCER W.

Hitting Walls Slows Down Vehicle
As a default name, enter NOWHEELS.

Four Players Linked Up
Link the PlayStations and change all players' default name to LINK. Pick the "Establish Link" option in the Options screen on all PlayStations.

WIPEOUT XL

Infinite Energy
Pause and hold L1+R1+Select while you press Triangle, X, Square, Circle, Triangle, X, Square, Circle.

Infinite Time
Pause and hold L1+R1+Select while you press Triangle, Square, Circle, X, Triangle, Square, Circle, X.

Infinite Weapons
Pause the game and hold L1+R1+Select while you press X (2), Square (2), Circle (2), Triangle.

Machine Guns
Pause and hold L1+R1+Select while you press Square, Circle, X, Square, Circle, X, Triangle.

Animal Team
Hold L1+R2+Start+Select while the game is loading.

Piranha Team
At the main menu, hold L1+R1+Select and press X (4), Circle, Triangle, Square.

Phantom Class
At the main menu, hold L1+R1+Select and press X (3), Circle (3).

Challenge 1 Mode
As a password, enter Square, Circle, Square, Triangle, Circle, Triangle (2), Circle, Square (3), Triangle, X, Square.

Challenge 2 Mode
As a password, enter Square, Circle, Square, Triangle, Circle, Triangle, X, Square, X, Triangle (2), X, Circle (2).

Unlock All Tracks
At the main menu, hold L1+R1+Select and press Square, Circle, Triangle, Circle, Square.

Piranha Craft and More Bonuses
At the Setup screen, hold L1+R1+Select and press Square, Circle, Square, Triangle, Circle, X, Square, X, Circle, Square, Triangle, X, Square.

Vostok Island and Spilskinanke Hidden Tracks
At the main menu, hold L1+R1+Select and press Square, Circle, Square, Triangle, Circle, Triangle, X, Triangle, Circle (2), Triangle, X (2), Square.

WORLD CUP '98

Sound Effects
Press Square, Circle, Triangle, or X after scoring a goal.

World Cup Classic Games
Using any team, win the World Cup to unlock World Cup Classics at the main menu. Then use one of the classic teams to win the World Cup again. This unlocks the next World Cup Classic match. Pick one of the new classic teams to keep unlocking more matches. You can do this eight times.

WORLD LEAGUE SOCCER

Real Player Names
Go into the English league and pick any team. Go into the Player Edit screen and modify the first player's name to "TEAMTWO." The hidden Default 2 option will be displayed. Enable this option.

WORLD'S SCARIEST POLICE CHASES

Unlock All Bonuses
At the main menu, press Left, Right, L1, R1, Circle, Square, R2, L2. This unlocks all bonuses.

Unlock All Missions
To unlock all missions, enter the following button presses at the main menu: Down, Up, Left, Right, X, Triangle, Circle, Square.

Unlock All Starting Locations (Patrol Mode)
To open all starting locations in patrol mode, push the following buttons at the main menu: Down, Up, L2, L1, Cross, Triangle, R2, R1.

Unlock Everything
At the main menu, press Left, Right, L1, R1, Circle, Square, R2, L2. If you enter the code correctly, you hear a meow. This unlocks all weapons in Free Patrol and all other cars and extras in the Bonus Items screen of the Options menu.

WORMS

Extra Weapons
Press X+Square (8) at the Weapon Options screen. You get banana bombs, sheep bombs, and a minigun, and the ninja rope will be bouncy.

Infinite Banana Bombs
Press Down, Right, X, Square (2), X, Square (2), X, Square (2) at the Weapon Options screen.

Boxing Ring
Start a fire punch or a dragonball. Then quickly hold Square and press R1, L1, Circle. One worm from each team is teleported to a boxing ring. All you can do is punch and use dragonballs. Defeat your opponent. You return to the normal game after you defeat one of the worms.

Hell Bonus Level
Hades/666

Woods Bonus Level
Forest

Candyland Bonus Level
Candy

Junkyard Bonus Level
Junk

Martian Bonus Level
Mars

H.R. Giger Type Bonus Level
Alien

Polar Bonus Level
Artic

WORMS ARMAGEDDON

Blood
Earn a gold in Basic Training mode.

Aqua Sheep
Earn a gold in Super Sheep Training mode.

Longbow Power-Up
Earn a gold on the Euthanasia Training mode.

Shotgun Power-Up
Earn a gold on the Rifle Range Training mode.

Grenade Power-Up
Earn a gold on the Artillery Range.

All Weapon Crates Have Sheep
Earn a gold in Crazy Crates.

Invincibility
Earn an Elite rank in Deathmatch mode.

Laser Sight
Beat Mission 4.

Jetpack
Beat Mission 8.

Fast Walk
Beat Mission 13.

Invisibility in Net Games
Beat Mission 16.

Low Gravity
Beat Mission 20.

Indestructible Landscape
Beat Mission 25.

Super Banana Bomb Power-Up
Beat Mission 33.

Full Wormage
Earn a gold medal and Elite rank in all modes.

WRECKIN CREW

Unlock Bonuses
Enter Circle (2), Square, Triangle (2), Square (3), X, Circle (3), Triangle, Square (2), X as a password.

WU TANG: SHAOLIN STYLE

Fatality and Blood Code
As a password, enter Triangle, Circle, X (2), Square, Triangle, Circle, Square.

All Characters
Press Right (4), Left (4), Square, Circle, Square, Circle at the main menu.

Secret Mode (1P Games)
Hold R1+R2 after you selected a level in a 1P game. A sound confirms correct entry.

Wu-Tang Songs
Put the game disk into an audio CD player.

Play Your Own Music
Pause the game. Open the PlayStation lid, take out the game, and insert your music CD. Unpause the game and your music plays.

Play as Hystrix
In Versus mode, highlight Method Man at the Character Selection screen. Hold Select and press X.

Play as Fearmentor
In Versus mode, highlight RZA at the Character Selection screen. Hold Select and press X.

Play as Otis
In Versus mode, highlight Ghostface Killer at the Character Selection screen. Hold Select and press X.

Play as Gasche
In Versus mode, highlight Masta Killa at the Character Selection screen. Hold Select and press X.

Play as Lecher
In Versus mode, highlight Old Dirty Bastard at the Character Selection screen. Hold Select and press X.

Play as Xin
In Versus mode, highlight Inspecta Deck at the Character Selection screen. Hold Select and press X.

Play as Sinesis
In Versus mode, highlight U-God at the Character Selection screen. Hold Select and press X.

Play as Cerith
In Versus mode, highlight GZA at the Character Selection screen. Hold Select and press X.

Play as Bone Gear
In Versus mode, highlight Raekwon at the Character Selection screen. Hold Select and press X.

WWF ATTITUDE

Alternate Costumes
In any mode besides Career mode, highlight a character at the Character Selection screen. For the first outfit, press X. For the second outfit, hold L1 and press X. For the third outfit, hold L2 and press X. For the fourth outfit, hold R2 and press X.

Unlock Sable, Marc Mero, Trainer mode, Squeaky mode, and Other Bonuses in Create Wrestler Mode
Win the European title in Career mode at any difficulty.

Unlock Chyna, Jacqueline, Big Head Mode, and Three Additional Points in Create Wrestler Mode
Win the Intercontinental title in Career mode at any difficulty.

Unlock Head Mode, Beep Mode, and Ego Mode
Win the Heavyweight title in Career mode at any difficulty.

Unlock Jerry Lawler and Paul Bearer
Win the Royal Rumble PPV in Career mode.

Unlock Sgt. Slaughter and Shawn Michaels
Win the Summerslam PPV in Career mode.

Unlock Kurrgan and Taka Michinoku
Win the King of the Ring PPV in Career mode.

Perform a Taunt
Hold Kick+Tie-up and press Up, Down, Left, or Right during a match.

New Chants
When the crowd starts chanting, pause. Unpause and the chant changes.

Random Select
Press R1 at the Character Selection screen.

Blood Matches
Go into the Utilities screen from the main menu and enable the blood option.

Alternate Animations and Music
Set the language to Teen or Bleeped. You hear different theme music and different comments by Billy Gunn, X-Pac, Triple H, Chyna, Mark Henry, and Road Dogg.

Call Partner Into the Ring
Hold X and press R1 to get your partner to come into the ring without being tagged during a Tag Team match.

Show Wrestling Moves
Enter Create Wrestler mode. Pick his move set. Go to edit to learn that character's moves, or pause while in the ring and go to the move list to see what kind of moves can be done in that situation.

WWF IN YOUR HOUSE

Quadruple-Damage Taunt
Press Up, Down, Up, Down to have your character perform a taunt. Your next attack (within a couple of seconds) deals quadruple damage.

Random Select
Hold Up and press Start at the Character Selection screen.

Automatic Super-Pins
Pause and press Down (4), Left. Reenter the code to revert to normal.

Freeze the CPU Players
Pause and press Left (2), Up, Down, R2. Reenter the code to revert to normal.

Extra Damage
Pause and press Up (2), L1, L2, Down. Reenter the code to revert to normal.

Enable Combos
Pause and press R1, L2, R2, L2, Right. Reenter the code to revert to normal.

Take Minor Damage
Pause and press Down, Up, L2, Right, Left. Reenter the code to revert to normal.

Take No Damage
Pause and press R2, L2, R2, L2, R1. Reenter the code to revert to normal.

WWF SMACKDOWN

Unlock Ivory
Play season mode for one year.

Unlock Prince Albert
Play season mode for two years.

Unlock Jacqueline
Play season mode for three years.

Unlock Viscera
Play season mode for four years.

Unlock Mideon
Play season mode for six years.

Unlock Gerald Brisco
Play season mode for seven years.

Unlock Pat Patterson
Play season mode for eight years.

Gain 80 Ability Points
Play season mode for five years.

Gain 90 Ability Points
Play season mode for 10 years.

Gain 100 Ability Points
Play season mode for 20 years.

Wealth Option
Complete one pre-season.

European Title and Ability
Complete two pre-seasons.

Women's Title and Ability
Complete three pre-seasons.

Tournament and Ability
Complete four pre-seasons.

Hardcore Title and Ability
Complete five pre-seasons.

Intercontinental Title and Ability
Complete six pre-seasons.

Tag Title and Ability
Complete seven pre-seasons.

Title Match and Ability
Complete eight pre-seasons.

Pre-Season Skip
Complete 10 pre-seasons.

Return to the Main Menu
Press Start+Select during a match.

WWF SMACKDOWN 2!: KNOW YOUR ROLE

Unlock Steve Austin
Play through the first year season's Backlash event to unlock one new move set, three standard parts, one new character, and one new titantron.

Unlock Shawn Michaels
Play through the first year season's Judgment Day event to unlock one new move set, three standard parts, one new character, one new titantron, and an Iron Man Referee match type.

Unlock Billy Gunn
Play through the first year season's King of the Ring event to unlock one new move set, three standard parts, two new characters, and one new titantron.

Unlock Cactus Jack
Play through the first year season's No Way Out event to unlock one new move set, three standard parts, two new characters, and one new titantron.

Unlock Mick Foley
Play through the first year season's Wrestlemania event to unlock one new move set, three standard parts, two new characters, one new titantron, and a Credits menu inside the Options menu.

Unlock Pat Patterson and Gerald Brisco
During the first year season, you see cutscenes with Vince McMahon, Pat Patterson, and Gerald Brisco. Then you get two new move sets, six standard parts, and four new characters.

Unlock Pete Gas, Rodney, Joey Abs
During the first year season, you see cutscenes with Pete Gas, Joey Abs, and Rodney. Then you get three new move sets, nine standard parts, six new characters, and one titantron.

Unlock Debra
During the first year season, you see cutscenes leading to a match involving Debra. Then you get one new move set, two new characters, and one titantron.

Unlock Table Tornado Tag Match
During the first year season, a Table Tornado Tag Match eventually appears on the event card and this type of match becomes unlocked. You don't have to compete in this match to unlock it.

Unlock a TLC Match
During the first year season, a TLC Match eventually appears on the event card and this type of match becomes unlocked. You don't have to compete in this match to unlock it.

Unlock Michael Cole
He is unlocked after the opening event of the second year. You also get one new move set and three new standard parts.

WWF WARZONE

Big Head Mode
Win the Challenge mode with the Rock or British Bulldog at Medium or Hard difficulty.

Additional Create-a-Wrestler Costumes
Win the Challenge mode with Kane at Medium or Hard difficulty.

Additional Goldust Costumes
Win the Challenge mode with Goldust at Medium or Hard difficulty. Highlight Goldust and press L2, R1, or R2 at the Character Selection screen.

Additional Stone Cold Costumes
Win the Challenge mode with Stone Cold at Medium or Hard difficulty. Highlight Stone Cold and press L2, R1, or R2 at the Character Selection screen.

Different Costumes
Hold L2 when you pick your character at the Character Selection screen.

Ego Mode
Win the Challenge mode with Ahmed Johnson at Medium or Hard difficulty. If the crowd chants, your character's head expands. If the crowd boos, your character's head shrinks.

No Meters Mode
Win the Challenge mode with Undertaker at Medium or Hard difficulty.

No Wimps Mode
Win the Challenge mode with Faarooq or Ken Shamrock at Medium or Hard difficulty. You won't be able to block anymore.

Beans Mode
Win the Challenge mode with the Headbangers at Medium or Hard difficulty. Characters belch and flatulate during matches.

Taunts
Press Punch+Block or Tie-up+Kick to perform two different taunts.

Unlock Female Body Type
Win the Challenge mode with Shawn Michaels or Triple H on Medium or Hard difficulty. The "Female" body type becomes available in Create a Wrestler mode.

Random Select
Hold Up and press Block at the Character Selection screen.

View Unlocked Characters and Mode
Press L1, R1 at the main menu to see a list of characters and modes that have been unlocked.

Dizzy Character
Hold Square at the Create a Wrestler screen. Keep holding it down until the character seems dizzy.

Unlock Cactus Jack and Dude Love
Win the Challenge mode with Mankind at Medium or Hard difficulty.

Unlock Sue the Ring Girl
Win the Challenge mode with Bret or Owen Hart at Medium or Hard difficulty. Sue becomes available as a custom character.

Unlock Trainer
Enter training mode at the Character Selection screen. Select "Custom," then "Trainer" to play as the trainer. The trainer becomes available as a custom character.

Unlock Rattlesnake
This gives you Stone Cold wearing only jeans. Win the Challenge mode at Medium or Hard difficulty with a user-created character with 30 attribute points or more.

View FMV Sequences
When the "Press Start" shows on the opening screen, press Up+Triangle, Right+Circle, Down+X, Left+Square, Left+Square, Left+Square, Left+Square, R1+L1, R2+L2, R1+L1, R2+L2. A new option, Movie 1, appears if you entered the code correctly. Press Up or Down to select an FMV sequence between 1 and 64. Press X to view it.

Steve Austin Interference
Press L1+L2+R1+R2+Up+Kick during a one-on-one match in Versus or Challenge mode. This changes the match to a handicap match and you automatically lose by disqualification. Steve Austin enters your match and fights your opponent.

Shawn Michaels Interference
Press L1+L2+R1+R2+Left+Punch during a one-on-one match in Versus or Challenge mode. This changes the match to a handicap match and you automatically lose by disqualification. Shawn Michaels enters your match and fights your opponent.

Triple H Interference
Press L1+L2+R1+R2+Right+Tie Up during a one-on-one match in Versus or Challenge mode. This changes the match to a handicap match and you automatically lose by disqualification. Triple H enters your match and fights your opponent.

The Undertaker Interference
Press L1+L2+R1+R2+Right+Block during a one-on-one match in Versus or Challenge mode. This changes the match to a handicap match and you automatically lose by disqualification. The Undertaker enters your match and fights your opponent.

Owen Hart Interference

Press L1+L2+R1+R2+Left+Block during a one-on-one match in Versus or Challenge mode. This changes the match to a handicap match and you automatically lose by disqualification. Owen Hart enters your match and fights your opponent.

The Rock Interference

Press L1+L2+R1+R2+Right+Kick during a one-on-one match in Versus or Challenge mode. This changes the match to a handicap match and you automatically lose by disqualification. The Rock enters your match and fights your opponent.

Faarooq Interference

Press L1+L2+R1+R2+Up+Punch during a one-on-one match in Versus or Challenge mode. This changes the match to a handicap match and you automatically lose by disqualification. Faarooq enters your match and fights your opponent.

Mankind Interference

Press L1+L2+R1+R2+Up+Tie Up during a one-on-one match in Versus or Challenge mode. This changes the match to a handicap match and you automatically lose by disqualification. Mankind enters your match and fights your opponent.

Goldust Interference

Press L1+L2+R1+R2+Right+Punch during a one-on-one match in Versus or Challenge mode. This changes the match to a handicap match and you automatically lose by disqualification. Goldust enters your match and fights your opponent.

Ken Shamrock Interference

Press L1+L2+R1+R2+Down+Kick during a one-on-one match in Versus or Challenge mode. This changes the match to a handicap match and you automatically lose by disqualification. Ken Shamrock enters your match and fights your opponent.

Bret Hart Interference

Press L1+L2+R1+R2+Left+Tie Up during a one-on-one match in Versus or Challenge mode. This changes the match to a handicap match and you automatically lose by disqualification. Bret Hart enters your match and fights your opponent.

The British Bulldog Interference

Press L1+L2+R1+R2+Left+Kick during a one-on-one match in Versus or Challenge mode. This changes the match to a handicap match and you automatically lose by disqualification. The British Bulldog enters your match and fights your opponent.

Ahmed Johnson Interference

Press L1+L2+R1+R2+Up+Block during a one-on-one match in Versus or Challenge mode. This changes the match to a handicap match and you automatically lose by disqualification. Ahmed Johnson enters your match and fights your opponent.

Kane Interference

Press L1+L2+R1+R2+Down+Punch during a one-on-one match in Versus or Challenge mode. This changes the match to a handicap match and you automatically lose by disqualification. Kane enters your match and fights your opponent.

Mosh Interference

Press L1+L2+R1+R2+Down+Block during a one-on-one match in Versus or Challenge mode. This changes the match to a handicap match and you automatically lose by disqualification. Mosh enters your match and fights your opponent.

Thrasher Interference

Press L1+L2+R1+R2+Down+Tie Up during a one-on-one match in Versus or Challenge mode. This changes the match to a handicap match and you automatically lose by disqualification. Thrasher enters your match and fights your opponent.

Random Interference

Press L1+L2+R1+R2+Kick+Punch during a one-on-one match in Versus or Challenge mode. This changes the match to a handicap match and you automatically lose by disqualification. Random enters your match and fights your opponent.

WWF WRESTLEMANIA: THE ARCADE GAME

Easy CPU

Pause, then press X, Triangle, R2, Triangle, X.

Infinite Combo Meter

At the Character Selection screen, press L1+R2, Square, X, Circle, Triangle. If you did this correctly, "Combo" appears beneath your character.

No Human Damage

Pause, then press X, Triangle, R2, Up.

Disable All Codes

Pause, then press Square, Circle, Triangle, X.

Stronger Hits

Pause, then press X, Triangle, L2, Down.

Stop Timer

Pause, then press X, Triangle, R2, Left.

Weaker Hits

Pause, then press X, Triangle, L2, Right.

Random Select

Hold Up and press Start at the Character Selection screen.

Hyper Mode

Hold L1+R2 and press Up, Down, Up, Down, Square, Triangle, Right, Left at the Character Selection screen.

X2

Nine Lives

Enter 220969 as a password in the Options screen.

Nine Continues

Enter 267776 as a password in the Options screen.

See Ending

Enter 300167 as a password in the Options screen.

Invisible Ships

Enter 180771 as a password in the Options screen.

Level 2

Enter 713948 as a password in the Options screen.

Level 3

Enter 900277 as a password in the Options screen.

Level 4

Enter 213490 as a password in the Options screen.

Level 5

Enter 866141 as a password in the Options screen.

Level 6

Enter 321904 as a password in the Options screen.

Level 7

Enter 196861 as a password in the Options screen.

Level 8

Enter 040186 as a password in the Options screen.

Level 9

Enter 841003 as a password in the Options screen.

Level 10

Enter 216409 as a password in the Options screen.

X-COM 2: TERROR FROM THE DEEP

More Money

Name your base AEIOU.

Super Soldiers

Name your base JUSTLIKEME.

XENA: WARRIOR PRINCESS

Invincibility

At the main menu, press: Up (3), Circle, Square, Up, Right, Left. A sound confirms correct entry.

Attack and Shield Power Up

At the main menu, press: Triangle, Square, Triangle, Square (2), Up (3). A sound confirms correct entry.

Level Select

At the main menu, highlight "New Game" and press Triangle, Square, Circle, Triangle, Square, Up (3). A sound confirms correct entry.

XEVIOUS 3D/G+

Play as Heihachi

At the title screen, highlight "Start" and press and hold X+Left+Circle+Start on controller one. Hold the buttons until the game begins and the ship turns to Heihachi.

Play as Paul

At the title screen, highlight "Start" and press and hold X+Right+Circle+Start on controller two. Hold the buttons until the game begins and the ship turns to Paul.

Play as Black Ship
Move your cursor to the "RESET" option on the title screen. Press and hold L1+L2+R1+R2. The "Game Start" should be highlighted. Now press Start while still holding down those buttons. Don't let go of the buttons until your ship changes color.

Unlimited Continues
At the Selection screen, press and hold L1+L2+R1+R2 and press Circle.

Xevious Debug Mode
Press Square+X+Start at the Xevious title screen.

Wide Ship
Enter the Play as the Black Ship code first. Go back to the title screen and highlight the "Exit" option of the Configuration Mode screen. Hold L1+L2+R1+R2+Start. Press Start after "Start" is highlighted and continue holding all the buttons until the ship changes shape.

Twisty Ship
Use Namco's NegCon controller to twist the ship.

X-GAMES PRO BOARDER

All Tracks and Circuits
As a password, enter Square, Triangle, X, Square, Circle (2).

Unlock Circuit Mode
As a password, enter X, Circle, X, Triangle (2), Square.

Unlock Super Circuit and Secret Boarder
As a password, enter Triangle, X, Square, X, Triangle, Circle.

Control X Logo
Use the D-Pad to control the X logo whenever the game is loading.

X-MEN: CHILDREN OF THE ATOM

Quick Continue
Hold L1+L2+R1+R2 and press Start at the continue screen. You quickly return to the game with the same character.

Play as Akuma (Player 1)
Go into the Character Selection screen. Highlight Spiral for three seconds. Then highlight these characters in this order: Silver Samurai, Psylocke, Colossus, Iceman, Colossus, Cyclops, Wolverine, Omega Red. Then, highlight Silver Samurai. Leave your cursor on Silver Samurai for three seconds, then press LK+HK+HP. Akuma appears in place of Silver Samurai.

Play as Akuma (Player 2)
Go into the Character Selection screen. Highlight Storm for three seconds. Highlight these characters in this order: Cyclops, Colossus, Iceman, Sentinel, Omega Red, Wolverine, Psylocke, Silver Samurai. Highlight Spiral. Leave your cursor on Spiral for three seconds, then press LK+HK+HP. Akuma appears in place of Spiral.

X-MEN: MUTANT ACADEMY

Unlock Everything
Go into the Option screen. Press Circle, Select, L1, R1, R2, L2, Square (2), Select. Every secret in the game becomes unlocked. Alternately, you can press Select, Up, L2, R1, L1, R2 at the main menu to unlock all secrets. A sound confirms correct entry.

Unlock Toad
Beat Arcade mode once with any character.

Unlock Mystique
Beat Arcade mode twice with any character.

Unlock Sabretooth
Beat Arcade mode three times with any character.

Unlock Magneto
Beat Arcade mode four times with any character.

Movie Outfits
Press Square at the Character Selection screen to gain the outfits from the X-Men movie.

Behind the Scenes Pictures
Beat Arcade mode with all the characters wearing their movie outfits to unlock behind the scenes images in Cerebro mode.

Character Intro FMV
Beat the game with any character in Arcade mode to unlock an Intro FMV option in Cerebro mode.

Character Movie Pictures
Beat 20 rounds with any character wearing the movie outfit in Survival mode to unlock a Movie Picture option in Cerebro mode.

Character Comic Pictures
Beat 10 rounds with any character wearing the normal outfit in Survival Mode to unlock a Comic Picture option in Cerebro mode.

Historical Comic Pictures
Beat the game with all characters wearing their regular costumes to unlock a Historical Comic Picture option in Cerebro mode.

Character Outro FMV
Graduate the Academy with any character to unlock an Outro FMV option in Cerebro mode.

Extra Third Costume
Graduate the Academy with all A's with any character to unlock his third costume. Select the third costume by pressing Circle at the Character Selection screen.

Movie Images
Beat 20 rounds with Gambit in Survival mode to unlock a Movie Picture option in Cerebro mode.

Lock Movies, Bosses, Survival Pictures 1 & 2
Hold Select+Start at the main menu or Character Selection screen. The game returns to the main menu. Everything is locked again in Cerebro mode, except for Academy mode rewards.

X-MEN VS. STREET FIGHTER

Play as Apocalypse
Beat the game with a difficulty of at least five stars. Select Versus mode. Then, highlight Akuma, hold Select for at least five seconds, and press any Punch button.

Play as Akuma
At the Character Selection screen, highlight Magneto, Juggernaut, Dhalsim, or Vega and press Up.

Original Costume Colors
When selecting a character, press LP or LK.

Play as *Street Fighter Alpha 2* Version of Chun Li
At the Character Selection screen, highlight Chun Li. Then, hold Select for at least five seconds and press any button.

EX Options Menu
At the main menu, press Triangle (2), Right, Circle, L1.

Reset Game
Hold R1+L1+Select+Start anytime during a game.

Random Select
Highlight the left-most character at the Character Selection screen. Press Left. Or go to the right most character and press Right to get a random character.

Continue the Beat Down
Press Start after you defeat your opponent.

X-RACING

Hidden Stages
Enter SFO as a password.

Y

YOU DON'T KNOW JACK

How to Use the Screw
Hit R1 then select. Choose which opponent you want to answer the question.

YU-GI-OH! FORBIDDEN MEMORIES

Getting Cards
You will need a certain amount of Starchips to get the cards when using the following passwords.

Ancient Elf
93221206

Ansatsu
48365709

Armaill
53153481

B. Skull Dragon
11901678

Baron Of The Fiend Sword
86325596

Battle Ox
05053103

Beaver Soldier
32452818

Bickuribox
25655502

Black Luster Ritual
81756897

Blue Eyes White Dragon
89631139

Book of Secret Arts
91595718

Call Of The Haunted
91536248

Card Destruction
72892473

Castle Walls
44209392

Celtic Guardian
91152256

Change of Heart
04031928

Claw Reacher
41218256

Crushcard
577728570

Curse of Dragon
28279543

Curse Of Trihorned Dragon
79699070

D. Human
81057959

Dark Hole
53129443

Dark Magician
46986414

Dark Rabbit
99261403

Dark World Thorns
43500484

Darkfire Dragon
17881964

Defense Paralas
63102017

De-Spell
19159413

Doma The Angel Of Silence
16972957

Dragon Capture Jar
50045299

Dragon Zombie
66672569

Drooling Lizard
16353197

Enchanting Mermaid
75376965

Feral Imp
41392891

Fiend Reflection #2
02863439

Fire Grass
53293545

Fissure
66788016

Flame Ghost
58528964

Flame Manipulator
34460851

Flame Swordsman
45231177

Frenzied Panda
98818516

Gaia The Fierce Knight
06368038

Gemini Elf
69140098

Giant Soldier of Stone
13039848

Great White
13429800

Green Phantom King
22910685

Gyakutenno Megami
31122090

Hane-Hane
07089711

Hard Armor
20060230

Harpie Lady Sisters
12206212

Hinotama Soul
96851799

Hitotsu-Me Giant
76184692

Judge Man
30113682

Kagemusha Of The Blue Flame
15401633

King Fog
84686841

Kojikocy
01184620

Koumori Dragon
67724379

Kumootoko
56283725

Kurama
85705804

Last Will
85602018

Lesser Dragon
55444629

Machine Chaser
07359741

Magical Ghost
46474915

Mammoth Graveyard
40374923

Man Eater
93553943

Man-Eater Bug
54652250

Man-Eating Treasure Chest
13723605

Masaki The Legendary Swordsman
44287299

Millennium Shield
32012841

Misairuzame
33178416

Monster Reborn
83764718

Monster-egg
36121917

M-warrior #1
56342351

M-Warrior #2
92731455

Mystic Clown
47060154

Mystic Horseman
68516705

Mystical Elf
15025844

Mystical Sheep #2
83464209

Nemuriko
90963488

Neo The Magic Swordsman
50930991

Ogre of the Black Shadow
45121025

Pale Beast
21263083

Parrot Dragon
62762898

Petit Dragon
75356564

Puppet Ritual
05783166

Red Eyes Black Dragon
74677422

Red Medicine
38199696

Reinforcements
17814387

Remove Trap
51482758

Reverse Trap
77622396

Rogue Doll
91939608

Root Water
39004808

Rude Kaiser
26378150

Salamandra
32268901

Sandstone
73051941

Silver Fang
90357090

Sogen
86318356

Sorcerer Of The Doomed
49218300

Soul Exchange
68005187

Spike Seadra
85326399

Steel Ogre Grotto #1
29172562

Summoned Skull
70781052

Sword Arm of Dragon
13069066

Sword of Dark Destruction
37120512

Swordstalker
50005633

Tera The Terrible
63308047

The 13th Grave
00032864

The Inexperience Spy (Magic Card)
81820689

The Stern Mystic
87557188

Toon World
15259793

Trap Hole
04206964

Trap Master
46461247

Turtle Tiger
37313348

Two-Pronged Attack
83887306

Ultimate Offering
80604091

Unknown Warrior of the Fiend
97360116

Uraby
01784619

Waboku
12607053

Wall of Illusion
13945283

Widespread Ruin
77754944

Winged Dragon, Guardian Of The Fortress #1
87796900

Witty Phantom
36304921

Yami
59197169

Z

Z

Level Select
Enter Triangle (2), X, Circle, Triangle (2), X, Circle as a password.

Level 2 Password
Square, Triangle, X, Circle, Triangle, Square, Circle, X

Level 3 Password
Square, X, Circle, Triangle (2), Square, X, Circle

Level 4 Password
Square, Triangle, X, Circle (2), Triangle, X, Circle

Level 5 Password
X, Circle, Square, X, Triangle, Square, X, Circle

Level 6 Password
Square, Circle, Triangle, X, Circle, X, Square, Circle

Level 7 Password
X, Circle, Square, X, Triangle (2), X, Circle

Level 8 Password
X (2), Circle, Triangle, X, Circle, Square, X

Level 9 Password
Circle, X, Circle, Square, X, Circle, Square, Circle

Level 10 Password
Circle, Triangle, Circle (2), Square, Triangle, X, Circle

Level 11 Password
X, Square, Circle, X (2), Square (2), Circle

Level 12 Password
X (2), Circle, X, Circle, X, Square, Circle

Level 13 Password
Circle, Triangle, X, Circle, Triangle, Square, X, Circle

Level 14 Password
Square, Triangle, X, Circle, Triangle, X, Circle, Square

Level 15 Password
Square, Triangle, X, Circle, Square, Triangle, X, Circle

Level 16 Password
Circle, X, Circle, Square (2), X, Square, X

Level 17 Password
Circle, Square, Triangle, X, Triangle, X, Circle, Square

Level 18 Password
Square, Circle, Square, X (2), Circle (2), Triangle

Level 19 Password
X, Circle, X, Circle, Triangle (2), X, Circle

Level 20 Password
Triangle (2), X, Circle, Triangle (2), X, Circle

ZEIRAM ZONE

Unlock Versus Mode
Rotate the joystick 360 degrees and press X, Square, Circle, Triangle at the main menu. A sound confirms correct entry. Versus mode becomes available.

Extra Hard Difficulty
Hold Left for three seconds, then press Right, Circle, Triangle at the main menu. The "Option" selection turns red if you entered the code correctly. Go into the Option menu and change the difficulty to extra hard.

Unlock All Characters
Press Right, Down, Down-Right, Down, Down-Left, Left, Triangle at the main menu. "Game Start" turns red if you entered the code correctly. Pick "Game Start" and a new menu appears. The menu will let you play as any character.

Extra Mode
At the main menu, hold Left for a couple seconds and then press Right, Circle, Triangle. A whacking sound confirms correct entry and the letters turn red. Enter the Options menu and choose Extra mode to discover additional features.

ZERO 4 CHAMP DOOZY J

Always Get 777 on Slots
Pause the game when the slot machine is spinning. Press Up, L1, Select.

Sound Novel Mode
Use NOVEL as your first name and SOUND! as your last name.

Development Staff
Press Down+L1+R1+Circle at the title screen.

ZERO DIVIDE

Phalanx Bonus Minigame
Hold Select+Start on controller two, then turn on your PlayStation. Keep holding the buttons for a while. A "Bonus Game" option appears if you entered the code correctly. Use controller two to play.

Phalanx MiniGame Invincibility
Go to the Phalanx option screen. Highlight "Speed" and press Up+Left+R2+L2+Triangle. The background turns red if you entered the code correctly.

Alternate Colors
Press Up when choosing a fighter at the Character Selection screen.

CPU vs. CPU
At the title screen, hold L1+L2+R1+R2. Highlight "Vs. Play" by pressing Down+Start, while still holding the previous buttons. Choose your fighters and the CPU will control them.

Play as Neco
Beat the game, without continuing, with Zulu and Xtal on Normal or Hard difficulty.

Play as Zulu
Go through the entire game and defeat Zulu with all eight characters. The announcer says "Wow" at the title screen after the last character beats Zulu.

Play as Xtal
Beat the entire game, without continuing, on the Normal or Hard difficulty setting and beat Xtal.

Play Against Xtal
Beat the entire game, without continuing, with all eight characters (including Zulu).

Play Against Neco
Beat the game, without continuing, with Xtal. Hold L1+L2+R1+R2 and press Select when Xtal's icon appears at the screen's top in the Pre-fight menu.

Neco Comic Strip
Beat the game on easy mode. You must win every round and never continue. Highlight the "Option" icon at the title screen. Hold L1+L2+R1+R2+Start+Select on controller two. A Neco comic is shown.

Area Select
Gather more than 30 hours of gameplay. The announcer says "Wow." Go into a Two-player Versus mode game with Zulu and Xtal. Win a round with a lap time of less than five seconds with both of them. Then you can choose your battle area.

PLAYSTATION

Flat Shaded Turbo Mode

Gather more than 100 hours of gameplay having used a five hit combo. Go into the Options menu and highlight "Match Point 3." Hold L1+L2+R1+R2 and press Down. A "Shadow Obj" option appears. Enable the option to see this code. Repeating this code to disable it.

Special Congratulations

Gather more than 200 hours of gameplay.

ZERO DIVIDE 2

Play as Eve and Nox

Beat the game with any character and difficulty setting.

Play as Neco and Modoki

Beat the game with Eve at any difficulty setting.

View Neco's Demo

Beat the game with any character. Hold Select+Start to restart.

Unlock Extra Levels

Beat the game on the three difficulty settings. You unlock two levels every time you beat the game under one of the three difficulty settings.

Alternate Colors

Hold Select and press any button on controller two at the Character Selection screen.

Z-GUNDAM

Play as GP-01Fb

Complete Battle mode with any robot.

Play as GP-02A

Use GP-01Fb to complete the Battle mode.

ZIG ZAG BALL

Full Energy

Don't press any buttons for more than two seconds during a game. Then press Right, Right, Up (2), Left, Down, Left, Down, X, Circle.

Open Exit Doors

Don't press any buttons for more than two seconds during a game. Then press Right, Up, Right, Up, Select (2), Start (2).

All Items

Don't press any buttons for more than two seconds during a game. Then press Right, Up, Down, Left, R2, L2, L1.

PlayStation2

AGGRESSIVE INLINE SKATING

Master Code
Enter P, L, Z, D, O, M, E as a code at the cheat screen.

Level Select, All Park Editor Objects, Full Stats
Enter Up, Up, Down, Down, Left, Right, Left, Right, B, A, B, A as a code at the cheat screen.

All Bonus Characters
Enter Down, Right, Right, Down, Left, Down, Left, Down, Right, Right, Right as a code at the cheat screen.

All Keys
Enter S, K, E, L, E, T, O, N as a code at the cheat screen.

Never Die
Enter K, H, U, F, U as a code at the cheat screen.

Low Gravity Wallride
Enter Up, Down, Up, Down, Left, Right, Left, Right, A, B, A, B, S as a code at the cheat screen.

Super Spin
Enter Left, Left, Left, Left, Right, Right, Right, Right, Left, Right, Left, Right, Up as a code at the cheat screen.

Perfect Manuals
Enter Q, U, E, Z, D, O, N, T, S, L, E, E, P as a code at the cheat screen.

Perfect Handplants
Enter J, U, S, T, I, N, Space, B, A, I, L, E, Y as a code at the cheat screen.

Perfect Grinds
Enter B, I, G, U, P, Y, A, S, E, L, F as a code at the cheat screen.

Juice Regeneration
Enter Left, Left, Right, Right, Left, Right, Down, Up, Up, Down, A, I as a code at the cheat screen.

Juice Bar Is Always Full
Enter B, A, K, A, B, A, K, A as a code at the cheat screen. Your juice bar will remain full, even if you crash.

FMV Sequences
Successfully complete the normal challenges in a level to unlock its FMV sequence.

ALL-STAR BASEBALL 2002

Unlock Bonus Teams
Unlock two special bonus teams, the Dingers and the Islanders, by going into the Exhibition mode and tapping R2+L2 at the team selection screen. Once you hear a gong sound, select either team. If you don't hear the tone at first, tap the buttons until you do.

Unlock Dingers in Batting Practice
To get the Austin Dingers bonus team in Batting Practice, enter that mode and then press R2+R1+L2+L1 at the team selection screen.

ARMORED CORE 2

Use Overweight Cores
Beat Mission mode and let the credits finish.

Set Camera Angle
Hold Start+Circle+X during gameplay and the game will pause. Press Start to resume playing. The camera is now fixed at the pre-location.

Default View
Pause the game and press Start to resume the game.

First-Person Angle
Hold Start+Square+Triangle during gameplay. The game will pause. Now press Start to resume the game.

Human Plus Cheats
Drop to -50,000 credits and an experiment will be done on you. Do this multiple times to get the full benefits of this code. Each time you do this code you restart your game. Do this code six times to unlock various cheats described below.

First Human Plus Cheat
Perform the Human Plus Cheats code once to unlock an automatic radar.

Second Human Plus Cheat
Perform the Human Plus Cheats code twice to unlock the ability to throw the laserblade.

Third Human Plus Cheat
Perform the Human Plus Cheats code three times to have heat taken away from attacks.

Fourth Human Plus Cheat
Perform the Human Plus Cheats code four times to gain the ability to walk while shooting back weapons.

Fifth Human Plus Cheat
Perform the Human Plus Cheats code five times to use half of the energy.

Sixth Human Plus Cheat
Perform the Human Plus Cheats code six times to have double energy.

ARMY MEN: AIR ATTACK 2

Level 2 Password
Up, X, Triangle, Right, Left, Square, Circle, X

Level 3 Password
Triangle, Circle, Down, Left, Square (2), Up (2)

Level 4 Password
X, Right, Left, X, Circle, Square (2), Triangle

Level 5 Password
Down (2), Circle, Square, Circle, Square, Right, X

Level 6 Password
Triangle, X, Up, Left, Right, Left, Circle, Triangle

Level 7 Password
Left, Square, Right, Down, Circle, X (2), Right

Level 8 Password
Triangle, Right, Square (2), Circle, Down (2), X

Level 9 Password
Up, X, Square, Left, Right, Circle, Left (2)

Level 10 Password
Triangle, Up, Circle, X, Square, Down (3)

Level 11 Password
Circle (2), Up, Left, Right, X, Triangle, Square

Level 12 Password
Right, Up, X, Right, Circle, Square, Triangle, Circle

Level 13 Password
Left (2), Triangle, Circle, X (2), Down, Right

Level 14 Password
Square, Right, Circle, Up, Down, Square, Down, X

Level 15 Password
Left, Right, Circle, X, Square, Down (2), Circle

Level 16 Password
Triangle, Circle, X, Right (2), Circle, Square, Down

Level 17 Password
Square, Up (2), Right, Left, Square, Down, X

Level 18 Password
Circle, X, Right, Triangle, Square, Up, X (2)

Level 19 Password
Down, Right, X, Square, Right, Up, Circle (2)

Level 20 Password
Up, X, Circle, Up, Left, Square, Circle, X

ARMY MEN: SARGE'S HEROES 2

Passwords
To enter Passwords, go to the Levels selection at the main menu. At the Input Code screen, insert the following codes to unlock the corresponding level.

Boot Camp
BOOTCAMP

Dinner Table
DINNER

Bridge
OVERPASS

Refrigerator
COOLER

Graveyard
NECROPOLIS

Castle
CITADEL

Tan Base
MOUSE

Revenge
ESCAPE

Desk
ESCRITOIRE

Bed
COT

Plasticville
BLUEBLUES

Toy Shelf
BUYME

Cashier
EXPRESS

Toy Train Town
LITTLEPEOPLE

Rocket Base
NUKEM

Pool Table
EIGHTBALL

Pinball Machine
BLACKKNIGHT

All Levels
FREEPLAY

Immortal
NODIE

All Weapons
GIMME

Invisible
NOSEEUM

Mini Mode
SHORTY

Super Sized
IMHUGE

Test Info
THDOTEST

BLOODY ROAR 3

Unlock Sudden Death Survival
If you want one-hit kills in Survival mode, survive through nine fights in Survival Mode to unlock Sudden Death. Be careful though, as you can also die with only one hit.

Unlock No Blocking Mode
To make it so you or your opponent cannot block attacks in Survival or Versus, gain first place in Arcade mode.

Unlock Super Difficulty
To make your opponents harder to defeat, complete Arcade mode once without continuing.

Unlock One Hit Knockdowns
Unlock a one-hit knockdown mode in Survival and Versus by getting first place in Sudden Death mode.

Unlock High Speed Mode
If you want your moves to move faster, win 100 battles in Survival with a single character, then record your name in the records.

Unlock Low Speed Mode
To move in slow motion, gain a ranking with each character in Arcade mode.

Unlock Hyper Beast Mode
To always play in Hyper Beast Mode, win 10 fights with a single character in Arcade mode and record your name.

Unlock One Fall Mode
In this mode, the first character to fall will lose, but he or she will be invincible to all other attacks. To unlock this cheat, win 20 rounds in Survival mode with a single character.

Unlock Kohryu
Win four rounds in Arcade mode without continuing, then defeat Kohryu in round five. You can now play as him.

Unlock Uranus
Complete Arcade mode without continuing once, then Uranus appears. Defeat him to play as him.

Debug Mode (Import Version)
From the main menu, enter the options menu. After you're at the options menu, press and hold L2 and hit the Circle button.

THE BOUNCER
Successfully complete the game to unlock more characters each time.

Unlock Leann Caldwell
Play through the entire game as Kou (you can't switch to any other character at any time).

Unlock MSF Kou
Play through the game as Kou, until he is infiltrating the Mikado building as a MSF soldier. Save your game and you can use that costume in Survival and Versus modes by holding L1+L2+R1+R2 when selecting Kou in those modes.

Alternate Costumes
Four different costumes for use in any mode other than Story are available for each character. To use one of these costumes, hold R1, R2, L1, or L2 while selecting the character of your choice.

Unlock Black-Hooded Sion
Access Sion's black hooded costume in Versus and Survival mode after you complete Survival mode once by holding L1+L2+R1+R2 when selecting Sion.

Unlock Wong Leung
Play through the game as any character. Battle Kaldea (the battle right before the final fight), with any character other than Sion. Then, use Sion to complete the game.

CITY CRISIS

Unlock Chase Mode
Earn an A rating on all missions and an S on the Bus Chase.

Unlock Disaster Mode
Achieve an S rating in Final Rescue Mode to unlock Disaster Mode.

Unlock Final Rescue Mode
To unlock the Final Rescue Mode, earn an S rating with the Sports Car.

CRAZY TAXI

Another View
To get another view of the *Crazy Taxi* proceedings, begin a game. While the game is in progress, press and hold L1 and R1, then press Circle to enter first-person driving mode. Press Triangle (while holding L1 and R1) to show things from a wider angle. Press Square (while holding L1 and R1) to see the speedometer.

Taxi Bike
At the character select screen, hit L1+R1 three times quickly. You can now drive a fast taxi bike. You can also gain access to the bike after you beat all Crazy Box challenges. Press D-Up at the select screen to get it.

Turn Off Arrow
To make the arrow that points you to your next destination disappear, hold R1 and press Start before you see the Character Selection screen. "No Arrows" appears on the screen if entered correctly.

Turn Off Destination Mark
To switch off the glowing square that indicates your destination, press and hold, then press Start before you see the Character Selection screen. "No Destination" appears onscreen if done correctly.

Unlock Another Day
To shake things up in the city and play "Another Day," press and hold R1. Keep holding it until you choose a taxi driver. After you do, "Another Day" appears onscreen, indicating correct code entry.

Unlock Expert Mode
To unlock the special Expert Mode, press and hold L1 and R1, then press Start before you see the Character Selection screen. "Expert" appears onscreen if done properly.

DANCE SUMMIT 2001 BUST-A-MOVE

Unlock Disco Estrus Team and Muscle Stadium Stage
Beat the game twice.

Unlock Far East Commanders Team and Iga Base Stage
Beat the game four times.

Unlock Galaxy 4 Team and Disco 21 Stage
Beat the game in Team mode.

Unlock Jumbo Max Team and 79 Street Stage
Beat the game three times.

DAVE MIRRA FREESTYLE BMX 2

Unlock All Bikes
To unlock all of the bikes in the game, enter the following code at the main menu: Up, Left, Down, Right, Down, Down, Right, Down, Down, Left, Square. All of the bikes for all of the riders are now available.

Unlock Amish Boy
To unlock Amish Boy, enter the following cheat at the main menu: Up, Left, Down, Right, Right, Left, Left, Down, Up, Left, Square. Now the bearded one will be available for Free play and ProQuest modes.

Unlock Colin Mackay's Competition Outfit
To unlock this rider's outfit, go to the main menu and press Up, Down, Right, Down, Up, Right, Right, Up, Square.

Unlock Dave Mirra's Competition Outfit
To unlock this rider's outfit, go to the main menu and press Up, Down, Up, Down, Right, Left, Up, Up, Square.

Unlock Joey Garcia's Competition Outfit
To unlock this rider's outfit, go to the main menu and press Up, Down, Up, Left, Down, Right, Down, Right, Square.

Unlock Kenan Harkin's Competition Outfit
To unlock this rider's outfit, go to the main menu and press Up, Down, Left, Down, Left, Up, Down, Up, Square.

Unlock Leigh Ramsdell's Competition Outfit
To unlock this rider's outfit, go to the main menu and press Up, Down, Down, Left, Down, Down, Down, Left, Square.

Unlock Luc-E's Competition Outfit
To unlock this rider's outfit, go to the main menu and press Up, Down, Left, Down, Left, Right, Left, Left, Square.

Unlock Mike Dias

To unlock Mike Dias, enter the following code at the main menu: Up, Left, Down, Right, Right, Left, Up, Down, Up, Right, Square. Mike Dias will be available for Free play and ProQuest modes.

Unlock Mike Laird's Competition Outfit

To unlock this rider's outfit, go to the main menu and press Up, Up, Down, Down, Left, Right, Right, Left, Square.

Unlock Rick Moliterno's Competition Outfit

To unlock this rider's outfit, go to the main menu and press Up, Down, Up, Up, Up, Up, Left, Up, Square.

Unlock Ryan Nyquist's Competition Outfit

To unlock this rider's outfit, go to the main menu and press Up, Down, Down, Left, Down, Up, Up, Down, Square.

Unlock Scott Wirch's Competition Outfit

To unlock this rider's outfit, go to the main menu and press Up, Down, Right, Down, Up, Right, Right, Up, Square.

Unlock Tim Mirra's Competition Outfit

To unlock this rider's outfit, go to the main menu and press Up, Down, Right, Left, Left, Up, Down, Up, Square.

Unlock Todd Lyons' Competition Outfit

To unlock this rider's outfit, go to the main menu and press Up, Down, Down, Right, Up, Left, Left, Down, Square.

Unlock Troy McMurray's Competition Outfit

To unlock this rider's outfit, go to the main menu and press Up, Down, Left, Down, Right, Left, Up, Left, Square.

Unlock Zack Shaw's Competition Outfit

To unlock this rider's outfit, go to the main menu and press Up, Down, Left, Right, Down, Down, Right, Down, Square.

DEAD OR ALIVE 2

Deluxe Credit Ending

Beat the game with every character in Very Hard mode.

Unlock Bayman

Beat Story mode with every character. Or complete Story mode using any combination of characters 30 times.

Unlock Tengu

Collect 10 stars in Survival mode. Or play as any combination of characters more than 200 times.

Ayane C3 Costume

Complete Story mode with Ayane on any setting.

Ayane C4 Costume

Complete Story mode with Ayane and without Continuing on default settings or higher. Or complete Story mode using Ayane five times on any setting.

Ayane C5 Costume

Earn 1.5 million points with Ayane in Survival mode on default settings or higher. Or play as Ayane more than 25 times.

Ayane C6 Costume

Beat more than 50 stages with Ayane in Survival mode on any setting. Or play as Ayane more than 50 times.

Ayane C7 Costume

Complete Time Attack mode with Ayane and in less than 4:15 on any setting. Or play as Ayane more than 100 times.

Ayane C8 Costume

Get the "Tiara" item with Ayane in Survival mode on any setting. Or play as Ayane more than 200 times.

Bass C3 Costume

Complete Story mode with Bass on any setting.

Bass C4 Costume

Complete Story mode with Bass and without Continuing on default settings or higher. Or complete Story mode using Bass five times on any setting.

Bass C5 Costume

Get the "Championship Belt" item with Bass in Survival mode on any difficulty setting. Or play as Bass more than 50 times.

Bayman C3 Costume

Play as Bayman more than 10 times.

Bayman C4 Costume

Get the "Bayman's Missile" item with Bayman in Survival mode on any setting. Or play as Bayman more than 30 times.

Ein C3 Costume

Complete Story mode with Ein on any setting.

Ein C4 Costume

Complete Story mode with Ein and without Continuing on default settings or higher. Or complete Story mode using Ein five times on any setting.

Ein C5 Costume

Get the "Scrolls" item with Ein in Survival mode on any setting. Or play as Ein more than 50 times.

Gen Fu C3 Costume

Complete Story mode with Gen on any setting.

Gen Fu C4 Costume

Complete Story mode with Gen and without Continuing on default settings or higher. Or complete Story mode using Gen five times on any setting.

Gen Fu C5 Costume

Earn 1 million points with Gen in Survival mode on default settings or higher. Or play as Gen more than 30 times.

Gen Fu C6 Costume

Win 48 matches in Survival mode on default settings or higher. Or play as Gen more than 75 times.

Gen Fu C7 Costume

Get the "Mah Jong Counter" item with Gen in Survival mode. Or play as Gen more than 100 times.

Helena C3 Costume

Complete Story mode with Helena on any setting.

Helena C4 Costume

Complete Story mode with Helena and without Continuing on default settings or higher. Or complete Story mode using Helena five times on any setting.

Helena C5 Costume

Earn 2 million points with Helena in Survival mode on default settings or higher. Or play as Helena more than 30 times.

Helena C6 Costume

Complete Time Attack mode with Helena in less than 4:15 on default settings or higher. Or play as Helena more than 75 times.

Helena C7 Costume

Get the "Rocket" item with Helena in Survival mode on any setting. Or play as Helena more than 150 times.

Jann Lee C3 Costume

Complete Story mode with Jann Lee on any setting.

Jann Lee C4 Costume

Complete Story mode with Jann Lee and without Continuing on default settings or higher. Or complete Story mode using Jann Lee five times on any setting.

Jann Lee C5 Costume

Earn 1 million points with Jann Lee without Continuing on default settings or higher. Or play as Jann Lee more than 50 times.

Jann Lee C6 Costume

Get the "Dragon" item with Jann Lee in Survival mode on any setting. Or play as Jann Lee more than 100 times.

Kasumi C3 Costume

Complete Story mode with Kasumi on any setting.

Kasumi C4 Costume

Complete Story mode with Kasumi and without Continuing on default settings or higher. Or complete Story mode using Kasumi three times on any setting.

Kasumi C5 Costume

Complete Story mode with Kasumi and without Continuing on default settings or higher. Or complete Story mode using Kasumi five times on any setting.

Kasumi C6 Costume

Earn 2 million points with Kasumi in Survival mode on default settings or higher. Or play as Kasumi more than 50 times.

Kasumi C7 Costume

Complete more than 50 stages with Kasumi in Survival mode on default settings or higher. Or play as Kasumi more than 100 times.

Kasumi C8 Costume

Get the "Cherry" item with Kasumi in Survival mode on any setting. Or play as Kasumi more than 200 times.

Lei Fang C3 Costume

Complete Story mode with Lei Fang on any setting.

Lei Fang C4 Costume

Complete Story mode with Lei Fang and without Continuing on default settings or higher. Or complete Story mode using Lei Fang three times on any setting.

Lei Fang C5 Costume

Earn 1 million points with Lei Fang in Survival mode on default settings or higher. Or complete Story mode five times with Lei Fang.

Lei Fang C6 Costume
Complete Tag Battle mode with Lei Fang in a C5 costume and partnering with Jann Lee in a C5 costume. Or play as Lei Fang more than 50 times.

Lei Fang C7 Costume
Complete Time Attack mode with Lei Fang in less that 4:15 on default settings or higher. Or play as Lei Fang more than 100 times.

Lei Fang C8 Costume
Get the "Decoration Cake" item with Lei Fang in Survival mode on any setting. Or play as Lei Fang more than 200 times.

Leon C3 Costume
Complete Story mode with Leon on any setting.

Leon C4 Costume
Complete Story mode with Leon and without continuing on default settings or higher. Or complete Story mode using Leon three times on any setting.

Leon C5 Costume
Get the "Missile" item with Leon in Survival mode on any setting. Or play as Leon more than 50 times.

Ryu Hayabusa C3 Costume
Complete Story mode with Ryu on any setting.

Ryu Hayabusa C4 Costume
Complete Story mode with Ryu and without Continuing on default settings or higher. Or complete Story mode using Ryu five times on any setting.

Ryu Hayabusa C5 Costume
Earn 1 million points with Ryu in Survival mode on default settings or higher. Or play as Ryu more than 50 times.

Ryu Hayabusa C6 Costume
Get the "Green Tea" item with Ryu in Survival mode on any setting. Or play as Ryu more than 100 times.

Tina C3 Costume
Complete Story mode with Tina on any setting.

Tina C4 Costume
Complete Story mode with Tina and without Continuing on default settings or higher. Or complete Story mode using Tina five times on any setting.

Tina C5 Costume
Earn 1.5 million points with Tina in Survival mode on default settings or higher. Or play as Tina more than 30 times.

Tina C6 Costume
Complete Time Attack mode with Tina in less than 4:15 on default settings or higher. Or play as Tina more than 75 times.

Tina C7 Costume
Get the "Roast Chicken" item with Tina in Survival mode on any setting. Or play as Tina more than 100 times.

Zack C3 Costume
Complete Story mode with Zack on any setting.

Zack C4 Costume
Complete Story mode with Zack and without Continuing on default settings or higher. Or complete Story mode using Zack five times on any setting.

Zack C5 Costume
Earn 1 million points with Zack in Survival mode on default settings or higher. Or play as Zack more than 50 times.

Zack C6 Costume
Get the "Parfait" item with Zack in Survival mode on any setting. Or play as Zack more than 100 times.

DEAD OR ALIVE 2: HARDCORE

Bonus Options
Pause the game. Press Triangle+X.

Longer Credits
Beat the Story mode with all the characters and on the Very Hard difficulty setting.

More Bounce
Go into the Options menu. Change your age between 13 and 99. The higher you set your age, the more bounce you will see from the female characters.

Unlock Bayman
Beat Story mode with every character on the Easy Difficulty setting. Bayman becomes unlocked in all modes except for Story mode.

Unlock the CG Gallery
Beat Team mode with five characters.

DEUS EX: THE CONSPIRACY

Activate Cheats
Enter the Goals/Notes/Images screen. Press L2, R2, L1, R1, Start(3) to display another tab on this screen with the following cheats that you can turn on and off: God, Full Health, Full Energy, Full Ammo, Full Mods, All Skills, Full Credits, and Tantalus. The Tantalus cheat allows you to destroy a highlighted object during gameplay.

DRUM MANIA

After you select "Start Game" you're taken to the Mode Select screen. At this screen, perform the following patterns:

Drums Mirror Mode
Snare (2), High Tom, Low Tom, High Tom, Bass

Drums Expert Mode
Hi-Hat (2), Snare (2), High Tom, Low Tom, High Tom, Bass, Bass

Drums Hidden Mode
Low Tom, High Tom, Low Tom, High Tom, Low Tom, Bass

Drums Speed Mode
Hi-Hat, Snare, Hi-Hat (2), Snare, Hi-Hat, Bass.

Guitar Hidden Mode
Red, Blue, Green, Blue, Red, Green

Guitar Fast Flow
Red, Green, Blue, Pick (2)

Guitar Super Fast Flow
Red, Green, Blue, Pick (2), Red, Green, Blue, Pick (2)

Guitar Blank Screen
Red, Blue, Green, Blue, Red, Green, Red, Blue, Green, Blue, Red, Green

Guitar Random Mode
Blue, Green (2), Red, Green, Pick

DYNASTY WARRIORS

Free Health
Find a save point even if you don't have a memory card. The game asks if you want to save. It doesn't matter if you save or not. When you return to your game all of your health will be restored.

Different Intro Sequence
Beat Mosou mode with any character.

Editing Mode
Beat Mosou mode with all the characters except for Diao Chan, Dong Zhuo, Yuan Shao, Lu Bu, and Zhang Jiao.

Unlock Side Selection and BGM Option
Beat Mosou mode with one member of each kingdom.

Unlock Ma Chao, Huang Zhong, and Jiang Wei
Beat Mosou mode with Zhao Yun, Zhang Fei, or Guan Yu.

Unlock Zhang Liao and Xiahou Yuan
Beat Mosou mode with Dian Wei, Xiahou Dun, or Xu Zhu.

Unlock Lu Meng, Taishi Ci, and Gan Ning
Beat Mosou mode with Lu Xun, Zhou Yu, or Sun Shang Xiang.

Unlock Sun Quan and Sun Jian
Beat Mosou mode with Lu Xun, Sun Shang Xiang, Zhou Yu, Lu Meng, Taishi Ci, and Gan Ning.

Unlock Dong Zhuo, Diao Chan, Yuan Chao, and Zhang Jiao in Free Mode
Beat Mosou mode with one member of each kingdom.

Unlock Lu Bu in Free Mode
Complete Stage 2, Hulao Gate, in Musou mode with at least 1,000 KOs.

Unlock Cao Cao
Beat Mosou mode with Dian Wei, Xiahou Dun, Xiahou Yuan, Xu Zhu, Zhang Liao, and Sima Yi.

Unlock Liu Bei
Beat Mosou mode with Zhao Yun, Huang Zhong, Guan Yu, Zhang Fei, Ma Chao, Jiang Wei, and Zhuge Liang.

Unlock Sima Yi
Beat Mosou mode with Dian Wei, Xiahou Dun, and Xu Zhu.

ESPN INTERNATIONAL TRACK & FIELD

Purple Player
Enter Seoul at the Name Entry screen in Trial mode. A sound confirms correct entry.

Orange Player
Enter Atlanta at the Name Entry screen in Trial mode. A sound confirms correct entry.

Gray Player
Enter Athens at the Name Entry screen in Trial mode. A sound confirms correct entry.

Red Player
Enter Tokyo at the Name Entry screen in Trial mode. A sound confirms correct entry.

Green Player
Enter Mexico at the Name Entry screen in Trial mode. A sound confirms correct entry.

Aluminum Player
Enter Munich at the Name Entry screen in Trial mode. A sound confirms correct entry.

Blue Player
Enter L.A. at the Name Entry screen in Trial mode. A sound confirms correct entry.

Cream Player
Enter Moscow at the Name Entry screen in Trial mode. A sound confirms correct entry.

Copper Player
Enter Roma at the Name Entry screen in Trial mode. A sound confirms correct entry.

Bronze Player
Enter Helsinki at the Name Entry screen in Trial mode. A sound confirms correct entry.

Silver Player
Enter Sydney at the Name Entry screen in Trial mode. A sound confirms correct entry.

Gold Player
Enter Montreal at the Name Entry screen in Trial mode. A sound confirms correct entry.

FANTAVISION

Unlock Bonus Option 1
Beat and save the game under the Normal difficulty setting.

Bonus Option 2
Beat and save the game under the Hard difficulty setting.

GAUNTLET DARK LEGACY

Enter the codes in the spot where you name new characters. You can only utilize one special character or game mode at a time. Choose the character type (i.e. Dwarf, Valkyrie, etc.), as well as naming that character according to the code. Use special game modes (i.e., Unlimited Supershot, Unlimited Invulnerably) with any character type.

Dwarf General
ICE600

S & M Dwarf
NUD069

Happy Face Jester
STX222

Chainsaw Jester
KJH105

Punkrock Jester
PNK666

Battle General (Knight)
BAT900

Ninja (Knight)
TAK118

Employee Stig (Knight)
STG333

Waitress (Knight)
KAO292

Ex-Employee Chris (Knight)
CSS222

Football Dude (Knight)
RIZ721

Manager Mike (Knight)
DIB626

Karate Steve (Knight)
SJB964

Created By Don (Knight)
ARV984

Town General (Valkyrie)
TWN300

School Girl (Valkyrie)
AYA555

Cheerleader (Valkyrie)
CEL721

Castle General (Warrior)
CAS400

Mountain General (Warrior)
MTN200

Rat Knight (Warrior)
RAT333

Regular Garm (Wizard)
GARM99

Sickly Garm (Wizard)
GARM00

Desert General (Wizard)
DES700

Sky General (Wizard)
SKY100

Sumner (Wizard)
SUM224

Unlimited Supershot
SSHOTS

Unlimited Invulnerability
INVULN

9 Keys and 9 Potions Per Level
ALLFUL

Unlimited Full Turbo
Purple

$10,000 Gold per level
10000K

Unlimited Halo and Levitate
1ANGLI

Unlimited Shrink Enemy and Growth
DELTA1

Unlimited Invisibility
000000

Unlimited X-Ray Glasses
PEEKIN

Unlimited Rapid Fire
QCKSHT

Unlimited 3 Way Shot
MENAGE

Unlimited Extra Speed
XSPEED

Unlimited Reflective Shot
REFLEX

Unlimited Play as Pojo
EGG911

GRADIUS 3 AND 4: MYTHOLOGY OF REVIVAL

Laser Power-Up
Pause the game. Press Up (2), Down (2), Left, Right, Left, Right, X, Circle. You can only do this a certain number of times.

Double Shot Power-Up
Pause the game. Press Up (2), Down (2), Left, Right, Left, Right, Square, Triangle. You can only do this a certain number of times.

Gran Turismo 3 A-Spec
Complete the races listed to unlock the corresponding automobiles.

Sunday Cup
Toyota Sprinter, Trueno GT-Apex (AE-86 Type I)

Clubman Cup
Mazda Eunos Roadster

FF Challenge
Toyota Vitz RS 1.5

FR Challenge
Nissan Silvia K's 1800cc

MR Challenge
Toyota MR-S S Edition

4WD Challenge
Suzuki Alto Works, Suzuki Sports Limited

Lightweight K Cup
Mini Cooper 1.3i

Stars and Stripes Grand Championship
Chevrolet Camaro SS

Spider/Roadster Cup
Mazda Miata Roadster RS

80's Sports Car Cup
Mazda Savanna RX7 Infini III

NA Race of NA Sports
Honda CRX Del Sol SiR

Turbo Race of Turbo Sports
Daihatsu Mira TR XX Avanzato R

Tourist Trophy Audi TT Race
Audi TT 1.8T Quattro

Legend of Silver Arrow Mercedes Benz
Mercedes SLK 230 Kompressor

Altezza Race
Toyota Celica SS-II

Vitz Race
4 cars, Toyota Vitz RS 1.5

Type R Meeting
Honda Civic SiR-II

Evolution Meeting
Mitsubishi Lancer Evolution IV GSR

Beetle Cup
Volkswagen New Beetle Rsi

Grand Turismo World Championship
Toyota Celica GT-Four, Mitsubishi Lancer Evolution VI GSR, Mazda Miata, Nissan Skyline GTR V-spec II

Get All Golds
Mitsubishi Lancer Evolution V GSR

Japanese Championship
Mazda RX7 Type RZ, Mitsubishi Evolution IV GSR, FTO GP Version R, Subaru Impreza WRX Sti Version VI Wagon

American Championship
Subaru Impreza Sedan WRX STi Version VI, Chevy Camaro Race Car, Audi TT 1.8T Quattro, Mazda RX7 Type RS

European Championship
Lotus Elise 190, Nissan GTR V-Spec, Gillet Vertigo Race Car, Mini Cooper 1.3i

Gran Turismo World Championship
Nissan C-West Razo Silvia, Nissan Z Concept car, Toyota GT1 Road Car, Mazda RX8

Deutsche Tourenwagen Challenge
Volkswagen Lupo Cup Car, Volkswagen Beetle Cup Racer, Astra Touring Car, RUF 3400S

FF Challenge
Celica TRD Sports M

FR Challenge
Toyota Sprinter Trueno GT-Apex Shigeno Version

MR Challenge
Honda NSX Type S Zero

4WD Challenge
Mitsubishi Lancer Evolution VII GSR

Stars & Stripes Grand Championship
Spoon Sports S2000 Race Car

Boxer Spirit
Subaru Legacy Blitzer B4

80s Sports Car Cup
Nismo Skyline GT-R S-tune

NA Race of NA Sports
Mazda RX8 Turbo

Race of Turbo Sports
Mines Lancer Evolution VI GSR

Gran Turismo All-Stars
Mine's GT-R-N1 V-spec, Raybrig NSX

All Japanese GT Championship
Honda Arta NSX JGTC, Denso Supra Race Car

Tourist Trophy
Audi S4

Race of Red Emblem
Nismo 400R

Legend of Silver Arrow
Mercedes Benz CLK Touring Car (D2 AMG Mercedes)

Altezza Championship Race
Tom's X540 Chaser, Toyota Vitz RS 1.5

Type R Meeting
4 cars, Honda NSX Type-R

Evolution Meeting
Mitsubishi Lancer Evolution VI Rally Car

Dream Car Championship
Mitsubishi FTO LM Race Car, Mazda RX7 LM Race Car

Get all Golds
Team ORECA Dodge Viper GTSR

British GT Car Cup
Aston Martin Vanquish

MR Challenge
Tommy Kaira ZZII

4WD Challenge
Mitsubishi Lancer Evolution VII Rally Car Prototype

Spider & Roadster Championship
Shelby Cobra

Dream Car Championship
Toyota GT1, Panoz Esperante GTR, FTO LM Race Car, F090/s

Like the Wind
Mazda 787B

Tahiti Challenge of Rally
Toyota Celica Rally Car

Tahiti Maze
Ford Escort Rally Car

Smokey Mountain Rally
Ford Focus Rally Car

Swiss Alps
Peugeot 206 Rally Car

Tahiti Challenge of Rally II
Toyota Corolla Rally Car

Tahiti Maze II
Impreza Rally Car

Smokey Mountain II
Mitsubishi Lancer Evolution VI Rally Car

Swiss Alps II
Mitsubishi Lancer Evolution VII Rally Car Prototype

Super Special Route 5 Wet
Citroen Xsara Rally Car

Super Special Route 5 Wet II
Subaru Impreza Rally Car Prototype

Get All Golds
Suzuki Escudo Pikes Peak Version

Super Speedway 150 Miles
Chevrolet Corvette C5R, Tickford Falcon XR8 Race Car, F090/S

All Golds on B License
Mazda Miata RS

All Golds on A License
Mazda RX8

All Golds on IB License
Nissan Z Concept Car

All Golds on IA License
Aston Martin Vanqish

All Golds on S License
Dodge Viper GTS-R Concept Car

All Golds on Rally License
Subaru Impreza Rally Car Prototype

Win Toyota Sprinter Truendo GT-Apex
To win the sprinty Toyota Truendo, complete the Sunday Cup with gold medals in each of the three races.

Win Mazda Eunos Roadster
To win the Eunos Roadster, complete the Cupman Cup with gold medals in each of the three races.

Unlock Blue Toyota MR-S S Edition
Win the Beginner MR Challenge to unlock the Blue Toyota MR-S S Edition.

Unlock Mazda Roadster RS
To unlock the Mazda Roadster RS, complete the Spider and Roadster cup with gold medals across the board.

Unlock Mitsubishi Lancer Evolution VI Rally Car
Win the Amateur Evolution Meeting to unlock the Mitsubishi Lancer Evolution VI Rally Car.

Unlock Nissan Silvia K's 1800cc
To unlock the Nissan Silvia K's 1800cc, win the Beginner FR Challenge series.

Unlock Silver Daihatsu Mira TRXX
Unlock Silver Daihatsu Mira TRXX Avanzato R by winning Beginner Race of Turbo Sports.

Unlock Silver Honda CRX Del Sol SiR
To unlock Silver Honda CRX Del Sol SiR, win the Beginner Race of NA Sports series.

Unlock Tan Nissan Skyline GT-R V-spec II R32
Win the Beginner GT World Championships to unlock Tan Nissan Skyline GT-R V-spec II R32.

Unlock Titanium Mitsubishi Lancer Evolution VII GSR
Win the Amateur 4WD Challenge to unlock the Titanium Mitsubishi Lancer Evolution VII GSR.

Unlock Tracks in Arcade Mode
Arcade mode track unlocking: Beat each tier of tracks on easy mode, and you unlock the next tier of tracks.

Tier 1 (start out with these):
Super Speedway, Midfield Raceway, Smokey Mountain, Swiss Alps, Trial Mountain, Midfield Raceway II

Tier 2:
Smokey Mountain II, Tokyo R246, Grand Valley Speedway, Laguna Seca Raceway, Rome Circuit, Tahiti Circuit.

Tier 3:
Swiss Alps II, Trial Mountain II, Deep Forest Raceway II, Special Stage Route 5, Seattle Circuit, Test Course.

Unlock White Mine's Lancer Evolution VI
Win the Amateur Race of Turbo Sports to unlock the White Mine's Lancer Evolution VI.

Unlock Yellow Honda Civic SiR-II EG
Win Beginner Type R Meeting to unlock Yellow Honda Civic SiR.

GRAND THEFT AUTO 3

Tank (Rhino)
Press Circle(6), R1, L2, L1, Triangle, Circle, Triangle during gameplay. A message will confirm correct code entry. The tank will appear in front of you. This may be repeated as many times as needed.

Flying Car (Low Gravity)
Press Right, R2, Circle, R1, L2, Down, L1, R1 during gameplay. A message will confirm correct code entry. Accelerate and press Up to fly.

No Wanted Level
Press R2(2), L1, R2, Up, Down, Up, Down, Up, Down during gameplay. A message will confirm correct code entry. Note: Saving the game will make the effects of this code permanent.

Higher Wanted Level
Press R2(2), L1, R2, Left, Right, Left, Right, Left during gameplay. A message will confirm correct code entry. Note: Saving the game will make the effects of this code permanent.

PLAYSTATION2

All Weapons

Press R2(2), L1, R2, Left, Down, Right, Up, Left, Down, Right, Up during gameplay. A message will confirm correct code entry. Repeat this code for more ammunition. To get unlimited ammunition, enable the "All Weapons" code continuously until whatever you want is at 9999 shots. The next time your clip runs out, it will reload automatically, but the magazine (9999) will stay the same. Note: If you are busted, your weapons will disappear and this code will have to be repeated.

Full Health

Press R2(2), L1, R1, Left, Down, Right, Up, Left, Down, Right, Up during gameplay. A message will confirm correct code entry. Note: If this code is enabled during a mission where there is damage on your car, the meter will reset to zero. If your vehicle is on fire, enable the "Full Health" code to extinguish it. This code also repairs your car. You can't see the repairs, but it acts like a new car. If you're on a mission where you need a mint-condition car, sometimes enabling the "Full Health" code will fulfill the requirements.

Full Armor

Press R2(2), L1, L2, Left, Down, Right, Up, Left, Down, Right, Up during gameplay. A message will confirm correct code entry.

More Money

Press R2(2), L1, L1, Left, Down, Right, Up, Left, Down, Right, Up during gameplay. A message will confirm correct code entry.

Destroy All Cars

Press L2, R2, L1, R1, L2, R2, Triangle, Square, Circle, Triangle, L2, L1. A message will confirm correct code entry.

Better Driving Skills

Press R1, L1, R2, L1, Left, R1(2), Triangle during gameplay. A message will confirm correct code entry. Press L3 or R3 to jump while driving. Note: Saving the game allows your car to never tip. Also, every car will have hydraulics that enable it to jump 15 feet in the air over other cars. After this code is enabled, any time you roll your car, press Square + X to flip back over. This works as long as your car is not on its roof.

Increased Gore

Press Square, L1, Circle, Down, L1, R1, Triangle, Right, L1, X during gameplay. No confirmation message will appear. You can shoot off pedestrians' arms, legs, and heads with some weapons (sniper rifle, assault rifle, explosives) with an increase in the overall amount of blood left behind. Note: Saving the game will make the effects of this code permanent.

Fog

Press L1, L2, R1, R2(2), R1, L2, X during gameplay. A message will confirm correct code entry.

Overcast Skies

Press L1, L2, R1, R2(2), R1, L2, Square during gameplay. A message will confirm correct code entry.

Rain

Press L1, L2, R1, R2(2), R1, L2, Circle during gameplay. A message will confirm correct code entry.

Normal Weather

Press L1, L2, R1, R2(2), R1, L2, Triangle during gameplay. A message will confirm correct code entry.

Invisible Cars

Press L1(2), Square, R2, Triangle, L1, Triangle during gameplay. A message will confirm correct code entry. Only your vehicle's wheels will be visible.

Faster Gameplay

Press Triangle, Up, Right, Down, Square, L1, L2 during gameplay. A message will confirm correct code entry. Repeat this code to increase its effect.

Slower Gameplay

Press Triangle, Up, Right, Down, Square, R1, R2 during gameplay. A message will confirm correct code entry. This cheat also continues the effect of an adrenaline pill.

Speed Up Time

Press Circle(3), Square(5), L1, Triangle, Circle, Triangle during gameplay. A message will confirm correct code entry. Repeat this code to increase its effect.

Different Costume

Press Right, Down, Left, Up, L1, L2, Up, Left, Down, Right during gameplay. A message will confirm correct code entry.

Pedestrians Riot

Press Down, Up, Left, Up, X, R1, R2, L2, L1 during gameplay. A message will confirm correct code entry. Note: Saving the game will make the effects of this code permanent.

All Pedestrians Have Weapons

Press R2, R1, Triangle, X, L2, L1, Up, Down during gameplay. A message will confirm correct code entry. Some pedestrians will throw bombs or shoot at you if you steal their car. Note: Saving the game will make the effects of this code permanent.

Pedestrians Attack You

Press Down, Up, Left, Up, X, R1, R2, L1, L2 during gameplay. A message will confirm correct code entry. Note: Saving the game will make the effects of this code permanent.

GUN GRIFFON BLAZE

Start With Different Weapons

Which country your pilot is from determines which set of weapons your mech is outfitted with. Change your pilot's origin to equip your mech with different weapons. From the main menu select Create New Pilot. From here, you can rename your pilot and change other statistics.

HEADHUNTER

Activate Cheat Mode

Hold R1 + Square and press Start during gameplay.

HOT SHOTS GOLF 3

In-Game Reset

Press L1 + R1 + L2 + R2 + Start + Select during gameplay.

Left-Handed Golfer

Press Start when selecting a golfer.

JAMES BOND 007: AGENT UNDER FIRE

Golden Gun

Successfully complete the Trouble in Paradise level with a "Gold" rank. This cheat unlocks the Golden P2K. With this gun, you receive a silencer that the normal P2K doesn't have.

Golden Gun in Multiplayer Mode

Successfully complete the Precious Cargo level with a "Platinum" rank and all 007 icons.

Golden CH-6

Successfully complete the Precious Cargo level with a "Gold" rank. When used, this cheat gives you unlimited rockets.

Golden Accuracy Power-Up

Successfully complete the Bad Diplomacy level with a "Gold" rank. This cheat enables you to have greater auto-aim.

Golden Clip Power-Up

Successfully complete the Cold Reception level with a "Gold" rank.

Golden Grenade Power-Up

Successfully complete the Night of the Jackal level with a "Gold" rank.

Golden Bullet Power-Up

Successfully complete the Poseidon level with a "Gold" rank.

Golden

Successfully complete the Forbidden Depths level with a "Gold" rank.

Unlimited Golden Gun Ammunition

Successfully complete the Evil Summit level with a "Gold" rank.

Unlimited Car Missiles

Successfully complete the Dangerous Pursuit level with a "Gold" rank.

Rocket Manor Multiplayer Level

Successfully complete the Trouble in Paradise level with a "Platinum" rank and all 007 icons. This cheat unlocks a new multiplayer level. It is a large, open area. The map settings allow only rockets.

Stealth Bond

Successfully complete the Dangerous Pursuit level with a "Platinum" rank and all 007 icons.

Guard Skin in Multiplayer Mode

Successfully complete the Cold Reception level with a "Platinum" rank and all 007 icons.

Alpine Guard Skin in Multiplayer Mode

Successfully complete the Streets of Bucharest level with a "Platinum" rank and all 007 icons.

Cyclops Oil Guard Skin in Multiplayer Mode

Successfully complete the Poseidon level with a "Platinum" rank and all 007 icons.

Poseidon Guard Skin in Multiplayer Mode
Successfully complete the Mediterranean Crisis level with a "Platinum" rank and all 007 icons.

Carrier Guard Multiplayer Skin
Successfully complete the Evil Summit level with a "Platinum" rank and all 007 icons.

Rapid Fire Power-Up
Successfully complete the Fire and Water level with a "Gold" rank.

Regenerative Armor Power-Up
Successfully complete the Mediterranean Crisis level with a "Gold" rank.

Calypso Gun in Multiplayer Mode
Successfully complete the Fire and Water level with a "Platinum" rank and all 007 icons.

Full Arsenal in Multiplayer Mode
Successfully complete the Forbidden Depths level with a "Platinum" rank and all 007 icons.

Gravity Boots in Multiplayer Mode
Successfully complete the Bad Diplomacy level with a "Platinum" rank and all 007 icons.

Viper Gun in Multiplayer Mode
Successfully complete the Night of the Jackal level with a "Platinum" rank and all 007 icons.

Lotus Esprit Car
Successfully complete the Streets of Bucharest level with a "Gold" rank.

JIKKYOU WORLD SOCCER 2000

Unlock the All-Stars Team
Press Up (2), Down (2), Left, Right, Left, Right, X, Circle, Start.

KLONOA 2: LUNATEA'S VEIL

Unlock Music Box
Complete both hidden levels to unlock the Music Box sound test. The first hidden level gives you the first 27 tracks, while the second one gives you the remaining songs.

Unlock Hidden Levels.
In each stage are six stars. If you collect all six, you gain a doll that appears on the R1 screen. Collect eight dolls to unlock the first hidden level, and all sixteen for the second.

Unlock Pictures in Image Gallery.
Each stage has 150 little gems scattered about. If you collect all 150, you'll open up more images in the special image gallery.

KNOCKOUT KINGS

Select "Modes" from the main menu, then choose "Career." Next choose "New" and type one of the names to unlock the corresponding boxer.

Unlock Ashy Knucks
MECCA

Unlock Ray Austin
AUSTIN

Unlock Trevor Nelson
NELSON

Unlock Jason Giambi
JGIAMBI

Unlock Charles Hatcher
HATCHER

Unlock Bernardo Osuna
OSUNA

Unlock David Defiagbon
DEFIAGBN

Unlock Barry Sanders
MRBARRY

Unlock Chuck Zito
ZITO

Unlock David Bostice
BOSTICE

Unlock David DeMartini
DEMART

Unlock Joe Mesi
BAILEY

Unlock John Botti
JBOTTI

Unlock Jr Seau
JRSEAU

Unlock Owen Nolan
OWNOLAN

Unlock Steve Francis
STEVEF

LE MANS 24 HOURS

See the Credits
To view the credits, enter your name as "HEINEY" in the Championship Mode name screen.

Unlock All Cars
To unlock all the cars in the game, enter your name as "ACO" at the Championship Mode name screen.

Unlock All Championships
To unlock all championships, enter your name as "NUMBAT" in the Championship Mode name screen.

Unlock All Tracks
To unlock all tracks, enter your name as "SPEEDY" at the Championship Mode name screen.

Unlock Le Mans
To unlock the Le Mans, enter your name as "WOMBAT" in the Championship Mode name screen.

MADDEN NFL 2001

Unlimited Creation Points
Create a player. Go into the "Edit Player" option at the Roster screen. Use Up or Down to choose the player you want to modify. Press Right to get to the speed category. Press X, X.

Slam Dunk Celebration
Score a touchdown and immediately hold L1+R2.

Shoulder Shake Celebration
Score a touchdown and immediately hold L1+R1.

Spike the Football Celebration
Score a touchdown and immediately hold L1+X.

Say a Prayer Celebration
Score a touchdown and immediately hold L1+Triangle.

Hip Thrust Celebration
Score a touchdown and immediately hold L1+Square.

Jump Spike Celebration
Score a touchdown and immediately hold L1+Circle.

MAXIMO

Gallery Mode
Collect the Sorceress kiss at the end of each level. Seat each of the four kisses to a power-up position. Once the game is completed, the art gallery will be unlocked.

Mastery Mode
Have a 100 percent mastery ranking at the end of the game for all levels except those in the Hub. To master a level, you must kill every enemy and find every hidden chest.

MDK2 ARMAGEDDON

Kurt in His Boxer Shorts
At the main menu, press and hold L2 + R2 and press: Square (2), Triangle, Square. As soon as Kurt is done skydiving and is on the ground, he'll be without his coil suit and sporting boxer shorts.

A Little Piece of Home
While playing through Level 5, take a moment to stop and look through the alien telescope. To activate the telescope, first destroy the BottRock Generator and the panel on the ledge above the telescope. Shoot the telescope lens to move it into a position where you can look through it and see crack animator Russ Rice on the Bioware balcony with some Conehead visitors.

Drop Camera
This makes a new camera effect. Hold L2+R2, press Circle, X, Circle, X and the camera drops in place. As you move, the perspective changes like in Resident Evil. To return the camera to normal, repeat the code.

Farting Doc
Doctor Hawkins needs a new diet. At any time while playing the Doctor hold down L2+R2, and press in on both control sticks.

Invincibility
First pause the game. Now while holding L2+R2, press Up (2), Down (2), Left (2), Right (2), Square, Triangle, Square, Triangle, Select, Start.

King of the Coneheads
In the Spider Room of Level 7, one of the Sniper Balls unleashes a pack of Coneheads. Rather than shooting them, stand around and wait. If you look carefully into the middle of the room while standing on the upper ledge, you may see the King of the Coneheads!

The *MDK 2* Development Team Are Stars

While playing through Level 4 don't forget to take a moment to gaze at the stars in the large arena with the three Poopsy Generators. Kill all of the enemies in this room first so you can star gaze without getting killed. Now, using Kurt Hectic's sniper scope, zoom in on certain special stars in the sky (they are usually slightly pinkish in color). There you find the crack team that made *MDK2* possible gazing back down at you, along with their Wu-Tang Clan names.

Matrix Camera Mode

Pause the game, then press L1+R1. This code removes the Pause menu, giving you an unobstructed view of the spinning Matrix Camera mode while the game is paused.

Max's Slo Mo Mode

While holding down Max's Shoot button, press Max's Equip Weapons button three times.

MEDAL OF HONOR FRONTLINE

Invincibility

Pause gameplay, then press Square, L1, Circle, R1, Triangle, L2, Select, R2. The game will automatically resume.

Unlimited Ammunition

Pause gameplay, then press Circle, L2, Square, L1, Select, R2, Triangle, Select. The game will automatically resume.

Master Code

Enter DAWOIKS at the Enigma Machine. Green lights will confirm correct code entry. Select the "Bonus" option under the Enigma Machine to enable/disable any desired cheat.

Information in this section was contributed by nmayse1.

Silver Bullet Mode

Enter WHATYOUGET at the Enigma Machine. Green lights will confirm correct code entry. Select the "Bonus" option under the Enigma Machine to enable/disable this cheat. Silver Bullet mode allows enemies to be killed with one shot.

Rubber Grenade Mode

Enter BOING at the Enigma Machine. Green lights will confirm correct code entry. Select the "Bonus" option under the Enigma Machine to enable/disable this cheat.

Snipe-O-Rama Mode

Enter LONGSHOT at the Enigma Machine. Green lights will confirm correct code entry. Select the "Bonus" option under the Enigma Machine to enable/disable this cheat. This cheat allows all guns to zoom like a sniper rifle.

Bullet Shield Mode

Enter BULLETZAP at the Enigma Machine. Green lights will confirm correct code entry. Select the "Bonus" option under the Enigma Machine to enable/disable this cheat. Any bullets fired at you will not damage you.

Mission 2 (A Storm in the Port)

Enter ORANGUTAN at the Enigma Machine. Green lights will confirm correct code entry. Select the "Bonus" option under the Enigma Machine to enable/disable this cheat.

Mission 3 (Needle in a Haystack)

Enter BABOON at the Enigma Machine. Green lights will confirm correct code entry. Select the "Bonus" option under the Enigma Machine to enable/disable this cheat.

Mission 4 (Several Bridges Too Far)

Enter CHIMPNZEE at the Enigma Machine. Green lights will confirm correct code entry. Select the "Bonus" option under the Enigma Machine to enable/disable this cheat.

Mission 5 (Rolling Thunder)

Enter LEMUR at the Enigma Machine. Green lights will confirm correct code entry. Select the "Bonus" option under the Enigma Machine to enable/disable this cheat.

Mission 6 (The Horten's Nest)

Enter GORILLA at the Enigma Machine. Green lights will confirm correct code entry. Select the "Bonus" option under the Enigma Machine to enable/disable this cheat.

Complete Current Mission with Gold Star

Enter MONKEY at the Enigma Machine. Green lights will confirm correct code entry. Select the "Bonus" option under the Enigma Machine to enable/disable this cheat.

Complete Previous Mission with Gold Star

Enter TIMEWARP at the Enigma Machine. Green lights will confirm correct code entry. Select the "Bonus" option under the Enigma Machine to enable/disable this cheat.

Perfectionist

Enter URTHEMAN at the Enigma Machine. Green lights will confirm correct code entry. Select the "Bonus" option under the Enigma Machine to enable/disable this cheat. This cheat allows the Nazis to kill you with one shot.

Mohton Torpedoes

Enter TPDOMOHTON at the Enigma Machine. Green lights will confirm correct code entry. Select the "Bonus" option under the Enigma Machine to enable/disable this cheat. Your bullets will change into "photon torpedoes."

Achilles' Head Mode

Enter GLASSJAW at the Enigma Machine. Green lights will confirm correct code entry. Select the "Bonus" option under the Enigma Machine to enable/disable this cheat. Nazis can be killed only with a headshot when this cheat is active.

Invisible Enemies

Enter WHERERU at the Enigma Machine. Green lights will confirm correct code entry. Select the "Bonus" option under the Enigma Machine to enable/disable this cheat. You will see only your enemies' guns and helmets.

Men with Hats

Enter HABRDASHR at the Enigma Machine. Green lights will confirm correct code entry. Select the "Bonus" option under the Enigma Machine to enable/disable this cheat. Characters will have various objects on their heads.

Making of D-Day FMV Sequence

Enter BACKSTAGEO at the Enigma Machine. Green lights will confirm correct code entry. Select the "Bonus" option under the Enigma Machine to enable/disable this cheat.

Making of Needle in a Haystack FMV Sequence

Enter BACKSTAGER at the Enigma Machine. Green lights will confirm correct code entry. Select the "Bonus" option under the Enigma Machine to enable/disable this cheat.

Making of Several Bridges Too Far FMV Sequence

Enter BACKSTAGEF at the Enigma Machine. Green lights will confirm correct code entry. Select the "Bonus" option under the Enigma Machine to enable/disable this cheat.

Making of The Horten's Nest FMV Sequence

Enter BACKSTAGES at the Enigma Machine. Green lights will confirm correct code entry. Select the "Bonus" option under the Enigma Machine to enable/disable this cheat.

Making of Storm in the Port FMV Sequence

Enter BACKSTAGET at the Enigma Machine. Green lights will confirm correct code entry. Select the "Bonus" option under the Enigma Machine to enable/disable this cheat.

Making of Rolling Thunder FMV Sequence

Enter BACKSTAGEI at the Enigma Machine. Green lights will confirm correct code entry. Select the "Bonus" option under the Enigma Machine to enable/disable this cheat.

Secret Medal

Successfully complete the game with a Gold Star in every mission to receive the EA LA Medal of Valor.

MIDNIGHT CLUB: STREET RACING

Dune Buggy Car

Use a memory card that has some saved data from the *Smugglers Run* game.

Bonus Cars

Keep an eye out for red circles that appear on levels. Stop your car on the circle until you hear a gurgling sound. That unlocks a new car. There are red circles on London and New York, but there could be a lot more from other levels.

MOBILE SUIT GUNDAM: JOURNEY TO JABURO

Unlock Tactics Battle Mode

To unlock Tactics Battle Mode, complete the Story Mode.

MOTO GP

Unlock Jurgen Vd Goorbergh

Beat 13"600 in Challenge mode on any difficulty setting.

Unlock Haruchika Aoki

Beat 24"000 in Challenge mode on any difficulty setting.

Unlock Juan Borja

Beat 22"200 in Challenge mode on any difficulty setting.

Unlock Jean Michel Bayle

Beat 8"280 in Challenge mode on any difficulty setting.

Unlock Nobuatsu Aoki

Beat 20"000 in Challenge mode on any difficulty setting.

Unlock Norick Abe
Place first at Suzuka in Arcade mode on Normal difficulty.

Unlock Simon Crafar
Place first at Donington in Arcade mode on Normal difficulty.

Unlock Alex Criville
Place first at Jerez in Arcade mode on Normal difficulty.

Unlock John Kocinski
Place first at Paul Ricard in Arcade mode on Normal difficulty.

Unlock Kenny Roberts
Place first at Motegi in Arcade mode on Normal difficulty.

Unlock Jose Luis Cardoso
Beat 20"300 in Challenge mode on any difficulty setting.

Unlock Mike Hale
Beat 22"000 in Challenge mode on any difficulty setting.

Unlock Regis Laconi
Beat 24"000 in Challenge mode on any difficulty setting.

Unlock Takuma Aoki
Beat 35"500 in Challenge mode on any difficulty setting.

Unlock Carlos Checa
Get one lap under 1'24"000 at Paul Ricardo stage in Time Trial mode on any difficulty setting.

Unlock Max Biaggi
Get one lap under 2'12"000 at Suzuka stage in Time Trial mode on any difficulty setting.

Unlock Alex Barros
Get one lap under 1'54"000 at Motegi stage in Time Trial mode on any difficulty setting.

Unlock Sete Gibernau
Get one lap under 1'47"000 at Jerez stage in Time Trial mode on any difficulty setting.

Unlock Tadayuki Okada
Get one lap under 1'36"000 at Donington stage in Time Trial mode on any difficulty setting.

Unlock Tetsuya Harada
Complete all five seasons in Season mode on Hard difficulty.

Unlock Mick Doohan
Get first overall at the end of five seasons in Season mode on Hard difficulty.

Unlock Klonoa
Beat 21"000 in Challenge mode on any difficulty setting.

Unlock K1
Get three laps under 1'22"500 in Time Trial mode on any difficulty setting.

Unlock Gun Koma
Complete one season under Season mode on Easy difficulty.

Unlock Photo
Complete all races in one season under Season mode on any difficulty setting.

Unlock Photo
Complete all races in one season under Season mode on Normal or Hard difficulty.

Unlock Suzuka Reverse
Place first at Suzuka in Arcade mode on Hard difficulty.

Unlock Jerez Reverse
Place first at Jerez in Arcade mode on Hard difficulty.

Unlock Paul Ricard Reverse
Place first at Paul Ricard in Arcade mode on Hard difficulty.

Unlock Motegi Reverse
Place first at Motegi in Arcade mode on Hard difficulty.

Unlock Photo
Beat 31"000 in Challenge mode on any difficulty setting.

Unlock Photo
Beat 24"000 in Challenge mode on any difficulty setting.

Unlock Photo
Beat 29"500 in Challenge mode on any difficulty setting.

Unlock Photo
Beat 36"700 in Challenge mode on any difficulty setting.

Unlock Photo
Beat 33"600 in Challenge mode on any difficulty setting.

Unlock Photo
Beat 33"000 in Challenge mode on any difficulty setting.

Unlock Photo
Beat 31"700 in Challenge mode on any difficulty setting.

Unlock Photo
Beat 56"200 in Challenge mode on any difficulty setting.

Unlock Photo
Beat 34"500 in Challenge mode on any difficulty setting.

Unlock Photo
Beat 20"500 in Challenge mode on any difficulty setting.

Unlock Photo
Beat 25"200 in Challenge mode on any difficulty setting.

Unlock Photo
Beat 35"200 in Challenge mode on any difficulty setting.

Unlock Photo
Race with all 12 teams in Season mode on Normal difficulty.

Unlock Photo
Race with all 12 teams in Season mode on Hard difficulty.

Unlock Photo
Use a Level C or D team and finish first overall at the end of one season in Season mode on Hard difficulty.

Unlock Photo
Pass 10 or more bikes in one lap in Arcade mode on any difficulty setting.

Unlock Photo
Beat 28"500 in Challenge mode on any difficulty setting.

Unlock Photo
Place first at Suzuka in Arcade mode on any difficulty setting. You must not touch another or go off road at any time.

Unlock Photo
Using all three Level A teams, place first on every circuit in Arcade mode on any difficulty setting.

Unlock Photo
Complete three consecutive laps where all the lap times are under 2'10"000 in Time Trial mode on any difficulty setting.

Unlock Photo
Complete every race over five seasons in Season mode on hard difficulty where the laps are set to full.

Unlock Photo
Get a Bronze or Silver on all the challenges above in Challenge mode on any difficulty setting.

Unlock Photo
Get a Gold on all the challenges above in Challenge mode on any difficulty setting.

MOTOR MAYHEM

Unlock Buzzsaw
To unlock Buzzsaw as a playable character, beat the Deathmatch, Endurance, and Eliminator modes with the same character on either Hard or Very Hard Difficulty.

NASCAR 2001

Unlock the EA.com Car
Win the Superspeedway Shootout at Veteran or Legend difficulty.

Unlock the EA Sports Car
Win the Road Course Challenge.

Unlock the Treasure Island Track
Under Veteran difficulty, win a season.

Unlock the Black Box Exotic Car
Win the Half Season.

Unlock the Black Box Classic Car
Win the Short Track Challenge.

NASCAR HEAT 2002

Hornball Enabled
At the Race Day screen in Single Race or Head-to-Head, the following cheats are present...Up, Down, Left, Right, R1, Up, Up: start a race with hornball enabled (press Up on D-Pad to fire a ball). To start a practice session with hornball enabled: Up, Down, Left, Right, R1, Down, Down.

Unlock Hardcore Realism Mode
To unlock Hardcore Realism Mode, earn a 100 point rating on any track. The Harcore Realism will be unlocked for the track on which you earned the rating.

Unlock Richard Petty
Complete all of the Heat Challenges and earn at least a Bronze rating on each to unlock the legendary Richard Petty.

NBA HOOPZ

At the Versus screen, use the following buttons to change the numbers for code entry: Square to change the first number, X to change the second number, and Circle to change the third number. Then use the D-Pad to enter the direction. If you entered the code correctly you'll see the name of the code displayed on the screen.

Infinite Turbo
3-1-2 Up

Beach Court
0-2-3 Left

Street Court
3-2-0 Left

Play as Dr. Atomic
5-4-4 Left

Home Uniform
0-1-4 Right

Away Uniform
0-2-4 Right

ABA Ball
1-1-1 Right

Granny Shots
1-2-1 Left

Show Shot Percent
0-1-1 Down

Show Hotspot
1-1-0 Down

No Goaltending
4-4-4 Left

No Fouls
2-2-2 Right

No Hotspots
3-0-1 Up

Big Heads
3-0-0 Right

Tiny Heads
3-3-0 Left

Tiny Players
5-4-3 Left

NBA LIVE 2001

Creating a Dream Team
Go into Season mode, hit Circle to bring up the menu bar and select "Roster" from the bar. From here, select "Create Player." When creating a player, load him up with maximum stats and save him into the Free Agent pool. Then, return to the menu bar, select "Roster" and Sign the player you've just made. If his rating is over 90, you can trade him for any player in the league (including Shaq and Allen Iverson). Repeat this process until you have all the talent you want.

Make a Super Star Even Better
At the main menu press Circle to open the Active menu. Select "Roster." Then select "Edit Player." A Super Star loads up if your Create-a-Player list is empty. Make the player's stats better (3 pointers, strength, dunking, etc.) by hitting R2 at the Edit Player screen. If you want a different player, go back to the empty Create-a-Player list by pressing L2. Press Start and change someone else.

NBA STREET

Activate Cheat Mode
After entering one of the icon codes, press Enter direction on the D-Pad to complete code entry.

Unlimited Turbo
Enter Shoe, Basketball, Backboard, Basketball as a code.

No Turbo
Enter Turntable, Microphone, Microphone, Backboard as a code.

Information in this section was contributed by JJ SPORTS.

Authentic Uniforms
Enter Basketball, Basketball, Turntable, Turntable as a code.

Casual Uniforms
Enter Turntable, Turntable, Basketball, Basketball as a code.

ABA Socks
Enter Microphone, Microphone, Microphone, Microphone as a code.

Tiny Players
Enter Microphone, Basketball, Microphone, Basketball as a code.

Big Heads
Enter Microphone, Turntable, Shoe, Turntable as a code.

Tiny Heads
Enter Microphone, Shoe, Basketball, Shoe as a code.

Less Blocks
Enter Backboard, Turntable, Shoe, Backboard as a code.

Less Steals
Enter Backboard, Turntable, Microphone, Basketball as a code.

No Player Indicators
Enter Microphone, Basketball, Basketball, Microphone as a code.

No Shot Indicator
Enter Microphone, Backboard, Shoe, Microphone as a code.

No Shot Clock
Enter Microphone, Microphone, Basketball, Backboard as a code.

No Alley-oops
Enter Backboard, Microphone, Turntable, Shoe as a code.

No Two-pointers
Enter Backboard, Backboard, Basketball, Backboard as a code.

No Auto Replays
Enter Turntable, Shoe, Turntable, Turntable as a code.

WNBA ball
Enter Basketball, Turntable, Shoe, Basketball as a code.

EA Big Ball
Enter Basketball, Turntable, Microphone, Basketball as a code.

Beach Ball
Enter Basketball, Turntable, Turntable, Shoe as a code.

Soccer Ball
Enter Basketball, Shoe, Turntable, Basketball as a code.

ABA Ball
Enter Basketball, Turntable, Turntable, Basketball as a code.

Medicine Ball
Enter Basketball, Turntable, Turntable, Backboard as a code.

NuFX Ball
Enter Basketball, Turntable, Backboard, Basketball as a code.

Volleyball
Enter Basketball, Turntable, Turntable, Microphone as a code.

Mega Dunking
Enter Backboard, Basketball, Turntable, Basketball as a code.

No Dunks
Enter Backboard, Basketball, Turntable, Shoe as a code.

More Gamebreakers
Enter Turntable, Microphone, Backboard, Shoe as a code.

Less Gamebreakers
Enter Turntable, Backboard, Microphone, Shoe as a code.

No Gamebreakers
Enter Turntable, Microphone, Microphone, Shoe as a code.

Springtime Joe "The Show"
Enter Turntable, Turntable, Basketball, Turntable as a code.

Summertime Joe "The Show"
Enter Turntable, Basketball, Basketball, Turntable as a code.

Athletic Joe "The Show"
Enter Turntable, Shoe, Basketball, Turntable as a code.

Captain Quicks
Enter Backboard, Basketball, Shoe, Turntable as a code.

Explosive Rims
Enter Turntable, Shoe, Microphone, Basketball as a code.

Harder Distance Shots
Enter Shoe, Shoe, Backboard, Basketball as a code.

Easy Distance Shots
Enter Shoe, Turntable, Backboard, Basketball as a code.

Ultimate Power
Enter Backboard, Turntable, Turntable, Basketball as a code.

Mad Handles
Enter Backboard, Shoe, Turntable, Basketball as a code.

Super Swats
Enter Backboard, Backboard, Turntable, Basketball as a code.

Sticky Fingers
Enter Backboard, Microphone, Turntable, Basketball as a code.

Player Names
Enter Basketball, Turntable, Shoe, Backboard as a code.

No HUD Display
Enter Turntable, Microphone, Turntable, Shoe as a code.

Disable All Cheats
Enter Turntable, Turntable, Turntable, Turntable as a code.

Team Big
Enter the "Enter User ID" screen, and get to the User Record box (displays either a user ID's record information, or "no user record"). Quickly hold L2 and press Up, Down(2), Left, X. Alternately, get 10 wins in any mode.

Team 3LW
Enter the "Enter User ID" screen, and get to the User Record box (displays either a user ID's record information, or "no user record"). Quickly hold R1 and press Left(2), Right, Down, X. Alternately, get 20 wins in any mode.

NYC Legends Team
Enter the "Enter User ID" screen, and get to the User Record box (displays either a user ID's record information, or "no user record"). Quickly hold L2 and press Down(3), Left, X. Alternately, get 30 wins in any mode.

Team Street Legends
Enter the "Enter User ID" screen, and get to the User Record box (displays either a user ID's record information, or "no user record"). Quickly hold R1 and press Right, Left, Up, Down, X. Alternately, win the City Circuit to unlock the Street Legends team. This team includes Biggs, Bonafide, Drake, DJ, Takashi, Stretch, and Michael Jordan.

Team Dream
Enter the "Enter User ID" screen, and get to the User Record box (displays either a user ID's record information, or "no user record"). Quickly hold R2 and press Up(2), Right(2), X. Alternately, win (complete all the objectives) Hold the Court mode to unlock a team that includes Graylien Alien, Magma Man, and Yeti Snowman.

All Courts
In Hold the Court mode, go to the screen where you choose your court. Hold R2 and press Up, Down, Left, Right, Right, Left, Down, Up, and while still holding Up, press X.

More Player Creation Points
Note: This code can only be used for new players that are created. Hold L1 + L2 and press Left, Down, Right, then press Square, Triangle, Circle at the Create Player menu.

Biggs and Beacon Hill Court
Play the City Circuit and reach the Region 1 City Challenge. Defeat Biggs' team to unlock him as a selectable player and to unlock the Beacon Hill court.

Bonafide and Broad Street Court
Play the City Circuit and reach the Region 2 City Challenge. Defeat Bonafide's team to unlock him as a selectable player and to unlock the Broad Street court.

Drake and the Yard Court
Play the City Circuit and reach the Region 3 City Challenge. Defeat Drake's team to unlock him as a selectable player and to unlock The Yard court.

DJ and Venice Beach Court
Play the City Circuit and reach the Region 4 City Challenge. Defeat DJ's team to unlock him as a selectable player and to unlock the Venice Beach court.

Takashi and Yakatomni Plaza Court
Play the City Circuit and reach the Region 5 City Challenge. Defeat Takashi's team to unlock him as a selectable player and to unlock the Yakatomni Plaza court.

Stretch and Rucker Park Court
Play the City Circuit and reach the Region 2 City Challenge. Defeat Stretch's team to unlock him as a selectable player and to unlock the Rucker Park court.

NBA Superstars
Play the City Challenge and defeat an NBA team to unlock a player from their roster.

Created Player Pieces
Successfully complete the Hold the Court challenges to unlock more pieces and development points for created players.

NFL GAMEDAY 2001

Unlock Super Bowl Teams
At the Team Selection screen, press Circle.

Unlock All-Star Teams
At the Team Selection screen, press Circle (2).

NHL 2001

Super Defense Players
Enter Sandis Ozolinsh or Chris Pronger as a name in the Create-a-Player screen. Choose "Yes" to use his ratings (you can still adjust them with NHL Challenge bonus points). Return to the previous screen and you can change his name to whatever you want, but don't change any other settings.

Super Goalies
Enter Patrick Roy, Dominik Hasek, or Ed Belfour as a name in the Create-a-Player screen. Choose "Yes" to use his ratings (you can still adjust them with NHL Challenge bonus points). Return to the previous screen and you can change his name to whatever you want, but don't change any other settings.

Super Forwards
Enter Peter Forsberg, Jaromir Jagr, Keith Tkachuk, Pavel Bure, Steve Yzerman, Owen Nolan, Olaf Kolzig, Nicklas Lidstrom, or Rob Blake as a name in the Create-a-Player screen. Choose "Yes" to use his ratings (you can still adjust them with NHL Challenge bonus points). Return to the previous screen and you can change his name to whatever you want, but don't change any other settings.

The Dude
Enter Bruce Willis as a name in the Create-a-Player screen. The announcer will call that player "The Dude" during the game.

The Hammer
Enter Hammer as a name in the Create-a-Player screen. The announcer will call that player "The Hammer" during the game.

Taunts
Hold Triangle after you score a goal, win a fight, win a game, or the opposing team gets a penalty.

ONI

Change the Character
During gameplay press the Select button, then highlight the "Help" button. Now press L2, L1, L2, Square, Circle, Square, L2 (4). Do not move your cursor yet. Hit the L2 button until you select your character.

One Shot, One Kill
During gameplay press the Select button, then highlight the "Help" button. Now enter L2, L1, L2, Square, Circle, Square, L3, R3, Circle, Square. A sound confirms correct entry.

Unlimited Health
During gameplay press the Select button, then highlight the "Help" button. Now enter L2, L1, L2, Square, Circle Square, R3, L3, R3, Circle. A sound confirms correct entry.

Extra Powerful Punches and Kicks
During gameplay press the Select button, then highlight the "Help" button. Now enter L2, L1, L2, Square, Circle, Square, R3, L3, Circle, Square. A sound confirms correct entry.

A sound confirms correct entry.

Itty Bitty Characters
During gameplay press the Select button, then highlight the "Help" button. Now enter L2, L1, L2, Square, Circle, Square, L3, R3, Square, Circle. A sound confirms correct entry.

Unlimited Phase Cloak
During gameplay press the Select button, then highlight the "Help" button. Now enter L2, L1, L2, Square, Circle, Square, L1, R3, L2, L3. A sound confirms correct entry. Stay invisible for as long as you want.

Big Head Mode
During gameplay press the Select button, then highlight the "Help" button. Now enter L2, L1, L2, Square, Circle, Square, Start, Square, Circle, Start. A sound confirms correct entry.

Godly Guns
During gameplay press the Select button, then highlight the "Help" button. Now enter L2, L1, L2, Square, Circle, Square, L2, L2, L1, L3. A sound confirms correct entry. This code gives you unlimited ammo and you never have to reload.

Huge Characters
During gameplay press the Select button, then highlight the "Help" button. Now enter L2, L1, L2, Square, Circle, Square, R3, Square, Circle, L3. A sound confirms correct entry.

Avoid Fall Damage
When you fall from high areas, you take damage. When you near the ground, press L2 to do a flip. This eliminates damage.

Hard Mode

During gameplay press the Select button, then highlight the "Help" button. Now enter L2, L1, L2, Square, Circle, Square, R3, L3, Circle, Square. A sound confirms correct entry.

Instant Level Completion

During gameplay press the Select button, then highlight the "Help" button. Now enter L2, L1, L2, Square, Circle, Square, L3, R3, L2, L1.

ONIMUSHA WARLORDS

Get the Bishamon Sword

Fight through all 20 levels of the Dark Realm. Kill all of the monsters on the 20th level, then open the treasure box to discover the Bishamon Ocarina. In the area just beyond the second Marcellus boss fight, use the Ocarina on the bone door to open it. Head inside and claim the prize—a sword with unlimited magic which kills any non-boss character in a single swipe. A powerful ally, indeed.

Beat Oni Spirits…Unlock An Arsenal

If you make it past all 12 levels of the challenging Oni Spirits mini-game, you unlock a gameplay option that allows you to start the regular game with a wonderful array of toys. Not only do you get to play through the game with the Bishamon Sword, but you get unlimited Arrows and Bullets, and begin with 99 Soul Absorbers in your inventory. In addition, any magic you use automatically respawns after the attack. With this at your disposal, beating the game again and unlocking everything else is a cinch!

Unlock Oni Spirits

If you collect all 20 Flourites and finish the game, the mini-game Oni Spirits will unlock.

Unlock *Onimusha 2* Trailer

Finish the game on any difficulty to unlock a sneak preview of *Onimusha 2*. When you go to the main menu after saving, go to Special Feature to view the preview footage.

Unlock the Panda Suit

If you collect 10 or more Flourites during the course of the game and successfully finish, there will be an extra costume available for Samanosuke when you begin a new game…a cuddly panda suit! When you restart, select Samanosuke-Extra to play as the big bear. Check out the daisy gauntlet and stuffed friend in the mucus pouch. During gameplay, use L2 to wear the head on or off.

Alternate Costumes

To make your character look different, complete the game one time, then start a new game after saving. You will see a "Normal/Special" option. If you select the Special option, you will appear in a special panda suit.

Preview for *Onimusha 2*

After you complete the game for the first time, it prompts you to save. Do so, then start a new game. View the "Special Report" to see a small preview of *Onimusha 2*, which takes place 10 years after the events in this game.

Unlock Easy Mode

There are two ways of unlocking the easy mode:

1. Beat the game 4 times to make the Easy Mode available.

2. If Osric beats you 5 times or more, the Easy Mode unlocks.

ORPHEN: SCION OF SORCERY

Restart the Battle

Pause the game before you get defeated. Pick "Equip" and resume the game at the start of the battle. All your energy will be restored.

PAC-MAN WORLD 2

Pac-Man Mini-Game

Collect 10 tokens during gameplay to unlock the classic Pac-Man arcade game.

Pac-Attack Mini-Game

Collect 30 tokens during gameplay to unlock the classic Pac-Attack arcade game.

Pac-Mania Mini-Game

Collect 100 tokens during gameplay to unlock the classic Pac-Mania arcade game.

Ms. Pac-Man Mini-Game

Collect 180 tokens during gameplay to unlock the classic Ms. Pac-Man arcade game.

Music Test

Collect 60 tokens during gameplay to unlock the "Jukebox" option.

Pre-Production Art and Programmers

Collect 150 tokens during gameplay to unlock the "Museum" option.

PARAPPA THE RAPPER 2

Unlock Blue Hat

Beat the game once, and Parappa dons a snazzy blue hat.

Unlock Dog House

Beat each level while wearing the yellow hat and Parappa gets a new dog house. Go there immediately to listen to some tunes. In the dog house, you can listen to tracks from any level on which you've earned a "Cool" rating.

Unlock Pink Hat

Beat each level while wearing the blue hat to give Parappa a new pink hat.

Unlock Yellow Hat

Beat each level while wearing the pink hat to give Parappa a new yellow hat.

PIRATES: THE LEGEND OF BLACK KAT

Invincibility for Katarina

Hold R1 + R2 and press X, Circle, L3, Triangle, R3, Select, R3, L1, L2, Square.

Invincibility for the Wind Dancer

Hold R1 + R2 and press Select, Triangle, L1, X, R3, L2, Square, R3, Circle, L3.

Reveal Buried Treasure Chests

Hold R1 + R2 and press Circle, X, Square, Triangle, L1, Select, L3, L2, L3, R3. Green Xs will appear on the captain's log maps to indicate the location of buried treasure chests.

Reveal All Treasure Chests

Hold R1 + R2 and press R3, X, Triangle, L3, Circle, L1, Select, L3, Square, L2.

All Treasure Chest Keys

Hold R1 + R2 and press Circle, Select, X, Square, R3, L1, L3, L2, Triangle, L3.

Wind Dancer

Hold R1 + R2 and press L2, Triangle, R3, L3, X, Square, R3, Select, L1, Circle.

Unlimited Items

Hold R1 + R2 and press Triangle, L1, Select, L2, R3, L3, Square, X, R3, Circle. Once found, an item will be available in unlimited amounts.

Extra Gold

Hold R1 + R2 and press Triangle, R3, L3, X, Square, R3, Select, L1, Circle. Sail to another map to get the Galleon.

Unlimited Wind Boost

Hold R1 + R2 and press Select, L1, R3, Circle, L2, Triangle, X, L3.

Advance to Katarina's Next Sword

Hold R1 + R2 and press R3, Select, L2, L3, Square, X, L1, Circle, L3, Triangle.

Alternate Glacial Gulf Music

Hold R1 + R2 and press L1, X, Triangle, L2, Square, Circle, L3, Select, R3, L3 to hear music from SSX when sliding down in Glacial Gulf.

High-Pitched Voices

Hold R1 + R2 and press R3, Circle, Select, X, R3, Triangle, L1, Square, L2, L3.

Kane Poison Head

Hold R1 + R2 and press Triangle, L2, L1, Square, L3, X, L3, Circle, R3, Select. The poison status will be indicated by the head of Kane from *Command and Conquer*.

Alternate Katarina Costumes

The following code requires two players and controllers. Simultaneously hold L1 + L2 + Up + Select + L3 on controller one and R1 + R2 + Triangle + Start + R3 on controller two. A short sequence of music will confirm correct code entry. Press R3 on controller one to change the value of the numbers that appear on screen, then start a new game or resume a saved game to view the corresponding costume. The costumes that can be accessed are as follows.

Original Costume and Hair Color
00000000

Blackbeard in Purple
00000001

Red Hair with Red and Orange Bikini
00000010

Blue Hair with Orange and Red Bikini
00000011

Tan, Brown Hair, Orange and Yellow Bikini
00000100

Blonde Hair, Orange and Yellow Bikini
00000101

Blonde Hair, Pink Bikini
00000110

Blue Hair, Shiny Silver Bikini
00000111

Red Hair, Black Bikini, Black Stockings
00001000

Pink Hair, Shiny Black Body Suit
00001001

Blue Hair, Shiny Copper Body Suit
00001010

Purple Hair, Shiny Silver Body Suit
00001011

RAYMAN 2: REVOLUTION

Extra Bonus Mini-Games
From the Press Start screen, press Start. Now, select your language. Next, select "Options." Then choose "Language." Select "Voices" and highlight "Raymanian." Now, press and hold L1+R1, then press L2, R2, L2, R2, L2, R2.

Cheat Menu
During Gameplay pause your game and then select "Sound." Now highlight the "Mute" selection. Do not Validate it, simply highlight it. Now, press and hold L1+L2, then press L2, R2, L2, R2, L2, R2.

Soccer Names
First enable the "Extra Bonus Mini-Games" cheat and select "Baby Soccer." While you play this game press and hold L1+R1, then press L2, R2, L2, R2, L2, R2.

RC REVENGE PRO

Unlock Every Track
At the main menu press L1, R1,R2, Square, Circle. When you enter the game, select your vehicle and then choose any track.

Unlock Every Vehicle
At the main menu press L1, L2, R1, R2, Circle, Square. When you start you will have every vehicle to choose from.

Unlock the Next Championship
At the main menu, press L1, R1, R2, L2 to unlock the next Championship. Keep typing the code to unlock more championships. A total of seven more championships can be opened.

READY 2 RUMBLE: ROUND 2

Play as Freak E. Deke and Michael Jackson
At the Character Selection screen, press R1 (13), R2, R1 (10), R2.

Unlock Freak E. Deke
Beat Arcade mode once.

Unlock Michael Jackson
Beat Arcade mode twice.

Unlock G.C. Thunder
Beat Arcade mode three times.

Unlock Wild "Stubby" Corley
Beat Arcade mode four times.

Unlock Shaquille O'Neal
Beat Arcade mode five times.

Unlock Freedom Brock
Beat Arcade mode six times.

Unlock Rocket Samchay
Beat Arcade mode seven times.

Unlock Bill Clinton
Beat Arcade mode eight times.

Unlock Hillary Clinton
Beat Arcade mode nine times.

Unlock Rumbleman
Beat Arcade mode 10 times.

Fat Boxer
At the Character Selection screen, press Right (2), Up, Down, Right, R1 (2), R2. A sound confirms correct entry.

Skinny Boxer
At the Character Selection screen, press Right, Right, Up, Down, Right, R1, R2. A sound confirms correct entry.

Big Gloves
At the Character Selection screen, press Left, Right, Up, Down, R1, R2. A sound confirms correct entry.

Undead Boxer
At the Character Selection screen, press Left, Up, Right, Down, R1 (2), R2. A sound confirms correct entry.

New Year's Costume
Set the system date to January 1. Joey T will be in a baby costume.

Valentine's Day Costume
Set the system date to February 14. Lulu will be in a sexy costume.

St. Patrick's Day Costume
Set the system date to March 17. The referee will be in a leprechaun costume.

Easter Costume
Set the system date to April 23. Mama Tua will be in a Playboy bunny costume.

Fourth of July Costume
Set the system date to July 4. G.C. Thunder will be in a Uncle Sam costume.

Halloween Costume
Set the system date to October 31. J.R. Flurry will be in a skeleton costume.

Christmas Costume
Set the system date to December 25. Selene Strike will be in an elf costume and Rumbleman will be in a snowman costume.

Unlock Champion Costumes
Complete Championship mode.

REDCARD SOCCER 2003

Cheat Mode
Enter BIGTANK as a name to unlock all teams, stadiums, and Finals mode.

Apes Team and Victoria Falls Stadium
Defeat the Apes team in World Conquest mode.

Dolphins Team and Nautilus Stadium
Defeat the Dolphins team in World Conquest mode.

Martians Team and USAFB001 Stadium
Defeat the Martians team in World Conquest mode.

Matadors Team and Coliseum Stadium
Defeat the Matadors team in World Conquest mode.

SWAT Team and Nova City Stadium
Defeat the SWAT team in World Conquest mode.

Samurai Team and Youhi Gardens Stadium
Defeat the Samurai team in World Conquest mode.

Finals Mode
Win all matches in World Conquest mode.

RED FACTION

Secret Roof Location in Lobby Multiplayer Map
You can get on the roof of the Lobby (where there is a giant skylight) to find a Fusion Rocket Launcher and a Rail Driver, as well as a great sniping spot. To get there, go up to the second level of the area where you are able to pick up the Rocket Launcher. Arm that weapon and aim for the corner of the wall where the skylight begins. Fire rockets to punch a hole into the ceiling and the wall. Continue to fire rockets until you form a small alcove where you can jump to, then up onto the roof. After you are there, grab a Fusion Rocket Launcher at one end of the skylight and a Rail Driver at the other end.

RESIDENT EVIL CODE VERONICA X

Get Special Journal
Go to the slot machine in the palace each time through the Battle Game (with the same character). On the third try, a special journal is there. It belongs to someone named D.I.J.

Unlock Linear Launcher for Battle Game
Get an A ranking with the two Claires, Steves, Chrises and Weskers in the Battle Game to unlock the Linear Launcher. After you gain it, it automatically appears in your inventory when you begin the Battle Game again.

Unlock Rocket Launcher
Complete the main game with an "A" Ranking to earn the Rocket Launcher. To do this, do not use First Aid Spray, do not save your game, do not retry. You must save Steve from the Luger room quickly, give the Medicine to your jailer Rodrigo, and finish in under 4:30. When you begin another game, the Launcher will be available from the first Item Box you run across.

Unlock Steve for Battle Game
Unlock Steve in Battle Game by solving a puzzle in the main game. In the underground Save Room in Chris's walkthrough, complete the drawer puzzle in the corner. Grab the Gold Luger to unlock Mr. Burnside.

Unlock Wesker for Battle Game
Unlock Albert Wesker for use in the Battle Game by beating the Battle game with Chris Redfield.

Unlock the Battle Game
Beat the game once to unlock the Battle Game. Chris and Claire Redfield are now available as playable characters.

RIDGE RACER V

Changing Saved Game Icon
Beat the game with all secrets unlocked. The saved game icon will change from a car to Ai Fukami, a programmer.

Unlock *Pac-Man* Mode
Race more than 3,000 kilometers in total distance. The *Pac-Man* race becomes available. Beat the *Pac-Man* race and the *Pac-Man* car and the ghosts on scooters become unlocked.

Modifying the Intro Sequence
Press L1+R1 during the intro sequence with the girl. Press R1 once for black-and-white graphics. Press R1 a second time and the game will have a yellow tint. Press R1 a third time to add a blur effect. That blur effect eliminates the jaggies in the graphics. You can press L1 to cycle back through the various effects.

Unlock Duel Mode
Enter Standard Time Attack GP and finish first in lap and overall time.

Onscreen Information
During a race, press and hold Select for a few seconds. A window shows up on the screen with various information. Press and hold Select again to make the information window go away.

Unlocking Bonus Cars
Beat each of the Grand Prix circuits. Or break the Time Attack high scores.

Unlock 50's Super Drift Caddy
Place first in the Danver Spectra race in Duel mode to unlock this car in Free Run, Duel, and Time Attack modes.

Unlock a Beetle
Place first in the Solort Rumeur race in Duel mode to unlock this car in Free Run, Duel, and Time Attack modes.

Unlock a McLaren Type Car
Place first in the Kamata Angelus race in Duel mode to unlock this car in Free Run, Duel, and Time Attack modes.

Unlock Devil Drift
Place first in the Rivelta Crinale race in Duel mode to unlock this car in Free Run, Duel, and Time Attack modes.

99 Lap Option
Get the top score in all the Time Attack GP races in Extra mode and finish in first place.

RUMBLE RACING
Go to the Game Options menu on the title screen. Then go to Load/Save and select "Passwords." Use the passwords below to open the corresponding vehicles and features.

Cataclysm Vehicle, Falls Down Track, and Pro Cup 2
P1PROC1PU

EsCargot Vehicle, the Gauntlet Track, and Pro Cup 3
Q2PROC2YT

Road Kill Vehicle, Elite Class Vehicles, Surf and Turf Vehicle, and Elite Cup
AEPPROPUC

Jolly Roger Vehicle, Coal Cuts Track, and Elite Cup 2
ILETEC1MB

Malice Vehicle, Wild Kingdom Track, and Elite Cup 3
ILCTEC2VB

Championship Mode
KOZIEC1PU

OORKIEPUC

KZOIEC2P1

Buckshot Vehicle
UBTCKSTOH

Gamecus Vehicle
BSUIGASUM

High Roller Vehicle
HGIROLREL

Redneck Rocket Vehicle
KCEROCTEC

Revolution Vehicle
PTOATRTO1

Road Trip Vehicle
ABOGOBOGA

Sporticus Vehicle
OPSRTISUC

Stinger Vehicle
AMHBRAAMH

Van Itty Vehicle
VTYANIYTT

Vortex Vehicle
1AREXT1AR

XXS Tomcat Vehicle
NALDSHHSD

Unlock So Refined Track
Win the Gold on Rookie Cup 1.

Unlock the Passing Through Track
Win the Gold on Rookie Cup 2.

Unlock the Sun Burn Track
Win the Gold on EA Rookie Cup.

Unlock the Falls Down Track
Win the Gold on Pro Cup 1.

Unlock the Gauntlet Track
Win the Gold on Pro Cup 2.

Unlock the Rookie Cup 2
Win the Gold on Rookie Cup 1.

Unlock the Rookie Cup 3
Win the Gold on Rookie Cup 2.

Unlock the EA Rookie Cup
Win the Gold on Rookie Cup 3.

Unlock the Pro Cup 1
Win the Gold on Rookie Cup 3.

Unlock the Pro Cup 2
Win the Gold on Pro Cup 1.

Unlock the Pro Cup 3
Win the Gold on Pro Cup 2.

Unlock the Dragon Vehicle
Win the Gold on Rookie Cup 1.

Unlock the Mandrake Vehicle
Win the Gold on Rookie Cup 2.

Unlock the Maelstrom Vehicle
Win the Gold on EA Rookie Cup.

Unlock the Pro Class of Vehicles
Win the Gold on EA Rookie Cup.

Unlock the Cataclysm Vehicle
Win the Gold on Pro Cup 1.

Unlock the Escargot Vehicle
Win the Gold on Pro Cup 1.

SHADOW OF DESTINY

Unlock the Extra Option
When you beat the game, you are graded on how well you played. This leads to one of five endings. After you complete the game once and earn an ending, an "Extra" feature appears on the main menu. Access it to see Movies, Ending Files, and the Result for each completed level.

Unlock an Extra Ending
Complete the game five times and earn all of the Ending Files, then play through once more to get a special, extra ending.

Unlocking Movies
Beat the game once and earn an Ending File, unlocking a Movie. Earn three Ending Files to unlock a movie from a European Konami show. Get the special "extra" ending to unlock a Movie from the Fall Tokyo Game Show.

SILENT SCOPE

Expert Mode
Hold the trigger button when you select Training or Arcade mode. Press Start (4). A second gunshot confirms correct entry. This removes the guide arrows and aiming rings.

Extra Options
Beat the game on any difficulty setting more than twice. This unlocks infinite credits, more health, and more time in the Options menu.

Night Vision Mode
Hold the trigger button when you select the Training or Arcade mode. Press Start (5). A second gunshot confirms correct entry. This makes the game always at night.

SILPHEED: THE LOST PLANET

All Nine Weapons
Start a new game. Enter XACALITE as your name.

SKY ODYSSEY

Hidden Plane
Right Wing: Land at the alternate landing strip in the Adventure Begins level.

Left Wing: Land at the alternate landing strip in the Labyrinth level.

Body: Land at the alternate landing strip in the Towers Of Terror level.

Jet Engine: Land at the alternate landing strip in The Great Divide level.

Swordfish Triple Wing
Land at the alternative landing strip in the level Mid-Air Rendezvous. The alternate landing strip is easier to find after you earn the Special Radar by playing through the Target mode.

Unlock Custom Parts
Earn custom parts for your aircraft by earning grades of B or higher in the Adventure mode missions.

Unlock the Pontoons
To earn a set of pontoons for your aircraft, allowing you to land in the water, complete the Stormy Seas level, landing on an aircraft carrier. The pontoons are required for a mission later in the game.

Unlock the Auto Gyro Plane
Clear every stage of the Sky Canvas mode with a score of at least 90 Points.

Unlock the ME 262
Beat the entire Adventure mode once (including the final level) to earn the ME 262, a very fast jet with two engines.

Unlock the Corsair
To unlock the Corsair you must be good enough at pulling acrobatic tricks to earn enough Acrobatic points in Adventure mode to get circles to appear around 10 of your mission grades.

Unlock the Silver UFO
Complete all Adventure mode missions with an A grade to unlock the silver UFO.

Unlock the Gold UFO
To earn the gold UFO, get gold on every mission in Target mode.

Unlock the Stealth Jet
Complete every mission in Adventure mode with a total time of 10 minutes.

Unlock Radio in Target Mode
Earn four gold medals.

Unlock Music Track in Target Mode
Earn one silver medal each (12 tracks total).

Unlock Special Radar in Target Mode
Earn two gold medals.

Unlock Emblems in Target Mode
Earn two silver medals. (Find the new emblems in the Customize Aircraft mode.)

Unlock Unlimited Boost in Target Mode
Earn two gold medals. (Once equipped, all jet planes will have an infinite amount of boost, but must recharge after every use.)

The Adventure Begins Card No. 1
Clear the Adventure Begins level two times. Picture displayed is MS+Swordfish.

The Desert Express Card No. 2
Clear the Desert Express level two times. Pictures displayed are MS+Bf-109.

Take the Low Road Card No. 3
Clear the Take the Low Road level two times. Pictures displayed are MS+Pulse Jet.

The Labyrinth Card No. 4
Clear the Labyrinth level two times. Pictures displayed are MS+Me262.

Stormy Seas Card No. 5
Clear the Stormy Seas level two times. Pictures displayed are MS+F4U Corsair.

Blown Away Card No. 6
Clear the Blown Away level two times. Pictures displayed are MS + Pulse Jet.

Great Divide Card No. 7
Clear the Great Divide level two times. Pictures displayed are MS+Shinden.

Relief from Above Card No. 8
Clear the Relief from Above level two times. Pictures displayed are MS+Shinden-kai.

The Ancient Forest Card No. 9
Clear the Ancient Forest level two times. Pictures displayed are MS+Autogyro.

Mid-Air Rendezvous Card No. 10
Clear the Mid-Air Rendezvous level two times. Pictures displayed are MS+F117.

Heart of the Mine Card No. 11
Clear the Heart of the Mine level two times. Pictures displayed are MS+Bf-109.

Towers of Terror Card No. 12
Clear the Towers of Terror level two times. Pictures displayed are MS+F4U Corsair.

S.O.S Card No. 13
Clear the S.O.S. level two times. Pictures displayed are MS+Shinden.

Over the Falls Card No. 14
Clear the Over the Falls level two times. Pictures displayed are MS+Floatplane.

Storm Before the Calm Card No. 15
Clear the Storm Before the Calm level two times. Pictures displayed are MS+Swordfish.

A Tight Squeeze Card No. 16
Clear the A Tight Squeeze level two times. Pictures displayed are MS+Me262.

The Valley of Fire Card No. 17
Clear the Valley of Fire level two times. Pictures displayed are MS+Bf-109.

The Great Falls Card No. 18
Clear the Great Falls level two times. Pictures displayed are MS+Pulse Jet.

Maximus Card No. 19
Clear the Maximus level two times. Pictures displayed are MS+Swordfish.

The Adventure Begins Card No. 20
Clear the Adventure Begins level one time. Picture displayed is Mission Scenery.

The Desert Express Card No. 21
Clear the Desert Express level one time. Picture displayed is Mission Scenery.

Take the Low Road Card No. 22
Clear the Take the Low Road level one time. Picture displayed is Mission Scenery.

The Labyrinth Card No. 23
Clear the Labyrinth level one time. Picture displayed is Mission Scenery.

Stormy Seas Card No 24
Clear the Stormy Seas level one time. Picture displayed is Mission Scenery.

Blown Away Card No. 25
Clear the Blown Away level one time. Picture displayed is Mission Scenery.

The Great Divide Card No. 26
Clear the Great Divide level one time. Picture displayed is Mission Scenery.

Relief from Above Card No. 27
Clear the Relief from Above level one time. Picture displayed is Mission Scenery.

The Ancient Forest Card No. 28
Clear the Ancient Forest level one time. Picture displayed is Mission Scenery.

Mid-Air Rendezvous Card No. 29
Clear the Mid-Air Rendezvous one time. Picture displayed is Mission Scenery.

Heart of the Mine Card No. 30
Clear the Heart of the Mine one time. Picture displayed is Mission Scenery.

Towers of Terror Card No. 31
Clear the Towers of Terror level one time. Picture displayed is Mission Scenery.

S.O.S Card No. 32
Clear the S.O.S. level one time. Picture displayed is Mission Scenery.

Over the Falls Card No. 33
Clear the Over the Falls level one time. Picture displayed is Mission Scenery.

Storm Before the Calm No. 34
Clear the Storm Before Calm level one time. Picture displayed is Mission Scenery.

A Tight Squeeze Card No. 35
Clear the A Tight Squeeze level one time. Picture displayed is Mission Scenery.

The Valley of Fire Card No. 36
Clear the Valley of Fire level one time. Picture displayed is Mission Scenery.

The Great Falls Card No. 37
Clear the Great Falls level one time. Picture displayed is Mission Scenery.

Maximus Card No. 38
Clear the Maximus level one time. Picture displayed is Mission Scenery.

Bf-109 Customized Card No. 39
Clear the Maximus level with Bf-109. The picture displayed is of a customized craft.

Bf-109 Customized Card No. 40
Clear the Maximus level with Bf-109. The picture displayed is of a customized craft.

Swordfish Customized Card No. 41
Clear the Maximus level with Swordfish. The picture displayed is of a customized craft.

Swordfish Customized Card No. 42
Clear the Maximus level with Swordfish. The picture displayed is of a customized craft.

Pulsejet Customized Card No. 43
Clear the Maximus level with Pulsejet. The picture displayed is of a customized craft.

Pulsejet Customized Card No. 44
Clear the Maximus level with Pulsejet. The picture displayed is of a customized craft.

Swordfish Custom Data Card No. 45
Get Swordfish triple wing. The picture displayed is of a CG Rendering.

Swordfish Custom Data Card No. 46
Get Swordfish triple wing. The picture displayed is of a Draft Illustration.

Bf-109 Custom Data Card No. 47
Get Bf-109 Custom parts. The picture displayed is of a CG Rendering.

Bf-109 Custom Data Card No. 48
Get Bf-109 Custom parts. The picture displayed is of a Draft Illustration.

Pulse Jet Test Type Data Card No. 49
Get Pulse Jet Custom parts. The picture displayed is of a CG Rendering.

Pulse Jet Test Type Data Card No. 50
Get Pulse Jet Custom parts. The picture displayed is of a Draft Illustration.

Me262 Data Card No. 51

Get Me262. The picture displayed is of a CG Rendering.

Me262 Data Card No. 52

Get Me262. The picture displayed is of a Draft Illustration.

F4U Corsair Data Card No. 53

Get F4U Corsair. The picture displayed is of a CG Rendering.

F4U Corsair Data Card No. 54

Get F4U Corsair. The picture displayed is of a Draft Illustration.

F117 Data Card No. 55

Get Stealth Jet. The picture displayed is of a CG Rendering.

F117 Data Card No. 56

Get Stealth Jet. The picture displayed is of a Draft Illustration.

Shinden Data Card No. 57

Get Shinden. The picture displayed is of a CG Rendering.

Shinden Data Card No. 58

Get Shinden. The picture displayed is of a Draft Illustration.

Shinden-Kai Data Card No. 59

Get Shinden-kai. The picture displayed is of a CG Rendering.

Shinden-Kai Data Card No. 60

Get Shinden-kai. The picture displayed is of a Draft Illustration.

Autogytro XG-1 Data Card No. 61

Get Autogytro. The picture displayed is of a CG Rendering.

Autogytro XG-1 Data Card No. 62

Get Autogytro. The picture displayed is of a Draft Illustration.

UFO Type Gold Data Card No. 63

Get UFO 2. The picture displayed is of a CG Rendering.

UFO Type Gold Data Card No. 64

Get UFO 2. The picture displayed is of a Draft Illustration.

UFO Type Silver Data Card No 65

Get UFO 1. The picture displayed is of a CG Rendering.

UFO Type Silver Data Card No 66

Get UFO 1. The picture displayed is of a Draft Illustration.

Pontoon Plane Data Card No. 67

Get Pontoons. The picture displayed is of a CG Rendering.

Pontoon Plane Data Card No. 68

Get Pontoons. The picture displayed is of a Draft Illustration.

Movie Card No. 69

Earn 2,000 Acrobatic Points. The picture displayed is of a CG Movie.

Movie Card No. 70

Earn 3,000 Acrobatic Points. The picture displayed is of a CG Movie.

Movie Card No. 71

Earn 4,000 Acrobatic Points. The picture displayed is of a CG Movie.

Movie Card No. 72

Earn 5,000 Acrobatic Points. The picture displayed is of a CG Movie.

Movie Card No. 73

Earn 6,000 Acrobatic Points. The picture displayed is of a CG Movie.

Special Card No. 74

All other cards earned. The picture displayed is of a Special Framed Card.

Special Card No. 75

All other cards earned. The picture displayed is of a Special Framed Card.

Special Card No. 76

All other cards earned. The picture displayed is of a Special Framed Card.

SMUGGLER'S RUN

Vehicles from *Midnight Club: Street Racing*

Use a saved game from *Midnight Club: Street Racing* to be able to use vehicles from that game.

Invisibility

Pause the game. Press R1, L1 (2), R2, L1 (2), L2. A sound confirms correct entry.

Less Time Warp

Pause the game. Press R2, L2, L1, R1, Left (3). A sound confirms correct entry.

More Time Warp

Pause the game. Press R1, L1, L2, R2, Right (3). A sound confirms correct entry.

Light Cars

Pause the game. Press L1, R1 (2), L2, R2 (2). A sound confirms correct entry.

No Gravity

Pause the game. Press R1, R2, R1, R2, Up (3). A sound confirms correct entry.

SPIDERMAN: THE MOVIE

Master Code

Enter the Specials menu and enter ARACHNID as a code. A laugh will confirm correct code entry. All levels in the level warp option, all gallery options (movie viewer/production art), and combo moves will be unlocked. Repeat code entry to return to normal.

Unlimited Webbing

Enter the Specials menu and enter ORGANICWEBBING as a code. A laugh will confirm correct code entry. Repeat code entry to return to normal. Alternately, accumulate 50,000 points during gameplay.

All Fighting Controls

Enter the Specials menu and enter KOALA as a code. A laugh will confirm correct code entry. Repeat code entry to return to normal.

Level Select

Enter the Specials menu and enter IMIARMAS as a code. A laugh will confirm correct code entry. Repeat code entry to return to normal.

Level Skip

Enter the Specials menu and enter ROMITAS as a code. A laugh will confirm correct code entry. Repeat code entry to return to normal. Pause gameplay and select the "Next Level" option to advance to the next level.

Bonus Training Levels

Enter the Specials menu and enter HEADEXPLODY as a code. A laugh will confirm correct code entry. Repeat code entry to return to normal.

Play as Mary Jane

Enter the Specials menu and enter GIRLNEXTDOOR as a code. A laugh will confirm correct code entry. Repeat code entry to return to normal.

Play as the Shocker

Enter the Specials menu and enter HERMANSCHULTZ as a code. A laugh will confirm correct code entry. Repeat code entry to return to normal.

Play as a Scientist

Enter the Specials menu and enter SERUM as a code. A laugh will confirm correct code entry. Repeat code entry to return to normal.

Play as a Police Officer

Enter the Specials menu and enter REALHERO as a code. A laugh will confirm correct code entry. Repeat code entry to return to normal.

Play as Captain Stacey (Helicopter Pilot)

Enter the Specials menu and enter CAPTAINSTACEY as a code. A laugh will confirm correct code entry. Repeat code entry to return to normal.

Play as Skulls Gang Thug

Enter the Specials menu and enter KNUCKLES as a code. A laugh will confirm correct code entry. Repeat code entry to return to normal.

Play as Uncle Ben's Killer

Enter the Specials menu and enter STICKYRICE as a code. A laugh will confirm correct code entry. Repeat code entry to return to normal.

Play as Shocker's Thug

Enter the Specials menu and enter THUGSRUS as a code. A laugh will confirm correct code entry. Repeat code entry to return to normal.

Matrix-Style Attacks

Enter the Specials menu and enter DODGETHIS as a code. A laugh will confirm correct code entry. Repeat code entry to return to normal.

Goblin-Style Costume

Enter the Specials menu and enter FREAKOUT as a code. A laugh will confirm correct code entry. Repeat code entry to return to normal.

Small Spider-Man

Enter the Specials menu and enter SPIDERBYTE as a code. A laugh will confirm correct code entry. Repeat code entry to return to normal.

Big Head and Feet for Spider-Man

Enter the Specials menu and enter GOESTOYOURHEAD as a code. A laugh will confirm correct code entry. Repeat code entry to return to normal.

Enemies Have Big Heads

Enter the Specials menu and enter JOELSPEANUTS as a code. A laugh will confirm correct code entry. Repeat code entry to return to normal.

First-Person View
Enter the Specials menu and enter UNDER-THEMASK as a code. A laugh will confirm correct code entry. Repeat code entry to return to normal.

Unlimited Green Goblin Glider Power
Enter the Specials menu and enter CHILLOUT as a code. A laugh will confirm correct code entry. Repeat code entry to return to normal.

Pinhead Bowling Mini-Game
Accumulate 10,000 points during gameplay to unlock the Pinhead bowling mini-game in the training menu.

Vulture FMV Sequence
Accumulate 20,000 points during gameplay to unlock a Vulture FMV sequence in the CG menu.

Shocker FMV Sequence
Accumulate 30,000 points during gameplay to unlock a Vulture FMV sequence in the CG menu.

Green Goblin FMV Sequence
Successfully complete the game under the hero or greater difficulty setting.

Play as Alex Ross
Successfully complete the game under the normal or higher difficulty setting to unlock the Alex Ross costume in the Specials menu.

Play as the Green Goblin
Successfully complete the game under the hero or superhero difficulty setting to unlock the Green Goblin costume option at the Specials menu. Select that option to play as Harry Osborn in the Green Goblin costume, including his weapons, in an alternate storyline in which he tries to correct the Osborn family's reputation. To unlock this easily, start a new game under the hero or superhero difficulty setting. At the first level, pause gameplay, then quit to the main menu. Enable the ARACHNID code, then go to the "Level Warp" option. Choose the "Conclusion" level (that features Norman revealing himself to Spider-Man followed by the glider sequence), then exit. This marks the game as completed under the selected difficulty setting. The Green Goblin costume option will be unlocked at the "Secret Store" screen.

Alternate Green Goblin Costume
If you are using the Alex Ross Spider-Man, play any level with the Green Goblin in it and he will have an alternate costume that more closely resembles his classic costume.

Play as Peter Parker
Successfully complete the game under the easy or higher difficulty setting to unlock the Peter Parker costume in the Specials menu.

Play as Wrestler
Successfully complete the game under the easy or higher difficulty setting to unlock the wrestler costume in the Specials menu. To unlock this easily, first unlock the "Unlimited Webbing" cheat. When you get to the ring, zip to the top and keep on shooting Spidey Bombs.

SSX

Unlock All Courses, Costumes, Characters, and Boards
Go into the Options menu. Hold R1+R2+L1+L2 and press Down, Left, Up, Right, X, Circle, Triangle, Square. A sound confirms correct entry.

Unlock the Running Man
Go into the Options menu. Hold R1+R2+L1+L2 and press Square, Triangle, Circle, X, Square, Triangle, Circle, X. A sound confirms correct entry.

Maximum Stats
Go into the Options menu. Hold R1+R2+L1+L2 and press X (7), Square. A sound confirms correct entry.

Unlocking All Course Hints
Go into the Options menu. Hold R1+R2+L1+L2 and press Circle, X, Circle, X, Circle, X, Circle, X. A sound confirms correct entry.

Unlocking the Third Board
Obtain the Rookie rank.

Unlocking the Fourth Board
Obtain the Sensei rank.

Unlocking the Fifth Board
Obtain the Contender rank.

Unlocking the Sixth Board
Obtain the Natural rank.

Unlocking the Seventh Board
Obtain the Star rank.

Unlocking the Eighth Board
Obtain the Veteran rank.

Unlocking the Ninth Board
Obtain the Champ rank.

Unlocking the 10th Board
Obtain the Superstar rank.

Unlocking the 11th Board
Obtain the Master rank.

Unlock the Third Costume
Complete all green circle tricks.

Unlock the Fourth Costume
Complete all blue square tricks.

Unlock Jurgen
Win one gold medal.

Unlock JP
Win two gold medals.

Unlock Zoe
Win three gold medals.

Unlock Hiro
Win four gold medals.

Unlock Mercury City Meltdown Track
Get a medal on Elysium.

Unlock Mesablanca Track
Get a medal on Mercury City Meltdown.

Unlock Tokyo Megaplex Track
Get a medal on Mesablanca.

Unlock Aloha Ice Jam Track
Get a medal on Tokyo Megaplex.

Unlock Pipedream Track
Get a medal on Tokyo Megaplex.

Unlock the Untracked Course
Get a medal on the Aloha Ice Jam.

SSX TRICKY

Master Code
Hold L1 + R1 and press X, Triangle, Right, Circle, Square, Down, Triangle, Square, Left, Circle, X, Up at the title screen. Release L1 + R1 and a sound will confirm correct code entry.

Full Stat Points
Hold L1 + R1 and press Triangle(2), Right, Triangle(2), Down, X(2), Left, X(2), Up at the title screen. Release L1 + R1 and a sound will confirm correct code entry. All the boarders will have full stat points.

Mallora Board
Hold L1 + R1 and press X(2), Right, Circle(2), Down, Triangle(2), Left, Square(2), Up at the title screen. Release L1 + R1 and a sound will confirm correct code entry. Choose Elise and start a track. Elise will have the Mallora Board and a blue outfit. This code only works for Elise.

Sticky Boards
Hold L1 + R1 and press Square(2), Right, Triangle(2), Down, Circle(2), Left, X(2), Up at the title screen. Release L1 + R1 and a sound will confirm correct code entry.

Running Man Mode
Hold L1 + R1 + R2 + L2 press Square, Triangle, Circle, X, Square, Triangle, Circle, X at the O9lptions screen.

Mix Master Mike
Hold L1 + R1 and press X(2), Right, X(2), Down, X(2), Left, X(2), Up at the title screen. Release L1 + R1 and a sound will confirm correct code entry. Choose any boarder at the Character Selection screen and he or she will be replaced by Mix Master Mike on the course. He has decks on his back and a vinyl board. Repeat the code to disable its effect.

Pipedream Course
Win a medal on all Showoff courses.

Untracked Course
Win a medal on all Race courses.

Uberboards
Unlock all of the tricks for a character to get their uberboard, which is their best board.

Fugi Board
Get a gold medal on every course with all boarders with their uberboard to unlock a Fugi board.

Alternate Costumes
To earn more costumes, complete all chapters in your trick book. To unlock the final chrome costume, complete World Circuit mode with a Master rank.

Play as Brodi
Win a gold medal in World Circuit mode.

Play as Zoe
Win two gold medals in World Circuit mode.

Play as JP
Win three gold medals in World Circuit mode.

Play as Kaori
Win four gold medals in World Circuit mode.

Play as Marisol
Win five gold medals in World Circuit mode.

Play as Psymon
Win six gold medals in World Circuit mode.

Play as Seeiah

Win seven gold medals in World Circuit mode.

Play as Luther

Win eight gold medals in World Circuit mode.

STAR WARS: STARFIGHTER

My Day at Work

To view this short slideshow, enter the Code screen from the Options screen then type JAMEZ.

Hidden Christmas Video

Enter the Options screen from the main menu and then enter the Code screen. Type WOZ.

Jar Jar Mode

Enter the Options screen from the main menu and then enter the Code screen. Type JARJAR.

View Hidden Picture

At the Code screen type SIMON. You'll be shown a picture of the LEC team.

Unlock Experimental N-1 Fighter

At the Code screen type BLUENSF.

Invincibility

At the Code screen type MINIME.

Unlock Everything

Enter the Options screen from the main menu and then enter the Code screen. Now type OVERSEER.

Director Mode

Enter the Options screen from the main menu and then enter the Code screen. Now type DIRECTOR.

Hidden Message

At the Code screen and type LTDJGD.

No Heads Up Display

Enter the Options screen from the main menu and then enter the Code screen. Now type NOHUD.

View Character Sketches

From the main menu select Options then choose the Code screen. Type HEROES.

View the Credits

Enter the Options screen from the main menu and then enter the Code creen. Now type CREDITS.

Default Message

At the Code screen type either SHOTS or SIZZLE.

Unlock the Gallery

Enter the Options screen from the main menu and then enter the Code screen. Now type SHIPS.

View Planet Sketch-Work

Enter the Options Screen from the main menu and then enter the Codes Screen. Now type PLANETS.

View the Dev Team

Enter the Options screen from the main menu and then enter the Code screen. Now type TEAM.

Unlock Multiplayer Mode

Enter the Options screen from the main menu and then enter the Code screen. Now type ANDREW.

Unlock the Outpost Attack Bonus Mission

To play the Outpost Attack Mission you must get Bronze in all 14 missions of the normal game.

Unlock the Space Sweep Bonus Mission

To play the Space Sweep Mission you must get Silver in all 14 missions of the normal game.

Unlock the *Guardian Mantis*

To use the *Guardian Mantis* ship in every mission, get gold in these three missions: Contract Infraction, Secrets On Eos, The New Resistance.

Unlock Canyon Sprint Bonus Mission

To play the Canyon Sprint Bonus Mission, get silver in these six missions: Naboo Proving Grounds, the Royal Escort, Taking the Offensive, Midnight Munitions Run, Rescue On the Solleu, the Final Assault.

Unlock Charm's Way Bonus Mission

To play the Charm's Way Bonus Mission, get a bronze medal in these six missions: the Royal Escort, Contract Infraction, Piracy Above Lok, Taking the Offensive, the New Resistance, the Final Assault.

Unlock the Havoc

To use the Havoc bomber in every mission, get gold in these five missions using the Havoc in the normal game: Piracy Above Lok, Valuable Goods, Eye Of the Storm, the Crippling Blow, Last Stand On Naboo.

Unlock the N-1 Starfighter

To use the N-1 Starfighter in every mission, get gold in these six missions using the N-1 in the regular game: Naboo Proving Grounds, the Royal Escort, Taking the Offensive, Midnight Munitions Run, Rescue on Solleu, the Final Assault.

Unlock Darth Maul's *Infiltrator*

To use the amazing and super-powerful *Infiltrator* ship in every mission, get gold in every mission in the normal game.

Unlock Two-Player Canyon Race

To play the hidden two-player games you must first beat the normal game on any difficulty level. Once unlocked, you must get gold in every level of the normal game to play the bonus level.

Unlock Two-Player Capture the Flag

To play the hidden two-player games you must beat the normal game on any difficulty level. Once unlocked, you must get gold in every level of the normal game to play the bonus level.

Grim Fandango Hotrod

Come in first in the Canyon Sprint Bonus Mission.

Outlaw Gallery

To view this Easter Egg, start the first level. Instead of following your instructor's ship, turn around and go the other way to fly into a large room and view artwork from a game called OUTLAW.

Burger Droid

To witness this Easter Egg, first type the DIRECTOR code. Then enter the Bonus Missions and select Fighter Training. After a few seconds you see an asteroid with an android on it barbecuing some hamburgers.

STAR WARS: SUPER BOMBAD RACING

Unlock Galaxy Circuit

To unlock the Galaxy Circuit, play through each individual race and finish in the top three on each track. Then the Galaxy Circuit will be available to race.

Unlock Reverse Mirror Tracks

To unlock the option to race the tracks in reverse, complete the Galaxy Circuit with any character and receive a gold medal.

Unlock Darth Vader

To play as the original Dark Lord of the Sith, play through the Galaxy Circuit as Anakin Skywalker and win a gold medal.

Everybody Is a Kaadu

At the main menu press L1,R1,L2, R2. You get the message: Poof! Everybody is a kaadu!

Unlock Boba Fett

Tap Square, Circle, Triangle, Circle, Square at the main menu. You get a message saying that Boba Fett has replaced your racer. Then start the game as normal, select your character, and you play as Boba Fett when the race starts.

Unlock Trade Federation Battle Tank

To race as a squished version of a Trade Federation Battle Tank, press Circle, Triangle, Square, Circle, Triangle, Square at the main menu. Next select your character as normal, and when the race starts you will be playing as the Tank.

STATE OF EMERGENCY

Invincibility

Press L1, L2, R1, R2, X during gameplay. A message will confirm correct code entry.

Unlimited Time in Kaos Mode

Press L1, L2, R1, R2, Circle during gameplay. A message will confirm correct code entry.

Unlimited Ammunition

Press L1, L2, R1, R2, Triangle during gameplay. A message will confirm correct code entry. You can't be holding a weapon for this to work.

All Weapons

Press L1(2), R2(2), X during gameplay. A message will confirm correct code entry.

Pistol

Press Left, Right, Down, L1, Triangle during gameplay.

Tazer

Press Left, Right, Down, L1, Circle during gameplay.

Pepper Spray

Press Left, Right, Down, L1, Square during gameplay.

Tear Gas

Press Left, Right, Down, L1, X during gameplay.

Shotgun

Press Left, Right, Down, L2, Triangle during gameplay.

Minigun

Press Left, Right, Down, R1, Triangle during gameplay.

Flame Thrower
Press Left, Right, Down, R1, Circle during gameplay.

Grenade Launcher
Press Left, Right, Down, R1, Square during gameplay.

Rocket Launcher
Press Left, Right, Down, R1, X during gameplay.

AK47
Press Left, Right, Down, R2, Triangle during gameplay.

M16
Press Left, Right, Down, R2, Circle during gameplay.

Grenade
Press Left, Right, Down, R2, Square during gameplay.

Molotov Cocktail
Press Left, Right, Down, R2, X during gameplay.

Mission Skip
Press Left(4), Triangle during gameplay. A message will confirm correct code entry.

Mission Select
Press L1, L2(3), L1, X during gameplay. A message will confirm correct code entry.

Punches Decapitate
Press L1, L2, R1, R2, Square during gameplay. A message will confirm correct code entry.

Little Player
Press R1, R2, L1, L2, X during gameplay. A message will confirm correct code entry.

Big Player
Press R1, R2, L1, L2, Triangle during gameplay. A message will confirm correct code entry.

Normal Player
Press R1, R2, L1, L2, Circle during gameplay. No confirmation message will appear. Alternately, press R1, R2, L1, L2, Square during gameplay.

Looting on the Rise
Press R1, L1, R2, L2, Triangle during gameplay. A message will confirm correct code entry.

Bull
Press Right(4), X during gameplay in Kaos mode. A message will confirm correct code entry. Alternately, successfully complete the East Side level in Revolution mode to unlock Bull in Kaos mode.

Freak
Press Right(4), Circle during gameplay in Kaos mode. A message will confirm correct code entry. Alternately, successfully complete the Chinatown level in Revolution mode to unlock Freak in Kaos mode.

Spanky
Press Right(4), Triangle during gameplay in Kaos mode. A message will confirm correct code entry. Alternately, successfully complete the Mall level in Revolution mode to unlock Spanky in Kaos mode.

Policeman
Hold L1, then press R2(2), L2, R1 during gameplay. A message will confirm correct code entry.

Unlimited Kaos Mode Time
Successfully complete all Kaos levels in Arcade mode.

Chinatown Level
Score 25,000 points in the Capitol City Mall level in Kaos mode.

East Side Level
Score 50,000 points in the Chinatown level in Kaos mode.

Corporation Central Level
Score 100,000 points in the East Side level in Kaos mode.

Last Clone Standing Levels
Successfully complete the three-minute and five-minute versions of a level to unlock the Last Clone Standing version of that map in Kaos mode.

STREET FIGHTER EX3

Bonus Characters
Beat the game with a regular character and without Continuing on normal difficulty to unlock one of the hidden characters. Do this nine times to unlock all the bonus characters. Each time you beat the game you must use a different regular character though. The order of bonus characters are: Sagat, Vega, Garuda, Shadow Geist, Kairi, Pullum, Area, Darun, and Vulcano.

Evil Ryu
Beat Original mode eight times with Ryu and without Continuing. Go to the Character Selection screen and highlight Ryu. Press X, Square, or Circle.

Narrator Sakura
Beat Original mode eight times with Sakura and without Continuing. Go to the Character Selection screen and highlight Sakura. Press Select.

M. Bison II
Beat Original mode eight times with M. Bison and without Continuing. Go to the Character Selection screen and highlight M. Bison. Press X, Square, or Circle.

SUPER BUST-A-WORLD

Bonus Characters
Press Triangle, Left, Right, Triangle at the "Push Start Button" screen. An icon in the upper left confirms correct entry.

More Puzzles
Press Triangle, Right, Left, Triangle at the "Push Start Button" screen. An icon in the upper right confirms correct entry. Enter Puzzle mode and choose "Arcade" to see more puzzles.

SURFING

Unlock Normal Boards and Riders
Beat the game on Normal difficulty to unlock six new boards, Tyrone King, Lara Barcella, and Gareos.

Unlock Semi-Pro Boards and Riders
Beat the game on Semi-Pro difficulty to unlock six new boards, Jojo, Morsa and Serena Knox.

Unlock Pro Boards and Riders
Beat the game on Pro difficulty to unlock five new boards, Largo, Lyco Sassa, and Mikey Sands.

Unlocks Master Boards and Riders
Beat the game on Master difficulty to unlock three new boards and Surfroid.

TEKKEN TAG TOURNAMENT

Play as Angel
Highlight Devil at the Character Selection screen. Press Start.

Play as Tiger
Highlight Eddy at the Character Selection screen. Press Start.

Bonus Characters
Beat Arcade mode with any character to unlock one of the hidden characters. A bonus character is revealed each time you beat the game. The bonus characters appear in this order: Kunimitsu, Bruce Irvin, Jack-2, Lee Chaolan, Wang Jinrey, Roger and Alex, Kuma and Panda, Kazuya Mishima, Ogre, True Ogre, Prototype Jack, Mokujin and Tetsujin, Devil and Angel, and Unknown.

Extra Armor King Costume
Beat Arcade mode with Armor King. Go to the Character Selection screen and highlight Armor King. Press Start to get his extra costume.

Extra Ling Ending
Beat Arcade mode with Ling. Then beat the game a second time with Ling in her school uniform.

Theater Mode
Beat Arcade mode once.

Tekken Bowl Mode
Once you unlock Ogre you have Tekken Bowl.

Gallery Mode
Once you unlock Devil you can access Gallery mode.

Tekken Bowl Jukebox
Score higher than 200 in Tekken Bowl. Press Start inside Tekken Bowl to access the Bowling menu. Choose "Bowling Options" and pick what song you want to listen to.

Change Partners Before a Fight
Hold the tag button before a match begins to let your partner start first.

Supercharging
During a match, press all buttons to charge up. Press X+Circle+Triangle+Square if you kept the default buttons.

Law's Stage (New)
Highlight Practice mode at the main menu. Hold L2 and press R2 (1).

Yoshimitsu's Stage (Light Snow)
Highlight Practice mode at the main menu. Hold L2 and press R2 (2).

Ling's Stage
Highlight Practice mode at the main menu. Hold L2 and press R2 (3).

Hwoarang's Stage
Highlight Practice mode at the main menu. Hold L2 and press R2 (4).

Lei's Stage
Highlight Practice mode at the main menu. Hold L2 and press R2 (5).

Ogre's Stage
Highlight Practice mode at the main menu. Hold L2 and press R2 (6).

School Stage (Evening)
Highlight Practice mode at the main menu. Hold L2 and press R2 (7).

Jin's Stage (Evening)
Highlight Practice mode at the main menu. Hold L2 and press R2 (8).

Nina's Stage (Day)
Highlight Practice mode at the main menu. Hold L2 and press R2 (9).

Eddy's Stage (Sunset)
Highlight Practice mode at the main menu. Hold L2 and press R2 (10).

King's Stage
Highlight Practice mode at the main menu. Hold L2 and press R2 (11).

Heihachi's Stage
Highlight Practice mode at the main menu. Hold L2 and press R2 (12).

Eddy's Stage (Day)
Highlight Practice mode at the main menu. Hold L2 and press R2 (13).

Unknown
Highlight Practice mode at the main menu. Hold L2 and press R2 (14).

Law's Stage (Old)
Highlight Practice mode at the main menu. Hold L2 and press R2 (15).

School Stage (Day)
Highlight Practice mode at the main menu. Hold L2 and press R2 (16).

Jin's Stage (Day)
Highlight Practice mode at the main menu. Hold L2 and press R2 (17).

Nina's Stage (Night)
Highlight Practice mode at the main menu. Hold L2 and press R2 (18).

Yoshimitsu's Stage (Heavy Snow)
Highlight Practice mode at the main menu. Hold L2 and press R2 (19).

Paul
Highlight Practice mode at the main menu. Hold L2 and press R2 (20).

THEME PARK ROLLER COASTER

All Items Researched
While you're in the park, press the combination Up, Down, Up, Down, Left, Up, Down, Up eight times.

Everything Is Free
While you are in the park press the combination Left, Down, X, Circle eight times.

Golden Tickets
While you are in the park press the combination Up, Down, Left, Right, Circle, Right, Left, Down, Up, Circle four times.

TIGER WOODS PGA TOUR 2001

Speed up Computer Players
Hold L1 and Triangle to fast forward through the CPU's turn.

Taunt Your Friends
Playing against one or more human opponents, press Square, Circle, Triangle or X to taunt the golfer while he is at the tee box. Hold down R1 or R2, then press the Square, Circle, Triangle or X for even more annoying sounds.

Unlock Red Shirt Tiger
Beat all 21 games in the Play Now feature to unlock Tiger's shirt. Play with the red shirt Tiger and his in-game stats will match his real-world stats, giving him a major advantage.

TIMESPLITTERS

Unlock the Living Dead
Complete challenge 1-A.

Unlock Green and Brown Zombies
Complete challenge 1-B.

Unlock Police, Skull and Jacket Zombies
Complete challenge 1-C.

Unlock Duckman Drake as a Bot
Complete challenge 2-A.

Unlock the All Enemies Are Ducks Cheat
Complete challenge 2-B.

Unlock Duckman Drake
Complete challenge 2-C.

Unlock Robofish as a Bot
Complete challenge 3-A.

Unlock the All Enemies Are Fish Cheat
Complete challenge 3-B.

Unlock Robofish
Complete challenge 3-C.

Unlock Enemy Bricks Cheat
Complete challenge 4-B.

Unlock Brick as an Arcade Mode Weapon
Complete challenge 4-C.

Unlock the Impersonator as a Bot
Complete challenge 5-A.

Unlock the All Enemies Are Impersonators Cheat
Complete challenge 5-B.

Unlock the Impersonator
Complete challenge 5-C.

Unlock Gasmask SWAT
Complete challenge 6-B.

Unlock Veiled SWAT
Complete challenge 6-C.

Unlock Ginger as a Bot
Complete challenge 7-A.

Unlock the All Enemies Are Gingerbreads Cheat
Complete challenge 7-B.

Unlock Gingerbread
Complete challenge 7-C.

Unlock Fun-Bunny as a Bot
Complete challenge 8-A.

Unlock the All Enemies Are Bunnies Cheat
Complete challenge 8-B.

Unlock Farrah Fun-Bunny
Complete challenge 8-C.

Unlock TimeSplitters as a Bot
Complete challenge 9-A.

Unlock Timesplitter
Complete challenge 9-B.

Unlock the Cultist
Beat the 1935 Tomb level on Easy.

Unlock the Eyes Mummy
Beat the 1935 Tomb level on Hard.

Unlock the Chinese Chef
Beat the 1970 Chinese level on Easy.

Unlock the Suit Hoodlum
Beat the 1970 Chinese level on Easy.

Unlock Peekaboo Jones
Beat the 2020 Planet X level on Easy.

Unlock Jacques Misere
Beat the 2020 Planet X level on Easy.

Unlock Olga Strom
Beat the 2020 Planet X level on Easy.

Unlock Gretel
Beat the 2020 Planet X level on Easy.

Unlock Mary-Beth Casey and R108
Beat the 2020 Planet X level on Easy.

Unlock Challenge Mode
Beat Story mode at any difficulty to unlock Challenge mode. Then defeat each successive Challenge to unlock the next.

Unlock Paintball Mode
Unlock the Paintball mode by beating the 1935 Tomb level on Easy in under one minute.

Unlock the Graveyard Arcade Level
Beat the 1935 Tomb level on Normal.

Unlock the Site Arcade Level
Beat the 1970 Chinese level on Normal.

Unlock the Streets Arcade Level
Beat the 2005 Cyberden level on Normal.

Unlock the 1950 Village Arcade Level
Beat the 1950 Village level on Easy.

Unlock the Castle Arcade Level
Beat the 1950 Village level on Normal.

Unlock the 1985 Chemical Plant Arcade Level
Beat the 1985 Chemical Plant level on Easy.

Unlock the Bank Arcade Level
Beat the 1985 Chemical Plant level on Normal.

Unlock the 2020 Planet X Arcade Level
Beat the 2020 Planet X level on Easy.

Unlock the Spaceship Arcade Level
Beat the 2020 Planet X level on Normal.

Unlock the 1965 Mansion Arcade Level
Beat the 1965 Mansion level on Easy.

Unlock the Mall Arcade Level
Beat the 1965 Mansion level on Normal.

Unlock the 2000 Docks Arcade Level
Beat the 2000 Docks level on Easy.

Unlock the Compound Arcade Level
Beat the 2000 Docks level on Normal.

Unlock the 2035 Spaceways Arcade Level
Beat the 2035 Spaceways level on Easy.

Unlock the Warzone Arcade Level
Beat the 2035 Spaceways level on Normal.

Unlock the Period Horror Bot Set
Beat the 1950 Village level on Easy.

Unlock the Usual Suspects Bot Set
Beat the 1985 Chemical Plant level on Easy.

Unlock the Space Opera Bot Set
Beat the 2020 Planet X level on Easy.

Unlock the Horror Shocker Bot Set
Beat the 1965 Mansion level on Easy.

Unlock the Law and Order Bot Set
Beat the 2000 Docks level on Easy.

Unlock the Space Opera Bot Set
Beat the 2035 Spaceways level on Easy.

Unlock the Badass Cyborg Bot Set
Beat the 2005 Cyberden level on Easy.

Female Cyborg Bot Set
Beat the 2005 Cyberden level on Easy.

Siamese Cyborg Bots
Beat the 2005 Cyberden level on Easy.

Unlock the Malehood Bots
Beat the 1985 Chemical Plant level on Easy.

Unlock the Waiter and Lumberjack Bots
Beat the 1985 Chemical Plant level on Easy.

Unlock the Tuxedo Cyborg Bot
Beat the 2020 Planet X level on Easy.

Unlock the Red and Green Alien Bots
Beat the 2020 Planet X level on Easy.

Unlock the Fishwife Mutant Bot
Beat the 1965 Mansion level on Easy.

Unlock Hick Hyde and Insect Mutant Bots
Beat the 1965 Mansion level on Easy.

Unlock Overall Mutant and Girl Zombie Bots
Beat the 1965 Mansion level on Easy.

Unlock the Male and Female Soldier Bots
Beat the 2000 Docks level on Easy.

Unlock the Gasmask Soldier, Male and Female SWAT Bots
Beat the 2000 Docks level on Easy.

Unlock the Gasmask SWAT Bots
Beat the 2000 Docks level on Easy.

TOKYO XTREME RACER: ZERO

Change Horn to Siren
Select rear spoiler type 5 for R30 and R30M to change the horn to a siren.

Clean Pause Screen
When Pausing, press Triangle+Square to remove the Pause menu. You can't unpause the game while removing the Pause menu. Press Triangle+Square to show the Pause menu.

Get a Special Nickname
Put a team sticker on the car you were driving for this team to get a special nickname.

Manipulate Parts Camera
In the Parts type select screen, selecting Aero parts or exhaust makes the camera move toward the car, but pressing Triangle will not cause the camera to move close to the parts (you'll see the entire car on your screen). Press Triangle again to see the close-up.

Reset Records
In Time Record screen, hold down L1+L2+R1+R2 with Start to reset the record data. (This also resets the Quick race high score.) These will not be saved, though.

See Meters During Replay
When viewing replay, press Select to show the meter(s).

See Other Car in One-on-One
When having one-on-one battle with a rival, hold down 1P controller's square button to show other cars on the course.

See Other Cars in Free Run
In "FREE RUN," press 1P's controller square button when you enter the course select to show other cars on the course.

Show Analyze Option
In Pause Menu (except in the VS mode), hold down Square while you move the cursor to the bottom to show "ANALYZE." Selecting this option (turning this ON) shows the ANALYZE meter.

Show Mirror Ornaments
Hold down L1/L2/R1/R2 when selecting the "Shift Assist" option, to show ornaments in Driver view.

Driver View Replay
When viewing replay in "DRIVER VIEW," press L1/R1 to move the camera left/right.

Watch Replay with Regular Angle
When you're about to see the replay, hold down 1P controller's Triangle to see the replay in regular camera angle. (You can't switch camera angles when you do this.)

TONY HAWK'S PRO SKATER 3

Cheat Menu
Enter the Options menu, then select "Cheats." Enter backdoor (case sensitive) to unlock the Cheat menu at the Pause screen. The sound of money being collected will confirm correct code entry. Press Start to pause gameplay in Career or Free Skate mode to access the Cheat menu. Press X to toggle the options. This does not unlock the hidden characters and bonus levels.

Master Code
Enter the Options menu, then select "Cheats." Enter MAGICMISSILE as a code to unlock all mode options, such as Snowboard, Giant, and First Person. This code also unlocks the "Super Stats," "Always Perfect," "Perfect Manuals," and "Perfect Rails" cheats. The sound of money being collected will confirm correct code entry.

All Characters
Enter the Options menu, then select "Cheats." Enter Yohomies (case sensitive) to unlock all characters. The sound of money being collected will confirm correct code entry. After activating this code, go to "select a level." Go to the one farthest to the left (the custom park) and select "pre-made parks" to get more secret parks.

Level Select
Enter the Options menu, then select "Cheats." Enter RoadTrip (case sensitive) to unlock all levels. The sound of money being collected will confirm correct code entry. This code also completes the game for the current skater and gives all stat points and decks. Play any level and, when you complete or exit it, the game will open a trick slot and unlock a new character, cheat, or level. Do this with every character to complete the entire game with everything unlocked.

Full Stats
Enter the Options menu, then select "Cheats." Enter PUMPMEUP for maximum stat points.

All Decks for Current Skater
Enter the Options menu, then select "Cheats." Enter givemesomewood (case sensitive) to unlock all decks for the current skater.

All FMV Sequences
Enter the Options menu, then select "Cheats." Enter Peepshow (case sensitive) to unlock all FMV sequences. The sound of money being collected will confirm correct code entry.

TOP GEAR DARE DEVIL

All Cars
Press Square, Up, Down, Right, Left, X, Circle, Square while the main screen is loading.

Alternate Colors
Press Down, Square, Down, R1, Right(2), Up, Left, Circle(2), L2, L1 at the main menu, then begin gameplay.

Drive a Blue Hot Rod
On the main menu screen, press main menu Down, Square, Down, R1, Right (2), Up, Left, Circle (2), L2, L1.

Turn on Motion Blur
On the main menu screen, press Up, Left, Circle, Down, Right, Square, Up, Down, Left, Right, Circle, Square. Then, go to the Options menu to use a slider bar at the bottom of the screen to increase Motion Blur.

TRIPLE PLAY BASEBALL

Always Hit the Grand Salami
Go to the Create Player screen in the Roster Menu. Create a player named "SLUGGER." Whenever he comes up with the bases loaded, he'll hit a home run.

TWISTED METAL: BLACK

Change Camera
To change the camera angle, press and hold Select, then press Down. To switch between horizontal and vertical, press and hold Select, then press Left.

Convert Weapons into Health
Here's a handy code that you can use to refill your health when you pick up some weapons. During the game, hold down all four shoulder buttons, then press Triangle, X, Square, Circle. Your weapons vanish and you're health fills up a little.

Decipher Minion
To understand what Minion's numbered codes mean on the load screens (when playing as him), match the number with its corresponding letter. A=1, B=2, and Z=26.

Different Weapons Display
Press and hold Select, then press Right during gameplay to change the weapons selection display.

Downtown Jackpot

On one side of the river in the downtown level is the R&D Chemicals Plant. On the left side of the main building are three giant balls, like the ones in the highway loop level. Shoot the one closest to the sign with a gas can, and it rolls into a building, knocking it down and revealing three healths (which are supplied throughout the level at this location). Shoot the ball on the far left and it rolls into the building directly behind the previous one, giving you six power missiles.

Elevator in Downtown

Find this elevator to pick up power-ups and escape the city hustle and bustle. Find the Atom Bank and face it. To its left is a building with glass doors. Shoot them and they'll blow to pieces. Use the elevator to drive up to the higher reaches of the building. There's one health power-up up there, and it's a great view!

Infinite Ammo

To have unlimited ammunition for your ride, press and hold the shoulder buttons (R1, R2, L1, L2) then press Up, X, Left, Circle.

Invincibility

During gameplay (this includes Story mode), press and hold all four shoulder buttons, then press Right, Left, Down, Up.

Mega Machine Guns

To enable the Mega Machine Guns feature, press and hold all four shoulder buttons (R1, R2, L1, L2) and press X, X, Triangle.

One Hit Kills

During gameplay, press and hold L1+R1+L2+R2 and quickly press X(2) and Up during gameplay. At the top of the screen, a message confirms you've done it right.

Open Elevators Level

Go the Highway Loop Level and kill off six or seven of the combatants. Drive to the raised, broken bridge (with the two health pick-ups and another pick-up in between), and find a power plant, directly off the road. There are two or three giant steel balls there. Shoot the one closest to the bridge with a Gas Can (the projectiles don't work well for this), and it breaks off and rolls. Stay clear of its path, or you'll be squashed. Follow the ball. When it crashes through a wall, follow into the newly opened area and find the Black Cube inside. Health and weapon pick-ups are also inside.

Open Freeway Level

To open the Freeway for multiplayer action, get 10 Kills in Survival Mode in the Snowy Roads arena.

Open Mini-Suburbs Level

To open the Mini-Suburbs for multiplayer action, get 10 Kills in Survival Mode in the Drive-In arena.

Unlock Axel

After beating the first level, choose the Freeway level, not Suburbs (and not the Highway Loop level). Drive to the middle of the level, where an entrance to the construction lot and a Repair Station are located. Of the two cranes located here, focus on the left one. Center your vehicle in the middle of the construction site and use the middle ridge to aim any kind of missile toward the orange control box near the center of the crane. Locate your vehicle halfway up the ledge for the perfect shot. Doing this takes time, and enemies are sure to throw a barrage of projectiles at you, so beat down several of them before trying this.

Unlock God Mode

During gameplay, press and hold L1+R1+L2+R2 and rapidly press Up, X, Left, Circle while playing. There is a message at the top of the screen that reads "God Mode On," confirming you did it right.

Unlock Manslaughter

Manslaughter, the giant dump-truck driven by Black, is located in the Prison Passage level. Down on the docks to the starboard side of the landed ship is a stack of crates holding a health power-up. Shoot the crates to blast open a ramp to the health, then shoot at the ship's hull above where the crates are stacked against it. A panel opens, and you can drive into a room inside the ship where Manslaughter is located. As per usual, destroy the control panel to unlock the new car.

Unlock Minion

To unlock the bad-ass truck Minion, beat the Story Mode with every character, including those you unlock in the game. In other words, beat the game with all starting characters plus Manslaughter, Warthog, Yellow Jacket, and Axel.

Unlock Warhawk's Level

To open Warhawk's multiplayer level in the first level (Zorko Bros. Scrap and Salvage, a.k.a. the Junkyard), focus your efforts on the vertical crusher. There are two ways to get up on top of the vertical crusher—this first way is easiest. Drive up the ramp to the broken freeway and drive halfway along it. Aim your car toward the Bob's Big Boy, and shoot it with a Power or a Fire, to avoid hitting any other cars. When that blows up, it creates a ramp to the vertical crusher. Drive down to the newly created green ramp and, when the crusher is down, drive onto it. Drive slowly onto it so you don't go over it. When it ascends, shoot the building on top of the deck, then drive onto the deck. On the left side is a Black Cube, which opens Warhawk's multiplayer level.

Unlock Warthog

In the Suburbia level, head to the carnival area. At the gate, take a left and head toward the smoke over the ridge. Aim your vehicle for that, speeding up and ramping off the angled dirt ridge here. You land on a building below with a large hole in its roof. Go inside and look for a control panel in the corner. Shoot it to unlock Warthog.

Unlock Yellow Jacket

In the first level, Zorko Brothers Scrap Salvage, there is an airplane circling around again and again. Use a homing missile and shoot it down. Lead the missile to the plane. Go to the wall near the giant magnetic slammer and shoot from there. After that's done, drive to the lower section of the level. The plane has crashed and you can drive in it. Go to the end, find the console and shoot it with machine gun fire. After four seconds, you can see Yellow Jacket's car lower down.

UNREAL TOURNAMENT

Level Advance

Pause the game. Press Up, Down, Left, Right (2), Left, Circle.

Level Select

Pick the "Resume Game" option. Highlight a previously saved game. Press Up, Down (2), Up, Left, Up, Right, Down.

Fatboy Mutation

Press Circle (3), Up, Down (2), Up, Circle (3) at the title screen. Enter multiplayer mode and choose the Fatboy Mutator. You get fatter as you get more frags. You get thinner as you get fragged more.

Stealth Mutation

Press Square (2), Circle (2), Square (2), Circle (2) at the title screen. Enter multiplayer mode and choose the Stealth Mutator.

God Mode

Pause the game. Press Square, Circle, Left, Right, Circle, Square and you will be invincible.

Max Ammo

Pause the game. Press Left, Right, Circle (3), Right, Left.

Firewire Multiplayer

Get a four-port Firewire PC hub. Get one to three more PS2 consoles and hook them up to the hub with Firewire cables. Start a two-person multiplayer game. Pause the game. Press Left, Circle, Left, Right, Square, Right. Then have all the other players press Start to join in.

USB Multiplayer

You need to use two USB keyboards, two USB mice, and two controllers. Set the third and fourth player configurations to the keyboard and mouse.

WILD WILD RACING

Secret Menu and Top Secret Menu

At the main menu highlight and select Options. At the Options menu hold down Square and press Up, Circle, Down, Circle, Left, Right, Left, Right, Circle. This will open the Secret menu option on the Options screen. Now enter Single Player and type your name as NORTHEND.

New Engines

Each country in Time Attack rewards you with an engine for one of the three initially-selectable buggies. Complete the three races per Time Attack (Uphill, Downhill, and Flat) to gain a new engine that ups the stats on your buggy.

WORLD DESTRUCTION LEAGUE: WAR JETZ

Add 10 Money
Enter WNNNGS.

Double Money
Enter TWFSTD.

Instantly Win
Enter SMSHNG.

Invincibility
Enter this code to become invincible: DNGDM.

Level Passwords
Enter the following passwords to take you to the corresponding level.

Panama 2
JBVKWNBBCBQM

Panama 3
MDKKWYFTKBQM

Australia 1
MHZKWTJMQBQM

Australia 2
ZBCKXPBHNBQM

Australia 3
LDRKXYFZTBQM

Thailand
ZHHKXJJTBBQM

Thailand 2
TBPKYZBVHBQM

Thailand 3
KFFPJRFNPBQN

Rhine River 1
YJVPJCJGVBQN

Rhine River 2
FCNPKXBVWBQN

Rhine River 3
PGDPKGFPDBQN

New York City 1
KKSPKRJHKBQN

New York City 2
VBFKPLHBWZBQN

New York City 3
WJYPLWFQGBQN

Antarctica 1
CMPPLHJJNBQN

Antarctica 2
RKFPMYBZHBQN

Antarctica 3
GNVPMQFSNBQN

San Francisco 1
TRLPMBJLVBQN

San Francisco 2
SVMPNFBFVBQN

San Francisco 3
RXDPNHFYDBQN

Valhalla 1
XBXPNGKRKBQN

Valhalla 2
LPXKVMCQZBQM

Valhalla 3
QSMKVSGKHBQM

Level Select
JMPTT

Plane Automatically Wins
SMSHNG

Show All Boxes
BXDRW

Super Armor
MRRMR

Unlock Faster Jets
ZPPY

Unlock Ghost mode
SNKY

Unlock Huge Guns
QD

Unlock Overlords mode
VRLRDS

Unlock Rapid Fire
FRHS

Unlock Spin Shots
DZZY

Unlock All Codes
TWLVCHTS

Unlock All Movies
GRTD

Unlock everything
SPRLZY

View All FMV
GRTD

X-SQUAD

Private Rank Code
Press Square, Circle, Triangle at the title screen. Start a new game. You'll start with the Michaels 9mmS and 99 clips, and bonus points will be shown.

Sergeant Rank Code
Press Triangle, Circle, Square at the title screen. Start a new game. You'll start with the Taylor M82, no weight limit, Michaels 9mmS, and 99 clips, and bonus points will be shown.

Lieutenant Rank Code
Press R1, L2, L1, R2 at the title screen. Start a new game. You'll start with a Level 2 shield and the items from the Sergeant Rank code. You'll also earn a 10,000-point bonus when you complete the level.

Captain Rank Code
Press Circle, R1, Circle, L1, Triangle, R2 at the title screen. Start a new game. You'll start with a radar and the rest of items from the Lieutenant Rank code.

Major Rank Code
Press L2, Square, R2, Triangle, L1, Circle, R1 at the title screen. Start a new game. You'll start with a Level 3 shield, Level 3 sensor, and the rest of the items from the Sergeant Rank code.

Colonel Rank Code
Press Triangle, Square, Circle, Square, Triangle, Circle at the title screen. Start a new game. You'll start with a Level 3 shield, Level 3 sensor, radar, no weight limit, 99 clips, and beginner level of all weapons, and bonus points will be shown.

General Rank Code
Press L1 (2), L2 (2), R1 (2), R2 (2) at the title screen. Start a new game. You'll start with the items from Colonel Rank code except that this one has intermediate level of all weapons.

Master of X-Squad Rank Code
Press Circle (4), Triangle, Square (4) at the title screen. Start a new game. You'll start with the items from the General Rank code except this one has a master level of all weapons.

ZONE OF THE ENDERS

Unlock Versus Mode
Complete the game to receive Versus mode. Your score (the amount of continues used, saves, and the amount of civilians you rescued) determines which frames you get to play.

Alternate Ending
Complete all of the S.O.S calls, ranking A in each of them, and you see a different ending sequence.

XG3 EXTREME G RACING

Unlimited Turbo
To get unlimited turbo, go to the title screen. Press R1+L1, R2+L2, R1+L1, R2+L2. When the code is entered correctly, you get a message confirming entry.

Unlock All Tracks
To unlock all of the tracks in the game, go to the main menu and press L1, L1, L2, L2, R2, R2, R1, R1, then L1+R1+L2+R2. If the code is entered correctly, a message appears.

Nintendo 64

NUMBERS

1080 DEGREE SNOWBOARDING

Manipulate View of Title Screen
At the title screen, press C-Up to adjust your view.

Deadly Fall Course
In Expert mode, select Match Race and complete all courses.

Dragon Cave Course
In Expert mode, select Match Race and complete all courses.

Ghost Playback During Demo
Save the Ghost while completing any course in Time Attack mode. Go back to the Demonstration screen with Kensuke Kimachi, and the demo will continue after he crosses the finish line.

Keep Going Past the Finish Line
With any character, board, and course, select "Match Race." Proceed to the finish line, press Start, and retire before you cross the line. Your character will continue snowboarding.

Gold Boarder
Complete Match Race in Expert difficulty with the "transparent" character. Select Kensuke Kimachi, hold C-Up, and press A at his Statistics screen.

Panda Boarder
In Expert difficulty, finish Match Race better than all the EAD scores on the Time Attack, Trick Attack, and Contest modes. Select Rob Haywood, hold C-Right, and press A at his Statistics screen.

Crystal Boarder
At Expert difficulty, win Race mode. Finish better than all the EAD scores on the Time Attack and Trick Attack modes. Select Akari Hayami, hold C-Left, and press A at his Statistics screen.

Penguin Snowboard
Execute all 24 Training mode tricks. At the Snowboard Selection screen, highlight any character's default board, hold C-Down, and press A.

Jam with Replay Music
Press the analog stick in any direction during a replay to add record scratches to the music.

Turbo Start
Press Up just as the number 1 starts to disappear at the Start of Race screen.

Unlock Tricks
Choose the Training option at the main menu. Pick any rider and board, and select an easy trick from the list. Take off from the jump or from the side of the half pipe and execute the trick. Quickly press C-Right twice while in midair. The trick list appears again. Choose a trick that hasn't been unlocked; then resume the game and land with the easy trick. The harder trick should now be unlocked.

A

AERO GAUGE

All Tracks and Vehicles
Hold Start on Controller 1 as the game turns on until the Press Start screen appears. Then use Controller 2 and press Up+C-Down+R+L+Z, and then release. Quickly press Start or A on Controller 1 to enter Grand Prix mode.

AEROFIGHTERS ASSAULT

Bonus Plane
Press C-Left, C-Down, C-Right, C-Up, C-Left, C-Right, C-Down at the Press Start screen.

AIDYN CHRONICLES 1ST MAGE

Faster Speed
To avoid an attack, press left, left (control stick) before the enemy attacks.

Make Money
Buy ingredients for inferno flasks and make them. With the alchemist ability, sell them to make money.

Acid Wand
It is located in the chest behind the Goblin King. To find the chest, find a hobgoblin in a tent with torches all around.

AIR BOARDER 64

Bonus Characters
Complete one of the following goals to unlock a bonus character: In Street mode, earn an A and S ranking on each level and track. In Time Attack mode, complete each level and track within the time limit. In Coin mode, earn a Perfect rank on each level and track.

Bonus Boards
Unlock all four bonus characters. Then press Up (2), Down (2), Left, Right, Left, B, A at the Board Selection screen.

Alien Team and Stadium
Enter ATEMYBUIK in the Cheat menu.

Flat Players
Enter PRPPAPLYR in the Cheat menu.

Oversized Feet and Heads
Enter BIGHELIUM in the Cheat menu.

ALL-STAR BASEBALL '99

Beach Ball Baseballs
Enter BBNSTRDS in the Cheat menu.

Big Heads, Big Bodies, Big Bats
Enter GOTHELIUM in the Cheat menu.

Credits Option
At the title screen press R, A, Z, R, C-Right, A, B.

Fat and Skinny Players
Enter ABBTNCSTLO in the Cheat menu.

Fireball
Enter GRTBLSFDST in Cheat menu.

Team of Lizards
Start an exhibition game and choose Kaufmann Stadium. Inside the stadium are two signs that say, "Win a lizard." If someone hits the sign, the team members turn into lizards.

Broken Bats
Enter BRKNBATS in the Cheat menu.

View Programmer Messages
Press C-Up, R, B (2) at the title screen.

ALL-STAR BASEBALL 2000

Flying Players
Enter FLYAWAY in the Cheat menu. Player flies back to the dugouts.

Baseball Trails
Enter WLDWLDWST in the Cheat menu.

Blackout Mode
Enter WTOTL in the Cheat menu.

Wire Frame Mode
Enter SKETCHY in the Cheat menu.

Fast Running
Enter SONIC in the Cheat menu.

Blurry Graphics
Enter MYEYES in the Cheat menu.

Large Baseball
Enter BCHBLKTPTY in the Cheat menu.

Tiny Baseball Players
Enter TOMTHUMB in the Cheat menu.

Super Fastball
Hold C-Down+A while pitching in Arcade mode.

Team of Lizards
Start an exhibition game and choose Kaufmann Stadium. Inside the stadium are two signs that say "Win a lizard." If someone hits the sign, the team members turn into lizards.

ALL-STAR BASEBALL 2001

Fly Back to Dugout
Enter FLYAWAY in the Cheat menu.

Small Players
Enter TOMTHUMB in the Cheat menu.

Big Baseball
Enter BCHBLKTPTY in the Cheat menu.

Baseball Trails
Enter WLDWLDWST in the Cheat menu.

Blackout Mode
Enter WTOTL in the Cheat menu.

Blurred Graphics
Enter MYEYES in the Cheat menu.

ARMORINES: PROJECT S.W.A.R.M.

All Cheats
Enter GOLDENPIE in the Cheat menu.

All Weapons
Enter LOADED in the Cheat menu.

God Mode
Enter GODLY in the Cheat menu.

Infinite Ammo
Enter SORTED in the Cheat menu.

Level Select
Enter SKIPPY in the Cheat menu.

Egypt Fodder in Multiplayer Mode
Enter CLAW in the Cheat menu. You may use only one multiplayer code at a time.

Female Trooper in Multiplayer Mode
Enter GODDESS in the Cheat menu. You may use only one multiplayer code at a time.

Hive Guard in Multiplayer Mode
Enter LEGGY in the Cheat menu. You may use only one multiplayer code at a time.

Volcano Guard in Multiplayer Mode
Enter RUBBER in the Cheat menu. You may use only one multiplayer code at a time.

Hive Fodder in Multiplayer Mode
Enter UGLY in the Cheat menu. You may use only one multiplayer code at a time.

Hive Level 1
PNRVPZ

Hive Level 2
NGQDCZ

Hive Level 3
VRGBNZ

Hive Level 4
SVPQQZ

Level 2
PNTNNP

Level 3
NGMLQP

Level 4
SPLGZW

Level 5
DQRFKW

Level 6
PSQQLW

Level 7
NBGJVX

Level 8
VKPDMX

Level 9
SDKNSX

Level 10
PVBWGJ

Level 11
NWVCHJ

ARMY MEN: AIR ATTACK

Unlock all Levels and Choppers
R, C-Left, Right, Up

Level 2
Up, Down, Left, Right

Level 3
Up, Down, Left, Up

Level 4
Down, Up, Left, Right

Level 5
Down, Up, Left, Down

Level 6
Down, Up, Right, Down

Level 7
Left, Down, L, Up

Level 8
Left, Down, L, Down

Level 9
Left, Up, L, Down

Level 10
L, Up, Left, Down

Level 11
L, Up, Left, Up

Level 12
L, Up, L, Down

Level 13
L, Down, Up, Left

Level 14
R, C-Left, Up, Right

Level 15
C-Down, L, Down (2)

Level 16
R, C-Left, Right, Up

ARMY MEN: AIR COMBAT

Unlock all Levels and Helicopters
Enter as password: R, C-Left, Right, Up.

Unlock Level 10
Enter as password: L, Up, Left, Down.

Unlock Level 11
Enter as password: L, Up, Left, Up.

Unlock Level 12
Enter as password: L, Up, L, Down.

Unlock Level 13
Enter as password: L, Down, Up, Left.

Unlock Level 14
Enter as password: R, C-Left, Up, Right.

Unlock Level 15
Enter as password: C-Down, L, Down, Down.

Unlock Level 16
Enter as password: R, C-Left, Right, Up.

ARMY MEN: SARGE'S HEROES

Debug Mode
Enter THDTST.

All Weapons
Enter NSRLS.

Maximum Ammo
Enter MMLVSRM.

Use General Plastro
Enter PLSTRLVSVG.

Use Vikki
Enter GRNGRLRX.

Unlock all Characters in Multiplayer Mode
Enter VRCLN.

Use Tin Soldier
Enter TNSLDRS after activating another character.

Mini Mode
Enter DRVLLVSMM.

Use Hoover
Enter PLYHVR.

Restart Level
Hold L+R+C-Down to restart the current level.

Attack Level
LNLGRMM

Spy Blue Level
TRGHTR

Bathroom Level
TDBWL

Riff Mission Level
MSTRMN

Forest Level
TLLTRS

Hoover Mission Level
SCRDCT

Thick Mission Level
STPDMN

Snow Mission Level
BLZZRD

Shrap Mission Level
SRFPNK

Fort Plastro Level
GNRLMN

Scorch Mission Level
HTTTRT

Showdown Level Password
ZBTSRL

Sandbox Level Password
HTKTTN

Kitchen Level
PTSPNS

Living Room Level
HXMSTR

The Way Home Level
VRCLN

ARMY MEN SARGE'S HEROES 2

Play As General Plastro
PLSTRLVSVG

Play As Vikki
GRNGRLRX

Play in Mini Mode
DRVLLVSMM

Play in High-Tech Armor
TNMN

Display Debug Information
THDTST

Level 2: Bridge
FLLNGDWN

Level 3: Fridge
GTMLK

Level 4: Freezer
CHLLBB

Level 5: Inside Wall
CLSNGN

Level 6: Graveyard
DGTHS

Level 7: Castle
FRNKNSTN

Level 8: Tan Base
BDBZ

Level 9: Revenge
LBBCK

Level 10: Desk
DSKJB

Level 11: Bed
GTSLP

Level 12: Blue Town
SMLLVLL

Level 13: Cashier
CHRGT

Level 14: Train
NTBRT

Level 15: Rockets
RDGLR

Level 16: Pool Table
FSTNLS

Level 17: Pinball
WHSWZRD

ASTEROIDS HYPER 64

Unlock Original Asteroids
Shoot the green asteroid in Zone 1, 15th level.

AUTOMOBILI LAMBORGHINI

Hidden Cars
Each time you beat Basic or Pro series in Arcade mode, you receive a new set of cars.

Reverse Tracks
Beat Championship mode at Novice and Expert difficulty levels.

All Cars
Press R (6) at the main screen.

BANJO-TOOIE

Activate Cheat Mode
Enter the witch's head on Spiral Mountain to find Cheato. One cheat is revealed for every five Cheato pages that you find. Other cheats are revealed by finding the various mystery eggs hidden throughout the game or are rewards for doing certain actions. The cheats are entered in the Mayahem Temple near Wumba's Wigwam. Note: Grenade eggs are required to enter the temple.

Spell out one of the following cheat codes inside the temple to activate the corresponding effect. Cheats prefixed with CHEATO are unlocked immediately without collecting the required number of Cheato pages.

Level Select
CHEATO JIGGYWIGGYSPECIAL

Double Feather Carrying Capacity
FEATHERS or CHEATO SREHTAEF

Double Egg Carrying Capacity
EGGS or CHEATO SGGE

Unlimited Eggs and Feathers
CHEATO NESTKING

Unlimited Air and Health
HONEYKING or CHEATO KCABYENOH

All Mini-Games, Bosses, and Movies in Replay Mode
CHEATO PLAYITAGAINSON

Banjo Moves Faster
CHEATO SUPERBANJO

Enemies Move Faster
CHEATO SUPERBADDY

Music Test Unlocked in Jolly Roger Bay Jukebox
JUKEBOX or CHEATO XOBEKUJ

Unlimited Health
CHEATO HONEYBACK

Unlimited Glowbos
GLOKING

Unlimited Mega Glowbos
SUPGLOKING

No Damage When Falling
FALLPROOF or CHEATO FOORPLLAF

Eggs Home in on Nearest Target
HOMING

Jiggy Hints Given by Signs in Master Jiggywiggy's House
GETJIGGY or CHEATO YGGIJTEG

All Replay Sub-Options Unlocked
CHEATO PLAYITAGAINSON

View Ending Sequence
CHEATO JIGGYSCASTLIST

BATTLETANX

Invincibility
Enter MSTSRVV as a password.

Frog Mode
Enter FRGZ as a password.

Toad Gang
Enter TDZ as a password.

All Gangs in Campaign Mode
Enter LTSLTSGNGS as a password.

Storm Ravens Gang
Enter WMNRSMRTR as a password.

Warp to State Street: 10 Lives, 1 Nuke, 5 Goliaths
Enter CLSKPFLGMH as a password.

Infinite Lives
Enter LVFRVR as a password.

Infinite Ammo
Enter LTSFBLLTS as a password.

All Weapons
Enter PLVRZM as a password.

Invisibility
Enter CRSTLCLR as a password.

Run Story Mode
Enter CDPLT as a password.

Psychedelic View
Enter CNCTHRTM as a password.

Spinning View
Enter HVRL as a password.

Suicide
Hold C-Left+C-Right+C-Up+C-Down.

End Game
During gameplay, hold C-Left+C-Right+C-Up+C-Down.

Multiplayer Weapons Power-Up
Collect at least 15 of one weapon while in Multiplayer mode. Then press A+B while aiming at an opponent.

Level 2
LHTTTBKRLS

Level 3
RCJRWPCLGM

Level 4
VVSLGGVHRF

Level 5
LPFFLNHJJF

Level 6
CTMGPRWGBH

Level 7
HPJMKGMCJV

Level 8
WHSNKNFRGS

Level 9
CRFPHGCTKP

Level 10
HHRBKPVWGB

Level 11
WFHMKCFWLB

Level 12
SPLJTFLRFS

Level 13
LTSLTSGNGS

Level 14
TMFNJMKJGF

Level 15
PPJLJHRCVV

Level 16
LNKNSWKGTH

Level 17
WMNRSMRTR

BATTLETANX: GLOBAL ASSAULT

All Weapons
Enter RCKTSRDGLR as a password.

God Mode
Enter HPPYHPPY as a password.

Level Select
Enter 8ODYS as a password.

Unlock Brandon Gang
Enter NNKNHCKS as a password.

Unlock Custom 1 Gang
Enter TRDDYBRRKS as a password.

Campaign Mode Bonus Level
Enter WRDRB as a password.

Self Destruction
Destroy your tank by holding C-Down+C-Up+C-Right+C-Left.

Weapon Power-Up
Collect at least 15 power-ups of one weapon, except grenades. Then press A+B to fire a stronger version of that weapon. If you're using guided missiles, press A+B+Z to fire a blue laser.

BATTLEZONE: RISE OF THE BLACK DOGS

Infinite Ammo
At the main menu, hold Z and press L, R, L, R.

Infinite Armor
At the main menu, hold Z and press Up, Left, Down, Left.

Unlock All Levels
First enter the Infinite Ammo and Infinite Armor codes. Then, at the main menu, hold Z and press C-Up, C-Right, C-Down, C-Left, Start.

Free Buildings
First enter the Infinite Ammo and Infinite Armor codes. Then, at the main menu, hold Z and press A, B, A, B.

Free Satellite
First enter the Infinite Ammo and Infinite Armor codes. Then, at the main menu, hold Z and press B, C-Left, C-Down, A.

BEAST WARS: TRANSMETALS 64

Play As Starscream
In Versus or Arcade mode, select Waspinator, hold A, and press Z at the Character Selection screen. Press right or left to locate and select Starscream.

NINTENDO 64

Play As Blackarachnia

In Versus or Arcade mode, select Tarantulas, hold A, and press Z at the Character Selection screen. Press Right or Left to locate and select Blackarachnia.

Play As Ravage or Tigatron

In Versus or Arcade mode, select Cheetor, hold A, and press Z at the Character Selection screen. Press Right or Left to locate and select Ravage and Tigatron.

Play As Megatron X

Without using any continues, defeat Megatron X in Arcade mode. This unlocks him as a playable character in Arcade mode.

Use Rattrap's Armor

Complete the game, defeating all enemies, including Megatron X.

BEETLE ADVENTURE RACING

Cheat Menu

Begin gameplay in single-player Championship mode on the Coventry Cove track. Locate the shortcut near the barn with the two haystacks. Drive into the haystack nearest the track and into the box inside. Groovy will appear, and a Cheat menu becomes available on the Options screen.

BIO F.R.E.A.K.S.

Alternate View

During gameplay, hold Left and press Start. To return to default view, hold Down and press Start.

BLADES OF STEEL NHL '99

Special Turbo

When you select ice conditions, press Left, Right, C-Up, C-Down, A+B and Start.

BLAST CORPS

Bonus Courses

Finish all missions and find all six scientists to unlock two bonus courses. A third bonus mission becomes available after you achieve a perfect score.

Quick Explosion

Drive your vehicle up to an obstacle and press Z. The driver yells but won't exit the vehicle because the obstacle is too close. Keep holding Z until the obstacle explodes. Use this to destroy buildings that require special demolition techniques.

Quick Start

Accelerate when you hear the last beep as the light turns green.

Ghost Vehicle

Finish a course, select a different vehicle and play that course again to race a ghost version of your previous vehicle.

BLUES BROTHERS 2000

Extra Lives

In the Chicago level, open the sewer cover with the gray wrench. Leave the sewer, then return to collect as many extra lives as you want.

BODY HARVEST

Weapon Power-Up

Enter ICHEAT as a name. Press C-Down, C-Up, Up, Z (2), Left, C-Right during a game.

Black Adam

Enter ICHEAT as a name. Press C-Left, C-Right, A, C-Down, C-Right, Left during a game.

Weak Boss

Enter ICHEAT as a name. Press Z, C-Right (2), B, Left, C-Right during a game.

Smart Bomb

Enter ICHEAT as a name. Press A, C-Up (2), Up, Left during a game.

Kill Adam

Enter ICHEAT as a name. Press B, Left, C-Right (2), Down during a game.

Short Adam

Enter ICHEAT as a name. Press Down, C-Left, A, Right, Z during a game.

Tall Adam

Enter ICHEAT as a name. Press B, A, C-Up, A, C-Up, A during a game.

Mutant Alien

Enter ICHEAT as a name. Press C-Down, Up, Z (2), C-Right, Right during a game.

Surreal Mode

Enter ICHEAT as a name. Press C-Down, Up, Right (2), C-Right, A, Left during a game.

Dancer

Enter ICHEAT as a name. Press Down, Up, C-Up, Down, C-Right (2) during a game.

Fat Legs

Enter ICHEAT as a name. Press Left, A, Right, Down during a game.

Increased Difficulty

Enter the Difficulty Selection screen and keep pressing Right until Very Hard appears.

All Artifacts

Enter ICHEAT as a name. Press Up, C-Down, C-Right, Z, Up, Left during a game.

Gain Health and Fuel

Enter ICHEAT as a name. Press Down, Up, Right, A, B, Left, C-Right during a game.

All Weapons

Enter ICHEAT as a name. Press A, Right, C-Down, C-Right, C-Up, A, Left during a game.

BOMBERMAN 64: THE SECOND ATTACK

Extra Characters

In Battle mode, hold Z and press A at the Character Selection screen.

BOMBERMAN HERO

Gold Bomber

Get five gold medals, and then look for the gold Bomber in the Options menu for three extra levels.

Ice Slider

Get three gold medals, and then look for "Minigame" in the Options menu. Play the minigame to get the slider.

Millan's Treasure Hunt

Get six gold medals to find "Treasure Hunt" in the Options menu.

Gossick World

Collect all Other-Dimension bombs to get a 5 on all stages.

Level Select

Press A+B+Z at the title or Options screen.

BUCK BUMBLE

Refill All Weapons and Health

Press Left, Right, Up, Down at the title screen. Next, hold Z and press Right (2), Left (2). While playing, press A+B+R.

Fast-Forward Text

Press Z to fast-forward text. Press A to skip text.

Level Select

At title screen, hold Z and press Right, Down (2), Right. Release Z and press Right, Up, Down, Left (2), Up, Right (2).

Play As Dark Stinger

Hold Z+analog stick-Up before title screen appears; then press C-Up, C-Right, C-Down, C-Left (5), B, A, B.

God Mode

At the title screen, hold Z and press R, L, Up, Down, Left, Right.

A BUG'S LIFE

Level Select

Hold Z+C-Up+C-Down+C-Left+C-Right and press R at the anthill on the main screen. A right-pointing arrow appears at the screen's bottom.

Invincibility

Hold Z+R+L at the level description. This only works for one level and must be repeated at the beginning of every level.

BUST-A-MOVE 2: ARCADE EDITION

Another World

At the main menu (Game Start, Time Attack, Options) press L, Up on the D-Pad, R, Down on the D-Pad.

Extra Puzzles

At the title screen, press A, Up, B, Down.

BUST-A-MOVE '99

Another World

At the title screen, press B, Left, Right, B. All the new puzzles become available in Arcade mode.

CALIFORNIA SPEED

Five-Oh Car

Place first in Sports Cup.

Mountain Dew Pickup

Win the Heavy Cup.

Predator Car

Use Five-Oh car to complete Sports series.

Semi Truck

Place first in California Cup.

Squirrel Car

Complete the Light Cup.

Insect Car

Use Squirrel car to complete the Light Cup.

California Track

Beat the entire Series mode.

Fuji Track

Play Sports series with 486SE car. Complete the fifth race of week two.

Clover Track

Unlock Fuji track first, then beat Fuji a second time during the third week.

Mano Car
Finish the Sports series with any car except Five-Oh.

Use Bulldozer
Play California Cup and win all races.

Adjust Fog Color
Choose a non-series race. When the screen fades, hold L+R+C-Up+C-Down+C-Left+C-Right+Down. When Track Select screen appears, press Right.

Change Screen Position
Hold L+R+Start on Controller 2 during Single-player race and move analog stick.

Oval Track
Finish second week of Heavy series.

San Andreas Track
Finish third week of Heavy series.

Forklift Car
Finish Light series with the Insect car.

Ol' Truck
Finish Heavy series with Mountain Dew pickup.

Camper Truck
Use Ol' Truck to finish Heavy series.

Mirrored Series Tracks
Choose a mirrored track in Practice mode. Exit right after getting on the track, choose Series mode, and start a new race.

CASTLEVANIA 64

Expert Mode
Beat the game and wait for the credits to end. Save the game and restart.

CASTLEVANIA: LEGACY OF DARKNESS

Alternate Costumes
Save two children as Henry; then finish and save the game to unlock a different costume for Cornell.

Fight Against Renon
During the game, spend more than 30,000 gold to buy items.

Hard Difficulty Setting
Save three children as Henry; then finish and save the game. Start a new game using the saved game.

Play As Henry
Complete the game with Cornell. Save the game after the credits roll. Load the saved game.

Play As Reinhardt
Complete the game as Henry. Save the game after the credits roll. Load the saved game.

CHAMELEON TWIST

Fight Every Level Boss
Get 20 crowns and defeat the boss for each level. A box labeled "...?" appears on the Level Selection screen.

CHAMELEON TWIST 2

Alternate Costumes
Collect all 20 coins and beat the boss on any level. Then press Start at the Level Selection screen to access a new "Costumes" option.

CHARLIE BLAST'S TERRITORY

Level 2 Select
4 Clubs, 5 Hearts, 10 Clubs, Queen Clubs, Queen Clubs

Level 3 Select
4 Clubs, 5 Hearts, 10 Spades, 9 Clubs, 4 Clubs

Level 4 Select
Ace Clubs, 7 Diamonds, 6 Hearts, 6 Spades, 2 Hearts

Level 5 Select
6 Hearts, 2 Hearts, Ace Spades, 5 Hearts, 8 Hearts

Level 6 Select
9 Diamonds, 10 Diamonds, Jack Diamonds, Jack Hearts, Queen Hearts

Level 7 Select
9 Diamonds, 10 Hearts, 10 Hearts, 7 Diamonds, 5 Hearts

Level 8 Select
Ace Clubs, 7 Diamonds, 8 Diamonds, 5 Clubs, 8 Hearts

Level 9 Select
6 Diamonds, 4 Hearts, 9 Hearts, 6 Hearts, Queen Clubs

Level 10 Select
7 Diamonds, 10 Hearts, Ace Hearts, 9 Spades, 6 Hearts

Level 11 Select
7 Diamonds, 4 Spades, 9 Diamonds, 7 Hearts, Queen Hearts

Level 12 Select
6 Diamonds, 4 Diamonds, 9 Clubs, 8 Clubs, 4 Clubs

Level 13 Select
5 Spades, 9 Spades, Jack Hearts, 6 Clubs, 4 Clubs

Level 14 Select
2 Hearts, 3 Diamonds, 9 Diamonds, 3 Diamonds, 2 Clubs

Level 15 Select
4 Clubs, 5 Hearts, Queen Spades, 4 Clubs, 8 Clubs

Level 16 Select
6 Diamonds, Jack Spades, 2 Hearts, Ace Diamonds, 6 Hearts

Level 17 Select
6 Hearts, 2 Hearts, Queen Clubs, 7 Spades, 3 Hearts

Level 18 Select
6 Clubs, King Hearts, 10 Hearts, Ace Clubs, 3 Spades

Level 19 Select
2 Hearts, 3 Diamonds, 7 Hearts, 6 Clubs, 10 Diamonds

Level 20 Select
6 Diamonds, Jack Clubs, 3 Hearts, 4 Clubs, 8 Hearts

Level 21 Select
Ace Clubs, Jack Spades, 3 Clubs, 7 Hearts, 9 Hearts

Level 22 Select
9 Hearts, 6 Clubs, 2 Hearts, 6 Spades, 2 Spades

Level 23 Select
2 Hearts, 3 Diamonds, 7 Clubs, Queen Diamonds, 8 Diamonds

Level 24 Select
Ace Clubs, 7 Diamonds, 6 Spades, Jack Clubs, 4 Hearts

Level 25 Select
Ace Clubs, Jack Clubs, 3 Diamonds, Jack Hearts, King Hearts

Study Levels While Paused
Pause game in Puzzle mode. Change camera view with C buttons.

CHOPPER ATTACK

President Eject
During gameplay, press Z+C-Up+C-Down; then launch a homing cluster at your opponent. The president will eject from the plane if the cluster hits it.

CLAYFIGHTER 63-1/3

300 Hit Combos
Perform any combo first. Then execute one of your character's special moves when your opponent's Life Meter turns red.

Alternate Colors
Press C-Down to select your character.

Stage Select
In Two-player mode, when the Versus screen appears, press C-Right or C-Left to change the fight stage.

Play As Boogerman
Hold L+Up, Right, Down, Left, Right, Left at the Character Selection screen.

Play As Dr. Kiln
At the Character Selection screen, hold L, and then press B, C-Left, C-Up, C-Right, C-Down, A.

Play As Sumo Santa
At the Character Selection screen, hold L, and then press A, C-Down, C-Right, C-Up, C-Left, B.

Secret Options
At the Character Selection screen, hold L, then press C-Up, C-Right, C-Left, C-Down, B, A (2). Go to the Options menu.

CLAYFIGHTER 63-1/3: SCULPTOR'S CUT

Play As Earthworm Jim
At the Character Selection screen, hold Z or R and choose LP, MP, HP, HK, MK, HP. Then press R on the controller to scroll through the characters.

Play As Boogerman
At the Character Selection screen, hold Z or R and choose LP, LP, HK, HK, MP, HK. Then press R on the controller to scroll through the characters.

Play As Sumo Santa
At the Character Selection screen, hold Z or R and choose LK, HK, LK, HK, MK, HP. Then press R on the controller to scroll through the characters.

Play As High Five
At the Character Selection screen, hold Z or R and choose HP, MK, MP, HK, LP, LK. Then press R on the controller to scroll through the characters.

COMMAND AND CONQUER

Easier Building
Highlight unit from toolbar and press A. To build duplicate units, hold Z and press A after viewing "Unit Ready" or "Construction Complete" message.

Get $1,000
Destroy village churches.

Build NOD Attack Chopper
Take over NOD's main base and find chopper option.

Gold NOD Weapons
Playing as GDI, take over NOD airstrip.

All Missions
Press B, A, R (2), A, Right, C-Right, Up, Down, A at the start screen. Press L at "Replay Mission."

Camera Zoom
Hold L and press C-Up or C-Down as you play.

CONKER'S BAD FUR DAY

50 Lives
Enter BOVRILBULLETHOLE as a code.

Easy Game Controls and Difficulty
Enter EASY as a code.

Very Easy Game Controls and Difficulty
Enter VERYEASY as a code.

Debug Mode
Enter XFYHIJERPWAL_IELWZS as a code. Note that the underscore indicates a space. This code allows the game to be played in debug mode on Nintendo 64 development systems. It has no useful function in the retail version of the game.

Play as Sergeant and Tedi Leader in Multiplayer Mode
Enter RUSTYSHERIFFSBADGE as a code.

Play as Cavemen in Multiplayer Mode
Enter EATBOX as a code.

Play as Conker in Multiplayer Mode
Enter WELLYTOP as a code.

Play as Gregg the Grim Reaper in Multiplayer Mode
Enter BILLYMILLROUNDABOUT as a code.

Play as "NEO" Conker in Multiplayer Mode
Enter EASTEREGGSRUS as a code.

Play as Weasel Henchmen in Multiplayer Mode
Enter CHINDITVICTORY as a code.

Play as Zombies and Villagers in Multiplayer Mode
Enter BEEFCURTAINS as a code.

Frying Pan in Race Mode
Enter DUTCHOVENS as a code.

Baseball Bat in Race Mode
Enter DRACULASTEABAGS as a code.

All Chapters and Scenes Unlocked
Enter WELDERSBENCH as a code.

Barn Boys Chapter
Enter PRINCEALBERT as a code.

Bats Tower Chapter
Enter CLAMPIRATE as a code.

The Heist Chapter
Enter CHOCOLATESTARFISH as a code for extra money and to unlock "The Heist" in Chapters mode.

It's War Chapter
Enter BEELZEBUBSBUM as a code.

Slopranos Chapter
Enter ANCHOVYBAY as a code.

Spooky Chapter
Enter SPANIELSEARS as a code.

Uga Buga Chapter
Enter MONKEYSCHIN as a code.

New Death Animation in Multiplayer Mode
Enter SPUNKJOCKEY as a code. Use a chain saw or katana to cut a Teddyz head off in the War level for a Matrix-type death animation.

Insult
Enter the same incorrect code twice in a row. You'll be insulted by the Fire Imp.

Unlimited Tails
Find the hook on a sign in Level 2. Intentionally die to start the hook tutorial. The hook will have a tail for extra lives. Take the tail and return to Level 1. Return and another tail will appear on the same hook. Repeat to get as many lives as needed.

CRUIS'N EXOTICA

Unlock All Extra Cars and Models
Win all the challenge races, finish Cruis'n Exotica mode twice, win all the freestyle races, and reach 40,000 miles to unlock the Heavyliftin, Lil Lightnin, Jalopie, Bad Mobile, Hunkajunk, Skidmarks, G Ride, Cooler, Piewagon, Boxcar, Scrapin By, Glide, Formula 2, Whiplash, Rail, and Rocket. Wacky and Insane modes are also unlocked.

Unlock the Glide Car
Reach 2,200 miles.

Unlock the Heavyliftin' (Forklift)
Reach 5,000 miles.

Unlock the Rocket Car
Reach 100,000 miles.

Unlock the Formula 2 Car
Reach 100,000 miles, placing first through third in all races.

Unlock the Whiplash Car
Win Exotica mode with Formula 2.

Unlock Lil Lightning
Win Freestyle mode.

Unlock Cooler
Win Challenge mode.

CRUIS'N USA

Bonus Cars
At the Vehicle Selection screen, highlight any car (except the Ferrari). Now press C-Up+C-Left+C-Down. The Devastator becomes a police car, La Bomba becomes a school bus, and the Muscle car becomes an all-terrain vehicle.

Golden Gate Park Track
Highlight the US 101 track and enter Left+C-Left+C-Down.

Indiana Track
Highlight the Beverly Hills track and enter Left+C-Right+C-Up.

San Francisco Track
Highlight the Grand Canyon track and enter Left+C-Right+C-Down.

Nitro Boost
Get a high score in any race; then enter your initials at the Hot Times screen. Scroll to the bottom of the High Scores list and hold Down-Left on the control pad. A conveyor belt moves, and after 30 seconds or so, a head scrolls by saying "I love this job!" Now start a game and press Brake (3), Gas, Brake, Gas following each checkpoint to accelerate faster.

Fallen Wheel
Finish a Two-player challenge game. The losing player loses a wheel if that player rotates the analog stick clockwise repeatedly. The wheel falls off after the car rotates four times.

Faster Car Upgrades
Start a Two-player game and race to Washington D.C. Press Start and quit the game once the Washington D.C. race begins. Save and reset the game. Have Player 1 beat the Washington D.C. course. Reset again. Have Player 2 beat the Washington D.C. course. This upgrades both cars.

Change Car Colors
Press C-Up on the Vehicle Selection screen.

Flashing Lights and Sirens (School Bus/Police Car)
Get a high score in any race and enter your initials. Scroll to the bottom of the Hot Times screen and hold Down-Left. After 30 seconds or so, a head scrolls by saying "I love this job!" Release the buttons and return to the Vehicle Selection screen. Enter the Bonus Cars code to choose the police car or school bus. To activate flashing lights and sirens, press Brake (2), Gas. Hold Gas to continue lights and sirens.

Windshield Stuff
Drive in In-car view through Iowa or Indiana. Flies or bird droppings will hit the windshield.

Change Paint Job
Press L+R when selecting a car.

Flips and Rolls
Press A (2) as you approach a jump.

Jump Over Cars
Press A (2) as you swiftly approach another car from behind.

Race on the Moon
Finish entire game and wait for credits to end.

Turbo Boost
Hold down accelerator immediately after "Set" at the starting line.

Bugs Splatter on Windshield
On the Mexico track, race using In-car view and press C-Up once.

Speed Demon Car
Get more than 9,999 points in Championship mode.

Power Level 1
Get 8 or more points in Championship mode, and press C-Up or C-Down on Vehicle Selection screen.

Power Level 3
Get 100 or more points in Championship mode, and press C-Up or C-Down on Vehicle Selection screen.

Power Level 4

Get 500 or more points in Championship mode, and press C-Up or C-Down on Vehicle Selection screen.

Power Level 5

Get 1,500 or more points in Championship mode, and press C-Up or C-Down on Vehicle Selection screen.

Two-Tone Colors

Get 150 or more points in Championship mode, and press L or R on Vehicle Selection screen.

Flip Roll

During a jump, execute a normal flip and press B (2), A, B, C-Up.

Unlock Bulldog

Beat 1:46.00 on England track.

Unlock Conductor

Beat 2:06.00 on Kenya track.

Unlock Enforcer

Beat 1:14.00 on China track.

Unlock Grass Hopper

Beat 2:11:00 on New York track.

Unlock Howler

Beat 1:46:00 on Mexico track.

Unlock Monsta

Beat 3:47.00 on Hawaii track.

Unlock Rocket

Beat 2:48.00 on Japan track.

Unlock Rocket

Beat 1.58:00 on Russia track.

Unlock Skool Bus

Beat 1:07:00 on Egypt track.

Unlock Surgeon

Beat 1:49.00 on Australia track.

Unlock Taxi

Beat 2:27.00 on Germany track.

Unlock Tommy

Beat 2:15:00 on France track.

CRUIS'N WORLD

Change Paint Job

When you select your car in one or two player mode, use L and R to change the car's body color.

Easy Mega Roll Bonus in New York

In order to do this trick, use a car that goes about 140 MPH. Enter a Championship race in New York, and as you are about to make a sharp turn, do a wheelie into the curved wall. You do a Mega Roll and bounce back on course! You should be at a fast speed when performing this trick.

Flips and Rolls

To do a flip off of a jump, press A twice when you come up to a jump.

Jump Over Cars

When you are coming up behind a car very fast, pop a wheelie (press A twice) to fly over them.

Power Boost

While racing, quickly press A twice to do a wheelie and speed up.

Race on the Moon

To race on the Moon, beat the whole game. Beat Florida to see the helicopter pick up your car and drop it into a rocket. It will show the rocket liftoff into space. You land on the Moon and hear a man say, "We're cruisn' now!" Wait for the credits to end. When they're finished, there is a tiny box that reads "Moon expert."

Unlock Surgeon

Beat 1:49 on Australia track.

Unlock Enforcer

Beat 1:14 on China track.

Unlock Skool Bus

Beat 1:07 on Egypt track.

Unlock Bulldog

Beat 1:46 on England track.

Unlock Tommy

Beat 2:15 on France track.

Unlock New York Taxi

Beat 2:27 on Germany track.

Unlock Monsta

Beat 3:47 on Hawaii track.

Unlock Rocket

Beat 2:48 on Japan track.

Unlock Conductor

Beat 2:06 on Kenya track.

Unlock Howler

Beat 1:46 on Mexico track.

Unlock Grass Hopper

Beat 2:11 on New York track.

Unlock Rocket

Beat 1.58 on Russia track.

Unlock Speed Demon.

Finish gaining all of the points in Champion mode.

Australia Shortcut

A little while after the 1st checkpoint, there is a dirt path on the left. Take it, bust through the fence, and get ready for another jump.

Great Wall of China Shortcut

When you see a lighthouse to the left, drive toward it and take the path. Go straight.

Hawaii Shortcut

Near the beginning of Hawaii, there are road signs telling you to turn. On the left side turn at the first sign, then there is another sign. Ram into that sign and go straight to get to the shortcut.

When you see a bunch of barrels on the left side of a turn without a curb, drive into the forest to go through a shortcut. You'll jump over all the cars.

Italy Shortcut

Go to the Italy track in Cruise the World mode. After you pass the 2nd or 3rd checkpoint, you drive down a tree-lined road. The second before you come out of that little alcove of trees, there is a ramp to your left. Drive up that ramp to save some time.

Kenya Shortcut

Go to Kenya in Practice Cruise the World mode. After the third checkpoint at the first right, turn. The road splits in two; veer right. Go straight at a ramp to see an elephant before you hit the jump. That's the shortcut!

Mexico Shortcut

In Mexico at the Aztec Temple, go into the brush to the left. There is a ramp and a shortcut.

New York Shortcut

In New York on the last two tunnels take any of the off-ramps on the side.

CYBERTIGER WOODS GOLF

Volcano Course

Select any character and change the name to Sthelens.

Play As an Alien

Select any character and change the name to Ufo.

Play As Ghost Miner

Select any character and change the name to Golddgr.

Play As a Biker

Select any character and change the name to Delvis.

Play As a Tiger

Select any character and change the name to Tigerrrr.

Play As Cindy

Select any character and change the name to Instyle.

Play As Kimmi

Select any character and change the name to Rapper.

Play As Tiger in '70s Costume

Select any character and change the name to Liltiger.

Play As Tiger in '80s Costume

Select any character and change the name to Prodigy.

Play As Little Mark in '70s Costume

Select any character and change the name to Brat.

Play As Little Mark in '80s Costume

Select any character and change the name to Marko.

Play As Billy in a Black Sweater

Select any character and change the name to Cybertw.

Play As Billy in White Shirt

Select any character and change the name to Willi.

Play As Inga in Flower Power Costume

Select any character and change the name to Retro.

Play As Chip with Goatee

Select any character and change the name to Ice.

Play As Traci in Leopard Costume

Select any character and change the name to Safari.

DAIKATANA

Unlock All Weapons
Press C-Left, C-Down, C-Right, C-Up, Z, L, R, C-Left, C-Down, C-Right, C-Up at Stage Select.

Unlock All Stages
Press C-Up, C-Right, C-Down, C-Left, R, L, Z, C-Up, C-Right, C-Down, C-Left at Stage Select. Use the analog stick to select stages.

DANCE DANCE REVOLUTION FEATURING DISNEY CHARACTERS

Unlock All Songs
Press Up, Left, Right, Down, Up, Right, Left, Down at the Password screen.

Mickey Mouse As Chorus Leader
Press Left, Up, Down, Right, Left, Down, Up, Right at the Password screen.

Unlock Disco Magic Mode
Press Up (2), Right, Left, Down, Up, Left, Right at the Password screen.

DARK RIFT

Play As Demitron
At the start screen, press A, B, R, L, C-Down, C-Up.

Play As Sonork Nezom
At the start screen, press Left, Right, C-Up, C-Down, C-Left, C-Right.

Fight Against Demitron
When "Start" appears on the title screen, press Up, C-Left, R, Right, Down, B (3), C-Up. A sound confirms correct entry.

View Aaron Ending
When "Start" appears on the title screen, press Up, C-Left, R, Right, Down, R (2), C-Left.

View Demonica Ending
When "Start" appears on the title screen, press Up, C-Left, R, Right, Down, R (2), C-Up.

View Demitron Ending
When "Start" appears on the title screen, press Up, C-Left, R, Right, Down, L (2), C-Down.

View Eve Ending
When "Start" appears on the title screen, press Up, C-Left, R, Right, Down, R (2), C-Right.

View Gore Ending
When "Start" appears on the title screen, press Up, C-Left, R, Right, Down, R (2), C-Down.

View Morphix Ending
When "Start" appears on the title screen, press Up, C-Left, R, Right, Down, R (2), B.

View Niiki Ending
When "Start" appears on the title screen, press Up, C-Left, R, Right, Down, R (2), A.

View Scarlet Ending
When "Start" appears on the title screen, press Up, C-Left, R, Right, Down, L (2), C-Left.

View Sonork Ending
When "Start" appears on the title screen, press Up, C-Left, R, Right, Down, L (2), C-Up.

View Zenmuron
When "Start" appears on the title screen, press Up, C-Left, R, Right, Down, L (2), C-Right.

DEADLY ARTS

Play As Gourki
At the title screen, press Up (2), Down (2), Left, Right, Left, Right, B, A.

Play As Reiji
At the title screen, press A, B, Right, Left, Right, Left, Down (2), Up (2).

Alternate Outfits
Before selecting your character, hold L and press Left or Right on the control pad. Continue to hold L and select your character.

Bonus Level
Beat Tag Team mode with only one character on Very Easy in less than 21 minutes, and don't let anyone join you.

Free Health
Keep pressing one of the C buttons when you get knocked down.

DESTRUCTION DERBY 64

Unlock the Street Rocket
Beat Novice Championship with Gold status using any car.

Unlock the Taxi
Beat Amateur championship with Gold status using the Street Rocket.

Unlock the Pickup Truck
Beat Pro Championship with Gold status using the Taxi.

Unlock the Ambulance
Beat Legend Championship with Gold status using the Pickup Truck.

Unlock the Baja Buggy
Beat Destruction Junction with the best time in Time Trial mode using the Street Rocket.

Unlock the Rag Top
Beat Alpine Ridge with the best time in Time Trial mode using the Baja Buggy.

Unlock the Blue Demon
Beat Seascape Sprint with the best time in Time Trial mode using the Rag Top.

Unlock the Hatchback
Beat Terminal Impact with the best time in Time Trial mode using the Rag Top.

Unlock the Low Rider
Beat Metro Challenge with the best time in Time Trial mode using the Rag Top.

Unlock the Woody Wagon
Beat Bayou Run with the best time in Time Trial mode using the Rag Top.

Unlock the Hot Rod
Beat Sunset Canyon with the best time in Time Trial mode using the Rag Top.

Unlock the Police Car
Beat Midnight Rumble with the best time in Time Trial mode using the Hot Rod.

Turbo Start
Press A immediately after the announcer says "Set" at the start of the race.

DOOM 64

Super Code
Enter W93M 7H2O BCYO PSVB.

Ultimate Code
Enter ?TJL BDFW BFGV JVVB.

Be Gentle! Level 02
cdp8 9bj2 68zt svk?

Be Gentle! Level 03
cxm8 9bjy 681t jvk?

Be Gentle! Level 04
ddk8 9bjt 683s 9vk?

Be Gentle! Level 05
dxh8 9bjp 685s 1vk?

Be Gentle! Level 06
fdf8 9bjk 687s svk?

Be Gentle! Level 07
fxc8 9bjf 689s jvk?

Be Gentle! Level 08
gd?8 9bc? 69br ?bk?

Be Gentle! Level 09
gx88 9bc6 69dr 2bk?

Be Gentle! Level 10
hd68 9bc2 69gr tbk?

Be Gentle! Level 11
hx48 9bcy 69jr kbk?

Be Gentle! Level 12
jd28 9bct 69lq ?bk?

Be Gentle! Level 13
jx08 9bcp 69nq 2bk?

Be Gentle! Level 14
kdy8 9bck 69qq tbk?

Be Gentle! Level 15
kxw8 9bcf 69sq kbk?

Be Gentle! Level 16
lft8 9bb? 69vp ?vk?

Be Gentle! Level 17
lyr8 9bb6 69xp 2vk?

Be Gentle! Level 18
mfp8 9bb2 69zp tvk?

Be Gentle! Level 19
mym8 9bby 691p kvk?

Be Gentle! Level 20
nfk8 9bbt 693n ?vk?

Be Gentle! Level 21
nyh8 9bbp 695n 2vk?

Be Gentle! Level 22
pff8 9bbk 697n tvk?

Be Gentle! Level 23
pyc8 9bbf 699n kvk?

Be Gentle! Level 24
qf?8 9bf? 6?bm ?bk?

Be Gentle! Level 25
qy88 9bf6 6?dm 2bk?

Be Gentle! Level 26
rf68 9bf2 6?gm tbk?

Be Gentle! Level 27
ry48 9bfy 6?jm kbk?

Be Gentle! Level 28
sf28 9bft 6?ll ?bk?

Be Gentle! Level 29
sy08 9bfp 6?nl 2bk?

Be Gentle! Level 30
tfy8 9bfk 6?ql tbk?

Be Gentle! Level 31
tyw8 9bff 6?sl kbk?

Be Gentle! Level 32
vbt8 9bd? 6?vk 9vk?

Bring it On! Level 02
cjpr 9bj1 68z? qvk?

Bring it On! Level 03
c1mr 9bjx 681? gvk?

Bring it On! Level 04
djkr 9bjs 6839 7vk?

Bring it On! Level 05
d1hr 9bjn 6859 zvk?

Bring it On! Level 06
fjfr 9bjj 6879 qvk?

Bring it On! Level 07
f1cr 9bjd 6899 gvk?

Bring it On! Level 08
gj?r 9bc9 69b8 8bk?

Bring it On! Level 09
g18r 9bc5 69d8 0bk?

Bring it On! Level 10
hj6r 9bc1 69g8 rbk?

Bring it On! Level 11
h14r 9bcx 69j8 hbk?

Bring it On! Level 12
jj2r 9bcs 69l7 8bk?

Bring it On! Level 13
j10r 9bcn 69n7 0bk?

Bring it On! Level 14
kjyr 9bcj 69q7 rbk?

Bring it On! Level 15
k1wr 9bcd 69s7 hbk?

Bring it On! Level 16
lktr 9bb9 69v6 8vk?

Bring it On! Level 17
l2rr 9bb5 69x6 0vk?

Bring it On! Level 18
mkpr 9bb1 69z6 rvk?

Bring it On! Level 19
m2mr 9bbx 6916 hvk?

Bring it On! Level 20
nkkr 9bbs 6935 8vk?

Bring it On! Level 21
n2hr 9bbn 6955 0vk?

Bring it On! Level 22
pkfr 9bbj 6975 rvk?

Bring it On! Level 23
p2cr 9bbd 6995 hvk?

Bring it On! Level 24
qk?r 9bf9 6?b4 8bk?

Bring it On! Level 25
q28r 9bf5 6?d4 0bk?

Bring it On! Level 26
rk6r 9bf1 6?g4 rbk?

Bring it On! Level 27
r24r 9bfx 6?j4 hbk?

Bring it On! Level 28
sk2r 9bfs 6?l3 8bk?

Bring it On! Level 29
s20r 9bfn 6?n3 0bk?

Bring it On! Level 30
tkyr 9bfj 6?q3 rbk?

Bring it On! Level 31
t2wr 9bfd 6?s3 hbk?

Bring it On! Level 32
vgtr 9bd9 6?v2 7vk?

I Own Doom! Level 02
cnn8 9bj0 680t nvk?

I Own Doom! Level 03
c5l8 9bjw 682t dvk?

I Own Doom! Level 04
dnj8 9bjr 684s 5vk?

I Own Doom! Level 05
d5g8 9bjm 686s xvk?

I Own Doom! Level 06
fnd8 9bjh 688s nvk?

I Own Doom! Level 07
f5b8 9bjc 68?s dvk?

I Own Doom! Level 08
gn98 9bc8 69cr 6bk?

I Own Doom! Level 09
g578 9bc4 69fr ybk?

I Own Doom! Level 10
hn58 9bc0 69hr pbk?

I Own Doom! Level 11
h538 9bcw 69kr fbk?

I Own Doom! Level 12
jn18 9bcr 69mq 6bk?

I Own Doom! Level 13
j5z8 9bcm 69pq ybk?

I Own Doom! Level 14
knx8 9bch 69rq pbk?

I Own Doom! Level 15
k5v8 9bcc 69tq fbk?

I Own Doom! Level 16
lps8 9bb8 69wp 6vk?

I Own Doom! Level 17
l6q8 9bb4 69yp yvk?

I Own Doom! Level 18
mpn8 9bb0 690p pvk?

I Own Doom! Level 19
m6l8 9bbw 692p fvk?

I Own Doom! Level 20
npj8 9bbr 694n 6vk?

I Own Doom! Level 21
n6g8 9bbm 696n yvk?

I Own Doom! Level 22
ppd8 9bbh 698n pvk?

I Own Doom! Level 23
p6b8 9bbc 69?n fvk?

I Own Doom! Level 24
qp98 9bf8 6?cm 6bk?

I Own Doom! Level 25
q678 9bf4 6?fm ybk?

I Own Doom! Level 26
rp58 9bf0 6?hm pbk?

I Own Doom! Level 27
r638 9bfw 6?km fbk?

I Own Doom! Level 28
sp18 9bfr 6?ml 6bk?

I Own Doom! Level 29
s6z8 9bfm 6?pl ybk?

I Own Doom! Level 30
tpx8 9bfh 6?rl pbk?

I Own Doom! Level 31
t6v8 9bfc 6?tl fbk?

I Own Doom! Level 32
vls8 9bd8 6?wk 5vk?

Watch Me Die! Level 02
csnr 9bjz 680? lvk?

Watch Me Die! Level 03
c9lr 9bjv 682? bvk?

Watch Me Die! Level 04
dsjr 9bjq 6849 3vk?

Watch Me Die! Level 05
d9gr 9bjl 6869 vvk?

Watch Me Die! Level 06
fsdr 9bjg 6889 lvk?

Watch Me Die! Level 07
f9br 9bjb 68?9 bvk?

Watch Me Die! Level 08
gs9r 9bc7 69c8 4bk?

Watch Me Die! Level 09
g97r 9bc3 69f8 wbk?

Watch Me Die! Level 10
hs5r 9bcz 69h8 mbk?

Watch Me Die! Level 11
h93r 9bcv 69k8 cbk?

Watch Me Die! Level 12
js1r 9bcq 69m7 4bk?

Watch Me Die! Level 13
j9zr 9bcl 69p7 wbk?

Watch Me Die! Level 14
ksxr 9bcg 69r7 mbk?

Watch Me Die! Level 15
k9vr 9bcb 69t7 cbk?

Watch Me Die! Level 16
ltsr 9bb7 69w6 4vk?

Watch Me Die! Level 17
l?qr 9bb3 69y6 wvk?

Watch Me Die! Level 18
mtnr 9bbz 6906 mvk?

Watch Me Die! Level 19
m?lr 9bbv 6926 cvk?

Watch Me Die! Level 20
ntjr 9bbq 6945 4vk?

Watch Me Die! Level 21
n?gr 9bbl 6965 wvk?

Watch Me Die! Level 22
ptdr 9bbg 6985 mvk?

Watch Me Die! Level 23
p?br 9bbb 69?5 cvk?

Watch Me Die! Level 24
qt9r 9bf7 6?c4 4bk?

Watch Me Die! Level 25
q?7r 9bf3 6?f4 wbk?

Watch Me Die! Level 26
rt5r 9bfz 6?h4 mbk?

Watch Me Die! Level 27
r?3r 9bfv 6?k4 cbk?

Watch Me Die! Level 28
st1r 9bfq 6?m3 4bk?

Watch Me Die! Level 29
s?zr 9bfl 6?p3 wbk?

Watch Me Die! Level 30
ttxr 9bfg 6?r3 mbk?

Watch Me Die! Level 31
t?vr 9bfb 6?t3 cbk?

Watch Me Die! Level 32
vqsr 9bd7 6?w2 3vk?

DUAL HEROES

Play As Gyn
Beat the game in Expert with any character.

Play As Ray
Set the difficulty to Hard and choose 2-round mode. Now beat Story mode with Hana.

Access Cheat Menu
At the main menu, press Left (2), L (2), Right (2), Left (2).

All Items
Turn on the Cheat menu; then return to the main menu and press R, C-Right, Right, L, C-Left, Left, C-Right, Right.

Level Warp
Turn on the Cheat menu and press L (3), C-Right, Right, Left (2), C-Left.

Invincibility
Turn on Cheat menu and press R (7), Left.

No Monsters
Turn on Cheat menu and press L, C-Left, Left, R, C-Right, Right, Left (2), Right.

DUKE NUKEM 64

Activate Cheat Codes
Press Left (2), L (2), Right (2), Left (2) to open the Cheat menu.

All Items Code
R, Right-C, Right, L, Left-C, Left, Right-C, Right

Invincibility
R (7), Left

No Enemies
L, Left-C, Left, R, Right-C, Right, Left (2), Right

Level Select
L (3), Right-C, Right, Left (2), Left-C

DUKE NUKEM: ZERO HOUR

Rifle with Unlimited Ammo
At the Start screen, press C-Up, C-Down, C-Left, C-Right, L, R.

Freeze Thrower
At the Start screen, press Down, Up, A, L, R, Z.

Group 1 MP Characters
At the Start screen, press A, L, R, Left, B, Down, Up.

Group 2 MP Characters
At the Start screen, press B, A (2), R, L.

Group 3 MP Characters
At the Start screen, press L (2), Up, Down, R, B, A.

Group 4 MP Characters
At the Start screen, press B (3), R, Left, A.

Group 5 MP Characters
At the Start screen, press Right, B, Left, L, A, Z.

Group 6 MP Characters
At the Start screen, press Up, Down, B, A (2), Left.

Skin Select
At the Start screen, press C-Left, R, Left, Up, Down, B, A, Z, and then select Single-player mode.

Action Nuk'em Mode
At the Start screen, press Down (2), A, Z (2), Left, A, or finish the entire game.

Big Head Mode
Save all the babes on Level 2.

Big Gun Mode
Kill all enemies on Level 3.

Flat Shade Map
Get every secret in the Wetworld secret level.

Ice Skin
Save all the babes on Level 5.

Weather
Get all the secrets on Level 6.

High Speed Zombies
Save all the babes on Level 8.

Maximum Blaster Ammo
Kill all enemies on Level 9.

Maximum Shotgun Ammo
Save all the babes on Level 10.

Maximum Rifle Ammo
Save all the babes on Level 11.

Maximum Revolver Ammo
Kill all enemies on Level 12.

Maximum Sawed-Off Shotgun Ammo
Kill all enemies on Level 13.

Maximum SMG Ammo
Get all the secrets on Level 15.

Maximum Gatling Gun Ammo
Kill all enemies on Level 16.

Maximum Volt C. Ammo
Get all the secrets on Level 17.

Maximum Sniper Ammo
On Going Down secret level, save all the babes.

Maximum Freezer Ammo
Kill all enemies on Level 20.

Maximum Gamma Ammo
Save all the babes on Level 21.

Refill Health
Destroy fire hydrant, stand in water, and hold A.

First-Person View
In the opening screen, press Down, Up, L, B, Z, Left, C-Up, C-Right, C-Left, Z.

DYNAMITE COP

Bonus Missions
Successfully complete missions 1, 2, and 3 to unlock missions 4, 5, and 6. Mission 4 is based on mission 1, with a single life, double damage weapons, and no continues. Mission 5 is based on mission 2, with a time limit in each room and no continues. Mission 6 is based on mission 3, with very little health, few health power-ups, no other power-ups, and no continues.

Play As the Monkey
Successfully complete missions 4, 5, and 6 to unlock the Monkey. The Monkey fights similarly to Bruno.

Play As Original Bruno
Collect all illustrations in the game to unlock the original Bruno from *Die Hard Arcade*.

Play As Cindy
At the character selection screen, highlight Ivy, then hold Start to unlock Cindy from *Die Hard Arcade*.

Tranquilizer Gun Mini-Game
Successfully complete the game once.

Infinite Credits (Tranquilizer Gun Mini-Game)
Successfully complete missions 1, 2, and 3 without using any continues to have infinite credits for the Tranquilizer Gun mini-game.

EARTHWORM JIM 3D

Small Jim
At the title screen, hold Z and press C-Up, C-Down, Left.

ECW: HARDCORE REVOLUTION

Big Feet Mode
Beat career mode with Balls Mahoney.

Big Hand Mode
Beat career mode with Jason.

Big Head Mode
Beat career mode with Rhino.

Custom Wrestler Textures
Beat career mode as Tommy Dreamer.

Ego Mode
Beat career mode as Chris Chetti.

Fat Man Mode
Beat career mode as Spike Dudley.

Hangman Mode
Beat career mode as Sal E. Graziano.

Headless Mode
Beat career mode with Taz.

Little Head Mode
Beat the career mode with Roadkill.

Play As Beulah McGillicutty
Play the career mode and win the ECW World Tag Team belt.

Play As Bill Alfonso.
Beat career mode with Rob Van Dam.

Play As Cyrus the Virus
Play the career mode and win the ECW World TV belt.

Play As Joel Gertner
Play the career mode and win the Acclaim belt.

Play As Joey Styles
Play the career mode and win the Acclaim belt.

Play As Judge Jeff Jones
Beat career mode with Mike Awesome.

Play As Louie Spicolli
Play the career mode and win the ECW World Heavyweight belt.

Play As Taz
Play the career mode and win the ECW World Heavyweight belt.

Play As the Sheik
Play the career mode and win the ECW World Tag Team belt.

Play As Tommy Rich
Play the career mode and win the ECW World TV belt.

Play As the Jobbers
Defend the ECW World Heavyweight belt five times.

Random Head Mode
Beat career mode as Louie Spicolli.

EXTREME-G

All Levels and Roach
Enter 51GG95 as a password.

All Tracks, Roach, Neon
Enter 61GGB5 as a password.

All Regular Tracks, Roach, Neon, Hidden Track
Enter 81GGD5 as a password.

Receive Weapons
In Contest mode, enter ARSENAL at the Name Selection screen.

Slippery Track
In Contest mode, enter BANANA at the Name Selection screen.

Unlimited Turbo Boosts
In Contest mode, enter NITROID at the Name Selection screen.

Extreme Speed
In Contest mode, enter XTREME at the Name Selection screen.

Extreme Ghostly
In Contest mode, enter GHOSTLY at the Name Selection screen.

Magnify Mode
In Contest mode, enter MAGNIFY at the Name Selection screen.

Race Upside Down
In Contest mode, enter ANTIGRAV at the Name Selection screen.

Stealth Mode
In Contest mode, enter STEALTH at the Name Selection screen.

Ugly Mode
In Contest mode, enter UGLYMODE at the Name Selection screen.

Wireframe Mode
In Contest mode, enter WIRED at the Name Selection screen.

All Bikes Are Boulders
In Contest mode, enter ROLLER at the Name Selection screen.

Fisheye Lens
In Contest mode, enter FISHEYE at the Name Selection screen.

Quit Race and Still Win
In Contest mode, enter RA50 at the Name Selection screen.

Shoot Fergus
Enter the name FERGUS and go into Shoot 'Em Up mode.

Race As the Extreme Team
Enter the name XGTEAM and change it to the first name of one of the game's programmers (Justin, Shawn, or John).

EXTREME-G 2

Venom Bike
Enter 68QCMH3H9HT.

Wasp Bike
Enter 55HZ1MH3H9H1.

Spectre Bike
Enter HSFDCCV611FV.

Extra Multiplayer Levels
Enter N31GG76CG9DZ.

Mirror Mode
Enter HS3B9BQ9DGPL.

Infinite Weapon, Shield Energy
In Bike Select screen of Extreme Contest mode, press R and enter the name XCHARGE.

Infinite Nitros
In Bike Select screen of Extreme Contest mode, press R and enter the name NITROID.

All Homing, Multiple Missiles
In Bike Select screen of Extreme Contest mode, press R and enter the name MISPLACE.

Complete Race
In Bike Select screen of Extreme Contest mode, press R and enter the name RA50.

WipeOut Mode
In Bike Select screen of Extreme Contest mode, press R and enter the name 2064.

Turbo Mode
In Bike Select screen of Extreme Contest mode, press R and enter the name XXX.

Tron Mode
In Bike Select screen of Extreme Contest mode, press R and enter the name NEUTRON.

Random Circuit Tracks
In Bike Select screen of Extreme Contest mode, press R and enter name JUGGLE.

Pixelated Graphics
In Bike Select screen of Extreme Contest mode, press R and enter the name PIXIE.

Wireframe Graphics
In Bike Select screen of Extreme Contest mode, press R and enter the name LINEAR.

Full Screen
In Bike Select screen of Extreme Contest mode, press R and enter the name FLICK or NOPANEL.

Spiraling Screen
In Bike Select screen of Extreme Contest mode, press R and enter the name SPIRAL.

Overhead View
In Bike Select screen of Extreme Contest mode, press R and enter the name SPYEYE.

Unlimited Weapons
In Bike Select screen of Extreme Contest mode, press R and enter the name MISTAKE.

All Bikes
Enter 3GP8ZKW76ZMW.

All Tracks
Enter 8KLSZKW76ZM7.

Duel Mode, All Tracks, All Bikes
Enter 27PVNM6F45S1.

FIFA 64

Control Crowd Taunts
During gameplay, press the control pad in any direction.

Scoring Animations
For a different scoring animation after a goal, press one of the C buttons.

FIFA: ROAD TO THE WORLD CUP '98

Ghost Players
Choose Slovakia as your team. At the Player Edit screen enter LASKO as a name.

Creations Programmers Team
Choose England as your team. At the Player Edit screen enter BURYFC as a name.

Invisible Players
Choose Sheffield as your team. At the Player Edit screen enter WAYNE as a name.

Black and White Mode
Choose Canada as your team. At the Player Edit screen enter MARC as a name.

No Stadium
Choose any team. At the Player Edit screen enter CATCH22 as a name.

Small Players
Choose Vancouver as your team. At the Player Edit screen enter KERRY as a name.

Full Upside-Down Screen
Choose Australia as your team. At the Player Edit screen enter NWODEDISPU as a name.

Partial Upside-Down Screen
Choose Vancouver as your team. At the Player Edit screen enter TED as a name.

View Victory Sequences
Choose Japan as your team. At the Player Edit screen enter NORIE as a name. Then press Z+C-Left+C-Up at the Round Select screen.

Hot Potato Mode
Choose Ireland, R Ireland, or UEFA as your team. At the Player Edit screen enter SPUD as a name.

Invisible Walls
Choose Wales as your team. At the Player Edit screen enter WARREN as a name.

Unlimited Player Attribute Points
Choose Vancouver as your team. At the Player Edit screen enter DAVE as a name.

World Cup Mode Round Select
Choose Japan as your team. At the Player Edit screen enter YUJI as a name.

Giant Players
Select Brazil in Season/League mode. Start a game and pause. Highlight "Music Volume" and press C-Up+C-Down+Start+B.

FIFA SOCCER '99

Atlanta Attack Team
Play as Brazil and win the Champion's Cup under Pro.

MLS Teams
Beat every country's league and the World League. Then play the U.S. League at Hardest difficulty and win. The MLS teams become available under U.S.

Find Ronaldo
He may be found on the Inter Milan team as Calcio.

Big Players
Select Canada. At the Player Edit screen, enter Joe as the first player's name. Now start a friendly game.

Booing Crowd
After the other team scores a goal, press B continuously during the intermission sequence.

No Goalie
Pause gameplay against the computer. Change the controller to the other team. Resume and wait for your original team to gain possession of the ball; then hold R to have the goalie run after the ball. Keep holding R and press Start. Switch controllers back and resume. The computer goalie won't return until next half.

FIGHTER'S DESTINY

Fight As Boro
Beat the game at Easy difficulty.

Fight As the Joker
Beat the game to earn a star. Then select Survival mode and defeat all 100 characters.

Fight As the Master
Beat the game to earn a star. Then select Master Challenge mode and defeat all opponents.

Fight As Robert
Beat the game to earn a star. Then select Fastest mode and defeat all fighters in less than one minute.

Fight As Ushi
Beat the game to earn a star. Then select Rodeo mode and remain undefeated for at least one minute.

Winning Poses
After defeating your opponent, press A or B repeatedly.

Alternate Costume
When selecting your character, press R.

Easy Money
Roll repeatedly against a wall. Money should appear.

Invincibility and Level Select
Hold L+Z+C-Up+C-Down at the main menu to go to the Character Select screen. Use C-Right and C-Left to choose your level.

FIGHTING FORCE 64

Air Base Gun
When you get to the Air Base, go left to find an A-10 plane. Destroy it and a huge gun falls out the front.

Car Engine
If you completely destroy a car (e.g., with a bazooka shot), you can grab the car's engine. This only works with Smasher.

Airplane Gun
On the Air Base stage, go inside the hanger and destroy the plane. After it is destroyed you will be able to use its gun.

Double Team
In the co-op mode ,when you throw an enemy or boss, the other player can hit the enemy that is being held.

Easy Money
Walk to the wall and roll. Make sure you roll against the wall and not by it. Money comes out.

Find Flare Guns
There are two black structures on either side of the hovercraft stage. Destroy those, and a flare gun drops out of each structure.

Level Select and Invincibility
At the main menu, press and hold L + Z + C-Up + C-Down. This takes you to the character select screen. From there, you may press C-Left or C-Right to choose your starting level. You start with invincibility.

Out of Change
When entering the subway in mission 4.1, toll machines stop you. There are two ways to get through them—either destroy them or pay the toll. To pay the toll, there is a payphone on the wall to your right. Hit the phone and grab a coin. Walk to one of the toll machines and the bar pops up. You are able to walk through

Rocket Launcher
If you break the police car on the car park stage, a rocket launcher comes out the trunk.

Special Moves
Each character lists a special move at the end of his or her character bio. Each of these button configurations works for all characters, giving each character four special moves.

Weapons on the First Stage
As soon as you start the level, there is a police car to your left. Destroy it, and a weapon comes out the trunk. Go through the gate to see a black car. Destroy it, and another weapon comes out of the trunk.

FLYING DRAGON

Very Easy Difficulty
Highlight the Easy difficulty option. Tap Left repeatedly until the Very Easy difficulty option appears.

Very Hard Difficulty
Highlight the Hard difficulty option. Tap Right repeatedly until the Very Hard difficulty option appears.

Unlock Platinum Fighters
Defeat 10 platinum characters to get all 10 medals in SD Hiryu mode.

Play in Ryumaou Tournament
Get nine medals.

Play As Ryumaou
Beat Ryumaou in the Ryumaou Tournament.

Play As Bokuchin
Defeat Bokuchin in a game.

Play As Virtual Ryumaou
Beat SD Hiryu mode as Ryumaou several times, until you receive the Skull of the Devil King prize. The prize unlocks Ryumaou in the Virtual Hiryu screen.

Dark Dragon Claw
Get nine medals and beat the Ryumaou Tournament as Yuka (Rank S), with Normal difficulty and two 60-second rounds per match option.

FORSAKEN 64

Frozen Enemies
While paused, press R, Z, Right (2), C-Up, C-Left, C-Right, C-Down.

Gore Mode
While paused, press Z, Down, C-Up, C-Left (4), C-Down.

Infinite Solaris Missiles
While paused, press B, L (2), Z, Up, Down, C-Up (2).

Infinite Titan Missiles
While paused, press A, B, L, Up (2), C-Up (2), C-Right.

One-Hit Kills
While paused, press B (3), L, R, Left, Down (2).

Psychedelic Mode
While paused, press A, R, Left, Right, Down, C-Up, C-Left, C-Down.

Stealth Mode
While paused, press Up (4), Right, Down, C-Left (2).

Nitro Mode
While paused, press B (2), R, Up, Left, Down, C-Up, C-Left.

Wire Frame Mode
While paused, press L (2), R, Z, Left, Right, C-Up, C-Right.

God Mode
While paused, press A, Z (2), Up, Left, C-Left (2), C-Down.

Level Select
While paused, press A, R, Z, Up (2), C-Up, C-Down (2).

Unlimited Main Weapon
While paused, press A, R, Z, Right, C-Up, C-Right, C-Down (2).

Unlimited Secondary Weapon
While paused, press B (2), Z, Left (2), C-Up, C-Left, C-Right.

Unlimited Weapon Energy
While paused, press L, Z, Left, Right, Down (2), C-Down (2).

FOX SPORTS COLLEGE HOOPS '99

1998 Cleveland Indians Team
Choose St. Joseph as a team in an Exhibition game.

No Crowd
Enter NOFANS in the Code menu.

Translucent Players
Enter GHOST in the Code menu.

Ball Trails
Enter TRAILS in the Code menu.

Z-Axis Court
Enter Z-WOOD in the Code menu.

Big Heads
Enter NOGGIN in the Code menu.

More Fouls Called on Home Team
Enter HOMIE in the Code menu.

Fox Interactive Team
Enter TEAM-Z in the Code menu.

Alternative Commentary
Enter MONKEY in the Code menu.

Invisible Players
Enter VIS in the Code menu.

Team Mascot
Enter MASCOTTS in the Code menu.

Final Four Stadium
Enter FFWOOD in the Code menu.

No Shot Clock
Enter BUZZZ in the Code menu.

One-Minute Game
Enter THIRTY in the Code menu.

F-ZERO X

Smaller Racers
Hold L+R+C-Up+C-Down+C-Left+C-Right at the Ship Selection screen.

Larger Racers
Hold L+R+Z+C-Up+C-Down+C-Left+C-Right at the Ship Selection screen.

Unlock Joker Cup Tracks
Beat Jack, Queen, and King cups at Standard difficulty to unlock the Joker Cup with six bonus tracks.

Unlock X Cup Tracks
Beat Jack, Queen, and King cups at Expert difficulty to unlock the X Cup with six randomly generated bonus tracks.

Master Difficulty Level
Beat Jack, Queen, and King cups at all three difficulty levels.

Preview Tracks
Press C-Up, C-Down, C-Left, or C-Right at the Track Selection screen.

Alternate Title Screens
Beat the game at Expert difficulty for the first title screen change. Then beat the game at Master difficulty to see the second title change.

Preview Cars
At the Customization screen, press C-Up, C-Down, C-Left, or C-Right.

Change Car Colors
Select a ship and press R or Z at the Statistics screen.

Unlock All Tracks, Levels, Ships
In Mode Selection screen, press L, Z, R, C-Up, C-Down, C-Left, C-Right, Start.

GAUNTLET LEGENDS

Permanent Anti-Death
Beat the game to receive Permanent Anti-death, which allows you to steal health from Death.

Turn Death into Food
Do not open the container where Death is hidden. Use a potion nearby and you'll hear Death scream. Then open the container to get a fruit.

Play As Sumner
On the last level of the battlefield, the Trench, exit through the secret door. Then, at the bonus level, collect 50 coins.

Play As the Minotaur
In the Mountain Kingdom, go to the cliff stage. Find every switch, and then go to the exit area. Avoid the exit portal. Instead, continue to a skull-and-crossbones trapdoor. Step on it to transport to a room with many coins. Collect 50 to unlock the Minotaur.

Play As the Falconess
In the Castle World, go to the bonus stage and collect 50 coins.

Play As the Jackal
At the end of the Ice World's second level, you'll find a pile of crates with a trapdoor on top. Open the door and collect 50 coins.

Play As the Tigress
Find all the main switches at the first town level and go to the portal. From there, backtrack a bit to a hill with a chest, a switch, and Death. Avoid Death and hit the switch. Go in the direction the switch is pointing until you reach a trapdoor. Stand on the trapdoor and collect 50 coins.

Start New Game with Secret Character
First, unlock a secret character and save the game. Then select the file with the secret character. Press B at the Rumble Pak screen. Select New to start a new game with the secret character.

Stop Time and Explore
At the first end boss, when you're about to die, use the Stop Time item. When you lose the life, make sure the Stop Time item is still running. Choose to continue and enter any level besides a boss level.

Max Stats
Play Level 1 in the Mountain World and complete it without using any items collected in the level. Sell your items at the Tower. Use the money to buy 20 points' worth of stats. Repeat as necessary.

GEX: ENTER THE GECKO

Super
Enter the password M758FQRW3J58FQRW4! for all remotes with 99 lives.

First Gate
DPXMDGVXCVLCG5WFL

Second Gate
C2G57FLRDQJV7FBTCN

Third Gate
FFY(Right Arrow)SJB5D5HCVJL8DV

Fourth Gate
GFT(Right Arrow)/M9BH56FBLMF2B

GEX 3: DEEP COVER GECKO

Turn into DracuGex Without A Code
Just before you enter the level "Clueless in Seattle" there is a painting of DracuGex. Look at it with C-Up to turn into DracuGex for 30 seconds. This helps you get the bonus and paw coin that are across from you.

GLOVER

Bonus Levels
While paused, press C-Down, C-Up, C-Right (2), C-Down, C-Left, C-Right (2).

Checkpoints
While paused, press C-Down (2), C-Right, C-Left, C-Up (2), C-Down, C-Left.

Open Portals
While paused, press C-Up, C-Right (2), C-Down, C-Left, C-Down, C-Up, C-Right.

Disable All Cheats
Pause and press C-Down (8).

Play As Froggy
While paused, press C-Up, C-Right, C-Down, C-Right, C-Up, C-Left (2), C-Up.

Big Glover
While paused, press C-Down (3), C-Left (2), C-Down, C-Right, C-Left.

Powerball
While paused, press C-Up, C-Down, C-Up, C-Down, C-Up, C-Down, C-Left, C-Up.

Turn Opponents into Frogs
While paused, press C-Down, C-Left, C-Down (2), C-Left, C-Down, C-Up, C-Left. Then press R to turn enemies into frogs.

Speed Increase for Glover
While paused, press C-Left (2), C-Right, C-Up, C-Right, C-Left, C-Down (2).

Summon the Ball
While paused, press C-Up, C-Left (2), C-Up, C-Right, C-Left, C-Down, C-Up after you lose the ball.

Big Ball Spell
While paused, press C-Down (2), C-Up, C-Down (2), C-Left, C-Right, C-Down.

Boomerang Ball
While paused, press C-Right, C-Up (4), C-Left (2), C-Down.

Control Ball
While paused, press C-Left, C-Right, C-Left, C-Right, C-Up, C-Down, C-Right (2).

Invisible Ball
While paused, press C-Down (2), C-Left (2), C-Up (2), C-Down, C-Up.

Enemy Ball
While paused, press C-Left, C-Down, C-Up, C-Right, C-Left (2), C-Down (2).

Rotate Camera Left
While paused, press C-Right, C-Down, C-Right, C-Down, C-Up (2), C-Right, C-Left.

Rotate Camera Right
While paused, press C-Left, C-Right, C-Up (2), C-Down, C-Right, C-Down, C-Right.

Low Gravity
While paused, press C-Left (2), C-Up, C-Left, C-Right, C-Up (3).

Fish Eyes
While paused, press C-Left, C-Right, C-Left, C-Right, C-Left, C-Right, C-Left, C-Right.

Mad Garibs
While paused, press C-Down, C-Right, C-Down, C-Up, C-Left, C-Down, C-Left, C-Up.

Locate Garibs
While paused, press C-Left, C-Up, C-Right, C-Down, C-Left, C-Up, C-Left (2).

Random Cheat
While paused, press C-Left, C-Down, C-Up, C-Right, C-Left (2), C-Down (2).

Open All Levels
While paused, press C-Down (2), C-Left, C-Up (3), C-Right, C-Down.

All Levels (in Uncovered Worlds)
While paused, press C-Down (2), C-Left, C-Up (3), C-Right, C-Down.

Level Select
While paused, press C-Up (3), C-Left (2), C-Right, C-Left, C-Right.

Open Portals
While paused, press C-Up, C-Right (2), C-Down, C-Left, C-Down, C-Up, C-Right.

Smart Bomb Spell
While paused, press C-Up, C-Left (4), C-Up, C-Right, C-Up, un-pause, and then press R.

Unlimited Energy
While paused, press C-Right (2), C-Down, C-Right (3), C-Up, C-Left.

Unlimited Lives
While paused, press C-Up (5), C-Right, C-Down, C-Right.

GOEMON'S GREAT ADVENTURE

Four-Player Mode
With four controllers inserted, play the game with one or two players. Get 44 hands from various levels. Then press C-Right+Start on controllers 3 and 4.

Alternate Outfits
Enable the Four-player mode code and go to the Prediction House.

Unlimited Lives (Requires Memory Card)
You need 100 coins in EDO before you advance to Lost'n Town. Head to the restaurant and buy sushi to gain an extra life. Then go to the inn and save your game. Reset the game. Load the saved game. Now you'll have the additional lives and 100 coins. Repeat for more lives.

Faster Hula-Hoop
Highlight "Try Again" at the Game Over screen. Then press A repeatedly to move the hula-hoop faster.

Infinite Items (Requires Memory Card)
Play a game and go to the Upgrade Store. Purchase any item. Go to the save location and save your game. Reset the game, and then load the saved game. You'll still have all your money and the item you bought. Repeat for more items.

Double Your Coins
Defeat an opponent at night to get two coins instead of the single coin you get for daytime victories.

GOLDEN NUGGET 64

Easy Money
Play the max in the Catch of the Day slot machine. Pause gameplay during the spin. Change the player name and reset the purse to receive $1,000. You net $700 each time you do this.

GRAND THEFT AUTO

All Guns, Body Armor, Get Out of Jail Free Card
suckmyrocket

No Police
iamthelaw

99999999999 Points
itcouldbeyou

Unlimited Lives
iamgarypenn

GT 64 CHAMPIONSHIP EDITION

Turbo Start
After the starting light turns yellow, press Accelerate.

Reversed Tracks
Beat Championship mode at Easy.

HEXEN

Enable Cheat Menu
Pause gameplay and press C-Up, C-Down, C-Left, C-Right. The Cheat menu appears at the bottom of the menu.

Invincibility
At the Cheat menu, quickly press C-Left, C-Right, C-Down.

Level Select
At the Cheat menu, quickly press C-Left (2), C-Right (2), C-Down, C-Up.

Kill All Visible Enemies
At the Cheat menu, quickly press C-Down, C-Up, C-Left (2).

Full Health
At the Cheat menu, quickly press C-Left, C-Up, C-Down (2).

No Clipping
At the Cheat menu, quickly press C-Up (20), C-Down.

All Keys
At the Cheat menu, quickly press C-Down, C-Up, C-Left, C-Right. Then enter the Collect menu to activate the code.

All Artifacts
At the Cheat menu, quickly press C-Up, C-Right, C-Down, C-Up. Then enter the Collect menu to activate the code.

All Weapons
At the Cheat menu, quickly press C-Right, C-Up, C-Down (2). Then enter the Collect menu to activate the code.

All Puzzle Items
At the Cheat menu, quickly press C-Up, C-Left (3), C-Right, C-Down (2). Then enter the Collect menu to activate the code.

HOT WHEELS: TURBO RACING

Tow Jam Car
At the main menu, highlight "Options." Then press C-Up, C-Down, Z, R, C-Left, C-Right, C-Up, C-Down.

Night Racing
At the main menu, highlight "Options." Then press C-Up (2), C-Down (2), C-Left, C-Right, C-Left, C-Right.

Stealth Mode
At the main menu, highlight "Options." Then press C-Left, Z (2), C-Up, C-Left, R, C-Down, C-Up.

Wireframe Mode
At the main menu, highlight "Options." Then press C-Up, Z, C-Down, C-Left, C-Up, Z, C-Down, C-Left.

Unlock Bonus Cars and Tracks
Win the Hot Wheels Cup, or enter 99T8DTY8VD D7BDDDDDD2 as a password.

Additional Bonus Cars
Enter 9PTNPTFN6P NMQPPNPPPL as a password.

All Tracks and Cars
Enter (Space)-WYZKZ1VDD OTX1TRGHSV as a password.

Mirror Tracks
At the main menu press Z, R, Z (2), R, Z (2).

Unlimited Turbo
At the main menu press C-Right, Z, C-Up, C-Down, R, C-Left, Z, C-Right.

HYBRID HEAVEN

Cheat Menu
Set screen resolution to High Resolution Letterbox. Begin a game. Reset the N64 system; after each save, toggle the screen resolution to the opposite setting.

Play As Alien
Beat the game at Ultimate. Then press L, R, L, R, Z at the title screen.

Play As President Weller
Beat the game at Ultimate. Then press L, R, L, R, Start at the title screen.

Extra Mode
Beat the game at Ultimate. Then press L, R, L, R, A at the title screen.

HYDRO THUNDER

Catacombs Track
Place first in the Hard tracks.

Hydro Speedway Track and Tiny Titanic Boat
Place first in the Catacombs track.

Castle Von Dandy Track and Armed Response Boat
Place first in the Hydro Speeday track.

Nile Adventure Track and Blowfish Boat
Place first in the Castle Von Dandy track.

Chumdinger Boat
Place first in the Nile Adventure track.

IGGY'S RECKIN' BALLS

Iggy's Girlfriend
Press R+Z at the opening screen, then enter ENTAROADUN.

Ice Platforms
Press R+Z at the opening screen, then enter ICEPRINCESS.

Higher Ball Bounce
Press R+Z at the opening screen, then enter TOOMUCHFUN.

Turok 2 Graphic Engine
Press R+Z at the opening screen, then enter 2ROKTOO.

Nonstop Roller Ball
Press R+Z at the opening screen, then enter NONSTOP.

Gooey and Ice Platforms
Press R+Z at the opening screen, then enter GOOEYICEPRINCESS.

Random Bombs
Press R+Z at the opening screen, then enter OHMY.

Pencil Sketch
Press R+Z at the opening screen, then enter PENCIL.

Black and White
Press R+Z at the opening screen, then enter ROLFHARRIS.

Full Turbos
Press R+Z at the opening screen, then enter GOBABY.

Gooey Platforms
Press R+Z at the opening screen, then enter GOOEYGOOGOO.

Different Accessories for Characters
Press R+Z at the opening screen, then enter SWOPSHOP.

Play As Lizzie
Set the game on Hard difficulty and then beat all the opponents in Iggy's Challenge at Tiki Woods.

Unlock Bonus Characters
Place first in each race.

Refill Boost Meter
Tap Jump while you are on a boost platform.

All Characters
Press R+Z at the opening screen, then enter HAPPYHEADS.

All Tracks
Press R+Z at the opening screen, then enter THEUNIVERSE.

Big Reckin' Balls
Press R+Z at the opening screen, then enter TOOMUCHPIE.

Level Select
Press R+Z at the opening screen, then enter JUMPAROUND.

Small Reckin' Balls
Press R+Z at the opening screen, then enter MICROBALLS.

Turbo Mode
Press R+Z at the opening screen, then enter 2TIMES.

INDIANA JONES AND THE INFERNAL MACHINE

Select Level
FORGEOFF

Access Expert Mode
REALHARD

View Development Team Picture
CHEESE!!

Unlock Hidden, Return to Peru Level
Get 1,500 I.Q. points.

INDY RACING LEAGUE 2000

Unlock All Tracks and Cars
Begin game in Gold Cup mode. Enter YOU DA MAN as player name.

Gallery
Begin game in Gold Cup mode. Enter WOODY COOKIES as player name.

IN-FISHERMAN BASS HUNTER 64

Extra Money
At the Options menu, select "Cheat Codes," and enter ALLDCASH.

Hard-to-Find Fish
At the Options menu, select "Cheat Codes," and enter WHEREDFISH.

Slow Boat
At the Options menu, select "Cheat Codes," and enter WHATADRAG.

Fast Boat
At the Options menu, select "Cheat Codes," and enter HYPERBOAT.

Bathtub Boat
At the Options menu, select "Cheat Codes," and enter RUBADUBDUB.

Win the Current Tournament
At the Options menu, select "Cheat Codes," and enter IWINIWIN.

Upgraded Depth Finder or Catch Al Linder
At the Options menu, select "Cheat Codes," and enter FISHMAN.

All Lures
At the Options menu, select "Cheat Codes," and enter ALLDLURES.

Big Heads on Fishermen
At the Options menu, select "Cheat Codes," and enter HEADADBIGA.

No Penalties in Tournament
At the Options menu, select "Cheat Codes," and enter NOPENALTY.

No Snags
At the Options menu, select "Cheat Codes," and enter BAGDSNAG.

Livewell Filled with Large Fish
At the Options menu, select "Cheat Codes," and enter GIMMIEDFISH.

Funny Noises
At the Options menu, select "Cheat Codes," and enter SILLYSOUND.

Easy to Catch Fish
At the Options menu, select "Cheat Codes," and enter SUPERLURE.

Alternate View
At the Options menu, select "Cheat Codes," and enter GIMMIEDVIEW.

Active Fish
At the Options menu, select "Cheat Codes," and enter HAPPYFISH.

All Lakes
At the Options menu, select "Cheat Codes," and enter ALLDLAKES.

Large Fish
At the Options menu, select "Cheat Codes," and enter MONDOFISH.

No Other Fishermen
At the Options menu, select "Cheat Codes," and enter NOCOMP.

Unbreakable Fishing Line
At the Options menu, select "Cheat Codes," and enter SUPERSTRING.

INTERNATIONAL SUPERSTAR SOCCER 64

Bonus Teams
At the title screen, press Up, L, Up, L, Down, L, Down, L, Left, R, Right, R, Left, R, Right, R, B, A, hold Z+Start. If you do it correctly, the announcer says, "What an incredible comeback!"

Big Heads
Press C-Up (2), C-Down (2), C-Left, C-Right, C-Left, C-Right, B, A, hold Z+Start at the title screen. If you do it correctly, the announcer says, "Goal."

INTERNATIONAL SUPERSTAR SOCCER '98

Bonus Teams
When "Press Start" flashes on the title screen, press Up, C-Up, Up, C-Up, Down, C-Down, Down, C-Down, Left, C-Left, Right, C-Right, Left, C-Left, Right, C-Right, B, A, hold Z, and press Start. A sound confirms correct entry.

World Stars Team
When "Press Start" flashes on the title screen, press Left, C-Left, Right, C-Right, Left, C-Left, Right, C-Right, Down, C-Down, Down, C-Down, Up, C-Up, Up, C-Up, B, A, hold Z, and press Start. A sound confirms correct entry.

Big Heads
When "Press Start" flashes on the title screen, press C-Down (2), C-Up (2), C-Right, C-Left, C-Right, C-Left, B, A, hold Z, and press Start. A sound confirms correct entry.

Call a Foul
When a player is tackled but doesn't fall, hold the D-Pad in any direction and press A+B+L+R.

INTERNATIONAL TRACK AND FIELD 2000

Unlock Pole Vault
Enter the name L.A. in Championship mode.

JEOPARDY!

Bonus Cash

After you answer a question correctly, press L, R, L (3), R (2), C-Down, C-Up.

Different Host

Press R (2), L, R in the Options screen.

JEREMY McGRATH SUPERCROSS

Invisible Rider

At the main menu, press L, C-Up, C-Down, C-Up, C-Down to access Cheat mode. Then type INVISORIDER.

KILLER INSTINCT GOLD

Unlock All Costume Colors

Press Z, B, A, Z, A, L when the story intro appears.

Play As Gargos

Press Z, A, R, Z, A, B when the story intro appears.

View Ending Credits

Press Z, L, A, Z, A, R when the story intro appears.

Random Team Select

After choosing the number of team members, hold Down on the control pad and press Start in either Team or Team Elimination mode.

Random Character Select

Hold Up and press Start when selecting a character.

All Options

Press Z, B, A, L, A, Z during story intro.

Two-Player Mode Level Select: Bridge

Hold Down+QP.

Two-Player Mode Level Select: Dojo

Hold Down+QK.

Two-Player Mode Level Select: Dungeon

Hold Down+MP.

Two-Player Mode Level Select: Helipad

Hold Up+FK.

Two-Player Mode Level Select: Jungle

Hold Up+MP.

Two-Player Mode Level Select: Museum

Hold Up+MK.

Two-Player Mode Level Select: Sky Stage

Hold Down+MK (on both controllers).

Two-Player Mode Level Select: Space Ship

Hold Up+FP.

Two-Player Mode Level Select: Spinal Ship

Hold Down+MK.

Two-Player Mode Level Select: Stonehenge

Hold Up+QK.

Two-Player Mode Level Select: Street

Hold Down+FP.

Two-Player Mode Level Select: Wolf Castle

Hold Up+QP.

KNIFE EDGE: NOSE GUNNER

Super Hard Difficulty

When the Kemco logo appears, hold L+R+C-Up and press C-Right, C-Left, B.

Level Select

Hold all C buttons and R. Press Right, Up, Left, Down when level number appears in Story mode.

KNOCKOUT KINGS 2000

Big Gloves

Pause gameplay and press C-Up, C-Down, C-Up (2), C-Down. A bell sound confirms correct entry. Re-enter the code to return to normal.

Big Heads

Pause gameplay and press C-Left, C-Right, C-Left (2), C-Right. A bell sound confirms correct entry. Re-enter the code to return to normal.

LEGO RACERS

Disable All Cheats

Make a license named NMRCHTS.

Faster Game

Make a license named FSTFRWRD.

Turbo Power-Ups Only

Make a license named PGLLGRN.

No Chassis

Make a license named NCHSSS.

Rocket Car

Make a license named FLYSKYHGH.

Rocket Racer Run Mirror Track

Make a license named LNFRRRM.

Grapple Power-Ups Only

Make a license named RPCRNLY.

Mine Power-Ups Only (Yellow)

Make a license named PGLLYLL.

Shooter Attacks Power-Ups Only (Red)

Make a license named PGLLRD.

No Wheels

Make a license named NWHLS.

No Driver

Make a license named NDRVR.

All Characters

Make license named HIDDNKARACTRS.

No Slow Down

Make a license named NSLWJ.

Pickups at Maximum

Make license named MXPMX.

LODE RUNNER 3-D

Bonus Levels

While paused, hold Z, press C-Down, L, R, L, R, L, R, L, R, L, R. Highlight the "Enter Secret Worlds" option and press A to play the new levels.

Level Select

While paused, hold Z, press R, B, A, B, A, C-Up, C-Down, C-Left, C-Right, C-Up, C-Down, C-Left, C-Right.

MACE: THE DARK AGE

Fight As Pojo

In One- or Two-player mode, perform Taria's execution. Begin another match. At the Character Selection screen, highlight "Taria" and hold Start. Keep holding Start and press Quick.

Fight As Grendal

In Two-player mode, win three times. Begin a another match, and at the Character Selection screen, highlight "Executioner" and hold Start. Keep holding Start and press Quick.

Fight As Gar Gunderson (War Mech) or Ichiro

When you turn on the N64 system, press Right, Up, Left, Down, Right, Up, Left, Down at the first screen. A sound confirms correct entry.

Center Screen

Hold L+R+Z and move the analog stick and D-Pad in the same direction.

Alternate Costumes

When selecting your character, press L, R, C-Up, C-Down, C-Left, or C-Right.

Grendal's Devil Costume

In Two-player mode, win three times to unlock Grendal. At the Character Selection screen, highlight "Executioner" and hold Start. Then press C-Down.

Two-Player Practice Mode

Highlight "Practice" and press Start on controllers 1 and 2 at the same time.

Stage Select

Highlight any fighter and press Start (4), to fight on that character's stage.

Refill Credits

Before you have one credit, press Start on Controller 2. Have Player 2 defeat Player 1 and go on to fight the computer. Press Start on Controller 1. Have Player 1 defeat Player 2.

Mini Golf Course Stage

Highlight Koyasha, Mordus Kull, Takeshi, and press Start after each.

Grendal's Stage

Highlight Namira, Koyasha, Taria, and press Start after each.

Grendal's Stage

Highlight Mordus Kull, Taria, Ragnar, and press Start after each.

Grendal's Stage

Highlight Ichiro, Xiao Long, Koyasha, and press Start after each.

Fight As Ned

Highlight Koyasha, Executioner, Lord Deimos, Xiao Long, and press Start after each.

Big Heads

Highlight Koyasha, Al' Rashid, Takeshi, and press Start after each.

Switch Heads

Highlight Al Rashid, Takeshi, Mordos Kull, Xio Long, Namira, and press Start after each.

Small Characters

Highlight Takeshi, Al' Rashid, Ragnar, Xiao Long, and press Start after each.

The Ultimate Code Book: Book of Secrets

Bunny Slippers
Highlight Ragnar, Dregan, Koyasha, and press Start after each.

Random AI
Highlight Hell Knight, Xiao Long, Dregan, Namira, and press Start after each.

Speed Grid
Highlight Ichiro, Xiao Long, Koyasha, and press Start after each.

San Francisco Rush
Highlight Xiao Long, Al Rashid, Koyasha, and press Start after each.

Macchu Picchu
Highlight Namira, Koyasha, Taria, and press Start after each.

MADDEN NFL 2001

Accessing Cheat Menu
Choose "Secret Codes" under the Settings menu.

Unlock 1957 49ers
Enter GOLDRUSH.

Unlock 1957 Lions
Enter LIONPOWER.

Unlock 1958 Colts
Enter STABLES.

Unlock 1958 Giants
Enter JOLLYGREEN.

Unlock 1962 Oilers
Enter THEREWASAMAN.

Unlock 1962 Texans
Enter GETEM.

Unlock 1966 Chiefs
Enter MEGIVEYOU.

Unlock 1966 Cowboys
Enter WHOSHOTJR.

Unlock 1966 Packers
Enter CHAMPS.

Unlock 1967 Cowboys
Enter TUNDRA.

Unlock 1967 Packers
Enter SNOWPLOW.

Unlock 1967 Rams
Enter BLITZER.

Unlock 1968 Colts
Enter SHOCKER.

Unlock 1968 Jets
Enter TVTIMEOUT.

Unlock 1968 Raiders
Enter HEIDI.

Unlock 1969 Chiefs
Enter NOFLUKE.

Unlock 1969 Vikings
Enter AIIFLUKE.

Unlock 1970 Browns
Enter MNF.

Unlock 1970 Vikings
Enter DAMYANKEES.

Unlock 1971 Chiefs
Enter OVERTIME.

Unlock 1971 Cowboys
Enter STARS.

Unlock 1971 Dolphins
Enter LONGESTGAME.

Unlock 1972 Colts
Enter AIRSHOW.

Unlock 1972 Dolphins
Enter PERFECT.

Unlock 1972 Jets
Enter AIRTIME.

Unlock 1972 Raiders
Enter SOUR.

Unlock 1972 Steelers
Enter LUCKY.

Unlock 1973 Bengals
Enter JUNGLECATS.

Unlock 1974 Dolphins
Enter DEFENDERS.

Unlock 1974 Raiders
Enter STRUGGLE.

Unlock 1974 Steelers
Enter STEELCURTAIN.

Unlock 1974 Vikings
Enter TARK.

Unlock 1975 Cowboys
Enter HAILMARY.

Unlock 1975 Steelers
Enter MIRACLELEAP.

Unlock 1975 Vikings
Enter PURPLE.

Unlock 1977 Colts
Enter GHOSTTOTHEPOST.

Unlock 1977 Raiders
Enter THEGHOST.

Unlock 1978 Chargers
Enter ROLLER.

Unlock 1978 Dolphins
Enter CANNEDTUNA.

Unlock 1978 Oilers
Enter EARL.

Unlock 1978 Raiders
Enter HOLY.

Unlock 1978 Steelers
Enter DYNASTY.

Unlock 1979 Buccaneers
Enter PIRATES.

Unlock 1979 Cowboys
Enter COMEBACK.

Unlock 1981 49ers
Enter THECATCH.

Unlock 1981 Bengals
Enter TIGERS.

Unlock 1981 Chargers
Enter IRONMAN.

Unlock 1981 Cowboys
Enter NOCHANCE.

Unlock 1983 Raiders
Enter HOMESICK.

Unlock 1984 All-Madden Team
Enter MADDEN84.

Unlock 1984 Dolphins
Enter DANTHEMAN.

Unlock 1985 All-Madden Team
Enter MAD1985.

Unlock 1985 Bears
Enter UPSET.

Unlock 1985 Falcons
Enter FLYAWAY.

Unlock 1985 Patriots
Enter BLOWOUT.

Unlock 1986 All-Madden Team
Enter 86MADDEN.

Unlock 1986 Broncos
Enter THEDRIVE.

Unlock 1987 All-Madden Team
Enter 1987MAD.

Unlock 1988 All-Madden Team
Enter MADDEN88.

Unlock 1988 Bengals
Enter NOHOPE.

Unlock 1989 All-Madden Team
Enter MAD1989.

Unlock 1989 Broncos
Enter CRUSHED.

Unlock 1990 All-Madden Team
Enter 90MADDEN.

Unlock 1990 Bills
Enter WIDERIGHT.

Unlock 1990 Raiders
Enter ONEEYE.

Unlock 1991 All-Madden Team
Enter 1991MAD.

Unlock 1991 Falcons
Enter NEONLIGHTS.

Unlock 1991 Lions
Enter TOOMUCH.

Unlock 1992 All-Madden Team
Enter MADDEN92.

Unlock 1992 Bills
Enter COMEBACKKID.

Unlock 1992 Cowboys
Enter HOWBOUTEM.

Unlock 1993 All-Madden Team
Enter MAD1993.

Unlock 1993 Bills
Enter NOTAGAIN.

Unlock 1994 49ers
Enter BYTHEBAY.

Unlock 1994 All-Madden Team
Enter 94MADDEN.

Unlock 1994 Broncos
Enter OUCH.

Unlock 1994 Chargers
Enter CHARGE.

Unlock 1995 All-Madden Team
Enter 1995MAD.

Unlock 1996 All-Madden Team
Enter MADDEN96.

Unlock 1996 Packers
Enter ALMOST.

Unlock 1997 All-Madden Team
Enter MAD1997.

Unlock 1998 49ers
Enter THECATCHTWO.

Unlock 1998 All-Madden Team
Enter 98MADDEN.

Unlock 1998 Packers
Enter NOLUCK.

Unlock 1998 Vikings
Enter MISSEDCHANCE.

Unlock 1999 All-Madden Team
Enter 1999MAD.

Unlock 1999 Rams
Enter NOWHEREMAN.

Unlock 1999 Titans
Enter MIRACLEPLAY.

Unlock 1960 Eagles
Enter GREENWINGS.

Unlock 1977 Cowboys
Enter USATEAM.

Unlock All 49ers Team
Enter GOLDNINERS.

Unlock All Bears Team
Enter BROWNBEAR.

Unlock All Bills Team
Enter BLUEBILLS.

Unlock All Broncos Team
Enter BUCKINGBRONCO.

Unlock All Chargers Team
Enter BLUECHARGERS.

Unlock All Chiefs Team
Enter REDCHIEFS.

Unlock All Colts Team
Enter WHITECOLTS.

Unlock All Cowboys Team
Enter BLUECOWBOYS.

Unlock All Dolphins Team
Enter AQUAFINS.

Unlock All Eagles Team
Enter GREENEAGLES.

Unlock All Falcons Team
Enter BLACKFALCONS.

Unlock All Giants Team
Enter BIGGIANTS.

Unlock All Jets Team
Enter GREENJETS.

Unlock All Lions Team
Enter SILVERLIONS.

Unlock All Packers Team
Enter YELLOWPACK.

Unlock All Panthers Team
Enter BIGCATS.

Unlock All Patriots Team
Enter REDPATS.

Unlock All Raiders Team
Enter SILVERRAID.

Unlock All Rams Team
Enter GOLDRAMS.

Unlock All Redskins Team
Enter REDINDIANS.

Unlock All Saints Team
Enter MARCHINGIN.

Unlock All Steelers team
Enter BLACKSTEEL.

Unlock All Vikings Team
Enter CONQUER.

Unlock EA Sports Team
Enter INTHEGAME.

Unlock Mummies Team
Enter KINGTUT.

Acquire the Final Madden Card
Buy all Gold, Silver, and Bronze Madden Cards in each set. After all 296 cards are obtained, a 297th card (number 000) with the All-Time Madden team is unlocked.

Unlimited Madden Card Use
Unlock a Madden Card and save your profile before adding the card to the loaded game. Then, select the "Add Player to Roster" option, and reset the Nintendo 64.

Always Receive
When playing against the CPU, press Start at the Coin Toss screen before anything appears.

MADDEN NFL 64

Large Players
In Season mode, enter the Front Office menu and create a player named Tiburon. Use Continue and save the player. Press B (2), and select Exhibition mode to return to the Game Selection screen.

Larger, More Powerful Players
In Season mode, enter the Front Office menu and create a player named Elec Arts. Use Continue and save the player. Press B (2), and select Exhibition mode to return to the Game Selection screen.

1960s Team
In Season mode, enter the Front Office menu and create a player named Sixties. Use Continue and save the player. Press B (2), and select Exhibition mode to return to the Game Selection screen.

1970s Team
In Season mode, enter the Front Office menu and create a player named Seventies. Use Continue and save the player. Press B (2), and select Exhibition mode to return to the Game Selection screen.

1980s Team
In Season mode, enter the Front Office menu and create a player named Eighties. Use Continue and save the player. Press B (2), and select Exhibition mode to return to the Game Selection screen.

1997 AFC Pro Bowl Team
In Season mode, enter the Front Office menu and create a player named B Howlie. Use Continue and save the player. Press B (2), and select Exhibition mode to return to the Game Selection screen.

1997 NFC Pro Bowl Team
In Season mode, enter the Front Office menu and create a player named Lei. Use Continue and save the player. Press B (2), and select Exhibition mode to return to the Game Selection screen.

All-Time Madden Team
In Season mode, enter the Front Office menu and create a player named AT Madden. Use Continue and save the player. Press B (2), and select Exhibition mode to return to the Game Selection screen.

Stats Leader Team
In Season mode, enter the Front Office menu and create a player named Stats Men. Use Continue and save the player. Press B (2), and select Exhibition mode to return to the Game Selection screen.

Tiburon Stadium
In Season mode, enter the Front Office menu and create a player named Maitland. Use Continue and save the player. Press B (2), and select Exhibition mode to return to the Game Selection screen.

EA Stadium
In Season mode, enter the Front Office menu and create a player named San Mateo. Use Continue and save the player. Press B (2), and select Exhibition mode to return to the Game Selection screen.

View Ending Sequence
As the game starts, hold L+R+Z at the EA logo.

Always Win Coin Toss
When the ref tosses the coin, press Down for tails. For heads, press Up two seconds before the coin lands.

MADDEN NFL '99

NFL Pro Bowl Team
At the Code Entry screen, press A on New Code. Enter BESTNFC and press A. Highlight "Add Code" and press A. Now begin a game in Exhibition mode.

AFC Pro Bowl Team
At the Code Entry screen, press A on New Code. Enter AFCBEST and press A. Highlight "Add Code" and press A. Now begin a game in Exhibition mode.

All-Madden Team
At the Code Entry screen, press A on New Code. Enter BOOM and press A. Highlight "Add Code" and press A. Now begin a game in Exhibition mode.

All-Time Stat Leaders Team
At the Code Entry screen, press A on New Code. Enter IMTHEMAN and press A. Highlight "Add Code" and press A. Now begin a game in Exhibition mode.

1960s Greats Team
At the Code Entry screen, press A on New Code. Enter PEACELOVE and press A. Highlight "Add Code" and press A. Now begin a game in Exhibition mode.

1970s Greats Team
At the Code Entry screen, press A on New Code. Enter BELLBOTTOMS and press A. Highlight "Add Code" and press A. Now begin a game in Exhibition mode.

1980s Greats Team
At the Code Entry screen, press A on New Code. Enter SPRBWLSHUFL and press A. Highlight "Add Code" and press A. Now begin a game in Exhibition mode.

1990s Greats Team
At the Code Entry screen, press A on New Code. Enter HEREANDNOW and press A. Highlight "Add Code" and press A. Now begin a game in Exhibition mode.

All-Time Greats Team
At the Code Entry screen, press A on New Code. Enter TURKEYLEG and press A. Highlight "Add Code" and press A. Now begin a game in Exhibition mode.

75th Anniversary Team
At the Code Entry screen, press A on New Code. Enter THROWBACK and press A. Highlight "Add Code" and press A. Now begin a game in Exhibition mode.

NFL Equipment Team
At the Code Entry screen, press A on New Code. Enter GEARGUYS and press A. Highlight "Add Code" and press A. Now begin a game in Exhibition mode.

1999 Cleveland Browns
At the Code Entry screen, press A on New Code. Enter WELCOMEBACK and press A. Highlight "Add Code" and press A. Now begin a game in Exhibition mode.

EA Sports Team
At the Code Entry screen, press A on New Code. Enter INTHEGAME and press A. Highlight "Add Code" and press A. Now begin a game in Exhibition mode.

Tiburon Team
At the Code Entry screen, press A on New Code. Enter HAMMERHEAD and press A. Highlight "Add Code" and press A. Now begin a game in Exhibition mode.

Tiburon Stadium
At the Code Entry screen, press A on New Code. Enter OURHOUSE and press A. Highlight "Add Code" and press A. Now begin a game in Exhibition mode.

EA Sports Stadium
At the Code Entry screen, press A on New Code. Enter EASTADIUM and press A. Highlight "Add Code" and press A. Now begin a game in Exhibition mode.

Tomato Quarterback
At the Code Entry screen, press A on New Code. Enter SPLAT and press A. Highlight "Add Code" and press A. Now begin a game in Exhibition mode.

Faster Runningbacks
At the Code Entry screen, press A on New Code. Enter TURBO_TIME and press A. Highlight "Add Code" and press A. Now begin a game in Exhibition mode. Press A during gameplay to run faster.

Random Stadiums
At the Stadium Select screen, press R or Z.

Dancing Ref
During the coin toss, press B (2), A, C-Up.

Always Receive
During the coin toss, keep pressing Start.

MADDEN NFL 2000

100-Yard Field Goals
Enter BIGFOOT in the Code screen.

5-Yard First Downs
Enter POPWARNER in the Code screen.

20-Yard First Downs
Enter FIRSTIS20 in the Code screen.

Clowns Fantasy Team
Enter SCARYCLOWN in the Code screen.

Comets Fantasy Team
Enter ONESMALLSTEP in the Code screen.

EA Sports Team
Enter WEARETHEGAME in the Code screen.

Madden Millennium Team
Enter TIMELESS in the Code screen.

Industrials Team
Enter INTHEFUTURE in the Code screen.

Marshall's Fantasy Team
Enter COWBOYS in the Code screen.

Junkyard Dog Team
Enter TETANUS in the Code screen.

Toymaker Team
Enter SANTATEAM in the Code screen.

Tiburon Fantasy Team
Enter SHARKATTACK in the Code screen.

Mummies Team
Enter YOMUMMY in the Code screen.

Sugarbuzz Team
Enter PANCAKE in the Code screen.

Praetorians Team
Enter WESALUTEYOU in the Code screen.

Circus Stadium
Enter 3RING in the Code screen.

Dodge City Stadium
Enter WILDWEST in the Code screen.

EA Sports Stadium
Enter ITSINTHEGAME in the Code screen.

X-Mas Rush Stadium
Enter XMASGIFT in the Code screen.

Quick Fatigue
Enter CHAINSMOKER in the Code screen.

Bullet Passes
Enter FASTFORWARD in Code screen.

Defensive Points I
Enter FRACORAS in the Code screen. Defense gets two points for sacks and one for interceptions.

Defensive Points II
Enter FRAPLAPRO in the Code screen. Defense gets one point for sacks and two for interceptions.

Electric Sidelines
Enter STATICCLING or WOOGAWOOGA in the Code screen.

Easier to Catch Football
Enter MAGNASAVE in the Code screen.

Big vs. Small Team
Enter MICEANDMEN in the Code screen.

Floating Heads
Enter GUILLOTINE in the Code screen.

Weird Ball Physics
Enter EMC2 in the Code screen.

More Injuries
Enter PAINFUL in the Code screen.

Harder to Tackle Players
Enter TEFLON in the Code screen.

Jump Farther
Enter SPRONG in the Code screen.

Run Faster
Enter NO2 in the Code screen.

No Interceptions
Enter VICEGRIP in the Code screen.

Fewer Penalties
Enter REFISBLIND in the Code screen.

Multiple Passes
Enter MULTIQB in the Code screen to throw the ball as many times forward and backward as you want in one play.

No Sacked Quarterbacks
Enter QBINTHECLUB in the Code screen.

Ball Camera
Enter VERTIGO in the Code screen.

Always Win Coin Toss
Keep pressing Start repeatedly at the Toss screen.

20-Yard First Down
Enter FIRSTIS20 in the Code screen.

100-Yard Passes
Enter PIGSKINSFLY in the Code screen.

All 1960s Team
Enter MOJOBABY in the Code screen.

All 1970s Team
Enter SIDEBURNS in the Code screen.

All 1980s Team
Enter REAGANOMICS in the Code screen.

All-Madden Team
Enter TEAMMADDEN in the Code screen.

More Fumbles
Enter ROLLERJAM in the Code screen.

More Interceptions
Enter PICKEDOFF in the Code screen.

Super Jump
Enter SUPERJUMPS in the Code screen.

Super Speed Burst
Enter GOTTHEROCK in the Code screen.

Super Stiff Arm
Enter SMACKDOWN in the Code screen.

TDs 10 points, FGs 7 points
Enter DRBENWAY in the Code screen.

MAGICAL TETRIS CHALLENGE

Tetris Status Bar
Start a gain in Endless mode. Tap A+B during gameplay. A Tetris status bar appears on the right side of the screen.

Magical Meter Shortening
Clear all the blocks. An "ALL CLEAR" message appears if you got it right.

NINTENDO 64

MAH-JONGG MASTER

Open All Characters
While the opening demo plays, enter the following code on the D-Pad: up (2), down (2), left, right, left, right, B, A, Start. Access the Free Battle Kulong Mode to use all 19 computer characters.

MAJOR LEAGUE BASEBALL FEATURING KEN GRIFFEY, JR.

Bonus Teams
Highlight Exhibition and keep pressing C-Left+C-Right+C-Up+C-Down. A sound confirms correct entry.

View Ending Sequence
In Exhibition mode, choose the same team for both home and visitor. Then press C-Left, C-Right, C-Left (2), C-Right, C-Down, C-Up, Z at the Stadium Selection screen. A sound confirms correct entry.

Dancing Batter
Press Up (2), Down, Left (2), Right (2), Left (2), Down, Up (2) while batting.

Dancing Pitcher
Press Up (2), Down, Left (2), Right (2), Left (2), Down, Up (2) while pitching.

Flying Outfielder
When a pop fly is hit to the outfield, let the ball drop. Then pick it up. Hold Z and press C-Up to run into the infield. Press C-Right, C-Up, C-Left, C-Down, C-Left, C-Up, C-Down, C-Right, C-Up, C-Left, C-Down to throw the ball around. The crowd will boo. The next time the ball is hit to the outfield, ignore it and press A or B to fly.

Exploding Batter
Quickly press Right, Left, Down, Right, Left, Up, Right, Left, Down while batting.

Fireworks
Go to View Stadium mode and press R+Z.

Automatic Home Run
When controlling Ken Griffey Jr. at bat, press Left (2), Right (3), Left (2). Griffey Jr. points his bat toward where the ball will be hit. Now just hit the next ball.

Alternate Uniform Color
In Exhibition mode, choose to be the home team. After selecting Play Ball, keep pressing C-Left+C-Right+C-Up+C-Down at the black screen until the players run onto the field.

Start a Fight

MEGAMAN 64

Unlock Hard Difficulty Level
Complete the Game.

Unlock Easy Difficulty Setting
Complete the game under the Hard difficulty level.

Complete Grade A
Play the Beast Hunter game at the Studio to get 4,000 gold.

Begin Game with Buster Max and Jet Skates
Complete the game in the Hard difficulty setting.

Color Change to Black Megaman
After defeating Bruno, turn on the TV, then go downtown. Shoot the red car coming toward you, and pick up the suitcase. Don't talk to the detective, and walk to the south door. Tell the character that you want to keep the money.

MICRO MACHINES 64 TURBO

Tanks on All Tracks
Type your name as ALLTANKS in the Character Select screen in Multiplayer mode.

Nine Lives in Challenge Mode
Enter the name MOGSLIFE in Character Select screen.

Maximum Bounce
While paused, press C-Left, Right (2), Down, Up, Down, Left, Down (2). Re-enter the code to disable it.

Computer Opponents Slowed Down
While paused, press C-Right, C-Up, C-Left, C-Down, C-Right, C-Up, C-Left, C-Down. Re-enter the code to disable it.

Speed Boost at Start
Press Z+B before the race begins.

Change Cars
While paused, press Down (2), Up (2), Right (2), Left (2) in Challenge mode.

Behind Car Perspective
While paused, press Left, Right, C-Left, C-Right, Left, Right, C-Left, C-Right. Re-enter the code to disable it.

Turbo Speed
While paused, press C-Left, C-Down, C-Right, C-Left, C-Up, C-Down (4). Re-enter the code to disable it.

Debug Mode
While paused, press C-Left, Up, Down (2), C-Left, C-Right (2), C-Up, C-Down. Then enter any of the following codes.

Instant Win
In Debug mode, press C-Down+Z. This can't be done during time trials.

Destroy All Cars
In Debug mode, hold Z and press C-Up+C-Right+C-Left during gameplay.

Change Camera Angle
In Debug mode, hold Z and press Left, Right, Up, or Down during gameplay.

Change Camera Depth
In Debug mode, hold Z and press L or R during gameplay.

CPU Controlled Car
In Debug mode, hold Z and press C-Left during gameplay.

MIKE PIAZZA'S STRIKEZONE

Access Cheat Mode
At the Pre-game menu, press L, R, L, R.

Devil's Thumb Stadium
Enable Cheat mode and press Right, A, C-Up, L, A.

Super Players
Enable Cheat mode and press B, A, R, B, A, L (2).

Better Throws
Enable Cheat mode and press B, A, L, Down, Z.

Better Plays
Enable Cheat mode and press B, A, R, Down, L, B.

Faster Fielders
Enable Cheat mode and press R, A, Z, L, Down, A, Z, L.

Better Pitches
Enable Cheat mode and press B, L, A, B, R, Z.

Faster Pitches
Enable Cheat mode and press R, A, Z, L, Down.

Crazy Pitches
Enable Cheat mode and press C-Right, A, Z, C-Up, R, B.

Varied Pitches
Enable Cheat mode and press C-Right, A, Z, C-Up, R, L.

Always Hit Home Runs
Enable Cheat mode and press L, A, Down, R.

Crazy Ball
Enable Cheat mode and press C-Right, A, Z, B, A, L (2).

Easy Steals
Enable Cheat mode and press C-Left, A, Down, C-Up, Z.

Aluminum Bats
Enable Cheat mode and press R, A, Z, B, A, L (2).

Red Bats
Enable Cheat mode and press R, Down, B, A, Right.

Blue Bats
Enable Cheat mode and press B, L, B, A, Right.

Psychedelic Bats
Enable Cheat mode and press Z, B, R, A.

Low Gravity
Enable Cheat mode and press Up, R, A, L.

Increased Gravity
Enable Cheat mode and press Up, Down, L, Up, R.

Fast Ball
Enable Cheat mode and press L, A, Z, R, B, A, L (2).

Slow Game
Enable Cheat mode and press Up, L (2), B, A, L (2).

Alternate Sky
Enable Cheat mode and press C-Right, A, Z, C-Up, L, R, Z.

Bonus Teams
Enable Cheat mode and press C-Right, A, Down, Left at the title screen.

Hidden Message
Enable Cheat mode and press C-Up, R, B (2) at the title screen.

View Credits
Enable Cheat mode and press R, A, Z, R, C-Right, A, B at the title screen.

MILO'S ASTRO LANES

Code Limits
You may enter only one code per turn and three codes per match.

Mega/Pea Ball
When your character's ball is rolling, press L (2), R (2), L, R.

White Dwarf/Spring Ball
When your character's ball is rolling, press R (2), R, L (3).

Turbo/Goo Ball
When your character's ball is rolling, press R (2), L (2), R, L.

Clone/Bomb Ball
When your character's ball is rolling, press L (3), R (3).

Green Screen
When it's your turn to bowl, press R, L, R, L (2), R. A sound confirms correct entry.

Swing Arm
When it's your turn to bowl, press L, R, L, R (2), L. A sound confirms correct entry.

Automatic Power-Ups
When it's your turn to bowl, press R (2), L, R (2), L. A sound confirms correct entry.

All Domes Available
When it's your turn to bowl, press Up (2), Down (2), L, R, L, R, B, A, B, A. A sound confirms correct entry.

MISCHIEF MAKERS

Sound Test
At the title screen, press Left+A+C-Left+C-Right+Start.

Bonus Levels
Get all 52 gold gems and watch the entire ending sequence. At the last screen with the stages, press R.

MISSION: IMPOSSIBLE

God Mode
Press R, Z, C-Down, R, C-Down at the Level Select screen.

Infinite Ammo
Press C-Up, Z, C-Left, Z, L at the Level Select screen.

Turbo Mode
Press C-Up, Z, C-Up, Z, C-Up at the Level Select screen.

Kid Mode
Press C-Down, C-Up, R, L, Z at the Level Select screen.

Big Head Mode
Press C-Down, R, C-Up, L, C-Left at the Level Select screen.

Giant Head Mode
Press C-Down, L, C-Up, C-Right, L at the Level Select screen.

Big Feet Mode
Press C-Down, R, Z, C-Right, C-Left at the Level Select screen.

Start with 7.65 Silenced Pistol
Press C-Up, L, C-Right, C-Left, C-Up at the Level Select screen.

Start with Uzi
Press C-Right, C-Left, C-Right, C-Down, R at the Level Select screen.

Start with Powerful 9mm Pistol
Press R, L, C-Down, C-Up (2) at the Level Select screen.

Start with Mini Rocket Launcher
Press R, L, C-Left, C-Right, C-Down at the Level Select screen.

Bonus Level
Beat the game and watch the credits. Do nothing until after the Infogrames logo disappears. You'll appear in the embassy. Production and design team members stand around. Talk to them all and Candice and Ethan will enter the room.

MONOPOLY

Mr. Potato Head Token
Rename the Moneybag token Potato.

Gold Token
Rename any token Aurum.

Control View
Rename any token Wander. Then, during gameplay, press Z. Press C-Up; then A to zoom in or B to zoom out.

Expert Mode
Rename any token Ace.

MONSTER TRUCK MADNESS 64

Low-Rider Trucks
Enter YRDR.

Full Time Missiles
Enter Y WNT T. Then press Left during gameplay.

Gut Bomb
Enter BRPS.

Turbo Mode
Enter CFFNYN.

Programmer Images
Enter JMPNG.

Weird Textures
Enter JMPR. Select Done; then press Start. Select New Game and choose Summit Rumble.

Jet Pack Power-Up
At the main menu, hold L+R+C-Left+C-Right+C-Up+C-Down and press Start.

Beginner Level Password: Ruins
G(Up Arrow)(Star)NJ2L0

Beginner Level Password: Junk Yard
J(Star)XQYN4G

Beginner Level Password: The Heights
M(Star)OT1Q9R(Left Arrow)

Beginner Level Password: Voodoo Island
P(Left Arrow)3W4TC(Star)(Left Arrow)F(Up Arrow)

Beginner Level Password: Greenhill Pass
5(Up Arrow)627WFX9(Left Arrow)23G

Beginner Level Password: Wasteland
V(Left Arrow)92(Up Arrow)2(Down Arrow)0CL56B5V

Beginner Level Password: Aztec Valley
YYC5D2L3F(Right Arrow)89(Down Arrow)8(Right Arrow)B7level

Intermediate Level Password: Ruins
GBGJ5MTL

Intermediate Level Password: Junk Yard
JNJMQL7S

Intermediate Level Password: The Heights
MJMPT(Right Arrow)XRN

Intermediate Level Password: Voodoo Island
PJPSWR0(Star)89R

Intermediate Level Password: Greenhill Pass
SBSV2(Star)3XBC(Up Arrow)4(Down Arrow)

Intermediate Level Password: Wasteland
VBVY2X60(Down Arrow)FD7B2M

Intermediate Level Password: Aztec Valley
YFY15093H(Left Arrow)G(Up Arrow)(Down Arrow)5675

Intermediate Level Password: Alpine Challenge
1N1483C6KLJDH89(Up Arrow)G4N

Expert Level Password: Ruins
GKGH(Up Arrow)G(Star)(Left Arrow)

Expert Level Password: Junk Yard
JGJKLJP(Star)

Expert Level Password: The Heights
MSMN(Right Arrow)M7QW

Expert Level Password: Voodoo Island
PKPQRP(Up Arrow)T793

Expert Level Password: Greenhill Pass
SKST(Star)SDW(Up Arrow)C61R

Expert Level Password: Wasteland
VOVWXVGZDF9463R

Expert Level Password: Aztec Valley
YGY209YJ2G(Left Arrow)C796462

Expert Level Password: Alpine Challenge
101231M5JLF(Up Arrow)C979S0D

Expert Level Password: Death Trap
404564P8M(Right Arrow)(Left Arrow)DFC(Up Arrow)CV32KC

MORTAL KOMBAT 4

Access Cheat Menu
Enter the Options screen and highlight "Continues." Then hold C-Left+C-Down until a sound confirms the code.

Play as Goro
Beat the game with Shinnok. Enable the Cheat menu code. Select Hidden on the Character Select screen. Now press Up (3), and Left. The cursor will be on Shinnok. Now press Run+Block to play as Goro.

Play as Meat
Go to Group mode. Win all your games using all 16 characters. After you play and win with the final character, pick any character. Your character will play as Meat with the same moves as the character you chose.

Play as Noob Saibot
Beat the game with Reiko. Enable the Cheat menu code. Select Hidden on the Character Select screen. Now press Up (2), Left. The cursor will be on Reiko. Now press Run+Block to play as Noob Saibot.

Different Ending with Cage

Highlight Johnny Cage in Character Select screen. Hold Start and press C-Up (3). Cage will be wearing a tuxedo. He has a different weapon. Complete the game with him to view a different ending.

Kai's New Weapon

Beat the game with Kai. Begin a new game to get Raiden's staff as a new weapon.

Alternate Costumes

Highlight a character in the Character Select screen. Hold Block and press any button to rotate the character's picture. Rotate a picture twice to get the second costume. Rotate Sonya and Tonya's pictures three times to get the second costume. Rotate other characters' pictures three times to get a third costume.

Alternate Weapons

Highlight a character in Character Select screen. Hold Block and press any button three times. The character will have an alternate weapon.

Endings

Enable the Endings option in the Cheat menu. Then start a game in Character mode and defeat one character.

Fatalities 1

Enable the Fatalities 1 option in the Cheat menu. To finish your opponent with a fatality, hold Down and press High Punch.

Fatalities 2

Enable the Fatalities 2 option in the Cheat menu. To finish your opponent with a fatality, hold Down and press High Punch.

Level Fatalities

Enable the level Fatalities option in the Cheat menu. To perform a level fatality, hold Down and press High Punch.

Unlimited Run

At the Two-player Vs. screen, first player Low Kick, second player Low Kick.

Weapon Kombat

At the Two-player Vs. screen, first player Low Kick (2), second player Low Kick (2).

Maximum Damage

At the Two-player Vs. screen, first player Block, second player Block.

Noob Saibot

At the Two-player Vs. screen, first player Block, Low Kick (2), second player Block, Low Kick (2).

Red Rain

At the Two-player Vs. screen, first player Block (2), second player Block (2).

Explosive Kombat

At the Two-player Vs. screen, first player Block (5), second player Block (5).

Throwing Disabled

At the Two-player Vs. screen, first player Low Punch, second player Low Punch.

Maximum Damage and Throwing Disabled

At the Two-player Vs. screen, first player Low Punch, Block, second player Low Punch, Block.

Free Weapon

At the Two-player Vs. screen, first player Low Punch, Block, Low Kick, second player Low Punch, Block, Low Kick.

No Power

At the Two-player Vs. screen, first player Low Punch, Block (2), Low Kick (3), second player Low Punch, Block (2), Low Kick (3).

Random Weapons

At the Two-player Vs. screen, first player Low Punch (2), Block (2), Low Kick (2), second player Low Punch (2), Block (2), Low Kick (2).

Big Head Mode

At the Two-player Vs. screen, first player Low Punch (3), Block (2), Low Kick, second player Low Punch (3), Block (2), Low Kick.

Randper Kombat

At the Two-player Vs. screen, first player Low Punch (3), Block (3), Low Kick (3), second player Low Punch (3), Block (3), Low Kick (3).

Armed and Dangerous

At the Two-player Vs. screen, first player Low Punch (4), Block (4), Low Kick (4), second player Low Punch (4), Block (4), Low Kick (4).

Many Weapons

At the Two-player Vs. screen, first player Low Punch (5), Block (5), Low Kick (5), second player Low Punch (5), Block (5), Low Kick (5).

Silent Kombat

At the Two-player Vs. screen, first player Low Punch (6), Block (6), Low Kick (6), second player Low Punch (6), Block (6), Low Kick (6).

Goro's Lair

At the Two-player Vs. screen, first player Block, Low Kick, second player Block, Low Kick.

The Well

At the Two-player Vs. screen, first player Block (2), Low Kick (2), second player Block (2), Low Kick (2).

Elder Gods

At the Two-player Vs. screen, first player Block (3), Low Kick (3), second player Block (3), Low Kick (3).

Tomb Stage

At the Two-player Vs. screen, first player Block (4), Low Kick (4), second player Block (4), Low Kick (4).

Rain Stage

At the Two-player Vs. screen, first player Block (5), Low Kick (5), second player Block (5), Low Kick (5).

Snake Stage

At the Two-player Vs. screen, first player Block (6), Low Kick (6), second player Block (6), Low Kick (6).

The Dojo

At the Two-player Vs. screen, first player Low Punch, Low Kick, second player Low Punch, Low Kick.

Living Forest

At the Two-player Vs. screen, first player Low Punch (2), Low Kick (2), second player Low Punch (2), Low Kick (2).

Prison

At the Two-player Vs. screen, first player Low Punch (3), Low Kick (3), second player Low Punch (3), Low Kick (3).

Snow Stage

At the Two-player Vs. screen, first player Low Punch (3), Block, Low Kick (3), second player Low Punch (3), Block, Low Kick (3).

MORTAL KOMBAT MYTHOLOGIES: SUB-ZERO

Unlimited Urns

Enter NXCVSR.

1,000 Lives

Enter GTTBHR.

View Credits

Enter CRVDTS.

Invincibility

Enter TDFCLT.

Final Battles

Enter ZCHRRY. Before Sub-Zero dies before a checkpoint, hold L+A to face Quan Chi, or hold L+B to face Shinnok.

Level 2, Wind Password

THWMSB

Level 3, Earth Password

CNSZDG

Level 4, Water Password

ZVRKDM

Level 5, Fire Password

JYPPHD

Level 6, Prison Password

RGTKCS

Level 7, Bridge Password

QFTLWN

Level 8, Fortress Password

XJKNZT

MORTAL KOMBAT TRILOGY

Unlimited Credits

At the Story screen, press Down (2), Up (2), Right (2), Left (2). Lose the next match for freeplay.

Extra Options

Press Up+Start at the Kombat Mode Selection screen.

Enable Both ? Menus

At the Story screen, quickly press Block, High Kick, Low Kick, Run, Low Punch, High Punch (3), Low Punch (2).

Bonus *Galaga*-Type Game

Fight 100 two-player matches in a row.

Bonus *Pong* Game

Fight 50 two-player matches in a row.

Bonus *Space Invaders*-Type Game

When playing in Two-player mode on the pit stage, press Z when an object appears over the moon. The winner cam play Invaders from Space.

Stage Select

Highlight Sonya and press Up+Start.

Random Character Select

Highlight Noob Saibot for Player 1, or Rain for Player 2. Then hold Up and press Start.

Fight Khameleon

When you hear "Toasty" on the Star Bridge, quickly press Down+Start.

Fight as Human Smoke

Select Cyber-Ninja. Before the Fight screen appears, hold Away+High Punch+High Kick+Run+Block.

The Ultimate Code Book: Book of Secrets

Fight as Motaro
Select any character and play on either Jade's Desert, Khan's Tower, or The Wasteland stages. Then before the match begins, hold Away+Low Kick+High Kick.

Fight as Shao Kahn
Select any character and play on either the Rooftop, Pit Three, or Khan's Cave stages. Then before the match begins, hold Down+High Punch+Low Punch.

Fight as Khameleon
At the story screen, press C-Right, C-Up, A, B, C-Down, C-Up, C-Right.

Super Endurance Mode
In Single-player, highlight "Kano" and press Down+Start. Now choose your character and select the hardest path.

Kombat Kodes Key
At the Vs. screen, press Low Punch, Block, and Low Kick to set the six boxes at the bottom of the screen. The numbers that follow represent the symbols that will appear in the boxes. Tap the button to advance, or hold the button to go back. Codes marked with an asterisk (*) are new for MKT: 0 = Dragon, 1 = MK, 2 = Yin-yang, 3 = 3, 4 = Question Mark, 5 = Lightning, 6 = Goro, 7 = Rayden, 8 = Shao Kahn, 9 = Skull.

Fast Uppercut Recovery
788-322

No Power
044-440

Silent Kombat
300-300

Throwing Disabled
100-100

Throwing Encouraged
010-010

Blocking Disabled
020-020

Winner Fights Smoke
205-205

Winner Fights Noob
769-342

Winner Fights Shao Kahn
969-141

Winner fights Motaro
033-564

Randper Kombat
444-444

No Fear
282-282

Flipper Message
987-666

Wavenet UMK3 Message
550-550

Version Number Message
999-999

Don't Jump at Me
448-844

Rain Is in the Graveyard
717-313

Skunky!
122-221

Ed Boon Message
004-400

No Powerbars
987-123

Dark Fighting
688-422

Psycho Kombat
985-125

Play Hidden Game
642-468

Uppercut Recovery
788-322

Unlimited Running
466-466

Super Run Jumps
321-789

Health Recovery
975-310

Combos Disabled
722-722

Special Moves Disabled
555-556

Super Endurance Kombat
024-689

Automatic Kombos*
484-484

Bloody Kombat*
109-901

Babalities Are Reversible*
202-808

Winner Fights Khameleon*
123-321

Play Pong*
246-246

Explosive Kombat/Throwing Disable (2-on-2 and 3-on-3)
022-220

Explosive Kombat (2-on-2 and 3-on-3)
227-227

Jade's Desert Zone
330-033

Scorpion's Lair Zone
666-444

Bell Tower Zone
091-190

Graveyard Zone
666-333

Scislac Busorez Zone
933-933

Subway Zone
880-088

Noob's Dorfen Zone
050-050

The Roof Zone
343-343

Pit III Zone
820-028

Kahn's Kave Zone
004-700

River Kombat Zone
002-003

Kombat Temple Zone
600-040

The Street Zone
079-035

The Soul Chamber Zone
123-901

The Bridge Zone
077-022

Kahn's Tower Zone
880-220

Dead Pool Zone*
222-222

The Armory Zone*
191-191

The Pit Zone*
919-919

Star Bridge Zone*
606-606

The Tower Zone*
101-010

The Portal Zone*
007-007

The Pit II Zone*
166-661

The Courtyard Zone*
121-121

The Wasteland Zone*
212-212

The Lair Zone*
000-666

MS. PAC-MAN: MAZE MADNESS

Unlock Bonus Multiplayer Map
Get a score of over 50,000 at the Pier Pressure round. Save the game, quit, then select the "Multiplayer" option on the main menu to find the new bonus map.

MULTI-RACING CHAMPIONSHIP

Use Locked Cars
In Two-player mode, select one of the inaccessible garages. Quit Two-player mode and start a one-player race without selecting another car.

Race Against Hannya
In Championship mode, win all three courses.

Race with Hannya Car
Defeat Hannya on all three courses. You also may race against Due.

Match Race Mode
Place first in Championship mode under each difficulty level.

Race with Dues Car and Reversed Tracks
Defeat Dues on all three courses.

Quick Start
When the timer reaches 1, hold Accelerate.

MYSTICAL NINJA STARRING GOEMON

Unlock Boss Mode in Options
Collect 45 Fortune Dolls.

Bonus Image
Enable the Boss mode code. Go into the Boss mode option and complete the Boss sequence.

Infinite Items and Gold
Find an area that contains multiple items or gold. Collect the items and leave the room. Re-enter and items become available again.

Rumble Pak Option
Boss mode can support the Rumble Pak, even though the game wasn't designed to handle it.

Move Impact's Head
Push the analog stick to move Impact's head at the end of Impact's intro sequence.

NAGANO OLYMPIC HOCKEY '98

Constant Fights
In Options, highlight "Fighting", hold L and press C-Right, C-Left (2), C-Right, C-Down, C-Up (2), C-Down, C-Left, C-Right (2), C-Left, C-Right, C-Left.

Multiplayer Practice Mode
With A held on Controllers 2, 3, and/or 4, use Controller 1 to highlight "Practice" and press A.

Quick Start
At the main menu, hold B and press Start.

Select Computer Opponent
Highlight the opponent you wish to play against and press C-Right (3). A click confirms correct entry.

Lose Game
Pause gameplay, hold L and press C-Left (9). Then resume gameplay. You may have to enter this code twice.

Invisible Players
During the face-off, pause gameplay and select Replay. Press L or R to make a player flash. Press Z to make that player invisible.

Change Player Appearance Key
At the Options screen, edit the first 6 bits of a 16-bit register. Use: C-Down+R (head size, alters bits 1 and 2); C-Left+R (body size, alters bits 3 and 4); C-Up+R (announcer's voice, alters bits 5 and 6).

Change Player Appearance: Stocky Players
100000

Change Player Appearance: Stocky Players, Big Heads
010000

Change Player Appearance: Stocky Players, Small Heads
110000

Change Player Appearance: Small Players, Small Announcer
001000

Change Player Appearance: Large Players, Large Announcer
000100

Change Player Appearance: Crunched Players, Small Announcer
000010

Change Player Appearance: Elongated Players, Large Announcer
000001

Change Player Appearance: Large Players, Small Heads, Large Announcer
110110

Change Player Appearance: Crunched Players, Large Heads, Small Announcer
010010

Change Player Appearance: Large Players, Large Heads, Large Announcer
010101

Change Player Appearance: Elongated Players, Large Heads, Large Announcer
010001

Special Medal Sequences
Win a medal in all events, then at the Awards screen, press Up (2), Down (2), Left, Right, Left, Right, B, A to view the first sequence. To view the second sequence, press Up (2), Down (2), L, R, L, R, B, A.

NAMCO MUSEUM 64

Two Fighters: *Galaga*
Shoot one of the green ships on top to turn it blue. When it dives alone, intentionally allow your fighter to be captured by its tractor beam. Then using your next ship, wait until that one dives again. Shoot the alien ship while avoiding your fighter. Now you'll have two fighters with twice the firepower.

Keep Enemies from Shooting: *Galaga*
On Level 1, allow the alien ships to get into formation. Kill all of them except for the bee in the bottom-left corner, then put your ship in the bottom-right corner. Allow him to fly around. After the first pass with him not firing, allow him to pass again. Shoot him during the second pass if he is still not firing. This keeps the enemy from firing for the rest of the game.

NASCAR '99

Race as Bobby Allison
Set the Controller Configuration to 3. Then select the Charlotte track, highlight "Select Car," and press C-Up, C-Left, C-Down, C-Right, L, R, L, R, Z (2) in less than four seconds. A sound confirms correct entry.

Race as Davey Allison
Set the Controller Configuration to 3. Then select the Talladega track, highlight "Select Car," and press C-Up, C-Left, C-Down, C-Right, L, R, L, R, L, R in less than four seconds. A sound confirms correct entry.

Race as Alan Kulwicki
Set the Controller Configuration to 3. Then select the Bristol track, highlight "Select Car," and press Z (8), R (2) in less than four seconds. A sound confirms correct entry.

Race as Benny Parsons
Set the Controller Configuration to 3. Then select the Richmond track, highlight "Select Car," and press C-Up, C-Right, C-Down, C-Left, Z (3), L, Z (2) in less than four seconds. A sound confirms correct entry.

Race as Richard Petty
Set the Controller Configuration to 3. Then select the Martinsville track, highlight "Select Car," and press C-Up (2), C-Down (2), C-Left, C-Right, C-Left, C-Right, L, R in less than four seconds. A sound confirms correct entry.

Race as Cale Yarborough
Set the Controller Configuration to 3. Then select the Darlington track, highlight "Select Car," and press L, R, L (3), R (2), Z in less than four seconds. A sound confirms correct entry.

Paintball Mode
In Single Race Mode, hold Left+R and press B, A, B, A, B, A, B, A at the Track Selection screen.

NASCAR 2000

Play as Alan Kulwicki
Select Bristol Motor Speedway. Highlight "Select Car" option and press Left, Right, C-Up (2), C-Down (2), C-Left (2), C-Right (2) in less than four seconds. A sound confirms correct entry. Or race in championship season with at least a 50 percent race length and place in the top five on the Bristol Motor Speedway.

Play as Benny Parsons
Select Richmond International Raceway. Highlight "Select Car" and press Right (2), Z (2), Left (2), C-Up (2), C-Down (2) in less than four seconds. A sound confirms correct entry. Or race in championship season with at least 50 percent race length and place in the top five on the Richmond International Raceway.

Play as Cale Yarborough
Select Darlington Raceway. Highlight "Select Car" and press C-Up, C-Left, C-Down, C-Right, C-Up, C-Left, C-Down, C-Right, Z (2) in less than four seconds. A sound confirms correct entry. Or race in championship season with at least 50 percent race length and place in the top five on the Darlington Raceway.

Play as Davey Allison
Select Talladega Superspeedway. Highlight "Select Car" and press C-Up, C-Down, C-Left, C-Right, C-Up, C-Down, C-Left, C-Right, Z (2) in under four seconds. A sound confirms correct entry. Another way of playing him is to race in championship season with at least 50 percent race length and place in the top five on the Talladega Superspeedway.

Play as David Pearson
Select Martinsville Speedway. Highlight "Select Car" and press Left, Z, Right, C-Right, C-Down, C-Left, C-Up, C-Right, Z (2) in less than four seconds. A sound confirms correct entry. Or race in championship season with at least 50 percent race length and place in the top five on the Martinsville Speedway.

Play as Will Smith
Pick Tony Labonte at the Select Car screen. Choose Talladega Superspeedway. Now press and hold C-Up+L+R+A+B+Up when the screen tells you where you are racing.

CPU Drives Car
Press L during a race.

NBA HANGTIME

Random Team
When selecting your team, hold Turbo+Up.

Outdoor Court
At Tonight's Matchup screen, press Turbo (6), Shoot (4).

Tournament Mode
At Tonight's Matchup screen, press Turbo, Shoot, Pass.

Baby Mode
At Tonight's Matchup screen, press Shoot (2), Pass (5).

No Music
At Tonight's Matchup screen, press Shoot (4), Pass (8).

No Goaltending
At Tonight's Matchup screen, press Turbo (9), Shoot (3), Pass (7).

Quick Hands
At Tonight's Matchup screen, press Turbo (7), Pass (9).

Maximum Power
At Tonight's Matchup screen, press Turbo (8), Pass (2).

Maximum Speed
At Tonight's Matchup screen, press Turbo (2), Shoot (8), Pass (4).

Hyper Speed
At Tonight's Matchup screen, press Turbo (5), Shoot (5), Pass (2).

Stealth Mode
At Tonight's Matchup screen, press Turbo (2), Shoot (7), Pass (3).

Unlimited Turbo
At Tonight's Matchup screen, press Turbo (4), Shoot (6), Pass.

No Pushing
At Tonight's Matchup screen, press Turbo (3), Shoot (9).

Fast Passing
At Tonight's Matchup screen, press Turbo, Shoot (2).

Block Power
At Tonight's Matchup screen, press Turbo (6), Shoot, Pass (6).

Shot Percentage
Press D-Pad clockwise in a full circle starting at Up at the Tonight's Matchup screen as the teams are announced. If done correctly, the code box will flash.

Big Heads
Hold Up and press Turbo+Pass at the Tonight's Matchup screen as the teams are announced. If done correctly, the code box will flash.

Huge Heads
Press Up (2), Pass, Turbo at the Tonight's Matchup screen as the teams are announced. If done correctly, the code box will flash.

No Tag Arrow
Press Left (2), Pass, Turbo at the Tonight's Matchup screen as the teams are announced. If done correctly, the code box will flash.

No Drifting
Press Down (2), Shoot, Turbo at the Tonight's Matchup screen as the teams are announced. If done correctly, the code box will flash.

Turbo ABA Ball
Hold Right and press Shoot, Turbo, Pass at the Tonight's Matchup screen as the teams are announced. If done correctly, the code box will flash.

No CPU Assistance
Hold Right and press Pass (2) at the Tonight's Matchup screen as the teams are announced. If done correctly, the code box will flash.

Rooftop Jam
Hold Left and press Turbo (2) at the Tonight's Matchup screen as the teams are announced. If done correctly, the code box will flash.

Unlock Penny Hardaway
Enter name/PIN: AHRDWY/0000

Unlock Dan Amrich
Enter name/PIN: AMRICH/2020

Unlock Hidden Character
Enter name/PIN: BARDO/6000

Unlock Hidden Character
Enter name/PIN: CARLOS/1010

Unlock Cliff Robinson
Enter name/PIN: CLIFFR/0000

Unlock Hidden Character
Enter name/PIN: DANIEL/0604

Unlock Dan Roan
Enter name/PIN: DANR/0000

Unlock David Robinson
Enter name/PIN: DAVIDR/0000

Unlock Sal Divita
Enter name/PIN: DIVITA/0201

Unlock Hakeem Olajuwon
Enter name/PIN: DREAM/0000

Unlock Hidden Character
Enter name/PIN: EDDIE/6213

Unlock Sean Eliot
Enter name/PIN: ELLIOT/0000

Unlock Hidden Character
Enter name/PIN: EUGENE/6767

Unlock Patrick Ewing
Enter name/PIN: EWING/0000

Unlock Development Team Picture
Enter name/PIN: FUNCOM/1993

Unlock Grant Hill
Enter name/PIN: GHILL/0000

Unlock Glen Rice
Enter name/PIN: GLENNR/0000

Unlock Horace Grant
Enter name/PIN: HGRANT/0000

Unlock Jamie Rivett
Enter name/PIN: JAMIE/1000

Unlock Hidden Character
Enter name/PIN: JAPPLE/6660

Unlock Hidden Character
Enter name/PIN: JASON/0729

Unlock Hidden Character
Enter name/PIN: JC/0000

Unlock Hidden Character
Enter name/PIN: JIGGET/1010

Unlock Hidden Character
Enter name/PIN: JFER/0503

Unlock Jon Hey
Enter name/PIN: JONHEY/6000

Unlock Larry Johnson
Enter name/PIN: JOHNSN/0000

Unlock Shawn Kemp
Enter name/PIN: KEMP/0000

Unlock Jason Kidd
Enter name/PIN: KIDD/0000

Unlock Ed Boon (Mortal Kombat Programmer)
Enter name/PIN: KOMBAT/0004

Unlock Karl Malone
Enter name/PIN: MALONE/0000

Unlock Hidden Character
Enter name/PIN: MARIUS/1003

Unlock Hidden Character
Enter name/PIN: MARTY/1010

Unlock Intro Rapper
Enter name/PIN: MDOC/2099

Unlock Hidden Character
Enter name/PIN: MEDNIK/6000

Unlock Reggie Miller
Enter name/PIN: MILLER/0000

Unlock Hidden Character
Enter name/PIN: MINIFE/6000

Unlock Air Morris
Enter name/PIN: MORRIS/6000

Unlock John Tobias (Mortal Kombat programmer)
Enter name/PIN: MORTAL/0004

Unlock Dikembe Motumbo
Enter name/PIN: MOTUMB/0000

Unlock Alonzo Mourning
Enter name/PIN: MOURNI/0000

Unlock Larry Munday
Enter name/PIN: MUNDAY/5432

Unlock Gheorghe Muresan
Enter name/PIN: MURSAN/0000

Unlock Hidden Character
Enter name/PIN: MXV/1014

Unlock Hidden Character
Enter name/PIN: NICK/7000

Unlock Announcer
Enter name/PIN: NFUNK/0101

Unlock Hidden Character
Enter name/PIN: NOBUD/1010

Unlock Hidden Character
Enter name/PIN: NORTH/5050

Unlock Hidden Character
Enter name/PIN: PATF/2000

Unlock Joe Perry
Enter name/PIN: PERRY/3500

Unlock Scottie Pippen
Enter name/PIN: PIPPEN/0000

Unlock Hidden Character
Enter name/PIN: QUIN/0330

Unlock Hidden Character
Enter name/PIN: RICE/0000

Unlock Dennis Rodman
Enter name/PIN: RODMAN/0000

Unlock John Root
Enter name/PIN: ROOT/6000

Unlock Hidden Character
Enter name/PIN: SHAWN/0123

Unlock Rik Smits
Enter name/PIN: SMITS/0000

Unlock S. Oursler
Enter name/PIN: SNO/0103

Unlock Jerry Stackhouse
Enter name/PIN: STACKH/0000

Unlock John Starks
Enter name/PIN: STARKS/0000

Unlock Mark Turmell
Enter name/PIN: TURMEL/0322

Unlock Spud Webb
Enter name/PIN: WEBB/0000

Unlock Chris Webber
Enter name/PIN: WEBBER/0000

NBA IN THE ZONE '98

Easy Free Throws
When shooting free throws, press the analog stick Up a couple times to slow the shot indicator.

NBA JAM '99

Large Players
Pause gameplay and press L (2), C-Right, L (2), C-Right, L (2), C-Right, Z.

Small Players
Pause gameplay and press L (2), C-Left, L (2), C-Left, L (2), C-Left, Z. Repeat to make the players smaller than the ball.

Long Distance Dunks
Pause gameplay and press L (2), C-Down, L (2), C-Down, L (2), C-Down, Z.

Perfect Shot
Pause gameplay and press L (2), C-Up, L (2), C-Up, L (2), C-Up, Z.

Large Ball
Pause gameplay and press L (2), C-Left, L (2), C-Up, L (2), C-Right, L (2), C-Down, Z.

Stronger Pushes
Pause gameplay and press L (2), Up, L (2), Up, L (2), Up, Z.

Tied Score
Pause gameplay and press L (2), Down, L (2), Down, L (2), Down, Z.

On-Fire Team
Pause gameplay and press L (2), Right, L (2), Right, L (2), Right, Z.

Disable Cheats
Pause gameplay and press L (2), Left, L (2), Left, L (2), Left, Z.

NBA JAM 2000

Run Faster
When you have the ball, hold L+Z or R+Z.

NBA LIVE '99

Bonus Team
Select Create Custom Team at the Rosters screen and enter EA Europals.

Bonus Team
Select Create Custom Team at the Rosters screen and enter Hitmen Coders.

Bonus Team
Select Create Custom Team at the Rosters screen and enter Hitmen Earplugs.

Bonus Team
Select Create Custom Team at the Rosters screen and enter Hitmen Idlers.

Bonus Team
Select Create Custom Team at the Rosters screen and enter Hitmen Pixels.

Bonus Team
Select Create Custom Team at the Rosters screen and enter Hitmen Rebounds.

NBA LIVE 2000

Unlock Isiah Thomas
Get 15 steals at the Superstar level.

Unlock Michael Jordan as a Free Agent
Beat Michael Jordan in a one-on-one game.

NBA SHOWTIME: NBA ON NBC

Play as Atlanta Hawks Mascot
HAWK/0322

Play as Charlotte Hornets Mascot
HORNET/1105

Play as Chicago Bulls Mascot
BENNY/0503

Play as Denver Nuggets Mascot
ROCKY 0201

Play as Houston Rockets Mascot
TURBO/1111

Play as Indiana Pacers Mascot
BOOMER/0604

Play as Minnesota Timberwolves Mascot
CRUNCH/0503

Play as New Jersey Nets Mascot
SLY/6765

Play as Phoenix Suns Mascot
GORILA/0314

Play as Seattle Sonics Mascot
SASQUA/7785

Play as Toronto Raptors Mascot
RAPTOR/1020

Play as Utah Jazz Mascot
BEAR/1228

Create-a-Player: Clown
CRISPY/2084

Create-a-Player: Kerri in Alternate Uniform
KERRI/1111

Create-a-Player: Kerri the Female Player
KERRI/0220

Create-a-Player: Large Alien
BIGGY/0958

Create-a-Player: Lia in Alternate Uniform
LIA/1111

Create-a-Player: Lia the Female Player
LIA/0712

Create-a-Player: Nikko the Devil Dog
NIKKO/6666

Create-a-Player: Old Man
OLDMAN/2001

Create-a-Player: Pinto Horse
PINTO/1966

Create-a-Player: Pumpkin
JACKO/1031

Create-a-Player: Referee
THEREF/7777

Create-a-Player: Retro Rob
RETRO/1970

Create-a-Player: Small Alien
SMALLS/0856

Create-a-Player: White Horse
HORSE/1966

Create-a-Player: Wizard
THEWIZ/1136

Midway Staff: Alex Gilliam, Midway Game Tester
LEX/0014

Midway Staff: Andy Eloff, Midway System Hardware
ELOFF/2181

Midway Staff: Beth Smukowski, Midway Creative Media
BETHAN/1111

Midway Staff: Brian LeBaron, Midway Game Tester
GRINCH/0222

Midway Staff: Chris Skrundz, Midway Creative Media
CMSVID/0000

Midway Staff: Dan Thompson, Midway Programmer
DANIEL/0604

Midway Staff: Dave Grossman, Midway Creative Media
DAVE/1104

Midway Staff: Eugene Geer, Midway Artist
EGEER/1105

Midway Staff: Jason Skiles, Midway Programmer
JASON/3141

Midway Staff: Jeff Johson, Midway Programmer
JAPPLE/6660

Midway Staff: Jennifer Hedrick, Midway Artist
JENIFR/3333

Midway Staff: Jennifer Hedrick (Alternate Uniform)
JENIFR/1111

Midway Staff: Jim Gentile, Midway Artist
GENTIL/1228

Midway Staff: Jim Tianis, Midway Creative Media
DIMI/0619

Midway Staff: John Root, Midway Artist
ROOT/6000

Midway Staff: Jon Hey, Midway Sound and Music
JONHEY/8823

Midway Staff: Larry Wotman, Midway Creative Media
STRAT/2112

Midway Staff: Mark Guidarelli, Midway Programmer
GUIDO/6765

Midway Staff: Mark Turmell, Midway Lead Programmer
TURMEL/0322

Midway Staff: Matt Gilmore, Midway Artist
MATTG/1006

Midway Staff: Mike Lynch, Midway System Hardware
LYNCH/3333

Midway Staff: Paul Martin, Midway PC Support
STENTR/0269

Midway Staff: Paulo Garcia, Midway Game Tester
PAULO/0517

Midway Staff: Rob Gatson, Midway Programmer
GATSON/1111

Midway Staff: Sal DiVita, Midway Lead Artist
SAL/0201

Midway Staff: Tim Bryant, Midway Artist
TIMMYB/3314

Midway Staff: Tim Moran, Midway Creative Media
TIMCRP/6666

Extra Player: Shawn Liptak, Programming Consultant
LIPTAK/0114

Extra Player: Isiah Thomas, NBC Sports Announcer
THOMAS/1111

Extra Player: Tim Kitzrow, Midway Sports Announcer
TIMK/7785

Extra Player: Willy Morris, Motion Capture Actor
WIL/0101

Extra Player: Greg Cutler, Motion Capture Actor
CUTLER/1111

Extra Player: Chad Edmunds, Motion Capture Actor
CHAD/0628

Show Shot
At the Tonight's Matchup screen, press Pass, Down.

Show Hotspot
At the Tonight's Matchup screen, press Turbo, Down.

Tournament Mode (No Power-Ups)
At the Tonight's Matchup screen, press Turbo, Shoot, Pass, Down.

Snow On
At the Tonight's Matchup screen, press Turbo, Shoot (2), Pass, Left.

Thick Fog On
At the Tonight's Matchup screen, press Turbo, Shoot (2), Pass (3), Down.

Night Fog On
At the Tonight's Matchup screen, press Turbo, Shoot (2), Pass (3), Left.

Swamp Fog On
At the Tonight's Matchup screen, press Turbo, Shoot (2), Pass (3), Right.

Fog On
At the Tonight's Matchup screen, press Turbo, Shoot (2), Pass (3), Up.

Blizzard On
At the Tonight's Matchup screen, press Turbo, Shoot (3), Pass, Left.

Rain On
At the Tonight's Matchup screen, press Turbo, Shoot (4), Pass, Left.

Big Head Mode
At the Tonight's Matchup screen, press Turbo (2), Right.

No Hotspots
At the Tonight's Matchup screen, press Turbo (2), Pass, Up.

No Fouls in Versus Mode
At the Tonight's Matchup screen, press Turbo (2), Shoot (2), Pass (2), Left.

No Fouls
At the Tonight's Matchup screen, press Turbo (2), Shoot (2), Pass (2), Right.

ABA Ball
At the Tonight's Matchup screen, press Turbo (2), Shoot (3), Pass (2), Right.

No Replays
At the Tonight's Matchup screen, press Turbo (3), Shoot (3), Pass, Left.

Team Uniform
At the Tonight's Matchup screen, press Turbo (4), Right.

Midway Uniform
At the Tonight's Matchup screen, press Turbo (4), Pass, Right.

Home Uniform
At the Tonight's Matchup screen, press Turbo (4), Shoot, Right.

Unlimited Turbo
At the Tonight's Matchup screen, press Turbo (4), Shoot, Pass, Up.

Away Uniform
At the Tonight's Matchup screen, press Turbo (4), Shoot (2), Right.

Alternate Uniform
At the Tonight's Matchup screen, press Turbo (4), Shoot (3), Right.

No Tip Off
At the Tonight's Matchup screen, press Turbo (4), Shoot (4), Pass (4), Up.

No Goal Tending
At the Tonight's Matchup screen, press Turbo (5), Shoot (5), Pass (5), Left

Bonus Court: Clown
CRISPY/2084

Bonus Court: Kerri in Alternate Uniform
KERRI/1111

Bonus Court: Kerri the Female Player
KERRI/0220

Bonus Court: Large Alien
BIGGY/0958

Bonus Court: Lia in Alternate Uniform
LIA/1111

Bonus Court: Lia the Female Player
LIA/0712

Bonus Court: Nikko the Devil Dog
NIKKO/6666

Bonus Court: Old Man
OLDMAN

Place Any Player on Any Team
Enter the first three letters of the player's team as initials and enter his jersey number as a PIN.

NEW TETRIS

Turbo Mode
In Single-player mode, enter the name 2FAST4U.

Turbo CPU Mode
In Single-player mode, enter the name AI2EZ4U?.

Delete Line Totals and Reset Wonders
In Single-player mode, enter the name O1DERS.

Delete Line Totals, Reset Wonders, Delete High Scores
In Single-player mode, enter the name 1N175R4M.

NFL BLITZ

Unlock Hidden Player
Select "Enter Name For Record Keeping" and enter name/PIN: BETH/7761.

Unlock Hidden Player
Select "Enter Name For Record Keeping" and enter name/PIN: BILLZ/0526.

Unlock Brain
Select "Enter Name For Record Keeping" and enter name/PIN: BRAIN/1111.

Unlock Hidden Player
Select "Enter Name For Record Keeping" and enter name/PIN: BRIAN/0818.

Unlock Headless Guy
Select "Enter Name For Record Keeping" and enter name/PIN: CARLTN/1111.

Unlock Dan Thompson
Select "Enter Name For Record Keeping" and enter name/PIN: DANIEL/0604.

Unlock Hidden Player
Select "Enter Name For Record Keeping" and enter name/PIN: DBN/6969.

Unlock Hidden Player
Select "Enter Name For Record Keeping" and enter name/PIN: ED/3246.

Unlock Dan Forden
Select "Enter Name For Record Keeping" and enter name/PIN: FORDEN/1111.

Unlock Hidden Player
Select "Enter Name For Record Keeping" and enter name/PIN: GATSON/1111.

Unlock Hidden Player
Select "Enter Name For Record Keeping" and enter name/PIN: GENE/0310.

Unlock Jim Gentile
Select "Enter Name For Record Keeping" and enter name/PIN: GENTIL/1111.

Unlock Hidden Player
Select "Enter Name For Record Keeping" and enter name/PIN: GRINCH/2220.

Unlock Hidden Player
Select "Enter Name For Record Keeping" and enter name/PIN: GUIDO/6765.

Unlock Jeff Johnson
Select "Enter Name For Record Keeping" and enter name/PIN: JAPPLE/6660.

Unlock Jason Skiles
Select "Enter Name For Record Keeping" and enter name/PIN: JASON/3141.

Unlock Jennifer Hedrick
Select "Enter Name For Record Keeping" and enter name/PIN: JENIFR/3333.

Unlock Hidden Player
Select "Enter Name For Record Keeping" and enter name/PIN: JIMK/5651.

Unlock Hidden Player
Select "Enter Name For Record Keeping" and enter name/PIN: JOHN/5158.

Unlock Hidden Player
Select "Enter Name For Record Keeping" and enter name/PIN: JOSH/4288.

Unlock Hidden Player
Select "Enter Name For Record Keeping" and enter name/PIN: LT/7777.

Unlock Luis Mangubat
Select "Enter Name For Record Keeping" and enter name/PIN: LUIS/3333.

Unlock Hidden Player
Select "Enter Name For Record Keeping" and enter name/PIN: MARKA/1112.

Unlock Mike Lynch
Select "Enter Name For Record Keeping" and enter name/PIN: MIKE/3333.

Unlock Hidden Player
Select "Enter Name For Record Keeping" and enter name/PIN: MITCH/4393.

Unlock Hidden Player
Select "Enter Name For Record Keeping" and enter name/PIN: MONTY/1836.

Unlock Hidden Player
Select "Enter Name For Record Keeping" and enter name/PIN: NICO/4440.

Unlock Hidden Player
Select "Enter Name For Record Keeping" and enter name/PIN: PAULA/0425.

Unlock Hidden Player
Select "Enter Name For Record Keeping" and enter name/PIN: PAULO/0517.

Unlock Raiden from Mortal Kombat
Select "Enter Name For Record Keeping" and enter name/PIN: RAIDEN/3691.

Unlock Hidden Player
Select "Enter Name For Record Keeping" and enter name/PIN: ROG/8148.

Unlock John Root
Select "Enter Name For Record Keeping" and enter name/PIN: ROOT/6000.

Unlock Hidden Player
Select "Enter Name For Record Keeping" and enter name/PIN: RYAN/1029.

Unlock Sal Divita
Select "Enter Name For Record Keeping" and enter name/PIN: SAL/0201.

Unlock Shinnok from Mortal Kombat
Select "Enter Name For Record Keeping" and enter name/PIN: SHINOK/8337.

Unlock Hidden Player
Select "Enter Name For Record Keeping" and enter name/PIN: SHUN/0530.

Unlock Skull
Select "Enter Name For Record Keeping" and enter name/PIN: SKULL/1111.

Unlock Hidden Player
Select "Enter Name For Record Keeping" and enter name/PIN: THUG/1111.

Unlock Hidden Player
Select "Enter Name For Record Keeping" and enter name/PIN: TODD/1122.

Unlock Mark Turmell
Select "Enter Name For Record Keeping" and enter name/PIN: TURMEL/0322.

Unlock Hidden Player
Select "Enter Name For Record Keeping" and enter name/PIN: VAN/1234.

Unlock Hidden Player
Select "Enter Name For Record Keeping" and enter name/PIN: ZZ/1221.

Allow Stepping OB
Turbo (2), Jump, Pass, Left

Fast Turbo Running
Jump (3), Pass (2), Left

Headless Team
Turbo, Jump (2), Pass (3), Right

Hide Receiver Name
Turbo, Pass (2), Right

Hyper Blitz
Turbo (5), Jump (5), Pass (5), Up

Infinite Turbo
Turbo (5), Jump, Pass (4), Up

Invisible
Turbo (4), Jump (3), Pass (3), Up

Invisible Receiver Highlight
Turbo (3), Jump (3), Pass (3), Left

Night Game
Turbo (2), Jump (2), Pass (2), Right

Late Hits
Jump, Up

Big head
Turbo (2), Right

Fast Passes
Turbo (2), Jump (5), Left

Fog On
Jump (3), Down

Huge Head
Jump (4), Up

Big Football
Jump (5), Right

Blood Mode
Turbo (2), Jump (5), Up

No CPU Assistance
Jump, Pass (2), Down

No First Downs
Turbo (2), Jump, Up

No Head
Turbo (3), Jump (2), Pass, Left

No Interceptions
Turbo (3), Jump (4), Pass (4), Up

No Play Selection
Turbo, Jump, Pass (5), Left

No Punting
Turbo, Jump (5), Pass, Up

No Random Fumbles
Turbo (4), Jump (2), Pass (3), Down

Power-Up Blockers
Turbo (3), Jump, Pass (2), Left

Power-Up Defense
Turbo (4), Jump (2), Pass, Up

Power-Up Offense
Turbo (3), Jump, Pass (2), Up

Power-Up Speed
Turbo (4), Pass (4), Left

Power-Up Teammates
Turbo (2), Jump (3), Pass (3), Up

Show Field Goal
Pass, Down

Show More Field
Jump (2), Pass, Right

Thick Fog On
Jump (4), Pass, Down

Super Blitzing
Jump (4), Pass (5), Up

Tournament Mode
Turbo, Jump, Pass, Down

Super Field Goals
Turbo, Jump (2), Pass (3), Left

Team Big Players
Turbo, Jump (4), Pass, Right

Team Big Heads
Turbo (2), Pass (3), Right

Clear Weather
Turbo (2), Jump, Pass (2), Left

Team Tiny Players
Turbo (3), Jump, Right

Smart CPU Opponent
Turbo (3), Jump, Pass (4), Down

Super Passing
Turbo (4), Jump (2), Pass (3), Right

Turn Off Stadium
Turbo (5), Left

Snow
Turbo (5), Jump (2), Pass (5), Down

Rain
Turbo (5), Jump (5), Pass (5), Right

Bonus Player
Name = BETH, PIN = 7761

Bonus Player
Name = BILLZ, PIN = 0526

Bonus Player
Name = BOXER, PIN = 2111

Bonus Player
Name = BRAIN, PIN = 1111

Bonus Player
Name = BRIAN, PIN = 0818

Bonus Player
Name = DANIEL, PIN = 0604

Bonus Player
Name = DBN, PIN = 6969

Bonus Player
Name = DINO, PIN = 1111

Bonus Player
Name = ED, PIN = 3246

Bonus Player
Name = FORDEN, PIN = 1111

Bonus Player
Name = GENE, PIN = 0310

Bonus Player
Name = GENTIL, PIN = 1111

Bonus Player
Name = GRINCH, PIN = 0222

Bonus Player
Name = GUIDO, PIN = 6765

Bonus Player
Name = JAPPLE, PIN = 6660

Bonus Player
Name = JASON, PIN = 3141

Bonus Player
Name = JENIFR, PIN = 3333

Bonus Player
Name = JIMK, PIN = 5651

Bonus Player
Name = JOHN, PIN = 5158

Bonus Player
Name = JOSH, PIN = 4288

Bonus Player
Name = JOVE, PIN = 6644

Bonus Player
Name = JULIA, PIN = 1234

Bonus Player
Name = KEVIN, PIN = 1234

Bonus Player
Name = LT, PIN = 7777

Bonus Player
Name = MARKA, PIN = 1112

Bonus Player
Name = MIKE, PIN = 3333

Bonus Player
Name = MITCH, PIN 4393

Bonus Player
Name = MONTY, PIN = 1836

Bonus Player
Name = PAULA, PIN = 0425

Bonus Player
Name = PAULO, PIN = 0517

Bonus Player
Name = RAIDEN, PIN = 3691

Bonus Player
Name = ROG, PIN = 8148

Bonus Player
Name = ROOT, PIN = 6000

Bonus Player
Name = RYAN, PIN = 1029

Bonus Player
Name = SAD, PIN = 1111

Bonus Player
Name = SAL, PIN = 0201

Bonus Player
Name = SHINOK, PIN = 8337

Bonus Player
Name = SHUN, PIN = 0530

Bonus Player
Name = SKULL, PIN = 1111

Bonus Player
Name = THUG, PIN = 1111

Bonus Player
Name = TODD, PIN = 1122

Bonus Player
Name = VAN, PIN = 1234

Bonus Player
Name = ZZ, PIN = 1221

Always Receiver
Turbo (2), Jump (2), Pass (2), Right. This code works when there are at least two human teammates.

Always Quarterback
Turbo (2), Jump (2), Pass (2), Left. This code works when there are at least two human teammates.

Big Football
Jump (5), Right

Big Heads
Turbo (2), Right

Field Goal Percentage Display
Pass, Down

Punt Hang Time Meter
Pass, Right

Fast Turbo
Jump (3), Pass (2), Left

Asphalt Field
Turbo (3), Pass, Up

Astroturf Field
Turbo (3), Pass (3), Up

Grass Field
Turbo (3), Up

Snow Field
Turbo (3), Pass (4), Up

Headless Players
Turbo (3), Jump (2), Pass, Left

Hidden Receiver Names
Turbo, Pass (2), Right

Huge Heads
Jump (4), Up

Hyper Blitzing
Turbo (5), Jump (5), Pass (5), Up. Both players have to enter this code for it to work.

Infinite Turbo
Turbo (5), Jump, Pass (4), Up

Invisible Player
Turbo (4), Jump (3), Pass (3), Up

Invisible Receiver Highlight
Turbo (3), Jump (3), Pass (3), Left

Late Hits
Jump, Up

No First Downs
Turbo (2), Jump, Up

No Fumbles
Turbo (4), Jump (3), Pass (2), Down

No Interceptions
Turbo (3), Jump (4), Pass (4), Up

No Out-of-Bounds
Turbo (2), Jump, Pass, Left

No Punting
Turbo, Jump (5), Pass, Up

Current Team Playbook
Turbo, Up

Power-Up Blockers
Turbo (3), Jump, Pass (2), Left

Power-Up Defense
Turbo (4), Jump (2), Pass, Up

Power-Up Teammates
Turbo (2), Jump (3), Pass (3), Up

Power-Up Offense
Turbo (3), Jump (2), Pass, Up

Smart CPU
Turbo (3), Jump, Pass (4), Down. This code can only be done in One-player mode.

City Stadium
Turbo (5), Pass, Left

Day Stadium
Turbo (5), Pass, Down

Night Stadium
Turbo (5), Pass (2), Down

Turn Off Stadium
Turbo (5), Left

Old Day Stadium
Turbo (5), Pass, Up

Old Night Stadium
Turbo (5), Pass (2), Up

Old Snow Stadium
Turbo (5), Pass (3), Up

Roman Stadium
Turbo (5), Pass (3), Left

Snow Stadium
Turbo (5), Pass (3), Down

Future Stadium
Turbo (3), Pass (2), Left

Dirt Stadium
Turbo (3), Pass (2), Up

Super Blitzing
Jump (4), Pass (5), Up

Super Field Goals
Turbo, Jump (2), Pass (3), Left

Super Passing
Turbo (2), Jump (5), Left

Team Big Heads
Turbo (2), Pass (3), Right

Team Big Players
Turbo, Jump (4), Pass, Right

Team Small Players
Turbo (3), Jump, Right

Night Time Game
Jump (2), Pass (2), Right

Tournament Mode
Turbo, Jump, Pass, Down. This code only works in Two-player games.

Clear Weather
Turbo (2), Jump, Pass (2), Left

Snow
Turbo (5), Jump (2), Pass (5), Down

Rain
Turbo (5), Jump (5), Pass (5), Right

Fog
Jump (3), Down

Heavy Fog
Jump (4), Pass, Down

No Play Selection
Turbo, Jump, Pass (5), Left. Both players have to enter this code for it to work.

Show More Field
Jump (2), Pass, Right. Both players have to enter this code for it to work.

No CPU Assistance
Jump, Pass (2), Down. Both players have to enter this code for it to work.

Power-Up Speed
Turbo (4), Pass (4), Left. Both players have to enter this code for it to work.

NFL QUARTERBACK CLUB '98

Eight Downs
On the Cheat menu, enter 8DWNDRV.

Tall, Skinny Players
On the Cheat menu, enter BBMNTBL.

Super Defense
On the Cheat menu, enter BGBFYDF.

Stronger Receivers
On the Cheat menu, enter BGBFYFF.

Further Dives
On the Cheat menu, enter BGSPRDV.

Spinning Receiver
On the Cheat menu, enter BGTWSTRS.

Better Quarterbacks
On the Cheat menu, enter BRDWYNMTH.

Farther Jumps
On the Cheat menu, enter CRLLWYS.

Unlimited Downs
On the Cheat menu, enter DWNDRV.

Slow Motion
On the Cheat menu, enter FRMBYFRM.

Large Players
On the Cheat menu, enter GLYTHMD.

Fumble Mode
On the Cheat menu, enter GTNHNDS.

Short Players
On the Cheat menu, enter JPNSMWR.

Instant Passes
On the Cheat menu, enter LDSTRTRK.

Disable All Cheats
On the Cheat menu, enter LLCHTSFF.

Poor Defense
On the Cheat menu, enter LLDFSCK.

Ball Tipped on Passes
On the Cheat menu, enter LWYSTPSS.

Fast Players
On the Cheat menu, enter MCHLJNSN.

Constant Dives
On the Cheat menu, enter MNFLDMD.

Never Tackle
On the Cheat menu, enter NBCTCKLS.

Crawling Players
On the Cheat menu, enter PBYBYMD.

Poor Players
On the Cheat menu, enter PWHYRMN.

Strong, but Slow Running Backs
On the Cheat menu, enter RNLDSWZNGR.

Small Players
On the Cheat menu, enter SMLMDGT.

Sled Mode
On the Cheat menu, enter SNWSLDS.

100 Passes, Kicks, Punts
On the Cheat menu, enter SPRBGRMS.

Always Tackle
On the Cheat menu, enter SPRDPRTCKL.

Slippery Field
On the Cheat menu, enter SPRSLYD.

Super Players
On the Cheat menu, enter SPRTMMD.

Turbo Running
On the Cheat menu, enter SPRTRBMD.

Acclaim and Iguana Teams
On the Cheat menu, enter STNTXTM.

Easier Catches
On the Cheat menu, enter STYCKYHNDS.

No Fumbles
On the Cheat menu, enter TGHTGRP.

Poor Quarterback
On the Cheat menu, enter TRNTDLFR.

Stronger Running Backs
On the Cheat menu, enter WLTRPYTN.

Electric Football Mode
On the Cheat menu, enter YLCTRCFB.

Max Discipline and Awareness Stats
On the Cheat menu, enter YNSTYNS.

Thin Players
On the Cheat menu, enter TTHPCK.

NFL QUARTERBACK CLUB '99

Fat Players
On the Cheat menu, enter MRSHMLLW.

Short Players
On the Cheat menu, enter SHRTGYS.

Big Feet
On the Cheat menu, enter REALBIGFEET.

Fumble Mode
On the Cheat menu, enter BTTRFNGRS.

No Fumbles
On the Cheat menu, enter STCKYBLL.

Big Coin During Toss
On the Cheat menu, enter BGMNY.

Big Football
On the Cheat menu, enter BCHBLL.

Increased Injuries
On the Cheat menu, enter HSPTL.

Eight Downs
On the Cheat menu, enter DBLDWNS.

Electric Football Mode
On the Cheat menu, enter XTRVLTG.

Rugby Mode
On the Cheat menu, enter RGBY.

Racquetball Mode
On the Cheat menu, enter RCQTBLL.

Slow Motion
On the Cheat menu, enter FRRSTGMP.

Turbo Mode
On the Cheat menu, enter TRBMN.

Kickers Never Miss
On the Cheat menu, enter PWRKCKR.

Flubber Ball
On the Cheat menu, enter FLBBR.

Slippery Field
On the Cheat menu, enter SLPNSLD.

Pylons on Field
On the Cheat menu, enter PWRPYLNS.

Players Bounce Like Pinballs
On the Cheat menu, enter PNBLL.

Players on Fire
On the Cheat menu, enter HSNFR.

Fire Stadium
On the Cheat menu, enter FIRFILD.

Unlock All Extra Teams
On the Cheat menu, enter XTRTMS.

Alien Stadium
On the Cheat menu, enter SCLLYMLDR.

Landmine Mode
On the Cheat menu, enter PPCRNRTRNS.

Opponents Score Set to 0
On the Cheat menu, enter RLSTN.

Start Game with 12 Points
On the Cheat menu, enter BLOWOUT.

Fat Players
On the Cheat menu, enter MRSHMLLW.

NFL QUARTERBACK CLUB 2000

Thin Players
Enter TTHPCK at Cheat menu.

Flubber Ball
Enter FLBBR at Cheat menu.

Alien Stadium
Enter SCLLYMLDR at Cheat menu.

Big Football
Enter BCHBLL at Cheat menu.

Easy Fumbles
Enter BTTRFNGRS at Cheat menu.

Landmines on the Field
Enter PPCRNRTRNS at Cheat menu.

Rugby Mode
Enter RGBY at Cheat menu.

More Injuries
Enter HSPTL at Cheat menu.

Football on Fire
Enter HSNFR at Cheat menu.

Small Players
Enter SHRTGYS at Cheat menu.

Large Coin in Coin Toss
Enter BGMNY at Cheat menu.

Slow Motion Mode
Enter FRRSTGMP at Cheat menu.

NFL Quarterback Club 2001

Rugby Mode
In the Cheat menu, enter RGBY.

More Fumbles
In the Cheat menu, enter BTTRFNGRS.

More Injuries
In the Cheat menu, enter HSPTL.

Big Football
In the Cheat menu, enter BCHBLL.

Extra-Bouncy Football
In the Cheat menu, enter FLBBR.

NHL '99

Big Players
Enter the code BIGBIG.

Big Heads
Enter the code BRAINY.

Larger Sticks
Enter the code STICKS.

View Ending Sequence
Enter the code VICTORY.

Fast Gameplay and Clock
Enter the code FAST.

Very Fast Gameplay and Clock
Enter the code FASTER.

Enable Camera Flashes
Enter the code FLASH.

No Goalies
Enter the code PULLED.

Harder Checking
Enter the code CHECK.

NHL 2000

Jersey Number 9
At the Create-a-Player screen, enter the name Wayne Gretzky.

Super Players
At the Create-a-Player screen, enter the name Joe Sakic or Peter Forsberg.

Super Goalie
At the Create-a-Player screen, enter the name Patrick Roy.

NHL Blades of Steel '99

Faster Ice
Before a game, when selecting the condition of the ice, press Left, Right, C-Up, C-Down, A+B.

NHL Breakaway '98

Cheat Mode
At the main menu, press C-Left, C-Right, C-Left, C-Right, R (2).

Extra Points
Enable Cheat mode, then press C-Left (2), C-Right (2), C-Left (2), C-Right (2), R at the main screen under Season mode. Repeat as much as necessary.

Extra Teams
Enable Cheat mode, then quickly press C-Up, L, C-Left at the Team Selection screen.

Player with Perfect Attributes
At the Player Creation screen, enter the case-sensitive name Jim Jung.

Small Player with Perfect Attributes
At the Player Creation screen, enter the case-sensitive name Simon Carbone.

Powerful Player
At the Player Creation screen, enter the case-sensitive name grEEn jeLLo.

NHL Breakaway '99

Cheat Mode
At the main menu, press C-Left, C-Right, C-Left, C-Right, R (2).

Extra Points
Enable Cheat mode, then press C-Left (2), C-Right (2), C-Left (2), C-Right (2), R (2) at the main menu. Repeat as needed.

Bonus Teams
At the Team Selection screen, quickly press C-Up, L, C-Left.

Full Player Attributes
At the Player Creation screen, enter the case-sensitive name Douglas Yellin.

Buffed Player
At the Player Creation screen, enter the case-sensitive name Jim Jung.

Small Player with Perfect Attributes
At the Player Creation screen, enter the case-sensitive name Simon Carbone.

Powerful Player
At the Player Creation screen, enter the case-sensitive name grEEn jeLLo.

Super Center
At the Player Creation screen, enter the case-sensitive name Perfect C.

Super Right Winger
At the Player Creation screen, enter the case-sensitive name Perfect RW.

Super Left Winger
At the Player Creation screen, enter the case-sensitive name Perfect LW.

Super Defensemen
At the Player Creation screen, enter the case-sensitive name Perfect D.

Super Goalie
At the Player Creation screen, enter the case-sensitive name Perfect G.

Nightmare Creatures

Cheat Mode
Enter the password C-Down, Up, C-Up, C-Left, C-Up, Left, C-Down, C-Left, then choose Start.

Nuclear Strike 64

God Mode
Use the password CPPLM.

50 Percent Increase in Armor
Use the password PCPNL.

Quad Damage
Use the password BDGFK.

Off-Road Challenge

Punisher Truck
At the Vehicle Selection screen, press C-Down.

4x4 Monster Truck
At the Vehicle Selection screen, press C-Up.

Thunderbolt Truck
At the Vehicle Selection screen, press C-Left.

Crusher Truck
At the Vehicle Selection screen, press C-Right.

El Cajon Track
At the Track Selection screen, hold Up and press L+R. The sound of an air wrench confirms correct entry. Then highlight El Paso and press Z+A.

Flagstaff Track
At the Track Selection screen, hold Left and press L. The sound of an air wrench confirms correct entry. Then highlight Mojave and press Z+A.

Guadalupe Track
At the Track Selection screen, hold Down and press R. The sound of an air wrench confirms correct entry. Then highlight Vegas and press Z+A.

Paperboy

Invincibility
Select Secret Codes on the Options menu. Then enter INVINC as a New Code.

Unlimited Papers on All Levels
Select Secret Codes on the Options menu. Then enter NOBUNDLE as a New Code.

Level Select
Select Secret Codes on the Options menu. Then enter OBVIOUS as a New Code.

View All Headlines
Select Secret Codes on the Options menu. Then enter HEADLINE as a New Code.

Big Newspapers
Select Secret Codes on the Options menu. Then enter SUNDAY as a New Code.

Super Jumps
Select Secret Codes on the Options menu. Then enter MOON as a New Code.

Super Jump Springs
Select Secret Codes on the Options menu. Then enter ALLJUMP as a New Code.

Rocket Boosters
Select Secret Codes on the Options menu. Then enter GOFAST as a New Code.

Turbo Mode
Select Secret Codes on the Options menu. Then enter RUSH as a New Code.

Slow Motion
Select Secret Codes on the Options menu. Then enter WAKING as a New Code.

Random Paper Tossing
Select Secret Codes on the Options menu. Then enter RANDOM as a New Code.

Frame-by-Frame Mode
Select Secret Codes on the Options menu. Then enter UNTIMED as a New Code. Then press C-Right to advance a frame.

Invisible Objects
Select Secret Codes on the Options menu. Then enter JUMBLE as a New Code.

Screaming Objects
Select Secret Codes on the Options menu. Then enter SCREAM as a New Code.

Throw Papers Backwards
Select Secret Codes on the Options menu. Then enter BACKWARD as a New Code.

Throw Papers Directly in Front
Select Secret Codes on the Options menu. Then enter FRONTS as a New Code.

Throw Papers at 90 Degree Angle
Select Secret Codes on the Options menu. Then enter SIDES as a New Code.

Small Paperboy
Select Secret Codes on the Options menu. Then enter LITTLE as a New Code.

Nearsighted Mode
Select Secret Codes on the Options menu. Then enter MAGOO as a New Code.

Cartoon Sounds
Select Secret Codes on the Options menu. Then enter THUMP or THUNK as a New Code.

PENNY RACERS

Bonus Mode B
Earn a medal on every track of Mode C.

Bonus Mode A
Earn a medal on every track of Mode B.

Bonus Mode AA
Earn a medal on every track of Mode A.

Turbo Starts
Press the acceleration button when the last light is about to turn green before the start of a race.

Fast Select
Press the A button repeatedly when the computer is choosing what parts to take. The computer selects faster and might not even take anything from you.

Always Trade Parts
Enter the Parts Option screen. Leave "Steal Parts" and "Trade Parts/Swap Parts" on. Now the CPU will steal one item from you at the most and the CPU will always give you something.

PGA EUROPEAN TOUR

Play with Big Head
Enter RTYNBRTYNNY as password.

Play with Big Hands
Enter RTYNMGRNY as password.

Play as Big Golfer
Enter TRYBFCKRYB as password.

Play as Small Golfer
Enter RTOCFCAMHCE as password.

Play with Small Head
Enter RNTYRNMYQDNB as password.

PILOTWINGS 64

Mt. Wario
Use the Gyro Copter, in class B, and fly to Mt. Rushmore. If you shoot Mario in the nose, he will morph into Wario.

New York and San Francisco Warp
This trick warps you from New York to San Francisco. Start on Little States Island using the Rocketbelt or Gyrocopter. Go inside the green building near the start of the level in New York. Fly past an N64 logo and look for the other door to exit. Exit that door and you'll be in San Francisco. This trick can be reversed to warp to New York using the same procedure.

Miami and Seattle Warp
This trick warps you from Miami to Seattle. Start by flying inside the space shuttle hanger in Florida. Fly toward the ceiling. Then turn around and fly out of the hangar to be in Seattle. This trick can be reversed to warp to Miami using the same procedure.

Gyrocopter Driving
Gyrocopters can be driven on the ground as long as they achieved enough forward momentum while in the air. After landing anywhere, keep the Gyrocopter moving forward. The Gyrocopter begins to fly again once the speed exceeds 40.

POWER LEAGUE 64

Hidden Teams
Enter the following code at the Open Team Select screen: After you press Start, enter up, left, right, down using the analog stick, then hit Start. This unlocks the Hu-Bees and Monsters teams.

POWER RANGERS: LIGHTSPEED RESCUE

Play as Titanium Ranger
Rescue the Titanium Ranger in Level 7. Complete the game, allow the credits to run, and then save. Restart, and the Titanium Ranger will be available.

Unlock Characters for Megazord Arena
Defeat characters in levels to unlock them in the arena.

Megazord Arena Special Attack
Charge your power meter to full and press C-Down.

QUAKE

Debug Mode
Enter QQQQ QQQQ QQQQ QQQQ as a password. Then go to the Options menu. A Debug menu will appear.

New Uniform Color
Enter Debug password and then clear the password. Enter S3TC OOLC OLOR S???. Play a two-player game to see the uniforms.

No Clipping
Enter NOCLIP as a password to pass through walls.

Level 2
H40X ZVVB HLBD 74DJ

Level 3
H0P3 2XBN WQ2B NZVK

Level 4
CWHX CH3B GDB3 14JY

Level 5
PQW4 9QVD Y8VY X21M

Level 6
PL24 XBBT YJLQ 32?6

Level 7
6JR3 KDDV 3SLG 9RFT

Level 8
GWY6 7BBB 23BD L4HK

Level 9
B8YN BBBB ZBBB SXR4

Level 10
55R6 0XCJ 2LBR QVV1

Level 11
51RZ ?6xQ RGBR NNJH

Level 12
5XRV SMXP B7BR LP5H

Level 13
5SR9 TPFG VQBR JBCT

Level 14
5NRV JF6G CVBR GBFL

Level 15
5JR6 HDXM 2ZBR DPN5

Level 16
5DR0 HW4N PZ?S 5Y2W

Level 17
49R6 XBBJ 2GBQ 932T

Level 18
45RZ ZF32 LZBQ 773R

Level 19
41R0 6PFG WGBQ 5BCH

Level 20
4XRV QBFG B3BQ 3BD3

Level 21
4SR5 DBBN ZGBQ 1628

Level 22
4NRV JBBF BRY5 744W

Level 23
4JR5 1BBB 0QBQ X4HX

Level 24
39R9 2PFG W7BQ SBCF

Level 25
4DR1 4XDD RVBQ VM1B

QUAKE II

Password Screen
To access the Password screen, either press B at the Load Game screen (when the list of saved games appears) or enter the Options and Set-up menu.

Multiplayer Infinite Ammo
Access the Password screen and enter S3T1 NF1N IT3S H0TS.

Additional Colors
Access the Password screen and enter S3TC 00LC 0L0R S???.

Bigger Jumps
Access the Password screen and enter S3T1 NF1N 1T3S HOTS. This only works in Multiplayer mode.

Reduced Gravity
Access the Password screen and enter S3TL 0WGR V1TY ????. This only works in Multiplayer mode.

Level 0: Twists (Easy)
Access the Password screen and enter FBBC VBBB FBBC VBF7.

Level 0: Twists (Medium)
Access the Password screen and enter FLBC ZBBB FLBC ZBB9.

Level 0: Twists (Hard)
Access the password screen and enter FVBS LBBB 7VBC 3BB5.

Level 2 (Easy)
6JBN SHFB 07BR X3J1

Level 3 (Easy)
1KLG VL2H LNBF F4LQ

Level 4 (Easy)
2KQD 2MSD Z9VM 4XYL

Level 5 (Easy)
VK7N Z?LY ?4V5 LJ4W

Level 6 (Easy)
VK3J HSW5 9GZN LQW9

Level 7 (Easy)
TK3T RN5N Q06W JV05

Level 8 (Easy)
S?WM H1G9 B46C WBOD

Level 9 (Easy)
R8WB 8X7J VGQ0 SJWR

Level 10 (Easy)
Q?WB BLW8 RP6Y XLSN

Level 11 (Easy)
P6P5 KYWX HB8R DJZH

Level 12 (Easy)
N520 KJFW Y681 VLMD

Level 13 (Easy)
M525 TZ35 HXW0 BXZ

Level 14 (Easy)
L56X 41DX ZKR8 VJV8

Level 15 (Easy)
K58V 01HJ V5K9 C3VK

Level 16 (Easy)
J584 W6NR D05B VDQ?

Level 17 (Easy)
H522 98MJ SM1C B82C

Level 18 (Easy)
G52W 300Z 561C W4HK

Level 19 (Easy)
F569 G2D6 HT6X SG5Y

Level 2 (Normal)
PGBR VK?B 65BH Y3HD

Level 3 (Normal)
1KLS DN5H 7NBF DWRQ

Level 4 (Normal)
2KLR SDRY ?VV4 YQ8X

Level 5 (Normal)
VK3T 7LFC 94B7 D3R3

Level 6 (Normal)
WK3H QNBW NLV5 XGL3

Level 7 (Normal)
TK7P 6LLP KWGY XD4V

Level 8 (Normal)
ST0N QPX4 2WGY JXTS

Level 9 (Normal)
R??P 7NY4 2WGX 99TX

Level 10 (Normal)
Q??K BBBV NBQ1 7GCV

Level 11 (Normal)
P64? ZM5B ?BM0 5YH6

Level 12 (Normal)
N664 SQ63 XB?K B7LF

Level 13 (Normal)
M682 M7QT 1215 8098

Level 14 (Normal)
L669 H8MD G8XB JNYV

Level 15 (Normal)
K681 X8CL H01K 1PF5

Level 16 (Normal)
J6?0 BT5M NRZ2 QXLL

Level 17 (Normal)
H6?0 XXFW PHV1 77P4

Level 18 (Normal)
G6?9 GYMK RWNK SMSL

Level 19 (Normal)
F6Y3 WXQK CHD0 8K4D

QUEST 64

Restore Health
Say you'll stay the night at a hotel. Go to the Save screen and press B to escape.

Hidden Library Room
Use the yellow wings and enter the castle after you have defeated Nepty at the Isle of Skye. Go to the library. Push against the left corners of the bookcases to open a hidden library.

Secret Castle
Play until you reach the desert section. Explore the southeast part of the desert with no walls until you see a gem floating in the air. Touch the gem to be teleported to Shamwood, a castle that doesn't appear on your map and is full of items.

Double Attack
Distance yourself so that the staff is within striking distance. Choose a spell and press A. You will cast your spell and hit the opponent with your staff at the same time.

RAINBOW SIX

Level Select for Recruit Difficulty
Enter VZRFTMQ2G8SQ as a password.

Level Select for Veteran Difficulty
Enter FZJFTMR2G8RQ as a password.

Level 2: Red Wolf (Recruit)
12D1S2Q22MQQ

Level 3: Sun Devil (Recruit)
BJDBC3Q22WQQ

Level 4: Eagle Watch (Recruit)
BZDBSMQZZ!QQ

Level 5: Ghost Dance (Recruit)
CJTCCQQ2FGSQ

Level 6: Fire Walk (Recruit)
K2TK65Q2F4SQ

Level 7: Lion's Den (Recruit)
T2TT68QGF!WQ

Level 8: Deep Magic (Recruit)
5JR5L1QGGGSQ

Level 9: Lone Fox (Recruit)
52T572Q4G4SQ

Level 10: Black Star (Recruit)
VJVVLJQGGWSQ

Level 11: Wild Arrow (Recruit)
VZVVXMQ26!SQ

Level 12: Mystic Tiger (Recruit)
VZRFTMQ2G8SQ

Level 2: Red Wolf (Veteran)
1ZL1S2RF2MQQ

Level 3: Sun Devil (Veteran)
BJJBC3RF25QQ

Level 4: Eagle Watch (Veteran)
BZJBSMRF28RQ

Level 5: Ghost Dance (Veteran)
CZBCS5RFFMRQ

Level 6: Fire Walk (Veteran)
DJBDCYRFF5RQ

Level 7: Lion's Den (Veteran)
DJDDC6R2FWR8

Level 8: Deep Magic (Veteran)
LZBDS8R2F8RQ

Level 9: Lone Fox (Veteran)
MJB2D1R2G2RQ

Level 10: Black Star (Veteran)
2ZB2T2R2GMQQ

Level 11: Wild Arrow (Veteran)
FJJFD3R2G5RQ

Level 12: Mystic Tiger (Veteran)
FZJFTMR2G8RQ

Level 2: Red Wolf (Elite)
1ZB1S2S22M??

Level 3: Sun Devil (Elite)
BJBBC3S225??

Level 4: Eagle Watch (Elite)
BZBBSMS22888

Level 5: Ghost Dance (Elite)
CJDCCQS2F288

Level 6: Fire Walk (Elite)
CZDCSWS2FMQ8

Level 7: Lion's Den (Elite)
DJBDCYS2F5??

Level 8: Deep Magic (Elite)
DZBDS8S2F???

Level 9: Lone Fox (Elite)
2JB2D1S2G2??

Level 10: Black Star (Elite)
2ZB2T2S2GM??

Level 11: Wild Arrow (Elite)
FJDFD3S2G5??

Level 12: Mystic Tiger (Elite)
FZDFTMS2G888

RAMPAGE WORLD TOUR

Level Select
At the Character Selection screen, hold L+C-Up+C-Down+C-Left+C-Right. A sound confirms correct entry. Begin a new game and press Up or Down to select a country and Left or Right to select a city at the Peoria Day 1 screen.

Turn Bad Food into Good Food

When the current level is over and when the name of the city in the US appears, hold Down and if playing as George press Jump (3). If playing as Lizzy, press Punch (3). If playing as Ralph, press Kick (3).

No Bad Food

When the current level is over and when the name of the city is Casablanca, Kiev, Kodiak, London, Moab, Nashville, Rio de Janeiro, or Washington DC, press Jump if playing as George. If playing as Lizzy, press Punch. If playing as Ralph, press Kick.

Level Skip

When the current level is over and Cleveland, Fargo, Oklahoma City, or Reno appear, press Jump, Punch, Kick if playing as George. If playing as Lizzy, press Punch, Kick, Jump. If playing as Ralph, press Kick, Jump, Punch.

Play as Tyrannosaurus Rex

Win all levels and start a new game. Highlight Lizzy, hold Z and keep pressing L, R, until a scream is heard.

RAMPAGE 2: UNIVERSAL TOUR

Play as Ralph
Enter the password LVPVS.

Play as George
Enter the password SM14N.

Play as Lizzy
Enter the password S4VRS.

Play as Myukus
Enter the password N0T3T.

Play as Alternate Myukus
Enter the password B1G4L.

Play as Noob Myukus
Enter the password SRY3D.

Unlock All Characters
Enter the password GOT3T.

Cheat Options
Enter the password BVGGY.

RAT ATTACK

Bonus Characters
Complete the game in normal mode to unlock the scratch cats Atomicat and Pearl.

RAYMAN 2: THE GREAT ESCAPE

75 Percent Trick
Find the first frog in the Aztec level. Go near it. You will get the code to 75 percent from the fairy.

READY 2 RUMBLE BOXING

Alternate Costumes
Press C-Up+C-Left at the Character Selection screen. This also changes the intro and ending sequence for the characters.

Unlock Bronze Class Boxers
Enter BRONZE as the gym name in Championship mode. This unlocks all the bronze class boxers and Kemo Claw in Arcade mode.

Unlock Silver Class Boxers
Enter SILVER as the gym name in Championship mode. This unlocks all silver class boxers and Bruce Blade in Arcade mode.

Unlock Gold Class Boxers
Enter GOLD as the gym name in Championship mode. This unlocks all gold class boxers and Nat Daddy in Arcade mode.

Unlock Championship Class Boxers
Enter CHAMP as the gym name in Championship mode. This unlocks all champ class boxers and Damien Black in Arcade mode.

Cheaper Training Equipment
Enter Championship mode and select the "Train Boxer" option. Go to Rumble Aerobics Training, press Left and then A immediately. If you did this correctly, then you should have purchased the $25,000 vitamins for $500. Try this with other training equipment.

Taunts
Hold C-Up+C-Right or C-Down+C-Left during a match to taunt your opponent.

Bonus Characters
Win the title fight at the Bronze, Silver, and Gold matches. When you win one of the title fights, a character will be unlocked in Championship and Arcade mode.

READY TO RUMBLE BOXING: ROUND 2

Unlock Overweight Boxer
At the Character Select screen, press Right (2), Up, Down, Right, R (2), L.

Unlock Thin Boxer
At the Character Select screen, press Right (2), Up, Down, Right, R, L.

Unlock Zombie Boxer
At the Character Select screen, press Left, Up, Right, Down, R (2), L.

Box with Giant Gloves
At the Character Select screen, press Left, Up, Right, Down, R, L.

Unlock Champion Costumes
Defeat all opponents in Championship mode.

Unlock New Characters
Defeat the game in Arcade mode.

RESIDENT EVIL 2

Unlimited Ammo
At the Load Game screen, press Up (4), Right (4), L, R, L, R, C-Right, C-Left. If done correctly, the game returns to the main menu.

Invincibility
At the Load Game screen, press Down (4), Left (4), L, R (2), L, C-Up, C-Down. If done correctly, the game returns to the main menu.

RE-VOLT

All Cars and Tracks
Enter the password B, A, Z (2), B, L, A, C.

Reversed Tracks
In Time Trial Challenge mode, beat all the times on all Normal tracks in all circuits.

Mirrored Tracks
In Time Trial Challenge mode, beat all the times on all Reversed tracks in all circuits.

Mirrored Reversed Tracks
In Time Trial Challenge mode, beat all the times on all Mirrored tracks in all circuits.

RIDGE RACER 64

Motion Blurring
During an instant replay, press C-Left.

Reversed Track
Begin a new game in Grand Prix mode. Play on the first course. When the race starts, turn around and drive into the wall. Keep driving into the wall until your car goes through it.

Golf Caddy Car
Enable the Reversed Track and place first in the race.

Blinky Ghost Car
In Free Run in Time Trial mode, drive 99 laps on any track.

Pooka
In Time Attack mode, choose Stage 7 or 8 and select "Set Record." Break the record to unlock Pooka.

Crazy Canuck
In Car Attack mode, choose Stage 8 in Mirror mode. Defeat the car.

00 Agent
With two players, select Team mode. Choose three teams and pick Stage 7 or 8. Place first and second.

Galaga '88 Minigame
Place first in Ridge Racer Extreme Extra. You can play one level of the game Galaga '88. Destroy all 40 aliens to unlock the Galaga '88 car and the Galaga Pac Jam song.

ROAD RASH 64

All Tracks and Motorcycles
Press C-Up, C-Left (2), C-Right, L, R, C-Down, Z at the main menu.

Insanity Level
Press C-Up, C-Left (2), C-Right, L, R, C-Down, Z at the Thrash Mode screen.

Play as Cop
Press Z, C-Left, C-Down, C-Left, Z, L, R, C-Down at the main menu.

Biker Girl
Press C-Right, C-Left, Z, L, R, C-Up at the main menu.

Change Bike and Rider Colors
Press Up or Down at the Bike Selection screen.

Scooters
Press C-Down, C-Right, C-Up, C-Left (2), L, C-Left at the main menu.

Quick Starts
Hold A to get a faster start at the beginning of a race.

Stage 2 Level
Press R, C-Right, Z, R, L, C-Up, C-Left, C-Up at the main menu. A sound confirms correct entry.

Stage 3 Level
Press R, C-Right (3), R, C-Left, C-Down, Z at the main menu. A sound confirms correct entry.

Stage 4 Level
Press R, C-Right, C-Down, C-Left, C-Right (2), Z, L at the main menu. A sound confirms correct entry.

Stage 5 Level
Press Z, C-Right, C-Down, C-Left, C-Right (2), Z, L at the main menu. A sound confirms correct entry.

ROADSTERS

Get $250,000
Rename any character to the case-sensitive name fastBUCKS.

Get $1,000,000
Rename any character to the case-sensitive name EasyMoney.

Hovercraft Cars
Rename any character to the case-sensitive name Skywalker.

Mini-Cars
Rename any character to the case-sensitive name Car Radio.

All Classes
Rename any character to the case-sensitive name Gimme ALL.

Big Tires
Rename any character to the case-sensitive name BigWheels.

High Resolution
Rename any character to the case-sensitive name Extra rez. Return to the Options screen.

Overhead View
Rename any character to the case-sensitive name Chopper.

High-Pitched Commentary
Rename any character to the case-sensitive name Smurfing.

Mirrored and Reversed Circuits
Rename any character to the case-sensitive name Anyway.

All Divisions
Rename any character to the case-sensitive name _Trophies (replace "_" with a space).

Disable All Cheats
Rename any character to the case-sensitive name CheatsOff.

ROBOTRON 64

Shield Power-Up
During gameplay, press Down, Left, C-Left, C-Right. This may only be used five times a level.

Turbo Power-Up
During gameplay, press Left (2), Right (2), C-Up. This may only be used five times a level.

Two-Way Shot Power-Up
During gameplay, press Up, C-Up, Up, C-Up. This may only be used five times a level.

Three-Way Shot Power-Up
During gameplay, press Right (2), C-Left, C-Down. This may only be used five times a level.

Four-Way Shot Power-Up
During gameplay, press Down (2), Up, C-Right. This may only be used five times a level.

Pulse Wave Power-Up
During gameplay, press Up, Down, C-Right, C-Left. This may only be used five times a level.

Flamethrower Power-Up
During gameplay, press Down, Right, Down, Right, C-Right. This may only be used five times a level.

Level Select
At the Setup screen, press Down, Up, C-Left, Down, C-Left, C-Right, Down, C-Right.

---

50 Lives
At the Setup screen, press Up (2), Down (2), Left, Right, Left, Right, C-Left, C-Right, C-Left, C-Right.

Monochrome Mode
At the Setup screen, press Up, Down, Right, C-Left, Down, Up, Left, C-Right, Up, Down.

CPU Control
While at the Setup screen, quickly press Left, Right, Up, Down, Left-C, Right-C, Left-C, Right-C, Left, Right, Up, Down, Left-C, Right-C, Left-C, Right-C, Left, Right, Up, Down, Left-C, Right-C, Left-C, Right-C.

Start with 110 Lives (Easy)
Enter the password BSBBBBTJBB.

Start with 110 Lives (Normal)
Enter the password BCBBLBTJBB.

Start with 110 Lives (Insane)
Enter the password BFBBBCTJBB.

Before Final Level
Enter the password BBBBNBFFBR.

ROCKET: ROBOT ON WHEELS

All Vehicles
Pause gameplay and press Up, Down, Z, R, Left, Up, Down, Left, Down (2).

Low Friction
Pause gameplay and press Up, R (2), Left, Z (2), Down, Left, Up, Right.

Low Gravity
Pause gameplay and press Z, R, Z, R, Down, R (2), Right (2), R.

Heavy Rocket
Pause gameplay and press Up, Right (2), R, Right, R, Z, R (2), Up.

Super Speed
Pause gameplay and press Z, Right, Down, Up, Down, R, Up, Down, Left, Up.

Super Jump
Pause gameplay and press Down, Up, Down, Z, Up (3), R, Up, Z.

Super Grab
Pause gameplay and press Down, Left, Right, Z, Down, Right, Down (3), Left.

Super Grapple
Pause gameplay and press R (2), Right, Up, Z, Left, R, Z, Left, Up.

Disable All Cheats
Pause gameplay and press Up, Z, Right, Up, Down, R, Up, Down (2), Up.

RUGRATS: SCAVENGER HUNT

Hidden Level
At the title screen, hold Z and press R, A to display the Password screen. Now enter the password Z, A (2), B, R, L.

RUSH 2: EXTREME RACING USA

Cheat Menu
At the Settings screen, hold C-Up+C-Down+C-Left+C-Right+L+R+Z to unlock a Cheat menu under Audio. Enter the Cheat menu and highlight a cheat you wish to unlock. Hold L+R+C-Up+C-Down+C-Right+C-Left+Z+A. Release the buttons and repeat until the code becomes activated.

SAN FRANCISCO RUSH

The Rock Bonus Track
Enter the password: 8DP5KG5L4G59P G92WVCQY0DRDQ or 9DQ6LH6M5H6$Q H$3XWCR01DTDR. Then start the race and let the timer expire. Return to the Start Game screen and select "One Race," then "Just Play." Press A to select a track. Then at the Car Selection screen, hold C-Left, then hold Z. Release both buttons and press Left. Press B (3), highlight "Setup," and press A to return to the Setup screen. Hold C-Up and then hold Z. Release the buttons again and press Up. Press B, highlight "One Race" and press A. Highlight "Just Play" and press A. Hold C-Right and then hold Z at the Track Selection screen. Release the buttons and press Right. Select the current track by pressing A. Hold C-Down and then hold Z. Release the buttons and press Down, L, R. A sound confirms correct entry. Press B and choose Track 7.

Mines
At the Setup screen, quickly press L, R, L, R, L, R.

Upside-Down Tracks
At the Setup screen, press Up, Right, Down, Left, Down, Right, Up, Left.

Race as a Mine
At the Car Selection screen, press C-Right (2), Z, C-Down, C-Up, Z, C-Left (2).

Race as a Taxi
If you get at least half of the six to eight keys hidden on any track, the taxi becomes unlocked for that track only.

Race as a Street Rod
If you get at least half of the six to eight keys hidden on any track, the street rod becomes unlocked for that track only.

Race as Formula 1 Car
Enter one of the passwords listed under The Rock Bonus Track.

Disable Stuck Car Help
At the Setup screen, press C-Up (4).

Change Rear Tire Size
At the Car Selection screen, hold C-Right, hold C-Left. Release both buttons, then hold C-Left, hold C-Right.

Change Front Tire Size
At the Car Selection screen, hold C-Left, hold C-Right. Release both buttons. Hold C-Right, hold C-Left.

Change Car Size
At the Car Selection screen, hold C-Down, hold C-Up. Release both buttons. Hold C-Up, hold C-Down.

Alternate Fog Color
At the Car Selection screen, hold Z and press C-Down (3).

Toggle Gravity
At the Setup screen, hold Z and press Up, Down. Release Z and press Up, Down, Up, Down.

Toggle Road Textures
At the Setup screen, hold C-Right and press L. Release both buttons and press Z. Hold C-Right and press L. Release C-Right and press Z.

Toggle Camera Distance and Height
During gameplay, hold L and press Up or Down.

Random High Score Entries
At the Records screen, when Fast Times or Best Laps is displayed, press L, R, L, R, L, R, L, R.

Toggle Car Collision Damage
At the Setup screen, press Left, hold Right and press C-Right. Release Right and press C-Up, C-Left, C-Down, Z.

Crashed Car Replay
Crash your car after crossing the finish line. Then when Game Over is flashing, hold L+R+Z. Release the buttons at the High Score screen.

Drive Crashed Car
At the Car Selection screen, hold C-Up and press Z (4).

Resume Race from Crash Location
At the Setup screen, hold Z, hold C-Left, hold C-Right. Release the buttons, except for Z. Hold C-Right, hold C-Left. Release all buttons.

Foggy Night
Enter Options and change "Fog" to the Heavy setting. Hold C-Right+C-Left+C-Down+C-Up and press Right.

Screen Adjustment
Hold L+R and move the analog stick to move the screen.

Reverse Controls
Enter Options and highlight "Mirror." Hold C-Right+C-Left+C-Down+C-Up and press Right. An extra option called "Extreme" appears. This mode changes your controls to the opposite: Right becomes left and vice versa.

Infinite Time
At the Car Selection screen, hold Z, hold C-Left, hold C-Right. Release the buttons, except for Z. Hold C-Up, hold C-Down. A small clock confirms correct entry.

Tag Mode
Abort the race during the countdown sequence of a Two-player Practice game. A timer is set to five minutes and the timer runs for the person who's "it." It's like a game of tag and Player 2 is always "it" first. Tag the other player to make him "it." The game ends when the timer runs out.

SAN FRANCISCO RUSH 2049

Access Cheat Menu
Highlight "Options" at the main menu, then tap Z as you hold down L+R+C-up+C-down.

Invincibility Cheat
From the Cheat menu, select "Invincible," and press C-Right, L, R (2), L, and then, while holding C-Left and C-Down, press Z.

All Parts
From the Cheat menu, select "All Parts," and hold R and L, and press Z. Release the buttons, press C-Down, C-Left, C-Up, C-Left, C-Right. Hold R and L and press Z.

Heavy Car Cheat
From the Cheat menu, select "Mass," and press R+C-Up, L+C-Down, R+C-Left, L+C-Right.

Super Speed
From the Cheat menu, select "Super Speed," and press Z. While holding L and R, press Z again. Release, and press C-Down. Press L+R and C-Down. Release, and press C-Up (3).

All Cars
From the Cheat menu, select "All Cars," and press C-Left (3), C-Up (3), C-Right (3), C-Down (3). While holding C-Up, C-Left, C-Right, C-Down, R, and L, press Z

Invisible Car
From the Cheat menu, select "Invisible Car," and press C-Up, C-Down, C-Left, C-Right, L, R, Z.

Invisible Track
From the Cheat menu, select "Invisible Track," and press C-Right (2). Then press C-Left while holding R and L. Release, and press C-Left (2). Hold R and L, and press C-Left.

Brakes
From the Cheat menu, select "Brakes," and press C-Down (2). Hold R and L, and press C-Up. Release and press C-Up (2). Release and press C-Down while holding R and L.

Super Tires
From the Cheat menu, select "Super Tires," and press Z (3), L, R, C-Up (2), C-Left, C-Right, C-Down.

Super Speed
From the Cheat menu, select "Super Speed," and press Z. Hold R and L, and press Z. Release, and press C-Down. Hold R and L and press C-Down. Release all and press C-Up (3).

Fog Color Change
From the Cheat menu, select "Fog Color," and press L while holding C-Up and C-Right. Release and press R while holding C-Left and C-Down. Release and press C-Right, C-Left, C-Right, C-Left.

Battle Paint Access
From the Cheat menu, select, "Battle Paint Shop," and press Z (3), C-Down (3), C-Left (3), C-Right, C-Up, C-Left, C-Down.

First Place, Race 4 (Beginner)
WX17QQ6FDC XBDWCLCTYC

First Place, Race 5 (Beginner)
BYI7QQBHWC YBFLD@CJFD

First Place, Race 6 (Beginner)
WYI7QQLJ8C 3WJWDGD6%C

First Place, Race 7 (Beginner)
BII7QQWK%C @BMLFLD@MD

First Place, Race 8 (Beginner)
WII7QQ6LLD FXNWFWDQ2D

First Place, Race 2 (Intermediate)
XB@#T3LCGB FWB6C2B42C

First Place, Race 3 (Intermediate)
CC@#T36WDLB LBCWFBCQ3C

First Place, Race 4 (Intermediate)
XC@#T36FNB VBD6GQC%2C

First Place, Race 5 (Intermediate)
CD@#T3BHQB YBFBJLDW9C

First Place, Race 6 (Intermediate)
XD@#T3LJTB 5BG6K2DWQD

First Place, Race 7 (Intermediate)
CF@#T3WKWB %WJWL@DYMD

First Place, Race 8 (Intermediate)
XF@#T36L2B HCK6MLF6LD

First Place, Race 9 (Intermediate)
CG@#t3BN4B KXLWP@FW#D

First Place, Race 10 (Intermediate)
XG@#T3LP6B MCPLRLGQVD

First Place, Race 2 (Extreme)
IWBBBWMCDB KWDWBQBN2B

First Place, Race 3 (Extreme)
FXBBBBYDJB TBH6B6BTFC

First Place, Race 4 (Extreme)
IXBBBB8FLB IWLLCGCBDC

First Place, Race 5 (Extreme)
FYBBBBDHQB 8BMBD6CGIC

First Place, Race 6 (Extreme)
IYBBBBNJTB ?WQ6DBD4WC

First Place, Race 7 (Extreme)
FIBBBWYKWB CCWBGQDYFC

First Place, Race 8 (Extreme)
IIBBBW8L4B JXILG2DNVC

First Place, Race 9 (Extreme)
F2BBBWDN6B MC56GLFQXC

First Place, Race 10 (Extreme)
I2BBBWNP@B QX8BH@FWDD

First Place, Race 11 (Extreme)
F3BBBWYQBC RC%LJLGJFD

First Place, Race 12 (Extreme)
I3BBBW8RDC WXCXKWGLDD

First Place, Race 13 (Extreme)
F4BBBWDVJC 5CD7L@GTCD

First Place, Race 14 (Extreme)
I4BBBWNWNC @XHXMBHG#C

First Place, Race 15 (Extreme)
F5BBBWYXYC ?CM7M2HLTD

First Place, Race 16 (Extreme)
I5BBBW8YYC GYMXNWJBFD

First Place, Race 17 (Extreme)
F6BBBWD24C HDRMPGK63C

First Place, Race 18 (Extreme)
I6BBBWN3@C NYW7PLKYWC

First Place, Race 19 (Extreme)
F7BBBWY4BD VDYCQGLNGC

First Place, Race 20 (Extreme)
I7BBBW85JD XY3MQ6LN3C

Access Disco Track
Get 100,000 points in Stunt mode.

Access Warehouse Track
Get 500,000 points in Stunt mode.

Access Oasis Track
Get 250,000 points in Stunt mode.

Access Obstacle Course
Get 1,000,000 points in Stunt mode.

Unlock Venom Car
Collect all silver coins in Stunt mode.

Unlock Crusher Car
Collect 16 gold coins in Stunt mode.

Unlock LX Car
Collect 24 gold coins in Stunt mode

Unlock GX2 Car
Collect 24 gold coins in Race mode.

Unlock Mini XS Car
Collect 36 gold coins in Race mode.

Unlock Panther Car
Collect all gold and silver coins in both Race and Stunt modes.

Access Downtown Battle Arena
Get 100 kills in Battle mode.

Access Plaza Battle Arena
Get 250 kills in Battle mode.

Access Roadkill Battle Arena
Get 500 kills in Battle mode.

Access Factory Battle Arena
Get 1000 kills in Battle mode.

S.C.A.R.S.

Crystal Cup
Enter the password LGSSSX.

Diamond Cup
Enter the password CRKKYY.

Zenith Cup
Enter the password DZPKKK.

Master Mode and All Bonus Cars
Enter the password PXPRTS.

Scorpion Car
Enter the password SDSSRT.

Cobra Car
Enter the password TRTTLL.

Cheetah Car
Enter the password NRNNRR.

Panther Car
Enter the password YMSTTR.

All Cars and Cups
Enter the password GGWWOO.

All Cars and Tracks
Enter the password WLLVDD or WLLYDD.

Enable All Codes
At the Player Selection screen, press Left, Up, Right, Down, Z, R, Down, Left, Up, Right.

SCOOBY-DOO: CLASSIC CREEPY CAPERS

Unlimited Courage
During gameplay with Shaggy, hold L and press C-Up, C-Left, C-Down, C-Up, C-Down, Up, Right, Down, Left, Up, Left, Down, Right, Up, Down.

Level Skip
During gameplay with Shaggy, hold L and press C-Up, C-Down, C-Up, C-Down, Up, Down, Up, Down, Left, Right, Left, Right.

SHADOW MAN

Play as Deadwing
In the Playhouse, go in a room with a Cyclops playing pool. Kill the Cyclops and jump on the pool table. The message "Cheat Actived" appears. Look in your inventory to find the Book of Shadows. When you open the book, Book of Cheats appears on top. Highlight Play as Deadwing and press Right.

Good and Longer Ending
You normally get the bad ending if you die or go near the chair. Get the better ending by standing on the opposite platform and shooting the Violator with powered-up Shadowgun shots. Defeat him without dying and you will see a longer ending.

Deadside Shotguns
Get off the tram into the Cathedral of Pain. Head straight to a ramp on the left, which leads down to a flow of coals between two platforms. Run on the coals to the left until you encounter some rotating spikes. Follow the path until you find a hole with a pole sticking out. Fall on the left side. You see and hear a "Cheat Activated" message. Now your inventory contains a Book of Shadows. Activate the cheat you just earned, "I like Deadside shotguns."

Play as a Dog
Kill the fat criminal. Explore around the nearby rooms. This enables a cheat where you can play as a Rottweiler.

Play as Duppie
Go to the Asylum: Undercity level. Look at the ceiling. Notice an arching pipe and an accessible ledge nearby. Get on the ledge and jump from the ledge to the pipe. This activates a cheat to let you play as Duppie.

Play as Bloodshot
Go to the third gad temple. Head to the room where you make the big hammer knock over the pillar. Knock the pillar over. Begin to walk across the pillar, but notice a small room to the right. Jump to the room. The "Cheat Activated" sign should appear. Now you can play as Bloodshot.

Play as Deadsider
Use the teddy bear to go to the Gateway by the Asylum. After that, you appear on a bridge over a pool of lava. While facing the door, drop off the left side of the bridge and onto the trail below. Follow the path until you find a dark soul in a room with rafters. Jump on the rafts and one of the crates activates the cheat that gives you Deadsider.

Play as Invisible Man
At Jack the Ripper's stage, go through the Cathedral of Pain and into Down St. Station. Go up the spiral staircase and you'll come to an actual station-looking area with a door directly across from where you enter. Go through the door. Walk down the hallway and go into the two bathrooms around there. When you walk into one of the bathrooms, the "Cheat Activated" message appears. Invisible mode now appears in the Book of Shadows.

Pea Soup Mode
Go to the room filled with small jail cells and a staircase in the Gardelle Jail level. The staircase leads down to more small jail cells. Go down the stairs. Enter the last small cell on the right to unlock Pea Soup mode and make all areas foggy green.

Wireframe Mode
Head to the top floor of Mordant Street, Queens. Enter the only door on the floor. Go right. When you are near the corner, notice the two odd-looking floor panels. Jump over the panels and the "Cheat Activated" message appears. This cheat is now unlocked in the Book of Shadows.

Stick Boy
Go through the flambeau maze. You enter a big chamber containing three voodoo sisters. Make your way up the large ramp. At the top of the ramp, look to the right to see a pathway. Jump on the railing and then jump over to the pathway. Eventually the "Cheat Activated" message appears and this cheat becomes unlocked in the Book of Shadows.

Flame Grilled
Go to the last room in the Temple of Life. There are five altars that let you extend your life meter. Run up to the second altar from the right to activate this cheat.

SIMCITY 2000

Bonus Map
At the title screen, press C-Up (2), C-Down, C-Left (2), C-Right (2), C-Up, C-Right, C-Left, C-Down, Start.

SNOWBOARD KIDS

All Snowboards, Characters, and Courses
At the Starting screen, press Analog-Stick Down, Analog-Stick Up, Down, Up, C-Down, C-Up, L, R, Z, Left, C-Right, Analog-Stick Up, B, Right, C-Left, Start.

Unlock Quicksand Valley Track
Earn gold cups on Tracks 1 through 6 to unlock Quicksand Valley and receive a new snowboard.

Unlock Silver Mountain Track
Earn a gold cup on Quicksand Valley to unlock Silver Mountain and a special ending sequence.

Unlock Ninja Land Track
Earn gold cups on Tracks 1 through 8. Then earn a gold medal on the Silver Mountain bonus track.

Turbo Start
Push Analog-Stick Up and rapidly tap A when the ref says "Ready."

Play as Sinobin
Earn a gold cup on Ninja Land.

SNOWBOARD KIDS 2

All Characters, Tracks, and Snowboards
At the title screen, press Z, B, C-Up, Down, Analog-Stick Left, Analog-Stick Right, Up, R, Z, A.

Expert Mode
Complete Story mode.

Turbo Start
Press B when the announcer says "Go."

Play as Damien
Beat Story mode.

Play as Mr. Penguin
Beat Mr. Penguin in the training session.

Play as Mr. Dog
Go to the Shot Cross and get a perfect score without missing one mailbox.

Play as Coach
Beat Coach in Training mode.

Play as Panda
Pick Mr. Dog with his space suit costume in Battle mode. The character changes to Panda when the race starts.

Unlock Poverty Snowboard
Beat the Sunny Mountain track in Expert mode. You lose money when you use this board.

Unlock Feather Snowboard
Beat the Turtle Island track in Expert mode. This board helps you get more air when jumping.

Unlock Ice Snowboard
Beat the Snowman Boss track in Expert mode. This board is slippery and hard to control.

Unlock Star Snowboard
Beat the Wendy's House track in Expert mode. This board has no special features, but it's a great all-around board.

Unlock Rich Snowboard
Beat the Linda's Castle track in Expert mode. You gain money while using this board.

Unlock Dragon Snowboard
Beat the Dinosaur Boss track in Expert mode. This board comes equipped with rockets and feathers.

Unlock Ninja Snowboard
Beat the Starlight Highway track in Expert mode. This board is invisible when you are using it.

Unlock Charm Snowboard
Beat the Haunted House track in Expert mode. This board gives you ghosting protection.

Unlock High-Tech Snowboard
Beat the Mecha-Damien track in Expert mode. This board comes with the Speed Fan.

SOUTH PARK

Play as Allen
Enter MAJESTIC as a password in the Cheat menu.

Play as Chef
Enter LOVEMACHINE as a password in the Cheat menu.

Play as Gay Al
Enter OUTRAGE as a password in the Cheat menu.

Play as Ike
Enter KICKME as a password in the Cheat menu.

Play as Jimbo
Enter STARINGFROG as a password in the Cheat menu.

Play as Mephisto
Enter GOODSCIENCE as a password in the Cheat menu.

Play as Mr. Garrison
Enter DORTHYSFRIEND as a password in the Cheat menu.

Play as Mr. Mackey
Enter CHEATINGISBAD as a password in the Cheat menu.

Play as Mrs. Cartman
Enter ALLWOMAN as a password in the Cheat menu.

Play as Ned
Enter HAWKING as a password in the Cheat menu.

Play as Officer Barbrady
Enter ELVISLIVES as a password in the Cheat menu.

Play as Phillip
Enter PHAERT as a password in the Cheat menu.

Play as Pip
Enter FISHNCHIPS as a password in the Cheat menu.

Play as Starvin Marvin
Enter SLAPupMEAL as a password in the Cheat menu.

Play as Terrance
Enter RAFT as a password in the Cheat menu.

Play as Wendy
Enter CHECKATACO as a password in the Cheat menu.

All Cheats
Enter BOBBYBIRD as a password in the Cheat menu.

Big Head Mode
Enter MEGANOGGIN as a password in the Cheat menu.

Pen and Ink Mode
Enter PLANEARIUM as a password in the Cheat menu.

Skinny Players
Enter VEGGIEHEAVEN as a password in the Cheat menu.

View Credits
Enter SCREWYOUGUYS as a password in the Cheat menu.

All Characters in Multiplayer
Enter OBGTKKYB as a password in the Cheat menu.

All Weapons
Enter FATKNACKER as a password in the Cheat menu.

God Mode
Enter ASSMAN as a password in the Cheat menu.

Level Select
Enter THEEARTHMOVED as a password in the Cheat menu.

Unlimited Ammo
Enter FATTERKNACKER as a password in the Cheat menu.

SOUTH PARK: CHEF'S LUV SHACK

Beefcake Bonus Animation
Eat all the cans of Weight Gain 4000 in the Beefcake mini-game to see a bonus animation at the end.

Variety of Minigames
Use Cartman to see a better variety of minigames. Cartman is the only character who can play the Beefcake and Rodeo minigames.

SOUTH PARK RALLY

Cheat Mode
Win Championship mode without using any tokens.

All Skins
Get the three hidden pick-ups in the Valentine's Day race.

Play as Bebe
Lose the Cow Days race and don't get any health power-ups.

Play as Big Gay Al
Win the Pink Lemonade race.

Play as Cartman Cop
In the Read a Book Day race, hit the Chicken Lover five times with the salty balls.

Play as Damian
Win the New Year's race, being the only racer to touch the millennium key.

Play as Death
In the Halloween race, drop off four candies at a time, then win the race.

Play as Grandpa
Win the Halloween race.

Play as Ike
In the Memorial Day race, get the hidden power-up on top of the airplane.

Play as Jesus
Win the Christmas race.

Play as Marvin
Win the Thanksgiving race and don't get any turkeys.

Play as Mephisto
Win the Independence Day race.

Play as Mr. Garrison
In the Rally Days 2 race, activate all four checkpoints.

Play as Mr. Mackey
Win the Spring Cleaning race.

Play as Mrs. Cartman
In Pink Lemonade race, drop off all lemonades without letting any other racer get to a checkpoint.

Play as Ned
In the Independence Day race, get more than 12 turbo pick-ups.

Play as Pip
In the Rally Days 2 race, activate Checkpoints 1 and 4.

Play as Satan
Win the New Year's race.

Play as Scuzzlebutt
In the Easter Egg Hunt race, get a Phillip Phart. Then find the waterfall and Phart your way to the Golden Cow next to the waterfall.

Play as Sheila Broflovski
In the Easter Egg Hunt race, get the Pot Pie next to the building.

Play as Shelly
Win the Valentine's Day race.

Play as Terrance and Phillip
In the Christmas race, get the four hidden power-ups.

Play as Tweak
In the Spring Cleaning race, get five caffeine pick-ups.

Play as Visitor
In the Memorial Day race, get the hidden power-up above Checkpoint 1 and another power-up between Checkpoint 4 and the wood bridge.

Random Checkpoints Option
Complete the entire Championship mode.

Speech Test Option
Complete the entire Championship mode.

Random Track Option
Complete the entire Championship mode.

Cheat Sheet Option
Don't collect any pick-ups and win the Rally Days 1 race.

SPACE DYNAMITES

Fight as Final Boss
Press A, B, R, L, C-Down at the title screen.

Secret Combo
Press C-Up+C-Down+C-Left when your combo meter is full.

SPACE INVADERS

Classic Mode
Beat the game under Normal, and Classic mode will appear at the main menu.

Maniac Mode
Beat the game under Expert and Maniac mode will appear at the main menu.

SPACE STATION SILICON VALLEY

Bonus Energy
Press C-Left, L, Z, Down, L, Z, C-Left, C-Right at the Level Select or Saved Game screen. A sound confirms correct entry. Select a saved game or level.

Asteroid Level
Press Down, Up, Z, L, Down, Left, Z, Down at the Level Select or Saved Game screen. A sound confirms correct entry. Start game and press Left.

Desert Level
Press Up, Down, L, Z, Down, Left, Z, Down at the Level Select or Saved Game screen. A sound confirms correct entry. Start game and press Left.

Europe Level
Press Up, Down, L, Z, Down, Up, Z at the Level Select or Saved Game screen. A sound confirms correct entry. Start a game and press Left.

Ice Level
Press Up, Down, Z, L, Down, C-Right, Z, Down at the Level Select or Saved Game screen. A sound confirms correct entry. Start a game and press Left.

Jungle Level
Press Up, Down, L, Z, Down, C-Left, Z, Down at the Level Select or Saved Game screen. A sound confirms correct entry. Start a game and press Left.

Final Level
Press Up, Down, L, Z, Down, Right, Z, Down at the Level Select or Saved Game screen. A sound confirms correct entry. Start a game and press Left.

Secret Level
Press Down, Up, Z, L, Down, Left, Z, Down at the Level Select or Saved Game screen. Start game and press Left.

Funny Effects 1
Press Up, L, Z, Down, Left, Z, Down, Up at the Level Select or Saved Game screen. A sound confirms correct entry. Select a saved game or level.

Funny Effects 2
Press L, Down, Z, L, Down, Up, L, Left at the Level Select or Saved Game screen. A sound confirms correct entry. Select a saved game or level.

Funny Effects 3
Press Z, Down, Up, L, Right, L, Left, Right at the Level Select or Saved Game screen. A sound confirms correct entry. Select a saved game or level.

Funny Effects 4
Press Left, Right, Z, L, Left, Z, Right, Left at the Level Select or Saved Game screen. A sound confirms correct entry. Select a saved game or level.

Golden Evo
Collect all 390 metal orbs on the last stage when you are playing as Evo. This turns Evo from silver to gold.

Different Intro Sequence
Hold A or B when you turn on the Nintendo 64. Two different intros appear depending on which button you are pressing.

Stop Camera in Wall Race
Press Down, A, C-Up, L, C-Down, L, Left at the Level Select or Saved Game screen. A sound confirms correct entry. Select a saved game or level.

SPIDER-MAN

Unlock Everything
Enter TRUBLEVR at the Special/Cheats menu.

Level Select
Enter LVLSKIPPER at the Special/Cheats menu.

Invincibility
Enter TURTLE at the Special/Cheats menu.

Full Health
Enter HELP ME at the Special/Cheat menu.

Sound Test
Enter LISTEN at the Special/Cheat menu.

Infinite Webbing
Enter STICKYSTUF at the Special/Cheat menu.

View All Comic Books
Enter CLTTHMALL at the Special/Cheat menu.

View All Game Covers
Enter COV VIEW at the Special/Cheat menu.

Access All Characters in Spidey's Gallery
Enter WHOSINTGM at the Special/Cheat menu.

Access Storyboard Viewer
Enter SMESTORY at the Special/Cheat menu.

Unlock Symbiote Costume
Enter SYMBSPID at the Special/Cheat menu.

Unlock Spider-Man 2099 Costume
Enter SPTWOKNN at the Special/Cheat menu.

Unlock Captain Universe Costume
Enter POWCOSMIC at the Special/Cheat menu.

Unlock Spider-Man: Unlimited Costume
Enter LIMITEDED at the Special/Cheat menu.

Unlock Scarlet Spider Costume
Enter SPIDINRED at the Special/Cheat menu.

Unlock Peter Parker Costume
Enter MISTERMJ at the Special/Cheat menu.

Unlock Ben Reilly Costume
Enter DACLONE at the Special/Cheat menu.

Unlock Quick Change Spider-Man Costume
Enter GTATNKFST at the Special/Cheat menu.

ST. ANDREWS OLD COURSE GOLF

Change Golfer's Clothes
When you tee up, press any of the four C-Buttons to change your golfer's clothes.

Mini and Giant Golfers
While you're in the Player Configuration Mode, put the cursor on top of your character, press and hold all four C-Buttons at the same time, then press A. You are now able to customize your player's stature and pick height data from 10 to 255 cm.

STARCRAFT 64

Shopping list Access
Press R and Z during gameplay.

Unlock Invincibility
Complete the final round of Episode 3 in Brood War.

Fog of War Off
Fly past the small island in Episode 3 in Brood War with a white flag on it. Touch the flag.

Mega Build/Faster Build Cheat
Save the first two hives in the first level of Episode 6 of Brood War. Explore the corners until you find the data disc. Touch it to unlock the cheat.

Info Mana Cheat
Complete the final round in Brood War.

Access Bonus Mission
Complete the Zerg mission of Brood War with at least five minutes remaining.

STARFOX 64

Control Title Screen
Beat the game on any path. When you return to the title screen, use the analog stick to move the 64 logo.

Play as Land Master
Win a medal on Vemon under Normal. The Land Master becomes available in Versus mode.

Alternate Title Screen
Win all 30 medals in the game: 15 under Normal and 15 under Expert.

Play on Foot
Win a medal on Vemon under Expert. Now you may play Falco, Fox, Peppy, or Slippy on foot in Versus mode.

Expert Mode
Win a medal on all 15 levels with the number of hits exceeding the following minimums and keeping all your wingmen alive: Aquas: 150, Area 6: 300, Corneria: 150, Fortuna: 50, Katina: 150, Macbeth: 150, Meteo: 200, Sector X: 150, Sector Y: 150, Sector Z: 100, Solar: 100, Titania: 150, Venom: 200, Boluse: 150, Zoness: 300.

Tanks in Versus Mode
Obtain a medal on Venom.

Disable the Crosshair
Press R when the game is paused.

STAR SOLDIER: VANISHING EARTH

Bonus Options
Beat the game under Regular difficulty.

Alternate Mode Selection Screen
Beat the game under Beginner difficulty.

STAR WARS: EPISODE I—THE BATTLE FOR NABOO

Unlock Hard Mode
NASTYMDE

Fly a Pink Fighter
RUAGIRL?

Unlock Advanced Shields
DROIDEKA

Unlock Graphics Gallery
KOOLSTUF

See the Development Team
LOVEHUTT

Unlock All Levels
TOOWEAK?

Unlock All Levels and One Bonus Level
LEC&FIVE

Infinite Lives
PATHETIC

Receive All Upgrades
OVERLOAD

Allow One-Hit Kills
EWERDEAD

Unlock Expert Mode
NASTYMDE

Unlock Developer Commentary of the Game
TALKTOME

Unlock Advanced Blasters
ADEGAN

Unlock Advanced Bombs
BOOM!?

Unlock Advanced Missiles
?NUNAPWR

Unlock Homing Torpedoes and Missiles
CANTMISS

Unlock Rapid Fire Lasers
OVERLOAD

STAR WARS: EPISODE I RACER

Six Pit Droids
In empty Tournament save spot, hold Z. Enter RRPITDROID by entering the letters with L. Select "End" and put in any initials. At Watto's shop, press Up, Down, Left, Right (2), Up.

Unlock All Cheats
Select an empty Tournament save spot. Hold Z and use L to enter RRTANGENT. Select "End" and press L, B. Select the same file, now hold Z and use L to enter ABACUS. Select "End" and press L, A. Begin a race on a Tournament track and pause the game. Now press Up, Left, Down, Right to access the Cheat menu.

Invincibility
In empty Tournament save spot, hold Z. Enter RRJABBA with L. Still hold Z down and press L to push the end button. Press A. Pause the game in a Tournament Track race and press Up, Left, Down, Right to access the Cheat menu. Turn on the Invincibility option for this code to work.

Turbo Start
Press A when the number one disappears during countdown for a quick start.

Debug Option
In empty Tournament save spot, hold down Z and use L to enter RRDEBUG as your name. Still hold Z down and use L to push the end button. Using the same process as before, enter RRTANGENTABACUS. Start a race and pause the game. Then push Up, Left, Down, Right. Cheat options should now show up.

CPU Controlled Racer
Enter the Unlock All Cheats code above. While playing, press R, Z. The computer controls the racer and the only thing you control is the speed. Press R, Z to regain control of the racer.

Dual Control Mode
In empty Tournament save spot, hold Z and use L to enter RRDUAL. Select "End" and press L followed by A. Now you can play the game with two controllers. You must have a controller in port 1 and 3 to play the game with two controllers.

Taunting Opponents
Pick Tournament mode. At the menu, highlight "Start Race." Hold Z and press A to begin the race. A sequence pops up showing your character and opponent taunting each other. Press R, R during the race to taunt your opponent more.

Mirror Mode
Select an empty game save. Hold Z down and use L to enter RRTHEBEAST. Select "End" and press L. Enter your name as usual. During a race, pause and enter Left, Down, Right, Up to enable Mirror mode.

Play as Cy Yunga
You must have Bullseye Navior to use this code. Select an empty game save. Hold down Z and use L to enter RRCYYUN. Highlight "End" and press L.

Play as Jinn Reeso
This code only works after you unlock Mars Guo. Select an empty game save. Hold down Z and use L to enter RRJINNRE. Highlight "End" and press L.

See Through Walls
Enter the Debug Option code and set the Debug Level option to any number except zero. Press Left+Z.

Invisible Racer
Enter the Debug Option code and set the Debug Level option to any number except zero. Press Left.

Destroy the Pod Racer
Enter the Debug Option code and set the Debug Level option to any number except zero. Press Right.

Fast Forward Level
Enter the Debug Option code and set the Debug Level option to any number except zero. Press Up.

Rewind Level
Enter the Debug Option code and set the Debug Level option to any number except zero. Press Down.

Unlock Sebulba
Place first on Boonta Classic, Galactic.

Unlock Aldar Beedo
Place first on Beedo's Wild Ride, Amateur.

Unlock Ark Bumpy Roose
Place first on Bumpy's Breakers, Semi-pro.

Unlock Ratts Tyerell
Place first on Howler Gorge, Semi-pro.

Unlock Slide Paramita
Place first on AP Centrum, Invitational.

Unlock Mawhonic
Place first on Andobi Mountain Run, Galactic.

Unlock Clegg Holdfast
Place first on Aquilaris Classic, Amateur.

Unlock Bullseye Navior
Place first on Sunken City, Semi-pro.

Unlock Bozzie Baranta
Place first on Abyss, Invitational.

Unlock Wan Sandage
Place first on Scrapper's Run, Semi-pro.

Unlock Neva Kee
Place first on Baroo Coast, Semi-pro.

Unlock Ben Quadinaros
Place first on Inferno, Invitational.

Unlock Teemto Pagalies
Place first on Mon Gazza Speedway, Amateur.

Unlock Mars Guo
Place first on Spice Mine Run, Amateur.

Unlock Boles Roor
Place first on Zugga Challenge, Semi-pro.

Unlock Fud Sang
Place first on Vengeance, Amateur.

Unlock Toy Dampner
Place first on Executioner, Galactic.

STAR WARS: ROGUE SQUADRON

All Levels and Ships
Enter DEADDACK as a code.

Unlimited Lives
Enter IGIVEup as a code.

Fly the Millennium Falcon
Enter FARMBOY as a code.

Fly the TIE Interceptor
Enter TIEDup as a code. The TIE Interceptor is hidden behind the Millennium Falcon in the hangar. Push Up on the analog stick for a couple seconds to be able to select the TIE Interceptor.

Fly the Naboo Starfighter
Enter HALIFAX? as a code. Then enter !YNGWIE! as a second passcode. To disable this code just enter HALIFAX? again.

Fly a Car
Enter KOELSCH as a code.

Play as AT-ST
Enter CHICKEN as a code.

Improved Radar
Enter RADAR as a code.

All Power-Ups
Enter TOUGHGUY as a code.

Music Menu
Enter MAESTRO as a code.

View Credits
Enter CREDITS as a code.

Development Team Photos
Enter BLAMEUS as a code.

Watch Cutscenes
Enter DIRECTOR as a code.

Beggar's Canyon
Earn a Bronze medal or better in all missions to fly a T-16 Skyhopper through Beggar's Canyon.

Death Star Trenches
Earn a Silver medal in all missions for a new level to fly in a Death Star trench run.

Battle of Hoth
Earn a Gold medal in all missions to fly a snowspeeder in the Battle of Hoth.

Ship Selections
Earn a Gold medal in the Battle of Hoth level. Now you can select most ships for any mission.

STAR WARS: SHADOWS OF THE EMPIRE

Make sure the codes are entered exactly. They are case sensitive.

All Weapons
Enter your name as _Jabba ("_" represents a space). Start a game on Jedi difficulty.

Control Enemies
Enter your name as _Wampa__Stompa ("_" represents a space).

Control an AT-ST
Enable the Control Enemies code. Go perform this code at the Battle of Hoth level once you see the AT-STs. Press Left+C-Right, Up. Press C-Right to change views until the AT-ST is displayed.

Control a Trooper
Enable the Control Enemies code. At the Echo Base, Gall Spaceport, or Imperial Freighter Suprosa levels, press Right+C-Right, Up. Press C-Right to change views until the Stormtrooper is displayed.

View Credits
Enter your name as _Credits ("_" represents a space).

View Development Staff
Enable the View Credits code first. After the credits are finished, the game returns to the title screen. Press Up on the analog stick.

Hidden Credits
Beat the game. During the entire ending sequence, hold C-Right. Look at the screen's bottom to see hidden text.

Fly X-Wing or TIE Fighter
Change the controller configuration to Traditional settings. Pause the game. Hold Left+C-Left+C-Down+C-Right+L+R+Z and press the analog stick Up or Down.

No Flight Sequences
Enter your name as "Joe," set the difficulty level to Easy, and start a game.

Wampa Sounds
Enter your name as R_Testers_ROCK ("_" represents a space). The Wampa sound effects play whenever a menu is displayed.

STUNT RACER 64

Access Snowboard Racer
Enter BUCKYB as player name.

Race Using Milk Truck
Enter MOOOOO as player name.

Money Cheat
Press B, Z (2), B, Up, C-Down, Z, Start on Controller 2 during gameplay.

Overhead View
Press Up (3), A, Left, A (3) on Controller 2 during gameplay.

Blurry View
Press B, Left, Up, Right (3), A, Start (2), Z, Right, A, up, Z, C-Down, Start on Controller 2 during gameplay.

SUPER ROBOT SPIRITS

All Characters
Press L (9), R (7), Z, C-Down (10), C-Right (5) at the opening screen before the Banpresto logo disappears.

Choose Victory Pose
Hold L or R at the end of a match, when the screen says "K.O."

Unlock Master Gundam
In Story mode, defeat Master Gundam three times in a row.

Unlock Super Mode Shining Gundam
In Versus mode, pick Shining Gundam and any other opponent. Defeat Shining Gundam 21 times in a row. Press Start the next time you highlight Shining Gundam for the next fight. It says something in Japanese if the code was entered correctly.

Unlock Devil Gundam
Beat Story mode with all the fighters. Use Master Gundam in 64 mode and defeat Devil Gundam.

Unlock Judecca
Accrue more than 300 hours of gameplay.

Different Walker Galliam and Dunbine Costumes
Accrue more than 50 hours of gameplay. Highlight Walker Galliam or Dunbine and press Start for their alternate costumes.

SUPERCROSS 2000

Cheat Screen
At the Select Event menu, press C-Up.

No Crashes
Enter N0CR4SH at the Cheat screen.

Big Bikes
Enter B1GB1K3S at the Cheat screen.

Giant Riders
Enter G14NTS at the Cheat screen.

Additional Views
Enter M0R3C4MS at the Cheat screen.

Headless Rider
Enter H34DL3SS at the Cheat screen.

No Riders
Enter N0R1D3RS at the Cheat screen.

Mercury Gravity
Enter M3RCVRY at the Cheat screen.

Venus Gravity
Enter V3NVS at the Cheat screen.

Moon Gravity
Enter M00N at the Cheat screen.

Mars Gravity
Enter M4RS at the Cheat screen.

Jupiter Gravity
Enter JVP1T3R at the Cheat screen.

Saturn Gravity
Enter S4TVRN at the Cheat screen.

Uranus Gravity
Enter VR4NVS at the Cheat screen.

Neptune Gravity
Enter N3PTVN3 at the Cheat screen.

Pluto Gravity
Enter PLVT0 at the Cheat screen.

Cancel Off Track Reset
Enter N00FFTR4CK at the Cheat screen.

Cancel Skipping Track Reset
Enter SK1PP1NG0K at the Cheat screen.

Big Dirt Sprays
Enter B1GSPR4Y at the Cheat screen.

All Riders Block You
Enter BL0CKM3 at the Cheat screen.

Hopping Bike
Enter H0P at the Cheat screen.

SUPERMAN

Level Select
Begin a Single-player game. Play until you can save your game on the controller pak; save and then reset. Load your saved game. A prompt asks you to insert a Rumble Pack. Hold L+B for a second and then press A. A level selection screen appears and you can play any levels on the current difficulty setting. You can still change the difficulty by changing it in the options menu.

Cheat Mode
Activate Cheat mode by pressing C-Up, C-Left, C-Down, C-Right at the main menu. A sound confirms correct entry.

Heat Vision
Activate Cheat Mode. Pause the game and press R, L.

Level Skip
Activate Cheat Mode. Pause the game and press C-Up, C-Down.

Refill Health
Activate Cheat Mode. Pause the game and press Z, R.

Super Speed
Activate Cheat Mode. Pause the game and press R, Z.

Super Punch
Activate Cheat Mode. Pause the game and press L, Z.

Super Breath
Activate Cheat Mode. Pause the game and press Z, L.

TARZAN

Cheat Mode
At the main menu, press Left (2), Right (2), Up, Down, Left, Right, Up (2), Down (2).

TETRISPHERE

Level Select
Enter the name Saturn, Spaceship, Rocket, Heart, Skull. Press L+C-Right+C-Down to enter the special characters.

Bonus Music
Enter the name G[Alien head]MEBOY. Press L+C-Right+C-Down to enter the special characters.

Lines Minigame
Enter the name LINES.

View Vortex Sequence
Enter the name VORTEX. Then hold the reset button.

View Credits
Enter the name CREDITS.

Secret Characters
Press L, C-Right, C-Down at the New Name screen to bring up the secret characters.

TOM AND JERRY IN FISTS OF FURY

Unlock Cheat Menu
Defeat the single-player game with every character on any difficulty.

Unlock Teamplay Mode
Complete the game with Spike.

Unlock Duckling
Complete the game with Tom or Jerry.

Unlock Butch
Complete the game with Duckling.

Unlock Spike Jr.
Complete the game with Butch.

Unlock Tuffy
Complete the game with Spike Jr.

Unlock Spike
Complete the game with Tuffy.

TONIC TROUBLE

Final Battle
Pause the game. Press A, B, A, B, A, Left, Right, Up, Down, Z.

High Energy
Beat the game using a memory card. Begin a new game and your energy level will be the same as when you beat the game.

All Items
Stand on mushroom and face the scientist when you first meet him. Press R (2), Analog-Stick Up, Analog-Stick Down, D-Pad Up, D-Pad Down, C-Up, C-Down, C-Left, C-Right, C-Up (2), C-Left (2), C-Right (2), C-Up (2), C-Down (2), Analog-Stick Up, Analog-Stick Down, Analog-Stick Left, Analog-Stick Right, Start. Press all those buttons quickly and if you entered the code correctly, after 30 to 45 seconds the scientist will say you have all the items.

TONY HAWK'S PRO SKATER

Random Starting Location
Pause gameplay, hold L and press C-Left, C-Right, C-Down, Up, Down. If you did it correctly, the screen will shake.

Perfect Balance
Pause gameplay, hold L and press C-Up, C-Right, Left, C-Right, Right, Up, Down. If you did it correctly, the screen will shake.

10 Times Trick Multiplier
Pause gameplay, hold L and press Down, Right, Up, Right, Up, Left, C-Left. If you did it correctly, the screen will shake.

Stats to 10
Pause gameplay, hold L and press C-Up, C-Left, Left, Up, C-Down. If you did it correctly, the screen will shake.

Stats to 13
Pause gameplay, hold L and press C-Up, C-Left, Left, Up, Down. If you did it correctly, the screen will shake.

Unlimited Special
Pause gameplay, hold L and press C-Down, C-Up, C-Left, Down, Up, Down. If you did it correctly, the screen will shake.

Fast Specials
Pause gameplay, hold L and press C-Up, Left, C-Down (2), Up, Down, Right. If you did it correctly, the screen will shake.

All Tapes
Pause gameplay, hold L and press C-Right, Left, Up, C-Up (2), Right, Down, Up. If you did it correctly, the screen will shake.

Slow Motion
Pause gameplay, hold L and press Down (2), C-Up, C-Right, Left. If you did it correctly, the screen will shake.

Turbo Mode
Pause gameplay, hold L and press Right, Up, Down (2), Up, Down. If you did it correctly, the screen will shake.

Girl's Picture
Pause gameplay, hold L and press C-Left, C-Down, C-Right, C-Left, C-Down, C-Right (2). If you did it correctly, the screen will shake.

Officer Dick
In Career Mode, get all 30 tapes.

Private Carrera
In any mode, start a game as Officer Dick. Then pause gameplay, hold L and press C-Left, C-Down, C-Right, C-Down, Up, Right, Left. If you did it correctly, the screen will not shake. Quit the game and go to the Character Selection screen. Officer Dick will be replaced with Private Carrera.

View Skaters Special Moves
Get a gold in all three competitions with any character. This unlocks a Trick Tutorial option in the Extras menu. The tutorial shows you how to perform that character's special moves.

TONY HAWK'S PRO SKATER 2

Enable Perfect Balance
This code has the potential to wreck your game. Press and hold L, then press C-down, right, down, C-left, C-down, C-up, C-right, C-left.

Make Skater's Stats 10
To make the current skater's stats 10, pause the game and hold L. Then press down, up, C-up, C-left, down, up, C-up.

Make Skater's Stats 13
To make the current skater's stats 13, pause the game and hold L. Then press C-down, C-right, C-right, C-up, up, down, right, left.

Make Your Skater Thin
To make your skater thinner, pause the game. Press and hold L, then press left, C-right, right, down, C-down, up, up.

Multiply Score by 10
To multiply your score by 10, pause the game and hold L. Press C-down, C-down, C-down, C-down, C-up, right, C-right, right.

Unlimited Special Meter
To get unlimited special meter, pause the game and hold L, then press C-left, C-down, C-up, right, C-right, right.

Unlock Flight Mode
To unlock flight mode, pause the game. Press and hold L, then press right, up, C-up, C-down, C-left, C-left, C-right.

Unlock McSqueeb
Complete Career Mode 100% with Tony Hawk to unlock McSqueeb as Tony's third costume.

Unlock Spider-Man
Complete the game 100% with a created skater.

Unlock Trixie
Find all of the gaps in the game to unlock Trixie as a playable character.

Unlock Turbo Mode
To unlock Turbo Mode, pause the game and hold L. Then press C-left, C-down, C-up, down, up, right.

TOP GEAR: HYPERBIKE

Unlock All Tracks
Press Up, Left, Right, L, Z, R at the Mode Selection screen.

Unlock All Bikes
Press Up, Left, Right, L, Z, R, Up, Down (2), Z, Down at the Mode Selection screen.

TOP GEAR: OVERDRIVE

All Standard Cars
Using the analog stick, highlight "Credits," "Championship," "Championship," "Versus," and press Z after each.

First Bonus Car
Using the analog stick, highlight "Credits," "Versus," "Setup," "Championship," "Versus," "Versus," and press Z after each.

Second Bonus Car
Using the analog stick, highlight "Championship," "Credits," "Versus," "Setup," "Versus," "Championship," "Setup," "Credits," and press Z after each.

Third Bonus Car
Using the analog stick, highlight "Versus," "Versus," "Championship," "Credits," "Championship," "Versus," "Championship," "Credits," "Setup," "Versus," "Setup," and press Z after each.

Dump Truck
Using the analog stick, highlight "Setup," "Versus," "Championship," "Setup," and press Z after each.

All Cars
Using the analog stick, highlight "Credits," "Credits," "Versus," "Credits," "Setup," "Championship," "Championship," "Championship," "Versus," and press Z after each.

Season Four
Using the analog stick, highlight "Versus," "Championship," "Championship," "Credits," "Setup," "Setup," "Championship," and press Z after each.

Season Five
Using the analog stick, highlight "Setup," "Championship," "Credits," "Versus," "Versus," "Setup," "Championship," "Versus," "Credits," "Championship," and press Z after each.

Season Six
Using the analog stick, highlight "Credits," "Setup," "Versus," "Championship," "Championship," "Credits," "Championship," "Versus," "Setup," "Championship," "Credits," "Setup," "Setup," and press Z after each.

Alternate Credits
Using the analog stick, highlight "Setup," "Setup," "Championship," "Versus," and press Z after each.

View Wienermobile Sequence
Using the analog stick, highlight "Credits," "Versus," "Setup," "Championship," "Versus," "Versus," and press Z after each.

View NP Car Sequence
Using the analog stick, highlight "Championship," "Credits," "Versus," "Setup," "Versus," "Championship," "Setup," "Credits," and press Z after each.

View Nintendo Logo Car Sequence
Using the analog stick, highlight "Credits," "Versus," "Versus," "Championship," "Credits," "Championship," "Versus," "Championship," "Credits," "Setup," "Versus," and press Z after each.

TOP GEAR RALLY

All Tracks
At the Arcade Mode screen, press A, Left (2), Right, Down, Z.

Mirror Tracks
After you start a race, press Right, Up, Left, C-Down, Right, Down, Z.

All Cars Except Bonus Cars
At the Arcade Mode screen, press A, Left (2), C-Down, A, Right, Z.

Beach Ball Car
At the Arcade Mode screen, press B (2), A, Left (2), C-Down, A, Right. You will enter and leave menus when you enter this code, but the car will be on the car select menu.

Cupra Car
At the Arcade Mode screen, press C-Down, Up, B, Right, A, C-Down, A, Right.

Helmet Car
At the Arcade Mode screen, press Up (2), Z, B, A, Left (2). You will enter and leave menus when you enter this code, but the car will be on the Car Select menu.

Milk Truck
Press Down, A, Right, Z, Right, Up, C-Down at the menu at the menu screens before the race.

Level Select
Go to practice. Play on the Mirror jungle. Press A, B (2), A, B, A, Z, A and then choose what level you want to go to.

View Real Credits
Go to the Options screen and click on the Credits icon. Press Left, C-Down, Right, Down, Z.

Remove Bi-Linear Filtering
Press B, Left, Right, Up, Left, Z, Right during gameplay. Enter the code again to disable this trick.

Rainbow Mode
Press C-Down, Z, B, Up (2), Right during gameplay.

Official Completion Date
Hold down C-Right+C-Left+C-Up+C-Down after you start the game. A date appears on the screen telling you the official completion date of Top Gear Rally.

TOP GEAR RALLY 2

No Damage or Failures
Press L, Z, Start, Up (2) at the title screen.

Bouncy Cars
Press C-Up, C-Left, R, L, Down at the title screen.

Repair Power
Press L, Z, R, L, Start at the Race Description screen.

High Resolution Mode
Press C-Left (2), Left, L (2) at the title screen. You need the 4MB expansion pak for this code to work.

Big Tire
Press C-Left, Z, R, Down (2) at the title screen.

Wobbly Tire
Press R, C-Right, Start, Down, Z at the title screen.

Speed Based Aspect Ratio
Press Z, C-Left, L, Up, Right at the title screen.

Speed Warp View
Press Z, C-Left, R, Up, Right at the title screen.

Upside-Down World
Press C-Up, Z, Start, Up, Down at the title screen.

Thin World
Press Z, C-Right, R, Up, Right at the title screen.

Fat World
Press Z, C-Right, L, Up, Right at the title screen.

Volcano Valley World
Press C-Left, Z, R, L, Down at the title screen.

Max Championship Points in Support Van
Press L, C-Up, Left, L (2) at the title screen.

100,000 Sponsor Credits in Support Van
Press L, Z, Start, L (2) at the title screen.

TOY STORY 2

Level Select
Press Up (4), Down (2), Up (2), Down (3) at the Options screen. A sound confirms correct entry.

Unlimited Lives
Give Potato Head his ear and then get the cosmic shield. Go to Al's Penthouse and run into the shield. Then run to the fireplace to grab the extra life inside there. Exit the level and re-enter Al's Penthouse to repeat this process.

TRANSFORMERS: BEAST WARS TRANSMETALS

Unlock Blackarachnia
Highlight Tarantulas at the character select screen and press Z and A. Then move left or right to select the new character.

Unlock Ravage
To unlock Ravage in Arcade or Versus Mode, stop on Cheetor at the Character Select screen. Hold Z and press A. Now, Use the Left and Right to cycle through the color selections until you see Ravage.

Unlock Starscream
To play as Starscream, highlight Waspinator at the character select screen and hit Z and A. Move left or right to select Starscream.

Unlock Tigatron and Ravage
To play as both Ravage and Tigatron, highlight Cheetor at the character select screen and press Z and A. Then move left or right to select the other two characters.

TRIPLE PLAY 2000

Instant Three Outs
Hold L+R+Z and press Down, Up while playing.

Instant Three Ball Count
Hold L+R+Z and press Up, Down while playing.

Home Run Sounds
Press any of the C buttons to make sounds while you are running around the bases after you hit a home run.

Hit a Homer
Hold L+R+Z and press Left, Up, Left, Up while you are in the batter's box.

Instant Strike Out

Hold L+R+Z and press Right, Up, Right, Up while you are on the pitcher's mound.

One Run for Home Team

Hold L+R+Z and press C-Left (2) during gameplay.

One Run for Away Team

Hold L+R+Z and press C-Right (2) during gameplay.

TUROK: DINOSAUR HUNTER

Ultimate Code

Start a game, pause, go to the Cheat menu, and enter NTHGTHDGDCRTDTRK. This gives you invincibility, infinite ammo, all weapons, infinite lives, maps, big head, warps, and level skip.

All Weapons

Start a game, pause, go to the Cheat menu, and enter CMGTSMMGGTS.

Unlimited Ammo

Start a game, pause, go to the Cheat menu, and enter BLLTSRRFRND.

Big Heads

Start a game, pause, go to the Cheat menu, and enter TSHNTTBNCTPRDCRD.

Dana's Cheat

Start a game, pause, go to the Cheat menu, and enter DNCHN to shrink enemies.

Flight Mode

Start a game, pause, go to the Cheat menu, and enter LKMBRD. Use R and L to move up and down.

Disco Mode

Start a game, pause, go to the Cheat menu, and enter SNFFRR. Colors flash onscreen and things start to dance.

Infinite Lives

Start a game, pause, go to the Cheat menu, and enter FRTHSTHTTRLSCK.

Gallery

Start a game, pause, go to the Cheat menu, and enter THBST to view the enemies in 3D.

Quack Mode

Start a game, pause, go to the Cheat menu, and enter CLLTHTNMTN to reduce the graphics and animations.

Rainbow Colors

Start a game, pause, go to the Cheat menu, and enter LLTHCLRSFTHRNB. The game environment becomes full of rainbow colors after the next cutscene or the use of a teleport portal.

Show All Enemies

Start a game, pause, go to the Cheat menu, and enter NSTHMNDNT. All enemies will be represented by red arrows on the map.

Robin's Cheat

Start a game, pause, go to the Cheat menu, and enter RBNSMTH as a code to enable big heads, all weapons, invincibility, and infinite ammo and credits.

Greg Mode

Start a game, pause, go to the Cheat menu, and enter GRGCHN to enable big heads, all weapons, and infinite ammo and credits.

Spirit Mode

Start a game, pause, go to the Cheat menu, and enter THSSLKSCL to enable invincibility with slow-moving enemies.

Display Credits

Start a game, pause, go to the Cheat menu, and enter FDTHMGS.

Pen and Ink Mode

Start a game, pause, go to the Cheat menu, and enter DLKTDR.

TUROK: RAGE WARS

Cheat Menu

Create a character and save it. Get more than 500 career kills with that character and save. Copy that character to the other three slots on the controller pak. Then load all four of these cloned players. The combined kill total will be more than 2,000 kills. All cheats are now available in the Cheat menu. Hit Z at the main menu to turn on the cheats.

Bonus Multiplayer Characters

Complete Single-player Trial mode with Turok. This unlocks a character for Single-player Trial mode and another character for Multiplayer mode. Keep using another character in Single-player Trials to unlock more characters.

TUROK 2: SEEDS OF EVIL

All Cheats

In Code entry, use BEWAREOBLIVIONISAT-HAND. Then go to the Cheat menu to enable the codes you want.

Big Hands and Feet

In Code entry use STOMPEM. Earn this cheat code by completing Level 4.

Big Head

In Code entry use UBERNOODLE. Earn this cheat code by defeating the Level 4 boss.

Small Enemies

In Code entry use PIPSQUEAK.

Small and Skinny Enemies

In Code entry use HOLASTICKBOY.

Blackout Mode

In Code entry use LIGHTSOUT. This makes the environments dark.

Fruit Stripes

In Code entry use FROOTSTRIPE. Earn this cheat code by completing Level 1.

Juan's Cheat

In Code entry use HEEERESJUAN. Juan's face will appear on the health icons.

Pen and Ink Mode

In Code entry use IGOTABFA. Earn this cheat code by completing Level 2.

View Credits

In Code entry use ONLYTHEBEST.

Zach Attack

In Code entry use AAHGOO. Zach's face will appear on the health icons.

Gouraud Shading

In Code entry use WHATSATEXTUREMAP. Earn this cheat code by completing level 3.

Play as Monkey

You can play as the monkey in Single-player mode only. Start a new frag-tag game in Single-player mode. Choose your character and become the monkey. Go to the Cheat menu and warp to the credits. Press Start during the credits. This takes you back to the main menu. Begin a new Single-player game and you should be playing as the monkey once you start playing.

TUROK 3: SHADOW OF OBLIVION

All Weapons

At the Enter New Secrets screen, enter owl, bear, owl, insect, hawk, owl.

All Keys

At the Enter New Secrets screen, enter lizard, dragonfly, bull, bear, wolf, eagle.

Invincibility

At the Enter New Secrets screen, enter raven, salmon, eagle, bear, lizard, rabbit.

Infinite Ammo

At the Enter New Secrets screen, enter salmon, elk, bull, snake, eagle, salmon.

Gasping Mode

At the Enter New Secrets screen, enter drag-onfly, bull, rabbit, salmon, eagle, raven.

Mannequin Mode

At the Enter New Secrets screen, enter snake, bull, snake, frog bear, elk.

Sketch Mode

At the Enter New Secrets screen, enter jaguar, horse, elk, salmon, jaguar, hawk.

Enlarged Head Mode

At the Enter New Secrets screen, enter cougar, wolf, snake, rabbit, lizard, coyote.

Stick Man Mode

At the Enter New Secrets screen, enter horse, eagle, snake, cougar, insect, salmon.

Mini-Mode

At the Enter New Secrets screen, enter frog, frog, salmon, insect, wolf, cougar.

Enlarged Hands and Feet Mode

At the Enter New Secrets screen, enter lizard, lizard, dragonfly, horse, lizard, coyote.

Headless Mode

At the Enter New Secrets screen, enter lizard, elk, eagle, owl, salmon, horse.

Credits

At the Enter New Secrets screen, enter elk (6).

Mad Menu

At the Enter New Secrets screen, enter rabbit, owl, horse, insect, bear (2).

Gouraud Graphics Mode

At the Enter New Secrets screen, enter lizard, salmon, insect, salmon, wolf, dragonfly.

Warp Level 1

At the Enter New Secrets screen, enter frog, elk, horse, dragonfly, wolf, rabbit.

Warp Level 2

At the Enter New Secrets screen, enter owl (2), horse, elk (3).

Warp Level 3

At the Enter New Secrets screen, enter owl, rabbit, bear, insect, frog, cougar.

Warp Level 4
At the Enter New Secrets screen, enter bear, horse, raven, eagle, horse, coyote.

Warp Level 5
At the Enter New Secrets screen, enter bear, dragonfly, horse, bear, frog, elk.

TWISTED EDGE EXTREME SNOWBOARDING

Unlock G
Complete Stunt mode and place first with a score of 28,000 points or higher.

Unlock Tiny
Get a medal on each difficulty level under Competition mode.

Quick Start
Press Up (2) after the word "Go" disappears.

Unlock Bob and Boss Board
Finish first on the mirror courses.

Master Mode
Complete the game on all three difficulty levels.

Twisted Mode
Complete the game on Master mode.

Mirror Mode
Complete the game on Twisted mode.

Unlock the Bucky Board
Complete Stunt Challenge mode.

Unlock the Twisty Board
On the Hard difficulty setting, defeat the ghost on Twisty Canyon under Practice mode.

Unlock the Flower Board
Place first in all three courses during the first round of Competition mode.

Unlock Bonus Boards
Get first place in all races to get the YYY6, Top Gear Rally, and Midway boards. The Top Gear Rally board can also be unlocked by having a custom paint job from Top Gear Rally on your memory pak.

Cheat Mode
Only one of the following cheats can be activated at a time.

All Players
At the Sound menu, set Speech: off, Music Vol: 4, SFX Vol: 1, Music Test: 2. Then highlight "SFX Vol" and press C-Right+C-Down.

Ant
At the Sound menu, set Speech: ON, Music Vol: 1, SFX Vol: 6, Music Test: 1. Then highlight "SFX Vol" and press Z+C-Right.

Art Boards
At the Sound menu, set Speech: on, Music Vol: 5, SFX Vol: 1, Music Test: 3. Then highlight "SFX Vol" and press C-Left+C-Up.

Board Only
At the Sound menu, set Speech: off, Music Vol: 7, SFX Vol: 5, Music Test: 2. Then highlight "SFX Vol" and press Z+C-Down.

BOSS Board
At the Sound menu, set Speech: off, Music Vol: 6, SFX Vol: 3, Music Test: 4. Then highlight "SFX Vol" and press C-Up.

Canada
At the Sound menu, set Speech: on, Music Vol: 4, SFX Vol: 0, Music Test: 7. Then highlight "SFX Vol" and press Z+C-Up+C-Left.

Easy Tracks
At the Sound menu, set Speech: on, Music Vol: 7, SFX Vol: 2, Music Test: 6. Then highlight "SFX Vol" and press L.

Ghost 1
At the Sound menu, set Speech: on, Music Vol: 4, SFX Vol: 6, Music Test: 5. Then highlight "SFX Vol" and press L+R.

Ghost 2
At the Sound menu, set Speech: off, Music Vol: 0, SFX Vol: 8, Music Test: 3. Then highlight "SFX Vol" and press R+C-Up+C-Down.

Ghost in Replay
At the Sound menu, set Speech: on, Music Vol: 8, SFX Vol: 8, Music Test: 7. Then highlight "SFX Vol" and press L+R+C-Down.

Grow
At the Sound menu, set Speech: off, Music Vol: 8, SFX Vol: 7, Music Test: 5. Then highlight "SFX Vol" and press Z+C-Left.

Hard Tracks
At the Sound menu, set Speech: on, Music Vol: 5, SFX Vol: 2, Music Test: 4. Then highlight "SFX Vol" and press Z.

Helium
At the Sound menu, set Speech: off, Music Vol: 0, SFX Vol: 7, Music Test: 1. Then highlight "SFX Vol" and press C-Left+C-Up+C-Down.

Light
At the Sound menu, set Speech: off, Music Vol: 5, SFX Vol: 1, Music Test: 6. Then highlight "SFX Vol" and press L+C-Up+C-Left.

Little Bob (Tiny)
At the Sound menu, set Speech: on, Music Vol: 7, SFX Vol: 7, Music Test: 5. Then highlight "SFX Vol" and press L.

Long Credits
At the Sound menu, set Speech: off, Music Vol: 2, SFX Vol: 2, Music Test: 3. Then highlight "SFX Vol" and press C-Up+Z.

Midway Board
At the Sound menu, set Speech: on, Music Vol: 8, SFX Vol: 4, Music Test: 5. Then highlight "SFX Vol" and press C-Left.

Midway Mode
At the Sound menu, set Speech: on, Music Vol: 2, SFX Vol: 4, Music Test: 3. Then highlight "SFX Vol" and press Z+L.

Mirror Tracks
At the Sound menu, set Speech: on, Music Vol: 7, SFX Vol: 6, Music Test: 6. Then highlight "SFX Vol" and press L+R.

Naked Dude (G)
At the Sound menu, set Speech: off, Music Vol: 6, SFX Vol: 4, Music Test: 6. Then highlight "SFX Vol" and press C-Left+C-Right+R.

Night Mode
At the Sound menu, set Speech: on, Music Vol: 2, SFX Vol: 8, Music Test: 5. Then highlight "SFX Vol" and press Z+C-Up.

No Board
At the Sound menu, set Speech: on, Music Vol: 0, SFX Vol: 8, Music Test: 4. Then highlight "SFX Vol" and press C-Up+C-Left+C-Right.

Normal Tracks
At the Sound menu, set Speech: off, Music Vol: 3, SFX Vol: 5, Music Test: 6. Then highlight "SFX Vol" and press R.

Stunt Credits
At the Sound menu, set Speech: on, Music Vol: 1, SFX Vol: 3, Music Test: 7. Then highlight "SFX Vol" and press C-Down+Z.

V-RALLY EDITION '99

Cheat Menu
Press L+R, C-Left, C-Right, L+R, Start at the Press Start screen. Then at the next screen, hold Z and keep pressing L until a Cheat menu appears.

Bonus Cars
Press L+R, C-Left, C-Right, L+R at the Press Start screen. Then go to the Options screen, hold Z and press L.

VIGILANTE 8

Play as Dave
Complete Quest mode with Chassey Blue and Slick Clyde.

Play as Convoy
Complete Quest mode with Sheila and John Torque.

Play as Molo
Complete Quest mode with Loki and Houston 3.

Play as Sid Burn
Complete Quest mode with Boogie and Beezwax.

Play as the Alien (Y)
Complete Quest mode with all characters.

Alien Vehicle
Enter GIMME_DA_ALIEN as a password.

All Vehicles Except the Alien
Enter GANGS_UNLOCKED as a password.

Big Wheels
Enter MONSTER_WHEELS as a password.

All Vehicles, Levels, Characters
Enter JTBT7CFD1LRMGW as a password.

High Resolution
Enter MAX_RESOLUTION as a password.

Better Missiles
Enter MISSILE_ATTACK as a password.

Same Cars in Multi-Player
Enter MIX_MATCH_CARS as a password.

Invincibility
Enter LIVING_FOREVER as a password.

Rapid Fire
Enter FIRE_NO_LIMITS as a password.

Low Gravity
Enter A_MOON_GETAWAY as a password.

No Enemies
Enter POPULATION_OUT as a password.

Slow Motion
Enter GO_REALLY_SLOW as a password.

All Endings
Enter LONG_SLIDESHOW as a password.

Super Hard Difficulty
Enter I_AM_TOUGH_GUY as a password.

Unlock Levels
Enter LEVEL_SHORTCUT as a password.

Unlock All Coyote Cars with Completed Quests
Enter CFG2ZW4TBT7CF7 as a password.

Super Dreamland 64 Level
Enter DDDDDDDDDDDDDD as a password or complete all of the Alien's missions in Quest mode.

VIGILANTE 8: SECOND OFFENSE

Unlock Lord Clyde
In Quest mode, complete all objectives with Nina, Molo, and Dallas 13.

Unlock Obake
In Quest mode, complete all objectives with Lord Clyde.

Unlock Boogie
In Quest mode, complete all objectives with Obake.

Unlock Houston
In Quest mode, complete all objectives with Sheila, John Torque, and the Flying All-Star Trio.

Unlock Convoy
In Quest mode, complete all objectives with Houston.

Unlock Dave's Cultsmen
In Quest mode, complete all objectives with Convoy.

Unlock Chassey Blue
In Quest mode, complete all objectives with Astronaut Bob O, Garbage Man, and Agent R. Chase.

Unlock Padre Destino
In Quest mode, complete all objectives with Chassey Blue.

Unlock Dusty Earth
In Quest mode, complete all objectives with Padre Destino.

Password Screen
Select "Game Status" in the Options screen. Highlight any of the characters and press L+R. Then enter one of the following codes.

Big Wheels
Enter GO_MONSTER at the Password screen.

Attract Enemies
Enter UNDER_FIRE at the Password screen.

Fast Action
Enter QUICK_PLAY at the Password screen.

No Enemies in Arcade Mode
Enter HOME_ALONE at the Password screen.

No Gravity
Enter NO_GRAVITY at the Password screen.

Faster Cars
Enter MORE_SPEED at the Password screen.

Heavy Cars
Enter GO_RAMMING at the Password screen.

Lighter Cars
Enter HI_CEILING at the Password screen.

High Suspensions
Enter JACK_IT_up at the Password screen.

Slow Motion
Enter GO_SLOW_MO at the Password screen.

Rapid Fire
Enter RAPID_FIRE at the Password screen.

No Wheel Attachment Icons
Enter DRIVE_ONLY at the Password screen.

High Resolution
Enter GO_MAX_REZ at the Password screen. This requires a 4MB expansion pak.

Same Cars in Multiplayer
Enter MIXED_CARS at the Password screen.

All Endings
Enter LONG_MOVIE at the Password screen.

Super Missiles
Enter BLAST_FIRE at the Password screen.

Disable Codes
Enter NO_CODES at the Password screen.

VIRTUAL CHESS 64

Debug Menu
Press C-Up, C-Down, C-Left, C-Right, Up, Down, Left, Right during gameplay.

Alternate Board
Press C-Left or C-Right during gameplay in Tutorial or 2D mode.

See CPU's Next Move
Press C-Up, C-Down, Up, Down, Left, Right during gameplay.

VIRTUAL POOL 64

Extra Rating Points
Beat the computer. View the replay and keep viewing your replay. Each time you watch a replay your rating points increase.

Make the Computer Miss
Press R to change to overhead when the CPU is taking a shot. Use the analog stick to move the CPU's cue stick.

Re-Power a Shot Against the CPU
Press Left during the CPU's turn. This takes you to instant replay, but before the replay starts hold R to change to the overhead view. Then hold A to rescue the shot. Keep holding A as you change the power level.

VIRTUAL PRO WRESTLING 2 (IMPORT)

Taunt Copying
Move the analog stick in a circle to copy the taunt when your opponent is performing his taunt.

VIRTUAL PRO WRESTLING 64 (IMPORT)

Camera Zoom
Move the analog stick while choosing your character.

Unlock Diamond Dallas Page
Go to League Challenge. Choose WCW. Play the game through and make sure to beat Diamond Dallas Page.

Unlock Glacier
Defeat IU in League Challenge mode.

Unlock Randy "Macho Man" Savage
Defeat NOW in League Challenge mode.

Unlock Joe Bruiser and Black Widow
Defeat all the different game modes first to unlock an extra menu called Whole World Wrestling. Defeat the heavyweight and cruiserweight titles to face a boss. Defeat the boss to unlock him.

Do an Opponent's Move
When your spirit meter is flashing "Special," perform a strong grapple on your opponent. Then press A+B to perform one of your opponent's moves.

WAIALAE COUNTRY CLUB: TRUE GOLF CLASSICS

Drive a Golf Cart
Press Z during gameplay and select the "Cart Cam" option.

Fly a Helicopter
Press Z during gameplay. Choose the "Cart Cam" option. Then, press C-Up to become the helicopter.

Faster Shots
Hold B after you hit the ball to speed up the shot. This doesn't affect shot distance, only the speed of the ball.

WAR GODS

Play as Exor
Press Left, Down (2), Right, Left, Up, Left, Up, Right, Down at the Character Selection screen. Choose any character.

Play as Grox
Press Down, Right, Left (2), Up, Down, Right, Up, Left (2) at the Character Selection screen. Choose any character.

Random Character Selection
Hold Up and press Start at the Character Selection screen.

Infinite Continues
Press C-Left (2), C-Right, A, B, C-Up, C-Right at the title screen. Go to the Options menu and highlight "Continues." Keep pressing Left until "Freeplay" appears.

Access Cheat Menu
Press Right (3), B (2), A (2) at the title screen before the start and option selections appear. A spoken phrase confirms correct entry. A Cheat menu appears in the Options menu.

Easy Fatalities
Enable the Cheat menu and choose Easy Fatalities. Press HP+LP+HK+LK to perform a fatality on an opponent.

WAYNE GRETZKY'S 3D HOCKEY

Bonus Teams
Go to the Options screen. Hold L and press C-Right, C-Left (2), C-Right, C-Left (2), C-Right, C-Left (2). If you entered the code correctly, you should see a "1" in the tenth digit of the Specials option.

Opponent Choice
Go to the Team Select screen. Highlight the team you wish to play against. Press C-Right (3). A clicking sound confirms correct entry.

Famous Female Players

Go to the Trade Player screen during a season. Hold A and press B, Left, Right, Up, Down, C-Down, C-Right, C-Left. A slapshot noise confirms correct entry. Go to Mike Modano on the Stars. He should be a woman. You can pick from five different women.

Invisible Players

Pause the game at the beginning face off. Select Replay. Press L or R to make a player flash. Press Z while the player is flashing to make him invisible. You can do this for your entire team.

Forfeit a Game

Pause the game. Enter the Options screen. Hold L and press C-Left (9). Resume your game and you should lose 1 to 0.

Constant Fights

Enter the Options screen. Hold L and press C-Right, C-Left (2), C-Right, C-Down, C-Up (2), C-Down, C-Left, C-Right (2), C-Left, C-Right, C-Left. Fights happen all the time now. The code has to be re-entered at each period.

Trading Players

Enter the Options screen. Hold L and press C-Down (2), C-Up (2), C-Down (2), C-Right (2), C-Down. Go back to the main menu and choose Records. Enter the Team Statistics screen. Press C-Up (10). Now you can start trading players. Highlight a team and press A. Then highlight a second team and press A. Then press Start to enter the trading screen.

View Credits

Press A (20) at the title screen.

Two-Player Practice Mode

Highlight Practice mode at the main menu. Press A simultaneously on both controllers 1 and 2.

View Sponsors

Enter the Options, Setup, or Audio screens and press Z multiple times to see all of the game's sponsors.

Controlling the Screen

Do this trick anytime, except during gameplay. Hold L+R and rotate the analog stick to move the screen. Release L+R to keep the screen in the new position. Hold L+R again to return the screen to normal.

Play a Quick Game

At the main menu, highlight the "Play Game" option. Hold down C-Left, C-Right, C-Up, or C-Down and press Start. You play against the New York Rangers.

Debug Mode

Go to the Options screen. Press C-Down+R, C-Left+R, or C-Up+R. Then you can modify a 16-bit register to change the game. Alter the bits by using these controls. C-Down+R changes the head size. C-Left+R changes the body size. C-Up+R changes the height of a player. Below are some examples of what you can do.

Stocky Players

Enter Debug mode and make the register 100000.

Stocky Players, Big Heads

Enter Debug mode and make the register 010000.

Stocky Players, Small Heads

Enter Debug mode and make the register 110000.

Small Players, Small Announcer

Enter Debug mode and make the register 001000.

Large Players, Large Announcer

Enter Debug mode and make the register 000100.

Crunched Players, Small Announcer

Enter Debug mode and make the register 000010.

Elongated Players, Large Announcer

Enter Debug mode and make the register 000001.

Large Players, Small Heads, Large Announcer

Enter Debug mode and make the register 110110.

Crunched Players, Large Heads, Small Announcer

Enter Debug mode and make the register 010010.

Large Players, Large Heads, Large Announcer

Enter Debug mode and make the register 010101.

Elongated Players, Large Heads, Large Announcer

Enter Debug mode and make the register 010001.

WAYNE GRETZKY'S 3D HOCKEY '98

Bonus Teams

Enter the Options screen. Hold L and press C-Right, C-Left (2), C-Right, C-Left (2), C-Right, C-Left (2). A "1" appears on the tenth digit of the Specials option.

Opponent Choice

Go to the Team Select screen. Highlight the team you wish to play against. Press C-Right (3). A clicking sound confirms correct entry.

Invisible Players

Pause the game at the beginning face off. Select Replay. Press L or R to make a player flash. Press Z while the player is flashing to make him invisible. You can do this for your entire team.

Controlling the Screen

Do this trick anytime, except during gameplay. Hold L+R and rotate the analog stick to move the screen. Release L+R to keep the screen in the new position. Hold L+R again to return the screen to normal.

Play a Quick Game

At the main menu, highlight the "Play Game" option. Hold C-Left, C-Right, C-Up, or C-Down and press Start. You will then play against the New York Rangers.

Forfeit a Game

Pause the game. Enter the Options screen. Hold L and press C-Left (9). Resume your game and you should lose 1 to 0.

Constant Fights

Enter the Options screen. Hold L and press C-Right, C-Left (2), C-Right, C-Down, C-Up (2), C-Down, C-Left, C-Right (2), C-Left, C-Right, C-Left. Fights happen all the time now. The code has to be re-entered each period.

Trading Players

Enter the Options screen. Hold L and press C-Down (2), C-Up (2), C-Down (2), C-Right (2), C-Down. Go back to the main menu and choose "Records." Enter the Team Statistics screen. Press C-Up (10). Highlight a team and press A. Then highlight a second team and press A. Then press Start to enter the Trading screen.

View Credits

Press A (20) at the title screen.

Two-Player Practice Mode

Highlight Practice mode at the main menu. Press A simultaneously on both Controllers 1 and 2.

View Sponsors

Enter the Options, Setup, or Audio screens and press Z multiple times to see all of the game's sponsors.

Debug Mode

Go to the Options screen. Press C-Down+R, C-Left+R, or C-Up+R. Then you can modify a 16-bit register to change the game. Alter the bits by using these controls. C-Down+R changes the head size. C-Left+R changes the body size. C-Up+R changes the height of a player. Below are some examples of what you can do.

Stocky Players

Enter Debug mode and make the register 100000.

Stocky Players, Big Heads

Enter Debug mode and make the register 010000.

Stocky Players, Small Heads

Enter Debug mode and make the register 110000.

Small Players, Small Announcer

Enter Debug mode and make the register 001000.

Large Players, Large Announcer

Enter Debug mode and make the register 000100.

Crunched Players, Small Announcer

Enter Debug mode and make the register 000010.

Elongated Players, Large Announcer

Enter Debug mode and make the register 000001.

Large Players, Small Heads, Large Announcer

Enter Debug mode and make the register 110110.

Crunched Players, Large Heads, Small Announcer

Enter Debug mode and make the register 010010.

Large Players, Large Heads, Large Announcer

Enter Debug mode and make the register 010101.

Elongated Players, Large Heads, Large Announcer

Enter Debug mode and make the register 010001.

WCW: BACKSTAGE ASSAULT

Unlimited Stamina

Press R (2), B, R (2), B at the main menu.

Unbreakable Weapons

Press L, R, L, R, C-Left (2) at the main menu.

Access Mini Wrestlers

Press R (2), L (2), C-Left, C-Right at the main menu.

Access Alternate Grunts

Press R, L, R, L, B (2) at the main menu.

Access Larger Female Wrestlers

Press R (2), B (2), L (2) at the main menu.

WCW MAYHEM

All Backrooms

Enter CBCKRMS as a PPV password. Choose the backstage you want to fight in by selecting "Match Options" at the Match Setup screen. Run to the entrance to fight in the backstage area when you are playing a one-on-one match.

Unlock All Characters

Enter PLYHDNGYS as a PPV password.

Alternate Characters

Enter NGGDYNLN as a PPV password.

Fight with the Same Characters

Enter DPLGNGRS as a PPV password. The code only works for Two-player Versus games.

Full Attribute Characters

Enter MKSPRCWS as a PPV password.

Classic TNT Nitro Set

Enter PLYNTRCLSC as a PPV password. Then, at the Ring Selection screen, choose "Nitro."

Halloween Havoc PPV

Enter td^pKRmZ-<yL as a PPV password.

World War III 1999 PPV

Enter yKh#J$=JQLmFs as a PPV password. After you enter the "Q" in this code, press Right to go to the next line because this code is longer than the top line.

Starcade PPV

Enter @KcXKF=W?j^pF as a PPV password.

Superbrawl 2000 PPV

Enter rJPmB6lfMlk$B as a PPV password. You might think the code has "1" in it, but it is actually a lowercase "L."

Uncensored 2000 PPV

Enter 2JJhKXdJFm4kB as a PPV password.

Spring Stampede 2000 PPV

Enter @JHkfylBwfQQF as a PPV password.

Momentum Meter

Enter PRNTMMNTM as a PPV password.

Stamina Meter

Enter PRNTSTMN as a PPV password.

Rank Advancement

Enter CHT4DBST as a PPV password. Then push Right when you are in Quest for the Best mode.

Unlock Mean Gene Okerland

Beat Quest for the Best mode with a non-Cruiserweight character on Medium difficulty.

Unlock Arn Anderson

Beat Quest for the Best mode with a Cruiserweight character on Hard difficulty.

Unlock Bam Bam Bigelow

Beat Quest for the Best mode with a non-Cruiserweight character on Medium difficulty.

Unlock Barry Windham

Beat Quest for the Best mode with a non-Cruiserweight character on Medium difficulty.

Unlock Bobby Eaton

Beat Quest for the Best mode with a Cruiserweight character on Easy difficulty.

Unlock Bobby Blayze

Beat Quest for the Best mode with a non-Cruiserweight character on Easy difficulty.

Unlock Chris Jericho

Play in all 13 backstage areas and beat the Quest for the Best mode.

Unlock Doug Dellinger

Beat Quest for the Best mode with a Cruiserweight character on Hard difficulty.

Unlock Eric Bischoff

Beat Quest for the Best mode with a non-Cruiserweight character on Hard difficulty.

Unlock Jimmy Hart

Beat Quest for the Best mode with any character on Hard difficulty.

Unlock Lash LeRoux

Beat Quest for the Best mode with a Cruiserweight character on Medium difficulty.

Unlock Rick Flair

Beat Quest for the Best mode with a non-Cruiserweight character on Hard difficulty.

Unlock Rick Steiner

Beat Quest for the Best mode with any character on Hard difficulty.

Unlock Scott Hall

Beat Quest for the Best mode with any character on Hard difficulty.

Unlock Sgt. Buddy Lee Parker

Beat Quest for the Best mode with any character on Easy difficulty.

Unlock Sony Onoo

Beat Quest for the Best mode with Earnest Miller on Easy difficulty.

Unlock Wolfpack Sting

Beat Quest for the Best mode with any character on Hard difficulty.

Bam Bam Bigelow Vs. Lex Luger (Main Event)

Enter td^NmPmQ-<xY as a PPV password.

Barry Windham Vs. Juvi (Cruiserweight Title)

Enter tdSJKRmZ-<yL as a PPV password.

Barry Windham Vs. Juvi (TV Title)

Enter tdSJKRmZ-<yL as a PPV password.

Barry Windham Vs. Rey Mysterio (Cruiserweight Title)

Enter tdSfKRmZ-<yL as a PPV password.

Barry Windham Vs. Rey Mysterio (TV Title)

Enter tdSfKRmZ-<yL as a PPV password.

Barry Windham Vs. Wrath (Cruiserweight Title)

Enter tdS4KRmZ-<yL as a PPV password.

Barry Windham Vs. Wrath (TV Title)

Enter tdS4KRmZ-<yL as a PPV password.

Bobby Blaze

Enter tdkDpKRmZ-<yL as a PPV password.

Booker T Vs. Scott Hall

Enter td^pKxmZ-<yL as a PPV password.

Buff Bagwell Vs. Kevin Nash

Enter td^pKRmZrhyP as a PPV password.

Cruiserweight (Main Event)

Enter td^pKRmZrbyP as a PPV password.

Curt Hennig Vs. Chris Jericho (Cruiserweight Title)

Enter tdQ6KRmZ-<yL as a PPV password.

Curt Hennig Vs. Chris Jericho (TV Title)

Enter tdQ6KRmZ-<yL as a PPV password.

Curt Hennig Vs. Eddy Guerrero (Cruiserweight Title)

Enter tdQGKRmZ-<yL as a PPV password.

Curt Hennig Vs. Eddy Guerrero (TV Title)

Enter tdQGKRmZ-<yL as a PPV password.

Curt Hennig Vs. Kidman (Cruiserweight Title)

Enter tdQhKRmZ-<yL as a PPV password.

Curt Hennig Vs. Kidman (TV Title)

Enter tdQhKRmZ-<yL as a PPV password.

Disco Inferno Vs. Bret Hart

Enter td^pmRmZ-<yL as a PPV password.

Disco Inferno Vs. Bret Hart, Booker T Vs. Hall, Sting Vs. Ric Flair, and Savage Vs. Steiner

Enter td^pmRmQ-<PY as a PPV password.

Disco Inferno Vs. Chavo

Enter td^NKRmZ-<yL as a PPV password.

Disco Inferno Vs. Chavo, Booker T Vs. Scott Hall, Rick Steiner Vs. Booker T

Enter td^NKxmZ-<ky as a PPV password.

Disco Inferno Vs. Chris Kanyon

Enter td^pZRmZ-<yL as a PPV password.

Disco Inferno Vs. Curt Hennig

Enter td^QmPmQ-<YX as a PPV password.

Disco Inferno Vs. Konnan, Hogan Vs. Luger, DDP Vs. Rick Flair, and Rick Steiner Vs. Booker T

Enter td^NmPmQ-<ky as a PPV password.

Disco Inferno Vs. La Parka

Enter td^QKRmQ-<ky as a PPV password.

Disco Inferno Vs. La Parka, Hogan Vs. Luger, and DDP Vs. Rick Flair

Enter td^QKPmQ-<yP as a PPV password.

Goldberg (World Champion)

Enter td^QKYgQrYyP as a PPV password.

Horace Hogan

Enter td7QKYgQr<yP as a PPV password.

Horace Hogan Vs. Mongo

Enter tdDpKRmZ-xp as a PPV password.

Hollywood Hogan

Enter td^QKYgQr<y* as a PPV password.

Randy Savage, Rick Steiner Vs. Sting, Ric Flair

Enter td^NKxmQ-<PY as a PPV password.

Randy Savage Vs. Diamond Dallas Page
Enter td^NmPmQ-< as a PPV password.

Randy Savage Vs. Diamond Dallas Page (Main Event)
Enter td^pKRmZ-<Yp as a PPV password.

Randy Savage Vs. Stevie Ray
Enter td^QKRmQ-<YY as a PPV password.

Rick Steiner (World Champ) Vs. Booker T
Enter td^pKRmZ-<kL as a PPV password.

Rick Steiner Vs. Diamond Dallas Page
Enter td^QKYgQ-<yP as a PPV password.

Rick Steiner Vs. Kevin Nash
Enter td^pKRmZ-<kP as a PPV password.

Rick Steiner Vs. Lex Luger
Enter td^pKYmz-<yL as a PPV password.

Scott Hall
Enter td^pKYmz-<yP as a PPV password.

Sting (First Match)
Enter td^DpKRmZ-<yL as a PPV password.

Sting Vs. Hogan
Enter td^QKYgQr<y* as a PPV password.

Sting Vs. Scott Hall
Enter td^pKYmz-<yP as a PPV password.

Sting Vs. Sting
Enter td^QKYgQr<yP as a PPV password.

WCW NITRO

Unlock All Superstars
Press C-Right (4), C-Left (4), R (4), L (4), Z at the title screen. A sound confirms correct entry.

Unlock All Rings
Press C-Left, L, C-Right, R, C-Left, L, C-Right, R, Z at the title screen. A sound confirms correct entry.

Ring Select
At the Options screen, press C-Right, R, C-Right, R, Z. A sound confirms correct entry. Press Z to advance to the next ring. Move in reverse by pressing C-Left, L, C-Left, L, Z.

Swelling Heads
Press C-Left (7), L, Z at the title screen. A sound confirms correct entry. Every time you get hit, your character's head will get bigger.

Big Heads
Press C-Right (7), R, Z at the title screen. A sound confirms correct entry.

Big Hands
Press L (7), C-Left (17) at the Mode Selection screen. A sound confirms correct entry.

Big Heads, Hands, and Feet
Press R (7), C-Right, Z at the title screen. A sound confirms correct entry.

YMCA Dancing
Press B+C-Left when you are on the Disco stage.

Wrestler Interference
Press Z during a match.

WCW/NWO REVENGE

Unlock TV Title Mode
Win the Cruiserweight belt.

Unlock World Heavyweight Mode
Win the US Heavyweight belt.

Unlock Curt Henning
Win the US Heavyweight competition.

Unlock Barbarian and Meng
Win the Tag Team belts.

Unlock Kidman
Win the Cruiserweight belt.

Unlock Rowdy Roddy Piper
Win the World Heavyweight belt.

Unlock Kanyon and Mortis
Win the TV Title. Pick Mortis by highlighting Kanyon and pressing C-Down.

Unlock THQ Man
At the Character Selection screen, highlight Aki and press C-Down.

Play as Managers
Start a one-on-one exhibition match. Pick the characters that have managers. Then press Z on Controller 3 and 4 after the beginning of a match.

Silver Belts
Watch the opening sequence once you turn on the game. Press A when you see Hogan, Bischoff, and Giant speaking at the microphone. Now gold belts will be silver. To turn them back, exit the Championship section and go back. Resetting the game also disables this code.

Do Opponent's Special Move
With your Special meter filled, perform a grapple and press A+B at the same time.

Do Opponent's Ground Moves
Press A+B when the opponent is on the ground.

Alternate Costumes
Press any of the C buttons during the Character Selection screen.

Alternate Intro Sequences
Change the costumes of any of the characters. Watch the beginning sequence again and the characters will be wearing the new costumes.

Do Opponent's Taunt
When your opponent performs a taunt, rotate the analog stick counterclockwise.

Weapons
Get out of the ring during a match. Go to the crowd and press C-Up.

WCW VS. NWO: WORLD TOUR

Unlock Diamond Dallas Page
Defeat WCW in League Challenge mode.

Unlock Randy "Macho Man" Savage
Defeat NWO in League Challenge mode.

Unlock Glacier
Defeat IU in League Challenge mode.

Unlock Wrath
Defeat DOA in League Challenge mode.

Unlock Joe Bruiser or Black Widow
Defeat DOA, NWO, and WCW in League Challenge mode. A "Whole World Wrestling" option opens up. Go in there and beat the Heavyweight and Cruiserweight classes to face Joe Bruiser and Black Widow. Defeat them to unlock them.

Change Uniform
Press C-Left or C-Right at the Character Selection screen.

WETRIX

Change Floor Tiles
Complete all 16 practice rounds. Enter the Options screen and find a new option called "Floor." You can now choose different floor sets and backgrounds.

Making Waves
Get the top score in Classic mode and enter imani as your name. Go to the main menu and hold C-Up or C-Down to control the level of water. Hold down one of those buttons and move the analog stick at the same time to move the water across the pool.

Changing Puzzle Shapes
Complete all the practice rounds. Next, obtain an OK rating in all modes except for Practice and Multiplayer. You will see a green background color if you did this right. Now pick any game mode except practice. You see a little blue guy. Pick him and he turns into a duck. Start a game and the tetrads have different shapes.

WINBACK: COVERT OPERATIONS

All Characters in Multiplayer
Press Up, Down (2), Right (3), Left (4). Hold C-Up and press Start while "Press Start" is on screen. A sound confirms correct entry.

Sudden Death Mode
Quickly press C-Left, C-Right, C-Left, C-Right, C-Up, C-Down, C-Up, C-Down, press and hold L, press Start at the Press Start screen. A gunshot sound confirms correct entry.

Trial Mode
Quickly press Up, Down (2), Right (3), Left (4), press and hold C-Down, press Start at the Press Start screen. A gunshot sound confirms correct entry.

Maximum Power
Quickly press L, C-Right, C-Left, C-Right, C-Left, C-Down, C-Up, C-Down, C-Up, press and hold L, press Start at the Press Start screen. A gunshot sound confirms correct entry.

Unlock Sudden Death, Trial, and Maximum Power Modes at Once
Beat the game on the hardest settings to unlock all three modes at once.

Multiplayer C4
Start a Multiplayer game in Factory-1 level. All characters can use C4 by pressing Down on the controller.

Flamethrower for Thunder (Multiplayer Only)
Select Thunder in Multiplayer mode. Press R in the middle of a game to activate laser sights. Now press B to fire the flamethrower.

WIPEOUT 64

All Ships
Hold L+R+Z and press C-Down (4), C-Right, C-Up, C-Left at the main menu.

Infinite Energy
Hold L+R+Z and press C-Up, C-Down, C-Left, C-Right, C-Up, C-Down, C-Left, C-Right at the main menu.

Infinite Ammo
Hold L+R+Z and press C-Down (2), C-Left (2), C-Right (2), C-Up at the main menu.

Infinite Time

Hold L+R+Z and press C-Up, C-Right, C-Left, C-Down, C-Up, C-Right, C-Left, C-Down at the main menu.

Double Your Weapon Damage

Hold L+R+Z and press C-Left, C-Right, C-Down, C-Left, C-Right, C-Down, C-Up at the main menu. Or complete Weapons Challenge mode with a bronze or higher.

Velocitar Course

Hold L+R+Z and press C-Left, C-Right, C-Up, C-Right, C-Left at the main menu. Or complete Race Competition mode with a bronze or higher.

Super Combo Challenge Mode

Complete all three Challenge modes.

Unlock Piranha II Ship

Place third or better in Time Challenge mode.

Gold Challenge Races

Get first in all races of a particular type of series to unlock that series' Gold Challenge.

WORLD CUP '98

Sound Effects

Press A, B, C-Down, or C-Left after you score a goal.

World Cup Classics

Using any team, win the World Cup. This unlocks World Cup Classics at the main menu. Then use one of the classic teams to win the World Cup again. This unlocks the next World Cup Classic match. You can do this eight times.

Developers Team

Enter BuryFC as a custom player's name in the Team Customization screen. The developers replace the players on the England team.

WORLD DRIVER CHAMPIONSHIP

Unlock All GT2 Cars

Start a Championship game and press Z, Analog-Stick Right, Z (2), Z, B, C-Down, A, Analog-Stick Right, Start at the Team Selection screen.

Changing Car Colors

Press Z at the Car Selection screen.

IGN64 Car

Begin a new game in Championship mode. Enter your name as IGN64. All vehicles in the game will be bright pink.

GT2 Ending Movie

Complete a GT2 season to unlock the GT2 ending sequence option.

Mirror Tracks

Instead of pressing A, press Z to select a mirror track.

Red Skid Marks

Press B, Left, Up, Down, Right (3), Down before the countdown to the start of a race. "Race" appears on your screen if you did the code correctly.

Unlock Sydney Tracks

Remove the memory card from the controller. Begin a new championship game. Enter FROZENSKY as the name. Accept an offer from one of the two teams. Return to the main menu and pick "Quick Race." Choose any race mode and pick the "Sydney Circuit." Return to the main menu and put your memory card back in. Load a saved game to restore all your settings. Then save the game.

Falcon Interceptor

Win all racing events with a gold medal. Return to the main menu and race in the novice cup. Beat the Falcon Interceptor in the novice cup races. The Interceptor becomes unlocked under "Boss Racing" at the Team Selection screen.

Unlock Sydney-CR Track

Win the Las Vegas-A track with a Manta (C-class).

Unlock Kyoto-AR Track

Win the Hawaii-C track with a Rage (A-class).

Unlock Kyoto-B Track

Win the Lisbon-CR track with a Swift (C-class).

Unlock Hawaii-C Track

Win the Lisbon-C track with a Rage (A-class).

Unlock Las Vegas-CR Track

Win the Hawaii-A track with a Stallion (C-class).

WORLD IS NOT ENOUGH

Change Gun Options

Hold B and press Z.

Unlock the Air Raid Scenario

Complete the Masquerade level on the Agent difficulty setting with a time less than 3:15.

Unlock the Capture the Briefcase Scenario

Complete the Turncoat level on the Secret Agent difficulty setting with a time less than 3:20.

Unlock the Castle Scenario

Complete the Subway level on the Agent difficulty setting with a time less than 2:15.

Unlock the Forest Scenario

Complete the Night Watch level on the 00 Agent difficulty setting with a time less than 2:20.

Unlock the Golden Gun Scenario

Complete the game on the 00 Agent difficulty setting.

Unlock the Sky Rail Scenario

Complete the Cold Reception level on the Secret Agent difficulty setting with a time less than 3:15.

Unlock the Team King Of The Hill Scenario

Complete the King's Ransom level on the Agent difficulty setting with a time less than 2:20.

Unlock the Civilian Skins

Complete the City Of Walkways 1 level on the Agent difficulty setting with a time less than 3:35.

Unlock the Classic Skins

Complete the game on the Secret Agent difficulty setting to unlock Tuxedo Bond, Baron Samedi, Oddjob, and Jaws.

Unlock the Contemporary Skins

Complete the game on the Agent difficulty setting to unlock Alec Trevlyan (006), Wai Lin, Max Zorin, May Day, and Christmas Jones (dress).

Unlock the Covert Skins

Complete the City of Walkways 1 level on the Secret Agent difficulty setting with a time less than 3:45.

Unlock the Exotic Skins

Complete the Cold Reception level on the 00 Agent difficulty setting with a time less than 3:25.

Unlock the Security Skins

Complete the King's Ransom level on the Secret Agent difficulty setting with a time less than 3:45.

Unlock the Scientist Skins

Complete the Masquerade level on the 00 Agent difficulty setting with a time less than 4:20.

Unlock the Soldier Skins

Complete the Midnight Departure level on the Agent difficulty setting with a time less than 3:05.

Unlock the Suit Skins

Complete the Curiour level on the Secret Agent difficulty setting with a time less than 2:00.

Unlock the Gadget War mode

Complete the Fallen Angel level on the Secret Agent difficulty setting with a time less than 2:45.

Unlock the Wildfire Mode

Complete the City of Walkways 2 level on the Agent difficulty setting with a time less than 3:40.

WORMS ARMAGEDDON

Cheat Mode

Turn on the following cheats at the Weapon or Game Option screens after the task is completed.

Laser Sighting

Beat mission 4.

Jetpack

Beat mission 8.

Faster Walking

Beat mission 13.

Invisibility in Net Games

Beat mission 16.

Low Gravity

Beat mission 20.

Invincible Landscape

Beat mission 25.

Super Banana Bomb Power-Up

Beat mission 33.

Full Wormage Options

Earn a gold medal and Elite rank in everything.

Invincibility

Get an Elite rank in Deathmatch mode.

Shotgun Power-Up

Get a gold medal in Rifle Range training mode.

Longbow Power-Up

Get a gold medal in Euthanasia training mode.

Grenade Power-Up

Get a gold medal in Artillery Range training mode.

Aqua Sheep

Get a gold medal in Super Sheep Racing training mode.

All Weapon Crates Have Sheep

Get a gold medal in Crazy Crates training mode.

Worms Bleed When Shot

Get a gold medal in Basic training mode.

WWF ATTITUDE

All Cheats
Beat Carrier mode using a created player on Medium or Hard difficulty.

Alternate Animations
Pick "Utilities" at the main menu. Set the language to "Teen." You see different entrances, maneuvers, and hear the character's theme song.

Perform a Taunt
Hold Kick+Tie-up and press Up, Down, Left, or Right during a match.

Random Select
Press R at the Character Selection screen.

New Chants
Wait for a chant to start up from the crowd, then pause. Unpause and the crowd will perform a different chant.

Alternate Costumes
Press C-Up, C-Down, C-Left, or C-Right at the Character Selection screen.

European Title (Career Mode)
Win the European title in Career mode on any difficulty setting to unlock Sable, Marc Mero, Trainer mode, Squeaky mode, and other bonuses in Create a Wrestler mode.

Intercontinental Title (Career Mode)
Win the Intercontinental title in Career mode on any difficulty setting to unlock Chyna, Jacqueline, Big Head mode, and three additional points in Create a Wrestler mode.

WWF Heavyweight Title (Career Mode)
Win the Heavyweight title in Career mode on any difficulty setting to unlock Head mode, Beep mode, and Ego mode.

Royal Rumble PPV (Career Mode)
Win the Royal Rumble PPV in Career mode to unlock Jerry Lawler and Paul Bearer.

King of the Ring PPV (Career Mode)
Win the King of the Ring PPV in Career mode to unlock Kurrgan and Taka Michinoku.

Summerslam PPV (Career Mode)
Win the Summerslam PPV in Career mode to unlock Sgt. Slaughter and Shawn Michaels.

WWF NO MERCY

Unlock Debra
Highlight Terri, then press either C-left or C-right.

Unlock Fabulous Moolah
Highlight, Mae Young, then press either C-left or C-right.

Unlock Funaki
Highlight Taka Michinoku, then press either C-left or C-right.

Unlock Gerald Brisco
Highlight, Pat Patterson, then press either C-left or C-right.

Unlock the Goodfather
Highlight Godfather, then press either C-left or C-right.

Unlock Jacqueline
Highlight Ivory, then press either C-left or C-right.

Unlock the King
Highlight JR, then press either C-left or C-right.

WWF WARZONE

Additional Create a Wrestler Costumes
Win the Challenge mode with Kane at Medium or Hard difficulty.

Additional Goldust Costumes
Win the Challenge mode with Goldust at Medium or Hard difficulty. Then highlight Goldust and press C-Right, R, or C-Up at the Character Selection screen.

Additional Stone Cold Costumes
Win the Challenge mode with Stone Cold at Medium or Hard difficulty. Then highlight Stone Cold and press C-Right, R, or C-Up at the Character Selection screen.

Big Head Mode
Win the Challenge mode with The Rock or British Bulldog at Medium or Hard difficulty.

Ego Mode
Win the Challenge mode with Ahmed Johnson at Medium or Hard difficulty. If the crowd chants, your character's head enlarges. If the crowd boos, your character's head shrinks.

No Meters Mode
Win the Challenge mode with Undertaker at Medium or Hard difficulty.

No Wimps Mode
Win the Challenge mode with Farooq or Ken Shamrock at Medium or Hard difficulty. You won't be able to block anymore.

Polished Mode
Win the Challenge mode with any character and at any difficulty level. You will have highly reflective surfaces.

Beans Mode
Win the Challenge mode with the Headbangers at Medium or Hard difficulty.

Taunts
Press Punch+Block or Tie-up+Kick to perform two different taunts.

Unlock Female Body Type
Win the Challenge mode with Shawn Michaels or Triple H. The "Female" body type becomes selectable inside the Create a Wrestler mode.

Random Select
Hold Up and press Kick at the Character Selection screen.

View Unlocked Characters and Mode
Press L+R at the main menu to see a list of characters and modes that have been unlocked.

Dizzy Character
Press L+R at the Create a Wrestler screen.

Unlock Cactus Jack and Dude Love
Win the Challenge mode with Mankind at Medium or Hard difficulty.

Unlock Sue the Ring Girl
Win the Challenge mode with Bret or Owen Hart at Medium or Hard difficulty.

Unlock Pamela
Win the Challenge mode with Sue the Ring Girl at Medium or Hard difficulty.

Unlock Trainer
Enter training mode at the Character Selection screen. Select "Custom" and then "Trainer" to be play as the trainer.

Unlock Rattlesnake
This will give you a Stone Cold wearing only jeans. Do not use any cheats or distribute attribute points to your user-created character. Win the Versus, Cage, Challenge, Weapons, and Tag modes with a user-created character at Hard difficulty.

WWF WRESTLEMANIA 2000

Random Select
Press C-Down at the Character Selection screen.

Different Costumes
Press C-Left or C-Right at the Character Selection screen.

Perform Opponent's Taunt
Spin the analog stick counterclockwise during a match.

Perform Opponent's Special Move
When your Special meter is full and flashing, do a strong grapple on your opponent. Then press the analog stick in any direction and press A+B to perform the opponent's special move.

Weapons
Exit the ring and head toward the crowd. Once you get to the barricades, press C-Up to get a weapon from the crowd.

Unmasked Kane
Go to edit and select "Kane." Go to the Appearance Edit and edit his mask. Set his mask at zero to see his face.

Unlock Paul Bearer
Use the Undertaker in a Road to Wrestlemania game. Paul Bearer will accompany the Undertaker after a few matches and become a selectable character.

Unlock Stephanie McMahon
Use Test in a Road to Wrestlemania game. Stephanie will accompany Test after a few matches and become a selectable character.

Unlock Shawn Michaels
Use any character in a Road to Wrestlemania game. Win the championship belt. Then Michaels's theme song begins playing and he challenges you to a match. Beat him and he becomes a selectable character.

Unlock Cactus Jack
Use any character in a Road to Wrestlemania game. Win the hard-core title. Defend the title a few times and Cactus Jack will come out and challenge you to a match. Cactus Jack is now a selectable character.

Unlock Dude Love
Use any character to win the WWF Heavyweight belt at Summerslam. Dude Love will appear and become a selectable character.

Unlock Jim Ross
Use any character in a Road to Wrestlemania game. Make it to Wrestlemania for the WWF World Championship match. Jim Ross will appear and become unlocked.

Unlock Jerry Lawler
Use any character in a Road to Wrestlemania game. Make it to Wrestlemania for the WWF World Championship match. Jerry Lawler will appear and become unlocked.

Never Lose in Road to Wrestlemania
Press Start and pick "Quit" to exit a Road to Wrestlemania match without losing.

Manager Interference
Start a one-on-one match and pick a character that has a manager or valet. Then pick an opponent that doesn't have a manager or valet. Start the match. Wait for an interfering character to run in and your manager will jump in. The manager will beat up the interfering character.

Manager Assistance
This only works for single matches. Be the first person in the ring. Hold C-Up+C-Down+Z on Controller 3 to have Player 3 control your manager. If your character is the second person in the ring, then hold C-Up+C-Down+Z on Controller 4. Then Player 4 will control your manager.

Mooning Woman
Choose a woman and pick your opponent to be Bad Ass Billy Gun. Rotate the analog stick counterclockwise to moon him.

D-Generation-X Appearance
Put X-Pac and Triple H with the DX music and video to make them appear together in a tag match with D-Generation-X being displayed.

Mark Henry & D'Lo Brown Appearance
Put Mark Henry with the D'Lo Brown music and video. They appear together in a tag match.

The Brood Appearance
Put Edge and Christian with the Brood music and video. Then have Gangrel placed in a tag match with Christian or Edge. They appear in tag team match with The Brood displayed.

New Age Outlaws Appearance
Put Billy Gunn with the Road Dogg's entrance and titantron. The two appear together and the New Age Outlaws will be displayed.

Union Appearance
Put Mankind, Ken Shamrock, Test, or Show with the Union music and no video. They appear together in a tag match with the Union being displayed.

Headbangers Appearance
Edit Chaz and change his clothes to Thrasher. Change his name to MOSH (case-sensitive). Change his music and video to the Headbangers. Then Mosh and Thrasher appear together as the Headbangers.

Corporate Ministry Appearance
Put Vince, Shane, or Undertaker with the Corporate Ministry music and video. They will appear together in a tag match and the Corporate Ministry will be displayed.

Smoking Skull Belt
Win the Road to Wrestlemania with Stone Cold Steve Austin. This unlocks the Smoking Skull Belt in Create a Belt mode.

See Entrance Costumes
Pick a character and then return to the Character Selection screen. Highlight the same character again and you should see him in his entrance costume.

Finishing Moves
Perform a grapple on the opponent when your Special meter is full and flashing. Then move the analog stick in any direction to perform the finishing move.

Slow Motion Moves
Enter the Edit Wrestler mode and go to the "Moves Edit" option. Preview a move, but then hold C-Right to see the move in slow motion.

Different Intro Sequence
Edit any character's first costume to a different outfit. Save the outfit change. Restart the game and do not press Start at the title screen. The character's new outfit will be shown during the intro sequence.

XENA: WARRIOR PRINCESS

God Mode
Hold A, Press Right (2), Left (2), Right, Left, Right, Strong Punch (3), Weak Kick (3), A while playing.

Instant Kills
Hold A, Press Right (2), Left (2), Right, Left, Right, Strong Punch (3), Weak Kick (3), R while playing.

Play as Despair
Press Right (2), Left (2), Right, Left, Right, at the main menu. A sound confirms correct entry. Or complete the game at any difficulty.

Play as Despair with Bunny Outfit
Press Right (2), Left (2), Right, Left, Right, C-Left, C-Up, C-Right, C-Down at the main menu. A sound confirms correct entry.

Big Feet
Hold A and press Right (2), Left (2), Right, Left, Right, R while playing.

Big Head
Hold A and press Right (2), Left (2), Right, Left, Right, Z while playing.

Smaller Fighters
Hold A and press Right (2), Left (2), Right, Left, Weak Punch, Strong Punch, Strong Kick, Weak Kick, A while playing.

Invisible Opponent
Hold A and press Right (2), Left (2), Right, Left, Right, Strong Kick (3), Weak Kick, Z while playing.

Invisible Fighters
Hold A and press Right (2), Left (2), Right, Left, Right, Strong Kick (3), Weak Kick, A while playing.

Polygon Fighters
Hold A and press Right (2), Left (2), Right, Left, Right, Strong Punch (2) while playing.

Fight Gabrielle Instead of Hope
Press Right (2), Left (2), Right, Left, Right, C-Left (4) at the main menu. A sound confirms correct entry.

Titan Mode
Press Right (2), Left (2), Right, Left, Right, C-Up, C-Down, C-Up, C-Down at the main menu. A sound confirms correct entry.

Take Less Damage
Hold A and press Right (2), Left (2), Right, Left, Right, Strong Punch (3), Weak Kick (3), Z while playing.

Take No Damage
Hold A and press Right (2), Left (2), Right, Left, Right, Strong Punch (3), Weak Kick (3), A while playing.

Snow Mode
Hold A and press Right (2), Left (2), Right, Left, Right, Strong Punch (2), Z while playing.

Slippery Stages
Hold A and press Right (2), Left (2), Right, Left, Right, Weak Punch (3), Weak Kick (3), A while playing.

Green Nose
Hold A and press Right (2), Left (2), Right, Left, Right, Weak Punch (2), R while playing.

Red Nose
Hold A and press Right (2), Left (2), Right, Left, Right, Weak Punch (2), A while playing.

Purple Nose
Hold A and press Right (2), Left (2), Right, Left, Right, Weak Punch (2), Z while playing.

Combos
A word is spoken when these combos are performed correctly. SP = Strong Punch, WP = Weak Punch, SK = Strong Kick, WK = Weak Kick.

Ares
Ring of Fire: SP+SK

Autolyus
Dropkick: Away, Toward+SK

Caesar
Archers Combo: Away, Toward+WP

Callisto
Roundhouse: Away, Toward+SK

Callisto
Spinning Slash Combo: Away+SP, SP, SK, SP, SP, SP, SK, WK

Callisto
Multislash Combo: WP, WP, SP, SP, SP, SK, WK

Despair
Blender: Crouch+SK, SK

Despair
Homing Fire Snake: Away, Toward+SP+SK

Ephiny
Super Cartwheel: Away, Toward+SK

Gabrielle
Speed Bag Combo: Away+WP, WP, WP, SP, SP, SP

Velasca
Blast Combo: Away+WP, SP, WK, SK, SP, SP

Xena
Big Swing Combo: Away+WP, WP, SP, WP, SK, SK, SK, SP

Xena
Flying Kick: Away, Toward+SK

YAKOUCHUU II

New Sub-Scenario
Save your game after you finish *Yakouchuu II* for the first time. You are now able to access a new sub-scenario when you get on the Pandora.

Nintendo GameCube

18 WHEELER: AMERICAN PRO TRUCKER

Bonus Parking Levels
Successfully complete each of the four parking levels to unlock an additional parking level. Successfully complete the bonus parking level to unlock a sixth parking level.

Nippon Maru
Successfully complete Arcade mode with all four characters.

Bonus Trailers
Successfully complete Arcade mode with all four characters to unlock two bonus trailers in Score Attack mode, Versus mode, and Arcade mode (if the Nippon Maru is selected).

AGGRESSIVE INLINE

FMV Sequences
Successfully complete the normal challenges in a level to unlock its FMV sequence.

Bonus Character
Successfully complete the normal and hidden challenges in a level to unlock a bonus character.

Cheats
Collect all juice boxes in a level to reveal a cheat code.

Power Skates
Complete all challenges (normal and hidden) on every level. The Power Skates give you one blue stat point for every attribute.

Ultra Skates
Complete all the levels with 100 percent. The Ultra Skates give you the other blue stat point for every attribute.

ALL-STAR BASEBALL 2003

Activate Cheat Menu
Press L at the controller selection screen to activate cheats that have been bought.

Alternate Uniforms
Hold L + R to select alternate jerseys.

Information in this section was contributed by John Erik Madsen.

Taunt Opponents
Hit a homerun and on the way to third (after replay), press L or R. Your player will taunt the other team's players.

Information in this section was contributed by LroyEnuff.

Credit Commentary
Press A during the credits to hear commentary about the person currently featured.

BATMAN VENGEANCE

Master Code
Press L, R, L, R, Y(2) at the main menu. A sound confirms correct code entry.

Invincibility
Press L, R, X, L, R, Y, L at the main menu. A sound confirms correct code entry.

All Power Moves and 120 Achievement Points
Press L(2), R(2), L, R, L, R at the main menu. A sound confirms correct code entry.

Unlimited Handcuffs
Press X, Y, X, Y, L, R(2), L(2) at the main menu. A sound confirms correct code entry.

Unlimited Batlauncher
Press Y, X, Y, X, L, R, L, R at the main menu. A sound confirms correct code entry.

Unlimited Batarangs
Press L, R, Y, B, L at the main menu. A sound confirms correct code entry.

Unlimited Electric Batarangs
Press L, R, Y, X at the main menu. A sound confirms correct code entry.

99 of All Items
Press L, R, Y(2) at the main menu. A sound confirms correct code entry.

Bruce in Warehouse-Level Disguise
Press L, R(2), L, R(2), L, R, L, R(2), L at the main menu, then hold L while selecting the level.

BLOODY ROAR: PRIMAL FURY

Fight as Cronos the Phoenix
Successfully complete the game two times to unlock Cronos the Phoenix.

Fight as Ganesha the Elephant
Successfully complete the game one time to unlock Ganesha the Elephant.

Fight as Kohryu
Play the game in Arcade mode. Win four consecutive rounds. You'll fight Kohryu in the next round. Defeat him, then complete Arcade mode to unlock Kohryu the Iron Mole as a selectable character.

Fight as Uranus
Defeat Uranus in Stage 16 of Survival mode. To make this easier, play as Kohryu and enable the "Beast mode," "No walls," and "No blocking" cheats. When the "Ready?" message appears, push them to the corner of the stage and step back. When the "Fight!" message appears, do Kohryu's Projectile move (Down, Down/Forward, Forward, Beast). They'll fly off for a ring out. This cheat also unlocks her stage.

Fight against Uranus
Successfully complete the game three times to unlock Uranus. She resembles a type of Minotaur. Alternately, complete Time Attack mode in under 20 minutes. Next, choose Versus mode, highlight the "Next Character" box, press A multiple times, then press B.

Chaos Lab Stage
Defeat Uranus in Survival mode to unlock her Chaos Lab stage.

Evil Laboratory Stage
Successfully complete the game two times to unlock Cronos the Phoenix's Evil Laboratory stage.

Indian Palace Stage
Successfully complete the game one time to unlock Ganesha the Elephant's Indian Palace stage.

Movie Player Option
Successfully complete the game one time to unlock the "Movie Player" option.

Com Battle Option
Successfully complete the game two times to unlock the "Com Battle" option.

Kid Mode
Successfully complete the game three times to unlock the "Kid Mode" option.

Big Kid Mode
Successfully complete the game four times to unlock the "Big Kid Mode" option.

Super Buff Mode
Successfully complete the game five times to unlock the "Super Buff" option.

No Walls Mode
Successfully complete the game six times to unlock the "Eliminate All Walls" option.

Weak Walls Mode
Successfully complete the game seven times to unlock the "Weaken All Walls" option.

Break Walls Only in Final Round
Successfully complete the game eight times to unlock the "Break Walls" option.

Slow Motion Mode
Successfully complete the game nine times to unlock the "Low Speed" option.

Turbo Mode
Successfully complete the game 10 times to unlock the "High Speed" option.

No Blocking Mode
Successfully complete the game 11 times to unlock the "No Blocking Mode" option.

Expert Mode
Successfully complete the game 12 times to unlock the "Max Difficulty" option.

Knock Down Battle Mode
Successfully complete the game 13 times to unlock the "Knock Down Battle Mode" option.

Human Mode
Successfully complete the game 14 times to unlock the "Human Mode" option.

Beast Mode
Successfully complete the game 15 times to unlock the "Beast Mode" option.

Hyper Mode
Successfully complete the game 16 times to unlock the "Hyper Mode" option. This also unlocks Kohryu the Iron Mole. Kohryu has no ending.

Alternate Costumes
Press Y at the Character Selection screen.

BOMBERMAN GENERATION

Play as MAX in Battle Mode
Obtain all Lightning Cards in Normal mode. Then, in Battle mode, press Z at the player selection screen to switch Bomberman to MAX.

Play as Golden Bomber in Battle Mode
Win any match in Battle mode, then replay the same match without changing any other options (except for the stage, if desired). You'll play as Golden Bomber during the replay.

Group A/B Options

Complete the game once in Normal mode to unlock the "Group A/B" option at the stage selection screen in Battle mode. Press Up or Down to toggle between Group A and Group B. Group A gives you access to the basic power-ups during standard Battle mode matches, while Group B gives you access to the more advanced power-ups. Note: The traps of most of the stages change when you select Group B.

Mini-Game Option

Successfully complete level 5-3 to unlock the Mini Game option at the main menu.

Change View in Battle Mode

This trick works for any Battle Game mode. Immediately before the battle game starts, when "Ready" appears, use the C-stick to change the angle of the field. You can't do this after the game starts.

BURNOUT

Ending Bonuses

Successfully complete the game to unlock the Free Run mode (no vehicles on the road), Free Run Twin mode (two-player Free Run), and Credits options.

Face Off Option

Successfully complete Championship mode once to unlock Face Off 1 against the Roadster.

Roadster

Defeat the Roadster in Face Off 1 to unlock it and Face Off 2 against another car.

Towtruck

Play in Championship mode until you unlock Face Off 2 in the Special Options screen. Defeat the Towtruck once to unlock it.

Saloon GT

Defeat the Saloon GT in Face Off 3.

Bus

Defeat the bus in Face Off 4.

CEL DAMAGE

Cheat Mode

Enter the Character Selection screen, select "Load," then enter FATHEAD as a name to unlock all cars, tracks, and modes. Enter PITA or SUSIE! as a name to unlock various combinations of features.

Information in this section was contributed by Richard Wagner.

Invincibility

Enter the Character Selection screen, select "Load," then enter CODY as a name.

Pen and Ink Graphics

Enter the Character Selection screen, select "Load," then enter PENCILS as a name.

Plastic Graphics

Enter the Character Selection screen, select "Load," then enter FANPLASTIC as a name. Enter the event selection screen and highlight "Smack Attack." Press Down and select the Event Settings button. Then, select the Options button and select the Rendering Modes button. Change this option to "Render Plastic." The message "Current mode plastic" will appear. Return to the event selection screen, then select a level and begin gameplay. To return to normal, repeat the steps and choose the cartoon renderer at the "Rendering Modes" screen.

Ranged Weapons

Enter the Character Selection screen, select "Load," then enter GUNSMOKE! as a name.

Melee Weapons

Enter the Character Selection screen, select "Load," then enter MELEEDEATH as a name.

Hazard Weapons

Enter the Character Selection screen, select "Load," then enter HAZARDOUS as a name.

Personal Weapons

Enter the Character Selection screen, select "Load," then enter UNIQUEWPNS as a name.

Movement Power-Ups

Enter the Character Selection screen, select "Load," then enter MOVEITNOW as a name.

All FMV Sequences

Enter the Character Selection screen, select "Load," then enter MULTIPLEX! as a name.

Brian the Brain and Space World

Enter the Character Selection screen, select "Load," then enter BRAINSALAD as a name.

Count Earl and Transylvania World

Enter the Character Selection screen, select "Load," then enter EARLSPLACE as a name.

Whack Angus and Desert World

Enter the Character Selection screen, select "Load," then enter WHACKLAND as a name.

T. Wrecks and Jungle World

Enter the Character Selection screen, select "Load," then enter TWRECKSPAD as a name.

Big Head Mode

Hold L + R + Up during gameplay.

Gate Rally Mode

Win once in Smack Attack mode.

Additional FMV Sequences

Successfully complete Smack Attack, Gate Relay, and Flag Relay with each character to unlock additional FMV sequences.

CRAZY TAXI

Secret Push Bike

Hold L + R at the Character Selection screen. Release L, then release R. Hold L + R again, then release them simultaneously. Then, press A. A ringing sound confirms correct code entry, and your character will mount the bicycle. To unlock the Push Bike in Another Day mode, select original mode. Then press R + L, R + L, R + L, R, R + A at the Character Selection screen.

Expert Mode

Hold L + R + Start at the main menu. Continue to hold the buttons until the Character Selection screen appears, then press A to select the game mode and variation. The phrase "Expert Mode" appears in the lower left corner to confirm correct code entry. No destination or arrow indicators appear in this mode.

Disable Arrow Indicators

Hold R + Start after choosing your time limit and before the Character Selection screen appears. The message "No Arrows" appears in the lower left corner to confirm correct code entry.

Disable Destination Indicator

Hold L + Start after choosing your time limit and before the Character Selection screen appears. The message "No Destination Markers" appears in the lower left corner to confirm correct code entry.

Another Day Mode

Press R at the Character Selection screen, then release it. Then, hold R and press A. The message "Another Day" appears in the lower left corner to confirm correct code entry. This mode modifies various positions in the game.

Alternate Display

Begin gameplay in Arcade or Original mode. Hold L + R and press the Y button on controller three to display a speedometer. Press other buttons on controller three to change to first-person perspective, change to camera view, or return to normal view.

ETERNAL DARKNESS

View Credits

Successfully complete the game to unlock the "Credits" option.

Level Select

Successfully complete the game twice on the same save file to unlock the "Jump to Game" option.

Invincibility

Successfully complete the game three times on the same save file to unlock the "Eternal Mode" option in the "Jump to Game" menu.

Alternate Ending

Successfully complete the game three times on the same save file, choosing a new story path each time.

Skeleton Screen

At the main menu screen, choose "Options," and the picture of Alex will turn into a skeleton.

EXTREME-G 3

Unlimited Shields and Turbos

Press L + R, Z, L + R, Z after "Press Start" appears at the title screen. A message confirms correct code entry. This effect lasts for only one race and must be re-enabled before the next one.

GAMECUBE

Unlimited AMMUNITION and STARCOM TEAM
Press L, R, L, R, L + R, Z after "Press Start" appears at the title screen. A message confirms correct code entry. This effect lasts for only one race and must be re-enabled before the next one.

Always Win XG Career Mode Races
Press R, L, Z, L, R, Z, R, L, Z after "Press Start" appears at the title screen. A message confirms correct code entry. This code allows you to win a race even if you quit, lose, or die. This effect lasts for only one race and must be re-enabled before the next one.

Win Next Race
Press L + R + Z, L + R, Z, L + R + Z after "Press Start" appears at the title screen. A message confirms correct code entry. This effect lasts for only one race and must be re-enabled before the next one.

Double Prize Money
Press L, R, Z, L, R, Z, L + R after "Press Start" appears at the title screen. A message confirms correct code entry. This effect lasts for only one race and must be re-enabled before the next one.

Extreme Lap Challenge
Press L, R, L, R, L, R, Z, L + R at the main menu. A message confirms correct code entry. This code unlocks an oval track for maximum speed. This effect lasts for only one race and must be re-enabled before the next one.

All Teams and Tracks
Press L(2), R(2), Z(2), L + R + Z after "Press Start" appears at the title screen. A message confirms correct code entry. This effect lasts for only one race and must be re-enabled before the next one.

GAUNTLET: DARK LEGACY

Invincibility
Enter INVULN as a name.

Permanent Super Shot with Large Crossbow
Enter SSHOTS as a name.

Permanent Pojo the Chicken
Enter EGG911 as a name.

Permanent Anti-Death
Enter 1ANGEL as a name.

Permanent Invisibility
Enter 000000 as a name.

Permanent X-Ray Vision
Enter PEEKIN as a name.

Permanent Full Turbo
Enter PURPLE as a name.

Permanent Triple Shot
Enter MENAGE as a name.

Permanent Reflect Shot
Enter REFLEX as a name.

Permanent Shrink Enemy and Growth
Enter DELTA1 as a name.

Always Have Nine Potions and Keys
Enter ALLFUL as a name.

Run Quickly
Enter XSPEED as a name.

Throw Quickly
Enter QCKSHT as a name.

10,000 Gold per Level
Enter 10000K as a name.

Dwarf Is a Large Jester
Enter ICE600 as a name.

Dwarf in S&M Costume
Enter NUD069 as a name.

Jester Is a Stick Figure with Smiley Face
Enter STX222 as a name.

Jester Is a Stick Figure with Baseball Cap Head
Enter KJH105 as a name.

Jester Is a Stick Figure with Mohawk Head
Enter PNK666 as a name.

Knight Is a Roman Centurion
Enter BAT900 as a name.

Knight Is a Ninja (Sword and Claws)
Enter TAK118 as a name.

Knight Is a Bald Man in Street Clothes (Sean Gugler)
Enter STG333 as a name.

Knight Is an Orange-Skirted Waitress
Enter KAO292 as a name.

Knight Wears Street Clothes (Chris Sutton)
Enter CSS222 as a name.

Knight Wears Street Clothes
Enter ARV984 as a name.

Knight Wears Street Clothes and Baseball Cap
Enter DIB626 as a name.

Knight Is a Quarterback
Enter RIZ721 as a name.

Knight Wears Black Karate Outfit with Twin Scythes
Enter SJB964 as a name.

Knight Wears Black Outfit and Cape
Enter DARTHC as a name.

Valkyrie as the Grim Reaper with Bloody Scythe
Enter TWN300 as a name.

Valkyrie as a Japanese School Girl
Enter AYA555 as a name.

Valkyrie as a Cheerleader with Baton
Enter CEL721 as a name.

Warrior with an Ogre Costume
Enter CAS400 as a name.

Warrior as an Orc Boss
Enter MTN200 as a name.

Warrior with a Rat Head
Enter RAT333 as a name.

Wizard with an Evil Appearance
Enter GARM99 as a name.

Wizard as an Undead Lich
Enter GARM00 as a name.

Wizard as a Pharaoh
Enter DES700 as a name.

Wizard as an Alien
Enter SKY100 as a name.

Wizard as Sumner
Enter SUM224 as a name.

Introduction Sequence
Press L at the Midway Games screen to see how the story begins.

JAMES BOND 007: AGENT UNDER FIRE

Golden Gun
Successfully complete the Trouble in Paradise level with a "Gold" rank. This cheat unlocks the Golden P2K. With this gun, you receive a silencer that the normal P2K doesn't have. To do this easily, get as much accuracy as you can, take as few hits as you can, and do all the Bond moves (shooting barrels to explode, shooting vital enemy characters, and finding secret areas).

Golden Gun in Multiplayer Mode
Successfully complete the Precious Cargo level with a "Platinum" rank and all 007 icons.

Golden CH-6
Successfully complete the Precious Cargo level with a "Gold" rank. When used, this cheat gives you unlimited rockets.

Golden Accuracy Power-Up
Successfully complete the Bad Diplomacy level with a "Gold" rank. This cheat enables you to have greater auto-aim.

Golden Clip Power-Up
Successfully complete the Cold Reception level with a "Gold" rank.

Golden Grenade Power-Up
Successfully complete the Night of the Jackal level with a "Gold" rank.

Golden Bullet Power-Up
Successfully complete the Poseidon level with a "Gold" rank.

Golden Armor Power-Up
Successfully complete the Forbidden Depths level with a "Gold" rank.

Unlimited Golden Gun Ammunition
Successfully complete the Evil Summit level with a "Gold" rank.

Unlimited Car Missiles
Successfully complete the Dangerous Pursuit level with a "Gold" rank.

Rocket Manor Multiplayer Level
Successfully complete the Trouble in Paradise level with a "Platinum" rank and all 007 icons. This cheat unlocks a new multiplayer level. It's a large open area. The map settings allow only rockets.

Stealth Bond Skin in Multiplayer Mode
Successfully complete the Dangerous Pursuit level with a "Platinum" rank and all 007 icons.

Guard Skin in Multiplayer Mode
Successfully complete the Cold Reception level with a "Platinum" rank and all 007 icons.

Alpine Guard Skin in Multiplayer Mode
Successfully complete the Streets of Bucharest level with a "Platinum" rank and all 007 icons.

Cyclops Oil Guard Skin in Multiplayer Mode
Successfully complete the Poseidon level with a "Platinum" rank and all 007 icons.

Poseidon Guard Skin in Multiplayer Mode
Successfully complete the Mediterranean Crisis level with a "Platinum" rank and all 007 icons.

Carrier Guard Multiplayer Skin
Successfully complete the Evil Summit level with a "Platinum" rank and all 007 icons.

Rapid Fire Power-Up
Successfully complete the Fire and Water level with a "Gold" rank.

Regenerative Armor Power-Up
Successfully complete the Mediterranean Crisis level with a "Gold" rank.

Calypso Gun in Multiplayer Mode
Successfully complete the Fire and Water level with a "Platinum" rank and all 007 icons.

Full Arsenal in Multiplayer Mode
Successfully complete the Forbidden Depths level with a "Platinum" rank and all 007 icons.

Gravity Boots in Multiplayer Mode
Successfully complete the Bad Diplomacy level with a "Platinum" rank and all 007 icons.

Viper Gun in Multiplayer Mode
Successfully complete the Night of the Jackal level with a "Platinum" rank and all 007 icons.

Lotus Esprit Car
Successfully complete the Streets of Bucharest level with a "Gold" rank.

JEREMY MCGRATH SUPERCROSS WORLD

Unlimited Turbo
Press Down(3), L, R, Z at the main menu. The lower left corner of the screen will flash and the message "Need for speed" will confirm correct code entry.

Moon Gravity
Press Left, Right, Up, Down, B(3) at the main menu. The lower left corner of the screen will flash and the message "Feel lighter" will confirm correct code entry.

Bouncy Bike
Press Up(2), Y(2), X(2) at the main menu. The lower left corner of the screen will flash and the message "Bouncy, bouncy" will appear to confirm correct code entry.

Big Heads
Press B, X, R, L, Right at the main menu. The lower left corner of the screen will flash and the message "Your head expands" will appear to confirm correct code entry.

Tiny Mode
Press L, Z, Left, Right, B(2) at the main menu. The lower left corner of the screen will flash and the message "Drink me" will confirm correct code entry.

Tag Mode
Press Z, X, Z, X at the main menu. The lower left corner of the screen will flash and the message "Tag you're it" will confirm correct code entry.

LEGENDS OF WRESTLING

All Wrestlers
Press Up(2), Down(2), Left, Right, Left, Right, Y(2), X at the main menu. A message confirms correct code entry. After enabling the code, go to the Options screen and save your options. This keeps all wrestlers unlocked if you start your game over.

Captain Lou Albano
Successfully complete Career mode with a wrestler in the "Hated" category.

David von Erich
Successfully complete Career mode as Kevin Von Erich.

Dory Funk
Successfully complete Career mode as Terry Funk.

Fritz von Erich
Successfully complete Career mode as Kerry von Erich.

Ivan Koloff
Win the versus tournament.

Jimmy Hart
Successfully complete Career mode with a wrestler in the "Loved" category.

King Kong Bundy
Win the Southeast Territory in Career mode.

Michael von Erich
Successfully complete career mode as David von Erich.

Mr. Fuji
Win the Tag Belts in Tournament mode.

Robert Gibson and Ricky Morton
Win the tag tournament.

Sabu
Successfully complete Career mode as The Sheik.

Bonus Arenas
Successfully complete the game in Career mode to unlock the Back Lot, Gym, Beach Resort, and Casino arenas in Exhibition mode.

Real Names
You can create wrestlers such as Ric Flair, Hall, Nash, and others, and the announcer will say their names.

NBA STREET

Cheat Mode
After entering one of the following icon codes, press enter direction on the D-Pad to complete code entry.

No Cheats
Enter Basketball, Shoe, Basketball, Shoe as a code at the Versus screen before a game.

Casual Uniforms
Enter Basketball, Shoe, Megaphone, Megaphone as a code at the Versus screen before a game.

Authentic Uniforms
Enter Basketball, Shoe, Turntable, Turntable as a code at the Versus screen before a game.

Player Names
Enter Turntable, Turntable, Basketball, Turntable as a code at the Versus screen before a game.

No Auto Replays
Enter Turntable, Turntable, Turntable, Turntable as a code at the Versus screen before a game.

No HUD display
Enter Turntable, Turntable, Shoe, Turntable as a code at the Versus screen before a game.

No Player Indicators
Enter Turntable, Turntable, Backboard, Turntable as a code at the Versus screen before a game.

Summertime Joe "The Show"
Enter Turntable, Turntable, Megaphone, Turntable as a code at the Versus screen before a game.

Springtime Joe "The Show"
Enter Turntable, Turntable, Turntable, Basketball as a code at the Versus screen before a game.

Athletic Joe "The Show"
Enter Turntable, Turntable, Turntable, Shoe as a code at the Versus screen before a game.

No Shot Indicator
Enter Turntable, Turntable, Turntable, Backboard as a code at the Versus screen before a game.

Explosive Rims
Enter Turntable, Turntable, Turntable, Megaphone as a code at the Versus screen before a game.

ABA Ball
Enter Basketball, Basketball, Turntable, Shoe as a code at the Versus screen before a game.

WNBA Ball
Enter Basketball, Basketball, Shoe, Backboard as a code at the Versus screen before a game.

Nufx Ball
Enter Basketball, Basketball, Back Board, Megaphone as a code at the Versus screen before a game.

EA Big Ball
Enter Basketball, Basketball, Megaphone, Turntable as a code at the Versus screen before a game.

Beach Ball
Enter Basketball, Basketball, Turntable, Turntable as a code at the Versus screen before a game.

Medicine Ball
Enter Basketball, Basketball, Shoe, Shoe as a code at the Versus screen before a game.

Volleyball
Enter Basketball, Basketball, Backboard, Backboard as a code at the Versus screen before a game.

Soccer Ball
Enter Basketball, Basketball, Megaphone, Megaphone as a code at the Versus screen before a game.

Tiny Players
Enter Shoe, Shoe, Shoe, Turntable as a code at the Versus screen before a game.

GAMECUBE

Big Heads

Enter Shoe, Shoe, Shoe, Backboard as a code at the versus screen before a game.

Tiny Heads

Enter Shoe, Shoe, Shoe, Megaphone as a code at the Versus screen before a game.

ABA Socks

Enter Shoe, Shoe, Shoe, Shoe as a code at the Versus screen before a game.

No Shot Clock

Enter Shoe, Shoe, Shoe, Basketball as a code at the Versus screen before a game.

Fewer Gamebreakers

Enter Shoe, Turntable, Turntable, Basketball as a code at the Versus screen before a game.

More Gamebreakers

Enter Shoe, Backboard, Backboard, Basketball as a code at the Versus screen before a game.

No Gamebreakers

Enter Shoe, Megaphone, Megaphone, Basketball as a code at the Versus screen before a game.

No Juice

Enter Turntable, Backboard, Backboard, Basketball as a code at the Versus screen before a game.

Unlimited Turbo

Enter Turntable, Shoe, Shoe, Basketball as a code at the Versus screen before a game.

Easy Distance Shots

Enter Basketball, Backboard, Backboard, Basketball as a code at the Versus screen before a game.

Harder Distance Shots

Enter Basketball, Turntable, Turntable, Basketball as a code at the Versus screen before a game.

Mega Dunking

Enter Basketball, Megaphone, Megaphone, Basketball as a code at the Versus screen before a game.

Ultimate Power

Enter Turntable, Shoe, Backboard, Basketball as a code at the Versus screen before a game.

Mad Hands

Enter Shoe, Backboard, Turntable, Basketball as a code at the Versus screen before a game.

Super Swats

Enter Backboard, Turntable, Shoe, Basketball as a code at the Versus screen before a game.

Sticky Fingers

Enter Backboard, Shoe, Turntable, Basketball as a code at the Versus screen before a game.

Captain Quicks

Enter Shoe, Turntable, Backboard, Basketball as a code at the Versus screen before a game.

No Dunks

Enter Turntable, Backboard, Shoe, Basketball as a code at the Versus screen before a game.

Fewer Blocks

Enter Basketball, Turntable, Shoe, Basketball as a code at the Versus screen before a game.

Fewer Steals

Enter Basketball, Shoe, Backboard, Basketball as a code at the Versus screen before a game.

No Alley-Oops

Enter Basketball, Backboard, Turntable, Basketball as a code at the Versus screen before a game.

No Two-Pointers

Enter Basketball, Turntable, Backboard, Basketball as a code at the Versus screen before a game.

Team Big

Get 10 wins in any mode.

Team 3LW

Get 20 wins in any mode.

NYC Legends Team

Get 30 wins in any mode.

Team Street Legends

Win the City Circuit to unlock the Street Legends team. This team includes Biggs, Bonafide, Drake, DJ, Takashi, Stretch, and the player that you did the best with throughout the season.

Team Dream

Win (complete all the objectives) Hold the Court mode to unlock a team that includes Graylien Alien, Magma Man, and Yeti Snowman.

Biggs and Beacon Hill Court

Play the City Circuit and reach the Region 1 City Challenge. Defeat Biggs' team to unlock him as a selectable player and to unlock the Beacon Hill court.

Bonafide and Broad Street Court

Play the City Circuit and reach the Region 2 City Challenge. Defeat Bonafide's team to unlock him as a selectable player and to unlock the Broad Street court.

Drake and the Yard Court

Play the City Circuit and reach the Region 3 City Challenge. Defeat Drake's team to unlock him as a selectable player and to unlock the Yard court.

DJ and Venice Beach court

Play the City Circuit and reach the Region 4 City Challenge. Defeat DJ's team to unlock him as a selectable player and to unlock the Venice Beach court.

Takashi and Yakatomni Plaza Court

Play the City Circuit and reach the Region 5 City Challenge. Defeat Takashi's team to unlock him as a selectable player and to unlock Yakatomni Plaza court.

Stretch and Rucker Park Court

Play the City Circuit and reach the Region 2 City Challenge. Defeat Stretch's team to unlock him as a selectable player and to unlock Rucker Park court.

EA Big Pacific Boulevard Court

Successfully complete Street School mode training.

NBA Superstars

Play the City Challenge and defeat an NBA team to unlock a player from their roster.

Custom Team

Successfully complete the game in Single-Player mode with the Street Legends team under the "expert difficulty" setting. You can now create a team of 16 players of your choice.

NHL HITZ 2002

Cheat Mode

Press B, Y, and X to change the icons in the first, second, and third boxes, respectively, at the match-up screen. The numbers in the following list indicate the number of times each button is pressed. After the icons have been changed, press the D-Pad in the indicated direction to enable the code. For example, to enter 1-2-3 Left, press B, Y(2), X(3), Left.

Big Head Player
2-0-0 Right

Huge Head Player
3-0-0 Right

Big Head Team
2-2-0 Left

Huge Head Team
3-3-0 Left

Big Hits
2-3-4 Down

Late Hits
3-2-1 Down

Hitz Time
1-0-4 Right

No Crowd
2-1-0 Right

Pinball Boards
4-2-3 Right

Show Shot Speed
1-0-1 Up

Show the Team's Hot Spot
2-0-1 Up

No Fake Shots
4-2-4 Down

No Puck Out
1-1-1 Down

No One-Timers
2-1-3 Left

Big Puck
1-2-1 Up

Huge Puck
3-2-1 Up

Bulldozer Puck
2-1-2 Left

Tennis Ball
1-3-2 Down

Snow Mode
1-2-1 Left

Rain Mode
1-4-1 Left

Domino Effect
0-1-2 Right

Turbo Boost
0-0-2 Up

Unlimited Turbo
4-1-3 Right

Win Fights for Goals
2-0-2 Left

Skills Versus
2-2-2 Down

First to Seven Wins
3-2-3 Left

More Time to Enter Codes
3-3-3 Right

Hockey Ball
1-3-3 Left

Disable Previous Code
0-1-0 Down

PAC-MAN WORLD 2

Pac-Man Mini-Game
Collect 10 tokens during gameplay to unlock the classic *Pac-Man* arcade game.

Pac-Attack Mini-Game
Collect 30 tokens during gameplay to unlock the classic *Pac-Attack* arcade game.

Pac-Mania Mini-Game
Collect 100 tokens during gameplay to unlock the classic *Pac-Mania* arcade game.

Ms. Pac-Man Mini-Game
Collect 180 tokens during gameplay to unlock the classic *Ms. Pac-Man* arcade game.

Music Test
Collect 60 tokens during gameplay to unlock the "Jukebox" option.

Pre-Production Art and Programmers
Collect 150 tokens during gameplay to unlock the "Museum" option.

REDCARD SOCCER 2003

Cheat Mode
Enter BIGTANK as a name to unlock all teams, stadiums, and finals mode.

Apes Team and Victoria Falls Stadium
Defeat the Apes team in World Conquest mode.

Dolphins Team and Nautilus Stadium
Defeat the Dolphins team in World Conquest mode.

Martians Team and USAFB001 Stadium
Defeat the Martians team in World Conquest mode.

Matadors Team and Coliseum Stadium
Defeat the Matadors team in World Conquest mode.

SWAT Team and Nova City Stadium
Defeat the SWAT team in World Conquest mode.

Samurai Team and Youhi Gardens Stadium
Defeat the Samurai team in World Conquest mode.

Finals Mode
Win all matches in World Conquest mode.

RESIDENT EVIL

Ending Bonuses
Successfully complete the game as Jill or Chris and save the game. A new background will appear on the main menu. Select the "Once Again" option when playing your completed saved game. You may now choose new difficulty settings for the replay. You also get a key that allows the character who completed the game to have a new costume. Enter the room with the large mirror on the second floor of the mansion. Unlock the door in the back. Enter the closet and go to the end of the clothes rack. A message asking "There is an outfit that fits you perfectly, do you want to put it on?" will appear. Select "Yes" to change your character's clothes. Complete the game again under a different difficulty setting to unlock a second costume. Jill's bonus costumes are a commando uniform and her costume from *Resident Evil 3*. Chris' bonus costumes are casual clothes and his costume from *Resident Evil: Code Veronica*.

Unlock Samurai Edge Gun
Successfully complete the game as Jill or Chris in Once Again mode under the normal difficulty setting with a time less than five hours. Save the game at the end, then start a new game to begin with the Samurai Edge gun.

Unlock Rocket Launcher
Successfully complete the game as Jill or Chris in Once Again mode with a time less than three hours. Save the game at the end, then start a new game to begin with the Rocket Launcher with unlimited ammunition.

Unlock Real Survivor Option
Successfully complete the game in Once Again mode under the normal difficulty setting with a time less than five hours. With this option, item boxes don't transfer items to each other and bonus costumes are available. Additionally, the aiming system is manual.

Unlock Invisible Enemy Option
Successfully complete the game two times as Jill or Chris in Once Again mode. All enemies are transparent in this mode.

Unlock One Dangerous Zombie Option
Successfully complete the game as both Jill and Chris one time. When this option is enabled, a special zombie follows you around during the first part of the game. Shooting the zombie will end the game, so you must avoid it during gameplay.

Unlock Gallery
Successfully complete the game in Invisible Enemy mode with a time less than five hours to unlock a "Special Features" option that displays a message from the game developers and a gallery of pre-production costumes.

THE SIMPSONS: ROAD RAGE

Activate Cheat Mode
Multiple cheats can be entered simultaneously. Cheats are only active for the next game session. All cheats are disabled once you return to the main menu. When any cheat is enabled, no money can be earned in Road Rage mode.

Horizontal Split Screen
Hold L + R and press Y(4) at the options menu. A sound confirms correct code entry. The screen is split horizontally instead of vertically in Two-Player mode.

Alternate Views
Hold L + R and press B(4) at the Options menu. A sound confirms correct code entry. Additional views are unlocked at the Pause screen. To unlock another set of views, hold L + R and press B, A(3) at the Options menu.

Nighttime
Hold L + R and press A(4) at the Options menu. A sound confirms correct code entry.

Flat Characters
Hold L + R and press X(4) at the Options menu. A sound confirms correct code entry. All the people (except the character you selected) are flat.

Show Collision Lines
Hold L + R and press B(2), A(2) at the Options menu. A sound confirms correct code entry.

No Map Display
Hold L + R and press Y, B(2), X at the Options menu. A sound confirms correct code entry.

Drive Red Brick Car
Hold L + R and press B(2), Y, X at the Options menu. A sound confirms correct code entry. This car is controlled by Homer and is small, fast, and heavy.

Drive as Smithers in Mr. Burns' Limousine
Hold L + R and press B(2), Y(2) at the Options menu. A sound confirms correct code entry.

Drive Nuclear Bus
Hold L + R and press B(2), Y, A at the Options menu. A sound confirms correct code entry.

Special Car Moves
Hold L1 + R1 and press A, B(2), A at the Options menu. A sound confirms correct code entry. Hold Gas + Brake + Handbrake while steering left or right while in mid-air to execute the Road Rage Roll. Hold Gas + Handbrake while stationary, then release Handbrake to execute the Speed Boost.

Time Trial Mode
Hold L + R and press X, B, Y, A at the Options menu. A sound confirms correct code entry. There are no passengers, pedestrians, or traffic in this mode. Press Horn to start, stop, and reset the timer.

Slow Motion
Hold L + R and press A, X, B, Y at the Options menu. A sound confirms correct code entry.

GAMECUBE

Halloween Mode

Hold L + R and press B(2), X, A at the Options menu. A sound confirms correct code entry. Select any character to play as Bart in a Frankenstein costume. Alternately, set the system date to October 31.

New Year's Day Mode

Hold L + R and press B(2), X, Y at the Options menu. A sound confirms correct code entry. Select any character to play as Krusty in a tuxedo, Alternately, set the system date to January 1.

Thanksgiving Mode

Hold L + R and press B(2), X(2) at the Options menu. A sound confirms correct code entry. Select any character to play as Marge in a pilgrim dress. Alternately, set the system date to the third Thursday in November.

Christmas Mode

Hold L + R and press B(2), X, B at the Options menu. A sound confirms correct code entry. Select any character to play as Apu in a Santa costume. Alternately, set the system date to December 25.

Disable All Active Codes

Hold L + R and press Start(4) at the Options menu. A sound confirms correct code entry.

Car Built for Homer

Complete all 10 levels in Mission mode to unlock the car built for Homer.

SMASHING DRIVE

Rush Hour Shift

Successfully complete the Early Bird shift.

Night Owl Shift

Successfully complete the Rush Hour shift.

Dusk and Wired Shift

Successfully complete the Night Owl shift.

SPIDERMAN: THE MOVIE

Master Code

Enter the Specials menu and enter ARACHNID as a code. A laugh confirms correct code entry. All levels in the level warp option, all gallery levels (movie viewer/production art), and combo moves are unlocked. Repeat code entry to return to normal.

Unlimited Webbing

Enter the Specials menu and enter ORGAN-ICWEBBING as a code. A laugh confirms correct code entry. Repeat code entry to return to normal. Alternately, accumulate 50,000 points during gameplay.

All Fighting Controls

Enter the Specials menu and enter KOALA as a code. A laugh confirms correct code entry. Repeat code entry to return to normal.

Level Select

Enter the Specials menu and enter IMIARMAS as a code. A laugh confirms correct code entry. Repeat code entry to return to normal.

Level Skip

Enter the Specials menu and enter ROMITAS as a code. A laugh confirms correct code entry. Repeat code entry to return to normal. Pause gameplay and select the "Next Level" option to advance to the next level.

Bonus Training Levels

Enter the Specials menu and enter HEADEX-PLODY as a code. A laugh confirms correct code entry. Repeat code entry to return to normal.

Play as Mary Jane

Enter the Specials menu and enter GIRL-NEXTDOOR as a code. A laugh confirms correct code entry. Repeat code entry to return to normal.

Play as the Shocker

Enter the Specials menu and enter HERMANSCHULTZ as a code. A laugh confirms correct code entry. Repeat code entry to return to normal.

Play as a Scientist

Enter the Specials menu and enter SERUM as a code. A laugh confirms correct code entry. Repeat code entry to return to normal.

Play as a Police Officer

Enter the Specials menu and enter REALHERO as a code. A laugh confirms correct code entry. Repeat code entry to return to normal.

Play as Captain Stacey (helicopter pilot)

Enter the Specials menu and enter CAPTAINSTACEY as a code. A laugh confirms correct code entry. Repeat code entry to return to normal.

Play as Skulls Gang Thug

Enter the Specials menu and enter KNUCKLES as a code. A laugh confirms correct code entry. Repeat code entry to return to normal.

Play as Uncle Ben's Killer

Enter the Specials menu and enter STICKYRICE as a code. A laugh confirms correct code entry. Repeat code entry to return to normal.

Play as Shocker's Thug

Enter the Specials menu and enter THUGSRUS as a code. A laugh confirms correct code entry. Repeat code entry to return to normal.

Matrix-Style Attacks

Enter the Specials menu and enter DODGETHIS as a code. A laugh confirms correct code entry. Repeat code entry to return to normal.

Goblin-Style Costume

Enter the Specials menu and enter FREAKOUT as a code. A laugh confirms correct code entry. Repeat code entry to return to normal.

Small Spider-Man

Enter the Specials menu and enter SPIDER-BYTE as a code. A laugh confirms correct code entry. Repeat code entry to return to normal.

Big Head and Feet for Spider-Man

Enter the Specials menu and enter GOESTOYOURHEAD as a code. A laugh confirms correct code entry. Repeat code entry to return to normal.

Enemies Have Big Heads

Enter the Specials menu and enter JOELSPEANUTS as a code. A laugh confirms correct code entry. Repeat code entry to return to normal.

First-Person View

Enter the Specials menu and enter UNDERTHEMASK as a code. A laugh confirms correct code entry. Repeat code entry to return to normal.

Unlimited Green Goblin Glider Power

Enter the Specials menu and enter CHILLOUT as a code. A laugh confirms correct code entry. Repeat code entry to return to normal.

Pinhead Bowling Mini-Game

Accumulate 10,000 points during gameplay to unlock the Pinhead bowling mini-game in the Training menu.

Vulture FMV Sequence

Accumulate 20,000 points during gameplay to unlock a Vulture FMV sequence in the CG menu.

Shocker FMV Sequence

Accumulate 30,000 points during gameplay to unlock a Vulture FMV sequence in the CG menu.

Green Goblin FMV Sequence

Successfully complete the game under the hero or greater difficulty setting.

Play as Alex Ross

Successfully complete the game under the normal or higher difficulty setting to unlock the Alex Ross costume in the Specials menu.

Play as the Green Goblin

Successfully complete the game under the hero or superhero difficulty setting to unlock the Green Goblin costume option at the Specials menu. Select that option to play as Harry Osborn in the Green Goblin costume, including his weapons, in an alternate storyline where he tries to correct the Osborn family's reputation. To unlock this easily, start a new game under the hero or superhero difficulty setting. At the first level, pause gameplay, then quit to the main menu. Enable the ARACHNID code, then go to the "Level Warp" option. Choose the Conclusion level (that features Norman revealing himself to Spider-Man followed by the glider sequence), then exit. This marks the game as completed under the selected difficulty setting. The Green Goblin costume option is unlocked at the Secret Store screen.

Alternate Green Goblin Costume

If you're using the Alex Ross Spider-Man, play any level with the Green Goblin in it and he'll have an alternate costume that more closely resembles his classic costume.

Play as Peter Parker

Successfully complete the game under the easy or higher difficulty setting to unlock the Peter Parker costume in the Specials menu.

Play as Wrestler

Successfully complete the game under the easy or higher difficulty setting to unlock the wrestler costume in the Specials menu. To unlock this easily, first unlock the "Unlimited webbing" cheat. When you get to the ring, zip to the top and keep on shooting Spidey Bombs.

SPY HUNTER

Activate Cheat Mode

Cheats are unlocked by completing all mission objectives (not just the primary objectives) within a set amount of time. To activate the cheats, enter "System Options," then choose "Extras," and "Cheat Grid." To play the FMV sequences unlocked in the Cheat menu, choose the "Movie Player" option that is above "Cheat Grid."

Saliva Spy Hunter Video
Complete Level 1 in 340.

Green HUD
Complete Level 2 in 335.

Saliva Your Disease Video
Complete Level 3 in 240.

Night Vision
Complete Level 4 in 315.

Early Test Animatic Video
Complete Level 5 in 325.

Extra Cameras
Complete Level 6 in 345.

Rainbow HUD
Complete Level 7 in 310.

Inversion Camera
Complete Level 8 in 305.

Concept Art Video
Complete Level 9 in 345.

Fisheye View
Complete Level 10 in 315.

Camera Flip
Complete Level 11 in 310.

Puke Camera
Complete Level 12 in 330.

Making of Video
Complete Level 13 in 215.

Tiny Spy
Complete Level 14 in 510.

Hover Spy
Complete the entire game.

Super Spy
Complete all 65 objectives in the game for unlimited ammunition and invincibility for your car.

The Making of Spy Hunter FMV Sequence
Choose an agent at the start of the game and select an empty slot. Enter MAKING or MODEL as a name. The name disappears and a clucking sound confirms correct code entry. After this is done, enter your own name and start the game. Select "System Options," then "Extras," then "Movie Player" to access the FMV sequence.

Saliva Spy Hunter Theme FMV Sequence
Choose an agent at the start of the game and select an empty slot. Enter GUNN as a name. The name disappears and a clucking sound confirms correct code entry. After this is done, enter your own name and start the game. Select "System Options," then "Extras," then "Movie Player" to access the FMV sequence.

Saliva Your Disease FMV Sequence
Choose an agent at the start of the game and select an empty slot. Enter SALIVA as a name. The name disappears and a clucking sound confirms correct code entry. After this is done, enter your own name and start the game. Select "System Options," then "Extras," then "Movie Player" to access the FMV sequence.

Spy Hunter Concept Art FMV Sequence
Choose an agent at the start of the game and select an empty slot. Enter SHAWN or SCW823 as a name. The name disappears and a clucking sound confirms correct code entry. After this is done, enter your own name and start the game. Select "System Options," then "Extras," then "Movie Player" to access the FMV sequence.

Early Test Animatic FMV Sequence
Choose an agent at the start of the game and select an empty slot. Enter WOODY or WWS413 as a name. The name disappears and a clucking sound confirms correct code entry. After this is done, enter your own name and start the game. Select "System Options," then "Extras," then "Movie Player" to access the FMV sequence.

Classic Spy Hunter Mini-Game
Choose an agent at the start of the game and select an empty slot. Enter OGSPY as a name. The name disappears and a clucking sound confirms correct code entry. After this is done, enter your own name and start the game.

SSX TRICKY

Master Code
Hold L + R and press A, B, Z, X, Y, Z, B, Y, Z, X, A, Z at the title screen. Release L + R and a sound confirms correct code entry.

Full Stat Points
Hold L + R and press B(2), Z, B(2), Z, A(2), Z, A(2), Z at the title screen. Release L + R and a sound confirms correct code entry. All the boarders have full stat points.

Mallora Board
Hold L + R and press A(2), Z, X(2), Z, B(2), Z, Y(2), Z at the title screen. Release L + R and a sound confirms correct code entry. Choose Elise and start a track. Elise will have the Mallora Board and a blue outfit. This code only works for Elise.

Mix Master Mike
Alternately, hold L + R and press A(2), Z, A(2), Z, A(2), Z, A(2), Z at the title screen. Release L + R and a sound confirms correct code entry. Choose Mac at the Character Selection screen and he's replaced by Mix Master Mike on the course, with Mac's übers. He has decks on his back and a vinyl board. Repeat the code to disable its effect.

Cheat Menu
Unlock all characters. Then successfully complete the world circuit using the following characters in order JP, Mac, Psymon, Zoe, Eddie, Mike, Brodi, Kaori, Luther, and Marisol. Go to the main menu, select "Single Event," and go to "Cheats." In this menu, you can turn on two different secret characters with full stats, extra boards and outfits for all of the characters, and extra trick chapters for each character. There's also an infinite tricky meter option.

Pipedream Course
Win a medal on all Showoff courses.

Untracked Course
Win a medal on all Race courses.

Überboards
Unlock all of the tricks for a character to get their überboard, which is their best board.

Fugi Board
Get a gold medal on every course with all boarders with their überboard to unlock a Fugi board.

Alternate Costumes
To earn more costumes, complete all chapters in your trick book. To unlock the final chrome costume, complete World Circuit mode with a "Master" rank.

Play as Brodi
Win a gold medal in World Circuit mode.

Play as Zoe
Win two gold medals in World Circuit mode.

Play as JP
Win three gold medals in World Circuit mode.

Play as Kaori
Win four gold medals in World Circuit mode.

Play as Marisol
Win five gold medals in World Circuit mode.

Play as Psymon
Win six gold medals in World Circuit mode.

Play as Seeiah
Win seven gold medals in World Circuit mode.

Play as Luther
Win eight gold medals in World Circuit mode.

STAR WARS: ROGUE LEADER: ROGUE SQUADRON 2

Unlimited Lives
Enter JPVI?IJC as a password. R2D2 doesn't beep for this password. Return to the Password screen and enter RSBFNRL as a second password. R2D2 beeps to confirm correct code entry.

Level Select
Enter !??QWTTJ as a password. R2D2 doesn't beep for this password. Return to the Password screen and enter CLASSIC as a second password. R2D2 beeps to confirm correct code entry. This doesn't unlock the bonus missions.

Asteroid Field Level
Enter TVLYBBXL as a password. R2D2 doesn't beep for this password. Return to the Password screen and enter NOWAR!!! as a second password. R2D2 beeps to confirm correct code entry.

Death Star Escape Level
Enter PYST?OOO as a password. R2D2 doesn't beep for this password. Return to the Password screen and enter DUCKSHOT as a second password. R2D2 beeps to confirm correct code entry.

Triumph of the Empire Level
Enter AZTBOHII as a password. R2D2 doesn't beep for this password. Return to the Password screen and enter OUTCAST! as a second password. R2D2 beeps to confirm correct code entry.

Revenge on Yavin Level

Enter OGGRWPDG as a password. R2D2 doesn't beep for this password. Return to the Password screen and enter EEKEEK! as a second password. R2D2 beeps to confirm correct code entry.

Endurance Level

Enter ?WCYBRTC as a password. R2D2 doesn't beep for this password. Return to the Password screen and enter ??MBC??? as a second password. R2D2 beeps to confirm correct code entry.

Naboo Starfighter

Enter CDYXF!?Q as a password. R2D2 doesn't beep for this password. Return to the Password screen and enter ASEPONE! as a second password. R2D2 beeps to confirm correct code entry.

Millennium Falcon

Enter MVPQIU?A as a password. R2D2 doesn't beep for this password. Return to the Password screen and enter OH!BUDDY as a second password. R2D2 beeps to confirm correct code entry.

Slave I

Enter PZ?APBSY as a password. R2D2 doesn't beep for this password. Return to the Password screen and enter IRONSHIP as a second password. R2D2 beeps to confirm correct code entry.

TIE Fighter

Enter ZT?!RGBA as a password. R2D2 doesn't beep for this password. Return to the Password screen and enter DISPSBLE as a second password. R2D2 beeps to confirm correct code entry.

TIE Advanced X1 Prototype
(Darth Vader's TIE)

Enter NYM!UUOK as a password. R2D2 doesn't beep for this password. Return to the Password screen and enter BLKHLMT! as a second password. R2D2 beeps to confirm correct code entry.

Imperial Shuttle

Enter AJHH!?JY as a password. R2D2 doesn't beep for this password. Return to the Password screen and enter BUSTOUR as a second password. R2D2 beeps to confirm correct code entry. The Imperial Shuttle can be piloted only in levels where an Imperial ship is normally used (for example, Revenge on Yavin). Press B when flying the Imperial Shuttle and an automatic gun on the ship will fire.

Car

Enter !ZUVIEL! as a password. R2D2 doesn't beep for this password. Return to the Password screen and enter !BENZIN! as a second password. R2D2 beeps to confirm correct code entry. Note: This code must be re-activated every time a new game session is started.

All Tech Upgrades

Enter AYZB!RCL as a password. R2D2 doesn't beep for this password. Return to the Password screen and enter WRKFORIT as a second password. R2D2 beeps to confirm correct code entry.

Ace Mode

Enter U!?!VWZC as a password. R2D2 doesn't beep for this password. Return to the Password screen and enter GIVEITUP as a second password. R2D2 beeps to confirm correct code entry. In Ace mode, you just need to complete a level to get a gold rank.

Monochrome Graphics

Enter LIONHEAD as a password.

Audio Commentary

Enter BLAHBLAH as a password. The "Audio Commentary" option is unlocked at the Special Features menu.

Sound Test

Enter COMPOSER as a password. The "Sound Test" option is unlocked at the Special Features menu.

Art Gallery

Enter EXHIBIT! as a password. The "Art Gallery" option is unlocked at the Special Features menu.

Documentary

Enter ?INSIDER as a password. The "Documentary" option is unlocked at the Special Features menu.

Credits

Enter THATSME! as a password. The "Credits" option is unlocked at the Special Features menu.

Quick Mission Start

Hold L + R while selecting a mission to start it immediately with the default ship.

In-Game Reset

Hold X + Y + B + Start for about one and a half seconds.

SUPER MONKEY BALL

Skip Credits

Hold L + R and repeatedly press A when you see the first words appear. Alternately, press A as soon as the credit scene appears.

Quick Finish in Monkey Race

During any Monkey Race on any setting, press L + R + A + X + Y to instantly finish the race.

Bonus Level

Select any difficulty setting and complete all normal levels. A bonus level will start during the credits. Get as many bananas as you can while avoiding the falling letters from the credits.

EX Levels

To unlock three EX levels, successfully complete Beginner mode without losing any lives.

Master Mode

Successfully complete the game in Expert mode without using any continues.

Unlimited Continues

After you buy all three mini-games, for every 2,500 play points you get, you'll gain an extra continue. After you reach nine continues, the game gives you unlimited continues.

TARZAN: UNTAMED

Jane

Successfully complete the Terk challenges in World 1 to unlock Jane in the waterskiing or river surfing challenges.

Porter

Successfully complete the Terk challenges in World 2 to unlock Porter in the waterskiing or river surfing challenges.

Terk the Monkey

Successfully complete the three Terk challenges in the final levels of the game to unlock Terk.

Ground Tumble Trick Move

Successfully complete the Terk challenges in World 1 to unlock the Ground Tumble trick move for jungle exploration.

Scarecrow Trick Move

Successfully complete the Terk challenges in World 2 to unlock the Scarecrow trick move for the waterskiing challenges.

Corkscrew Trick Move

Successfully complete the Terk challenges in World 3 to unlock the Corkscrew trick move for the river surfing challenges.

TONY HAWK'S PRO SKATER 3

Master Code

Enter the Options menu, then select "Cheats." Enter MarkedCards as a code to unlock all mode options, such as "Snowboard," "Giant," and "First Person." This also unlocks the "Super Stats," "Always Perfect," "Perfect Manuals," and "Perfect Rails" cheats. The sound of money being collected confirms correct code entry.

All FMV Sequences

Enter the Options menu, then select "Cheats." Enter Popcorn as a code to unlock all FMV sequences. The sound of money being collected confirms correct code entry. Alternately, get gold medals in all three competitions in Career mode.

Super Stats

Enter the Options menu, then select "Cheats." Enter MaxMeOut as a code. The sound of money being collected confirms correct code entry. Alternately, complete all the goals in the game and get gold medals in all three competitions 14 times in Career mode with a different skater each time.

Unlimited Specials

Enter the Options menu, then select "Cheats." Enter Unlimited as a code. The sound of money being collected confirms correct code entry. Alternately, complete all the goals in the game and get gold medals in all three competitions 12 times in Career mode with a different skater each time.

All Characters

Enter the Options menu, then select "Cheats." Enter Freakshow as a code. The sound of money being collected confirms correct code entry. All characters are unlocking, including Darth Maul, Wolverine, Officer Dick, Private Carrera, Ollie the Magic Bum, Kelly Slater, Demoness, and the Neversoft Eyeball Man.

All Created Skaters

Enter the Options menu, then select "Cheats." Enter WEEATDIRT as a case-sensitive code to unlock all created skaters.

Perfect Record

To get a perfect record for a skater, enable the following codes in order: "Level select," "All characters," "All FMV sequences," and "Master code."

Perfect Balance for Manuals

Complete all the goals in the game and get gold medals in all three competitions 17 times in Career mode with a different skater each time.

Perfect Balance for Rails

Complete all the goals in the game and get gold medals in all three competitions 13 times in Career mode with a different skater each time.

Slow Motion

Complete all the goals in the game and get gold medals in all three competitions 16 times in Career mode with a different skater each time.

Moon Physics

Complete all the goals in the game and get gold medals in all three competitions 19 times in Career mode with a different skater each time.

Snowboard Mode

Complete all the goals in the game and get gold medals in all three competitions 11 times in Career mode with a different skater each time.

Expert Mode

Complete all the goals in the game and get gold medals in all three competitions 20 times in Career mode with a different skater each time.

First-Person Mode

Complete all the goals in the game and get gold medals in all three competitions 22 times in Career mode with a different skater each time.

Demoness

Complete all the goals in the game and get gold medals in all three competitions 10 times in Career mode with a different skater each time.

Darth Maul

Complete all the goals in the game and get gold medals in all three competitions one time with any character in Career mode.

Kelly Slater

Complete all the goals in the game and get gold medals in all three competitions eight times in Career mode with a different skater each time.

Neversoft Mascot

Complete all the goals in the game and get gold medals in all three competitions 21 times in Career mode with a different skater each time.

Officer Dick

Complete all the goals in the game and get gold medals in all three competitions three times in Career mode with a different skater each time.

Ollie the Magic Bum

Complete all the goals in the game and get gold medals in all three competitions seven times in Career mode with a different skater each time.

Private Carrera

Complete all the goals in the game and get gold medals in all three competitions five times in Career mode with a different skater each time.

Wolverine

Complete all the goals in the game and get gold medals in all three competitions two times in Career mode with a different skater each time.

Small Skater

Complete all the goals in the game and get gold medals in all three competitions 18 times in Career mode with a different skater each time.

Huge Skater

Complete all the goals in the game and get gold medals in all three competitions 15 times in Career mode with a different skater each time.

Burnside Level from Tony Hawk's Pro Skater

Complete all the goals in the game and get gold medals in all three competitions six times in Career mode with a different skater each time.

Roswell Level from Tony Hawk's Pro Skater

Complete all the goals in the game and get gold medals in all three competitions nine times in Career mode with a different skater each time.

Warehouse Level from Tony Hawk's Pro Skater

Complete all the goals in the game and get gold medals in all three competitions three times in Career mode with a created skater.

Cruise Ship Level

Get any medal on all three competition levels.

All Highlight Tapes

Get gold medals in all three competitions in Career mode with a skater to unlock his or her tape.

A Day in the Life FMV Sequence

Complete all the goals in the game and get gold medals in all three competitions in Career mode with the Neversoft Eyeball.

Kickflip Contest FMV Sequence

Complete all the goals in the game and get gold medals in all three competitions in Career mode with Private Carrera.

Neversoft Bails FMV Sequence

Complete all the goals in the game and get gold medals in all three competitions in Career mode with Darth Maul.

Neversoft Friends FMV Sequence

Complete all the goals in the game and get gold medals in all three competitions three times in Career mode using five bonus or created skaters.

Neversoft Friends FMV Sequence

Complete all the goals in the game and get gold medals in all three competitions in Career mode with Ollie the Magic Bum.

Neversoft Makes FMV Sequence

Complete all the goals in the game and get gold medals in all three competitions in Career mode with Wolverine.

Neversoft Old School FMV Sequence

Complete all the goals in the game and get gold medals in all three competitions in Career mode with Demoness.

Pro Bails 2 FMV Sequence

Complete all the goals in the game and get gold medals in all three competitions in Career mode with a created skater.

Pro Bails FMV Sequence

Get medals (gold, silver, or bronze) in all three competitions in Career mode.

Pro Retro FMV Sequence

Complete all the goals in the game and get gold medals in all three competitions in Career mode with Officer Dick.

Slater Surf FMV Sequence

Complete all the goals in the game and get gold medals in all three competitions in Career mode with Kelly Slater.

TOP GUN: COMBAT ZONES

Unlock All Aircraft and Levels

Enter SHPONGLE as a name to unlock all aircraft and levels. The effects of the code are disabled if the game is saved.

UNIVERSAL STUDIOS PARK ADVENTURE

Attraction Mode

Get all eight stamps, then talk to Woody Woodpecker near the globe. Select the magic show when you talk to him. Allow the credits to finish, then return to the title screen. The option for Attraction mode will be unlocked.

Night Mode

Complete five attractions and the sun goes down.

Easy Points

Repeatedly watch the Waterworld Show to get 100 points each time.

Easy Money

Walk around the park, picking up trash and throwing it away.

WAVE RACE: BLUE STORM

Time Attack Tournament Mode

Press X + Z + Start at the Options menu to unlock the "Password" selection. Passwords for various time attack tournaments may now be entered.

Lost Temple Lagoon Time Attack Track

Enter LQ3TRKTE as a password to unlock this track under Time Attack mode. Enter J784WMHF as a password in the Japanese version of the game.

La Razza Canal Time Attack Track

Enter MJV8LKL6 as a password to unlock this track under Time Attack mode.

Dolphin Park Stunt Track

Enter KTUPWNPD as a password to unlock this track in the normal difficulty setting under Stunt mode. Enter 463YWNX3 as a password in the Japanese version of the game.

Southern Island Stunt Track

Enter WCX5WP5A as a password to unlock this track in Stunt mode.

Expert Championship Tournament

Enter AJXY8P53 as a password to unlock an expert championship tournament on seven tracks.

Ride a Dolphin

Enter DLPHNMOD as a password to ride on the back of a dolphin in Free Run mode. You can still perform tricks on the dolphin, but you can only do back flips and barrel rolls.

Control Loading Screen

Press the left analog stick while a track loads to control the water.

Control Title Screen

Press the left analog stick when "Start" appears on the title screen to move it on the water. Press Z at the title screen to change the Start button into a magnifying lens. Press Z again to change it back.

Control Replay

Use the right analog stick during a replay to control the view: Analog-Stick Up to change camera angles. Analog-Stick Right to pan the camera around your character. Analog-Stick Down to bring the view to water level. Analog-Stick Left to switch to a first-person view.

Alternate Visualizations

Go to the Options screen, then select the audio settings. Press Z to change visualizations.

Information in this section was contributed by migge.

Alternate Costumes

Highlight a racer, and press Z at the Character Selection screen.

Ghost Rider

To make the rider appear as a ghost, press the C-Stick up. Press the C-Stick down to return to normal.

In-Game Reset

Hold X + B + Start during gameplay.

Arctic Bay Track

Successfully complete the game in Championship mode under the normal difficulty setting. This track is named Cool Ocean in the Japanese version of the game.

La Razza Canal Track

Successfully complete the game in Championship mode under the advanced difficulty setting. This track is named Aqua Maze in the Japanese version of the game.

Strongwater Keep Track

Successfully complete the game in Championship mode under the expert difficulty setting. This track is named Victory Gate in the Japanese version of the game.

Weather

Successfully complete the Expert Championship in first, second, or third place, respectively, to unlock the weather conditions in Time Trial mode under the expert, advanced, or normal difficulties.

Trial Mode

Successfully complete Tutorial mode under the beginner and master difficulty settings to unlock the "Trial" option on the tutorial menu.

WWE WRESTLEMANIA X8

Unlock Chris Benoit

Win the WWE Undisputed Championship.

Unlock Vince McMahon

Win the WWE Intercontinental Championship.

Unlock Ric Flair

Win the WWE European Championship.

Unlock Rhyno

Win the WWE Hardcore Championship.

Unlock Raven

Win the WWE Light Heavyweight Championship.

Unlock Stacy Keibler

Win the WWE Tag Team Championship.

Unlock Original WWE SmackDown Arena

Win the WWE Undisputed Championship as The Rock.

Unlock WWE WrestleMania X7 Arena

Wrestle in all other arenas in Exhibition mode.

Unlock WWE Royal Rumble 2001 Arena

Win the Royal Rumble with any Superstar.

ZOOCUBE

Ending Bonuses

Successfully complete the Pacific Ocean level under the classic difficulty setting to unlock the gold difficulty setting and the Gulf of Mexico bonus level. Successfully complete the Pacific Ocean level under the gold difficulty setting to unlock the platinum difficulty setting for the Gulf of Mexico level.

Warp Speed Setting

Successfully complete the Pacific Ocean level under the platinum difficulty setting.

Game Boy

NUMBERS

102 DALMATIANS: PUPPIES TO THE RESCUE

Unlock Garage Level
At the password entry screen, enter: BONE, BONE, PAWPRINT, TANK.

Unlock Cafeteria Level
At the password entry screen, enter: DOMINO, BONE, KEY, PAW PRINT.

Unlock Cruella Level
At the password entry screen, enter: TOY, BONE, BONE, BONE. If you beat Cruella, you are given two more passwords. Use them to unlock mini-games.

1942

Enter the following icons in the password screen to be taken to the corresponding level.

Level 4
Medal, Medal, Your Plane, Enemy Plane

Level 8
Your Plane, Enemy Plane, Enemy Plane, Medal

Level 12
Bullet, Enemy Plane, Your Plane, Your Plane

Level 16
Enemy Plane, Enemy Plane, Bullet, Enemy Plane

Level 20
Your Plane, Medal, Bullet, Your Plane

Level 24
Bullet, Your Plane, Medal, Medal

Level 28
Medal, Enemy Plane, Medal, Enemy Plane

ACTION MAN

All Stages Unlocked
At the Password screen, type "7!B!".

ALL-STAR BASEBALL 2000

Invisible Base-Runners
Hold A for 30 seconds, hold Up for 13 seconds, then press A, B, Down, and Start.

ANTZ

Level 2
BCCB

Level 3
DQGH

Level 4
HGGF

Level 5
KGBF

Level 6
QGJJ

Level 7
QGJJ

Level 8
GQHG

Level 9
FLDP

Level 10
KGQQ

Level 11
DLGQ

Level 12
CBHG

Level 13
JBJG

Level 14
PLDP

Level 15
LFGB

Level 16
DQLD

Level 17
CLPG

Level 18
DLHD

Level 19
LFQG

ARMORINES: PROJECT S.W.A.R.M.

Cheat Mode
Enter BBBBBBBB.

ARMY MEN

Desert, Cactus Flats, Caution
Grenade, Machine Gun, Helicopter, Jeep

Desert, Cactus Flats, En Route
Jeep, Helicopter (2), Jeep

Desert, Cactus Flats, Clean Up
Machine Gun, Grenade, Machine Gun, Grenade

Desert, Casa Flats, Enter Town
Machine Gun, Helicopter, Jeep, Machine Gun

Desert, Casa Flats, To the Bank
Grenade (2), Helicopter (2)

Desert, Casa Flats, Stop the Tans
Machine Gun, Jeep, Machine Gun, Helicopter

Desert, Casa Flats, Tan's HQ
Jeep (2), Grenade, Machine Gun

Desert, Winding Canyon, Find that Jeep
Machine Gun, Plane, Jeep, Helicopter

Desert, Winding Canyon, Clear Patrols
Tank, Helicopter, Jeep, Machine Gun

Desert, Winding Canyon, Clear the Radar
Mortar, Tank, Helicopter, Jeep

Desert, Winding Canyon, Play It Again
Machine Gun, Helicopter, Tank, Mortar

Desert, Winding Canyon, To the Helipad
Machine Gun, Mortar, Machine Gun, Helicopter

Alpine, Winding River, Patrol
Mortar (2), Grenade, Machine Gun

Alpine, Winding River, Defense
Helicopter, Grenade, Jeep, Machine Gun

Alpine, Winding River, Radar Round Up
Jeep, Mortar, Machine Gun (2)

Alpine, Winding River, House Call
Helicopter, Jeep, Grenade, Plane

Alpine, Winding River, Movin' On
Plane, Tank, Mortar, Jeep

Alpine, Prison Camp, Assault Prep
Machine Gun, Tank, Helicopter, Jeep

Alpine, Prison Camp, Assault Start
Machine Gun, Mortar, Plane, Mortar

Alpine, Prison Camp, Destroy Camp
Mortar, Machine Gun, Grenade, Mortar

Alpine, Prison Camp, Escape
Plane, Machine Gun, Grenade, Machine Gun

Alpine, Construction, Secure Region
Mortar, Plane, Machine Gun, Plane

Alpine, Construction, Get the Tank
Helicopter, Jeep, Grenade, Tank

Alpine, Construction, Sack the Base
Machine Gun, Helicopter (2), Jeep

Alpine, Construction, Final Assault
Mortar, Helicopter, Machine Gun, Jeep

Alpine, Construction, Victory
Plane, Tank, Plane, Machine Gun

ARMY MEN 2

Level 2
Jeep (2), Mortar, Plane

Level 3
Tank, Grenade, Tank, Mortar

Level 4
Rifle, Mortar, Jeep, Plane

Level 5
Mortar, Rifle, Plane, Jeep

Level 6
Mortar, Grenade, Rifle, Chopper

Level 7
Plane, Grenade, Rifle, Tank

Level 8
Grenade, Mortar, Chopper, Mortar

Level 9
Tank, Mortar, Rifle, Tank

Level 10
Jeep, Chopper, Tank, Mortar

Level 11
Rifle, Mortar, Grenade, Mortar

Level 12
Jeep, Chopper, Grenade, Chopper

Level 13
Plane (2), Grenade, Mortar

Level 14
Plane, Rifle, Plane, Chopper

Level 15
Rifle, Chopper (2), Tank

Level 16
Chopper (2), Rifle, Grenade

Level 17
Rifle, Tank, Plane, Mortar

Level 18
Rifle (2), Grenade, Jeep

Level 19
Rifle, Jeep, Chopper, Grenade

Level 20
Chopper, Grenade, Rifle, Jeep

Level 21
Mortar, Grenade, Chopper, Jeep

The Ultimate Code Book: Book of Secrets

Level 22
Rifle, Tank, Chopper, Rifle

Level 23
Plane, Jeep, Tank, Mortar

Level 24
Chopper, Rifle, Jeep, Mortar

Level 25
Tank, Grenade, Plane, Grenade

Level 26
Plane, Tank, Rifle, Mortar

Level 27
Tank (2), Jeep, Tank

Level 28
Jeep, Tank, Jeep, Mortar

ARMY MEN: AIR COMBAT

Level 2
Box, Cross, Box (2)

Level 3
Rocket (3), Cross

Level 4
Patch, Rocket, Box (2)

Level 5
Cross, Patch, Cross, Rocket

Level 6
Helmet, Rocket, Patch, Helmet

Level 7
Box, Cross, Rocket, Cross

Level 8
Rocket, Patch, Cross, Helmet

Level 9
Patch (2), Rocket (2)

Level 10
Cross, Helmet, Cross, Helmet

Level 11
Helmet, Patch, Cross, Helmet

Level 12
Box, Cross, Patch (2)

Level 13
Rocket, Cross, Helmet (2)

Level 14
Patch, Cross, Box, Patch

Level 15
Cross, Box, Patch, Helmet

Level 16
Helmet, Cross, Rocket, Patch

ASTERIX: SEARCH FOR DOGMATIX

Level 2
CQPSJ

Level 3
MLSPS

Level 4
RSFMS

Level 5
TPPGN

ASTEROIDS (GAME BOY COLOR)

Cheat Mode
Enter CHEATONX as a password. Then, while in game, press Select to bring up a Cheat menu. Press Left or Right to pick zone, Up or Down to select a level, or press A for invincibility.

Excalibur Ship
Enter PROJECTX as a password.

Level 2
SPACEVAC

Level 3
STARSBRN

Level 4
WORMSIGN

Level 5
INCOMING

ATLANTIS: THE LOST EMPIRE

Skip Levels
Type in the following passwords to skip to the indicated level.

Submarine
DCNC

Cove
XDKV

Fire
CFCS

Ice
DHCV

Volcano
TJJT

Internal
JMFJ

Palace
QNFS

B

BABE AND FRIENDS

Level 2
B0B

Level 3
RN6

Level 4
G5M

Level 5
RM1

Level 6
N6W

Level 7
TYQ

BATMAN: CHAOS IN GOTHAM

Level 2
Batman, Batmobile, Batman, Batcycle

Level 3
Batman, Batcycle, Batgirl, Batcycle

Level 4
Batmobile (2), Batman, Batmobile

Level 5
Batmobile, Batcycle, Batgirl (2)

Level 6
Batcycle (2), Batman, Batgirl

Level 7
Batcycle, Batgirl (2), Batman

Level 8
Batgirl, Batcycle, Batman, Batmobile

Level 9
Batgirl (2), Batmobile, Batcycle

BATMAN BEYOND: RETURN OF THE JOKER

Level 2
C76564J

Level 3
L88R8TC

Level 4
Y539WZG

Level 5
NTTJ9KY

BATTLESHIP

Mission 2
QYBGTK

Mission 3
QYGZXK

Mission 4
GKPQZP

Mission 5
QRKGTD

Mission 6
QPDGYM

Mission 7
QQLGTD

Mission 8
QXFGTL

Mission 9
QNMGTK

Mission 10
NPGGYM

Mission 11
NXHGTL

Mission 12
NQBGYD

Mission 13
NQZGPD

Mission 14
NNCGYK

Mission 15
HJXQCN

Mission 16
NYDGTK

Mission 17
NWLGTM

Mission 18
NTFGTB

Mission 19
NRMGTD

Mission 20
BBQQBP

Mission 21
YPHGTM

Mission 22
YRBGTD

Mission 23
YRZGXD

Mission 24
YQCGTD

Mission 25
YSKGPC

Mission 26
BCSQBV

Mission 27
BDVQJQ

Mission 28
YYFGPK

Mission 29
BJRQZN

Mission 30
TRGGTD

Mission 31
JDNQJQ

Mission 32
TXBGTL

Mission 33
ZKTQKP

Mission 34
ZHPQCW

Mission 35
JCXQJV

Mission 36
TVDGTL

Mission 37
TTLGPB

Mission 38
JZWQKX

Mission 39
JMRQCQ

Mission 40
PXGGTL

Mission 41
CHNQBW

Mission 42
CGYQJS

Mission 43
CDTQZQ

Mission 44
CBPQBP

Mission 45
CMXQCQ

Mission 46
CKSQJP

Mission 47
CLVQZV

Mission 48
PPFGYM

Ending
Enter PQMGTD to see the ending cutscene.

BILLY BOB'S HUNTIN' AND FISHIN'

Hunt For Turkey and Pike
At password screen, enter: Pig, Boat, Bag, Deer, Bag, Deer.

BLADE

View Ending Sequence
Enter 9?!1N?BKT?51G as a password.

BLACK BASS LURE FISHING

Get Both Lakes
At the Password screen enter "K" for every space.

BLAST MASTER: ENEMY BELOW

Level 1
E6C3D3KF

Level 2
E6D3D3KG

Level 3
E7C3D3KH

Level 4
E7D3D3KI

Level 5
F6C3D3KQ

Level 6
F6D3D3KR

Level 7
F7C3D3KU

Level 8
F7D3D3KT

BOARDER ZONE

Bonus Track
Enter 020971 as the password.

Challenge Mode Tracks
Enter 290771 as the password.

BOMBERMAN POCKET

Forest 1
7693

Forest 2
3905

Forest 3
2438

Forest 4
8261

Forest Boss
1893

Ocean 1
2805

Ocean 2
9271

Ocean 3
1354

Ocean 4
4915

Ocean Boss
8649

Wind 1
0238

Wind 2
5943

Wind 3
6045

Wind 4
2850

Wind Boss
8146

Cloud 1
9156

Cloud 2
2715

Cloud 3
4707

Cloud 4
7046

Cloud Boss
0687

Evil 1
3725

Evil 2
0157

Evil 3
5826

Evil 4
9587

Evil Boss
3752

All Power-Ups
5656

BUBBLE BOBBLE (GAME BOY COLOR)

Level 1
BBBB

Level 2
CBCB

Level 3
DBBD

Level 4
FFBB

Level 5
GGBB

Level 6
HBHB

Level 7
JBBJ

Level 8
KKBB

Level 9
LLBB

Level 10
MBMB

Level 11
NBBN

Level 12
PPBB

Level 13
QQBB

Level 14
RBRB

Level 15
SBBS

Level 16
TTBB

Level 17
CCBB

Level 18
FCCC

Level 19
FDBC

Level 20
GFBC

Level 21
JCCG

Level 22
JBCH

Level 23
LJCC

Level 24
MCKC

Level 25
NCCL

Level 26
PMCC

Level 27
QNCC

Level 28
RCPC

Level 29
SCCQ

Level 30
TRCC

Level 31
VSCC

Level 32
WCTC

Level 33
DBDB

Level 34
XBXB

Level 35
GDBD

Level 36
JCDF

Level 37
KGCD

Level 38
LHCD

Level 39
MDJC

Level 40
NCDK

Level 41
PLCD

Level 42
QMCD

Level 43
RDNC

Level 44
SCDP

Level 45
TQCD

Level 46
VRCD

Level 47
WDSC

Level 48
XCDT

Level 49
GBCF

Level 50
HFCC

Level 51
JCFD

Level 52
JBFF

Level 53
KGBF

Level 54
LHBF

Level 55
MFJB

Level 56
NBFK

Level 57
PLBF

Level 58
QMBF

Level 59
RFNB

Level 60
SBFP

Boss Level 1
VVBB

Boss Level 2
FCBD

BUFFY THE VAMPIRE SLAYER

Level 2
9MD1WV

Level 3
XTN4F7

Level 4
5BVPL2

Level 5
9D6FOS

Level 6
TSCNB4

Level 7
CSJTQZ

Level 8
BNPXZ9

End of Game Animation
GH9MRY

BUG'S LIFE

Level 1
9LKK

Level 2
BL26

Level 3
5P9K

Level 4
6652

Level 5
BKK2

Level 6
2PLB

Level 7
6562

Level 8
L59B

BURAI FIGHTER (GAME BOY COLOR)

Eagle Level 2
BRFG

Eagle Level 3
KTDC

Eagle Level 4
DRMF

Eagle Level 5
SRSD

Albatross Level 2
NKMR

Albatross Level 3
TCKP

Albatross Level 4
NQTK

Albatross Level 5
MQFH

Ace Level 2
KDMT

Ace Level 3
SNNS

Ace Level 4
KMGT

Ace Level 5
MSKD

BUST-A-MOVE 4

Bonus Characters
From the main menu, press Up, Down, Left (2), Right, Up, A, B (2), A.

Bonus Levels
When "Push Start" appears, press A, Left, Right, Left, A.

BUZZ LIGHTYEAR OF STAR COMMAND

Level 2
BBVBB

Level 3
CVVBB

Level 4
XBVBB

Level 5
YVVBB

Level 6
GBVBB

Level 7
HVVBB

Level 8
3BVBB

Level 9
4VVBB

Level 10
LBVBB

Level 11
MVVBB

Level 12
7BVBB

Level 13
8VVBB

CATWOMAN

Level 2
At the password entry screen enter: K6T@1

Level 3
At the password entry screen enter: 1QT@@

Level 4
At the password entry screen enter: KQYXY

Level 5
At the password entry screen enter: 1@FVQ

Level 6
At the password entry screen enter: K@FVP

Level 7
At the password entry screen enter: @JFV4

Level 8
At the password entry screen enter: KJFZR

Level 9
At the password entry screen enter: 16TJV

CARMEGEDDON

All Cars and Tracks
Enter 0Z6SZD[Skull]V as a password.

CARROT CRAZY

Level Skip
Put Taz, Elmer Fudd, Daffy Duck as a password. Pause the game and press Select. Press A to skip to next stage.

CHASE HQ: SECRET POLICE

Level 2
NDHQ

Level 3
WVLF

Level 4
JD1S

Level 5
NC4Z

Level 6
BHKT

Level 7
ZDKW

Level 8
14FQ

Level 9
XVNP

Level 10
MMQG

CHICKEN RUN

Enter the following medals at the Password screen:

Level 3
Diamond, Bravery, Honor, Bronze

Level 4
Cross, Bravery, Bronze (2)

Level 5
Honor, Crown, Diamond, Crown

Level 6
Valor, Diamond, Cross, Silver

Invisibility
Crown, Bronze, Honor, Valor

Unlimited Time
Diamond, Honor, Cross, Crown

Skip Stages
Honor, Valor, Bronze, Silver (press Select at Pause screen)

CONKER'S POCKET TALES

More Health
Save the game when health is low, then restart to continue with more health.

Bonus Music
Stop playing without pausing the game to eventually have Conker play music from Banjo-Kazooie.

DAVE MIRRA FREESTYLE BMX

Game Completed
Enter R6KZBS7L1CTQMH as a password.

DISNEY'S ATLANTIS: THE LOST EMPIRE

Jump to Submarine Level
At the password screen, enter DCNC.

Jump to Cove Level
At the password screen, enter XDKV.

Jump to Fire Level
At the password screen, enter CFCS.

Jump to Ice Level
At the password screen, enter DHCV.

Jump to Volcano Level
At the password screen, enter TJJT.

Jump to Internal Level
At the password screen, enter JMFJ.

Jump to Palace Level
At the password screen, enter QNFS.

DISNEY'S THE JUNGLE BOOK: MOWGLI'S WILD ADVENTURE

Level Select
Enter BMHG as password.

Unlock Cheat Mode
Press Select during gameplay, then choose "Music/Effects." Play the following sounds in order: 40, 30, 20, 19, 18, 17, 16, 15.

DISNEY'S TARZAN

Level 2-1
Cross, X, Moon, Cross

Level 3-1
Vertical Lines (2), Maze, Swirl

Level 4-1
X, Moon, Triangles, Cross

Level 5-1
Triangles (2), Moon, Vertical Lines

Level 6-1
Swirl, Maze, Cross, Triangles

DEXTER'S LABORATORY: ROBOT RAMPAGE

PlayCheat menuSuper Robot
Go to the title screen and press A 10 times, then B 10 times. Press SELECT.

DOGZ

Get All Dogs
Retire a dog immediately after you get it, after it gets in the playpen. It retires as a happy dog. Repeat to get all the dogs.

DRAGON DANCE

Level 1
3128

Level 2
1497

Level 3
7434

Level 4
4136

Level 5
9224

Level 6
6230

Level 7
4592

Level 8
7271

Level 9
2315

Level 10
2042

Level 11
9913

Level 12
9354

Level 13
1720

Level 14
3310

Level 15
0170

Level 16
5108

Level 17
6482

Level 18
1277

Level 19
2460

Level 20
4838

DRAGON WARRIOR MONSTERS

Get Orchie
Breed a monster from Dragon family with a Dracolord, with the Dragon as the pedigree.

Get Dragon Lord
Breed a Servant and Great Drak, with the Servant being the pedigree.

Get Gophecada
Breed a Madcat and a Giantslug to get a Gophecada egg.

Get the Key to the Labyrinth
In the Labyrinth go up, up, up, left, down, down, and left. Beat the monster and receive the key.

DRIVER

Access Cheat Mode
At main menu, select "Undercover," and press Up (2), Down (2), Up, Down, Up, Down, Up (2), down (2). Choose "Cheat" as the option.

Level 1
face (4)

Level 2
tire tread, badge, cone, red siren

Level 3
stoplight, key (2), blue siren

Level 4
cone (3), badge

Level 5
key, red siren (2), stoplight

Level 6
key, badge, tire tread, blue siren

Level 7
badge, cone, badge, red siren

Level 8
red siren, badge, key, tire tread

Level 9
cone, blue siren, red siren (2)

Level 10
badge (2), stoplight, cone

Level 11
blue siren, key (3)

Level 12
stoplight, tire tread, red siren, badge

Level 13
key, badge, badge, cone

Level 14
red siren, blue siren, red siren, blue siren

Level 15
tire tread, key, cone, stoplight

DUKE NUKEM

Level Select
At the title screen, press Left, Right, Up (2), Down, Up, Right, Left.

Invincibility
At the title screen, press Up, Down (2), Left, Right, Left, Up (2).

EARTHWORM JIM: MENACE 2 THE GALAXY

Level 6
ebdnkg 3bbbbb bb3hbl

EVEL KNIEVEL

Snake River Canyon
Enter LASTSTAGE as a password.

Grand Finale mode
Enter LEVELS as a password.

FLINTSTONES: BURGERTIME IN BEDROCK

Level 2
Enter the following icons at the password screen: Fly, Blue Dinosaur, Gazoo, Snaggletooth.

Level 3
Enter the following icons at the password screen: Alligator, Alligator, Snake, Gazoo.

Level 4
Enter the following icons at the password screen: Frog, Fly, Snake, Gazoo.

Level 5
Enter the following icons at the password screen: Alligator, Snaggletooth, Snaggletooth, Snake.

Level 6
Enter the following icons at the password screen: Gazoo, Dinosaur, Fly, Crocodile.

FORCE 21

Level 2
Enter password LXCR

Level 3
Enter password PTKL

Level 3
Enter password LSGY

Level 4
Enter password DUSM

FROGGER

Cheat Mode
Run out of lives during the game. Then at the High Scores, press A, B, A, B, Select, Start. A Cheat option becomes available at the main menu.

GHOSTS 'N GOBLINS

Quest 1 Level 2
Enter L, Heart, K, Heart, Heart, Heart, B, L as the password.

Quest 1 Level 3
Enter Q, Zero, M, Heart, Heart, Heart, 1, H as the password.

Quest 1 Level 4
Enter P, S, 5, Heart, 7, Heart, B, 4 as the password.

Quest 1 Level 5
Enter T, J, R, Heart, 7, Heart, 2, Heart as the password.

Quest 1 Level 6
Enter J, J, T, Heart, 7, Heart, 7, L as the password.

Quest 1 Boss
Enter K, D, C, Heart, H, Heart, S, H as the password.

Quest 2 Level 1
Enter G, N, Heart, Heart, K, 0, 0, H as the password.

Quest 2 Level 2
Enter G, N, 1, Heart, 5, 0, 8, J as the password.

Quest 2 Level 3
Enter X, 4, 3, Heart, 5, 0, M, R as the password.

Quest 2 Level 4
Enter L, S, 5, Heart, 9, 1, 1, 4 as the password.

Quest 2 Level 5
Enter 5, D, N, 7, Heart, 9, 3, Heart, 7 as the password.

Quest 2 Level 6
Enter 6, X, N, 9, Heart, 9, 3, 3, 3 as the password.

Quest 2 Level Boss
Enter N, 8, C, Heart, K, 4, 0, N as the password.

GODZILLA: THE SERIES

Level 2
GL6T

Level 3
C47?

Level 4
8W2H

Level 5
WT7Q

Level 6
B#QGGH4/

Level 7
39TN

Level 8
JHJ/

Level 9
=M3K

Level 10
T94/

Level 11
HB2/

Level 12
1XPK

Level 13
71CL

Level 14
C?#2

Level 15
GG1C

Level 16
?KGQ9T4M

Level 17
L&=7

Level 18
SC/W

Level 19
Q41M

Level 20
8QH=

Level 21
=65=

Level 22
T8CJ

Level 23
?7QG

Level 24
LC/W

Level 25
?=5Q

Level 26
MXRT

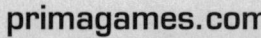

Go to Boss Level
To see the end, enter JXRB7K&948HPD32#JN as the password.

GRAND THEFT AUTO

Episode Skip
This code advances the game to the next episode of the current level. Die or get arrested until you have no lives remaining. When the screen displaying your stats appears, press A to restart and use the same character. The next episode in the level will be unlocked. Repeat this procedure to unlock all the levels.

Level Select
Rename any character to LEVELS or WENDY to unlock all cities.

Infinite Ammunition
Rename any character to FULL.

Hidden Characters
Rename the character KELLY to SUMNER to unlock the game's developers.

THE GRINCH

Level 1
9, 7, +, 2, 4, 2, 8, -, 3

Level 2
4, 8, -, 4, Max, Grinch, Max, X, 2

Level 3
3, 7, -, 2, 6, 2, Cindy Loo Who, X, 3

Level 4
4, X, 0, 2, +, 7, 4, +, 8

Level 5
Max, 4, 6, 0, 6, +, 8, Cindy Loo Who, 9

Level 6
0, 8, -, Cindy Lou Who, 1, Grinch, 8, X, 4

Level 7
-, X, o, Grinch, +, 7, 1, 7, 0

Level 7-6
7, 4, 2, 0, 6, + (2), X (2)

HALLOWEEN RACER

Hard Tracks
Enter 2!!MT9 as a password.

HARVEST MOON

Good Cows
To get cows that grow faster and give good milk, add a symbol at the beginning of their name. This only works if you did it to your first cow.

HARVEST MOON GB (RE-RELEASE)

Infinite Eggs
Find a watering can and water an egg close to the shipping box. It changes to a fence. Grab the fence and it changes into an egg. The fence remains and unlimited eggs are yours for the taking.

Automatic Watering
Water your crops and go to sleep. When the screen turns white, power off your Game Boy. Turn your Game Boy on again and your crops are watered.

Cool Cow
Get your first cow and use a heart symbol to start its name. It will give good milk and grow up faster.

Free $1,000
Start the game and go into the cupboard to find $1,000.

Infinite Egg
Let one of your chickens lay an egg above the shipping box. Water the egg to change it into a block. Grab the block to get infinite eggs and a ton of money.

More Eggs
Buy a chicken. During the same year, grab the egg your chicken has laid in the barn. Hurl it against the wall. The egg will lodge itself inside the wall. Cut the egg from the wall with your sickle, then put it in a shipping box. Extract another egg the same way. You can grab 100 eggs before the wall is exhausted.

Sell Egg at Chicken Prices
Grab an egg (laid by one of your chickens) and put it in an incubator. Walk to the animal shop, choose "Sell a Chicken," and highlight your egg. You'll get chicken prices for your egg.

The Name Game
Capitalize the first letter of your name and you'll be able to grow eggplants and carrots. Leave the first letter of your name lowercase to grow peanuts and broccoli. To grow everything, start your name with a symbol, such as a heart.

HELLO KITTY'S CUBE FRENZY

Unlock All Levels
Press down, left, right, up, B, A, B, up, down, up, down, right, left.

HERCULES

Level 2
B7FG4

Level 3
XTV5P

Level 4
TV5DP

Level 5
FX6NL

Level 6
HGRSV

Level 7
K7DGR

Level 8
FTXCG

Level 9
GSJ4H

View Credits
CRDTS

HOME ALONE

Final Level with All Items
At the title screen, press Up, Down, Right, Left, and Select.

HOME ALONE 2

Extra Life
On the first floor (at the start of the game), go right until you see the Vacuum cleaner. Jump over the cleaner and get on the couch. A man behind a desk to your right is throwing keys. Keep jumping in the middle of the couch. You'll end up on the rafters. Go right until you see the pizzas.

Extra Dart Gun
When you get to the 12th floor, proceed until you come to a door with a tag on it and a plant in front of it. A dart gun pops out if you jump into the plant.

HONG KONG

Sound Test
Press B+Start at the game's second screen.

Test Mode
Press A+B+Start at the game's second screen.

View Ending
Press A+Start at the game's second screen.

HOT WHEELS STUNT TRACK DRIVER

All Cars and Tracks Password
Down, Left, Up, A, Down, Right

Shadow Jet 2 Password
Left, Up, Left, Down, Up, A

Shadow Jet 3 Password
Right, Up, Right, Down, Up, A

Shadow Jet 4 Password
Up, B, Up (2), Left, A

Shadow Jet 5 Password
B, Left, B, Up (2), Left

Shadow Jet 6 Password
Down, Left, Up, A, Up (2)

Shadow Jet End Password
Down, Left, Up, A, Down, Right

Tow Jam 2 Password
B (2), Left, Up, A, B

Tow Jam 3 Password
Left (2), Up, A, Right (2)

Tow Jam 4 Password
Left (2), Up, Left, A, Left

Tow Jam 5 Password
Down, Up, Left, Down (2), A

Tow Jam 6 Password
B (3), Right (2), Up

Tow Jam End Password
Down, Left, Up, A, Down, Right

Way Too Fast 2 Password
Right, A, Right, B, Left, Down

Way Too Fast 3 Password
Down, Right, B, Right, Down, B

Way Too Fast 4 Password
Right (2), Down, A, Down, A

Way Too Fast 5 Password
Up, A (2), Down, Left, Up

Way Too Fast 6 Password
Left, Up, A, B (2), Right

Way Too Fast End Password
Down, Left, Up, A, Down, Right

Slide Out 2 Password
Down, A, Up, A, B (2)

Slide Out 3 Password
Left, B, Left, Right, Down, B

Slide Out 4 Password
Down, B (3), Right, Down

Slide Out 5 Password
A (2), Right (2), B, Down

Slide Out 6 Password
Right, Up, Left, Up, Left, Right

Slide Out End Password
Down, Left, Up, A, Down, Right

Twin Mill 2 Password
Down, Left, B (2), Right, B

Twin Mill 3 Password
Up, B, Down (2), Right, Left

Twin Mill 4 Password
Right, Up, Right, B (2), Right

Twin Mill 5 Password
Right, Up, Right, Down, A, Right

Twin Mill 6 Password
Right, Left, Up, A, Up, Down

Twin Mill End Password
Down, Left, Up, A, Down, Right

HUMANS

Level 2
C V B M

Level 3
Q W S D

Level 4
P L K P

Level 5
M N B V

Level 6
V B C D

Level 7
Z X V Z

Level 8
K J H R

Level 9
P Y S T

Level 10
L K L Q

Level 11
H D Z W

Level 12
N B G F

Level 13
S W Q R

Level 14
T Y T L

Level 15
X R T D

Level 16
C D S R

Level 17
J H Y T

Level 18
M J H N

Level 19
T R W M

Level 20
P L M N

Level 21
S S X C

Level 22
K L L Y

Level 24
V B S R

Level 25
T V Y P

Level 26
L K M V

Level 27
Q V C X

Level 28
P M H R

HUNT FOR RED OCTOBER

25 Extra Fuel Units
Hold A+B, then press Select, Left, Right when the sub course is displayed.

25 Extra Missiles
Hold A+B, then press Up, Down when the sub course is displayed.

25 Extra Ships
Hold A+B, then press Select, Up, Down when the sub course is displayed.

25 Extra Silent Runnings
Hold A+B then press Left, Right on the Mission Select screen.

Level Select
From the main menu, press B, Select, Left, Right then press Start.

HYPER LODE RUNNER

Level Select
Enter the password QM-0388.

INDIANA JONES: THE LAST CRUSADE

Level 2
011031158

Level 3
D912H4133D

Level 4
0313B51330

Level 5
20153612JF

INDIANA JONES AND THE INFERNAL MACHINE

Level 2
DDJHQQKM

Level 3
MGHXUPSS

Level 4
FDMJWPJW

Level 5
BGKKQKST

Level 6
GDFFWPPP

Level 7
KFGFWLSS

Level 8
HFJJZKN3

Level 9
HDDNSKZW

Level 10
BKGHXKJL

Level 11
FJGJZPSM

Level 12
DLFLSQJZ

Level 13
HKMKTPNS

Level 14
KLKTLTQ

Level 15
HLKHRHN3

INSPECTOR GADGET

Plasma Heart
FH2KBH

Volcano
FM!PQM

The Vats
FRVTLR

Underground
FWQZ!?

IRON MAN/XO MANOWAR IN HEAVY METAL

Level 1
TYCKPQ

Level 2
TJYPDF

Level 3
ZXCVBM

Level 4
KDZCPL

Level 5
MGHQZS

Level 6
SPLHRJ

Level 7
YPMBCK

Level 8
SDWZCM

Level 9
DPWMQZ

Level 10
LKLPDX

Level 11
XCSQSS

Level 12
MPQPRY

Level 13
JKRTSC

Level 14
DXCMGH

Level 15
LPJKHX

GAME BOY

Level 16
XCSMMN

Level 17
VNTMZS

Level 18
SXZPLK

Level 19
MPKHKG

Level 20
BMQZHL

JAMES BOND 007

Black Jack Sub-Game
Enter the name: BJACK.

Baccarat Sub-Game
Enter the name: BACCR.

Red Dog Sub-Game
Enter the name: REDOG.

JEREMY MCGRATH SUPERCROSS 2000

Unlock 250cc Class
At password, enter SHJBBCGB.

JUDGE DREDD

Level Select
At the title screen, press A, Left, Right, B, Start.

JUNGLE STRIKE

Level 2
4975200968

Level 3
2922502918

Level 4
6505068908

Level 5
0540524815

Level 6
0550792954

Level 7
0950035298

Level 8
0155908131

Level 9
1185402550

JURASSIC PARK

Level Skip
With the dinosaur mouth open and the options available, press Up, Down, Left, Up, Down, Right, Select. Repeat this to hear a crash. Start the game, then pause and press Select to skip to the next level.

KEN GRIFFEY JR. PRESENTS MAJOR LEAGUE BASEBALL

Easy Home Run Derby Win
Hold Down and B as the computer bats in the home run derby. The computer skips its turn and ends up with a low score.

KID DRACULA

Level 2
5613

Level 3
3272

Level 4
7283

Level 5
5346

Level 6
7225

Level 7
5539

Level 8
7158

KILLER INSTINCT

Level Select
At the title screen, hold Up and press A, B, Start, or Select.

No Combo Breaker for Computer
At the Vs. screen, hold Left then press B, A, B, A. You should hear a sound.

PlayCheat menuEyedol
Go to the Player Vs. Player screen. Hold Right and press Select, Start, B, A.

Random Select
Hold Up and press Start on the player select screen.

KING OF FIGHTERS '95

Bonus Characters
Turn on the game. Press Select (25) when the Takara logo appears.

Computer Vs. Computer
Press B before choosing Single or Team Play. Next, press A to start the game.

Desperation Attacks
You can pull off super special moves with no energy in your power meter if your health meter is flashing.

Ryo's Desperation Move
Away, Down, Toward (2), Down, Away, Punch

Fight Nakoruru
Defeat the game on Hard difficulty. Wait for the credits to end. Nakoruru will challenge you.

PlayCheat menuNakoruru
Press Select (20) at the Takara logo.

PlayCheat menuSaisyu and Rugal
Press Select (3) at the Takara logo.

PlayCheat menuSame Player
At the Takara screen, press A+B, then press Select.

Random Character Select
Press Start+A+B on the Character Select screen.

Rugal Move: Reppu Ken
D, F+Punch

Rugal Move: Keiser Wave
F, B, D, F+Punch

Rugal Move: Genocide Cutter
D, B+Kick

Rugal Move: Dark Barrier
D, F+Kick

Rugal Move: God Press
F, D, B+Punch

Rugal Super Special Move: Gigantic Pressure
F, D, B, F, D, B+Kick

Saisyu Move: Dark Thrust
D, F+Punch

Saisyu Move: Fire Ball
F, D, F+Punch

Saisyu Move: Fire Tackle
F, D, B+Punch

Saisyu Super Special Move: Serpent Wave
D, B, D, F+Punch

Nakoruru Move: Amube Yatoro
F, D, B+Punch

Nakoruru Move: Anna Mutsube
B, D+Punch

Nakoruru Move: Lela Mutsube
D, F+Punch

Nakoruru Move: Kamui Ryuse
B, D, B+Punch

Nakoruru Move: Mamahaha Flight
D, B+Kick

Nakoruru Move: Kamui Mutsube
In Mamahaha flight: Punch. When jumping: D, F+Punch

Nakoruru Move: Yatoru Bokku
In Mamahaha flight: D+Punch. When jumping: D, B+Punch

Nakoruru Super Special Move: Elelyu Kamui Rise
F, D, B, F, D, B+Punch

Benimaru's Dive (When Jumping)
D+Kick

Joe's TNT Punch Extender
Punch (6)+D, F+Punch

KING OF FIGHTERS '96

Battle: Kyo and Chizuru vs. Orochi Iori
Defeat Goenitz with Kyo, Iori, Chizuru.

Battle: The Rest of Your Team
Defeat Goenitz with Kyo, Terry, Ryo.

Battle: Geese Vs. the Rest of the Team
Defeat Goenitz with Geese, Krauser, Mr. Big.

Battle: Terry and Andy Vs. Geese
Defeat Goenitz with Terry, Andy, Geese.

Battle: Ryo and Robert Vs. Mr.Big
Defeat Goenitz with Ryo, Robert, Mr. Big.

Battle: Iori and Mature Vs. Orochi Leona
Defeat Goenitz with Iori, Leona, Mature.

Computer Vs. Computer
At the Battle Select screen, hold B and press A.

Fight Mr. Karate
Finish the game in Hard mode without losing a match.

Hidden Ending
Use Mr. Big, Geese, and Krauser vs. Iiro, Chizuru, and Kyo as a team.

PlayCheat menuCrazy Iiro/Leona
Enter the code for Play as Mr. Karate. At the Player Select screen, highlight Iiro/Leona and press Start.

PlayCheat menuGoenitz

Press Select (3) at the Takara logo.

PlayCheat menuKagura

Enter the code for Play as Mr. Karate. At the Player Select screen, highlight Chizuru and press Start.

PlayCheat menuMr. Karate

Press Select (20) at the Takara logo.

PlayCheat menuSame Player

At the Takara screen, press A+B, then press Select.

Random Character Select

Press Start+A+B on the Character Select screen.

Slow Motion

Pause the game and quickly tap Select.

KINGDOM CRUSADE

Raise the Dead

You need a character with a checkmark as a spell. From the map, hold Select and move your cursor over the character with the checkmark. Pres B until the checkmark flashes. Press Select and A and a screen will appear with every dead character you have. Select one and choose any free space of your land to put him or her on.

KLAX

Furd Herder Minigame

Enter Green Alien (2), Square, Green Alien as a password.

Snake Minigame

Enter Circle, Diamond, Square, Green Alien as a password.

View Klax History

Enter Yellow Alien, Pillar (2), Green Alien as a password.

View Klax Myth

Enter Square, Pillar, Diamond, Green Alien as a password.

View Programmers

Enter Green Alien (2), Circle, Square as a password.

View Credits

Enter Pillar, Yellow Alien, Diamond (2) as a password.

Adventure Mode (European Version)

Enter Square, Yellow Alien, Green Alien, Yellow Alien as a password.

Level 1

Yellow Alien, Pillar (2), Circle

Level 6

Circle, Yellow Alien, Square, Yellow Alien

Level 11

Yellow Alien (2), Square, Green Alien

Level 16

Diamond, Yellow Alien, Green Alien, Diamond

Level 21

Diamond, Square, Diamond, Green Alien

Level 26

Pillar, Yellow Alien, Square, Pillar

Level 31

Green Alien, Circle, Pillar (2)

Level 36

Circle (2), Yellow Alien (2)

Level 41

Pillar, Diamond (2), Circle

Level 46

Yellow Alien, Diamond, Circle, Pillar

Level 51

Square, Diamond, Yellow Alien, Square

Level 56

Pillar, Square (2), Yellow Alien

Level 61

Circle, Square, Circle, Green Alien

Level 66

Circle, Diamond (2), Green Alien

Level 71

Circle, Square (2), Pillar

Level 76

Green Alien (2), Yellow Alien, Circle

Level 81

Pillar, Circle (2), Pillar

Level 86

Square, Green Alien, Diamond, Circle

Level 91

Yellow Alien, Green Alien, Circle, Diamond

Level 96

Pillar (2), Green Alien, Square

KNIGHT'S QUEST

Final Level

To skip to the final level, enter the password [Hourglass] n7nB dc!Zc SHhhn.

KONAMI GB COLLECTION VOL. 1

Contra Level Select

At the title screen, enter up, up, down, down, left, right, left, right, B, A, B, A, Start.

KORODICE

Level 4 Easy

94347

Level 5 Easy

68890

Level 6 Easy

24486

Level 7 Easy

49320

Level 8 Easy

28076

Level 9 Easy

96545

Level 10 Easy

83193

Level 4 Normal

22307

Level 5 Normal

64422

Level 6 Normal

43059

Level 7 Normal

46403

Level 8 Normal

50136

Level 9 Normal

17443

Level 10 Normal

99007

KRUSTY'S FUN HOUSE

Level 2

MC BAIN

Level 3

MILHOUSE

Level 4

CMBURNS

Level 5

PRINCESS

LEGEND OF THE RIVER KING (RE-RELEASE)

Bonus level

Catch one of each kind of fish before catching the guardian. The phrase "Funland Unlocked" appears following the credits. Restart the game and stay at the inn on Level 1 to reach Level 5. Level 5 contains an inn and a small lake that has every type of fish.

LION KING

Level Skip

Pause the game and press B, A (2), B, A (2).

LITTLE NICKY

Unlock a Far Better Place

At the password screen enter Evilray—Evilray—innerlight—possession.

LOCK 'N' CHASE

Warp to Level 7.1

At the title screen, press A (2), B (2), A, B (2). The word "Extra" appears in the screen's upper right. Press Start.

LOONEY TOONS: CARROT CRAZY

Level 01: Treasure Island

Marvin Martian, Elmer Fudd, Daffy Duck

Level 02: Crazy Town

Daffy Duck, Taz, Elmer Fudd

Level 04: Space Station

Yosemite Sam, Daffy Duck, Elmer Fudd

Level (Hard) 2: Crazy Town

Taz, Marvin Martian, Yosemite Sam

Level (Hard) 4: Space Station

Marvin Martian, Taz, Yosemite Sam

Skip Stage

Enter Taz, Elmer Fudd, Daffy Duck as a password. Pause game and press Select. Then push A to skip stage.

LOONEY TUNES (RE-RELEASE)

Faster Frisbees

At the first water in Level 1, jump in and jump out on the right (onto land). Walk through the wall into a room. You'll find an item that makes your Frisbees faster.

GAME BOY

LOONEY TUNES: TWOUBLE!

Level 1
Hector, Tweety, Taz, Granny, Sylvester

Level 2
Taz, Sylvester, Tweety, Hector, Granny

Level 3
Granny, Tweety, Hector, Sylvester, Taz

Level 4
Sylvester, Tweety, Taz, Granny, Hector

Level 5
Taz, Hector, Tweety, Sylvester, Granny

LOST WORLD: JURASSIC PARK

Level 2
kqtv

Level 3
nplx

Level 4
bgmd

Level 5
hrty

Level 6
jfcd

Level 7
mrbm

Level 8
xgnt

LUCKY LUKE

Level 1
Luke, Horse, Horse, Old Man, Luke

Level 2
Coyote, Horse, Luke, Old Man, Old Man

Level 3
Old Man, Coyote, Luke, Horse, Coyote

Level 4
Coyote, Horse, Luke, Old Man, Coyote

M&M MINI MADNESS

Level Passwords
Enter the following codes at the password screen to select your level of choice.

World 1
Level 2
yellow, red, blue, blue, green, blue

Level 3
green, blue, yellow, red, yellow, yellow

World 2
Level 1
green, blue, green, red, green, yellow

Level 2
red, yellow, orange, yellow, brown, blue

Level 3
brown, green, red, blue, orange, blue

MADDEN NFL '96

Bonus Teams
Highlight the All-Madden team but don't choose it. Press B+Right+Select for Team Halestorm. Repeat for Da Funhouse.

MADDEN NFL 2000

Begin Season with Winning Record
Enter jcBhDXJPFNSgLXdQBD as password.

MARU'S MISSION

Bonus Bubbles
Shoot the first tree stump in the first level repeatedly.

MATCHBOX CATERPILLAR CONSTRUCTION ZONE

Level Select
Enter BG6S as the password.

MEGA MAN

Elec Man Defeated
A2, A4, B3, D1, D2

Ice Man Defeated
A1, A2, B2, B3, D4

Fire Man Defeated
A1, B1, B2, C4, D2

Dr. Wily's Castle
A2, A3, B4, C2, C3

Fire Man and Cut Man Defeated
A2, B2, C3, D1, D3

Fire Man, Cut Man, and Elec Man Defeated
A3, B2, B3, B4, C4

Dr. Wiley's Castle
A2, A3, B4, C2, C3

Fire Man and Ice Man Defeated
A2, B3, D2, D3, D4

Ice Man and Elec Man Defeated
A1, B4, C1, D2, D4

Fire Man, Ice Man, and Elec Man Defeated
A2, A3, C1, D2, D3

MEGA MAN 2

Password for Last Four Robots (Needle, Hard, Magnet, and Top)
B1, A2, A3, B4, C3, D1, and D4

MEGA MAN 3

Start with Shadow Man, Spark Man, Gemini Man, and Snake Man Beaten
Enter the password A3, B3, C3, C2, D2.

Start with Shadow Man, Spark Man, Gemini Man, Snake Man and Dr. W's First Guy Beaten
Enter the password A2, B1, B2, C1, D2.

Start on the Last Stage with Only Sawman Left to Fight
Enter the password A0, B0, C1, C2, B2.

MEGA MAN 4

All Weapons, B-E-A-T, W-I-L-Y, 4 Energy Tanks, 4 Weapon Tanks, a Super Tank, an Energy Balancer, and 999 P-Chips
--RRB-, -E-RE-, B---E-, -BR--B

MEGA MAN 5

All Power-Ups and Items
RRT--, ET--T, -E-RT, TTRRE, TRTRR

Reduced Energy Usage
Collect the four jewels on Jupiter, Saturn, Uranus, and Pluto. Dr. Light can combine them to form an item that reduces the amount of energy consumed by your special weapons.

Turbo Buster
On any stage, get Mega Man nailed. Repeat the procedure until Dr. Light takes pity on you and grants you the Turbo Buster. This makes your shots and charges faster.

MEGA MAN EXTREME

Hard Mode
Successfully complete the game to unlock a harder version of the game.

Extreme Mode
Successfully complete the game under Hard mode. Extreme mode consists of the eight bosses without the story version of the game.

MEGA MAN EXTREME 2

Xtreme Mode
Successfully complete the game with either Zero or X. Iris will talk to you and the game will end. When you load that saved game, you will be in Xtreme mode. Xtreme mode will also be one of the options in the mission selection screen. In Xtreme mode, you start with both X and Zero and can go to any of the levels. You can get different weapons if you defeat one of X's bosses with Zero and vice versa.

MEN IN BLACK

Level 2
2710

Level 3
1807

Level 4
309

Level 5
2705

Level 6
3107

Level Skip
To skip levels, enter 2409 as a password. Now begin a new game and Pause. Press Select to skip to the next level or press A to skip to the next stage within the current level.

Cheat Mode
Enter 0601 as a password. Don't mind the "Invalid Password" message. Press Start to return to the command center. Start a game and hold Select+Up to move up vertically. Press Left or Right to move in that direction, or Select+Down to move down vertically. Hold Select+A to get the Noisy Cricket super-gun. A lightning bolt appears next to the number of lives remaining.

View Ending Sequence
Enter 1943 as a password.

Get Noisy Cricket!
Enter the Fly code. Next, hold Select+A. There is a lightning symbol next to the number of lives. Stand back and press the shoot button. You fire off an incredibly powerful blast.

Flying

Enter the password 0601. An error message appears. Press start to return to the Command Center screen. Start playing the game. While motionless, press and hold Select+Up to fly. Press Left or Right while in the air to move. Press Down or Select to land.

MERCENARY FORCE

Easy Money

Press Up+Select+A+B at the title screen to start with 50,000 yen.

Level Select

Enter the Easy Money code and choose your men. Press Start to begin a game. When "Round 1" appears, press Right to select your starting round.

META FIGHT FX

Stage 1
E6C3D3KF

Stage 2
E6D3D3KG

Stage 3
E7C3D3KH

Stage 4
E7D3D3KI

Stage 5
F6C3D3KQ

Stage 6
F6D3D3KR

Stage 7
F7C3D3KU

Stage 8
F7D3D3KT

METAL GEAR SOLID

Sound Menu

Complete all the VR training missions ranking 100 percent. At the Options screen, a sound menu becomes available.

Special Stage Select

Finish the game on the Easy (or higher) difficulty setting. Use the Special Stage Select to play with altered mission objectives.

Plot Revelation

Finish the stages in the Special Stage Select. No. 4 reveals pieces of the plot.

Automatic Ration Use

If you equip rations but don't use them, Snake automatically consumes them when needed.

MICKEY MOUSE MAGIC WANDS!

Stage 2
BVCK

Stage 3
FXLL

Stage 4
GRWN

Stage 5
WHVT

Stage 6
BZSS

Stage 7
CZCK

Stage 8
DRWP

Stage 9
BXLK

Stage 10
HWNT

Boss 1
SLVP

Stage 11
SPZT

Stage 12
BLZW

Stage 13
GRWP

Stage 14
TRVP

Stage 15
BWLL

Stage 16
WVLK

Stage 17
DRZP

Stage 18
FLVG

Stage 19
HZST

Stage 20
TQPY

Boss 2
JXMP

Stage 21
MQLT

Stage 22
FRYT

Stage 23
RQNT

Stage 24
LQST

Stage 25
JXRY

Stage 26
MQND

Stage 27
SQLL

Stage 28
TWCK

Stage 29
NWCK

Stage 30
SZFT

Boss 3
PQCK

Stage 31
YVRD

Stage 32
RQST

Stage 33
SZLD

Stage 34
FRZM

Stage 35
THVN

Stage 36
CQNT

Stage 37
PZST

Stage 38
HQRS

Stage 39
SWLK

Stage 40
CHWP

Boss 4
JZWL

MICKEY'S RACING ADVENTURE

Switch Characters

Go to the racing levels and exit. After getting back to the home town, go to Minnie's house. To change to Pluto, proceed to his doghouse.

MICRO MACHINES

Extra Life

In the first race of sports cars on desktops, jump the notebook onto the other desk and pause the game. A noise sounds and you gain an extra life.

MIGHTY MORPHIN POWER RANGERS

Level 2
1001

Level 3
1012

Level 4
175

Level 5
1387

MIGRAIN ACCLAIM

Level 2
742

Level 3
X480

Level 4
586Y

Level 5
3081

MILON'S SECRET CASTLE

All Items

Go to the password screen and enter all M's.

MONSTER MAX

Level 4
-8?-35R-

Level 5
273?35RZ

Level 6
JZVHMV3D

Level 7
L5VP79N7

Level 8
PL1H17P-

Level 9
MQLYTY2D

Level 10
-J#X5DKP

MONTEZUMA'S RETURN

Infinite Lives
Enter Elephant as the password.

All Doors Open
Enter Sunshine as the password.

End
Enter 6JYBSPPJ as the password.

Levels
Enter NQXZJ9?K for the top and 2N4ZQWZM for the bottom.

MORTAL KOMBAT

PlayCheat menuGoro
Defeat the game and watch the credits. When "The End" appears, hold Up+Left+Select+A. Enter your initials and press A.

MORTAL KOMBAT 2

Fight Jade
Use only the kick button to win the fight before the question mark fight.

Fight Smoke
When the small guy comes up in the corner of the screen, press Down+Start. You'll find the passage to fight Smoke.

One Credit
Press Down twice on the Choose Your Destiny screen.

Random Character
Hold Up and press Start on the Character Selection screen.

MORTAL KOMBAT 3

Extra Credits
When the Choose Your Destiny screen appears, press Up to increase your credits to five.

PlayCheat menuSmoke
When the icon screen comes up, enter the code 192234 (move up 1 box, move to the next box, move up 9 boxes, etc.). Smoke's fatality is a step inside full screen or closer then press Up (2), Toward, Down. This code must be done in one continuous motion.

MORTAL KOMBAT 4

Kodes
Put these in before a match starts. A number is assigned to each character. Here is how they convert: Dragon=0, MK Logo=1, Ying-Yang=2, Four=3, Question Mark=4, Lightning Bolt=5, Goro=6, Raiden=7, Shao Kahn=8, Skull=9.

FightCheat menuReptile
192-234

Fight Against Reptile
205-205

Disable Throws
100-100

Swicharoo
460-460

Dark Kombat
688-422

Psycho Kombat
985-125

No Blocking
020-020

Player 1, 25% Life
707-000

Player 1, 50% Life
033-000

CPU, 25% Life
000-707

CPU, 50% Life
000-033

One-Hit Win
123-123

Noob Saibot Mode
012-012

Explosive Kombat
050-050

Disable Max Damage
010-010

No Throw, Disable Max Damage
110-110

Weapons Never Dropped
002-002

Many Weapons
555-555

Random Weapon Appears
111-111

Start with Random Weapon
222-222

Randper Kombat
333-333

Start with Weapons Drawn
444-444

Silent Kombat
666-666

Big Heads
321-321

Programmer's Message
987-666

Programmer's Message
123-926

MOTOCROSS MANIACS

Underground Shortcut
Find the loop halfway through the first lap of route 2A. (There is dirt on the left and a ramp to the right.) Hit B (4) while on the loop. After you exit the loop, you go underground.

Hitchhikers
Flip off of some jumps, and some little hitch-hikers will follow you. Finish with them to gain extra points. If you crash, you'll lose them.

Invisible Power-Ups
Doing a flip off certain jumps gets you an invisible power-up box called a Jet.

MOTOCROSS MANIACS 2

Pick Up Hitchhikers
On certain ramps do a flip and pick up hitchhikers.

MULAN

Level 2
JSFPW

Level 3
QGHXB

Level 4
TZDML

Level 5
RCVNJ

Level 6
PGDSH

THE MUMMY RETURNS

Level 1
71P4KW

Level 2
8K371J

Level 3
P3C664

Level 4
CXS0N0

Level 5
1N0F1N

Level 6
7B4L6S

Level 7
8148W4

Level 8
TNMN5Q

Level 9
HTS0ZX

Level 10
1RD10V

Level 11
T6415P

MR. NUTZ

Level 2
DDMMNN

Level 3
NNRRGG

Level 4
CCLLRS

Level 5
JJMPPR

Level 6
SWWTCH

NBA HOOPZ

Infinite Turbo
At the Play Match screen, enter BALL, A, B, and press Up.

Show Hot Spot
At the Play Match screen, enter A, BALL, BALL, and press Down.

Disable "On Fire"
At the Play Match screen, enter B, B, B, and press Left.

Island Court
At the Play Match screen, enter N, B, A and press Right.

Stadium Court
At the Play Match screen, enter B, B, N, and press Left.

Factory Court
At the Play Match screen, enter N, A, B, and press Down.

Future Court
At the Play Match screen, enter BALL, N, B, and press Up.

Night Club Court
At the Play Match screen, enter N, BALL, A, and press Left.

Oil Rig Court
At the Play Match screen, enter B, A, BALL, and press Right.

Practice Court
At the Play Match screen, enter A, A, B, and press Down.

Prison Court
At the Play Match screen, enter B, BALL, N, and press Right.

Rooftop Court
At the Play Match screen, enter N, N, N, and press Up.

Volcano Court
At the Play Match screen, enter A, B, N, and press Left.

NBA JAM

Bill Clinton
Enter the first two initials of the player, then highlight the letter to the right of the last letter of the hidden person's initials: USA Left+A+B.

Jamie Rivett
Enter the first two initials of the player, then highlight the letter below the last letter of the hidden person's initials: BAT Up+A+B.

Chow Cow
Enter the first two initials of the player, then highlight the letter above the last letter of the hidden person's initials: AMX Down+A+B.

Air Dog
Enter the first two initials of the player, then highlight the letter below the last letter of the hidden person's initials: JAM Up+B.

George Clinton
Enter the first two initials of the player, then highlight the letter to the right of the last letter of the hidden person's initials: FNK Left+B.

Mark Turmell
Enter the first two initials of the player, then highlight the letter to the right of the last letter of the hidden person's initials: WIM Left+B.

Al Gore
Enter the first two initials of the player, then highlight the letter below the last letter of the hidden person's initials: EXC Up+Start+B.

Weasel
Enter the first two initials of the player, then highlight the letter below the last letter of the hidden person's initials: MAN Up+Start+A+B.

Sal Davita
Enter the first two initials of the player, then highlight the letter above the last letter of the hidden person's initials: SDT Down+B.

Unknown
Enter the first two initials of the player, highlight the last letter of the hidden person's initials: VIK Right+A+B.

Unknown
Enter the first two initials of the player, then highlight the letter to the right of the last letter of the hidden person's initials: FRD Left+B.

Interception Power-Up
At the Match-Up screen, hold Right while tapping any button 15 times.

Power-Up Defense
At the Tonight's Match-Up screen press A (5), then hold Up until the game starts.

Power-Up Dunks
At the Tonight's Match-Up screen press A (10), then hold A+Down until you see the words "Power-up Dunks."

Power-Up Fire
Tap A or B (7), then hold Left on the D-Pad.

NBA JAM: TOURNAMENT EDITION

Always Get the Jump Ball
At the Tonight's Match-Up screen press B rapidly.

Display Shot Percentage
Press Up (2), Down (2), B at the Tonight's Match-Up screen. "SHOT %" flashes on the screen.

Goaltending
Press Right, Up, Down, Right, Down, Up at the Tonight's Match-Up screen. "GOALTEND" flashes across the screen.

High Shots
Press Up, Down, Up, Down, Right, Up, A (4), Down at the Tonight's Match-Up screen.

Juice Mode
Press Up (4), Left (4), B, A at the Tonight's Match-Up screen for an extra fast game.

Maximum Power
Press Right (2), Left, Right, B (2), Right at the Tonight's Match-Up screen to increase your players' Power stats. "MAX PLYR" flashes on the screen.

Permanent On-Fire
Press Down, Right (2), B, A, Left at the Tonight's Match-Up screen. "FIRE" flashes on the screen.

PlayCheat menuan Alien
At the Tonight's Match-Up screen, press Up, Down, Right (2), Down, Left.

Power-Up Dunks
Press Left, Right, A, B (2), A at the Tonight's Match-Up screen to be able to dunk from anywhere on the court. "ULTRA JAM" flashes on the screen before the game starts.

Power-Up Offense
Press A, B, Up, A, B, Up, Down at the Tonight's Match-Up screen to increase your offensive capability. "OFFENSE" flashes on the screen.

Power-Up Push
Press Down, Right, A, B, A, Right, Down at the Tonight's Match-Up screen to increase your pushing power. "PUSH" flashes on the screen.

Power-Up Turbo
Press B (3), A, Down (2), Up, Left at the Tonight's Match-Up screen to get unlimited turbo power. "TURBO" flashes on the screen.

Quick Hands
Press Left (4), A, and Right at the Tonight's Match-Up screen to improve your chances of making a steal. "QUICK HND" flashes on the screen.

Slippery Court
Press A (5), Right (5) at the Tonight's Match-Up screen.

Three-Point Shots
Press Up, Down, Left, Right, Left, Down, Up at the Tonight's Match-Up screen to improve your chances of making your three-point shots. "3PT" flashes on the screen.

NBA JAM '99

Championship Game
In playoff, enter MIK in the main window. Then enter R4QKFCWCDG.

NBA SHOWTIME

Unlimited Turbo
Press Up, B, A, Up, B, A, Up, B, A .

Extra Courts
Press Left, Left, A, A, Left, Down, Right, B, A .

Extra Teams
Press Up, A, Down, B, Right, Left, Right, Left, B, A

NEMESIS

Full Weapons and Shields
Pause your game and press Up (2), Down (2), Left, Right, Left, Right, B, A, Start.

Power No More
Pause the game and press Up, Select, Down, Select, Left, Select, Right, Select (3), Start.

Power Up Drain
Pause the game and press A, Left (5), Start.

Secret Level
In stage 4, right below the third skull that shoots balls at you, fly to the screen's bottom left and stay there for two seconds. You'll go to the secret stage.

Speed and Shields
For greater speed and protection, pause the game and press B (5), A (5).

NEW ADVENTURES OF MARY-KATE & ASHLEY

Volcano Mystery
Enter password CBTHPM

Haunted Camp
Enter password GMQTCK

Funhouse Mystery
Enter password LHDDQJ

Hotel Who-Done-It
Enter password MDGKMQ

NINJA GAIDEN SHADOW

Sound Test
At the title screen, hold A+B and press Start.

NFL BLITZ

Emerysville Eclipse Team
Enter 00606744 as the password.

Midway Blitzers Team
Enter 06267545 as the password.

Start SeasonCheat menuthe Bills
Enter 75566677 as the password.

Random Play
Press Left+B.

Desert Field
At the Match-Up screen in Exhibition mode, press Start (2), A (2), Right.

Night Game
At the Match-Up screen in Exhibition mode, press Start (2), B (2), A (2), Right.

Parking Lot
At the Match-Up screen in Exhibition mode, press Start (3), B (2), A (3), Down.

No Pointer
At the Match-Up screen in Exhibition mode, press Start (3), B (3), A (3), Left.

No Fumbles
At the Match-Up screen in Exhibition mode, press Start (4), B (2), A (3), Down.

Invisible Receiver
At the Match-Up screen in Exhibition mode, press Start (4), B (3), A (3), Up.

Infinite Turbo
At the Match-Up screen in Exhibition mode, press Start (5), B, A (4), Up.

Strange Colors
At the Match-Up screen in Exhibition mode, press Start (5), B (5), A, Up.

Start in Overtime
At the Match-Up screen in Exhibition mode, press A (6), Up.

Brick Field in Deep Space
At the Match-Up screen in Exhibition mode, press Start (2), A (2), Right. This code cancels the effect of the Night Game code.

Fast Turbo Running
At the Match-Up screen in Exhibition mode, press B (3), A (2), Left.

Onside Kick
After you score the P.A.T. or a field goal, hold down A, B, and Up. You go for an onside kick.

Predator Mode
At the Match-Up screen in Exhibition mode, press Start (5), B (5), A, Up.

Super Star Team
Enter 75566677 as a password.

NFL BLITZ 2000

Hidden Plays
At the Match-Up screen in Exhibition mode, press Start (3), B (3), A (3), Down.

Infinite Turbo
At the Match-Up screen in Exhibition mode, press B, A (3), Up.

No Fumbles
At the Match-Up screen in Exhibition mode, press Start (3), B, A (2), Down.

No First Downs
At the Match-Up screen in Exhibition mode, press Start (2), B, Up.

No Interceptions
At the Match-Up screen in Exhibition mode, press Start (2), B (3), A (3), Left.

No Punting
At the Match-Up screen in Exhibition mode, press Start, B (3), A, Up.

Super Defense
At the Match-Up screen in Exhibition mode, press Start (3), B (2), A, Up.

Super Offense
At the Match-Up screen in Exhibition mode, press Start (3), B, A (2), Up.

Super Passing
At the Match-Up screen in Exhibition mode, press Start (3), B, A (2), Right.

Super Team
At the Match-Up screen in Exhibition mode, press Start (2), B (3), A (3), Up

NHL BLADES OF STEEL

Skip the Opening
Hold Start after you turn on the system to go straight to the 1 or 2 Player Select screen.

ODDWORLD ADVENTURES

High Jump
Pause the game in the middle of a jump. Un-pause and press B to jump again while still in the air. Jump as high as you need to. Caution: Jumping too high can crash the game.

Level 2-0
JCBCM

Level 2-1
JMBCC

Level 2-2
JMCCB

Level 2-3
JPCCD

Level 2-4
JTCCJ

Level 2-5
STCCS

Level 2-6
SBCCT

Level 2-7
TBFCQ

Level 3-1
TBKCL

Level 3-2
TBTCB

Level 3-3
TBTDC

Level 3-4
TBTGF

Level End
TBTBT

Door at the Lower Left
JCBCM

Door at the Lower Left, Door at the Lower Right
JCCCL

Door at the Lower Left, Door at the Upper Left
SCBCC

Door at the Lower Left, Second Door in from the Upper Left
JDBCL

Door at the Lower Left, Second Door in from the Upper Right
JFBCP

Door at the Lower Left, Door at the Upper Right
JHBCR

Door at the Lower Left, Second Door in from the Lower Right
JMBCC

Door at the Lower Left, Door at the Upper Left, Door at the Lower Right
SCCCB

Door at the Lower Left, Door at the Upper Left, Second Door in from the Upper Left
SDBCB

Door at the Lower Left, Second Door in from the Upper Left, Door at the Lower Right
JDCCM

Door at the Lower Left, Second Door in from the Upper Right, Door at the Lower Right
JFCCN

Door at the Lower Left, Second Door in from the Lower Right, Door at the Lower Right
JMCCB

Door at the Lower Left, Door at the Upper Right, Door at the Lower Right
JHCCQ

Door at the Lower Left, Second Door in from the Upper Left, Second Door in from the Upper Right
JGBCN

Door at the Lower Left, Second Door in from the Upper Left, Door at the Upper Right
JJBCQ

Door at the Lower Left, Second Door in from the Upper Left, Second Door in from the Lower Right
JNBCB

Door at the Lower Left, Second Door in from the Upper Right, Door at the Upper Right
JKBCT

Door at the Lower Left, Second Door in from the Upper Right, Second Door in from the Lower Right
JPBCF

Door at the Lower Left, Door at the Upper Right, Second Door in from the Lower Right
JRBCH

Door at the Lower Left, Door at the Upper Left, Door at the Upper Right
SHBCH

Door at the Lower Left, Door at the Upper Left, Second Door in from the Upper Right
SFBCF

Door at the Lower Left, Door at the Upper Left, Second Door in from the Lower Right
SMBCM

Door at the Lower Left, Door at the Upper Left, Second Door in from the Upper Left, Door at the Lower Right
SDCCC

Door at the Lower Left, Door at the Upper Left, Second Door in from the Upper Right, Door at the Lower Right
SFCCD

Door at the Lower Left, Door at the Upper Left, Door at the Upper Right, Door at the Lower Right
SHCCG

Door at the Lower Left, Door at the Upper Left, Second Door in from the Lower Right, Door at the Lower Right
SMCCL

Door at the Lower Left, Door at the Upper Left, Second Door in from the Upper Left, Second Door in from the Upper Right
SGBCD

Door at the Lower Left, Door at the Upper Left, Second Door in from the Upper Left, Door at the Upper Right
SJBCG

Door at the Lower Left, Door at the Upper Left, Second Door in from the Upper Left, Second Door in from the Lower Right
SNBCL

Door at the Lower Left, Door at the Upper Right, Second Door in from the Lower Right, Door at the Lower Right
JRCCG

Door at the Lower Left, Second Door in from the Upper Right, Second Door in from the Lower Right, Door at the Lower Right
JPCCD

Door at the Lower Left, Second Door in from the Upper Left, Second Door in from the Lower Right, Door at the Lower Right
JNCCC

Door at the Lower Left, Second Door in from the Upper Right, Door at the Upper Right, Door at the Lower Right
JKCCS

Door at the Lower Left, Second Door in from the Upper Left, Door at the Upper Right, Door at the Lower Right
JJCCR

Door at the Lower Left, Second Door in from the Upper Left, Second Door in from the Upper Right, Door at the Lower Right
JGCCP

Door at the Lower Left, Second Door in from the Upper Left, Second Door in from the Upper Right, Door at the Upper Right
JLBCS

Door at the Lower Left, Second Door in from the Upper Left, Second Door in from the Upper Right, Second Door in from the Lower Right
JQBCD

Door at the Lower Left, Second Door in from the Upper Left, Door at the Upper Right, Second Door in from the Lower Right
JSBCG

Door at the Lower Left, Second Door in from the Upper Right, Door at the Upper Right, Second Door in from the Lower Right
JTBCK

Door at the Lower Left, Door at the Upper Left, Door at the Upper Right, Second Door in from the Lower Right
SRBCR

Door at the Lower Left, Door at the Upper Left, Second Door in from the Upper Right, Door at the Upper Right
SKBCK

Door at the Lower Left, Door at the Upper Left, Second Door in from the Upper Right, Second Door in from the Lower Right
SPBCP

Door at the Lower Left, Door at the Upper Left, Second Door in from the Upper Left, Second Door in from the Lower Right, Door at the Lower Right
SNCCM

Door at the Lower Left, Door at the Upper Left, Second Door in from the Upper Left, Second Door in from the Upper Right, Door at the Lower Right
SGCCF

Door at the Lower Left, Door at the Upper Left, Second Door in from the Upper Left, Door at the Upper Right, Door at the Lower Right
SJCCH

Door at the Lower Left, Door at the Upper Left, Second Door in from the Upper Right, Door at the Upper Right, Door at the Lower Right
SKCCJ

Door at the Lower Left, Door at the Upper Left, Second Door in from the Upper Right, Second Door in from the Lower Right, Door at the Lower Right
SPCCN

Door at the Lower Left, Door at the Upper Left, Door at the Upper Right, Second Door in from the Lower Right, Door at the Lower Right
SRCCQ

Door at the Lower Left, Door at the Upper Left, Second Door in from the Upper Left, Second Door in from the Upper Right, Door at the Upper Right
SLBCJ

Door at the Lower Left, Door at the Upper Left, Second Door in from the Upper Left, Second Door in from the Upper Right, Second Door in from the Lower Right
SQBCN

Door at the Lower Left, Door at the Upper Left, Second Door in from the Upper Left, Door at the Upper Right, Second Door in from the Lower Right
SSBCQ

Door at the Lower Left, Second Door in from the Upper Right, Door at the Upper Right, Second Door in from the Lower Right, Door at the Lower Right
JTCCJ

Door at the Lower Left, Second Door in from the Upper Right, Door at the Upper Right, Second Door in from the Lower Right, Door at the Lower Right
JSCCH

Door at the Lower Left, Second Door in from the Upper Left, Second Door in from the Upper Right, Second Door in from the Lower Right, Door at the Lower Right
JQCCF

Door at the Lower Left, Second Door in from the Upper Left, Second Door in from the Upper Right, Door at the Upper Right, Door at the Lower Right
JLCCT

Door at the Lower Left, Second Door in from the Upper Left, Second Door in from the Upper Right, Door at the Upper Right, Second Door in from the Lower Right
JBBCJ

Door at the Lower Left, Door at the Upper Left, Second Door in from the Upper Right, Door at the Upper Right, Second Door in from the Lower Right
STBCT

Door at the Lower Left, Door at the Upper Left, Second Door in from the Upper Left, Door at the Upper Right, Second Door in from the Lower Right, Door at the Lower Right
SSCCR

Door at the Lower Left, Door at the Upper Left, Second Door in from the Upper Right, Door at the Upper Right, Second Door in from the Lower Right, Door at the Lower Right
STCCS

Door at the Lower Left, Door at the Upper Left, Second Door in from the Upper Left, Second Door in from the Upper Right, Door at the Upper Right, Door at the Lower Right
SLCCK

Door at the Lower Left, Door at the Upper Left, Second Door in from the Upper Left, Second Door in from the Upper Right, Second Door in from the Lower Right, Door at the Lower Right
SQCCP

Door at the Lower Left, Door at the Upper Left, Second Door in from the Upper Left, Second Door in from the Upper Right, Door at the Upper Right, Second Door in from the Lower Right
SBBCS

Door at the Lower Left, Second Door in from the Upper Left, Second Door in from the Upper Right, Door at the Upper Right, Second Door in from the Lower Right, Door at the Lower Right
JBCCK

All (Start in Big Door)
SBCCT

In the Big Door: 2nd Part
TBCCS

In the Big Door: 3rd Part
TBHCN

In the Big Door: 4th Part
TBRCD

In the Big Door: 5th Part
TBRDF

In the Big Door: 6th Part, Last Level
TBTBT

Chant in the Password Screen
Go to the Gamespeak screen and chant by pressing Left. Proceed into password, and press Left, Right, Up, or Down rapidly to hear Abe chant.

OPERATION C

10 Lives
At the title screen press Up four times, Down four times, Left four times, Start.

Level Select
At the title screen press Up (2), Down (2), Left, Right, Left, Right, B, A, B, A, Start.

Powerful Weapons
The more often you collect the same gun, the more powerful it will be!

Sound Test
At the title screen press Up, Down, Left, Right, Start.

PAC-MAN (GB)

Full Screen Mode
Press Left or Right on the title screen until a 1/2 symbol appears next to the "1 Player" option. Now press Start.

PAC-MAN (GBC)

Level 1
STR

Level 2
HNM

Level 3
KST

Level 4
TRT

Level 5
MYX

Level 6
KHL

Level 7
RTS

Level 8
SKB

Level 9
HNT

Level 10
SRY

PAPERBOY

All Bikes
Immediately after you start on Easy Street, turn your bike sharply to the left. Then, press Start, A(3), B, Select, A, B, Start. The screen flashes if you entered the code correctly.

PAPYRUS

Boy Level 1
F+51

Boy Level 2
3DTS

Boy Level 3
F80W

Boy Level 4
9N87

Boy Level 5
WX-0

Boy Level 6
1-SN

Boy Level 7
H1WR

Boy Level 8
C2VX

Boy Level 9
1-KS

Boy Level 10
GTCP

Boy Level 11
X9M-

Boy Level 12
8Q63

Boy Level 13
8NRR

Boy Level 14
1KK2

Boy Level 15
-07L

Boy Level 16
VTGT

Boy Level 17
ZHNK

Boy Level 18
X3FB

Girl Level 1
KN4K

Girl Level 2
1-QB

Girl Level 3
GND9

Girl Level 4
JV-B

Girl Level 5
CR73

Girl Level 6
RPD9

Girl Level 7
JNTX

Girl Level 8
F-T-

Girl Level 9
3BWX

Girl Level 10
DS+Q

Girl Level 11
TB81

Girl Level 12
7R+D

Girl Level 13
59GN

Girl Level 14
R4PX

Girl Level 15
9NWN

Girl Level 16
92B0

Girl Level 17
5SNC

Girl Level 18
N0-3

PARODIUS

All Weapons and Power-Ups
Pause the game, then press Up (2), Down (2), Left, Right, Left, Right, B, A, Start.

PENGUIN

Level Select
Press Left+B, then press A and choose your level.

PIPE DREAM

Level 5
haha

Level 9
grin

Level 13
reap

Level 17
seed

Level 21
grow

Level 25
tall

Level 29
yali

PIT FIGHTER

Superpower
Select Ty. After reaching a level, hold Select and tap A continuously. You'll kick three times as fast as you normally do during a fight.

PITFALL: BEYOND THE JUNGLE

Underground Level
FLTYWTRS

Volcano Level
GNGDWN

Prison Level
SLTHHRNG

The Scourge Level
SWPNGBLW

PLANET OF THE APES

Skip Levels
Enter the following passwords to skip to a specific level.

Desert 2
1C6YPT

Cave
0RK01D

Jungle 1
6PC49G

Jungle 2
JMF69J

Medical Center
0F1BR8

Ape City 1
LY7VRQ

Ape City 2
2TMQ1V

Ape City 3
V!TG14

Beach
DTRZ1L

Mountains
XZPFR0

Underground City 1
06H91V

Underground City 2
G!WN9Z

PLAY ACTION FOOTBALL

Power Boost
Press A rapidly to speed up while running.

POCAHONTAS

Level 2
KPGXH4T8

Level 3
CMQZB6R1

Level 4
JWDLF7K5

Level 5
TGNDX3V9

Level 6
HFSBD2M6

Level 7
QZJRL1W4

Level 8
BPXCV7Z3

Level 9
SDLFT8G2

Level 10
RWHJX9Z5

Level 11
MVNGB4C6

Level 12
KCQTD3W1

Level 13
TBPRG5H8

Level 14
QFCMX2B9

Level 15
VDHKS6L7

Level 16
BNJHZ1R9

POCKET BOMBERMAN

Boss Mode with Full Power
Enter 9437 as a password.

Ocean Level with All Items
Enter 4622 as a password.

All Power-Ups
Enter 5656 as password.

Forest 1
7693

Forest 2
3905

Forest 3
2438

Forest 4
8261

Forest Boss
1893

Ocean 1
2805

Ocean 2
9271

Ocean 3
1354

Ocean 4
4915

Ocean Boss
8649

Wind 1
0238

Wind 2
5943

Wind 3
6045

Wind 4
2850

Wind Boss
8146

Cloud 1
9156

Cloud 2
2715

Cloud 3
4707

Cloud 4
7046

Cloud Boss
0687

Evil 1
3725

Evil 2
0157

Evil 3
5826

Evil 4
9587

Evil Boss
3752

PONG

Two Balls in Arctic Pong
When hit by one of the specials, your paddle slants and is able to catch the ball. If you hit one of the penguins, it throws another ball at you.

POWER RANGERS: THE MOVIE

Ivan Ooze
411

Pig
5989

Rat
936

Goldar
3713

Lord Zedd
3500

Queen Tengu
3999

View Credits
3844

POWER QUEST

National Tournament, Level 2 Parts and Power Pack
1SZK-DRT2-QFY5

National Tournament, Level 2 Parts, Power Pack, Heal Pack
32RY-DVNS-D2SP

Level 3 Attacks, Super Parts, Power Pack
PV9S-040G-0140

National Tournament, Level 4 Parts, Heal Pack, Power Pack, Super Parts
5X7Q-RLD8-JF67

Level 4 Parts And All Items
9996-G889-899S

One Level 4 Part, All Items, 999,990 Credits
XHP3-Z6P9-5XQT

999,990 Credits
1R75-FLVD-FKVC

POWERPUFF GIRLS: BAD MOJO JOJO

Unlimited Super Attack
Enter GIRLPOWER at "Enter cheat."

Unlock Buttercup
Enter CHEMICALX at "Enter cheat."

POWERPUFF GIRLS: BATTLE HIM

Power-Up
Enter ELBO at the Enter Secrets option at the main menu.

Extra Legal Pads
Enter CLIPP at the Enter Secrets option at the main menu.

Utonium Chateau Level
Enter GOGETBUTCH at the Enter Secrets option at the main menu.

Townsville Skies Level
Enter BEATBRICK at the Enter Secrets option at the main menu.

Townsville Dump Level
Defeat Butch at the Utonium Chateau level, then go to the hearts. Select the Play option, and press Left.

Access Buttercup Graphics
Enter LUMPKINS at the Enter Secrets option at the main menu.

Access Blossom Graphics
Enter MISSKEANE at the Enter Secrets option at the main menu.

Access Mayor Graphics
Enter MCCRACKEN at the Enter Secrets option at the main menu.

Get the Art Museum Trading Card
Enter MALPHS at the Enter Secrets option at the main menu.

Get the Boogie Man Trading Card
Enter HOTLINE at the Enter Secrets option at the main menu.

Get the Boomer Trading Card
Enter ICEBREATH at the Enter Secrets option at the main menu.

Get the Evil Cat Trading Card
Enter POWERPUFF at the Enter Secrets option at the main menu.

Get the Rainbow the Clown Trading Card
Enter MRSBELLUM at the Enter Secrets option at the main menu.

Get the Talking Dog Trading Card
Enter RUFFBOYS or BIGBILLY at the Enter Secrets option at the main menu.

Get the Townsville Trading Card
Enter TOYSPOWER at the Enter Secrets option at the main menu.

Get the Townsville City Hall Trading Card
Enter PRINCESS at the Enter Secrets option at the main menu.

POWERPUFF GIRLS: PAINT THE TOWNSVILLE GREEN

Power-Up
Enter EBSTORE at the Enter Secrets option at the main menu.

Utonium Chateau Level
Enter BEATBRICK at the Enter Secrets option at the main menu.

Bonsai Garden Level
Enter DUSTBOOMER at the Enter Secrets option at the main menu.

Access Bubbles Graphics
Enter UTONIUM at the Enter Secrets option at the main menu.

Access Blossom Graphics
Enter POKEYOAKES at the Enter Secrets option at the main menu.

Access Mayor Graphics
Enter OCTIEVIL at the Enter Secrets option at the main menu.

Get the Big Billy Trading Card
Enter KABOOM at the Enter Secrets option at the main menu.

Get the Broccloid Emperor Trading Card
Enter MOJOJOJO at the Enter Secrets option at the main menu.

Get the Butch Trading Card
Enter ROWDYRUFFS at the Enter Secrets option at the main menu.

Get the Fuzzy Lumpkins Trading Card
Enter RZONE at the Enter Secrets option at the main menu.

Get the Grubber Trading card
Enter GRUBBER at the Enter Secrets option at the main menu.

Get the Little Arturo Trading Card
Enter TARGETPOWR at the Enter Secrets option at the main menu.

Get the Mrs. Keane Trading Card
Enter SEARSRULE at the Enter Secrets option at the main menu.

Get the Powerpuff Girls Trading Card
Enter GOCIRCUIT at the Enter Secrets option at the main menu.

Get the Snake Trading Card
Enter SQUID at the Enter Secrets option at the main menu.

Get the Townsville Dump Trading Card
Enter AMOEBABOYS at the Enter Secrets option at the main menu.

PREHISTORIK MAN

Cheat Mode
During the introduction, press Down, A, Up, B, Left, Right, B, A, B, A, B, A, Up, Down. Cheat mode becomes activated on the next screen. You are invincible and can skip levels by pressing Select.

PRINCE OF PERSIA

Level 2
6769075

Level 3
28611065

Level 4
92117015

Level 5
87019105

Level 6
46308135

Level 7
65903195

Level 8
70914195

Level 9
68813685

Level 10
1414654

Level 11
32710744

Level 12
26614774

Jaffar
98119464

Ending
89012414

PROJECT S-11

Mission 2—Kenhull Badlands
At the password entry screen, enter H0!3.

Mission 3—Lewap Forest
At the password entry screen, enter 3!!F.

Mission 4—Bern Jungle
At the password entry screen, enter SZPP.

Mission 5—Ma'akai Jungle
At the password entry screen, enter 0237.

Mission 6—Giel Glacial Park
At the password entry screen, enter G!ZT.

Mission 7—Notav Space Quadrant
At the password entry screen, enter GFGF.

PUZZLE MASTER

Level 1
KING

Level 2
FAIRY

Level 3
WIZARD

Level 4
CHAMPION or MOUSE

Q*BERT

See All Movies
At the title screen, press Right, Up, B, A, Down, Up, B, Down, Up, B.

QIX

No Sound
At the title screen, hold Left and press Start.

QUEST FOR CAMELOT (GBC)

Free Health
Have at least 30 jewels before you attempt this. Get down to your last heart and save the game. Restart the game, then reload your saved game. You have full health.

Print Intermission Scenes
Press Select during an intermission scene to print to the Game Boy Printer.

Easily Kill Bosses
Trap a boss against a wall. Then hit it with your sword.

R-TYPE

Drawing Mode
At the High Score screen, press Down-Left+A+B. You enter a drawing program. Use A to draw, B to erase, Start to clear the screen, and the D-Pad to move the cursor around.

R-TYPE DX (GBC)

Invincibility
Beat R-Type DX using fewer than 10 credits. Then press Select+A during a R-Type standard game.

Restart Level
Hold B and turn the Game Boy off when you are playing a game. Continue holding B and turn the Game Boy on again. The game resumes at the last level. You have five ships, no points, and no power-ups.

Level Skip
Pause the game. Press B to advance through previously played levels.

Drawing Mode
Beat R-Type I Enhanced, R-Type II Enhanced, and R-Type DX. At the main menu, press Right until the De Souza drawing editor opens.

RAGING FIGHTER

Player vs. Player
At the title screen, press Up (2), Down (2), Left, Right, Left, Right, A, B. A bell confirms correct entry.

1P Game, Same Color
At the title screen, press Up (2), Down (2), Left, Right, Left, Right, B (2).

1P Game, Alternate Color
At the title screen, press Up (2), Down (2), Left, Right, Left, Right, B, A.

2P Game, Same Color
At the title screen, press Up (2), Down (2), Left, Right, Left, Right, A (2).

2P Game, Alternate Color
At the title screen, press Up (2), Down (2), Left, Right, Left, Right, A, B.

RAMPAGE: WORLD TOUR (GBC)
Play As Tiny
Choose Ralph, then let him die. Then press Select, A, B (2), Up, Down, Forward, Back when you turn into a person.

Link Mode
At the Options menu, hold Select and press Up, Down, Left, Right, Down, Up. This unlocks the "Players 1 or 2" option, where two players can play the Two-player mode with a link cable.

RAMPAGE 2: UNIVERSAL TOUR (GBC)
Play As George
Enter SM14N1230 at the password screen.

Play As Ralph
Enter LVPVS7890 at the password screen.

Play As Myukus
Enter N0T3T3210 at the password screen.

Play As Lizzie
Enter S4VRS4560 at the password screen.

RATS! (GBC)
Level 2
WYH4TFGR9J

Level 3
MMQ1DXXLT5

Level 4
C7CDSFVRTQ

Level 5
CW6F2FBLPG

Level 6
LBBWQVDJJR

Level 7
WRGSCD8QPN

Level 8
BWBK8CBQQ4

Level 9
4XLG-WJRD3

Level 10
M1CS4YNKKW

Level 11
5YMJFYJBC3

Level 12
5TWKTYJCF7

Level 13
CD588DDJ5L

Level 14
BJR9XBLS4Q

Level 15
5VLDPYJ8W?

Level 16
WV4M3FRQKD

Level 17
WDP6PDRM-N

Level 18
VMF7YB9BND

Level 19
BW7Z2CMKS8

Level 20
VXXSTCRBD2

Level 21
W8M-TF1MPX

Level 22
CT3L4DWQ5B

Level 23
MCVRJXPB7W

Level 24
M12?BYFG7H

Level 25
CXCPSFMJ3G

Level 26
VD5H7BRQQ2

Level 27
BWTTZCMM48

Level 28
VWYMTC1NN?

Level 29
V6D61B9SJN

Level 30
BR5GGBMYSG

Level 31
VW1TFC2GX-

Level 32
4TRZ1VQDDK

Level 33
5DYHMXZN5S

Level 34
4Y4J1WZKJ3

Level 35
M6R-DYBNMV

Level 36
5BJDYXZSYS

Level 37
WCY39D2T7P

Level 38
L8NGVWBTJ5

Level 39
MWH2VY4HF1

Level 40
4JC-CVZPBT

Level 41
L1CWSWVMJ5

Level 42
BMJ2BBNTVG

Level 43
M-?YSYBCYW

Level 44
W3NBFF2DPJ

Level 45
VQ2C5BJYX7

Level 46
4W1WRW9GXJ

Level 47
B7S??CPKDM

Level 48
C2FBZDPTT4

Level 49
VT?6KC-BLN

Level 50
4ZYT3VRC8X

Level 51
VKLSTCTKNS

Level 52
B4?LJBYCXV

Level 53
W2VCKDTHPJ

Level 54
MSXT4Y5DRB

Level 55
43WCTVRT66

Level 56
WWTK-DKB7-

Level 57
L-1GZVWN?W

Level 58
W9HN5D3CRX

Level 59
M5DKJX5CKW

Level 60
5QJ5FY179J

Level 61
BGJ48CGCXQ

Level 62
LB1?8WSC2M

Level 63
LS84SW2CBG

Level 64
57MWWX6R7X

Level 65
MZ36JXJMM8

Level 66
WXMLTDVNFD

Level 67
WZ?MPD4NRJ

Level 68
BVJDZBZQQG

Level 69
4MZL1WDP86

Level 70
CVNJGDZJW8

Level 71
VNYVYCBSQJ

Level 72
VDFDPCVRQS

Level 73
V5SF1BBL6Y

Level 74
MC256Y2K1H

Level 75
CQFTZFQ75G

RAYMAN (GBC)
99 Lives
Pause the game. Press A, Right, B, Up, A, Left, B, Down, A, Right, B, Up, A, Left, B.

All Powers
Pause the game, Press Right, Left, Up, Down, A, Up (2), Down (2), B, Right (2), Left (2), A.

World Map

Pause the game. Press A, Left, A, Left, A, B, Right, B, Up, B, A, Left, A, Down, A.

Full Energy

Pause the game. Press B, Right, A, Up, B, Left, A, Down, B, Right.

Level Select

Type CH5G4mS1jD as a password.

RAZOR FREESTYLE SCOOTER

Level 2

At the Password screen enter Y2QXMZNHNL-LQLBLM9L.

Level 3

At the Password screen enter GJ9ZP35TR0-QQLBCV1N.

Level 4

At the Password screen enter YWGBRDTTT0-0LLBHXWS.

Level 5

At the Password screen enter H0SQTNVTW0-00VBHYNS.

Level 6

At the Password screen enter 2111YQ7TY0-10ZBHVFS.

Level 7

At the Password screen enter M2D98XBT002-02BHWBS.

READY 2 RUMBLE BOXING (GBC)

Play As Damien Black

Highlight "Arcade Mode" from the main menu. At the main menu, press Right, Left, Right (2), Left (2), Right (3), Left (3).

Play As Nat Daddy

Highlight "Arcade Mode" from the main menu. At the main menu, press Right (3), Left (3), Right, Left, Right, Left.

Play As Kemo Claw

Highlight "Arcade Mode" from the main menu. At the main menu, press Left (3), Right (3), Left, Right, Left, Right.

REAL BOUT FATAL FURY SPECIAL

Bonus Option

Go to the Options screen and highlight the "Sound Test" option. Press Left+A. A "Soft Dip" option appears.

Secret Characters

Beat the game. At the Player Select screen, highlight Billy or Krauser's face. Press Start. You can play as Geese or Iori.

REAL GHOSTBUSTERS

Level 2

LFBD

Level 3

VCSB

Level 4

TRFF

Level 5

ZFRG

Level 6

NFSF

Level 7

QDCZ

Level 8

KCNG

Level 9

TRBD

Level 10

LGCK

Level 11

WGRD

Level 12

TCMF

Level 13

RBCN

Level 14

NBMF

Level 15

GPBL

Level 16

RBCT

Level 17

RCNG

Level 18

FCRF

Level 19

YBRD

Level 20

SGNG

Level 21

GGLD

Level 22

LBMP

Level 23

TWCN

Level 24

FDSF

Level 25

SPGT

Level 26

NFWS

Level 27

RGSF

Level 28

RBCF

Level 29

DCSK

Level 30

HBCR

Level 31

JBZZ

Level 32

GBMF

Level 33

HGLD

Level 34

BCRD

Level 35

DGLL

Level 36

WGRM

Level 37

STBR

Level 40

HFLP

Level 41

CTRL

Level 42

FMHX

Level 43

PCGR

Level 44

LGSK

Level 45

PRPY

Level 46

NPTF

Level 47

MSDP

Level 48

MJCY

Level 49

MFHD

Level 50

CCNK

Level 51

FNDG

REVELATIONS: THE DEMON SLAYER (GBC)

Lucifer Joins Team

Beat Lucifer to complete the game. You can then explore the game freely. Find Lucifer in the Cave of Oasis and talk to him.

Michael Joins Team

Beat Lucifer to complete the game. Go back to Nova and talk to Uncle Hata. He turns out to be Michael and he joins you.

ROAD CHAMPS BXS STUNT BIKING

Unlock The Training, Career and Tournament Modes

At the password entry screen enter QGF7

ROAD RASH

Level 4

9DGG-BB9F-FFKK

Level 5

9CBK-632C-88KO

ROADSTERS '98

Level 2

GMBY

Level 3

DMG

Level 4

BRK

Level 5

TRCK

Level 6

SPKR

Level 7

XTL

Level 8

JPN

Level 9

WNDW

Level 10
MNKY

Level 11
SCRP

Level 12
XFMR

Level 13
VHSVCR

Level 14
PNP

Level 15
FLPY

Level 16
NTRY

Level 17
TTLCMS

Level 18
CHR

Level 19
RDY

Level 20
STRT

Level 21
HTML

Level 22
JMPR

Level 23
GLSSY

Level 24
SRC

Level 25
HLT

Level 26
PTH

Level 27
PCK

Level 28
TRP

Level 29
BDY

Level 30
STP

Level 31
JCT

Level 32
DRP

ROBOCOP 2
See the Ending
At the title screen, press A+B+Select+Start, Left.

RUGRATS: THE MOVIE
Level Skip
Reach the second level. When you get to the third fireplace, skip all of the balloons and head toward the front of the fireplace. Press Up (2), Down(2), B, Right, Left. The screen shows a "level skip?" phrase if you entered the code correctly.

Level 2
TQMMY QK

Level 3
RQVDHJVV

Level 4
BVBYFJND

Level 5
RJDBCVRT

Level 6
VNGBLJCV

Level 7
BJGSMVSH

Level 8
LJTBWQQD

RUGRATS: TIME TRAVELERS (GBC)
Level 1
PVCJFJFR

Level 2
BVBYMJLK

Level 3
TPJCKLFS

Level 4
TQYCLQWN

Level 5
DJDJ*STW

Level 6
DJVPFRSS

Level 7
SPJKFDQG

Level 8
FLWFFJFS

Level 9
SVNDPJTS

Level 10
PHJL*LJL

Level 11
CQQKJFSS

Level 12
CRVWLJNG

Level 13
PLVYPFNS

Level 14
TQYBQXFS

Level 15
TRVJNAFT

SABRINA THE ANIMATED SERIES: ZAPPED!
Level 1-2
At the password screen, enter the following characters: Sabrina, Sabrina, Salem, Jem.

Level 1-3
At the password screen, enter the following characters: Sabrina, Salem, Salem, Red Head Boy.

Level 1-4
At the password screen, enter the following characters: Sabrina, Harvey, Salem, Harvey.

Level 2-1
At the password screen, enter the following characters: Salem, Cloey, Sabrina, Salem.

Level 2-2
At the password screen, enter the following characters: Harvey, Salem, Red Head Boy, Red Head Boy.

Level 2-3
At the password screen, enter the following characters: Harvey, Harvey, Red Head Boy, Sabrina.

Level 2-4
At the password screen, enter the following characters: Harvey, Cloey, Red Head Boy, Salem.

Level 3-1
At the password screen, enter the following characters: Cloey, Jem, Jem, Harvey.

Level 3-2
At the password screen, enter the following characters: Jem, Harvey, Cloey, Sabrina.

Level 3-3
At the password screen, enter the following characters: Jem, Cloey, Cloey, Salem.

Level 3-4
At the password screen, enter the following characters: Jem, Jem, Cloey, Salem.

Level 4-1
At the password screen, enter the following characters: Red Head Boy, Red Head Boy, Harvey, Cloey.

Level 4-2
At the password screen, enter the following characters: Sabrina, Cloey, Jem, Salem.

Level 4-3
At the password screen, enter the following characters: Sabrina, Jem, Jem, Harvey.

Level 4-4
At the password screen, enter the following characters: Sabrina, Red Head Boy, Jem, Cloey.

SAMURAI SHODOWN
Secret Characters
Press Select (4) on the third screen of the opening to access Kuroko, Amakusa, and Hikyaku.

SAN FRANCISCO RUSH
Level 2
MADTOWN

Level 3
FATCITY

Level 4
SFRISCO

Level 5
GASWRKZ

Level 6
SKYWAYZ

Level 7
INDSTRL

Level 8
NEOCHGO

Level 9
RIPTIDE

SAN FRANCISCO RUSH 2049
Track 2
MADTOWN

Track 3
FATCITY

Track 4
SFRISCO

Track 5
GASWRKZ

Track 6
SKYWAYZ

Track 7
INDSTRL

Track 8
NEOCHGO

Track 9
RIPTIDE

SHADOWGATE CLASSIC (GBC)

Hints
During a game, press Select to get a hint in most rooms.

SHREK: FAIRY TALE FREAKDOWN

All Characters
Enter VGHVGTVRQ or LDHCJMSXG as a password.

Gingerbread Man
Enter TFGKWLSJJ as a password to play as the Gingerbread Man.

Dragon
Enter VLLZSYYZK as a password and you will fight with the dragon. You can play with the dragon after the fight is over.

Lord Farkfawd
Enter WCKUSTVZX as a password.

Skip Level
Enter one of the following passwords to skip to a specific level as a certain character.

Village (As Thelonius)
LRSVGTLXM

Dungeon (As Thelonius)
YFSVGTLXK

Village (As Shrek)
SMHTVKCQR

Dungeon (As Shrek)
TQDFNHGGM

Swamp (As Shrek), Gingerbread Man unlocked
TFGKWLSJJ

Dark Forest (As Shrek), Invincibility Power-Up Unlocked
KDNBQGKVY

Bridge (As Shrek), Speed Power-Up Unlocked
KWJPYXCQC

Castle (As Shrek) ,Ogre Strength Power-Up, the Dragon Unlocked
YNNHLBMBY

SIMPSONS: BART AND THE BEANSTALK

Bonus Energy
Find a place where there are three coins in a row. Jump and get all three coins; your energy goes up.

SIMPSONS: BART VS. THE JUGGERNAUTS

Secret Board
Get maximum speed and jump over the juggernaut at Captain Murdock's skateboard jump. On the side is the special board.

SIMPSONS: ESCAPE

Change Music
Pause the game and press B.

SIMPSONS: NIGHT OF THE LIVING TREEHOUSE OF HORROR

Level 2
FWXCKJXGLWN

Level 3
TNSLRYSJGWW

Level 4
BXPGCFPYJWB

Level 5
WSQJLTQFYWK

Level 6
NPKYGBKTFWQ

Level 7
XQRFJWRBTWP

SMALL SOLDIERS

Level 4
Archer, Brick, Kip, Chip

Level 5
Kip, Chip, Archer, Brick

SMURFS

Level Select
Beat the game once and watch the credits. There is a Level Select menu at the end. You can replay most of the levels again.

Level 5
pbsp

Level 10
zrms

SMURFS NIGHTMARE (GBC)

Level 2
Glasses, Pencil, Mouth

Level 3
Soap Bell, Mouth, Glasses

Level 4
Shy, Chief, Glasses

SNOOPY TENNIS

Unlock Woodstock
At Password screen, input WHGX.

SNOW BROS. JR.

Secret Levels
At the title screen, hold Up+B+Select and press Start.

Invulnerability
At the title screen, hold Down-Left+A+B and press Start. You must finish the code before the "JR." logo appears.

SOCCER MANIA

Invisible Opponents
At the title screen, hold Up (2), Down (2), Left, Right, Left, Right, B, A, Start.

SOLOMON'S CLUB

All Keys
At the title screen, press A, B, A, B (2), A, Up. Do this before the Start and options appear.

Level 1-1
O8__ 8888

Level 1-2
CVJB 8888

Level 1-3
GVJD 8888

Level 1-4
RVJH 8888

Level 1-5
XVJS 8888

Level 1-6
XVJY 8888

Level 1-7
8VBY 8888

Level 1-8
CYDY 8888

Level 1-9
MYHY 8888

Level 1-10
TYSY 8888

Level 2-1
TZ__ 8888

Level 2-2
QZVJ B888

Level 2-3
OZVJ D888

Level 2-4
8ZVJ H888

Level 2-5
?ZVJ S888

Level 2-6
?ZVJ Y888

Level 2-7
CZVB Y888

Level 2-8
QZYD Y888

Level 2-9
4ZYH Y888

Level 2-10
KZYS Y888

Level 3-1
KZ__ Z888

Level 3-2
6ZZV JB88

Level 3-3
TZZV JD88

Level 3-4
CZZV JH88

Level 3-5
2ZZV JS88

Level 3-6
2ZZV JY88

Level 3-7
QZZV BY88

Level 3-8
6ZZY DY88

Level 3-9
XZZY HY88

Level 3-10
RZZY SY88

Level 4-1
RZ__ZZ88

Level 4-2
JZZZ VJB8

Level 4-3
KZZZ VJD8

Level 4-4
QZZZ VJH8

Level 4-5
VZZZ VJS8

Level 4-6
VZZZ VJY8

Level 4-7
6ZZZ VBY8

Level 4-8
JZZZ YDY8

Level 4-9
?ZZZ YHY8

Level 4-10
8ZZZ YSY8

Level 5-1
8Z__ ZZZ8

Level 5-2
MZZZ ZVJB

Level 5-3
RZZZ ZVJD

Level 5-4
6ZZZ ZVJH

Level 5-5
6ZZZ ZVJS

Level 5-6
GZZZ ZVJY

Level 5-7
JZZZ ZVBY

Level 5-8
MZZZ ZYDY

Level 5-9
2ZZZ ZYHY

Level 5-10
CZZZ ZYSY

Solomon
CZ__ ZZZZ

SPACE INVADERS (GBC)

Classic Mode
Enter CLSS1281999DBM as a password.

Level Password Note
The following passwords may vary depending on some game factors such as lives, ships, and shields.

Venus Level
RTJNPBKCX2RJPW

Earth Level
WWYXTC2NQW79VY

Mars Level
?WZ4VCLN4W81V?

Jupiter Level
RSSN3QJ78?GJMC

Saturn Level
WSPZMSO8N?H8NF

Uranus Level
CV1?QWKGJ3X8R5

Neptune Level
HV27RW1GN3YOR7

Pluto Level
MV7HRCLHS3ZSR9

Invader Homeworld Level
RV8RRC2HX3?RJC

SPANKY'S QUEST

Music Menu
Enter 1007 as a password.

Level Select
Enter 0119 as a password.

SPAWN (GBC)

Level 2
Spawn, Heart, Skull, Heart

Level 3
Heart, Skull (2), Flame

Level 4
Heart, Spawn, Skull, Spawn

Level 5
Heart, Skull, Spawn (2)

Level 6
Skull, Spawn (2), Heart

Level 7
Skull, Spawn (2), Heart

SPEEDBALL II

Start with 10 Points
Start a new game and choose Cup mode. Quickly press A, B, A, B, A, Select, A, B, A, B, A, Select when the screen says "Round One."

SPEEDY GONZALES

Mexico Level
500999

Island Level
522472

Country Level
812171

Forest Level
343003

Desert Level
830637

SPEEDY GONZALES: AZTEC ADVENTURE (GBC)

Level 2
6483

Level 3
2397

Level 4
9853

Level 5
5629

Level 6
5141

SPIDER-MAN

Join Game After Defeating Venom
Enter GVCBF as password.

Join Game After Defeating Venom and Lizard
Enter QVCLF as password.

Join Game at Lab Entrance
Enter S8KR6 as password.

SPIDER-MAN 2: THE SINISTER SIX

Infinite Health
At the title screen, press Up, Down, Right, A.

Infinite Web
At the title screen, press Left, Down, B, Up.

After Mysterio
C3K23M

After Sandman
T4Q59J

After Vulture
MM947F

After Scorpion
TS6!96

After Kraven
LR6!9G

Level Skip
At the title screen, press B, A, Left, Down, Up, Right. You are taken to a screen where you can select your level—from 1 to 18.

Unlock Bonus Teddies Game
At the title screen, press A, B, A, B, Down. You are taken to a game where Spidey and Doc Ock have to move around a trampoline, bouncing teddy bears from one side of the screen to the other.

Unlock Nightmare Mode
At the title screen, press A, B, Select, Up, Right, Down.

Web O' Death
At the title screen press Down, A, B, A, A.

SPONGEBOB SQUAREPANTS: THE LEGEND OF THE LOST SPATULA

Level Select
Enter D3BVG-M0D3 at the Continue screen. After you press pause during gameplay, you see a Level Select option.

SPUD'S ADVENTURE

Level Select
Enter BANCHOU as a password. A "MAP Select 000" message appears. Press Down to choose stages and press Start to select the level.

SPY HUNTER/MOON PATROL

Unlimited Ammunition
At the game selection screen, press Up, Down, Left, Right, Up, Down, Left, Right, Up, Left, Down, B.

Unlimited lives
At the game selection screen, press Up, Down, Left, Right, Up, Down, Left, Right, Up, Left, Down, A.

SPY VS. SPY (GBC)

Final Level
Enter 15Y24 as a password.

Level Select
Enter Z4W4P as a password.

SPY VS. SPY: OPERATION BOOBY TRAP

Level 2
ZKP

Level 3
YPT

Level 4
MMD

STAR TREK: 25TH ANNIVERSARY

First Planet
0523.4

Second System
7552.3

Second Planet
6541.2

Third System
5570.1

Third Planet
4567.0

Last System
3516.7

STAR TREK: THE NEXT GENERATION

Level Select
Enter Override as a password. Start a new game. Press Up when Captain Picard explains your mission to select another level.

Captain Rank
Locutus

Commander Rank
Ro Laren

Lt. Commander Rank
Tomalak

Lieutenant Rank
Barclay

Ensign Rank
Q

STAR WARS: EPISODE I—RACER (GBC)

Faster Anakin
Unlock all the racers. Anakin's max speed will reach 735 mph.

Turbo Start
Press A as the "1" fades during the countdown sequence.

Get Sebulba's Pod
Race against Sebulba and win.

STAR WARS: EPISODE I—OBI-WAN ADVENTURES

Level 2
BQVQK

Level 3
WNLRM

Level 4
SDGNK

Level 5
CNLML

Level 6
BXGTG

Level 7
QSRVJ

Level 8
TKGJZ

Level 9
LPZCP

STAR WARS: RETURN OF THE JEDI

Dance Hall Level
SNKMTD

Sail Barge Level
RWVJBC

Endor Level
TFGBMN

Ewok Village Level
HJMKPL

Power Generator Level
QGTHGD

Death Star Level
PSVZKL

Tower Level
SFPYSW

Death Star Mission 1 Level
CGGYQM

Death Star Mission 2 Level
KFGZXQ

STREET FIGHTER ALPHA (GBC)

Fight Against Akuma
Pick your character in Arcade mode. Press and hold A+B when you choose either "Manual" or "Auto" option for your character. Hold the buttons until a fight begins.

Fight Against M. Bison
Pick your character in Arcade mode. Press and hold A+B+Select when you choose either "Manual" or "Auto" option for your character. Hold the buttons until a fight begins.

SUMO FIGHTER

Level 2-1
532773

Level 2-2
753442

Level 2-3
362459

Level 3-1
355530

Level 3-2
526158

Level 3-3
085530

Level 4-1
524358

Level 4-2
780554

Level 4-3
546127

Level 5-1
650594

Level 5-2
105960

Level 5-3
155965

Finals
968158

SURVIVAL KIDS

Access Fishing Minigame
Go near the main river and take the big rock. After getting it, use it where you see fish.

Access Big Berry Minigame
Go to the big berry tree(after the river, near where you get the big stick) when you have the monkey. Check the tree to access the big berry minigame.

Access Egg Catcher Minigame
Go into the desert, near the northern ashes. Take the monkey with you.

TAMAGOTCHI

Music Mode
Win any tournament with an adult Tamagotchi. At the Stat screen, a symbol appears above your Tamagotchi's picture. Go to the Options menu. Music mode becomes unlocked there.

TARZAN (GBC)

Level 2-1
Cross, X, Moon, Cross

Level 3-1
Vertical Lines (2), Maze, Swirl

Level 4-1
X, Moon, Triangles, Cross

Level 5-1
Triangles (2), Moon, Vertical Lines

Level 6-1
Swirl, Maze, Cross, Triangles

TAZ-MANIA

Level 2
345371

Level 3
745577

Level 4
367123

Level 5
662077

TECHMO BOWL

San Francisco vs. Denver Championship Game Password
1DAFF7A6

L.A. vs. Washington Championship Game Password
967FBFA5

Washington vs. Chicago Championship Game Password
587BFFA0

Indianapolis vs. Los Angeles Championship Game Password
438FDFAD

Seattle vs. Washington Championship Game Password
937FBFA5

New York vs. Miami Championship Game Password
24AFFDAD

Los Angeles vs. Miami Championship Game Password
94BFFDAI

Invisible Team vs. Chicago Championship Game Password
397BFFA5

Chicago vs. Los Angeles Championship Game Password
A89FDFA8

Miami vs. San Francisco Championship Game Password
072F7FAA

Dallas vs. San Francisco Championship Game Password
202F7FAE

Denver vs. Los Angeles Championship Game Password
0C8FDFA9

Cleveland vs. New York Championship Game Password
098DFFA9

Minnesota vs. Los Angeles Championship Game Password
2E9FDEA3

Washington Same Team Password
5B7FBFA3

Indianapolis Same Team Password
43AFFEAC

Cleveland Same Team Password
49AFFBA9

Miami Same Team Password
46AFFDAB

Los Angeles Same Team Password
969FDFA5

Dallas Same Team Password
63AEFFA5

New York Same Team Password
269DFFA1

San Francisco Same Team Password
9C3F7FA5

Chicago Same Team Password
697BFFA5

Minnesota Same Team Password
AC#&FFA9

Denver Same Team Password
CFBFF7A0

TEENAGE MUTANT NINJA TURTLES III: RADICAL RESCUE

2 Continues
Always put a 2 in the last spot of your passwords.

16 Hearts on Shredder's Level
Enter 1HHHHH2 as a password.

Before Scratch Level Password
1000002

After Scratch Level Password
2100002

After Card 1 Level Password
4110102

Before Dirtbag Level Password
1111102

After Dirtbag Level Password
2311102

After Raphael Level Password
3311302

After Card 2 Level Password
4331302

Before Triceraton Level Password
1311302

After Triceraton Level Password
2711302

After Donatello Level Password
3711702

After Card 3 Level Password
4773702

Before Scale Tail Level Password
1777702

After Scale Tail Level Password
2H77702

After Splinter Level Password
3H77HO2

After Card 4 Level Password
4HH7HO2

Before Shredder Level Password
1HHHH02

TEENAGE MUTANT NINJA TURTLES: FALL OF THE FOOT CLAN

Refill Health
Pause the game. Press Up (2), Down (2), Left, Right, Left, Right, B, A, Start. You can only use this once per game.

Bonus Games
At the Level Select screen, press Select+A+B. A tone confirms correct entry. A "?" appears on the screen's right side. Click on it to play the extra games.

TENNIS

Easy Win
When you are serving, toss the ball up and walk under the ball so that the ball lands on your head. This should bring up a screen that shows that you just scored. Repeat for the win.

TERMINATOR 2: THE ARCADE GAME

Slow Time on Level 3
Hold Select during gameplay on Level 3. This slows down your cursor and timer and also disables the music.

TEST DRIVE 6 (GBC)

Unlock the Mega Cup Tournament
Win all the tournaments.

Bonus Cars
Win the Mega Cup Tournament to unlock two cars at the Purchase Car screen.

TETRIS

Hard Mode
At the title screen, hold Down and press Start to make the game run much faster.

Secret Ending
Play Tetris Mode B. With an initial height of five, score 25 lines on Level 9. New music and a new title picture become unlocked if you do that correctly.

Secret Rockets
In Tetris Mode A, score 100,000 points to get a small rocket. Score 200,000 points to get a large rocket. In Tetris Mode B, you can get a space shuttle if you beat the game at Level 9 and Height 5.

No Piece Preview
Hit Start to pause a game. Press Select. When you resume playing the preview piece is gone. Disable this by pausing and pressing Select again.

TETRIS 2

Easy Mode
At the title screen, hold Up+Start until the title screen disappears. In Easy mode, bricks fall slower and there are fewer bombs.

TETRIS ATTACK

Fight Bowser
Enter 78RN5B?8 as a password.

Bonus Puzzles
Enter JO!JOO6O as a password.

Extra Hard Games
In Vs. Com mode, highlight "Hard." Hold Up+Select+A or Up+Select+Start. When you start playing a game, the difficulty level reads "SPHard."

(Hard Mode) Passwords
Enter these passwords to jump to specific levels in Hard mode.

Level 2
?4XJ700N

Level 3
?28J71HN

Level 4
Q1LK51ZN

Level 5
JCCK82TP

Level 6
!WML12!P

Level 7
PZ5LQCZP

Level 8
KJXMJXXP

Level 9
YKHMJYWP

Level 10
ZPPM5YWP

Level 11
RN9NRZUP

(Versus Computer) Passwords
Enter these passwords to jump to specific levels against the computer.

Level 2
63QJJ05Q

Level 3
6FDJJ1CQ

Level 4
65MJK1ZN

Level 5
2HBJN2TP

Level 6
1PQK22TP

Level 7
4!9L1C?P

Level 8
2ZRLRXXP

Level 9
8LCL8YXP

Level 10
B!YL8YWP

Level 11
8JFL8ZWP

TETRIS BLAST

Fight Mode
At the One-player/Two-player screen, press B (5), Start. A "Fight 2" option appears on the next screen.

Change Music
Pause the game. Press Select to change the music.

Level 20
DOVGYKHD or DMSDTFCL

Level 40
ZCYXJVMH

TETRIS DX (GBC)

Reset Game
During a game, press Start+Select+A+B.

Expert Mode
Pause the game. Press Select. The preview window doesn't show the next piece when the game resumes.

Continue Game
Pause the game in Single-player mode. Turn the Game Boy Color off. Turn the Game Boy Color on and a Continue screen appears.

Alternate Screens
Let the Demonstration mode begin and get ready to enter the code when you see an Aquarium screen. Press A (2) to display a confetti screen. Press B (2) and a chalkboard appears.

Reverse Movement
Hold Left or Right until the piece touches the wall. Continue to hold that Left or Right to keep it against the wall and rapidly tap A. This works on all the pieces except for the square and straight bar.

TETRIS PLUS

Level Select
Beat stage 100, which is Atlantis World Stage 20. Select "Puzzle" and then "Continue." Your continued game will say "Stage Clear." While you are playing a puzzle game, pause the game and press B. You can choose to play any level from 1 to 100.

TINY TOON ADVENTURES: MONTANA'S MOVIE MADNESS

Minigames
Hold A+B before the Konami screen appears. Then, press Start at the Press Start screen while still holding A+B.

Options Menu
At the title screen, press Start+B.

Hard Mode
At the title screen, press Start+A.

TINY TOON ADVENTURES: WACKY SPORTS

Event Select
At the title screen, press Up (2), Down (2), Left, Right, Left, Right, B, A, Start.

TOM & JERRY

Level 4
Heart, Cheese, Soda, Clock

Level 7
Blank, Clock, Soda, Heart

Level 10
Jerry, Heart, Blank Soda

TOM & JERRY: FRANTIC ANTICS

Level 5
Fish, Star, Cracker, Potato, Heart

Level 8
Heart (2), Watermelon (2), Fish

TOM AND JERRY IN MOUSE ATTACKS

Level 2
Mouse (2), Cat, Mouse, Cat, Dog, Duck, Cat, Mouse

Level 3
Cat, Duck, Cat, Mouse (3), Duck, Dog, Cat

Level 4
Duck (2), Cat, Mouse, Cat, Mouse, Duck, Dog (2)

Level 5
Dog (2), Cat, Mouse, Dog (2) Duck, Cat, Mouse

TONY HAWK'S PRO SKATER 2

Play As Bucky Lasek
22LCVVFCPDBV

Play As Kareem Campbell
ZGPWVVPFPBVB

Play As Andrew Renolds
MF7CVVPFPBVB

Play As Rodney Mullen
KD8WVVFFPDBB

Play As Bob Burnquist
C4CDVVPFPDVB

Play As Jeff Rowley
6?GWVVFFPBBV

Play As Ellisa Steamer
P?GWVVFFPBBB

Play As Eric Coston
H8GCVVFFPBBB

Play As Tony Hawk, Fully Equipped
VZMLPTBBBBVV

Play As Tony Hawk with Maximum Cash
VZ?QZTTTTFDW

Play As Tony Hawk with All Boards and Levels
B58LPTGBBBBV

Play As Tony Hawk with $50,000
V!T!MBBBBBVV

Play As Steve Caballero
DPJBVWFCPDBV

TOONSYLVANIA

Level 3
4F627

Level 4
XVJRL

Level 5
NMVN3

TOP GEAR POCKET (GBC)

Extra Cars and Pole Track
Enter YQX+%Y as a password.

Improved Cornering
While you are rounding a corner, hold Up and tap A or B.

All Cars and Courses
Enter YQX-%ZD as a password.

Slug Bug
At the title screen, press A, B, A (2), B (2), Select (2), Start.

TOP GUN: GUTS AND GLORY

Level 2
WN7WQQT

Level 3
8NQSQQL

Level 4
PNQZQQP

Level 5
KNKQWQQ

Level 6
CN4XWQQ

Level 7
SN7TWQP

Level 8
XN778Q4

Level 9
7N7FPQF

Level 10
FN2FKQF

TOY STORY

Select Stages
Go to the Options screen. Turn off the "Story" option. Pick "9 Hats" and press Start.

TOY STORY 2 (GBC)

Level 2
PBPP

Level 3
BJWJ

Level 4
PJBW

Level 5
WBPP

Level 6
JBPJ

Level 7
JJWW

Level 8
PBWJ

Level 9
BPWW

TRUE LIES

Secret Level
RSSHLS

Construction Site Level
QFFCSS

TRUMP BOY

See Opponent's Hand
Press Up, Down, Left, Right, Up, Down, Left, Right, Start (2) while opening.

TUMBLE POP

Level 2
4qp9nnqqq

Level 3
4gpbnx304

Level 4
42pbpxzom

Level 5
4gp1p=376

Level 6
4d809xo=x

TUROK 2: SEEDS OF EVIL (GBC)

Infinite Lives
Enter DLVTRKBLVS as a password.

Infinite Health
Enter DLVTRKBNRG as a password.

Skip Levels
Enter DLVTRKBLVL as a password. To skip a level, pause the game. Press A+B.

All Weapons
Enter DLVTRKBWPS as a password.

Bird Mode
Enter DLVTRKBBRD as a password. During gameplay, hold Select and press A.

Alternate Ending
Press Down when the enemy appears in Level 9. You enter a secret tunnel. Shoot the computer and destroy the incubator.

Level 2 (Easy)
DVYLWKVYYZ

Level 3 (Easy)
GRYLWKWVVN

Level 4 (Easy)
DRYLSRWVVZ

Level 5 (Easy)
GVZLSRSQVV

Level 6 (Easy)
DVZLBVSQQT

Level 7 (Easy)
GRZLBVBQQQ

Level 8 (Easy)
DRZLBVBQQT

Level 9 (Easy)
GVYNBVBQWC

Level 2 (Medium)
QVYLWKVYYC

Level 3 (Medium)
TRYLWKWVYY

Level 4 (Medium)
QRYLSRWVPT

Level 5 (Medium)
TRZLSRSQPS

Level 6 (Medium)
QVZLBVSQVN

Level 7 (Medium)
TRZLBVBQVL

Level 8 (Medium)
QRZLBVBQVN

Level 9 (Medium)
TVYNBVBQQD

Level 2 (Hard)
DLTLWKVYYC

Level 3 (Hard)
GNYLWKWVPP

Level 4 (Hard)
DNYLSRWVPT

Level 5 (Hard)
GLZLSRSVPW

Level 6 (Hard)
DLZLBVSVVB

Level 7 (Hard)
GNZLBVBQVL

Level 8 (Hard)
DNZLBVBQVN

Level 9 (Hard)
GLYNBVBQQD

TUROK: BATTLE OF THE BIONOSAURS

Level 2
GRZNNPCRDB

Level 3
DVZNDPBTNG

Level 4
GVZNDPBTNG

Level 5
PCVYGRBTDK

Level 6
RCVYGRSTDR

Level 7
VSVYTRSQDG

Level 8
RSQPTNSQNW

TUROK: RAGE WARS

All Weapons
5lm2fb

Level 2 (Easy)
K14QF4

Level 3 (Easy)
3T5L31

Level 4 (Easy)
SMJ54M

Level 2 (Medium)
3MQTL1

Level 3 (Medium)
Z1KMQ1

Level 4 (Medium)
2TQCMR

Level 2 (Hard)
DT5JV1

Level 3 (Hard)
2F5QZM

Level 4 (Hard)
MQ5LRS

TUROK 3: SHADOW OF OBLIVION

Unlimited Ammo
ZXLCPMZ

Unlimited Lives
FJVHDCK

Skip Level
XCDSDFS

TURRICAN

Invincibility
At the title screen, press A, B (2), A, B, A (2), B, A (2), B, A (2).

Level Skip
Enable Invincibility and start a game. Pause the game and press Select to go to the next level.

Level Select
At the title screen, hold Select and press Start.

TWOUBLE! (GBC)

Granny's House Part 1
Enter Dog, Granny, Tweety, Taz, Sylvester at the Password screen.

Granny's Cellar Part 1
Enter Taz, Sylvester, Tweety, Dog, Granny at the Password screen.

Toy Shop Part 1
Enter Taz, Dog, Tweety, Sylvester, Granny at the Password screen.

Out in the Streets Part 1
Enter Dog, Tweety, Taz, Granny, Sylvester at the Password screen.

Garden Part 1
Enter Sylvester, Tweety, Dog, Taz, Granny at the Password screen.

ULTIMATE PAINTBALL

Level 2
1SQMJY2K

Level 3
1XDMJJET

Level 4
1TQMJWTO

URBAN STRIKE

Baja Oil Rigs Level
L82WFV8KK9L

Mexico Level
PH4L5V4WRDL

Las Vegas Level
DHJ3KD2JMCC

Underground Level
M5L2G6XMJL7

End Level
HFM7HDQJNGB

V-RALLY EDITION '99 (GBC)

Medium Difficulty Courses
Enter FAST as a password.

Hard Difficulty Courses
Enter FOOD as a password.

WACKY RACES

Unlock All Tracks and Racers
Input MUTTLEY as password.

WARIO LAND 3

Extra Lives
Press Start to pause gameplay, then press Select(16). If you do it correctly, a blinking square appears around the last digit of the number of your remaining lives. Hold A + B, then press Left, Up to change the number.

In-Game Reset
Press Start + Select + A + B during gameplay.

Free Wario Golf Play
Before you enter a Wario Golf game, save the game. Reload the game and enter the door. If you do badly in Wario Golf, shut down the Game Boy Color. Reload the game and you will be outside the door. Keep repeating this until you win.

Time Attack Mode
Successfully complete the game after collecting all 100 treasures.

WAYNE'S WORLD

Level Select
Pause the game. Hold A+B and press Left (2), Select.

View Programmer Picture
In the game, hold Start and press A, B, A, Down, Left, A, Down.

View Programmer's Girlfriend
In the game, hold Start and press Select, A, Left, A, Down, Left, A, Select (2).

View Programmer's Friend
Pause the game. Hold Start and press Right, A, Down, A, Right, B, Right, A.

WHO FRAMED ROGER RABBIT?

Level 2
DLT3QYBY

Level 3
GPLDMSRC

Level 4
MMCFGWXJ

Level 5
BGQTVKJP

Level 6
RTJBWN43

WIZARDS & WARRIORS X

Extra Lives
Enter W, Heart, W as initials on the High Score screen. You start the next game with six lives.

WORLD HEROES 2 JET

Play As the Boss
At the Takara screen, press Right, Left, A, B, Down, A, B, Up.

THE WORLD IS NOT ENOUGH

Activate Cheat Mode
Pause gameplay and press Up, Right, Left. When the cheat screen appears, line up the following icons to activate each effect.

Invincibility
Enter Taser, Grenade, Key, Goggles as a code at the cheat screen.

Unlimited Ammo
Enter Pistol, Rifle, Taser, Grenade as a code at the cheat screen.

Dim Match (One Hit Kills)
Enter Grenade, Key, Goggles, Pistol as a code at the cheat screen.

Undetectable
Enter Goggles, Grenade, Pistol, Rifle as a code at the cheat screen.

Level 2
Briefcase, Camera, Watch, Triangles in Circle

Level 3
Camera, Triangles in Circle, Two Circles, Watch

Level 4
Briefcase, Aim, Aim, Rectangle Chip

Level 5
Aim, Briefcase, Camera, Briefcase

Level 6
Card, Gun, Watch, Aim

Level 7
Card, Biohazard Symbol, Two Circles, Camera

Level 8
Rectangle Chip, Rectangle Chip, Aim, Two Circles

WORMS ARMAGEDDON (GBC)

Jungle Level
Pink Worm, Banana Bomb, Skeletal Worm, Pink Worm

Cheese Level
Pink Worm, Banana Bomb, Blue Worm, Dynamite

Medical Level
Skeletal Worm, Blue Worm, Banana Bomb (2)

Desert Level
Red Worm, Pink Worm, Skeletal Worm, Blue Worm

Tools Level
Banana Bomb, Pink Worm (2), Blue Worm

Egypt Level
Skeletal Worm, Pink Worm, Red Worm, Banana Worm

Hell Level
Pink Worm, Blue Worm, Red Worm, Dynamite

Treehut Level
Red Worm, Skeletal Worm, Dynamite, Blue Worm

Garden Level
Banana Bomb, Red Worm, Skeletal Worm, Dynamite

Snow Level
Dynamite, Pink Worm, Blue Worm, Blue Worm

Construction Yard Level
Pink Worm (2), Banana Bomb (2)

Pirate Level
Dynamite, Blue Worm, Dynamite, Skeletal Worm

Fruit Level
Skeletal Worm, Red Worm, Banana Bomb, Skeletal Worm

Alien Level
Dynamite, Blue Worm, Red Worm (2)

Circuit Level
Red Worm, Dynamite (3)

Medieval Level
Blue Worm, Dynamite, Skeletal Worm, Blue Worm

WWF: ATTITUDE (GBC)

Stone Cold Steve Austin Level 1
CBFPCQJC

Stone Cold Steve Austin Level 2
BCDNBRKB

Stone Cold Steve Austin Level 3
FDCMFSGF

Stone Cold Steve Austin Level 4
DFBCDTHD

Stone Cold Steve Austin Level 5
RQTKRBNR

Stone Cold Steve Austin Level 6
QRSJQCPQ

Stone Cold Steve Austin Level 7
TSRHTDLT

Stone Cold Steve Austin Level 8
STQGSFMS

Stone Cold Steve Austin Level 9
MLPFMGSM

Stone Cold Steve Austin Level 10
LMNDLHTL

Stone Cold Steve Austin Level 11
PNMCPJQP

Stone Cold Steve Austin Level 12
NPLBNKAN

Stone Cold Steve Austin Level 13
HQKTHLDH

Stone Cold Steve Austin Level 14
GRJSGMFG

Stone Cold Steve Austin Level 15
KSHRKNBK

The Rock Level 1
GHKRCSCG

The Rock Level 2
KJGSDRDK

The Rock Level 3
JKHPFRFJ

The Rock Level 4
CBDQGNGC

The Rock Level 5
BCFRHPHB

The Rock Level 6
FDBSJLJF

The Rock Level 7
DFCTKMKD

The Rock Level 8
RQSBLJLR

The Rock Level 9
QRTCMKMQ

The Rock Level 10
TSQDNGNT

The Rock Level 11
STRFPHPS

The Rock Level 12
MLNGQDQM

The Rock Level 13
LMPGRFRL

The Rock Level 14
PHLJSBSP

The Rock Level 15
NPMKTCTN

The Rock Level 16
HQJLBSBH

The Rock Level 17
GRKMCTCG

The Rock Level 18
KSGNDQDK

Kane Level 2
JBKBGRGG

Kane Level 3
GDHDKSKK

Kane Level 4
FHDHCLCC

Kane Level 5
DGFGBMBB

Kane Level 6
CKBKFNFF

Kane Level 7
BJCJDPDD

Kane Level 8
TMSMRGRR

Kane Level 9
SLTLQHQQ

Kane Level 10
RPQPTJTT

Kane Level 11
QNRNSKSS

Kane Level 12
PRNRMBMM

Kane Level 13
NQPQLCLL

Kane Level 14
MTLTPDPP

Kane Level 15
LSMSNFNN

Kane Level 16
KMJCHQHH

Kane Level 17
JLKBGRGG

Kane Level 18
HPGFKSKK

Sable Level 2
QCGMAKHG

Sable Level 3
TDKNSGJK

Sable Level 4
SFJPTHKJ

Sable Level 5
MGCQLDBC

Sable Level 6
NKDTPCFD

Sable Level 7
HLRBGSQP

Sable Level 8
GMQCHTRQ

Sable Level 9
JPSFKRTS

Sable Level 10
BRLHCPML

Sable Level 11
FSPJDLNP

Sable Level 12
DTNKFMPN

Sable Level 13
RLHLQJGH

Sable Level 14
FSNNFNQP

Sable Level 15
DTPPDPRN

Sable Level 16
RLGGRGDH

Sable Level 17
QMHHQHFG

Sable Level 18
TNJJTJBK

The Undertaker Level 1
SGKTCRHG

The Undertaker Level 2
RKGQDSJK

The Undertaker Level 3
QJHRFTKJ

The Undertaker Level 4
PCDNGLBC

The Undertaker Level 5
NBFPHMCB

The Undertaker Level 6
MFBLJNDF

The Undertaker Level 7
LDCMKPFD

The Undertaker Level 8
KRSJLGQR

The Undertaker Level 9
JQTKMHRQ

The Undertaker Level 10
HTQGNJST

The Undertaker Level 11
GSRHPKTS

The Undertaker Level 12
FMNDQBLM

The Undertaker Level 13
DLPFRCML

The Undertaker Level 14
CPLBSDNP

The Undertaker Level 15
BNMCTFPN

The Undertaker Level 16
TRJSBQGH

The Undertaker Level 17
SQKTCRHG

The Undertaker Level 18
RTGQDSJK

Edge Level 1
SHTPLMJG

Edge Level 2
BJQLPNHK

Edge Level 3
QKRMNPGJ

Edge Level 4
PBNSRQEC

Edge Level 5
NCPTQRDB

Edge Level 6
MDLQTSCF

Edge Level 7
LFMRSTDD

Edge Level 8
KQJDCBTR

Edge Level 9
JRKFBCSQ

Edge Level 10
HSGBFDRT

Edge Level 11
GTHCDFQS

Edge Level 12
FLDJHGPM

Edge Level 13
DMFKGHNL

Edge Level 14
CNBGKJMP

Edge Level 15
BPCHJKLM

Edge Level 16
TQSNMLKH

Edge Level 17
SRTPLMJG

Edge Level 18
RSQLPNHK

The Godfather Level 1
NGHNGDHG

The Godfather Level 2
MKJMKCJK

The Godfather Level 3
LJKLJBKJ

The Godfather Level 4
TCBTCKBC

The Godfather Level 5
SBCSBJCB

The Godfather Level 6
RFDRFHDF

The Godfather Level 7
QDFQDGFD

The Godfather Level 8
FRQFRPQR

The Godfather Level 9
DQRDQNRQ

The Godfather Level 10
CTSCTMST

The Godfather Level 11
BSTBSLTS

The Godfather Level 12
KMLKMTLM

The Godfather Level 13
JLMJLSML

The Godfather Level 14
HPNHPRNP

The Godfather Level 15
GNPGNQPN

The Godfather Level 16
PRGPHFGH

The Godfather Level 17
NQHNGDHG

The Godfather Level 18
MTJMKCJK

Taka Michinoku Level 1
DHJRMMGG

Taka Michinoku Level 2
CJHSNNKK

Taka Michinoku Level 3
BKGTPPJJ

Taka Michinoku Level 4
KBFLQQCC

Taka Michinoku Level 5
JCDMRRBB

Taka Michinoku Level 6
HDCNSSFF

Taka Michinoku Level 7
GFBPTTDD

Taka Michinoku Level 8
PQTGBBRR

Taka Michinoku Level 9
MRSHCCQQ

Taka Michinoku Level 10
MSRJDDTT

Taka Michinoku Level 11
LTQKFFSS

Taka Michinoku Level 12
TLPBGGMM

Taka Michinoku Level 13
SMNCHHLL

Taka Michinoku Level 14
RNMDJJPP

Taka Michinoku Level 15
QPLFKKNN

Taka Michinoku Level 16
FQKQLLHH

Taka Michinoku Level 17
DRJRMMGG

Taka Michinoku Level 18
CSHSNNKK

Jeff Jarrett Level 1
LGJCRMHG

Jeff Jarrett Level 2
PKHDSNJK

Jeff Jarrett Level 3
NJGFTPKJ

Jeff Jarrett Level 4
RCFGLQBC

Jeff Jarrett Level 5
QBDHMRCB

Jeff Jarrett Level 6
TFCJNSDF

Jeff Jarrett Level 7
SDBKPTFD

Jeff Jarrett Level 8
CRTLGBQR

Jeff Jarrett Level 9
BQSMHCRQ

Jeff Jarrett Level 10
FTRNJDST

Jeff Jarrett Level 11
DSQPKFTS

Jeff Jarrett Level 12
HMPQBGLM

Jeff Jarrett Level 13
GLNRCHML

Gangrel Level 1
TPSTPTHK

Gangrel Level 2
QLRQLQJG

Gangrel Level 3
RMQRMRKH

Gangrel Level 4
DSFDJDLN

Gangrel Level 5
FTDFKFMP

Gangrel Level 6
BQCBGBNL

Gangrel Level 7
CRBCHCPM

Gangrel Level 8
JNKJDJQS

Gangrel Level 9
KPJKFKRT

Gangrel Level 10
GLHGBGSQ

Gangrel Level 11
HMGHCHTR

Gangrel Level 12
NJPNSNBD

Gangrel Level 13
PKNPTPCF

Gangrel Level 14
LGMLQLDB

Gangrel Level 15
MHLMRMFC

Gangrel Level 16
SDTSNSGJ

Gangrel Level 17
TFSTPTHK

Gangrel Level 18
QBRQLQJG

WWF BETRAYAL

Unlock Debug Mode
Enter 4232 as a password. You can then change several options in the game.

WWF RAW

One Hit Knock Downs
Press A for five seconds at the Player Selection screen.

WWF SUPERSTARS 2: STEEL CAGE CHALLENGE

Fight Outside Ring
At the Ring Selection screen, press A, B, Up, Down, Left, Right, Start.

WWF WARZONE

Stone Cold vs. Goldust
JGTCDGK

Stone Cold vs. Goldust in Feud
HKQFCKG

Stone Cold vs. Bulldog
RKQFCTG

Stone Cold vs. Owen Hart
JJRFBJH

Stone Cold vs. Mankind
CCNHKCD

Stone Cold vs. Undertaker
DGFHJBF

Stone Cold vs. Undertaker in Feud
CKBKHFB

Stone Cold vs. Ahmed J.
MKBKHPB

Stone Cold vs. the Rock
DJCKGDC

Stone Cold vs. the Rock in Feud
RMSMPRS

Stone Cold vs. Shawn M.
HMSHPHS

Stone Cold vs. Shamrock for IC Title
SQTMNQT

Stone Cold vs. Shamrock in Feud
RTQPMTQ

Stone Cold vs. Farooq
HJQPMKQ

Stone Cold vs. Kane in a Cage
SSRPLSR

Mankind vs. Ahmed J.
DHRFNGG

Mankind vs. the Rock
CJSCMKK

Mankind vs. Shawn Michaels
DKTCLJJ

Mankind vs. Shawn Michaels in Feud
HBLKTCC

Mankind vs. Kane
RBLKTMC

Mankind vs. Shamrock
JHCKSSB

Mankind vs. Farooq
HJDHRFF

Mankind vs. Farooq in Feud
JKFHQDD

Mankind vs. Triple H
SKFHQND

Mankind vs. Stone Cold
MLQPFRR

Mankind vs. Stone Cold in Feud
NRRPDQQ

Mankind vs. Owen Hart for IC Title
DRRPDGQ

Mankind vs. Owen Hart in Feud
MSSMCTT

Mankind vs. Goldust
CSSMCKT

Mankind vs. Bulldog in a Cage
NTTMBSS

Undertaker vs. Kane
DRSCBGH

Undertaker vs. Triple H
CSRFFKJ

Undertaker vs. Triple H in Feud
DTQFDJK

Undertaker vs. Stone Cold
NTQFDSK

Undertaker vs. Owen Hart
HLPHHCB

Undertaker vs. Goldust
JRDHGBC

Undertaker vs. the Rock
HSCKKFD

Undertaker vs. the Rock in Feud
JTBKJDF

Undertaker vs. Mankind
STBKJNF

Undertaker vs. Mankind in Feud
MBTMMRQ

Undertaker vs. Ahmed J.
CBTMMHQ

Undertaker vs. Bulldog for IC Title
NHSMLQR

Undertaker vs. Bulldog in Feud
MJRPPTS

Undertaker vs. Shawn Michaels in Cage
NKQPNST

Kane vs. Stone Cold
JHRFGGK

Kane vs. Goldust
HJSCKKG

Kane vs. Owen Hart
JKTCJJH

Kane vs. Owen Hart in Feud
CBLKCCD

Kane vs. Bulldog
MBLKCMD

Kane vs. the Rock
DHCKBBF

Kane vs. the Rock in Feud
CJDHFFB

Kane vs. Shawn Michaels
DKFHDDC

Kane vs. Mankind
MJDHFBB

Kane vs. Ahmed J.
RLQPRRS

Kane vs. Ahmed J. in Feud
SRRPQQT

Kane vs. Undertaker for IC Title
JRRPQGT

Kane vs. Undertaker in Feud
RSSMTTQ

Kane vs. Shamrock
HSSMTKQ

Kane vs. Farooq in Cage
STTMSSR

Triple H vs. Bulldog
DGSCDHG

Triple H vs. Bulldog in Feud
CKRFCJK

Triple H vs. Mankind
MKRFCSK

Triple H vs. Undertaker
DJQFBKJ

Triple H vs. the Rock
HCPHKBC

Triple H vs. Shawn Michaels
JGDHJCB

Triple H vs. Shawn Michaels in Feud
HKCKHDF

Triple H vs. Shamrock
RKCKHNF

Triple H vs. Kane
JJBKGFD

Triple H vs. Kane in Feud
MMTMPQR

Triple H vs. the Rock
CMTMPGR

Triple H vs. Farooq for IC Title
NQSMNRQ

Triple H vs. Stone Cold
CTRPMJT

Triple H vs. Owen Hart in Cage
NSQPLTS

WWF WRESTLEMANIA 2000 (GBC)

The Rock vs. Ken Shamrock
FSDM

The Rock vs. Jeff Jarrett
FSH4

The Rock vs. Road Dogg
FSKN

The Rock vs. X-Pac
FSLH

The Rock vs. Mr. Ass
FSPL

The Rock vs. Val Venis
FSR6

The Rock vs. Big Boss Man
FSS3

The Rock vs. X-Pac
FSW9

The Rock vs. Triple H
FSXP

The Rock vs. Shawn Michaels
FSZ7

The Rock vs. the Big Show
FS2K

The Rock vs. Kane
FS30

The Rock vs. Mankind
FS6L

The Rock vs. Undertaker
FS7Z

The Rock vs. Steve Austin
FS!P

The Rock vs. Mankind
FTB8

The Rock vs. Big Boss Man
FTD8

Steve Austin vs. Ken Shamrock
CSD7

Steve Austin vs. Jeff Jarrett
CSGQ

Steve Austin vs. Road Dogg
CSK8

Steve Austin vs. X-Pac
CSL3

Steve Austin vs. Mr. Ass
CSP6

Steve Austin vs. Val Venis
CSQS

Steve Austin vs. Big Boss Man
CSTP

Steve Austin vs. X-Pac
CSVW

Steve Austin vs. Triple H
CSX9

Steve Austin vs. Shawn Michaels/Val Venis
CS0T

Steve Austin vs. the Big Show
C525

Steve Austin vs. Kane
CS4L

Steve Austin vs. Mankind
CS66

Steve Austin vs. the Rock
CS8K

Steve Austin vs. the Undertaker
CS!9

Steve Austin vs. Mankind
CTCV

Steve Austin vs. Big Boss Man
CTFV

The Undertaker vs. Val Venis
2BDM

The Undertaker vs. Road Dogg
2BH4

The Undertaker vs. X-Pac
2BKN

The Undertaker vs. Billy Gunn
2BLH

The Undertaker vs. Ken Shamrock
2BPL

The Undertaker vs. Big Boss Man
2BRN

The Undertaker vs. Shawn Michaels
2BS3

The Undertaker vs. Mr. Ass
2BW9

The Undertaker vs. Triple H
2BKP

The Undertaker vs. Kane
2B2K

The Undertaker vs. the Big Show
2B30

The Undertaker vs. Mankind
2B6L

The Undertaker vs. the Rock
2B7Z

The Undertaker vs. Steve Austin
2B!P

The Undertaker vs. Mankind
2CB8

The Undertaker vs. Shawn Michaels
2CD8

Billy Gunn vs. Road Dogg
PJH!

Billy Gunn vs. Val Venis
PJHT

Billy Gunn vs. Jeff Jarrett
PJKB

Billy Gunn vs. Shawn Michaels
PJM6

Billy Gunn vs. Big Boss Man
PJN9

Billy Gunn vs. Ken Shamrock
PJRW

Billy Gunn vs. the Big Show
PJSS

Billy Gunn vs. Shawn Michaels
PJWZ

Billy Gunn vs. Triple H
PJXC

Billy Gunn vs. X-Pac/Ken Shamrock
PJZX

Billy Gunn vs. Steve Austin
PJ18

Billy Gunn vs. the Undertaker
PJ3P

Billy Gunn vs. Kane
PJ59

Billy Gunn vs. the Rock
PJ7N

Billy Gunn vs. Mankind
PJ!C

Billy Gunn vs. Kane
PKBY

Billy Gunn vs. the Big Show
PKDY

X-MEN MUTANT ACADEMY

Fight As Phoenix
Press Down, Right, Down, up, Left, Right, B, and A at the title screen.

Fight As Apocalypse
Press Right, Left, Up, Down, Left, Up, B, and A at the title screen.

X-MEN: MUTANT WARS

Level 2
0KNG6HWB

Level 3
0LNG6HXQ

Level 4
0LNF7HYP

Level 5
0KPF7HZG

Level 6
1KPF7H0D

Level 7
1KPG7H19

Level 8
1KPF7J2C

Level 9
1KPF7J3L

X-MEN: WOLVERINE'S RAGE

Level 3
Wolverine Head, Claws, X, Wolverine Body

XTREME SPORTS

View Ending and Play Winner's Level
Start a new game, and enter name as "staff." Leave the sign-in hut and head left to the snack shop.

400 Medals
Choose New Game and go to the sign-in hut. Enter name as "xyzzy." After exiting the hut, Hold A and press Select. You can toggle back and forth between having 400 Medals and No Medals.

Secret Path Through the Credits
Beat the game. During the end credits, which are actually a playable level, look for a low building immediately before the programmer's credit. Double jump on top of it, and jump up onto on a series of invisible clouds that lead to the right. If you make it all the way, you'll see a special message!

View Scrapbook and Debug Menu
At the title screen, press Left (5),Up (5), Right (5), Down (5), Select (5).

YODA STORIES (GBC)

Level 2
XKJ

Level 3
GJP

Level 4
TDM

Level 5
WTM

Level 6
ZBV

Level 7
QTC

Level 8
TGR

Level 9
VDP

Level 10
BFG

Level 11
FNP

Level 12
STJ

Level 13
FTG

Level 14
BLP

Level 15
YSF

YUU YUU HAKUSHO 4

Play As Raizen
In Vs. Comp mode, highlight Enki. Hold B+Select and press Right.

Play As Lei Zhang
In Vs. Comp mode, highlight Enki. Hold B+Select and press Right.

ZEN: INTERGALACTIC NINJA

Level 1: After Smog
[Blank], Bottle, Tire, Can

Level 2: After Water
Newspaper, [Blank], Newspaper, Tire

Level 3: After Dust
Tire, Newspaper, [Blank], Can

Final
Bottle, Tire, Can (2)

Game Boy Advance

ADVANCE GTA

Hidden Go-Kart Mode
To access the extra Go-Kart mode, play through the Championship mode and beat the beginner, middle, and high-speed classes. You get a new car (a go-kart) after the last race you win. Go to the main menu and the first option that was unlockable will read extra.

Formula 1 Mode
To access the extra Formula 1 mode, play through the Championship mode and beat all four of the classes with a first place in each race. You get a new car (Formula 1 racecar) after the last race. At the Menu screen, the Extra 2 option will be available.

ADVANCE RALLY

Co-Driver Mode
Win first place in all races in World Rally mode.

Information in this section was contributed by nileriver.

Hidden Track
Win first place in Co-Driver mode.

ADVANCE WARS

In-Game Reset
Press Start + Select + B + A during gameplay. Note: Do not use this while the Game Boy Advance is linked to a Gamecube or it may cause data loss.

Deleted Saved Games
Hold L + Right + Select when turning on the Game Boy Advance.

Ghost Mode
Hold B during your turn.

Advance Campaign Mode
Successfully complete Campaign mode. Enter the Battle Maps screen and buy the "Advance Campaign" item for one coin. Hold Select and choose Campaign mode to begin an advanced campaign, with a more difficult CPU opponent.

Field Training Bonuses
Successfully complete field training mode to unlock the "War Room," "Campaign," "Design Maps," "Stats," and "Special Intel" options.

Quickly Finish Field Training
Select the final battle in Field Training. Win that battle to unlock all options that normally require Field Training to be completed.

ALIENATORS: EVOLUTION CONTINUES

Full Ammunition
Enter RBJPXCKC as a password.

Skip Level
Enter the following codes as passwords to skip to specific levels.

Level 2
MDKMZKCC

Level 3
BHSZSKTC

Level 4
ZKTSHKMC

Level 5
JLPFDKHB

Level 6
HMDBRKCB

Level 7
GLDKLKZB

Level 8
GLPKLKRB

Level 9
GLDJBKKF

Level 10
GLPJBKFF

Level 11
GLDKBKZF

Level 12
GLPKBKRF

Level 13
GLDJLKHD

ARMY MEN ADVANCE

All Levels Unlocked
At the Password screen, enter NQRDGTPB.

ARMY MEN: OPERATION GREEN

Skip Level
Enter the following passwords to skip to a specific level.

Level 2: Workin' 9 til 5
5VKPR6*B

Level 3: With a Bucket, a Spade, and a Hand Grenade
5PK5LL*4

Level 4: Goin' Downtown
Y8DTF4HK

Level 5: Down on the Farm
62BVXHXY

Level 6: Baby, Light My Fire
MQ5310VP

Level 7: Here a Tan, There a Tan
SZQR6W1J

Level 8: The Rumble in the Jungle
44BQQCWH

Level 9: The Donkey Ride
F4J1ZRWG

Level 10: Top Brass in Trouble
FFOOWP36

Level 11: Jungle Fever
*HBNVVV4

Level 12: Spider's Web
85M3QCF*

ATLANTIS: THE LOST EMPIRE

Skip Level
Enter the following passwords to skip to a specific level.

Level 2
BMQDNPJS

Level 3
BRZSGZDY

Level 4
BVMJFYLG

Level 5
B7JHPMHC

Level 6
C6XQLUNF

Final Level
COCNQQIY

BATMAN VENGEANCE

View All Animations
Enter NORA as a password.

Unlimited Smoke Bombs
Enter LSMRTG as a password in a story or in Advance mode.

Skip Level
Enter one of the following passwords to skip to a specific level.

Level 2 (Normal)
GOTHAM

Level 3 (Normal)
BATMAN

Level 4 (Normal)
BARBARA

Level 5 (Normal)
GRAYSON

Level 6 (Normal)
ROBIN

Level 7 (Normal)
TIM

Level 8 (Normal)
BATGIRL

Level 9 (Normal)
FRIES

Level 10 (Normal)
VICTOR

Level 11 (Normal)
ALFRED

Level 12 (Normal)
CATWOMAN

Level 13 (Normal)
JAMES

Level 14 (Normal)
DRAKE

Level 15 (Normal)
HARVEY

Level 16 (Normal)
SELINA

Level 17 (Normal)
BATARANG

Level 18 (Normal)
BRUCE

Level 19 (Normal)
QUINZEL

Level 20 (Normal)
JACK

Level 21 (Normal)
EDWARD

Level 1 (Advanced)
ARKHAM

Level 2 (Advanced)
WAYNE

Level 3 (Advanced)
AMY

Level 4 (Advanced)
NYGMA

Level 5 (Advanced)
CARRIE

Level 6 (Advanced)
WESKER

Level 7 (Advanced)
BULLOCK

Level 8 (Advanced)
GORDON

Level 9 (Advanced)
JONES

Level 10 (Advanced)
OSWALD

Level 11 (Advanced)
TALIA

Level 12 (Advanced)
MONTOYA

Level 13 (Advanced)
SCARFACE

Level 14 (Advanced)
CREEPER

Level 15 (Advanced)
DENT

Level 16 (Advanced)
KYLE

BRITNEY'S DANCE BEAT

Activate Cheat Mode
Enter HMNFK as a password to unlock all levels and bonuses.

CASTLEVANIA: CIRCLE OF THE MOON

Unlock Magician Mode
To unlock Magician mode after you beat the game, enter the name "FIREBALL" at the Data screen. You will begin the game with all DSS Cards available right away.

Get the Shining Armor
To get the Shining Armor, beat the Battle Arena. It is in the chapel tower.

Unlock Fighter Mode
To enable Fighter mode, beat the game twice (the second time in Magician mode). Your stats are higher then usual, but there are no DSS cards to collect.

CASTLEVANIA: HARMONY OF DISSONANCE

Play as Maxim Kischine
Enter MAXIM as a name after completing the game at least once. He is faster and jumps higher than Belmont.

No Magic
Enter NO MAGIC as a name after completing the game at least once.

Hard Mode
Enter HARDGAME as a name after completing the game at least once. A voice at the start of the introduction confirms correct code entry.

Boss Rush Mode
Successfully complete the game to unlock the Boss Rush option. There are three levels (easy, normal, and hard) that must be unlocked by playing each in succession, starting with easy.

Classic Simon
Unlock Boss Rush mode, then press Up(2), Down(2), Left, Right, Left, Right, B, A, Select at the Konami logo. Select Boss Rush mode to play as the NES version of Simon.

Sound Test Mode
Successfully complete the game with the good ending (where you rescue Maxim and Lydie).

CASTLEVANIA: WHITE NIGHT CONCERTO

Play as Maxim Kischine
Enter MAXIM as a name after completing the game at least once. He is faster and jumps higher than Belmont.

No Magic
Enter NO MAGIC as a name after completing the game at least once.

Hard Mode
Enter HARDGAME as a name after completing the game at least once. A voice at the start of the introduction confirms correct code entry.

Boss Rush Mode
Successfully complete the game to unlock the Boss Rush option. There are three levels (easy, normal, and hard) that must be unlocked by playing each in succession, starting with easy.

Classic Simon
Unlock Boss Rush mode, then press Up(2), Down(2), Left, Right, Left, Right, B, A, Select at the Konami logo. Select Boss Rush mode to play as the NES version of Simon.

Sound Test Mode
Successfully complete the game with the good ending (where you rescue Maxim and Lydie).

CHU CHU ROCKET

Unlock New Modes
Chu Chu Rocket has three additional modes. Complete Normal mode to unlock Hard mode. Complete Hard mode to unlock Special mode. Complete Special mode to unlock Mania mode.

CRASH BANDICOOT: THE HUGE ADVENTURE

Turbo
Successfully complete the game to unlock the ability to run faster in subsequent games. Hold L during gameplay to move faster.

Double Jump
Defeat N. Gin on the boss stage on the second floor to get the Double Jump.

Super Belly Flop
Get all the items and you will receive the Super Belly Flop.

Tornado Spin
Defeat Tiny on the boss stage on the third floor to get the Tornado Spin.

Bonus level
Finish the game with a 100 percent completion. Play again and fight the final boss. Win the battle to play a level featuring mutated bosses.

CRUIS'N VELOCITY

Skip Level
Enter one of the following passwords to skip to a specific level.

Level 1
HLDDRTSN

Level 2
HLDDSNST

Level 3
HLDDNRLN

Level 4
HLDDHVGD

CT SPECIAL FORCES

Unlock Special Characters
Enter 0202 as a password.

Skip Level
Enter one of the following passwords to skip to a specific level.

Level 2
1608

Level 3
2111

Final Level
1705

DARK ARENA

All Keys
Enter KNGHTSFR as a password.

All Maps
Enter LMSPLLNG as a password.

All Weapons
Enter THRBLDNS as a password.

Unlimited Ammunition
Enter NDCRSDRT as a password.

Unlimited Health
Enter HLGNDSBR as a password.

Level Skip
Enter NFTRWLLH as a password. Go to the Map screen, and press Select to advance to the next level.

Sound Effects Test
Enter CRSDR as a password. Enter the Game Options menu, then set "Sound FX" to Off, then back On to hear a random sound.

God Mode
Enter S_X_N as a password. Note that the underscore ("_") indicates a space. This code activates unlimited health, all weapons, all keys, unlimited ammunition, all maps, and the level skip features.

DEXTER'S LABORATORY: DEESASTER STRIKES!

Invincibility
Pause gameplay, then press L(3), R(5), L, R(4), L(3).

Extra Life
Pause gameplay, then press L(2), R(2), L, R, L(3), R, L(2), R(2), L(2). Repeat to get more lives for a maximum of nine.

Extra Ray Gun Ammunition
Pause gameplay, then press L, R(3), L(2), R(2), L(4), R, L(2), R.

Faster Movement
Pause gameplay, then press L, R(4), L, R, L, R(2), L(2), R, L, R(2).

GAME BOY ADVANCE

Less Damage

Pause gameplay, then press L, R(4), L(3), R, L(6), R.

Higher Jumps

Pause gameplay, then press L(2), R(6), L(2), R(2), L(3), R.

Faster Opponents

Pause gameplay, then press L, R(5), L(4), R(4), L(2).

Slower Opponents

Pause gameplay, then press L(2), R(3), L, R(3), L(2), R(2), L(2), R.

Stronger Opponents

Pause gameplay, then press L(2), R(4), L, R(3), L(6).

Stronger Dexter

Pause gameplay, then press L(2), R(3), L(2), R, L(2), R(2), L, R, L, R. Dexter can destroy robots more easily by punching or kicking for a limited amount of time.

Reverse Controls

Pause gameplay, then press L, R(6), L, R, L(2), R(2), L(3).

DOOM

God Mode

Press Start to pause gameplay, then hold L + R and press A(2), B, A(5).

Disable God Mode

Press Start to pause gameplay, then hold L + R and press A(2), B, A, B(4).

Level Skip

In single-player games, press Start to pause gameplay, then hold L + R and press A, B, A(2), B(3), A.

Advance Ten Levels

In single-player games, press Start to pause gameplay, then hold L + R and press A, B, A(2), B(2), A(2). You will advance ten levels, depending on the current level. Note that there are only 24 maps in single-player games; therefore, this code won't work when starting from maps higher than 14, "Halls of the Damned".

Computer Map

Press Start to pause gameplay, then hold L + R and press B, A(7).

Information in this section was contributed by manakin8000.

Radiation Suit

Press Start to pause gameplay, then hold L + R and press B(2), A(6).

Invincibility

Press Start to pause gameplay, then hold L + R and press B(3), A(5).

Berserk

Press Start to pause gameplay, then hold L + R and press B, A, B, A(5).

All Weapons, Items, Keys

Press Start to pause gameplay, then hold L + R and press A, B(2), A(5).

DRIVEN

All Cars and Tracks

Enter 29801 as a code.

Game Stop Car

Enter 07913 as a code.

Master Car

Enter 62972 as a code.

EARTHWORM JIM

Skip to Buttville

Pause the game and enter: L, A, Up, R, A, R, A, Select.

Skip to Down the Tubes

Pause the game and enter Up, L, Down, A, R, A.

Skip to For Pete's Sake

Pause the game and enter R, L, R, L, A, R.

Skip to Level 5

Pause the game and enter R, L, A, B, B, A, L, R.

Skip to Snot a Problem

Pause the game and enter R, Up, Select, L, R, Left.

Skip to What the Heck

Pause the game and enter Select, R, B, Down, L.

E.T.: THE EXTRA-TERRESTRIAL

Skip Level

Enter the following passwords to skip to a specific level.

Level 2

Up, Up, A, Down, Down, B, R, L

Level 3

Left, Up, Right, Down, L, A, R, B

Level 4

A, Left, B, Right, L, Up, R, Down

Level 5

L, R, R, L, A, Up, B, Left

Level 6

L, Left, R, Right, A, A, B, A

Level 7

B, R, B, L, A, Up, B, Up

Level 8

Up, Up, A, Down, Down, Left, A, B

Level 9

Right, B, B, Left, Up, R, R, L

Level 10

Left, Left, A, L, Right, Right, B, R

F-14 TOMCAT

Skip Level

Enter one of the following passwords to skip to a specific level.

Level 2 (Novice)
DHGJ KLFF

Level 3 (Novice)
GSDF BFPT

Level 4 (Novice)
RRHC FDVM

Level 5 (Novice)
BPSX FDNF

Level 6 (Novice)
LDFS DTKQ

Level 7 (Novice)
PXSB SZNJ

Level 8 (Novice)
DKXZ GZQK

Level 9 (Novice)
GKQB GHCT

Level 10 (Novice)
DTRH RPFJ

Level 11 (Novice)
WZPK JYZX

Level 12 (Novice)
JDZFLKFV

Level 13 (Novice)
SPNG DRRG

Level 14 (Novice)
SFGF JHDH

Level 15 (Novice)
LPFH PRFZ

Level 16 (Novice)
TDKZ XSHX

Level 17 (Novice)
DGBV KMNB

Level 18 (Novice)
KJHG RJCB

Level 19 (Novice)
VBMQ RWTP

Level 20 (Novice)
LKFD SPBV

Level 21 (Novice)
NHDC DKPM

Level 2 (Ace)
DHGJ

Level 3 (Ace)
KJTR DBPT

Level 4 (Ace)
RVBP ZJVM

Level 5 (Ace)
BMNQ YLNF

Level 6 (Ace)
LFMS DNBQ

Level 7 (Ace)
PGHP CZNJ

Level 8 (Ace)
DKDG BPQK

Level 9 (Ace)
GSYP ZLCT

Level 10 (Ace)
DCZX RPQR

Level 11 (Ace)
WRTN JYSX

Level 12 (Ace)
JDPQ MLRT

Level 13 (Ace)
SPBX BMRG

Level 14 (Ace)
SPXP RGDH

Level 15 (Ace)
LPFG NBGZ

Level 16 (Ace)
TQWJ GZHN

Level 17 (Ace)
BGJK SZPQ

Level 18 (Ace)
PLMN HRTY

Level 19 (Ace)
GLMR TRRC

Level 20 (Ace)
NHDJ PBCX

Level 21 (Ace)
LCML FLTC

FINAL FIGHT ONE

Change Control Settings
Pause gameplay and hold L + R + B + A.

Alpha Cody and Alpha Guy
Press Left or Right at the Character Selection screen to choose these fighters. Alpha Cody is bigger, and Alpha Guy is stronger.

FIRE PRO WRESTLING

Unlock All Wrestlers
Here's a trick to unlock all of the grapplers in the game. Edit a player. On the Name Entry screen, go to Name Entry and begin editing the name. For the nickname, put "ALL." For first name enter "STYLE." For last name put "CLEAR." Put Exchange to "OFF" and at Middle, enter a space. Press start and return to the main menu. All wrestlers will be unlocked.

F-ZERO

Faster Vehicles
Press A, B, L, A(2), R, B at the title screen.

Alternate Vehicles
Press A(2), B, A, L, R, A, B, L at the title screen.

Slower Opponents
Press A, R, L, B, A(2), B, L at the title screen.

All Tracks
Press B, L, B, A, R, B(2), A(2) at the title screen.

Password Screen
Press L, R, Start, R, L, Select at the machine selection screen in Grand Prix mode.

In-Game Reset
Press Select + Start + A + B during gameplay.

GRADIUS GALAXIES

All Power-Ups
Press Start to pause gameplay, then press Up(2), Down(2), L, R, L, R, B, A, Start. This cheat can be used only a limited number of times until it causes your ship to self-destruct.

Self-Destruct
Press Start to pause gameplay, then press Up(2), Down(2), Left, Right, Left, Right, B, A, Start.

Delete Saved Game
Enter the Options screen, highlight "Exit," then hold L + R + B and press Start.

Challenge A Mode
Successfully complete the game to unlock the Challenge A option at the main menu.

Challenge B Mode
Successfully complete the game in Challenge A mode.

GT ADVANCE 2: RALLY RACING

All Cars
Hold L + B and press Left at the title screen.

All Tracks
Hold L + B and press Right at the title screen.

All Tune Ups
Hold L + B and press Up at the title screen.

Extra Modes
Hold L + B and press Down at the title screen.

GT ADVANCE CHAMPIONSHIP RACING

Unlock F1 Mode
At the title screen, press and hold L + R, press Left, then B. The Extra 2 option will be available. This allows you to race with F1 cars.

Unlock Go-Kart Mode
At the title screen, press and hold L + R, then press Right, then B. The Extra 1 option will be available. This allows you to race with go-karts.

View Credits
At the title screen, press and hold L + R, press Up, B. This allows you to see the Credits at the end of the game.

GUILTY GEAR X

Alternate Costumes
Press Start or Select when choosing a fighter at the Character Selection screen.

Fight as Dizzy or Testament
Press Down, Right(2), Up, Start at the Press Start screen.

Dizzy
Defeat Dizzy's daredevil version in Survival mode. Alternately, defeat Dizzy on Stage 10 in Arcade mode.

Testament
Defeat Testament's daredevil version in Survival mode. Alternately, defeat Testament in Stage 9 and Dizzy on Stage 10 in Arcade mode.

Extra Mode
Defeat a fighter's daredevil version in Survival mode to unlock the extra mode for that fighter. The fighter's extra version can execute new moves and supers.

Original Mode
Successfully complete the game in Survival mode to unlock the "Original Mode" selection at the Options screen.

HARRY POTTER AND THE SORCERER'S STONE

Get 10 Extra Lives
Press Select, B, A, B, A, B(2), A(2) during gameplay.

ICE AGE

Level Select
Enter NTTTTT as a password.

Art Gallery
Enter MFKRPH as a password.

INSPECTOR GADGET: ADVANCE MISSION

Skip Level
Enter one of the following passwords to skip to a specific level.

Statue of Liberty: In the Statue
*7*MM14

Statue of Liberty: The Flame of Liberty
*3HMLI4

The Tower: The Tower Keeps Watch
R3*3M64

The Tower: The Lift
R7H3L64

The Tower: Higher than Anything
*CH3L24

The Great Wall: At the Foot of the Great Wall
*H*3M24

The Great Wall: On the Great Wall
R5*3MR4

Big Ben: The Palace
*3RM33P

Big Ben: The Top
RHRM37P

Egypt: The Valley of the Kings
RC7M27P

Egypt: The Great Pyramid
*9R33XP

IRIDION 3D

Unlock All Levels
Go to the Password screen and enter S3L3CT0N. Press OK. Go to the Password screen from the main menu and enter SH0WT1M3, then press OK.

View All Bosses
To view an end level boss, go to the Game Options screen and highlight Start Level. Select your level, then highlight the option for Start at Boss. Select Yes, then OK and you will be at the boss fight!

JACKIE CHAN ADVENTURES: LEGEND OF THE DARK HAND

Activate Cheat Mode
Hold R and press B, A, Left, Down, Up, Right at the Press Start screen to unlock all levels and scrolls. Alternately, hold R and press B, A, Up, Down, Left, Right.

KAO THE KANGAROO

Skip Level
Enter one of the following icon passwords to skip to a specific level.

Ancient Ruins
Flag, Bomb, Kao's Face, Boxing Glove, Kao's Face

Bear Peak
Frog, Frog, Kao's Face, Boxing Glove, Kao's Face

Big Blizzard
Lamp, Palm Tree, Heart, Boxing Glove, Kao's Face

Crocodile Island
Heart, Palm Tree, Lamp, Boxing Glove, Kao's Face

Deadly Waterfall
Boxing Glove, Mushroom, Evergreen, Boxing Glove, Kao's Face

Evil Descent
Owl, Butterfly, Bird, Boxing Glove, Kao's Face

Frozen Lake
Bird, Key, Frog, Boxing Glove, Kao's Face

Holy Temple
Bomb, Kao's Face, Boxing Glove, Boxing Glove, Kao's Face

Hunter
Palm Tree, Lamp, Frog, Boxing Glove, Kao's Face

Hypnodjin
Bomb, Flag, Coin, Boxing Glove, Kao's Face

Ice Caves
Key, Key, Kao's Face, Boxing Glove, Kao's Face

Island Shores
Coin, Heart, Palm Tree, Boxing Glove, Kao's Face

Lightning Speed
Palm Tree, Heart, Coin, Boxing Glove, Kao's Face

Little Valley
Butterfly, Bird, Key, Boxing Glove, Kao's Face

Lost Village
Evergreen, Fish, Owl, Boxing Glove, Kao's Face

Megasaurus Ferocious
Fish, Owl, Butterfly, Boxing Glove, Kao's Face

Mythical Caves
Mushroom, Evergreen, Fish, Boxing Glove, Kao's Face

Neverending Slide
Flag, Coin, Heart, Boxing Glove, Kao's Face

Peril Desert
Heart, Coin, Flag, Boxing Glove, Kao's Face

Trade Village
Coin, Flag, Bomb, Boxing Glove, Kao's Face

KONAMI KRAZY RACERS

Unlock Bear
Bear is a secret character hidden within one of the courses in the game. To get him, begin a race (not a free race, but an actual competition) on Cyber Field 2. As you approach the finish line, grab the blue diamond that sits between the two gaps. Complete the race and save. Bear is now available on the Character Selection screen.

Unlock King
King is a secret character hidden within the Sky Bridge 2 course. To get him, begin a race (not a free race, but an actual competition) on Sky Bridge 2. Grab the Blue Bell and use it to make a blind leap to the right at the first large gap, landing on a distant platform. Here is the blue diamond. Grab it, finish the race, and save. King is now available on the Character Selection screen.

Unlock Vic Viper
Vic Viper is a secret character hidden within the Moon Road course. To get him, begin a race (not a free race, an actual competition) on the Moon Road. At the first long gap, use a boost to make a blind jump to the right. Land on a long platform with the blue diamond on it. After you collect it, finish the race and save the game. Vic Viper is now selectable on the Character Selection screen.

LEGO BIONICLE

Activate Cheat Mode
Enter one of the following codes as a name and select "End." Press A, Start, B, Start, then select "Quit Game," "Yes," then "No."

Master Code
Enter B9RBRN as a name.

Gali Mini-Game
Enter 9MA268 as a name. Alternately, successfully complete the game as Gali.

Kopaka Snow Ball Sling Mini-Game
Enter V33673 as a name. Alternately, successfully complete the game as Kopaka.

Lewa Mini-Game
Enter 3LT154 as a name. Alternately, successfully complete the game as Lewa.

Onua Crab Dig Mini-Game
Enter 8MR472 as a name. Alternately, successfully complete the game as Onua.

Pohatu Football Mini-Game
Enter 5MG834 as a name. Alternately, successfully complete the game as Pohatu.

Tahu Lava Surf Mini-Game
Enter 4CR487 as a name. Alternately, successfully complete the game as Tahu.

LILO AND STITCH

Skip Level
Use the following icon combinations as passwords to skip to specific levels.

Beach
Stitch, Stitch, Stitch, Stitch, Stitch, Stitch, Stitch

Mothership
UFO, Scrump, Stitch, Rocket, UFO, Stitch, UFO

Space Cruiser
Lilo, Rocket, Stitch, Rocket, Rocket, Scrump, Stitch

Junkyard Planet
UFO, Rocket, Stitch, Rocket, Rocket, Scrump, Stitch

Escape!
Stitch, Scrump, UFO, Gun, Rocket, Scrump, UFO

Rescue
Flower, Scrump, UFO, Gun, Gun, Gun, UFO

Final Challenge
Lilo, Pineapple, Flower, Pineapple, Gun, Gun, Stitch

End
Pineapple, Pineapple, Pineapple, Pineapple, Stitch, Stitch, Stitch

---

MARIO KART SUPER CIRCUIT

Delete Game
Hold L + R + B + Start and power on the system to delete the current saved data.

Special Cup Circuit
Win a gold cup in all races to unlock the Special Cup circuit.

Super Mario Kart tracks
Get 100 coins or more by the end of the cup to unlock extra tracks. Press L or R to view and play them. Once you get an "A" rank on every cup on every class you will unlock all of the original courses from Super Mario Kart.

Alternate Title Screen
Successfully complete all circuits in all classes to change the background color of the title screen.

Waluigi
Win every cup (50, 100, 150) and get gold medals in everything, including the secret levels.

Control Player Selection Screen
Press L to shoot a green shell or press R to jump at the Character Selection screen.

MEN IN BLACK: THE SERIES

Invincibility
Enter LVFRVRDD as a password.

All Weapons
Enter LLWPNSDD as a password.

Unlimited Ammunition
Enter NFNTMMDD as a password. Note: This code also unlocks the game's ending.

Skip Level
Enter one of the following passwords to skip to a specific level.

Episode 2: Forest Landing Site
FCHTRMNS

Episode 3: Alien Technology Lab
HSDSHSBS

Episode 4: Rocket Silo
MXNMSNNG

Episode 5: MIB Safehouse
THXBXSCK

Episode 6: Halloween in Manhattan
NNTNDWNY

Ending
NFNTMMDD

MONSTERS, INC.

Skip Level
Enter one of the following passwords to skip to a specific level.

Level 2
SJBOGS

Level 3
MKB2Z7

Level 4
VPB971

Level 5
LLCOBK

Level 6
8PW2DY

Level 7
NQWOJF

Level 8
WRC9SQ

Level 9
3RC!94

Level 10
XRDZB1

Level 11
YRX2DQ

Level 12
3NX2JX

Level 13
LTD!SK

Level 14
ZTFZD8

Level 15
BYY2NL

Level 16
M2F9S7

Level 17
LYGOBO

Level 18
1FZ2CJ

Level 19
F2Z2FM

Level 20
F2Z2KR

Level 21
PNG!TL

Level 22
WRG!!C

NBA JAM 2002

Beach and Street Courts
Enter LHNGGDBLBJGT as a password.

Playoffs
Enter MKJLBFQBLDGH as a password to be in the playoffs as the Toronto Raptors.

Extra Points
When you're shooting the ball, go to center court and throw. Sometimes you'll get lucky and get up to nine points if you sink it. However, you could get as little as one point.

NFL BLITZ 2002

Activate Cheat Mode
Press L, B, and A to enter the following codes on the match-up screen in Exhibition mode. The numbers in the following list indicate the number of times each button is pressed. After the first part of the code has been entered, press the D-Pad in the indicated direction to enable it. Example, to enter 1-2-3 Right, press L, B(2), A(3), Right.

No Random Fumbles
3-2-1 Right

Unlimited Turbo
4-3-2 Right

Ogre Field
1-3-2 Right

Snow Field
2-2-5 Right

Shadow Players
3-1-3 Right

NHL 2002

Zamboni in Introduction Sequence
Hold R + L and power on the Game Boy Advance. Hold the buttons until the Zamboni appears (instead of the puck) during the introduction sequence.

Bonus Teams and Extra Creation Points
Wait for Demo mode to begin, then hold Select and rapidly tap L, R repeatedly. When the demonstration is about to end press Start but keep Select held while tapping L and R. Keep tapping them until you hear a voice say "It's in the game." If you do it correctly, you should get the Budcat and Tiburon teams in Exhibition mode and 1,000 points for creating a player.

NO RULES

Skip Level
Enter one of the following passwords to skip to a specific level.

Boss 1
13TYNLP18J34

Level 2
DPTYNLP17ZM!

Boss 2
PPTDDLS18J26

Level 3
NKTDDLS18J24

Boss 3
K7RFNLKH8J39

Level 4
JTRFNLKH8J3v

Boss 4
TFQFNL9H8J2R

PAC-MAN COLLECTION

Pac Attack Passwords
Here are the passwords for the last five levels of *Pac Attack*:

96: YLW

97: PNN

98: SPR

99: CHB

100: LST

PETER PAN: RETURN TO NEVERLAND

Skip Level
Enter one of the following passwords to skip to a specific level.

Jungle
RGCKYD

Beach
PGCMMD

Forest
CNCGKG

Ship
ZGWYCR

PITFALL: THE MAYAN ADVENTURE

Infinite Continues
In order to continue forever, use all of your lives in the first level, then tap B, B, B when the Continue screen comes up. The counter stops counting down and you're able to continue forever.

View All Levels
To view all levels, enter the following button presses at the title screen: L, Select, A, Select, R, A, L, Select. Press Select and R or L to scroll through the levels. Press Left to make the boomerang appear around the word "Start."

PLANET OF THE APES

Skip Level
Enter the following passwords to skip to a specific level.

Level 2
64N4HY

Level 3
F5BMGF

Level 4
B1SKZR

Level 5
76FNHB

Level 6
P7GRXK

Level 7
6B7VM#

Level 8
QK6293

Level 9
JDDUTJ

Level 10
046PJ#

Level 11
3#9QLS

Level 12
C12KYY

Level 13
CBCYPH

POWER RANGERS: TIME FORCE

Skip Level
Enter one of the following passwords to skip to a specific level.

Level 2
DBBR

Level 3
GCB5

Level 4
HCB9

Final Battle
8QSD

RAYMAN ADVANCE

Unlimited Continues
To continue without losing a continue in the process, go to the Continue screen and press Up, Down, Right, Left, then Start.

RAZOR FREESTYLE SCOOTER

Skip Level
Enter one of the following passwords to skip to a specific level.

Aircraft Carrier Completed
VDY3ZJ6LJVCQBF

Circus Completed
ZBF4GJ5VJVCQBF

Construction Site Completed
QHY4LJ2LHZCQBF

Scooter Park Completed
SBY5VJ4BJVCQBF

Shopping Mall Completed
QLY67J3BJVCQBF

Sports Stadium Completed
7JY4GJZBJVCQBF

READY 2 RUMBLE BOXING: ROUND 2

Unlock Michael Jackson
At the main menu, highlight the Arcade option, then press Left(2), Right (2), Left, Right, L + R to get Michael Jackson. You'll hear a cheering noise if you entered the code correctly.

Unlock Rumble Man
When you go to the menu, highlight CHAMPIONSHIP. Press Left(2), Right, Left, Right(2), Left, Right, and Left. Then, press L and R at the same time. You'll hear some cheering, then you can play as Rumble Man.

Unlock Shaquille O'Neal
At the main menu, highlight the Survival option, then press Left(4), Right(2), Left(2), Right, then press L + R to get O'Neal.

ROCKET POWER: DREAM SCHEME

Skip Level
Enter one of the following passwords to skip to a specific level.

After Ocean Shores Beach
4GWD!KL1

After Mad Town
MFKGTB!R

After Elementary School
2V74BFDG

After Town Square
6!LN99V5

After Neighborhood
?FXX6BLJ

After Spooky Woods
2L!DZHS8

Dr. Stepatone's Hideout
TW1ST3R!

End
B!P356BT

RUGRATS: CASTLE CAPERS

Skip Level
Enter one of the following passwords to skip to a specific level.

Level 2
QGPCJNWXGWCB

Level 3
QQTKJYWLGKGF

Level 4
CTKLJKGLSCQR

Level 5
RLPTKKGLWKWP

Level 6
FZLDVHMMDQRB

End
JSJRJKSLXCFJ

THE SCORPION KING

Play as Cassandra
Enter Mathayus, Menmon, Isis, Mathayus as a password to play as Cassandra with all runes.

Level Select
Enter the following character colors at the Password screen: Blue, Green, Green, Blue.

SONIC THE HEDGEHOG ADVANCE

Tails as Partner
Highlight Sonic at the Character Selection screen and press Up. Next, highlight Tails and press Down. Then, highlight Knuckles and press L. Finally, highlight Amy and press R. Highlight Sonic and press A to select him. Tails will follow you during the game, but can't be controlled.

Moon Zone
Collect all seven Emeralds for all characters. Successfully complete the game as Sonic to unlock the Moon Zone.

Hidden Sound Test Mode Songs
To get more than the 39 default songs in Sound Test mode, successfully complete The Moon Zone, Extra mode, or unlock the Super Sonic Ending. Three additional songs will be available.

SPIDERMAN: THE MOVIE

Unlock Cheat Mode
Successfully complete the game, collecting all of the small red spiders and taking the pictures on each stage to unlock the cheats (armor upgrade, strength enhancement, and level cheat) in the Secrets menu.

Ending Bonus
Successfully complete the game to unlock the level select option at the main menu. Press Start during gameplay to choose a new level.

Movie Clips
Take pictures on every level to unlock all movie clips.

SPONGE BOB SQUAREPANTS: SUPERSPONGE

Skip Level
Enter the following passwords to skip to a specific level.

Level 1
BGNR

Level 2
CLMB

Level 3
KVNF

Level 4
WKGA

Level 5
DFVJ

Level 6
NGPS

Level 7
WMCV

Level 8
XNAD

Level 9
HPJQ

Level 10
QHDG

Level 11
WFXM

Level 12
MNTL

Level 13
QGAV

Level 14
LXHK

Level 15
HGCD

Level 16
CNXK

Level 17
LKKV

Level 18
PVHS

Level 19
JAST

Final Level
WMBT

SPY HUNTER

Arcade Mode
Enter EDACRA as a name.

Delete Saved Games
Press Left(2), Right, Left, R(2) at the Copyright screen.

Delete High Scores
Press Up(2), Down, L, R, L at the Copyright screen.

Super Agent Mode
Successfully complete the game with all Primary Objectives and Secondary Objectives.

SPYRO: SEASON OF ICE

Level Portals Opened
Press Up(2), Down(2), Left, Right, Up, Down, A when "Press Start" appears at the title screen. All level portals can be opened without collecting the required fairies.

99 Lives
Press Left, Right(3), Down, Up, Right, Up, A when "Press Start" appears at the title screen.

Warp
Press Left, Right(2), Left, Up, Left(2), Right, A when "Press Start" appears at the title screen.

Warp Unlock All Levels
Press Down, Up, Down, Left, Right, Up, Left, Up, A when "Press Start" appears at the title screen.

Unlock All Levels
Press Down(2), Up(2), Left, Right, Up, Down, A when "Press Start" appears at the title screen.

Unlimited Health in Sparx Worlds
Press Down, Up(2), Down, Left, Right(2), Left, A when "Press Start" appears at the title screen.

Unlimited Weapons in Sparx Worlds
Press Down, Right, Up, Left(2), Up, Right, Down, A when "Press Start" appears at the title screen.

Extra Sparx Weapons
Press Right, Up, Right, Left, Down, Up, Left, Down, A when "Press Start" appears at the title screen. Then, use one of the following commands during gameplay in Sparx worlds.

Invincibility Shield
Press Up + Select.

Smart Bomb
Press Right + Select.

Rapid Fire
Press Left + Select.

Homing Bombs
Press Down + Select.

All Keys
Press L + Select.

STAR WARS: EPISODE 2 - ATTACK OF THE CLONES

Skip Level
Enter the following passwords to skip to a specific level.

Level 2 as Padawan
BHDBGJ

Level 3 as Padawan
BHFBHJ

Level 4 as Padawan
BHGBDJ

Level 5 as Padawan
BHHBFJ

Level 6 as Padawan
BGKBCK

Level 7 as Padawan
BGLBSK

Level 8 as Padawan
BGMBTK

Level 9 as Padawan
BGNBQK

Level 10 as Padawan
BGPBRK

Level 11 as Padawan
BGQBNK

Final Level as Padawan
BGRBPK

Level 2 as Jedi Knight
BJDGGM

Level 3 as Jedi Knight
BJFGHM

Level 4 as Jedi Knight
BJGGDM

Level 5 as Jedi Knight
BJHGFM

Level 6 as Jedi Knight
BJKGCM

Level 7 as Jedi Knight
BJLGSM

Level 8 as Jedi Knight
BJMGTM

Level 9 as Jedi Knight
BJNGQM

Level 10 as Jedi Knight
BJPGRM

Level 11 as Jedi Knight
BGQGNP

STAR WARS: JEDI POWER BATTLES

Skip Level
Enter the following passwords to skip to a specific level.

Level 2 as Obi-Wan
WFJ3BPG

Level 3 as Obi-Wan
XFJ3BYG

Level 4 as Obi-Wan
YFJ3B6G

Level 5 as Obi-Wan
ZFJ3BFH

Level 6 as Obi-Wan
0FJ3BPH

Level 7 as Obi-Wan
1FJ3BYH

Level 8 as Obi-Wan
2FJ3B6H

Level 9 as Obi-Wan
3FJ3BFJ

Level 10 as Obi-Wan
4FJ3BPJ

Level 2 as Qui Gon
VHS3BFG

Level 3 as Qui Gon
VMN3BFG

Level 4 as Qui Gon
VRL3BFG

Level 5 as Qui Gon
VWL3BFG

Level 6 as Qui Gon
V0L3BYG

Level 7 as Qui Gon
V4N3BFH

Level 8 as Qui Gon
V8N3BPH

Level 9 as Qui Gon
VCP3BYH

Level 10 as Qui Gon
VHR3BFJ

Level 2 as Mace Windu
VC1LCGF

Level 3 as Mace Windu
VCJCC6F

Level 4 as Mace Windu
VC1CCFG

Level 5 as Mace Windu
VCJDCPG

Level 6 as Mace Windu
VC1DCYG

Level 7 as Mace Windu
VCJPCFH

Level 8 as Mace Windu
VC1FCFH

Level 9 as Mace Windu
VCJGCPH

Level 10 as Mace Windu
VC1GCYH

Level 2 as Darth Maul
VCJ0D2J

Level 3 as Darth Maul
VCJ0G*J

Level 4 as Darth Maul
VCJ0JKK

Level 5 as Darth Maul
VCJ0LTK

Level 6 as Darth Maul
VCJ0N2K

Level 7 as Darth Maul
VCJ0Q1K

Level 8 as Darth Maul
VCJ0SFK

Level 9 as Darth Maul
VCJ0VPK

Level 10 as Darth Maul
VCJ0XYK

Final Battle
Enter NBJ3L6H as a password.

Level Select
Enter G1V34LL as a password to unlock the upper levels for all three characters.

SUPER DODGE BALL ADVANCE

Rank Climbing Tip
To climb the ranks quickly during Championship mode, always challenge the top team. If you win, you'll move halfway up the list each time. In four matches, you could be playing for Number One!

Unlock Dream Team B: the Rockets
Win Championship mode once.

Unlock Dream Team C: Iron Men
Win Special Championship mode once.

Unlock Dream Team A: the Shooters
Win Special Championship for the second time.

Unlocking the Special Championship
To unlock the Special Championship, beat the Rocket team in the finals of Championship mode.

SUPER STREET FIGHTER II TURBO REVIVAL

Easy Special Moves
During a 1p game, quickly tap Up, Up, Down, Down, Left, Right, Left, Right, B, A without pausing the game. After you enter the code, you can pull off special moves by tapping a direction on the D-Pad and the correct button.

Unlock Survival Mode and Time Attack
Two additional modes appear on the main menu after you beat the game a couple of times. The first mode is Survival mode; the second is Time Attack.

TEKKEN

All Modes and Characters
Hold A + B and press L, R(2), L(2), Up(2), R at the main menu. Note: You may need to repeat this two or three times before it activates.

Alternate Costumes
Press L, R, or Start at the character selection screen.

Fight as Heihachi
Successfully complete the game with all nine characters. Heihachi will appear next to Hworang and Paul at the Character Selection screen.

Team Battle Modes
Successfully complete Arcade mode as Heihachi to unlock the Versus Team Battle options.

TONY HAWK'S PRO SKATER 2

Unlock Spider-Man
To unlock Spider-Man as a playable character, enter the following button presses at the main menu or while paused during gameplay. Press and hold R, then press Up, Up, Down, Down, Left, Right, Left, Right, B, A, Start.

All Levels Unlocked and Maximum Money
Enter the following button presses at the main menu or while paused during gameplay. Press and hold R, then press B, A, Left, Down, B, Left, Up, B, Up, Left, Left.

Happy Face Blood
Enter the following button presses at the main menu or while paused during gameplay. Press and hold R, then press Start, A, Down, B, A, Left, Left, A, Down.

Set Time to Zero
To set the time to zero, enter the following button presses at the main menu or while paused during gameplay. Press and hold R, then press Left, Up, Start, Up, Right.

Turn Off the Blood!
Enter the following button presses at the main menu or while paused during gameplay. Press and hold R, then press B, Left, Up, Down, Left, Start, Start.

Unlock All Levels
Enter the following button presses at the main menu or while paused during gameplay. Press and hold R, then press A, Start, A, Right, Up, Up, Down, Down, Up, Up, Down.

Unlock Cheats
To unlock all of the cheats in the Cheat menu (in the Options screen), enter the following button presses at the main menu or while paused during gameplay. Press and hold R, then press B, A, Down, A, Start, Start, B, A, Right, B, Right, A, Up, Left. The following cheats are now available: Perfect Balance, Always Special, Stud Mode, Sim Mode, Moon Physics, and Always Zoom.

Unlock Disco Zoom
Enter the following button presses at the main menu or while paused during gameplay. Press and hold R, then press Left, A, Start, A, Right, Start, Right, Up, Start.

Unlock Mindy
To unlock Mindy, the female cop, hold R and press A, Left, Left, Up, Right, B, A, and Start at the main menu.

Unlock Unlimited Air
While holding the R button, press Left, A, Start, A, Right, Up, Start. Now every time you ollie, hold B to fly. It's hard to control at first, but you can use L and R to go left and right, Up and Down to go forward and back, B to rise, and A to hover.

WARIO LAND 4

Super Hard Difficulty Setting
Successfully complete the game under the hard difficulty setting. Start a new game, and the super hard difficulty setting can now be selected.

Wario Karaoke
Enter the sound room and highlight the Exit option. Press Select + Start + R + L + Up to unlock Wario Karaoke. Alternately, get gold crowns by collecting over 10,000 coins in all levels to unlock the Wario Karaoke (music test) option.

Wario Karaoke Control
Press Up or Down to change the pitch of the song. Press Left or Right to change the tempo of the song. Press L or R to toggle between a green CD, yellow CD, or just the lyrics.

WILD THORNBERRYS: CHIMP CHASE

Skip Level
Enter one of the following passwords to skip to a specific level.

Jungle 2
4S7JXTJ3

Jungle 3
473H1SZD

Plains 1
B147T3B2

Plains 2
4DZZFB7F

Plains 3
Y5TSGWK2

Arctic 1
6GRHJ74W

Arctic 2
KF3W?6Jr

Arctic 3
MR8594NJ

Outback 1
8!YJCDH4

Outback 2
!!2VKJFS

Outback 3
NDC4SJ3S

End
M661M8LB

WOLFENSTEIN 3D

God Mode
Press Start to pause gameplay, then hold L + R and press A(2), B, A(5). A sound confirms correct code entry.

All Weapons, Keys, Ammo, and Health
Press Start to pause gameplay, then hold L + R and press A, B(2), A(5). A shout confirms correct code entry. All weapons and keys are unlocked, and your health and ammunition are restored.

Skip Level
Press Start to pause gameplay, then hold L + R and press A, B, A(2), B(3), A. The sound of a door opening confirms correct code entry. When the game is resumed, you start on the next level. Note: If this code is enabled on Level 1, you go to the secret floor.

Advance to Boss Level
Press Start to pause gameplay, then hold L + R and press A, B, A(2), B(2), A(2). The sound of a siren confirms correct code entry. When the game is resumed, you start at the current boss.

Xbox

AGGRESSIVE INLINE

FMV Sequences
Successfully complete the normal challenges in a level to unlock its FMV sequence.

Bonus Characters
Successfully complete the normal and hidden challenges in a level to unlock a bonus character.

Cheats
Collect all juice boxes in a level to reveal a cheat code.

Power Skates
Complete all challenges (normal and hidden) on every level. The Power Skates give you one blue stat point for every attribute.

Ultra Skates
Complete all the levels with 100 percent. The Ultra Skates give you the other blue stat point for every attribute.

AMPED: FREESTYLE SNOWBOARDING

Level Select, All Costumes, Gear, and Snowboards
Select "Options" at the main menu, then "Cheats." Enter GimmeGimme as a case-sensitive code. A sound confirms correct code entry. Press B to exit the Cheat menu.

Perfect Jumps
Select "Options" at the main menu, then "Cheats." Enter StickiT as a case-sensitive code. A sound confirms correct code entry. Press B to exit the Cheat menu.

Super Spins
Select "Options" at the main menu, then "Cheats." Enter WhirlyGig as a case-sensitive code. A sound confirms correct code entry. Press B to exit the Cheat menu.

Super Statistics
Select "Options" at the main menu, then "Cheats." Enter BigsteeZ as a case-sensitive code. A sound confirms correct code entry. Press B to exit the Cheat menu.

Low Gravity
Select "Options" at the main menu, then "Cheats." Enter MegaLeg as a case-sensitive code. A sound confirms correct code entry. Press B to exit the Cheat menu.

Play as Raven
Select "Options" at the main menu, then "Cheats." Enter RidinwRaven as a case-sensitive code to unlock Raven, the girl from the original Xbox tech demos, and an Xbox snowboard. A sound confirms correct code entry. Press B to exit the Cheat menu.

Play as Steezy
Select "Options" at the main menu, then "Cheats." Enter ChillinwSteezy as a case-sensitive code. A sound confirms correct code entry. Press B to exit the Cheat menu.

Disable Tree Collisions
Select "Options" at the main menu, then "Cheats." Enter buzzsaW as a case-sensitive code. A sound confirms correct code entry. Press B to exit the Cheat menu.

Bouncy Terrain
Select "Options" at the main menu, then "Cheats." Enter MegabOUnce as a case-sensitive code. A sound confirms correct code entry. Press B to exit the Cheat menu.

Harder to Do Flips and Spins
Select "Options" at the main menu, then "Cheats." Enter KeepnReal as a case-sensitive code. A sound confirms correct code entry. Press B to exit the Cheat menu.

Free Movement
Select "Options" at the main menu, then "Cheats." Enter ZiPster as a case-sensitive code. A sound confirms correct code entry. Press B to exit the Cheat menu. You can move anywhere quickly, even going uphill.

View Programmer Replays
Enter the "Replay Theater" and highlight "Hard Disk." Press Right until "Game Disc" appears to find replays generated by the programmers. To play one of those levels, select a replay, then highlight "Watch Replay." Press Right until you see "Challenge," then select it.

AZURIK: RISE OF PERATHIA

God Mode
Quickly press X, Black, White, R + L, click Left Analog-Stick + Right Analog-Stick. A sound confirms correct code entry. Repeat this code to disable its effect.

Level Select
Press Left Analog-Stick Right + Right Analog-Stick Left, Left Analog-Stick Left + Right Analog-Stick Right, A, B, click Right Analog-Stick, click Left Analog-Stick. This cheat also allows you to change your stats and view all FMV sequences. However, you must power off the Xbox to exit an FMV sequence.

Full Power and Health
Hold Left and rotate the Right Analog-Stick from right counter-clockwise to Right Analog-Stick Left. Release Left, then press A, X. You can now restore your health and elemental power.

Save at Any Point
Quickly press White, Up, Down, A, B, click Right Analog-Stick during the "swing" animation. A click confirms that the game has been saved. This may be done at any time during the game, but choose your save point carefully. Avoid saving on moving platforms, in areas where enemies respawn, while falling, or while dying.

Gem Mode
Quickly press Right, Left, A, B, A, B, Right, Left. You can get Earth, Air, Fire, Water, and Obsidian gems by pressing A, B, X, Y, or Black. Any other button exits Gem mode. You can increase your elemental power storage and get all the Obsidians through this mode. However, you also might create more gems than are supported and crash the game.

Big Heads
Quickly click Right Analog-Stick, press R, Down, Up, A. A sound confirms correct code entry.

Afro Hairstyle
Quickly press Down, Right, Black + White, click Right Analog-Stick, click Left Analog-Stick, press Left Analog-Stick Right + Right Analog-Stick Left, B, Y. A sound confirms correct code entry.

Adjust Camera
Quickly press R, Down, Up, Down, Up, click Right Analog-Stick, click Left Analog-Stick. The game stops, allowing you to alter the view. Press L or R to move the view up or down. Press Left Analog-Stick or Right Analog-Stick to move the view forward and back. Press the D-Pad to zoom in and out. Press A to view and remove the elemental power display. Press Back to resume the game.

Adjust Lighting
Quickly press A, click Right Analog-Stick, B, click Right Analog-Stick, click Left Analog-Stick. Darker areas become easier to see, but at the expense of having less dramatic lighting. Repeat this code to return to normal.

BATMAN VENGEANCE

Master Code
Press L, R, L, R, X(2), Y(2) at the main menu. A sound confirms correct code entry.

Unlimited Electric Batarangs
Press L, R, B, White, L at the main menu. A sound confirms correct code entry.

Unlimited Batarangs
Press L, R, White, Y at the main menu. A sound confirms correct code entry.

Bonus Characters
Press Left, Right, Down, White, L + R, then press Start at the main menu.

BLOOD WAKE

Unlimited Ammunition
Press Black, White, L, R, click Right Analog-Stick(2), press Y, X at the Start Game screen, then press Start. A sound confirms correct code entry.

Unlimited Turbo
Press Up(2), Down(2), Left, Right, Left, Right, B, A at the Start Game screen, then press Start. A sound confirms correct code entry.

Invincibility
Click Left Analog-Stick, click Right Analog-Stick, press Down, Left, Down, Left, B, Y at the Start Game screen, then press Start. A sound confirms correct code entry.

All Boats
Press Up, Down, Left, Right, L, B, X(2), click Right Analog-Stick at the Start Game screen, then press Start. A sound confirms correct code entry.

All Levels
Press X, Y, Up, Right, Left, Down, Up, Down, click Left Analog-Stick, L at the Start Game screen, then press Start. A sound confirms correct code entry.

Blood Ball Mode
Press X, Y, White, Black, B, A, Left, Up, Right, Down at the Start Game screen, then press Start. A sound confirms correct code entry.

Puffer Fish
Press A, B, Black, White, Y, X, click Right Analog-Stick(2), click Left Analog-Stick(2) at the Start Game screen, then press Start. A sound confirms correct code entry.

Rubber Duck Mode
Click Right Analog-Stick, click Left Analog-Stick, R, L, Black, White, Up, Down, Left, Right at the Start Game screen, then press Start. A sound confirms correct code entry.

Import Boat Mode
Press Y, B, X, A, L, R, Left, Right, click Left Analog-Stick, click Right Analog-Stick at the Start Game screen, then press Start. A sound confirms correct code entry.

All Battle Modes
Press Y, A, X, B, click Left Analog-Stick, click Right Analog-Stick, Black, White, R(2) at the Start Game screen, then press Start. A sound confirms correct code entry.

Basilisk
Successfully complete the "Protection Racket" level under the captain difficulty setting.

Fireshark
Successfully complete the "Up the Nagau" level under the ensign difficulty setting.

Guncat Catamaran
Successfully complete the "Protection Racket" level under the ensign difficulty setting.

Gunshark
Successfully complete the "Ships in the Night" level under the ensign difficulty setting.

Hellcat Catamaran
Successfully complete the "The Gauntlet" level under the ensign difficulty setting.

Hydroplane Switchblade
Successfully complete the "Gladiator" level under the ensign difficulty setting.

Jackal
Successfully complete the "Assault on Black Moon" level under the ensign difficulty setting.

Lightning
Successfully complete the "A Friend in Need" level under the ensign difficulty setting.

Pike
Successfully complete the "Payment Is Due" level under the ensign difficulty setting.

Salamander
Successfully complete the "Fish in a Barrel" level under the ensign difficulty setting.

Tigershark
Successfully complete the "Sampan Surprise" level under the ensign difficulty setting.

Switchblade Hydroplane
Successfully complete the "Gladiator" level under the ensign difficulty setting.

Kingdom Come Battle Mode
Successfully complete the "Baptism of Fire" level under the ensign difficulty setting.

Clanbake Battle Mode
Successfully complete the "A Poke in the Eye" level under the ensign difficulty setting.

Metal Massacre Battle Mode
Successfully complete the "Hurricane of Fire" level under the ensign difficulty setting.

CRASH BANDICOOT: THE WRATH OF CORTEX

Alternate Ending Sequence
Collect all 46 gems.

DARK SUMMIT

Extra Points
Hold Back + Start and press Y, L, X, B, R, A, R, A at the main menu. A sound confirms correct code entry. You'll get 9,100,000 lift points, which unlock all lifts except for the Moon Gate. You'll also get 9,100,000 equipment points, which unlock all boards, accessories, and special tricks.

All Boarders
Hold Back + Start and press Y, L, X, B, R, A, R, B at the main menu. A sound confirms correct code entry.

Challenges Completed
Hold Back + Start and press Y, L, X, B, R, A, R, Y at the main menu. A sound confirms correct code entry. All challenges except for 43 (Race the Chief), 48 (Bomb #5), 49 (Alien Half Pipe), and 50 (Storm HQ) will be completed. You'll also have all Bomb Pieces, with the exception of Bomb #5.

Alien Unlocked
Hold Back + Start and press Y, L, X, B, R, A, R, X at the main menu. A sound confirms correct code entry. Challenges 43 (Race the Chief), 48 (Bomb #5), 49 (Alien Half Pipe), and 50 (Storm HQ) will be completed. You'll also have Bomb Piece #5.

Shoot Projectile
Hold Back + Start and press Y, X, B, R at the main menu. A sound confirms correct code entry. Press L + R to shoot a barrel with a projectile.

Slow Motion
Hold Back + Start and press Y, X, B, L at the main menu. A sound confirms correct code entry. Press L + R when in the air or during a railslide to activate Slow Motion mode. This mode automatically ends when you reach the ground.

DEAD OR ALIVE 3

Control Victory View
Press R3 or R4 and use the Left Analog-Stick or Right Analog-Stick during the victory scene after a battle to change the camera angle. The Left Analog-Stick pans the camera, and the Right Analog-Stick zooms in and out.

Control Replays
Hold A + B + X after winning a match. When the replay starts, press Y to slow it down or go back.

Taunts
Each character has at least one taunt. All characters do this with Back, Forward, Back, then Black or X + A + B. Some characters have more, such as Hayabusa, Brad, Ayane, and Lei Fang. To do these extra taunts, press Down(2), Black or X + A + B. Another one is done by pressing Forward, Back, Forward (Black or X + A + B). Yet another is done by pressing Back(2), (Black or X + A + B). Note: Only one or two characters have the last two sets of taunt moves.

Alternate Snow Stage Appearance
Select Versus or Training mode and highlight the snow stage. Press X for a light snow, press Y for a blizzard, or press A for a random effect.

FUZION FRENZY

First-Person Mode
Press Start to pause gameplay. Then hold L and press Y, B, Y, B. Repeat the code to disable its effect.

Turbo Mode
Press Start to pause gameplay during a mini-game. Then hold L and press Y, B, X(2). Repeat the code to disable its effect.

Welsh Mode
Press Start to pause gameplay. Then hold L and press Y(4). Repeat the code to disable its effect.

Enable "Real Controls"
Press Start to pause gameplay. Then hold L and press Y(3), B. Repeat the code to disable its effect.

Squeaky Voices
Press Start to pause gameplay. Then hold L and press Y, X, Y(2). Repeat the code to disable its effect.

Mutant Mode
Press Start to pause gameplay. Then hold L and press Y, B, X(2). To get Mutant mode two, repeat the code. To return to Mutant mode, repeat the code again. To disable the code, repeat it one more time.

GAUNTLET: DARK LEGACY

Invincibility
Enter INVULN as a name.

Permanent Super Shot with Large Crossbow
Enter SSHOTS as a name.

Permanent Pojo the Chicken
Enter EGG911 as a name.

Permanent Anti-Death
Enter 1ANGEL as a name.

Permanent Invisibility
Enter 000000 as a name.

Permanent X-Ray Vision
Enter PEEKIN as a name.

Permanent Full Turbo
Enter PURPLE as a name.

Permanent Triple Shot
Enter MENAGE as a name.

XBOX

Permanent Reflect Shot
Enter REFLEX as a name.

Permanent Shrink Enemy and Growth
Enter DELTA1 as a name.

Always Have Nine Potions and Keys
Enter ALLFUL as a name.

Run Quickly
Enter XSPEED as a name.

Throw Quickly
Enter QCKSHT as a name.

10,000 Gold per Level
Enter 10000K as a name.

Dwarf Is a Large Jester
Enter ICE600 as a name.

Dwarf in S&M Costume
Enter NUD069 as a name.

Jester Is a Stick Figure with Smiley Face
Enter STX222 as a name.

Jester Is a Stick Figure with Baseball Cap Head
Enter KJH105 as a name.

Jester Is a Stick Figure with Mohawk Head
Enter PNK666 as a name.

Knight Is a Roman Centurion
Enter BAT900 as a name.

Knight Is a Ninja (Sword and Claws)
Enter TAK118 as a name.

Knight Is a Bald Man in Street Clothes (Sean Gugler)
Enter STG333 as a name.

Knight Is an Orange-Skirted Waitress
Enter KAO292 as a name.

Knight Wears Street Clothes (Chris Sutton)
Enter CSS222 as a name.

Knight Wears Street Clothes
Enter ARV984 as a name.

Knight Wears Street Clothes and Baseball Cap
Enter DIB626 as a name.

Knight Is a Quarterback
Enter RIZ721 as a name.

Knight Wears Black Karate Outfit with Twin Scythes
Enter SJB964 as a name.

Knight Wears Black Outfit and Cape
Enter DARTHC as a name.

Valkyrie as the Grim Reaper with Bloody Scythe
Enter TWN300 as a name.

Valkyrie as a Japanese School Girl
Enter AYA555 as a name.

Valkyrie as a Cheerleader with Baton
Enter CEL721 as a name.

Warrior with an Ogre Costume
Enter CAS400 as a name.

Warrior as an Orc Boss
Enter MTN200 as a name.

Warrior with a Rat Head
Enter RAT333 as a name.

Wizard with an Evil Appearance
Enter GARM99 as a name.

Wizard as an Undead Lich
Enter GARM00 as a name.

Wizard as a Pharaoh
Enter DES700 as a name.

Wizard as an Alien
Enter SKY100 as a name.

Wizard as Sumner
Enter SUM224 as a name.

Introduction Sequence
Press L at the Midway Games screen to see how the story begins.

HUNTER: THE RECKONING

All Weapons
Press B, Up, Left, Down, Right, B(2) during gameplay.

Sound Test
Press Left(2), B or Right(2), B during gameplay.

Nightmare Mode
Successfully complete the game to unlock the "Nightmare Mode" option at the Special Features screen.

Alternate Hunter Mode
Successfully complete the game to unlock the "Alternate Hunter Mode" option at the Special Features screen.

Alternate Ending Sequence
Save at over 50 Innocents before returning to the train to unlock the good ending.

JAMES BOND 007: AGENT UNDER FIRE

Golden Gun
Successfully complete the Trouble in Paradise level with a "Gold" rank. This cheat unlocks the Golden P2K. With this gun, you receive a silencer that the normal P2K doesn't have. To do this easily, get as much accuracy as you can, take as few hits as you can, and do all the Bond moves (shooting barrels to explode, shooting vital enemy characters, and finding secret areas).

Golden Gun in Multiplayer Mode
Successfully complete the Precious Cargo level with a "Platinum" rank and all 007 icons.

Golden CH-6
Successfully complete the Precious Cargo level with a "Gold" rank. When used, this cheat gives you unlimited rockets.

Golden Accuracy Power-Up
Successfully complete the Bad Diplomacy level with a "Gold" rank. This cheat enables you to have greater auto-aim.

Golden Clip Power-Up
Successfully complete the Cold Reception level with a "Gold" rank.

Golden Grenade Power-Up
Successfully complete the Night of the Jackal level with a "Gold" rank.

Golden Bullet Power-Up
Successfully complete the Poseidon level with a "Gold" rank.

Golden Armor Power-Up
Successfully complete the Forbidden Depths level with a "Gold" rank.

Unlimited Golden Gun Ammunition
Successfully complete the Evil Summit level with a "Gold" rank.

Unlimited Car Missiles
Successfully complete the Dangerous Pursuit level with a "Gold" rank.

Rocket Manor Multiplayer Level
Successfully complete the Trouble in Paradise level with a "Platinum" rank and all 007 icons. This cheat unlocks a new multiplayer level, a large, open area. The map settings allow only rockets.

Stealth Bond Skin in Multiplayer Mode
Successfully complete the Dangerous Pursuit level with a "Platinum" rank and all 007 icons.

Guard Skin in Multiplayer Mode
Successfully complete the Cold Reception level with a "Platinum" rank and all 007 icons.

Alpine Guard Skin in Multiplayer Mode
Successfully complete the Streets of Bucharest level with a "Platinum" rank and all 007 icons.

Cyclops Oil Guard skin in Multiplayer Mode
Successfully complete the Poseidon level with a "Platinum" rank and all 007 icons.

Poseidon Guard Skin in Multiplayer Mode
Successfully complete the Mediterranean Crisis level with a "Platinum" rank and all 007 icons.

Carrier Guard Multiplayer Skin
Successfully complete the Evil Summit level with a "Platinum" rank and all 007 icons.

Rapid Fire Power-Up
Successfully complete the Fire and Water level with a "Gold" rank.

Regenerative Armor Power-Up
Successfully complete the Mediterranean Crisis level with a "Gold" rank.

Calypso Gun in Multiplayer Mode
Successfully complete the Fire and Water level with a "Platinum" rank and all 007 icons.

Full Arsenal in Multiplayer Mode
Successfully complete the Forbidden Depths level with a "Platinum" rank and all 007 icons.

Gravity Boots in Multiplayer Mode
Successfully complete the Bad Diplomacy level with a "Platinum" rank and all 007 icons.

Viper Gun in Multiplayer Mode
Successfully complete the Night of the Jackal level with a "Platinum" rank and all 007 icons.

Lotus Esprit Car
Successfully complete the Streets of Bucharest level with a "Gold" rank.

MAX PAYNE

Cheat Mode

Start a game. Press Back during gameplay to display the main menu. Then, hold L + R + click Left Analog-Stick + click Right Analog-Stick, and quickly press White, Black(2), White(2), Black at the main menu. A cheat option will appear.

The Cheat menu will have "All Weapons" and "Refill" (restores ammunition, painkillers, and bullet time) options. To use these cheats, press Back during gameplay and select the desired options at the Cheat menu. Then, press Back to resume gameplay. Note: Other cheats in the Cheat menu must be unlocked during gameplay.

Level Skip

Press Start during gameplay. Then, hold L and press Black(4), X(6), Y(3), Back. When you're at the main menu, go back. A sound confirms that the current chapter has been completed.

Additional Difficulty Settings

Successfully complete the game under the "Fugitive" difficulty setting to unlock the "Dead on Arrival" and "New York Minute" settings.

Bonus Level

Successfully complete the game in New York Minute mode to unlock a new bonus level in which you have to kill a lot of enemies, all in bullet time.

Last Challenge Bonus Level

Successfully complete the game under the "Dead on Arrival" difficulty setting to unlock the Last Challenge bonus level.

Secret Programmer Room

Successfully complete the Last Challenge level. The doors in the back of the room will open up to the Remedy Room.

NBA 2K2

Cheat Menu

Enter the Options menu and select "Gameplay." Hold D-Pad Left + Left Analog-Stick Right and press Start. The "Codes" selection is now unlocked at the Options menu.

Bonus Teams

Enter MEGASTARS as a case-sensitive code to unlock the Sega Sports, Visual Concepts, and Team 2K2 in Exhibition and Street modes.

Muhammad Ali and Michael Jackson

Press Start and hold L during an Exhibition game. The screen shakes to confirm correct code entry. Go onto the Sixers and they should be on the starting lineup.

Airball

Select "Street" at the main menu. Press White, then hold L and press Y(2). Press Start and "Airball" appears to confirm correct code entry.

NBA INSIDE DRIVE

Unlimited Turbo

Enter the Options screen and select "Codes." Enter CARDIOMAN as a code. Repeat the code to disable its effect.

ABA Basketball

Enter the Options screen and select "Codes." Enter OLDSCHOOL as a code. Repeat the code to disable its effect.

WNBA Basketball

Enter the Options screen and select "Codes." Enter GOTGAME as a code. Repeat the code to disable its effect.

Soccer Ball

Enter the Options screen and select "Codes." Enter HOOLIGAN as a code. Repeat the code to disable its effect.

Volleyball

Enter the Options screen and select "Codes." Enter SPIKEIT as a code. Repeat the code to disable its effect.

Beach Ball

Enter the Options screen and select "Codes." Enter SANDINMYSHORTS as a code. Repeat the code to disable its effect.

8-Ball

Enter the Options screen and select "Codes." Enter GAMEOVER as a code. Repeat the code to disable its effect.

Xbox Ball

Enter the Options screen and select "Codes." Enter BACHMAN as a code. Repeat the code to disable its effect.

Chicago Rooftop Court

Enter the Options screen and select "Codes." Enter WINDYCITY as a code, then start an Exhibition game. Repeat the code to disable its effect.

More Three Pointers

Enter the Options screen and select "Codes." Enter THREE4ALL as a code. Repeat the code to disable its effect.

More Alley-Oops

Enter the Options screen and select "Codes." Enter IGOTHOPS as a code. Repeat the code to disable its effect.

Little Players

Enter the Options screen and select "Codes." Enter SMALLSHOES as a code. Repeat the code to disable its effect.

Disable Trade Rules

Enter the Options screen and select "Codes." Enter GIMMETHAT as a code. Repeat the code to disable its effect.

NHL HITZ 2002

Activate Cheat Mode

Press X, Y, and B to change the icons in the first, second, and third boxes respectively at the Match-Up screen. The numbers in the following list indicate the number of times each button is pressed. After the icons have been changed, press the D-Pad in the indicated direction to enable the code. For example, to enter 1-2-3 Left, press X, Y(2), B(3), Left.

Big Head Player
2-0-0 Right

Huge Head Player
3-0-0 Right

Big Head Team
2-2-0 Left

Huge Head Team
3-3-0 Left

Big Hits
2-3-4 Down

Late Hits
3-2-1 Down

Hitz Time
1-0-4 Right

No Crowd
2-1-0 Right

Pinball Boards
4-2-3 Right

Show Shot Speed
1-0-1 Up

Show the Team's Hot Spot
2-0-1 Up

No Fake Shots
4-2-4 Down

No Puck Out
1-1-1 Down

No One-Timers
2-1-3 Left

Big Puck
1-2-1 Up

Huge Puck
3-2-1 Up

Bulldozer Puck
2-1-2 Left

Tennis Ball
1-3-2 Down

Snow Mode
1-2-1 Left

Rain Mode
1-4-1 Left

Domino Effect
0-1-2 Right

Turbo Boost
0-0-2 Up

Unlimited Turbo
4-1-3 Right

Win Fights for Goals
2-0-2 Left

Skills Versus
2-2-2 Down

First to Seven Wins
3-2-3 Left

More Time to Enter Codes
3-3-3 Right

Hockey Ball
1-3-3 Left

Disable Previous Code
0-1-0 Down

OUTLAW GOLF

Master Code

Start a new game and enter Golf_Gone_Wild as a case-sensitive name, including underscores, to unlock all characters, clubs, and stages.

Bonus Costumes
Hold L and press Y(2), White, Y, Black, Y at the character selection screen.

Distract Opponent
Start a game with two or more players. While the other person is hitting the ball, press A to say things to distract them.

Atlas Driver
Complete the Stroke Me event.

Atlas Fairway Woods
Complete the Not-So-Goodfellas event.

Atlas Irons
Complete the High Rollers event.

Atlas Putter (Black)
Complete the All the Marbles event.

Atlas Putter Gold
Complete the Suave's Revenge event.

Atlas Wedge
Complete the Pretty in Pink event.

Boiler Maker Fairway Woods
Complete the Hole Lotta Luv event.

Boiler Maker Irons
Complete the Jersey Ball Bash event.

Boiler Maker Putter
Complete the Sun Stroke event.

Boiler Maker Wedge
Complete the Back 9 Shuffle event.

C.C.
Complete the Hot, Hot, Hot event.

Cincinnati Balls
Complete the Rough Riders event.

Cincinnati Driver
Complete the Ol' Blood and Guts event.

Cincinnati Fairway Woods
Complete the Full Frontal event.

Cincinnati Irons
Complete the Stroke Me Again event.

Cincinnati Wedge
Complete the Blister in the Sun event.

Coiler Maker Driver
Complete the Money Talks event.

Doc Diggler
Complete the Ladies Night event.

Ecstasy Balls
Complete the Scorched Earth Classic event.

Ecstasy Putter
Complete the Motley Crew event.

Killer Miller
Complete the Test Drive event.

Nelson Balls
Complete the Different Strokes event.

Python Driver
Complete the Heat Rash Invitational event.

Python Fairway Woods
Complete the Tough Crowd event.

Python Irons
Complete the A Hole in the Sun event.

Python Wedge
Complete the Garden State Stroke Fest event.

Scrummy
Complete the Odd Ball Classic event.

Suave's Balls
Complete the Garden State Menage a Trois event.

Suki
Complete the Baked on the Bone event.

Trixie
Complete the Chicks with Sticks event.

PIRATES: THE LEGEND OF BLACK KAT

Invincibility for Katarina
Hold L + R and press A, Y, click Left Analog-Stick, press B, click Right Analog-Stick, press Back, click Right Analog-Stick, press White, Black, X.

Invincibility for the Wind Dancer
Hold L + R and press Back, B, White, A, click Right Analog-Stick, press Black, X, click Right Analog-Stick, press Y, click Left Analog-Stick.

Reveal Buried Treasure Chests
Hold L + R and press Y, A, X, B, White, Back, click Left Analog-stick, Black, click Left Analog-Stick, click Right Analog-Stick. Green Xs appear on the captain's log maps to indicate the location of buried treasure chests.

Reveal All Treasure Chests
Hold L + R and click Right Analog-Stick, press A, B, click Left Analog-Stick, press Y, White, Back, click Left Analog-Stick, press X, Black.

All Treasure Chest Keys
Hold L + R and press Y, Back, A, X, click Right Analog-Stick, press White, click Left Analog-Stick, press Black, B, click Left Analog-Stick.

Wind Dancer
Hold L + R and press Black, B, click Right Analog-Stick, click Left Analog-Stick, press A, X, click Right Analog-Stick, press Back, White, Y.

Unlimited Items
Hold L + R and press B, White, Back, Black, click Right Analog-Stick, click Left Analog-Stick, press X, A, click Right Analog-Stick, press Y. Once found, an item becomes available in unlimited amounts.

Extra Gold
Hold L + R and press B, click Right Analog-Stick, press White, X, A, click Right Analog-Stick, press Back, click Left Analog-Stick, press Y, Black. Sail to another map to get the Galleon.

Unlimited Wind Boost
Hold L + R and press Back, White, click Right Analog-Stick, press X, click Left Analog-Stick, press Y, Black, B, A, click Left Analog-Stick.

Advance to Katarina's Next Sword
Hold L + R and click Right Analog-Stick, press Back, Black, click Left Analog-Stick, press X, A, White, Y, click Left Analog-Stick, press B.

Alternate Glacial Gulf Music
Hold L + R and press White, A, B, Black, X, Y, click Left Analog-Stick, press Back, click Right Analog-Stick, click Left Analog-Stick to hear music from SSX when sliding down in Glacial Gulf.

High-Pitched Voices
Hold L + R and click Right Analog-Stick, press Y, Back, A, click Right Analog-Stick, press B, White, X, Black, click Left Analog-Stick.

Kane Poison Head
Hold L + R and press B, Black, White, X, click Left Analog-Stick, press A, click Left Analog-Stick, press Y, click Right Analog-Stick, press Back. The poison status will be indicated by the head of Kane from *Command and Conquer*.

Alternate Katarina Costumes
Press L + R, click Left Analog-Stick, press Back, Up. A short sequence of music confirms correct code entry. Click Right Analog-Stick to change the value of the numbers that appear on screen, then start a new game or resume a saved game to view the corresponding costume. The costumes that can be accessed are listed below.

Original Costume and Hair Color
00000000

Blackbeard in Purple
00000001

Red Hair with Red and Orange Bikini
00000010

Blue Hair with Orange and Red Bikini
00000011

Tan, Brown Hair, Orange and Yellow Bikini
00000100

Blonde Hair, Orange and Yellow Bikini
00000101

Blonde Hair, Pink Bikini
00000110

Blue Hair, Shiny Silver Bikini
00000111

Red Hair, Black Bikini, Black Stockings
00001000

Pink Hair, Shiny Black Body Suit
00001001

Blue Hair, Shiny Copper Body Suit
00001010

Purple Hair, Shiny Silver Body Suit
00001011

REDCARD SOCCER 2003

Cheat Mode
Enter BIGTANK as a name to unlock all teams, stadiums, and finals mode.

Apes Team and Victoria Falls Stadium
Defeat the Apes team in World Conquest mode.

Dolphins Team and Nautilus Stadium
Defeat the Dolphins team in World Conquest mode.

Martians Team and USAFB001 Stadium
Defeat the Martians team in World Conquest mode.

Matadors Team and Coliseum Stadium
Defeat the Matadors team in World Conquest mode.

SWAT Team and Nova City Stadium
Defeat the SWAT team in World Conquest mode.

Samurai Team and Youhi Gardens Stadium
Defeat the Samurai team in World Conquest mode.

Finals Mode
Win all matches in World Conquest mode.

SMASHING DRIVE

Rush Hour Shift
Successfully complete the Early Bird shift.

Night Owl Shift
Successfully complete the Rush Hour shift.

Dusk and Wired Shift
Successfully complete the Night Owl shift.

SPIDERMAN: THE MOVIE

Master Code
Enter the Specials menu and enter ARACHNID as a code. A laugh confirms correct code entry. All levels in the Level Warp option, all Gallery options (movie viewer/production art), and combo moves are unlocked. Repeat code entry to return to normal.

Unlimited Webbing
Enter the Specials menu and enter ORGAN-ICWEBBING as a code. A laugh confirms correct code entry. Repeat code entry to return to normal. Alternately, accumulate 50,000 points during gameplay.

All Fighting Controls
Enter the Specials menu and enter KOALA as a code. A laugh confirms correct code entry. Repeat code entry to return to normal.

Level Select
Enter the Specials menu and enter IMIARMAS as a code. A laugh confirms correct code entry. Repeat code entry to return to normal.

Level Skip
Enter the Specials menu and enter ROMITAS as a code. A laugh confirms correct code entry. Repeat code entry to return to normal. Pause gameplay and select the "Next Level" option to advance to the next level.

Bonus Training Levels
Enter the Specials menu and enter HEADEX-PLODY as a code. A laugh confirms correct code entry. Repeat code entry to return to normal.

Play as Mary Jane
Enter the Specials menu and enter GIRL-NEXTDOOR as a code. A laugh confirms correct code entry. Repeat code entry to return to normal.

Play as the Shocker
Enter the Specials menu and enter HERMAN-SCHULTZ as a code. A laugh confirms correct code entry. Repeat code entry to return to normal.

Play as a Scientist
Enter the Specials menu and enter SERUM as a code. A laugh confirms correct code entry. Repeat code entry to return to normal.

Play as a Police Officer
Enter the Specials menu and enter REALHERO as a code. A laugh confirms correct code entry. Repeat code entry to return to normal.

Play as Captain Stacey (Helicopter Pilot)
Enter the Specials menu and enter CAPTAIN-STACEY as a code. A laugh confirms correct code entry. Repeat code entry to return to normal.

Play as Skulls Gang Thug
Enter the Specials menu and enter KNUCKLES as a code. A laugh confirms correct code entry. Repeat code entry to return to normal.

Play as Uncle Ben's Killer
Enter the Specials menu and enter STICKYRICE as a code. A laugh confirms correct code entry. Repeat code entry to return to normal.

Play as Shocker's Thug
Enter the Specials menu and enter THUGSRUS as a code. A laugh confirms correct code entry. Repeat code entry to return to normal.

Matrix-Style Attacks
Enter the Specials menu and enter DODGETHIS as a code. A laugh confirms correct code entry. Repeat code entry to return to normal.

Goblin-Style Costume
Enter the Specials menu and enter FREAKOUT as a code. A laugh confirms correct code entry. Repeat code entry to return to normal.

Small Spider-Man
Enter the Specials menu and enter SPIDER-BYTE as a code. A laugh confirms correct code entry. Repeat code entry to return to normal.

Big Head and Feet for Spider-Man
Enter the Specials menu and enter GOESTOY-OURHEAD as a code. A laugh confirms correct code entry. Repeat code entry to return to normal.

Enemies Have Big Heads
Enter the Specials menu and enter JOELS-PEANUTS as a code. A laugh confirms correct code entry. Repeat code entry to return to normal.

First-Person View
Enter the Specials menu and enter UNDER-THEMASK as a code. A laugh confirms correct code entry. Repeat code entry to return to normal.

Unlimited Green Goblin Glider Power
Enter the Specials menu and enter CHILLOUT as a code. A laugh confirms correct code entry. Repeat code entry to return to normal.

Pinhead Bowling Mini-Game
Accumulate 10,000 points during gameplay to unlock the Pinhead bowling mini-game in the Training menu.

Vulture FMV Sequence
Accumulate 20,000 points during gameplay to unlock a Vulture FMV sequence in the CG menu.

Shocker FMV Sequence
Accumulate 30,000 points during gameplay to unlock a Vulture FMV sequence in the CG menu.

Green Goblin FMV Sequence
Successfully complete the game under the hero or greater difficulty setting.

Play as Alex Ross
Successfully complete the game under the normal or higher difficulty setting to unlock the Alex Ross costume in the Specials menu.

Play as the Green Goblin
Successfully complete the game under the hero or superhero difficulty setting to unlock the Green Goblin Costume option at the Specials menu. Select that option to play as Harry Osborn in the Green Goblin costume, including his weapons, in an alternate storyline in which he tries to correct the Osborn family's reputation. To unlock this easily, start a new game under the hero or superhero difficulty setting. At the first level, pause gameplay, then quit to the main menu. Enable the ARACHNID code, then go to the Level Warp option. Choose the Conclusion level (that features Norman revealing himself to Spider-Man followed by the glider sequence), then exit. This marks the game as completed under the selected difficulty setting. The Green Goblin costume option will be unlocked at the Secret Store screen.

Alternate Green Goblin Costume
If you're using the Alex Ross Spider-Man, play any level with the Green Goblin in it and he'll have an alternate costume that more closely resembles his classic costume.

Play as Peter Parker
Successfully complete the game under the easy or higher difficulty setting to unlock the Peter Parker costume in the Specials menu.

Play as Wrestler
Successfully complete the game under the easy or higher difficulty setting to unlock the wrestler costume in the Specials menu. To unlock this easily, first unlock the Unlimited Webbing cheat. When you get to the ring, zip to the top and keep on shooting Spidey Bombs.

SPY HUNTER

Activate Cheat Mode
Cheats are unlocked by completing all mission objectives (not just the primary objectives) within a set amount of time. To activate the cheats, enter "System Options," then choose "Extras," and "Cheat Grid." To play the FMV sequences unlocked in the Cheat menu, choose the Movie Player option that is above "Cheat Grid."

Saliva Spy Hunter Video
Complete Level 1 in 340.

Green HUD
Complete Level 2 in 335.

Saliva Your Disease Video
Complete Level 3 in 240.

Night Vision
Complete Level 4 in 315.

Early Test Animatic Video
Complete Level 5 in 325.

Extra Cameras
Complete Level 6 in 345.

Rainbow HUD
Complete Level 7 in 310.

Inversion Camera
Complete Level 8 in 305.

Concept Art Video
Complete Level 9 in 345.

Fisheye View
Complete Level 10 in 315.

Camera Flip
Complete Level 11 in 310.

Puke Camera
Complete Level 12 in 330.

Making of Video
Complete Level 13 in 215.

Tiny Spy
Complete Level 14 in 510.

Hover Spy
Complete the entire game.

Super Spy
Complete all 65 objectives in the game for unlimited ammunition and invincibility for your car.

The Making of Spy Hunter FMV Sequence
Choose an agent at the start of the game and select an empty slot. Enter MAKING or MODEL as a name. The name disappears and a clucking sound confirms correct code entry. Next, enter your own name and start the game. Select "System Options," then "Extras," then "Movie Player" to access the FMV sequence.

Saliva Spy Hunter Theme FMV Sequence
Choose an agent at the start of the game and select an empty slot. Enter GUNN as a name. The name disappears and a clucking sound confirms correct code entry. Next, enter your own name and start the game. Select "System Options," then "Extras," then "Movie Player" to access the FMV sequence.

Saliva Your Disease FMV Sequence
Choose an agent at the start of the game and select an empty slot. Enter SALIVA as a name. The name disappears and a clucking sound confirms correct code entry. Next, enter your own name and start the game. Select "System Options," then "Extras," then "Movie Player" to access the FMV sequence.

Spy Hunter Concept Art FMV Sequence
Choose an agent at the start of the game and select an empty slot. Enter SHAWN or SCW823 as a name. The name disappears and a clucking sound confirms correct code entry. Next, enter your own name and start the game. Select "System Options," then "Extras," then "Movie Player" to access the FMV sequence.

Early Test Animatic FMV Sequence
Choose an agent at the start of the game and select an empty slot. Enter WOODY or WWS413 as a name. The name disappears and a clucking sound confirms correct code entry. Next, enter your own name and start the game. Select "System Options," then "Extras," then "Movie Player" to access the FMV sequence.

Classic Spy Hunter Mini-Game
Choose an agent at the start of the game and select an empty slot. Enter OGSPY as a name. The name disappears and a clucking sound confirms correct code entry. Next, enter your own name and start the game.

SSX TRICKY

Master Code
Hold L + R and press A, Y, Right, B, X, Down, Y, X, Left, B, A, Up at the main Options screen, with the "Start Game" and "DVD Extras" option. Release L + R and a sound confirms correct code entry.

Full Stat Points
Hold L + R and press Y(2), Right, Y(2), Down, A(2), Left, A(2), Up at the main Options screen, with the "Start Game" and "DVD Extras" option. Release L + R and a sound confirms correct code entry. All the boarders will have full stat points.

Mallora Board
Hold L + R and press A(2), Right, B(2), Down, Y(2), Left, X(2), Up at the main Options screen, with the "Start Game" and "DVD Extras" option. Release L + R and a sound confirms correct code entry. Choose Elise and start a track. Elise will have the Mallora Board and a blue outfit. This code only works for Elise.

Annette Board
Hold L + R and press X, A, Right, X, A, Down, X, A, Left, X, A, Up at the main Options screen, with the "Start Game" and "DVD Extras" option. Release L + R and a sound confirms correct code entry. Choose Kaori and start a track. Kaori will have a full Tricky meter, and a faster board.

Sticky Boards
Hold L + R and press X(2), Right, Y(2), Down, B(2), Left, A(2), Up at the main Options screen, with the "Start Game" and "DVD Extras" option. Release L + R and a sound confirms correct code entry.

Mix Master Mike
Hold L + R and press A(2), Right, A(2), Down, A(2), Left, A(2), Up at the main Options screen, with the "Start Game" and "DVD Extras" option. Release L + R and a sound confirms correct code entry. Choose any boarder at the character selection screen, and he or she will be replaced by Mix Master Mike on the course, with the übers of the character that was originally selected. He has decks on his back and a vinyl board. Repeat the code to disable its effect.

Pipedream Course
Win a medal on all Showoff courses.

Untracked Course
Win a medal on all Race courses.

Überboards
Unlock all of the tricks for a character to get his or her überboard, which is that character's best board.

Fugi Board
Get a gold medal on every course with all boarders with their überboards to unlock a Fugi board.

Alternate Costumes
To earn more costumes, complete all chapters in your trick book. To unlock the final chrome costume, complete World Circuit mode with a "Master" rank.

Play as Brodi
Win a gold medal in World Circuit mode.

Play as Zoe
Win two gold medals in World Circuit mode.

Play as JP
Win three gold medals in World Circuit mode.

Play as Kaori
Win four gold medals in World Circuit mode.

Play as Marisol
Win five gold medals in World Circuit mode.

Play as Psymon
Win six gold medals in World Circuit mode.

Play as Seeiah
Win seven gold medals in World Circuit mode.

Play as Luther
Win eight gold medals in World Circuit mode.

STAR WARS: JEDI STARFIGHTER

Master Code
Enter LONGO as a code.

Invincibility
Enter SOLID as a code.

Mara Jade's Z-95 Headhunter Ship
Enter HUNT as a code. The Z-95 has homing missiles and a strong dual laser.

Alternate Camera Angles
Enter DARON as a code.

Advanced Freefall Ship
Achieve the bonus objective in Act 3, Mission 1.

Advanced Havoc Ship
Achieve the bonus objective in Act 3, Mission 3.

Advanced Jedi Starfighter
Achieve the bonus objective in Act 2, Mission 4.

Advanced Zoomer Ship
Achieve the bonus objective in Act 2, Mission 3.

Republic Gunship
Achieve the bonus objective in Act 3, Mission 5.

Sabaoth Fighter
Achieve the bonus objective in Act 2, Mission 5.

TIE Fighter
Achieve the bonus objective in Act 1, Mission 4.

X-Wing
Achieve the bonus objective in Act 1, Mission 3.

Slave 1 Ship
Achieve the hidden objective in all missions.

STAR WARS: OBI-WAN

Level Select
Select the "New Game" option at the main menu, then enter GREYTHERAT as saved game name. All levels, including the bonus levels, will be unlocked. Enter M1A2U3L4!? as a saved game name to unlock all levels until Darth Maul.

Battle Royal Mission
Defeat Darth Maul in Level 25 to unlock the Battle Royal mission, where you have to fight eight other Jedi Masters in the Saber Arena.

Additional Versus Mode Characters
Defeat a character in the Jedi Arena during gameplay to unlock him or her in Versus mode.

STAR WARS: STARFIGHTER: SPECIAL EDITION

Master Code
Enter EUROPA as a code. Everything except the multiplayer levels will be unlocked.

Information in this section was contributed by touchomagic.

Invincibility
Enter EARCHIPS as a code. The message "Invincibility" confirms correct code entry.

Bruiser Gun
Enter BRUISER as a code.

Trade Federation Freighter
Enter UTILITY as a code.

Secret Spaceship for Bonus Missions
Enter FSNEULB as a code to unlock the Experimental N-1 Fighter. Alternately, earn a gold medal in the Naboo Proving Grounds, the Royal Escort, Taking the Offensive, Midnight Munitions Run, Rescue on the Solleu, and the Final Assault missions.

Enemy Ship Gallery
Enter SHIPS as a code.

Pre-Production Art
Enter PLANETS as a code.

Spaceship and Cast Pictures
Enter HEROES as a code.

Programmer FMV Sequence
Enter LATEAM as a code.

Secret Level Programmers
Enter SLTEAM as a code.

Disable Cockpit Displays
Enter NOHUD as a code.

Alternate Camera Angles
Enter DIRECTOR as a code. The message "Director Mode" confirms correct code entry.

Reversed Controls
Enter JARJAR as a code. The message "Jar Jar Mode" confirms correct code entry.

Default Screen
Enter SIZZLE as a code.

View Credits
Enter CREDITS as a code.

Charm's Way Mission
Earn a bronze medal in the Royal Escort, Contract Infraction, Piracy above Lok, Taking the Offensive, the New Resistance, and the Final Assault missions.

Outpost Attack Mission
Earn a bronze medal in all default missions.

Canyon Sprint Mission
Earn a silver medal in the Naboo Proving Grounds, the Royal Escort, Taking the Offensive, Midnight Munitions Run, Rescue on the Solleu, and the Final Assault missions.

Space Sweep Mission
Earn a silver medal in all default missions.

Guardian Mantis Ship
Earn a gold medal in the Contract Infraction, Secrets on Eos, and the New Resistance missions.

Havoc Ship
Earn a gold medal in the Piracy above Lok, Valuable Goods, Eye of the Storm, the Crippling Blow, and Last Stand on Naboo missions.

Darth Maul's Infiltrator Ship
Earn a gold medal in all default missions.

TEST DRIVE: OFF-ROAD WIDE OPEN

Pro Class Trucks
Successfully complete the first nine tracks in single-race mode.

Unlimited Class Trucks
Successfully complete the first of 27 tracks in Single Race mode.

Monster Truck
Successfully complete the 27 tracks in Single Race mode in first place.

Humvee
Finish in first place in the first three seasons of Career mode in all divisions.

Shelby Dodge Durango
Finish in first place in season four of Career mode in the speed division.

Dodge T-Rex
Finish in first place in season four of Career mode in the power division.

Rod Hall Hummer
Finish in first place in all divisions in Career mode. The Rod Hall Hummer is good for speed. It handles poorly and is average in climbing. It can be a power vehicle if needed and it works well for single race on the blitz races.

Moon Level and Moon Buggy
Collect all nine Blue Moon cafe signs in Free Roam or Career mode. There are three signs in each level. The Moon Buggy is the best all-around vehicle and can reach speeds of 132 mph. It's the vehicle to use on all the other races in single race.

WORLD SERIES BASEBALL

Batting Champ Medal
Complete Franchise mode in the top three teams in batting averages.

Big Spender Medal
Complete Franchise mode in the top three teams in BP spent.

Cellar Dweller Medal
Complete Franchise mode in the bottom three teams in wins.

Dominant Team Medal
Complete Franchise mode in the top three teams in wins.

Golden Slugger Medal
Complete Franchise mode in the top three teams in homeruns.

Great Glove Medal
Complete Franchise mode in the top three teams in fielding percentages.

Pitching Ace Medal
Complete Franchise mode in the top three teams in earned run averages.

Speed Demon Medal
Complete Franchise mode in the top three teams in stolen bases.

Strikeout King Medal
Complete Franchise mode in the top three teams in strikeouts.

Tightwad Medal
Complete Franchise mode in the bottom three teams in BP spent.

WRECKLESS

Missions A-2 to A-4
Successfully complete mission A-1.

Missions B-2 to B-4
Successfully complete mission B-1.

AUV
Successfully complete mission A-9.

Dragon-SPL Car
Successfully complete mission A-1.

Super Car
Successfully complete mission B-1.

Tank-90
Successfully complete mission B-8.

Tiger-SPL
Successfully complete mission A-8 to unlock the car that Tiger Tagachi drives.

Yakuza Car
Successfully complete mission B-9.

Music Test
Successfully complete all 20 missions to unlock the "Music Test" selection at the Options screen.

Alternate View
Press Down to cycle through different screen effects during gameplay and replays. To unlock more effects, successfully complete missions A-9, A-10, B-9, and B-10.

WWE RAW

Fred Durst
Win all the championship belts.

Shane McMahon
Win the Hardcore title.

Stephanie McMahon-Helmsley
Win the Women's title.

Vince McMahon
Win the WWF Heavyweight title.

Bubba Ray Dudley's Glasses
Attack Bubba Ray Dudley during his entrance.

Christian's Glasses
Fight Christian during his entrance. Keep hitting him until his glasses fall off.

Crash Holly's Hat
Fight Crash Holly during his entrance.

D-Von Dudley's Glasses
Attack D-Von Dudley during his entrance.

Edge's Glasses
Attack Edge during his entrance.

Fred Durst's Hat

Fight Fred Durst in a one-on-one hardcore match and knock it off. Play as Fred Durst and let another wrestler knock your hat off. Pick it up and you'll have the item.

K-Kwik's Mic

Attack K-Kwik during his entrance.

Kurt Angle's Real Gold Medals

Fight Kurt Angle during his entrance and steal his medals after they fall off his head. Hit him with them 64 times, and the real medals appear. They're gold and have a green band.

Perry Saturn's Moppy

Attack Perry Saturn during his entrance. Alternately, fight Perry Saturn in a one-on-one hardcore match.

Spike Dudley's Glasses

Choose a one-on-one match and fight with Spike Dudley during his entrance.

Tazz's Glasses

Fight Tazz during his entrance until his glasses fall off.

Triple H's Water Bottle

Fight Triple H during his entrance.

Undertaker's Bandanna

Fight Undertaker during his entrance until he drops his bandanna.

Undertaker's Glasses

Fight Undertaker during his entrance until his glasses fall off.

X-Pac's Bandanna

Fight X-Pac during his entrance until he drops his bandanna.